FAMILY LAW IN A CHANGING AMERICA

ASPEN CASEBOOK SERIES

FAMILY LAW IN A CHANGING AMERICA

DOUGLAS NEJAIME
Anne Urowsky Professor of Law
Yale Law School

RALPH RICHARD BANKS
Jackson Eli Reynolds Professor of Law
Stanford Law School

JOANNA L. GROSSMAN
Ellen K. Solender Endowed Chair in Women and the Law & Professor of Law
SMU Dedman School of Law

SUZANNE A. KIM
Professor of Law & Judge Denny Chin Scholar
Rutgers Law School

Published by Wolters Kluwer in New York.

Wolters Kluwer Legal & Regulatory U.S. serves customers worldwide with CCH, Aspen Publishers, and Kluwer Law International products. (www.WKLegaledu.com)

To contact Customer Service, e-mail customer.service@wolterskluwer.com, call 1-800-234-1660, fax 1-800-901-9075, or mail correspondence to:

Wolters Kluwer
Attn: Order Department
PO Box 990
Frederick, MD 21705

Printed in the United States of America.

3 4 5 6 7 8 9 0

ISBN 978-1-5438-1591-7

Library of Congress Cataloging-in-Publication Data

Names: NeJaime, Douglas, author. | Banks, Ralph Richard, author. |
  Grossman, Joanna L., author. | Kim, Suzanne A., author.
Title: Family law in a changing America / Douglas NeJaime, Anne Urowsky
  Professor of Law, Yale Law School; Ralph Richard Banks, Jackson Eli Reynolds
  Professor of Law, Stanford Law School; Joanna L. Grossman, Ellen K. Solender
  Endowed Chair in Women and the Law & Professor of Law, SMU Dedman
  School of Law; Suzanne A. Kim, Professor of Law & Judge Denny Chin Scholar,
  Rutgers Law School.
Description: New York : Wolters Kluwer, [2021] | Series: Aspen casebook
  series | Includes bibliographical references and index. | Summary: "This
  casebook reflects the changes in family law in recent years" — Provided
  by publisher.
Identifiers: LCCN 2020029775 (print) | LCCN 2020029776 (ebook) | ISBN
  9781543815917 (hardcover) | ISBN 9781543823219 (ebook)
Subjects: LCSH: Domestic relations — United States. | Parent and child
  (Law) — United States. | Children — Legal status, laws, etc — United
  States. | Adoption — Law and legislation — United States.
Classification: LCC KF505 .N45 2021 (print) | LCC KF505 (ebook) | DDC
  346.7301/5 — dc23
LC record available at https://lccn.loc.gov/2020029775
LC ebook record available at https://lccn.loc.gov/2020029776

About Wolters Kluwer Legal & Regulatory U.S.

Wolters Kluwer Legal & Regulatory U.S. delivers expert content and solutions in the areas of law, corporate compliance, health compliance, reimbursement, and legal education. Its practical solutions help customers successfully navigate the demands of a changing environment to drive their daily activities, enhance decision quality and inspire confident outcomes.

Serving customers worldwide, its legal and regulatory portfolio includes products under the Aspen Publishers, CCH Incorporated, Kluwer Law International, ftwilliam.com and MediRegs names. They are regarded as exceptional and trusted resources for general legal and practice-specific knowledge, compliance and risk management, dynamic workflow solutions, and expert commentary.

Summary of Contents

Contents

CHAPTER 6
Parents, Children, and the State

Preface

Changing Families and Family Law

During the last several decades, families and family law in the United States have changed in fundamental ways. Families have been, simultaneously, reshaped by egalitarian law reform and riven by economic and racial inequality. Families thus have become both more *and* less equal. Each of these changes is unprecedented and calls for a casebook that centrally reflects their significance.

Throughout much of American history, family law doctrines formally reinforced gender inequality, white supremacy, and heterosexuality. Marriages across racial lines were, in many jurisdictions, a criminal offense, a prohibition meant to signify the inferiority of non-whites. Married women had no independent legal identity and instead were controlled through law by their husbands. Children were treated as property. Adults who dared to form families without marrying were invisible in the eyes of the law, given few of the legal entitlements that marital families took for granted. These hierarchies—white over nonwhite, men over women, heterosexuals over gays and lesbians, adults over children, and married over unmarried—were written into formal law.

Now, thankfully, the law has, in significant ways, repudiated these status hierarchies. The law, formally at least, accords more equality and autonomy than ever before. People are more free now to form the families they want, without their choices being devalued or disfavored. Same-sex couples are permitted to marry. Penalties and prohibitions no longer attach to loving across racial lines. Women no longer sacrifice their legal identity when they marry. Individuals no longer must marry to be recognized as legal parents, and the law protects the rights of non-marital children.

Even as egalitarian aspirations have infused family law doctrines, however, legally enforced inequality persists and, as importantly, social and economic inequalities dramatically shape families. The inequalities of the broader society are now reflected acutely in family patterns. As our society has grown more economically unequal, so too have family patterns diverged. Mass incarceration, the opioid epidemic, the intensification of economic inequality and residential segregation, the persistence of the privatization of care, and even advances in reproductive technologies have all contributed to disparities in the family patterns between the advantaged and the marginalized.

Some inequalities reflect the fact that traditional status hierarchies have been repudiated only partially. The law continues to privilege marriage and to extend rights and benefits to marital families that it withholds from non-marital families. This has consequences beyond the married-unmarried divide, given the race and class dimensions of marriage and non-marriage in contemporary society and the pressures placed on families to undertake caregiving work without public support. Within families, status hierarchies — some connected to caregiving work — continue as well. In disadvantaged communities, adults, compared to their more affluent counterparts, are less likely to marry, and more likely to bear and raise children without being married, often while in an intimate relationship with a non-marital partner. The consequences are multi-generational. Children in disadvantaged families are more likely than children in privileged families to come into contact with the child welfare system and to have parents who have been incarcerated, drug addicted, homeless, or indigent. Given the government's relatively limited role in directly supporting families and children, these children grow up with limited opportunities and resources — a reality that shapes their own family lives as adults.

These arrangements are not natural or self-evident. Rather, law shapes them, participating in the production and perpetuation of inequality even as, along some dimensions, it aspires to and generates equality. Accordingly, this book aims to illuminate the complicated and dynamic relationship between family law and family life by attending to law's role in both producing and challenging growing equality *and* inequality in American society.

Organizational Structure

These reconfigurations of family law and life have informed our approach to this casebook. We aim to enable students to understand the nature of the shifts that have remade families and family law, and to appreciate the sources and consequences of these shifts. Thus, the casebook is interdisciplinary, highlighting the social, legal, and economic influences that shape families.

We depart from other casebooks in our conceptual approach. Rather than append new developments onto existing frameworks, we have taken the opportunity, in creating a new casebook, to start fresh. In our account of existing law, we deliberately reject the centrality of the dominant organizing principle of past eras: heterosexual marriage. Our goal is to structure the materials in a way that highlights law and family patterns as they are now, rather than as they were decades ago, in part to give a better sense of the challenges and choices ahead.

Rather than accord centrality to marriage, we organize the presentation of the law around i) adult relationships and ii) parent-child relationships. And within each, we integrate types of cases that would have been previously separated. With adult relationships, for example, we do not treat marriage as the unquestioned starting point and then, as most casebooks do, separately consider "nontraditional" relationships. Instead, we deliberately situate marriage as a social institution, as one of a series of legally legitimate adult relationships, and as a legal institution among many potential ways of regulating intimate relationships. Moreover, we consider divorce, for example, as part of a broader discussion about relationship dissolution.

The aim of this approach is not to deny or overlook the legal and social significance of marriage, for it remains unquestionably an important legal and social institution. Rather, we hope to highlight, rather than presume answers to, the normative questions posed by the intersection of the traditional centrality of marriage, on one hand, and the unprecedented changes of recent decades, on the other. The materials prompt students and instructors to consider: What significance, if any, should be accorded the fact of marriage when, say, a couple's relationship dissolves? Are the rationales for preferring marriage to alternative ways of regulating intimate relationships persuasive, such that marriage will and should persist?

With parent-child relationships, we view non-marital, non-biological, and same-sex parenting as central, rather than peripheral. We group the material not based on the status of the parents, but instead based on the nature of the legal decision at issue: identifying a parent, custody, visitation, child support, and abuse and neglect determinations.

Just as the changes of the last several decades have put into question the long-standing legal centrality of heterosexual marriage, so too have latent assumptions about the legal regulation of the parent-child relationship been put into question. These changes highlight provocative and fundamental inquiries: What makes a person a parent in the eyes of the law? What should make one a parent? And how are the legal entitlements that flow from being a parent limited by the interests of children, or of other adults?

Scope and Sources of Law

We have assembled materials that expose students to the myriad sources of family law. Just as we depart from the tendency to privilege marriage, so too do we decline to privilege constitutional law, which is one among many sources shaping legal regulation of the family. Rather than supply an overarching constitutional framework at the outset, we incorporate constitutional law into relevant substantive areas. Doing this allows us to challenge the idea of constitutional law and family law as separate spheres and to resist the temptation to view constitutional law as shaping family law in a top-down, one-way direction.

We emphasize the importance of statutory law and analysis throughout the casebook. We include relevant federal legislation, representative state statutes, and Uniform Acts. In addition, we integrate questions of ethics and practice, rather than treat professional responsibility or lawyering in a separate chapter. At various points, we consider questions of representation and ethics, and we address systemic issues shaping family law collaborative practice, and other forms of alternative dispute resolution. We also selectively address family law in comparative perspective to illuminate salient aspects of our American system.

As important as courts and legislatures are, the law takes shape outside of those domains too. This casebook addresses a range of legal actors, not only lawyers, legislators, and judges, but also administrators of various sorts, caseworkers, and ordinary people who decide to work to improve our society.

As part of our effort to consider how the system shapes the lives of some of the most disadvantaged people in our society, we include materials on abuse and neglect proceedings, foster care, and reunification. And we address the child welfare system's troubling race, gender, and class dimensions.

In devoting significant attention to the child welfare system, we deliberately expand the scope of what constitutes family law. We do so as well by including legal questions at the intersection of work and family, to illuminate the privatization of care as a central family law concern. This leads us to include materials on the Family and Medical Leave Act, paid leave, workplace discrimination, and the gendered division of labor.

The casebook includes a number of practical problems and exercises (typically based on actual cases or events) that explore the implications of existing doctrine and illuminate gaps and tensions in the law. Many of the problems give students an opportunity to evaluate or formulate new rules to govern particular situations. They help students to develop a range of legal analytical skills by having them occupy a rich mix of roles: judge, litigator, legislator, institutional decisionmaker, activist. By assuming such diverse roles, students will develop a deeper appreciation of the multifaceted nature of particular controversies.

Ultimately, we have two broad goals for this book. We aim to equip students who want to practice family law with knowledge about the law and institutions that regulate the family. For these students, as well as those who do not intend to practice family law, we also want the book to provide an opportunity to think deeply about some of the fundamental conceptual, doctrinal, and practical problems that arise where law meets life.

Acknowledgments

Writing a new casebook is a daunting task. We would not have completed this project without the guidance, support, and assistance of our families, friends, colleagues, students, and institutions. Our family law work is made possible because of the support we receive from our own families. We are sustained by our respective spouses and children. We are also indebted to our scholarly families, including our colleagues at our home institutions and our colleagues in the family law community. We are also grateful to our students, who have shaped our approach to teaching and writing about family law. This book would not have been possible without excellent research and faculty support. Our research assistants and faculty assistants helped us to produce materials that are lively, detailed, and comprehensive. We want to express special gratitude to: Grace Choi, Tyler Dang, Sam Davis, Kyla Eastling, Carolina Yamamoto Eguchi, Elaine Emmerich, Zach Fields, Leanne Gale, Max Goldberg, Hilary Hogan, Juliana Moraes Liu, Ahmad Maaz, Madison Needham, Cara Newlon, Sonia Qin, Arjun Ramamurti, Cara Reichard, Sara Sampoli, Becca Steinberg, Anna Wherry, and Kath Xu; Inez Asante, Andrew Hoy, Christina La Bruno, Heather McLinn, Alexandria Silva, Sofia Ucles, Nicole Virella, and Samantha Weckenman; Stephen Chance, Anne Dzurilla, Mackenzie Fitzgerald, Ali Siller, and Hailey Swanson; and Gilat Bachar and Ginny Smith. Colleagues, students, and research assistants have taught each of us — leading us to see old topics in new ways and to notice other issues for the first time. Professor Khiara Bridges, Sara Bronin, Courtney Joslin, and Elizabeth Katz made special contributions on particular topics. We also thank our home institutions, Rutgers Law School, SMU Dedman School of Law, Stanford Law School, and Yale Law School, and our deans, Jennifer Collins, Heather Gerken, Jenny Martinez, Ron Chen, Kimberly Mutcherson, and David Lopez, for generous support. We are grateful to our editors at Wolters Kluwer, who helped us translate an idea into a casebook. Finally, we thank all of you — those who are reading, teaching, and using this casebook.

FAMILY LAW IN A
CHANGING AMERICA

CHAPTER 1

Justifying the Legal Treatment of Family and Marriage

I. Changing Family Patterns in Contemporary America

During the last several decades, family patterns in the United States have changed in fundamental and unprecedented ways, raising questions about how law should respond. The next several pages describe some of the key changes in family forms that you need to understand in order to engage with current and emerging legal issues.

Family life used to be a package deal, with most children being raised by married couples, most couples who lived together being married, and most sexual activity (in theory at least) being confined to marriage. Through the middle decades of the twentieth century, less than 10 percent of children were born to unmarried mothers.[1]

Now, family life is more à la carte. Marriage is no longer the exclusive means of structuring people's family lives. People marry later than they used to and get divorced more frequently, with 4 in 10 marriages ending in divorce.[2] Similarly, roughly 4 in every 10 children are born to unmarried mothers.[3] Many of these children are born to parents who are cohabiting.[4] Some of those couples will marry after their children are born; others will split up. And some will remain unmarried cohabitants as they raise their children. In addition to these shifts, more unmarried

---

1. Carmen Solomon-Fears, Cong. Research Serv., Nonmarital Births: An Overview 8 (2014); Stephanie J. Ventura et al., Nonmarital Childbearing in the United States, 1940–99, 48 Nat'l Vital Stat. Rep. 1, 17 (2000).

2. See Kira S. Birditt et al., Implications for Divorce over 16 Years, 72 J. Marriage & Fam. 1188, 1188 (2010).

3. Joyce A. Martin et al., Births: Final Data for 2018, 68 Nat'l Vital Stat. Rep. 1, 5 (2019).

4. See Esther Lamidi, Nat'l Ctr. for Family & Marriage Research, A Quarter Center Change in Nonmarital Births, Family Profiles, FP-16–03 (2016).

but committed couples are "living apart together," maintaining separate and independent residences, with about 10 percent of the adult population falling into this category.[5]

Overall trends in family formation do not tell the whole story. Race and class differences in marriage and childbearing have widened in recent decades.[6] Low-income Americans are both less likely to marry, and more likely to divorce when they do (compared either to their counterparts from earlier generations or to higher-income couples today).[7] As a result, their children are especially likely to grow up not living with both of their parents.

Divergences in family patterns due to disadvantage are especially apparent among African Americans. Compared to other groups, African Americans are least likely to marry, most likely to divorce, and most likely to bear children without being married.[8] Roughly 7 in 10 black children are born to unmarried parents.[9]

Affluent, highly educated couples adhere most closely to the conventional script of marrying first and then having children. But they too are arriving at parenthood differently.[10] Reproductive technologies, such as in vitro fertilization, create a broad array of possibilities for reproduction. Once used simply to help infertile, married, different-sex couples have children, reproductive technologies increasingly have been used by same-sex couples and single individuals. Many same-sex couples are raising children from previous different-sex relationships,[11] but an increasing number have engaged in assisted reproduction to have a child together. Of course, for same-sex couples, (at least) one of the parents is not genetically related to the child. (In addition, many same-sex couples adopt children, with one-fifth of gay or lesbian parents having adopted, compared to only 3 percent of heterosexual parents.[12])

Changes in family patterns stem from other changes in society. One key change is the growth of gender equality norms that were driven by, and in turn drove, the entry of women into the workforce. More than half of women now work for pay outside the home, with mothers' workforce participation varying based on their

---

5. Cynthia Grant Bowman, Living Apart Together, Women, and Family Law, 24 Cardozo J. Equal Rts. & Soc. Just. 47, 48–49 (2017); Cynthia Grant Bowman, How Should the Law Treat Couples Who Live Apart Together?, 29 Child and Fam. L.Q. 335, 345 (2017).

6. See, e.g., Ralph Richard Banks, Is Marriage for White People? How the African American Marriage Decline Affects Everyone (2011); June Carbone & Naomi R. Cahn, Marriage Markets: How Inequality Is Remaking the American Family (2014).

7. See Benjamin R. Karney, What's (Not) Wrong With Low-Incomes Marriages, 74 J. Marriage & Fam. 413, 415 (2012); R. Kelly Raley & Larry Bumpass, The Topography of the Divorce Plateau Levels & Trends in Union Stability in the United States After 1980, 8 Demographic Res. 245, 256 (2003).

8. Pew Res. Ctr., The Decline of Marriage & Rise of New Families 9, 11, 111 (2010).

9. Id. at 9.

10. See generally Carbone & Cahn, supra note 6.

11. Shoshana K. Goldberg & Kerith J. Conron, Williams Inst., How Many Same-Sex Couples in the U.S. are Raising Children? (2018).

12. Id.

marital status and the age of their children.[13] The increased ability of women to support themselves has made marriage less of an economic necessity, but greater workforce participation by unmarried mothers than married ones suggests some continued connection between marriage and financial support.[14] Moreover, income gaps between men and women persist, especially between men and women with children.[15] Legal reforms have mattered, too. The Civil Rights Act of 1964, prohibiting discrimination by employers on the basis of sex and other characteristics, for instance, helped to usher women into workplaces on terms more equal to men.[16] And society continues to debate the need for family leave policies that allow men and women, the latter of whom continue to bear disproportionate caretaking burdens, to balance work and family.

Just as medical and legal developments altered how some women have children, these developments also expanded women's ability to separate sex and childbearing. As the Supreme Court acknowledged in protecting women's access to birth control and abortion, women's ability to control their reproductive decision-making — whether and when to have children — relates to their ability to participate in public life.[17] The ability to control reproduction enabled women not only to work without interruption but also to complete the long educational process that some professions require.

As momentous as these changes in family patterns have been, there are divergent assessments about their desirability, and conflict persists over the proper role of law in response to these changes. Whereas some commentators view the liberation of sex and childbearing from marriage as a welcome affirmation of individual freedom, autonomy, and pluralism, others see the so-called breakdown of the family as undermining the welfare of adults and children alike. Whether the reconfiguration of family patterns is, on balance, desirable or worrisome, and how law should respond, depends partly on one's perspective.

What seems less controvertible is that widening economic inequality and the lack of a safety net has left the disadvantaged in dire family situations.[18] The rise of mass incarceration and, more recently, the opioid crisis have wreaked havoc within many families. More than 1.2 million incarcerated persons are parents of

13. Bureau of Lab. Stat., Employment Characteristics of Families — 2018 2 (2018).

14. Bureau of Lab. Stat., Employment Characteristics of Families — 2019 2 (2020).

15. Gender pay gaps are wider among married people and even more so with the arrival of children. Claudia Goldin et al., The Expanding Gender Earnings Gap: Evidence from the LEHD-2000 Census, 107 Am. Econ. Rev. 110, 113 (2017); Erling Barth, Sari Pekkala Kerr, Claudia Olivetti, The Dynamics of Gender Earnings Differentials: Evidence from Establishment Data 27 (Nat'l Bureau Econ. Research, Working Paper No. 23381, 2019).

16. 42 U.S.C. §2000 et seq. (2018).

17. See Planned Parenthood of Se. Pa. v. Casey, 505 U.S. 833, 856 (1992).

18. For discussion of impacts on families of economic inequality in the U.S., see Maxine Eichner, The Free-Market Family: How the Market Crushed the American Dream (and How It Can Be Restored) (2020).

children under 18.[19] Communities of color are disproportionately affected, with many children having parents who are or have been incarcerated.[20] Women's incarceration has grown at twice the pace of men's in the past four decades, increasing 834 percent since 1978 nationwide; fifty-two percent of incarcerated women, more than 120,000, are mothers.[21] The opioid crisis has resulted in many children losing parents to death or drug addiction.[22] Parental incarceration or drug addiction can result in children being placed in foster care and their parents being subject to state investigation for abuse or neglect.[23] This occurs alongside longstanding scrutiny of single mothers, particularly those of color, who face the prospect of separation from their children due to circumstances associated with poverty.

Much of this book considers how the law has responded, and should respond, to shifting family forms. The law does not passively reflect family patterns; it helps shape people's intimate and family lives, a task made more daunting by the absence of any consensus about what defines the "ideal" family form.

* * *

The cases and materials in the next section consider the question of how the law does and should define family. That inquiry necessarily focuses on two questions: whether the law should accord any special status to *families*, and if so, *how the law should define family*. As you read these cases, you should ask: What are the governmental interests asserted in defense of the proposed regulation? What individual interests are burdened? How best should those competing interests be reconciled? What definition of "family" does the applicable law use? How are tensions between state and local regulation, on the one hand, and federal constitutional rights, on the other, resolved?

19. See Pew Charitable Trs., Collateral Costs: Incarceration's Effect on Economic Mobility 6 (2010); see also Lauren E. Glaze & Laura M. Maruschak, U.S. Dep't of Justice, Parents in Prison and Their Minor Children 1 (2008).

20. See Pew Charitable Trs., supra note 19, at 4; Sarah Schirmer et al., The Sentencing Project, Incarerated Parents & Their Children 2 (2009); Jean M. Kjellstrand & J. Mark Eddy, Parental Incarceration During Childhood, Family Context, & Youth Behavior Across Adolescence, 50 J. Offender Rehabilitation 18, 27–29 (2011).

21. Wendy Sawyer, The Gender Divide: Tracking Women's State Prison Growth (2018); Pew Charitable Trs., supra note 19; Spencer K. Beall, "Lock Her Up!: How Women Have Become the Fastest-Growing Population in the American Carceral State, 23:2 Berkeley J. Crim. L. 1, 6 (2018).

22. See Rania Gihleb, Osea Giuntella, & Ning Zhang, Inst. of Lab. Econ., The Effects of Mandatory Prescription Drug Monitoring Programs on Foster Care Admissions 2 (2018).

23. See Suzanne C. Brundage & Carol Levine, United Hosp. Fund, The Ripple Effect: The Impact of the Opiod Epidemic on Children & Families 17 (2019); see also Robin Ghertner et al., U.S. Dep. of Health & Human Servs., The Relationship Between Substance Use Indicators & Child Welfare Caseloards 7 (2018).

II. How Does, and Should, the Law Define Family?

"Family" is a common, yet loaded, term. As the materials that follow make clear, significant legal consequences often turn on whether the law treats a particular group of people as a family. The U.S. Constitution never mentions the word "family," but the Supreme Court has held that the Fourteenth Amendment nonetheless protects the right of certain groups to live together. As you read the next two cases, consider how the Court makes that determination.

VILLAGE OF BELLE TERRE V. BORAAS
416 U.S. 1 (1974)

MR. JUSTICE DOUGLAS delivered the opinion of the Court.

Belle Terre is a village on Long Island's north shore of about 220 homes inhabited by 700 people. Its total land area is less than one square mile. It has restricted land use to one-family dwellings excluding lodging houses, boarding houses, fraternity houses, or multiple-dwelling houses. The word "family" as used in the ordinance means, "one or more persons related by blood, adoption, or marriage, living and cooking together as a single housekeeping unit, exclusive of household servants. A number of persons but not exceeding two (2) living and cooking together as a single housekeeping unit though not related by blood, adoption, or marriage shall be deemed to constitute a family."

Appellees the Dickmans are owners of a house in the village and leased it in December 1971 for a term of 18 months to Michael Truman. Later Bruce Boraas became a colessee. Then Anne Parish moved into the house along with three others. These six are students at nearby State University at Stony Brook and none is related to the other by blood, adoption, or marriage. When the village served the Dickmans with an "Order to Remedy Violations" of the ordinance, the owners plus three tenants thereupon brought this action under 42 U.S.C. § 1983 for an injunction and a judgment declaring the ordinance unconstitutional. The District Court held the ordinance constitutional and the Court of Appeals reversed. . . .

The present ordinance is challenged on several grounds: that it interferes with a person's right to travel; that it interferes with the right to migrate to and settle within a State; that it bars people who are uncongenial to the present residents; that it expresses the social preferences of the residents for groups that will be congenial to them; that social homogeneity is not a legitimate interest of government; that the restriction of those whom the neighbors do not like trenches on the newcomers' rights of privacy; that it is of no rightful concern to villagers whether the residents are married or unmarried; that the ordinance is antithetical to the Nation's experience, ideology, and self-perception as an open, egalitarian, and integrated society.

We find none of these reasons in the record before us. It is not aimed at transients. It involves no procedural disparity inflicted on some but not on others. It involves no "fundamental" right guaranteed by the Constitution, such as voting, the right of association, the right of access to the courts, or any rights of privacy. We deal with economic and social legislation where legislatures have historically drawn lines which we respect against the charge of violation of the Equal Protection Clause if the law be "reasonable, not arbitrary" and bears "a rational relationship to a [permissible] state objective."

It is said, however, that if two unmarried people can constitute a "family," there is no reason why three or four may not. But every line drawn by a legislature leaves some out that might well have been included. That exercise of discretion, however, is a legislative, not a judicial, function.

It is said that the Belle Terre ordinance reeks with an animosity to unmarried couples who live together. There is no evidence to support it; and the provision of the ordinance bringing within the definition of a "family" two unmarried people belies the charge.

The ordinance places no ban on other forms of association, for a "family" may, so far as the ordinance is concerned, entertain whomever it likes.

The regimes of boarding houses, fraternity houses, and the like present urban problems. More people occupy a given space; more cars rather continuously pass by; more cars are parked; noise travels with crowds.

A quiet place where yards are wide, people few, and motor vehicles restricted are legitimate guidelines in a land-use project addressed to family needs. This goal is a permissible one . . . . The police power is not confined to elimination of filth, stench, and unhealthy places. It is ample to lay out zones where family values, youth values, and the blessings of quiet seclusion and clean air make the area a sanctuary for people. . . .

Mr. Justice Marshall, dissenting.

This case draws into question the constitutionality of a zoning ordinance of the incorporated village of Belle Terre, New York, which prohibits groups of more than two unrelated persons, as distinguished from groups consisting of any number of persons related by blood, adoption, or marriage, from occupying a residence within the confines of the township. Lessor-appellees, the two owners of a Belle Terre residence, and three unrelated student tenants challenged the ordinance on the ground that it establishes a classification between households of related and unrelated individuals, which deprives them of equal protection of the laws. In my view, the disputed classification burdens the students' fundamental rights of association and privacy guaranteed by the First and Fourteenth Amendments. Because the application of strict equal protection scrutiny is therefore required, I am at odds with my Brethren's conclusion that the ordinance may be sustained on a showing that it bears a rational relationship to the accomplishment of legitimate governmental objectives.

I am in full agreement with the majority that zoning is a complex and important function of the State. It may indeed be the most essential function performed by local government, for it is one of the primary means by which we protect that sometimes difficult to define concept of quality of life. I therefore continue to adhere to the principle of *Euclid v. Ambler Realty Co.*, 272 U.S. 365 (1926), that deference should be given to governmental judgments concerning proper land-use allocation. That deference is a principle which has served this Court well and which is necessary for the continued development of effective zoning and land-use control mechanisms. Had the owners alone brought this suit alleging that the restrictive ordinance deprived them of their property or was an irrational legislative classification, I would agree that the ordinance would have to be sustained. Our role is not and should not be to sit as a zoning board of appeals.

I would also agree with the majority that local zoning authorities may properly act in furtherance of the objectives asserted to be served by the ordinance at issue here: restricting uncontrolled growth, solving traffic problems, keeping rental costs at a reasonable level, and making the community attractive to families. The police power which provides the justification for zoning is not narrowly confined. And, it is appropriate that we afford zoning authorities considerable latitude in choosing the means by which to implement such purposes. But deference does not mean abdication. This Court has an obligation to ensure that zoning ordinances, even when adopted in furtherance of such legitimate aims, do not infringe upon fundamental constitutional rights. . . .

My disagreement with the Court today is based upon my view that the ordinance in this case unnecessarily burdens appellees' First Amendment freedom of association and their constitutionally guaranteed right to privacy. Our decisions establish that the First and Fourteenth Amendments protect the freedom to choose one's associates. Constitutional protection is extended, not only to modes of association that are political in the usual sense, but also to those that pertain to the social and economic benefit of the members. The selection of one's living companions involves similar choices as to the emotional, social, or economic benefits to be derived from alternative living arrangements.

The freedom of association is often inextricably entwined with the constitutionally guaranteed right of privacy. The right to "establish a home" is an essential part of the liberty guaranteed by the Fourteenth Amendment. And the Constitution secures to an individual a freedom "to satisfy his intellectual and emotional needs in the privacy of his own home." *Stanley v. Georgia*, 394 U.S. 557, 565 (1969). Constitutionally protected privacy is, in Mr. Justice Brandeis' words, "as against the Government, the right to be let alone . . . the right most valued by civilized man." *Olmstead v. United States*, 277 U.S. 438, 478 (1928) (dissenting opinion). The choice of household companions — of whether a person's "intellectual and emotional needs" are best met by living with family, friends, professional associates, or others — involves deeply personal considerations as to the kind and quality of intimate relationships within the home. That decision surely falls within the ambit of the right to privacy protected by the Constitution.

The instant ordinance discriminates on the basis of just such a personal lifestyle choice as to household companions. It permits any number of persons related by blood or marriage, be it two or twenty, to live in a single household, but it limits to two the number of unrelated persons bound by profession, love, friendship, religious or political affiliation, or mere economics who can occupy a single home. Belle Terre imposes upon those who deviate from the community norm in their choice of living companions significantly greater restrictions than are applied to residential groups who are related by blood or marriage, and compose the established order within the community. The village has, in effect, acted to fence out those individuals whose choice of lifestyle differs from that of its current residents.

This is not a case where the Court is being asked to nullify a township's sincere efforts to maintain its residential character by preventing the operation of rooming houses, fraternity houses, or other commercial or high-density residential uses. Unquestionably, a town is free to restrict such uses. Moreover, as a general proposition, I see no constitutional infirmity in a town's limiting the density of use in residential areas by zoning regulations which do not discriminate on the basis of constitutionally suspect criteria. This ordinance, however, limits the density of occupancy of only those homes occupied by unrelated persons. It thus reaches beyond control of the use of land or the density of population, and undertakes to regulate the way people choose to associate with each other within the privacy of their own homes. . . .

Because I believe that this zoning ordinance creates a classification which impinges upon fundamental personal rights, it can withstand constitutional scrutiny only upon a clear showing that the burden imposed is necessary to protect a compelling and substantial governmental interest. . . .

A variety of justifications have been proffered in support of the village's ordinance. It is claimed that the ordinance controls population density, prevents noise, traffic and parking problems, and preserves the rent structure of the community and its attractiveness to families. As I noted earlier, these are all legitimate and substantial interests of government. But I think it clear that the means chosen to accomplish these purposes are both overinclusive and underinclusive, and that the asserted goals could be as effectively achieved by means of an ordinance that did not discriminate on the basis of constitutionally protected choices of lifestyle. The ordinance imposes no restriction whatsoever on the number of persons who may live in a house, as long as they are related by marital or sanguinary bonds — presumably no matter how distant their relationship. Nor does the ordinance restrict the number of income earners who may contribute to rent in such a household, or the number of automobiles that may be maintained by its occupants. In that sense the ordinance is underinclusive. On the other hand, the statute restricts the number of unrelated persons who may live in a home to no more than two. It would therefore prevent three unrelated people from occupying a dwelling even if among them they had but one income and no vehicles. While an extended family of a dozen or more might live in a small bungalow, three elderly and retired persons could not occupy the large manor house next door. Thus the statute is also grossly overinclusive to accomplish its intended purposes.

There are some 220 residences in Belle Terre occupied by about 700 persons. The density is therefore just above three per household. The village is justifiably concerned with density of population and the related problems of noise, traffic, and the like. It could deal with those problems by limiting each household to a specified number of adults, two or three perhaps, without limitation on the number of dependent children. The burden of such an ordinance would fall equally upon all segments of the community. It would surely be better tailored to the goals asserted by the village than the ordinance before us today, for it would more realistically restrict population density and growth and their attendant environmental costs. Various other statutory mechanisms also suggest themselves as solutions to Belle Terre's problems — rent control, limits on the number of vehicles per household, and so forth, but, of course, such schemes are matters of legislative judgment and not for this Court. Appellants also refer to the necessity of maintaining the family character of the village. There is not a shred of evidence in the record indicating that if Belle Terre permitted a limited number of unrelated persons to live together, the residential, familial character of the community would be fundamentally affected.

By limiting unrelated households to two persons while placing no limitation on households of related individuals, the village has embarked upon its commendable course in a constitutionally faulty vessel. I would find the challenged ordinance unconstitutional. But I would not ask the village to abandon its goal of providing quiet streets, little traffic, and a pleasant and reasonably priced environment in which families might raise their children. Rather, I would commend the village to continue to pursue those purposes but by means of more carefully drawn and evenhanded legislation.

I respectfully dissent.

NOTES AND QUESTIONS

1. *Governmental Objectives.* What objectives is the town of Belle Terre seeking to advance with its zoning ordinance? Are these objectives legitimate? Assuming that they are, how do the majority and Justice Marshall's dissent reach different outcomes? The majority assumes the reasonableness of the connection between the concept of "family" and the ordinance's objectives. Why doesn't the Court pursue

a more searching review? Justice Marshall suggests more even-handed regulations to address concerns underlying the ordinance. Do you think this type of approach makes sense?

2.   *What Is a Family?* Family might be defined in any of three ways: i) on the basis of formal ties such as marriage or adoption, ii) on the basis of biological ties, or iii) on the basis of whether a group functions as a family. Which of these approaches does the town of Belle Terre use? Why does Justice Douglas assume it is reasonable for the locality to assume that families are different from other groups of people? Are the Court's assumptions warranted? What are the advantages and disadvantages, for both the government and the individuals, of these different approaches to defining family?

3.   *The Fundamental Rights Branch of Equal Protection.* In dissent, Justice Marshall asserts that "the disputed classification burdens the students' fundamental rights of association and privacy" and concludes that "the application of strict equal protection scrutiny is therefore required." This type of statement may look unfamiliar from the perspective of contemporary Fourteenth Amendment jurisprudence, but in the era in which *Village of Belle Terre* was decided, courts sometimes reasoned about fundamental rights within the context of equal protection. The Equal Protection Clause has been understood to protect citizens against unequal access to fundamental rights. This reasoning has mattered in cases involving the right to vote, the right to access the courts, and the right to marry.[24] You will see this type of reasoning recur across cases in this chapter, as well as in other chapters.

4.   *Individual Autonomy Versus Relationships.* Justice Marshall's dissent suggests that the Court should focus less on the type of relationship at issue, and more on the individual's autonomy to choose "one's living companions." Is that a sensible approach? Would it properly balance the interests of the individual and the government? How could a government define family in a way that fosters individual autonomy?

MOORE v. CITY OF EAST CLEVELAND
431 U.S. 494 (1977)

MR. JUSTICE POWELL announced the judgment of the Court, and delivered an opinion in which MR. JUSTICE BRENNAN, MR. JUSTICE MARSHALL, and MR. JUSTICE BLACKMUN joined.

East Cleveland's housing ordinance, like many throughout the country, limits occupancy of a dwelling unit to members of a single family. But the ordinance

---

24. See Zablocki v. Redhail, 434 U.S. 374 (1978) (marriage); Harper v. Va. Bd. of Elections, 383 U.S. 663 (1966) (voting); Douglas v. California, 372 U.S. 353 (1963) (courts).

contains an unusual and complicated definitional section that recognizes as a "family" only a few categories of related individuals. Because her family, living together in her home, fits none of those categories, appellant stands convicted of a criminal offense. The question in this case is whether the ordinance violates the Due Process Clause of the Fourteenth Amendment.

I

Appellant, Mrs. Inez Moore, lives in her East Cleveland home together with her son, Dale Moore, Sr., and her two grandsons, Dale, Jr., and John Moore, Jr. The two boys are first cousins rather than brothers; we are told that John came to live with his grandmother and with the elder and younger Dale Moores after his mother's death.

In early 1973, Mrs. Moore received a notice of violation from the city, stating that John was an "illegal occupant" and directing her to comply with the ordinance. When she failed to remove him from her home, the city filed a criminal charge. . . .

II. . .

East Cleveland . . . has chosen to regulate the occupancy of its housing by slicing deeply into the family itself. This is no mere incidental result of the ordinance. On its face it selects certain categories of relatives who may live together and declares that others may not. In particular, it makes a crime of a grandmother's choice to live with her grandson in circumstances like those presented here.

When a city undertakes such intrusive regulation of the family, the usual judicial deference to the legislature is inappropriate. This Court has long recognized that freedom of personal choice in matters of marriage and family life is one of the liberties protected by the Due Process Clause of the Fourteenth Amendment. A host of cases . . . have consistently acknowledged a "private realm of family life which the state cannot enter." Of course, the family is not beyond regulation. But when the government intrudes on choices concerning family living arrangements, this Court must examine carefully the importance of the governmental interests advanced and the extent to which they are served by the challenged regulation. When thus examined, this ordinance cannot survive. The city seeks to justify it as a means of preventing overcrowding, minimizing traffic and parking congestion, and avoiding an undue financial burden on East Cleveland's school system. Although these are legitimate goals, the ordinance before us serves them marginally, at best. For example, the ordinance permits any family consisting only of husband, wife, and unmarried children to live together, even if the family contains a half dozen licensed drivers, each with his or her own car. At the same time it forbids an adult brother and sister to share a household, even if both faithfully use public transportation. The ordinance would permit a grandmother to live with a single dependent son and children, even if his school-age children number a dozen, yet it forces Mrs. Moore to find another dwelling for her grandson John, simply because of the presence of his uncle and cousin in the same household. . . .

Our decisions establish that the Constitution protects the sanctity of the family precisely because the institution of the family is deeply rooted in this Nation's history and tradition. It is through the family that we inculcate and pass down many of our most cherished values, moral and cultural. Ours is by no means a tradition limited to respect for the bonds uniting the members of the nuclear family. The tradition of uncles, aunts, cousins, and especially grandparents sharing a household along with parents and children has roots equally venerable and equally deserving of constitutional recognition. Over the years millions of our citizens have grown up in just such an environment, and most, surely, have profited from it. Even if conditions of modern society have brought about a decline in extended family households, they have not erased the accumulated wisdom of civilization, gained over the centuries and honored throughout our history, that supports a larger conception of the family. Out of choice, necessity, or a sense of family responsibility, it has been common for close relatives to draw together and participate in the duties and the satisfactions of a common home. Decisions concerning child rearing, which [our] cases have recognized as entitled to constitutional protection, long have been shared with grandparents or other relatives who occupy the same household — indeed who may take on major responsibility for the rearing of the children. Especially in times of adversity, such as the death of a spouse or economic need, the broader family has tended to come together for mutual sustenance and to maintain or rebuild a secure home life. This is apparently what happened here.

Whether or not such a household is established because of personal tragedy, the choice of relatives in this degree of kinship to live together may not lightly be denied by the State. . . . [T]he Constitution prevents East Cleveland from standardizing its children — and its adults — by forcing all to live in certain narrowly defined family patterns.

MR. JUSTICE BRENNAN, with whom MR. JUSTICE MARSHALL joins, concurring. . . .

I agree that the Constitution is not powerless to prevent East Cleveland from prosecuting as a criminal and jailing a 63-year-old grandmother for refusing to expel from her home her now 10-year-old grandson who has lived with her and been brought up by her since his mother's death when he was less than a year old. I do not question that a municipality may constitutionally zone to alleviate noise and traffic congestion and to prevent overcrowded and unsafe living conditions, in short to enact reasonable land-use restrictions in furtherance of the legitimate objectives East Cleveland claims for its ordinance. But the zoning power is not a license for local communities to enact senseless and arbitrary restrictions which cut deeply into private areas of protected family life. East Cleveland may not constitutionally define "family" as essentially confined to parents and the parents' own children.[3] The plurality's opinion conclusively demonstrates that classifying family patterns in this eccentric way is not a rational means of achieving the ends East Cleveland claims for its ordinance, and further that the ordinance unconstitutionally abridges the "freedom of personal choice in matters of . . . family life [that] is one of the liberties protected by the Due Process Clause of the Fourteenth Amendment." I write only to underscore the cultural myopia of the arbitrary boundary drawn by the East Cleveland ordinance in the light of the tradition of the American home that has been a feature of our society since our beginning as a Nation — the "tradition" in the plurality's words, "of uncles, aunts, cousins, and especially grandparents sharing a household along with parents and children. . . ." The line drawn by this ordinance displays a depressing insensitivity toward the economic and emotional needs of a very large part of our society.

In today's America, the "nuclear family" is the pattern so often found in much of white suburbia. The Constitution cannot be interpreted, however, to tolerate the imposition by government upon the rest of us of white suburbia's preference in patterns of family living. The "extended family" that provided generations of early Americans with social services and economic and emotional support in times of hardship, and was the beachhead for successive waves of immigrants who populated our cities, remains not merely still a pervasive living pattern, but under the goad of brutal economic necessity, a prominent pattern — virtually a means of survival — for large numbers of the poor and deprived minorities of our society. For them compelled pooling of scant resources requires compelled sharing of a household.

The "extended" form is especially familiar among black families.[6] We may suppose that this reflects the truism that black citizens, like generations of white immigrants before them, have been victims of economic and other disadvantages that would worsen if they were compelled to abandon extended, for nuclear, living

---

3. The East Cleveland ordinance defines "family" to include, in addition to the spouse of the "nominal head of the household," the couple's childless unmarried children, but only one dependent child (married or unmarried) having dependent children, and one parent of the nominal head of the household or of his or her spouse. Thus an "extended family" is authorized in only the most limited sense, and "family" is essentially confined to parents and their own children. Appellant grandmother was charged with violating the ordinance because John, Jr., lived with her at the same time her other grandson, Dale, Jr., was also living in the home; the latter is classified as an "unlicensed roomer" authorized by the ordinance to live in the house.

6. B. Yorburg, The Changing Family 108 (1973). "Within the black lower-class it has been quite common for several generations, or parts of the kin, to live together under one roof. Often a maternal grandmother is the acknowledged head of this type of household which has given rise to the term 'matrifocal' to describe lower-class black family patterns." See J. Scanzoni, The Black Family in Modern Society 134 (1971).

The extended family often plays an important role in the rearing of young black children whose parents must work. Many such children frequently "spend all of their growing-up years in the care of extended kin. . . . Often children are 'given' to their grandparents, who rear them to adulthood. . . . Many children normally grow up in a three-generation household and they absorb the influences of grandmother and grandfather as well as mother and father." J. Ladner, Tomorrow's Tomorrow: The Black Woman 60 (1972).

patterns.[7] Even in husband and wife households, 13% of black families compared with 3% of white families include relatives under 18 years old, in addition to the couple's own children. In black households whose head is an elderly woman, as in this case, the contrast is even more striking: 48% of such black households, compared with 10% of counterpart white households, include related minor children not offspring of the head of the household.

I do not wish to be understood as implying that East Cleveland's enforcement of its ordinance is motivated by a racially discriminatory purpose. The record of this case would not support that implication. But the prominence of other than nuclear families among ethnic and racial minority groups, including our black citizens, surely demonstrates that the "extended family" pattern remains a vital tenet of our society. It suffices that in prohibiting this pattern of family living as a means of achieving its objectives, appellee city has chosen a device that deeply intrudes into family associational rights that historically have been central, and today remain central, to a large proportion of our population. . . .

The choice of the "extended family" pattern is within the "freedom of personal choice in matters of . . . family life [that] is one of the liberties protected by the Due Process Clause of the Fourteenth Amendment." . . .

MR. JUSTICE STEWART, with whom MR. JUSTICE REHNQUIST joins, dissenting. . . .

I would hold, for the reasons that follow, that the existence of blood ties does not elevate either the appellant's claim of associational freedom or her claim of privacy to a level invoking constitutional protection. . . .

The "association" in this case is not for any purpose relating to the promotion of speech, assembly, the press, or religion. And wherever the outer boundaries of constitutional protection of freedom of association may eventually turn out to be,

---

7. The extended family has many strengths not shared by the nuclear family.

"The case histories behind mounting rates of delinquency, addiction, crime, neurotic disabilities, mental illness, and senility in societies in which autonomous nuclear families prevail suggest that frequent failure to develop enduring family ties is a serious inadequacy for both individuals and societies." D. Blitsten, The World of the Family 256 (1963).

Extended families provide services and emotional support not always found in the nuclear family:

"The troubles of the nuclear family in industrial societies, generally, and in American society, particularly, stem largely from the inability of this type of family structure to provide certain of the services performed in the past by the extended family. Adequate health, education, and welfare provision, particularly for the two nonproductive generations in modern societies, the young and the old, is increasingly an insurmountable problem for the nuclear family. The unrelieved and sometimes unbearably intense parent-child relationship, where childrearing is not shared at least in part by others, and the loneliness of nuclear family units, increasingly turned in on themselves in contracted and relatively isolated settings, is another major problem." Yorburg, supra, n. [6], at 194.

they surely do not extend to those who assert no interest other than the gratification, convenience, and economy of sharing the same residence.

The appellant is considerably closer to the constitutional mark in asserting that the East Cleveland ordinance intrudes upon "the private realm of family life which the state cannot enter." *Prince v. Massachusetts,* 321 U.S. 158, 166 (1944). Several decisions of the Court have identified specific aspects of what might broadly be termed "private family life" that are constitutionally protected against state interference. Although the appellant's desire to share a single-dwelling unit also involves "private family life" in a sense, that desire can hardly be equated with any of the interests protected in the case just cited. The ordinance about which the appellant complains did not impede her choice to have or not to have children, and it did not dictate to her how her own children were to be nurtured and reared. The ordinance clearly does not prevent parents from living together or living with their unemancipated offspring. . . .

[handwritten margin note: attacking "private life" interest arg]

When the Court has found that the Fourteenth Amendment placed a substantive limitation on a State's power to regulate, it has been in those rare cases in which the personal interests at issue have been deemed "'implicit in the concept of ordered liberty.'" The interest that the appellant may have in permanently sharing a single kitchen and a suite of contiguous rooms with some of her relatives simply does not rise to that level. To equate this interest with the fundamental decisions to marry and to bear and raise children is to extend the limited substantive contours of the Due Process Clause beyond recognition. *[handwritten: line drawing]*

The appellant also challenges the single-family occupancy ordinance on equal protection grounds. Her claim is that the city has drawn an arbitrary and irrational distinction between groups of people who may live together as a "family" and those who may not. While acknowledging the city's right to preclude more than one family from occupying a single-dwelling unit, the appellant argues that the purposes of the single-family occupancy law would be equally served by an ordinance that did not prevent her from sharing her residence with her two sons and their sons.

[handwritten margin note: attacking the eq pro arg]

This argument misconceives the nature of the constitutional inquiry. In a case such as this one, where the challenged ordinance intrudes upon no substantively protected constitutional right, it is not the Court's business to decide whether its application in a particular case seems inequitable, or even absurd. The question is not whether some other ordinance, drafted more broadly, might have served the city's ends as well or almost as well. The task, rather, is to determine if East Cleveland's ordinance violates the Equal Protection Clause of the United States Constitution. And in performing that task, it must be borne in mind that "[we] deal with economic and social legislation where legislatures have historically drawn lines which we respect against the charge of violation of the Equal Protection Clause if the law be 'reasonable, not arbitrary' and bears 'a rational relationship to a [permissible] state objective.'" "[E]very line drawn by a legislature leaves some out that might well have been included. That exercise of discretion, however, is a legislative, not a judicial, function."

Viewed in the light of these principles, I do not think East Cleveland's definition of "family" offends the Constitution. The city has undisputed power to ordain single-family residential occupancy. And that power plainly carries with it the power to say what a "family" is. . . .

Obviously, East Cleveland might have as easily and perhaps as effectively hit upon a different definition of "family." But a line could hardly be drawn that would not sooner or later become the target of a challenge like the appellant's. If "family" included all of the householder's grandchildren there would doubtless be the hard case of an orphaned niece or nephew. If, as the appellant suggests, a "family" must include all blood relatives, what of longtime friends? The point is that any definition would produce hardships in some cases without materially advancing the legislative purpose. That this ordinance also does so is no reason to hold it unconstitutional, unless we are to use our power to interpret the United States Constitution as a sort of generalized authority to correct seeming inequity wherever it surfaces. . . .

NOTES AND QUESTIONS

1. Belle Terre *Versus* Moore. How does *Belle Terre* provide support for *Moore*? How can *Moore* be distinguished? How do these differences affect the outcomes in the cases? How do understandings of "family" compare in these two cases?

2. *Family Pluralism.* Justice Brennan's concurring opinion emphasizes the historical role of extended family in American life, especially for immigrant and minority families. What is the significance of pluralism in the plurality's analysis? How does the social reality of how families — across socioeconomic, racial, and ethnic categories — live factor into the Court's analysis?

3. *Multigenerational Households, Race and Ethnicity, and Immigration Status.* Even today, research reveals the prevalence of extended and multigenerational households in the U.S., many with grandparents helping to raise grandchildren. In 2016, roughly 20 percent of the U.S. population lived in multigenerational households, a figure that has increased from previous years. The percentages of multigenerational households differ across racial and ethnic groups. In 2016, 29 percent of Asian Americans and 26 percent of African Americans lived in multigenerational households, compared to only 16 percent of white Americans.[25] Moreover, foreign-born Americans are more likely to live with multiple generations of family, and "before Asians so it's "Asians and Hispanics are more likely than whites to be immigrants."[26]

4. *Race and Class.* Justice Brennan notes racial and ethnic differences in household composition, although he says the record does not support the claim

---

25. D'Vera Cohn & Jeffrey S. Passel, A Record 64 Million Americans Live in Multigenerational Households, Pew Res. Ctr. (Apr. 5, 2018).
    26. Id.

that the city was motivated by racial animus in passing the zoning ordinance. What if the city was motivated by class-based interests? According to Professor Peggy Cooper Davis, the zoning ordinance was part of a detailed plan to preserve the middle-class character of the city after an enormous rise in the number of black families — from 2 to 44 percent in just 7 years.[27] As this makes clear, though, race and class intersect. As Professor Nancy Dowd explains, zoning codes like the one in East Cleveland "were both race and class focused," seeking "to 'manage' and resist integration and to prevent white flight."[28] Obscuring these dimensions, a formal report commissioned by the city emphasized the need to build "a community of achievement," where "upward-mobile groups develop their own capabilities and develop the standards and values of a new kind of life."[29] The plan was ultimately unsuccessful, and the city became one of the state's poorest by the 1980s.

PROBLEMS

1. You have been approached by Suresh Singh, an immigrant from India, who lives in the local town and has been served with a notice of zoning violation by the city housing department. The City has threatened legal action if Mr. Singh does not remedy the zoning violation within 30 calendar days. Mr. Singh lives in a four-bedroom, single-family home with his wife and two children, one boy and one girl. The home is also occupied by Mr. Singh's cousin and his wife, who have one daughter. Each couple has one bedroom, and the children's bedrooms are split by sex, with the two girls in one bedroom and the one boy in the other. The zoning ordinance applicable to this neighborhood limits occupancy of each dwelling to a "single family." City officials state that Mr. Singh has violated that restriction. Mr. Singh is convinced that the City's enforcement action against him is a form of ethnic or racial bias, as the City recently has experienced an influx of Indian immigrants, who often live with members of their extended families. He states that his family has lived in this sort of arrangement for generations, from before they came to the U.S., and sees no reason why they should not be allowed to continue to do so. Your job is to convince the city housing department that Mr. Singh should not be required to move. What arguments would be most persuasive?

---

27. Peggy Cooper Davis, Moore v. City of East Cleveland: Constructing the Suburban Family, in Family Law Stories (Carol Sanger ed., 2008).

28. Nancy E. Dowd, John Moore Jr.: Moore v. City of East Cleveland and Children's Constitutional Arguments, 85 Fordham L. Rev. 2603, 2606 (2017).

29. Davis, supra note 27, at 84 (citing City of East Cleveland & Arthur D. Little, Inc., East Cleveland: Response to Urban Change (1969)).

2. In the U.S., average life expectancy for women is almost five years longer than for men.[30] A group of four retired women who are lifelong best friends have decided to grow old together. Each of their husbands has passed away. They would like to purchase a four-bedroom house and live together, contributing equally to the household expenses and mortgage. Their jurisdiction has an ordinance that restricts homes to single-family dwellings and defines a family as: "No more than three individuals who are not related by blood, adoption, or marriage, living and cooking together as a single housekeeping unit." They come to you for legal advice about whether they could live together and, if not, how they might challenge the ordinance. What advice would you give them?

CITY OF LADUE v. HORN
720 S.W.2d 745 (Mo. Ct. App. 1986)

CRANDALL, JUDGE.

Defendants, Joan Horn and E. Terrence Jones, appeal from the judgment of the trial court in favor of plaintiff, City of Ladue (Ladue), which enjoined defendants from occupying their home in violation of Ladue's zoning ordinance and which dismissed defendants' counterclaim. . . .

Certain zones were designated as one-family residential. The zoning ordinance defined family as: "One or more persons related by blood, marriage or adoption, occupying a dwelling unit as an individual housekeeping organization." The only authorized accessory use in residential districts was for "[a]ccommodations for domestic persons employed and living on the premises and home occupations." The purpose of Ladue's zoning ordinance was broadly stated as to promote "the health, safety, morals and general welfare" of Ladue.

In July, 1981, defendants purchased a seven-bedroom, four-bathroom house which was located in a single-family residential zone in Ladue. Residing in defendants' home were Horn's two children (aged 16 and 19) and Jones's one child (age 18). The two older children attended out-of-state universities and lived in the house only on a part-time basis. Although defendants were not married, they shared a common bedroom, maintained a joint checking account for the household expenses, ate their meals together, entertained together, and disciplined each other's children. Ladue made demands upon defendants to vacate their home because their household did not comprise a family, as defined by Ladue's zoning ordinance, and therefore they could not live in an area zoned for single-family dwellings. . . .

---

30. Elizabeth Arias et al., United States Life Tables, 66 Nat'l Vital Stats. Reps. 1, 2 (2017).

Capsulated, defendants' attack on Ladue's ordinance is three-pronged. First, the zoning limitations foreclose them from exercising their right to associate freely with whomever they wish. Second, their right to privacy is violated by the zoning restrictions. Third, the zoning classification distinguishes between related persons and unrelated persons. Defendants allege that the United States and Missouri Constitutions grant each of them the right to share his or her residence with whomever he or she chooses. They assert that Ladue has not demonstrated a compelling, much less rational, justification for the overly proscriptive blood or legal relationship requirement in its zoning ordinance.

Defendants posit that the term "family" is susceptible to several meanings. They contend that, since their household is the "functional and factual equivalent of a natural family," the ordinance may not preclude them from living in a single-family residential Ladue neighborhood. Defendants argue in their brief as follows:

> The record amply demonstrates that the private, intimate interests of Horn and Jones are substantial. Horn, Jones, and their respective children have historically lived together as a single family unit. They use and occupy their home for the identical purposes and in the identical manners as families which are biologically or maritally related.

To bolster this contention, defendants elaborate on their shared duties.... Defendants acknowledge the importance of viewing themselves as a family unit, albeit a "conceptual family" as opposed to a "true non-family," in order to prevent the application of the ordinance.

The fallacy in defendants' syllogism is that the stipulated facts do not compel the conclusion that defendants are living as a family. A man and woman living together, sharing pleasures and certain responsibilities, does not *per se* constitute a family in even the conceptual sense. To approximate a family relationship, there must exist a commitment to a permanent relationship and a perceived reciprocal obligation to support and to care for each other. Only when these characteristics are present can the conceptual family, perhaps, equate with the traditional family. In a traditional family, certain of its inherent attributes arise from the legal relationship of the family members. In a non-traditional family, those same qualities arise in fact, either by explicit agreement or by tacit understanding among the parties....

[W]e cannot assume that the trial court's perception of defendants' familial status comported with defendants' characterization of themselves as a conceptual family.... [Nonetheless, w]e assume, *arguendo*, that the sole basis for the judgment entered by the trial court was that defendants were not related by blood, marriage or adoption, as required by Ladue's ordinance.

We first consider whether the ordinance violates any federally protected rights of the defendants. Generally, federal court decisions hold that a zoning classification based upon a biological or a legal relationship among household members is justifiable under constitutional police powers to protect the public health, safety, morals or welfare of the community.

More specifically, the United States Supreme Court has developed a two-tiered approach by which to examine legislation challenged as violative of the equal protection clause. If the personal interest affected by the ordinance is fundamental, "strict scrutiny" is applied and the ordinance is sustained only upon a showing that the burden imposed is necessary to protect a compelling governmental interest. If the ordinance does not contain a suspect class or impinge upon a fundamental interest, the more relaxed "rational basis" test is applied and the classification imposed by the ordinance is upheld if any facts can reasonably justify it. Defendants urge this court to recognize that their interest in choosing their own living arrangement inexorably involves their fundamental rights of freedom of association and of privacy. . . .

Here, because we are dealing with economic and social legislation and not with a fundamental interest or a suspect classification, the test of constitutionality is whether the ordinance is reasonable and not arbitrary and bears a rational relationship to a permissible state objective.

Ladue has a legitimate concern with laying out guidelines for land use addressed to family needs. "It is ample to lay out zones where family values, youth values, and the blessings of quiet seclusion and clean air make the area a sanctuary for people." The question of whether Ladue could have chosen more precise means to effectuate its legislative goals is immaterial. Ladue's zoning ordinance is rationally related to its expressed purposes and violates no provisions of the Constitution of the United States. Further, defendants' assertion that they have a constitutional right to share their residence with whomever they please amounts to the same argument that was made and found unpersuasive by the court in *Belle Terre*. . . .

For purposes of its zoning code, Ladue has in precise language defined the term family. It chose the definition which comports with the historical and traditional notions of family; namely, those people related by blood, marriage or adoption. That definition of family has been upheld in numerous Missouri decisions. . . .

[M]aintenance of a traditional family environment constitutes a reasonable basis for excluding uses that may impair the stability of that environment and erode the values associated with traditional family life. The essence of zoning is selection; and, if it is not invidious or discriminatory against those not selected, it is proper. There is no doubt that there is a governmental interest in marriage and in preserving the integrity of the biological or legal family. There is no concomitant governmental interest in keeping together a group of unrelated persons, no matter how closely they simulate a family. Further, there is no state policy which commands that groups of people may live under the same roof in any section of a municipality they choose.

The stated purpose of Ladue's zoning ordinance is the promotion of the health, safety, morals and general welfare in the city. Whether Ladue could have adopted less restrictive means to achieve these same goals is not a controlling factor in considering the constitutionality of the zoning ordinance. Rather, our focus is on whether there exists some reasonable basis for the means actually employed. In making such a determination, if any state of facts either known or which could reasonably be assumed is presented in support of the ordinance, we must defer to the legislative judgment. We find that Ladue has not acted arbitrarily in enacting its zoning ordinance which defines family as those related by blood, marriage or adoption. Given the fact that Ladue has so defined family, we defer to its legislative judgment. . . .

NOTES AND QUESTIONS

1. *Arguing from Precedent.* *Belle Terre* and *Moore* represent precedents for the *City of Ladue* court. If you represented the couple in their appeal of the court's ruling, what arguments would you make that the enforcement of the statute against them is unconstitutional?

2. *State Interests.* The *City of Ladue* court asserts that "[t]here is no doubt that there is a governmental interest in marriage and in preserving the integrity of the biological or legal family." What precisely is the state's interest in marriage? How, if at all, would a zoning ordinance like Ladue's further that interest? What is the state's interest in preserving the "legal family"? What about the "biological family"? Conversely, the court asserts that "[t]here is no concomitant governmental interest in keeping together a group of unrelated persons, no matter how closely they simulate a family." Why not? Could you identify such a state interest?

3. *Formal Versus Functional Versus Biological Approaches.* After reading *Village of Belle Terre*, we considered the difference between functional, biological, and formal definitions of family. Which approach is exemplified in *City of Ladue*? What would you identify as some of the strengths and weaknesses of this approach?

A classic example of the functional approach is Braschi v. Stahl Associates Co.[31] In that case, a man sought to retain occupancy of a rent-controlled apartment in New York City where he had lived for eleven years with his same-sex partner until the partner's death. Under the applicable city ordinance, a surviving spouse or any "family member" who was living in the apartment at the time of the tenant's death was entitled to non-eviction protection. The ordinance provided no definition of family. The state's highest court rejected a legal definition of family that would have included only those related by blood, marriage, or adoption in favor of a "more realistic" functional definition that would require a fact-intensive, individualized determination of eligibility. Whether someone qualifies as a "family

---

31. 543 N.E.2d 49 (N.Y. 1989).

member" should be based, the court held, "on realities of family life" and should include "two adult lifetime partners whose relationship is long term and characterized by an emotional and financial commitment and interdependence." The court listed "familial characteristics" that might support a claim of family relationship, including longevity of relationship, exclusivity, the manner in which the household is conducted, reputation in society, reliance on one another for family services, and an interwoven social life. Is this a good approach? A dissenting opinion in *Braschi* argued that the court's approach requires much greater judicial intervention than a more formal definition. Is that a valid concern? The dissent also argued that courts are not in a good position to examine the level of emotional commitment between two people without formal ties. Do you agree?

4.   *Co-Housing.* Combining single-family homes with shared common areas, "co-housing" represents a recent trend. More dense than typical single-family zoned areas, co-housing communities are more popular outside the U.S., but have gained increased attention here, especially from policymakers interested in exploring supportive housing models for older adults to "age in place."[32] Co-housing is thought to balance residents' desire for privacy, community, and mutual support.[33] Variances to zoning ordinances as well as alternative zoning structures support these types of communities.[34] How do co-housing units conform to or depart from the view of the family embodied by conventional zoning schemes?

PROBLEMS

1. Two families participated in a new version of the reality show "Wife Swap," in which the wives switch places for one year. In each family, the wife is a homemaker who cooks, cleans, and serves as the primary caretaker for the children. One of the families — the Smiths — lives in a neighborhood subject to a "single family dwelling" zoning ordinance. A neighbor has threatened to report the "Smiths" (Mr. Smith, his swapped "wife," and their children) to the zoning board, alleging that they are not a "single family." What arguments will the Smiths make when called before the zoning board? Will they be allowed to stay in their house?

2. The "Scarborough 11" are a group of eight adults and three children — two couples with children, one couple with no children, and two single adults. What ties them

---

32. AARP Pub. Policy Inst., Cohousing for Older Adults (Mar. 2010); Ronda Kaysen, Cohousing: A Growing Concept in Communal Living, AARP (Feb. 1, 2018); Vera Prosper, N.Y. State Office for the Aging, Livable New York Resource Manual, Cohousing (2010).

33. Prosper, Livable New York Resource Manual, Cohousing, supra note 32; AARP Pub. Policy Inst., Cohousing for Older Adults, supra note 32.

34. Paul Beyer, Governor's Smart Growth Cabinet, Livable New York Resource Manual, Retirement Housing Zoning (2010).

together is lifelong friendship and a desire to intermingle their lives. They pooled their money to buy a nine-bedroom house in one of the wealthiest neighborhoods in Hartford, Connecticut. They share expenses and chores, and they provide one another with emotional support. The local zoning board served them with a cease-and-desist order on grounds that the group does not meet the definition of a family; the zoning board of appeals upheld the order. The chair of the zoning board said the group "seemed like nice people," but that to let them stay would open up a "Pandora's box."[35] Assume the zoning board might allow this group to stay if it could do so without allowing other unrelated groups, such as college students, to move into the neighborhood. Draft a definition of family that might accomplish this.

POSTSCRIPT

In 2016, the city of Hartford withdrew the suit it had brought to enforce its zoning ordinance against the Scarborough 11, thus allowing them to continue to live in the home.[36] The city also overhauled its zoning regulations, replacing the definition of family with a reference to a "household unit," defined as:

> A collection of individuals occupying the entire dwelling unit, sharing a household budget and expenses, preparing food and eating together regularly, sharing in the work to maintain the premises, and legally sharing in the ownership or possession of the premises.[37]

The regulations then define "dwelling unit" as:

> A room or group of rooms connected together that include a bathroom and facilities for living, sleeping, cooking, and eating that are arranged, designed, or intended to be used as living quarters for one household, whether owner occupied, rented, or leased.[38]

Does this help the Scarborough 11? Do you think this represents a better approach to zoning?[39]

---

35. See Vanessa de la Torre, 8 Adults, 3 Children, 1 House — And a Big Zoning Dispute in Hartford, Hartford Courant (Nov. 20, 2014).

36. See Vanessa de la Torre, City of Hartford Withdraws Suit in 'Scarborough 11' Case, Hartford Courant (Oct. 27, 2016).

37. City of Hartford, Zoning Regulations 51 (effective Jan. 19, 2016). The regulations are regularly amended.

38. Id. at 49.

39. The chair of Hartford's Planning and Zoning Commission at the time of these changes has written about how cities can revise their codes in ways that accommodate functional families. See Sara C. Bronin, Zoning for Families, 95 Ind. L.J. 1 (2020).

David D. Haddock and Daniel D. Polsby, Family as a Rational Classification
74 Wash. U. L.Q. 15 (1996)

Does a legislative preference for "family" amount to an irrational classification?

The question was squarely raised in City of Santa Barbara v. Adamson. According to the California Supreme Court, the city violated the state's constitution by pegging its residential land use regulations to the subsistence of a "family" (as traditionally and legally constituted). . . .

[W]hy should organized society care, one way or another, about the family? If most people want to live in families, fine; if others do not, so what? . . .

[A] good deal of modern family law appears to accept the subtly inconsistent premise that how a person chooses to live, and with whom, is essentially a private matter into which the community intrudes as a hostile and officious stranger. According to our argument, that premise is specious. A matter, even a sensitively intimate one like a person's domestic living arrangements, can hardly be "private" if seen as threatening to result in important external harm. . . .

What is the basis for the fireside induction that "families" behave differently from a demographically matched group of non-family members? The answer is largely one of the stability of relationships, and the costs that members of any relational group will ordinarily encounter when they try to control the behavior of other group members. Our argument is summarized in the following four paragraphs.

There does exist a probabilistic difference between family, as that term is ordinarily understood, and non-family, and it has to do with the relative probabilities of exit, emotional as well as physical, from the household. The ease or difficulty of exit carries implications for the ability of the domestic unit to acquire and preserve reputational capital, which in turn affects the stake that household members have in investing in the household's "brand name."

There is thus a logical non-religious rationale that explains why families, as producers of collective goods, are encouraged (although not necessarily compelled) by the communities they benefit. Conversely, non-familial domestic morphs will be discouraged (not necessarily forbidden) by the state because expectationally, they produce collective "bads." They are more often nuisances, in a real sense, to the neighbors.

Family members have incentives to constrain one another's behavior in order to maximize the family's equity in such reputational assets as honesty, virtue, trustworthiness, community-mindedness, and so on, because "having a good name" will translate into increased latitude for the members of the family as they function in the larger community. The full value of reputation emerges only over time. Short-term players have very different incentives, an insight that is reflected, among other ways, by the insinuation of malevolence that goes with the term drifter. Private markets display the same horse-sense when they ordain discernibly higher rental rates for transients than for a long-term tenant of the same abode. It often makes more sense to tax nuisances expectationally than to try to punish only that subset of actors that ultimately proves to be miscreant. When deterrence is unacceptably costly, a "misbehavior premium" is pooled across all the individuals in a risk category. The unavoidable downside of such a procedure is that certain unoffending people will end up bearing added costs to which their behavior will not at all have contributed. . . .

Communities can be expected to prefer stable to unstable households because virtually everyone is benefitted if the prisoners' dilemma can be undone through repeat playing. Stable households have stronger incentives to support community-regarding and oppose community-dissipating behavior by their members. Contractual quasi-marital domestic households, because of their at-will characteristics, are more susceptible both to instability and the production of negative externalities. Society can be expected therefore to be somewhere between wary and disapproving of such arrangements, as, of course it traditionally has been.

III. Questioning Marriage and Its Centrality

A. What Is Marriage?

Whereas the previous section asked, "What is a family?", the following material asks, "What is marriage?" Marriage is at once religious and civil; private and public; an agreement and an institution; social and legal; and formal and functional. In the following cases, you should consider how these different facets of marriage recede or come to the fore in particular circumstances or disputes.

But first, consider your own hopes and expectations for marriage. Even though marriage is no longer the exclusive domain for family life, its salience as a cultural symbol remains high. While Americans have delayed marrying, most continue to want to marry, and their expectations of marriage are multifaceted.

Most people who marry have a ceremony (indeed, most states require one). Marriage ceremonies can take many different forms.[40] Consider the following selection of vows and descriptions of different wedding rituals. To what extent are these passages describing the same institution? Do these vows or pronouncements by an officiant reflect common expectations for marriage? Might they shape understandings of marriage? What is the relationship between religious vows or rituals and the civil law of marriage? Consider the fact that only 30 percent of Americans feel that having one's relationship recognized in a religious ceremony is a very important reason to marry.[41]

---

40. For a concise summary of different religious wedding traditions, see Malini Bhatia, Wedding Vows from Across Religions, Huffington Post (Feb. 19, 2017).

41. A.W. Geiger & Gretchen Livingston, 8 Facts About Love and Marriage in America, Pew Research Ctr. (Feb. 13, 2019).

THE BOOK OF COMMON PRAYER

The Celebrant, facing the people and the persons to be married, with the woman to the right and the man to the left, addresses the congregation and says

Dearly beloved: We have come together in the presence of God to witness and bless the joining together of this man and this woman in Holy Matrimony. The bond and covenant of marriage was established by God in creation, and our Lord Jesus Christ adorned this manner of life by his presence and first miracle at a wedding in Cana of Galilee. It signifies to us the mystery of the union between Christ and his Church, and Holy Scripture commends it to be honored among all people.

The union of husband and wife in heart, body, and mind is intended by God for their mutual joy; for the help and comfort given one another in prosperity and adversity; and, when it is God's will, for the procreation of children and their nurture in the knowledge and love of the Lord. Therefore marriage is not to be entered into unadvisedly or lightly, but reverently, deliberately, and in accordance with the purposes for which it was instituted by God.

Into this holy union *N.N.* and *N.N.* now come to be joined. If any of you can show just cause why they may not lawfully be married, speak now; or else for ever hold your peace.

The Celebrant says to the woman

N., will you have this man to be your husband; to live together in the covenant of marriage? Will you obey him and serve him, love him, comfort him, honor and keep him, in sickness and in health; and, forsaking all others, be faithful to him as long as you both shall live?

The Woman answers I will.

The Celebrant says to the man

N., will you have this woman to be your wife; to live together in the covenant of marriage? Will you love her, comfort her, honor and keep her, in sickness and in health; and, forsaking all others, be faithful to her as long as you both shall live?

The Man answers I will.

The Celebrant then addresses the congregation, saying

Now that *N.* and *N.* have given themselves to each other by solemn vows, with the joining of hands and the giving and receiving of a ring, I pronounce that they are man and wife, in the Name of the Father, and of the Son, and of the Holy Spirit. Those whom God has joined together let no one put asunder.

SOCIETY FOR ETHICAL CULTURE

The wedding ceremony reflects the humanistic values of Ethical Culture, and the joy and significance of the occasion. The focus is on the couple — their values, commitments and styles — and on the ideals of Ethical Culture as they pertain to marriage.

A successful way of giving the ceremony this personal dimension is by inviting the couple to collaborate with the Leader in its creation. Among elements that couples may include in the ceremony are the following: An initial greeting to a guest; brief talks by friends and relatives (no more than six is best); an instrumental or vocal piece as part of the ceremony; a ceremony within the ceremony such as lighting a single candle, drinking wine from a common goblet, etc.; composing and speaking vows that they have created; recommending concepts to be included by the Leader in his or her presentation.

Values are the foundation of an Ethical Culture wedding or commitment ceremony: respect for the worth and uniqueness of each person and the importance of making and keeping commitments are two key values that an Ethical Culture ceremony stresses.

Ethical Culture wedding ceremonies express a warm and simple dignity, with values and personalism that can be appreciated by all. However, it must be emphasized that Ethical Culture wedding ceremonies are humanistic ceremonies. It is therefore outside the scope of Ethical Culture to include prayer or theistic references. Ethnic and cultural expressions conveying the backgrounds of the couple may be factored into the ceremony. The professional association of Ethical Culture Leaders is committed to the legalization of gay and lesbian marriage.

Our ceremonies are often described as "spiritual but not religious" or even "non-religious" by the families and friends who attend the ceremonies. The words used in the ceremonies are focused on the commitments that the couple is making to each other, on the uniqueness of their responsibilities and future together in this world. With some narrow understanding of the word "religious" (focus on a Supreme Being, the presence of a priest or rabbi, taking place in a church, etc[.])[,] people might perceive an Ethical Culture ceremony to be "non–religious." However, Ethical Culture ceremonies, for legal purposes, are considered religious, not civil, ceremonies.

Ethical Societies consider themselves religious organizations, and their legal status as religious organizations has been confirmed in several court cases. There is no required creed or statement of belief in an Ethical Society, and there is considerable diversity of beliefs, particularly about metaphysical truths. The unifying factor for members of Ethical Societies is a commitment to ethical living: respect for all persons and the creation of a more humane world.[42]

---

42. This excerpt is a combination of text from the websites of two chapters of the Society for Ethical Culture. See The Ethical Culture Wedding Ceremony, Ethical Culture Soc'y of Bergen Cty. (Apr. 8, 2012), https://ethicalfocus.org/wedding-ceremony; and Your Commitment to Each Other: Weddings the Ethical Culture Way, N.Y. Soc'y for Ethical Culture, http://ethical.nyc/wp-content/uploads/2019/06/Your-Commitment-to-Each-Other-brochure.pdf.

MAHA ALKHATEEB, ISLAMIC MARRIAGE CONTRACTS (2012)

Once the couple agrees to pursue the marriage, the next step is to sign the Islamic marriage contract in an official ceremony frequently referred to as *nikah*. In traditional Islamic jurisprudence, the Islamic marriage contract solemnizes the physical connection between a man and woman, and serves as the foundation for their marriage. By signing the Islamic marriage contract, couples commit to nurturing an environment of love and mercy that is conducive to Islamic growth. Although the marriage contract falls under civil contract laws in traditional Islamic jurisprudence, it is considered to be a sacred covenant involving two consenting (*qubool*) parties making an agreement in the presence of two witnesses. Most schools of thought in traditional Islamic jurisprudence require women to have a guardian (*wali*), based upon the rationale that male family members will protect the interests of the bride. . . . In traditional Islamic jurisprudence, men proposing to women represented by *walis* must seek permission from the guardian to marry their daughter or female relative. The *wali* then asks the bride whether she consents to the marriage.

The marriage contract ceremony must include the consenting and competent couple (who are of marriageable age), the person solemnizing the marriage (typically an imam or *khateeb* in the U.S.), and two witnesses. . . . Before signing the contract the solemnizer asks the couple whether they consent and for the amount of the *mahr*. Under traditional Islamic law grooms must provide a *mahr*, or marital gift, for their wives (Qur'an 4:20). There is no minimum or maximum amount specified for the *mahr*, and the gift can range from cash to gold to property. The *mahr* can be given at the onset of marriage, during the marriage, or divided into immediate and deferred portions, and is payable upon demand, divorce, or the husband's death. . . .

In addition to determining the *mahr*, Islamic law allows stipulations to be added to the marriage contract. The traditional Islamic schools of jurisprudence are diverse in their legal opinions regarding the types of stipulations that can be included in the Islamic marriage contract. . . . [T]ypical stipulations tend to protect women's rights by bringing couples to an agreement regarding an equal right to initiate divorce, an agreement to remain monogamous, the right to education and work, equal division of domestic responsibilities, and living conditions.

NOTES AND QUESTIONS

1. *Marriage Vows.* The Book of Common Prayer is a liturgical book used by the Anglican Church. The book was first authorized for use by the Church of England in 1549. In 1979, the book was revised and updated with modern language.[43] What

---

43. Encyclopedia Britannica, Book of Common Prayer (2017).

are the key features of marriage as reflected in these vows? What would be a valid basis for a guest to raise an objection to the marriage? Would it be important to you to agree with all the components of a ceremony before choosing it for your wedding?

2.   *Marriage as Contract.* The Islamic marriage ceremony does not feature vows and instead focuses on the contractual aspect of marriage. As one commentator describes, "Unlike in some Christian denominations, marriage in Islam is not a 'sacrament' but a contractual agreement. . . . As in all contracts, both parties must agree to the terms, and the parties have the option to cancel the marriage plans if they cannot agree. This businesslike negotiation may seem odd under the traditional American concept of marriage involving two people who date, fall in love, and recite romantic vows."[44] Does the Islamic approach strike you as a more accurate description of the marital relation? What are the consequences of having the marriage ceremony reflect the contractual, more than the romantic, dimensions of marriage?

3.   *Solemnization.* Most states require a ceremony for a couple to be married. For example, Michigan law provides:

> In the solemnization of marriage, no particular form shall be required, except that the parties shall solemnly declare, in the presence of the person solemnizing the marriage and the attending witnesses, that they take each other as husband and wife; and in every case, there shall be at least 2 witnesses, besides the person solemnizing the marriage, present at the ceremony.[45]

Do you think it is important for a couple to have a ceremony? Why or why not? Does it matter whether the marriage is solemnized by a judge, religious figure, or Elvis impersonator in Las Vegas?

4.   *Witnesses.* Is there any particular significance to the fact that the vows contemplate (and most states require) people present for the wedding other than the bride and groom? What role do the witnesses play? Would a wedding without witnesses be any less legitimate?

B. Marriage at the Supreme Court

The following cases show how the Supreme Court approached marriage in the late nineteenth century and again in the 1960s. The first case involves the validity of a divorce granted to a husband by a legislature and the effect of that divorce on the

---

44. Tracie Rogalin Siddiqui, Interpretation of Islamic Marriage Contracts by American Courts, 41 Fam. L.Q. 639, 642 (2007).

45. Mich. Comp. Laws § 551.9 (2020); see also La. Civ. Code Ann. Art. 91 (2020); Ariz. Rev. Stat. Ann. § 25-111 (2020); N.C. Gen. Stat. § 51-1 (2020).

rights of his wife. The excerpt focuses not on the specific controversy, but instead on the Court's understanding of marriage. The second case involves the rights of married couples to use contraception. As you read the excerpts, consider how the Court conceptualizes the marital relationship and how judicial understandings of marriage have changed over time. In what ways is the Court responding to shifts in social attitudes toward marriage? How might the Court be shaping those attitudes? Does the Court's approach suggest why marriage receives preferential treatment in our society and in our law?

MAYNARD V. HILL
125 U.S. 190 (1888)

MR. JUSTICE FIELD . . . delivered the opinion of the court. . . .

Marriage, as creating the most important relation in life, as having more to do with the morals and civilization of a people than any other institution, has always been subject to the control of the legislature. That body prescribes the age at which parties may contract to marry, the procedure or form essential to constitute marriage, the duties and obligations it creates, its effects upon the property rights of both, present and prospective, and the acts which may constitute grounds for its dissolution. . . .

[W]hile marriage is often termed by text writers and in decisions of courts a civil contract — generally to indicate that it must be founded upon the agreement of the parties, and does not require any religious ceremony for its solemnization — it is something more than a mere contract. The consent of the parties is of course essential to its existence, but when the contract to marry is executed by the marriage, a relation between the parties is created which they cannot change. Other contracts may be modified, restricted, or enlarged, or entirely released upon the consent of the parties. Not so with marriage. The relation once formed, the law steps in and holds the parties to various obligations and liabilities. It is an institution, in the maintenance of which in its purity the public is deeply interested, for it is the foundation of the family and of society, without which there would be neither civilization nor progress. This view is well expressed by the Supreme Court of Maine in *Adams v. Palmer.* Said that court, speaking by Chief Justice Appleton:

> When the contracting parties have entered into the married state, they have not so much entered into a contract as into a new relation, the rights, duties, and obligations of which rest not upon their agreement, but upon the general law of the State, statutory or common, which defines and prescribes those rights, duties, and obligations. They are of law, not contract. It was of contract that the relation should be established, but, being established, the power of the parties as to its extent or duration is at an end. Their rights under it are determined by the will of the sovereign, as evidenced by law. They can

neither be modified nor changed by any agreement of parties. It is a relation for life, and the parties cannot terminate it at any shorter period by virtue of any contract they may make. The reciprocal rights arising from this relation, so long as it continues, are such as the law determines from time to time, and none other.

And again:

It is not, then, a contract within the meaning of the clause of the Constitution which prohibits the impairing the obligation of contracts. It is, rather, a social relation, like that of parent and child, the obligations of which arise not from the consent of concurring minds, but are the creation of the law itself; a relation the most important, as affecting the happiness of individuals, the first step from barbarism to incipient civilization, the purest tie of social life and the true basis of human progress.

And the Chief Justice cites in support of this view the case of *Maguire v. Maguire,* and *Ditson v. Ditson.* In the first of these, the Supreme Court of Kentucky said that marriage was more than a contract; that it was the most elementary and useful of all the social relations, was regulated and controlled by the sovereign power of the state, and could not, like mere contracts, be dissolved by the mutual consent of the contracting parties, but might be abrogated by the sovereign will whenever the public good, or justice to both parties, or either of the parties, would thereby be subserved; that being more than a contract, and depending especially upon the sovereign will, it was not embraced by the constitutional inhibition of legislative acts impairing the obligation of contracts. In the second case the Supreme Court of Rhode Island said that

marriage, in the sense in which it is dealt with by a decree of divorce, is not a contract, but one of the domestic relations. In strictness, though formed by contract, it signifies the relation of husband and wife, deriving both its rights and duties from a source higher than any contract of which the parties are capable, and as to these uncontrollable by any contract which they can make. When formed, this relation is no more a contract than "fatherhood" or "sonship" is a contract.

In *Wade v. Kalbfleisch,* the question came before the Court of Appeals of New York whether an action for breach of promise of marriage was an action upon a contract within the meaning of certain provisions of the Revised Statutes of that State, and in disposing of the question the court said:

The general statute, "that marriage, so far as its validity in law is concerned, shall continue in this State a civil contract, to which the consent of parties, capable in law of contracting, shall be essential," is not decisive of the question. This statute declares it a civil contract, as distinguished from a religious sacrament, and makes the element of consent necessary to its legal validity, but its nature, attributes, and distinguishing features it does not interfere with or attempt to define. It is declared a civil contract for certain purposes, but it is not thereby made synonymous with the word contract employed in the common law or statutes. . . . The relation is always regulated by government. It is more than a contract. It requires certain acts of the parties to constitute marriage independent of and beyond the contract. It partakes more of the character of an institution regulated and controlled by public authority, upon principles of public policy, for the benefit of the community. . . .

GRISWOLD V. CONNECTICUT
381 U.S. 479 (1965)

MR. JUSTICE DOUGLAS delivered the opinion of the Court.

Appellant Griswold is Executive Director of the Planned Parenthood League of Connecticut. Appellant Buxton is a licensed physician and a professor at the Yale Medical School who served as Medical Director for the League at its Center in New Haven — a center open and operating from November 1 to November 10, 1961, when appellants were arrested.

They gave information, instruction, and medical advice to *married persons* as to the means of preventing conception. They examined the wife and prescribed the best contraceptive device or material for her use. Fees were usually charged, although some couples were serviced free.

The statutes whose constitutionality is involved in this appeal are §§ 53-32 and 54-196 of the General Statutes of Connecticut (1958 rev.). The former provides:

> Any person who uses any drug, medicinal article or instrument for the purpose of preventing conception shall be fined not less than fifty dollars or imprisoned not less than sixty days nor more than one year or be both fined and imprisoned.

Section 54-196 provides:

> Any person who assists, abets, counsels, causes, hires or commands another to commit any offense may be prosecuted and punished as if he were the principal offender.

The appellants were found guilty as accessories and fined $100 each. . . .

Coming to the merits, we are met with a wide range of questions that implicate the Due Process Clause of the Fourteenth Amendment. Overtones of some arguments suggest that *Lochner v. New York*, 198 U.S. 45 (1905), should be our guide. But we decline that invitation. . . . We do not sit as a super-legislature to determine the wisdom, need, and propriety of laws that touch economic problems, business affairs, or social conditions. This law, however, operates directly on an intimate relation of husband and wife and their physician's role in one aspect of that relation. . . .

[T]he right of privacy which presses for recognition here is a legitimate one.

The present case, then, concerns a relationship lying within the zone of privacy created by several fundamental constitutional guarantees. And it concerns a law which, in forbidding the *use* of contraceptives rather than regulating their manufacture or sale, seeks to achieve its goals by means having a maximum destructive impact upon that relationship. Such a law cannot stand in light of the familiar principle, so often applied by this Court, that a "governmental purpose to control or prevent activities constitutionally subject to state regulation may not be achieved by means which sweep unnecessarily broadly and thereby invade the area of protected freedoms." Would we allow the police to search the sacred precincts of marital bedrooms for telltale signs of the use of contraceptives? The very idea is repulsive to the notions of privacy surrounding the marriage relationship.

We deal with a right of privacy older than the Bill of Rights — older than our political parties, older than our school system. Marriage is a coming together for better or for worse, hopefully enduring, and intimate to the degree of being sacred. It is an association that promotes a way of life, not causes; a harmony in living, not political faiths; a bilateral loyalty, not commercial or social projects. Yet it is an association for as noble a purpose as any involved in our prior decisions.

Reversed.

MR. JUSTICE GOLDBERG, whom THE CHIEF JUSTICE and MR. JUSTICE BRENNAN join, concurring.

I agree with the Court that Connecticut's birth-control law unconstitutionally intrudes upon the right of marital privacy. . . .

The Connecticut statutes here involved deal with a particularly important and sensitive area of privacy — that of the marital relation and the marital home. . . .

I agree with Mr. Justice Harlan's statement in his dissenting opinion in *Poe v. Ullman*, 367 U.S. 497, 551–552:

> Certainly the safeguarding of the home does not follow merely from the sanctity of property rights. The home derives its pre-eminence as the seat of family life. And the integrity of that life is something so fundamental that it has been found to draw to its protection the principles of more than one explicitly granted Constitutional right. . . . Of this whole "private realm of family life" it is difficult to imagine what is more private or more intimate than a husband and wife's marital relations.

The entire fabric of the Constitution and the purposes that clearly underlie its specific guarantees demonstrate that the rights to marital privacy and to marry and raise a family are of similar order and magnitude as the fundamental rights specifically protected.

Although the Constitution does not speak in so many words of the right of privacy in marriage, I cannot believe that it offers these fundamental rights no protection. The fact that no particular provision of the Constitution explicitly forbids the State from disrupting the traditional relation of the family — a relation as old and as fundamental as our entire civilization — surely does not show that the Government was meant to have the power to do so. Rather, as the Ninth Amendment expressly recognizes, there are fundamental personal rights such as this one, which are protected from abridgment by the Government though not specifically mentioned in the Constitution. . . .

[I]t should be said of the Court's holding today that it in no way interferes with a State's proper regulation of sexual promiscuity or misconduct. As my Brother Harlan so well stated in his dissenting opinion in *Poe v. Ullman.*

> Adultery, homosexuality and the like are sexual intimacies which the State forbids . . . but the intimacy of husband and wife is necessarily an essential and accepted feature of the institution of marriage, an institution which the State not only must allow, but which always and in every age it has fostered and protected. It is one thing when the State exerts its power either to forbid extra-marital sexuality . . . or to say who may marry, but it is quite another when, having acknowledged a marriage and the intimacies inherent in it, it undertakes to regulate by means of the criminal law the details of that intimacy. . . .

Mr. Justice White, concurring in the judgment. . . .

[T]his is not the first time this Court has had occasion to articulate that the liberty entitled to protection under the Fourteenth Amendment includes the right "to marry, establish a home and bring up children," *Meyer v. Nebraska*, 262 U.S. 390, 399 (1923), and "the liberty . . . to direct the upbringing and education of children," *Pierce v. Society of Sisters*, 268 U.S. 510, 534 (1925), and that these are among "the basic civil rights of man." *Skinner v. Oklahoma*, 316 U.S. 535, 541 (1942). These decisions affirm that there is a "realm of family life which the state cannot enter" without substantial justification. *Prince v. Massachusetts*, 321 U.S. 158, 166 (1944). Surely the right invoked in this case, to be free of regulation of the intimacies of the marriage relationship, "come[s] to this Court with a momentum for respect lacking when appeal is made to liberties which derive merely from shifting economic arrangements." *Kovacs v. Cooper*, 336 U.S. 77, 95 (1949) (opinion of Frankfurter, J.).

The Connecticut anti-contraceptive statute . . . forbids all married persons the right to use birth-control devices, regardless of whether their use is dictated by considerations of family planning, health, or indeed even of life itself. The anti-use statute, together with the general aiding and abetting statute, prohibits doctors from affording advice to married persons on proper and effective methods of birth control. . . .

There is no serious contention that Connecticut thinks the use of artificial or external methods of contraception immoral or unwise in itself, or that the anti-use statute is founded upon any policy of promoting population expansion. Rather, the statute is said to serve the State's policy against all forms of promiscuous or illicit sexual relationships, be they premarital or extramarital, concededly a permissible and legitimate legislative goal. . . .

[O]ne is rather hard pressed to explain how the ban on use by married persons in any way prevents use of such devices by persons engaging in illicit sexual relations and thereby contributes to the State's policy against such relationships. Neither the state courts nor the State before the bar of this Court has tendered such an explanation. It is purely fanciful to believe that the broad proscription on use facilitates discovery of use by persons engaging in a prohibited relationship or for some other reason makes such use more unlikely and thus can be supported by any sort of administrative consideration. Perhaps the theory is that the flat ban on use prevents married people from possessing contraceptives and without the ready availability of such devices for use in the marital relationship, there will be no or less temptation to use them in extramarital ones. This reasoning rests on the premise that married people will comply with the ban in regard to their marital relationship, notwithstanding total nonenforcement in this context and apparent nonenforcibility, but will not comply with criminal statutes prohibiting extramarital affairs and the anti-use statute in respect to illicit sexual relationships, a premise whose validity has not been demonstrated and whose intrinsic validity is not very evident. At most the broad ban is of marginal utility to the declared objective. A statute limiting its prohibition on use to persons engaging in the prohibited relationship would serve the end posited by Connecticut in the same way, and with the same effectiveness, or ineffectiveness, as the broad anti-use statute under attack in this case. I find nothing in this record justifying the sweeping scope of this statute, with its telling effect on the freedoms of married persons, and therefore conclude that it deprives such persons of liberty without due process of law.

MR. JUSTICE BLACK, with whom MR. JUSTICE STEWART joins, dissenting. . . .

The Court talks about a constitutional "right of privacy" as though there is some constitutional provision or provisions forbidding any law ever to be passed which might abridge the "privacy" of individuals. But there is not. There are, of course, guarantees in certain specific constitutional provisions which are designed in part to protect privacy at certain times and places with respect to certain activities. . . .

"Privacy" is a broad, abstract and ambiguous concept which can easily be shrunken in meaning but which can also, on the other hand, easily be interpreted as a constitutional ban against many things other than searches and seizures. I have expressed the view many times that First Amendment freedoms, for example, have suffered from a failure of the courts to stick to the simple language of the First Amendment in construing it, instead of invoking multitudes of words substituted for those the Framers used. For these reasons I get nowhere in this case by talk about a constitutional "right of privacy" as an emanation from one or more constitutional provisions. I like my privacy as well as the next one, but I am nevertheless compelled to admit that government has a right to invade it unless prohibited by some specific constitutional provision. For these reasons I cannot agree with the Court's judgment and the reasons it gives for holding this Connecticut law unconstitutional. . . .

MR. JUSTICE STEWART, whom MR. JUSTICE BLACK joins, dissenting.

Since 1879 Connecticut has had on its books a law which forbids the use of contraceptives by anyone. I think this is an uncommonly silly law. As a practical matter, the law is obviously unenforceable, except in the oblique context of the present case. As a philosophical matter, I believe the use of contraceptives in the relationship of marriage should be left to personal and private choice, based upon each individual's moral, ethical, and religious beliefs. As a matter of social policy, I think professional counsel about methods of birth control should be available to all, so that each individual's choice can be meaningfully made. But we are not asked in this case to say whether we think this law is unwise, or even asinine. We are asked to hold that it violates the United States Constitution. And that I cannot do. . . .

I can find no such general right of privacy in the Bill of Rights, in any other part of the Constitution, or in any case ever before decided by this Court. . . .

NOTES AND QUESTIONS

1. *Contract Versus Status. Maynard* famously raises the issue of how to understand marriage: as contract or status? Which is it? Or is it both? Why does this distinction matter?

2. *What Is the Marriage Contract?* What do you think you are agreeing to when you agree to marry? Consider this question further when you explore the materials in Chapters 3 and 5. If the government establishes the rights and obligations that inhere in marriage, which of these, if any, should the parties be allowed to change? Which, if any, would you want to change? Why should you be able to do so, or why not?

3. *Ending Marriage.* If individuals enter marriage with the expectation that it is a lifelong commitment, why should they be allowed to end the marriage? What grounds should justify ending the marriage? We explore these questions in Chapter 4.

4. *Gender and Marriage.* How does the Court's understanding of gender — and specifically the roles of women and men — shape understandings of marriage in *Maynard* and *Griswold*? How might married women's right to use contraception relate to gender equality? What is the significance of the fact that condoms were widely available in Connecticut at the time *Griswold* was decided?

5. *Married Couples Versus Unmarried Individuals. Griswold* suggests that some aspects of the marital relationship are beyond state regulation. To whom does this right to privacy attach? Each individual spouse or the couple as a unit? Why

should married couples have a special right to privacy? Is the interest of married persons in using contraception weightier than the interest of unmarried persons? Eventually, the Court extended the right to use contraception to unmarried individuals in *Eisenstadt v. Baird*, which is excerpted in Chapter 2.[46] How would you assess the government's interest in regulating unmarried persons as opposed to married persons?

6. *Marriage and Children.* Many associate marriage with childrearing. Is procreation a core purpose of marriage? Does *Griswold* have anything to say about this? Consider this question further as you read Chapters 2 and 3.

C. Contemporary Litigation over Marriage

In recent years, the greatest controversy over marriage's meaning has grown out of conflict over the right of same-sex couples to marry. The following cases represent critical precedents on the constitutional regulation of marriage and same-sex couples (an issue considered in detail in Chapter 2). But the excerpts here focus simply on how courts think about marriage. As you read, consider the following questions: What is the purpose of marriage? Who decides what marriage means? How has marriage changed over time? What is the government's interest in defining marriage in a particular way?

PERRY V. SCHWARZENEGGER
704 F. Supp. 2d 921 (N.D. Cal. 2010)

VAUGHN R. WALKER, CHIEF JUDGE.

Plaintiffs challenge a November 2008 voter-enacted amendment to the California Constitution ("Proposition 8" or "Prop 8"). In its entirety, Proposition 8 provides: "Only marriage between a man and a woman is valid or recognized in California." Plaintiffs allege that Proposition 8 deprives them of due process and of equal protection of the laws. . . .

Plaintiffs are two couples. Kristin Perry and Sandra Stier reside in Berkeley, California and raise four children together. Jeffrey Zarrillo and Paul Katami reside in Burbank, California. Plaintiffs seek to marry their partners and have been denied marriage licenses by their respective county authorities on the basis of Proposition 8. No party contended, and no evidence at trial suggested, that the county authorities had any ground to deny marriage licenses to plaintiffs other than Proposition 8.

---

46. 405 U.S. 438 (1972).

Having considered the trial evidence and the arguments of counsel, the court . . . finds that Proposition 8 is unconstitutional and that its enforcement must be enjoined. . . .

All four plaintiffs testified that they wished to marry their partners, and all four gave similar reasons. Zarrillo wishes to marry Katami because marriage has a "special meaning" that would alter their relationships with family and others. Zarrillo described daily struggles that arise because he is unable to marry Katami or refer to Katami as his husband. Zarrillo described an instance when he and Katami went to a bank to open a joint account, and "it was certainly an awkward situation walking to the bank and saying, 'My partner and I want to open a joint bank account,' and hearing, you know, 'Is it a business account? A partnership?' It would just be a lot easier to describe the situation — might not make it less awkward for those individuals, but it would make it — crystalize it more by being able to say . . . 'My husband and I are here to open a bank account.'" To Katami, marriage to Zarrillo would solidify their relationship and provide them the foundation they seek to raise a family together, explaining that for them, "the timeline has always been marriage first, before family."

Perry testified that marriage would provide her what she wants most in life: a stable relationship with Stier, the woman she loves and with whom she has built a life and a family. To Perry, marriage would provide access to the language to describe her relationship with Stier: "I'm a 45-year-old woman. I have been in love with a woman for 10 years and I don't have a word to tell anybody about that." Stier explained that marrying Perry would make them feel included "in the social fabric." Marriage would be a way to tell "our friends, our family, our society, our community, our parents . . . and each other that this is a lifetime commitment . . . we are not girlfriends. We are not partners. We are married."

Plaintiffs and proponents presented expert testimony on the meaning of marriage. Historian Nancy Cott testified about the public institution of marriage and the state's interest in recognizing and regulating marriages. . . . The state's primary purpose in regulating marriage is to create stable households.

Think tank founder David Blankenhorn testified that marriage is "a socially-approved sexual relationship between a man and a woman" with a primary purpose to "regulate filiation." Blankenhorn testified that others hold to an alternative and, to Blankenhorn, conflicting definition of marriage: "a private adult commitment" that focuses on "the tender feelings that the spouses have for one another." To Blankenhorn, marriage is either a socially approved sexual relationship between a man and a woman for the purpose of bearing and raising children who are biologically related to both spouses or a private relationship between two consenting adults. . . .

Psychologist Letitia Anne Peplau testified that couples benefit both physically and economically when they are married. Peplau testified that those benefits would accrue to same-sex as well as opposite-sex married couples. To Peplau, the desire of same-sex couples to marry illustrates the health of the institution of marriage and not, as Blankenhorn testified, the weakening of marriage. Economist Lee Badgett provided evidence that same-sex couples would benefit economically if they were able to marry and that same-sex marriage would have no adverse effect on the institution of marriage or on opposite-sex couples. . . .

FINDINGS OF FACT

Having considered the evidence presented at trial, the credibility of the witnesses and the legal arguments presented by counsel, the court now makes the following findings of fact. . . .

19. Marriage in the United States has always been a civil matter. Civil authorities may permit religious leaders to solemnize marriages but not to determine who may enter or leave a civil marriage. Religious leaders may determine independently whether to recognize a civil marriage or divorce but that recognition or lack thereof has no effect on the relationship under state law. . . .

21. California, like every other state, has never required that individuals entering a marriage be willing or able to procreate. . . .

26. Under coverture, a woman's legal and economic identity was subsumed by her husband's upon marriage. The husband was the legal head of household. Coverture is no longer part of the marital bargain. . . .

27. Marriage between a man and a woman was traditionally organized based on presumptions of a division of labor along gender lines. Men were seen as suited for certain types of work and women for others. Women were seen as suited to raise children and men were seen as suited to provide for the family. . . .

28. The development of no-fault divorce laws made it simpler for spouses to end marriages and allowed spouses to define their own roles within a marriage. . . .

32. California has eliminated marital obligations based on the gender of the spouse. Regardless of their sex or gender, marital partners share the same obligations to one another and to their dependents. As a result of Proposition 8, California nevertheless requires that a marriage consist of one man and one woman. . . .

34. Marriage is the state recognition and approval of a couple's choice to live with each other, to remain committed to one another and to form a household based on their own feelings about one another and to join in an economic partnership and support one another and any dependents. . . .

36. States and the federal government channel benefits, rights and responsibilities through marital status. Marital status affects immigration and citizenship, tax policy, property and inheritance rules and social benefit programs. . . .

37. Marriage creates economic support obligations between consenting adults and for their dependents. . . .

38. Marriage benefits both spouses by promoting physical and psychological health. Married individuals are less likely to engage in behaviors detrimental to

health, like smoking or drinking heavily. Married individuals live longer on average than unmarried individuals. . . .

39. Material benefits, legal protections and social support resulting from marriage can increase wealth and improve psychological well-being for married spouses. . . .

40. The long-term nature of marriage allows spouses to specialize their labor and encourages spouses to increase household efficiency by dividing labor to increase productivity. . . .

41. The tangible and intangible benefits of marriage flow to a married couple's children. . . .

52. Domestic partnerships lack the social meaning associated with marriage, and marriage is widely regarded as the definitive expression of love and commitment in the United States. . . .

54. The availability of domestic partnership does not provide gays and lesbians with a status equivalent to marriage because the cultural meaning of marriage and its associated benefits are intentionally withheld from same-sex couples in domestic partnerships. . . .

56. The children of same-sex couples benefit when their parents can marry. . . .

58. Proposition 8 places the force of law behind stigmas against gays and lesbians, including: gays and lesbians do not have intimate relationships similar to heterosexual couples; gays and lesbians are not as good as heterosexuals; and gay and lesbian relationships do not deserve the full recognition of society. . . .

60. Proposition 8 reserves the most socially valued form of relationship (marriage) for opposite-sex couples. . . .

61. Proposition 8 amends the California Constitution to codify distinct and unique roles for men and women in marriage. . . .

66. Proposition 8 increases costs and decreases wealth for same-sex couples because of increased tax burdens, decreased availability of health insurance and higher transactions costs to secure rights and obligations typically associated with marriage. Domestic partnership reduces but does not eliminate these costs. . . .

67. Proposition 8 singles out gays and lesbians and legitimates their unequal treatment. Proposition 8 perpetuates the stereotype that gays and lesbians are incapable of forming long-term loving relationships and that gays and lesbians are not good parents. . . .

OBERGEFELL V. HODGES
135 S. Ct. 2584 (2015)

JUSTICE KENNEDY delivered the opinion of the Court.

The Constitution promises liberty to all within its reach, a liberty that includes certain specific rights that allow persons, within a lawful realm, to define and express their identity. The petitioners in these cases seek to find that liberty by marrying someone of the same sex and having their marriages deemed lawful on the same terms and conditions as marriages between persons of the opposite sex. . . .

From their beginning to their most recent page, the annals of human history reveal the transcendent importance of marriage. The lifelong union of a man and a woman always has promised nobility and dignity to all persons, without regard to their station in life. Marriage is sacred to those who live by their religions and offers unique fulfillment to those who find meaning in the secular realm. Its dynamic allows two people to find a life that could not be found alone, for a marriage becomes greater than just the two persons. Rising from the most basic human needs, marriage is essential to our most profound hopes and aspirations.

The centrality of marriage to the human condition makes it unsurprising that the institution has existed for millennia and across civilizations. Since the dawn of history, marriage has transformed strangers into relatives, binding families and societies together. Confucius taught that marriage lies at the foundation of government. This wisdom was echoed centuries later and half a world away by Cicero, who wrote, "The first bond of society is marriage; next, children; and then the family." There are untold references to the beauty of marriage in religious and philosophical texts spanning time, cultures, and faiths, as well as in art and literature in all their forms. It is fair and necessary to say these references were based on the understanding that marriage is a union between two persons of the opposite sex.

That history is the beginning of these cases. The respondents say it should be the end as well. To them, it would demean a timeless institution if the concept and lawful status of marriage were extended to two persons of the same sex. Marriage, in their view, is by its nature a gender-differentiated union of man and woman. This view long has been held — and continues to be held — in good faith by reasonable and sincere people here and throughout the world.

The petitioners acknowledge this history but contend that these cases cannot end there. Were their intent to demean the revered idea and reality of marriage, the petitioners' claims would be of a different order. But that is neither their purpose nor their submission. To the contrary, it is the enduring importance of marriage that underlies the petitioners' contentions. This, they say, is their whole point. Far from seeking to devalue marriage, the petitioners seek it for themselves because of their respect — and need — for its privileges and responsibilities. And their immutable nature dictates that same-sex marriage is their only real path to this profound commitment. . . .

The ancient origins of marriage confirm its centrality, but it has not stood in isolation from developments in law and society. The history of marriage is one of both continuity and change. That institution — even as confined to opposite-sex relations — has evolved over time.

For example, marriage was once viewed as an arrangement by the couple's parents based on political, religious, and financial concerns; but by the time of the Nation's founding it was understood to be a voluntary contract between a man and a woman. As the role and status of women changed, the institution further evolved.

Under the centuries-old doctrine of coverture, a married man and woman were treated by the State as a single, male-dominated legal entity. As women gained legal, political, and property rights, and as society began to understand that women have their own equal dignity, the law of coverture was abandoned. These and other developments in the institution of marriage over the past centuries were not mere superficial changes. Rather, they worked deep transformations in its structure, affecting aspects of marriage long viewed by many as essential. . . .

Justice Alito, with whom Justice Scalia and Justice Thomas join, dissenting.

Until the federal courts intervened, the American people were engaged in a debate about whether their States should recognize same-sex marriage. The question in these cases, however, is not what States *should* do about same-sex marriage but whether the Constitution answers that question for them. It does not. The Constitution leaves that question to be decided by the people of each State. . . .

For today's majority, it does not matter that the right to same-sex marriage lacks deep roots or even that it is contrary to long-established tradition. The Justices in the majority claim the authority to confer constitutional protection upon that right simply because they believe that it is fundamental. . . .

Noting that marriage is a fundamental right, the majority argues that a State has no valid reason for denying that right to same-sex couples. This reasoning is dependent upon a particular understanding of the purpose of civil marriage. Although the Court expresses the point in loftier terms, its argument is that the fundamental purpose of marriage is to promote the well-being of those who choose to marry. Marriage provides emotional fulfillment and the promise of support in times of need. And by benefiting persons who choose to wed, marriage indirectly benefits society because persons who live in stable, fulfilling, and supportive relationships make better citizens. It is for these reasons, the argument goes, that States encourage and formalize marriage, confer special benefits on married persons, and also impose some special obligations. This understanding of the States' reasons for recognizing marriage enables the majority to argue that same-sex marriage serves the States' objectives in the same way as opposite-sex marriage.

This understanding of marriage, which focuses almost entirely on the happiness of persons who choose to marry, is shared by many people today, but it is not the traditional one. For millennia, marriage was inextricably linked to the one thing that only an opposite-sex couple can do: procreate.

Adherents to different schools of philosophy use different terms to explain why society should formalize marriage and attach special benefits and obligations to persons who marry. Here, the States defending their adherence to the traditional understanding of marriage have explained their position using the pragmatic vocabulary that characterizes most American political discourse. Their basic argument is that States formalize and promote marriage, unlike other fulfilling human relationships, in order to encourage potentially procreative conduct to take place within a lasting unit that has long been thought to provide the best atmosphere for raising children. They thus argue that there are reasonable secular grounds for restricting marriage to opposite-sex couples.

If this traditional understanding of the purpose of marriage does not ring true to all ears today, that is probably because the tie between marriage and procreation has frayed. Today, for instance, more than 40% of all children in this country are born to unmarried women. This development undoubtedly is both a cause and a result of changes in our society's understanding of marriage.

While, for many, the attributes of marriage in 21st-century America have changed, those States that do not want to recognize same-sex marriage have not yet given up on the traditional understanding. They worry that by officially abandoning the older understanding, they may contribute to marriage's further decay. It is far beyond the outer reaches of this Court's authority to say that a State may not adhere to the understanding of marriage that has long prevailed, not just in this country and others with similar cultural roots, but also in a great variety of countries and cultures all around the globe.

NOTES AND QUESTIONS

1. *What Is Marriage?* The *Perry* court relied on expert testimony — from historians and social scientists — to make findings of fact about the nature of marriage. Do you think the meaning of marriage is susceptible to this type of fact finding? Do the opinions of the expert witnesses and the conclusions the court draws from those opinions match your views about marriage? Whose views should matter when judges are asked to adjudicate claims like those at issue in *Perry*?

2. *Different Views of Marriage.* Both the district court in *Perry* and the Supreme Court in *Obergefell* understood marriage as an institution that can include both different-sex and same-sex couples. What are the core attributes of this understanding of marriage? In his dissent in *Obergefell*, Justice Alito contrasted two different views of marriage: a modern, revisionist view focused on the romantic and committed relationship of spouses and a traditional, conjugal view focused on channeling procreative conduct into stable unions for childrearing. Is his characterization of the majority's approach to marriage accurate? Did same-sex couples in *Perry* and *Obergefell* advance the modern view that Justice Alito describes?

3. *Marriage, Children, and Same-Sex Couples.* Is an approach to marriage that includes same-sex couples necessarily adult-centered? Or may it also be child-centered? If so, what is the view of procreation and childrearing embedded in an approach to marriage that includes same-sex couples? Consider this perspective:

> Over the many years of litigation leading up to *Obergefell*, child-centered arguments constituted the central justification for those defending same-sex marriage bans. . . .

LGBT advocates responded with child-centered arguments of their own. Same-sex couples, they argued, are similarly situated to different-sex couples specifically with regard to parenting. The commonality emerges not from biology or gender, but from functional and intentional relationships. Just like different-sex couples, same-sex couples have and raise children.

In considering same-sex couples' claims, courts faced a choice between competing models of parenthood — one prioritizing biological, dual-gender childrearing, and the other focusing on chosen, functional families. In accepting same-sex couples' claims, courts validated the latter model, and thereby centered a model of parenthood that includes same-sex-couple-headed families.[47]

4. *The Demographics of Same-Sex Couples.* According to the Williams Institute, a UCLA-based research center that focuses on LGBT law and policy, just a few months after *Obergefell*, nearly half of all same-sex couples were married.[48] A pre-*Obergefell* Williams Institute report found that married same-sex couples are more likely to be female and that married female couples are more likely than their male counterparts to be raising children. The report also found that although married and unmarried different-sex couples are raising children at similar rates, married same-sex couples are more likely to be raising children than unmarried same-sex couples.[49] What do you think explains this difference?

D. Should the State Sponsor Marriage?

LAW COMMISSION OF CANADA, BEYOND CONJUGALITY: RECOGNIZING AND SUPPORTING CLOSE PERSONAL ADULT RELATIONSHIPS (2001)

The Legal Organization of Personal Relationships . . .

[W]e set out to address the nature of the state's role and interest in assigning rights and responsibilities within committed personal adult relationships. . . .

The Role of the State

Many people long for stability and certainty in their personal relationships just as they do in other areas of their lives, at work or in business. The state does have

---

47. Douglas NeJaime, Marriage Equality and the New Parenthood, 129 Harv. L. Rev. 1185, 1236–37 (2016).

48. See Gary J. Gates & Taylor N.T. Brown, Williams Inst., Marriage and Sex-Sex Couples After Obergefell 1 (Nov. 2015).

49. See Gary J. Gates, Williams Inst., Demographics of Married and Unmarried Same-Sex Couples: Analyses of the 2013 American Community Survey 1–2 (March 2015).

a role in providing legal mechanisms for people to be able to achieve such private understandings. It must provide an orderly framework in which people can express their commitment to each other and voluntarily assume a range of legal rights and obligations.

In attempting to provide for adequate legal structures or mechanisms that may support the relationships that people develop, the state must respect . . . equality, autonomy and choice.

For a long time, the state has focused on marriage as the vehicle of choice for adults to express their commitment. Marriage provides parties with the ability to state publicly and officially their intentions toward one another. . . . It also provides for certainty and stability since the marriage cannot be terminated without legal procedures. Marriage as a legal tool demonstrates characteristics of voluntariness, stability, certainty and publicity that made it attractive as a model to regulate relationships.

But it is no longer a sufficient model to respond to the variety of relationships that exist in Canada today. Whether we look at older people living with their adult children, adults with disabilities living with their caregivers, or siblings cohabiting in the same residence, the marriage model is inadequate. Some of these other relationships are also characterized by emotional and economic interdependence, mutual care and concern and the expectation of some duration. All of these personal adult relationships could also benefit from legal frameworks to support people's need for certainty and stability.

Throughout our consultations, it became clear that simply allowing people the option to enter into private contracts, such as cohabitation agreements or caregiving arrangements, was insufficient because it did not always have the official or public aspect that was needed, nor did it offer sufficient guarantee of certainty. In addition, the lack of official record of such private arrangements prevents the efficient administration of laws and programs where relationships could be relevant. . . .

We must therefore examine ways for the state to offer all Canadians appropriate legal frameworks that respond to their needs for certainty and stability in their personal relationships. . . . These legal frameworks must keep pace with the ways in which adults organize their lives.

It is in this context that one must look at the mechanisms currently developed to allow Canadians to organize their private lives.

Legal Frameworks for Personal Relationships

In this section, we review four legal models of regulation of personal relationships. . . .

Private Law

People are always at liberty to express their commitments through contracts. . . . Expressly or implicitly, people who reside together, who help each other or who have an intimate relationship organize their lives around shared expectations that are more or less well defined. When such expectations are not fulfilled, they may seek remedy in court under various theories of private law, unjust enrichment, constructive trust, or the creation of an implicit partnership, to name a few.

Parties may choose to state explicitly in a written document their shared expectations and demand execution of such a contractual arrangement through the civil courts. . . .

But it is a tool beyond the reach of many people. Leaving the parties to design their own contractual or private law arrangements imposes too high a burden on people who do not have time, energy or the requisite knowledge to do so. The possible involvement of a lawyer to design such arrangements is also too costly or inconvenient for the majority of people. Furthermore, there is also a concern that the stronger or wealthier party may impose unfavourable terms on the poorer or weaker party.

Although contracts will continue to remain an important method for individuals to determine their mutual rights and obligations, they are not a sufficient remedy in and of themselves. The contractual model may respect the value of autonomy but often falls short of fulfilling other values such as equality or efficiency. . . .

In the absence of a contract, people will also continue to use the courts and private law remedies. . . . However, this mechanism, used in the aftermath of a relationship, is uncertain, expensive and requires that people be able to afford and endure costly and difficult court proceedings. . . .

Ascription

Ascription refers to treating unmarried cohabitants as if they were married, without their having taken any positive action to be legally recognized. In most Canadian provinces and at the federal level, governments have moved to extend policies and legislation aimed at married couples to common-law partners. For example, the *Modernization of Benefits and Obligations Act* extended to both same-sex and opposite-sex couples living in a conjugal relationship for at least one year, a wide array of rights and obligations previously available only to married couples.

Ascription is generally heralded as a way for governments to prevent the risks of exploitation inherent in a contractual model. It imposes a set of obligations on people in conjugal relationships which are presumed to correspond to the expectations of the majority of people. It has hence allowed governments to respond to the changes in Canadian society, particularly with respect to the regulation of the relationships of unmarried conjugal relationships. It also supplies a default arrangement for couples who have not provided for any arrangements and who would otherwise have to resort to cumbersome traditional private law models.

However, ascription as a model has limits. First, it is a blunt policy tool in that it treats all conjugal relationships alike, irrespective of the level of emotional or economic interdependency that they may present. Second, it infringes upon the value of autonomy. Although people may opt out of certain statutory provisions governing their relationships, they are not always aware of this possibility. In addition, ascription is not the best way to respond to the needs of non-conjugal relationships. . . . Governments . . . should also provide Canadians with appropriate tools to define for themselves the terms of their relationships. . . .

Registration

Recently, there has been a move toward the creation of a new status, often called registered partnership (or Registered Domestic Partnership or RDP). . . . Often RDPs were introduced as a means of recognizing same-sex relationships. However, as these schemes developed in other jurisdictions, they have been extended to also allow opposite-sex couples to register their relationships. . . .

The objective of these registration schemes is to provide an alternative way for the state to recognize and support close personal relationships. When people register their relationships, they are then included within a range of rights and responsibilities often similar to marriage. It is a regime that has begun to develop as a parallel to marriage. . . .

First, a registration scheme is worthy of consideration because it would enable a broader range of relationships to be recognized. It would therefore provide both conjugal and non-conjugal unions with a way to formalize their relationship and to voluntarily assume rights and responsibilities toward each other. In this way, a registration system would promote the equality of non-conjugal relationships. The second major advantage of a registration scheme is that it affirms the autonomy and choices of Canadians in their close personal relationships. There is value in encouraging people to make their relationship commitments clear and in recognizing the choices that people make in their close personal relationships. . . .

A registration system may also promote the values of equality and autonomy within relationships without compromising the value of privacy. The ascription model described above, if it were to use more functional definitions, would require that governments examine individual relationships to decide whether they fit the definition. It is an approach that necessarily involves some degree of invasion of privacy. A registration scheme, on the other hand, by leaving the choice entirely up to the individuals within relationships and then respecting that choice, provides a way of recognizing conjugal and non-conjugal relationships without compromising the values of autonomy or privacy. . . .

Designing a Registration Scheme

There are many challenging questions that governments will have to address in deciding how a registration scheme should be designed and implemented. . . .

Formal Attributes

The first question that must be addressed in designing a registration scheme involves its formal attributes, that is, who may register? . . .

One of the greatest advantages of a registration scheme is that it provides an opportunity to recognize the formal commitment of individuals in any relationship. There is no reason for governments to restrict a registration scheme to conjugal couples or to same-sex couples or, indeed, only to couples. . . .

A few jurisdictions have introduced registration schemes which include non-conjugal couples. . . .

[A] number of jurisdictions have considered whether registrations should be limited to couples who live together. . . . In our view, there is no reason to impose a residential requirement on registrations. There is no similar restriction on marriage: married couples do not have to live together for the marriage to be valid. . . .

Another question that governments will have to address is how registrations should be terminable; that is, how can partners decide to end their registration? In our view, registrations should be terminable by mutual agreement. . . . Furthermore, given that married spouses can end their marriage unilaterally by making an application for divorce after living separate and apart for one year, it would not be justifiable to impose a more rigorous standard on domestic partners. Partners in a registered relationships [sic] should similarly be able to register a dissolution of their registration. . . .

Legal Implications of Registrations

The legal consequences of registration might be limited to the private rights and responsibilities within the relationship. It could involve such issues as property and support obligations both during and after the relationship. It could involve determinations for care arrangements, consent to treatment or other aspects of the relationship. The commitment of entering into a registration would be about the voluntary assumption of mutual responsibilities. It would be about clarifying this commitment of mutual responsibility in law, both for the parties themselves and for potentially interested third parties. . . .

[T]he number of people who choose to register their relationships may not be significant. It also seems clear that registration schemes could not completely replace the ascription model which has taken root in Canadian law, particularly when the care of children is involved. . . .

Marriage

[This section provides] an assessment as to whether our marriage laws continue to meet the needs of our evolving society. . . .

We begin with a fundamental question as to whether there needs to be marriage laws at all. One could imagine that in order to achieve equality toward the range of relationships that exist in Canada, the state could simply institute a system of registration as recommended above that could replace marriage, for all legal purposes. What would be the implications of such a model? Would it better serve the objectives of the state?

Registration Instead of Marriage

Creating a registration scheme that would permit all relationships, conjugal and other, to benefit from the characteristics of voluntariness, publicity, certainty and stability now afforded only to marriage could eliminate the need for marriage. It would not prevent people from marrying religiously or calling themselves "married" in addition to "registering" their unions. However, the religious marriage would not carry legal connotations nor would the public identification as "married" be of any legal consequence. In order to have legal consequences, people would have to register their relationship. . . .

By removing the link between marriage and legal consequences, the spheres of religious and secular authority would be more clearly delineated. By establishing a civil registration scheme . . . , the state could focus more clearly and effectively on accomplishing the underlying objective currently accomplished incompletely by marriage, namely, recognizing and supporting committed personal adult relationships by facilitating an orderly regulation of their affairs.

However, one disadvantage of leaving the solemnization of marriage to religious authorities is that the option of marrying in a secular ceremony would be lost. This may be a serious disadvantage given that civil marriage ceremonies constitute a growing proportion of marriages solemnized in many Canadian jurisdictions. . . .

While there are many principled advantages to this model, it is not likely an option that would appear very attractive to a majority of Canadians. . . .

The Case for Civil Marriage

In many countries, only a civil marriage has legal consequences. Religious institutions conduct religious marriages. However, a couple must enter a civil marriage in order for the marriage to have legal consequences. . . .

This model of civil marriage is one that completely separates the respective roles of church and state. Churches continue to have authority over the religious aspects of marriage, but the state alone has jurisdiction over the civil aspects of marriage. Only civil marriages have legal consequences.

The only disadvantage to adopting a model of civil marriage as it exists in France and other European countries is the duplication it entails. . . . A mandatory civil ceremony would require the additional visit to state officials, and the appropriate personnel and facilities for such celebrations. . . .

Conclusion

The state has a role in providing a legal framework to help people fulfill the responsibilities and rights that arise in close personal relationships. . . . Instead of focusing mainly on married couples and couples deemed to be "marriage-like," governments should establish registration schemes to facilitate the private ordering of both conjugal and non-conjugal relationships. . . .

NOTES AND QUESTIONS

---

1.   *Private Law.* The Law Commission of Canada (LCC) assumed that individuals in intimate relationships lacking formal recognition could make private agreements governing their mutual rights and obligations and could also seek equitable remedies in the event of dissolution. While that may accurately reflect the law in Canada, courts in the U.S. continue to debate this issue. Why might courts hesitate to enforce a contract between unmarried cohabitants? Why might courts refuse to entertain equitable claims? We address this issue in Chapter 5.

2.   *Marriage and Same-Sex Couples.* The LCC released *Beyond Conjugality* in 2001. At this relatively early point in the modern fight for same-sex marriage, the LCC weighed in, asserting that "the capacity to form conjugal relationships characterized by emotional and economic interdependence has nothing to do with sexual orientation."[50] Accordingly, "[i]f governments are to continue to maintain an institution called marriage, they cannot do so in a discriminatory fashion."[51] As Canadian scholars Brenda Cossman and Bruce Ryder explain, the LCC's views appeared to influence the debate. "In the years immediately following the release of *Beyond Conjugality*, . . . court rulings legaliz[ed] same-sex marriage in British Columbia, Ontario, and Quebec."[52] Ultimately, in 2005, the Civil Marriage Act opened marriage to same-sex couples across Canada.

3.   *What Kind of Functional Approach?* The state may operationalize a functional approach in different ways. It could ask whether the individuals look and act like a "traditional" family or a married couple. Or it could look beyond relationships that appear to replicate formal family structures. As Cossman and Ryder explain, the LCC "sought to put the power to determine which relationships are most important in individuals' hands."[53] But when this is not feasible, it

> encouraged governments and legislatures to rethink the functional definitions they use to ascribe relational status so that the focus is on relevant criteria. In particular, the report focused on emotional intimacy and economic interdependence as two functional relational attributes important across a number of contexts.[54]

---

50. Law Comm'n of Canada, Beyond Conjugality: Recognizing and Supporting Close Adult Relationships 130 (2001).

51. Id.

52. Brenda Cossman & Bruce Ryder, Beyond Beyond Conjugality, 30 Canadian J. Fam. L. 227, 230 (2017).

53. Id. at 229.

54. Id.

How would the approach advanced by the LCC lead legislators to alter existing laws regulating family relations? How would it affect judges adjudicating disputes that implicate the meaning of "family"?

PROBLEMS

1. You work for a state senator who serves in a legislature in which the following bill has been introduced:

AN ACT TO PROMOTE MARRIAGE

The legislature of this jurisdiction enacts the proposed legislation in light of the following findings:

* Rates of non-marital childbearing have risen dramatically during the past half century. Nearly 40 percent of all children born in the U.S. are born to unmarried parents. Among African Americans, approximately 70 percent of children are born to unmarried parents.
* Children born to unmarried parents fare less well than children born to married parents with respect to a number of important outcomes. The children of unmarried parents are more likely to: be abused, perform poorly in school, drop out of school, be unemployed as adults, and commit crimes.
* Children with unmarried parents are economically disadvantaged, compared to children in married-couple households. For example, a child raised by a never-married mother is seven times more likely to live in poverty. Eighty percent of child poverty occurs among children whose parents either never married or divorced. Single-parent families are disproportionately represented among recipients of government "welfare" programs.
* The increase in unmarried childbearing during the past four decades is counter to the moral values that have sustained this nation. Those values emphasize the importance of family, and of marriage as the proper setting within which to bear and rear children.
* Unmarried childbearing disadvantages adults as well. Marriage has been shown to relate to a variety of beneficial outcomes for both men and women. Health, wealth, earnings, and happiness have all been positively associated with marriage. Unwed childbearing, in contrast, has been associated with myriad negative outcomes for adults.

The legislature hereby resolves that:

* All children deserve the benefit of two married parents so that they may reach their fullest potential.

- All adults should be made aware of the many benefits of marriage, both for the individual and for any children that are born to a couple.
- The nation has an important interest in preserving and bolstering the institution of marriage.

In light of the foregoing, the legislature will, in a companion bill, allocate substantial funding for the following programs:

- Marriage education programs that teach the value of marriage to high school students across the state.
- Public education campaigns: Pro-marriage messages shall be disseminated through public service announcements that make people aware of the benefits of marriage.
- Marriage mentoring programs that provide unmarried and married couples with information on how to build and maintain strong marriages. Emphasis should be placed on offering such programs to low-income couples at risk of bearing children out of wedlock. These voluntary programs shall be made available to all couples who apply for a marriage license, to all women who give birth to a child, and through churches that perform marriage ceremonies.
- Pro-marriage counseling offered to all pregnant women and unmarried mothers receiving Medicaid services.
- Divorce education that helps couples resolve problems and preserve their marriage. If the marriage cannot be preserved, the counseling will assist the couple in establishing a functional post-marriage relationship if children are involved. Any couple that files for divorce will be required to undergo divorce education counseling with a state-approved counselor.

The state senator for whom you work is considering what position to take on the bill. She wants your advice about whether she should support the legislation. Is such legislation justified? What concerns does it raise? Does it pose constitutional problems? What advice will you give the senator?

2. You work for a state representative planning to introduce the following bill in the new legislative session:

AN ACT TO END CIVIL MARRIAGE AND INSTITUTE REGISTERED PARTNERSHIPS

Marriage is hereby abolished as a legal institution. While individuals may continue to marry in religious ceremonies, such ceremonies would carry no legal implications. In place of state-sanctioned marriage, the government hereby establishes a registration system for those who wish to be considered "domestic partners." Any two adults may register as "domestic partners," provided that they: (i) share the same residence, (ii) agree to be responsible for each other's living expenses,

(iii) have established what they view as a long-term, interdependent relationship, and (iv) are both unmarried and not a member of another domestic partnership. "Domestic partners" are to be accorded substantially the same legal rights and obligations that married couples currently enjoy, including with respect to property rights and children. A domestic partnership shall be established by the filing of a registration form, completed by both parties and notarized, with the Secretary of State. A domestic partnership ends by the death of either partner, or by the filing of a dissolution, signed by both parties and notarized, with the Secretary of State. The state shall prescribe procedures for dissolution when the partners do not mutually agree to end the partnership.

The representative for whom you work asks for your own opinion on the proposed legislation. She also asks what objections she should anticipate from colleagues, interest groups, and the public. What will you tell her?

3. Today, marriage is often not for life. Many couples divorce within the first few years of marriage. Even marriages that are for life are not necessarily happy marriages. In light of these emerging social realities, a state legislator introduces a bill providing couples with the option of entering into a limited-term marriage, one in which the goal is not longevity.

AN ACT PROVIDING FOR LIMITED-TERM MARRIAGES

Couples applying for a marriage license are permitted to choose the term of their marriage. A couple may choose an indefinite term (the traditional approach) or they may specify a 2, 3, or 5 year term. If they select a term of years, the marriage will automatically dissolve at the end of the term, without the need for any legal proceedings, unless they elect in writing to renew.

Do you find the bill's approach appealing? Consider the proposal in light of the different rationales justifying the government's interest in promoting marriage.

Access to Relationships

I. State Control over Adult Relationships

The freedom people have today in the United States to determine whether, when, and how to engage in intimate relationships is the product of important social changes, as well as some hard-fought court and legislative battles over state control. Legal restrictions on people's intimate relationships have diminished significantly during the past century, but some prohibitions remain. As you read the following materials, consider the scope of the relevant constitutional rights and the ways in which states continue to control access to intimate relationships. Consider also the civil law consequences that can operate in tandem or in lieu of criminal punishments. Think about what social and technological changes might have helped shift the law so dramatically — and whether more shifts are likely or desirable.

A. Criminal and Civil Regulation of Sexual Relationships

THOMAS V. STATE
22 So. 725 (Fla. 1897)

TAYLOR, C.J.

The plaintiffs in error, upon information filed, were tried and convicted in the criminal court of record of Volusia county at its April term, 1897, of the crime of lewd and lascivious cohabitation, and sentenced to 18 months' imprisonment in the state penitentiary, and seek reversal on writ of error.

Their motion for new trial, the denial of which is assigned as error, was upon the ground, among others, "that the evidence introduced by the state was totally insufficient to convict them of the crime charged." The information upon which they were ried was predicated upon the first paragraph of the following section (2596) of the Revised Statutes: "If any man and woman, not being married to each other, lewdly and lasciviously associate and cohabit together, or if any man or woman, married or unmarried, is guilty of open and gross lewdness and lascivious behavior, they shall be punished by imprisonment in the state prison not exceeding two years, or in the county jail not exceeding one year, or by fine not exceeding three hundred dollars."

The evidence upon which such conviction was had was substantially as follows, as appears from the transcript of the record: J. R. Turner, for the state, testified: That he knew both of the defendants. That he was sheriff of Volusia county. That about the 21st of February, 1897, between 12 and 1 o'clock at night, he went to the house where Mary Long resided. That when he got there he had reason to believe Thomas was in there with the woman Mary, and he heard them get out of bed, and called to them to come out. Henry said, "All right," and apparently was trying to get a light. That he heard a racket on the floor, and looked beneath, and saw some one getting through a trap door, and he called to them to come out, and they jumped back in the room. That he then ran against the door, and broke it in, and struck some matches, and saw Henry and Mary in the room together. It was on Sunday night. Neither of them were in bed when he got in the room. Only one bed was in the room. Henry was partly dressed, and she was in her night clothes. That as he pushed the door down he struck a match, and Henry said, "Don't shoot me," and fanned out the match with his coat, and he (the witness) fired. Henry Thomas then struck him in the breast, and he sprang back to recover, and as he did so Henry went over him, and jumped and fell on the ground and lay there. Mr. W. P. Edwards, who was with him at the time, searched the house, and found a revolver close to the trap door. We got Mary then. It all happened in Volusia county, Fla. After Henry was arrested, he finished dressing. W. P. Edwards testified that he was a deputy sheriff of Volusia county, and assisted in arresting Henry Thomas and Mary Long. He reiterated, substantially, the testimony of the sheriff. Aaron Adams, for the state, testified that he knew both of the defendants; that he had never seen them associated together, — no further than being in the yard; that he had seen them together in the yard; that he had seen Henry there quite a lot of times; that he had never seen him in the house there, but saw him there in the yard about 10 o'clock at night on the Saturday before he was arrested; that he was in the yard, talking, and he called him; that he had seen him there before at night quite a lot of times; that he (witness) was only passing by when he saw him there; that he had never seen them in that house and in bed together. Allen Long, for the state, testified that he knew both of the defendants; that he was a brother to the defendant Mary Long, and lived on Lake Helen; that he had seen Henry and Mary together, but not so many times. After first denying it, this witness then stated that late on the Saturday before Henry was arrested he brought groceries there, and gave them to Mary, and he and she went in the room and cooked and ate them, and did not come out of there; that he had seen Henry there a number of times, and that he had brought groceries, and went into the room, and they shut the door, and stayed there shut up together; that he lived with his father, and that he, his father, an older sister, and Mary, the defendant, lived there together in that house. Lucy Suber, for the state, testified that she lived in Lake Helen village, about a quarter of a mile from the house of old man Long; that she went by there, but never at any time saw Henry Thomas there, nor in the yard. This comprised the whole of the state's evidence.

Nathan Irving, for the defendants, testified that he lived in Lake Helen, about 400 yards from Mary Long's house, and was about as near a neighbor to her as any one; that he and Thomas had worked together pretty much, and in going to work and leaving their work they passed by there, and he had never seen him stop by; that he had never seen them together, sleeping together, or cohabiting together, and if they had done so he would have been likely to have seen it. This constitutes the substance of the entire evidence in the cause.

In Luster v. State, 23 Fla. 339, 2 South. 690, this court, construing this statute, says: "The evidence must show a dwelling or living together, or cohabitation, that is lewd or lascivious; it must show that the parties dwell together as if the conjugal relation existed between them. The object of the statute was to prohibit the public scandal and disgrace of such living together by persons of opposite sexes, and unmarried to each other; to prevent such evil and indecent examples, with their tendency to corrupt public morals. Proofs of occasional acts of incontinency will not of themselves sustain the charge." . . . According to these authorities, — and we do not hesitate to indorse their correctness, — the testimony presented to us in the record is wholly insufficient to sustain a conviction. It tends to show one act of secret lewdness between the defendants, but there is an entire absence of any proof even tending to show that open dwelling or cohabiting together as though the marriage relation existed between the parties that is essential to be proved, in conjunction with illicit sexual intercourse between them, in order to make out the offense under this statute.

The judgment of the court below is reversed, and a new trial awarded.

PACE V. STATE OF ALABAMA
106 U.S. 583 (1883)

In Error to the Supreme Court of Alabama.

Section 4184 of the Code of Alabama provides that "if any man and woman live together in adultery or fornication, each of them must, on the first conviction of the offense, be fined not less than $100, and may also be imprisoned in the county jail or sentenced to hard labor for the county for not more than six months. . . ."

Section 4189 of the same Code declares that "if any white person and any negro, or the descendant of any negro to the third generation, inclusive, though one ancestor of each generation was a white person, intermarry or live in adultery or fornication with each other, each of them must, on conviction, be imprisoned in the penitentiary or sentenced to hard labor for the county for not less than two nor more than seven years."

In November, 1881, the plaintiff in error, Tony Pace, a negro man, and Mary J. Cox, a white woman, were indicted under section 4189, in a circuit court of Alabama, for living together in a state of adultery or fornication, and were tried, convicted, and sentenced, each to two years' imprisonment in the state penitentiary. . . .

FIELD, J.

The counsel of the plaintiff in error compares sections 4184 and 4189 of the Code of Alabama, and assuming that the latter relates to the same offense as the former, and prescribes a greater punishment for it, because one of the parties is a negro, or of negro descent, claims that a discrimination is made against the colored person in the punishment designated, which conflicts with the clause of the fourteenth amendment prohibiting a state from denying to any person within its jurisdiction the equal protection of the laws.

The counsel is undoubtedly correct in his view of the purpose of the clause of the amendment in question, that it was to prevent hostile and discriminating state legislation against any person or class of persons. Equality of protection under the laws implies not only accessibility by each one, whatever his race, on the same terms with others to the courts of the country for the security of his person and property, but that in the administration of criminal justice he shall not be subjected, for the same offense, to any greater or different punishment. Such was the view of congress in the re-enactment of the civil-rights act, after the adoption of the amendment. . . .

The defect in the argument of counsel consists in his assumption that any discrimination is made by the laws of Alabama in the punishment provided for the offense for which the plaintiff in error was indicted when committed by a person of the African race and when committed by a white person. The two sections of the Code cited are entirely consistent. The one prescribes, generally, a punishment for an offense committed between persons of different sexes; the other prescribes a punishment for an offense which can only be committed where the two sexes are of different races. There is in neither section any discrimination against either race. Section 4184 equally includes the offense when the persons of the two sexes are both white and when they are both black. Section 4189 applies the same punishment to both offenders, the white and the black. Indeed, the offense against which this latter section is aimed cannot be committed without involving the persons of both races in the same punishment. Whatever discrimination is made in the punishment prescribed in the two sections is directed against the offense designated and not against the person of any particular color or race. The punishment of each offending person, whether white or black, is the same.

Judgment affirmed.

NOTES AND QUESTIONS

1. *Criminal Regulation of Intimacy.* State control of sexual morality peaked in the early twentieth century and reflected the view that sex was only legitimate within marriage.[1] Although longstanding, that belief found new advocates in the anti-vice movement of the so-called Progressive Era and was enshrined in the criminal laws. As Professor Melissa Murray puts it, "criminal law historically has worked in tandem with family law to define, elaborate, and organize the normative content of intimate life."[2] Although states varied in their efforts to restrict nonmarital sexual behavior, many criminalized fornication (sex by unmarried persons), cohabitation (living with a non-marital intimate partner), bastardy (fathering a child out of wedlock), and adultery (sex by a married person with someone other than the person's spouse).[3]

2. *Public Mores.* In *Thomas*, the Florida Supreme Court drew a distinction between "one act of secret lewdness," which the law could tolerate, and "cohabiting together as though the marriage relation existed," which it could not. Why is the latter deemed more objectionable?

3. *Racial Equality?* How does the Supreme Court justify upholding the Alabama law that punished interracial sex significantly more harshly than intraracial sex? Note that *Pace* was decided more than a decade before the Supreme Court's decision in Plessy v. Ferguson,[4] which is commonly thought to inaugurate the era of separate but equal. Why do you think that *Plessy* has received so much attention and *Pace*, in comparison, so little?

4. *Heartbalm Laws.* "Heartbalm" laws refer to a cluster of torts thought to remedy "broken hearts." These claims included criminal conversation, alienation of affections, wrongful seduction, and breach of the promise to marry, which was the most common and typically brought by a woman. Wrongful seduction permitted a woman to sue for having been tricked or manipulated into sex outside of marriage. Criminal conversation was, despite its name, a civil cause of action that permitted one spouse to sue a person who had sex with the other spouse. Alienation of affections also permitted a suit against a spouse's paramour, but extended further to permit lawsuits against any third party who caused a spouse to lose interest in the other spouse — e.g., a meddling mother-in-law or a friend. Criminal conversation and alienation of affections

---

1. For a more detailed history, see Ariela R. Dubler, Immoral Purposes: Marriage and the Genus of Illicit Sex, 115 Yale L.J. 756 (2006); Joanna L. Grossman & Lawrence M. Friedman, Inside the Castle: Law and the Family in 20th Century America (2011).

2. Melissa Murray, Strange Bedfellows: Criminal Law, Family Law, and the Legal Construction of Intimate Life, 94 Iowa L. Rev. 1253, 1257 (2009).

3. See Bishop, Commentaries on the Criminal Law (1858).

4. 163 U.S. 537 (1896).

claims were typically brought by men. What do you think explains gender differences in who pursued these different claims?

Beginning in the 1930s, states began to abolish heartbalm causes of action as concerns about fabricated claims and "gold-digging" began to outweigh concerns for women's reputations. In most states today, there is no available cause of action related to seduction, adultery, or broken engagements. Alienation of affections has survived as a claim in a few states and occasionally results in large verdicts that attract media attention. In a 2010 North Carolina case, a jury awarded $9 million to Cynthia Shackelford in her suit against Anne Lundquist, whom Shackelford sued for breaking up her 33-year marriage. Shackelford told reporters she hoped the verdict would be a cautionary tale for "would-be homewreckers," and that they would "lay off."[5] Similarly, the Mississippi Supreme Court upheld a jury verdict of $642,000 for alienation of affections in 2007, rejecting pleas to abolish the cause of action.[6] Should this cause of action be available today? Why or why not?

The most common controversies arising from a broken engagement these days relate to whether an engagement ring must be returned and whether non-refundable wedding expenses must be shared by both parties. Expensive rings became common during the 1930s, as heartbalm laws were being repealed.[7] Current law varies from state to state, but the majority approach treats an engagement ring as a conditional gift that must be returned if the wedding does not occur.[8] In some states, courts only require the ring to be returned if the recipient is at fault and allow it to be kept if the donor caused the broken engagement.[9]

In contrast, in most states, courts will not order reimbursement of expenses incurred for a wedding that did not occur. (New York is an exception to the dominant approach, insofar as a state statute gives courts discretion to order recoupment of a share of wedding expenses where the parties had made a "genuine contract" to share the cost.[10]) Given the social norm that, in different-sex relationships, the man gives an engagement ring and the woman's family often pays for the wedding, the combination of the legal rules regarding rings and wedding expenses means that women, and often their families, end up bearing a disproportionate burden of a broken engagement. Professor Rachel Moran argues that the

---

5. Alice Gomstyn & Lee Ferran, Wife's $9M Message to Mistress: "Lay Off," abcnews.com (Mar. 23, 2010); see also Joanna L. Grossman & Lawrence M. Friedman, Elizabeth Edwards v. Andrew Young: Can He Be Held Liable for Contributing to the Failure of the Edwardses' Marriage?, FindLaw's Writ (Feb. 19, 2010).

6. Fitch v. Valentine, 959 So. 2d 1012 (Miss. 2007).

7. Margaret F. Brinig, Rings and Promises, 6 J.L. Econ. & Org. 203, 206 (1990) (noting success of the diamond industry after 1935 and the near universal choice of diamond engagement rings by 1960).

8. Lindh v. Surman, 742 A.2d 643 (Pa. 1999); Heiman v. Parrish, 942 P.2d 631 (Kan. 1997); Vigil v. Haber, 888 P.2d 455 (N.M. 1994).

9. See Rebecca Tushnet, Rules of Engagement, 107 Yale L.J. 2583, 2592 (1998).

10. DeFina v. Scott, 755 N.Y.S.2d 587 (N.Y. Sup. Ct. 2003); N.Y. Civ. Rights Law § 80-b (McKinney 2020) (enacted 1965).

prevailing rules treat men's sense of loss as "real and deserving of compensation," while the "disappointed bride to be who spends money on wedding preparations or makes herself sexually available because she has been promised marriage cannot seek compensation of any kind."[11] Should the law try to equalize the burden on men and women for broken engagements?

5. *The Age of Consent.* Every state has established an age at which individuals can legally consent to sex. This age was as low as 10 or 12 at common law, but states increased it in the early twentieth century, setting the age as high as 18 or 21.[12] Today, almost all states set 16 or 17 as the age of consent,[13] below which even consensual sexual activity with an adult can subject the adult to charges of "statutory rape." Although in most states the age of consent is the same for boys and girls, the Supreme Court has upheld a statutory rape law that only applied when men had sex with a minor female.[14] The Court reasoned: "Only women may become pregnant, and they suffer disproportionately the profound physical, emotional and psychological consequences of sexual activity. The statute at issue here protects women from sexual intercourse at an age when those consequences are particularly severe."[15] Do you agree that sex-based biological differences justify different ages of consent based on gender? The dissenting justices argued that a gender-neutral law would have been as effective in achieving the state's aims.[16]

Many consent statutes apply special rules to minors who are close in age to one another. Some of these so-called Romeo and Juliet provisions apply a lesser penalty to the criminal sexual act, while others render the sexual act itself lawful. In Texas, for example, the age of consent is 17, but consensual sex with a person who is at least 14 is permitted if the other party is no more than three years older.[17] Some of these laws apply only to different-sex relations or vaginal intercourse, leaving a teenager engaging in same-sex relations or non-vaginal intercourse with a younger person vulnerable to a statutory rape charge. In one case, the Kansas Supreme Court invalidated the exclusion of same-sex sexual activity from the state's Romeo and Juliet law that provided lesser sanctions for sex between teens.[18] In another case, the North Carolina Supreme Court upheld the application of the state's "crime against nature" law to a 14-year-old boy who engaged in oral sex with a 12-year-old girl.[19] While

---

11. Rachel F. Moran, Law and Emotion, Love and Hate, 11 J. Contemp. Leg. Issues 747, 781 (2001).

12. Frances Olsen, Statutory Rape: A Feminist Critique of Rights Analysis, 63 Tex. L. Rev. 387, 403 (1984).

13. See Marci A. Hamilton, 50-State Age of Majority v. Age of Consent, SOL Reform (2015).

14. Michael M. v. Superior Court of Sonoma County, 450 U.S. 464 (1981).

15. Id. at 471–72.

16. See id. at 488–94 (Brennan, J., dissenting).

17. Tex. Penal Code § 21.11 (2020).

18. State v. Limon, 122 P.3d 22 (Kan. 2005).

19. In re R.L.C., 643 S.E.2d 920 (N.C. 2007).

laws relating to vaginal intercourse included a minimum age differential, the law prohibiting oral and anal sex did not. The court reasoned: "Besides the goal of promoting proper notions of morality among our State's youth, the government's desire for a healthy young citizenry underscores the legitimacy of the government's interest in prohibiting the commission of crimes against nature by minors.[20] Does the law's enforcement vindicate an interest in "a healthy young citizenry"? Is "promoting proper notions of morality" a legitimate justification for the law? Does the state have a different interest in sexual morality when minors, rather than adults, are at issue? Should it matter how old the minors are? Consider the fact that, of American teens (ages 13 to 17) who have had romantic or dating relationship experience, those ages 15 to 17 are significantly more likely to be sexually active (36 percent) than younger teens, ages 13 to 14 (12 percent).[21] Consider these questions as you read the cases that follow in this section.

6. *From Criminal to Civil Penalties for Non-Marital Sexual Relationships.* Criminal bans on non-marital sex remain on the books in many states but were rarely enforced after the 1940s. Police and prosecutors had lost interest in enforcing these laws, even though the moral norms hadn't much changed. When the American Law Institute put forth the Model Penal Code in 1962, it deliberately omitted the crime of cohabitation based on common criticism that the criminal law should not be used to enforce a moral code.[22] Many states formally repealed their cohabitation bans during the 1970s and 1980s, retaining criminal bans only on sexual behavior in public. Civil consequences for "immoral" relationships remained. For example, in 1977, Jacqueline Jarrett lost custody of her three children because she was cohabiting with a man after her divorce, a ruling the Illinois Supreme court upheld, despite her presentation of evidence that cohabitation had become much more common.[23] The court relied on the fact that there was a criminal ban on fornication still on the books in the state and that Jarrett was open and honest with her children and neighbors about the fact that she was not married to her cohabiting partner. Her openness, the court wrote, "encourages others to violate [prevailing] standards, and debases public morality."[24] The U.S. Supreme Court declined to review a similar case in 1978, in which a federal court had upheld the firing of a couple from their jobs at a public library because they were living together and had a child without being married.[25] Justice Marshall wrote a dissent to the denial

---

20. Id. at 925.

21. Amanda Lenhart et al., Pew Research Ctr., Teens, Technology & Romantic Relationships 17 (2015).

22. See generally Martha L. Fineman, Law and Changing Patterns of Behavior: Sanctions of Non-Marital Cohabitation, 1981 Wis. L. Rev. 275; see also Fort v. Fort, 425 N.E.2d 754, 758 (Mass. App. Ct. 1981).

23. Jarrett v. Jarrett, 400 N.E.2d 421, 424 (Ill. 1979).

24. Id.

25. Hollenbaugh v. Carnegie Free Library, 578 F.2d 1374 (3d Cir.), cert. denied, 439 U.S. 1052 (1978).

of certiorari, arguing that the Court should give more scrutiny to a governmental action that "permits a public employer to dictate the sexual conduct and family living arrangements of its employees, without a meaningful showing that these private choices have any relation to job performance."[26] As the next section explores, both civil and criminal penalties for non-marital sexual relationships have diminished. Still, civil penalties remain in some settings.[27]

B. The Development of Sexual and Relationship Freedom

The regulation of sexuality developed largely at the state level until the 1960s, when the Supreme Court first weighed in on the constitutionality of various state laws relating to sexual and reproductive health. The Court's opinion in *Griswold v. Connecticut*,[28] excerpted in Chapter 1, was the launching point for situating reproductive decision-making within the Fourteenth Amendment's right to privacy. As you read the next case, consider its import in relation to *Griswold*. How do these two Supreme Court decisions treat marital and nonmarital sex, and how do they treat the gender dynamics within heterosexual relations? To what extent do they reallocate power from men, who always had easy access to condoms, to women, who need doctors and sometimes pharmacists to facilitate access to the birth control they use?

EISENSTADT V. BAIRD
405 U.S. 438 (1972)

MR. JUSTICE BRENNAN delivered the opinion of the Court.

Appellee William Baird was convicted at a bench trial in the Massachusetts Superior Court under Massachusetts General Laws Ann., c. 272, § 21, first, for exhibiting contraceptive articles in the course of delivering a lecture on contraception to a group of students at Boston University and, second, for giving a young woman a package of Emko vaginal foam at the close of his address. The Massachusetts Supreme Judicial Court unanimously set aside the conviction for exhibiting contraceptives on the ground that it violated Baird's First Amendment rights, but by a four-to-three vote sustained the conviction for giving away the foam. . . .

---

26. Hollenbaugh v. Carnegie Free Library, 439 U.S. 1052 (1978) (Marshall, J., dissenting).

27. Melissa Murray, Rights and Regulation: The Evolution of Sexual Regulation, 116 Colum. L. Rev. 573 (2016).

28. 381 U.S. 479 (1965).

Massachusetts General Laws Ann., c. 272, § 21, under which Baird was convicted, provides a maximum five-year term of imprisonment for "whoever . . . gives away . . . any drug, medicine, instrument or article whatever for the prevention of conception," except as authorized in § 21A. Under § 21A, "[a] registered physician may administer to or prescribe for any married person drugs or articles intended for the prevention of pregnancy or conception. [And a] registered pharmacist actually engaged in the business of pharmacy may furnish such drugs or articles to any married person presenting a prescription from a registered physician." As interpreted by the State Supreme Judicial Court, these provisions make it a felony for anyone, other than a registered physician or pharmacist acting in accordance with the terms of § 21A, to dispense any article with the intention that it be used for the prevention of conception. The statutory scheme distinguishes among three distinct classes of distributees — first, married persons may obtain contraceptives to prevent pregnancy, but only from doctors or druggists on prescription; second, single persons may not obtain contraceptives from anyone to prevent pregnancy; and, third, married or single persons may obtain contraceptives from anyone to prevent, not pregnancy, but the spread of disease. . . .

We agree that the goals of deterring premarital sex and regulating the distribution of potentially harmful articles cannot reasonably be regarded as legislative aims of §§ 21 and 21A. And we hold that the statute, viewed as a prohibition on contraception per se, violates the rights of single persons under the Equal Protection Clause of the Fourteenth Amendment. . . .

The question for our determination in this case is whether there is some ground of difference that rationally explains the different treatment accorded married and unmarried persons under Massachusetts General Laws Ann., c. 272, §§ 21 and 21A. For the reasons that follow, we conclude that no such ground exists. . . .

It would be plainly unreasonable to assume that Massachusetts has prescribed pregnancy and the birth of an unwanted child as punishment for fornication, which is a misdemeanor under Massachusetts General Laws Ann., c. 272, § 18. Aside from the scheme of values that assumption would attribute to the State, it is abundantly clear that the effect of the ban on distribution of contraceptives to unmarried persons has at best a marginal relation to the proffered objective. What Mr. Justice Goldberg said in *Griswold v. Connecticut*, 381 U.S. 479 (1965), concerning the effect of Connecticut's prohibition on the use of contraceptives in discouraging extramarital sexual relations, is equally applicable here. "The rationality of this justification is dubious, particularly in light of the admitted widespread availability to all persons in the State of Connecticut, unmarried as well as married, of birth-control devices for the prevention of disease, as distinguished from the prevention of conception." Like Connecticut's laws, §§ 21 and 21A do not at all regulate the distribution of contraceptives when they are to be used to prevent, not pregnancy, but the spread of disease. Nor, in making contraceptives available to married persons without regard to their intended use, does Massachusetts attempt to deter married persons from engaging in illicit sexual relations with unmarried persons. Even on the assumption that the fear of pregnancy operates as a deterrent to fornication, the Massachusetts statute is thus so riddled with exceptions that deterrence of premarital sex cannot reasonably be regarded as its aim. . . .

The Supreme Judicial Court . . . held that the purpose of the amendment was to serve the health needs of the community by regulating the distribution of potentially harmful articles. . . . [But] we must agree with the Court of Appeals[:] . . . "If the prohibition (on distribution to unmarried persons) . . . is to be taken to mean that the same physician who can prescribe for married patients does not have sufficient skill to protect the health of patients who lack a marriage certificate, or who may be currently divorced, it is illogical to the point of irrationality." Furthermore, we must join the Court of Appeals in noting that not all contraceptives are potentially dangerous. As a result, if the Massachusetts statute were a health measure, it would not only invidiously discriminate against the unmarried, but also be overbroad with respect to the married, a fact that the Supreme Judicial Court itself seems to have conceded. . . .

[Furthermore,] whatever the rights of the individual to access to contraceptives may be, the rights must be the same for the unmarried and the married alike. If under *Griswold* the distribution of contraceptives to married persons cannot be prohibited, a ban on distribution to unmarried persons would be equally impermissible. It is true that in *Griswold* the right of privacy in question inhered in the marital relationship. Yet the marital couple is not an independent entity with a mind and heart of its own, but an association of two individuals each with a separate intellectual and emotional makeup. If the right of privacy means anything, it is the right of the individual, married or single, to be free from unwarranted governmental intrusion into matters so fundamentally affecting a person as the decision whether to bear or beget a child.

On the other hand, if *Griswold* is no bar to a prohibition on the distribution of contraceptives, the State could not, consistently with the Equal Protection Clause, outlaw distribution to unmarried but not to married persons. In each case the evil, as perceived by the State, would be identical, and the underinclusion would be invidious. . . .

We hold that by providing dissimilar treatment for married and unmarried persons who are similarly situated, Massachusetts General Laws Ann., c. 272, §§ 21 and 21A, violate the Equal Protection Clause. The judgment of the Court of Appeals is affirmed.

NOTES AND QUESTIONS

---

1. *A Right to Privacy?* Recall the constitutional basis for the Court's majority opinion in *Griswold*. Are you persuaded that it supports the holding in *Eisenstadt*? To what extent is *Eisenstadt* supported by the reasoning in Justice Goldberg's concurrence in *Griswold*?

2. *The Role of Marriage.* The majority in *Griswold* focused heavily on the impact of the contraceptive ban on married couples. Its reference to the marital bedroom as a "sacred precinct" suggests an exalted reverence for marital relationships. Should marital relationships be given more constitutional protection than non-marital ones when it comes to sex and sexuality? Why or why not?

3. *The Constitution and Social Change.* *Griswold* marked the end of an era in which the government tried to restrict access to contraception. Women's reproductive choices had not been broadly regulated in the United States until the nineteenth century, when moral reformers and physicians sought control in the face of an increase in demand for contraception and abortion. The professionals asserted technical, ethical, and social superiority over their competitors, particularly midwives, and the result was a labyrinth of legal regulations about who could prescribe and dispense contraceptives and who could perform abortions. In 1873, Congress passed the Comstock Law, which prohibited dissemination of information about abortion and contraception.[29] Challenges to this law were rooted in women's rights to control their own bodies, as well as now-repudiated eugenic arguments. Margaret Sanger was a powerful advocate for greater access to contraceptives, but her motivations were mixed. Throughout the twentieth century, fertility control emerged as a right for the privileged and a duty for the poor.

Social, legal, and technological developments in the second half of the twentieth century made it difficult for the government to retain its control over reproduction. The birth control pill was first approved for use in 1960, and the number of women relying on it for contraception greatly increased with the passage in 1970 of Title X, a law that led to the creation of federally supported family planning clinics.[30] At the same time, more liberal sexual mores, opportunities for women in paid employment, economic pressure within families to control fertility, and the availability of oral contraception helped liberalize public attitudes and practices. What would have happened if *Griswold* or *Eisenstadt* had come out the other way? Would some states today still ban access to prescription birth control?

4. *Privacy and Domestic Violence.* Are there unintended consequences for guarding privacy within a sexual relationship? Does the Court's treatment of intimate relationships make it more difficult to address intimate partner violence?[31] Reconsider this question after reading the materials on domestic violence in Chapter 3.

---

29. On this history, see Priscilla J. Smith, Contraceptive Comstockery: Reasoning from Immorality to Illness in the Twenty-First Century, 47 Conn. L. Rev. 971 (2015).

30. Public Health Service Act of 1970 Tit. X, Pub. L. 91–572 (1970).

31. See, e.g., Reva B. Siegel, "The Rule of Love": Wife Beating as Prerogative and Privacy, 105 Yale L.J. 2117 (1996).

5. *Beyond* Griswold *and* Eisenstadt. In the decades following *Griswold*, the Supreme Court expanded the right to privacy to include other aspects of reproduction such as abortion. Those cases are discussed at length in Chapters 3 and 9.

* * *

As of 1961, all 50 states prohibited sodomy, which most statutes defined to include any type of oral-genital contact and anal sex. Sodomy bans were first challenged on constitutional grounds in the early 1970s; plaintiffs in these cases argued unsuccessfully that the bans were unduly vague and thus violated the Due Process Clause.[32] Advocates eventually shifted to arguments rooted in the right of privacy. In 1976, the Supreme Court first considered the constitutionality of a sodomy statute in Doe v. Commonwealth's Attorney.[33] The lower court in *Doe* determined that the Supreme Court's privacy cases only "condemn[] State legislation that trespasses upon the privacy of the incidents of marriage, upon the sanctity of the home, or upon the nurture of family life."[34] The court concluded that there is "no authoritative judicial bar to the proscription of homosexuality . . . since it is obviously no part of marriage, home or family life. . . ."[35] The Supreme Court summarily affirmed the ruling, over a dissent by Justices Brennan, Marshall, and Stevens.

A decade later, the Supreme Court would consider the question again in Bowers v. Hardwick.[36] That case arose after an Atlanta police officer, who appeared to have been targeting Michael Hardwick, entered Hardwick's apartment while he was engaged in oral sex with another man. The officer arrested both men for committing sodomy. The Supreme Court upheld their convictions, finding no constitutional violation in the law as written or applied. As the Court explained:

> This case does not require a judgment on whether laws against sodomy between consenting adults in general, or between homosexuals in particular, are wise or desirable. It raises no question about the right or propriety of state legislative decisions to repeal their laws that criminalize homosexual sodomy, or of state-court decisions invalidating those laws on state constitutional grounds. The issue presented is whether the Federal Constitution confers a fundamental right upon homosexuals to engage in sodomy and hence invalidates the laws of the many States that still make such conduct illegal and have done so for a very long time. The case also calls for some judgment about the limits of the Court's role in carrying out its constitutional mandate.

---

32. See, e.g., Wainwright v. Stone, 414 U.S. 21, 22–23 (1973) (per curiam).
33. 425 U.S. 901 (1976).
34. 403 F. Supp. 1199, 1200 (E.D. Va. 1975).
35. Id. at 1202.
36. 478 U.S. 186 (1986).

We first register our disagreement with the Court of Appeals and with respondent that the Court's prior cases have construed the Constitution to confer a right of privacy that extends to homosexual sodomy and for all intents and purposes have decided this case. The reach of this line of cases was sketched in *Carey v. Population Services International*, 431 U.S. 678 (1977). *Pierce v. Society of Sisters*, 268 U.S. 510 (1925), and *Meyer v. Nebraska*, 262 U.S. 390 (1923), were described as dealing with child rearing and education; *Prince v. Massachusetts*, 321 U.S. 158 (1944), with family relationships; *Skinner v. Oklahoma ex rel. Williamson*, 316 U.S. 535 (1942), with procreation; *Loving v. Virginia*, 388 U.S. 1 (1967), with marriage; *Griswold v. Connecticut*, 381 U.S. 479 (1965), and *Eisenstadt v. Baird*, 405 U.S. 438 (1972), with contraception; and *Roe v. Wade*, 410 U.S. 113 (1973), with abortion. The latter three cases were interpreted as construing the due process clause of the Fourteenth Amendment to confer a fundamental individual right to decide whether or not to beget or bear a child.

Accepting the decisions in these cases and the above description of them, we think it evident that none of the rights announced in those cases bears any resemblance to the claimed constitutional right of homosexuals to engage in acts of sodomy that is asserted in this case. No connection between family, marriage, or procreation on the one hand and homosexual activity on the other has been demonstrated, either by the Court of Appeals or by respondent. Moreover, any claim that these cases nevertheless stand for the proposition that any kind of private sexual conduct between consenting adults is constitutionally insulated from state proscription is unsupportable. . . .

States remained free after *Bowers*, as a federal constitutional matter, to criminalize same-sex sexual activity — though sodomy laws in eleven states were struck down by state courts on state constitutional grounds or were repealed by state legislatures after *Bowers*.[37] Enforcement of sodomy laws was relatively rare but the criminal bans, like the cohabitation bans discussed above, were also used, to justify discrimination against lesbians, gay men, and bisexuals in other contexts, such as employment and family law.[38] For instance, in 1998, the Alabama Supreme Court cited the state's sodomy law as it upheld a trial court decision transferring custody from a lesbian mother to her ex-husband, the child's father.[39] The court explained: "While the evidence shows that the mother loves the child and has provided her with good care, it also shows that she has chosen to expose the child continuously to a lifestyle that is 'neither legal in this state, nor moral in the eyes

---

37. See, e.g., Jegley v. Picado, 80 S.W.3d 332 (Ark. 2002); Powell v. State, 510 S.E.2d 18 (Ga. 1998) (striking down the same statute upheld in *Bowers*); Gryczan v. State, 942 P.2d 112 (Mont. 1997); Nev. Rev. Stat. § 201.190 (amended 1993).

38. See generally Diana Hassel, The Use of Criminal Sodomy Laws in Civil Litigation, 79 Tex. L. Rev. 813 (2001); Christopher R. Leslie, Creating Criminals: The Injuries Inflicted by "Unenforced" Sodomy Laws, 35 Harv. C.R.-C.L. L. Rev. 103 (2000).

39. Ex parte J.M.F., 730 So. 2d 1190 (Ala. 1998).

of most of its citizens.' "[40] In 1995, the Virginia Supreme Court upheld a trial court decision removing custody from a lesbian mother and placing the child not with another parent but with the child's grandmother.[41] In doing so, it stated: "Conduct inherent in lesbianism is punishable as a Class 6 felony in the Commonwealth; thus, that conduct is another important consideration in determining custody."[42]

The Supreme Court returned to the question of sodomy laws just seventeen years after its ruling in *Bowers*.

LAWRENCE V. TEXAS
539 U.S. 558 (2003)

JUSTICE KENNEDY delivered the opinion of the Court.

Liberty protects the person from unwarranted government intrusions into a dwelling or other private places. In our tradition the State is not omnipresent in the home. And there are other spheres of our lives and existence, outside the home, where the State should not be a dominant presence. Freedom extends beyond spatial bounds. Liberty presumes an autonomy of self that includes freedom of thought, belief, expression, and certain intimate conduct. The instant case involves liberty of the person both in its spatial and in its more transcendent dimensions.

The question before the Court is the validity of a Texas statute making it a crime for two persons of the same sex to engage in certain intimate sexual conduct.

In Houston, Texas, officers of the Harris County Police Department were dispatched to a private residence in response to a reported weapons disturbance. They entered an apartment where one of the petitioners, John Geddes Lawrence, resided. The right of the police to enter does not seem to have been questioned. The officers observed Lawrence and another man, Tyron Garner, engaging in a sexual act. The two petitioners were arrested, held in custody overnight, and charged and convicted before a Justice of the Peace.

The complaints described their crime as "deviate sexual intercourse, namely anal sex, with a member of the same sex (man)." The applicable state law is Tex. Penal Code Ann. § 21.06(a) (2003). It provides: "A person commits an offense if he engages in deviate sexual intercourse with another individual of the same sex." The statute defines "[d]eviate sexual intercourse" as follows:

"(A) any contact between any part of the genitals of one person and the mouth or anus of another person; or

"(B) the penetration of the genitals or the anus of another person with an object." § 21.01(1). . . .

---

40. Id. at 1196.
41. Bottoms v. Bottoms, 457 S.E.2d 102 (Va. 1995).
42. Id. at 108.

The petitioners were adults at the time of the alleged offense. Their conduct was in private and consensual.

We conclude the case should be resolved by determining whether the petitioners were free as adults to engage in the private conduct in the exercise of their liberty under the Due Process Clause of the Fourteenth Amendment to the Constitution. For this inquiry we deem it necessary to reconsider the Court's holding in *Bowers v. Hardwick*, 478 U.S. 186 (1986).

There are broad statements of the substantive reach of liberty under the Due Process Clause in earlier cases . . . but the most pertinent beginning point is our decision in *Griswold v. Connecticut*, 381 U.S. 479 (1965).

In *Griswold* the Court invalidated a state law prohibiting the use of drugs or devices of contraception and counseling or aiding and abetting the use of contraceptives. The Court described the protected interest as a right to privacy and placed emphasis on the marriage relation and the protected space of the marital bedroom.

After *Griswold* it was established that the right to make certain decisions regarding sexual conduct extends beyond the marital relationship. In *Eisenstadt v. Baird*, 405 U.S. 438 (1972), the Court invalidated a law prohibiting the distribution of contraceptives to unmarried persons. The case was decided under the Equal Protection Clause . . . ; but with respect to unmarried persons, the Court went on to state the fundamental proposition that the law impaired the exercise of their personal rights. . . .

The opinions in *Griswold* and *Eisenstadt* were part of the background for the decision in *Roe v. Wade*, 410 U.S. 113 (1973). . . . *Roe* recognized the right of a woman to make certain fundamental decisions affecting her destiny and confirmed once more that the protection of liberty under the Due Process Clause has a substantive dimension of fundamental significance in defining the rights of the person. . . .

This was the state of the law with respect to some of the most relevant cases when the Court considered *Bowers v. Hardwick*. . . .

The Court began its substantive discussion in *Bowers* as follows: "The issue presented is whether the Federal Constitution confers a fundamental right upon homosexuals to engage in sodomy and hence invalidates the laws of the many States that still make such conduct illegal and have done so for a very long time." That statement, we now conclude, discloses the Court's own failure to appreciate the extent of the liberty at stake. To say that the issue in *Bowers* was simply the right to engage in certain sexual conduct demeans the claim the individual put forward, just as it would demean a married couple were it to be said marriage is simply about the right to have sexual intercourse. The laws involved in *Bowers* and here are, to be sure, statutes that purport to do no more than prohibit a particular sexual act. Their penalties and purposes, though, have more far-reaching consequences, touching upon the most private human conduct, sexual behavior, and in the most private of places, the home. The statutes do seek to control a personal relationship that, whether or not entitled to formal recognition in the law, is within the liberty of persons to choose without being punished as criminals.

This, as a general rule, should counsel against attempts by the State, or a court, to define the meaning of the relationship or to set its boundaries absent injury to a person or abuse of an institution the law protects. It suffices for us to acknowledge that adults may choose to enter upon this relationship in the confines of their homes and their own private lives and still retain their dignity as free persons. When sexuality finds overt expression in intimate conduct with another person, the conduct can be but one element in a personal bond that is more enduring. The liberty protected by the Constitution allows homosexual persons the right to make this choice. . . .

At the outset it should be noted that there is no longstanding history in this country of laws directed at homosexual conduct as a distinct matter. . . . [E]arly American sodomy laws were not directed at homosexuals as such but instead sought to prohibit nonprocreative sexual activity more generally. This does not suggest approval of homosexual conduct. It does tend to show that this particular form of conduct was not thought of as a separate category from like conduct between heterosexual persons. . . .

It was not until the 1970's that any State singled out same-sex relations for criminal prosecution, and only nine States have done so. . . . Over the course of the last decades, States with same-sex prohibitions have moved toward abolishing them.

In summary, the historical grounds relied upon in *Bowers* are more complex than the majority opinion and the concurring opinion by Chief Justice Burger indicate. Their historical premises are not without doubt and, at the very least, are overstated.

It must be acknowledged, of course, that the Court in *Bowers* was making the broader point that for centuries there have been powerful voices to condemn homosexual conduct as immoral. The condemnation has been shaped by religious beliefs, conceptions of right and acceptable behavior, and respect for the traditional family. For many persons these are not trivial concerns but profound and deep convictions accepted as ethical and moral principles to which they aspire and which thus determine the course of their lives. These considerations do not answer the question before us, however. The issue is whether the majority may use the power of the State to enforce these views on the whole society through operation of the criminal law. "Our obligation is to define the liberty of all, not to mandate our own moral code." *Planned Parenthood of Southeastern Pa. v. Casey*, 505 U.S. 833 (1992). . . .

In all events we think that our laws and traditions in the past half century are of most relevance here. These references show an emerging awareness that liberty gives substantial protection to adult persons in deciding how to conduct their private lives in matters pertaining to sex. "[H]istory and tradition are the starting point but not in all cases the ending point of the substantive due process inquiry." *County of Sacramento v. Lewis*, 523 U.S. 833, 857 (1998) (Kennedy, J., concurring).

This emerging recognition should have been apparent when *Bowers* was decided. In 1955 the American Law Institute promulgated the Model Penal Code and made clear that it did not recommend or provide for "criminal penalties for consensual sexual relations conducted in private." . . . In 1961 Illinois changed its laws to conform to the Model Penal Code. Other States soon followed. [By the time of the Court's decision in *Bowers*,] 24 States and the District of Columbia had sodomy laws. Justice Powell pointed out that these prohibitions often were being ignored, however. . . .

[T]he deficiencies in *Bowers* became even more apparent in the years following its announcement. The 25 States with laws prohibiting the relevant conduct referenced in the *Bowers* decision are reduced now to 13, of which 4 enforce their laws only against homosexual conduct. In those States where sodomy is still proscribed, whether for same-sex or heterosexual conduct, there is a pattern of nonenforcement with respect to consenting adults acting in private. The State of Texas admitted in 1994 that as of that date it had not prosecuted anyone under those circumstances. *State v. Morales*, 869 S.W.2d 941, 943 (Tex. 1994).

Two principal cases decided after *Bowers* cast its holding into even more doubt. In *Planned Parenthood of Southeastern Pa. v. Casey*, 505 U.S. 833 (1992), the Court reaffirmed the substantive force of the liberty protected by the Due Process Clause. The *Casey* decision again confirmed that our laws and tradition afford constitutional protection to personal decisions relating to marriage, procreation, contraception, family relationships, child rearing, and education. . . . Persons in a homosexual relationship may seek autonomy for these purposes, just as heterosexual persons do. The decision in *Bowers* would deny them this right.

The second post-*Bowers* case of principal relevance is *Romer v. Evans*, 517 U.S. 620 (1996). There the Court struck down class-based legislation directed at homosexuals as a violation of the Equal Protection Clause. . . .

As an alternative argument in this case, counsel for the petitioners and some *amici* contend that *Romer* provides the basis for declaring the Texas statute invalid under the Equal Protection Clause. That is a tenable argument, but we conclude the instant case requires us to address whether *Bowers* itself has continuing validity. Were we to hold the statute invalid under the Equal Protection Clause some might question whether a prohibition would be valid if drawn differently, say, to prohibit the conduct both between same-sex and different-sex participants.

Equality of treatment and the due process right to demand respect for conduct protected by the substantive guarantee of liberty are linked in important respects, and a decision on the latter point advances both interests. If protected conduct is made criminal and the law which does so remains unexamined for its substantive validity, its stigma might remain even if it were not enforceable as drawn for equal protection reasons. When homosexual conduct is made criminal by the law of the State, that declaration in and of itself is an invitation to subject homosexual persons to discrimination both in the public and in the private spheres. The central holding of *Bowers* has been brought in question by this case, and it should be addressed. Its continuance as precedent demeans the lives of homosexual persons.

The stigma this criminal statute imposes, moreover, is not trivial. The offense, to be sure, is but a class C misdemeanor, a minor offense in the Texas legal system. Still, it remains a criminal offense with all that imports for the dignity of the persons charged. The petitioners will bear on their record the history of their criminal convictions. . . . We are advised that if Texas convicted an adult for private, consensual homosexual conduct under the statute here in question the convicted person would come within the registration laws of a least four States were he or she to be subject to their jurisdiction. This underscores the consequential nature of the punishment and the state-sponsored condemnation attendant to the criminal prohibition. Furthermore, the Texas criminal conviction carries with it the other collateral consequences always following a conviction, such as notations on job application forms, to mention but one example. . . .

The doctrine of *stare decisis* is essential to the respect accorded to the judgments of the Court and to the stability of the law. It is not, however, an inexorable command. . . .

The rationale of *Bowers* does not withstand careful analysis. In his dissenting opinion in *Bowers*, Justice Stevens came to these conclusions:

> Our prior cases make two propositions abundantly clear. First, the fact that the governing majority in a State has traditionally viewed a particular practice as immoral is not a sufficient reason for upholding a law prohibiting the practice; neither history nor tradition could save a law prohibiting miscegenation from constitutional attack. Second, individual decisions by married persons, concerning the intimacies of their physical relationship, even when not intended to produce offspring, are a form of "liberty" protected by the Due Process Clause of the Fourteenth Amendment. Moreover, this protection extends to intimate choices by unmarried as well as married persons.

Justice Stevens' analysis, in our view, should have been controlling in *Bowers* and should control here.

Bowers was not correct when it was decided, and it is not correct today. It ought not to remain binding precedent. *Bowers v. Hardwick* should be and now is overruled.

The present case does not involve minors. It does not involve persons who might be injured or coerced or who are situated in relationships where consent might not easily be refused. It does not involve public conduct or prostitution. It does not involve whether the government must give formal recognition to any relationship that homosexual persons seek to enter. The case does involve two adults who, with full and mutual consent from each other, engaged in sexual practices common to a homosexual lifestyle. The petitioners are entitled to respect for their private lives. The State cannot demean their existence or control their destiny by making their private sexual conduct a crime. Their right to liberty under the Due

Process Clause gives them the full right to engage in their conduct without intervention of the government. "It is a promise of the Constitution that there is a realm of personal liberty which the government may not enter." *Casey*, 505 U.S. at 47. The Texas statute furthers no legitimate state interest which can justify its intrusion into the personal and private life of the individual.

Had those who drew and ratified the Due Process Clauses of the Fifth Amendment or the Fourteenth Amendment known the components of liberty in its manifold possibilities, they might have been more specific. They did not presume to have this insight. They knew times can blind us to certain truths and later generations can see that laws once thought necessary and proper in fact serve only to oppress. As the Constitution endures, persons in every generation can invoke its principles in their own search for greater freedom.

JUSTICE O'CONNOR, concurring in the judgment.

The Court today overrules *Bowers*. I joined *Bowers*, and do not join the Court in overruling it. Nevertheless, I agree with the Court that Texas' statute banning same-sex sodomy is unconstitutional. Rather than relying on the substantive component of the Fourteenth Amendment's Due Process Clause, I base my conclusion on the Fourteenth Amendment's Equal Protection Clause. . . .

The statute at issue here makes sodomy a crime only if a person "engages in deviate sexual intercourse with another individual of the same sex." Sodomy between opposite-sex partners, however, is not a crime in Texas. That is, Texas treats the same conduct differently based solely on the participants. Those harmed by this law are people who have a same-sex sexual orientation and thus are more likely to engage in behavior prohibited by § 21.06.

The Texas statute makes homosexuals unequal in the eyes of the law by making particular conduct — and only that conduct — subject to criminal sanction. . . . [P]etitioners' convictions, if upheld, would disqualify them from or restrict their ability to engage in a variety of professions, including medicine, athletic training, and interior design. Indeed, were petitioners to move to one of four States, their convictions would require them to register as sex offenders to local law enforcement.

And the effect of Texas' sodomy law is not just limited to the threat of prosecution or consequence of conviction. Texas' sodomy law brands all homosexuals as criminals, thereby making it more difficult for homosexuals to be treated in the same manner as everyone else. Indeed, Texas itself has previously acknowledged the collateral effects of the law, stipulating in a prior challenge to this action that the law "legally sanctions discrimination against [homosexuals] in a variety of ways unrelated to the criminal law," including in the areas of "employment, family issues, and housing." *State v. Morales*, 826 S.W.2d 201, 203 (Tex. App. 1992).

Texas attempts to justify its law, and the effects of the law, by arguing that the statute satisfies rational basis review because it furthers the legitimate governmental interest of the promotion of morality. In *Bowers*, we held that a state law criminalizing sodomy as applied to homosexual couples did not violate substantive due process. We rejected the argument that no rational basis existed to justify the law, pointing to the government's interest in promoting morality. . . . *Bowers* did not hold that moral disapproval of a group is a rational basis under the Equal Protection Clause to criminalize homosexual sodomy when heterosexual sodomy is not punished. *but, uphold Bowers b/c no EP issue*

This case raises a different issue than *Bowers*: whether, under the Equal Protection Clause, moral disapproval is a legitimate state interest to justify by itself a statute that bans homosexual sodomy, but not heterosexual sodomy. It is not. Moral disapproval of this group, like a bare desire to harm the group, is an interest that is insufficient to satisfy rational basis review under the Equal Protection Clause. . . .

Moral disapproval of a group cannot be a legitimate governmental interest under the Equal Protection Clause because legal classifications must not be "drawn for the purpose of disadvantaging the group burdened by the law." . . . The Texas sodomy law "raises the inevitable inference that the disadvantage imposed is born of animosity toward the class of persons affected." . . .

Whether a sodomy law that is neutral both in effect and application would violate the substantive component of the Due Process Clause is an issue that need not be decided today. I am confident, however, that so long as the Equal Protection Clause requires a sodomy law to apply equally to the private consensual conduct of homosexuals and heterosexuals alike, such a law would not long stand in our democratic society. . . .

JUSTICE SCALIA, with whom the CHIEF JUSTICE and JUSTICE THOMAS join, dissenting.

I begin with the Court's surprising readiness to reconsider a decision rendered a mere 17 years ago in *Bowers v. Hardwick*. . . .

Having decided that it need not adhere to *stare decisis*, the Court still must establish that *Bowers* was wrongly decided and that the Texas statute, as applied to petitioners, is unconstitutional.

Texas Penal Code Ann. § 21.06(a) (2003) undoubtedly imposes constraints on liberty. So do laws prohibiting prostitution, recreational use of heroin, and, for that matter, working more than 60 hours per week in a bakery. But there is no right to "liberty" under the Due Process Clause, though today's opinion repeatedly makes that claim. The Fourteenth Amendment *expressly allows* States to deprive their citizens of "liberty," *so long as "due process of law" is provided*. . . .

Our opinions applying the doctrine known as "substantive due process" hold that the Due Process Clause prohibits States from infringing *fundamental* liberty interests, unless the infringement is narrowly tailored to serve a compelling state interest. We have held repeatedly, in cases the Court today does not overrule, that *only* fundamental rights qualify for this so-called "heightened scrutiny" protection — that is, rights which are "deeply rooted in this Nation's history and tradition." All other liberty interests may be abridged or abrogated pursuant to a validly enacted state law if that law is rationally related to a legitimate state interest.

Bowers held, first, that criminal prohibitions of homosexual sodomy are not subject to heightened scrutiny because they do not implicate a "fundamental right" under the Due Process Clause. . . .

The Court today does not overrule this holding. Not once does it describe homosexual sodomy as a "fundamental right" or a "fundamental liberty interest," nor does it subject the Texas statute to strict scrutiny. Instead, having failed to establish that the right to homosexual sodomy is "deeply rooted in this Nation's history and tradition," the Court concludes that the application of Texas's statute to petitioners' conduct fails the rational-basis test, and overrules *Bowers*' holding to the contrary. . . .

After discussing the history of antisodomy laws, the Court proclaims that, "it should be noted that there is no longstanding history in this country of laws directed at homosexual conduct as a distinct matter." . . . It is (as *Bowers* recognized) entirely irrelevant whether the laws in our long national tradition criminalizing homosexual sodomy were "directed at homosexual conduct as a distinct matter." Whether homosexual sodomy was prohibited by a law targeted at same-sex sexual relations or by a more general law prohibiting both homosexual and heterosexual sodomy, the only relevant point is that it *was* criminalized — which suffices to establish that homosexual sodomy is not a right "deeply rooted in our Nation's history and tradition." . . .

Bowers' conclusion that homosexual sodomy is not a fundamental right "deeply rooted in this Nation's history and tradition" is utterly unassailable.

Realizing that fact, the Court instead says: "[W]e think that our laws and traditions in the past half century are of most relevance here. These references show *an emerging awareness* that liberty gives substantial protection to adult persons in deciding how to conduct their private lives *in matters pertaining to sex*." Apart from the fact that such an "emerging awareness" does not establish a "fundamental right," the statement is factually false. States continue to prosecute all sorts of crimes by adults "in matters pertaining to sex": prostitution, adult incest, adultery, obscenity, and child pornography. Sodomy laws, too, have been enforced "in the past half century," in which there have been 134 reported cases involving prosecutions for consensual, adult, homosexual sodomy. . . .

In any event, an "emerging awareness" is by definition not "deeply rooted in this Nation's history and tradition[s]," as we have said "fundamental right" status requires. Constitutional entitlements do not spring into existence because some States choose to lessen or eliminate criminal sanctions on certain behavior. . . .

I turn now to the ground on which the Court squarely rests its holding: the contention that there is no rational basis for the law here under attack. This proposition is so out of accord with our jurisprudence — indeed, with the jurisprudence of *any* society we know — that it requires little discussion.

The Texas statute undeniably seeks to further the belief of its citizens that certain forms of sexual behavior are "immoral and unacceptable" — the same interest furthered by criminal laws against fornication, bigamy, adultery, adult incest, bestiality, and obscenity. *Bowers* held that this *was* a legitimate state interest. The Court today reaches the opposite conclusion. . . . This effectively decrees the end of all morals legislation. If, as the Court asserts, the promotion of majoritarian sexual morality is not even a *legitimate* state interest, none of the above-mentioned laws can survive rational-basis review. . . .

Today's opinion is the product of a Court, which is the product of a law-profession culture, that has largely signed on to the so-called homosexual agenda, by which I mean the agenda promoted by some homosexual activists directed at eliminating the moral opprobrium that has traditionally attached to homosexual conduct. I noted in an earlier opinion the fact that the American Association of Law Schools (to which any reputable law school *must* seek to belong) excludes from membership any school that refuses to ban from its job-interview facilities a law firm (no matter how small) that does not wish to hire as a prospective partner a person who openly engages in homosexual conduct.

One of the most revealing statements in today's opinion is the Court's grim warning that the criminalization of homosexual conduct is "an invitation to subject homosexual persons to discrimination both in the public and in the private spheres." It is clear from this that the Court has taken sides in the culture war, departing from its role of assuring, as neutral observer, that the democratic rules of engagement are observed. Many Americans do not want persons who openly engage in homosexual conduct as partners in their business, as scoutmasters for their children, as teachers in their children's schools, or as boarders in their home. They view this as protecting themselves and their families from a lifestyle that they believe to be immoral and destructive. The Court views it as "discrimination" which it is the function of our judgments to deter. So imbued is the Court with the law profession's anti-anti-homosexual culture, that it is seemingly unaware that the attitudes of that culture are not obviously "mainstream"; that in most States what the Court calls "discrimination" against those who engage in homosexual acts is perfectly legal. . . .

Let me be clear that I have nothing against homosexuals, or any other group, promoting their agenda through normal democratic means. Social perceptions of sexual and other morality change over time, and every group has the right to persuade its fellow citizens that its view of such matters is the best. That homosexuals have achieved some success in that enterprise is attested to by the fact that Texas is one of the few remaining States that criminalize private, consensual homosexual acts. But persuading one's fellow citizens is one thing, and imposing one's views in absence of democratic majority will is something else. . . .

At the end of its opinion — after having laid waste the foundations of our rational-basis jurisprudence — the Court says that the present case "does not involve whether the government must give formal recognition to any relationship that homosexual persons seek to enter." Do not believe it. . . . Today's opinion dismantles the structure of constitutional law that has permitted a distinction to be made between heterosexual and homosexual unions, insofar as formal recognition in marriage is concerned. If moral disapprobation of homosexual conduct is "no legitimate state interest" for purposes of proscribing that conduct, and if, as the Court coos (casting aside all pretense of neutrality), "[w]hen sexuality finds overt expression in intimate conduct with another person, the conduct can be but one element in a personal bond that is more enduring," what justification could there possibly be for denying the benefits of marriage to homosexual couples exercising "[t]he liberty protected by the Constitution"? Surely not the encouragement of procreation, since the sterile and the elderly are allowed to marry. This case "does not involve" the issue of homosexual marriage only if one entertains the belief that principle and logic have nothing to do with the decisions of this Court. Many will hope that, as the Court comfortingly assures us, this is so. . . .

NOTES AND QUESTIONS

1. *From Sodomy Bans to Same-Sex Marriage.* In *Lawrence*, Justice Kennedy distinguished between sodomy laws and bans on same-sex marriage when he noted that the case did "not involve [the question of] whether the government must give formal recognition to any relationships that homosexual persons seek to enter."[43] Justice O'Connor went further by suggesting that while sodomy laws are unconstitutional, same-sex marriage bans are not because "unlike the moral disapproval of same-sex relations — the asserted state interest in this case — other reasons exist to promote the institution of marriage beyond mere moral disapproval of an excluded group."[44] Justice Scalia, on the other hand, concluded that once sodomy statutes fall, so too would marriage bans.[45]

Five months after *Lawrence*, the Massachusetts Supreme Judicial Court ruled that, under the state constitution, same-sex couples could not be excluded from marriage. The decision, *Goodridge v. Department of Public Health*, is discussed in this chapter.[46] As you read the materials in Subsection C, below, consider whether Justice Scalia was right that *Lawrence* necessarily undermined states' ability to exclude same-sex couples from marriage. Is there a difference between criminalizing sexual relations and withholding state benefits based on sexual relations?

2. *Liberty Versus Privacy.* The *Lawrence* Court gave relatively little attention to the notion of privacy that had animated the Court's prior opinions in *Griswold*,

---

43. *Lawrence*, 539 U.S. at 578.
44. Id. at 585 (O'Connor, J., concurring).
45. See id. at 604–05 (Scalia, J., dissenting).
46. 798 N.E.2d 941 (Mass. 2003).

Eisenstadt, and *Roe* (as well as Justice Blackmun's dissent in *Bowers*). Althoug
Lawrence falls squarely in that line of cases, the focus of the majority opinion was
on "liberty," which more directly invokes the text of the Fourteenth Amendment. In
the family context, are notions of "privacy" and "liberty" likely to protect the same
things? Does one concept seem more appropriate than the other when thinking
about family or intimate relationships?

3. *Due Process Versus Equal Protection.* Justice Kennedy justified choosing
to rely on due process rather than equal protection grounds because the former
would directly address the ability of states to prohibit sodomy at all, while the latter
would simply require states to regulate sodomy in non-discriminatory ways (potentially infringing on the privacy rights of even more people).[47] Justice O'Connor, in
contrast, would have left *Bowers* in place, but invalidated the Texas law because it
represented impermissible moral disapproval of lesbians and gay men as a group,
and as such, violated the Equal Protection Clause.[48] Why, though, should moral
disapproval constitute a sufficient government interest for due process purposes
but not for equal protection?

4. *A Fundamental Right?* Justice Scalia criticized the majority for striking
down the Texas law under what he took to be rational basis review. He assumed
that the majority did not regard the right at stake as a fundamental right merit-
ing heightened scrutiny under the Due Process Clause. Did *Lawrence* implicate a
fundamental right? What level of scrutiny did the Court apply? Many courts have
puzzled over these questions.[49] In *Obergefell v. Hodges*, which we read later in the
chapter, the Court, in an opinion by Justice Kennedy, appeared to treat *Lawrence* as
part of the fundamental rights line of cases.[50]

5. *A Right to Have Sex?* In *Bowers*, the Court held that even though states
were restricted in their ability to regulate fertility, contraception, and abortion,
they were free to regulate sexual activity. When *Lawrence* was decided, roughly
one fifth of states had laws regulating private consensual adult sexual behavior.[51]
In *Lawrence*, the Court protected the right of consenting adults to engage in voluntary, non-commercial sexual activity in private, although the language of the
opinion is couched more in terms of protecting the relationship than the sexual
activity per se. *Lawrence* produced a variety of constitutional challenges to state

---

47. See *Lawrence*, 539 U.S. at 574–75.

48. See id. at 582–83 (O'Connor, J., concurring).

49. Compare Williams v. Att'y Gen. of Alabama, 378 F.3d 1232 (11th Cir. 2004) (reasoning that
Lawrence did not find a fundamental right and applied rational basis review), with Witt v. Dep't of Air
Force, 527 F.3d 806 (9th Cir. 2008) (reasoning that *Lawrence* applied heightened scrutiny).

50. See, e.g., 135 S. Ct. 2584, 2589 (2015) (citing *Lawrence* in a passage about "[t]he identification and
protection of fundamental rights").

51. Sara Sun Beale, The Many Faces of Overcriminalization: From Morals and Mattress Tags to
Overfederalization, 54 Am. U. L. Rev. 747 (2005).

...e or otherwise restrict sexual activity.[52] Those legal challenges ... results. The Virginia Supreme Court invalidated its criminal ...on.[53] North Carolina's criminal ban on cohabitation was struck ... As discussed above, the Kansas Supreme Court invalidated a law ... same-sex statutory rape more harshly than different-sex statutory ...fth Circuit invalidated a Texas ban on the use of sex toys, but the ...cuit upheld a similar one in Alabama.[56] Can criminal bans on adultery or p... gamy survive after *Lawrence*? What about other restrictions on sexual conduct? The following materials consider the impact of *Lawrence* on laws prohibiting incest.

LOWE V. SWANSON
663 F.3d 258 (6th Cir. 2011)

GRIFFIN, CIRCUIT JUDGE.

Petitioner Paul Lowe appeals the district court's denial of his petition for a writ of habeas corpus, arguing that the Ohio Supreme Court unreasonably applied federal law as clearly established by the Supreme Court in *Lawrence v. Texas*, 539 U.S. 558 (2003), when it upheld his incest conviction for engaging in sexual conduct with his stepdaughter. We disagree and therefore affirm.

Lowe was charged with one count of sexual battery for engaging in sexual conduct by means of sexual intercourse with his 22-year-old stepdaughter, in violation of Ohio Rev. Code § 2907.03(A)(5), which makes it a crime to "engage in sexual conduct with another, not the spouse of the offender, when ... [t]he offender is the other person's natural or adoptive parent, or a stepparent, or guardian, custodian, or person in loco parentis of the other person." Lowe moved to dismiss the charge in the trial court, arguing that the facts alleged in the indictment did not constitute an offense under Ohio Rev. Code § 2907.03(A)(5) because there was a "clear legislative intent to have the law apply to children, not adults." Lowe also argued that the statute was unconstitutional as applied to him because the government had no legitimate interest in regulating sexual activity between consenting adults. . . .

---

52. On the scope and meaning of *Lawrence*, see Cass R. Sunstein, What Did *Lawrence* Hold? Of Autonomy, Desuetude, Sexuality, and Marriage, 2003 Sup. Ct. Rev. 27; Ariela R. Dubler, From McLaughlin v. Florida to Lawrence v. Texas: Sexual Freedom and the Road to Marriage, 106 Colum. L. Rev. 1165 (2006).

53. Martin v. Ziherl, 607 S.E.2d 367 (Va. 2005).

54. Hobbs. v. Smith, No. 05 CVS 267, 2006 WL 3103008 (N.C. Super. Ct. Aug. 25, 2006).

55. State v. Limon, 122 P.3d 22 (Kan. 2005).

56. Reliable Consultants, Inc. v. Earle, 517 F.3d 738 (5th Cir. 2008); Williams v. Morgan, 478 F.3d 1316 (11th Cir. 2007).

The Ohio Court of Appeals upheld Lowe's conviction on direct review. . . . On discretionary review, the Ohio Supreme Court also affirmed. It determined that "*Lawrence* did not announce a 'fundamental' right to all consensual adult sexual activity, let alone consensual sex with one's adult children or stepchildren" and that "the statute in *Lawrence* was subjected to a rational-basis rather than a strict-scrutiny test." . . .

Lowe then filed a 28 U.S.C. § 2254 petition for habeas relief with the federal district court, arguing that the Ohio Supreme Court unreasonably applied federal law as clearly established by the Supreme Court in *Lawrence*. . . .

Lowe argues that he is entitled to habeas relief because the Ohio Supreme Court "unreasonably applied the federal law announced in *Lawrence*." According to Lowe, the Ohio Supreme Court "made the same mistake as the *Bowers* Court by framing the issue as 'whether [Mr.] Lowe is guaranteed a fundamental right to engage in sexual intercourse with his consenting adult stepdaughter,' " rather than framing the issue more broadly as "the recognition of the right, as between consenting adults, to engage in private sexual conduct." Lowe also contends that this broad right is a fundamental one requiring strict scrutiny. . . .

Lowe's arguments have some support. In *Cook v. Gates*, 528 F.3d 42 (1st Cir. 2008), the First Circuit, considering a challenge by members of the United States Armed Forces who claimed that the "Don't Ask, Don't Tell" statute, violated their substantive due process rights, found that *Lawrence* announced a broad Fourteenth Amendment right to sexual privacy. The court noted that "[t]he *Lawrence* Court characterized the constitutional question as whether petitioners' criminal convictions for adult consensual sexual intimacy in the home violate their vital interests in liberty and privacy protected by the Due Process Clause"; and it further explained that "[t]aking into account the precedent relied on by *Lawrence*, the tenor of its language, its special reliance on Justice Stevens' *Bowers* dissent, and its rejection of morality as an adequate basis for the law in question, we are convinced that *Lawrence* recognized that adults maintain a protected liberty interest to engage in certain 'consensual sexual intimacy in the home.' " The Fifth Circuit came to a similar conclusion in *Reliable Consultants, Inc. v. Earle*, 517 F.3d 738 (5th Cir. 2008), asserting that "[t]he right the Court recognized [in *Lawrence*] was not simply a right to engage in the sexual act itself, but instead a right to be free from governmental intrusion regarding 'the most private human contact, sexual behavior.' " *Id.* at 744.

Also, were *Lawrence* applicable, there is authority for Lowe's position that a heightened standard, greater than a rational basis, may govern. Again, Lowe relies on *Cook*, where the First Circuit held that *Lawrence* "applies a standard of review that lies between strict scrutiny and rational basis" because it "balanced the strength of the state's asserted interest in prohibiting immoral conduct against the degree of intrusion into the petitioners' private sexual life caused by the statute in order to determine whether the law was unconstitutionally applied." *Cook*, 528 F.3d at 56. . . .

Other circuit courts, however, have concluded just the opposite. In *Seegmiller v. La Verkin City*, 528 F.3d 762 (10th Cir. 2008), the Tenth Circuit considered a plaintiff's claim that her employer . . . "violated her fundamental liberty interest to 'engage in a private act of consensual sex.'" The court noted that "[b]roadly speaking, no one disputes a right to be free from government interference in matters of consensual sexual privacy. But as the case law teaches us, a plaintiff asserting a substantive due process right must both (1) carefully describe the right and its scope; and (2) show how the right as described fits within the Constitution's notions of ordered liberty." *Id.* at 769 (citing *Washington v. Glucksberg*, 521 U.S. 702, 721 (1997)). Applying that standard, the court concluded that *Lawrence* did not announce a fundamental right, noting that "nowhere in *Lawrence* does the Court describe the right at issue in that case as a fundamental right or a fundamental liberty interest. It instead applied rational basis review to the law and found it lacking."

The Court of Appeals for the Eleventh Circuit has similarly construed *Lawrence*. In *Lofton v. Sec'y of Dep't of Children & Family Servs.*, 358 F.3d 804 (11th Cir. 2004), it held that "it is a strained and ultimately incorrect reading of *Lawrence* to interpret it to announce a new fundamental right" when the *Lawrence* opinion "contains virtually no inquiry into the question of whether the petitioners' asserted right is one of those fundamental rights and liberties which are, objectively, deeply rooted in this Nation's history and tradition and implicit in the concept of ordered liberty . . ."; "never provides the careful description of the asserted fundamental liberty interest that is to accompany fundamental-rights analysis"; and "[m]ost significant[ly] . . . never applied strict scrutiny, the proper standard when fundamental rights are implicated, but instead invalidated the Texas statute on rational basis grounds. . . ."

In the present case, as the magistrate judge and district court correctly concluded, this split of authority provides strong support . . . to affirm the decision of the Ohio Supreme Court. In light of the disagreement among the circuits and the well-reasoned authority in favor of respondent, we hold that the Ohio Supreme Court did not unreasonably apply clearly established federal law in reviewing Ohio Rev. Code § 2907.03(A)(5) for a rational basis.

Furthermore, assuming that *Lawrence* clearly established a fundamental right and/or a higher standard of review, we hold that neither the right nor standard is implicated in the present case. In this regard, we agree with the Seventh Circuit's decision in *Muth v. Frank*, 412 F.3d 808 (7th Cir. 2005). There, the defendant was convicted of incest in a Wisconsin state court and argued that "Wisconsin's incest statute is unconstitutional insofar as it seeks to criminalize a sexual relationship between two consenting adults." The defendant filed a petition for habeas corpus relief that the federal district court denied. On appeal, the Seventh Circuit affirmed. . . .

A similar conclusion applies here. As the Seventh Circuit held, *Lawrence* did not address or clearly establish federal law regarding state incest statutes. Indeed, the *Lawrence* Court expressly distinguished statutes like Ohio Rev. Code § 2907.03(A)(5) when it emphasized that "[t]he present case does not involve ... persons who might be injured or coerced or who are situated in relationships where consent might not easily be refused." Unlike sexual relationships between unrelated same-sex adults, the stepparent-stepchild relationship is the kind of relationship in which a person might be injured or coerced or where consent might not easily be refused, regardless of age, because of the inherent influence of the stepparent over the stepchild.

Moreover, the State of Ohio's interest in criminalizing incest is far greater and much different than the interest of the State of Texas in prosecuting homosexual sodomy. Ohio's paramount concern is protecting the family from the destructive influence of intra-family, extra-marital sexual contact. This is an important state interest that the *Lawrence* Court did not invalidate. For these reasons, we hold that the Ohio Supreme Court's decision was not contrary to and did not involve an unreasonable application of clearly established federal law.

Lowe's remaining arguments are meritless. His claim that the Ohio law is contrary to *Lawrence* because it is morality-based fails for two reasons. First, the state has a legitimate and important interest in protecting families. Second, the *Lawrence* Court did not categorically invalidate criminal laws that are based in part on morality. Finally, Lowe's assertion that Ohio's "generalized interest in protecting the family unit" cannot support the statute as applied in this case because "there is no evidence in the record that beyond [his] technical status as stepfather an actual family unit even existed" is also without merit. Ohio has an interest in protecting *all* families against destructive sexual contacts irrespective of the particular factual family dynamic. . . .

For these reasons, we affirm the judgment of the district court.

NOTES AND QUESTIONS

1. *Regulating Incest.* Incest regulations work in two ways. They prohibit certain marriages, and, as in *Lowe*, they prohibit sexual conduct between family members. Are the justifications for the two sets of laws the same? While incest prohibitions are universal, the specific relationships that are prohibited have varied across societies and even now across jurisdictions in the U.S. Incest prohibitions might be based on affinity (i.e., relationships through marriage or adoption) or consanguinity (i.e., relationships based on genetic ties). What rationales support each type of prohibition? Is it possible to justify incest prohibitions — based on both affinity and consanguinity — without endorsing the same sort of moral judgment that Justice O'Connor declared impermissible in *Lawrence*? Consider these questions as you explore impediments to marriage below.

2. *The Role of Consent.* What is the proper role of consent in the legal regulation of adult incest? What justifies vitiating the consent, for example, of adult

stepchildren to have sexual relations with their stepparents or of adult siblings to have sex with each other? Is the problem that consent in intra-family contexts cannot be meaningful (analogous perhaps to the ways in which a minor lacks the capacity to consent to have sex with an adult)? Or is the problem that, even if consent to sex can be meaningful in at least some intra-family circumstances, there are other societal interests that outweigh considerations of consent and personal liberty?

3. *Incest Between Adults?* What is the danger of permitting adult relatives to engage in consensual sexual relationships? Consider the following argument by political scientist Stephen Macedo:

> The distinctive forms of love and trust that characterize healthy family relations . . . depend on the exclusion of sexual relations. For siblings or parents and children to consider each other as eligible sexual partners *prospectively* is inherently corrupting of norms that sustain healthy and valuable family relations, and these are vital to human well-being. If we were to announce permission for adult siblings, or parents and their adult children, past a certain age to have sexual relations, this would reshape the way that siblings and parents and children regard one another generally, including from the time children are very young. . . . Once the idea becomes socially acceptable, it becomes a prospective possibility, available to all, shaping . . . the imaginations of the young and older family members. It becomes thinkable for parents to consider raising their children to be prospective sexual partners, but of course, only at the proper age. How could we trust, if ever this happened, that the parent had not manipulated and subverted the education for independence and equal freedom that every child is owed (like Humbert Humbert's rearing of Lolita)?[57]

4. Lawrence *and Incest.* The courts have consistently rejected the claim that *Lawrence* requires striking down incest bans.[58] Are they correct to do so even when the sexual activity is between two consenting adults?

PROBLEM

The highest court in a state has consolidated the appeals in two cases. In the first, a married woman challenges the constitutionality of her criminal conviction for adultery, a charge brought after her soon-to-be ex-husband reported her behavior

57. Stephen Macedo, Just Married: Same-Sex Couples, Monogamy and the Future of Marriage 195 (2016).

58. In addition to the court's ruling in *Lowe,* see, e.g., Muth v. Frank, 412 F.3d 808 (7th Cir. 2005); People v. McEvoy, 154 Cal. Rptr. 3d 914 (Cal. Ct. App. 2013); People v. Scott, 68 Cal. Rptr. 3d 592 (Cal. Ct. App. 2007); Prather v. Commonwealth, No. 2012-CA-001725-MR, 2014 WL 2536866 (Ky. Ct. App. June 6, 2014); State v. Freeman, 801 N.E.2d 906 (Ohio Ct. App. 2003).

to the police. In the second, a 50-year-old man challenges the constitutionality of his conviction for incest after his wife discovered and reported that he was having a consensual, sexual relationship with his 19-year-old biological daughter, who had been raised exclusively by her mother. How should the court rule on these constitutional claims? Must they be resolved in the same way? Is it relevant that adultery is an extremely common behavior and consensual incest is relatively rare?

II. Eligibility to Marry

This section considers three substantive restrictions on the choice of marriage partner: (i) the requirement that the spouses be different sexes (the same-sex marriage prohibition), (ii) the requirement that the spouses be unrelated (the incest prohibition), and (iii) the requirement that there be only two spouses (the polygamy prohibition). For most of American history, every state enforced each of these prohibitions.

As a result of the Supreme Court's ruling in Obergefell v. Hodges in 2015, no state is constitutionally permitted to bar same-sex couples from marrying. Yet states continue to enforce prohibitions on incestuous and bigamous marriages. Does the Court's decision to strike down bans on same-sex marriage mean that restrictions on incestuous and polygamous marriages should be overturned as well? Or is the issue of same-sex marriage sufficiently unlike the issue of incestuous or polygamous marriage — doctrinally, conceptually, politically, or culturally?

In the following cases, courts consider the constitutionality of state restrictions of the choice of marital partner. Such restrictions might be evaluated under either the Due Process Clause doctrine that has accorded constitutional protection to certain family relationships (including marriage), or under the Equal Protection Clause doctrine that disfavors laws that promote inequality among identity-based groups. As you read, consider how courts do and should apply each doctrinal framework to these distinct restrictions.

In addition to analyzing the constitutionality of these restrictions, you should also think about them as matters of social policy. What are the costs and benefits of these restrictions? How, if at all, *should* the state restrict the choice of a marital partner? What are the individual interests at stake? Do the courts' analyses of the constitutionality of these restrictions promote or undermine good social policy?

In thinking through both the constitutional and policy issues, it will be helpful to keep in mind two broad questions. First, to what extent does the restriction burden an individual's choice of a marital partner? Put differently, how are people harmed by the restriction? Second, on the other side of the balance, how would the state justify its restriction on individual choice? What is the legitimacy and weight

:erest, and how well does the challenged restriction further the gov-
ctives?

:ase below, Loving v. Virginia, concerns the constitutionality of racial
n the choice of marital partner. It is a foundational case that continues
ıking about all sorts of state marriage restrictions.

A. The Constitutional Framework

LOVING V. VIRGINIA
388 U.S. 1 (1967)

MR. CHIEF JUSTICE WARREN delivered the opinion of the Court.

This case presents a constitutional question never addressed by this Court: whether a statutory scheme adopted by the State of Virginia to prevent marriages between persons solely on the basis of racial classifications violates the Equal Protection and Due Process Clauses of the Fourteenth Amendment.

In June 1958, two residents of Virginia, Mildred Jeter, a Negro woman, and Richard Loving, a white man, were married in the District of Columbia pursuant to its laws. Shortly after their marriage, the Lovings returned to Virginia and established their marital abode in Caroline County. At the October Term, 1958, of the Circuit Court of Caroline County, a grand jury issued an indictment charging the Lovings with violating Virginia's ban on interracial marriages. On January 6, 1959, the Lovings pleaded guilty to the charge and were sentenced to one year in jail; however, the trial judge suspended the sentence for a period of 25 years on the condition that the Lovings leave the State and not return to Virginia together for 25 years. He stated in an opinion that:

> Almighty God created the races white, black, yellow, malay and red, and he placed them on separate continents. And but for the interference with his arrangement there would be no cause for such marriages. The fact that he separated the races shows that he did not intend for the races to mix. . . .

The two statutes under which appellants were convicted and sentenced are part of a comprehensive statutory scheme aimed at prohibiting and punishing interracial marriages. The Lovings were convicted of violating § 20-58 of the Virginia Code:

> Leaving State to evade law.-If any white person and colored person shall go out of this State, for the purpose of being married, and with the intention of returning, and be married out of it, and afterwards return to and reside in it, cohabiting as man and wife, they shall be punished as provided in § 20-59, and the marriage shall be governed by the same law as if it had been solemnized in this State. The fact of their cohabitation here as man and wife shall be evidence of their marriage.

Section 20-59, which defines the penalty for miscegenation, provides:

> Punishment for marriage.-If any white person intermarry with a colored person, or any colored person intermarry with a white person, he shall be guilty of a felony and shall be punished by confinement in the penitentiary for not less than one nor more than five years.

Other central provisions in the Virginia statutory scheme are § 20-57, which automatically voids all marriages between "a white person and a colored person" without any judicial proceeding,[3] and §§ 20-54 and 1-14 which, respectively, define "white persons" and "colored persons and Indians" for purposes of the statutory prohibitions.[4] The Lovings have never disputed in the course of this litigation that Mrs. Loving is a "colored person" or that Mr. Loving is a "white person" within the meanings given those terms by the Virginia statutes. Virginia is now one of 16 States which prohibit and punish marriages on the basis of racial classifications.[5] Penalties for miscegenation arose as an incident to slavery and have been common in Virginia since the colonial period. The present statutory scheme dates from the adoption of the Racial Integrity Act of 1924, passed during the period of extreme nativism which followed the end of the First World War. The central features of this Act, and current Virginia law, are the absolute prohibition of a "white person" marrying other than another "white person," a prohibition against issuing marriage licenses until the issuing official is satisfied that the applicants' statements as to their race are correct, certificates of "racial

---

3. Section 20-57 of the Virginia Code provides: "Marriages void without decree.-All marriages between a white person and a colored person shall be absolutely void without any decree of divorce or other legal process." Va. Code Ann. § 20-57 (1960 Repl. Vol.).

4. Section 20-54 of the Virginia Code provides: "Intermarriage prohibited; meaning of term 'white persons.'-It shall hereafter be unlawful for any white person in this State to marry any save a white person, or a person with no other admixture of blood than white and American Indian. For the purpose of this chapter, the term 'white person' shall apply only to such person as has no trace whatever of any blood other than Caucasian; but persons who have one-sixteenth or less of the blood of the American Indian and have no other non-Caucasic blood shall be deemed to be white persons. All laws heretofore passed and now in effect regarding the intermarriage of white and colored persons shall apply to marriages prohibited by this chapter." Va. Code Ann. § 20-54 (1960 Repl. Vol.).

The exception for persons with less than one-sixteenth "of the blood of the American Indian" is apparently accounted for, in the words of a tract issued by the Registrar of the State Bureau of Vital Statistics, by "the desire of all to recognize as an integral and honored part of the white race the descendants of John Rolfe and Pocahontas . . . Section 1-14 of the Virginia Code provides:

Colored persons and Indians defined.-Every person in whom there is ascertainable any Negro blood shall be deemed and taken to be a colored person, and every person not a colored person having one fourth or more of American Indian blood shall be deemed an American Indian; except that members of Indian tribes existing in this Commonwealth having one fourth or more of Indian blood and less than one sixteenth of Negro blood shall be deemed tribal Indians." Va. Code Ann. § 1-14 (1960 Repl.Vol.).

5. . . . Over the past 15 years, 14 States have repealed laws outlawing interracial marriages: Arizona, California, Colorado, Idaho, Indiana, Maryland, Montana, Nebraska, Nevada, North Dakota, Oregon, South Dakota, Utah, and Wyoming. The first state court to recognize that miscegenation statutes violate the Equal Protection Clause was the Supreme Court of California.

composition" to be kept by both local and state registrars, and the carrying forward of earlier prohibitions against racial intermarriage.

I.

In upholding the constitutionality of these provisions in the decision below, the Supreme Court of Appeals of Virginia referred to its 1955 decision in Naim v. Naim, 87 S.E.2d 749 (Va. 1955), as stating the reasons supporting the validity of these laws. In *Naim*, the state court concluded that the State's legitimate purposes were "to preserve the racial integrity of its citizens," and to prevent "the corruption of blood," "a mongrel breed of citizens," and "the obliteration of racial pride," obviously an endorsement of the doctrine of White Supremacy. . . .

While the state court is no doubt correct in asserting that marriage is a social relation subject to the State's police power, Maynard v. Hill, 125 U.S. 190 (1888), the State does not contend in its argument before this Court that its powers to regulate marriage are unlimited notwithstanding the commands of the Fourteenth Amendment. Nor could it do so in light of Meyer v. State of Nebraska, 262 U.S. 390 (1923), and Skinner v. State of Oklahoma, 316 U.S. 535 (1942). Instead, the State argues that the meaning of the Equal Protection Clause, as illuminated by the statements of the Framers, is only that state penal laws containing an interracial element as part of the definition of the offense must apply equally to whites and Negroes in the sense that members of each race are punished to the same degree. Thus, the State contends that, because its miscegenation statutes punish equally both the white and the Negro participants in an interracial marriage, these statutes, despite their reliance on racial classifications do not constitute an invidious discrimination based upon race. The second argument advanced by the State assumes the validity of its equal application theory. The argument is that, if the Equal Protection Clause does not outlaw miscegenation statutes because of their reliance on racial classifications, the question of constitutionality would thus become whether there was any rational basis for a State to treat interracial marriages differently from other marriages. On this question, the State argues, the scientific evidence is substantially in doubt and, consequently, this Court should defer to the wisdom of the state legislature in adopting its policy of discouraging interracial marriages.

Because we reject the notion that the mere "equal application" of a statute containing racial classifications is enough to remove the classifications from the Fourteenth Amendment's proscription of all invidious racial discriminations, we do not accept the State's contention that these statutes should be upheld if there is any possible basis for concluding that they serve a rational purpose. The mere fact of equal application does not mean that our analysis of these statutes should follow the approach we have taken in cases involving no racial discrimination where the Equal Protection Clause has been arrayed against a statute discriminating between the kinds of advertising which may be displayed on trucks in New York City, or an exemption in Ohio's ad valorem tax for merchandise owned by a non-resident in a storage warehouse. In these cases, involving distinctions not drawn according to race, the Court has merely asked whether there is any rational foundation for the discriminations, and has deferred to the wisdom of the state legislatures. In the case at bar, however, we deal with statutes containing racial classifications, and the fact of equal application does not immunize the statute from the very heavy burden of justification which the Fourteenth Amendment has traditionally required of state statutes drawn according to race.

The State finds support for its "equal application" theory in the decision of the Court in Pace v. State of Alabama, 106 U.S. 583 (1883). In that case, the Court upheld a conviction under an Alabama statute forbidding adultery or fornication between a white person and a Negro which imposed a greater penalty than that of a statute proscribing similar conduct by members of the same race. The Court reasoned that the statute could not be said to discriminate against Negroes because the punishment for each participant in the offense was the same. However, as recently as the 1964 Term, in rejecting the reasoning of that case, we stated "*Pace* represents a limited view of the Equal Protection Clause which has not withstood analysis in the subsequent decisions of this Court." McLaughlin v. Florida, 379 U.S. 184, 188 (1964). As we there demonstrated, the Equal Protection Clause requires the consideration of whether the classifications drawn by any statute constitute an arbitrary and invidious discrimination. The clear and central purpose of the Fourteenth Amendment was to eliminate all official state sources of invidious racial discrimination in the States.

There can be no question but that Virginia's miscegenation statutes rest solely upon distinctions drawn according to race. The statutes proscribe generally accepted conduct if engaged in by members of different races. Over the years, this Court has consistently repudiated "(d)istinctions between citizens solely because of their ancestry" as being "odious to a free people whose institutions are founded upon the doctrine of equality." At the very least, the Equal Protection Clause demands that racial classifications, especially suspect in criminal statutes, be subjected to the "most rigid scrutiny," Korematsu v. United States, 323 U.S. 214 (1944), and, if they are ever to be upheld, they must be shown to be necessary to the accomplishment of some permissible state objective, independent of the racial discrimination which it was the object of the Fourteenth Amendment to eliminate. Indeed, two members of this Court have already stated that they "cannot conceive of a valid legislative purpose which makes the color of a person's skin the test of whether his conduct is a criminal offense." There is patently no legitimate overriding purpose independent of invidious racial discrimination which justifies this classification. The fact that Virginia prohibits only interracial marriages involving white persons demonstrates that the racial classifications must stand on their own justification, as measures designed to maintain White Supremacy.[11] We have consistently denied the constitutionality of measures which restrict the rights of citizens on account of race. There can be no doubt that restricting the freedom to marry solely because of racial classifications violates the central meaning of the Equal Protection Clause.

II.

These statutes also deprive the Lovings of liberty without due process of law in violation of the Due Process Clause of the Fourteenth Amendment. The freedom to marry has long been recognized as one of the vital personal rights essential to the orderly pursuit of happiness by free men.

Marriage is one of the "basic civil rights of man," fundamental to our very existence and survival. To deny this fundamental freedom on so unsupportable a basis as the racial classifications embodied in these statutes, classifications so directly subversive of the principle of equality at the heart of the Fourteenth Amendment, is surely to deprive all the State's citizens of liberty without due process of law. The Fourteenth Amendment requires that the freedom of choice to marry not be restricted by invidious racial discriminations. Under our Constitution, the freedom to marry or not marry, a person of another race resides with the individual and cannot be infringed by the State.

NOTES AND QUESTIONS

1. *Liberty and Equality.* Note that the Court in *Loving* addresses the claim on both due process and equal protection grounds. The Court says that "the Equal Protection Clause requires the consideration of whether the classifications drawn by any statute constitute an arbitrary and invidious discrimination." In what way is the Virginia law "arbitrary and invidious"? Is the problem that such laws restricted individual freedom to marry (a due process violation)? Or is it that they contributed to group-based inequality (an equal protection violation)? Or are the equality and liberty dimensions related in important ways?

---

11. Appellants point out that the State's concern in these statutes, as expressed in the words of the 1924 Act's title, "An Act to Preserve Racial Integrity," extends only to the integrity of the white race. While Virginia prohibits whites from marrying any nonwhite (subject to the exception for the descendants of Pocahontas), Negroes, Orientals, and any other racial class may intermarry without statutory interference. Appellants contend that this distinction renders Virginia's miscegenation statutes arbitrary and unreasonable even assuming the constitutional validity of an official purpose to preserve "racial integrity." We need not reach this contention because we find the racial classifications in these statutes repugnant to the Fourteenth Amendment, even assuming an even-handed state purpose to protect the "integrity" of all races.

2. *The Economics of Miscegenation Bans.* The consequences of miscegenation statutes such as the Virginia law were far reaching. As the Court notes, such laws expressed an ideology of white supremacy. Miscegenation laws also contributed to racial inequality in a more practical way. By prohibiting marriages between whites and non-whites, such laws might also have contributed to whites' maintenance of their dominant economic position. If black women and white men could not marry, then neither could black women inherit or otherwise lay claim to any of the property of their white male partners. Indeed, miscegenation statutes were often invoked to invalidate a marriage and preclude a black woman from inheriting from her husband or benefiting from the financial support that marriage required husbands to provide.[59]

3. *The Construction of Race.* The transition from the Court's decision in *Pace* to its decision in *Loving* partly reflects changes in understandings of race.[60] In the nineteenth century, racial groups were believed to be biologically distinct and ineradicably different; some races were "better" than others. By the middle of the twentieth century, in the aftermath of the Holocaust, such thinking had begun to be discredited. Indeed, the term "racism" first came into being in Germany in the Nazi era to discredit racial ideas that had once been accepted as common sense. As a result, race came to be understood as an artificial, rather than natural, basis on which to regulate marriage.[61]

4. *Post-Loving Marriage Cases.* After *Loving*, the Supreme Court's 1978 decision in Zablocki v. Redhail struck down a state statute that precluded non-custodial parents with unpaid child support obligations from marrying unless they first received a court order permitting them to marry.[62] Describing marriage as a "fundamental right" and as "the foundation of the family in our society," the Court explained that "the decision to marry has been placed on the same level of importance as decisions relating to procreation, childbirth, child rearing, and family relationships."[63] The Court also relied on the Equal Protection Clause in striking down the law, finding a violation because the state had provided unequal access to a fundamental right. The Court viewed the law as creating three classifications that burdened the right to marry: between parents with and without support obligations, between the affluent and the

---

59. See Peggy Pascoe, Miscegenation Law, Court Cases, and Ideologies of "Race" in Twentieth-Century America, 83 J. Am. Hist. 44, 50 (1996).

60. For discussion of anti-miscegenation laws as they applied to different racial and ethnic groups, see Rachel F. Moran, Love with A Proper Stranger: What Anti-Miscegenation Laws Can Tell Us About the Meaning of Race, Sex, and Marriage, 32 Hofstra L. Rev. 1663, 1664 (2004); Deenesh Sohoni, Unsuitable Suitors: Anti-Miscegenation Laws, Naturalization Laws, and the Construction of Asian Identities, 41 Law & Soc'y Rev. 587, 587 (2007).

61. See George M. Fredrickson, Racism: A Short History (2002).

62. 434 U.S. 374 (1978).

63. Id. at 386.

d, and between custodial and noncustodial parents.[64] (Today, as we
pter 1, it is rare to see a court reason expressly in this way. Instead,
o separate the due process analysis of fundamental rights from the
ion analysis of impermissible classifications.) Although a majority
ki Court concurred in the ruling, the Justices agreed on no single
rationale, with four Justices writing concurring opinions. The opinion for the
Court noted that:

> By reaffirming the fundamental character of the right to marry, we do not
> mean to suggest that every state regulation which relates in any way to the
> incidents of or prerequisites for marriage must be subjected to rigorous scru-
> tiny. To the contrary, reasonable regulations that do not significantly inter-
> fere with decisions to enter into the marital relationship may legitimately be
> imposed.[65]

Less than a decade later, in Turner v. Safley, the Court struck down a state regulation that allowed prisoners to marry only if they first received the permission
of the warden, which would be granted only for compelling reasons.[66] Although
inmates would not necessarily be permitted to sexually consummate their marriages, the Court, in an opinion by Justice O'Connor, reasoned that:

> Many important attributes of marriage remain, however, after taking into
> account the limitations imposed by prison life. First, inmate marriages,
> like others, are expressions of emotional support and public commitment.
> These elements are an important and significant aspect of the marital
> relationship. In addition, many religions recognize marriage as having
> spiritual significance; for some inmates and their spouses, therefore, the
> commitment of marriage may be an exercise of religious faith as well as
> an expression of personal dedication. Third, most inmates eventually will
> be released by parole or commutation, and therefore most inmate mar-
> riages are formed in the expectation that they ultimately will be fully con-
> summated. Finally, marital status often is a precondition to the receipt of
> government benefits (e.g., Social Security benefits), property rights (e.g.,
> tenancy by the entirety, inheritance rights), and other, less tangible ben-
> efits (e.g., legitimation of children born out of wedlock). These incidents
> of marriage, like the religious and personal aspects of the marriage com-
> mitment, are unaffected by the fact of confinement or the pursuit of legit-
> imate corrections goals.[67]

---

64. Id. at 388–89.
65. Id. at 386.
66. 482 U.S. 78 (1987).
67. Id. at 95–96.

B. Marriage for Same-Sex Couples

Throughout American history, every state defined marriage, either explicitly or implicitly, as a relationship between a man and a woman. In the 1970s, same-sex couples challenged the different-sex marriage requirement in court and were consistently rebuffed.[68] Courts failed to engage seriously with the plaintiffs' arguments, rejecting claims based on the circular reasoning that the very definition of marriage precludes marriage between individuals of the same sex. After the Minnesota Supreme Court, in Baker v. Nelson, rejected a same-sex couple's challenge to their exclusion from marriage,[69] the U.S. Supreme Court, in 1972, dismissed the couple's appeal "for want of a substantial federal question."[70]

While marriage litigation subsided over the subsequent two decades, by the 1990s, marriage claims confronted courts again. To insulate decisions from Supreme Court review (not only because of the Supreme Court's cursory rejection of the plaintiffs' claim in Baker v. Nelson but also because of the general hostility the Court had shown to gay rights claims), litigants brought suit in state courts under state constitutional provisions.

In its groundbreaking 1993 ruling in *Baehr v. Lewin*, the Hawaii Supreme Court ruled that the different-sex requirement in the state's marriage law classified based on sex and thus needed to satisfy strict scrutiny under the state constitution's Equal Rights Amendment.[71] On remand, the trial court held that the marriage restriction failed that demanding standard.[72] Yet, before the decision went into effect, voters approved an amendment to the state constitution that allowed the state to "reserve marriage to opposite-sex couples."[73] Accordingly, no same-sex couple actually married in Hawaii in light of *Baehr*. Nonetheless, while the *Baehr* litigation was proceeding, the prospect that same-sex couples might travel to Hawaii to marry and then return to their home states alarmed many legislatures.[74] States passed laws to ban same-sex marriage and prohibit recognition of such marriages from other jurisdictions.[75] In 1996, Congress passed the Defense of Marriage Act (DOMA), which limited marriage to different-sex couples for purposes of federal law and declared that states need not recognize same-sex marriages entered into in other states.[76]

---

68. For a fascinating history of these cases, see Michael Boucai, Glorious Precedents: When Gay Marriage Was Radical, 27 Yale J.L. & Human. 1 (2015).

69. 191 N.W.2d 185 (Minn. 1971).

70. 409 U.S. 810 (1972).

71. 852 P.2d 44 (Haw. 1993).

72. Baehr v. Miike, CIV No. 91-1394, 1996 WL 694235 (Haw. Cir. Ct. Dec. 3, 1996).

73. Haw. Const. art. I, § 23.

74. For a review of this history, see, e.g., Joanna L. Grossman, Fear and Loathing in Massachusetts: Same-Sex Marriage and Some Lessons from the History of Marriage and Divorce, 14 B.U. Pub. Int. L.J. 87 (2004).

75. See Thomas M. Keck, Beyond Backlash: Assessing the Impact of Judicial Decisions on LGBT Rights, 43 Law & Soc'y Rev. 151, 172 tbl.5 (2009).

76. 1 U.S.C. § 7 and 28 U.S.C. § 1738C (Pub. L. 104–199).

Mobilization for and against same-sex marriage continued. By the first decade of the new millennium, state courts were taking a more serious look at constitutional challenges to laws that excluded same-sex couples from marriage.

Below are two cases, one from Massachusetts, the other from New York, which resolve the issue differently. As you read, consider each court's understanding of the individual interests burdened, and of the state's justifications for limiting marriage to different-sex couples.

GOODRIDGE V. DEPARTMENT OF PUBLIC HEALTH

798 N.E.2d 941 (Mass. 2003)

MARSHALL, C.J.

Marriage is a vital social institution. . . .

Without question, civil marriage enhances the "welfare of the community." It is a "social institution of the highest importance" . . . encouraging stable relationships over transient ones. . . .

Marriage also bestows enormous private and social advantages on those who choose to marry. Civil marriage is at once a deeply personal commitment to another human being and a highly public celebration of the ideals of mutuality, companionship, intimacy, fidelity, and family. . . . Because it fulfils yearnings for security, safe haven, and connection that express our common humanity, civil marriage is an esteemed institution, and the decision whether and whom to marry is among life's momentous acts of self-definition. . . .

The benefits accessible only by way of a marriage license are enormous, touching nearly every aspect of life and death. The department states that "hundreds of statutes" are related to marriage and to marital benefits. . . .

The department posits three legislative rationales for prohibiting same-sex couples from marrying: (1) providing a "favorable setting for procreation"; (2) ensuring the optimal setting for child rearing, which the department defines as "a two-parent family with one parent of each sex"; and (3) preserving scarce State and private financial resources. We consider each in turn.

The judge in the Superior Court endorsed the first rationale, holding that "the state's interest in regulating marriage is based on the traditional concept that marriage's primary purpose is procreation." This is incorrect. Our laws of civil marriage do not privilege procreative heterosexual intercourse between married people above every other form of adult intimacy and every other means of creating a family. General Laws c. 207 contains no requirement that the applicants for a marriage license attest to their ability or intention to conceive children by coitus. Fertility is not a condition of marriage, nor is it grounds for divorce. People who have never consummated their marriage, and never plan to, may be and stay married. People who cannot stir from their deathbed may marry. While it is certainly true that many, perhaps most, married couples have children together (assisted or unassisted), it is the exclusive and permanent commitment of the marriage partners to one another, not the begetting of children, that is the sine qua non of civil marriage.

Moreover, the Commonwealth affirmatively facilitates bringing children into a family regardless of whether the intended parent is married or unmarried, whether the child is adopted or born into a family, whether assistive technology was used to conceive the child, and whether the parent or her partner is heterosexual, homosexual, or bisexual. If procreation were a necessary component of civil marriage, our statutes would draw a tighter circle around the permissible bounds of nonmarital child bearing and the creation of families by noncoital means. The attempt to isolate procreation as "the source of a fundamental right to marry," overlooks the integrated way in which courts have examined the complex and overlapping realms of personal autonomy, marriage, family life, and child rearing. Our jurisprudence recognizes that, in these nuanced and fundamentally private areas of life, such a narrow focus is inappropriate.

The "marriage is procreation" argument singles out the one unbridgeable difference between same-sex and opposite-sex couples, and transforms that difference into the essence of legal marriage. . . .

The department's first stated rationale, equating marriage with unassisted heterosexual procreation, shades imperceptibly into its second: that confining marriage to opposite-sex couples ensures that children are raised in the "optimal" setting. Protecting the welfare of children is a paramount State policy. Restricting marriage to opposite-sex couples, however, cannot plausibly further this policy. . . .

The department has offered no evidence that forbidding marriage to people of the same sex will increase the number of couples choosing to enter into opposite-sex marriages in order to have and raise children. There is thus no rational relationship between the marriage statute and the Commonwealth's proffered goal of protecting the "optimal" child rearing unit. Moreover, the department readily concedes that people in same-sex couples may be "excellent" parents. These couples have children for the reasons others do—to love them, to care for them, to nurture them. But the task of child rearing for same-sex couples is made infinitely harder by their status as outliers to the marriage laws. . . . Excluding same-sex couples from civil marriage will not make children of opposite-sex marriages more secure, but it does prevent children of same-sex couples from enjoying the immeasurable advantages that flow from the assurance of "a stable family structure in which children will be reared, educated, and socialized."

No one disputes that the plaintiff couples are families, that many are parents, and that the children they are raising, like all children, need and should have the fullest opportunity to grow up in a secure, protected family unit. Similarly, no one disputes that, under the rubric of marriage, the State provides a cornucopia of substantial benefits to married parents and their children. . . .

The third rationale advanced by the department is that limiting marriage to opposite-sex couples furthers the Legislature's interest in conserving scarce State and private financial resources. . . .

An absolute statutory ban on same-sex marriage bears no rational relationship to the goal of economy. First, the department's conclusory generalization — that same-sex couples are less financially dependent on each other than opposite-sex couples — ignores that many same-sex couples, such as many of the plaintiffs in this case, have children and other dependents (here, aged parents) in their care. The department does not contend, nor could it, that these dependents are less needy or deserving than the dependents of married couples. Second, Massachusetts marriage laws do not condition receipt of public and private financial benefits to married individuals on a demonstration of financial dependence on each other; the benefits are available to married couples regardless of whether they mingle their finances or actually depend on each other for support. . . .

The marriage ban works a deep and scarring hardship on a very real segment of the community for no rational reason. The absence of any reasonable relationship between, on the one hand, an absolute disqualification of same-sex couples who wish to enter into civil marriage and, on the other, protection of public health, safety, or general welfare, suggests that the marriage restriction is rooted in persistent prejudices against persons who are (or who are believed to be) homosexual. . . .

We declare that barring an individual from the protections, benefits, and obligations of civil marriage solely because that person would marry a person of the same sex violates the Massachusetts Constitution. . . .

HERNANDEZ V. ROBLES
855 N.E.2d 1 (N.Y. 2006)

R.S. SMITH, J.:

We hold that the New York Constitution does not compel recognition of marriages between members of the same sex. . . .

[T]here are at least two grounds that rationally support the limitation on marriage that the Legislature has enacted. Others have been advanced, but we will discuss only these two, both of which are derived from the undisputed assumption that marriage is important to the welfare of children.

First, the Legislature could rationally decide that, for the welfare of children, it is more important to promote stability, and to avoid instability, in opposite-sex than in same-sex relationships. Heterosexual intercourse has a natural tendency to lead to the birth of children; homosexual intercourse does not. Despite the advances of science, it remains true that the vast majority of children are born as a result of a sexual relationship between a man and a woman, and the Legislature could find that this will continue to be true. The Legislature could also find that such relationships are all too often casual or temporary. It could find that an important function of marriage is to create more stability and permanence in the relationships that cause children to be born. It thus could choose to offer an inducement — in the form of marriage and its attendant benefits — to opposite-sex couples who make a solemn, long-term commitment to each other.

The Legislature could find that this rationale for marriage does not apply with comparable force to same-sex couples. These couples can become parents by adoption, or by artificial insemination or other technological marvels, but they do not become parents as a result of accident or impulse. The Legislature could find that unstable relationships between people of the opposite sex present a greater danger that children will be born into or grow up in unstable homes than is the case with same-sex couples, and thus that promoting stability in opposite-sex relationships will help children more. This is one reason why the Legislature could rationally offer the benefits of marriage to opposite-sex couples only.

There is a second reason: The Legislature could rationally believe that it is better, other things being equal, for children to grow up with both a mother and a father. . . .

Plaintiffs . . . argue that the proposition asserted is simply untrue: that a home with two parents of different sexes has no advantage, from the point of view of raising children, over a home with two parents of the same sex. Perhaps they are right, but the Legislature could rationally think otherwise.

To support their argument, plaintiffs refer to social science literature reporting studies of same-sex parents and their children. Some opponents of same-sex marriage criticize these studies, but we need not consider the criticism, for the studies on their face do not establish beyond doubt that children fare equally well in same-sex and opposite-sex households. What they show, at most, is that rather limited observation has detected no marked differences. More definitive results could hardly be expected, for until recently few children have been raised in same-sex households, and there has not been enough time to study the long-term results of such child-rearing. . . .

In the absence of conclusive scientific evidence, the Legislature could rationally proceed on the common-sense premise that children will do best with a mother and father in the home. And a legislature proceeding on that premise could rationally decide to offer a special inducement, the legal recognition of marriage, to encourage the formation of opposite-sex households.

In sum, there are rational grounds on which the Legislature could choose to restrict marriage to couples of opposite sex. . . . If we were convinced that the restriction plaintiffs attack were founded on nothing but prejudice — if we agreed with the plaintiffs that it is comparable to the restriction in *Loving v. Virginia*, 388 U.S. 1 (1967), a prohibition on interracial marriage that was plainly "designed to maintain White Supremacy" — we would hold it invalid, no matter how long its history. . . .

But the historical background of *Loving* is different from the history underlying this case. Racism has been recognized for centuries — at first by a few people, and later by many more — as a revolting moral evil. This country fought a civil war to eliminate racism's worst manifestation, slavery, and passed three constitutional amendments to eliminate that curse and its vestiges. *Loving* was part of the civil rights revolution of the 1950's and 1960's, the triumph of a cause for which many heroes and many ordinary people had struggled since our nation began. . . .

[T]he traditional definition of marriage is not merely a by-product of historical injustice. Its history is of a different kind.

The idea that same-sex marriage is even possible is a relatively new one. Until a few decades ago, it was an accepted truth for almost everyone who ever lived, in any society in which marriage existed, that there could be marriages only between participants of different sex. A court should not lightly conclude that everyone who held this belief was irrational, ignorant or bigoted. We do not so conclude.

Our conclusion that there is a rational basis for limiting marriage to opposite-sex couples leads us to hold that that limitation is valid under the New York Due Process and Equal Protection Clauses, and that any expansion of the traditional definition of marriage should come from the Legislature. . . .

NOTES AND QUESTIONS

---

1. *Children's Interests.* Each of these decisions discusses the different-sex marriage requirement in light of the interests of children. Should the state have to prove that, as the *Hernandez* court put it, "it is better . . . for children to grow up with both a mother and a father"? Or should the court defer to legislative judgments about children's well-being? Is the state's interest in having children raised by different-sex couples legitimate? Does the exclusion of same-sex couples from marriage further that interest? Should children's welfare figure so prominently in a case about whether adults must be permitted to marry?

2. *Procreation.* Another justification for the different-sex marriage requirement is that it provides a symbolic link between marriage and procreation — a link the state seeks to maintain. Consider Justice Cordy's dissenting opinion in *Goodridge*:

> So long as marriage is limited to opposite-sex couples who can at least theoretically procreate, society is able to communicate a consistent message to its citizens that marriage is a (normatively) necessary part of their procreative endeavor; that if they are to procreate, then society has endorsed the institution of marriage as the environment for it and for the subsequent rearing of their children; and that benefits are available explicitly to create a supportive and conducive atmosphere for those purposes. If society proceeds similarly to recognize marriages between same-sex couples who cannot procreate, it could be perceived as an abandonment of this claim, and might result in the

mistaken view that civil marriage has little to do with procreation: j[...]
potential of procreation would not be necessary for a marriage to [...]
marriage would not be necessary for optimal procreation and chil[...]
to occur.[77]

Is this a tenable argument? How does the *Goodridge* majority resp[...]
Justice Cordy's view relate to the *Hernandez* court's reasoning?

As *Hernandez* demonstrates, the argument from procreation eventually became more focused on a specific claim about "accidental" (or "responsible") procreation.[78] The stability of marriage is needed more in different-sex relationships, according to this argument, because only in those relationships can the couple procreate unintentionally. Marriage, in other words, channels procreative sex into stable family units. Does this argument justify same-sex couples' exclusion from marriage?

State and federal litigation regarding same-sex couples' claims to marriage continued after *Goodridge* and *Hernandez*. Over time, more courts accepted same-sex couples' claims. Legislatures too began to extend marriage to same-sex couples. And, in 2012, same-sex marriage prevailed at the ballot box, with voters in Maine, Maryland, and Washington voting to open marriage to same-sex couples.[79]

Eventually, in Obergefell v. Hodges, the Supreme Court resolved the question of the constitutionality of state laws limiting marriage to different-sex couples. The case consolidated appeals from Kentucky, Michigan, Ohio, and Tennessee.[80] (A different portion of *Obergefell* was excerpted in Chapter 1.)

OBERGEFELL V. HODGES

135 S. Ct. 2584 (2015)

JUSTICE KENNEDY delivered the opinion of the Court. . . .

[F]our principles and traditions . . . demonstrate that the reasons marriage is fundamental under the Constitution apply with equal force to same-sex couples.

A first premise of the Court's relevant precedents is that the right to personal choice regarding marriage is inherent in the concept of individual autonomy. This abiding connection between marriage and liberty is why *Loving v. Virginia*, 388 U.S. 1 (1967), invalidated interracial marriage bans under the Due Process Clause. Like

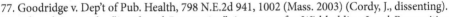

---

77. Goodridge v. Dep't of Pub. Health, 798 N.E.2d 941, 1002 (Mass. 2003) (Cordy, J., dissenting).

78. Edward Stein, The "Accidental Procreation" Argument for Withholding Legal Recognition for Same-Sex Relationships, 84 Chi.-Kent L. Rev. 403 (2009).

79. Edith Honan, Maryland, Maine, Washington Approve Gay Marriage, Reuters, Nov. 7, 2012.

80. DeBoer v. Snyder, 772 F.3d 388 (6th Cir. 2014).

choices concerning contraception, family relationships, procreation, and childrearing, all of which are protected by the Constitution, decisions concerning marriage are among the most intimate that an individual can make. Indeed, the Court has noted it would be contradictory "to recognize a right of privacy with respect to other matters of family life and not with respect to the decision to enter the relationship that is the foundation of the family in our society." . . .

A second principle in this Court's jurisprudence is that the right to marry is fundamental because it supports a two-person union unlike any other in its importance to the committed individuals. This point was central to *Griswold v. Connecticut*, 381 U.S. 479 (1965), which held the Constitution protects the right of married couples to use contraception. Suggesting that marriage is a right "older than the Bill of Rights," *Griswold* described marriage this way:

> Marriage is a coming together for better or for worse, hopefully enduring, and intimate to the degree of being sacred. It is an association that promotes a way of life, not causes; a harmony in living, not political faiths; a bilateral loyalty, not commercial or social projects. Yet it is an association for as noble a purpose as any involved in our prior decisions.

And in *Turner v. Safley*, 482 U.S. 78, 95–96 (1987), the Court again acknowledged the intimate association protected by this right, holding prisoners could not be denied the right to marry because their committed relationships satisfied the basic reasons why marriage is a fundamental right. . . . Marriage responds to the universal fear that a lonely person might call out only to find no one there. It offers the hope of companionship and understanding and assurance that while both still live there will be someone to care for the other. . . .

A third basis for protecting the right to marry is that it safeguards children and families and thus draws meaning from related rights of childrearing, procreation, and education. The Court has recognized these connections by describing the varied rights as a unified whole: "[T]he right to 'marry, establish a home and bring up children' is a central part of the liberty protected by the Due Process Clause." *Zablocki v. Redhail*, 434 U.S. 374, 384 (1978) (quoting *Meyer v. Nebraska*, 262 U.S. 390, 399 (1923)). Under the laws of the several States, some of marriage's protections for children and families are material. But marriage also confers more profound benefits. By giving recognition and legal structure to their parents' relationship, marriage allows children "to understand the integrity and closeness of their own family and its concord with other families in their community and in their daily lives." *United States v. Windsor*, 133 S. Ct. 2675, 2694–95 (2013). Marriage also affords the permanency and stability important to children's best interests.

As all parties agree, many same-sex couples provide loving and nurturing homes to their children, whether biological or adopted. And hundreds of thousands of children are presently being raised by such couples. Most States have allowed gays and lesbians to adopt, either as individuals or as couples, and many adopted and foster children have same-sex parents. This provides powerful confirmation from the law itself that gays and lesbians can create loving, supportive families.

Excluding same-sex couples from marriage thus conflicts with a central premise of the right to marry. Without the recognition, stability, and predictability marriage offers, their children suffer the stigma of knowing their families are somehow lesser. They also suffer the significant material costs of being raised by unmarried parents, relegated through no fault of their own to a more difficult and uncertain family life. The marriage laws at issue here thus harm and humiliate the children of same-sex couples. . . .

Fourth and finally, this Court's cases and the Nation's traditions make clear that marriage is a keystone of our social order. Alexis de Tocqueville recognized this truth on his travels through the United States almost two centuries ago:

> "There is certainly no country in the world where the tie of marriage is so much respected as in America. . . . [W]hen the American retires from the turmoil of public life to the bosom of his family, he finds in it the image of order and of peace. . . . [H]e afterwards carries [that image] with him into public affairs." 1 Democracy in America 309 (H. Reeve transl., rev. ed. 1990).

In *Maynard v. Hill*, 125 U.S. 190 (1888), the Court echoed de Tocqueville, explaining that marriage is "the foundation of the family and of society, without which there would be neither civilization nor progress." Marriage, the *Maynard* Court said, has long been " 'a great public institution, giving character to our whole civil polity.' " This idea has been reiterated even as the institution has evolved in substantial ways over time, superseding rules related to parental consent, gender, and race once thought by many to be essential. Marriage remains a building block of our national community.

For that reason, just as a couple vows to support each other, so does society pledge to support the couple, offering symbolic recognition and material benefits to protect and nourish the union. Indeed, while the States are in general free to vary the benefits they confer on all married couples, they have throughout our history made marriage the basis for an expanding list of governmental rights, benefits, and responsibilities. These aspects of marital status include: taxation; inheritance and property rights; rules of intestate succession; spousal privilege in the law of evidence; hospital access; medical decisionmaking authority; adoption rights; the rights and benefits of survivors; birth and death certificates; professional ethics rules; campaign finance restrictions; workers' compensation benefits; health insurance; and child custody, support, and visitation rules. Valid marriage under state law is also a significant status for over a thousand provisions of federal law. The States have contributed to the fundamental character of the marriage right by placing that institution at the center of so many facets of the legal and social order.

There is no difference between same- and opposite-sex couples with respect to this principle. Yet by virtue of their exclusion from that institution, same-sex couples are denied the constellation of benefits that the States have linked to marriage. This harm results in more than just material burdens. Same-sex couples are consigned to an instability many opposite-sex couples would deem intolerable in their own lives. As the State itself makes marriage all the more precious by the significance it attaches to it, exclusion from that status has the effect of teaching that gays and lesbians are unequal in important respects. It demeans gays and lesbians for the State to lock them out of a central institution of the Nation's society. Same-sex couples, too, may aspire to the transcendent purposes of marriage and seek fulfillment in its highest meaning.

The limitation of marriage to opposite-sex couples may long have seemed natural and just, but its inconsistency with the central meaning of the fundamental right to marry is now manifest. With that knowledge must come the recognition that laws excluding same-sex couples from the marriage right impose stigma and injury of the kind prohibited by our basic charter. . . .

The Due Process Clause and the Equal Protection Clause are connected in a profound way, though they set forth independent principles. Rights implicit in liberty and rights secured by equal protection may rest on different precepts and are not always co-extensive, yet in some instances each may be instructive as to the meaning and reach of the other. In any particular case one Clause may be thought to capture the essence of the right in a more accurate and comprehensive way, even as the two Clauses may converge in the identification and definition of the right. This interrelation of the two principles furthers our understanding of what freedom is and must become.

The Court's cases touching upon the right to marry reflect this dynamic. In *Loving* the Court invalidated a prohibition on interracial marriage under both the Equal Protection Clause and the Due Process Clause. . . .

Here the marriage laws enforced by the respondents are in essence unequal: same-sex couples are denied all the benefits afforded to opposite-sex couples and are barred from exercising a fundamental right. Especially against a long history of disapproval of their relationships, this denial to same-sex couples of the right to marry works a grave and continuing harm. The imposition of this disability on gays and lesbians serves to disrespect and subordinate them. . . .

These considerations lead to the conclusion that the right to marry is a fundamental right inherent in the liberty of the person, and under the Due Process and Equal Protection Clauses of the Fourteenth Amendment couples of the same-sex may not be deprived of that right and that liberty. . . .

CHIEF JUSTICE ROBERTS, with whom JUSTICE SCALIA and JUSTICE THOMAS join, dissenting. . . .

Although the policy arguments for extending marriage to same-sex couples may be compelling, the legal arguments for requiring such an extension are not. The fundamental right to marry does not include a right to make a State change its definition of marriage. And a State's decision to maintain the meaning of marriage that has persisted in every culture throughout human history can hardly be called irrational. In short, our Constitution does not enact any one theory of marriage. The people of a State are free to expand marriage to include same-sex couples, or to retain the historic definition. . . .

This universal definition of marriage as the union of a man and a woman is no historical coincidence. Marriage did not come about as a result of a political movement, discovery, disease, war, religious doctrine, or any other moving force of world history — and certainly not as a result of a prehistoric decision to exclude gays and lesbians. It arose in the nature of things to meet a vital need: ensuring that children are conceived by a mother and father committed to raising them in the stable conditions of a lifelong relationship.

The premises supporting this concept of marriage are so fundamental that they rarely require articulation. The human race must procreate to survive. Procreation occurs through sexual relations between a man and a woman. When sexual relations result in the conception of a child, that child's prospects are generally better if the mother and father stay together rather than going their separate ways. Therefore, for the good of children and society, sexual relations that can lead to procreation should occur only between a man and a woman committed to a lasting bond.

Society has recognized that bond as marriage. And by bestowing a respected status and material benefits on married couples, society encourages men and women to conduct sexual relations within marriage rather than without. As one prominent scholar put it, "Marriage is a socially arranged solution for the problem of getting people to stay together and care for children that the mere desire for children, and the sex that makes children possible, does not solve." J. Q. Wilson, The Marriage Problem 41 (2002). . . .

[T]he privacy cases provide no support for the majority's position, because petitioners do not seek privacy. Quite the opposite, they seek public recognition of their relationships, along with corresponding government benefits. Our cases have consistently refused to allow litigants to convert the shield provided by constitutional liberties into a sword to demand positive entitlements from the State. Thus, although the right to privacy recognized by our precedents certainly plays a role in protecting the intimate conduct of same-sex couples, it provides no affirmative right to redefine marriage and no basis for striking down the laws at issue here. . . .

JUSTICE THOMAS, with whom JUSTICE SCALIA Joins, dissenting.

The Court's decision today is at odds not only with the Constitution, but with the principles upon which our Nation was built. Since well before 1787, liberty has been understood as freedom from government action, not entitlement to government benefits. The Framers created our Constitution to preserve that understanding of liberty. Yet the majority invokes our Constitution in the name of a "liberty" that the Framers would not have recognized, to the detriment of the liberty they sought to protect. Along the way, it rejects the idea—captured in our Declaration of Independence—that human dignity is innate and suggests instead that it comes from the Government. This distortion of our Constitution not only ignores the text, it inverts the relationship between the individual and the state in our Republic. I cannot agree with it. . . .

Petitioners cannot claim, under the most plausible definition of "liberty," that they have been imprisoned or physically restrained by the States for participating in same-sex relationships. To the contrary, they have been able to cohabitate and raise their children in peace. They have been able to hold civil marriage ceremonies in States that recognize same-sex marriages and private religious ceremonies in all States. They have been able to travel freely around the country, making their homes where they please. Far from being incarcerated or physically restrained, petitioners have been left alone to order their lives as they see fit. . . .

Petitioners do not ask this Court to order the States to stop restricting their ability to enter same-sex relationships, to engage in intimate behavior, to make vows to their partners in public ceremonies, to engage in religious wedding ceremonies, to hold themselves out as married, or to raise children. The States have imposed no such restrictions. Nor have the States prevented petitioners from approximating a number of incidents of marriage through private legal means, such as wills, trusts, and powers of attorney. . . .[81]

NOTES AND QUESTIONS

1. *Principles of Marriage.* Justice Kennedy offers four principles that justify the special constitutional status of marriage: autonomy, marriage's importance to individuals, marriage's role in safeguarding children and families, and the centrality of marriage to the social order. What do you think about each of these principles? Is any of them more important than the others?

Justice Kennedy conceptualizes marriage in a way that resonates with the claims of same-sex couples. What view of marriage do the dissenting Justices take, and how does that view relate to same-sex couples' claims?

2. *A Right to Recognition?* Both Chief Justice Roberts and Justice Thomas assert that the privacy cases provide no support for petitioners' claim because petitioners seek formal state recognition of their relationships, rather than protection against state intervention. On this view, the Constitution limits state power and should not be interpreted to compel affirmative state recognition of same-sex couples' relationships. Is this distinction persuasive? What about previous

---

81. An excerpt from Justice Alito's dissenting opinion appears in Chapter 1.

right-to-marry decisions? Does constitutional protection for *hood necessarily entail a right to state recognition?

3. *Liberty and Equality.* Remember that in *Loving t*' due process and equal protection grounds. In *Obergefell* that the marriage restriction violates both due process ar. tees. How does the Court understand the relationship between . Why does the marriage restriction violate the equal protection rig.. couples? Does the Court find that those who voted for the restrictions we. by animus? Or is the Court more concerned with the laws' effects?

4. *Harms of Marriage Exclusion.* In describing the harms of the different-sex requirement, Justice Kennedy refers both to material harms and stigmatic harms. Can you give examples of each? How important are the stigmatic harms? For example, if a state created domestic partnerships with all the legal rights associated with marriage, how would same-sex couples be harmed?[82]

C. Incest

Earlier in the chapter we examined prohibitions on incestuous sex. Now we address prohibitions on incestuous marriage. Incest is a crime, but whether a relationship is incestuous often arises in non-criminal contexts as well (e.g., immigration or inheritance). As the following case shows, the contours of the incest prohibition may determine the validity of a marriage.

ISRAEL V. ALLEN
577 P.2d 762 (Colo. 1978)

PRINGLE, CHIEF JUSTICE.

This is an appeal from a decision of the District Court of Jefferson County holding a provision of the Colorado Uniform Marriage Act unconstitutional as violative of equal protection of the laws. We affirm.

Plaintiffs, Martin Richard Israel and Tammy Lee Bannon Israel, are brother and sister related by adoption and are not related by either the half or the whole blood.

Raymond Israel (the natural father of Martin Richard Israel) and Sylvia Bannon (the natural mother of Tammy Lee Bannon Israel) were married on November 3, 1972. At the time of their marriage, Martin was 18 years of age and was living in the

---

82. Perry v. Schwarzenegger, 704 F. Supp. 2d 921 (N.D. Cal. 2010), excerpted in Chapter 1, explores this question. See also In re Marriage Cases, 183 P.3d 384 (Cal. 2008) (holding California's domestic partnership regime insufficient to satisfy state constitutional obligations of liberty and equality).

e of Washington; Tammy was 13 years of age and was living with her mother in enver, Colorado. Raymond Israel adopted Tammy on January 7, 1975.

Plaintiffs desire to be married in the State of Colorado. Defendant, Clerk and Recorder of Jefferson County, however, denied plaintiffs a license to marry based on section 14-2-110(1)(b), C.R.S. 1973:

> *Prohibited marriages.* (1) The following marriages are prohibited: ...
> (b) A marriage between an ancestor and a descendant or between a brother and sister, whether the relationship is by the half or the whole blood or by adoption; ...

Since we find ... that the provision prohibiting marriage between adopted children fails even to satisfy minimum rationality requirements, we need not determine whether a fundamental right is infringed by this statute.

While the practice of adoption is an ancient one, the legal regulation of adoptive relationships in our society is strictly statutory in nature. The legislative intent in promulgating statutes concerning adoption was, in part, to make the law affecting adopted children in respect to equality of inheritance and parental duties *in pari materia* with that affecting natural children. It is clear, however, that adopted children are not engrafted upon their adoptive families for all purposes. *See, e.g.,* the criminal incest statute, section 18-6-301, C.R.S. 1973, which does not include sexual relationships between adopted brother and sister.

Nonetheless, defendant argues that this marriage prohibition provision furthers a legitimate state interest in family harmony. We do not agree. As the instant case illustrates, it is just as likely that prohibiting marriage between brother and sister related by adoption will result in family discord. While we are not, strictly speaking, dealing with an affinity based relationship in this case, we find the following analysis equally applicable to the situation presently before us:

> "According to the English law, relationship by affinity was an impediment to marriage to the same extent and in the same degree as consanguinity. While this principle, derived from the ecclesiastically administered canon law, still strongly persists in England, in the United States the statutory law governing the marriage relationship nowhere so sweepingly condemns the marriage of persons related only by affinity. . . . The objections that exist against consanguineous marriages are not present where the relationship is merely by affinity. The physical detriment to the offspring of persons related by blood is totally absent. The natural repugnance of people toward marriages of blood relatives, that has resulted in well-nigh universal moral condemnation of such marriages, is quite generally lacking in application to the union of those related only by affinity. It is difficult to construct any very logical case for the prohibition of marriage on grounds of affinity . . ." 1 *Vernier, American Family Laws* 183.

We hold that it is just as illogical to prohibit marriage between adopted brother and sister. . . .

NOTES AND QUESTIONS

1. *Beyond Genetics.* In striking down only the "or by adoption" component of the statute, the court suggests that the reasons for prohibiting incest have to do with the risk of physical detriment to the offspring of a couple related by blood. The marriage of siblings related by adoption does not implicate that risk and so is viewed by the court as an irrational restriction. Are there other justifications for restricting marriage by adopted siblings? The court also discusses the family harmony rationale for the incest prohibition. The court's logic seems to be that thwarting the desires of the siblings who want to marry promotes family discord. Is that reasoning sound? Should the interests of family members other than the couple play any role in the analysis?

2. *The Incest "Taboo."* Consider the following passage from famed anthropologist Margaret Mead describing a version of the family harmony rationale for the incest prohibition:

> Our present frequency of divorce has coincided with the development of a new set of attitudes and beliefs about incest. Incest taboos are among the essential mechanisms of human society, permitting the development of children within a setting where identification and affection can be separated from sexual exploitation, and a set of categories of permitted and forbidden sex can be established. . . . Close ties may be formed with forbidden sex partners without the intrusion of inappropriate sexuality; trust and affection, dependence and succorance, can exist independently of a sexual tie. Grown to manhood and womanhood, individuals are thus equipped to mate, and to continue strong, affectional ties with others than their own mates. . . .
>
> If the incest taboos are seen to make an essential contribution to the rearing of children within a situation where their own immature emotions are respected, and where they are at the same time prepared for both sexual and non-sexual relationships as adults, it is then obvious that the taboo must be extended to include all members of the household. No matter what the size of the household, sex relations must be rigorously limited to the sets of marital couples — parents, grandparents, married aunts and uncles–who live within its confines. When these rigorous limitations are maintained, the children of both sexes can wander freely, sitting on laps, pulling beards, and nestling their heads against comforting breasts — neither tempting nor being tempted beyond their years. . . .[83]

How, if at all, does the incest taboo shape childrearing practices? Would repealing incest laws change the social norms around the behavior?

---

83. Margaret Mead, Anomalies in American Post-Divorce Relationships, in Divorce and After 4–8 (Bohannan ed., 1970).

3.   *How Close Is Too Close?* Every state prohibits marriages between parents and children, biological siblings, and ancestors and descendants. Most prohibit aunt-nephew, uncle-niece marriages as well. States are evenly split on the legality of marriages between first cousins. Twenty-four states have laws forbidding first cousins from marrying.[84] A small number permit first-cousin marriages only if either or both partners are sterile. No countries in Europe prohibit cousin marriage, and in parts of the Middle East, Africa, and Asia, marriages between cousins are considered preferable. "In some parts of the world," one report says, "20 to 60 percent of all marriages are between close biological relatives."[85]

4.   *Relative Harm.* How do the interests of two cousins who want to marry compare to those of a same-sex couple who wants to marry? Is the cousins' interest less weighty than that of the same-sex couple?

5.   *Children's Interests.* Justifications for the incest prohibition often invoke health and the risk to the couple's offspring of genetic deformity. Yet the risks of genetic deformity as a result of incest are much less than most people suppose. Relationships between first cousins, for example, only increase the risk of genetic deformity by 2-3 percent compared to unrelated couples.[86] The risk of genetic defects for incestuous couples is also substantially less than the risk of such defects for parents with known genetic conditions such as Huntington's disease, which has a 50 percent chance of being passed on to a child.[87] Given the availability of extensive genetic testing for prospective parents, and the fact that no other couples are barred from marrying based on genetic risk to their children, should genetic considerations be accorded any weight in justifying the incest prohibition?

6.   *Creating New Families.* Consider this justification for the prohibition of marriage between relatives:

> Geneticists have shown that while consanguineous marriages are likely to bring ill effects in a society which has consistently avoided them in the past, the danger would be much smaller if prohibition had never existed, since this would have given ample opportunity for the harmful hereditary characters to become apparent and be automatically eliminated through selection: as a matter of fact this is the way breeders improve the quality of their subjects. Therefore, the dangers of consanguineous marriages are the outcome of the incest prohibition rather than actually explaining it. . . .

---

84. See Marriage Facts, CousinCouples.com; William Saletan, The Love That Dare Not Speak Its Surname, Slate (Apr. 10, 2002).

85. Denise Grady, Few Risks Seen to the Children of 1st Cousins, N. Y. Times, Apr. 4, 2002, at A1.

86. Hanan Hamamy, Consanguineous Marriages: Preconception Consultation in Primary Health Care Settings, 3 J. Community Genetics 185 (2012).

87. See Having Children, Huntington's Disease Youth Org. (Feb. 24, 2013), https://en.hdyo.org/eve/articles/45.

[T]he prohibition of incest established a mutual dependency between families, compelling them in order to perpetuate themselves, to give rise to new families. . . .

[T]he ultimate explanation is probably that mankind has understood very early that, in order to free itself from a wild struggle for existence, it was confronted with the very simple choice of "either marrying-out or being killed-out." The alternative was between biological families living in juxtaposition and endeavoring to remain closed, self-perpetuating units, over-ridden by their fears, hatreds, and ignorances, and the systematic establishment, through the incest prohibition, of links of intermarriage between them, thus succeeding to build, out of the artificial bonds of affinity, a true human society, despite, and even in contradiction with, the isolating influence of consanguinity. . . .[88]

PROBLEMS

1. John Johnson married Helen Wilson in 2013. At that time, Helen had an 18-year-old daughter, Jeannine, from a prior marriage, and John had a 22-year-old son, Peter. In 2018, Helen took ill, and in 2020 she died. During the course of caring for Helen, John and Jeannine got to know each other and gradually became very close. Now, John and Jeannine want to marry. Should they be allowed to do so?

   Now assume that the relevant statute prohibits marriage "to a current or former stepchild or stepparent," but that John and Jeannine do not disclose their relation when obtaining a marriage license; they marry and live together until John's death. John dies intestate. The intestacy law of the jurisdiction directs that half of the estate go to the surviving spouse, if any, and otherwise to any surviving children. Should John's only child, Peter, prevail on his claim that Jeannine cannot be John's widow because their marriage was incestuous and hence void? Or should Jeannine inherit her spousal share of John's estate?

2. Valerie and Vincent met at college when he was 21 and she was 19. After graduation, they married and over the next three years had two children. Valerie and Vincent then discovered that they were related prior to marriage. Vincent's half-sister (the child of his father, and who is 20 years his senior) is Valerie's mother. The incest statute in the jurisdiction (which is modeled on the Uniform Marriage and Divorce Act) prohibits marriage "between ancestors and descendants, between brothers and sisters, whether by the half or whole blood or by adoption, and between uncles and nieces and aunts and nephews." What arguments would you make that this

---

88. Claude Levi-Strauss, The Family, in Man, Culture and Society 261, 267–78 (Shapiro ed., 1956).

marriage should be declared void? What arguments would you make that the marriage does not violate the statute?

3. In the late 1990s, film director Woody Allen married Soon-Yi Previn, who was the adopted daughter of Allen's long-term intimate partner, Mia Farrow. When Allen and Farrow began their relationship, Previn was a teenager. There was no sexual contact between Allen and Previn until Previn turned 18. Should Allen and Previn be permitted to marry? Should they be permitted to marry if Allen and Farrow had been married and then divorced? Would it matter whether Previn had ever lived in the home with Allen and Farrow?

D. Polygamy

While polygamous marriages are not recognized in any state in the United States, they are accepted in many other nations. Some Muslim-majority countries in Africa and Asia, for example, permit polygamy.[89] And even some countries that do not allow the formation of polygamous marriages will recognize polygamous unions from countries where the practice is legal.[90] Although precise figures are impossible to obtain, according to estimates there are at least 50,000 people living in polygamous arrangements in the United States.[91]

Contemporary prohibitions on polygamous marriage have not produced a national controversy. Yet, the invalidation of the different-sex marriage requirement raises questions about justifications for the two-person marriage requirement. Chief Justice John Roberts in dissent in *Obergefell* framed the issue as follows:

> One immediate question invited by the majority's position is whether States may retain the definition of marriage as a union of two people. Although the majority randomly inserts the adjective "two" in various places, it offers no reason at all why the two-person element of the core definition of marriage may be preserved while the man-woman element may not. Indeed, from the standpoint of history and tradition, a leap from opposite-sex marriage to same-sex marriage is much greater than one from a two-person union to plural unions, which have deep roots in some cultures around the world. If the majority is willing to take the big leap, it is hard to see how it can say no to the shorter one.

---

89. Jaime M. Gher, Polygamy and Same-Sex Marriage—Allies or Adversaries Within the Same-Sex Marriage Movement, 14 Wm. & Mary J. Women & L. 559 (2008). Other countries also have historically permitted polygamy. See Kim Chu-Su, The Marriage System in Korea, Korea Journal 17 (July 1976).

90. Gher, supra note 89.

91. Barbara Bradley Hagerty, Some Muslims in U.S. Quietly Engage in Polygamy, NPR.com (May 27, 2008).

II. Eligibility to Marry

It is striking how much of the majority's reasoning would apply with equal force to the claim of a fundamental right to plural marriage. If "[t]here is dignity in the bond between two men or two women who seek to marry and in their autonomy to make such profound choices," why would there be any less dignity in the bond between three people who, in exercising their autonomy, seek to make the profound choice to marry? If a same-sex couple has the constitutional right to marry because their children would otherwise "suffer the stigma of knowing their families are somehow lesser," why wouldn't the same reasoning apply to a family of three or more persons raising children? If not having the opportunity to marry "serves to disrespect and subordinate" gay and lesbian couples, why wouldn't the same "imposition of this disability," serve to disrespect and subordinate people who find fulfillment in polyamorous relationships?

I do not mean to equate marriage between same-sex couples with plural marriages in all respects. There may well be relevant differences that compel different legal analysis. But if there are, petitioners have not pointed to any. When asked about a plural marital union at oral argument, petitioners asserted that a State "doesn't have such an institution." But that is exactly the point: the States at issue here do not have an institution of same-sex marriage, either.[92]

The only case in which the Supreme Court has considered the validity of the prohibition of polygamy is Reynolds v. United States, decided in 1878.[93] That case concerned a prosecution for polygamy in the Territory of Utah, where the practice had been made illegal by Congress. In unanimously upholding the prohibition, the *Reynolds* Court reasoned as follows:

> Polygamy has always been odious among the northern and western nations of Europe, and, until the establishment of the Mormon Church, was almost exclusively a feature of the life of Asiatic and of African people. At common law, the second marriage was always void (2 Kent, Com. 79), and from the earliest history of England polygamy has been treated as an offense against society. After the establishment of the ecclesiastical courts, and until the time of James I., it was punished through the instrumentality of those tribunals, not merely because ecclesiastical rights had been violated, but because upon the separation of the ecclesiastical courts from the civil the ecclesiastical were supposed to be the most appropriate for the trial of matrimonial causes and offences against the rights of marriage, just as they were for testamentary causes and the settlement of the estate of Deceased persons. . . .

> [W]e think it may safely be said there never has been a time in any State of the Union when polygamy has not been an offence against society, cognizable by the civil courts and punishable with more or less severity. In the face of

---

92. 135 S. Ct. 2584, 2621–22 (2015) (Roberts, J., dissenting).
93. 98 U.S. 145 (1878).

all this evidence, it is impossible to believe that the constitutional guaranty of religious freedom was intended to prohibit legislation in respect to this most important feature of social life. Marriage, while from its very nature a sacred obligation, is nevertheless, in most civilized nations, a civil contract, and usually regulated by law. Upon it society may be said to be built, and out of its fruits spring social relations and social obligations and duties, with which government is necessarily required to deal. . . . [T]here cannot be a doubt that, unless restricted by some form of constitution, it is within the legitimate scope of the power of every civil government to determine whether polygamy or monogamy shall be the law of social life under its dominion.[94]

The territory of Utah was only permitted to become a state once the Mormon Church officially prohibited polygamy and on the condition that the state constitution irrevocably prohibit polygamy. The conflict about polygamous marriage was intertwined with concern about Mormon religion and the power of the church. As Sarah Barringer Gordon notes in her account of the nineteenth century polygamy conflict, "polygamy was, avowedly, the extension of a theocracy into marriage. Certainly, prejudice against Mormons and their alternative faith played a role in the decision" in *Reynolds*. Gordon also notes the racist tinge of the *Reynolds* Court's opinion, whose "analogy of Mormon practices to those of Asia and Africa invoked the two continents whose peoples were most frequent targets of American prohibitions against interracial marriage. Such labeling, inevitably, carried racial and racist messages, as well as religious ones."[95]

Fundamentalist splinter groups continue to practice polygamy today and, as the following case indicates, are sometimes subject to prosecution.[96]

STATE V. HOLM
137 P.3d 726 (Utah 2006)

JUSTICE DURRANT for the majority

In this case, we are asked to determine whether Rodney Hans Holm was appropriately convicted for bigamy and unlawful sexual conduct with a minor. . . .

BACKGROUND

Holm was legally married to Suzie Stubbs in 1986. Subsequent to this marriage, Holm, a member of the Fundamentalist Church of Jesus Christ of

---

94. Id. at 164–66.

95. Id.

96. Sarah Barringer Gordon, The Mormon Question: Polygamy and Constitutional Conflict in Nineteenth-century America 142 (2002).

Latter-day Saints (the "FLDS Church"), participated in a religious marriage ceremony with Wendy Holm. Then, when Rodney Holm was thirty-two, he participated in another religious marriage ceremony with then-sixteen-year-old Ruth Stubbs, Suzie Stubbs's sister. After the ceremony, Ruth moved into Holm's house, where her sister Suzie Stubbs, Wendy Holm, and their children also resided. By the time Ruth turned eighteen, she had conceived two children with Holm, the second of which was born approximately three months after her eighteenth birthday. . . .

ANALYSIS

I. WE AFFIRM HOLM'S CONVICTION FOR BIGAMY . . .

Holm was convicted pursuant to Utah's bigamy statute, which provides that "[a] person is guilty of bigamy when, knowing he has a husband or wife or knowing the other person has a husband or wife, the person purports to marry another person or cohabits with another person." Utah Code Ann. § 76-7-101 (2003). The jury weighing the case against Holm indicated on a special verdict form its conclusion that Holm had both "purported to marry another person" and "cohabited with another person" knowing that he already had a wife. . . .

A. The "Purports to Marry" Provision of Utah's Bigamy Statute Is Applicable to Holm's Solemnization of His Relationship with Stubbs . . .

The "purports to marry" provision of Utah's bigamy statute declares that "[a] person is guilty of bigamy when, knowing he has a husband or wife or knowing the other person has a husband or wife, the person purports to marry another person." Both parties to this appeal agree that "purport" means "[t]o profess or claim falsely; to seem to be." Black's Law Dictionary 1250 (7th ed. 1999).

The definition of "marry," however, is disputed. The State argues that "marry" should not be construed as limited to legally recognized marriages. Holm argues that the word "marry" in subsection one refers only to a legally recognized marriage and that, therefore, there is no violation of the "purports to marry" provision unless an individual purports to enter into a legally valid marriage. We hold that the term "marry," as used in the bigamy statute, includes both legally recognized marriages and those that are not state-sanctioned because such a definition is supported by the plain meaning of the term, the language of the bigamy statute and the Utah Code, and the legislative history and purpose of the bigamy statute. . . .

Specifically, the bigamy statute does not require a party to enter into a second marriage (however defined) to run afoul of the statute; cohabitation alone would constitute bigamy pursuant to the statute's terms. . . .

Applying the definition of "marry" outlined above to the facts presented in this case, there can be no doubt that Holm purported to marry Stubbs. The undisputed facts establish that Holm stood before an official of the FLDS Church, Warren Jeffs (son of then-FLDS prophet Rulon Jeffs), with Stubbs at his side and responded affirmatively to a vow asking the following question:

> Do you Brother [Holm], take Sister [Stubbs] by the right hand, and receive her unto yourself to be your lawful and wedded wife, and you to be her lawful and wedded husband, for time and all eternity, with a covenant and promise, on your part that you will fulfill all the laws, rites and ordinances pertaining to this holy bond of matrimony in the new and everlasting covenant, doing this in the presence of God, angels, and these witnesses, of your own free will and choice?

At the ceremony, Stubbs wore a white dress, which she considered a wedding dress. Throughout her testimony at the trial court, Stubbs referred to the ceremony as a marriage. As mentioned, the ceremony was officiated by a religious leader and involved vows typical of a traditional marriage ceremony. In short, the ceremony in which Holm and Stubbs participated appeared, in every material respect, indistinguishable from a marriage ceremony to which this State grants legal recognition on a daily basis.

At trial, Stubbs testified that following the ceremony she considered herself married. The facts show that Stubbs lived in a house with Holm, that Holm and Stubbs considered themselves husband and wife, and that Holm and Stubbs regularly engaged in sexual intercourse. Although no one of these factors is itself indicative of marriage, looking at the cumulative effect of the factors present in this case it is clear that the relationship formed by Holm and Stubbs was a marriage, as that term is used in the bigamy statute. . . .

The crux of marriage in our society, perhaps especially a religious marriage, is not so much the license as the solemnization, viewed in its broadest terms as the steps, whether ritualistic or not, by which two individuals commit themselves to undertake a marital relationship. Certainly Holm, as a result of his ceremony with Stubbs, would not be entitled to any legal benefits attendant to a state-sanctioned marriage, but there is no language in the bigamy statute that implies that the presence of or desire for such benefits should be determinative of whether bigamy has been committed. Holm, by responding in the affirmative to the question placed to him by his religious leader, committed himself to undertake all the obligations of a marital relationship. The fact that the State of Utah was not invited to register or record that commitment does not change the reality that Holm and Stubbs formed a marital bond and commenced a marital relationship. The presence or absence of a state license does not alter that bond or the gravity of the commitments made by Holm and Stubbs. . . .

B. The Utah Constitution Does Not Shield Holm's Polygamous Behavior from State Prosecution . . .

Holm argues that the State of Utah is foreclosed from criminalizing polygamous behavior because the freedom to engage in such behavior is a fundamental liberty interest that can be infringed only for compelling reasons and that the State has failed to identify a sufficiently compelling justification for its criminalization of polygamy. We disagree and conclude that there is no fundamental liberty interest to engage in the type of polygamous behavior at issue in this case. . . .

In marked contrast to the situation presented to the Court in *Lawrence v. Texas*, 539 U.S. 558 (2003), this case implicates the public institution of marriage, an institution the law protects, and also involves a minor. In other words, this case presents the exact conduct identified by the Supreme Court in *Lawrence* as outside the scope of its holding.

First, the behavior at issue in this case is not confined to personal decisions made about sexual activity, but rather raises important questions about the State's ability to regulate marital relationships and prevent the formation and propagation of marital forms that the citizens of the State deem harmful. . . . Our State's commitment to monogamous unions is a recognition that decisions made by individuals as to how to structure even the most personal of relationships are capable of dramatically affecting public life. . . .

II. WE AFFIRM HOLM'S CONVICTION FOR UNLAWFUL SEXUAL CONDUCT . . .

Holm's . . . argument regarding his unlawful sexual conduct convictions is that section 7[6]-5-401.2 [the unlawful sexual conduct statute] violates his federal right to equal protection under the law because it impermissibly distinguishes between married and unmarried individuals. . . .

Section 76-5-407 exempts a married individual from operation of the unlawful sexual conduct statute where the individual engages in the proscribed conduct with his or her spouse. . . .

Holm argues that the State has no rational justification for endorsing consensual sexual conduct between a sixteen- or seventeen-year-old girl and a man ten years her elder where the two have entered a legal marriage with the consent of one of the girl's parents, . . . while criminalizing such conduct where the two are not legally married. He points out that if the distinction is based solely on the minor's inability to give valid consent, such a concern would not apply in this case because Stubbs's father consented to her religious union with Holm. Contrary to Holm's suggestion, we agree with the State that its interest in the distinction goes beyond any concern with obtaining parental consent. The state-determined framework within which the legal status of marriage exists provides a minor with certain protections under the law that are absent where the union is not a legal marriage and thus falls outside this framework. . . .

While the State's power to interfere with the private relationships of consenting adults is limited, it is well established that the same is not true where one of the individuals involved in the relationship is a minor. We believe the State has a legitimate interest in criminalizing the conduct at issue and that the Legislature's decision to criminalize the conduct only where the parties involved are not married to each other does not render the statute invalid under equal protection principles. We therefore uphold the constitutionality of Holm's convictions under section 76-5-401.2. . . .

We conclude that Holm was properly convicted of both bigamy and unlawful sexual conduct with a minor. . . .

CHIEF JUSTICE DURHAM, concurring in part and dissenting in part

I join the majority in upholding Holm's conviction for unlawful sexual conduct with a minor. As to the remainder of its analysis, I respectfully dissent. . . .

I do not believe it is appropriate to interpret the term "marry" when it appears in a state statute as providing what is essentially an anthropological description of human relationships. To do so is to ignore the fact that the law of our state and our nation has traditionally viewed marriage as denoting a legal status as well as a private bond. . . .

Undoubtedly, a couple may feel it is their commitment before God that gives their relationship its legitimacy or permanence. However, it is beyond dispute that such private commitments alone, even when made before God, do not constitute "marriage" in our state or in our legal system. Any two people can make private pledges to each other, with or without the assistance of a religious official, but these private commitments are not equivalent to marriage absent a license or an adjudication of marriage. . . .

I therefore interpret the "purports to marry" prong of section 76-7-101 as referring to an individual's claim of entry into a legal union recognized by the state as marriage. The phrase does not encompass an individual's entry into a religious union where there has been no attempt to elicit the state's recognition of marital status or to procure the attendant benefits of this status under the law, and where neither party to the union believed it to have legal import. . . .

I agree that the state has an important interest in regulating marriage, but only insofar as marriage is understood as a legal status. . . . In my view, the criminal bigamy statute protects marriage, as a legal union, by criminalizing the act of purporting to enter a second legal union. Such an act defrauds the state and perhaps an innocent spouse or purported partner. . . .

Those who choose to live together without getting married enter a personal relationship that resembles a marriage in its intimacy but claims no legal sanction. They thereby intentionally place themselves outside the framework of rights and obligations that surrounds the marriage institution. While some in society may feel that the institution of marriage is diminished when individuals consciously choose to avoid it, it is generally understood that the state is not entitled to criminally punish its citizens for making such a choice, even if they do so with multiple partners or with partners of the same sex. The only distinction in this case is that when Holm consciously chose to enter into a personal relationship that he knew would not be legally recognized as marriage, he used religious terminology to describe this relationship. . . .

The second state interest served by the bigamy law . . . is in preventing "marriage fraud," whereby an already-married individual fraudulently purports to enter a legal marriage with someone else, "or attempts to procure government benefits associated with marital status." . . . This interest is simply not implicated here, where no claim to the legal status of marriage has been made. . . .

"[P]rotecting vulnerable individuals from exploitation and abuse" [is claimed] as the third state interest served by the bigamy statute. . . . The State has provided no evidence of a causal relationship or even a strong correlation between the practice of polygamy, whether religiously motivated or not, and the offenses of "incest, sexual assault, statutory rape, and failure to pay child support." Moreover, even assuming such a correlation did exist, neither the record nor the recent history of prosecutions of alleged polygamists warrants the conclusion that section 76-7-101 is a necessary tool for the state's attacks on such harms. For one thing, I am unaware of a single instance where the state was forced to bring a charge of bigamy in place of other narrower charges, such as incest or unlawful sexual conduct with a minor, because it was unable to gather sufficient evidence to prosecute these other crimes. The State has suggested that its initial ability to file bigamy charges allows it to gather the evidence required to prosecute those engaged in more specific crimes. Even if there were support for this claim in the record, I would consider it inappropriate to let stand a criminal law simply because it enables the state to conduct a fishing expedition for evidence of other crimes. Further, the State itself has indicated that it does not prosecute those engaged in religiously motivated polygamy under the criminal bigamy statute unless the person has entered a religious union with a girl under eighteen years old. Such a policy of selective prosecution reinforces my conclusion that a blanket criminal prohibition on religious polygamous unions is not necessary to further the state's interests, and suggests that a more narrowly tailored law would be just as effective.

I do not reach this conclusion lightly. I acknowledge the possibility that other criminal conduct may accompany the act of bigamy. Such conduct may even . . . be correlated with the practice of polygamy in a community that has isolated itself from the outside world, at least partially in fear of criminal prosecution for its religious practice. Indeed, the FLDS community in its current form has been likened to a cult, with allegations focusing on the power wielded by a single leader who exerts a high degree of control over followers, ranging from ownership of their property to the determination of persons with whom they may enter religious unions. In the latter regard, reports of forcible unions between underage girls and older men within the FLDS community have recently appeared in the media. Yet, the state does not criminalize cult membership, and for good reason. To do so would be to impose a criminal penalty based on status rather than conduct — long considered antithetical to our notion of criminal justice. . . . The State of Utah has criminal laws punishing incest, rape, unlawful sexual conduct with a minor, and domestic and child abuse. Any restrictions these laws place on the practice of religious polygamy are almost certainly justified. However, the broad criminalization of the religious practice itself as a means of attacking other criminal behavior is not. . . .

I note that for similar reasons I could not uphold Holm's bigamy conviction on the basis that the religiously motivated conduct at issue is inherently harmful to children who grow up in polygamous homes, and are thereby exposed to the "culture" of polygamy. Our previous rulings and legislative policy support this conclusion. For example, this court has previously held that those engaged in the practice of polygamy are not automatically disqualified from petitioning for adoption of a child. Rather, a trial court must hold an evidentiary hearing to consider on a case-by-case basis whether the best interests of the child would be promoted by an adoption by the prospective parents.

We have also held that a parent's custody petition could not be denied solely because she practiced polygamy. . . . [T]he legislature's policy regarding child custody and parental rights termination issues has shifted in the past half-century, and now requires that courts focus on the "best interests of the child" rather than passing judgment on the morality of its parents. Given these developments, and the existence of legal mechanisms for protecting the interests of abused or neglected children apart from criminally prosecuting their parents for bigamy, I do not believe the criminalization of religiously motivated polygamous conduct is necessary to further these interests. . . .

NOTES AND QUESTIONS

1. *Green's Case.* The *Holm* decision relied in part on the court's prior ruling in *State v. Green*. In that case, the court upheld the prosecution of the widely-known polygamist, Tom Green, who had fathered twenty-five children through conjugal-type relationships with nine women, four of whom were pregnant during his trial. In upholding the bigamy statute, the court reasoned as follows:

> We conclude that Utah's bigamy statute is rationally related to several legitimate government ends. First, this state has an interest in regulating marriage. . . .
>
> The State of Utah's interest in regulating marriage has resulted in a network of laws, many of which are premised upon the concept of monogamy. . . .
>
> Utah's bigamy statute serves additional legitimate government ends. Specifically, prohibiting bigamy implicates the State's interest in preventing the perpetration of marriage fraud, as well as its interest in preventing the misuse of government benefits associated with marital status.
>
> Most importantly, Utah's bigamy statute serves the State's interest in protecting vulnerable individuals from exploitation and abuse. The practice

of polygamy, in particular, often coincides with crimes targeting women and children. Crimes not unusually attendant to the practice of polygamy include incest, sexual assault, statutory rape, and failure to pay child support. Moreover, the closed nature of polygamous communities makes obtaining evidence of and prosecuting these crimes challenging.[97]

2. *Law Reform in Utah.* The Utah state courts have consistently upheld the prosecution of polygamists and rejected claims that the relevant statutes are unconstitutional. The Utah legislature nonetheless has amended the state's bigamy statute in 2017 and 2020. It redefined bigamy to occur if an "individual purports to marry another individual" and "knows or reasonably should know that one or both of the individuals . . . are legally married to another individual."[98] This change eliminated the cohabitation prong of the definition discussed in Justice Durham's dissent in *Holm*. Before the amendment, this provision had been challenged by Kody Brown, the star of the reality television show *Sister Wives*, which chronicles his life with four wives (one legal, three religious) and the 21 children they are raising. They lived first in Utah, but relocated to Nevada for fear of prosecution under the cohabitation prong of Utah's bigamy law. In Brown v. Buhman, a federal district court struck down the cohabitation provision and interpreted the "purports to marry" provision to apply only to marriages for which state recognition is sought.[99] On appeal, that decision was vacated as moot because the government announced limits on how it would enforce the law and closed its file on the Browns.[100] Is it rational to prohibit cohabitation with four partners if one is a spouse, but not if none is a spouse? Why do you think Utah originally defined bigamy this way, and why would it shift to a narrower definition? How does the change accord with the position of the majority and the dissent in *Holm*? The amendments also distinguished among different types of bigamy.[101] Consensual bigamy, where all parties know of the existence of the other marriage or marriages, is now an infraction akin to a speeding ticket. Bigamy that is induced by fraud, false pretenses, threat, or coercion is a third degree felony. Bigamy that involves other criminal conduct such as homicide, kidnapping, trafficking, rape, child abuse, or domestic violence is a second degree felony—the most serious of the three types of bigamy. The following notes consider justifications for prohibiting polygamy. As you think about these justifications, consider whether you prefer the approach of the former law at issue in *Holm* or the current Utah law, which draws a distinction based on the type of conduct at issue.

3. *Polygamy and Fraud.* A common reason offered for the prohibition of polygamy is the prevention of marriage fraud. Is the discussion of that rationale in *Green* and *Holm* persuasive?

---

97. State v. Green, 99 P.3d 820, 829–30 (Utah 2004).

98. Utah Code § 76-7-101 (2020).

99. 947 F. Supp. 2d 1170 (D. Utah 2013).

100. Brown v. Buhman, 822 F.3d 1151, 1155 (10th Cir. 2016).

101. Utah Code § 76-7-101 (2020).

4. *Polygamy and Abuse.* Another justification for the continued prohibition of polygamy is the protection of vulnerable individuals from abuse. Who is being protected? Does polygamy necessarily subjugate women? Does polygamy undermine the state's interest in gender equality? Does it matter how equal the broader society in which polygamous marriages occurs is? Consider this perspective from a woman in a polygamous union:

> I married a married man.
>
> In fact, he had six wives when I married him 17 years ago. Today, he has nine. . . .
>
> While polygamists believe that the Old Testament mandates the practice of plural marriage, compelling social reasons make the life style attractive to the modern career woman. . . .
>
> In a monogamous context, the only solutions [to juggling career, motherhood and marriage] are compromises. . . . But why must women only embrace a marital arrangement that requires so many trade-offs?
>
> When I leave for the 60-mile commute to court at 7 A.M., my 2-year-old daughter, London, is happily asleep in the bed of my husband's wife, Diane. . . . When London awakes . . . she is surrounded by family members. . . .
>
> [On] Mondays . . . [my husband] Alex eats with us. The kids, excited that their father is coming to dinner, are on their best behavior. We often invite another wife or one of his children. . . .
>
> Most evenings . . . all I want to do is collapse into bed and sleep. But there is also the longing for intimacy and comfort that only he can provide, and when those feelings surface, I ask to be with him.
>
> Plural marriage is not for everyone. But it is . . . for me. . . . I believe American women would have invented it if it didn't already exist.[102]

Polygyny, a husband married to multiple wives, is significantly more common than polyandry, a woman married to more than one husband.[103] Anthropologists have found that polyandry has been more common in egalitarian societies.[104]

5. *Polygamy and the Interests of Children.* States ban polygamy to protect not only women but also children. The *Green* court, for example, asserted that polygamy is associated with incest, sexual assault, statutory rape, and failure to pay child support. Consider, though, the possibility that the polygamy prohibition may exacerbate these harms, as the following commentator suggests:

> [T]he ban on polygamy doesn't prevent thousands of polygamists from practicing their beliefs in the shadows, where they won't attract official scrutiny.

---

102. Elizabeth Joseph, My Husband's Nine Wives, N. Y. Times, May 23, 1991.

103. Katherine E. Starkweather & Raymond A. Hames, A Survey of Non-Classical Polyandry, 23 Human Nature 149 (2012).

104. Id.

By forcing them underground, in fact, the law breeds the very abuses decried by opponents, since the victims may fear that going to authorities will destroy the family. . . .[105]

6. *Polygamy and Romantic Love.* Yet another reason for the opposition to polygamy, one that does not make its way into judicial reasoning, is that polygamy is contrary to an American commitment that romantic love should be the core of a spousal relationship. Consider the following view:

> Why were [nineteenth century] Americans outraged by polygamy? In a word, because of love. . . . [R]omantic love as the fundamental pillar of marriage (alongside parenthood, of course) truly came into its own in the mid-nineteenth century. Polygamy was an offense against love, the structural glue of American marriage. . . .
>
> Far from denying this, Mormon theorists openly attacked the romantic sensibility. Polygamist leaders called on Mormons to sacrifice selfish and disruptive romantic desires, building marriages instead on simple friendship and piety. . . . Like Muslims today, Mormons touted polygamy as an alternative to prostitution and out-of-wedlock births, and a boon to women facing a dearth of truly marriageable men. And like today's proponents of same-sex marriage, polygamists and their apologists chided opponents as hypocrites bent on the "consecutive polygamy" of divorce and remarriage.
>
> Yet these arguments fell flat with most Americans, for whom romantic and companionate love was a cardinal aspiration. . . .
>
> In polygamous societies, where marriages are arranged and wives and children live collectively, too much individualized love (for spouses or children) endangers group solidarity. Yet in a democratic society, individualized love is praised and cultivated as the foundation of family stability. So take your pick. You can have a love-based democratic culture of monogamy, or an authority-based hierarchical culture of polygamy. But—as the *Reynolds* Court knew—you can't have both.[106]

7. *Polygamy and Democracy.* A final argument against polygamy, one that loomed large in *Reynolds*, is that polygamous unions are in some sense antithetical to democracy and its ideals. However legitimate that concern at the time of the *Reynolds* decision, does it provide any basis for the continued prohibition of polygamous marriage? Consider the position of the district court in Brown v. Buhman, discussed above in Note 2:

> The social harms implied by *Reynolds* arising from Mormon polygamy—that it introduced practices of Asiatic and African peoples into Christian

---

105. Steven Chapman, It's Not Our Place to Persecute Polygamists, Balt. Sun, Sept. 4, 2001.
106. Stanley Kurtz, Polygamy Versus Democracy; You Can't Have Both, Weekly Standard, Jun. 5, 2006.

Western civilization and assisted the Mormon Church in maintaining despotic, anti-democratic patriarchal control over the entire region, threatening all of American democracy — are no longer relevant, to say the least. . . .[107]

8. *Polyamory.* This material has focused on polygamy. What about polyamory or other plural arrangements? Do the various justifications put forward to prohibit polygamy also provide persuasive reasons to deny legal recognition to polyamorous arrangements? Are polyamorous arrangements likely to feature abuse? Might they be more likely to involve fraud? Do they disserve the interests of children?

Consider this portrait of a polyamorous family in Oakland, California:

An Oakland family has found what they think is the key to a happy household: three parents.

Two women named Melinda and Dani Phoenix and the man they both consider their husband, Jonathan Stein, are in a polyamorous relationship and parenting two babies together under the same roof.

Melinda and Dani began their relationship as a lesbian couple and became domestic partners in 2010. A year later, Jonathan joined them as the third partner and the three married last summer in a ceremony that is not legally recognized. . . .

Now the three are working as a team and sharing the responsibilities of caring for two babies. While many new parents are sleep-deprived and overwhelmed, this trio are gliding through parenthood as they take turns with childcare, diaper changes and nighttime feedings. . . .[108]

9. Obergefell *and Plural Marriage. Holm* was decided prior to the Supreme Court's decision in *Obergefell.* Given the Court's ruling that the different-sex requirement violates the Constitution, is there any justification for not striking down the two-partner limitation? How, if at all, can the two restrictions be distinguished?

10. *Marriage and Age. Holm* also raises an issue regarding age. The defendant's conviction for unlawful sex with a minor required both that his sexual partner be underage and that he not be married to her. Holm contended that the statute unconstitutionally distinguished between married and unmarried sexual partners. The statute permitted a 16-year-old, with the consent of the child's parent, to marry an adult, and yet it subjected Holm to criminal prosecution because he had sex with a 16-year-old who (in the eyes of the state) was not his spouse. The court rejected Holm's argument, reasoning that marriage provides the minor legal protections and

---

107. 947 F. Supp. 2d at 1220 n. 64.
108. Amy Graff, Polyamorous Oakland Family Finds Parenting Easier with Two Moms and a Dad, SFGate.com (Mar. 11, 2015).

enforces spousal obligations that do not extend to unmarried sexual partners. Is the state's use of marriage to confer legitimacy on what would otherwise be statutory rape justifiable?

The statute at issue in *Holm* illustrates more general points about age and the regulation of marriage. Courts have not extended to minors the right to marry that is enjoyed by adults. In Moe v. Dinkins, for example, a federal appeals court upheld a New York statute that permitted teenagers under the age of 18 to marry only with the consent of a parent.[109] The court subjected the statute to rational basis review.

Nearly every state has a similar scheme in which minors within a certain age range are permitted to marry only with parental consent.[110] Some states also require judicial approval of marriages involving minors.[111] Some states permit the marriage of children of any age, with parental consent and/or judicial approval, if the girl is pregnant or has a child.[112] The state interests asserted in support of the restriction in *Moe* included the protection of minors whose immaturity might lead them into ill-advised marriages that are likely to fail. Does this reasoning seem persuasive to you? Should 16- and 17-year-olds be permitted to marry without their parents' consent?[113]

Alternatively, one might ask why minors should be permitted to marry at all. Child marriage has been recognized as a human rights abuse and a problem in many parts of the world.[114] Some human rights groups argue that no one under age 18 should be permitted to marry:

> Child marriage . . . is a violent and abusive practice that stems from and sustains discrimination against women and girls. It not only excludes girls from decisions regarding the timing of marriage and the choice of spouse and is an abrupt and violent initiation into sexual relations, but also subjects them to other human rights violations such as . . . domestic violence, trafficking, exploitation, [and] curtailed education. . . . Child brides are often isolated and because of

---

109. 669 F.2d 67 (2d Cir. 1982).

110. Delaware, New Jersey, and Pennsylvania are the only states that do not allow minors to marry. See Tahirih Justice Center, Falling Through The Cracks: How Laws Allow Child Marriage to Happen in Today's America (July 2019) (table summarizing child marriage laws) see also Pa. Cons. Stat. § 1304 (effective July 7, 2020).

111. Id.

112. Nicholas L. Syrett, American Child Bride: A History of Minors and Marriage in the United States (2016).

113. See Legal Information Inst., Marriage Laws of the Fifty States, District of Columbia and Puerto Rico.

114. See United Nations Human Rights Office of the High Comm'r Child, Early and Forced Marriage, Including in Humanitarian Settings; United Nations Fund for Population Activities (UNFPA), Marrying Too Young: End Child Marriage (2012).

their marital status have little access to education and other services generally provided to children in the community.[115]

Different minimum ages for marriage by girls and boys were common nationwide until the last quarter of the twentieth century.[116] The New York state statute at issue in *Moe*, for example, allowed parental consent for the marriage of a girl as young as 14 and a boy as young as 16.[117] Today, Mississippi is the only state with a statute that expressly sets different minimum marriage ages based on sex.[118] Is there any valid justification for allowing girls to marry at a younger age than boys? Could such a law survive intermediate scrutiny under the Equal Protection Clause?

PROBLEM

At the age of 15, Jane wanted to marry her 48-year-old guitar teacher. Her parents were divorced and shared legal custody. Her mother consented to the marriage. The law in her state required the consent of both parents, but the law of a neighboring state required the consent of only one. Jane, her teacher, and her mother traveled to the other state, where the wedding took place. When her father learned of the marriage, he sought to have it invalidated. What statutory and constitutional arguments should he make? How should the court rule?

III. Establishing a Valid Marriage

In addition to being legally eligible to marry, individuals must possess the requisite legal capacity, consent to marry, and follow the formalities prescribed by the state in order to create a valid marriage. When these requirements are not satisfied, the remedy is often an annulment — a decree declaring that the marriage never existed due to a defect at the time of marriage. This is different from a divorce, which recognizes that a once-valid marriage has failed. Like divorce, however, annulments may be sought and granted only on enumerated statutory grounds.

---

115. Equality Now, Protecting the Girl Child 7 (2014).
116. Syrett, supra note 113.
117. *Moe*, 669 F.2d. at 68.
118. Miss. Code. Ann. § 93-1-5 (2020).

A. Capacity to Marry

Marriages can only be established with the consent of both parties, and meaningful consent is conditioned on an individual's capacity. What makes someone capable of consenting to marriage?

EDMUNDS V. EDWARDS
287 N.W.2d 420 (Neb. 1980)

BRODKEY, JUSTICE.

This case involves an action brought in the District Court for Douglas County on May 23, 1977, by Renne Edmunds, guardian of the estate of Harold Edwards, against Inez Edwards, to annul the marriage of his ward Harold to Inez, which occurred on May 10, 1975. In his petition, the guardian alleged that the marriage was void for the reason that Harold did not have the mental capacity to enter into a marriage contract on that date, which allegation was specifically denied by Inez. . . .

Harold was born on August 7, 1918, and was institutionalized at the Beatrice State Home as mentally retarded on September 25, 1939. He was a resident at the Beatrice State Home for a period of approximately 30 years. It was during this period that he first met Inez, who was also a patient of the home, and Bill Lancaster, who lived with Harold in Omaha after their release from the Beatrice State Home, and who has continued to reside with Harold and Inez since their marriage. Harold was placed in Omaha on November 14, 1969, and started a new life under the auspices of the Eastern Nebraska Community Office of Retardation (ENCOR), which was established in 1968 to provide alternatives for institutionalization of retarded persons at the Beatrice State Home and to assist in the normalization of the retarded in local communities. After coming to Omaha, Harold obtained employment as a food service worker in the Douglas County Hospital on February 16, 1970, and lived in a staffed ENCOR apartment from that time until shortly before his marriage in 1975. As will later be made apparent, he has functioned satisfactorily in that employment, and has received promotions and salary increases since commencing on that job. While under the auspices of ENCOR, Harold and Inez developed a romantic interest in each other and eventually decided to get married. The date of the marriage was postponed in order to afford the couple the opportunity to have premarital sex counseling and marriage counseling from the pastor of their church in Omaha. They were married by Reverend Verle Holsteen, pastor of the First Baptist Church in Omaha, Nebraska, and their friends, staff members of ENCOR, and out-of-state relatives attended the wedding in that church. The guardian did not bring this action to annul the marriage for a period of approximately 2 years after the date of the marriage ceremony. . . .

There is no question but that Harold was mentally retarded at the date of his marriage. The question in this case is the degree of his mental retardation, and whether it was such as to prevent him from entering into a valid marriage contract.

According to testimony in the record, mental retardation refers basically to delayed intellectual function and developmental delays usually associated from the time early in life and persisting throughout life. There are various degrees of mental retardation according to the official diagnostic system or nomenclature of the American Medical Association. . . . The expert medical witnesses for both parties agree that Harold falls within the classification of mild mental retardation.

The guardian first called his medical expert, Dr. Robert Mitchell, a psychologist connected with Creighton University in Omaha. Dr. Mitchell expressed the opinion that he did not believe Harold was competent to enter into a valid marriage, but admitted on cross-examination that being mildly mentally retarded did not automatically preclude a person from marriage. He also testified that he had asked Harold during his examinations and consultations what marriage meant, to which Harold responded "For life," and also "You stay married forever." Harold told Dr. Mitchell during the interview that he wanted to get married. . . .

The medical expert witness called by the defendant was Dr. Frank J. Menolascino, a psychiatrist specializing in the field of mental retardation, and author of numerous books and articles upon the subject. He was well acquainted with Harold, having first met him in 1959 when he was doing work at the Beatrice State Home, and had seen Harold many times since that time. . . . Harold told him he was marrying a lady he had known at the Beatrice State Home and that he had had premarital counseling from the minister of his church and also sexual counseling. Dr. Menolascino also testified that he had asked Harold why he wanted to get married, and Harold replied, "I don't want to be lonely." Harold had been married approximately 2 1/2 years before Dr. Menolascino saw him in December of 1977, and his mental status was "remarkably similar to the one I had seen in the past in the '60s." Dr. Menolascino was asked: "Doctor, do you believe that you have an opinion as to whether Mr. Edwards was capable of understanding the nature of a marriage within the paradigm you have discussed in May of 1975?" and he answered: "Yes, he was able to." . . . On cross-examination Dr. Menolascino was asked: "In your opinion, do you think that Harold Edwards understands the fact that he is liable for Mrs. Edwards' bills if she goes to a store and runs up some bills?" to which he replied: "Yes." He was then asked: "Do you think he understands the fact that if he gets a divorce he might have to pay alimony?" His reply to that question was: "I am not sure. I am not sure. . . ."

In addition to the medical witnesses who testified, there was also evidence adduced from various lay witnesses. Renne Edmunds, the guardian, testified that he first met Harold about April 8, 1975, although the date of the inception of the guardianship was October 18, 1972. At that time Harold was already under the care and guidance of ENCOR. Edmunds testified: "It was my conclusion that he (Harold) could not not only manage a fund of thirty thousand, he couldn't manage the small purchases, as well." . . . Harry John Naasz, an adviser for ENCOR, who was Harold's supervisor, testified that he had assisted Harold in making preparations for the marriage including obtaining of blood tests and the marriage certificate. He had discussed the forthcoming wedding with Harold: "Can you tell us what you discussed concerning the marriage? A. We discussed what it would mean, what it would mean living together, sharing their lives. Q. And what did Harold express to you? A. He wanted to get married. Q. What did he say that led you to believe that he might understand marriage? A. He mentioned to me that he understood, too that it was a commitment to each other, that Inez would be living there." . . .

David Bones, an employee of planned parenthood in Omaha and Council Bluffs, and also an ordained minister in the United Methodist Church, testified with reference to premarital sex counseling he had given to Harold and Inez on April 16, 1975. He testified: "As I recall, we talked some about the responsibility of economics, we talked about what kind of things they liked to do together, which is the common things we talk to most folks about. Q. Was there a response from Harold as to what kind of things they liked to do together? A. Well, the thing that I recall and I cannot swear that it is a specific specifically a statement made that, you know, Harold and Inez together talked about their enjoying just being together and being together in the sense of arms around each other, holding each other, holding hands, kidding one another, those things were a nice part of their experience as they were, and it appeared to us." Bones testified that he basically completed his premarital sex course with Harold and Inez and that Harold appeared to understand it and nodded his head.

Reverend Verle Holsteen, who was the pastor of the First Baptist Church on Park Avenue in Omaha, and who was the officiating officer at the marriage between Harold and Inez, testified that he had known Inez since 1971 and Harold since 1974, and they attended his church regularly. He gave them premarital counseling and recalls having had three sessions with them. He asked Harold if he understood what they were talking about and Harold said yes. . . . Reverend Holsteen testified on cross-examination: "I felt that Harold understood that if things followed through that he would be married to Inez." He was asked whether he had some doubt in his mind as to whether Harold understood what a marriage contract was all about and he replied: "By observing him I would say that he would not understand as much as other people what a marriage contract would be about. But I recognized, and I stand by this, that they would get along well together." . . .

Also testifying at the trial was Elizabeth Cartwright, an employee of ENCOR, who monitors Harold and Inez' finances. She testified that when Harold gets paid at the Douglas County Hospital he signs his check, takes it to the bank, deposits all the money except $40, and gives Inez $20 and he keeps $20. She does not have to go to the bank with him. Elizabeth Cartwright also testified that Inez is quite a bit sharper than Harold and she helps him around. . . . She also testified, however, that Harold cannot figure his finances and needs assistance. . . .

We now examine some established rules of law which we believe are applicable to this case. We first consider the nature of the marriage contract. Section 42-101, R.R.S.1943, provides: "In law, marriage is considered a civil contract, to which the consent of the parties capable of contracting is essential." Although by statute, marriage is referred to as a "civil contract," we have held: "That it is not a contract resembling in any but the slightest degree, except as to the element of consent, any other contract with which the courts have to deal, is apparent upon a moment's reflection. . . . What persons establish by entering into matrimony, is not a contractual relation, but a social Status; and the only essential features of the transactions are that the participants are of legal capacity to assume that Status, and freely consent so to do." University of Michigan v. McGuckin, 89 N.W. 778 (1902). . . . [W]hile our law defines marriage as a civil contract, it differs from all other contracts in its consequences to the body politic, and for that reason in dealing with it or with the status resulting therefrom the state never stands indifferent, but is always a party whose interest must be taken into account.

Another statutory provision of which we must take cognizance in this appeal is section 42-103, R.R.S.1943, which provides: "Marriages are void . . . (2) when either party, at the time of marriage, is insane or mentally incompetent to enter into the marriage relation;" . . .

A marriage is valid if the party has sufficient capacity to understand the nature of the contract and the obligations and responsibilities it creates. . . .

It is the general rule that the existence of a valid marriage is a question of fact. . . . Concededly, much of the evidence with reference to the capacity of Harold to enter into the marriage contract was conflicting and disputed. . . . [W]here the evidence on material questions of fact is in irreconcilable conflict, this court will, in determining the weight of the evidence, consider the fact that the trial court observed the witnesses and their manner of testifying, and therefore must have accepted one version of the facts rather than the opposite. . . . Applying this rule to the present case, we conclude, therefore, that the trial court was correct in dismissing the guardian's petition to annul the marriage of his ward, and that its action in this regard should be and hereby is affirmed.

NOTES AND QUESTIONS

1. *Legal Standards for Capacity.* Mental capacity is relevant to a number of different legal issues, and the standard varies by context.[119] Courts typically require the highest level of capacity to enter into contracts, or to buy and sell property; they require less to write a will, and even less to contract a valid marriage. Indeed,

---

119. See Lawrence A. Frolik & Mary F. Radford, "Sufficient" Capacity: The Contrasting Capacity Requirements for Different Documents, 2 NAELA J. 303 (2006).

it is not uncommon for courts to hold a will invalid but a marriage valid even when they occurred at the same time.[120] Why might courts reserve the lowest standard of capacity for marriage? Why have any capacity requirement at all? (You will consider this question in relation to the discussion in Chapters 3 and 5 about rights and obligations associated with marriage and its dissolution.) The court in *Edmunds* held that a marriage is valid if the party "has sufficient capacity to understand the nature of the contract and the obligations and responsibilities it creates." Is that a good standard? Why not ask for proof that the party is capable of fulfilling the obligations of marriage rather than simply capable of understanding them?

Sufficient mental capacity is required at the moment of solemnization. A person with intermittent incapacity due to a medical condition or use of intoxicating substances can still enter a valid marriage if done during a so-called lucid interval.

2. *Void Versus Voidable Marriages.* An annulment is a decree that the marriage was never valid, but an annulment is not always necessary. Some marriages are deemed *void ab initio*, which means that the parties are entitled to act as if the marriage never took place without seeking any decree of dissolution. Void marriages are typically those contracted despite significant impediments such as incest between close relatives or bigamy — impediments that violate a state's public policy. A void marriage is invalid even if the parties do not wish to set it aside, although, as a practical matter, they are often the only ones who know of the impediment. A third party can seek a decree that the marriage is void, even after the death of the parties, if it is relevant to a collateral proceeding such as probate of an estate. And a party to a void marriage may seek a decree of nullity for purposes of clarifying their legal status.

Other marriages are merely *voidable*, which means one party can seek to have the marriage annulled, but unless and until that happens, the marriage remains valid. An annulment is a decree that the marriage never existed in the eyes of the law, as opposed to a divorce, which decrees that a valid marriage existed and then failed. Most marriage impediments and irregularities are remedied through the annulment process, which is described in more detail in Chapter 4.[121] Depending on the grounds of annulment, the right to seek it may belong to both parties, only to one, or to a third party. For example, if a marriage was contracted between a person lacking sufficient capacity and a person possessing sufficient capacity, only

---

120. See, e.g., Hoffman v. Kohns, 385 So. 2d 1064 (Fla. Dist. Ct. App. 1980) (upholding marriage of housekeeper and her elderly employer, but invalidating his will executed the following day).

121. The void/voidable distinction is largely an artifact of English law and conflicts between civil and ecclesiastical courts. See Paul J. Goda, The Historical Evolution of the Concepts of Void and Voidable Marriages, 7 J. Fam. L. 297 (1967). Today, the distinction is determined primarily by the significance of the defect.

capacity, or that person's legal representative (e.g., Harold Edwards's seek to annul it. The same would be true for a marriage between a minor — only the minor or the minor's parent could seek to nullify . Voidable marriages typically cannot be annulled after the death of

sical Incapacity. A marriage may be annulled by one party because of the other party's inability to consummate the marriage through sexual intercourse, as long as the impotence was not known to the other party at the time the marriage was celebrated.[122] Most physical incapacity cases involve male impotence, but a man could seek an annulment based on his wife's physical inability to have sexual intercourse.[123]

B. Consent to Marry

Marriage requires mutual assent of the parties. A showing of legal capacity is necessary, but not sufficient, to satisfy this requirement. When the parties say "I do" during a wedding ceremony, they are expressing their assent to marry. But is their expression free of fraud and duress? Courts will only recognize certain types of misrepresentations as sufficient to invalidate a marriage.

In re Marriage of Meagher and Maleki
31 Cal. Rptr. 3d 663 (Cal. Ct. App. 2005)

Ruvolo, J.

The law in California has long been that an annulment of marriage may be granted on the basis of fraud only "in an extreme case where the particular fraud goes to the very essence of the marriage relation." Based on that settled rule, in this case we reverse a judgment granting an annulment to a wife whose husband, prior to the marriage, misrepresented his financial status and fraudulently induced her to invest in a business venture with him, with the intent to gain control of her assets. . . .

Appellant Ann Marie Meagher is a physician licensed as a psychiatrist. Respondent Malekpour Maleki is a real estate broker and investor, and has also been an importer and wholesaler of jewelry and Persian rugs. Meagher and Maleki first met socially in October 1997. At the time, Meagher was partially disabled and nearing retirement age, but was still working part time for the City and County of San Francisco. Maleki was in his late sixties and was living on the income from

---

122. See, e.g., Unif. Marriage and Divorce Act § 208(a)(2); Rickards v. Rickards, 166 A.2d 425 (Del. 1960); Eldredge v. Eldredge, 43 N.Y.S.2d 796 (N.Y. Sup. Ct. 1943); Harding v. Harding, 118 P.2d 789 (Wash. 1941).

123. See, e.g., T. v. M., 242 A.2d 670 (N.J. Super. Ct. Ch. Div. 1968).

some real property he owned. Meagher believed Maleki to be a well-educated millionaire with expertise in real estate and finance.

Meagher and Maleki developed a romantic relationship, and became engaged in February 1998. They also entered into a business relationship, in the course of which Meagher bought three residential properties as an investment. Meagher bought the first property (in San Francisco) through Maleki as broker, and the other two (in Daly City and Concord) directly from him. With respect to the properties that Meagher bought directly from Maleki, he promised her that when they were sold, he would reimburse her for their purchase price. Meagher thought that he had done so, but realized later that the reimbursement had not been complete. . . .

On August 28, 1999, after entering into the agreements for the business venture, Meagher and Maleki married. . . .

Meagher continued to believe that Maleki was wealthy until sometime in February 2002, when Maleki told Meagher that the couple did not have enough money to cover either their living expenses or their business expenses, which included a large tax bill. At that point, Meagher began to doubt what Maleki had been telling her about his financial situation and about how he was running their business venture. She revoked a power of attorney she had given him, and demanded more information about the business venture. At that point, Maleki became hostile and began talking about getting a divorce. Meagher still wanted to make the marriage work, however, because she did not want a divorce for religious reasons.

In mid-April 2002, however, Maleki told Meagher that he would divorce her if she did not put all her assets, including her home and pension, into joint tenancy and give him total control. At that point, Meagher began to suspect that Maleki had married her just for her money. She asked Maleki to buy out her share of the business venture, as he had always represented to her he had the means to do, but he told her that he could not and did not want to do so.

The parties separated in April or May 2002, and on May 6, 2002, Meagher filed a petition for dissolution of the marriage. She requested that various items of real property be confirmed as her separate property. Maleki's response asserted that "[a]ll property is community property or commingled joint, separate and community property," and contended that "[a]ll of [Meagher's] separate property claims should be denied."

On November 4, 2002, Meagher filed a motion seeking a summary adjudication annulling her marriage. . . .

On January 21, 2004, after protracted pretrial and trial proceedings, the trial court entered a judgment of nullity on the ground of fraud. . . . The court determined that. . . the parties' "marriage was based . . . on [Meagher's] reliance upon [Maleki's] representation that he had great wealth [and] that [he] would take care of her[,] and not that he expected through a series of transactions to divest her of at least half an interest in several million dollars' worth of property."

Based on these findings, the court concluded that "there was never a marriage" and that a judgment of nullity should be entered, and therefore that all the assets at issue were Meagher's sole and separate property. . . .

On this appeal, Maleki does not challenge the trial court's factual findings that he fraudulently misrepresented his financial circumstances to Meagher prior to the marriage, and that he deceived her in connection with the business venture. He argues, however, that, as a matter of law, a prospective spouse's fraud regarding financial matters is not a proper basis upon which to order an annulment.

The long-standing general rule in California is that "a marriage may only be annulled for fraud if the fraud relates to a matter which the state deems vital to the marriage relationship. As one court explained,

> because of its peculiar position as a silent but active party in annulment pro-
> ceedings . . . the state is particularly interested in seeing that no marriage is
> declared void as the result of fraud unless the evidence in support thereof
> is both clear and convincing. Thus[,] . . . [because] "[t]he state has a right-
> ful and legitimate concern with the marital status of the parties[,] . . . the
> fraud relied upon to secure a termination of the existing status must be such
> fraud as directly affects the marriage relationship and *not merely such fraud
> as would be sufficient to rescind an ordinary civil contract.*" . . .

The most recent published opinion upholding an annulment on the basis of fraud dates from 1987, and involves the paradigm example of a spouse who "harbors a secret intention at the time of the marriage not to engage in sexual relations with [the other spouse]." Similarly, "the secret intention of a woman concealed from her husband at the time of marriage never to live with him in any home provided by him would be a fraud going to the very essence of the marriage relation and of such a vital character as to constitute a ground for annulment." Annulment has also been held justified based on a wife's concealment that at the time of marriage she was pregnant by a man other than her husband or on a party's concealment of his or her sterility or intent to continue in an intimate relationship with a third person.

As these cases illustrate, annulments on the basis of fraud are generally granted only in cases where the fraud related in some way to the sexual or procreative aspects of marriage. The only California case of which we are aware that granted an annulment on a factual basis not directly involving sex or procreation is Douglass v. Douglass, 307 P.2d 674 (Cal. Ct. App. 1957). In *Douglass,* the Court of Appeal reversed a judgment denying an annulment to a woman whose husband, prior to their marriage, had "falsely and fraudulently represented to her that he was an honest, law abiding, respectable and honorable man" and that he had only one child from a prior marriage, who was "'well provided for.'" In fact, the husband had been convicted of grand theft only a few years earlier and was still on parole, and three months after the marriage he was arrested for parole violation due to his failure to support his two children from his prior marriage.

The *Douglass* court acknowledged that the test for annulment based on fraud is "whether the false representations or concealment were such as to defeat the essential purpose of the injured spouse inherent in the contracting of a marriage." The opinion in *Douglass* went on to state in rather general terms that because "the fraud of the [husband] in concealing his criminal record and true character was a deceit so gross and cruel as to prove him to [the wife] to be a man unworthy of trust," refusing her request for an annulment would be "unjust and intolerable." The facts of *Douglass* make clear, however, that the court did not grant an annulment based merely on the husband's general untrustworthiness. In holding the wife entitled to an annulment, the court relied in part on the fact that she already had two children from a former marriage, and that because of this, the "essentials of the marital relationship," from the wife's perspective, necessarily included having "husband of honorable character whom she could respect and trust, . . . and who would be a suitable stepfather for her children." When the wife learned the truth about the husband's failure to provide for his own children, her "hopes were shattered and her purposes defeated." Thus, even in *Douglass,* the fraud that the court found to be sufficient grounds for annulment had some nexus with the child-rearing aspect of marriage.

In the absence of fraud involving the party's intentions or abilities with respect to the sexual or procreative aspect of marriage, the long-standing rule is that neither party "may question the validity of the marriage upon the ground of reliance upon the express or implied representations of the other with respect to such matters as character, habits, chastity, *business or social standing, financial worth or prospects,* or matters of similar nature." In Marshall v. Marshall, 300 P. 816 (Cal. 1931), for example, the court expressly held that the trial court properly denied relief to a wife who sought an annulment on the basis of her husband's "fraudulent representation as to his wealth and ability to support and maintain" her, when in fact he was "impecunious" and subject to "harassment by creditors."

More recent case law has not changed this long-standing rule. In 1993, for example, the Fourth District reversed a judgment granting an annulment to a wife who discovered after the marriage that her husband had concealed the facts that he had a severe drinking problem for which he declined to seek help, and that he did not intend to work for a living. Even though the wife also alleged that the couple's "sex life after marriage was unsatisfactory," the court still found that the fraud did not "go to the *very essence* of the marital relation" and therefore was not sufficient as a basis for an annulment.

In the present case, Meagher does not contend that there is any evidence that Maleki lied to her about his marital history, or that he concealed an intention not to have sexual relations with her, not to live with her after the marriage, or not to discontinue an intimate relationship with a third party. On the contrary, the parties began living together even before their marriage and continued to do so for well over two years thereafter, and Meagher cites to no evidence in the record that she ever expressed any dissatisfaction with the intimate aspects of their relationship.

ırgues that the financial fraud at issue in this case is "at least as contrary
:e of marriage" as the types of fraud that have been held sufficient to jus-
ıent. She cites no authority, however, either in California or elsewhere,
position that annulment can be granted based on fraud or misrepresen-
ı purely financial nature. As already noted, the cases are entirely to the
contraı y. Accordingly, we agree with Maleki that the fraud established in this case,
as a matter of law, was not of the type that constitutes an adequate basis for granting
an annulment.

LEAX V. LEAX

305 S.W.3d 22 (Tex. App. 2009)

KEYES, JUSTICE.

Appellant, Elaine Leax, appeals the trial court's decree annulling her marriage
to appellee, Robert Leax. In three issues, Elaine contends that (1) the evidence
was legally and factually insufficient to support the trial court's decree granting an
annulment. . . .

Elaine and Robert were married on July 1, 2001 and moved into Robert's
home. . . . They separated on March 12, 2007, when Elaine moved out while Robert
was away on a cruise with his youngest daughter. Robert and Elaine did not have
any children together. Elaine took the majority of the household items from their
home, and she removed approximately $33,000.00 from a shared checking account,
leaving approximately $1,700.00 in the account.

Elaine then filed a petition for divorce. In her petition, Elaine alleged that the
marriage had become insupportable because of discord or conflict of personalities
between herself and Robert and that Robert was guilty of cruel treatment toward
her. . . . Robert denied Elaine's allegation of cruelty.

In response to some interrogatories, Elaine disclosed the existence of eight previous marriages. This prompted Robert to file his "Second Amended Counterpetition
for Annulment and Counterpetition for Divorce," asking for annulment on the basis
of fraud. . . .

Robert testified that he had been married to his previous wife for 25 years until she
died of cancer. He met Elaine, fell in love with her, and proposed to her. He testified
that he knew when they were dating that she had been married and divorced twice
before. He also testified that, just prior to their marriage, she admitted to a third previous marriage when it became obvious that Robert was likely to find out through other
means. Elaine told Robert that she did not tell him about the third marriage because
she knew Robert would not like the fact that she had had another marriage. Robert
testified that he specifically asked Elaine whether there were any other marriages in
her past, and she told him that there were not. Robert testified that he would not have
married Elaine if he had known that she had previously been married eight times. . . .

The trial court issued its decree declaring the marriage void and granting the annulment on December 19, 2007. . . .

The trial court found that Elaine misled Robert concerning the number of her previous marriages and intentionally withheld from him the existence of five previous marriages. The trial court also found that Elaine's misrepresentation was material and was made for the purpose of inducing Robert to enter into the marriage, that Robert did rely on Elaine's representations regarding the number of her previous marriages when he entered the marriage with Elaine, and that his reliance was reasonable and resulted in harm to him. The trial court concluded that Robert was entitled to an annulment of the marriage on the basis of fraud pursuant to section 6.107 of the Texas Family Code.

Section 6.107 provides:

> The court may grant an annulment of a marriage to a party to the marriage if:
> (1) the other party used fraud, duress, or force to induce the petitioner to enter into the marriage; and
> (2) the petitioner has not voluntarily cohabited with the other party since learning of the fraud or since being released from the duress or force.

TEX. FAM. CODE ANN. § 6.107 (Vernon 2006).

We were unable find any cases from Texas courts specifically articulating the proof necessary to warrant annulling a marriage on the basis of fraud. Fraudulent inducement is a type of fraud. . . . American courts generally have held that marriages can be annulled on the basis of fraud only if the fraud concerns an issue essential to the marriage. . . .

Several courts have held that the nondisclosure of a prior marriage and divorce does not qualify as an extreme enough fraud to annul a marriage. . . . However, at least one jurisdiction has held that the wife's concealment of five of her previous seven marriages on the application for a marriage license was sufficient fraud to serve as a basis to annul the marriage. Mayo v. Mayo, 617 S.E.2d 672 (N.C. Ct. App. 2005).

Here, Robert testified that while he and Elaine were dating she told him that she had been married twice. Just before their marriage, Elaine was compelled to reveal a third previous marriage to Robert. At this time, Robert asked Elaine directly whether she had had any other prior marriages, and she told him that she had not. Robert testified that if he had known Elaine had actually been married eight times previously, he would not have married her. He testified that he did not discover the other five marriages until after Elaine had moved out of the house. . . .

Elaine testified that Robert knew about all of her previous marriages at the time that they got married. . . .

The findings of fact clearly show that the trial court found Robert's testimony to be more credible than Elaine's. In light of Robert's testimony at trial, we conclude that there was legally sufficient evidence to support the trial court's finding of Elaine's fraud. . . . Therefore the evidence was legally sufficient to support the trial court's annulment of the marriage based on fraud. . . .

Robert testified that he was unaware of five of Elaine's eight previous marriages. This is certainly more significant than a spouse concealing only one previous marriage and divorce and clearly goes to the essentials of the marriage. . . .

NOTES AND QUESTIONS

1. *The "Essentials of the Marriage" Test.* An annulment requires proof of a defect at the outset of the marriage — one that has been recognized by the legislature as a basis for nullifying the union. Fraud is a standard ground in annulment statutes, but what constitutes sufficient fraud in this context has been determined primarily by courts. Many people tell plenty of lies during courtship, but courts typically take a "buyer beware" approach to fraud.[124] Annulment fraud doctrine developed based on a Massachusetts case from 1862, Reynolds v. Reynolds,[125] where the husband sought an annulment because the wife, during their six-week courtship, had passed herself off as "chaste and virtuous," despite being pregnant with another man's child. Ruling for the husband, the court concluded that the wife was "incapable of bearing a child to her husband at the time of the marriage," and thus unable to perform an important part of the marriage contract. *Reynolds* is cited for establishing the "essentials of the marriage" test, according to which the misrepresentation must relate to the sexual or procreative aspects of the marriage — those deemed "essential" to the very nature of marriage itself. Courts have used annulment as a remedy for fraud related to sexual capacity, intent to consummate the marriage, fertility, willingness to have children, pregnancy, and sexually transmitted disease, but generally refuse to use it for misrepresentations related to wealth, class, character, habits, or lifestyle.[126] Why restrict the types of fraud in this context? Why not allow any material misrepresentation, as with other contracts, to provide a basis for rescinding the agreement?

The courts in *Meagher* and *Leax* purport to adopt and apply the essentials of the marriage test but reach different conclusions about whether the particular misrepresentation qualifies. Why does the Texas court grant the annulment, while the California court does not? Is the problem in *Leax* that the wife specifically

---

124. On the most common lies and their legal consequences, see Jill Elaine Hasday, Intimate Lies and the Law (2019).

125. 85 Mass. 605 (1862).

126. See, e.g., Marshall v. Marshall, 300 P. 816 (Cal. 1931) (refusing to annul marriage based on husband's lies about his money and his ability to support his wife in the style to which she was accustomed); Adler v. Adler, 805 So. 2d 952 (Fla. Dist. Ct. App. 2001) (misrepresentations about prior marriages insufficient to constitute fraud). See generally Max Rheinstein, Marriage Stability, Divorce and Law 95 (1972).

misrepresented her past marital history when asked about it?[127] Is a spouse's financial status less central to a marriage than one's marital history? Wouldn't financial status have a greater effect on the course of the marriage than prior marriages that were validly dissolved? The standard for annulment is typically stated in objective terms, as some defect or misrepresentation going to the essence of the marriage. But why shouldn't an aggrieved spouse be able to obtain an annulment based on a misrepresentation that went to the essence of *their* marriage, as they subjectively viewed and valued it?

Annulment fraud doctrine was stretched in the early twentieth century in New York because divorce, as will be discussed in Chapter 4, was notoriously difficult to obtain. In the modern era, divorce is more accessible, and annulment rarely serves as a backstop. Nonetheless, annulment fraud doctrine has loosened over time, with many courts permitting annulment to be used as a remedy for fraud that was significant to a particular spouse, even if the fraud would not have had the same effect on every marriage.[128]

What if one party misrepresented the reason for marriage? In some cases, courts have granted annulments based on proof that one party pretended to be interested in the usual aspects of married life, but was secretly motivated by the desire for marital status because it came with some benefit such as eligibility for a green card or legitimacy for a child. (Importantly, the validity of the marriage under state law is independent of whether the marriage is recognized for federal immigration law purposes.[129]) The results in these cases are not uniform. Some courts have annulled marriages based on a misrepresentation about a spouse's motivations for marrying, while others have not.[130]

2. *Drunk at the Altar?* Can a couple assent to marry while drunk? What if they marry as a joke? These questions have arisen many times in annulment law. They do not neatly fit the statutory law of annulment, which has enumerated grounds like mental and physical incapacity, nonage, duress, and fraud. But marriage is premised on mutual assent, and intoxication can certainly affect one's ability to give meaningful consent. Courts have annulled marriages on this basis.

---

127. In re Marriage of Igene, 35 N.E.3d 1125 (Ill. App. Ct. 2015) (husband's concealment of previous marriages not sufficient to warrant annulment when he simply made no representations about his marital history).

128. See, e.g., Wolfe v. Wolfe, 389 N.E.2d 1143 (Ill. 1979) (granting husband an annulment based on wife's lie about a previous divorce, which was important to him as a strict Catholic).

129. United States v. Lutwak, 344 U.S. 604 (1953) (upholding criminal conviction for immigration fraud regardless of whether underlying marriage was valid).

130. Compare Desta v. Anyaoha, 371 S.W.3d 596 (Tex. App. 2012) (granting annulment based on evidence that wife induced marriage but her true motivation was to obtain green card); In re Marriage of Joel and Roohi, 404 P.3d 1251 (Colo. App. 2012) (same), with Johl v. United States, 370 F.2d 174 (9th Cir. 1967) (denying annulment despite evidence marriage was based on a fraudulent purpose); Roe v. Immigration & Naturalization Serv., 771 F.2d 1328 (9th Cir. 1985) (same). See generally John H. Wade, Limited Purpose Marriages, 45 Mod. L. Rev. 159 (1982).

Marriages undertaken in jest or in great haste are an even worse fit for annulment law, as the parties might have been perfectly capable of giving consent when they said "I do," but had their fingers crossed behind their backs. Pop singer Britney Spears married her childhood friend, Jason Alexander, in Las Vegas in 2004 and filed for annulment the next day. She claimed she "lacked understanding of her actions" and was "incapable of agreeing to the marriage;" moreover, her complaint stated that the two did not "know each other's likes and dislikes," their wishes about children, and were generally "incompatible." Her annulment was granted, even though none of what she described fit neatly into one of Nevada's grounds for annulment.[131] How should courts handle such cases? Does it strengthen or undermine the institution of marriage when such marriages are annulled? Is there a reason to grant annulment petitions when divorce is readily available in most cases?

PROBLEMS

1. Darva Conger and 49 other would-be brides on Fox's "Who Wants to Marry a Millionaire?" signed an "annulment agreement" before going on stage to compete for the hand of Rick Rockwell, the promised millionaire. The agreement provided that either party would consent to an annulment sought by the other. Rockwell selected Conger to be his bride, and they got married live on television at the end of the show, less than two hours after meeting on stage. They had a disastrous honeymoon, and Conger petitioned for an annulment in Nevada when they returned. She checked the box for "fraud" on the annulment petition, citing his failure to disclose his "history of problems with prior girlfriends," which included at least one restraining order taken out against Rockwell. How should the court evaluate her annulment petition? Is the agreement the parties signed in advance likely to be of any relevance?

2. In 1999, Larry and Joy divorced after 30 years of marriage. In 2004, Larry contacted Joy and told her he had been diagnosed with a terminal illness and asked whether she would remarry him so he would not have to die alone. They met for coffee, and he presented her with a folder of medical records, ostensibly documenting his diagnosis with a prognosis of less than a few years to live. Joy relied on Larry's representations about his health and agreed to his proposal; she felt sorry for him. After they remarried, Joy learned that although Larry did have a

---

131. See Spears v. Alexander, No. D311371 (Nev. Dist. Ct. Clark. Co. Jan. 5, 2004). Courts sometimes deny annulments in similar circumstances. See, e.g., Hand v. Berry, 154 S.E. 239 (Ga. 1930).

blood disorder, it was not as advanced as he had represented, and that his death was no more imminent than anyone else's. In 2007, she sued to annul the marriage on grounds of fraud.[132] Should the decree be granted?

C. Marriage Formalities

In addition to determining whether couples are eligible to marry, states prescribe *how* they get married. To create a valid, ceremonial marriage, states generally require: (1) a marriage license, and (2) solemnization of the marriage by a qualified officiant. As you read the materials that follow, pay attention to the variations among state marriage laws, the purposes ostensibly served by marriage formalities, and the response from courts when requirements are not satisfied.

1. Marriage Licenses

Every state requires couples to obtain a marriage license before participating in a marriage ceremony, but courts disagree about how to handle the failure to obtain the license. Compare the reasoning in the next two cases.

ESTATE OF DEPASSE

118 Cal. Rptr. 2d 143 (Cal. Ct. App. 2002)

BAMATTRE-MANOUKIAN, ACTING P.J.

Jack Harris appeals from an order in a probate proceeding denying his spousal property petition. . . .

Derrel DePasse was hospitalized at Stanford University Medical Center with a terminal illness. . . . Prior to her hospitalization, DePasse had resided with Jack Harris in his home in Saratoga, California. The record does not indicate how long the couple lived together. . . .

On July 5, 2000, while in the hospital, DePasse executed a holographic [handwritten] will appointing her brother, John DePasse, executor of her estate and instructing him to donate all of her artwork to one of three museums. . . . The will did not mention Harris.

---

132. This example is based on In re Marriage of Farr, 228 P.3d 267 (Colo. App. 2010).

On July 7, 2000, two days after DePasse executed the holographic will, she and Harris asked the hospital chaplain to perform a marriage ceremony for them. According to the chaplain, both DePasse and Harris told her that they wanted to be married before DePasse died and that there was no time for them to obtain a marriage license. The chaplain performed the marriage ceremony at Stanford University Medical Center. According to Harris, the couple had planned to be married in a large ceremony in late 2000 or in 2001.

DePasse died the day after the marriage ceremony. She was 52 years old. She is survived by her brother, John DePasse; her mother, Josephine DePasse; and Jack Harris. . . .

Harris admits that he and DePasse did not have a marriage license when the chaplain conducted the marriage ceremony. In addition, neither the parties nor the chaplain made any effort to obtain a license after the ceremony. Harris does not claim that a license was not required. He asserts instead that his failure to obtain a license was a curable defect that did not invalidate the marriage. . . .

Harris's arguments require us to determine, as a matter of law, whether a marriage license is required for a valid marriage. . . .

The state has a vital interest in the institution of marriage and plenary power to fix the conditions under which the marital status may be created or terminated. The regulation of marriage is solely within the province of the Legislature. In view of the Legislature's role in regulating marriage, we begin by reviewing the statutes governing marriage in California. . . .

Family Code section 300 provides: "Marriage is a personal relation arising out of a civil contract between a man and a woman, to which the consent of the parties capable of making that contract is necessary. Consent alone does not constitute marriage. *Consent must be followed by the issuance of a license* and solemnization as authorized by this division, except as provided by Section 425 and Part 4 (commencing with Section 500)."

Section 306 provides: "Except as provided in Section 307, *a marriage shall be licensed,* solemnized, and authenticated, and the certificate of registry of marriage shall be returned as provided in this part. Noncompliance with this part by a nonparty to the marriage does not invalidate the marriage."

Section 350 provides: "Before entering a marriage, or declaring a marriage pursuant to Section 425, the parties *shall first obtain a marriage license from a county clerk.*" The marriage license shall show the parties' identities, real and full names, places of residence, and ages. The applicants may be required to present identification and the clerk may examine them under oath or request additional documentary proof as to the facts stated. A marriage license shall not be granted if either of the applicants lacks the capacity to enter into a valid marriage or is under the influence of alcohol or drugs at the time he or she applies for the license. A marriage license expires 90 days after it is issued.

Section 421 provides: "*Before solemnizing a marriage, the person solemnizing the marriage shall require the presentation of the marriage license.* If the person solemnizing the marriage has reason to doubt the correctness of the statement of facts in the marriage license, the person must be satisfied as to the correctness of the statement of facts before solemnizing the marriage. For this purpose, the person may administer oaths and examine the parties and witnesses in the same manner as the county clerk does before issuing the license." Penal Code section 360 provides that every person who solemnizes a marriage "without first being presented with the marriage license, as required by Section § 21" is guilty of a misdemeanor. . . .

According to the statutory scheme, there are five steps in the marriage process. First, the parties must consent. Second, the parties must obtain a license from the county clerk. Since the license and certificate of registry are combined into one form, the parties also obtain the certificate of registry at that time. Third, the marriage must be solemnized. Before solemnizing the marriage, the person conducting the ceremony must ensure that the parties have obtained a marriage license. Fourth, the person solemnizing the marriage must authenticate the marriage by signing the certificate of registry and arranging for at least one witness to sign the certificate. Finally, the person solemnizing the marriage must return the certificate of registry to the county clerk for filing.

In this case . . . Harris admits that he never obtained a marriage license. . . .

In some jurisdictions, a marriage will be deemed valid even though no license was obtained where the statutes providing for the procurement of a license are viewed as directory rather than mandatory. Other jurisdictions view the licensing requirement as mandatory and hold that the absence of a license is a fatal flaw to the validity of a marriage. The California courts have never authoritatively determined whether a license is an absolute requirement for a valid marriage. However, the Legislature addressed the issue in 1945 by amending former Civil Code section 55 (now Fam. Code § 300) to provide that the parties' consent to marriage "must be followed by the issuance of a license." Other statutory provisions governing marriage reinforce the mandatory nature of the licensing requirement in California. Section 306 provides that "a marriage shall be licensed." Section 350 provides that "[b]efore entering a marriage, . . . the parties shall first obtain a marriage license" and section 421 provides that the person solemnizing the marriage "shall require the presentation of the marriage license."

We are cognizant of the fact that our courts have held that the use of the word "must" in a statute "does not necessarily and *ipso facto* make statutory provisions mandatory." Likewise the word "shall" has been held in some cases to be merely directory. Whether the words "must" or "shall" should be construed as mandatory or directory depends on the intention of the Legislature in enacting the particular code section. In 1992 the Legislature reorganized the major family law statutes into a new code, entitled the "Family Code." The new code specifically addressed the question of whether the term "shall" is directory or mandatory. Section 12 provides that the use of the term "shall" in the Family Code indicates that the required action is mandatory. Sections 306, 350, and 421 all employ the word "shall." Thus according to the plain language of the statutes, a license is a mandatory requirement for a valid marriage in California. . . .

Affirmed.

CARABETTA V. CARABETTA
438 A.2d 109 (Conn. 1980)

PETERS, ASSOCIATE JUSTICE. . . .

The plaintiff and the defendant exchanged marital vows before a priest in the rectory of Our Lady of Mt. Carmel Church of Meriden, on August 25, 1955, according to the rite of the Roman Catholic Church, although they had failed to obtain a marriage license. Thereafter they lived together as husband and wife, raising a family of four children, all of whose birth certificates listed the defendant as their father. Until the present action, the defendant had no memory or recollection of ever having denied that the plaintiff and the defendant were married.

The issue before us is whether, under Connecticut law, despite solemnization according to an appropriate religious ceremony, a marriage is void where there has been noncompliance with the statutory requirement of a marriage license. This is a question of first impression in this state. . . .

In determining the status of a contested marriage, we are bound . . . to examine with care the relevant legislative enactments that determine its validity. Such an examination must be guided by the understanding that some legislative commandments, particularly those affecting the validity of a marriage, are directory rather than mandatory. "The policy of the law is strongly opposed to regarding an attempted marriage . . . entered into in good faith, believed by one or both of the parties to be legal, and followed by cohabitation, to be void." Hames v. Hames, supra, 163 Conn. 599.

The governing statutes at the time of the purported marriage between these parties contained two kinds of regulations concerning the requirements for a legally valid marriage. One kind of regulation concerned substantive requirements determining those eligible to be married. . . . The other kind of regulation concerns the formalities prescribed by the state for the effectuation of a legally valid marriage. These required formalities, in turn, are of two sorts: a marriage license and a solemnization. . . .

As to licensing, the governing statute in 1955 was a section entitled "Marriage licenses." It provided, in subsection (a): "No persons shall be joined in marriage until both have joined in an application . . . for a license for such marriage." Its only provision for the consequence of noncompliance with the license requirement was contained in subsection (e): "... any person who shall join any persons in marriage without having received such (license) shall be fined not more than one hundred dollars." Neither this section, nor any other, described as void a marriage celebrated without license. . . .

In the absence of express language in the governing statute declaring a marriage void for failure to observe a statutory requirement, this court has held in an unbroken line of cases . . . that such a marriage, though imperfect, is dissoluble rather than void. We see no reason to import into the language "(n)o persons shall be joined in marriage until (they have applied for) a license," a meaning more drastic. . . . In sum, we conclude that the legislature's failure expressly to characterize as void a marriage properly celebrated without a license means that such a marriage is not invalid. . . .

The conclusion that a ceremonial marriage contracted without a marriage license is not null and void finds support, furthermore, in the decisions in other jurisdictions. In the majority of states, unless the licensing statute plainly makes an unlicensed marriage invalid, "the cases find the policy favoring valid marriages sufficiently strong to justify upholding the unlicensed ceremony. This seems the correct result. Most such cases arise long after the parties have acted upon the assumption that they are married, and no useful purpose is served by avoiding the long-standing relationship. Compliance with the licensing laws can better be attained by safeguards operating before the license is issued, as by a more careful investigation by the issuing authority or the person marrying the parties." Clark, Domestic Relations, p. 41 (1968).

Since the marriage that the trial court was asked to dissolve was not void, the trial court erred in granting the motion to dismiss for lack of jurisdiction over the subject matter. . . .

NOTES AND QUESTIONS

1. *Mandatory versus Discretionary "Requirements."* As the court noted in *Carabetta,* many state courts have ruled that while marriage laws require that the parties obtain a license to marry, the failure to do so does not invalidate the resulting marriage. Others, like in *DePasse,* insist on strict compliance. What purpose is served by a requirement that is often not enforced? Are there any disadvantages to requiring strict compliance?

2. *Waiting Periods.* Many states impose a waiting period of one to three days between the time a license is obtained and the time the ceremony can take place. Why? Some states provide that the waiting period can be waived by a judge upon a showing of special circumstances, such as an imminent birth.[133] What is the

---

133. See, e.g., W. Va. Code § 48-2-103(b) (2020).

function of this exception? Many states also provide that licenses are only valid for a short period, typically 30 to 60 days. Why? A small number of states encourage couples to obtain premarital counseling but typically do not require it. Should they?[134] Georgia law requires six hours of "premarital education" if either party is 17 years old; for adult couples, completion of the requisite hours results in a waiver of the marriage license fee.[135] Is this a good approach? What interest does the state have in premarital education?

3. *Purpose of Licensure.* Most states require that both parties to a marriage apply for a license in person at a designated government office. The parties will be asked to provide a variety of pieces of information about themselves, including facts necessary for the clerk to determine whether the parties appear eligible to marry under the state's laws. The parties will provide, at a minimum, their full names, ages, and marriage history, and they will state whether they are related to one another. If either party is underage, the application must be signed by a consenting parent. The role of this screening process was on display in cases challenging restrictions on marriage by same-sex couples, most of which originated from a clerk's refusal to issue a license to a couple.

4. *Healthy Enough to Marry?* Early in the twentieth century, many states passed statutes to require that couples undergo a medical exam prior to applying for a marriage license. Laws at the time routinely prohibited marriage by individuals with diseases that were believed, often incorrectly, to be hereditary. The state of Washington, for example, passed a law in 1909 that ruled out marriage for any "common drunkard, habitual criminal, epileptic, imbecile, feeble-minded person, idiot or insane person," and those with "hereditary insanity" or "pulmonary tuberculosis in its advanced stages."[136] The statute applied only to women under age 45, and the men who married them — the couples most likely to reproduce. Many states also prohibited people with sexually transmitted infections (referred to then as "venereal disease") from marrying; some statutes specifically required tests for syphilis and gonorrhea. Given the strong taboo on sex outside of marriage, states treated marriage as the launching point for legitimate sexual activity. But they feared men might have contracted diseases from "illegitimate" relationships, which might then be passed on to innocent wives and perhaps children via birth defects. Courts generally upheld these statutes. In Peterson v. Widule, the Wisconsin Supreme Court upheld a law that required men to get a medical certificate, stating that they were free from venereal disease, before a marriage license could issue.[137] "Society," wrote Chief

---

134. Premarital education programs typically focus on relationship skills, like communication. Tiffany L. Clyde, et al., The Effects of Premarital Education Promotion Policies on U.S. Divorce Rates, 26 Psychol. Pub. Pol'y & L. 105, 106 (2020).

135. Ga. Code § 19-3-30.1 (2020).

136. 1909 Wash. Sess. Laws, ch. 174.

137. 147 N.W. 966 (Wis. 1914).

Justice Winslow, "has a right to protect itself from extinction and its members from a fate worse than death."[138] The state was entitled to focus on men, since it was, in its view, "common knowledge . . . that the great majority of women who marry are pure, while a considerable percentage of men have had illicit sexual relations before marriage."

The requirements for blood tests and medical exams have been largely repealed. Pennsylvania dropped the requirement of a test for syphilis in 1997; Oklahoma in 2004; and the District of Columbia in 2008.[139] These repeals are part of a consistent trend away from state control over marriage, at least as a gateway to reproduction. Some states require the distribution of a pamphlet or other literature advising couples about the prevention and treatment of sexually transmitted infections.[140] Ohio does not require a blood test, but provides that a marriage license shall not be granted if either applicant "is infected with syphilis in a form that is communicable or likely to become communicable."[141] Washington requires couples to sign an affidavit stating that neither of them has a contagious sexually transmitted disease or that they are both aware of any such infection.[142] New York requires applicants who are not "of the Caucasian, Indian or Oriental race" to be tested for sickle cell anemia, but says that the failure to do so does not prevent or invalidate a marriage. In the late 1980s, Illinois briefly required marriage license applicants to undergo an HIV-AIDS test, but backed off because of public objection and the exorbitant cost.[143] Given the expense of the testing and the low rate of positive results, the state was spending "approximately $243,000 for each HIV-positive identification." The requirement also had a stark impact on marriage practices; Illinois residents went elsewhere to marry rather than submit to the mandatory test.[144]

5. *Racial Disclosure.* Eight states still have laws on the books that require marriage license applicants to disclose their race.[145] Some localities provide a list of race code options, including "mulatto," "octaroon," and other categories once used in the law but now widely denounced as racist.[146] The race disclosure law in Virginia is under challenge in a pending case. Does the state have any legitimate

---

138. Id. at 968.

139. Pa. Cons. Stat. Ann. §§ 23-1304 and 1305 contained the requirement until abolition. See Okla. Laws 2004, c. 333, sec. 3, which repealed 43 Okla. St. § 31; D.C. Law 15-154 (2003).

140. Mich. Laws Ann. § 333.5119 (2020); Ill. Stat. Ann. § 5/204 (2020).

141. Ohio Rev. Code § 3101.06 (2020).

142. Wash. Rev. Code § 26.04.210 (2020).

143. See Isabel Wilkerson, Illinoisans Fault Prenuptial AIDS Tests, N.Y. Times, Apr. 16, 1988, at A6.

144. See Margaret Brinig and Steven L. Nock, Marry Me, Bill: Should Cohabitation be the (Legal) Default Option?, 64 La. L. Rev. 403, 442 n.76 (2004).

145. These states are Alabama, Connecticut, Delaware, Kentucky, Louisiana, Minnesota, New Hampshire, and Virginia.

146. Jacey Fortin, Couples in Virginia Can Marry Without Disclosing Their Race, N.Y. Times, Sept. 17, 2019.

interest in collecting racial information if it lacks the ability to restrict marriage on this basis?[147]

2. Solemnization

States do not mandate any particular form of ceremony for a valid marriage. The common features of weddings in the United States are largely a function of custom rather than law. But the law does require that the parties express consent to marry ("I do") before an officiant who has been authorized by law to preside over the ceremony. The state delegates authority to an officiant to make sure the legal requirements are met — that the parties are there voluntarily, they both consent to be married, and the paperwork is completed so the state has a record of the change in their legal status. Only after the officiant returns the paperwork — signed by the parties and witnesses — does the state issue the "marriage certificate" that can be used as proof of marriage. The officiant's power comes with responsibility; the officiant in *DePasse* was guilty of a misdemeanor for performing a marriage ceremony without the requisite license. Who should have the legal power to officiate a wedding? State statutes typically delegate authority to a list of secular officials (e.g., judges, mayors, and certain clerks) and religious officials. These rules have given rise to a variety of disputes, including a recurring one over the validity of marriages solemnized by a minister who was ordained by mail or online. In reading the next case, consider why states grant the power to officiate over a civil wedding to religious officials and whether state goals are satisfied by empowering ministers ordained online.

In the Matter of Last Will and Testament of Robert C. Blackwell
531 So. 2d 1193 (Miss. 1988)

Robertson, Justice, for the Court:

At issue this day is whether a minister of the California-based — and not uncontroversial — Universal Life Church (ULC) may in this state solemnize the rites of matrimony so that the persons participating in those rites are legally married. The case turns on whether the Universal Life minister is a "spiritual leader" of a "religious body" within the meaning of our statute law. . . .

---

147. See Rogers v. Virginia State Registrar et al., No. 1:19-cv-01149-RDA-IDD, 2020 WL 3246327 (E.D. Va. Jan. 23, 2020); see also N.H. Rev. Stat. Ann. § 5-C:14 (2020); Del. Code Ann. tit. 13, § 103 (2020); Conn. Gen. Stat. Ch. § 46b-25 (2020); Ky. Rev. Stat. Ann. §§ 402.100, 110 (2020); La. Stat. Ann. § 9:224 (2020); Minn. Stat. § 144.223 (2020).

In 1984, Cobert C. Blackwell was a 58-year-old widower living in Walthall County, Mississippi. Blackwell and Nadine B. Fortenberry became enamored of one another and on November 8, 1984, the two obtained a marriage license in Walthall County.

The next day, a Friday, our couple set sail for Jackson (of all places) in search of legal blessing for their bliss. They checked into the Holiday Inn Southwest at around 4:00 or 4:30. Blackwell called a Hinds County Justice Court Judge, Jack Bass, and talked to the Judge's wife. Apparently Blackwell requested that the judge come to the motel room and marry them there but was told the judge would only marry people at his office.

Mrs. Bass referred the two to Claude Clark, suggesting that Clark was authorized to perform the marriage. They then contacted Clark who agreed to perform the marriage. On the following morning, Saturday, November 10, 1984, Clark performed the marriage ceremony and signed the marriage license. Shortly thereafter, the newlyweds returned to Walthall County and began living together and holding themselves out as man and wife.

As fate would have it, on February 7, 1985, Cobert Blackwell died. . . . Thereafter, on March 4, 1985, Nadine, the new Mrs. Blackwell, renounced the will, requested a widow's allowance and her share of the estate under the statute of descent and distribution.

Blackwell's brothers and sisters promptly challenged Nadine's rights, claiming that she and Blackwell were not lawfully married because Claude Clark was not a person qualified under state law to perform marriages. Specifically, we are told that the Universal Life Church is not a "religious body" and that Clark is not a "spiritual leader" within the meaning and contemplation of the statute. Miss. Code Ann. § 93–1–17 (1972). . . .

[T]he Chancery Court . . . ruled that Claude Clark was not a minister fitting within the requirements of Miss. Code Ann. § 93–1–17 (1972). . . .

Whatever its historical, cultural or religious origins, marriage is a function of the positive enabling laws of the state. Whether a man and woman be married turns upon their compliance with state imposed prerequisites and forms. Where an "i" has been left undotted or a "t" uncrossed, the parties are simply not married, common law marriages having long ago been abolished.

This state takes no neutral stance regarding marriage, and in this regard we are not unaware of many policy pronouncements which on their face appear of relevance. For example, we find it written more than once that

> The law favors marriage, and, when once solemnized according to the forms
> of law, will not declare its nullity upon anything less than clear and certain tes-
> timony, especially after it has been dissolved by the death of one of the parties.

See Whitman v. Whitman, 41 So.2d 22, 25 (1949). But this begs the question, which is whether the Blackwells' marriage was ever "solemnized according to the forms of law."

Only a select few have been empowered to perform with legal effect rites of matrimony, and we look to our statute law to identify those. Among those so empowered are "any . . . spiritual leader of any . . . religious body. . . ." The Chancery Court held that Claude Clark was not one within the statute and, accordingly, declared the Blackwells' purported marriage *void ab initio*. Nadine's appeal requires that we carefully examine the point.

Our focus is upon Claude Clark and the Universal Life Church. Clark is, by occupation, a constable of Hinds County, and by religion, a practicing Methodist. His only basis for any claim that he is a person authorized to perform marriages in Mississippi is his "Credentials of Ministry" secured in September of 1984 from the Universal Life Church of Modesto, California.

About two months before he "celebrated the rites of matrimony" between Cobert and Nadine, Clark had written to the ULC inquiring what was required to become one of its ministers. He received in the mail from it a paper entitled "Credentials of Ministry" by which the ULC certified that the bearer was an authorized minister. The space for the name of the bearer was blank, and Clark filled in his name.

The Universal Life Church was established by Kirby J. Hensley, an illiterate Baptist minister from North Carolina. He undertook to educate himself and in the process was influenced by his reading in world religion. Over the years, he conceived the idea of the universal church that would bring people of all religions together instead of separating them.

In 1962, Hensley founded the Universal Life Church having previously opened a "church" in his garage in Modesto, California. Though Hensley had his own ideas about theology, he felt others had a right to their own theories. He began to ordain ministers free, for life, without question. He would present a signed ordination certificate and a one-page information sheet on the ordination merely for the asking. Though ordination was free, a doctor of divinity later cost $20.00, and was offered with ten lessons on how to set up and operate a church.

California, however, enjoined Hensley from issuing a degree from an unaccredited institution, so the Department of Education was moved to Phoenix, Arizona. ULC has since made a not insignificant contribution to federal income tax jurisprudence.

Beyond this, Hensley has initiated several "reforms" by marrying a couple in a trial marriage, and marrying two girls at the 1971 Universal Life Church festival. A newspaper, *Universal Life*, is issued irregularly from the Modesto, California, headquarters. An annual convention is held. Over 16,000 were present in 1971. By 1977, the Universal Life Church claimed to have ordained more than 6,000,000 ministers. Some 25,000 of those had formed congregations that meet regularly, usually small groups in house-churches.

All in all, ULC is hardly a conventional church by Bible Belt standards.

Constable Clark became a minister of the Universal Life Church in September of 1984. As Clark explained, one of the deciding factors was that the Justice Court

Judges had gone on salary and therefore were no longer receiving fees for performing weddings. The judges in Hinds County therefore had discontinued performing weddings away from the office on nights or on weekends.

Clark knew some friends who had credentials of ministry with the Universal Life Church and, as a result, he wrote the church, having previously checked with the Attorney General's office which told him that this would be legal. He also checked with his attorney who gave his approval. He wrote the church a letter, asked them what they required and in return, they sent him the credentials of ministry, an I.D. card. Clark is still a Methodist layman and active in the Methodist church. From his testimony, his religious administrations as a minister of the Universal Life Church were restricted to performing weddings and giving devotions.

According to Clark, the church has no set doctrine per se, but one can worship God in the way that one sees fit and is comfortable with as long as it does not infringe on the rights of others. One is not required to express a belief in God or any deity before he can be a minister of the Universal Life Church. Before becoming a minister, Clark was not required to learn anything about the Universal Life Church or any religious belief that they had.

Clark, at the time of the marriage disputed here, had already performed several marriage ceremonies, a number of them in churches in the Jackson area and the chapel at the Mississippi Agricultural Museum, although it was not clear which of these weddings was performed before and after the wedding in controversy. On cross-examination, he estimated that he had performed twelve to fifteen marriage ceremonies before he conducted this one. The marriage ceremony he used was from the Abington Marriage Manual which he purchased at the Baptist Book Store in Jackson.

We are not unaware that the power of ULC ministers to perform marriage ceremonies has been litigated in at least three other states. New York rejects ULC ministers but under a statute far more restrictive than ours. Virginia has done likewise.

North Carolina originally held a ULC officiated marriage void in the context of a prosecution for bigamy. *State v. Lynch*, 272 S.E.2d 349 (N.C. 1980). The year after the *Lynch* decision, however, the North Carolina General Assembly passed an act which validated marriages performed by Universal Life Ministers prior to that date, unless they had already been invalidated by a court of competent jurisdiction. . . .

The experience in other states in matters such as this is always of value. We find the North Carolina experience particularly intriguing. In the end, however, we are confronted with our own statute[,] ultimate construction of which is our non-delegable duty. We confront this day no imperative that we establish some hard-edged line of demarcation prescribing minimum qualifications for one authorized to solemnize rites of matrimony under Section 93–1–17. Claude Clark is enough of a "spiritual leader", and the Universal Life Church is enough of a "religious body" that, in the eyes of the law of this state, Cobert C. Blackwell and Nadine B. Fortenberry became husband and wife on November 8, 1984, and this is sufficient unto the day.

The judgment of the Chancery Court is reversed and this matter is remanded for further proceedings not inconsistent with this opinion.

SULLIVAN, JUSTICE, specially concurring:

I concur in the result reached by the majority in this case but would find that Claude Clark meets the requirements of a spiritual leader and that the Universal Life Church meets the requirements of a religious body in the eyes of the laws of this State.

My concern is with the language of the majority that Claude Clark is "enough of a spiritual leader" and that the Universal Life Church is "enough of a religious body." The majority continues its new school of legal interpretation which I prefer to call the "horseshoes school". . . .

It is difficult enough for the bench and bar to anticipate and predict future rulings of this Court when we limit ourselves to simple statements of what the law does and does not allow. It is an impossible task when, by the use of "horseshoe jurisprudence," we begin to apply our new "close enough to count" standard as to what is lawful and to what is not. Close counts in horseshoes and hand grenades. . . .

NOTES AND QUESTIONS

---

1. *Variation in Officiant Laws.* State marriage laws vary in how restrictively they define "clergy" for purposes of delegating the power to perform weddings. Courts in New York have refused to validate marriages solemnized by a minister ordained online.[148] The applicable statute is stricter than in most states; it allows a "clergyman or minister of any religion" to solemnize marriages, but defines "religion" to be an "ecclesiastical denomination" and "minister" to be a person who presides over a congregation. A trial court rejected a claim by a group of ULC ministers that the statute violated the First Amendment's guarantee of free exercise of religion.[149] Can a state constitutionally define what makes something a religion or someone a clergy person? Is this a problem of religious liberty as well as religious establishment? Statutes also vary in the range of secular officials who are empowered to preside over civil ceremonies.[150] What qualities are public officials or religious officiants likely to possess that make them appropriate delegees of the power to conduct weddings? Should states tightly control the pool of officiants? Is there

---

148. Ranieri v. Ranieri, 146 A.D.2d 34 (N.Y. App. Div. 1989); Ravenal v. Ravenal, 338 N.Y.S.2d 324 (N.Y. Sup. Ct. 1972).

149. Matter of Rubino v. City of New York, 480 N.Y.S.2d 971 (N.Y. Super. Ct. 1984).

150. For a summary of the variations, see Robert E. Rains, Marriage in the Time of Internet Ministers: I Now Pronounce You Married, but Who Am I to Do So?, 64 U. Miami L. Rev. 809 (2010).

any limit on their power to do so?[151] Massachusetts permits any person who is not otherwise authorized to perform weddings to apply for permission from the governor to receive a one-day designation certification, which allows that person to officiate at a specific marriage ceremony.[152] Is that a better approach? Is it relevant that data show a decrease in the percentage of weddings that take place in religious settings and an increase in demand for friends or relatives to perform wedding ceremonies?[153] Does it matter that some couples, such as same-sex couples, may seek alternative officiants because of a lack of support of their marriage by more established institutions?[154]

2. *Proxy Marriages.* State marriage laws generally require that both parties participate in person in the wedding ceremony, but some permit "proxy" marriages in certain circumstances where it is difficult for one to be present. California, for example, requires both parties to appear in person to apply for a license and to declare their consent to marry before an authorized officiant, but creates an exception for "a member of the Armed Forces of the United States who is stationed overseas and serving in a conflict or a war."[155] Only Montana permits a "double-proxy" marriage.[156] Would a looser approach to proxy marriages create problems?[157]

3. *Wedding Traditions.* In 1973, two couples filed a federal civil rights suit against the City Clerk of New York, challenging the mandatory dress guidelines then in place for weddings at City Hall. Those guidelines provided, among other things, that "the bride must wear a dress or skirt or blouse — no slacks — and the groom must wear a coat and tie," and that "one or two rings must be exchanged." The challenge was explained as follows:

> Plaintiff Rappaport wished to wear pants to her wedding but was told to present herself in a skirt. She did, but was unhappy that she did not wear her green velvet pants suit for her wedding. Plaintiff Dibbell states that she

---

151. On a lawsuit against the State of Tennessee, which recently passed a ban on marriages solemnized by online-ordained officiants, see Joanna L. Grossman, When Friends Preside Over Weddings: Tennessee Fights the Online Ministers, Justia's Verdict (Sept. 10, 2019).

152. Mass. Gen. Laws 207, § 39 (2020).

153. See, e.g., Samuel G. Freedman, Couples Personalizing Role of Religion in Wedding Ceremonies, N.Y. Times, June 26, 2015, at A22.

154. See, e.g., Christine Hauser, Tennessee Says Internet-Ordained Ministers and Marriage Don't Mix, N.Y. Times, July 20, 2019.

155. Cal. Fam. Code § 420(b) (2020).

156. Mont. Code Ann. § 40-1-301 (2020) (permitting proxy marriages as long as one party is either a member of the armed forces on active duty or a resident of Montana); see also Tshiani v. Tshiani, 56 A.3d 311, 322 (Md. Ct. Spec. App. 2012) (giving effect to foreign marriage despite fact that one party participated by phone, which would have made the marriage invalid if celebrated in Maryland).

157. For an argument to expand proxy marriage, see Adam Candeub & Mae Kuykendall, Modernizing Marriage, 44 U. Mich. J.L. Reform 735 (2011); see also Kerry Abrams, Peaceful Penetration: Proxy Marriage, Same-Sex Marriage, and Recognition, 2011 Mich. St. L. Rev. 141 (2011) (history of proxy marriage).

wishes to wear pants to her wedding, and she and her intended spouse say they do not wish to exchange either one or two rings as part of their wedding ceremony. The couple to be married are a freelance journalist and a music critic. The bride-to-be says: 'I find dressing in pants . . . protects me from much of the sex-role stereotyping to which women continue to be subjected both professionally and socially.' The groom-to-be says: 'Because marriage has traditionally been an unequal yoke, it is essential to me that my marriage ceremony emphasize the equality of the partnership. For this reason, our dress at this ceremony must be virtually identical.' The plaintiffs charge that defendant's guidelines put them to the choice between their statutory right to be married by the City Clerk and their fundamental right to marry free of unwarranted governmental intrusion on their privacy and with free expression. . . .[158]

The court dismissed the lawsuit without ruling on the merits of the guidelines because federal courts should not "supervise marriage forms and procedures in City Clerk's offices." Though the court seemed sympathetic to the challenge — referring to skirts as "an accoutrement of diminishing use for many" — it did not believe federal courts should interfere in a "locally prescribed and directed function in an area fundamentally of state concern." Should the court have ruled on the merits? What are the consequences of leaving such matters to clerks' offices around the country?

4. *A Comparative Law Perspective.* In the United States, we permit religious traditions surrounding marriage to be intertwined with the acts necessary to create a legally valid marriage. In some countries, greater care is taken to separate church and state. In France, for example, marriages can only be celebrated at a government office. Religious ceremonies can be conducted afterwards, but they have no legal meaning. Is that a better approach?

PROBLEM

Anya, a clothing designer, and Wylie, a lawyer, began dating in 2004. In 2009, while on vacation in Tulum, Mexico, they decided to marry. They returned to the same spot the following year for a destination wedding. In thank-you notes sent to guests after the event, the couple recalled that "100 friends and family joined us for ten days in February 2010" and "lounged on the beach, shared steak sandwiches and lunch tables, and made memories that will last a lifetime." Beyond the lounging and sandwiches, the event involved a wedding of sorts. It drew on some Jewish

---

158. Rappaport v. Katz, 380 F. Supp. 808 (S.D.N.Y. 1974).

traditions — a chuppah, certain Hebrew prayers, and the breaking of a glass — but was not conducted by a rabbi. The officiant was Wylie's cousin, a New York dentist, who was ordained online as a Universal Life Church minister. He couldn't remember how or when he completed the ordination process, but told guests during the ceremony: "I am an ordained minister — this will be a legal union." (Anya's lawyer later produced a certificate from the ULC showing that the dentist was a minister in good standing.)

Before heading to Tulum for the wedding, the couple filled out forms provided by the resort about their planned nuptials. On the question about "type of ceremony," which gave a choice between (A) Civil and (B) Religious/symbolic, the couple crossed out "civil" and "religious" and wrote in all caps "SYMBOLIC" next to choice (B). The resort materials went on to detail legal requirements for civil marriage in Mexico, including the statement that "a religious ceremony that is not performed in a Catholic Church in compliance with the stated requirements for a Catholic wedding does not create a legally valid marriage," and in order for a civil marriage to be valid, "the judge must perform the ceremony." The parties disagreed about who knew what about the legalities of the ceremony. Anya said she never read these materials, and focused instead on the catering and making sure all the attendants dressed in white. According to her, only Wylie knew that there was a difference between a symbolic and a legal wedding, and he made the choice to go for the symbolic one.

What factors are relevant to a determination whether the couple is validly married?[159]

Mary Anne Case, Marriage Licenses
89 Minn. L. Rev. 1758 (2005)

First I want to examine more generally the ways in which the institution of civil marriage functions as a licensing scheme and the things marriage licenses. I will do this in part by drawing analogies to the licensing the state provides for the drivers of automobiles and the owners of dogs and, most importantly, to its provision of corporate charters. In all four of these cases, the underlying activities involved could be and were at times carried on without state involvement, but the state at one point asserted monopoly control over licensing and, because, *inter alia*, of efficiency advantages from its involvement, the state is unlikely to retreat completely from the field.

---

159. Ponorovskaya v. Stecklow, 987 N.Y.S.2d 543 (N.Y. Sup. Ct. 2014).

Marriage has always licensed, but what marriage licenses has changed over time. Marriage once licensed a husband's control over his wife, her body, and the products of her labor, from the children she bore to her earnings and property. Marriage was also once the exclusive means of licensing sex and all that went with it — procreation, cohabitation, and the control of children. While it once bound couples together indissolubly for life in a heavily regulated status relationship, virtually all of whose terms were mandatory and imposed by the state, marriage now licenses in a new way — a married couple is by and large free to have or not have sex, vaginal or not, procreative, contracepted, or otherwise; to be faithful or not, to divorce and remarry, to commingle their finances or keep them separate, to live together or separately, to differentiate roles or share all tasks, to publicize their relationship or be discreet about it, while still having their commitment to one another recognized by third parties including the state. . . .

[A] marriage license can be seen as analogous to a driver's license. First, just as the precondition for the lawful operation of a motor vehicle is these days ordinarily the possession of a valid driver's license, so, until quite recently, a valid marriage was the prerequisite to engaging lawfully in most any form of sexual activity. . . . Marriage was also seen as a prerequisite to licensed cohabitation, with both criminal laws and zoning ordinances prohibiting unmarried persons from sharing a dwelling. Today, although not yet in 1970, every constitutionally recognized aspect of liberty legal marriage formerly monopolized (sex, cohabitation, reproduction, parenting, etc.) seems, as a matter of constitutional right, no longer within the state's or marriage's monopoly control. . . .

A marriage license, like a driver's license, also has taken on functions far removed from its central core of authorizing the holder to engage in potentially dangerous, heavily regulated activities. . . . As Paula Ettelbrick observed, marriage "has become a facile mechanism for employers to dole out benefits, for businesses to provide special deals and incentives, and for the law to make distinctions in distributing meager public funds." Just as a valid driver's license will help get you onto a plane even if you have not driven in thirty years, so "a simple certificate of the state, regardless of whether the spouses love, respect, or even see each other on a regular basis, dominates and is supported." . . .

For good, as well as for ill, marriage now licenses couples to structure their lives as best suits them without losing recognition for their relationship. Some may find it disturbing that a couple that does not "even see each other on a regular basis" is still licensed by marriage to receive a host of benefits or that "marriage laws do not condition receipt of public and private financial benefits to married couples on a demonstration of financial dependence on each other; the benefits are available to married individuals regardless of whether they mingle their finances or actually depend on each other for support." Although I find it unfortunate that so many public and private benefits depend on marriage, I, by contrast, find much that is

good in the fact that a marriage certificate now allows heterose*
an open marriage, to live in different cities or in different apa*
city, to structure their finances as they please, without having t
the legal benefits that follow from it challenged.

PROBLEM

During the 2020 COVID-19 pandemic, many states restricted activity in order to reduce the likelihood and speed of transmission of the virus. Non-essential businesses were ordered closed and people were forbidden to gather with those outside their households. Courts continued to perform some essential functions, such as the arraignment of people after arrest, and handled some matters remotely where possible. Dallas County, home to more than two million people, stopped issuing marriage licenses completely during this period. Does this infringe on the fundamental right to marry? If not generally, are there circumstances in which the ban might be unconstitutional as applied to a particular couple? As you read the next set of materials, consider whether your answer might change because Texas recognizes common-law marriage, which can be created without a license and later verified by a filing with the state.

IV. Common-Law Marriage

We have seen the formalities required to establish a valid marriage — and the uncertainty that comes with the failure to observe them. But those formalities co-exist with an entirely different approach to creating a valid union: the common-law marriage. Where the doctrine is recognized, two people can become legally married simply by agreeing to be married, without any of the usual pomp and circumstance or any of the paperwork. Common-law marriage is different from ceremonial marriage only in the way it is established. Once contracted (and if recognized), the two types of marriage have precisely the same legal consequences, including the necessity of divorce or annulment to dissolve it. This type of marriage was established in a series of court decisions in the early nineteenth century. During its heyday in the early twentieth century, common-law marriage was permitted by about half the states.[160] Today, only nine states and the District of Columbia permit couples to

---

160. Otto E. Koegel, Common Law Marriage and Its Development in the United States 164–66 (1922).

blish common-law marriages.[161] As you read the following cases, think about what circumstances might lead a party to go to court to prove the existence of a common-law marriage. When does marital status matter? For what purposes? Consider also what we learn about society's expectations for marriage from cases in which people try to prove they acted like married people.

HARGRAVE v. DUVAL-COUETIL
777 N.W.2d 380 (S.D. 2010)

MEIERHENRY, JUSTICE.

Nathalie Duval–Couetil and Orielle Duval–Georgiades (Daughters) appeal the circuit court's judgment that Karen Hargrave (Hargrave) was the common-law wife of their father, Paul A. Duval (Duval). Daughters contend the circuit court erred when it held that Duval and Hargrave entered into a common-law marriage under the laws of Mexico and Oklahoma. We agree and reverse the circuit court....

Duval and Hargrave began living together in Massachusetts in 1994. In 1995, Duval acquired a home in Custer, South Dakota. Hargrave moved from Massachusetts to Duval's home in South Dakota in 1996. In 1997, Duval and Hargrave began a yearly routine of spending the summer months in Custer and the winter months in Mexico. In 1998, Duval and Hargrave bought a home together in Nuevo Leon, Mexico, as husband and wife.

In 2005, Duval was assaulted while in Mexico and placed in an intensive care unit for his injuries. Hargrave lived with Duval at the hospital while he was being treated. She later took Duval to Oklahoma for rehabilitation at a hospital in the Tulsa area and eventually to Rochester, Minnesota, for medical treatment at Mayo Clinic. Duval and Hargrave subsequently returned to Oklahoma for a period of time; and then, resumed their annual routine of spending winters in Mexico and summers in Custer. Duval was killed as a result of a rock climbing accident on June 24, 2008, in Custer County, South Dakota.

Duval and Hargrave never formally married. Hargrave testified that she and Duval had discussed a formal wedding ceremony, but mutually decided against it. She said they did not think they needed to marry because they held themselves out as husband and wife and felt like they were married. The circuit court specifically found that over the course of Duval and Hargrave's relationship, Duval referred to Hargrave as his wife on an income tax return form, designated her as the

---

161. The states are Alabama, Colorado, Iowa, Kansas, Montana, Rhode Island, South Carolina, Texas, Utah, and the District of Columbia. See John B. Crawley, Is the Honeymoon Over for Common-Law Marriage: A Consideration of the Continued Viability of the Common-Law Marriage Doctrine, 29 Cumb. L. Rev. 399 (1999).

beneficiary on his VA health benefits application, and executed a general power of attorney in her favor.

The circuit court ultimately concluded that Hargrave had established that she and Duval met the requirements for a common-law marriage under the laws of both Mexico and Oklahoma. As such, Hargrave was treated as Duval's surviving spouse for inheritance purposes in South Dakota. Daughters appeal. . . .

The relevant facts are not in dispute. . . . The first issue centers on whether South Dakota will give effect to a common-law marriage established by South Dakota domiciliaries while living in a jurisdiction that recognizes common-law marriage.

Common-law marriages were statutorily abrogated in South Dakota in 1959 by an amendment to SDCL 25–1–29. Notwithstanding, Hargrave contends that South Dakota continues to recognize valid common-law marriages entered into in other jurisdictions. Hargrave relies on SDCL 19–8–1, which provides that "[e]very court of this state shall take judicial notice of the common law and statutes of every state, territory, and other jurisdiction of the United States." In addition to taking judicial notice of the common-law of other states, the South Dakota Legislature specifically addressed the validity of marriages entered into in other jurisdictions in SDCL 25–1–38. This statute provides that "[a]ny marriage contracted outside the jurisdiction of this state . . . which is valid by the laws of the jurisdiction in which such marriage was contracted, is valid in this state." In view of these statutes, we conclude that a common-law marriage validly entered into in another jurisdiction will be recognized in South Dakota. . . .

Concubinage in Mexico

The parties agree that Nuevo Leon, Mexico, has no common-law on which a common-law marriage could be established. Nuevo Leon does, however, have a law that gives certain rights to persons who have entered into a concubinage. Hargrave provided the state law of Nuevo Leon, which defines a concubinage as:

> [T]he union of a man and woman, free from formal matrimony, who for more than five years make a marital life without being united in a formal matrimony unto the other as long as there is no legal impediment to their contracting it. The concubine's gender union can have rights and obligations in reciprocal form, of support and inheritance, independently of all others recognized by this code or other laws.

Compilacion Legislativa del Estado de Nuevo Leon, p 50, Book I of Persons, Title V of Matrimony, Ch 11 of Concubinage, Art 291. The circuit court concluded that concubinages were to be given the same legal effect as common-law marriages validly entered into in the United States. Daughters argue, however, that a concubinage is not the legal equivalent of a common-law marriage.

Other courts that have addressed this issue have declined to equate a concubinage with a common-law marriage. In *Nevarez v. Bailon*, 287 S.W.2d 521 (Tex. Civ.

App. 1956), the court held a woman who cohabited with a man within the definition of a concubinage was not entitled to claim any of the man's property after his death as his common-law wife because common-law marriage was not recognized in that Mexican state. The court noted that under Mexican law a concubinage was a "'legal union' but not a legal marriage." Because the woman met the definition of a concubine, she was entitled to certain rights, but was not a common-law wife under the laws of Mexico. Consequently, she was not entitled to the benefits given to a common-law wife in Texas "for such a relationship [was] non-existent in [Mexico]," and she would not "qualify in her home jurisdiction as a surviving wife." . . .

We are persuaded by the reasoning of *Nevarez* . . . and also conclude that a Mexican concubinage is not the legal equivalent of a common-law marriage in the United States. Consequently, the circuit court erred in concluding the concubinage between Duval and Hargrave, if one existed, had the same legal effect as a common-law marriage. Therefore, we reverse on this issue.

Common-Law Marriage in Oklahoma

The circuit court concluded that Duval and Hargrave entered into a valid common-law marriage while they lived in Oklahoma. The Oklahoma Court of Civil Appeals recently reaffirmed its recognition of common-law marriages and its requirements. The court stated:

> [T]his Court recognizes in accordance with established Oklahoma case law that, absent a marital impediment suffered by one of the parties to the common-law marriage, a common-law marriage occurs upon the happening of three events: a declaration by the parties of an intent to marry, cohabitation, and a holding out of themselves to the community of being husband and wife.

Brooks v. Sanders, 190 P.3d 357, 362 (Okla. Civ. App. 2008). . . .

[I]t appears that Oklahoma requires (1) a mutual agreement or declaration of intent to marry, (2) consummation by cohabitation, and (3) publicly holding themselves out as husband and wife. Oklahoma law requires the party alleging a common-law marriage satisfy these elements by clear and convincing evidence.

Thus, the first requirement Hargrave had to satisfy by clear and convincing evidence was that she and Duval had mutually agreed and/or declared their intent to marry while in Oklahoma. . . . The circuit court made no finding on mutual agreement or declaration of intent to marry, yet concluded that Duval and Hargrave entered into a common-law marriage. . . . A finding on whether the couple mutually agreed or declared their intent to marry while in Oklahoma was essential to support the circuit court's conclusion that they entered into a common-law marriage. A review of the testimony may explain why the circuit court was unable to enter a finding of a mutual agreement or declaration of intent to enter into a marital relationship.

Hargrave testified that she and Duval entered into an "implicit agreement" to be married while they were in Oklahoma. She also testified that "nobody said, okay, so we should agree to be married and write it down and put the date on it." When asked on cross-examination if there was ever a point when she and Duval made an agreement to be married, Hargrave stated in the negative, and said the couple just decided "well, I guess we are [married]."

The Oklahoma Supreme Court addressed this issue under a similar situation and recognized the importance of establishing a clear intent to marry. In *Standefer v. Standefer*, 26 P.3d 104 (Okla. 2001), the court stated the "evidence [wa]s clear and convincing that both parties assented to a marriage on Thanksgiving Day of 1988." Both the husband and wife in *Standefer* agreed that they were common-law spouses as a result of their mutual assent to marry on that day. Significantly, the couple was able to identify an instance where they mutually assented to a marriage. This fact stands in contrast to the present case where Hargrave's testimony established that no specific time existed when the couple mutually agreed or declared their intent to be married. To meet Oklahoma's requirements, their mutual agreement or declaration to marry would have to be more than an implicit agreement. This consent requirement is consistent with SDCL 25-1-38, which sets forth the requirement that a marriage must be "contracted" in the other jurisdiction before South Dakota will recognize the marriage as valid. SDCL 25-1-38 provides "[a]ny marriage *contracted* outside the jurisdiction of this state . . . which is valid by the laws of the jurisdiction in which such marriage was *contracted,* is valid in this state." Failing to establish that mutual assent or a declaration to marry took place, Hargrave could not meet the first requirement for entering into a common-law marriage in Oklahoma as outlined by *Brooks.*

The absence of a finding of fact on this issue, coupled with Hargrave's testimony, leads to a conclusion that as a matter of law Hargrave could not prove by clear and convincing evidence that the couple entered into a valid common-law marriage while in Oklahoma. Thus, no legal basis existed to support the circuit court's conclusion that the parties entered into a common-law marriage in Oklahoma. . . .

Based on the foregoing, we conclude that Duval and Hargrave were not validly married under either Mexico or Oklahoma law. Consequently, Hargrave cannot be considered a surviving spouse for purposes of inheriting from Duval's estate.

In re Estate of Carter

159 A.3d 970 (Pa. Super. Ct. 2017)

Moulton, J.:

Michael Hunter appeals from the July 8, 2016 order of the Beaver County Court of Common Pleas denying Hunter's petition for a declaration that he and his late partner, Stephen Carter, had entered into a common law marriage prior to January 1, 2005.[1] Because the United States Constitution mandates that same-sex couples

---

1. The Pennsylvania legislature abolished the doctrine of common law marriage effective January 24, 2005, but also provided that "[n]othing in this part shall be deemed or taken to render any common-law marriage otherwise lawful and contracted on or before January 1, 2005, invalid." 23 Pa. C.S. § 1103 (2020).

have the same right to prove a common law marriage as do opposite-sex couples, and because we conclude that Hunter met his burden of proving a common law marriage, we reverse and remand.

Hunter and Carter met in February 1996 at a social event in Philadelphia and began dating a few days later. During the course of their ensuing 17-year relationship, they shared a mutual enjoyment of rock climbing, canoeing, kayaking, and hiking. In July 1996, Hunter and Carter began living together in Carter's home in Philadelphia.

On Christmas Day 1996, Hunter proposed to Carter and gave him a diamond ring. Hunter bent down on one knee and asked, "Will you marry me?" to which Carter replied, "Yes." Two months later, on February 18, 1997, Carter gave Hunter a ring in return; the ring was engraved, "February 18, 1997." One year later, Hunter and Carter celebrated their first wedding anniversary, a ritual they repeated on February 18 of each year for the next 16 years.

In March 1999, Hunter and Carter purchased a home together in Philadelphia with a joint mortgage in both of their names. They prepared and executed mutual wills, in which each named the other as executor. They executed mutual financial and health care powers of attorney, in which each designated the other as his agent-in-fact. They also supported each other financially and held joint banking and investment accounts. At various points in their relationship, each served as the sole wage earner while the other advanced his education. The couple later moved to the Pittsburgh area and jointly purchased a home there.

Both of their families treated Hunter and Carter as spouses, with Carter's nieces referring to Hunter as "Uncle Mike." Hunter and Carter considered themselves married as of February 18, 1997 and referred to each other as spouses from that day forward.

In April 2013, Carter died from injuries sustained in a motorcycle accident. His death occurred less than two months before the United States Supreme Court's landmark decision in *United States v. Windsor*, 133 S. Ct. 2675 (2013), which struck down the provision of the federal Defense of Marriage Act ("DOMA") defining "marriage" as only between one man and one woman.

On May 17, 2016, Hunter filed a petition seeking a declaration that he and Carter had entered into a common law marriage prior to January 1, 2005, the date after which common law marriages were no longer recognized in Pennsylvania. On July 5, 2016, the trial court held an evidentiary hearing, at which Hunter, Carter's sister, and a friend of the couple testified in support of the petition. Notably, the petition was unopposed. . . . Despite the lack of opposition, on July 8, 2016, the trial court entered an order denying the petition. . . .

The Right of Same-Sex Couples to Common Law Marriage

First, Hunter asserts that the trial court erred in concluding that it was "legally impossible" for him and Carter to enter into a pre-2005 common law marriage because, at that time, the Pennsylvania Marriage Law defined marriage as a union "between one man and one woman." 23 Pa. C. S. § 1102. Hunter contends that because these provisions so defining marriage have been declared unconstitutional, they cannot preclude the recognition of his pre-2005 common law marriage to Carter. We agree.

Historically, Pennsylvania defined marriage as "a civil contract made between parties with the capacity to so contract." *In re Estate of Garges*, 378 A.2d 307, 308 (Pa. 1977). Pennsylvania has recognized two types of marriage: ceremonial and common law. . . .

As noted above, the Pennsylvania legislature abolished the doctrine of common law marriage effective January 1, 2005. However, section 1103 of the Marriage Law permits the legal recognition of common law marriages contracted before January 1, 2005.

The proper procedure for obtaining legal recognition of a common law marriage is the filing of a declaratory judgment action. . . .

This procedure is necessarily retrospective and often difficult, given the absence of a formal ceremony marking the occasion of the marriage.

In order to assess the trial court's "legal impossibility" reasoning, we will briefly review the relevant developments in Pennsylvania and federal law. In September 1996, the United States Congress enacted DOMA, which defined "marriage" as "only a legal union between one man and one woman as husband and wife," and which provided that states are not required to recognize a same-sex marriage or civil union established in another state. One month later, Pennsylvania amended its Marriage Law "to add anti-ceremony and anti-recognition provisions applicable to same-sex couples." As a result of those amendments, section 1102 of the Marriage Law defined "marriage" as "[a] civil contract by which one man and one woman take each other for husband and wife." Section 1704 of the Marriage Law provided:

> It is hereby declared to be the strong and longstanding public policy of this
> Commonwealth that marriage shall be between one man and one woman.
> A marriage between persons of the same sex which was entered into in
> another state or foreign jurisdiction, even if valid where entered into, shall be
> void in this Commonwealth.

Read together, sections 1102 and 1704 of the Marriage Law prevented same-sex couples from marrying in Pennsylvania and barred recognition in Pennsylvania of the marriages of same-sex couples legally married elsewhere.

In 2013, however, just two months after Carter's untimely death, there began a "tectonic shift in the law regarding same-sex marriage." *Neyman v. Buckley*, 153 A.3d 1010, 1018 (Pa. Super. 2016). This shift started with *Windsor*. . . .

Following *Windsor*, the United States District Court for the Middle District of Pennsylvania, addressing a challenge to Pennsylvania's Marriage Law, held "that the fundamental right to marry as protected by the Due Process Clause of the

Fourteenth Amendment to the United States Constitution encompasses the right to marry a person of one's own sex." *Whitewood v. Wolf*, 992 F. Supp. 2d 410, 423-24 (M.D. Pa. 2014). . . .

The district court held that "same-sex couples who seek to marry in Pennsylvania may do so, and already married same-sex couples will be recognized as such in the Commonwealth." Therefore, the court declared both sections 1102 and 1704 of the Marriage Law unconstitutional and issued an order permanently enjoining their enforcement.

Subsequently, in *Obergefell v. Hodges*, 135 S. Ct. 2584 (2015), the United States Supreme Court declared that all state laws prohibiting marriage between same-sex partners are unconstitutional violations of the Due Process and Equal Protection Clauses of the Fourteenth Amendment. . . .

Accordingly, following *Whitewood* and *Obergefell*, same-sex couples in Pennsylvania can legally marry and must be afforded the same rights and protections as opposite-sex married couples, including inheritance rights and survivor benefits.

Despite these clear pronouncements by the United States Supreme Court and the federal district court in Pennsylvania, the trial court in this case concluded that it was bound by the unconstitutional provisions of the Marriage Law, finding that because "same-sex couples did not have the right to marry in Pennsylvania until May of 2014 . . . it was never legal for same-sex couples to enter into a common law marriage." Thus, the trial court concluded that "it was legally impossible for [Hunter and Carter] to enter into a common law marriage before common law marriages were abolished in Pennsylvania [in 2005]." We conclude that the trial court erred.

The premise of the trial court's analysis was that sections 1102 and 1704 of the Marriage Law, though now declared unconstitutional, were legally binding during the time that Carter and Hunter might otherwise have entered into a common law marriage. This premise misreads the fundamental import of *Windsor*, *Whitewood*, and *Obergefell*. As the *Whitewood* court observed: "The right Plaintiffs seek to exercise is not a new right, but is rather a right that these individuals have always been guaranteed by the United States Constitution." . . .

Together, *Windsor*, *Whitewood*, and *Obergefell* teach that same-sex couples have precisely the same capacity to enter marriage contracts as do opposite-sex couples, and a court today may not rely on the now-invalidated provisions of the Marriage Law to deny that constitutional reality. Consequently, because opposite-sex couples in Pennsylvania are permitted to establish, through a declaratory judgment action, the existence of a common law marriage prior to January 1, 2005, same-sex couples must have that same right. To deprive Hunter of the opportunity to establish his rights as Carter's common law spouse, simply because he and Carter are a same-sex couple, would violate both the Equal Protection and Due Process Clauses of the Fourteenth Amendment.

Proving the Elements of Same–Sex Common Law Marriage

Next, Hunter asserts that the trial court erred in concluding that even if a same-sex couple were permitted to establish the existence of a pre-2005 common law marriage, Hunter failed to prove a common law marriage under controlling Pennsylvania law. After careful review of the record and the trial court's opinion, we conclude that Hunter satisfied his burden of proving that he and Carter agreed in February 1997 "to enter into the legal relationship of marriage at the present time." *Staudenmayer v. Staudenmayer*, 714 A.2d 1016, 1020 (1998).

Even before it was abolished in 2005, common law marriage was generally disfavored in Pennsylvania. As our Supreme Court explained: "Because claims for the existence of a marriage in the absence of a certified ceremonial marriage present a 'fruitful source of perjury and fraud,' Pennsylvania courts have long viewed such claims with hostility." The perceived motivation for such perjury and fraud lies in the set of potential benefits of an after-the-fact recognition of a marriage not otherwise established by tangible proof such as a marriage certificate or formal wedding ceremony.

As a result, the party seeking to establish the existence of a common law marriage has what has been described as "a heavy burden." The precise contours of that burden, however, have not always been clear, in part because the understandable concern about unchecked perjury has been tempered by the recognition of the inherent difficulty in proving a relationship not accompanied by formal ceremony. Our Supreme Court's most recent guidance on this subject came in 1998:

> A common law marriage can only be created by an exchange of words in the present tense, spoken with the specific purpose that the legal relationship of husband and wife is created by that. Regarding this requirement for an exchange of words in the present tense, this Court has noted:
>
>> It is too often forgotten that a common law marriage is a marriage by the express agreement of the parties without ceremony, and almost invariably without a witness, by words — not in futuro or in postea, but — in praesenti, uttered with a view and for the purpose of establishing the relationship of husband and wife. The common law marriage contract does not require any specific form of words, and all that is essential is proof of an agreement to enter into the legal relationship of marriage at the present time.
>
> The burden to prove the marriage is on the party alleging a marriage, and we have described this as a "heavy" burden where there is an allegation of a common law marriage. When an attempt is made to establish a marriage without the usual formalities, the claim must be viewed with "great scrutiny." Generally, words in the present tense are required to prove common law marriage. Because common law marriage cases arose most frequently because of claims for a putative surviving spouse's share of an estate, however, we developed a rebuttable presumption in favor of a common law marriage

where there is an absence of testimony regarding the exchange of *verba in praesenti*. When applicable, the party claiming a common law marriage who proves: (1) constant cohabitation; and, (2) a reputation of marriage "which is not partial or divided but is broad and general," raises the rebuttable presumption of marriage. . . .

At the hearing, Hunter testified that on December 25, 1996, he proposed to Carter and gave him a diamond ring. He asked, "Will you marry me?" to which Carter replied, "Yes." At this point, any reasonable reading of the facts would lead to the conclusion that Hunter and Carter were engaged to be married.

Two months later, on February 18, 1997, Carter completed the ring exchange by giving Hunter a ring in return. The ring bears the engraving, "February 18, 1997." Each year thereafter, Hunter and Carter celebrated their anniversary on February 18. Both of their families treated Hunter and Carter as spouses, with Carter's nieces referring to Hunter as "Uncle Mike." Hunter testified that he and Carter considered themselves married as of February 18, 1997 and referred to each other as spouses from that day forward. Hunter also submitted affidavits from his brother, several friends, and Carter's sisters, each of whom stated that Hunter and Carter had considered themselves married and held themselves out as a married couple.

Thus, the uncontradicted evidence established that Hunter and Carter had a present intent to marry on February 18, 1997. As prior cases have recognized, the exchange of rings is particularly strong evidence of such an intent. Moreover, unlike the many cases in which the declaration of common law marriage is sought for use as a sword against competing claims to an estate, Hunter's petition not only was uncontested but indeed was supported by Carter's family. Nothing about the facts of this case suggests that it is "a fruitful source for perjury or fraud."

That Hunter and Carter had the present intent to marry is further corroborated by their conduct after February 18, 1997. After their exchange of rings, both men considered themselves married to each other, held themselves out to others as a married couple, and lived together as such for more than 16 years. They purchased homes together, prepared and executed mutual wills, supported each other financially, and held joint banking and investment accounts. They also celebrated their anniversary on February 18 every year until Carter's death. . . . Therefore, we conclude that Hunter proved, by clear and convincing evidence, that he and Carter had entered into a common law marriage on February 18, 1997. . . .

Accordingly, because we conclude that Hunter satisfied his burden of proving that he and Carter had entered into a common law marriage before January 1, 2005, the trial court erred in denying his petition.

NOTES AND QUESTIONS

1. *Nineteenth-Century Relic?* In England, common-law marriage was abolished by Lord Hardwicke's Act in 1753, which provided that marriages had to be solemnized in church and in front of two witnesses in order to be valid.[162] But common-law marriage was widely practiced in the American colonies. Some states began abolishing it as early as 1895, while others did so more than a century later. The early abolitions reflected lawmakers' concern (prompted in part by some very ugly public trials) that many claims of common-law marriage were loosely tied to the facts at best and outright fabrications at worst. A salacious trial in New York in 1935, in which a 27-year-old woman claimed to be the common-law wife of a recently deceased 65-year-old man, might have been the last straw for the doctrine in New York. The trial included evidence that the man had stayed in the room while the woman undressed to be examined by a doctor before having an appendectomy, behavior she suggested was proof that he was her husband, but the court ruled against her.[163] Abolitions were also driven by the state's desire to exercise control over marriage and reproduction — and to have clearer evidence of marital status.[164] Pennsylvania, as discussed in *Carter*, did not abolish common-law marriage until 2005.[165] Several of the states that abolished common-law marriage did not make the rule retroactive, leaving open the possibility that couples could still prove that a common-law marriage had been established in the jurisdiction before the date of abolition.

2. *Common-Law Marriage in the Modern World.* Why would states require a license, solemnization, witnesses, and other formalities, but also permit marriages to be established without any of those steps? Historically, common-law marriage served a few different purposes. It made marriage possible for couples who might have lived far from governmental offices that issued licenses or who were unable to find an authorized officiant. (These obstacles were more significant for pioneers settling new land and before modern transportation was invented.[166]) It could also be used as a backstop for a ceremonial marriage with a defect in required

---

162. See Cynthia Grant Bowman, Social Science and Legal Policy: The Case of Heterosexual Cohabitation, 9 J. L. Fam. Stud. 1, 38 (2007) (citing Anne Barlow and Grace James, Regulating Marriage and Cohabitation in 21st Century Britain, 67 Mod. L. Rev. 143, 161–63 (2004)).

163. On the reasons for the decline of common-law marriage, see Joanna L. Grossman & Lawrence M. Friedman, Inside the Castle: Law and the Family in 20th Century America 78–89 (2011).

164. For more on the history of common-law marriage and its declining popularity, see id. at 84–89; Koegel, supra note 161, at 85–160.

165. Alabama, Georgia, Idaho, Ohio, and Oklahoma have abolished common-law marriage since 1991.

166. Nancy Cott, Public Vows: A History of Marriage and the Nation 30–31 (2000).

formalities, or to clarify property ownership in a messy estate battle. But it also served a social purpose in that it permitted a court, retroactively in most cases, to "authorize" what was likely an illegal, and certainly taboo, non-marital sexual relationship. As one commentator wrote in 1928, some "meretricious" relationships grow "insensibly into permanent unions," and it is "sound public policy to accept the final compliance" while ignoring the "initial disregard of the law."[167] Calling a cohabiting couple "married" ironically operated to preserve the deeply entrenched norm that legitimate sex occurred only within marriages. It might also have saved a child of the union from the stigmatizing label of "illegitimate." Might the same impulse explain why courts often refuse to invalidate marriages despite the lack of required formalities?[168] How well do these reasons hold up today? Do states have different reasons for allowing common-law marriage in the twenty-first century?

3. *Same-Sex Common-Law Marriage.* After the Supreme Court's ruling in Obergefell v. Hodges gave same-sex couples access to marriage nationwide, common-law marriage took on increasing importance as couples litigated the status of their relationship in the years before formal marriage was legally permitted. Professor Rocky Rhodes argues that states are required to grant retroactive access to common-law marriage because:

> same-sex couples in common-law marriage jurisdictions are entitled to government recognition of the legal consequences of past events on the same terms and conditions as opposite-sex couples. To this extent, common-law marriage recognition materially differs from the ceremonial marriage right. A ceremonial marriage necessitates official participation in its formation, and *Obergefell* neither attempted nor mandated a remedy for the states' past participation failures. In contrast, a common-law marriage merely requires the government's current recognition of the couple's past marital capacity, intent, cohabitation, and outward manifestations. Due to the retroactive application of *Obergefell's* legal principles, states cannot, in future disputes, employ an unconstitutional exclusion to deny recognition to informal same-sex marriages while recognizing common-law marriages between opposite-sex couples.[169]

Most court rulings to date are consistent with this approach. For example, a federal district court in Texas held that *Obergefell* permitted the retroactive authorization of standing in a wrongful death suit, brought by one partner to an informal same-sex marriage.[170]

---

167. Robert Black, Common Law Marriage, 2 U. Cin. L. Rev. 113, 133 (1928).

168. See Michael Grossberg, Governing the Hearth: Law and Family in Nineteenth-Century America (1985).

169. Charles W. "Rocky" Rhodes, Loving Retroactivity, 45 Fla. St. L. Rev. 383 (2018).

170. Ranolls v. Dewling, 223 F. Supp. 3d 613 (E.D. Tex. 2016); see also In re Powell, No. C-1-PB-14-001695 (Tex. Cty. Prob. Ct. Feb. 17, 2015) (approving family settlement agreement of decedent's estate, which required retroactive recognition of an informal marriage between a same-sex couple who had a religious marriage ceremony when marriage was not legal and held themselves out as married).

4. *Proving a Common-Law Marriage.* There are some common features among the states that continue to permit common-law marriage. First, because a common-law marriage is a legal marriage apart from the method of establishing it, the same substantive impediments to marriage apply.[171] A common-law marriage cannot, for example, be bigamous or incestuous. Courts have held, however, that a common-law marriage can arise when an impediment is lifted.[172] Second, states require the traditional elements be established: (1) intention to marry; (2) a present agreement to marry; and (3) holding out as married. A few states have codified the rules, deviating in small ways from the common-law doctrine. (Contrary to popular myth, there is no state that requires a seven-year cohabitation as an element; under most variations of the doctrine, a common-law marriage can be created in an instant.) In Texas, for example, an "informal marriage" can arise based on the standard elements, but if a proceeding to prove the marriage is not instigated within two years of when the couple ceased to cohabit, a rebuttable presumption arises that no agreement to marry was made.[173] In New Hampshire, a couple is deemed legally married if they cohabited and held each other out as spouses for three years — and continued to do so until one of their deaths.[174] Why should rights only accrue at death? Some states have a statute that makes clear that the rules regarding ceremonial marriage do not preclude proof of a common-law marriage, but does not provide any guidance on how to prove one.[175]

Common-law marriage requires that both parties intend to be married; the state does not impose the status, in general, on unwilling partners. But what if the decision not to marry has consequences for public benefits? Utah passed a common-law marriage statute in 1987, at the same time other states were poised to abolish it, which provides that a couple who are capable of marrying, cohabit, assume marital duties, and hold themselves out as married are considered married regardless of whether they intended to marry.[176] Utah was motivated in part by a desire to reduce public assistance to families who would be ineligible if the cohabiting adults were married.[177] (The recipient of public assistance would qualify

---

171. Nonetheless, age minimums, which are often contained in the marriage licensing law, do not necessarily apply to common-law marriages unless the legislature has expressly so provided. See, e.g., Kan. Stat. Ann. § 23-2502 (2020). The legislature adopted this provision in response to a court ruling that the age minimum did not apply to common-law marriages. In re Pace, 989 P.2d 297 (Kan. Ct. App. 1999).

172. Unif. Marriage & Divorce Act § 207(b) ("Parties to a marriage prohibited under this section who cohabit after removal of the impediment are lawfully married as of the date of the removal of the impediment.").

173. Tex. Fam. Code § 2.401 (2020); Utah Stat. § 30-1-4.5 (2020) (common-law marriage must be proved within one-year of termination of relationship).

174. N.H. Rev. Stat. § 457:39 (2020).

175. S.C. Code Ann. § 20-1-360 (2020).

176. Utah Stat. § 30-1-4.5 (2020).

177. See David F. Crabtree, Note, Recognition of Common-Law Marriages: Recent Development in Utah Law, 1988 Utah L. Rev. 273, 280–81.

based on her own income but would lose eligibility when her spouse's income was taken into account.) The federal government has adopted a similar approach for purposes of determining eligibility for means-tested disability benefits under the federal Social Security Income program.[178] Does it make sense to treat people as married even when they have decided not to formally marry?

5.   *Expectations for Marriage.* Most common-law marriage cases revolve around "holding out" evidence. The plaintiff in *Carter* was able to offer very concrete proof of the date the common-law marriage began and faced no opposition; in most cases, there is no evidence of a present agreement to be married. The factfinder is asked to draw an inference of intent and present agreement from the couple's conduct after the date of the alleged agreement. Did they act married? Ironically, our understanding of the expectations for marriages comes in part from common-law marriage cases in which judges wrote at length about how *real* husbands and wives behave, as the benchmark for assessing whether the couple acted married.[179] As you consider cases in Chapter 3, consider why we rely on cases like these to provide a glimpse into legal expectations of marriage. What behavior did the courts in *Hargrave* and *Carter* find important? Were they focusing on the right facts? What does it mean to "act married"? If you had to compile a list of ten things that differentiate a married couple from an unmarried couple, what would be on it? Was the court in *Hargrave* right to distinguish concubinage from marriage? What are the key differences?

6.   *Interstate Recognition.* Although most jurisdictions do not currently permit couples to establish common-law marriages, most of those will give effect to a common-law marriage validly created elsewhere. In *Hargrave,* the court considered the validity of a common-law marriage that might have been created in Oklahoma or Mexico and therefore would be valid in South Dakota despite the state's statutory abolition of such marriages. In a part of the opinion not included above, the court held that non-domiciliaries could validly create a common-law marriage in another jurisdiction.[180] Interstate recognition questions arise from the fact that states do not impose a residency requirement on marriages (though they do on divorce, as discussed in Chapter 4). This is highly consistent with social demand (as many couples seek to marry somewhere other than where they currently live), but has raised complicated questions of marriage recognition throughout

---

178. 20 C.F.R. §§ 416.1806(1)(3), 416.1826 (2020).

179. See Ariela R. Dubler, Wifely Behavior: A Legal History of Acting Married, 100 Colum. L. Rev. 957 (2000); see also Hendrik Hartog, Man and Wife in America: A History 136 (2000) (showing how separation cases established the standards for intact marriage).

180. Some courts have held that they will not recognize a common-law marriage unless the couple was domiciled in the state when the marriage was established. Others do not require proof of domicile, but do require residency, which is easier to prove and focuses on intent to reside rather than physical presence. See Homer H. Clark, Jr., The Law of Domestic Relations in the United States § 2.4, at 57–59 (2d ed. 1988).

this country's history. As we saw in *Hargrave*, courts would be wi nize a common-law marriage that was created during a vacation stay in a validating state. Actor William Hurt defended himself aga common-law marriage based on the time he and his girlfriend, Sa spent on a movie set in South Carolina, while filming *The Big C* had abolished common-law marriage in 1935 but would have given .... a marriage if it met the requirements of South Carolina law. Although Hurt had told Jennings that they had a "spiritual marriage in the eyes of God," and that they "were more married than most people," the court found it fatal to her claim that the other members of the cast knew they were *not* married.[181]

PROBLEM

Edi and Marcia began dating in 2001 and entered into a long-term, committed relationship. They exchanged rings in an impromptu ceremony at a bar — neither friends nor family attended the event. They laughed at the bar about the fact that society did not approve of their relationship; they knew they could not legally marry but believed it was symbolically important to participate in the usual wedding rituals. They lived together, referred to each other as "partner," maintained joint accounts, engaged in joint financial planning, and built a custom home together. When the relationship ended in 2016, Edi petitioned to dissolve a common-law marriage. Marcia filed a motion to dismiss, arguing that even if a common-law marriage could be recognized retroactively because of *Obergefell*, the couple did not meet the legal standard for establishing one.[182] Who should prevail? Why?

What should be done when a couple genuinely, but erroneously, believes they are married? What about when an individual believes in good faith she is married but only because of the other party's deceit? The rules regarding ceremonial and common-law marriage can be applied to determine whether a marriage is valid, but should spouses be protected when it is invalid? If so, under what circumstances?

---

181. Jennings v. Hurt, 1989 N.Y. Misc. LEXIS 868 (N.Y. Sup. Ct. 1989).
182. See In re Marriage of Hogsett & Neale, No. 17CA1484, 2018 WL 6564880 (Colo. App. 2018).

WILLIAMS V. WILLIAMS

97 P.3d 1124 (Nev. 2004)

PER CURIAM.

This is a case of first impression involving the application of the putative spouse doctrine in an annulment proceeding. Under the doctrine, an individual whose marriage is void due to a prior legal impediment is treated as a spouse so long as the party seeking equitable relief participated in the marriage ceremony with the good-faith belief that the ceremony was legally valid. A majority of states recognize the doctrine when dividing property acquired during the marriage, applying equitable principles, based on community property law, to the division. However, absent fraud, the doctrine does not apply to awards of spousal support. While some states have extended the doctrine to permit spousal support awards, they have done so under the authority of state statutes.

We agree with the majority view. Consequently, we adopt the putative spouse doctrine in annulment proceedings for purposes of property division and affirm the district court's division of the property. However, we reject the doctrine as a basis of awarding equitable spousal support. Because Nevada's annulment statutes do not provide for an award of support upon annulment, we reverse the district court's award of spousal support. . . .

On August 26, 1973, appellant Richard E. Williams underwent a marriage ceremony with respondent Marcie C. Williams. At that time, Marcie believed that she was divorced from John Allmaras. However, neither Marcie nor Allmaras had obtained a divorce. Richard and Marcie believed they were legally married and lived together, as husband and wife, for 27 years. In March 2000, Richard discovered that Marcie was not divorced from Allmaras at the time of their marriage ceremony.

In August 2000, Richard and Marcie permanently separated. In February 2001, Richard filed a complaint for an annulment. Marcie answered and counterclaimed for one-half of the property and spousal support as a putative spouse. In April 2002, the parties engaged in a one-day bench trial to resolve the matter.

At trial, Richard testified that had he known Marcie was still married, he would not have married her. He claimed that Marcie knew she was not divorced when she married him or had knowledge that would put a reasonable person on notice to check if the prior marriage had been dissolved. Specifically, Richard stated that Marcie should not have relied on statements from Allmaras that he had obtained a divorce because Marcie never received any legal notice of divorce proceedings. In addition, Richard claimed that in March 2000, when Marcie received a social security check in the name of Marcie Allmaras, Marcie told him that she had never been divorced from Allmaras. Marcie denied making the statement.

Marcie testified that she believed she was not married to her former husband, John Allmaras, and was able to marry again because Allmaras told her they were divorced. Marcie further testified that in 1971, she ran into Allmaras at a Reno bus station, where he specifically told her that they were divorced and he was living with another woman. According to Marcie, she discovered she was still married to Allmaras during the course of the annulment proceedings with Richard. Marcie testified that if she had known at any time that she was still married to Allmaras, she would have obtained a divorce from him.

During the 27 years that the parties believed themselves to be married, Marcie was a homemaker and a mother. From 1981 to 1999, Marcie was a licensed child-care provider for six children. During that time, she earned $460 a week. At trial, Marcie had a certificate of General Educational Development (G.E.D.) and earned $8.50 an hour at a retirement home. She was 63 years old and lived with her daughter because she could not afford to live on her own. . . .

The district court found that Marcie had limited ability to support herself. The district court also concluded that both parties believed they were legally married, acted as husband and wife, and conceived and raised two children. Marcie stayed home to care for and raise their children. Based upon these facts, the district court granted the annulment and awarded Marcie one-half of all the jointly-held property and spousal support. . . . Richard timely appealed the district court's judgment.

Annulment

A marriage is void if either of the parties to the marriage has a former husband or wife then living. Richard and Marcie's marriage was void because Marcie was still married to another man when she married Richard. Although their marriage was void, an annulment proceeding was necessary to legally sever their relationship. An annulment proceeding is the proper manner to dissolve a void marriage and resolve other issues arising from the dissolution of the relationship. . . .

Putative spouse doctrine

Under the putative spouse doctrine, when a marriage is legally void, the civil effects of a legal marriage flow to the parties who contracted to marry in good faith. That is, a putative spouse is entitled to many of the rights of an actual spouse. A majority of states have recognized some form of the doctrine through case law or statute. States differ, however, on what exactly constitutes a "civil effect." The doctrine was developed to avoid depriving innocent parties who believe in good faith that they are married from being denied the economic and status-related benefits of marriage, such as property division, pension, and health benefits.

The doctrine has two elements: (1) a proper marriage ceremony was performed, and (2) one or both of the parties had a good-faith belief that there was no impediment to the marriage and the marriage was valid and proper. "Good faith" has been defined as an "honest and reasonable belief that the marriage was valid at the time of the ceremony." Good faith is presumed. . . . Unconfirmed rumors or mere suspicions of a legal impediment do not vitiate good faith "'so long as no certain or authoritative knowledge of some legal impediment comes to him or her.'" However, when a person receives reliable information that an impediment exists, the individual cannot ignore the information, but instead has a duty to investigate further. Persons cannot act "'blindly or without reasonable precaution.'" Finally, once a spouse learns of the impediment, the putative marriage ends.

We have not previously considered the putative spouse doctrine, but we are persuaded by the rationale of our sister states that public policy supports adopting the doctrine in Nevada. Fairness and equity favor recognizing putative spouses when parties enter into a marriage ceremony in good faith and without knowledge that there is a factual or legal impediment to their marriage. Nor does the doctrine conflict with Nevada's policy in refusing to recognize common-law marriages or palimony suits. In the putative spouse doctrine, the parties have actually attempted to enter into a formal relationship with the solemnization of a marriage ceremony, a missing element in common-law marriages and palimony suits. As a majority of our sister states have recognized, the sanctity of marriage is not undermined, but rather enhanced, by the recognition of the putative spouse doctrine. We therefore adopt the doctrine in Nevada.

We now apply the doctrine to the instant case. The district court found that the parties obtained a license and participated in a marriage ceremony on August 26, 1973, in Verdi, Nevada. The district court also found that Marcie erroneously believed that her prior husband, Allmaras, had terminated their marriage by divorce and that she was legally able to marry Richard. In so finding, the district court also necessarily rejected Richard's argument that Marcie acted unreasonably in relying on Allmaras' statements because she had never been served with divorce papers and that she had a duty to inquire about the validity of her former marriage before marrying Richard. . . .

The district court was free to disregard Richard's testimony, and substantial evidence supports the district court's finding that Marcie did not act unreasonably in relying upon Allmaras' representations. The record reflects no reason for Marcie to have disbelieved him and, thus, no reason to have investigated the truth of his representations. Although older case law suggests that a party cannot rely on a former spouse's representation of divorce, more recent cases indicate this is just a factor for the judge to consider in determining good faith. We conclude that the district court did not err in finding that Marcie entered into the marriage in good faith. She therefore qualifies as a putative spouse. We now turn to the effect of the doctrine on the issues of property division and alimony.

Property division . . .

In this case, the district court treated the parties' property as quasi-community property and equally divided the joint property between the parties. Substantial evidence supports the district court's division, and we affirm the district court's distribution of the property.

Spousal support

States are divided on whether spousal support is a benefit or civil effect that may be awarded under the putative spouse doctrine. Although some states permit the award of alimony, they do so because their annulment statutes permit an award of rehabilitative or permanent alimony. At least one state, however, has found alimony to be a civil effect under the putative spouse doctrine even in the absence of a specific statute permitting an award of alimony. . . .

Nevada statutes do not provide for an award of alimony after an annulment. Thus, the cases in which alimony was awarded pursuant to statute are of little help in resolving this issue. . . .

The putative spouse doctrine did not traditionally provide for an award of spousal support. Extensions of the doctrine have come through statute or findings of fraud and bad faith. As neither is present in this case, we decline to extend the doctrine to permit an award of spousal support when both parties act in good faith. . . .

Conclusion

We conclude that an annulment proceeding is the proper method for documenting the existence of a void marriage and resolving the rights of the parties arising out of the void relationship. We adopt the putative spouse doctrine and conclude that common-law community property principles apply by analogy to the division of property acquired during a putative marriage. However, the putative spouse doctrine does not permit an award of spousal support in the absence of bad faith, fraud or statutory authority. Therefore, we affirm that portion of the district court's order equally dividing the parties' property and reverse that portion of the order awarding spousal support.

NOTES AND QUESTIONS

---

1. *The Putative Spouse Doctrine.* What policies underlie the putative spouse doctrine? What rights does a putative spouse have? Does the court's approach in *Williams* reflect the right approach?

2. *Applying Law to Facts.* Although a majority of states recognize the putative spouse doctrine, it takes many different forms. Consider whether it should apply in each of the following situations and explain why:

- A couple did not participate in any formal wedding ceremony nor obtain a license because they were too busy, but conducted themselves in every possible way like husband and wife.[183]

---

183. See UMDA § 209.

- A man reassured his fiancée that their state permitted common-law marriage and that they could marry without undertaking any formalities, knowing that the status had been abolished decades earlier.
- A couple participated in a traditional religious ceremony when they were too young to marry; after turning 18, they obtained a marriage license but did not participate in another ceremony.[184]

V. Recognition of Prohibited Marriages

In re May's Estate
117 N.Y.S.2d 345 (N.Y. App. Div. 1952)

BREWSTER, JUSTICE.

Respondent petitioner had been granted Letters of Administration upon the estate of the deceased, her mother, over the objections of the appellants, her father, brothers, and a sister, upon a holding that her father was not a lawful surviving husband of deceased in that their intermarriage in the state of Rhode Island on January 21, 1913, while valid under the laws of that jurisdiction may not be recognized when brought into question here. Deceased was appellant father's half niece. Under our statute they were forbidden to intermarry and penal consequences were provided for its violation. Domestic Relations Law, § 5; Penal Law, § 1110. The sole issue is whether such marriage of an uncle and his niece which is pronounced incestuous and void by our statute is to be so regarded when validly contracted in another state.

Relevant provisions of the aforecited statutes are:

Domestic Relations Law, Article 2 — Marriages

§ 5. Incestuous and void marriages

A marriage is incestuous and void whether the relatives are legitimate or illegitimate between either: . . .

3. An uncle and niece or an aunt and nephew.

If a marriage prohibited by the foregoing provisions of this section be solemnized it shall be void, and the parties thereto shall each be fined not less than fifty nor more than one hundred dollars and may, in the discretion of the court in addition to said fine, be imprisoned for a term not exceeding six months.

---

184. Xiong v. Xiong, 800 N.W.2d 187 (Minn. Ct. App. 2011).

Penal Law. Article 102 — Incest

§ 1110. Incest

When persons, within the degrees of consanguinity, within which marriages are declared by law to be incestuous and void, intermarry . . . with each other, each of them is punishable by imprisonment for not more than ten years.

The question is as to what recognition our law is to give to the civil status which was acquired by deceased and the appellant upon their marriage in Rhode Island, validly contracted there under the laws of that jurisdiction. As to "its validity in law" a marriage is deemed a civil contract, despite its many differences from an ordinary contract, and the general rule, too long and widely established to need much citation of authority, is that when contracted in another state or country, if valid there under the law of that place, it is valid everywhere. The rule is *jus gentium*. The only exceptions to this rule which obtain in our jurisdiction and which merit consideration in the instant case are: (1) cases coming within the inhibitions of *natural law* as it is recognized by countries adhering to the concepts of Christian culture and its antecedents, e.g., those which are polygamous or so incestuous in degree as to have been regarded with abhorrence since time immemorial, and (2) those prohibited by such of our positive laws as have extra-territorial force and bind the violator when he comes within or returns to our jurisdiction.

The blood relationship of an uncle and a niece is not sufficiently close to render their marital union so repugnant to our concept of the *natural law* as to bring it within the first class of exceptions aforestated. It was never so regarded either anciently or at common law. Indeed, it is still lawful in many jurisdictions in our country and abroad throughout Christendom. It was not interdicted by Levitical or Talmudical law and is presently sanctioned by the Jewish faith and doctrine. It was not forbidden in our own state until the enactment of our present statute in 1893, since which time, when lawfully contracted in a foreign jurisdiction it has been authoritatively recognized here.

Next, then, is there anything in the prohibitory statute, Domestic Relations Law, § 5, which gives it any extra-territorial force? Manifestly its highly criminal provisions as well as those of the Penal Law, supra, are not enforcible [sic] when the forbidden act is committed out of the state and he who thus acted comes or returns here. To so extend it as to enforce its other provisions would entail punishment equally or more severe than those provided for the crime, at least in some cases of which the instant one is an example. Here the marital union subsisted for over 32 years and until sundered by the death of the wife, with the issue of six children, adults now surviving. . . . It is well settled that for a statute to so operate as to give any of its provisions the extraterritorial force which, in effect, has been accorded by the decree in question, an expressed legislative design therefor is necessary. Such we do not find expressed, and its omission is in consonance with a public policy which marks its significance in view of the consequences which would follow if it were to be supplied by implication, viz: the abrogation of vested rights and the disruption and confusion of family order and establishment, including the bastardizing of children.

The decree should be reversed and the matter remitted for an award of the letters to appellant father.

NOTES AND QUESTIONS

1. *Marriage and Federalism.* As you have seen throughout this chapter, marriage is regulated primarily at the state level. Subject to constitutional constraints, states can impose restrictions on who can marry. Historically, states had significant disagreements about such restrictions. Many, but not all, states banned interracial marriage. Some states permitted common-law marriage, while others did not. Some states permitted first cousins to marry, while others did not. States varied in the minimum age for marriage. At the same time, states did not (and do not) impose residency requirements for marriage. Any couple who satisfies the procedural requirements (e.g., license and solemnization) and who meets the substantive eligibility requirements can marry in any state. But what happens if a couple is eligible to marry in the state where they celebrate the wedding but not in the state they call home? A nationally uniform marriage law would have solved these interstate conflicts, but states were simply unwilling to relinquish their control over marriage. Efforts early in the twentieth century to adopt a uniform marriage law failed.[185] There were also several unsuccessful attempts to amend the Constitution, either to give Congress general authority to regulate marriage and divorce, or specifically to ban polygamy, interracial marriage, or same-sex marriage nationwide.[186]

2. *Interstate Marriage Recognition Principles.* Conflicts that arose by virtue of different marriage laws were addressed through a set of marriage recognition rules that tried to balance respect for the laws of sister states (and foreign countries) with the ability of states to protect themselves from "lax" marriage laws. Because states sometimes imposed different restrictions on marriage, questions arose about marriage recognition — whether a marriage would be recognized as valid in a state that would have prohibited its celebration in the first instance. In *May's Estate*, the court articulates and applies the general rule of marriage

---

185. See Report of the Committee on Marriage and Divorce, in Proceedings of the Seventeenth Annual Conference of Commissioners on Uniform State Laws 122 (1907). The 1911 Uniform Marriage and Marriage License Act focused solely on procedural aspects of marriage law. See Unif. Marriage and Marriage License Act § 5, 9 U.L.A. 257 (1911).

186. See Edward Stein, Past and Present Proposed Amendments to the United States Constitution Regarding Marriage, 82 Wash. U. L.Q. 611 (2004).

recognition: a marriage valid where celebrated is valid everywhere.[187] And a logical corollary to this rule is that a marriage that is void where celebrated is void everywhere. Under the so-called "place of celebration" rule, most out-of-state marriages will be given effect in every jurisdiction. Indeed, as one conflict of laws scholar has observed, under the current approach "it should take *an exceptional case* for a court to refuse recognition of a valid foreign marriage of one of its domiciliaries even in the face of a local prohibition."[188] Why might courts have developed such a tolerant approach to marriage, even during eras when they resisted a uniform law and expressed a strong desire to control access to marriage? What practical problems might arise from a less tolerant approach? Is Professor Andrew Koppelman right that it "would be ridiculous to have people's marital status blink on and off like a strobe light" as they travel or move across state lines?[189]

The general rule was traditionally subject to exceptions for out-of-state marriages that violated the state's "positive law" (e.g., a statute that expressly bars extraterritorial recognition of a particular type of marriage) or "natural law" (virtually always described in the modern era as "public policy"). These exceptions are recited in numerous cases over two centuries, but rarely applied to avoid recognition. The positive-law exception was most likely to be applied to an evasive marriage — one in which the couple deliberately went out of state to marry because their home state would not permit the marriage — in a state that had adopted a statute against evasion. Mildred and Richard Loving were charged under such a law — Virginia prohibited interracial marriage and separately prohibited evasive marriages.[190] But when the Lovings prevailed at the Supreme Court, Virginia could no longer enforce either statute. The second exception has been applied even less often, in part because the two types of marriages generally thought to fall within the exception — bigamous and closely incestuous marriages — are not valid anywhere in the United States.[191] And although many courts have "cited the public policy exception, many have never actually used it

---

187. See, e.g., Joseph Story, Commentaries on the Conflict of Laws § 113 at 187 (8th ed. 1883); Fletcher W. Battershall, The Law of Domestic Relations in the State of New York 7–8 (1910) (describing "the universal practice of civilized nations" that the "permission or prohibition of particular marriages, of right belongs to the country where the marriage is to be celebrated").

188. Eugene Scoles et al., Conflicts of Laws § 13.9 at 575 (4th ed. 2004) (emphasis added).

189. Andrew Koppelman, Same Sex, Different States 17 (2006); see also Williams v. North Carolina, 317 U.S. 287, 299 (1942) (describing being married in one state but not another as one of "the most perplexing and distressing complication[s] in the domestic relations of . . . citizens"); In re Lenherr's Estate, 314 A.2d 255, 258 (Pa. 1974) ("In an age of widespread travel and ease of mobility, it would create inordinate confusion and defy the reasonable expectations of citizens whose marriage is valid in one state to hold that marriage invalid elsewhere.").

190. 388 U.S. 1 (1967).

191. Andrew Koppelman, Same-Sex Marriage, Choice of Law, and Public Policy, 76 Tex. L. Rev. 921 (1998).

to invalidate a marriage."[192] Many courts gave effect to interracial marriages even though they were prohibited.[193] Why did the court give effect to the couple's marriage in *May's Estate*, given that it met the definition of a prohibited incestuous marriage under New York law?

3. *Same-Sex Couples and the Defense of Marriage Act.* State marriage laws gradually converged over the course of the twentieth century. Interracial marriage bans were declared unconstitutional, most states raised the minimum age for marriage to 16 with parental consent (and 18 without), and restrictions based on disease were uniformly lifted.[194] Like family law in general, marriage laws headed toward more freedom for individuals — in this case, freedom to choose whom to marry. As a result, there were fewer cases involving marriage recognition principles. But as states began to consider recognizing marriages by same-sex couples, old controversies were resurrected.[195]

As we explained earlier in this chapter, when Hawaii made the first move in the direction of authorizing same-sex marriage, states and the federal government began to enact laws to fend off marriages by same-sex couples should they become lawful in one or more states. In 1996, Congress passed, and President Bill Clinton signed, the Defense of Marriage Act (DOMA).[196] Section 2 of DOMA amended the Full Faith and Credit Act to provide that states would not be required to give effect to same-sex marriages from sister states. The interstate marriage recognition rules discussed above were rooted in comity, or the principle of respect for sister states.[197] Comity provides a good reason for states to give effect to one another's marriages, but not a mandate. Courts have never applied full faith and credit principles to marriages. Roughly speaking, Section 2 of DOMA tracked the public policy exception to the general rule of recognition, although Congress wrongly couched it in terms of "full faith and credit." In any event, it granted states no power that they did not already have. Whether legally necessary or not, more than 40 states adopted mini-DOMAs, in which they expressly prohibited not only the licensing of same-sex marriages in the state but also the recognition of same-sex marriages validly celebrated in other states.

---

192. Id. at 923.

193. See, e.g., Bonds v. Foster, 36 Tex. 68, 70 (1871) (validating interracial marriage from Ohio despite Texas statute criminalizing such marriages); Pearson v. Pearson, 51 Cal. 120, 125 (1875) (same); State v. Ross, 76 N.C. 242, 246 (1877) (upholding interracial marriage from South Carolina despite conceding the marriage was "revolting to us").

194. See Legal Info. Inst., Marriage Laws of the Fifty States, District of Columbia and Puerto Rico; Guide to Legal Impediments to Marriage for 57 Registration Jurisdictions (July 30, 2004).

195. See Joseph William Singer, Same Sex Marriage, Full Faith and Credit, and the Evasion of Obligation, 1 Stan. J. C.R. & C.L. 1, 40 (2005); Andrew Koppelman, Interstate Recognition of Same-Sex Marriages and Civil Unions: A Handbook for Judges, 153 U. Pa. L. Rev. 2143, 2148 (2005).

196. Pub. L. No. 104-199, 110 Stat. 2419 (1996).

197. James Schouler, Law of the Domestic Relations 47 (2d ed. 1874).

Section 3 of DOMA was more consequential. It defined marriage for all federal-law purposes as a union between one man and one woman. This definition applied to a wide variety of laws and federal programs, singling out married couples of the same sex for adverse treatment in everything from tax to immigration to social security. Moreover, this provision was a significant departure from past practice because most federal programs do not contain their own definition of marriage or other family status relations. They defer, instead, to the law of the couple's home state.

After some states began to permit same-sex couples to marry, DOMA meant that couples had a different marital status at the federal level than they did at the state level. Beginning in 2009, same-sex couples filed a number of lawsuits challenging Section 3 of DOMA. In 2010, a federal court in Massachusetts became the first to hold this provision of DOMA unconstitutional.[198] Another lawsuit that was filed in federal court in New York would eventually reach the Supreme Court and lead to the Court's invalidation of Section 3 of DOMA on constitutional grounds. In that case, Edith Windsor and Thea Spyer had gone to Canada in 2007 to get married and then returned to New York. Spyer died two years later and left her estate to Windsor. Even though New York did not license marriage for same-sex couples at the time of Spyer's death, it would recognize the couple's marriage based on the "place of celebration" rule. Still, pursuant to Section 3 of DOMA, the federal government refused to recognize Windsor and Spyer as married. Under federal tax law, all transfers to a surviving spouse are tax free. But since the IRS did not treat the women as married, it handed Windsor a tax bill of $365,000 based on her inheritance from Spyer. She filed a lawsuit, which claimed that this provision of DOMA is unconstitutional.[199] The Supreme Court sided with Windsor. As you read the following excerpt from Justice Kennedy's opinion, consider the role played by marriage recognition principles. How did the history of marriage recognition influence the constitutional analysis?

United States v. Windsor
570 U.S. 744 (2013)

Justice Kennedy delivered the opinion of the Court. . . .

By history and tradition the definition and regulation of marriage . . . has been treated as being within the authority and realm of the separate States. Yet it is further established that Congress, in enacting discrete statutes, can make determinations that bear on marital rights and privileges. . . . Congress has the power both to

---

198. See Gill v. Office of Pers. Mgmt., 699 F. Supp. 2d 374 (D. Mass. 2010).
199. See Windsor v. United States, 833 F. Supp. 2d 394 (S.D.N.Y. 2012).

ensure efficiency in the administration of its programs and to choose what larger goals and policies to pursue. . . .

Though . . . discrete examples establish the constitutionality of limited federal laws that regulate the meaning of marriage in order to further federal policy, DOMA has a far greater reach; for it enacts a directive applicable to over 1,000 federal statutes and the whole realm of federal regulations. And its operation is directed to a class of persons that the laws of New York, and of 11 other States, have sought to protect.

In order to assess the validity of that intervention it is necessary to discuss the extent of the state power and authority over marriage as a matter of history and tradition. State laws defining and regulating marriage, of course, must respect the constitutional rights of persons, see, *e.g., Loving v. Virginia*, 388 U.S. 1 (1967); but, subject to those guarantees, "regulation of domestic relations" is "an area that has long been regarded as a virtually exclusive province of the States." *Sosna v. Iowa*, 419 U.S. 393, 404 (1975).

The recognition of civil marriages is central to state domestic relations law applicable to its residents and citizens. The definition of marriage is the foundation of the State's broader authority to regulate the subject of domestic relations with respect to the "[p]rotection of offspring, property interests, and the enforcement of marital responsibilities." "[T]he states, at the time of the adoption of the Constitution, possessed full power over the subject of marriage and divorce . . . [and] the Constitution delegated no authority to the Government of the United States on the subject of marriage and divorce." . . .

The significance of state responsibilities for the definition and regulation of marriage dates to the Nation's beginning; for "when the Constitution was adopted the common understanding was that the domestic relations of husband and wife and parent and child were matters reserved to the States." Marriage laws vary in some respects from State to State. . . .

Against this background DOMA rejects the long-established precept that the incidents, benefits, and obligations of marriage are uniform for all married couples within each State, though they may vary, subject to constitutional guarantees, from one State to the next. . . . The State's power in defining the marital relation is of central relevance in this case quite apart from principles of federalism. Here the State's decision to give this class of persons the right to marry conferred upon them a dignity and status of immense import. When the State used its historic and essential authority to define the marital relation in this way, its role and its power in making the decision enhanced the recognition, dignity, and protection of the class in their own community. DOMA, because of its reach and extent, departs from this history and tradition of reliance on state law to define marriage. "'[D]iscriminations of an unusual character especially suggest careful consideration to determine whether they are obnoxious to the constitutional provision.'" *Romer v. Evans*, 517 U.S. 620, 633 (1996).

The Federal Government uses this state-defined class for the opposite purpose—to impose restrictions and disabilities. That result requires this Court now to address whether the resulting injury and indignity is a deprivation of an essential part of the liberty protected by the Fifth Amendment. . . .

DOMA seeks to injure the very class New York seeks to protect. By doing so it violates basic due process and equal protection principles applicable to the Federal Government. The Constitution's guarantee of equality "must at the very least mean that a bare congressional desire to harm a politically unpopular group cannot" justify disparate treatment of that group. In determining whether a law is motived by an improper animus or purpose, "'[d]iscriminations of an unusual character'" especially require careful consideration. DOMA cannot survive under these principles. The responsibility of the States for the regulation of domestic relations is an important indicator of the substantial societal impact the State's classifications have in the daily lives and customs of its people. DOMA's unusual deviation from the usual tradition of recognizing and accepting state definitions of marriage here operates to deprive same-sex couples of the benefits and responsibilities that come with the federal recognition of their marriages. This is strong evidence of a law having the purpose and effect of disapproval of that class. The avowed purpose and practical effect of the law here in question are to impose a disadvantage, a separate status, and so a stigma upon all who enter into same-sex marriages made lawful by the unquestioned authority of the States. . . .

DOMA's operation in practice confirms this purpose. When New York adopted a law to permit same-sex marriage, it sought to eliminate inequality; but DOMA frustrates that objective through a system-wide enactment with no identified connection to any particular area of federal law. DOMA writes inequality into the entire United States Code. The particular case at hand concerns the estate tax, but DOMA is more than a simple determination of what should or should not be allowed as an estate tax refund. Among the over 1,000 statutes and numerous federal regulations that DOMA controls are laws pertaining to Social Security, housing, taxes, criminal sanctions, copyright, and veterans' benefits.

DOMA's principal effect is to identify a subset of state-sanctioned marriages and make them unequal. The principal purpose is to impose inequality, not for other reasons like governmental efficiency. Responsibilities, as well as rights, enhance the dignity and integrity of the person. And DOMA contrives to deprive some couples married under the laws of their State, but not other couples, of both rights and responsibilities. By creating two contradictory marriage regimes within the same State, DOMA forces same-sex couples to live as married for the purpose of state law but unmarried for the purpose of federal law, thus diminishing the stability and predictability of basic personal relations the State has found it proper to acknowledge and protect. . . .

DOMA divests married same-sex couples of the duties and responsibilities that are an essential part of married life and that they in most cases would be honored to accept were DOMA not in force. . . .

What has been explained to this point should more than suffice to establish that the principal purpose and the necessary effect of this law are to demean those persons who are in a lawful same-sex marriage. This requires the Court to hold, as it now does, that DOMA is unconstitutional as a deprivation of the liberty of the person protected by the Fifth Amendment of the Constitution.

———————

Two years after *Windsor*, the Supreme Court issued its ruling in Obergefell v. Hodges, holding that it is unconstitutional for a state to refuse to license or recognize marriages by same-sex couples. The Court's ruling mooted the interstate recognition questions that had arisen during the prior decade. when some states permitted same-sex couples to marry but many expressly prohibited both celebration and recognition of such unions. Can you think of any change to marriage law that might set off the next interstate controversy?

Regulating Ongoing Relationships

This chapter examines the legal regulation of ongoing intimate adult relationships, particularly marital ones. Tracing the evolution of legal treatment of ongoing relationships, the materials in this chapter reflect approaches to the substance of marriage as well as assumptions about its boundaries, considered through the law's treatment of ongoing marital relationships with respect to support, companionship, and caregiving; owning and controlling property; family naming; healthcare decision-making; violence; tort; and evidence. These materials highlight the tension between viewing marriage as an entity deserving of protection from the outside world versus viewing it as a partnership between two autonomous individuals, whose interests may not always align. Relatedly, while gender hierarchy has been formally eradicated from the law of marriage, do the effects of legally enforced patriarchy remain, and in what ways? How willing are courts to dictate the terms of marriage? To enforce those terms? Consider, also, how this chapter's materials express, by way of contrast, the law's attitudes about non-marital relationships, which have been decriminalized but do not enjoy extensive civil recognition. What does the law's treatment of married couples say about its understanding of unmarried couples?

One strand running through marriage law is the common-law doctrine of coverture, under which the wife's legal identity was covered by her husband's during marriage. This doctrine shaped the substance of marriage, its relationship with other areas of law, and the willingness of courts to intervene in spousal disputes. The following reading describes coverture, which American law borrowed from England.

William Blackstone, Commentaries on the Laws of England, Vol. 1 (1765)

By marriage, the husband and wife are one person in law: that is, the very being or legal existence of the woman is suspended during the marriage, or at least is incorporated and consolidated into that of the husband; under whose wing, protection, and *cover*, she performs every thing; and is therefore called in our law-French a *feme-covert, foemina viro co-operta*; is said to be *covert-baron*, or under the protection and influence of her husband, her *baron*, or lord; and her condition during her marriage is called her *coverture*.

Upon this principle, of a union of person in husband and wife, depend almost all the legal rights, duties, and disabilities, that either of them acquire by the marriage. I speak not at present of the rights of property, but of such as are merely *personal*. For this reason, a man cannot grant anything to his wife, or enter into covenant with her: for the grant would be to suppose her separate existence; and to covenant with her, would be only to covenant with himself: and therefore it is also generally true, that all compacts made between husband and wife, when single, are voided by the intermarriage. A woman indeed may be attorney for her husband; for that implies no separation from, but is rather a representation of, her lord. And a husband may also bequeath any thing to his wife by will; for that cannot take effect till the coverture is determined by his death. The husband is bound to provide his wife with necessaries by law, as much as himself; and, if she contracts debts for them, he is obliged to pay them; but for anything besides necessaries he is not chargeable. Also if a wife elopes, and lives with another man, the husband is not chargeable even for necessaries; at least if the person who furnishes them is sufficiently apprized of her elopement. If the wife be indebted before marriage, the husband is bound afterwards to pay the debt; for he has adopted her and her circumstances together. If the wife be injured in her person or her property, she can bring no action for redress without her husband's concurrence, and in his name, as well as her own: neither can she be sued without making the husband a defendant. . . . In criminal prosecutions, it is true, the wife may be indicted and punished separately; for the union is only a civil union. But in trials of any sort, they are not allowed to be evidence for, or against, each other: partly because it is impossible their testimony should be indifferent; but principally because of the union of person. But, though our law in general considers man and wife as one person, yet there are some instances in which she is separately considered; as inferior to him, and acting by his compulsion. And therefore any deeds executed, and acts done, by her, during her coverture, are void; except it be a fine, or the like manner of record, in which case she must be solely and secretly examined, to learn if her act be voluntary. She cannot by will devise lands to her husband, unless under special circumstances; for at the time of making it she is supposed to be under his coercion. And in some felonies, and other inferior crimes, committed by her, through constraint of her husband, the law excuses her; but this extends not to treason or murder.

The husband also, by the old law, might give his wife moderate correction. For, as he is to answer for her misbehavior, the law thought it reasonable to intrust him with this power of restraining her, by domestic chastisement, in the same moderation that a man is allowed to correct his apprentices or children; for whom the master or parent is also liable in some cases to answer. But this power of correction was confined within reasonable bounds, and the husband was prohibited from using any violence to his wife. . . .

These are the chief legal effects of marriage during the coverture; upon which we may observe, that even the disabilities, which the wife lies under, are for the most part intended for her protection and benefit. So great a favourite is the female sex of the laws of England.

What are the key features of coverture as envisioned by Blackstone? As you read the materials in the chapter, think about how those features matter. What convergence or divergence in interest between spouses do the materials below assume? Are these assumptions well placed? How does coverture influence ideas about the relationship between families and the state?

I. Care, Companionship, and Support

A. The Traditional Model of Marriage

As you read the next two cases, think about the legal ramifications of the model of marriage described by Blackstone.

McGUIRE v. McGUIRE
59 N.W.2d 336 (Neb. 1953)

Messmore, Justice.

The plaintiff, Lydia McGuire, brought this action in equity in the district court for Wayne County against Charles W. McGuire, her husband, as defendant, to recover suitable maintenance and support money, and for costs and attorney's fees. . . .

The district court decreed that the plaintiff was legally entitled to use the credit of the defendant and obligate him to pay for certain items in the nature of improvements and repairs, furniture, and appliances for the household in the amount of several thousand dollars; required the defendant to purchase a new automobile with an effective heater within 30 days; ordered him to pay travel expenses of the plaintiff for a visit to each of her daughters at least once a year; that the plaintiff be entitled in the future to pledge the credit of the defendant for what may constitute necessaries of life; awarded a personal allowance to the plaintiff in the sum of $50 a month; awarded $800 for services for the plaintiff's attorney; and as an alternative to part of the award so made, defendant was permitted, in agreement with plaintiff, to purchase a modern home elsewhere. . . .

The record shows that the plaintiff and defendant were married in Wayne, Nebraska, on August 11, 1919. At the time of the marriage the defendant was a bachelor 46 or 47 years of age and had a reputation for more than ordinary frugality, of which the plaintiff was aware. She had visited in his home and had known him for about 3 years prior to the marriage. After the marriage the couple went to live on a farm of 160 acres located in Leslie precinct, Wayne County, owned by the defendant and upon which he had lived and farmed since 1905. The parties have lived on this place ever since. The plaintiff had been previously married. Her first husband died in October 1914, leaving surviving him the plaintiff and two daughters. He died intestate, leaving 80 acres of land in Dixon County. The plaintiff and each of the daughters inherited a one-third interest therein. At the time of the marriage of the plaintiff and defendant the plaintiff's daughters were 9 and 11 years of age. By working and receiving financial assistance from the parties to this action, the daughters received a high school education in Pender. One daughter attended Wayne State Teachers College for 2 years and the other daughter attended a business college in Sioux City, Iowa, for 1 year. Both of these daughters are married and have families of their own.

On April 12, 1939, the plaintiff transferred her interest in the 80-acre farm to her two daughters. The defendant signed the deed.

At the time of trial plaintiff was 66 years of age and the defendant nearly 80 years of age. No children were born to these parties. The defendant had no dependents except the plaintiff.

The plaintiff testified that she was a dutiful and obedient wife, worked and saved, and cohabited with the defendant until the last 2 or 3 years. She worked in the fields, did outside chores, cooked, and attended to her household duties such as cleaning the house and doing the washing. For a number of years she raised as high as 300 chickens, sold poultry and eggs, and used the money to buy clothing, things she wanted, and for groceries. She further testified that the defendant was the boss of the house and his word was law; that he would not tolerate any charge accounts and would not inform her as to his finances or business; and that he was a poor companion. The defendant did not complain of her work, but left the impression to her that she had not done enough. On several occasions the plaintiff asked the defendant for money. He would give her very small amounts, and for the last 3 or 4 years he had not given her any money nor provided her with clothing, except a coat about 4 years previous. The defendant had purchased the groceries the last 3 or 4 years, and permitted her to buy groceries, but he paid for them by check. There is apparently no complaint about the groceries the defendant furnished. The defendant had not taken her to a motion picture show during the past 12 years. They did not belong to any organizations or charitable institutions, nor did he give her money to make contributions to any charitable institutions. . . . For the past 4 years or more, the defendant had not given the plaintiff money to purchase furniture or other household necessities. Three years ago he did purchase an electric, wood-and-cob combination stove which was installed in the kitchen, also linoleum floor covering for the kitchen. The plaintiff further testified that the house is not equipped with a bathroom, bathing facilities, or inside toilet. The kitchen is not modern. She does not have a kitchen sink. . . . She related that the furniture was old and she would like to replenish it, at least to be comparable with some of her neighbors. . . . The plaintiff was privileged to use all of the rent money she wanted to from the 80-acre farm, and when she goes to see her daughters, which is not frequent, she uses part of the rent money for that purpose, the defendant providing no funds for such use. . . . The plaintiff has had three abdominal operations for which the defendant has paid. She selected her own doctor, and there were no restrictions placed in that respect. When she has requested various things for the home or personal effects, defendant has informed her on many occasions that he did not have the money to pay for the same. She would like to have a new car. She visited one daughter in Spokane, Washington, in March 1951 for 3 or 4 weeks, and visited the other daughter living in Fort Worth, Texas, on three occasions for 2 to 4 weeks at a time. She had visited one of her daughters when she was living in Sioux City some weekends. The plaintiff further testified that she had very little funds, possibly $1,500 in the bank which was chicken money and money which her father furnished her, he having departed this life a few years ago; and that use of the telephone was restricted, indicating that defendant did not desire that she make long distance calls, otherwise she had free access to the telephone.

It appears that the defendant owned 398 acres of land with 2 acres deeded to a church, the land being of the value of $83,960; that he has bank deposits in the sum of $12,786.81 and government bonds in the amount of $104,500; and that his income, including interest on the bonds and rental for his real estate, is $8,000 or $9,000 a year. There are apparently some Series E United States Savings Bonds listed and registered in the names of Charles W. McGuire or Lydia M. McGuire purchased in 1943, 1944, and 1945, in the amount of $2,500. Other bonds seem to be in the name of Charles W. McGuire, without a beneficiary or co-owner designated. The plaintiff has a bank account of $5,960.22. . . .

While there is an allegation in the plaintiff's petition to the effect that the defendant was guilty of extreme cruelty towards the plaintiff . . . the plaintiff made no attempt to prove [this] allegation and the fact that she continued to live with the defendant is quite incompatible with the same. . . .

In the instant case the marital relation has continued for more than 33 years, and the wife has been supported in the same manner during this time without complaint on her part. The parties have not been separated or living apart from each other at any time. . . . [T]o maintain an action such as the one at bar, the parties must be separated or living apart from each other.

The living standards of a family are a matter of concern to the household, and not for the courts to determine, even though the husband's attitude toward his wife, according to his wealth and circumstances, leaves little to be said in his behalf. As long as the home is maintained and the parties are living as husband and wife it may be said that the husband is legally supporting his wife and the purpose of the marriage relation is being carried out. Public policy requires such a holding. It appears that the plaintiff is not devoid of money in her own right. She has a fair-sized bank account and is entitled to use the rent from the 80 acres of land left by her first husband, if she so chooses.

YEAGER, J., dissenting. . . .

I do not question the correctness of the statement of facts set forth in the majority opinion. I, however, do not think some important considerations have received appropriate emphasis. Therefore I shall present the dissent as I think the opinion should be, including a statement of facts. . . .

From the beginning of the married life of the parties the defendant supplied only the barest necessities and there was no change thereafter. He did not even buy groceries until the last 3 or 4 years before the trial, and neither did he buy clothes for the plaintiff.

As long as she was able plaintiff made a garden, raised chickens, did outside chores, and worked in the fields. From the sale of chickens and eggs she provided groceries, household necessities, and her own clothing. These things she is no longer able to do, but notwithstanding this the defendant does no more than to buy groceries. He buys her no clothing and does not give her any money at all to spend for her needs or desires. Only one incident is mentioned in the record of defendant ever buying plaintiff any clothing. He bought her a coat over 3 years before the trial.

The house in which the parties live is supplied with electricity and there is a gas refrigerator, otherwise it is decidedly not modern.

On these facts the district court decreed that plaintiff was legally entitled to use the credit of defendant and to obligate him to pay for a large number of items, some of which were in the nature of improvements and repairs to the house and some of which were furniture and appliances to be placed in the home. . . .

There is and can be no doubt that, independent of statutes relating to divorce, alimony, and separate maintenance, if this plaintiff were living apart from the defendant she could in equity and on the facts as outlined in the record be awarded appropriate relief. . . .

In the light of what the decisions declare to be the basis of the right to maintain an action for support, is there any less reason for extending the right to a wife who is denied the right to maintenance in a home occupied with her husband than to one who has chosen to occupy a separate abode?

If the right is to be extended only to one who is separated from the husband equity and effective justice would be denied where a wealthy husband refused proper support and maintenance to a wife physically or mentally incapable of putting herself in a position where the rule could become available to her. . . .

In primary essence the rule contemplates the enforcement of an obligation within and not without the full marriage relationship. . . .

GRAHAM V. GRAHAM
33 F. Supp. 936 (E.D. Mich. 1940)

TUTTLE, DISTRICT JUDGE.

This is a suit by a man against his former wife upon the following written agreement alleged to have been executed September 17, 1932, by the parties:

> This agreement made this 17th day of September, 1932, between Margrethe Graham and Sidney Graham, husband and wife. For valuable consideration Margrethe Graham hereby agrees to pay to Sidney Graham the sum of Three Hundred ($300.00) Dollars per month each and every month hereafter until the parties hereto no longer desire this arrangement to continue. Said Three Hundred ($300.00) Dollars per month to be paid to Sidney Graham by said Margrethe Graham directly to said Sidney Graham.
>
> This agreement is made to adjust financial matters between the parties hereto, so that in the future there will be no further arguments as to what money said Sidney Graham shall receive.

The parties were divorced on July 11, 1933. While the writing itself recites no consideration but merely states that it is made to prevent future arguments as to the amount of money the husband is to receive from his wife, the complaint alleges that the plaintiff had quit his job in a hotel at the solicitation of the defendant who wanted him to accompany her upon her travels, she paying his expenses, and that he was desirous of returning to work but that the defendant in order to induce him not to do so entered into this agreement. The total amount claimed until November 7, 1939, is $25,500, with interest at five per cent per annum from the time each monthly installment of $300 became due. The defendant in her answer alleges that she has no recollection of entering into the agreement; and she denies that she ever induced plaintiff to give up his hotel work, alleging that on the contrary his abandonment of work and continued reliance upon her for support was always distasteful to her. The answer further alleges that at the time of divorce the parties entered into a written settlement agreement under which defendant (plaintiff in the divorce suit) paid plaintiff (defendant in the divorce suit) $9,000 and each party surrendered any and all claims he or she might have in the property of the other. . . .

In the first place, it is highly doubtful if the alleged contract is within the capacity of a married woman to make under Michigan law. The degree of emancipation of married women with respect to contract and property rights varies widely in the different states. However, it has been repeatedly stated by the Michigan Supreme Court that under the Michigan statutes a married woman has no general power to contract, but can ~~contract only in relation to~~ her separate property. This is admitted by both parties and has been so frequently repeated by the Supreme Court of Michigan that an extended citation of authorities is unnecessary. The limitation applies to contracts of married women with their husbands as well as with third parties. . . .

However, I do not rest my decision on this ground, but rather upon the broader ground that ~~even if the contract is~~ otherwise within the contractual power of the parties it is void because it contravenes public policy. Under the law, marriage is not merely a private contract between the parties, but creates a status in which the state is vitally interested and under which certain rights and duties incident to the relationship come into being, irrespective of the wishes of the parties. As a result of the marriage contract, for example, the husband has a duty to support and to live with his wife and the wife must contribute her services and society to the husband and follow him in his choice of domicile. The law is well settled that a private agreement between persons married or about to be married which attempts to change the essential obligations of the marriage contract as defined by the law is contrary to public policy and unenforceable. While there appears to be no Michigan decision directly in point, the principle is well stated in the Restatement of the Law of Contracts, as follows:

Obligations of Marriage

A bargain between married persons or persons contemplating marriage to change the essential incidents of marriage is illegal.

> Illustrations:
> 1. A and B who are about to marry agree to forego sexual intercourse. The bargain is illegal.
> 2. In a state where the husband is entitled to determine the residence of a married couple, A and B who are about to marry agree that the wife shall not be required to leave the city where she then lives. The bargain is illegal.

Thus, it has been repeatedly held that a provision releasing the husband from his duty to support his wife in a contract between married persons, or those about to be married, except in connection with a pre-existing or contemplated immediate separation, makes the contract void. Similarly, the cases hold that an antenuptial agreement that the parties will not live together after marriage is void. Even in the states with the most liberal emancipation statutes with respect to married women, the law has not gone to the extent of permitting husbands and wives by agreement to change the essential incidents of the marriage contract.

The contract claimed to have been made by the plaintiff and defendant in the case at bar while married and living together falls within this prohibition. Under its terms, the husband becomes obligated to accompany his wife upon her travels;

while under the law of marriage the wife is obliged to follow the husband's choice of domicile. Indeed, it is argued by the plaintiff's attorney that this relinquishment by the husband of his rights constitutes consideration for the promise of his wife; but, by the same token it makes the contract violative of public policy. The situation is virtually identical with that set forth in Illustration 2 of Section 587 of the Restatement quoted above. The contract, furthermore, would seem to suffer from a second defect by impliedly releasing the husband from his duty to support his wife, and thereby making it fall directly within the rule of the cases cited supra holding that a contract between married persons living together which contains such a release is void. The present contract does not expressly contain such a release, but if the husband can always call upon his wife for payments of $300 per month he is in practical effect getting rid of his obligation to support his wife. The plaintiff seems to place this construction on the contract since his claim makes no deduction from the promised $300 per month for support of his wife. It is unnecessary to consider in detail the second alleged basis of consideration, namely, the promise of the husband to refrain from working, but it would seem again that a married man should have the right to engage in such work as he sees fit to do, unrestrained by contract with his wife.

The law prohibiting married persons from altering by private agreement the personal relationships and obligations assumed upon marriage is based on sound foundations of public policy. If they were permitted to regulate by private contract where the parties are to live and whether the husband is to work or be supported by his wife, there would seem to be no reason why married persons could not contract as to the allowance the husband or wife may receive, the number of dresses she may have, the places where they will spend their evenings and vacations, and innumerable other aspects of their personal relationships. Such right would open an endless field for controversy and bickering and would destroy the element of flexibility needed in making adjustments to new conditions arising in marital life. There is no reason, of course, why the wife cannot voluntarily pay her husband a monthly sum or the husband by mutual understanding quit his job and travel with his wife. The objection is to putting such conduct into a binding contract, tying the parties' hands in the future and inviting controversy and litigation between them. The time may come when it is desirable and necessary for the husband to cease work entirely, or to change to a different occupation, or move to a different city, or, if adversity overtakes the parties, to share a small income. It would be unfortunate if in making such adjustments the parties should find their hands tied by an agreement between them entered into years before.

It is important to note that the contract here was entered into between parties who were living together at the time and who obviously contemplated a continuance of that relationship. The case is to be distinguished in this respect from those cases which hold that a contract made after separation or in contemplation of an immediate separation which takes place as contemplated is legal, if the contract is a fair one, even though it contains a release of the husband's duty of support. . . . One reason why the courts uphold such separation contracts is that under the laws of most states married persons can secure a judicial separation with a judicial division of their property and a release of the husband's duty of support; and it is therefore felt that the parties should be permitted to enter into a fair agreement between themselves covering the same things upon which they could obtain relief in court. The problem is entirely different, however, where the parties are living together and contemplate a continuance of that relationship.

The case is also to be distinguished from a group of cases which hold that a married woman can properly contract with her husband to work for him outside the home and be compensated by him for her services. The ground on which the contract has been upheld in those cases is that it covered services outside the scope of the marriage contract; the promises did not, as here, involve the essential obligations of the marriage contract, and no question of public policy was therefore involved. There is certainly less reason to hold that a married woman cannot lease property owned by her to her husband for a fair consideration than to hold that the parties cannot contract to refrain from intercourse during marriage; in the former case no abridgement of marital rights or obligations is involved.

While, as stated, there are no Michigan cases exactly in point, there is nothing in them inconsistent with a holding that this contract is invalid, but on the contrary they point toward the same conclusion. . . .

NOTES AND QUESTIONS

1.   *Marital Privacy.* The *McGuire* court reasoned that the standard of living is "a matter for the household to determine," and declared that courts should decline to intervene in an intact marriage, unless the parties are living apart. Does respect for marital privacy justify the doctrine of nonintervention that the court applies, even if one party does not live up to an obligation that the law clearly imposes? What purposes are served by this doctrine? Does it, as some courts suggest, promote marital harmony? How might intervention undermine marital harmony? Professor Twila Perry observes that married couples are left to make their own agreements and rules about the level of support based on "a strong belief that judicial intervention into disputes of such nature would violate principles of marital autonomy, hopelessly entangle the courts in the day-to-day marital relationship and place an undue burden on judicial resources."[1] Does leaving couples to resolve disputes about support and spending between themselves increase or reduce the

---

1. Twila Perry, The Essentials of Marriage: Reconsidering the Duty of Support and Services, 15 Yale J.L. & Feminism 1, 14 (2003); see also Anita Bernstein, Toward More Parsimony and Transparency in "The Essentials of Marriage," 2011 Mich. St. L. Rev. 83 (2011).

likelihood of divorce? How would the prospect of judicial intervention shape the couple's relationship? The court's decision in *McGuire* does not mean the law will play no role in the couple's relationship, but it will play a different role than Mrs. McGuire sought. What laws will shape their relationship in the aftermath of the court's decision?

2.   *Four Pillars of Traditional Marriage.* In part because of the doctrine of marital privacy, courts rarely have occasion to discuss the behavior of parties to an intact marriage. We thus learn how the law conceives of marriage from cases at the margins — common-law marriage cases, where one party must prove the couple has acted married; fault-based divorce cases, where one party must prove that the other has breached the marriage contract; and annulment fraud cases, where one party must prove the other misrepresented their ability to carry out "essentials of the marriage."[2] Combined with expositions in treatises like Blackstone's Commentaries, we can construct a model of traditional marriage envisioned by the common law. The traditional model had four pillars: marital unity (e.g., coverture); fixed gender roles; standard obligations set by the state; and marital privacy. As you read the materials in this chapter, think about where and how these concepts continue to be relevant in modern marriage law.

3.   *Gender Roles in Marriage.* At common law, the doctrine governing marriage was known as the "law of husband and wife." Marriage law conceived of the rights and obligations of husbands very differently from the rights and obligations of wives. In its simplest form, marriage law imposed a set of reciprocal rights and obligations, sometimes referred to as the "incidents of marriage." The husband had the right to: choose the couple's domicile; have sexual and reproductive access to his wife; have his children cared for and house tended; have a faithful wife; and "correct" his wife's behavior when necessary. The wife had the obligation to ensure these rights were satisfied — she had to: follow him if he chose to move; make herself sexually available and be willing to bear his children; cook, clean, and raise the couple's children; be monogamous; and behave herself. Balanced against the wife's obligations was her right to be supported, and the right to a cohabiting, faithful husband (although the standard for fidelity often was applied differently for men and women); the husband had an obligation to provide food, clothes, shelter, and medical care. How well or poorly does this description fit married couples you know today? Which aspects of the traditional model of marriage have had staying power? How might you expect same-sex couples to deviate from a paradigm in which one party takes on a larger role in the home and the other in the workforce?

---

2. For discussion of the essential obligations that cannot be waived or altered because of marital status, see Bernstein, supra note 1. On the features of traditional marriage, see Hendrik Hartog, Man and Wife in America: A History (2000); Joanna L. Grossman, Separated Spouses, 53 Stan. L. Rev. 1613 (2001).

Given that Mrs. McGuire was seeking to enforce an accepted obligation of marriage, why did she lose?

4. *Intact Marriage.* In *McGuire*, the couple was still married at the time of the suit, but in *Graham* the couple had already divorced when the husband brought his claim. Does that distinction matter to the courts? Should it?

5. *Contracting about Marriage.* Why exactly did the *Graham* court refuse to enforce the contract between the parties? Did the court suggest that all the rights and obligations of marriage are determined by the state and set in stone? Would the court have been more accepting of a contract that aligned with traditional gender roles? The court suggested that enforcing contracts between parties to an intact marriage will create problems. What kinds of problems concerned the court? What if the parties in *Graham* were dating, but not married? Could they have entered into a binding contract with the same terms? Should married couples be precluded from entering contracts that would be permissible between unmarried individuals? For example, should contracts for housework or childcare be enforceable between spouses?

In *Graham*, the court held that the incidents of marriage are set by the state; in *McGuire*, the court recognized the unalterable obligations of marriage but refused to intervene when they were breached. What purposes do the rights and obligations of marriage serve if they cannot be enforced? Should couples be able to change any of the incidents of marriage?

6. *Necessaries Doctrine.* What are Mrs. McGuire options, given the court's decision? Will she be able to get the upgrades to her home and the new furniture she wants? In refusing to enter an order requiring Mr. McGuire to spend more money to satisfy his wife's needs, the court noted that she could buy things on credit, obligating him to pay the bills. The "necessaries" doctrine provides this right. According to the traditional doctrine, wives could purchase things they needed from merchants, who could then sue the husbands to collect on the debt. What problems might the court encounter if it intervened to enforce the necessaries doctrine?

NOTE: SEX EQUALITY UNDER THE CONSTITUTION

The traditional model of marriage was developed and enforced in an era in which there were no positive rights of sex equality in American law. To the contrary, separate spheres ideology, which posited that men and women had important but different roles in society, was in full force throughout the nineteenth century and well into the twentieth.[3] State codes and constitutions were littered with rules that

---

3. For discussions of "separate spheres" ideology, see, e.g., Linda K. Kerber, Separate Spheres, Female Worlds, Woman's Place: The Rhetoric of Women's History, 75 J. Am. Hist. 9 (1988); Joan C. Williams, Deconstructing Gender, 87 Mich. L. Rev. 797, 823–25 (1989); Alice Kessler-Harris, Women, Work and the Social Order, in Liberating Women's History 330, 333–37 (Berenice A. Carroll ed., 1976).

differentiated on the basis of sex, and the federal Constitution made no mention of women's rights until passage of the Nineteenth Amendment, which gave women the right to vote in federal elections, in 1920. The Supreme Court was asked several times between 1870 and 1970 to invalidate sex-based laws, but the Court did not oblige. It upheld a law restricting women's ability to practice law;[4] a law that imposed a restriction on the hours women, but not men, could work;[5] a law prohibiting women from working as a bartender unless their father or husband owned the bar;[6] and a law presuming women were unavailable for jury service and allowing them to be called only if they asked to be put on the juror roll.[7] Through all these cases, the Supreme Court accepted the idea that women's biological and social role in reproduction and childrearing could be used as a justification for limiting their participation in other aspects of civil society. Voting to allow the Illinois Bar to deny admission to a qualified woman, Justice Bradley explained the prevailing gender ideology as follows:

> [T]he civil law, as well as nature herself, has always recognized a wide difference in the respective spheres and destinies of man and woman. Man is, or should be, woman's protector and defender. The natural and proper timidity and delicacy which belongs to the female sex evidently unfits it for many of the occupations of civil life. The constitution of the family organization, which is founded in the divine ordinance, as well as in the nature of things, indicates the domestic sphere as that which properly belongs to the domain and functions of womanhood. The harmony, not to say identity, of interests and views which belong, or should belong, to the family institution is repugnant to the idea of a woman adopting a distinct and independent career from that of her husband. So firmly fixed was this sentiment in the founders of the common law that it became a maxim of that system of jurisprudence that a woman had no legal existence separate from her husband, who was regarded as her head and representative in the social state; and, notwithstanding some recent modifications of this civil status, many of the special rules of law flowing from and dependent upon this cardinal principle still exist in full force in most States. . . .
>
> It is true that many women are unmarried and not affected by any of the duties, complications, and incapacities arising out of the married state, but these are exceptions to the general rule. The paramount destiny and mission of woman are to fulfil the noble and benign offices of wife and mother. This is the law of the Creator. And the rules of civil society must be adapted to the general constitution of things, and cannot be based upon exceptional cases.[8]

---

4. Bradwell v. Illinois, 83 U.S. (16 Wall.) 130 (1873).

5. Muller v. Oregon, 208 U.S. 412 (1908).

6. Goesart v. Cleary, 335 U.S. 464 (1948).

7. Hoyt v. Florida, 368 U.S. 57 (1961).

8. Bradwell, 83 U.S. at 130, 141–42 (Bradley, J., concurring).

The constitutional tide did not turn in favor of sex equality until 1971, when the Supreme Court first invalidated a sex-based classification on equal protection grounds.[9] In that case, Reed v. Reed, the Court held that an Idaho probate law could not arbitrarily prefer male relatives to female ones for the position of intestate administrator. Although the statute at issue was relatively unimportant, it gave the Supreme Court the opportunity to consider the constitutionality of a legal system that reflexively and routinely differentiated among citizens on the basis of sex. The Court's willingness to start down this path was the product of the women's movement of the 1960s, which caused many to question the wisdom of this traditional system — though women had been mobilizing for change for decades.[10] The law had operated in many respects as if women's entire lives were consumed by marriage and motherhood, but as life spans lengthened and divorce became more accessible, women would live two-thirds of their lives on average with no minor children and many with no husband. These and other forces pushed women into the paid labor force in greater numbers than ever before and led to frustration with rampant barriers to their full participation in society.

Once the Court got into the business of gender equality, it moved at a fast clip, dismantling the legal system that had starkly differentiated between men and women for more than a century. Because gender roles were nowhere more entrenched than in the family, this process upended a wide variety of laws affecting marriage, divorce, and parenthood. In just the first decade, the Court held that Congress could not presume male servicemembers to have dependent wives while requiring female servicemembers to provide proof of a dependent husband;[11] that Georgia could not require only men to pay alimony and allow only women to receive it;[12] and that Utah could not require child support to be paid for boys until 21, but for girls only until 18.[13] These holdings resulted from the Court's recognition that sex-based classifications, like race-based ones, were inherently suspicious and deserved closer judicial scrutiny than ordinary pieces of social and economic legislation.

Many sex-based classifications were animated by archaic and overbroad generalizations about women, which meant they were descriptively inaccurate in many cases and operated prescriptively to limit the opportunities of women. In Craig v. Boren, the Court held that sex-based classifications merit intermediate scrutiny

---

9. 404 U.S. 71 (1971). For an account of these early cases and the role of early advocates such as Ruth Bader Ginsburg, see Fred Strebeigh, Equal: Women Reshape American Law (2009).

10. See Reva B. Siegel, The Nineteenth Amendment and the Democratization of the Family, 129 Yale L.J.F. 450 (2020).

11. Frontiero v. Richardson, 411 U.S. 677 (1973).

12. Orr v. Orr, 440 U.S. 268 (1979).

13. Stanton v. Stanton, 421 U.S. 7 (1975).

under the Equal Protection Clause, which means the government must justify such a classification by showing that it is substantially related to an important governmental interest.[14] The adoption of heightened scrutiny for sex-based classifications has had far-reaching implications in family law. It has forced states to craft rules that depend less on generalizations and require more individualized determinations. It also forces them to abandon long-held assumptions about the relative abilities, roles, and responsibilities of men and women in the family.

B. Modernizing Marriage?

CHESHIRE MEDICAL CENTER V. HOLBROOK
663 A.2d 1344 (N.H. 1995)

JOHNSON, JUSTICE.

This [case] poses several questions relating to the common law doctrine of necessaries, under which a husband is bound to pay for necessary medical services furnished to his wife. . . .

The facts are not in dispute. In March 1993, the defendants, Rachel R. Holbrook and Robert W. Holbrook, were married and shared a residence. During this time, Mrs. Holbrook received medical services from the plaintiff, Cheshire Medical Center. Cheshire Medical Center charged her $7,080.40 for her treatment. Mrs. Holbrook, who was subsequently incarcerated, could not pay the amount due. She offered to pay the medical center ten dollars each month until her release from prison in 1996, at which time she would "make more substantial payments, provided [she is] in good health and working."

Dissatisfied with this proposed payment schedule, Cheshire Medical Center filed a petition to attach real property owned by Mrs. Holbrook's husband. During a superior court hearing on the matter, her husband questioned whether the "doctrine of necessaries" remains the law of New Hampshire. . . .

The . . . questions of law are: (1) whether the necessaries doctrine as articulated in our common law violates the equal protection clauses of the New Hampshire and United States Constitutions, and if so, (2) whether the doctrine should be abolished; and if not, (3) whether the liability imposed under the doctrine is sole, joint and several, or primary and secondary. We find that as traditionally formulated, the necessaries doctrine is unconstitutional, and should be revised to impose reciprocal responsibilities upon husbands and wives. We also hold that the spouse who receives the necessary goods or services is primarily liable for payment; however, the other spouse is secondarily liable.

---

14. 429 U.S. 190 (1976).

I. The Common Law Doctrine of Necessaries

At common law, upon marriage a woman forfeited her legal existence and became the property of her husband:

> A man has as good a right to his wife, as to the property acquired under a marriage contract; and to divest him of that right without his default, and against his will, would be as flagrant a violation of the principles of justice as the confiscation of his estate.

"Personal chattels in possession which belonged to the wife at the time of the marriage, or which fell to her afterwards, became instantly the absolute property of the husband, . . . her choses in action became his . . . by his asserting title to them and reducing them to possession." Moreover, "the services and earnings of the wife belong[ed] to the husband, as much as his own; in law, they [were] his own." As she had no legal identity, "the married woman's contracts were absolutely void, — not merely voidable, like those of infants and lunatics."

Because the wife could not contract for food, clothing, or medical needs, her husband was obligated to provide her with such "necessaries" (at common law, married woman could not contract because marriage extinguished her "legal personality"; married woman was "under the protection and influence" of her husband). If the husband failed to do so, the doctrine of necessaries made him legally liable for essential goods or services provided to his wife by third parties. The husband's liability did not exceed his reasonable ability to pay.

In the mid-nineteenth century, the enactment of the married woman's act partly dissipated the marital disabilities of women, the common law preventing married women from retaining their earnings and owning property was abolished. In 1951, the legislature finally accorded married women the unrestricted right to contract that they possess today. In 1955, the legislature enacted RSA 546-A:2, which imposes a gender-neutral obligation of spousal support. Despite these developments, the common law rule of necessaries has endured.

II. Equal Protection

Our [state] constitution guarantees that "equality of rights under the law shall not be denied or abridged by this state on account of . . . sex." In order to withstand scrutiny under this provision, a common law rule that distributes benefits or burdens on the basis of gender must be necessary to serve a compelling State interest.

We find no compelling justification for the gender bias embodied in the traditional necessaries doctrine. . . .

> The old notion that generally it is the man's primary responsibility to provide a home and its essentials can no longer justify a [law] that discriminates on the basis of gender. No longer is the female destined solely for the home and the rearing of the family, and only the male for the marketplace and the world of ideas.

The traditional formulation of the necessaries doctrine, predicated on anachronistic assumptions about marital relations and female dependence, does not withstand scrutiny under the compelling interest standard. . . .

III. Modification of the Common Law Doctrine

Having determined that the gender bias in the necessaries rule violates our constitution's equal protection guarantees, we must determine whether the doctrine should be abolished or revised.

We conclude that imposing a reciprocal obligation on both parties to the marital contract is consistent with the policy underlying New Hampshire's gender-neutral support laws. Accordingly, we hereby expand the common law doctrine to apply to all married individuals equally, regardless of gender. We also hold that a medical provider must first seek payment from the spouse who received its services before pursuing collection from the other spouse.

BORELLI V. BRUSSEAU

16 Cal. Rptr. 2d 16 (Cal. Ct. App. 1993)

PERLEY, ASSOCIATE JUSTICE.

Plaintiff (and appellant) Hildegard L. Borelli appeals from a judgment of dismissal of her complaint against defendant and respondent Grace G. Brusseau, as executor of the estate of Michael J. Borelli. The complaint sought specific performance of a promise by appellant's deceased husband, Michael J. Borelli (decedent), to transfer certain property to her in return for her promise to care for him at home after he had suffered a stroke. . . .

FACTS . . .

On April 24, 1980, appellant and decedent entered into an antenuptial contract. On April 25, 1980, they were married. Appellant remained married to decedent until the death of the latter on January 25, 1989.

In March 1983, February 1984, and January 1987, decedent was admitted to a hospital due to heart problems. As a result, "decedent became concerned and frightened about his health and longevity." He discussed these fears and concerns with appellant and told her that he intended to "leave" [various] property to her. . . .

In August 1988, decedent suffered a stroke while in the hospital. "Throughout the decedent's August, 1988 hospital stay and subsequent treatment at a rehabilitation center, he repeatedly told [appellant] that he was uncomfortable in the hospital and that he disliked being away from home. The decedent repeatedly told [appellant] that he did not want to be admitted to a nursing home, even though it meant he would need round-the-clock care, and rehabilitative modifications to the house, in order for him to live at home."

"In or about October, 1988, [appellant] and the decedent entered an oral agreement whereby the decedent promised to leave to [appellant] . . . [various] property . . . , including a one hundred percent interest in the Sacramento property. . . . In exchange for the decedent's promise to leave her the property . . . [appellant] agreed to care for the decedent in his home, for the duration of his illness, thereby avoiding the need for him to move to a rest home or convalescent hospital as his doctors recommended. The agreement was based on the confidential relationship that existed between [appellant] and the decedent."

Appellant performed her promise but the decedent did not perform his. Instead his will bequeathed her the sum of $100,000 and his interest in the residence they owned as joint tenants. The bulk of decedent's estate passed to respondent, who is decedent's daughter.

DISCUSSION

"It is fundamental that a marriage contract differs from other contractual relations in that there exists a definite and vital public interest in reference to the marriage relation." . . .

"The laws relating to marriage and divorce have been enacted because of the profound concern of our organized society for the dignity and stability of the marriage relationship. This concern relates primarily to the status of the parties as husband and wife. The concern of society as to the property rights of the parties is secondary and incidental to its concern as to their status."

"Marriage is a matter of public concern. The public, through the state, has interest in both its formation and dissolution. . . . The regulation of marriage and divorce is solely within the province of the Legislature except as the same might be restricted by the Constitution."

In accordance with these concerns the following pertinent legislation has been enacted: Civil Code section 242 — "Every individual shall support his or her spouse. . . ." Civil Code section 4802 — "[A] husband and wife cannot, by any contract with each other, alter their legal relations, except as to property. . . ." Civil Code section 5100 — "Husband and wife contract toward each other obligations of mutual respect, fidelity, and support." Civil Code section 5103 — "[E]ither husband or wife may enter into any transaction with the other . . . respecting property, which either might if unmarried." Civil Code section 5132 — "[A] married person shall support the person's spouse while they are living together. . . ."

The courts have stringently enforced and explained the statutory language. "Although most of the cases, both in California and elsewhere, deal with a wife's right to support from the husband, in this state a wife also has certain obligations to support the husband."

"Indeed, husband and wife assume mutual obligations of support upon marriage. These obligations are not conditioned on the existence of community property or income." "In entering the marital state, by which a contract is created, it must be assumed that the parties voluntarily entered therein with knowledge that they have the moral and legal obligation to support the other."

Moreover, interspousal mutual obligations have been broadly defined. "[Husband's] duties and obligations to [wife] included more than mere cohabitation with her. It was his duty to offer [wife] his sympathy, confidence . . . , and fidelity." When necessary, spouses must "provide uncompensated protective supervision services for" each other. . . .

[A] wife is obligated by the marriage contract to provide nursing-type care to an ill husband. Therefore, contracts whereby the wife is to receive compensation for providing such services are void as against public policy; and there is no consideration for the husband's promise. . . .

[T]he marital duty of support under Civil Code sections 242, 5100, and 5132 includes caring for a spouse who is ill. They also establish that support in a marriage means more than the physical care someone could be hired to provide. . . . Marital duties are owed by the spouses personally. This is implicit in the definition of marriage as "a personal relation arising out of a civil contract between a man and a woman." (Civ. Code, § 4100.) . . .

Whether or not the modern marriage has become like a business, and regardless of whatever else it may have become, it continues to be defined by statute as a personal relationship of mutual support. Thus, even if few things are left that cannot command a price, marital support remains one of them. . . .

POCHE, J., dissenting.

A very ill person wishes to be cared for at home personally by his spouse rather than by nurses at a health care facility. The ill person offers to pay his spouse for such personal care by transferring property to her. The offer is accepted, the services are rendered and the ill spouse dies. . . . [T]his court holds that the contract was not enforceable because — as a matter of law — the spouse who rendered services gave no consideration. Apparently, in the majority's view she had a preexisting or precontract nondelegable duty to clean the bedpans herself. . . .

[M]odern attitudes toward marriage have changed almost as rapidly as the economic realities of modern society. The assumption that only the rare wife can make a financial contribution to her family has become badly outdated in this age in which many married women have paying employment outside the home. A two-income family can no longer be dismissed as a statistically insignificant aberration. Moreover today husbands are increasingly involved in the domestic chores that make a house a home. . . .

Restraints on interspousal litigation are almost extinct. With the walls supposedly protecting the domestic haven from litigation already reduced to rubble, it hardly seems revolutionary to topple one more brick. Furthermore, in situations such as this, where one spouse has died, preserving "'domestic life [from] discord and mischief'" seems an academic concern that no modern academic seems concerned with. . . .

California [has] enact[ed] a statute specifying that "either husband or wife may enter into any transaction with the other, or with any other person, respecting property, which either might if unmarried." This is but one instance of "the utmost freedom of contract [that] exists in California between husband and wife. . . ."

Had there been no marriage and had they been total strangers, there is no doubt Mr. Borelli could have validly contracted to receive her services in exchange for certain of his property. The mere existence of a marriage certificate should not deprive competent adults of the "utmost freedom of contract" they would otherwise possess. . . .

No one doubts that spouses owe each other a duty of support or that this encompasses "the obligation to provide medical care." There is nothing cited by the majority which requires that this obligation be *personally* discharged by a spouse except the decisions themselves. However . . ., before World War II it made sense for those courts to say that a wife could perform her duty of care only by doing so personally. That was an accurate reflection of the real world for women years before the exigency of war produced substantial employment opportunities for them. . . . So to the extent those decisions hold that a contract to pay a wife for caring personally for her husband is without consideration they are correct only because at the time they were decided there were no other ways she could meet her obligation of care. Since that was the universal reality, she was giving up nothing of value by agreeing to perform a duty that had one and only one way of being performed. . . .

Presumably, in the present day husbands and wives who work outside the home have alternative methods of meeting this duty of care to an ill spouse. Among the choices would be: (1) paying for professional help; (2) paying for nonprofessional assistance; (3) seeking help from relatives or friends; and (4) quitting one's job and doing the work personally.

A fair reading of the complaint indicates that Mrs. Borelli initially chose the first of these options, and that this was not acceptable to Mr. Borelli, who then offered compensation if Mrs. Borelli would agree to personally care for him at home. To contend in 1993 that such a contract is without consideration means that if Mrs. Clinton becomes ill, President Clinton must drop everything and personally care for her.

According to the majority, Mrs. Borelli had nothing to bargain with so long as she remained in the marriage. This assumes that an intrinsic component of the marital relationship is the *personal* services of the spouse, an obligation that cannot be delegated or performed by others. The preceding discussion has attempted to demonstrate many ways in which what the majority terms "nursing-type care" can be provided without either husband or wife being required to empty a single bedpan. It follows that, because Mrs. Borelli agreed to supply this personal involvement, she was providing something over and above what would fully satisfy her duty of support. That personal something — precisely because it was something she was not required to do — qualifies as valid consideration sufficient to make enforceable Mr. Borelli's reciprocal promise to convey certain of his separate property.

Not only does the majority's position substantially impinge upon couples' freedom to come to a working arrangement of marital responsibilities, it may also foster the very opposite result of that intended. . . . Moral considerations notwithstanding, no legal force could have stopped plaintiff from leaving her husband in his hour of need. Had she done so, and had Mr. Borelli promised to give her some of his separate property should she come back, a valid contract would have arisen upon her return. Deeming them contracts promoting reconciliation and the resumption of marital relations, California courts have long enforced such agreements as supported by consideration. Here so far as we can tell from the face of the complaint, Mr. Borelli and plaintiff reached largely the same result without having to endure a separation. . . . It makes no sense to say that spouses have greater bargaining rights when separated than they do during an unruptured marriage.

What, then, justifies the ban on interspousal agreements of the type refused enforcement by the majority? At root it appears to be the undeniable allure of the thought that, for married persons, "to attend, nurse, and care for each other . . . should be the natural prompting of that love and affection which should always exist between husband and wife." All married persons would like to believe that their spouses would cleave unto them through thick and thin, in sickness and in health. Without question, there is something profoundly unsettling about an illness becoming the subject of interspousal negotiations conducted over a hospital sickbed. Yet sentiment cannot substitute for common sense and modern day reality. Interspousal litigation may be unseemly, but it is no longer a novelty. . . . The majority's rule leaves married people with contracting powers which are more limited than those enjoyed by unmarried persons or than is justified by legitimate public policy. In this context public policy should not be equated with coerced altruism. Mr. Borelli was a grown man who, having amassed a sizeable amount of property, should be treated . . . as competent to make the agreement alleged by plaintiff. The public policy of California will not be outraged by affording plaintiff the opportunity to try to enforce that agreement. . . .

NOTES AND QUESTIONS

1. *Continued Vitality of the Necessaries Doctrine.* The *Holbrook* court, given the state constitutional prohibition of sex discrimination, had three options with respect to the common law necessaries doctrine: (i) abandon it, (ii) impose joint and several liability, or (iii) impose secondary spousal liability. Which option did the court embrace? Which seems preferable to you? Does the doctrine seem useful in the modern era?

Many state courts have been asked to consider whether the traditional formulation of the necessaries doctrine is constitutional and whether the doctrine continues to serve a useful purpose. These cases have produced a range of results. A few states have abolished the doctrine, concluding that it has either outlived its usefulness or can no longer be justified now that spouses do not have legally nder roles in marriage.[15] But most states continue to recognize the ther its traditional or a modified form. In Wisconsin, the state's high-eld the traditional doctrine, extending it to provide that a merchant e wife directly for payment, but only after trying and failing to get m the husband.[16] How does the holding in *Holbrook* differ from the Wisconsin approach? In other states, courts have held that spouses are jointly and severally liable for debts for necessaries, which means that a merchant could sue either or both for the full amount owed. Is that a better approach?

Today, much of the work that might be done by the necessaries doctrine is covered by family support statutes instead. Most states impose by statute an obligation on each spouse to support the other. The failure to support can give rise in most states to civil and criminal consequences.[17]

2. *Direct Versus Indirect Enforcement of Support Obligations*. *Holbrook* considers the same marital obligation of support as in *McGuire*. The difference is that in *Holbrook*, a third party was attempting indirectly to enforce the husband's obligation to support his wife. How does that fact change the decisional calculus of the court in deciding whether to enforce the doctrine?

3. *Scope of the Necessaries Doctrine*. What expenses are necessary? In *Holbrook*, what if the husband sought treatment that the wife opposed (e.g., for cosmetic surgery)? What if the husband had told the hospital personnel that he did not intend to be liable for the expenses of the wife's treatment?

4. *Duty of Care*. What are the implications of the ruling in *Borelli*? Is one spouse obligated to provide personal care for the other as part of the marital duty of support? Why was the court reluctant to enforce the contract the couple made? Are the reasons similar to those given in *McGuire*? In *Borelli*, the court denied enforcement of the husband's promise because the personal care that was ostensibly part of the wife's promise was already required by the marital contract. Therefore, there was no consideration to justify enforcement of the husband's promise. Beneath the consideration analysis is the substantive question of whether the court should enforce this sort of agreement. Is this a case where the husband took advantage of the wife by not holding up his end of the bargain? Or is this a case where the wife took advantage of her sick husband?

5. *Conceptions of Marriage*. How does the sort of promise at issue in *Borelli* fit with our conception of marriage? Should a wife freely change her husband's bedpans without compensation? What if she refuses? Is marriage a setting where we expect people to sacrifice for each other without compensation? Or is it a setting where we expect people to negotiate with each other?

---

15. See, e.g., Condore v. Prince George's County, 425 A.2d 1011, 1019 (Md. 1981); Medical Center Hosp. of Vermont v. Lorrain, 675 A.2d 1326, 1329 (Vt. 1996).

16. See, e.g., Sharpe Furniture, Inc. v. Buckstaff, 299 N.W.2d 219 (Wis. 1980); Marshfield Clinic v. Discher, 314 N.W.2d 326 (Wis. 1982); Davis v. Baxter County Hospital, 855 S.W. 2d 303 (Ark. 1993).

17. See, e.g., Cal. Penal Code § 270a (West 2020).

6. *Gender Roles.* Does the sex of the parties matter in *Borelli*? Would the court have reasoned exactly the same way if the wife were sick and the husband were providing the personal care?

PROBLEM

Clifford and Katherine had both been married before. They had many discussions before marrying each other about how they would conduct their marital relationship. Among other agreements, the couple decided they would have sex no more than once per week. Clifford claimed that Katherine did not stick to their agreement, but rather pressured him to engage in sexual activity sometimes more than once per day. Katherine says she has stuck to their agreement despite being frustrated that she is not permitted to have sex with her husband more than once per week. Does Clifford have any remedies for the alleged breach of their agreement? What reasons might a court give for not intervening to enforce the agreement? Does Katherine have any remedies for Clifford's refusal to permit sexual contact beyond the agreed upon frequency? Would a modern court and a traditional court reach the same conclusions about this case? Why or why not?

C. Caregiving Across Contexts

The previous section explored the legal treatment of care, companionship, and support in the marital context, tracing legal duties and obligations and their enforceability. How does the caregiving done within families, marital or not, shape experiences in other domains of life, such as the workplace?

The formal law of marriage no longer explicitly requires women to tend to the sphere of the home. Women continue to shoulder a greater burden of domestic and care work, however, even as women's and mothers' participation in the paid workforce has markedly increased over the past several decades.[18] Both law and workplace policies, however, tend to proceed from an assumption that workers have

---

18. Bureau of Labor Statistics, Dep't of Labor, Am. Time-Use Survey tbl. 8. (2006) (in 2005, in households with children under 6, working women spent an average of 2.17 hours per day providing care for household members compared with 1.31 hours for working men; in households with children 6 to 17, working women spent an average of .99 hours per day providing care for household members compared with .50 for working men); Bureau of Labor Statistics, Dep't of Labor, Women in the Labor Force: A Databook 1 (2006) (showing increase from 43 to 59 percent of women in the paid labor force from 1970 to 2005); id. at tbl. 7. (34 percent of mothers with children under three participated in the paid labor force in 1975 compared to 59 percent in 2005). This work force trend has recently stalled after peaking in 1999. See, e.g, Mitra Toossi & Teresa L. Morisi, Women In The Workforce Before, During, And After The Great Recession, U.S. Bureau of Labor Statistics (July 2017).

no care responsibilities, and that families will manage such needs on their own. The typical worker is often assumed to be in a marital family with a parent who is focused on the unpaid labor of childcare and other work at home.[19] Other systems, like the tax code, similarly assume, and reward, a model of specialization between market work and unpaid care work.[20] This model, however, is an increasingly stark mismatch for the profile of the labor force in the United States.[21]

Pregnancy, becoming a parent, caring for children, or needing to care for an ill or elderly family member are contexts that reveal underlying assumptions about how care gets done in families. They also expose attitudes in the workplace about pregnant workers, mothers, fathers, and other caregivers. The social penalty that women experience in the workplace from becoming mothers is matched by a marked wage penalty for mothers over the course of their working lives. Job instability due to pregnancy or other caregiver discrimination poses serious economic consequences for individual caregivers and families, with two incomes becoming a necessity for families to make ends meet, especially among lower-wage workers.[22] Single parents face greater economic instability and a structural mismatch between policy and the realities of care and dependency.

1. Pregnancy

For most of U.S. history, women's reproductive capacity was used as the basis to restrict women's participation in the labor force and other aspects of public life. Since the 1970s, however, efforts have aimed to eliminate pregnancy discrimination and permit women to participate fully in civil society despite their unique role in the reproductive process. Yet women who are pregnant face pervasive biases, including in the workplace — at the point of hire, in pay, and in advancement.[23] An estimated 250,000 pregnant women yearly are denied the accommodations they need at work.[24]

---

19. See generally Joan C. Williams, Reshaping the Work-Family Debate: Why Men and Class Matter (2010); see also Joan C. Williams, Unbending Gender: Why Family and Work Conflict and What To Do About It 61–72, 81–84 (2000).

20. See generally Lily Kahng, The Not-So-Merry Wives of Windsor: The Taxation of Women in Same-Sex Marriages, 101 Cornell L. Rev. 325, 332 (2016).

21. Testimony of Heather Boushey, Ctr. for Econ. & Pol'y Research, to the EEOC, Apr. 17, 2007 ("For many families, having a working wife can make the difference between being middle class and not. . . . The shift in women's work participation is not simply about women wanting to work, but it is also about their families needing them to work.").

22. Testimony of Heather Boushey, supra note 21; see also U.S. Equal Emp. Opportunity Comm'n, Notice No. 915.002, Enforcement Guidance: Unlawful Disparate Treatment of Workers with Caregiving Responsibilities (May 23, 2007).

23. See, e.g., Jennifer Cunningham & Therese Macan, Effects of Applicant Pregnancy on Hiring Decisions and Interview Ratings, 57 Sex Roles 497, 504–06 (2007); Stephen Benard et al., Cognitive Bias and the Motherhood Penalty, 59 Hastings L.J. 1359, 1368–72 (2008); Amy J.C. Cuddy et al., When Professionals Become Mothers, Warmth Doesn't Cut the Ice, 60 J. Soc. Issues 701, 701, 714 (2004).

24. Nat'l P'ship for Women & Families, Fact Sheet: The Pregnant Workers Fairness Act 2 (2019).

The Supreme Court's early cases on pregnancy reflected ambivalence about how to treat this type of discrimination. In Cleveland Board of Education v. LaFleur, the Court held that the state could not irrebuttably presume that pregnant teachers could not work and force them to take unpaid maternity leave; women had a due process right to be treated based on their individual capacity rather than stereotyped assumptions. But the same year, the Court held, in Geduldig v. Aiello, that pregnancy discrimination is not sex discrimination under the Equal Protection Clause and does not merit heightened scrutiny.[25] Upholding a state disability insurance plan that covered virtually every condition other than pregnancy, the Court wrote:

> The California insurance program does not exclude anyone from benefit eligibility because of gender but merely removed one physical condition — pregnancy — from the list of compensable disabilities. While it is true that only women can become pregnant, it does not follow that every legislative classification concerning pregnancy is a sex-based classification. . . . The program divides potential recipients into two groups — pregnant women and nonpregnant persons. While the first group is exclusively female, the second includes members of both sexes. The fiscal and actuarial benefits of the program thus accrue to members of both sexes.[26]

The Court applied the same reasoning two years later to Title VII, the federal employment discrimination statute, holding in General Electric v. Gilbert that pregnancy discrimination was not an actionable type of employment discrimination.[27] Congress overruled *Gilbert* by enacting the Pregnancy Discrimination Act (PDA) of 1978, which provides that sex discrimination includes discrimination on the basis of pregnancy, childbirth, and related medical conditions.[28] The PDA played a significant role in increasing women's labor force participation and normalizing pregnant women's presence in the workplace.[29]

In a second clause, the PDA also provides that "women affected by pregnancy, childbirth, or related medical conditions shall be treated the same for all employment-related purposes, including receipt of benefits under fringe benefit programs, as other persons not so affected but similar in their ability or inability to work."[30] What does it mean to be treated the same? Against whom should the treatment of pregnant workers be compared? In California Federal Savings & Loan

---

25. Cleveland Bd. of Educ. v. LaFleur, 414 U.S. 632, 651 (1974); Geduldig v. Aiello, 417 U.S. 484, 496–97 n.20 (1974).

26. 417 U.S. at 496–97 n.20.

27. 429 U.S. 125, 127–33 (1976).

28. 42 U.S.C. § 2000e(k) (2020).

29. Sankar Mukhopadhyay, The Effects of the 1978 Pregnancy Discrimination Act on Female Labor Supply, 53 Int'l Econ. Rev. 1133 (2012); Deborah Dinner, The Costs of Reproduction: History and the Legal Construction of Sex Equality, 46 Harv. C.R.-C.L. L. Rev. 415, 464 (2011).

30. 42 U.S.C. § 2000e(k) (2020).

Association v. Guerra, the U.S. Supreme Court concluded that the PDA operates as a floor and not a ceiling for pregnant workers, which means that an employer could choose, or a state law could require, that the physical effects of pregnancy be accommodated whether or not the same is done for comparably disabled workers.[31] At the same time, courts have concluded that the PDA does not impose any absolute right to accommodation of pregnancy or childbirth; employers can treat pregnant workers as badly as they treat those with comparable disabilities.[32] But employers cannot broadly exclude women from work because of their reproductive capacity. In UAW v. Johnson Controls, Inc., the Supreme Court invalidated a "fetal protection" policy that prevented fertile women, but not fertile men, from working in jobs in a battery-manufacturing business that involved exposure to lead.[33]

The Supreme Court again considered the scope of the second clause of the PDA in Young v. United Parcel Service, Inc.[34] There, a UPS driver challenged her employer's refusal to grant her a light-duty position transfer for the duration of her pregnancy. UPS had a policy that allowed employees to obtain light-duty assignments because they were injured on the job, were eligible for accommodations under the Americans with Disabilities Act, or had lost their commercial driver's license because of illness, injury, or even a DUI conviction. Pregnant women were among the only employees who could not seek light-duty assignments under this policy. Peggy Young argued that the second clause of the PDA required UPS to extend her the same accommodations it was making available to comparably disabled employees.[35] UPS defended its treatment of Young by arguing that its policy was pregnancy-blind and therefore non-discriminatory.[36]

UPS argued that it was free to deny accommodations to pregnant workers as long as it did not do so because of pregnancy per se.[37] Young argued that she was entitled to any accommodation that her employer provided (or would have provided) to another worker with similar limitations from another cause.[38] The Supreme Court rejected both interpretations of the second clause offered by the parties. Justice Breyer, writing for the majority, rejected Young's argument that she was entitled to any accommodation available to another temporarily disabled

31. 479 U.S. 272 (1987).

32. Troupe v. May Dep't Stores Co., 20 F.3d 734 (7th Cir. 1994) (rejecting pregnancy discrimination claim by worker terminated day before maternity leave was due to begin after tardiness that worker alleged was related to morning sickness).

33. 499 U.S. 187, 197 (1991).

34. 575 U.S. 206 (2015).

35. Id. at 211.

36. Id. at 212 ("[I]t had not discriminated against Young on the basis of pregnancy but had treated her just as it treated all 'other' relevant 'persons.'").

37. Id. at 1349. The Fourth Circuit had adopted this approach in Young's case. See Young v. United Parcel Serv., Inc., 707 F.3d 437, 446–47 (4th Cir. 2013), amended and superseded by 784 F.3d 192 (4th Cir. 2015).

38. Young, 575 U.S. at 220.

employee, deeming it too broad.[39] But he deemed UPS's interpretation too narrow and inconsistent with the text and history of the PDA, which made clear that employers cannot maintain a policy that broadly provides benefits but denies them to pregnant women.[40]

The majority in *Young* crafted an entirely new approach to the second clause of the PDA that, in its view, "minimizes the problems [of the parties' interpretations], responds directly to *Gilbert*, and is consistent with longstanding interpretations of Title VII."[41] This approach incorporates the *McDonnell-Douglas* test, which is used to smoke out evidence of unadmitted, but intentional discrimination by employers.[42] Under so-called pretext analysis, a plaintiff must first satisfy the prima facie case by showing she was treated differently from someone similarly situated but outside the protected class.[43] The Court modified the traditional test to fit failure-to-accommodate claims. Now, a plaintiff can raise an inference of discrimination that shifts the evidentiary burden to the employer by showing that "she belongs to the protected class, that she sought accommodation, that the employer did not accommodate her, and that the employer did accommodate others 'similar in their ability or inability to work.'"[44] The prima facie case, the majority wrote, is neither "onerous" nor "burdensome."[45] Moreover, it does not require the plaintiff to "show that those whom the employer favored and those whom the employer disfavored were similar in all but the protected ways."[46] The burden of production then shifts to the employer who must articulate a legitimate, nondiscriminatory reason for denying the accommodation to the pregnant worker. Under the Court's ruling, cost is not a legitimate reason. Then, the plaintiff gets the opportunity to prove discrimination by "providing sufficient evidence that the employer's policies impose a significant burden on pregnant workers, and that the employer's 'legitimate, nondiscriminatory' reasons are not *sufficiently strong* to justify the burden, but rather — when considered along with the burden imposed — give rise to an inference of intentional discrimination."[47] By way of example, the Court suggests that such inference could be drawn when an "employer accommodates a large percentage of nonpregnant workers while failing to accommodate a large percentage

---

39. Id. at 222.
40. Id. at 221–22.
41. Id. at 228.
42. See McDonnell Douglas Corp. v. Green, 411 U.S. 792 (1973).
43. *Young*, 575 U.S. at 212–13.
44. Id. at 229. Among the modified prima facie case's benefits is the elimination of the *McDonnell-Douglas* test's second prong — i.e., the plaintiff was "qualified" — which some pre-*Young* courts had found could not be satisfied by a pregnant worker needing accommodation. See, e.g., Spivey v. Beverly Enters., Inc., 196 F.3d 1309, 1312 (11th Cir. 1999); Urbano v. Continental Airlines, Inc., 138 F.3d 204, 206 (5th Cir. 1998).
45. *Young*, 575 U.S. at 228.
46. Id.
47. Id. at 229 (emphasis added).

of pregnant workers."[48] This approach invites a more searching inquiry into the circumstances surrounding accommodation claims and the reasons offered by employers.

Young's claim was a disparate treatment claim, but workers may also pursue disparate impact claims to address pregnancy discrimination. While disparate impact claims have often been viewed as less fruitful for addressing pregnancy discrimination, Professor Reva Siegel has argued that *Young* holds promise for disparate impact claims as well as disparate treatment ones.[49] In addition to breaking from a "rigid comparative framework," *Young* "rejects reflexive cost justifications, and reasons more flexibly about disparate treatment and disparate impact claims of pregnancy discrimination."[50] The analysis in *Young* contemplates a way to challenge "rigid job descriptions" and claim "reasonable accommodations," even under disparate impact.[51]

Although *Young* has made it easier for employees to exercise the right of comparative accommodation guaranteed under the PDA, employers are still free to deny accommodations as long as they do it "equally." Should pregnant employees have a right to reasonable accommodation? In an effort to establish such a right, patterned after the Americans with Disability Act, the Pregnant Workers Fairness Act was introduced in Congress in 2012 and has been reintroduced regularly since then.[52] As of April 2020, 25 states and 5 cities require some employers to provide accommodations to pregnant workers.[53] Is this a better approach than merely providing a way to address overt discrimination? Why might employers resist such a law?

Despite the law's protections, pregnancy bias remains common. Social science research demonstrates the pervasive nature of hostility to pregnant workers and stereotyped assumptions about their commitment, with pronounced negative employment outcomes for pregnant workers.[54] The economic effects of pregnancy discrimination and failure to accommodate are felt particularly by lower-income

---

48. Id. at 229–30.

49. See Reva B. Siegel, Pregnancy as a Normal Condition of Employment: Comparative and Role-Based Accounts of Discrimination, 59 Wm. & Mary L. Rev. 969, 999, 1005 (2018). For a discussion of disparate impact prior to *Young*, see Joan C. Williams & Nancy Segal, Beyond the Maternal Wall: Relief for Family Caregivers Who Are Discriminated Against on the Job, 26 Harv. Women's L.J. 77, 134–36 (2003).

50. Siegel, Pregnancy as a Normal Condition, supra note 49.

51. Id. at 1004.

52. H.R. 5647, 112th Cong. (2012), H.R. 1975, 113th Cong. (2013), H.R. 2654, 114th Cong. (2015), S. 1101, 115th Cong. (2017), H.R. 2694, 116th Cong. (2019).

53. A Better Balance, State Pregnant Workers Fairness Laws (Apr. 14, 2020).

54. See, e.g., Jennifer Bennett Shinall, The Pregnancy Penalty, 103 Minn. L. Rev. 749 (2018); Michelle R. Hebl et al., Hostile and Benevolent Reactions Toward Pregnant Women: Complementary Interpersonal Punishments and Rewards that Maintain Traditional Roles, 92 J. Applied Psychol. 1499 (2007); Shelley J. Correll et al., Getting a Job: Is There a Motherhood Penalty?, 112 Am. J. Soc. 1297, 1306 (2007).

women, immigrant women, and women of color, who are concentrated in lower-wage work with little workplace flexibility and greater economic vulnerability.[55]

Reproduction disproportionately burdens women beyond the workplace, and women of color fare worse across many dimensions. Research shows, for example, stark race-based disparities in maternal mortality rates in the United States.[56] According to the Centers for Disease Control, "Black, American Indian, and Alaska Native (AI/AN) women are two to three times more likely to die from pregnancy-related causes than white women — and this disparity increases with age. . . . Pregnancy-related deaths per 100,000 live births . . . for black and AI/AN women older than 30 was four to five times as high as it was for white women."[57] Can pregnancy discrimination doctrine address such disparities? How?

PROBLEM

A community center runs after-school programs for teenage girls, focused on fostering skills for adulthood. The center has a policy against hiring unmarried pregnant women, on the theory that these individuals present negative role models. Does the policy impermissibly discriminate on the basis of sex?

2. Family Leave

Among high-income nations around the world, the United States is an outlier in failing to guarantee broadly paid parental leave.[58] The federal Family Medical Leave Act of 1993 (FMLA) provides job protection and unpaid leave for up to twelve weeks for workers to care for a newborn or a newly adopted or foster child; to care for a child, spouse or parent with a serious health condition; or for the serious health condition of the employee, including maternity-related

---

55. Joanna L. Grossman &. Gillian L. Thomas, Making Pregnancy Work: Overcoming the Pregnancy Discrimination Act's Capacity-Based Model, 21 Yale J.L. & Feminism 15, 22 (2009); see also Laura Schlichtmann, Comment, Accommodation of Pregnancy-Related Disabilities on the Job, 15 Berkeley J. Emp. & Lab. L. 335, 338 (1994); Nat'l Latina Inst. for Reproductive Health & Nat'l Women's L. Ctr., Accommodating Pregnancy on the Job: The Stakes for Women of Color and Immigrant Women (May 2014).

56. Ctrs. for Disease Control & Prevention, Racial and Ethnic Disparities Continue in Pregnancy-Related Deaths (2019); see also Andreea A. Creanga et al., Racial and Ethnic Disparities in Severe Maternal Morbidity: A Multistate Analysis, 2008-10, 210 Am. J. Obstetrics & Gynecology 435 (2014).

57. Ctrs. for Disease Control & Prevention, supra note 56.

58. See Amy Raub et al., WORLD Pol'y Analysis Ctr., Paid Parental Leave: A Detailed Look at Approaches Across OECD Countries (2018); Gretchen Livingston & Deja Thomas, Among 41 Countries, Only U.S. Lacks Paid Parental Leave (Pew Res. Ctr., Dec. 16, 2019); see also Int'l Labour Org., Maternity and Paternity at Work: Law and Practice Across the World (2014).

disability.[59] The FMLA applies to employers with more than 50 employees, covering employees who have worked for at least 12 months and for 1,250 hours for a year before the leave.[60] Due to the FMLA's coverage restrictions, about 40 percent of workers are ineligible.[61] Even if a worker is eligible, because the leave is unpaid, many workers cannot afford to take it. This is especially the case for single parents, workers in lower-wage jobs, or parents of color — due to economic disparities these groups of workers are more likely to face.[62] Many employees are fearful that they will be retaliated against or otherwise treated negatively for taking leave.[63] Both women and men report such fears.[64] If employees are eligible for leave, and can afford to take it, gender plays a role in who takes it, with men doing so less frequently than women.[65] This may relate not only to stereotypes about work and care but also to the gender wage gap; the lower earner in a couple is more likely to take unpaid leave.[66] Does the FMLA vindicate sex equality principles or undermine them, or both? Consider the relationship between the gender wage gap and workplace penalties for taking leave.

The U.S. Supreme Court addressed the constitutionality of the FLMA as applied to state employers in Nevada Department of Human Resources v. Hibbs. The case involved a father and provided an opportunity for the Court to highlight gender-based discrimination against male caregivers.

> The FMLA aims to protect the right to be free from gender-based discrimination in the workplace. . . . The history of the many state laws limiting women's employment opportunities is chronicled in — and, until relatively recently, was sanctioned by — this Court's own opinions. . . . Congress responded to this history of discrimination by abrogating States' sovereign immunity in Title VII of the Civil Rights Act of 1964. . . . According to evidence that was before Congress when it enacted the FMLA, States continue to rely on invalid gender stereotypes in employment context, specifically in the administration of leave benefits. . . . Congress . . . heard testimony

---

59. Family and Medical Leave Act of 1993, 29 U.S.C §§ 2612(a)(1)(A-D) (2018).

60. Id. at §§ 2611(4)(A)(i); id. at §§ 2611(2)(A)(ii).

61. U.S. Dep't Labor, Family and Medical Leave in 2012: Technical Report 21 (2014); Wage and Hour Division (WHD), Fact Sheet #28: The Family and Medical Leave Act (2012); A Better Balance, 27 Years After FMLA It's Time For Paid Leave For All (Feb. 5, 2020).

62. See, e.g., Nat'l Women's Law Ctr., Half in Ten Report 2014 — Poverty and Opportunity Profile — Mothers (2014).

63. See Catherine R. Albiston, Bargaining in the Shadow of Social Institutions: Competing Discourses and Social Change in the Workplace Mobilization of Civil Rights, 39 Law & Soc'y Rev. 11, 23–27, 31–38 (2005); see also Catherine Albiston & Lindsey Trimble O'Connor, Just Leave, 39 Harv. J.L. & Gender 1 (2016).

64. Albiston, supra note 63, at 43–45; Sylvia Ann Hewlett & Carolyn Buck Luce, Off-Ramps and On-Ramps: Keeping Talented Women on the Road to Success, 83 Harv. Bus. Rev. 43 (Mar. 2005).

65. Lisa Bornstein, Inclusions and Exclusions in Work-Family Policy: The Public Values and Moral Code Embedded in the Family and Medical Leave Act, 10 Colum. J. Gender & L. 77, 94–95 (2000).

66. See generally Catherine R. Albiston, Institutional Inequality and the Mobilization of the Family and Medical Leave Act: Rights on Leave (2010).

that . . . "Even . . . [w]here child-care leave policies do exist, men, *both in the public and private sectors*, receive notoriously discriminatory treatment in their requests for such leave." . . . Many States offered women extended "maternity" leave that far exceeded the typical 4- to 8-week period of physical disability due to pregnancy and childbirth, but very few States granted men a parallel benefit: Fifteen States provided women up to one year of extended maternity leave, while only four provided men with the same. . . . This and other differential leave policies were not attributable to any differential physical needs of men and women, but rather to the pervasive sex-role stereotype that caring for family members is women's work.[67]

Hibbs' focus on a male plaintiff corresponds with Ruth Bader Ginsburg's strategy for litigating the earliest gender equality cases when she directed the American Civil Liberties Union Women's Rights Project in the 1970s.[68] She focused on attacking "gender lines" in the law, often those based on the ideology of separate spheres, in which men made money and women were homemakers.[69] Why did Justice Ginsburg seek to eliminate seemingly "benign" gender classifications, even those that might have looked helpful to women? By suggesting that family leave, including leave for pregnant workers, vindicates sex equality principles, does *Hibbs* have anything to say about *Geduldig*?[70]

The vast majority of Americans support paid family leave.[71] Through recent changes at the federal and state level, some workers are gaining access to paid leave. Significantly, Congress enacted legislation, effective October 2020, to provide paid leave to eligible federal employees who are new parents.[72] The Federal Employee Paid Leave Act gives twelve weeks of paid leave to each parent of a new child.[73] Some states have included paid family leave for workers in general as part of their disability or employment insurance programs.[74] In 2002, California became the first state to amend a state disability program to include up to six weeks of paid leave

---

67. Nevada Dep't of Human Res. v. Hibbs, 538 U.S. 721, 728–31 (2003).

68. We discuss some of these cases in Chapter 3.

69. See Jennifer Yatskis Dukart, *Geduldig* Reborn: *Hibbs* as a Success (?) of Justice Ruth Bader Ginsburg's Sex-Discrimination Strategy, 93 Calif. L. Rev. 541, 557 (2005).

70. See Reva Siegel, The Pregnant Citizen, from Suffrage to the Present, Geo. L.J. 19th Amend. Special Edition (2020); Reva B. Siegel, "You've Come a Long Way, Baby": Rehnquist's New Approach to Pregnancy Discrimination in *Hibbs*, 58 Stan. L. Rev. 1871 (2006).

71. See, e.g., Audrey Goodson Kingo, A New Survey Shows Paid Family Leave Is Popular Across Party Lines . . . So Why Isn't It Happening?, Working Mother (Aug. 9, 2018).

72. See Federal Employee Paid Leave Act, enacted as part of National Defense Authorization Act for Fiscal Year 2020, Pub. L. No. 116–92, § 1121 et seq., 113 Stat. 1198 (2019).

73. Id. at § 1122(a). For a detailed discussion of paid leave developments, see Deborah A. Widiss, Equalizing Parental Leave, 105 Minn. L. Rev. __ (forthcoming, 2021).

74. See Kingo, supra note 71; Sarah Fass, Nat'l Ctr. for Children in Poverty, Paid Leave in the States: A Critical Support for Low-Wage Workers and Their Families (2009); Gillian Lester, A Defense of Paid Family Leave, 28 Harv. J.L. & Gender 1, 3 (2005).

for the birth, adoption, or foster care placement of a new child or to care for an ill family member. New Hampshire, New Jersey, Rhode Island, Washington, and the District of Columbia followed suit, and a handful of other states have expanded their unemployment insurance programs to provide wage replacement for parental leave.[75] Support for paid family and medical leave has grown in recent years on both sides of the legislative aisle. The Family and Medical Insurance (FAMILY) Act was reintroduced in Congress in 2019 and would provide up to twelve weeks of paid leave for employees for becoming a parent, pregnancy, childbirth recovery, or caring for a close family member.[76] Should the government require *paid* family leave for all employees? If so, who should subsidize it?

Despite this increased support, at the onset of the COVID-19 pandemic, 30 million Americans lacked paid sick leave for when they were ill or needed to care for a family member.[77] In spring 2020, Congress passed emergency measures to fill gaps in employment leave for workers affected by the novel coronavirus. The Families First Coronavirus Response Act (FFCRA), effective on April 1, 2020 and set to expire on December 31, 2020, generally provides two weeks of coronavirus-related emergency paid sick leave to employees of public agencies or private employers with fewer than 500 employees, for workers subject to government-required or medically-advised quarantine or isolation orders or caring for those under such orders; those with coronavirus symptoms and seeking a medical diagnosis; and those caring for a child whose schools or places of care are closed or whose childcare providers are unavailable.[78] The act also expands the FMLA temporarily to provide up to twelve weeks of a combination of paid and unpaid leave to an employee who cannot work due to childcare responsibilities created by the coronavirus public health emergency.[79] The act provides tax credits for employers required to provide emergency sick or FMLA leave.[80] Due to exclusions and waiver provisions based on employer size, at least 6.5 million employees are not covered by FFCRA's leave provisions.[81]

---

75. Fass, supra note 74; see also Lester, supra note 74, at 3.

76. Maya Salam, Could the U.S. Get Paid Family Leave? It's Looking Better Than Ever, N.Y. Times (Feb. 15, 2019).

77. Families First Coronavirus Response Act, Pub. L. No. 116-127, §§ 5101-5111, 134 Stat. 178, 195–201 (2020); See also A Better Balance, Federal Emergency Coronavirus Paid Leave Laws: The Families First Coronavirus Response Act (FFCRA) and the Coronavirus Aid, Relief and Economic Security (CARES) Act (Apr. 9, 2020).

78. Families First Coronavirus Response Act, Pub. L. No. 116-127, §§ 5101-5111, 134 Stat. 178, 195–201 (2020) .

79. Families First Coronavirus Response Act, supra note 77, at §§ 3101-3106, 134 Stat. at 189–92.

80. Id. at §§ 7001-7005, 134 Stat. at 210–219. Congress subsequently passed the Coronavirus Aid, Relief, and Economic Security Act (CARES Act), which includes, among other provisions, expanded unemployment insurance benefits and some amendments to FFCRA leave provisions. Coronavirus Aid, Relief, and Economic Security Act, Pub. L. No. 116-136, §§ 2101-2116, 3605, and 3606, 134 Stat. 281, 411–412 (2020).

81. A Better Balance, We Applaud the Passage of the Families First Coronavirus Response Act & Call for Further, Immediate Action to Protect All Workers & Families (Mar. 18, 2020).

What barriers exist to more widespread coverage? Does the recent congressional action to address COVID-19 suggest the possibility of lasting change in mandated employee leave?

The FMLA and other leave laws in the United States have been framed in gender-neutral terms in support of greater gender equality in caregiving between men and women.[82] Leave is given to individual eligible employees, and not to families as a whole or individual children. Professor Deborah Widiss has critiqued the current system for disadvantaging single parents, who effectively receive half of the support of two-parent families.[83] As Widiss argues, "This is a significant problem, as forty percent of new mothers in the United States are unmarried."[84] Consider ways to remedy this through the following problem.

PROBLEM

Imagine you work as a legislative aide for a United States Senator asked to consider supporting newly proposed paid leave legislation. The senator is particularly concerned about protecting children and different types of families, including single-parent headed families. The proposed legislation would modify the existing FMLA to require that family leave be paid and apply to a broader range of employees. It would, like the FMLA, provide: a total of 12 workweeks of leave during any 12-month period for one or more of the following: (A) Because of the birth of a son or daughter of the employee and in order to care for such son or daughter; (B) Because of the placement of a son or daughter with the employee for adoption or foster care; (C) In order to care for the spouse, or a son, daughter, or parent, of the employee, if such spouse, son, daughter, or parent has a serious health condition; (D) Because of a serious health condition that makes the employee unable to perform the functions of the position of such employee. Is the law sufficiently supportive of nonmarital parents? What changes or additions would you propose for the law to be more helpful? What additional systemic changes might be necessary?

3. Caregiver Discrimination

Workers with caregiving responsibilities face various types of discrimination. These generally revolve around expectations about how workers with care responsibilities

---

82. Widiss, supra note 73.
83. Id.
84. Id.

will act or how they should act.[85] What scholars, courts, and lawyers call "family responsibilities discrimination" may be viewed as a type of gender discrimination.[86] Indeed, studies have established that motherhood plays a driving role in the wage gap between women and men; women face a wage penalty of approximately 5 percent per child that men do not experience.[87]

Researchers have documented barriers to women's advancement in the workplace, known as the "maternal wall," produced from biases about mothers' dedication, ability, or competence, especially that of mothers of young children and also of pregnant women.[88] Men may also experience bias as a result of their caregiving, where they will receive a benefit from the fact of being a father but suffer workplace penalties from visibly seeking to engage in the work of parenting.[89] Family responsibilities also extend to caring for aging or ill parents, ill or disabled partners, grandchildren, or other relatives.[90] Patterns of extended caregiving are more prevalent in communities of color and in immigrant families.[91] As the population ages, care needs of parents, in-laws, and partners will increase.

Family responsibilities cases might include discrimination because of pregnancy, for being a parent, or for having other caregiving duties.[92] In the following case, consider the importance of evidence of gender stereotyping in establishing the plaintiff's theory of caregiver discrimination.

BACK V. HASTINGS ON HUDSON UNION FREE SCHOOL DISTRICT
365 F.3d 107 (2d Cir. 2004)

CALABRESI, CIRCUIT JUDGE.

In 1998, Plaintiff-Appellant Elana Back was hired as a school psychologist at the Hillside Elementary School ("Hillside") on a three-year tenure track. At the

---

85. Cynthia Thomas Calvert, WorkLifeLaw, Caregivers in the Workplace: Family Responsibilities Discrimination Litigation Update 2016, at 9 (2016).

86. See Joan Williams, Unbending Gender, supra note 19, at 101–10.

87. Tamar Kricheli-Katz, Choice, Discrimination, and the Motherhood Penalty, 46 Law & Soc'y Rev. 557, 557 (2012); see also Michelle J. Budig & Paula England, The Wage Penalty for Motherhood, 66 Am. Soc. Rev. 204 (2001).

88. See, e.g., Stephen Benard et al., Cognitive Bias and the Motherhood Penalty, 59 Hastings L.J. 1359, 1360 (2008); Shelley J. Correll, Stephen Benard & In Paik, Getting a Job: Is There a Motherhood Penalty?, 112 Am. J. Sociology 1297, 1316 (2007); The Maternal Wall: Research and Policy Perspectives on Discrimination Against Mothers, 60 J. Soc. Issues (Special Issue) 667 (Monica Biernat et al. eds., 2004).

89. See, e.g., Knussman v. Maryland, 272 F.3d 625, 628 (4th Cir. 2001); Joan C. Williams & Stephanie Bornstein, The Evolution of "FReD": Family Responsibilities Discrimination and Developments in the Law of Stereotyping and Implicit Bias, 59 Hastings L.J. 1311, 1313 (2008).

90. See generally Peggie R. Smith, Elder Care, Gender, and Work: The Work-Family Issue of the 21st Century, 25 Berkeley J. Emp. & Labor L. 351, 355–60 (2004).

91. Id. at 396–97, D'vera Cohn & Jeffrey S. Passel, A Record 64 Million Americans Live in Multigenerational Households, Pew Reserach Ctr (Apr. 5, 2018).

92. Williams & Bornstein, supra note 89, at 1313.

end of that period, when Back came up for review, she was denied tenure and her probationary period was terminated. She alleged that the termination violated her constitutional right to equal protection of the laws. Defendants-Appellees contend that Back was fired because she lacked organizational and interpersonal skills. Back asserts that the real reason she was let go was that the defendants presumed that she, as a young mother, would not continue to demonstrate the necessary devotion to her job, and indeed that she could not maintain such devotion while at the same time being a good mother.

This appeal thus poses an important question, one that strikes at the persistent "fault line between work and family — precisely where sex-based overgeneralization has been and remains strongest." Nev. Dep't of Human Res. v. Hibbs, 538 U.S. 721 (2003). It asks whether stereotyping about the qualities of mothers is a form of gender discrimination, and whether this can be determined in the absence of evidence about how the employer in question treated fathers. We answer both questions in the affirmative. . . .

A. Background

i. Back's Qualifications

As the school psychologist at Hillside Elementary School, Elana Back counseled and conducted psychological evaluations of students, prepared reports for the Committee on Special Education, assisted teachers in dealing with students who acted out in class, worked with parents on issues related to their children, and chaired the "Learning Team," a group made up of specialists and teachers which conducted intensive discussions about individual students. Defendant-Appellee Marilyn Wishnie, the Principal of Hillside, and defendant-appellee Ann Brennan, the Director of Pupil Personnel Services for the District, were Back's supervisors. They were responsible for establishing performance goals for her position, and evaluating Back's work against these standards.

In the plaintiff's first two years at Hillside, Brennan and Wishnie consistently gave her excellent evaluations. . . . In her first annual evaluation, on a scale where the highest score was "outstanding," and the second highest score was "superior," Back was deemed "outstanding" and "superior" in almost all categories, and "average" in only one. . . .

In her second year at Hillside, Back took approximately three months of maternity leave. After she returned, she garnered another "outstanding" evaluation from Brennan, who noted that she was "very pleased with Mrs. Back's performance during her second year at Hillside." Other contemporaneous observations also resulted in strongly positive feedback, for example, that Back "demonstrate[d] her strong social/emotional skills in her work with parents and teachers, and most especially with students," and that she was "a positive influence in many areas, and continues to extend a great deal of effort and commitment to our work." In her annual evaluation, Back received higher marks than the previous year, with more "outstandings" and no "averages." The narrative comments noted that she "continues to serve in an outstanding manner and provides excellent support for our students," and that her "commitment to her work and to her own learning is outstanding." At the beginning of Back's third year at Hillside, she again received "outstanding" and "superior" evaluations from both Brennan and Wishnie.

Defendant-Appellant John Russell, the Superintendent of the School District, also conducted ongoing evaluations of Back's performance. In January 1999, he . . . rated her performance "superior." In February 2000, he again sat in on a Learning Team meeting, and again indicated that Back's performance was "superior." He also noted that she was effective without being overly directive, and worked well with the other members of the team. In addition, according to Back, all three individual defendants repeatedly assured her throughout this time that she would receive tenure.

ii. Alleged Stereotyping

Back asserts that things changed dramatically as her tenure review approached. The first allegedly discriminatory comments came in spring 2000, when Back's written evaluations still indicated that she was a very strong candidate for tenure. At that time, shortly after Back had returned from maternity leave, the plaintiff claims that Brennan, (a) inquired about how she was "planning on spacing [her] offspring," (b) said " '[p]lease do not get pregnant until I retire,' " and (c) suggested that Back "wait until [her son] was in kindergarten to have another child."

Then, a few months into Back's third year at Hillside, on December 14, 2000, Brennan allegedly told Back that she was expected to work until 4:30 p.m. every day, and asked " 'What's the big deal. You have a nanny. This is what you [have] to do to get tenure.' " Back replied that she did work these hours. And Brennan, after reportedly reassuring Back that there was no concern about her job performance, told her that Wishnie expected her to work such hours. But, always according to Back, Brennan also indicated that Back should "maybe . . . reconsider whether [Back] could be a mother and do this job which [Brennan] characterized as administrative in nature," and that Brennan and Wishnie were "concerned that, if [Back] received tenure, [she] would work only until 3:15 p.m. and did not know how [she] could possibly do this job with children."

A few days later, on January 8, 2001, Brennan allegedly told Back for the first time that she might not support Back's tenure because of what Back characterizes as minor errors that she made in a report. According to Back, shortly thereafter Principal Wishnie accused her of working only from 8:15 a.m. to 3:15 p.m. and never working during lunch. When Back disputed this, Wishnie supposedly replied that "this was not [Wishnie's] impression and . . . that she did not know how she could perform my job with little ones. She told me that she worked from 7 a.m. to 7 p.m. and that she expected the same from me. If my family was my priority, she stated, maybe this was not the job for me." A week later, both Brennan and Wishnie reportedly told Back that this was perhaps not the job or the school district for her if she had "little ones," and that it was "not possible for [her] to be a good mother and have this job." The two also allegedly remarked that it would be harder to fire Back if she had tenure, and wondered "whether my apparent commitment to my job was an act. They stated that once I obtained tenure, I would not show the same level of commitment I had shown because I had little ones at home. They expressed concerns about my child care arrangements, though these had never caused me conflict with school assignments." They did not — as Back told the story — discuss with her any concerns with her performance at that time. . . .

On April 30, 2001, Brennan and Wishnie purportedly repeated the same concerns about her ability to balance work and family, and told Back that they would recommend that she not be granted tenure and that Superintendent Russell would follow their recommendation. They reportedly also "stated they wanted another year to assess the child care situation." . . .

iii. Denial of Tenure

Back retained counsel in response to Brennan and Wishnie's alleged statements, and in a letter dated May 14, 2001, informed [Superintendent] Russell of these comments, and of her fear that they reflected attitudes that would improperly affect her tenure review. On May 29, 2001, Brennan and Wishnie sent a formal memo to Russell informing him that they could not recommend Back for tenure. . . .

On or around June 13, 2001, Wishnie and Brennan filed the first negative evaluation of Back, which gave her several "below average" marks and charged her with being inconsistent, defensive, difficult to supervise, the source of parental complaints, and inaccurate in her reports. Their evaluation, which was submitted to Russell, concluded that Back should not be granted tenure. Around the same time, several parents who had apparently complained about Back were encouraged by Russell to put their concerns in writing. Several parents submitted letters, reporting a range of complaints about Back's work, including that she was defensive, immature, unprofessional, and had misdiagnosed children. . . .

In September 2001, the Board notified Back that her probationary appointment would be terminated. . . .

Plaintiff presses three arguments on appeal. First, she contends that an adverse employment consequence imposed because of stereotypes about motherhood is a form of gender discrimination which contravenes the Equal Protection Clause. . . .

Discussion

A. Theory of Discrimination

Individuals have a clear right, protected by the Fourteenth Amendment, to be free from discrimination on the basis of sex in public employment. . . .

To make out such a claim, the plaintiff must prove that she suffered purposeful or intentional discrimination on the basis of gender. Discrimination based on gender, once proven, can only be tolerated if the state provides an "exceedingly persuasive justification" for the rule or practice. The defendants in this case have made no claim of justification; thus our inquiry revolves solely around the allegation of discrimination. . . .

To show sex discrimination, Back relies upon a *Price Waterhouse* "stereotyping" theory. *Price Waterhouse v. Hopkins*, 490 U.S. 228 (1989). Accordingly, she argues that comments made about a woman's inability to combine work and motherhood are direct evidence of such discrimination. . . .

It is the law, then, that "stereotyped remarks can certainly be evidence that gender played a part" in an adverse employment decision. The principle of *Price Waterhouse*, furthermore, applies as much to the supposition that a woman *will* conform to a gender stereotype (and therefore will not, for example, be dedicated to her job), as to the supposition that a woman is unqualified for a position because she does *not* conform to a gender stereotype.

The instant case, however, foregrounds a crucial question: What constitutes a "gender-based stereotype"? *Price Waterhouse* suggested that this question must be answered in the particular context in which it arises, and without undue formalization. We have adopted the same approach, as have other circuits. Just as "[i]t takes no special training to discern sex stereotyping in a description of an aggressive female employee as requiring 'a course at charm school,'" *Price Waterhouse*, 490 U.S. at 256, so it takes no special training to discern stereotyping in the view that a woman cannot "be a good mother" and have a job that requires long hours, or in the statement that a mother who received tenure "would not show the same level of commitment [she] had shown because [she] had little ones at home." These are not the kind of "innocuous words" that we have previously held to be insufficient, as a matter of law, to provide evidence of discriminatory intent.

Not surprisingly, other circuit courts have agreed that similar comments constitute evidence that a jury could use to find the presence of discrimination . . . .

The defendants argue that stereotypes about pregnant women or mothers are not based upon gender, but rather, "gender plus parenthood," thereby implying that such stereotypes cannot, without comparative evidence of what was said about fathers, be presumed to be "on the basis of sex." *Nevada Department of Human Resources v. Hibbs*, 538 U.S. 721 (2003), makes pellucidly clear, however, that, at least where stereotypes are considered, the notions that mothers are insufficiently devoted to work, and that work and motherhood are incompatible, are properly considered to be, themselves, gender-based. *Hibbs* explicitly called the stereotype that "women's family duties trump those of the workplace" a "*gender* stereotype," and cited a number of state pregnancy and family leave acts — including laws that provided *only* pregnancy leave — as evidence of "pervasive sex-role stereotype that caring for family members is women's work."

Defendants are thus wrong in their contention that Back cannot make out a claim that survives summary judgment unless she demonstrates that the defendants treated similarly situated men differently. Back has admittedly proffered no evidence about the treatment of male administrators with young children. Although her case would be stronger had she provided or alleged the existence of such evidence, there is no requirement that such evidence be adduced. Indeed we have held that,

> In determining whether an employee has been discriminated against "because of *such individual's* . . . sex," the courts have consistently emphasized that the ultimate issue is the reasons for *the individual plaintiff's* treatment, not the relative treatment of different *groups* within the workplace. As a result, discrimination against one employee cannot be cured, or disproven, solely by favorable, or equitable, treatment of other employees of the same race or sex.

Brown v. Henderson, 257 F.3d 246, 252 (2d Cir. 2001). . . .

Because we hold that stereotypical remarks about the incompatibility of motherhood and employment "can certainly be *evidence* that gender played a part" in an employment decision, we find that *Brown* applies to this case. As a result, stereotyping of women as caregivers can by itself and without more be evidence of an impermissible, sex-based motive. . . .

[W]e hold that Back has clearly produced sufficient evidence to defeat summary judgment as to Brennan and Wishnie. . . . We conclude that a jury could find, on the evidence proffered, that Brennan and Wishnie's cited justifications for their adverse recommendation and evaluation were pretextual, and that discrimination was one of the "motivating" reasons for the recommendations against Back's tenure. . . .

NOTES AND QUESTIONS

1. *Caregiver Stereotyping.* Note how the court observes that stereotyping alone may support a claim of discrimination even in the absence of comparator evidence. This is reinforced by enforcement guidance on caregiver discrimination issued by the Equal Employment Opportunity Commission.[93] In another case, Plaetzer v. Borton Auto., Inc., a federal district court held that a female plaintiff need not provide evidence that an employer treated fathers more favorably, as "an employer's objection to an employee's parental duties is actually a veiled assertion that mothers, because they are women, are insufficiently devoted to work, or that work and motherhood are incompatible."[94]

2. *Trends in Family Responsibilities Cases.* Cases brought under Title VII by employees facing discrimination due to their responsibilities to care for family members, originally described by Professor Joan Williams as "family responsibilities

---

93. EEOC, supra note 22, at 8-9.
94. Plaetzer v. Borton Auto., Inc., No. Civ. 02-3089 JRT/JSM, 2004 WL 2066770, at *6 n.3 (D. Minn. Aug. 13, 2004).

discrimination," have become more frequent and successful.[95] Between 1998 and 2012, caregiver discrimination cases increased 590 percent, when the number of employment discrimination cases in federal courts decreased by 13 percent.[96] Employees win in 52 percent of cases, particularly unusual for employment discrimination cases, known to be difficult to win.[97]

3.   *Aging and Care.* Caregiver discrimination suits concerning care of aging relatives is a rapidly growing area. Claims in this context increased more than 650 percent from 2006 to 2016.[98] By 2030, all baby boomers will be older than age 65.[99] This will expand the size of the older population so that 1 in every 5 U.S. residents will be retirement age. Given these trends, more workers will likely be involved in elder care. By 2060, it is expected that there will be two-and-a-half working-age adults for every retirement-age person, an increase from a ratio of three-and-a-half working-age adults for each retirement-age person in 2020. According to the nationally representative American Time Use Survey, in 2011, an estimated 39.8 million people in the U.S., or 16 percent of the population age 15 and over, provided unpaid care to a person over the age of 65.[100] Fifty-six percent of these caregivers were women, and people ages 45 to 64 were most likely to care for elders.[101] Employees in the so-called "sandwich generation" (ages 30 to 60) will increasingly find themselves simultaneously caring for children and elders while also working in the labor force.[102] Gender plays a role in who does the caring and who is cared for. Women undertake elder care work more often than men.[103] And women's longer life expectancy means they will need care longer. In 2016, among the population age 65 and over, there were 126 women for every 100 men. At age 85 and over, this ratio increased to 187 women for every 100 men.[104]

4.   *Is Caregiving Work?* Legal reform concerning work and family involves determining whether care is "work" and, relatedly, how to measure it. This issue arises, for instance, in the context of whether and how domestic work and childcare

---

95. See Joan Williams, Unbending Gender, supra note 19, at 101–10; see also Williams & Bornstein, supra note 89, at 1313; Williams & Segal, supra note 49, at 79.

96. Calvert, supra note 85, at 14.

97. Id. at 21.

98. Id. at 14.

99. Julie Iriondo, Older People Projected to Outnumber Children for First Time in U.S. History, U.S. Census Bureau (Mar. 13, 2018).

100. U.S. Dep't of Labor, Statistical Am. Time Use Survey, Eldercare in 2011 (2011).

101. Id.

102. EEOC, supra note 94, at 1–2, 4 n.20.

103. See Smith, supra note 90, at 360 (women provide about 70 percent of unpaid elder care); Cathy D. Martin, More Than the Work: Race and Gender Differences in Caregiving Burden, 21 J. Fam. Issues 986, 989–90 (2000).

104. Admin. for Cmty. Living, U.S. Dep't of Health and Human Servs., 2017 Profile of Older Americans 2 (Apr. 2018).

are valued in property division and spousal support. Consider the question of whether domestic work (including childcare) is work, raised in State v. Bachmann.[105] Suzanne Margie Bachmann pleaded guilty to burglary in the second degree and to check forgery.[106] While serving her 90-day sentence in the county jail, she sought "work-release privileges" pursuant to a state statute that allowed for continuation of employment without interruption during incarceration. Although Bachmann did not engage in paid labor outside of the home, she asked to be released from jail on weekdays to care for her four children and do homemaking services for her husband and her children (for which her husband would pay her $1.50). In considering whether "homemaking" was employment, the court drew on interpretations in other contexts like workers' compensation:

> Bachmann's homemaking services clearly have economic value. Nevertheless, homemaking is generally not considered employment....
>
>> The upkeep and care of a home for one's self and family are not in the category of a trade, business, profession or occupation, as generally understood. A home is not established and maintained in the expectation of pecuniary gain.... [W]e think a housewife is not an occupation within the meaning of the compensation act, since that work pertains exclusively to the management of the home. Furthermore, in the maintenance of the home the husband and wife are one. The one acts for the other.... [Eichholz v. Shaft, 208 N.W. 18, 19–20 (Minn. 1926).]
>>
>> And the same result was reached in Anderson v. Ueland, 267 N.W. 517, 518 (Minn. 1936), where we said: "the home is a sacred place for people to go and be quiet and at rest and not be bothered with the turmoil of industry," and that as such it is "a sanctuary of the individual and should not be interfered with by industrial disputes." We think [this] conception of "home" as "a sanctuary of the individual" is sound. The word is defined as, "the abiding place of the affections, esp. domestic affections"; as "the social unit formed by a family residing together in one dwelling," and as "an organized center of family life." [State v. Cooper, 285 N.W. 903, 904–05 (Minn. 1939).]
>
> The fact that Bachmann's husband has offered to pay an hourly wage to her does not change our conclusion.... Bachmann has an obligation to care for her children regardless of whether she is paid to do so.[107]

Are you persuaded by the court's distinction between homemaking ("the upkeep and care of a home and for one's self and family") and "trade, business, profession or occupation"? What is the significance of the court relying on conceptions of "home"? How does this ideal of home contrast with ideas about other

---

105. 521 N.W.2d 886 (Minn. Ct. App. 1994).
106. Id. at 887.
107. Id. at 887–88.

space in which employment happens? Consider this in relation to the idea of "separate spheres" we raised in the beginning of this chapter. Notice the court's observation that Bachmann is "obligated to care for her children regardless of whether she is paid to do so." How does this compare to the court's reasoning in Borelli v. Brusseau, discussed in the previous section?[108] If *Borelli* turns on expectations of what spouses are expected to do, how do expectations for Suzanne Bachmann shape the outcome here? Should the reasoning on Bachmann's eligibility for work release to care for her four children and to do homemaking services turn on whether she is obligated to care for her children as a parent?

5.   *Beyond the Workplace — Public Accommodations.* Caregivers can experience discrimination not just in the workplace but also in public accommodations. Professor Holning Lau has argued that physical environments in public spaces reproduce gendered assumptions about who engages in caregiving:

> The physical infrastructure around us plays a large role in the reproduction of cultural norms. For example, the lack of changing tables in men's restrooms reinforces the cultural practice of conflating caregiving with motherhood. Regulating men's access to changing tables is one way that the state could help to reshape our cultural environment. . . . The federal government very recently enacted the Bathrooms Accessible in Every Situation ("BABIES") Act, which requires federal government buildings to provide diaper changing facilities in both men's and women's restrooms. This is an important piece of public policy, but it only covers a very limited scope of buildings. Some municipal governments have gone further by requiring new and renovated public accommodations to provide men and women equal access to diaper changing facilities, either by placing diaper changing tables in both men's and women's restrooms or by placing changing tables in family restrooms. These ordinances cover not only government buildings but also other public accommodations, such as restaurants and retail stores. . . .[109]

What other areas of physical infrastructure reflect cultural norms about caregiving? How might they be regulated? Consider the design of physical spaces and organization of the workplace in relation to breastfeeding.[110] How might the law support breastfeeding in public or expression of breast milk during the day?

---

108. 16 Cal. Rptr. 2d 16 (Cal. Ct. App. 1993).

109. Holning Lau, Shaping Expectations About Dads As Caregivers: Toward an Ecological Approach, 45 Hofstra L. Rev. 183, 205–06 (2016).

110. For a critique of existing lactation laws for reinforcing traditional notions of motherhood, see Meghan Boone, Lactation Law, 106 Calif. L. Rev. 1827 (2018).

II. Owning and Controlling Property and Wealth

The status of marriage has significant implications for pro$_r$
quences, in general, are uniform for all couples, rather than determ..
uals. The rules, however, have shifted dramatically over time.

Under the principles of coverture, a married woman had fundamentally different rights regarding property and wealth than a single woman.[111] A married woman
was a "covered" woman, such that her legal identity was suspended for the duration
of the marriage. Coverture was a "principle of the common law, by which the husband and wife are regarded as one person, and her legal existence and authority in
a degree lost or suspended, during the continuance of the matrimonial union."[112]
This conception of a married woman's status reverberated throughout the law. As
Justice Bradley observed in an infamous nineteenth-century case in which the
Court rejected a woman's claim to the right to practice law in Illinois, "a woman
had no legal existence separate from her husband, who was regarded as her head
and representative in the social state."[113]

Coverture and the concept of unity had significant consequences for the control and ownership of family wealth and earnings. As described in the Blackstone
excerpt with which we began this chapter, a married woman, during her marriage,
had no legal capacity to enter into contracts, to own, sell, or exchange property, or to
keep any income she earned.[114] The rules of coverture gave the husband full responsibility, during marriage, for managing property that had belonged to the wife. He
assumed ownership of the personal property she brought to the marriage, except for
personal items like clothes. He also took control of any real property she owned as
a single woman, gained the right to rent or profits generated from the property, and
had the right to sell it. In addition, the husband had the legal right to any wages his
wife earned.

The harsh principles of coverture were not absolute and, in any event, were not
always as strict in practice as in theory. Historians have discovered practices that

---

111. See William Blackstone, 1 Commentaries on the Laws of England 430–32 (1765); see also
Richard H. Chused, Married Women's Property Law: 1800-1850, 71 Geo. L.J. 1359, 1361 (1983); Joanna
L. Grossman & Lawrence M. Friedman, Inside the Castle: Law and the Family in 20th Century America
73 (2011).

112. Kent, 2 Commentaries 106 (2d ed., 1832).

113. Bradwell v. Illinois, 83 U.S. 130, 141 (1872) (Bradley, J., concurring).

114. In English law, the doctrine of coverture was narrow and dealt only with ownership of property,
not the identities of husbands and wives, and applied only in royal courts. But when American courts
borrowed the concept, they stripped it of this context and applied it much more expansively. Hartog, supra
note 2, at 118–19.

otected women's property after marriage in some cases.[115] It was not uncommon, for example, for propertied spouses to enter into an arrangement to permit the wife to retain a "separate estate." This device, sometimes called a "*feme sole* estate," was designed to protect some money for the wife from her husband's creditors (and his wastefulness).[116] Early on, separate estates were created as trusts; a father or other male relative would put money in trust for the benefit of the soon-to-be wife and give exclusive control to a trustee. But by the seventeenth century, these trusts gave beneficiary-wives the power to control the assets directly, and by the end of the eighteenth century, separate estates were usually created by contract between husband and wife before marriage.[117] Although separate estates violated a core aspect of coverture, courts of equity consistently approved and enforced them.[118] Courts did not reject the underlying principles of coverture, but rather recognized the pragmatic need to deal with the situation of wives who were not adequately supported or who had informally separated from their husbands; these women "remained otherwise in the law in a state of coverture, subject to their absent husbands and without the legal capacity to contract or act in this world."[119] Courts also sometimes permitted women who were separated but not divorced to regain *feme sole* status, which allowed them to operate a business and keep their earnings, among other benefits.

As this makes clear, for a married woman to retain property rights, she had to ask to be treated like a single woman (*feme sole*) in some respects. As historian Hendrik Hartog has argued, "the fundamental contrast" was "not that between men and women but that between single women and married women. . . . A single woman's legal status was, for the most part, indistinguishable from the legal status of many men."[120]

Beginning in the 1840s, the ad hoc decisions of courts of equity that allowed married women some control over property were codified by legislatures. In three waves, a series of state statutes, collectively known as the Married Women's Property Acts, lifted the property-related disabilities of coverture.[121] The first wave simply

---

115. See, e.g., Norma Basch, Relief in the Premises: Divorce as a Woman's Remedy in New York and Indiana, 1815-1870, 8 Law & Hist. Rev. 1, 9 (1990) (noting that the idea that the gifts or dowry a wife brought to marriage should be returned if it was dissolved was never popular).

116. These devices are discussed in Hartog, supra note 2; Grossman, supra note 2, at 1627; Basch, supra note 116, at 9; Marylynn Salmon, Women and the Law of Property in Early America 116 (1986); Homer C. Clark, Jr., The Law of Domestic Relations in the United States 288–89 (2d ed. 1988).

117. Hartog, supra note 2, at 172; Salmon, supra note 1, at 116; Lawrence M. Friedman, A History of American Law 208 (2d ed. 1985).

118. Hartog, supra note 2, at 117.

119. Id. at 33.

120. Id. at 118.

121. Chused, supra note 112, at 1398–1400. See Joan Hoff, Law, Gender, & Injustice: A Legal History of US Women 377–82 (1991) (compiling married women's property acts and specific rights granted); see also Reva B. Siegel, The Modernization of Marital Status Law: Adjudicating Wives' Rights to Earnings, 1860-1930, 82 Geo. L.J. 2127 (1994); Amy Dru Stanley, Conjugal Bonds and Wage Labor: Rights of Contract in the Age of Emancipation, 75 J. Am. Hist. 471 (1988).

protected women's premarital property from their husbands' creditors, the same practice previously sanctioned by courts of equity. Later statutes gave women the ability to manage and dispose of their property, and, eventually, gave them control over their own earnings. The disabilities of coverture were largely abolished in full by 1950. The married women's property provision in Michigan is typical:

> Sec. 1. (1) If a woman acquires real or personal property before marriage or becomes entitled to or acquires, after marriage, real or personal property through gift, grant, inheritance, devise, or other manner, that property is and shall remain the property of the woman and be a part of the woman's estate. She may contract with respect to the property, sell, transfer, mortgage, convey, devise, or bequeath the property in the same manner and with the same effect as if she were unmarried. The property shall not be liable for the debts, obligations, or engagements of any other person, including the woman's husband, except as provided in this act.
>
> (2) A married woman has the absolute right to have, hold, own, retain, and enjoy earnings acquired by the married woman as the result of her personal efforts and those earnings shall be considered the property of the married woman as described in subsection (1).[122]

The abolition of coverture by state statute meant that married women could retain ownership of separate property, but it did not entitle them to share in the property or earnings of their husbands. Moreover, as you will see later in the chapter, even after coverture was abolished, the concept of marital unity retained rhetorical power and often shaped other aspects of the law of marriage.

What rights of ownership and control govern marriage *today*? States generally follow one of two approaches to property ownership during marriage. Most states follow a common-law system (also called a separate property system) of marital property in which each spouse solely owns all the property that spouse earned or otherwise acquired. Nine states have a community property system in which spouses equally share ownership of property acquired during the marriage through either spouse's efforts.[123] That is, regardless of title, spouses acquire an immediate and equal interest in the "community property" of the marriage. Each retains sole ownership of property acquired before the marriage or acquired by gift, inheritance, or other non-earning means during the marriage.[124]

The difference between the common-law approach and the community property approach is most apparent during an intact marriage. In the common-law

---

122. Mich. Comp. L. Ann. § 557.21 (West 2020).

123. The community property states are Arizona (2020), California, Idaho, Louisiana (2020), New Mexico, Nevada, Texas, Washington, Wisconsin.

124. See, e.g., Cal. Fam. Code § 751 (West 2020); Ariz. Rev. Stat. Ann. § 25-214 (2020); La. Civ. Code Ann. art. 2336 (2020); Nev. Rev. Stat. Ann. § 123.225 (West 2020); Tex. Fam. Code Ann. § 3.102(c) (West 2020); see also Carolyn J. Frantz & Hanoch Dagan, Properties of Marriage, 104 Colum. L. Rev. 75, 125 (2004).

system, unless the assets are titled otherwise, everything is separate property regardless of the timing or source of acquisition. If a man brings substantial property to a marriage, it remains his and his alone, unless he takes some action to transform its ownership. The same is true of the wages he earns during the marriage, any inheritance he receives, as well as gifts, lottery winnings, and personal injury judgments. The same would be true for a woman's property. Either could decide to make a gift of separate property to the other, or to use separate property to buy a jointly titled asset. But no joint ownership or interest arises from the status of marriage itself.

In contrast, the community property system assumes that once married, both parties labor on behalf of the community. While property brought to the marriage or property acquired by gift or inheritance remains separate, property earned by either spouse is owned 50/50 from the moment of acquisition.[125] This inchoate interest may or may not be reflected in the way assets are titled or held but is enforceable nonetheless. From the outset, then, there are three piles — spouse A's separate property, spouse B's separate property, and the couple's community property. Spouses in a community property state can also take actions that change the nature of separate property so that it becomes the separate property of the other spouse or becomes community property.

Note that in this section we are addressing questions of ownership *during* marriage. As we will see in Chapter 5, when a marriage ends in divorce or death, special rules come into play that determine who will walk away with the spoils (or debts) of the marriage. Historically, in common-law states, when a married couple *divorced*, courts would follow a title-based approach to awarding property — awarding property based on who had acquired it. The husband would leave the marriage with property he had brought to the marriage or acquired during it through earnings or other means; the wife would do the same. But these were rarely comparable spoils, given the disabilities of coverture and gender-based differences in property ownership and wage-earning activity. The disparities were lessened by the Married Women's Property Acts, which permitted women to earn wages in their own right as well as to buy and sell property. But those acts did nothing to address the differences that accrued from "separate spheres" ideology and the relegation of women to the domestic sphere.[126] Long after coverture was abolished, women faced continued legal, social, and economic constraints on earning and the acquisition of property at least until the emergence of constitutional sex equality principles in the 1960s and 1970s.

---

125. See, e.g., Cal. Fam. Code § 751 (West 2020) ("The respective interests of each spouse in community property during continuance of the marriage relation are present, existing, and equal interests."); Ariz. Rev. Stat. Ann. § 25-214 (2020); see also Frantz & Dagan, supra note 125, at 125.

126. In *Bradwell*, 83 U.S. 130, the Supreme Court affirmed Illinois's rejection of Myra Bradwell's application to practice law, based on the concept of women's and men's separate spheres.

The title-based system in common-law states continued to disadvantage women economically upon divorce until the 1970s, when states began to authorize redistribution of property through equitable distribution laws.[127] The title-based system for distributing property at divorce was eventually replaced in all common-law states. The new approach, which is fully explored in Chapter 5, permits a court to retroactively designate property to be shared based on principles of fairness. In community property states, the principles themselves dictate division at divorce or the death of the first spouse. In principle, each party retains the right to their separate property; and each retains a one-half interest in community property. Some but not all community property states permit equitable deviation from the 50/50 division.

While title no longer dictates how property earned during marriage is distributed at *divorce*, it still matters greatly during marriage. Who has title affects spouses' ownership, control, and management of property during an intact marriage. In common-law states, the spouse with title possesses power over the property during the marriage, and any shared property rights do not vest until dissolution.[128] For instance, in Hejailan-Amon v. Amon, a wife sought injunctive relief, return of property, and money damages against her husband and other defendants based on their removal of twenty items of artwork from the marital residence.[129] She alleged that the art was "marital property," which presumably established her "legal ownership or a superior right to the property at issue," and asserted claims of replevin and conversion against the defendants.[130] The court concluded that the wife's claims for conversion and replevin must fail. Although she might be able to assert a claim based on the property rules that arise at divorce, she could not do so during the marriage. "Indeed, [the wife's] claim that the art is 'marital property' can only be determined at the time of divorce. Under New York law, marital property 'is a statutory creature, is of no meaning whatsoever during the normal course of a marriage and arises full-grown, like Athena, upon the signing of a separation agreement or the commencement of a matrimonial action' in New York. . . ."[131]

Unlike in common-law states, spouses share property interests during the marriage in community property states. Regardless of title, spouses acquire an immediate and equal interest in the "community property" of the marriage, which includes

---

127. These disparities were also evident if the husband died first and had the power to give his property to someone other than his surviving wife. Separate property states addressed this inequity first through the law of dower and later through elective share statutes, which were adopted beginning in the 1930s. See generally Ariela R. Dubler, In the Shadow of Marriage: Single Women and the Legal Construction of the Family and State, 112 Yale L.J. 1641 (2003).

128. See also Frantz & Dagan, supra note 125, at 124. J. Thomas Oldham, Management of the Community Estate During an Intact Marriage, 56 Law & Contemp. Probs. 99, 100 (1993).

129. 160 A.D.3d 481, 482 (N.Y. App. Div. 2018).

130. Id. at 482–83.

131. Id. at 483.

property earned by either spouse. Although community property states have always recognized shared ownership of earnings, many assigned control and management to husbands in the days before such gendered rules were subject to constitutional challenge. Today, community property states follow one of three approaches to the management of the "community property" during marriage — "joint management" that requires the spouses to manage through joint action, "sole management" by one spouse over some parts of the community, or "equal management" that allows either spouse to control.[132] Some states impose fiduciary duties or duties of "good faith" on spouses in connection with management and control of the community property.[133]

As we have seen, in the common-law system, property acquired with one spouse's earnings would ordinarily be the property of that spouse, who would also have control over the property. But married couples often take ownership of property *together*, regardless of who earned the income that contributed to the property. There are three legal ways that a married couple can share ownership of property: tenancy by the entirety; joint tenancy; and tenancy in common. Tenancy by the entirety is a form of ownership available only to a married couple. It gives each spouse an undivided, one-half interest in the property, and includes a right of survivorship, which means when the first spouse dies, the second becomes the sole owner of the property. Neither spouse has the unilateral right to sell or otherwise dispose of or encumber the property, and neither can force a partition. This form of ownership is typically protected against the individual creditors of either spouse. Not all separate property states recognize this form of joint ownership, and those that do differ in some of the particulars.[134]

Another form of joint ownership that is common and not limited to married couples is joint tenancy. Joint tenants must have a unity of interests, such that they are situated vis-à-vis the property in the same way with respect to time, interest, title, and possession. Joint tenancies can come with rights of survivorship, but states

---

132. See, e.g., Cal. Fam. Code § 751 (West 2020); Ariz. Rev. Stat. Ann. § 25-214(B) (2020) ("The spouses have equal management, control and disposition rights over their community property and have equal power to bind the community."); La. Rev. Stat. Ann. § 2336 (2020) ("Each spouse owns a present undivided one-half interest in the community property."); Tex. Fam. Code Ann. § 3.102(c) (West 2020) ("Except as provided by Subsection (a), community property is subject to the joint management, control, and disposition of the spouses unless the spouses provide otherwise by power of attorney in writing or other agreement."). See also Oldham, supra note 129, at 101–04, 106, 116–17.

133. Some states expressly articulate a fiduciary duty that spouses owe one another regarding handling of community property during marriage. See, e.g., Idaho Code Ann. § 32-912 (West 2020); Cal. Fam. Code Ann. § 721 (West 2020); La. Civ. Code Ann. art. 2354 (2020); In re Marriage of Prentis-Margulis & Margulis, 130 Cal. Rptr. 3d 327 (Cal. Ct. App. 2011); Wheeling v. Wheeling, 546 S.W.3d 216 (Tex. App. 2017); Compton v. Compton, 612 P.2d 1175 (Idaho 1980); see also Lisa R. Mahle, A Purse of Her Own: The Case Against Joint Bank Accounts, 16 Tex. J. Women & L. 45, 54 (2006); Alexandra Streich, Spousal Fiduciaries in the Marital Partnership: Marriage Means Business but the Sharks Do Not Have a Code of Conduct, 34 Idaho L. Rev. 367, 368 n.2 (1998).

134. See Am. Coll. Trusts & Estates Counsel, Tenancy by the Entireties (2012).

differ as to whether they do by default or only upon express creation. Unlike a tenancy by the entirety, a joint tenancy can be unilaterally severed by either party, although some states limit the ability to do so when the asset is held jointly by spouses. Married couples hold many financial assets in this form, including joint bank accounts and joint investment accounts.

The third form of joint ownership is tenancy in common. This is the default arrangement in most states and not the preferred form for married couples. A tenancy in common can be unilaterally severed, and there is no right of survivorship.

Regardless of the formal law of separate and marital property, there are myriad ways in which the outside world views a married couple as a single economic entity. This view is sometimes enshrined in formal laws and policies, which can result in penalties for couples who do not operate in that manner. Consider, for example, the federal income tax. The federal income tax dates to 1913, when the Sixteenth Amendment to the Constitution authorized it. From 1918 on, married people were entitled to file a joint income tax return, pooling and aggregating their incomes. This put them more or less in the same position as couples in community property states. In these states, income of husband and wife was *community* income and taxed accordingly. This was a great advantage if the wife had no income; she was treated as if she had earned half, and the couple often paid less than if each had filed separately.[135]

In many other ways, government and third parties treat married couples as an economic unit. Spouses are entitled to a wide range of special economic protections. For example, any money left by one spouse to the other at the first spouse's death is exempt from the federal estate tax, regardless of amount, because it is assumed to have belonged to both of them.[136] Under the Social Security Act, any person married for at least ten years can collect on the basis of the other spouse's contribution.[137] This holds even if the collecting spouse never engaged in paid labor or earned enough credits to get payment on their own and even if the couple divorces. The Employee Retirement Income Security Act (ERISA), a complicated federal law regulating private pensions, makes spouses the primary beneficiaries of pension rights and does not permit the employee to waive those rights on behalf of a spouse.[138]

Although the law in separate property states does not force married couples to share either what they bring to the marriage or what they acquire during it, many married couples function as an economic partnership. They are more likely to pool their resources than unmarried couples.[139] The vast majority of married couples

---

135. See Marjorie E. Kornhauser, Wedded to the Joint Return: Culture and the Persistence of the Marital Unit in the American Income Tax, 11 Theor. Inq. Law 631 (2010).

136. 26 U.S.C. § 2056 (2018).

137. See 42 U.S.C. §§ 402(c),(d), 416(d) (2018).

138. See 29 U.S.C. § 1055(c)(2) (2018). This can, in some cases, be waived.

139. Dana Hamplova & Céline Le Bourdais, Pot or Two Pot Strategies? Income Pooling in Married and Unmarried Households in Comparative Perspective, 40 J. Comp. Fam. Stud. 355, 357 (2009).

use joint checking accounts.[140] Many of them do so exclusively, while others use a combination of joint and separate accounts.[141] This voluntary behavior means that the title-based system of property ownership may have little meaning for many married couples. Indeed, the joint bank account has arguably "become the primary mode through which spouses share property as economic partners."[142]

The sharing model may be less common among younger generations, or simply becoming less common in general.[143] Moreover, financial pooling is not equally prevalent among all couples.[144] For instance, sociologist Catherine Kenney has found that African American women in different-sex unions are less likely to pool income and more likely to manage finances separately than white women in different-sex unions, even when controlling for other factors like income and marital status. As she observes, "it seems possible that in the United States, the joint pooling system associated as it was with the male breadwinner-female homemaker division of labor never took hold among African American couples to the same extent as among other groups because of the considerable degree of employment among married women in this group."[145]

Moreover, it is still unknown how trends in economic behavior within marriage may shift, if at all, with the nationwide advent of same-sex marriage, given that the broader studies on joint finances predate this legal change.[146] For instance, some studies have shown greater emphasis on financial independence among same-sex couples in the U.S.[147] What factors might influence more or less financial sharing? How might marital status shape these choices among couples?

---

140. Kristen R. Heimdal & Sharon K. Houseknecht, Cohabiting and Married Couples' Income Organization: Approaches in Sweden and the United States, 65 J. Marriage & Fam. 525, 532 (2003) (less than 20 percent of married couples in the U.S. keep their money separate from one another).

141. Fenaba R. Addo & Sharon Sassler, Financial Arrangements and Relationship Quality in Low-Income Couples, 59 Fam. Rel. 408, 413 (2010) (over 60 percent of couples reported having only a joint account); Judith Treas, Money in the Bank: Transaction Costs and the Economic Organization of Marriage, 58 Amer. Soc. Rev. 723, 729 (1993) (64 percent of couples with accounts had only joint accounts, while another 18 percent had a combination of joint and separate accounts).

142. Mahle, supra note 134, at 52.

143. Liz Knueven, More Married Baby Boomers Combine Finances Than Any Generation after Them, and It Speaks to One of the Ways Money and Marriage are Changing, Bus. Insider (Nov. 17, 2019) ("Overall, 64% of all married people [in survey] had combined their finances. About 37% of married millennials kept their finances separate from their partner's, as did about 36% of Gen Xers. However, only 27% of baby boomers did the same."); Press Release, TD Bank, TD Bank Survey Finds Many Couples Maintain Separate Bank Accounts (Mar. 24, 2014) (finding that 42 percent of couples that maintain joint bank accounts also maintain separate accounts).

144. Suzanne A. Kim, The Common Place of Equality (forthcoming, manuscript on file with author).

145. Catherine T. Kenney, The Power of the Purse: Allocative Systems and Inequality in Couple Households, 20 Gender & Soc'y 354, 376 (2006).

146. For further discussion, see Kim, supra note 145.

147. See, e.g., Gabrielle Gotta et al., Heterosexual, Lesbian, and Gay Male Relationships: A Comparison of Couples in 1975 and 2000, 50 Fam. Process 353, 354 (2011).

Another means by which married couples voluntarily share property is through joint home ownership. It is extremely common for married couples to own real property as tenants by the entireties, which protects the interests of both parties during the marriage and consolidates them in the surviving spouse upon the first spouse's death.[148]

At the same time as the separate property rules belie significant property-sharing behavior, the community property rules do the opposite. Although equal management is envisioned as the legal norm underlying community property, equal control over finance eludes at least many different-sex couples. In a 2015 article, Professor Elizabeth Carter describes these dynamics:

> Several studies suggest that truly equal management of pooled income is not common. Qualitative studies have found that "among male breadwinner-female homemaker couples using joint accounts, inequalities remain in access to money because nonearning women feel uncomfortable spending on themselves using money they did not earn or because breadwinning men retain primary decision-making power over money that is nominally pooled." A 1997 study based on data collected by telephone interviews found that, although wives are primarily responsible for shopping and paying the bills, "financial decision making is a domain in which husbands report, on average, that they exercise greater control than is reported by wives." Nearly three-fourths of the husbands surveyed reported that they were responsible for making major financial decisions. Yet, the same survey showed a widespread belief in gender equality and shared decision-making. In the view of the study's authors, "when it comes to gender equality in the division of household chores and responsibilities, beliefs appear to have outrun practice."[149]

Do you think things have changed significantly since 1997, the year of the study that Carter discusses?

III. Marital Naming

Until the 1970s, the practice of wives' taking their husbands' surnames was not only common but also sometimes required.[150] In Forbush v. Wallace, for example,

---

148. Gregory S. Alexander, Governance Property, 160 U. Pa. L. Rev. 1853, 1860–61 (2012) (describing prevalence of joint ownership among married couples and domestic partners); Damaris Rosich-Schwartz, Tenancy by the Entirety: The Traditional Version of the Tenancy Is the Best Alternative for Married Couples, Common Law Marriages, and Same-Sex Partnerships, 84 N.D. L. Rev. 23, 23 (2008) (noting common nature of property ownership under tenancy by the entirety for married couples).

149. Elizabeth R. Carter, The Illusion of Equality: The Failure of the Community Property Reform to Achieve Management Equality, 48 Ind. L. Rev. 853, 871–72 (2015).

150. On marital naming, see Suzanne A. Kim, Marital Naming/Naming Marriage: Language and Status in Family Law, 85 Ind. L.J. 893, 915–19 (2010); Grossman & Friedman, supra note 112, at 72; Elizabeth F. Emens, Changing Name Changing: Framing Rules and the Future of Marital Names, 74 U. Chi. L. Rev. 761 (2007).

a federal district court upheld an unwritten Alabama policy that prohibited married women from obtaining a driver's license under their maiden names.[151] The ruling was affirmed without opinion by the U.S. Supreme Court.[152] Today, despite the absence of formal requirements regarding marital naming, the vast majority of women who marry men adopt their husband's surname or a hyphenated name that includes both surnames. Men rarely adopt their wife's surname upon marriage.[153] Couples may also decide to create a new last name entirely,[154] which most states generally do not permit without going through a legal name-change process.[155] There is less data about naming practices for same-sex couples, as their ability to legally marry is relatively new. Would you expect one spouse to take the other's name, or would you expect another practice?

Naming conventions in which women take their husbands' names upon marriage might seem to be a natural consequence of the common law's treatment of marriage. Coverture treated a husband and wife as having only one legal identity — and that identity was his. The next reading, however, suggests a more complicated relationship between the common law and marital naming practices.

Suzanne A. Kim, Marital Naming/Naming Marriage: Language and Status in Family Law
85 Ind. L.J. 893 (2010)

Until the 1970s and 1980s, American law supported the assumption that women must take their husbands' last names upon marriage. . . . [T]his standard was predicated on a misunderstanding of common law and the confusion of custom for law.

English common law, which all but one American state followed for marital names purposes, traditionally contemplated a fluid approach to names. . . . Common law established that all persons had the right to use and be known for all legal and social purposes by surnames they chose as long as they did not do so for fraudulent purposes. . . .

Although cases on marital names have frequently referred to a married woman's "legal name," the concept of a "legal name" was traditionally irrelevant in common law. . . . Common law allowed a man or woman to change his or her name at will, without a legal proceeding, by simply adopting a new name and becoming known by that name. A woman who acquired her husband's name did so by assumption

---

151. 341 F. Supp. 217 (M.D. Ala. 1971).

152. 405 U.S. 970 (1972).

153. Claudia Goldin & Maria Shim, Making a Name: Women's Surnames at Marriage and Beyond, 18 J. Econ. Persp. 143 (2004); see also Kif Augustine-Adams, The Beginning of Wisdom is to Call Things by Their Right Names, 7 S. Cal. Rev. L. & Women's Stud. 1 (1997).

154. Hannah Haksgaard, Blending Surnames at Marriage, 30 Stan. L. & Pol'y Rev. 307 (2019).

155. Id.

and general use. Name-change statutes, such as those in current existence in many states, are meant to aid the common law right by providing a mechanism for a formal record of a name change, but such records are not generally required for a legally effective name change.

Despite common law's flexible attitude toward naming, the common law principle of coverture could have been interpreted to vitiate any incentive for women to maintain an identity independent of their husbands, thus effectively imposing a requirement for women to assume their husbands' names. . . . The adoption of her husband's name was key to the merger of the wife's identity into the husband's. . . .

The disincentive imposed by coverture to attempt to forge a separate identity from one's husband through name retention evolved into a legal rule in case law originating in the late nineteenth century, which affirmatively stated that women adopted their husbands' last names upon marriage pursuant to common law. . . .

Building on precedent from the late nineteenth and early twentieth centuries, a number of state courts up to the 1970s and 1980s concluded that women adopted their husbands' surnames as a matter of law. . . .

Although the law may formally confer freedom on women to choose what to do with their names, social norms about naming influence the exercise of that choice. . . . Women in studies on marital naming point to the desire to follow tradition as a justification for adopting traditional name practice. . . . Many describe name change as "the thing to do," or "a conventional practice." Others say they "never considered doing anything else." . . .

Studies show that familial and spousal expectations also motivate women's name changes. Some women who change their names do so in compliance with their husbands' wishes. . . . Many women report that their husbands would have viewed their wives' decision not to take their names as a "rejection."

In some cases, men's name preferences for their wives may be related to widely held personal views on names. For example, in their study on college students' attitudes about marital-name practices, sociologists Laurie Scheuble and David Johnson found that males were more likely than females to believe that a woman should take her husband's last name when she marries if her relatives think she should, and to believe that women should always change their last names to that of their husbands. Males were also more likely than females to believe that a man should never change his last name to his wife's. . . .

Studies show that naming practices affect perceptions of women. Women who take their husband's names are perceived as more "communal" than women who either kept their birth names or hyphenated their names. The main stereotypes associated with a woman who maintains her birth name at marriage are "assertiveness," "orientation towards a job," and "urban upbringing." . . .

Men and women generally perceive women with hyphenated names as career oriented and bearing a more androgynous gender role and gender identity.

Conversely, men with hyphenated names are perceived as "highly committed" to the marriage. . . .

The social costs for men taking their wives' names include the perception of being nongender conforming and implicitly "unmasculine." . . .

NOTES AND QUESTIONS

1.   *Naming Procedures and Alternatives.* Upon marriage, a woman can adopt her husband's surname simply by putting it on the marriage certificate and using that document to change the name on identity documents like a driver's license or social security card.[156] What if a man wants to take his wife's surname? Some women choose to use one surname for family purposes and another professionally; this is legal as long as the name is not designed to defraud a creditor or other interested party. For couples seeking to blend — rather than simply hyphenate — their names to make a new last name,[157] state law creates obstacles. Only four states permit surname blending upon marriage; in others, the couple would have to file a name change petition in court.[158]

2.   *Name Changes for Same-Sex Couples.* Before same-sex couples had access to marriage, some sought to assume names that reflected their committed union. In In re Application for Change of Name by Bacharach,[159] the petitioner sought to hyphenate her surname with her partner's. The trial court denied the application out of a concern that the name change would "give the appearance of approval of a same-sex marriage" or concern about fraud on the public about the status of same-sex unions in the jurisdiction.[160] The appellate court reversed, however, deeming it "farfetched and inherently discriminatory" to deny a name change simply because some might be misled about the couple's legal status.[161] The idea of a name change was important to the petitioner in *Bacharach* because, as she said in the trial court hearing, "it will give me a more satisfying feeling that I have cultivated family."[162] Other courts have also permitted name changes based on the lack of fraud or misrepresentation.[163] Why are names considered so

---

156. Id. at 335.

157. Id. at 309.

158. Id.

159. 780 A.2d 579 (N.J. Super. Ct. App. Div. 2001).

160. Id. at 580–81.

161. Id. at 585.

162. Id. For discussion of the public policy implications of name changes in the same-sex marriage context, see In re Miller, 824 A.2d 1207 (Pa. Super Ct. 2003).

163. See, e.g., In re Hunter, 81 Va. Cir. 275 (Va. Cir. Ct. 2011); In re Daniels, 773 N.Y.S.2d 220 (N.Y. Civ. Ct. 2003).

important to family unity? What are some reasons for the gen
in naming practices in different-sex marriages?

3. *Name Change and Discrimination.* Surname changes,
by law, may result in discrimination. In Koren v. Ohio Bell
married a man and changed his last name to his husband's.[164] He alle
discriminated against at work because he asked to be called by his new las.
His name change, he alleged, violated gender norms, with name changing viewed a
"a 'traditionally' feminine practice."[165] The court allowed his sex-stereotyping claim
to proceed to trial.[166]

4. *Name Change upon Divorce.* Upon divorce, parties who changed their
name upon marriage may want to revert back to their former name. States may
allow women to request name restoration as part of the divorce decree, but men
who have changed their names may need to file a name-change petition in a stand-
alone proceeding.[167]

PROBLEM

Malcolm, who is planning to marry Jasmine, wants to change his last name to
Jasmine's last name. But a state statute allows a woman to change her surname on
a marriage certificate but not a man. With the help of a civil rights organization,
Malcolm brings suit against the state. What are his best constitutional arguments?

POSTSCRIPT

This problem is based on an ACLU case brought by a man named Mike Buday, who
filed suit against the State for unlawful discrimination on the basis of sex under
the Fourteenth Amendment. The case eventually settled but prompted the enactment of the California Name Equality Act of 2007.[168] The Act grants the parties in
a marriage the specific right to choose the name that each party will be referred to
after the marriage. Each party to the marriage may adopt any of the following last
names: (1) the current last name of the other spouse; (2) the last name of either

---

164. 894 F. Supp. 2d 1032 (N.D. Ohio 2012).

165. Id. at 1038.

166. Id. at 1039.

167. See, e.g., Mich. Comp. Laws Ann. § 552.391 (West 2020). For discussion of gender-differentiated
approach, see Tim Cordes, Four Years After *Obergefell*, and Michigan's Laws Are Still in Disarray, Mich.
B.J., Dec. 2019, at 14, 16.

168. Carla Hall, Take Your Wife's Name? That'll Cost You — so ACLU Steps In, L.A. Times (Dec. 15,
2006); see also Name Equality Act, 2007 Cal Stats. ch. 567.

pouse given at birth; (3) a name combining into a single last name all or a segment of the current last name or the last name of either spouse given at birth; or (4) a combination of last names.

IV. Healthcare Decision-Making

Marriage does not automatically confer the ability to make medical decisions for one's spouse. Legal disputes arise most often in the context of reproductive decisions and when one spouse becomes incapacitated and unable to make his or her own medical decisions.

A. Reproductive Decision-Making and Spousal Notification

PLANNED PARENTHOOD OF SOUTHEASTERN PENNSYLVANIA V. CASEY
505 U.S. 833 (1992)

JUSTICE O'CONNOR, JUSTICE KENNEDY, and JUSTICE SOUTER announced the judgment of the Court and delivered the opinion of the Court with respect to Parts I, II, III, V–A, V–C, and VI, an opinion with respect to Part V–E, in which JUSTICE STEVENS joins, and an opinion with respect to Parts IV, V–B, and V–D. . . .

I . . .

It must be stated at the outset and with clarity that *Roe*'s essential holding [Roe v. Wade, 410 U.S. 113 (1973)[169]], the holding we reaffirm, has three parts. First is a recognition of the right of the woman to choose to have an abortion before viability and to obtain it without undue interference from the State. Before viability, the State's interests are not strong enough to support a prohibition of abortion or the imposition of a substantial obstacle to the woman's effective right to elect the procedure. Second is a confirmation of the State's power to restrict abortions after fetal viability, if the law contains exceptions for pregnancies which endanger the woman's life or health. And third is the principle that the State has legitimate interests from the outset of the pregnancy in protecting the health of the woman and the life of the fetus that may become a child. These principles do not contradict one another; and we adhere to each.

---

169. *Roe* is excerpted in Chapter 9.

II

Constitutional protection of the woman's decision to terminate her pregnancy derives from the Due Process Clause of the Fourteenth Amendment. . . .

Our law affords constitutional protection to personal decisions relating to marriage, procreation, contraception, family relationships, child rearing, and education. . . . These matters, involving the most intimate and personal choices a person may make in a lifetime, choices central to personal dignity and autonomy, are central to the liberty protected by the Fourteenth Amendment. At the heart of liberty is the right to define one's own concept of existence, of meaning, of the universe, and of the mystery of human life. Beliefs about these matters could not define the attributes of personhood were they formed under compulsion of the State. . . .

V . . .

C

Section 3209 of Pennsylvania's abortion law provides, except in cases of medical emergency, that no physician shall perform an abortion on a married woman without receiving a signed statement from the woman that she has notified her spouse that she is about to undergo an abortion. The woman has the option of providing an alternative signed statement certifying that her husband is not the man who impregnated her; that her husband could not be located; that the pregnancy is the result of spousal sexual assault which she has reported; or that the woman believes that notifying her husband will cause him or someone else to inflict bodily injury upon her. A physician who performs an abortion on a married woman without receiving the appropriate signed statement will have his or her license revoked, and is liable to the husband for damages.

The District Court heard the testimony of numerous expert witnesses, and made detailed findings of fact regarding the effect of this statute. These included:

273. The vast majority of women consult their husbands prior to deciding to terminate their pregnancy. . . .

279. The "bodily injury" exception could not be invoked by a married woman whose husband, if notified, would, in her reasonable belief, threaten to (a) publicize her intent to have an abortion to family, friends or acquaintances; (b) retaliate against her in future child custody or divorce proceedings; (c) inflict psychological intimidation or emotional harm upon her, her children or other persons; (d) inflict bodily harm on other persons such as children, family members or other loved ones; or (e) use his control over finances to deprive of necessary monies for herself or her children. . . .

282. A wife may not elect to notify her husband of her intention to have an abortion for a variety of reasons, including the husband's illness, concern

about her own health, the imminent failure of the marriage, or the husband's absolute opposition to the abortion. . . .

286. Married women, victims of battering, have been killed in Pennsylvania and throughout the United States. . . .

287. Battering can often involve a substantial amount of sexual abuse, including marital rape and sexual mutilation. . . .

288. In a domestic abuse situation, it is common for the battering husband to also abuse the children in an attempt to coerce the wife. . . .

289. Mere notification of pregnancy is frequently a flashpoint for battering and violence within the family. The number of battering incidents is high during the pregnancy and often the worst abuse can be associated with pregnancy. . . . The battering husband may deny parentage and use the pregnancy as an excuse for abuse. . . .

290. Secrecy typically shrouds abusive families. Family members are instructed not to tell anyone, especially police or doctors, about the abuse and violence. Battering husbands often threaten their wives or her children with further abuse if she tells an outsider of the violence and tells her that nobody will believe her. A battered woman, therefore, is highly unlikely to disclose the violence against her for fear of retaliation by the abuser. . . .

294. A woman in a shelter or a safe house unknown to her husband is not "reasonably likely" to have bodily harm inflicted upon her by her batterer, however her attempt to notify her husband pursuant to section 3209 could accidentally disclose her whereabouts to her husband. Her fear of future ramifications would be realistic under the circumstances.

296. It is common for battered women to have sexual intercourse with their husbands to avoid being battered. While this type of coercive sexual activity would be spousal sexual assault as defined by the Act, many women may not consider it to be so and others would fear disbelief. . . .

297. The marital rape exception to section 3209 cannot be claimed by women who are victims of coercive sexual behavior other than penetration. The 90–day reporting requirement of the spousal sexual assault statute, further narrows the class of sexually abused wives who can claim the exception, since many of these women may be psychologically unable to discuss or report the rape for several years after the incident. . . .

298. Because of the nature of the battering relationship, battered women are unlikely to avail themselves of the exceptions to section 3209 of the Act, regardless of whether the section applies to them.

These findings are supported by studies of domestic violence. The American Medical Association (AMA) has published a summary of the recent research in this field, which indicates that in an average 12–month period in this country, approximately two million women are the victims of severe assaults by their male partners.

In a 1985 survey, women reported that nearly one of every eight husbands had assaulted their wives during the past year. The AMA views these figures as "marked underestimates," because the nature of these incidents discourages women from reporting them, and because surveys typically exclude the very poor, those who do not speak English well, and women who are homeless or in institutions or hospitals when the survey is conducted. According to the AMA, "[r]esearchers on family violence agree that the true incidence of partner violence is probably *double* the above estimates; or four million severely assaulted women per year. Studies on prevalence suggest that from one-fifth to one-third of all women will be physically assaulted by a partner or ex-partner during their lifetime." Thus on an average day in the United States, nearly 11,000 women are severely assaulted by their male partners. Many of these incidents involve sexual assault. . . . In families where wifebeating takes place, moreover, child abuse is often present as well.

Other studies fill in the rest of this troubling picture. Physical violence is only the most visible form of abuse. Psychological abuse, particularly forced social and economic isolation of women, is also common. Many victims of domestic violence remain with their abusers, perhaps because they perceive no superior alternative. Many abused women who find temporary refuge in shelters return to their husbands, in large part because they have no other source of income. Returning to one's abuser can be dangerous. Recent Federal Bureau of Investigation statistics disclose that 8.8 percent of all homicide victims in the United States are killed by their spouses. . . . Thirty percent of female homicide victims are killed by their male partners. . . .

The vast majority of women notify their male partners of their decision to obtain an abortion. In many cases in which married women do not notify their husbands, the pregnancy is the result of an extramarital affair. Where the husband is the father, the primary reason women do not notify their husbands is that the husband and wife are experiencing marital difficulties, often accompanied by incidents of violence.

This information and the District Court's findings reinforce what common sense would suggest. In well-functioning marriages, spouses discuss important intimate decisions such as whether to bear a child. But there are millions of women in this country who are the victims of regular physical and psychological abuse at the hands of their husbands. Should these women become pregnant, they may have very good reasons for not wishing to inform their husbands of their decision to obtain an abortion. Many may have justifiable fears of physical abuse, but may be no less fearful of the consequences of reporting prior abuse to the Commonwealth of Pennsylvania. Many may have a reasonable fear that notifying their husbands will provoke further instances of child abuse; these women are not exempt from § 3209's notification requirement. Many may fear devastating forms of psychological abuse from their husbands, including verbal harassment, threats of future violence, the destruction of possessions, physical confinement to the home, the withdrawal of financial support, or the disclosure of the abortion to family and friends. These methods of psychological abuse may act as even more of a deterrent to notification than the possibility of physical violence, but women who are the victims of the abuse are not exempt from § 3209's notification requirement. And many women who are pregnant as a result of sexual assaults by their husbands will be unable to avail themselves of the exception for spousal sexual assault, § 3209(b)(3), because the exception requires that the woman have notified law enforcement authorities within 90 days of the assault, and her husband will be notified of her report once an investigation begins, § 3128(c). If anything in this field is certain, it is that victims of spousal sexual assault are extremely reluctant to report the abuse to the government; hence, a great many spousal rape victims will not be exempt from the notification requirement imposed by § 3209.

The spousal notification requirement is thus likely to prevent a significant number of women from obtaining an abortion. It does not merely make abortions a little more difficult or expensive to obtain; for many women, it will impose a substantial obstacle. We must not blind ourselves to the fact that the significant number of women who fear for their safety and the safety of their children are likely to be deterred from procuring an abortion as surely as if the Commonwealth had outlawed abortion in all cases.

Respondents attempt to avoid the conclusion that § 3209 is invalid by pointing out that it imposes almost no burden at all for the vast majority of women seeking abortions. . . . [R]espondents argue [that] the effects of § 3209 are felt by only one percent of the women who obtain abortions. . . . For this reason, it is asserted, the statute cannot be invalid on its face. . . .

The analysis does not end with the one percent of women upon whom the statute operates; it begins there. Legislation is measured for consistency with the Constitution by its impact on those whose conduct it affects. . . . The proper focus of constitutional inquiry is the group for whom the law is a restriction, not the group for whom the law is irrelevant. . . .

The unfortunate yet persisting conditions we document above will mean that in a large fraction of the cases in which § 3209 is relevant, it will operate as a substantial obstacle to a woman's choice to undergo an abortion. It is an undue burden, and therefore invalid.

This conclusion is in no way inconsistent with our decisions upholding parental notification or consent requirements. Those enactments, and our judgment that they are constitutional, are based on the quite reasonable assumption that minors will benefit from consultation with their parents and that children will often not realize that their parents have their best interests at heart. We cannot adopt a parallel assumption about adult women.

We recognize that a husband has a "deep and proper concern and interest . . . in his wife's pregnancy and in the growth and development of the fetus she is carrying." With regard to the children he has fathered and raised, the Court has recognized his "cognizable and substantial" interest in their custody. If these cases concerned a State's ability to require the mother to notify the father before taking some action with respect to a living child raised by both, therefore, it would be reasonable to conclude as a general matter that the father's interest in the welfare of the child and the mother's interest are equal.

Before birth, however, the issue takes on a very different cast. It is an inescapable biological fact that state regulation with respect to the child a woman is carrying will have a far greater impact on the mother's liberty than on the father's. . . . "[T]he marital couple is not an independent entity with a mind and heart of its own, but an association of two individuals each with a separate intellectual and emotional makeup. If the right of privacy means anything, it is the right of the *individual*, married or single, to be free from unwarranted governmental intrusion into matters so fundamentally affecting a person as the decision whether to bear or beget a child." The Constitution protects individuals, men and women alike, from unjustified state interference, even when that interference is enacted into law for the benefit of their spouses.

There was a time, not so long ago, when a different understanding of the family and of the Constitution prevailed. In *Bradwell v. State*, three Members of this Court reaffirmed the common-law principle that "a woman had no legal existence separate from her husband, who was regarded as her head and representative in the social state; and, notwithstanding some recent modifications of this civil status, many of the special rules of law flowing from and dependent upon this cardinal principle still exist in full force in most States." Only one generation has passed since this Court observed that "woman is still regarded as the center of home and family life," with attendant "special responsibilities" that precluded full and independent legal status under the Constitution. These views, of course, are no longer consistent with our understanding of the family, the individual, or the Constitution.

In keeping with our rejection of the common-law understanding of a woman's role within the family, the Court held in *Planned Parenthood of Mo. v. Danforth*, 428 U.S. 52 (1976), that the Constitution does not permit a State to require a married woman to obtain her husband's consent before undergoing an abortion. The principles that guided the Court in *Danforth* should be our guides today. For the great many women who are victims of abuse inflicted by their husbands, or whose children are the victims of such abuse, a spousal notice requirement enables the husband to wield an effective veto over his wife's decision. Whether the prospect of notification itself deters such women from seeking abortions, or whether the husband, through physical force or psychological pressure or economic coercion, prevents his wife from obtaining an abortion until it is too late, the notice requirement will often be tantamount to the veto found unconstitutional in *Danforth*. The women most affected by this law — those who most reasonably fear the consequences of notifying their husbands that they are pregnant — are in the gravest danger. . . .

Section 3209 embodies a view of marriage consonant with the common-law status of married women but repugnant to our present understanding of marriage and of the nature of the rights secured by the Constitution. Women do not lose their constitutionally protected liberty when they marry. The Constitution protects all individuals, male or female, married or unmarried, from the abuse of governmental power, even where that power is employed for the supposed benefit of a member of the individual's family. These considerations confirm our conclusion that § 3209 is invalid. . . .

CHIEF JUSTICE REHNQUIST, with whom JUSTICE WHITE, JUSTICE SCALIA, and JUSTICE THOMAS join, concurring in the judgment in part and dissenting in part.

The joint opinion . . . retains the outer shell of *Roe v. Wade,* but beats a wholesale retreat from the substance of that case. We believe that *Roe* was wrongly decided, and that it can and should be overruled consistently with our traditional approach to *stare decisis* in constitutional cases. We would . . . uphold the challenged provisions of the Pennsylvania statute in their entirety. . . .

II . . .

C . . .

Pennsylvania has not imposed a spousal *consent* requirement of the type the Court struck down in *Planned Parenthood of Central Mo. v. Danforth.* Missouri's spousal consent provision was invalidated in that case because of the Court's view that it unconstitutionally granted to the husband "a veto power exercisable for any reason whatsoever or for no reason at all." But the provision here involves a much less intrusive requirement of spousal *notification,* not consent. Such a law requiring only notice to the husband "does not give any third party the legal right to make the [woman's] decision for her, or to prevent her from obtaining an abortion should she choose to have one performed." *Danforth* thus does not control our analysis. Petitioners contend that it should, however; they argue that the real effect of such a notice requirement is to give the power to husbands to veto a woman's abortion choice. The District Court indeed found that the notification provision created a risk that some woman who would otherwise have an abortion will be prevented from having one. For example, petitioners argue, many notified husbands will prevent abortions through physical force, psychological coercion, and other types of threats. But Pennsylvania has incorporated exceptions in the notice provision in an attempt to deal with these problems. For instance, a woman need not notify her husband if the pregnancy is the result of a reported sexual assault, or if she has reason to believe that she would suffer bodily injury as a result of the notification. Furthermore, because this is a facial challenge to the Act, it is insufficient for petitioners to show that the notification provision "might operate unconstitutionally under some conceivable set of circumstances." Thus, it is not enough for petitioners to show that, in some "worst case" circumstances, the notice provision will operate as a grant of veto power to husbands. Because they are making a facial challenge to the provision, they must "show that no set of circumstances exists under which the [provision] would be valid." This they have failed to do.

The question before us is therefore whether the spousal notification requirement rationally furthers any legitimate state interests. We conclude that it does. First, a husband's interests in procreation within marriage and in the potential life of his unborn child are certainly substantial ones. The State itself has legitimate interests both in protecting these interests of the father and in protecting the potential life of the fetus, and the spousal notification requirement is reasonably related to advancing those state interests. By providing that a husband will usually know of his spouse's intent to have an abortion, the provision makes it more likely that the husband will participate in deciding the fate of his unborn child, a possibility that might otherwise have been denied him. This participation might in some cases result in a decision to proceed with the pregnancy. As Judge Alito observed in his dissent below, "[t]he Pennsylvania legislature could have rationally believed that some married women are initially inclined to obtain an abortion without their husbands' knowledge because of perceived problems — such as economic constraints, future plans, or the husbands' previously expressed opposition — that may be obviated by discussion prior to the abortion."

The State also has a legitimate interest in promoting "the integrity of the marital relationship." . . . [T]he spousal notice requirement is a rational attempt by the State to improve truthful communication between spouses and encourage collaborative decisionmaking, and thereby fosters marital integrity. . . . The spousal notice provision will admittedly be unnecessary in some circumstances, and possibly harmful in others, but "the existence of particular cases in which a feature of a statute performs no function (or is even counter-productive) ordinarily does not render the statute unconstitutional or even constitutionally suspect." The Pennsylvania Legislature was in a position to weigh the likely benefits of the provision against its likely adverse effects, and presumably concluded, on balance, that the provision would be beneficial. Whether this was a wise decision or not, we cannot say that it was irrational. We therefore conclude that the spousal notice provision comports with the Constitution. . . .

NOTES AND QUESTIONS

---

1. *Spousal Consent and Notification.* The Court held in Planned Parenthood v. Danforth that the Constitution does not permit a state to require a married woman to obtain her husband's consent before undergoing an abortion.[170] Does

---

170. 428 U.S. 52 (1976).

the notification requirement present the same problems? What interest does a man have in knowing about or having control over his spouse's decision to terminate a pregnancy?

2. *Married and Unmarried Women.* Why does the state statute only require married women to notify their husbands and not unmarried women to notify their sexual partners? What assumptions about marital and non-marital relationships are built into this approach?

B. Decision-Making for Incapacitated Adults

In the event that an adult becomes unable to make decisions about their care, legal presumptions give that power to others, who can then legally act as surrogate decisionmakers. State statutes generally give first priority to an individual's spouse, followed by adult children, parents, siblings, and other relatives.[171] For unmarried people, some statutes will give first priority to non-marital partners—those in domestic partnerships,[172] civil unions,[173] or spouse-like relationships.[174] If there is no partner or qualifying relative, some states may give authority to a close friend.[175] These presumptions would apply in the absence of written instructions from the patient designating someone else, such as through an advance medical directive, living will, or health care proxy,[176] or the adjudication by a court of a guardian or conservator.[177] In the following case, who should make medical decisions for an incapacitated man—his parents or his same-sex partner?[178]

In re Guardianship of Atkins
868 N.E.2d 878 (Ind. Ct. App. 2007)

BAKER, CHIEF JUDGE. . . .

Patrick and Brett met and became romantically involved beginning in 1978 when they attended Wabash College together. Since that time—for twenty-five

---

171. Am. Bar Ass'n, Default Surrogate Consent Statutes (Sept. 2019).

172. See, e.g., Cal. Health & Safety Code § 24178 (West 2020).

173. See, e.g., N.H. Rev. Stat. Ann. § 137-J:34 to J:37 (2020).

174. See, e.g., N.M. Stat. Ann. § 24-7A-5 (2020).

175. See, e.g., Wis. Stat. Ann. § 50.06 (West 2020); Wyo. Stat. §35-22-406 (2020).

176. See, e.g., W. Va. Code § 16-30-4 (2019); N.Y. Pub. Health Law § 2981 (Consol. 2020); Colo. Rev. Stat. § 15-18.7-110 (2020).

177. See, e.g., Idaho Code Ann. § 15-5-312(1)(c) (West 2020); Haw. Rev. Stat. § 560:5-314(a) (2020).

178. For overview of state statutes pertaining to guardianship, see ABA Comm'n on Law & Aging, Adult Guardianship Statutory Table of Authorities (July 2019).

years—the men have lived together and have been in a committed and loving relationship.

Patrick's family vehemently disapproves of his relationship with Brett. Patrick, however, was able to reconcile his religious faith with his homosexuality and in 2000, Patrick wrote a letter to his family, begging them to accept him and welcome Brett:

> I want you all to know that Brett is my best friend in the whole world and I love him more than life itself. I beg all of you to reach out to him with the same love you have for me, he is extremely special and once you know him you will understand why I love him so much. Trust me, God loves us all so very much, and I know he approves of the love that Brett and I have shared for over 20 years.

Patrick's family, however, has steadfastly refused to accept their son's lifestyle. Jeanne believes that homosexuality is a grievous sin and that Brett and his relatives are "sinners" and are "evil" for accepting Brett and Patrick's relationship. She testified that no amount of evidence could convince her that Patrick and Brett were happy together or that they had a positive and beneficial relationship.

Neither Patrick nor Brett earned a degree from Wabash College. In 1982, Patrick began working for the family business, Atkins, Inc. d/b/a Atkins Elegant Desserts and Atkins Cheesecake, and he ultimately became the CEO of that business. . . . Brett is a waiter, has been working for Puccini's restaurants for the past ten years. . . . Patrick and Brett pooled their earnings, depositing them into a checking account that was titled solely in Patrick's name but was used as a joint account for payment of living expenses. They used some of their accumulated savings to make extra mortgage payments and periodically transferred the remaining savings into a Charles Schwab account that was titled solely in Patrick's name.

Between 1980 and 1992, Brett and Patrick lived together in various apartments. In 1992, they bought a house together in Fishers as joint tenants, and the home is still titled jointly.

On March 11, 2005, Patrick was on a business trip in Atlanta when he collapsed and was admitted to a hospital. Doctors determined that he had suffered a ruptured aneurysm and an acute subarachnoid hemorrhage. Patrick remained in the Intensive Care Unit (ICU) of the Atlanta hospital for six weeks. At some point during his stay in the ICU, Patrick suffered a stroke.

Brett traveled to the Atlanta hospital to be with Patrick; Patrick's family did as well. Patrick's brother testified that Brett's mere presence in the hospital was "hurting" Jeanne and offending her religious beliefs. Jeanne told Brett that if Patrick was going to return to his life with Brett after recovering from the stroke, she would prefer that he not recover at all.

Shortly after Brett's first visit with Patrick in the ICU, Patrick's family restricted the times and duration of Brett's visits. Subsequently, Brett was allowed to see Patrick for only fifteen minutes at a time after the close of regular visiting hours so that Patrick's family would not have to see Brett at all. Eventually, a sign was placed in Patrick's ICU space reading "immediate family and clergy only," purporting to exclude Brett altogether. Nevertheless, hospital staff defied the family's instructions and allowed Brett to continue to visit with Patrick early in the morning and in the evenings, outside of regular visiting hours.

On April 27, 2005, Patrick was moved from the Atlanta hospital to . . . Summer Trace, a nursing facility in Carmel. In May and June 2005, Brett visited Patrick daily at Summer Trace, with his visits usually taking place after regular visiting hours so that Patrick's relatives would not see him. Brett was well-received by the Summer Trace staff, who observed that his visits had a positive impact on Patrick's recovery.

On June 20, 2005, Brett filed a guardianship petition, requesting that he be appointed guardian of Patrick's person and property. The Atkinses filed an answer to the petition, a motion to intervene, and a cross-petition requesting that they be appointed co-guardians of Patrick's person and property. Brett eventually voluntarily withdrew his request to be appointed guardian of Patrick's property, seeking only to be named as guardian of Patrick's person.

In mid-August 2005, Patrick was admitted to Zionsville Meadows, another nursing facility, for physical rehabilitation and speech therapy. Brett continued to visit Patrick after regular visiting hours. . . . [I]n early November 2005, the Atkinses moved Patrick into their home and have refused to allow Brett to visit with Patrick since that time. The Atkinses have refused phone calls from Brett and requests from Brett and his family members to visit Patrick.

At the time of trial, Patrick was able to walk, dress, bathe, and feed himself with some supervision or prompting, to read printed matter aloud with good accuracy but only 25% comprehension, to engage in simple conversations, to communicate his basic wants and needs, and to answer questions with some prompting. He still required close and constant supervision and had significant problems with short-term memory, attention span, problem-solving, multi-step commands, reacting in urgent situations, and decision-making. The Atkinses took turns supervising or caring for Patrick in their Carmel home and were assisted by a certified home health aide. . . .

On January 11, 2006, Brett filed a petition for an order requiring the Atkinses to allow him to visit and have contact with Patrick. . . .

On May 10, 2006, the trial court entered two orders, making very limited findings of fact and disposing of the case by:

- Appointing the Atkinses as co-guardians of Patrick's person and estate;
- Denying Brett's visitation petition and ordering that "it is and shall be the ultimate and sole responsibility of [the Atkinses] to determine and control visitation with and access of visitors to Patrick Atkins in his best interest"; . . .

Brett now appeals. . . .

I. Guardianship

Brett first argues that the trial court erroneously appointed the Atkinses as Patrick's guardian. A guardianship action is initiated by filing a petition seeking appointment to serve as guardian of an incapacitated person. The guardianship statutes provide that the following are entitled to consideration for appointment as a guardian . . . in the order listed:

(1) a person designated in a durable power of attorney;

(2) the spouse of an incapacitated person;

(3) an adult child of an incapacitated person;

(4) a parent of an incapacitated person, or a person nominated by will of a deceased parent of an incapacitated person . . . ;

(5) any person related to an incapacitated person by blood or marriage with whom the incapacitated person has resided for more than six (6) months before the filing of the petition;

(6) a person nominated by the incapacitated person who is caring for or paying for the care of the incapacitated person.

With respect to persons having equal priority, however, "the court shall select the person it considers best qualified to serve as guardian." Additionally, the trial court is authorized to "pass over a person having priority and appoint a person having a lower priority or no priority" if the trial court believes that action to be in the incapacitated person's best interest. The trial court's paramount consideration in making its determination of the person to be appointed guardian is "the best interest of the incapacitated person."

Patrick did not designate Brett for guardianship consideration in a durable power of attorney. Therefore, only if the trial court concluded that it was in Patrick's best interest that Brett be appointed his guardian would his appointment have been proper. Brett makes a sincere and compelling argument that, based on his long-term relationship with Patrick and his heartfelt desire to take care of his life partner, "Patrick's best interest will be served by appointing Brett as guardian over Patrick's person." Under these circumstances, however, our standard of review does not permit us to conduct a de novo analysis of what is in Patrick's best interest. Instead, we must assess whether the trial court abused its discretion when it found that it was in Patrick's best interest that the Atkinses be appointed co-guardians of his person and estate.

The evidence presented established that the Atkinses' home was appropriate for Patrick's care. . . . The Atkinses were committed to providing Patrick with the best possible care by applying their own personal efforts, employing outside assistance, and pursuing potentially helpful therapies.

We conclude that there is sufficient evidence in the record supporting a conclusion that the Atkinses and Brett are equally well-equipped to care for Patrick's physical needs. Given the Atkinses' lack of support of their son's personal life through the years and given his mother's astonishing statement that she would rather that he *never recover* than see him return to his relationship with Brett, we are extraordinarily skeptical that the Atkinses are able to take care of Patrick's emotional needs. But we cannot conclude that the record shows that the trial court abused its discretion in denying Brett's guardianship petition. . . .

NOTES AND QUESTIONS

---

1. *Best Interests Standard.* The appellate court was "extraordinarily skeptical . . . that the Atkinses are able to take care of Patrick's emotional needs." Why, then, did they affirm the trial court's guardianship decision? How did the trial court make its decision in reference to the guardianship statute's list of priority individuals? What standard did the court use in applying the statute? How does this standard compare to what you might expect in a child custody decision?

2. *Same-Sex Couples and Guardianship.* *Atkins* was not the first case of its kind. The landmark case of In re Guardianship of Kowalski was the culmination of a decade-long battle by Karen Thompson, during which she repeatedly sought guardianship of her partner, Sharon Kowalksi, who had sustained a traumatic brain injury when she was hit in a car accident by a drunk driver.[179]

> Sharon was 27-years-old when the car accident left her severely disabled. . . . Sharon had been living for four years with her partner Karen, who was a teacher of physical education and a coach at St. Cloud State University. . . . The two women had exchanged rings and named each other as beneficiaries of their life insurance policies. Sharon's parents and siblings were not aware of the women's intimate relationship.
>
> The aftermath of the accident reveals the depths of the prejudice that gays and lesbians traditionally faced in their daily lives. . . . Upon learning of her partner's accident, Karen rushed to the hospital to discover Sharon's fate. . . . Because she was not a "family" member, Karen was prevented from knowing whether her beloved partner was living or dying. . . .
>
> Preceding the accident, relations between Karen and her partner's parents had been cordial. Afterwards, however, hostility soon developed because of Karen's devotion to her partner. Sharon's family members became increasingly suspicious and resentful of Karen's frequent hospital visits. Based on a

---

179. 478 N.W.2d 790, 797 (Minn. Ct. App. 1991).

psychologist's advice, Karen finally disclosed the nature of the women's intimate relationship to the Kowalskis.

The family responded with disbelief and horror. They immediately limited Karen's visitation. Animosity escalated as Karen disagreed with the Kowalskis about Sharon's medical treatment. Karen advocated aggressive treatment in a rehabilitation facility with state-of-the-art brain injury services. Instead, Sharon's parents placed her in a nursing home where Sharon vegetated. She was refused access to an electric wheelchair, typewriter, or computer to enable her to type short sentences; confined to a bed; refused visitation by friends; and denied competency testing. Impelled by intense concern about the quality of the medical care received by her partner, Karen instituted the first of three legal challenges that would consume her life for almost a decade.[180]

Karen Thompson was finally appointed as Sharon Kowalksi's guardian after her suitability was deemed "overwhelmingly clear."[181] While spouses are given priority under guardianship laws, Professor Nancy Polikoff has argued that cases like Karen Thompson's highlight the need for law that "values all families," not just marital ones.[182] Do you agree? Why might someone object to such an approach?

3. *Treatment Disputes.* What if close relatives disagree with the decision-maker about whether to continue life-sustaining treatment? This was the issue in the famous case involving Terry Schiavo, a woman who had been in a permanent vegetative state and whose parents and husband disagreed on whether to have her feeding tube removed.[183] After a trial, Florida granted the husband's petition to have the feeding tube removed. Her parents then pursued various appeals unsuccessfully, sought intervention from then-Florida Governor Jeb Bush, the Florida state legislature, and Congress. Terry Schiavo died four years after the original order to remove the feeding tube, based on her husband's decision as her proxy.[184]

---

180. D. Kelly Weisberg, Karen Thompson's Role in the Movement for Marriage Equality, 25 Hastings Women's L.J. 3, 3–4 (2014).

181. Kowalski, 478 N.W.2d at 797.

182. Nancy D. Polikoff, Law That Values All Families: Beyond (Straight and Gay) Marriage, 22 J. Am. Acad. Matrimonial Law. 85 (2009); see also Nancy D. Polikoff, Beyond (Gay and Straight) Marriage (2009).

183. In re Schiavo, No. 90-2908GD-003, 2000 WL 34546715 (Fla. Cir. Ct. Feb. 11, 2000); see Maura A. Flood, Treatment of the "Vegetative" Patient: The Legacies of Karen Quinlan, Nancy Cruzan and Terri Schiavo, 1 J. Health & Biomedical L. 1, 27–29 (2005).

184. In re Schiavo, 780 So. 2d 176, 180 (Fla. Dist. Ct. App. 2001) (affirming the Schiavo Original 2000 Order), review denied sub nom. Schindler v. Schiavo ex. rel. Schiavo, 789 So. 2d 348 (Fla. 2001). For discussion of the controversy, see Lois Shepherd, Terri Schiavo: Unsettling the Settled, 37 Loy. U. Chi. L.J. 297, 306–12 (2006).

V. Violence

The concept of marital privacy historically influenced legal approaches to violence within marriage.[185] Until the 1960s and 1970s, marital privacy served to cloak domestic violence from legal scrutiny. As Professor Reva Siegel explains:

> The Anglo-American common law originally provided that a husband, as master of his household, could subject his wife to corporal punishment or "chastisement" so long as he did not inflict permanent injury upon her. During the nineteenth century, an era of feminist agitation for reform of marriage law, authorities in England and the United States declared that a husband no longer had the right to chastise his wife. Yet, for a century after courts repudiated the right of chastisement, the American legal system continued to treat wife beating differently from other cases of assault and battery. While authorities denied that a husband had the right to beat his wife, they intervened only intermittently in cases of marital violence: Men who assaulted their wives were often granted formal and informal immunities from prosecution, in order to protect the privacy of the family and to promote "domestic harmony."[186]

Eventually, as Siegel observes, "In the late 1970s, the feminist movement began to challenge the concept of family privacy that shielded wife abuse, and since then, it has secured many reforms designed to protect women from marital violence."[187] Concerns about domestic violence arose not only within but outside of marriage. As Professor Sally Goldfarb explains:

> Women's rights advocates campaigned against domestic violence beginning in the nineteenth century, but it was not until the second wave of the feminist movement gave rise to the battered women's movement of the 1970s that their efforts brought about what one scholar has called "the domestic violence revolution." Feminists organized to break the silence on domestic violence, provide services and support to its victims, and define battering within a larger framework of gender subordination.[188]

Eventually, states reformed civil and criminal laws to better address intimate partner violence. Until this time, "[n]o term for intimate abuse existed in the

---

185. A husband's common law rights included the ability to "chastise" his wife. See, e.g., Bradley v. State, 1 Miss. (1 Walker) 156, 157 (1824) (husband may "use salutary restraints in every case of [his wife's] misbehaviour, without being subjected to vexatious prosecutions, resulting in the mutual discredit and shame of all parties concerned"); State v. Black, 60 N.C. (1 Win.) 262 (1864) (husband may "use towards his wife such a degree of force as is necessary to control an unruly temper and make her behave herself").

186. Reva B. Siegel, "The Rule of Love": Wife Beating as Prerogative and Privacy, 105 Yale L.J. 2117, 2118 (1994).

187. Id.

188. Sally F. Goldfarb, Reconceiving Civil Protection Orders for Domestic Violence: Can Law Help End the Abuse Without Ending the Relationship?, 29 Cardozo L. Rev. 1487, 1496 (2008).

national lexicon; virtually no shelters or safe houses devoted to battered women had been established; no civil laws had been enacted to deal with the emergency aftermath of an abusive incident; and the government had a long track record of ignoring the problem or even protecting perpetrators."[189] As discussed below, both the civil and criminal justice system provide mechanisms for addressing domestic violence, which occurs in marital and non-marital relationships.

Intimate partner violence persists, despite this growing awareness and legal response. In the United States, one in four women and one in seven men will experience violence from an intimate partner in their lifetime.[190] It affects both different-sex and same-sex relationships.[191] In 2010, the rate of intimate partner violence for married women was about 4 times lower than for women who had never married, about 3 times lower than for divorced or widowed females, and about 30 times lower than for separated females.[192] Intimate partner violence includes physical, emotional, and financial abuse.

Sexual violence is a distinct form of intimate partner violence. Again, marital privacy traditionally shielded such violence from legal scrutiny. Professor Jill Hasday explains, "At common law, husbands were exempt from prosecution for raping their wives."[193] While the law has been modified in ways that protect individuals who are raped by their spouses, "[a] majority of states still retain some form of the common law regime: They criminalize a narrower range of offenses if committed within marriage, subject the marital rape they do recognize to less serious sanctions, and/or create special procedural hurdles for marital rape prosecutions."[194] With sexual violence, then, unmarried women have been regarded as more legitimate subjects of legal protection than married women. What is the vision of marriage embodied by the legal treatment of marital rape? Hasday argues that there is a "cultural aversion to envisioning marriage (and marital intercourse in particular) as a potential site of disharmony, antagonism, and danger."[195] What arguments would be made to defend the differential treatment of marital rape? Instead of sex-based

---

189. Deborah Epstein, Procedural Justice: Tempering the State's Response to Domestic Violence, 43 Wm. & Mary L. Rev. 1843, 1845 (2002).

190. Michele C. Black et al., Nat'l Ctr. for Injury Prevention and Control, The National Intimate Partner and Sexual Violence Survey (NISVS): 2010 Summary Report 2 (2011).

191. See Luca Rollé et al., When Intimate Partner Violence Meets Same Sex Couples: A Review of Same Sex Intimate Partner Violence, 9 Frontiers in Psychol. 50 (2018).

192. Shannan Catalano, Intimate Partner Violence 1993-2010 2 (U.S Dep't of Justice Nov. 2012).

193. Jill Elaine Hasday, Contest and Consent: A Legal History of Marital Rape, 88 Calif. L. Rev. 1373, 1375 (2000).

194. Id.; see also Teresa M. Garvey et al., Charging Considerations in the Prosecution of Marital Rape, 34 AEquitas Strategies in Brief 2 (2019). For example, Minnesota maintained a "voluntary relationship defense" that reduced the severity of the crime when a husband sexually assaulted his wife. The defense was removed by statute only in 2019. See Minn. Stat. § 609.349, repealed by 2019 Minn. H.F. No. 15.

195. Hasday, supra note 94, at 1486.

arguments that reflect the legacy of coverture, contemporary arguments "speak about protecting the privacy of the marital relationship that husband and wife share," and "facilitat[ing] marital reconciliation."[196] Are such arguments persuasive?

We now consider legal approaches to domestic violence. Be advised that the following materials include descriptions of domestic violence and sexual assault.

A. Civil Protection Orders

All fifty states have passed laws providing for civil protection orders (often also called "restraining orders" or "orders of protection") to protect against domestic violence,[197] which may be issued ex parte on a temporary basis and permanently after a hearing.[198] Courts have broad discretion to award other relief, including stay-away orders, child custody and visitation orders, and restrictions on possession of firearms.[199] In the following case, the respondent, Jessica Gonzalez, who had obtained a restraining order against her estranged husband, asserted a constitutional right to have the order enforced.

TOWN OF CASTLE ROCK V. GONZALES
545 U.S. 748 (2005)

JUSTICE SCALIA delivered the opinion of the Court.

We decide in this case whether an individual who has obtained a state-law restraining order has a constitutionally protected property interest in having the police enforce the restraining order when they have probable cause to believe it has been violated.

I

The horrible facts of this case are contained in the complaint that respondent Jessica Gonzales filed in Federal District Court. Respondent alleges that petitioner,

---

196. Id. at 1487.

197. Caroline Bettinger-Lopez et. al., Domestic Violence in the United States: A Preliminary Report prepared for Rashida Manjoo, U.N. Special Rapporteur on Violence Against Women, at 15–16 (Apr. 18, 2011).

198. For an overview of state civil protection order statutes, see American Bar Ass'n Comm'n on Domestic and Sexual Violence, Domestic Violence Civil Protection Orders (CPOs) (Mar. 2014).

199. Goldfarb, supra note 189, at 1506–07.

the town of Castle Rock, Colorado, violated the Due Process Clause of the Fourteenth Amendment to the United States Constitution when its police officers, acting pursuant to official policy or custom, failed to respond properly to her repeated reports that her estranged husband was violating the terms of a restraining order.

The restraining order had been issued by a state trial court several weeks earlier in conjunction with respondent's divorce proceedings. The original form order, issued on May 21, 1999, and served on respondent's husband on June 4, 1999, commanded him not to "molest or disturb the peace of [respondent] or of any child," and to remain at least 100 yards from the family home at all times. The bottom of the preprinted form noted that the reverse side contained "IMPORTANT NOTICES FOR RESTRAINED PARTIES AND LAW ENFORCEMENT OFFICIALS." The preprinted text on the back of the form included the following **"WARNING"**:

> **A KNOWING VIOLATION OF A RESTRAINING ORDER IS A CRIME.** . . . . A VIOLATION WILL ALSO CONSTITUTE CONTEMPT OF COURT. **YOU MAY BE ARRESTED** WITHOUT NOTICE IF A LAW ENFORCEMENT OFFICER HAS PROBABLE CAUSE TO BELIEVE THAT YOU HAVE KNOWINGLY VIOLATED THIS ORDER."

The preprinted text on the back of the form also included a **"NOTICE TO LAW ENFORCEMENT OFFICIALS,"** which read in part:

> YOU SHALL USE EVERY REASONABLE MEANS TO ENFORCE THIS RESTRAINING ORDER. YOU SHALL ARREST, OR, IF AN ARREST WOULD BE IMPRACTICAL UNDER THE CIRCUMSTANCES, SEEK A WARRANT FOR THE ARREST OF THE RESTRAINED PERSON WHEN YOU HAVE INFORMATION AMOUNTING TO PROBABLE CAUSE THAT THE RESTRAINED PERSON HAS VIOLATED OR ATTEMPTED TO VIOLATE ANY PROVISION OF THIS ORDER AND THE RESTRAINED PERSON HAS BEEN PROPERLY SERVED WITH A COPY OF THIS ORDER OR HAS RECEIVED ACTUAL NOTICE OF THE EXISTENCE OF THIS ORDER.

On June 4, 1999, the state trial court modified the terms of the restraining order and made it permanent. The modified order gave respondent's husband the right to spend time with his three daughters (ages 10, 9, and 7) on alternate weekends, for two weeks during the summer, and, "'upon reasonable notice,'" for a midweek dinner visit "'arranged by the parties'"; the modified order also allowed him to visit the home to collect the children for such "parenting time."

According to the complaint, at about 5 or 5:30 p.m. on Tuesday, June 22, 1999, respondent's husband took the three daughters while they were playing outside the family home. No advance arrangements had been made for him to see the daughters that evening. When respondent noticed the children were missing, she suspected her husband had taken them. At about 7:30 p.m., she called the Castle Rock Police Department, which dispatched two officers. The complaint continues: "When [the officers] arrived. . . , she showed them a copy of the TRO and requested that it be enforced and the three children be returned to her immediately. [The officers] stated that there was nothing they could do about the TRO and suggested that [respondent] call the Police Department again if the three children did not return home by 10:00 p.m."

At approximately 8:30 p.m., respondent talked to her husband on his cellular telephone. He told her "he had the three children [at an] amusement park in Denver." She called the police again and asked them to "have someone check for" her husband or his vehicle at the amusement park and "put out an [all points bulletin]" for her husband, but the officer with whom she spoke "refused to do so," again telling her to "wait until 10:00 p.m. and see if" her husband returned the girls.

At approximately 10:10 p.m., respondent called the police and said her children were still missing, but she was now told to wait until midnight. She called at midnight and told the dispatcher her children were still missing. She went to her husband's apartment and, finding nobody there, called the police at 12:10 a.m.; she was told to wait for an officer to arrive. When none came, she went to the police station at 12:50 a.m. and submitted an incident report. The officer who took the report "made no reasonable effort to enforce the TRO or locate the three children. Instead, he went to dinner."

At approximately 3:20 a.m., respondent's husband arrived at the police station and opened fire with a semiautomatic handgun he had purchased earlier that evening. Police shot back, killing him. Inside the cab of his pickup truck, they found the bodies of all three daughters, whom he had already murdered.

On the basis of the foregoing factual allegations, respondent brought an action under Rev. Stat. § 1979, 42 U.S.C. § 1983, claiming that the town violated the Due Process Clause because its police department had "an official policy or custom of failing to respond properly to complaints of restraining order violations" and "tolerate[d] the non-enforcement of restraining orders by its police officers." The complaint also alleged that the town's actions "were taken either willfully, recklessly or with such gross negligence as to indicate wanton disregard and deliberate indifference to" respondent's civil rights. . . .

The District Court granted [Defendants' motion to dismiss], concluding that, whether construed as making a substantive due process or procedural due process claim, respondent's complaint failed to state a claim upon which relief could be granted.

A panel of the Court of Appeals affirmed the rejection of a substantive due process claim, but found that respondent had alleged a cognizable procedural due process claim. On rehearing en banc, a divided court reached the same disposition, concluding that respondent had a "protected property interest in the enforcement of the terms of her restraining order" and that the town had deprived her of due process because "the police never 'heard' nor seriously entertained her request to enforce and protect her interests in the restraining order." We granted certiorari.

II

The Fourteenth Amendment to the United States Constitution provides that a State shall not "deprive any person of life, liberty, or property, without due process of law." In 42 U.S.C. § 1983, Congress has created a federal cause of action for "the deprivation of any rights, privileges, or immunities secured by the Constitution and laws." Respondent claims the benefit of this provision on the ground that she had a property interest in police enforcement of the restraining order against her husband; and that the town deprived her of this property without due process by having a policy that tolerated nonenforcement of restraining orders. . . .

The procedural component of the Due Process Clause does not protect everything that might be described as a "benefit": "To have a property interest in a benefit, a person clearly must have more than an abstract need or desire" and "more than a unilateral expectation of it. He must, instead, have a legitimate claim of entitlement to it." Such entitlements are, " 'of course, . . . not created by the Constitution. Rather, they are created and their dimensions are defined by existing rules or understandings that stem from an independent source such as state law.' "

A

Our cases recognize that a benefit is not a protected entitlement if government officials may grant or deny it in their discretion. . . . The Court of Appeals in this case determined that Colorado law created an entitlement to enforcement of the restraining order because the "court-issued restraining order . . . specifically dictated that its terms must be enforced" and a "state statute command[ed]" enforcement of the order when certain objective conditions were met (probable cause to believe that the order had been violated and that the object of the order had received notice of its existence)." . . .

We do not believe that these provisions of Colorado law truly made enforcement of restraining orders *mandatory*. A well established tradition of police discretion has long coexisted with apparently mandatory arrest statutes. . . .

[A] true mandate of police action would require some stronger indication from the Colorado Legislature than "shall use every reasonable means to enforce a restraining order" (or even "shall arrest . . . or . . . seek a warrant"). That language is not perceptibly more mandatory than the Colorado statute which has long told municipal chiefs of police that they "shall pursue and arrest any person fleeing from justice in any part of the state" and that they "shall apprehend any person in the act of committing any offense . . . and, forthwith and without any warrant, bring such person before a . . . competent authority for examination and trial." . . .

The dissent correctly points out that, in the specific context of domestic violence, mandatory-arrest statutes have been found in some States to be more mandatory than traditional mandatory-arrest statutes. . . . Even in the domestic-violence context, however, it is unclear how the mandatory-arrest paradigm applies to cases in which the offender is not present to be arrested. As the dissent explains, much of the impetus for mandatory-arrest statutes and policies derived from the idea that it is better for police officers to arrest the aggressor in a domestic-violence incident than to attempt to mediate the dispute or merely to ask the offender to leave the scene. Those other options are only available, of course, when the offender is present at the scene.

As one of the cases cited by the dissent recognized, "there will be situations when no arrest is possible, *such as when the alleged abuser is not in the home.*" That case held that Washington's mandatory-arrest statute required an arrest only in "cases where the offender is on the scene," and that it "d[id] not create an on-going mandatory duty to conduct an investigation" to locate the offender. . . .

Respondent does not specify the precise means of enforcement that the Colorado restraining-order statute assertedly mandated — whether her interest lay in having police arrest her husband, having them seek a warrant for his arrest, or having them "use every reasonable means, up to and including arrest, to enforce the order's terms." Such indeterminacy is not the hallmark of a duty that is mandatory. Nor can someone be safely deemed "entitled" to something when the identity of the alleged entitlement is vague. . . .

Even if the statute could be said to have made enforcement of restraining orders "mandatory" because of the domestic-violence context of the underlying statute, that would not necessarily mean that state law gave *respondent* an entitlement to *enforcement* of the mandate. Making the actions of government employees obligatory can serve various legitimate ends other than the conferral of a benefit on a specific class of people. The serving of public rather than private ends is the normal course of the criminal law because criminal acts, "besides the injury [they do] to individuals, . . . strike at the very being of society; which cannot possibly subsist, where actions of this sort are suffered to escape with impunity." This principle underlies, for example, a Colorado district attorney's discretion to prosecute a domestic assault, even though the victim withdraws her charge. . . .

C

Even if we were to think otherwise concerning the creation of an entitlement by Colorado, it is by no means clear that an individual entitlement to enforcement of a restraining order could constitute a "property" interest for purposes of the Due Process Clause. Such a right would not, of course, resemble any traditional conception of property. Although that alone does not disqualify it from due process protection, . . . the right to have a restraining order enforced does not "have some ascertainable monetary value." . . . Perhaps most radically, the alleged property interest here arises *incidentally,* not out of some new species of government benefit or service, but out of a function that government actors have always performed — to wit, arresting people who they have probable cause to believe have committed a criminal offense. . . .

III

We conclude, therefore, that respondent did not, for purposes of the Due Process Clause, have a property interest in police enforcement of the restraining order against her husband. . . .

JUSTICE STEVENS, with whom JUSTICE GINSBURG joins, dissenting. . . .

The central question in this case is . . . whether, as a matter of Colorado law, respondent had a right to police assistance comparable to the right she would have possessed to any other service the government or a private firm might have undertaken to provide. . . .

Three flaws in the Court's rather superficial analysis of the merits highlight the unwisdom of its decision to answer the state-law question *de novo*. First, the Court places undue weight on the various statutes throughout the country that seemingly mandate police enforcement but are generally understood to preserve police discretion. As a result, the Court gives short shrift to the unique case of "mandatory arrest" statutes in the domestic violence context; States passed a wave of these statutes in the 1980's and 1990's with the unmistakable goal of eliminating police discretion in this area. Second, the Court's formalistic analysis fails to take seriously the fact that the Colorado statute at issue in this case was enacted for the benefit of the narrow class of persons who are beneficiaries of domestic restraining orders, and that the order at issue in this case was specifically intended to provide protection to respondent and her children. Finally, the Court is simply wrong to assert that a citizen's interest in the government's commitment to provide police enforcement in certain defined circumstances does not resemble any "traditional conception of property," in fact, a citizen's property interest in such a commitment is just as concrete and worthy of protection as her interest in any other important service the government or a private firm has undertaken to provide. . . .

[W]hen Colorado passed its statute in 1994, it joined the ranks of 15 States that mandated arrest for domestic violence offenses and 19 States that mandated arrest for domestic restraining order violations.

Given the specific purpose of these statutes, there can be no doubt that the Colorado Legislature used the term "shall" advisedly in its domestic restraining order statute. While "shall" is probably best read to mean "may" in other Colorado statutes that seemingly mandate enforcement, it is clear that the elimination of police discretion was integral to Colorado and its fellow States' solution to the problem of underenforcement in domestic violence cases. Since the text of Colorado's statute perfectly captures this legislative purpose, it is hard to imagine what the Court has in mind when it insists on "some stronger indication from the Colorado Legislature."

While Colorado case law does not speak to the question, it is instructive that other state courts interpreting their analogous statutes have not only held that they eliminate the police's traditional discretion to refuse enforcement, but have also recognized that they create rights enforceable against the police under state law. . . .

Indeed, the Court fails to come to terms with the wave of domestic violence statutes that provides the crucial context for understanding Colorado's law. The Court concedes that, "in the specific context of domestic violence, mandatory-arrest statutes have been found in some States to be more mandatory than traditional mandatory-arrest statutes," but that is a serious understatement. The difference is not a matter of degree, but of kind. Before this wave of statutes, the legal rule was one of discretion; as the Court shows, the "traditional," general mandatory arrest statutes have always been understood to be "mandatory" in name only. The innovation of the domestic violence statutes was to make police enforcement, not "more mandatory," but simply *mandatory*. If, as the Court says, the existence of a protected "entitlement" turns on whether "government officials may grant or deny it in their discretion," the new mandatory statutes undeniably create an entitlement to police enforcement of restraining orders.

Perhaps recognizing this point, the Court glosses over the dispositive question — whether the police enjoyed discretion to deny enforcement — and focuses on a different question — which "precise means of enforcement" were called for in this case. But that question is a red herring. The statute directs that, upon probable cause of a violation, "a peace officer shall arrest, or, if an arrest would be impractical under the circumstances, seek a warrant for the arrest of a restrained person." Regardless of whether the enforcement called for in this case was arrest or the seeking of an arrest warrant (the answer to that question probably changed over the course of the night as the respondent gave the police more information about the husband's whereabouts), the crucial point is that, under the statute, the police were *required* to provide enforcement; *they lacked the discretion to do nothing*. . . .

Given that Colorado law has quite clearly eliminated the police's discretion to deny enforcement, respondent is correct that she had much more than a "unilateral expectation" that the restraining order would be enforced; rather, she had a "legitimate claim of entitlement" to enforcement. Recognizing respondent's property interest in the enforcement of her restraining order is fully consistent with our precedent. . . .

Police enforcement of a restraining order is a government service that is no less concrete and no less valuable than other government services, such as education. The relative novelty of recognizing this type of property interest is explained by the relative novelty of the domestic violence statutes creating a mandatory arrest duty; before this innovation, the unfettered discretion that characterized police enforcement defeated any citizen's "legitimate claim of entitlement" to this service. Novel or not, respondent's claim finds strong support in the principles that underlie our due process jurisprudence. In this case, Colorado law *guaranteed* the provision of a certain service, in certain defined circumstances, to a certain class of beneficiaries, and respondent reasonably relied on that guarantee. . . . Surely, if respondent had contracted with a private security firm to provide her and her daughters with protection from her husband, it would be apparent that she possessed a property interest in such a contract. Here, Colorado undertook a comparable obligation, and respondent — with restraining order in hand — justifiably relied on that undertaking. Respondent's claim of entitlement to this promised service is no less legitimate than the other claims our cases have upheld, and no less concrete than a hypothetical agreement with a private firm. The fact that it is based on a statutory enactment and a judicial order entered for her special protection, rather than on a formal contract, does not provide a principled basis for refusing to consider it "property" worthy of constitutional protection. . . .

NOTES AND QUESTIONS

1. *Postscript.* After exhausting her domestic remedies, Jessica Gonzales (later Jessica Lenahan) pursued a claim against the United States for violation of international human rights law in the Inter-American Commission of Human Rights (IACHR) and won. In a decision issued in 2011, the IACHR found a violation because the United States "fail[ed] to exercise due diligence to protect Jessica Lenahan and her daughters from acts of domestic violence perpetrated by the ex-husband of the former and the father of the latter, even though Ms. Lenahan held a restraining order against him."[200] This failure violated the State's obligations "not to discriminate and to provide for equal protection before the law," "to undertake reasonable measures to protect the life of Leslie, Katheryn and Rebecca Gonzales in violation of their right to life," and "the right to judicial protection of Jessica Lenahan and her next-of-kin."[201] The IAHCR made recommendations for comprehensive law and policy reform in the U.S. The U.S. does not generally treat decisions of international human rights bodies as binding and enforceable, and the federal government did not implement the IAHCR recommendations.[202] Still, an increasing number of local government bodies have issued statements that freedom from domestic violence is a human right.[203]

2. *Domestic Violence, Access to Justice, and Divorce.* Domestic violence exacerbates the legal difficulties those seeking divorce may already experience in accessing the judicial system. These may include the cost of attorney representation, the

---

200. Lenahan v. United States, Case 12.626, Inter-Am. Comm'n H.R., Report No. 80/11 (2011).

201. Id.

202. See Lenora M. Lapidus, Justice for Jessica: Holding the U.S. Accountable for Protecting Domestic Violence Survivors, ACLU (Oct. 27, 2014), https://www.aclu.org/blog/womens-rights/violence-against-women/justice-jessica-holding-us-accountable-protecting-domestic.

203. Columbia Law School's Human Rights Institute, University of Miami School of Law Human Rights Clinic, and Cornell Law School's Gender Justice Clinic, Freedom from Domestic Violence as a Fundamental Human Right Resolutions, Presidential Proclamations, and Other Statements of Principle (Feb. 2018).

difficulty of navigating the court system without an attorney, and the need to serve the abusing spouse with divorce papers.[204] Recent research by the Legal Services Corporation, the country's largest funder of civil legal aid, found that one in four low-income households had experienced civil legal problems in the past year, including 67 percent of households with survivors of domestic violence or sexual assault.[205] These were needs apart from those related to domestic violence.[206]

3. *Immigration, Asylum, and Domestic Violence.* Immigrant women are particularly at risk for domestic violence.[207] Language barriers, financial dependence, lack of understanding of the legal system, and insecure immigration status affect immigrants' experiences in addressing domestic violence. U Visas provide immigration protection for eligible immigrants who have been abused, but demand far outpaces availability.[208] Within the past few years, police departments in areas with larger immigrant populations have been reporting declines in domestic violence reporting, which they attribute to changes in U.S. immigration policy and related fears of deportation.[209] Such fears have been fueled by instances like that of a transgender woman who had received a civil protection order for domestic violence but was arrested at a courthouse on an immigration charge.[210] In the asylum context, it was unclear until the 2014 case of Matter of A-R-C-G whether domestic violence could be a basis for asylum.[211] In 2018, the Trump administration took the view that "[g]enerally, claims by aliens pertaining to domestic violence or gang violence perpetrated by non-governmental actors will not qualify for asylum."[212] Then-Attorney General Jeff Sessions distinguished between "members of a distinct group in society," who may qualify for asylum protections, and women claiming domestic violence, who are "each . . . a victim of a particular abuser in highly individualized circumstances."[213]

---

204. Zoe Greenberg, Their Husbands Abuse Them. Shouldn't Divorce Be Easy?, N.Y. Times, May 11, 2018, at MB1.

205. Legal Servs. Corp., The Justice Gap: Measuring the Unmet Civil Legal Needs of Low-Income Americans 7 (2017).

206. Id. at 27.

207. Natalie Nanasi, The U Visa's Failed Promise for Survivors of Domestic Violence, 29 Yale J. L & Feminism 273, 283–285 (2018).

208. Id. at 277.

209. Cora Engelbrecht, Fewer Immigrants are Reporting Domestic Abuse, Police Blame Fear of Deportation, N.Y. Times, June 3, 2018, at A12.

210. Aaron Martinez, Transgender Woman Gets Time Served, Stays Jailed, El Paso Times (Apr. 13, 2017).

211. 26 I. & N. Dec. 388 (B.I.A. 2014).

212. Matter of A-B-, 27 I & N Dec. 316 (A.G. 2018); Katie Benner & Caitlin Dickerson, Sessions Says Domestic and Gang Violence Are Not Grounds for Asylum, N.Y. Times, June 11, 2018, at A1.

213. A-R-C-G, 26 I & N. Dec. at 336, 339.

This approach has been criticized for contravening international human rights law's understanding of domestic violence.[214]

4. *Domestic Violence and COVID-19.* Since the outbreak of COVID-19 around the world, advocates and agencies have observed increased domestic violence in the United States and abroad.[215] This change corresponds with rises in family violence during times of large-scale natural disasters or crises.[216] U.S. law enforcement agencies reported rises in domestic violence calls in March 2020, up to 18 percent or more in some jurisdictions.[217] According to the National Domestic Violence Hotline, callers have spoken of COVID-19 being used by abusers as a means to exert control — physically, socially, financially, and medically.[218] The World Health Organization points to increased "[s]tress, disruption of social and protective networks, and decreased access to services" as factors exacerbating the risk of violence for women.[219] In a time when individuals are confined to their homes, "[s]ocial norms and attitudes that suggest there is a 'sanctity' to family life — to home, in a social rather than physical sense — can also make it difficult for people to speak out about, let alone leave, abusive situations as a result of feelings of shame and embarrassment."[220]

B. Mandatory Interventions

As described in *Gonzales*, legal reform in the criminal justice system has included a variety of mandatory interventions to address domestic violence. As summarized by Professor Deborah Epstein, these include "mandatory arrests, which require police to arrest in domestic violence cases; no-drop prosecutions, which require that a criminal case go forward regardless of the victim's wishes; and mandatory stay-away orders, which require perpetrators to stay away from victims during the pendency of a prosecution."[221] Can a court constitutionally mandate that a husband

---

214. See, e.g., Caroline Bettinger-López, Human Rights at Home: Domestic Violence as a Human Rights Violation, 40 Colum. Hum. Rts. L. Rev. 19 (2008); Blaine Bookey, Domestic Violence as a Basis for Asylum: An Analysis of 206 Case Outcomes in the United States from 1994 to 2012, 24 Hastings Women's L.J. 107, 148 (2013).

215. See World Health Org., COVID-19 and Violence Against Women: What the Health Sector/System Can Do (Apr. 7, 2020); Caroline Bradbury-Jones & Louise Isham, The Pandemic Paradox: The Consequences of COVID-19 on Domestic Violence, 29 J. Clinical Nursing 2047, 2048 (2020); Emma Graham-Harrison et al., Lockdowns Around the World Bring Rise in Domestic Violence, Guardian (Mar. 28, 2020).

216. Bradbury-Jones & Isham, supra note 216; World Health Org., supra note 216.

217. Tyler Kingkade, Police See Rise in Domestic Violence Calls Amid Coronavirus Lockdown, NBC News (Apr. 5, 2020).

218. Mélissa Godin, As Cities Around the World Go on Lockdown, Victims of Domestic Violence Look for a Way Out, Time.com (Mar. 18, 2020).

219. World Health Org., supra note 216, at 1.

220. Bradbury-Jones & Isham, supra note 216, at 2047.

221. Epstein, Procedural Justice, supra note 190, at 1846.

stay away from the family home as a condition of pre-trial release? Does it matter if his wife wants him to return home?

WILLIAMS V. STATE

151 P.3d 460 (Alaska Ct. App. 2006)

COATS, CHIEF JUDGE.

This petition raises constitutional challenges to a statute, AS 12.30.027(b), that prohibits all persons charged with domestic violence from returning to the residence of the alleged victim while on pre-trial release—regardless of the circumstances of the offense and without any opportunity for judicial review. . . .

Facts and Proceedings

On April 21, 2004, the police responded to a report by a passerby that a man was strangling a woman in a house on Henderson Loop in Anchorage. When the police arrived at the house, they contacted Terese Williams. Williams said her husband, Thomas Williams, had grabbed her around the neck during an argument and pushed her to the ground. She said he kept a firm grip on her throat and squeezed for several minutes and that she was very scared. Then he let go and she got up. She was shaken and went to smoke a cigarette; her husband grabbed his bags and left. She said her husband worked in Point Mackenzie and stayed with a friend while he was there. She also told the police her husband had consumed some cough medicine and beers before the incident. The investigating officer noted that Terese Williams was "visibly shaken" and had a scratch on her chin, a finger impression under her right ear, and a small red mark on the left of her neck.

Based on these allegations, Thomas Williams was charged with fourth-degree assault. The conditions of his pre-trial release barred him from contacting his wife or returning to the residence they had shared.

Several weeks after his release, Williams asked the court to modify his release conditions so he could have contact with his wife. His attorney said Williams and his wife had been together for more than twenty years and that both parties wished to renew contact. The State did not oppose the request. The prosecutor told the court that "in looking at Mr. Williams's record and the facts in this case, the State [is] confident or at least hopeful that it was an isolated incident." The court modified the bail conditions to allow contact, but emphasized that, by statute, Williams was still barred from the residence.

Several months later, Williams asked the court for permission to stay in the residence to care for the house and dog while his wife and daughter were in London. Williams's wife supported the request, and the State did not oppose. The court also granted that request.

On December 23, 2004 — eight months after the incident — Williams, again with his wife's support, asked the court for permission to return to the residence for Christmas. He also filed a motion challenging the constitutionality of AS 12.30.027(b). Williams argued that the statute infringed his fundamental right to maintain his marital relationship and violated his rights to both due process and equal protection of the laws. He also argued that the statute violated the constitutional right of victims to be treated with dignity and fairness.

In support of Williams's request to return home for Christmas, Terese Williams told the court that she and Williams had been in contact for seven months, that they had seen each other regularly, and that maintaining separate residences was a financial burden. She said she and her husband had taken vacations together outside Alaska while this case was pending and that she did not feel her husband was a threat. She said their older daughter was coming home for the holidays and that it would be costly to find a place outside the residence for the family to be together.

Relying on AS 12.30.027(b), District Court Judge Sigurd E. Murphy denied Williams's request to return to the residence. . . .

Discussion . . .

Why AS 12.30.027(b) violates Alaska's guarantee of equal protection to the extent that it categorically forbids a person on pre-trial release for domestic violence from returning to the home of the alleged victim. . . .

Williams asserts that he has a fundamental right to live at home with his wife and family while on pre-trial release and that any government infringement of that right must be strictly scrutinized.

We have previously subjected restrictions on marital association to heightened scrutiny. In Dawson v. State, we observed that "[a] condition of probation restricting marital association plainly implicates the constitutional rights of privacy, liberty, and freedom of association and . . . must be subjected to special scrutiny." 894 P.2d 672, 680 (Alaska Ct. App. 1995).

The State[, defending the statute's constitutionality,] argues that no fundamental right is at stake in this case because Williams's conditions of release permit him to see his wife — just not in their home. Hence, the State argues, the residence restriction has "at most a modest, incidental, and temporary effect" on the marital relationship. This argument understates the integral relationship between cohabitation and marriage. Moreover, apart from any burden imposed on Williams's relationship with his wife and family, Williams has a liberty interest in choosing his family living arrangements. . . .

This liberty interest does not disappear because a person has been charged with a crime. We hold based on this authority that Williams has an important, if not fundamental, right to live in his home with his wife and family while on pre-trial release, and that any state infringement of that right must be carefully scrutinized. . . .

[T]he State undoubtedly has a legitimate and compelling interest in preventing domestic violence — and in preventing a person accused of domestic violence from tampering with the alleged victim's testimony. On the other hand, the government has no legitimate interest in barring a person who poses no appreciable risk of harming or intimidating the victim from returning to a shared residence. Given the importance of the right to live with a member of one's family, we will invalidate the classification if we find an insufficiently tight fit between the purposes of the statute and the means used to accomplish those purposes and if less restrictive alternatives are available.

The State argues that a blanket prohibition on returning to the alleged victim's residence is necessary because of the peculiar dynamics of domestic violence — in particular, the well-documented tendency of victims to remain with their abusers. The State argues that the victims of domestic violence are influenced by psychological and emotional forces that "too often make impossible an accurate assessment of whether the victim's safety can be assured if the defendant is allowed to return to [the] residence." . . .

We agree that it can be difficult for judges to accurately predict whether a particular defendant will be dangerous in the future. But judges confront this task "countless times each day throughout the American system of criminal justice." . . .

As the State points out, courts are not obliged to credit a victim's assertion that her abuser is no threat — even if that testimony is undisputed. . . .

Under the Alaska Statutes, once a court determines that a person charged with domestic violence poses a risk to the alleged victim, the court is authorized to impose numerous conditions of release (including removing the person from the victim's residence). . . . Before imposing any of these conditions, the court must assess the risk the accused person poses to the alleged victim, taking into account the possibility — perhaps the likelihood — that the victim has understated the risk of more violence. The State has advanced no evidence, and no convincing argument, that Alaska courts have failed, or must necessarily fail, at this task. . . .

Furthermore, because of the broad definition of "a crime involving domestic violence," there is a substantial risk that the statute will burden the liberty interests of persons who pose no appreciable risk of future violence. Although "domestic violence" is normally understood to mean an assault committed by one domestic partner against the other, the offense actually encompasses a much broader range of persons and conduct. In Alaska, a wide variety of crimes — extortion, reckless endangerment, trespass, and criminal mischief, to name a few — are domestic violence crimes if they are committed by one household member against another. And "household member" does not only mean people who are, or have been, involved in a sexual relationship; it also includes individuals who once lived together in any context or who dated in the past, or who are related by marriage or within the fourth degree of consanguinity. . . .

[U]nder Alaska's far-reaching definition of domestic violence, probable cause to believe a person has committed a domestic violence offense cannot necessarily be equated with probable cause to believe that the person poses an ongoing risk to the alleged victim's safety.

Even in Williams's case, which involves the more typical assault of a husband against a wife, it is possible to see how AS 12.30.027(b) might infringe an important liberty interest without advancing any significant governmental interest. . . .

Ultimately, Judge Murphy found that the release condition barring Williams from returning to the residence was appropriate in this case. But given the unrestricted contact Williams and his wife had outside the home, it is at least arguable that the prohibition on Williams returning to the residence was no longer serving its intended purpose. . . .

[I]ndividuals charged with, but not yet convicted of, a crime involving domestic violence retain an important liberty interest in choosing their family living arrangements. Moreover, far more disparate individuals are burdened by this statute. . . . Given the reach of the statute, and the importance of the right infringed, even if the State could show (which it has not) that the average person charged with domestic violence poses an ongoing danger to the alleged victim, the statute would likely still burden enough people who are not dangerous to violate our constitution. . . .

We therefore hold that AS 12.30.027(b), as applied to individuals on pre-trial release, violates article I, section 1 of the Alaska Constitution. . . .

NOTES AND QUESTIONS

1. *Mandatory Interventions.* Mandatory interventions may be viewed as a result of the success of the domestic violence movement. They include the type of mandatory stay-away order like the one in *Williams,* "which require[s] perpetrators to stay away from victims during the pendency of a prosecution."[222] Nonetheless, some domestic violence experts have come to criticize mandatory interventions for improperly restricting women's autonomy. Professor Sally Goldfarb argues:

> If orders permitting ongoing contact are not available (and for many women today, they are not), the result is that the law of civil protection orders gives a battered woman only two choices. If she obtains a protection order, her partner will be prohibited from seeing or contacting her. If she does not obtain a protection order, the law will do nothing to help redress the imbalance of power between herself and her partner. This all-or-nothing approach

---

222. Id.

excludes the middle ground that many women would prefer: an order that would help restructure the relationship without ending it.[223]

Mandatory interventions also include no-drop prosecution policies whereby cases proceed regardless of the victim's wishes — and "even if she recants her original story and testifies for the defense."[224] Such policies have resulted in increased conviction rates for batterers and send "a strong symbolic message that the community will not tolerate domestic violence."[225] Professor Deborah Epstein criticizes such policies for failing to prioritize victims' long-term safety in lieu of a short-term conviction and punishment.[226] The victim and the batterer may have a continued relationship, which may bring new and escalating risks, and yet the victim may not feel respected and trusted by the legal system and therefore will not seek necessary protection.[227] Mandatory arrest policies are subject to similar critiques.[228] Are mandatory interventions necessary to adequately address domestic violence? What is the alternative?

2. *De Facto Divorce.* Professor Jeannie Suk criticizes domestic violence enforcement for producing "'state-imposed de facto divorce,' wherein prosecutors use the routine enforcement of misdemeanor DV to seek to end (in all but name) intimate domestic relationships."[229] For the government, ending the intimate relationship provides a solution to the domestic violence problem. Is this a constitutional way to terminate individuals' private relationships? Does it matter what safeguards are in place? Suk asserts:

> The criminal court routinely issues the order of protection at arraignment, the defendant's first court appearance. The brief, formulaic, and compressed nature of arraignments in criminal court, which run around the clock to ensure that all defendants are arraigned within twenty-four hours of arrest, means that courts often issue orders with little detailed consideration of the particular facts. DV orders are generally requested and issued as a matter of course.
>
> When the protection order goes into effect, the defendant cannot go home or have any contact with the victim (usually his wife) and his children. If the defendant does go home or contact the protected parties, he could be arrested, prosecuted, and punished for a fresh crime. This is so even if the victim initiates contact or invites the defendant to come home. Police officers

---

223. Goldfarb, supra note 189, at 1501–02.
224. Deborah Epstein et al., Transforming Aggressive Prosecution Policies: Prioritizing Victims' Long-Term Safety in the Prosecution of Domestic Violence Cases, 11 Am. U. J. Gender Soc. Pol'y & L. 465, 466 (2003).
225. Id.
226. Id. at 468.
227. Id. at 469.
228. See Epstein, Procedural Justice, supra note 190, at 1891–92.
229. Jeannie Suk, Criminal Law Comes Homes, 116 Yale L.J. 2, 8 (2006).

then make routine unannounced visits to homes with a history of domestic violence. If a defendant subject to a protection order is present there, he is arrested. . . .[230]

Does the "state-imposed de facto divorce" deprive individuals of constitutionally protected relationship rights? Does it deprive both the alleged abuser and victim of such rights? Is the deprivation justified? Are there other problems with this practice? Suk argues that "state-imposed de facto divorce is so class-contingent that it could be called poor man's divorce. The initial DV arrest that sets the wheels in motion is much more likely to occur if people live in close quarters in buildings with thin walls, and neighbors can easily hear a disturbance and call the police."[231]

3. *Domestic Violence and Tort Law.* In the absence of common law impediments and interspousal tort immunity, which we address in the next section, domestic violence survivors may bring tort claims against their abusers. (A majority of interspousal tort cases involve domestic violence.[232]) As Professor Camille Carey explains, claims include "traditional common law claims like assault, battery, and intentional infliction of emotional distress . . . [as well as] several local and state tort claims for domestic violence and gender-motivated violence."[233] Tort suits not only may yield "financial compensation for harms," but also may allow the victim to "assume a position of control over legal claims addressing the abuse, experience both power and agency in an otherwise subordinating relationship, and seek deterrence of an abuser's abusive conduct."[234]

PROBLEM

Imagine that you serve on the State Governor's Task Force on Domestic Violence. You have been tasked with reviewing the existing domestic violence protection order enforcement system. The Commission is charged with addressing the serious harm of domestic violence. It is also asked to consider critiques that the system wrongly encroaches on family relationships. What further information might you want to seek? What reforms might you propose?

---

230. Id. at 48–50.

231. Id. at 59–60; see also Jeannie Suk, At Home in the Law: How the Domestic Violence Revolution Is Transforming Privacy (2009).

232. Jason Palmer, Domestic Violence, 11 Geo. J. Gender & L. 97, 149 (2010).

233. Camille Carey, Domestic Violence Torts: Righting A Civil Wrong, 62 U. Kan. L. Rev. 695, 696 (2014).

234. Id.

VI. Tort

At common law, spouses were historically not permitted to sue one another for personal injuries under the doctrine of interspousal tort immunity.[235] Because the wife's identity was merged into the husband's, it was doctrinally impossible for a wife (lacking legal identity) to sue a husband. As the law repudiated the system of coverture, justifications for interspousal tort immunity weakened. But the doctrine persisted. Courts justified interspousal tort immunity as necessary to avoid fraudulent collusion between spouses for financial gain, preserve marital harmony, and shield the marriage from prying public eyes.[236] In the case below, Maryland followed the overwhelming contemporary trend to abolish interspousal tort immunity.

BOZMAN v. BOZMAN
830 A.2d 450 (Md. 2003)

BELL, CHIEF JUDGE....

The doctrine of interspousal immunity in tort cases is a rule of law existing in the common law of Maryland.... "The rule at common law [was] that a married woman cannot maintain an action against her husband for injuries caused by his negligent or tortious act."...

"The reason usually given for that rule is the presumed legal identity of the husband and wife." A more complete statement of the rationale was provided [by this Court], with attribution to Blackstone:

> By marriage, the husband and wife are one person in the law: that is, the very being of legal existence of the woman is suspended during the marriage, or at least is incorporated and consolidated into that of the husband: under whose wing, protection, and cover, she performs everything; and is therefore called in our law french a *feme-covert, foemina viro co-operta;* is said to be a *covert-baron,* or under the protection and influence of her husband, her *baron,* or *lord;* and her condition during her marriage is called *coverture.* Upon this principle, of a union of person in husband and wife, depend almost all the legal rights, duties and disabilities, that either of them acquire by the marriage.

He adds, in discussing the consequences of this union of husband and wife, "If the wife be injured in her person or her property, she can bring no action for redress without her husband's concurrence, and in his name, as well as her own: neither can she be sued without making the husband a defendant."...

---

235. Carl Tobias, Interspousal Tort Immunity in America, 23 Ga. L. Rev. 359, 359 (1989).
236. Id. at 364, 389, 441.

That the Court uniformly applied the doctrine, without exception, did not mean that it did not recognize its flaws. . . . In fact, the Court did not hesitate to criticize the application of the doctrine and the rationale supporting it. . . . The Court . . . labeled the domestic tranquility rationale for the interspousal immunity doctrine "as artificial as" the unity of husband and wife rationale. Expounding on that theme, it pointed out:

> It applies to a post-bellum situation a theory which is clearly only applicable to conditions prior to the difficulty which caused the bringing of the legal action. After discord, suspicion and distrust have entered the home, it is idle to say that one of the parties shall not be allowed to sue the other because of fear of bringing in what is already there. . . .

The respondent argues that alternative remedies, already provided by the courts, are adequate for "garden-variety intentional torts between spouses." . . . In particular, the respondent emphasizes that Maryland is a marital property State, in which equity, rather than title controls property distribution. She also notes that the statutory scheme provides for the consideration of eleven factors when the equities and rights of the parties are being adjusted, and asserts that tortious conduct may be considered in granting alimony or making a monetary award. . . . . Finally, the respondent states that the aggrieved spouse has the benefit of the criminal law; he or she may charge the offender and seek restitution for any medical treatment required. . . .

The "remedies" the respondent proffers are, in the same sense, not compensation for tort damages. . . .

The overwhelming weight of authority supports the petitioner's argument that the interspousal immunity doctrine should be abrogated. Joining the many of our sister States that have already done so, we abrogate the interspousal immunity rule, a vestige of the past, whose time has come and gone, as to all cases alleging an intentional tort. . . .

NOTES AND QUESTIONS

1. *Marital Unity?* In *Bozman*, a man pursued an action for malicious prosecution against his wife, whose criminal charges against him resulted in his incarceration. The need to protect marital harmony historically has been a key rationale for interspousal tort immunity. In Counts v. Counts, a man whose wife had hired a hitman to kill him sought to sue his wife in tort, and requested that the Virginia court set aside the doctrine of interspousal tort immunity.[237] The court refused to

---

237. 266 S.E.2d 895 (Va. 1980).

do so on the theory that allowing living spouses to sue for torts would contribute to the destruction of marriages — "the mere availability of such an interspousal action injects into the marriage relationship just one more abrasive and unnecessary ingredient to be added to existing criminal and divorce remedies. . . . We refuse to add by judicial fiat this further impediment to the unity of marriage."[238] How well founded was the court's concern that abolishing interspousal tort immunity would imperil the marriage?[239] A small number of states have retained vestiges of interspousal tort immunity.[240]

2. *Unmarried Couples and Claims Against Third Parties.* In matters involving marriage, we have been examining whether spouses can sue *each other*. There was no doubt that a spouse could sue *a third party* for injuries sustained by the other spouse. For example, if a man was killed in a car accident, the man's spouse could sue the driver for wrongful death. For non-marital relationships, the questions are reversed: An unmarried person can sue her partner — there is no analogue to interspousal immunity. But can an unmarried person sue a third party based on injuries sustained by her partner?

Should third-party liability turn on marital status? If the purpose of a wrongful death statute is to compensate the person who is dependent on the deceased party, does it make sense to allow recovery for spouses? For all spouses? Only for spouses? Or might it make sense to allow non-marital partners to recover? If so, under what circumstances? When the surviving partner can show she was dependent on the decedent? When the non-marital partners had a marriage-like relationship?

In Graves v. Estabrook, the New Hampshire Supreme Court considered this issue.[241] Catrina Graves and Brett Ennis were engaged and had lived together for seven years. While riding a motorcycle, Ennis was severely injured by the defendant when the defendant ran a stop sign. Graves, who was following in a car, rushed to her fiancé's side, witnessed his injuries, and accompanied him to the hospital in the ambulance. Ennis died within a day. Graves sued to recover for negligent infliction of emotional distress, leading the court to consider whether bystander liability should extend to unmarried cohabitants. In order to satisfy the standard for bystander liability, the claimant has to show that she is "closely related" to the victim.[242] Was the relationship between Graves and Ennis

---

238. Id. at 898.

239. For historical discussion of interspousal tort immunity, see Carl Tobias, The Imminent Demise of Interspousal Tort Immunity, 60 Mont. L. Rev. 101 (1999); Carl Tobias, Interspousal Tort Immunity, supra note 236.

240. Jill Elaine Hasday, The Canon of Family Law, 57 Stan. L. Rev. 825, 838 (2004).

241. 818 A.2d 1255 (N.H. 2003).

242. Id. at 1258.

sufficient? The court said it was and rejected the argument that denying recovery is necessary to protect the state's interest in marriage. Does tort recovery provide an incentive to marry? Do ordinary people know whether they can sue based on injuries to a spouse or unmarried partner?

The court adopted a functional approach, focusing on the duration of the relationship, the degree of mutual dependence between the parties, and their shared experience. The relationship between Graves and Ennis, the court determined, was sufficiently close to satisfy the standard for bystander liability. Graves could thus pursue her claim.[243]

Proponents of progressive family law reform view decisions like *Graves* favorably, as the decision focuses on function over form. The court refused " 'to foreclose [an unmarried cohabitant] from making a claim based upon emotional harm' " because doing so would " 'work a potential injustice . . . where the emotional injury is genuine and substantial and is based upon a relationship of significant duration that . . . is deep, lasting and genuinely intimate.' "[244] Yet, some commentators point to the limits of this approach, arguing that the functional approach requires that the couple look sufficiently marriage-like to qualify for protection. In other words, marriage remains the dominant model, and the rights of unmarried people turn on how closely their relationships approximate marriage.[245]

While *Graves* involved a different-sex couple, much of the reform on non-marital partners grew out of claims by same-sex couples, who were excluded from marriage. For example, in the landmark case of Braschi v. Stahl Associates Co., which we discussed in Chapter 1, Miguel Braschi sought protection from eviction under New York City's rent-control law, after his partner Leslie Blanchard died.[246] Only Blanchard had been on the lease. The court determined that Braschi qualified as a "family member" protected by the law. Rejecting a formal definition of family limited by marriage, biology, and adoption, the court instead adopted a functional definition that examines "the totality of the relationship as evidenced by the dedication, caring and self-sacrifice of the parties."[247] Do you think this is the right approach? What problems does it present? How are courts to decide who qualifies? How are third parties expected to know who can claim the benefit of a statute if it doesn't turn on a formal family status?

---

243. Id. at 1261–62.

244. Id.

245. See Alice Ristroph & Melissa Murray, Disestablishing the Family, 119 Yale L.J. 1236, 1256 n.89 (2010).

246. 543 N.E.2d 49 (N.Y. 1989).

247. Id. at 55.

VII. Evidence

Under evidence law, spouses may not be required to testify against each other (the adverse testimony privilege), nor may they be required to testify as to private communications during marriage (the spousal communications privilege). On what vision of marriage are these privileges based? The following case addresses the scope of the adverse testimony privilege, asserted by a husband when his wife testified against him in a criminal prosecution.

Trammel v. United States
445 U.S. 40 (1980)

Mr. Chief Justice Burger delivered the opinion of the Court.

We granted certiorari to consider whether an accused may invoke the privilege against adverse spousal testimony so as to exclude the voluntary testimony of his wife. This calls for a re-examination of Hawkins v. United States, 358 U.S. 74 (1958).

On March 10, 1976, petitioner Otis Trammel was indicted with two others, Edwin Lee Roberts and Joseph Freeman, for importing heroin into the United States from Thailand and the Philippine Islands and for conspiracy to import heroin. . . . The indictment also named six unindicted co-conspirators, including petitioner's wife Elizabeth Ann Trammel.

According to the indictment, petitioner and his wife flew from the Philippines to California in August 1975, carrying with them a quantity of heroin. Freeman and Roberts assisted them in its distribution. Elizabeth Trammel then traveled to Thailand where she purchased another supply of the drug. On November 3, 1975, with four ounces of heroin on her person, she boarded a plane for the United States. During a routine customs search in Hawaii, she was searched, the heroin was discovered, and she was arrested. After discussions with Drug Enforcement Administration agents, she agreed to cooperate with the Government.

Prior to trial on this indictment, petitioner moved to sever his case from that of Roberts and Freeman. He advised the court that the Government intended to call his wife as an adverse witness and asserted his claim to a privilege to prevent her from testifying against him. At a hearing on the motion, Mrs. Trammel was called as a Government witness under a grant of use immunity. She testified that she and petitioner were married in May 1975 and that they remained married. She explained that her cooperation with the Government was based on assurances that she would be given lenient treatment. She then described, in considerable detail, her role and that of her husband in the heroin distribution conspiracy. . . .

At trial, Elizabeth Trammel testified within the limits of the court's pretrial ruling; her testimony, as the Government concedes, constituted virtually its entire case against petitioner. He was found guilty on both the substantive and conspiracy charges and sentenced to an indeterminate term of years. . . .

The privilege claimed by petitioner has ancient roots. Writing in 1628, Lord Coke observed that "it hath beene resolved by the Justices that a wife cannot be produced either against or for her husband." This spousal disqualification sprang from two canons of medieval jurisprudence: first, the rule that an accused was not permitted to testify in his own behalf because of his interest in the proceeding; second, the concept that husband and wife were one, and that since the woman had no recognized separate legal existence, the husband was that one. From those two now long-abandoned doctrines, it followed that what was inadmissible from the lips of the defendant-husband was also inadmissible from his wife.

Despite its medieval origins, this rule of spousal disqualification remained intact in most common-law jurisdictions well into the 19th century. . . .

The modern justification for this privilege against adverse spousal testimony is its perceived role in fostering the harmony and sanctity of the marriage relationship. Notwithstanding this benign purpose, the rule was sharply criticized. Professor Wigmore termed it "the merest anachronism in legal theory and an indefensible obstruction to truth in practice." The Committee on Improvements in the Law of Evidence of the American Bar Association called for its abolition. In its place, Wigmore and others suggested a privilege protecting only private marital communications, modeled on the privilege between priest and penitent, attorney and client, and physician and patient. . . .

[T]he long history of the privilege suggests that it ought not to be casually cast aside. That the privilege is one affecting marriage, home, and family relationships — already subject to much erosion in our day — also counsels caution. . . .

Since 1958, . . . support for the privilege against adverse spousal testimony has been eroded further. . . . The trend in state law toward divesting the accused of the privilege to bar adverse spousal testimony has special relevance because the laws of marriage and domestic relations are concerns traditionally reserved to the states. . . .

It is essential to remember that the *Hawkins* privilege is not needed to protect information privately disclosed between husband and wife in the confidence of the marital relationship — once described by this Court as "the best solace of human existence." Those confidences are privileged under the independent rule protecting confidential marital communications. The *Hawkins* privilege is invoked, not to exclude private marital communications, but rather to exclude evidence of criminal acts and of communications made in the presence of third persons.

No other testimonial privilege sweeps so broadly. The privileges between priest and penitent, attorney and client, and physician and patient limit protection to private communications. . . .

The *Hawkins* rule stands in marked contrast to these three privileges. Its protection is not limited to confidential communications; rather it permits an accused to exclude all adverse spousal testimony. As Jeremy Bentham observed more than a century and a half ago, such a privilege goes far beyond making "every man's house his castle," and permits a person to convert his house into "a den of thieves." It "secures, to every man, one safe and unquestionable and every ready accomplice for every imaginable crime."

The ancient foundations for so sweeping a privilege have long since disappeared. Nowhere in the common-law world — indeed in any modern society — is a woman regarded as chattel or demeaned by denial of a separate legal identity and the dignity associated with recognition as a whole human being. Chip by chip, over the years those archaic notions have been cast aside so that "[n]o longer is the female destined solely for the home and the rearing of the family, and only the male for the marketplace and the world of ideas."

The contemporary justification for affording an accused such a privilege is also unpersuasive. When one spouse is willing to testify against the other in a criminal proceeding — whatever the motivation — their relationship is almost certainly in disrepair; there is probably little in the way of marital harmony for the privilege to preserve. In these circumstances, a rule of evidence that permits an accused to prevent adverse spousal testimony seems far more likely to frustrate justice than to foster family peace. Indeed, there is reason to believe that vesting the privilege in the accused could actually undermine the marital relationship. For example, in a case such as this the Government is unlikely to offer a wife immunity and lenient treatment if it knows that her husband can prevent her from giving adverse testimony. If the Government is dissuaded from making such an offer, the privilege can have the untoward effect of permitting one spouse to escape justice at the expense of the other. It hardly seems conducive to the preservation of the marital relation to place a wife in jeopardy solely by virtue of her husband's control over her testimony. . . .

[W]e conclude that the existing rule should be modified so that the witness-spouse alone has a privilege to refuse to testify adversely; the witness may be neither compelled to testify nor foreclosed from testifying. This modification — vesting the privilege in the witness-spouse — furthers the important public interest in marital harmony without unduly burdening legitimate law enforcement needs.

Here, petitioner's spouse chose to testify against him. That she did so after a grant of immunity and assurances of lenient treatment does not render her testimony involuntary. . . .

NOTES AND QUESTIONS

1. *Evidentiary Privilege for Non-Marital Couples.* Courts have not extended similar testimonial or communications privileges to non-marital couples.[248] Should they? Does the availability of marriage to both same-sex and different-sex couples make the case for such an expansion stronger or weaker?

2. *Parent-Child Testimonial Privilege?* We have been discussing an adverse testimonial privilege between spouses. Should there be a parent-child privilege? Some countries, like France and Germany, have such a privilege, but in the United States, most federal and state courts have rejected it.[249] If we were going to recognize such a privilege, should it apply to both parents and children, such that neither would have to testify against the other? Or should it only allow children to refuse to testify against their parents, or parents to refuse to testify against their children? The few states that impose a parent-child privilege usually apply it only in one direction — with only children not having to testify against parents, or only parents not having to testify against children.[250]

---

248. See, e.g., United States v. Acker, 52 F.3d 509, 514–15 (4th Cir. 1995); United States v. White, 545 F.2d 1129, 1130 (8th Cir. 1976).

249. See Amee A. Shah, The Parent-Child Testimonial Privilege — Has the Time for It Finally Arrived, 47 Clev. St. L. Rev. 41, 42 (1999); see, e.g., In re Grand Jury Proceedings, 103 F.3d 1140 (3d Cir. 1997); Under Seal v. United States, 755 F.3d 213 (4th Cir. 2014); People v. Dixon, 411 N.W.2d 760 (Mich. Ct. App. 1987).

250. See, e.g., Mass. Ann. Laws ch. 233, § 20 (LexisNexis 2020); Idaho Code § 9-203 (2020); see also Catherine J. Ross, Implementing Constitutional Rights for Juveniles: The Parent-Child Privilege in Context, 14 Stan. L. & Pol'y Rev. 85 (2003).

CHAPTER 4

Dissolution and Divorce

This chapter considers the legal regulation of the ending of intimate relationships. It also addresses the constitutional right to access courts to do so and the power of courts over divorce actions.

I. Non-Marital Relationship Dissolution

For most of American history, non-marital sexual relationships were, as discussed in Chapter 2, regarded as illegitimate, immoral, and illegal. Though not frequently prosecuted, fornication was a crime, and was punished especially harshly if the partners were of different races.[1]

By the 1960s, however, things were changing. Sexual relationships between unmarried partners became more widely accepted. The Supreme Court overturned precedent and struck down state laws that applied harsher penalties in the case of sexual relationships between partners of different races.[2] More generally, the Court's decisions cast doubt on the constitutionality of laws prohibiting non-marital sexual relationships.[3]

Same-sex couples' struggles to have their relationships recognized as legitimate led the Supreme Court to strike down laws prohibiting intimate conduct between same-sex partners, overruling precedent that was less than 20 years old.[4] As state courts grappled with the question whether to extend the right to marry to same-sex couples (examined closely in Chapter 2), some states created the means for same-sex couples to have their relationships formally recognized.

---

1. Pace v. State of Alabama, 106 U.S. 583 (1883).
2. McLaughlin v. Florida, 379 U.S. 184 (1964).
3. See, e.g., Eisenstadt v. Baird, 405 U.S. 438 (1972).
4. Lawrence v. Texas, 539 U.S. 558 (2003) (overruling Bowers v. Hardwick, 478 U.S. 186 (1986)).

These formal relationship structures include domestic partnerships, civil unions, reciprocal beneficiaries, and designated beneficiaries. For the dissolution of these statuses, the degree of state involvement varies; there may be administrative state involvement, but often no judicial involvement. Domestic partnerships, for example, can often be ended by the filing of a notice of dissolution with the appropriate governmental office.[5] Civil unions, in contrast, typically must be dissolved in the same manner as a marriage.[6] Prior to the Supreme Court's ruling in Obergefell v. Hodges, many of the legal issues surrounding dissolution of these alternative statuses arose from interstate conflicts of law.[7]

Intimate relationships that are not formalized entail no state mandated procedure for dissolution; the process usually occurs without any state oversight unless one party asserts economic claims against the other, the nature and resolution of which are examined in Chapter 5.[8] As discussed in Chapter 2, some states preclude proof of a common law marriage more than a few years after a couple ceases to cohabit, rendering the passage of time a form of legal dissolution for informal relationships. In some other countries, even informal cohabiting relationships may require some legal procedure to be ended. But in the United States, generally, if there was no formal state involvement in the creation of a non-marital relationship, there need be no state involvement in its dissolution.[9]

II. Fault-Based Divorce

Traditionally, the law has not readily released people from marital bonds. The common law of England did not even allow divorce as we know it today.[10] Until 1857 in England, full divorces required an Act of Parliament, an option realistically available only to a select few.[11] American law in the colonies initially followed the English lead, requiring legislative action for a full divorce.[12] But after the American Revolution, states began to adopt judicial divorce laws. By the end of the nineteenth century, every state but South Carolina had provided for absolute divorce at least under some

---

5. See, e.g., Velez v. Smith, 48 Cal. Rptr. 3d 642 (Cal. Ct. App. 2006).

6. See, e.g., Groh v. Groh, 106 A.3d 1286 (N.J. Super. Ct. Ch. Div. 2014).

7. See, e.g., Rosengarten v. Downes, 802 A.2d 170 (Conn. App. Ct. 2002) (refusing to dissolve Vermont civil union); see generally Joanna L. Grossman, Resurrecting Comity: Revisiting the Problem of Non-Uniform Marriage Laws, 84 Or. L. Rev. 433, 484-86 (2005).

8. Comparative for discussion of dissolution, see Brienna Perelli-Harris & Nora Sánchez Gassen, How Similar Are Cohabitation and Marriage? Legal Approaches to Cohabitation Across Western Europe, 38 Population & Dev. Rev. 435 (2012).

9. An exception to this rule is common law marriage, which still exists in several U.S. jurisdictions and is discussed in Chapter 2.

10. Lawrence Friedman, A History of American Law (4th ed. 2019).

11. Lawrence Stone, The Family, Sex, and Marriage in England 1500-1800 (1977).

12. Nelson Blake, The Road to Reno: A History of Divorce in the United States (1962); Lawrence M. Friedman, Rights of Passage: Divorce Law in Historical Perspective, 63 Or. L. Rev. 649 (1984).

circumstances.[13] When the judiciary assumed control of divorce, it still limited the ability to exit a marriage. The party seeking a divorce had to file a suit in an adversarial proceeding showing that they were innocent and blameless *and* that the other spouse was a wrongdoer. Statutes enumerated the specific matrimonial offenses—marital "fault"—that would warrant a divorce. If none of the specific offenses could be shown, then no divorce could be granted. "Easier" divorce states included more grounds than "harder" ones. And a variety of defenses sometimes precluded a decree of dissolution even when fault had been proven. For example, if both parties were guilty of marital misconduct, then neither party would be entitled to a divorce.

In the 1970s, the fault-based regime began to cede some authority to an alternative approach: no-fault divorce. No-fault did not require a designation of one party as guilty, nor the other as innocent. Rather, no-fault directed attention to the question of whether the marriage was viable. Even after the advent of no-fault divorce, though, the fault-based approach remained important. Although California repealed its fault grounds when it moved to a no-fault system, most states added no-fault grounds to the existing fault-based grounds for divorce. Spouses seeking a divorce have multiple incentives to pursue a fault-based divorce, notwithstanding the availability of no-fault grounds. In some cases, a spouse may want the sense of moral vindication—confirmation that they behaved honorably, and that the other spouse did not. In other cases, the motivations for pursuing a fault-based divorce may be more practical. In many states, fault is still considered in property distribution and spousal support (discussed in Chapter 5). Thus, a finding that the other spouse was at-fault could afford a significant advantage with respect to these important determinations.

A. Fault-Based Grounds

The first two cases below are representative of the era when legally exiting a marriage through divorce meant prevailing in a fault-based system; the third case comes from the modern era.

BENSCOTER V. BENSCOTER
188 A.2d 859 (Pa. Super. Ct. 1963)

Opinion by ERVIN, J.

In this case the husband filed a complaint in divorce on the ground of indignities to the person....

[I]t is the duty of the appellate court to make an independent investigation of the evidence in order to determine whether in truth it does establish a legal cause

---

13. See Blake, supra note 12.

for divorce: We have accordingly reviewed the entire testimony and record in this case and have arrived at an independent conclusion that the husband is not entitled to a divorce.

The parties were married on August 21, 1946 in West Nanticoke, Pennsylvania. Four sons were born as a result of the marriage. . . . At the time of the hearing in January 1962 the plaintiff was 39 years of age and the defendant was 37 and she was suffering from multiple sclerosis.

The main indignity of which the husband complains is that the wife expressed her disappointment in failing to have a female child and that she verbally abused him and blamed him for this failure. The wife's alleged misconduct was sporadic in nature and did not constitute a course of conduct as required by law. It must be pointed out that the parties lived together for 15 years and it was not until August of 1961 that the plaintiff complained about the defendant. Therefore, the plaintiff's condition could not have been as intolerable nor his life so burdensome as he now alleges.

In August of 1958 the defendant-wife was stricken with the incurable disease, multiple sclerosis. As a result of this disease she has double vision, slurred speech, weakness of the muscles and she cannot walk without the assistance of another person or a cane. She falls down frequently. She lost weight and at the time of the hearing weighed only 86 pounds. She is subject to the frustrations that are attendant to this progressive disease. Even the plaintiff testified that in September of 1961 the defendant attempted to commit suicide three times. These circumstances cannot be blindly disregarded. Ill health both explains and excuses a wife's conduct and the acts of a spouse resulting from ill health do not furnish a ground for divorce.

During the summer of 1961 the defendant noticed that the plaintiff was taking more pride in his appearance, shaving every other day, using deodorants and changing clothes more frequently. Defendant's suspicions of another woman were aroused when she found prophylactics in the plaintiff's wallet and stains on his underclothes. Plaintiff offered a unique explanation of the presence of the prophylactics by stating that as game commissioner he used them for making turkey calls. The evidence clearly is that the plaintiff did accompany the other woman while trapping wild game and that he went swimming with her. We agree with the court below that plaintiff's interest in the other woman was above and beyond the call of duty. While the defendant was not able to prove adultery, certainly, under such circumstances, her suspicions were not unfounded. It was incumbent upon the plaintiff to show clearly and indubitably his status as the injured and innocent spouse. We do not believe that the plaintiff was the innocent and injured spouse.

The parties to a marriage take each other for better or for worse, in sickness and in health: The conclusion is inescapable that the plaintiff did not become dissatisfied with his wife until she became ill with multiple sclerosis. He cannot now discard her.

RANKIN V. RANKIN

124 A.2d 639 (Pa. Super. Ct. 1956)

WRIGHT, J.

On February 3, 1953, Michael J. Rankin instituted an action in divorce against his wife, Edith L. Rankin. The parties were at that time aged 58 and 43 years, respectively. The complaint originally alleged cruel and barbarous treatment and indignities to the person, but was subsequently amended to include a charge of desertion. . . . [The lower court accepted and adopted the master's report recommending a decree on all three grounds.]. . .

That the marriage of the parties . . . was not harmonious is clearly derived from the evidence in the case. . . .

Miss Powers testified that she saw appellee threaten appellant with a gun, that she saw Mrs. Rankin after she had been beaten by appellee, that her arms were injured, her knees bruised, and she had a black eye. James Morrison, Pastor of the Beallsville Presbyterian Church and a close neighbor of the parties, testified that he had heard appellee speak disrespectfully of his wife, that he had heard appellee say that if his money would save him he would kill his wife, and that he saw Mrs. Rankin when her face was "beat up". . . .

Considering first the question of cruel and barbarous treatment, we note that the master was "of the opinion that this ground has been established by clear and satisfactory evidence." However, the lower court said: "We have some doubt as to whether there is sufficient [evidence] in the case to sustain the cause of cruel and barbarous treatment". The term cruel and barbarous treatment comprises actual personal violence or a reasonable apprehension thereof, or such a course of treatment as endangers life or health and renders cohabitation unsafe. A single instance of cruelty may be so severe, and with such attending circumstances of atrocity, as to justify a divorce: The master bases his recommendation solely upon an incident which allegedly occurred when the parties were riding together in an automobile. As related in the master's report: "On one occasion, while they were riding in a car with defendant driving, she stated: 'I am going to kill you, you son of a bitch', and proceeded to drive the car at a high rate of speed. On this occasion plaintiff succeeded in slowing down the car by turning the ignition key, following which he jumped from the car; thereupon defendant attempted to run him down." This circumstance was categorically denied by appellant, was entirely uncorroborated, and is utterly improbable in the light of appellee's testimony that he "jerked the key out to slow the car down", that he got out of the car, and that appellant then "turned the car" and endeavored "to get me along the road."

Next considering the question of indignities, the findings of the master which the lower court deemed important may be thus summarized: Appellant's "attitude toward plaintiff was one of marked antipathy; she called him vile and opprobious names without provocation"; she refused to have children; she "had the furniture, with the exception of the box springs and mattress, removed from plaintiff's bedroom"; she "was frequently absent from the home without explanation . . . spit in his face and tried to strike him with a chair; that she threw hot water on plaintiff; and another time threatened him with a butcher knife." The lower court also considered the alleged incident in the automobile in connection with the charge of indignities. Appellee testified that his wife had him arrested "a lot of times" for assault and battery. It should be here noted that much of appellee's testimony consisted of similar general expressions and was vague and indefinite throughout. Sidney A. Grubbs testified that, at the insistence of appellee, he went to see appellant in an effort to effect a reconciliation, but appellant said "there was no use to try to get along with that dumb hunky". Mollie M. Leathers testified that she frequently heard appellant use profanity and remark that she hated to see her husband come home. . . .

As we pointed out in our opinion filed this day in *Moyer v. Moyer*, 124 A.2d 632, 637 (Pa. Super. 1956): "In a proceeding for divorce on the grounds of indignities, it must clearly appear from the evidence that the plaintiff was the injured and innocent spouse". . . . It is well established that indignities provoked by the other party do not constitute ground for a divorce, unless the retaliation is excessive.

In her testimony appellant admitted using profanity and calling her husband names. By way of explanation, she alleged that she had acquired her knowledge of profanity from appellee, and that, in calling her husband "a dumb hunky", she was only repeating his own words. She flatly denied that she ever threw hot water on him, or threatened him with a butcher knife. . . . In answer to appellee's charge that she refused to have children, appellant testified that in 1949 it was necessary for her to undergo a hysterectomy. This was corroborated by Dr. Krosnoff, who referred appellant to Dr. Fisher for the operation. Catherine Reeves and Florence Mills, two other witnesses for appellant, testified that appellee frequently used vile language toward his wife. Both testified that appellant was a good cook and a good housekeeper, and that she tried to get along with her husband. As already noted, several witnesses testified that appellee threatened to kill his wife. When asked if he had not said that he "would like to shoot that God Damn Crummy", appellee's reply was: "I don't know if I did or not."

The fact that married people do not get along well together does not justify a divorce. Testimony which proves merely an unhappy union, the parties being high strung temperamentally and unsuited to each other and neither being wholly innocent of the causes which resulted in the failure of their marriage, is insufficient to sustain a decree. If both are equally at fault, neither can clearly be said to be the innocent and injured spouse, and the law will leave them where they put themselves. At the very best, appellee's evidence might establish such a situation. A less favorable view of the evidence indicates that appellee was the principal offender, and that appellant was actually the innocent and injured spouse. In neither event has appellee established his right to a divorce on the ground of indignities.

Coming finally to the charge of desertion, in the words of the lower court, the "type of desertion" in the case at bar is "sometimes loosely and inappropriately called 'constructive desertion'". Appellee testified that, on the day he left home, he and his wife had an argument; that appellant's father and brother subsequently came to the house; that he refused to admit them; that they left the premises but later returned; that he (appellee) was then in his car; and that the father and brother pursued him for ten or fifteen miles. Appellee finally arrived in Windber, where he had a room, and never lived in Washington County again. . . . The master found that this testimony was sufficient to establish desertion by the wife, saying: "While the testimony brings the case within the category of 'constructive desertion', a somewhat vague concept in Pennsylvania jurisprudence and one of limited application, it is nevertheless clear that desertion may be said to exist where the plaintiff has been willfully and maliciously put out of the common habitation by force or justifiable fear of immediate bodily harm, or locked out against his will and without his consent." . . .

But we have not found a scintilla of evidence to support the proposition that appellee failed to return because of fear of harm from his wife's family. Moreover, we have searched the record in vain for evidence of an actual desire on appellee's part to return to the home. On the contrary, the testimony shows that he was satisfied with the separation. That appellee was not interested in a reconciliation is indicated by a letter to his wife dated July 2, 1953, reading in part as follows: "You say you want to talk to me. I don't have anything to talk about. . . . The most it will cost me now is $1,000.00 to get rid of you". An alleged desertion is reduced to the status of separation if the deserted spouse manifests his consent. . . .

We conclude by emphasizing that a divorce decree must be founded upon compelling reasons, and upon evidence that is clear and convincing, which necessary essentials are not disclosed by this record.

RICKETTS V. RICKETTS

903 A.2d 857 (Md. 2006)

BELL, C.J.

The issues presented by this case are: first, whether a spouse's complaint for a limited divorce alleging constructive desertion based on lack of marital relations may be maintained when both parties continue to live under the same roof, albeit not in the same bedroom and without cohabitation. . . .

The appellant, Robert M. Ricketts, Jr., and Mary C. Ricketts, the appellee, were married on June 13, 1981 and that union produced three children: Robert III, now emancipated and, thus, not subject to this Court's jurisdiction, Kathryn, who was born in 1987 and is emancipated, and Lawrence, who was born in 1989. It is unclear from the record when the parties' relationship began to deteriorate, but at some point, according to Mr. Ricketts, Mrs. Ricketts "forced [him] out of the bedroom, thus terminating their marital relationship." Since that time, he alleges, the parties have not had marital relations, although they have continued to reside in the marital household with their children, albeit in separate bedrooms.

On July 16, 2002, Mr. Ricketts filed a complaint seeking a limited divorce and custody of their two minor children. He alleged, as grounds for the divorce, constructive desertion, offering in support, Mrs. Ricketts's alleged denial of marital relations. On October 16, 2002, Mrs. Ricketts filed a Motion to Dismiss, arguing that because the parties continued to live under the same roof, had not separated and, therefore, were not living separate and apart, Mr. Ricketts's complaint for divorce was "fatally defective" and, thus, "must be dismissed." . . . Responding to the appellee's motion, the appellant admitted that the parties were still living together in the same house, under the same roof, but stated that this did not affect the validity of his complaint or the availability of the relief sought, i.e. limited divorce and custody. . . .

A limited divorce, which may be decreed for a limited or an indefinite period, Md. Code § 7-102(c), is "one from bed and board. It grants unto the injured spouse the right to live separate and apart from the one at fault. However, the parties remain *man* and *wife,* and there is no severance of the marital bonds." . . . This is in contrast to an absolute divorce, which effects a complete severance of the marital bond and entitles either of the parties, or both, to remarry.

Among the grounds for a limited divorce is desertion. Desertion may be constructive or actual. . . . We have defined actual desertion as:

> the voluntary separation of one of the married parties from the other, or the refusal to renew suspended cohabitation, without justification either in the consent or the wrongful conduct of the other party. . . . [Furthermore,] the separation and intention to abandon must concur, and desertion does not exist without the presence of both. The two need not begin at the same time, but desertion begins whenever to either one the other is added.

What is required to constitute constructive desertion was addressed in Scheinin v. Scheinin, 89 A.2d 609 (1952). In that case, we said:

> It is accepted that any conduct of a husband that renders the marital relation intolerable and compels the wife to leave him may justify a divorce on the ground of constructive desertion, even though the conduct may not justify a divorce on the ground of cruelty. Any misconduct of the husband will justify the wife in leaving him when it makes it impossible for her to live with him without loss of her health or self-respect, or gives her reasonable apprehension of bodily injury. If the husband's misconduct has been such as to render continuance of the marriage relation unbearable, justifying the wife in leaving him, he is the one who is guilty of desertion. . . .

Unlike actual desertion, where it is the party deserted who has the cause for divorce, in instances of constructive desertion, it is the departing party who has the cause of action for divorce.

To be sure, both actual desertion and constructive desertion generally require that one of the spouses physically leave the marital home. We have held, however, that constructive desertion may occur where both parties continue to live under the same roof. In *Scheinin,* we were emphatic and clear:

> It is beyond question that there may be a desertion although the husband and wife continue to live under the same roof. For desertion, as applied to husband and wife, signifies something more than merely ceasing to live together. It means ceasing to live together as husband and wife.

We have explained:

> the true doctrine is believed to be that the statutory term "desertion," as applied to husband and wife, means a cessation of the marital relation; and this doctrine is in accord with the general principles of the divorce law . . . [d]esertion implies something more than merely ceasing to cohabit or live together; for, as applied to husband and wife, it means the ceasing to live together as husband and wife.

Thus, "it is unquestionably the law in this State that permanent refusal of either the husband or the wife to have sexual intercourse with the other spouse, from no consideration of health or other good reason, constitutes matrimonial desertion although the parties continue to live in the same house." The fact that the spouses sleep in separate bedrooms or that they have ceased engaging in sexual relations does not per se establish constructive desertion, however. Additionally, when a husband and wife continue to live together without marital relations and yet neither makes any effort towards reconciliation, it is presumed that both spouses prefer to live under such circumstances, and, therefore, neither has a cause for divorce on the grounds of constructive desertion.

In the instant case, it is alleged by the appellant that Mrs. Ricketts denied him marital relations and forced him from the marital bedroom. Under Md. Code § 7-102(a)(3) of the Family Law Article and, pursuant to the aforementioned case law, if those allegations are established, . . . Mr. Ricketts has cause for a limited divorce, notwithstanding that he and Mrs. Ricketts are still living under the same roof, those allegations, and the necessary inferences, may sufficiently establish, for pleading purposes, constructive desertion. . . .

NOTES AND QUESTIONS

1. *Marriage, Divorce, and Morality.* The *Benscoter* case accurately reflects the sense of moral judgment that to some extent pervades family law even today. Even if the husband was innocent of wrongdoing, the court would not have granted the divorce because the wife, in the court's view, was not at fault. The court views the husband's marital obligation as a moral one, one from which he would be

released if his wife had been engaged in wrongdoing, but not here — as a result of her illness, need for his caretaking, or inability to be the wife he wanted her to be. How justifiable is the intuition that the husband should not divorce his sick wife? Even if it would be immoral for him to leave her, should it be the place of the law to stop him from doing so? Courts do not stop people from breaking contracts in other settings, so why do so here? What purpose is served by trying to force someone to continue a marriage in which that person is no longer invested?

2. *Extreme Cruelty.* The husband in *Benscoter* sought a divorce on the basis of "indignities to the person," described as the "most comprehensive ground for divorce in Pennsylvania" at the time.[14] That ground encompassed a wide range of behavior that could be placed in the category of "mental cruelty," everything from ridicule and abusive language to hate and estrangement.[15] Historically, courts equated cruelty with physical harm.[16] But by the 1860s, courts began to accept that cruelty could constitute fault even "though operating primarily upon the mind only," as long as the verbal abuse produced physical effects on the target spouse's health or life.[17] The concept of cruelty continued to expand in most states to include mental cruelty with no physical effects.[18] This shift rendered cruelty the most popular ground for divorce, as it gave spouses some ability to assert more individualized complaints.[19]

The *Rankin* court applied a traditional definition of cruelty, requiring proof of "actual personal violence or a reasonable apprehension thereof, or such a course of treatment as endangers life or health and renders cohabitation unsafe." Did the wife seem to have engaged in any behavior that would satisfy this standard? What if the "cruel" behavior was provoked? With regard to the husband's claim of indignities, the court noted that behavior provoked by the other party cannot constitute a ground for divorce, unless the retaliation is excessive. Was all the wife's offensive behavior provoked?

Even a broader definition of cruelty can still be a high bar. Courts have been consistent over time in refusing to grant divorces on the basis of complaints they deem trivial. As a Texas court recently explained its standard, "To be considered cruel treatment, the conduct of the accused spouse must rise to such a level that it

---

14. Robert A. Ebeustein, Grounds and Defenses in Pennsylvania, 15 Vill. L. Rev. 155, 163 (1969).

15. Id. at 164.

16. Cf. Elizabeth Pleck, Domestic Tyranny: The Making of Social Policy Against Family Violence from Colonial Times to the Present (1987); Reva B. Siegel, "The Rule of Love," Wife Beating as Prerogative and Privacy, 105 Yale L.J. 2117 (1996).

17. Powelson v. Powelson, 22 Cal. 358, 360–61 (1863).

18. See, e.g., Barnes v. Barnes, 30 P. 298 (Cal. 1892) (noting the "tendency of modern decisions, reflecting the advanced civilization of the present age," to "view marriage from a different standpoint than as a mere physical relation").

19. See generally Robert Griswold, The Evolution of Mental Cruelty in Victorian American Divorce, 1790–1900, 20 J. Soc. Hist. 127 (1986); Elaine Tyler May, Great Expectations: Marriage and Divorce in Post-Victorian America (1980).

renders the couple's living together insupportable. Insupportable for purposes of cruel treatment means incapable of being borne, unendurable, insufferable, or intolerable. Mere trivial matters or disagreements do not justify the granting of divorce for cruel treatment."[20] The challenge is to distinguish the ordinary ups and downs of a marriage from behavior that should justify divorce. Statutes and judicial opinions have tried to impose some kind of objective standard for the level of cruelty required. But can such a standard ever be articulated? The applicable Pennsylvania statute in a case excerpted in the next section required that the spouse's behavior be so severe "as to render [the innocent spouse's] condition intolerable and life burdensome."[21] Is it clear what conduct would meet that standard? The appeals court in *Rankin* reversed the trial court's judgment granting the divorce, explaining that unhappiness does not justify a grant of divorce. The question in fault-era divorce cases was not what a particular spouse wanted to put up with but rather what judges believed the spouse should be forced to tolerate. Is that the type of determination that courts are well-equipped to make?

3.   *Other Fault-Based Grounds.* In addition to the grounds discussed in *Rankin*, states provided a variety of other fault-based grounds for divorce. In Massachusetts, for example, "A divorce from the bond of matrimony may be adjudged for adultery, impotency, utter desertion continued for one year next prior to the filing of the complaint, gross and confirmed habits of intoxication caused by voluntary and excessive use of intoxicating liquor, opium, or other drugs, cruel and abusive treatment, or, if a spouse being of sufficient ability, grossly or wantonly and cruelly refuses or neglects to provide suitable support and maintenance for the other spouse."[22] In New York, the fault-based grounds for divorce include: cruel and inhuman treatment; the abandonment of the plaintiff by the defendant for a period of one or more years; the confinement of the defendant in prison for a period of three or more consecutive years; and adultery.[23] In Texas, the statute provides that a spouse may obtain a fault-based divorce on the ground of adultery, cruelty, abandonment that has persisted for at least one year, or felony conviction with a sentence of at least one year in prison.[24] Let's consider some of these grounds in more detail.

a.   *Actual or Constructive Desertion.* Desertion or abandonment is a common ground for divorce.[25] Desertion as a ground for divorce usually refers to the offending spouse having left the marital home or otherwise withdrawn from the relationship. However, as *Ricketts* indicates, desertion need not be limited

---

20. In re Marriage of Garcia and Garcia, No. 14-17-00444-CV, 2019 WL 1523483, *7 (Tex. App. Apr. 9, 2019) (internal citations omitted).

21. 23 Pa. Cons. Stat. § 3301 (2020).

22. Mass. Gen. Laws ch. 208, § 1 (West 2020).

23. N.Y. Dom. Rel. Law § 170 Tex. App. should be Tex. Ct. App. (McKinney 2020).

24. Tex. Fam. Code Ann. § 6.001-07 (West 2020).

25. See, e.g., N.Y. Dom. Rel. Law § 170 (McKinney 2020); Mo. Rev. Stat. § 452.320 (2020).

to physical desertion. As a New York court stated in a different case, "To establish abandonment as a ground for divorce, the plaintiff must prove that the defendant refused to fulfill the basic marital obligations for a period of one year or more, without consent by the abandoned spouse and without justification."[26] The refusal to have sexual relations for an extended period of time often constituted constructive desertion under most divorce statutes. In *Rankin*, the husband claimed the wife essentially forced him out of the home, leaving no real option other than to leave. Did the court sustain the husband's claim of constructive desertion? Why? In *Ricketts*, the husband's claim was one of constructive desertion, that his wife's behavior left him no choice but to abandon the relationship. But if her behavior was insufficient to constitute a ground for divorce, should he be able to convert it into a divorce claim through the concept of constructive desertion?

b. *Adultery.* Adultery was available as a ground for divorce in every state during the fault-based era,[27] and was commonly cited.[28] Where the spouse denies having engaged in adultery, the court confronts the difficult issue of proof. Typically, adultery will occur in private and may be difficult to prove even when it does occur. Courts have responded to this challenge by not requiring direct evidence of adultery. In Mississippi, for example, the state supreme court has explained that "one seeking a divorce on the grounds of adulterous activity must show by clear and convincing evidence both an adulterous inclination and a reasonable opportunity to satisfy that inclination. . . . Adultery may be shown by evidence or admissions[,] and either [is] sufficient to support a decree of divorce."[29] What facts might be offered to show a spouse's "inclination" and "opportunity" to commit adultery? It was not uncommon for alleged adultery to form the basis of a cruelty claim — e.g., "he cruelly taunted me with his affairs." Courts often applied a different standard to adultery by men (had to be flagrant or repeated) versus adultery by women (could be the mere suggestion of infidelity). Why? Are such double standards still reflected in modern attitudes about adultery?

In addition to being a ground for fault-based divorce in a majority of states, adultery is still a crime in twenty-one states.[30] According to Professor Edward Stein, treating sex with someone other than one's spouse as adultery sweeps too broadly, in that it would include consensual non-monogamy.[31] This

---

26. Dodd v. Colbert, 64 A.D.3d 982, 983 (N.Y. App. Div. 2009).

27. See Isabel Drummond, Getting a Divorce (1930); Chester G. Vernier, 2 American Family Laws 242 (1932) (noting that adultery was the most common ground available, followed by desertion and cruelty).

28. See Paul R. Amato & Denise Previti, People's Reasons for Divorcing: Gender, Social Class, the Life Course, and Adjustment, 24 J. Fam. Issues 602 (2003).

29. Gerty v. Gerty, 265 So. 3d 121, 131 (Miss. 2018).

30. Edward Stein, Adultery, Infidelity, and Consensual Non-Monogamy, 55 Wake Forest L. Rev. 147, 148–49 (2020).

31. Id. at 150–51.

might occur, for instance, in polyamorous relationships, including marital ones. Should the law treat consensual non-monogamy the same way as non-monogamy without one's spouse's consent? Is the problem the deception or simply having a sexual partner other than one's spouse?

c. *Willful Neglect.* Early divorce laws recognized neglect as a ground for divorce, but only women were permitted to claim it. As discussed in Chapter 3, marriage was gendered by law and social norms, both of which charged the husband with the duty to provide.[32] Recall McGuire v. McGuire from Chapter 3. Would Lydia have been able to prevail in a divorce action on grounds of neglect?

4.   *Legal Separation Versus Divorce. Ricketts* concerned a claim for a limited divorce, which is to say a formal, court-ordered, legal separation. Also known as a "divorce from bed and board" or a "divorce a mensa et thoro," legal separation was and is available only in some states.[33] The key difference between separation and divorce is that the former does not enable the parties to remarry. Historically, many divorce laws imposed restrictions on remarriage such as a one-year waiting period after divorce or a ban on remarriage during the lifetime of the other spouse. But today, most states treat divorce as a clean break. Many couples who separate enter into agreements governing property, support, and custody; courts also have the authority to impose orders concerning all aspects of the separation.

Legal separation requires grounds, just as divorce does. The grounds for separation are typically very similar to those for divorce, except that requirements (such as how long a particular type of fault, like abandonment, must have lasted) are less onerous.[34] Separation is sometimes a transitional phase before a couple gets divorced, but it can also be a permanent choice for couples who oppose divorce or have some other reason to stay married as a matter of formal status.

PROBLEM

Novel Davis filed for divorce against her husband, Shepherd Davis, on grounds of abandonment lasting at least one year, one of the available fault-based grounds in New York.[35] In her complaint, she alleged "social abandonment" — stating that her husband refused to celebrate or acknowledge major holidays or birthdays with her; refused to "eat meals together;" refused to "attend family functions or accompany [her] to movies, shopping, restaurants, and church services;" once left her "at

---

32. See generally Naomi Cahn, Faithless Wives and Lazy Husbands: Gender Norms in Nineteenth Century Divorce Law, 2002 U. Ill. L. Rev. 651. (2002).

33. See generally Vernier, supra note 27, at 242; Henrik Hartog, Man and Wife in America: A History (2000).

34. See, e.g., N.Y. Dom. Rel. Law § 200 (McKinney 2020).

35. Davis v. Davis, 71 A.D.3d 13 (N.Y. App. Div. 2009).

a hospital emergency room;" removed her "belongings from the marital bedroom;" and just generally "ignor[ed] her." Shepherd argued that even if all the facts alleged were true, it did not constitute marital fault. Prior cases have recognized that "abandonment" includes one party's leaving the marital home, refusing to have sexual relations, locking the other out of the home, or behaving in such a way as to force the other to leave the home. Should social abandonment be accepted as sufficient fault to justify a divorce? If it was accepted as sufficient grounds, how should it be defined, and how would a court measure whether it had occurred?

B. Fault-Based Defenses

The fault-based system was premised on the idea that an innocent spouse was entitled to a divorce upon proof of an enumerated ground of fault. The system was designed to be adversarial. Accordingly, the spouse accused of fault could assert a defense. The following two cases feature both fault-based grounds and defenses. (Be advised that these materials include descriptions of domestic violence.)

FULTON V. FULTON
918 So. 2d 877 (Miss. Ct. App. 2006)

CHANDLER, J., for the Court.

The Adams County Chancery Court granted a divorce to October and Anitra Fulton on the grounds of October's habitual cruel and inhuman treatment. Anitra was awarded custody of the children. October appeals, raising the following issues: (i) whether the Chancellor properly granted a divorce on the grounds of October's habitual cruel and inhuman treatment and (ii) whether the chancellor properly denied October's complaint for divorce on the grounds of adultery.

Finding no error, we affirm.

FACTS

October and Anitra Fulton were married on May 25, 1999, but they had lived together since May of 1991. The parties had three children, all of whom were born before the marriage. On May 23, 2002, October filed a complaint for divorce on the grounds of irreconcilable differences. Anitra filed a counterclaim, alleging that she was entitled to a divorce based on October's habitual cruel and inhuman treatment. October amended his complaint and alleged that he was entitled to divorce on the grounds of adultery and habitual cruel and inhuman treatment. The Fulton family lived together, and October and Anitra slept in the same bed, until Anitra and the children moved out in late February of 2003.

Anitra admitted that she had engaged in an adulterous relationship while she was married to October. The adulterous relationship ended in November of 2001, and in December of 2001 she confessed to her husband that she had an affair and that she had ended it. After Anitra admitted to the affair, the couple continued to live together and eventually resumed sexual relations.

Anitra testified that October physically abused her throughout the marriage. Anitra alleged three specific instances of cruel and inhuman treatment. When Anitra was pregnant with her third child, October, then a live-in boyfriend, kicked her from behind and bruised her tailbone. In June of 2002, October scratched the inside of her mouth and hit her in the back. Anitra filed criminal charges against October, to which October pleaded guilty. At trial, Anitra called corroborating witnesses who verified the injuries. In October of 2002, after the divorce had been filed, Anitra saw her husband in a car with Ms. Gaylor, October's girlfriend at the time, and followed them. When they stopped, Anitra attempted to take a picture of October with Ms. Gaylor. Ms. Gaylor took the camera out of Anitra's hand and hit her. Anitra hit her back, and the two of them started fighting. Ms. Gaylor's friends and sister came to Ms. Gaylor's aid and severely injured Anitra. October watched the incident in his car and did nothing to help. Anitra received treatment for her injuries at a hospital emergency room.

The chancellor awarded Anitra a divorce on the grounds of habitual cruel and inhuman treatment and denied October a divorce on all grounds he alleged. . . .

I. WHETHER THE CHANCELLOR PROPERLY GRANTED A DIVORCE ON THE GROUNDS OF OCTOBER'S HABITUAL CRUEL AND INHUMAN TREATMENT

Conduct that evinces habitual cruel and inhuman treatment must be such that it either (1) endangers life, limb, or health, or creates a reasonable apprehension of such danger, rendering the relationship unsafe for the party seeking relief, or (2) is so unnatural and infamous as to make the marriage revolting to the non-offending spouse and render it impossible for that spouse to discharge the duties of marriage, thus destroying the basis for its continuance. This ground for divorce must be proven by the preponderance of credible evidence. Although the cruel and inhuman treatment usually must be shown to have been systematic and continuous, a single incident may provide grounds for divorce.

Anitra testified to three specific instances of cruel and inhuman treatment on the part of October. One instance occurred before the parties were married and one instance occurred after the parties' separation. Anitra claimed that there were many other instances in which she called the police on October but never pressed charges. October denied that he had ever hit Anitra, but he did admit that he pleaded guilty to a charge of simple assault, and he did admit that he did nothing to help Anitra when his then-girlfriend attacked her.

Anitra called three witnesses that were able to verify October's abuse against Anitra. Jeanie Johnson, Anitra's mother, testified that there were two occasions that she saw bruises on Anitra. Christine Green, a close friend of Anitra's, testified that there were many instances in which Anitra called her late at night and talked about the altercations that she had with October. There was one occasion in which Anitra came over to Green's house after an argument with October where she was nervous, extremely upset, and crying. Loretta Herbert, Anitra's cousin, testified that in June of 2002 Anitra called her to take pictures of the bruises Anitra had on her face and scratches she had inside her mouth. Herbert also testified that she visited the Fultons' house several times a month and noticed the tension in the household. Specifically, she noted that October refused to speak to his wife. Herbert also testified that Anitra asked Herbert to take her to the emergency room when October's then-girlfriend attacked Anitra because October refused to help.

Although Anitra testified only to three specific instances of physical abuse on the part of October, and only one instance occurred during the course of the parties' marriage, her own testimony and her corroborating witnesses' testimony demonstrated a pattern of abuse that enabled the chancellor to grant a divorce on the grounds of habitual cruel and inhuman treatment.

II. WHETHER THE CHANCELLOR PROPERLY DENIED OCTOBER'S COMPLAINT FOR DIVORCE ON THE GROUNDS OF ADULTERY

Although a complainant is entitled to divorce on the grounds of adultery, the defense of condonation is recognized in our law. Condonation is the express or implied forgiveness of a marital wrong on the part of the wronged party. The mere resumption of residence does not constitute condonation, and condonation is conditioned on the offending spouse's good behavior.

Anitra testified that she ended her adulterous affair in November of 2001 and did not engage in another extramarital relationship after that time. October testified that he tried to make the marriage work after he learned of the affair. He was initially upset about Anitra's affair but resumed sexual relations with her approximately two months after he learned of the affair. Both parties testified that the sexual relations continued until July of 2002. The chancellor was presented with sufficient evidence that October condoned Anitra's adultery.

GILMARTIN V. GILMARTIN
822 S.E.2d 771 (N.C. Ct. App. 2018)

STROUD, JUDGE. . . .

[O]n 28 June 2016, plaintiff-wife filed a complaint against defendant-husband alleging that the parties married in 2006, had one child, and separated in June of 2016. . . .

Wife's claim was based upon North Carolina General Statute § 50-16.3A, and she alleged Husband had engaged in "marital misconduct," specifically "[i]llict sexual behavior" "and "[i]ndignities". . . .

Husband . . . contends "the trial court erred when it did not find that [Wife] condoned the [Husband's] illicit sexual behavior." Whether marital misconduct has been condoned is a question of fact. . . .

The North Carolina Pattern Jury Instructions succinctly and accurately summarize the law regarding condonation:

> In order to condone or forgive marital misconduct, a spouse must know that such marital misconduct occurred. This means that before marital misconduct can be forgiven, the spouse must have actual knowledge of the marital misconduct or have knowledge of facts which would satisfy a reasonably prudent person that the marital misconduct had been committed. . . .
>
> A spouse condones or forgives marital misconduct when he voluntarily elects to [continue] [resume] the marital relationship with the spouse who has committed marital misconduct. [Continuation] [Resumption] of the marital relationship means voluntary [continuation] [renewal] of the husband and wife relationship, as shown by the totality of the circumstances.
>
> [Evidence that the plaintiff and defendant engaged in sexual intercourse after the [plaintiff] [defendant] forgave his spouse for act(s) of marital misconduct is not required.]
>
> [Evidence of voluntary sexual intercourse between the plaintiff and the defendant after the [plaintiff] [defendant] has actual knowledge of the adultery of his spouse, or has knowledge of facts which would satisfy a reasonably prudent person that his spouse had committed adultery, is considered evidence of a spouse's forgiveness of adultery on the part of the offending spouse, and should be considered with all the other facts and circumstances in evidence.]
>
> Forgiveness may be express or implied. Express forgiveness is when a [husband] [wife] states to his spouse who has committed marital misconduct, "I forgive you for (state alleged marital misconduct)" or similar words to that effect.
>
> Forgiveness is implied when a husband and wife [continue] [resume] the marital relationship after a spouse has knowledge of marital misconduct by his spouse. [However, forgiveness is not implied simply because spouses live in the same residence.] [Isolated incidents of sexual intercourse between the parties do not constitute resumption of marital relations.]

N.C.P.I. — Civil 815.71 (footnotes omitted).

The trial court's findings relevant to marital fault and condonation, or the lack thereof, were as follows:

> Throughout the course of the parties' marriage the defendant was addicted to pornography. The plaintiff discovered this issue early in the marriage and she told the defendant it bothered her. The defendant exchanged pornographic

photos with others, including a nude picture of the plaintiff which was sent to a co-worker at the Coast Guard base without the plaintiff's knowledge or consent, and solicited sexual encounters with others on the internet. He also left a digital trail of pornographic websites on computers and tablets accessible to the children. . . .

Throughout the marriage the defendant repeatedly sought out online sexual encounters with other women and saw other women for sexual reasons. He admits having two affairs during the course of the marriage, one of which was with an exotic dancer and other with the teacher of one of the plaintiff's children.

The plaintiff confronted the defendant about his use of pornography and online sexual solicitations during the marriage, to no avail. The defendant's conduct continued. When confronted, the defendant would at first deny his conduct, then become angry and defensive and accuse the plaintiff of being nosey. He would then become contrite and say he was sorry. At one point the defendant agreed to go to counseling for his addiction to pornography but he stopped attending after a short time. At times the plaintiff believed the defendant had changed his ways but he never did and this pattern repeated itself throughout the marriage.

The defendant's conduct . . . had a devastating effect upon the plaintiff. At one point she thought she was going to have a nervous breakdown and she began to see a therapist, which she continues to do through the present. . . .

Just prior to the parties' separation their relationship appeared to the plaintiff to be on an upswing and they had sexual relations about a month prior to the separation. However, at this time the defendant was deceiving the plaintiff.

On the date of separation, the parties argued over whether the defendant would attend a middle school graduation for one of the children. This led to a larger argument. Then, with no other forewarning, the defendant told the plaintiff that he hated her and that their marriage was over.

Husband does not contest the findings of fact, but rather argues that the trial court erred in also failing to make "a finding of condonation on the part of" Wife. Husband contends that because Wife was aware of his illicit sexual behavior — the two affairs in 2008 — but the parties remained together and had intercourse after 2008, including approximately a month before separation, the trial court erred when it failed to make a finding of condonation of his illicit sexual behavior. But Husband fails to note almost all of the findings of fact regarding fault address indignities, not illicit sexual behavior. . . . The findings focus mostly on Husband's addiction to pornography and communications with women online, noting that these were problems "throughout the marriage." Even if we assume the trial court tacitly found Wife had condoned Husband's illicit sexual behavior in 2008, the marital fault of indignities remains.

Husband's argument fails to recognize that he had the burden of proof of condonation for *both* illicit sexual behavior *and* indignities, and these are separate and independent grounds for marital fault. Even if the affairs in 2008 were condoned as Husband contends, he did not show condonation of indignities. . . .

[T]he trial court's findings of fault are based upon the indignities, and Husband has not directed us to any evidence of condonation of his addictive use of pornography and seeking other women on social media websites. Instead, the evidence and findings show just the opposite: Husband was deceiving Wife regarding his continuing use of pornography and online sexual solicitations. Whenever Wife discovered what Husband was doing and objected, he would first deny and then acknowledge his actions and promise to stop. The fact that Husband and Wife continued to live together and even have sexual relations would not condone these indignities, since Wife would have had to have full knowledge of Husband's continuing pornography use and online solicitations to condone these actions. . . .

Even if Wife condoned the 2008 affairs, Wife could not have condoned Husband's continuing "use of pornography and online sexual solicitations" because Husband "deceiv[ed]" her into believing he had ceased the behavior. Husband does not contend that Wife had full knowledge at all times of his continuing pornography use and online solicitations nor that she ever acquiesced to his actions. Wife testified about finding pornography on their home computer, iPad, and cell phone, where their children could be exposed to it, and the oldest child did see it. Wife also testified about finding that Husband was "[r]egistering on dating sites. Searching for sex on Craig's List. Other women exchanging photos." Wife was upset about these findings and felt "[h]orrible." . . . .

The evidence and findings indicate that Husband denied the indignities, and when Wife confronted him with proof, he would admit what he had done and agree to counseling, but then he stopped the counseling and continued the misconduct, and "[a]t times the plaintiff believed the defendant had changed his ways but he never did and this pattern repeated itself throughout the marriage." The trial court further found that Husband "lied to and deceived" Wife "throughout the marriage[.]" The evidence supports the trial court's findings of fact regarding indignities, and the trial court did not make any findings regarding condonation of the indignities because Husband did not present any evidence that Wife ever had sufficient knowledge of his actions to condone them. When Wife did become aware of Husband's actions, she objected and asked him to stop, but he continued his behavior surreptitiously. . . .

NOTES AND QUESTIONS

1. *Timing of Misconduct.* The appeals court in *Fulton* upheld the lower court's grant of divorce to the wife based on cruel and inhuman treatment. There were three relevant instances offered in support of that ground: (i) when he kicked her while she was pregnant, (ii) when he scratched and hit her, and (iii) when he failed to intervene as she was attacked by his girlfriend. The first incident occurred before they were married, and the third happened after the filing of the petition for

divorce. Should that timing matter? If the question is what caused the marriage to end, shouldn't the first and third incidents be irrelevant?

The relevance of pre-marriage or, more commonly, post-petition behavior frequently arises, and courts have not been consistent in their approach, even within the same jurisdiction. One New York court, for example, considered adultery that occurred after the filing of the petition of divorce, while another New York court denied the relevance of acts of cruelty that occurred after the filing of the petition.[36] A New Hampshire court similarly allowed adultery to support a defense of recrimination, even though the adultery occurred after the filing of the divorce petition, and eleven months after the couple's separation.[37] Is there any justification for treating adultery differently than cruelty? More generally, should post-petition behavior be accorded any relevance in a divorce proceeding?

2. *Classifying Misconduct.* The court in *Gilmartin* addressed the husband's use of pornography and online sexual solicitations. To which ground for divorce should this behavior relate: indignities or illicit sexual behavior? The North Carolina statute defines illicit sexual behavior as "acts of sexual or deviate sexual intercourse, deviate sexual acts, or sexual acts . . . voluntarily engaged in by a spouse with someone other than the other spouse."[38] Indignities refers to behavior that is "intolerable." Does the husband's online behavior meet either standard?

3. *Fault-Based Defense: Collusion.* The fault-based system treats divorce as an adversarial proceeding. In the earlier era in which no-fault divorce was unavailable, the law sought to prevent spouses from manufacturing fault as a way to mutually end their marriage. Accordingly, courts themselves could raise defenses with the purpose of defeating the fault-based claim and thus denying the divorce. More specifically, the defense of collusion addressed situations in which the couple conspired to get divorced — fraudulently claiming that one spouse was innocent, while the other was the wrongdoer. To prevent collusion, courts sometimes required third-party corroboration of the claimed grounds for divorce.[39] Nonetheless, collusive divorces became the norm as demand for dissolution exceeded the law's willingness to tolerate it.[40] In a typical case, the wife filed for divorce; the husband did not respond to the complaint or appear in court; the wife put on a corroborating witness such as her sister or mother; and the court rubber-stamped the divorce. Where divorce laws were stricter,

---

36. Compare Golub v. Ganz, 22 A.D.3d 919 (N.Y. App. Div. 2005), with Hallingby v. Hallingby, 607 N.Y.S.2d 555 (N.Y. Sup. Ct. 1993).

37. In re Ross, 146 A.3d 1232 (N.H. 2016).

38. N.C. Gen. Stat. § 50-16.1A(3)a (2020).

39. Gayle v. Thompson, 41 N.Y.S.3d 853 (N.Y. Sup. Ct. 2016) (discussing the history of the corroboration requirement).

40. See Joanna L. Grossman & Lawrence M. Friedman, Inside the Castle: Law and Family in 20th Century America 163–68 (2011).

the collusion often involved more extensive perjury, fabrication of evidence, and a complicit legal system.[41]

4.   *Fault-Based Defense: Condonation.* The adversarial nature of fault-based divorce also meant that the accused spouse could assert a defense. Unlike defenses raised by courts, defenses raised by spouses retain their importance in the modern era. (Note that courts have treated defenses to divorce as equally applicable to defenses to legal separation.[42])

As *Fulton* and *Gilmartin* illustrate, condonation is a common defense to divorce. Condonation refers to the innocent spouse's forgiveness of the marital offense. What constitutes forgiveness? The husband in *Fulton* testified that he "tried to make the marriage work" after his wife's affair. The court concluded that the evidence was sufficient to prove condonation. Does this defense promote marital harmony? In *Gilmartin*, the court concluded that the wife forgave the husband's sexual affairs but that the condonation defense did not apply to the wife's claim of indignities. Therefore, the wife was entitled to a fault-based divorce on the ground of indignities. Does adultery invite forgiveness more than cruelty?

Although the concept of forgiveness might seem intuitive, the condonation defense raises a number of issues. First, how much knowledge of the misconduct is necessary before a resumption of the relationship constitutes condonation? In one Illinois case, the court upheld the husband's claim of condonation when the wife resumed the relationship after learning of his adultery, despite the wife's claim that she did not realize that the husband had actually borne a child with another woman.[43] Second, does the resumption of a marital relationship constitute forgiveness of all types of misconduct, giving the misbehaving spouse a clean slate? Many courts speak of condonation as restoring the offending spouse to the original position of innocence. A Pennsylvania court stated that "[c]ondonation means the blotting out of the offense imputed, so as to restore the offending party to the same position he or she occupied before the offense was committed."[44] The Mississippi Supreme Court, however, has taken a different view, explaining: "In practical effect, condonation places the offending spouse on a form of temporary probation."[45] Third, how should courts think about the line between toleration and forgiveness? In *Gilmartin*, the wife knew generally about the husband's online activities and continued the relationship. In *Fulton*, the husband said he wanted to make the relationship "work" after learning of his wife's adultery.

---

41. See William J. Goode, After Divorce 133 (1956); Leon C. Marshall & Geoffrey May, 2 The Divorce Court: Ohio 312 (1932).

42. Some courts, for example, have denied a plaintiff's claim for legal separation based on the plaintiff having engaged in adultery. See, e.g., Silverman v. Silverman, 632 N.Y.S.2d 393 (N.Y. Sup. Ct. 1995).

43. In re Marriage of Hightower, 830 N.E.2d 862 (Ill. App. Ct. 2005).

44. Talley v. Talley, 64 A. 523 (Pa. 1906).

45. Gerty v. Gerty, 265 So. 3d 121 (Miss. 2018).

Should the courts distinguish between grudging toleration and affirmative forgiveness? Fourth, what conduct constitutes evidence of condonation? Courts often have looked at the resumption of sexual relations. Is sexual intercourse a reliable indicator of forgiveness? Don't people have sex for reasons other than to express love and affection? What other behavioral indicators might be relevant to a claim of condonation? Why does sex play such a central role in the law's definition of forgiveness? A Pennsylvania court offered this justification for finding condonation based on a single act of sexual intercourse:

> It is the policy of the courts to promote reconciliation and keep families together whenever possible. It may seem a harsh result that a single act of intercourse would equate to condonation of the adulterous conduct. However, this Court must have an objective and conclusive test to utilize in determining whether condonation has occurred. Once one party to the marriage has knowledge of the other party's adultery, which is a very serious issue in a marital relationship, then that party must decide whether he or she thinks the marriage can be saved. Once that party decides to attempt to reconcile with the adulterous spouse, he or she may decide to resume sexual relations. The resumption of sexual intercourse in this situation is an objective standard by which to judge the condonation of that behavior by the other spouse. The surrounding circumstances, such as the state of mind of that spouse, are subjective and cannot be accurately gauged.[46]

5. *Fault-Based Defense: Connivance.* Though rarely asserted, the defense of connivance allows a court to deny the divorce despite proof of fault based on the "the plaintiff's consent, express or implied, to the misconduct alleged as a ground for divorce."[47] While condonation occurs after the misconduct, connivance occurs before the misconduct. In one Virginia case, for example, the court found connivance based on evidence that the "wife had urged [the husband] to date the other woman and that he had entered into a relationship only after his wife encouraged it . . . [because] she wished to be free from her marriage. . . ."[48]

6. *Fault-Based Defense: Recrimination.* The affirmative defense of recrimination allows the court to deny a divorce if the complaining spouse has also committed acts that could constitute grounds for divorce. In *Fulton,* after the wife counterclaimed that she was entitled to a divorce based on cruel and inhuman treatment, the husband amended his petition to seek divorce on the fault-based ground of adultery. If both grounds were proven, then the couple would not be able to obtain a fault-based divorce, because neither party would be innocent. Why might a spouse who also wants a divorce counterclaim on a different ground?

---

46. Hoffman v Hoffman, 762 A.2d 766, 771 (Pa. Super. Ct. 2000).
47. Greene v. Greene, 190 S.E.2d 258, 260 (N.C. Ct. App. 1972).
48. Hollis v. Hollis, 427 S.E.2d 233, 234 (Va. Ct. App. 1993).

Prior to the rise of no-fault divorce, every state permitted the defense of recrimination. More recently, some jurisdictions have eliminated the defense of recrimination, either by statute or judicial decision, while other jurisdictions have otherwise limited the defense.[49]

7. *Fault-Based Defense: Insanity.* Insanity can be both a ground for a no-fault divorce and a defense to a fault-based divorce. According to a Louisiana court, "Actions and behavior which should normally be construed as fault contributing to the separation are excused when involuntarily induced by a preexisting mental illness. However, the mental illness must be shown to have caused the objectionable actions or behavior."[50] As we saw in Chapter 2, insanity can also be grounds for an annulment.

8. *Causation or Condemnation?* In *Fulton*, was the court seeking to place moral blame or to identify who caused the divorce? Which type of inquiry should a court pursue? The court in *Gilmartin* noted that the relationship appeared to be on the "upswing" even after the husband's affairs and online activities and then soured after an argument during which the husband told the wife that he hated her and the marriage was over. If that account of how the marriage came to an end is correct, can it be said that the husband's prior misconduct "caused" the marriage to end? Does causation matter?

III. No-Fault Divorce

Upon the recommendation of the Report of the Governor's Commission on the Family, the California legislature in 1969 repealed the pre-existing fault-based grounds for divorce and replaced them with only two bases for divorce: incurable insanity and irreconcilable differences.[51] The new law made California the first state to adopt so-called no-fault divorce.

The no-fault approach is animated by multiple aims. As the Commission Report stated, the reform was intended to:

> eliminate much of the adversary aspect of divorce litigation, by removing the need for specific accusation and answer. It will prevent the use of misconduct not formally alleged as a bludgeon (by threat of its disclosure) in obtaining extortionate concessions concerning support and the division of property from the opposing spouse — concessions which are frequently inequitable and unworkable, and which do not represent any true agreement. Moreover,

---

49. See, e.g., Singer v. Singer, 391 N.E.2d 1239 (Mass. App. Ct. 1979); Thomason v. Thomason, 355 So. 2d 908 (La. 1978).

50. Scarengos v. Scarengos, 606 So. 2d 9, 10 (La. Ct. App. 1992).

51. Family Law Act of 1969, ch. 1608, § 4506; Report of the Governor's Commission on the Family (1966).

it will put an end to the dissimulation, hypocrisy — and even outright perjury — which is engendered by the present system of particular charge and
corroboration.[52]

The new no-fault system was also originally envisioned to include, along with
the principle that divorce should be available in the case of marital breakdown,
therapeutic support for couples.[53] This included a plan for marriage and divorce
counseling as part of a unified family court.[54] The family court reforms, however,
did not get implemented in the legislative process. Why do you think the legislature
failed to act on these reforms? In the end, the statutory change was simply to make
divorce easier to obtain. Every state eventually followed California's lead by adopting at least one no-fault ground for divorce — though the grounds were phrased
differently.

The general idea of no-fault was to eschew the search for a wrongdoer and
instead ask courts to assess whether a marriage had truly failed and was beyond
rehabilitation. The following cases highlight courts' interpretation and application
of the new no-fault grounds for divorce.

Desrochers v. Desrochers

347 A.2d 150 (N.H. 1975)

Kenison, Chief Justice. . . .

The [trial court found that]: "[T]he action was originally brought because the
defendant did not work steadily and stated that he, when he learned that the plaintiff was pregnant, wanted a boy instead of a girl; if the plaintiff bore a girl he would
like to put the child up for adoption. After the birth of the child [a daughter] the
defendant became very attached to the child, has visited the child weekly except on
two occasions, and has been faithfully making support payments under the temporary order of $25.00 a week. The defendant claims that he loves his wife, does not
want a divorce. The wife claims that she no longer loves her husband, but since the
filing of the divorce he has been an industrious worker and is very attached to the
child." . . .

RSA 458:7-a (Supp. 1973) provides: "A divorce from the bonds of matrimony
shall be decreed, irrespective of the fault of either party, on the ground of irreconcilable differences which have caused the irremediable breakdown of the marriage.
In any pleading or hearing of a libel for divorce under this section, allegations or
evidence of specific acts of misconduct shall be improper and inadmissible, except

---

52. Report of the Governor's Commission on the Family, supra note 51.
53. Herma Hill Kay, A Family Court: The California Proposal, 56 Cal. L. Rev. 1205, 1225 (1968).
54. Id. at 1225, 1226.

where child custody is in issue and such evidence is relevant to establish that parental custody would be detrimental to the child or at a hearing where it is determined by the court to be necessary to establish the existence of irreconcilable differences. If, upon hearing of an action for divorce under this section, both parties are found to have committed an act or acts which justify a finding of irreconcilable differences, a divorce shall be decreed and the acts of one party shall not negate the acts of the other nor bar the divorce decree." This section must be applied in conjunction with RSA 458:7-b (Supp. 1973) which precludes divorce when "there is a likelihood for rehabilitation of the marriage relationship" or when "there is a reasonable possibility of reconciliation."

RSA 458:7-a (Supp. 1973) is the product of a national discussion regarding the proper grounds for divorce. It follows in important respects the California Family Law Act of 1969. That statute, and others following it, have been criticized for vagueness, but have been held to be sufficiently definite to afford due process of law. A consensus has emerged that a period of separation due to marital difficulties is strong evidence of the irremediable breakdown of a marriage. . . .

The existence of irreconcilable differences which have caused the irremediable breakdown of the marriage is determined by reference to the subjective state of mind of the parties. While the desire of one spouse to continue the marriage is evidence of "a reasonable possibility of reconciliation," it is not a bar to divorce. If one spouse resolutely refuses to continue and it is clear from the passage of time or other circumstances that there is no reasonable possibility of a change of heart, there is an irremediable breakdown of the marriage. The defendant may attempt to impeach the plaintiff's evidence of his or her state of mind regarding the relationship. If the trial court doubts plaintiff's evidence that the marriage has irremediably broken down, the court may continue the action to determine if reconciliation is possible. However, if the parties do not reconcile, dissolution should be granted.

Knowledge of the sources of marital discord is helpful in determining whether a breakdown is irremediable or whether there is a reasonable possibility of reconciliation. Yet the statutory test is the existing state of the marriage. The statute authorizes the trial court to receive evidence of specific acts of misconduct where it is determined by the court to be necessary to establish the existence of irreconcilable differences. This authority is an exception to the general rule of the statute excluding such evidence, and the intent of the statute to minimize the acrimony attending divorce proceedings.

The question whether a breakdown of a marriage is irremediable is a question to be determined by the trial court. RSA 458:7-a contemplates the introduction of factual testimony sufficient to permit a finding of irreconcilable differences which have caused the irremediable breakdown of the marriage. Nevertheless there are limits to the inquiry. "In the first place, there is the natural tendency to withhold information of a personal nature from anyone but a trusted and discreet adviser; secondly, any probing into personal matters against the wishes of the party examined would be objectionable . . .; and thirdly, the parties have come to court for a purpose. Their answers, which may be perfectly honest ones, will inevitably be slanted in the direction of their ultimate goal, which is divorce." Within these limits the trial court must be adequately informed before acting in matters of such importance. But the statute does not contemplate a complete biopsy of the marriage relationship from the beginning to the end in every case. This is a difficult task, but judges face similar problems in other cases.

The separation of the parties for two and one-half years and the plaintiff's persistence in seeking a divorce during that period is evidence from which the trial court could find that this marriage has irremediably broken down.

NIETERS V. NIETERS
815 S.W.2d 124 (Mo. Ct. App. 1991)

PUDLOWSKI, PRESIDING JUDGE.

Wife, Gayle Nieters, appeals the trial court's dissolution of marriage decree that was modified in response to husband, Russell Nieter's, motion to amend the judgment. We reverse and remand.

Husband filed his verified petition for dissolution of marriage on June 12, 1989. The petition stated husband and wife separated around November, 1988, and there was no reasonable likelihood the marriage could be preserved. Based upon wife's default and failure to answer, an initial decree of dissolution was entered on November 3, 1989. This initial decree incorporated a separation agreement signed by both husband and wife. The separation agreement contained provisions for child custody, visitation rights, child support, division of marital property, and other issues. . . .

Wife petitioned to reopen the case, asserting that the separation agreement was coerced and, denying that the marriage was irretrievably broken. . . .

On September 19, 1990, a trial was held in the St. Louis County Circuit Court. At trial, husband testified that the couple had been separated since September, 1988. He also testified concerning the problems the couple had during the marriage and his current relationship with a woman named Cindy Yates. Wife testified that husband left in October, 1988, and that the marriage was not irretrievably broken. She also stated that there were differences about how the children should be raised and that she donated some money she earned to televangelists. . . .

Under the Missouri Dissolution of Marriage Statute § 452.320.2, RSMo 1986, when one party denies that the marriage is irretrievably broken, the court after considering all the relevant factors and hearing the evidence, must be satisfied that petitioner has established one of the following five facts in order to find that the marriage is irretrievably broken:

(a) That the respondent has committed adultery and the petitioner finds it intolerable to live with the respondent;

(b) That the respondent has behaved in such a way that the petitioner cannot reasonably be expected to live with the respondent;

(c) That the respondent has abandoned the petitioner for a continuous period of at least six months preceding the presentation of the petition;

(d) That the parties to the marriage have lived separate and apart by mutual consent for a continuous period of twelve months immediately preceding the filing of the petition;

(e) That the parties to the marriage have lived separate and apart for a continuous period of at least twenty-four months preceding the filing of the petition.

The trial court is not required to make specific findings of fact warranting dissolution. Although fact issues are deemed to accord with the result when no findings of fact are requested, the decree of the trial court must be supported by substantial evidence, must not be against the weight of the evidence, and must not erroneously declare or apply law.

In her first point, wife argues that the trial court erred in finding the marriage irretrievably broken. She contends that there was no substantial evidence to support a finding that one of the five facts was established.

We agree that the trial court's decree was against the weight of the evidence and unsupported by substantial evidence. The trial court should not have found the marriage irretrievably broken because the evidence does not establish any of the five fact situations necessary when one party denies that the marriage is irretrievably broken.

The first three fact situations require wrongdoing by the respondent. . . . Husband's trial testimony, that there were "several occasions where we just could not get along" and that "it got somewhat violent on both parts" over the last three or four years, does not provide substantial evidence of these three situations. Also, the fact that there were differences about raising the children and wife's donating some of her own money to televangelists is not behavior that one could not be reasonably expected to live with. In fact, husband's behavior, concerning his new companion and living arrangements, is more characteristic of behavior one would not be reasonably expected to live with.

The last two situations for rendering the marriage irretrievably broken are not supported by the record. There is no evidence that the parties lived apart by mutual consent for twelve months preceding the filing of the petition. Also, there is no evidence that husband and wife lived separate for a continuous period of at least twenty-four months preceding the filing of the petition. Even if the trial court believed the husband, who testified that the couple separated in September of 1988, the two year requirement was not satisfied because the petition was filed on June 12, 1989. The parties' separation for, at the most, ten months, was clearly not sufficient to satisfy either of the last two circumstances for finding the marriage irretrievably broken. . . .

We hold that the record does not provide substantial evidence that the marriage of the parties was irretrievably broken . . . and the decree of the trial court was against the weight of the evidence. . . .

Sinha v. Sinha
526 A.2d 765 (Pa. 1987)

Hutchinson, Justice.

Appellant, Chandra Prabha Sinha . . . argues that a unilateral divorce under our Divorce Code of 1980 requires formulation of an intent to dissolve the marriage before the statute's three year separation requirement begins to run. We agree with appellant that the reconciliation goals of the Divorce Code will be furthered by requiring an independent showing of intent to end the marriage before commencement of the three year period. Because this record shows appellee formed his intent to terminate the marital bonds only fourteen months before his filing suit in Common Pleas, we reverse the order of Superior Court.

On March 11, 1974, appellant and appellee, Shrikant Nandan Prasad Sinha, were married pursuant to a Hindu marriage ritual in Patna, Bihar, India. Appellee came to America in August of 1976 to pursue a master's degree in city and regional planning at Rutgers University in New Jersey. Due to appellant's inability to obtain a visa, she was unable to join or visit her husband in the United States. The parties corresponded regularly and, as late as September 26, 1978, the husband professed his love for his wife. In August 1979, the appellee filed a complaint in New Jersey Superior Court seeking a divorce. This action was voluntarily dismissed subsequent to appellee's move to Media, Delaware County. Appellee then renewed his efforts to secure a divorce with the filing of a complaint in Delaware County Common Pleas on October 15, 1980. The complaint alleged that the parties had lived separate and apart for three years and that the marriage was irretrievably broken. . . .

Appellee first revealed his intention to end the marriage with the filing of the New Jersey complaint in August, 1979. Pennsylvania's unilateral divorce provision, 23 P.S. § 201(d), requires that the parties live separate and apart for three years and that the marriage be irretrievably broken. Physical separation alone will not satisfy the requirements of the statute. The demands placed on marriage by modern society will often force a spouse to leave the marital abode for long periods of time. These separations should not be interpreted as an intent to terminate the marriage. Accordingly, § 201(d) of the Divorce Code requires an intent to terminate the marital relation independent of the physical separation mandated by the statute. As appellee's intent to dissolve the marriage clearly manifested itself only fourteen months before the filing of the Pennsylvania complaint, the three year requirement of § 201(d) has not been satisfied. . . .

Noting that the definitional section of the 1980 Divorce Code, 23 P.S. § 104, interprets "separate and apart" as the "[c]omplete cessation of any and all cohabitation," Superior Court affirmed Common Pleas' grant of a divorce to appellee based upon the parties' physical separation which commenced with appellee's departure for the United States in August 1976. This was error. Physical separation alone does not satisfy the separate and apart requirement of § 201(d). There must be an independent intent on the part of one of the parties to dissolve the marital union before the three year period commences. This intent must be clearly manifested and communicated to the other spouse. Any other interpretation would allow one spouse to depart the marital home for apparently benign purposes, remain away for the statutory period, and then sue for a divorce. The granting of a divorce under such circumstances would deprive the unknowing party an opportunity to attempt reconciliation, a specific policy goal of the legislature. All too often the exigencies of modern life require a spouse to leave the marital home for extended periods. The demands of one's employment, education and military service may not be utilized to secure a divorce, absent an independent intent to dissolve the marriage. . . .

In the context of another separation engendered by military service, the Supreme Court of Louisiana opined:

> Business and other necessities may require the husband to live in one place and the wife at another. . . . The separation intended by the statute is a separation by which the marital association is severed. It means the living asunder of the husband and wife. It is a voluntary act, and the separation must be with the intent of the married persons to live apart because of their mutual purpose to do so, or because one of the parties with or without the acquiescence of the other intends to discontinue the marital relationship.

Our research reveals many appellate decisions defining the "separate and apart" proviso of a unilateral divorce statute to require an intent to dissolve the marital union apart from mere physical separation. The results reached by those courts are in accord with what we believe our legislature intended in precluding a unilateral no-fault divorce until after a three year separation.

Our holding today, that the "separate and apart" language of 23 P.S. § 201(d) requires both physical separation and a clear intent on the part of at least one of the parties to dissolve the marital ties at the beginning of the three year period, requires us to reverse Superior Court. . . .

NOTES AND QUESTIONS

1.   *Mutual Consent Divorce.* Even as states permitted no-fault divorce, reformers were reluctant to permit a couple to divorce simply because they wanted to. As the California Governor's Commission Report had stated:

> We cannot overemphasize that this standard does not permit divorce by consent, wherein marriage is treated as wholly a private contract terminable at the pleasure of the parties without any effective intervention by society. The standard we propose requires the community to assert its interest in the status of the family, and permits dissolution of the marriage only after it has been subjected to a penetrating scrutiny and the judicial process has provided the parties with all of the resources of social science in aid of conciliation. . . .[55]

An obvious question follows: what evidence is sufficient for a court to grant a divorce that both spouses want based on a no-fault ground such as irretrievable breakdown? Should the couple's desire to end the marriage always be sufficient *by itself* for the court to grant the divorce? Or must the judge conduct some factual inquiry to convince herself that the marriage has broken down to the point that reconciliation will be impossible? Can or should a marriage be saved if both parties insist it cannot be?

2.   *Mutual Separation.* Rather than simply allow the word of the parties to warrant the granting of the divorce, many state statutes use a period of separation as a proxy for marital breakdown. For instance, Illinois permits divorce after a six-month separation, while Texas only after three years (although there is no durational requirement for the no-fault ground of "insupportability").[56] As evidenced by *Nieters*, some states require longer periods of separation when the separation and desire for the divorce are not mutual. In D.C., for instance, a 6-month separation period is required when the separation is mutual and voluntary, while a 1-year period is required when the desire for divorce is not mutual.[57] Is it sensible to have different durational requirements based on whether there is mutual consent for the separation? The justification for separation as a ground for divorce is that it provides a proxy for marital breakdown — after a certain point, it is unlikely that the parties will reconcile.

3.   *Length of Separation.* The court in *Sinha* found that in considering whether the parties have satisfied the statutory period for separation, the clock doesn't start to run until one of the spouses has formed an intent to end the marriage. Similarly, some courts have held that the separation period is tolled if parties resume a sexual relationship during that period, even if they don't resume actually living together.[58]

4.   *Cohabitation After Separation.* The paradigmatic case of separation is where one spouse moves out of the family home. The *Sinha* court required "cessation of any and all cohabitation." In the view of some other courts, though, physically

---

55. Report of the Governor's Commission on the Family, supra note 51.
56. Charts, 2017: Family Law in the Fifty States, D.C., and Puerto Rico, 51 Fam. L.Q. 543, 560–68 (2018).
57. D.C. Code § 16-904 (2020).
58. Pitts v. Pitts, 282 S.E.2d 488 (N.C. Ct. App. 1981). But see Prather v. Prather, 459 N.E.2d 234 (Ohio Ct. App. 1983).

departing the home is not always required to satisfy the separation requirement. (Indeed, for some couples, actually moving out of the home may not be financially feasible.) Some courts have found the statutory requirement for separation satisfied even if the spouses remain in the family home, provided that they lead separate lives and do not maintain a sexual relationship.[59] How do married couples who might "live apart together" pose a challenge to this legal requirement?

5. *Unilateral Divorce.* In each of the above cases, the courts confronted a situation in which divorce was sought by one spouse, yet resisted by the other. Should a no-fault divorce be available when one spouse wants to remain married? Consider this view offered by a New York court:

> Insofar as the phrase "broken down such that it is irretrievable" is nowhere defined in the statute, the determination of whether a breakdown of a marriage is irretrievable is a question to be determined by the finder of fact. This Court does hold, however, that whether a marriage is so broken that it is irretrievable need not necessarily be so viewed by both parties. Accordingly, the fact finder may conclude that a marriage is broken down irretrievably even though one of the parties continues to believe that the breakdown is not irretrievable and/or that there is still some possibility of reconciliation.[60]

In the court's view, unilateral divorce is permitted but not required. A court may conclude that the marriage is not irretrievably broken when one spouse wants to divorce and the other does not. What purpose, if any, would be served by a court making such a determination?

6. *Judicial Inquiry.* Both *Desrochers* and *Nieters* raise the question of how a court should go about determining whether the irretrievable breakdown of the marriage has occurred, when one spouse opposes the divorce petition. The *Nieters* court identified specific factors indicating breakdown, while the *Desrochers* court declined to specify particular factors. Which approach is preferable? In either case, would or should it matter how the spouse who wants to stay married has behaved?

PROBLEMS

1. John and Myra have been married for 15 years. They have three children, ages 2, 5, and 7. Myra has filed a petition for divorce. She states that the marriage is "irretrievably broken" in that she no longer loves her husband in the way she did

---

59. See, e.g., Camp v. Camp, 331 S.E.2d 163 (N.C. Ct. App. 1985); In re Marriage of Kenik, 536 N.E.2d 982 (Ill. App. Ct. 1989).

60. Strack v. Strack, 916 N.Y.S.2d 759 (N.Y. Sup. Ct. 2011).

when they married. John has provided financially for the family but, according to Myra, has ceased to be emotionally open. Myra feels that their marriage has become emotionally barren and unsatisfying. John would like to remain married. He feels that he has tried to be the best husband he can be and doesn't understand what would make Myra happy. Would the courts in *Desrochers* and *Nieters* grant her petition for divorce? Should the law allow her to obtain a divorce in such circumstances? If the divorce is granted, should a judge, in deciding child custody and property distribution, take account of the fact that Myra was the one who wanted to end the marriage?

2. Nick and Jeanine married in Maryland in 2006. In June 2010, Jeanine sought and received a restraining order against Nick, which led him to move out. After the order expired six months later, the couple continued to reside in separate residences, yet resumed an intermittent sexual relationship. In March 2011, the sexual relationship ended, and thereafter the parties had no in-person intimate contact. But they did communicate via telephone calls and text messages that "were of an explicit or provocative sexual nature."

In March 2012, the husband requested a divorce based on the ground of their 12-month uninterrupted separation. The wife moved to dismiss the complaint, arguing that the couple's sexually explicit phone calls and text messages constituted "cohabitation" and "marital relations" during the supposed period of separation. Should the court find that Nick and Jeanine satisfied the requirement of a 12-month period of uninterrupted separation? Or is their telephone communication enough of a sexual relationship to interrupt the separation period and start the clock running again? Should it matter whether telephone communication of a sexual nature would meet the standard for adultery in a fault-based divorce?

POSTSCRIPT

In the actual case, the court determined that the couple's sexually provocative telephone communication did not constitute cohabitation or marital relations. Thus, the required 12-month period of separation had been met and could provide a basis for the divorce.[61]

---

61. Bergeris v. Bergeris, 90 A.3d 553 (Md. Ct. Spec. App. 2014).

NOTE ON LEGAL ETHICS IN DIVORCE

Fault-based divorce aligned with traditional models of adversarial litigation in which a lawyer represents only one party to the marriage. But with the shift to no-fault divorce, the role of lawyers shifted as well. While many divorces remain adversarial, some divorcing couples may be in agreement about not only whether to divorce but also how to order their affairs. May a lawyer then attempt to represent both spouses? Would that be a good idea for the lawyer? For the spouses? Adversarial divorce litigation can be expensive.[62] In fact, one study found that, on average, litigated adversarial divorces cost $77,746.[63]

Under the ABA Model Rules of Professional Conduct, which have been widely adopted by states, lawyers may engage in joint representation if they reasonably believe that they will be able to provide "competent and diligent representation to each affected client," provided that each client gives written informed consent after full disclosure of the risks of such representation.[64] If an actual conflict develops between spouses represented by a single attorney, the Model Rules provide that the lawyer ordinarily cannot continue to represent either party.[65] For example, if one party confided that she had hidden money in an offshore account before the couple sat down to appraise and then equally divide their assets, a conflict exists and the lawyer should withdraw. Why? Would continued representation violate the lawyer's duty of loyalty? Would it violate her duty of confidentiality?

While some states simply adopt the approach of the Model Rules, which address joint representation generically without explicitly identifying divorce, other states make specific reference to family law matters. For example, the Comment to California's ethical rule on conflicts of interest provides that joint representation may occur in "the resolution of an 'uncontested' marital dissolution."[66] In contrast, the Comment to Virginia's rule explains that a "lawyer can never adequately provide joint representation in certain matters relating to divorce, annulment or separation — specifically, child custody, child support, visitation, spousal support and maintenance

---

62. Attorneys are generally prohibited by ethical rules from handling divorce matters on a contingent-fee basis. Model Rules of Prof'l Conduct r. 1.5 (Am. Bar Ass'n 2018).

63. Martha Neil, Kinder, Gentler Collaborative Divorce Also Costs Less, A.B.A. Journal (2007). One expert in divorce law estimated that the combined legal fees for dividing an estate valued at $500,000 typically average between $25,000 to $50,000. Mark P. Gergen, A Thoroughly Modern Theory of Restitution the Law and Ethics of Restitution 84 Tex. L. Rev. 173, 186 (2005) (reviewing Hanoch Dagan, The Law and Ethics of Restitution (2004)). Another study found that couples who obtained independent representation in adversarial divorce proceedings spent, on average, 134% more in total fees than couples who dissolved their marriages through comprehensive divorce mediation. Joan B. Kelly, Is Mediation Less Expensive? Comparison of Mediated and Adversarial Divorce Costs, 8 Mediation Q. 15 (1990-91).

64. Model Rules of Prof'l Conduct r. 1.7 (2018).

65. See id. and cmt. [4].

66. Cal. Rules of Prof'l Conduct r. 1.7 cmt. [2] (Cal. Bar Ass'n 2018).

or division of property."[67] Which state's approach do you prefer? Can a lawyer adequately represent both parties to a divorce in which the parties have a child? Can a lawyer adequately represent both parties to a premarital agreement? Should there be different rules for joint representation in the family law context than in others?

Ethics questions may also arise when one party in a divorce proceeding is self-represented. This is relatively common.[68] A study of eleven courts in large cities found that both spouses were self-represented in approximately 33% of contested divorce proceedings and 62% of uncontested ones.[69] Ethics opinions in several states expressly prohibit a lawyer for one spouse from preparing answers, complaints, or other documents for the unrepresented spouse to file pro se, even if the divorce is amicable or uncontested.[70] However, authorities in at least one state have opined that it is ethical for a lawyer to draft and submit responsive pleadings on behalf of the opposing unrepresented party, at least in circumstances where "all aspects of the marriage regarding property, custody and support have been previously settled and only the divorce remains.[71] Should the lawyer be allowed to communicate with the unrepresented spouse, other than to advise that spouse to seek legal representation?[72] If you were the represented spouse, would you consent to your lawyer communicating with your spouse? What about preparing documents for your spouse?

Issues may also arise when a lawyer serves as a mediator in a divorce. In Illinois, an ethics opinion provides that a lawyer who mediated a divorce matter should not then draft a proposed judgment of dissolution, a separation agreement, or a joint parenting agreement for the parties to the divorce, reasoning that this would represent a conflict of interest.[73] Why?

---

67. Va. State Bar Prof'l Guidelines r. 1.7 cmt. 8 (Va. Bar Ass'n 2009).

68. A report in Michigan, for example, found that 68% of divorce cases involved one or more self-represented parties. Michigan Legal Help Revaluation Report 6 (2015). In the District of Columbia, 83% of plaintiffs and 93% of respondents proceeded pro se in divorce, custody, and other miscellaneous family court cases. D.C. Access to Justice Commission, Delivering Justice: Addressing Civil Legal Needs in the District of Columbia (2019). A study comparing self-representation rates in domestic relations cases across states found that the proportion of divorce or dissolution cases involving self-represented parties varied widely, between 19% and 80% in the five states studied. See Richard Schauffler & Shauna Strickland, The Case for Counting Cases, 51 Ct. Rev. 52, 52 (2015).

69. However, both parties were more likely to obtain independent legal counsel when the proceedings involved custody of minor children. Nat'l Ctr. for State Courts, Family Justice Initiative: The Landscape of Domestic Relations Cases in State Courts 20, 21 (2018).

70. See, e.g., North Carolina State Bar, 2002 Formal Ethics Op. 6 (2013) (lawyer may not represent one party in divorce and prepare pleadings for the other pro se party to sign, even if both parties agree); Missouri Bar Ass'n Advisory Op. 940049 (lawyer may not prepare an answer for an unrepresented opposing party in divorce).

71. South Carolina Bar Ethics Advisory Op. 90-18 (1990).

72. See Model Rules of Prof'l Conduct r. 4.3 (Am. Bar Ass'n 2018) ("The lawyer shall not give legal advice to an unrepresented person, other than the advice to secure counsel, if the lawyer knows or reasonably should know that the interests of such a person are or have a reasonable possibility of being in conflict with the interests of the client.").

73. Illinois State Bar Ass'n Advisory Opinion on Professional Conduct, Op. No. 04-03 (Apr. 2005).

PROBLEM

Cynthia and Roland, a married couple, agree to divorce in a state where the ethical rules permit joint representation. They wish to resolve their divorce amicably and jointly obtain the services of an attorney to inform them about the law in their state and to draft their dissolution agreement. In their first meeting with the attorney, Cynthia and Roland each state that they want to divide all marital property equitably, but that each spouse should keep their own separate property. Both Cynthia and Roland repeatedly emphasize their desire to avoid the costs and stresses of adversarial litigation.

Cynthia and Roland both have graduate degrees and both make roughly $100,000 annually in income. They are co-signers on a 30-year mortgage for their home. After reviewing the couple's financial records, the attorney learns that Cynthia is the sole named beneficiary of a trust her godmother established in her name as a wedding present. However, Cynthia automatically deposits the monthly income from the trust in a joint savings account which Cynthia and Roland jointly draw upon to pay a portion of their monthly expenses, including their mortgage.

Cynthia and Roland ask the attorney for her opinion as to whether the trust is separate or marital property. The attorney responds that the trust would likely be categorized as separate property, but that it is a close call that could go either way if it went to court. Cynthia seems eager to move on, but Roland seems reluctant to do so. How should the attorney advise the couple?

IV. Re-Assessing No-Fault Divorce

No-fault divorce remains controversial. While the problems of the fault-based system were undeniable, no-fault may have created problems of its own. A core criticism is that no-fault, by making it easier to exit a marriage, has increased divorce rates to the detriment of the children, women, and men in families that have endured divorce. The intuition that no-fault would increase divorce rates is straightforward: by not requiring a showing that one spouse was at fault and that the other was not, no-fault makes it easier for a spouse who wants to leave the marriage to do so. Yet that effect may be counteracted by another effect of no-fault. Knowing that the other spouse can unilaterally decide to end the marriage gives each spouse a stronger incentive to treat their partner well, so that they will choose to stay in the relationship. While the divorce rate rose in the 1970s after the onset of no-fault, it has been declining since 1986.[74]

---

74. See W. Bradford Wilcox et al., Nat'l Marriage Project, State of Our Unions 2019, at 19 (2019).

What are the social consequences of a rise in divorce rates with no-fault? Put simply, is an increase in divorce socially undesirable? More specifically, can the gains for the person who wanted the divorce be outweighed by the costs imposed on the other spouse and children?

Divorce has both economic and psychological effects, and a common intuition is that divorce harms children on both dimensions. The economic impact of divorce is, to some extent, unavoidable, as families that previously maintained one household have to transition to maintaining two. Thus, the parents will have fewer resources available for the child if they divorce compared to if they had stayed together.

What about the psychological effects of divorce? While some commentators view divorce as traumatic for children with long-lasting deleterious effects,[75] others emphasize children's resilience and their ability to thrive in new family arrangements.[76] The best available research suggests that the effect of divorce on children depends on the level of conflict in their parents' marriage. In high-conflict marriages, children may benefit from their parents' divorce — even if high-conflict divorces also inflict harms on children.[77] In contrast, if the marriage was low conflict, the child might benefit more from the parents remaining together.[78]

There is also a question about whether the economic losses associated with divorce are shared equitably. Extensive evidence shows that women's standard of living declines more after divorce than does that of men.[79] An important cause of the differential decline in the standard of living is the specialization, or division of labor, within the family.[80] Women tend to assume responsibility for household and family

---

75. See, e.g., Judith S. Wallerstein et al., The Unexpected Legacy of Divorce: A 25 Year Landmark Study (2000).

76. See, e.g., Judith Stacey, Brave New Families: Stories of Domestic Upheaval in Late Twentieth Century America (1990).

77. See, e.g., Janet Weinstein & Ricardo Weinstein, "I Know Better Than That": The Role of Emotions and the Brain in Family Law Disputes, 7 J.L. & Fam. Stud. 351, 371–73 (2005); ABA, Family Law Section, The Wingspread Report and Action Plan, High-Conflict Custody Cases: Reforming the System for Children, 39 Fam. Ct. Rev. 146, 146–47 (2001).

78. Paul R. Amato, Good Enough Marriages: Parental Discord, Divorce, and Children's Long-Term Well-Being, 9 Va. J. Soc. Pol'y & L. 71 (2001).

79. See, e.g., Pamela J. Smock et al., The Effect of Marriage and Divorce on Women's Economic Well-Being, 64 Am. Soc. Rev. 794 (1999); Suzanne M. Bianchi et al., The Gender Gap in the Economic Well-Being of Nonresident Fathers and Custodial Mothers, 36 Demography 195 (1999); see also David de Vaus et al., The Economic Consequences of Divorce in Six OECD Countries, 52 Austl. J. of Soc. Issues 180 (2017).

80. Despite movements toward more parity, women continue to shoulder a greater domestic burden than men. See Bureau of Labor Statistics, Dep't of Labor, Am. Time-Use Survey-2006 Results, Tbl. 8 (2006) (in 2005, in households with children under 6, working women spent an average of 2.17 hours per day providing care for household members compared with 1.31 hours for working men; in households with children 6 to 17, working women spent an average of .99 hours per day providing care for household members compared with .50 for working men); see also Karen C. Holden & Pamela J. Smock, The Economic Costs of Marital Dissolution: Why Do Women Bear a Disproportionate Cost?, 17 Ann. Rev. Soc. 51 (1991). In addition, after decades of increases in labor force participation by women, this rate has stalled. Mitra Toossi & Teresa L. Morisi, U.S. Bureau of Labor Stats., Women In The Workforce Before, During, And After The Great Recession (July 2017).

labor, while men are more likely to work for pay outside the home in ways that develop marketable skills.[81] This differential standard-of-living decline affects children too, as the mother typically has primary custody. (Chapter 5 will examine how other changes associated with the rise of no-fault may have disadvantaged women.)

The effects of the rise of no-fault, and of divorce more generally, are complicated. Whatever the effects of no-fault on divorce rates, it is clear that family instability is a significant social issue. Some commentators also contend that no-fault divorce has had a diffuse yet deep effect by changing people's understanding of marriage. Whether a cause of changed views of marriage *or* an effect, no-fault was unquestionably intertwined with a changed cultural understanding of marriage, one in which moral norms receded and ideas of psychological health and fulfillment moved to the fore. In considering the following excerpt from one commentator, ask yourself: Does her assessment seem correct? And is the ethical shift she identifies one to welcome, to bemoan, or neither?

Barbara Dafoe Whitehead, The Divorce Culture (1997)

Beginning in the late 1950s, Americans began to change their ideas about the individual's obligations to family and society . . . away from an ethic of obligation to others and toward an obligation to self. . . . At least as important as the moral obligation to look after others, the new thinking suggested, was the moral obligation to look after oneself.

This ethical shift had a profound impact on ideas about the nature and purpose of the family [which had] been the realm defined by voluntary commitment, duty, and self-sacrifice. With the greater emphasis on individual satisfaction in family relationships, however, family well-being became subject to a new metric. More than in the past, satisfaction in this sphere came to be based on subjective judgments about the content and quality of individual happiness. . . . People began to judge the strength and "health" of family bonds according to their capacity to promote individual fulfillment and personal growth. . . . Once the domain of the obligated self, the family was increasingly viewed as yet another domain for the expression of the unfettered self.

These broad changes figured centrally in creating a new conception of divorce. . . . Once regarded mainly as a social, legal, and family event in which there were other stakeholders, divorce now became an event closely linked to the pursuit of individual satisfactions, opportunities, and growth.

---

81. Holden & Smock, supra note 80, at 51–78; Grossman & Friedman, supra note 40, at 144.

PROBLEMS

1. A mathematician has devised a formula that he claims to have a 94 percent success rate when it comes to forecasting whether a married couple will stay married or get divorced. The couples are observed during a 15-minute conversation just after being married. The observers award scores to the couples based on language, communication, body language, and other observable behavior (e.g., minus 3 for scorn, plus 2 for humor). Consider a legislative proposal to require couples to undergo the evaluation as a prerequisite to obtaining a marriage license. Pursuant to the proposal, couples who "fail" would not be barred from marrying, but would be forced to wait six months <u>and</u> undergo a 12-week premarital counseling program before obtaining a license. Would you support this bill? Why or why not?

2. Whatever the effects of no-fault specifically, it is clear that families in the United States have become less stable during the past half century. In light of that fact, consider whether you would support any of these proposals.

THE FAMILY PRESERVATION ACT

The bill allows dissolution based on irreconcilable differences only upon the mutual consent of the parties and only upon completion of an education or counseling program, either separately or together. If the parties do not consent to the dissolution, a party must prove fault by a preponderance of the evidence in order for the court to grant the dissolution, unless the party opposing the dissolution has been convicted of domestic abuse or a protective order has been granted.

THE BETTER MARRIAGES ACT

The bill requires all applicants for a marriage license to complete a course of premarital orientation, of not less than four hours, as condition precedent to obtaining a marriage license. The course can be provided by a licensed therapist or counselor or by a religious official authorized to perform marriage ceremonies.

THE CHILD PROTECTION ACT

The bill authorizes couples to seek an immediate divorce on a no-fault ground only if the parties consent and there are no minor children. If both parties do not consent or if there are minor children, then the divorce may be granted only on a showing of fault or, in the absence of fault, one year after the filing of the petition. In the absence of fault, the divorce will be granted only if the couple has completed six hours of pre-divorce counseling to ensure the children's welfare after the divorce.

THE COOLING OFF ACT

The bill requires a waiting period of three years between the filing of a petition for divorce and the entry of the decree of divorce, for any couple with a child below the age of 16 at the time of the filing of the petition. This waiting period shall be waived if either spouse has been convicted of domestic abuse or a protective order has been granted.

NOTE ON COVENANT MARRIAGE

In a partial response to no-fault divorce and concerns about divorce rates, between 1997 and 2001, three states — Arkansas, Arizona, and Louisiana — enacted "covenant marriage" laws.[82] The purpose of the covenant marriage laws is to provide an alternative to the no-fault vision of marriage, one that provides additional protections against divorce, with the goal of strengthening the institution of marriage.[83] Covenant marriage requires the couple to undergo premarital counseling and counseling during marriage before seeking to dissolve it. According to the Louisiana statute, those who elect to enter into a covenant marriage must understand and agree that the marriage between them is a lifelong relationship.[84]

Divorce from a covenant marriage is only permitted where "there has been a complete and total breach of the marital covenant commitment."[85] A divorce can be granted only on proof of one of the statutorily specified grounds. The Louisiana law, for example, lists adultery, abandonment, physical or sexual abuse of the spouse or the spouse's child, and felony conviction with a sentence of death or imprisonment.[86] In addition to these fault-based grounds, the Louisiana law permits a covenant marriage to be dissolved after a two-year informal separation or one year after a decree of separation.[87] In other words, a no-fault ground is still

---

82. See La. Rev. Stat. Ann. § 9:272 (2020); Ark Code Ann. § 9-11-803 (2020); Ariz. Rev. Stat. § 25-901 (2020).

83. Peter Feuerherd, Why Covenant Marriage Failed to Take Off, JStor Daily (Feb. 11, 2019).

84. La. Rev. Stat. Ann. § 9:272 (2020).

85. Id.; see also Developments in the Law — Marriage as Contract and Marriage as Partnership: The Future of Antenuptial Agreement Law, 116 Harv. L. Rev. 2075, 2087 (2003).

86. La. Rev. Stat. Ann. § 9:307 (2020).

87. Id.

included, but requires a much longer period of separation than under the state's no-fault system.

Covenant marriage statutes were controversial when they were enacted:

> Time magazine called covenant marriage [in Louisiana] the "no-way-out version" dissoluble "for the most part, only [by] impediments of biblical proportion — adultery, abandonment, abuse, imprisonment for a felony." . . . The Act's advocates regard the obstacles it places in the way of quick, easy divorce — especially unilateral no-fault divorce — as one of its virtues, while critics believe that those same obstacles will trap couples in bad, or even abusive, marriages.[88]

The effect of covenant marriage has been very small. In the three states with the option, fewer than 5 percent of marriages have been registered as covenant marriages.[89] Most who choose covenant marriage do so for religious reasons.[90] There is disagreement about whether covenant marriage laws have reduced divorce rates or produced better marriages, due in part to the fact that couples' choosing covenant marriage are not a random sample of the marrying population.[91]

Would you want to enter a covenant marriage? Would you support legislation to allow covenant marriages for those couples who want one? Why do you think so few couples elect to enter one?

V. Access to Divorce and Dissolution

Do individuals possess a *right* to access the courts to seek a divorce? Barriers to court access for the purpose of enforcing or adjusting family status raise procedural and substantive due process questions. The issue of court access also puts into focus the status of a constitutional right to divorce. If the right to marry is fundamental, what about the right to divorce? How should economic inequality affect access to the legal system to adjust one's marital status? What power should courts have to adjudicate divorces? In our interstate system, how much can one state's courts affect the status of parties in other states? Consider these questions as you read this section.

---

88. Jeanne Louise Carriere, "It's Déjà Vu All Over Again": The Covenant Marriage Act in Popular Cultural Perception and Legal Reality, 72 Tul. L. Rev. 1701, 1704 (1998).

89. Feuerherd, supra note 83; David White, Divorce Option May Be Harder to Reach Under Covenant Bill in Alabama Legislature, Birmingham News, Mar. 19, 2012; Steven Nock et al., Covenant Marriage: The Movement to Reclaim Tradition in America (2008).

90. See Elizabeth H. Baker et al., Covenant Marriage and the Sanctification of Gendered Marital Issues, 30 J. Fam. Issues 147, 152 (2009).

91. Feuerherd, supra note 83.

A. Access to Courts

BODDIE V. CONNECTICUT
401 U.S. 371 (1971)

MR. JUSTICE HARLAN delivered the opinion of the Court.

Appellants, welfare recipients residing in the State of Connecticut, brought this action in the Federal District Court for the District of Connecticut on behalf of themselves and others similarly situated, challenging, as applied to them, certain state procedures for the commencement of litigation, including requirements for payment of court fees and costs for service of process, that restrict their access to the courts in their effort to bring an action for divorce.

It appears from the briefs and oral argument that the average cost to a litigant for bringing an action for divorce is $60. . . . An additional $15 is usually required for the service of process by the sheriff, although as much as $40 or $50 may be necessary where notice must be accomplished by publication. . . .

There is no dispute as to the inability of the named appellants in the present case to pay either the court fees required by statute or the cost incurred for the service of process. The affidavits in the record establish that appellants' welfare income in each instance barely suffices to meet the costs of the daily essentials of life and includes no allotment that could be budgeted for the expense to gain access to the courts in order to obtain a divorce. . . .

Our conclusion is that, given the basic position of the marriage relationship in this society's hierarchy of values and the concomitant state monopolization of the means for legally dissolving this relationship, due process does prohibit a State from denying, solely because of inability to pay, access to its courts to individuals who seek judicial dissolution of their marriages.

I . . .

It is to courts, or other quasi-judicial official bodies, that we ultimately look for the implementation of a regularized, orderly process of dispute settlement. . . . Without th[e] guarantee that one may not be deprived of his rights, neither liberty nor property, without due process of law, the State's monopoly over techniques for binding conflict resolution could hardly be said to be acceptable under our scheme of things. . . . It is upon this premise that this Court has through years of adjudication put flesh upon the due process principle.

Such litigation has, however, typically involved rights of defendants — not, as here, persons seeking access to the judicial process in the first instance. This is because our society has been so structured that resort to the courts is not usually the only available, legitimate means of resolving private disputes. Indeed, private structuring of individual relationships and repair of their breach is largely encouraged in

American life, subject only to the caveat that the formal judicial process, if resorted to, is paramount. Thus, this Court has seldom been asked to view access to the courts as an element of due process. The legitimacy of the State's monopoly over techniques of final dispute settlement, even where some are denied access to its use, stands unimpaired where recognized, effective alternatives for the adjustment of differences remain. But the successful invocation of this governmental power by plaintiffs has often created serious problems for defendants' rights. For at that point, the judicial proceeding becomes the only effective means of resolving the dispute at hand and denial of a defendant's full access to that process raises grave problems for its legitimacy.

Recognition of this theoretical framework illuminates the precise issue presented in this case. As this Court on more than one occasion has recognized, marriage involves interests of basic importance in our society. It is not surprising, then, that the States have seen fit to oversee many aspects of that institution. . . . [W]e know of no instance where two consenting adults may divorce and mutually liberate themselves from the constraints of legal obligations that go with marriage, and more fundamentally the prohibition against remarriage, without invoking the State's judicial machinery.

Thus, although they assert here due process rights as would-be plaintiffs, we think appellants' plight, because resort to the state courts is the only avenue to dissolution of their marriages, is akin to that of defendants faced with exclusion from the only forum effectively empowered to settle their disputes. . . . For both groups this process is . . . the only available one. . . .

II . . .

A

Prior cases establish, first, that due process requires, at a minimum, that absent a countervailing state interest of overriding significance, persons forced to settle their claims of right and duty through the judicial process must be given a meaningful opportunity to be heard. . . .

B

Our cases further establish that a statute or a rule may be held constitutionally invalid as applied when it operates to deprive an individual of a protected right although its general validity as a measure enacted in the legitimate exercise of state power is beyond question. . . .

Just as a generally valid notice procedure may fail to satisfy due process because of the circumstances of the defendant, so too a cost requirement, valid on its face, may offend due process because it operates to foreclose a particular party's opportunity to be heard. The State's obligations under the Fourteenth Amendment are not simply generalized ones; rather, the State owes to each individual that process which, in light of the values of a free society, can be characterized as due.

III . . .

The arguments for this kind of fee and cost requirement are that the State's interest in the prevention of frivolous litigation is substantial, its use of court fees and process costs to allocate scarce resources is rational, and its balance between the defendant's right to notice and the plaintiff's right to access is reasonable.

In our opinion, none of these considerations is sufficient to override the interest of these plaintiff-appellants in having access to the only avenue open for dissolving their allegedly untenable marriages. . . . [T]here [is] no necessary connection between a litigant's assets and the seriousness of his motives in bringing suit. . . . Moreover, other alternatives exist to fees and cost requirements as a means for conserving the time of courts and protecting parties from frivolous litigation, such as penalties for false pleadings or affidavits, and actions for malicious prosecution or abuse of process, to mention only a few. In the same vein we think that reliable alternatives exist to service of process by a state-paid sheriff if the State is unwilling to assume the cost of official service. This is perforce true of service by publication which is the method of notice least calculated to bring to a potential defendant's attention the pendency of judicial proceedings. We think in this case service at defendant's last known address by mail and posted notice is equally effective as publication in a newspaper.

We are thus left to evaluate the State's asserted interest in its fee and cost requirements as a mechanism of resource allocation or cost recoupment. Such a justification was offered and rejected in *Griffin v. Illinois*, 351 U.S. 12 (1956). In *Griffin* it was the requirement of a transcript beyond the means of the indigent that blocked access to the judicial process. While in *Griffin* the transcript could be waived as a convenient but not necessary predicate to court access, here the State invariably imposes the costs as a measure of allocating its judicial resources. Surely, then, the rationale of *Griffin* covers this case.

IV

In concluding that the Due Process Clause of the Fourteenth Amendment requires that these appellants be afforded an opportunity to go into court to obtain a divorce, we wish to re-emphasize that we go no further than necessary to dispose of the case before us, a case where the bona fides of both appellants' indigency and desire for divorce are here beyond dispute. We do not decide that access for all individuals to the courts is a right that is, in all circumstances, guaranteed by the Due Process Clause of the Fourteenth Amendment so that its exercise may not be placed beyond the reach of any individual, for, as we have already noted, in the case before us this right is the exclusive precondition to the adjustment of a fundamental human relationship. The requirement that these appellants resort to the judicial process is entirely a state-created matter. Thus we hold only that a State may not, consistent with the obligations imposed on it by the Due Process Clause of the Fourteenth Amendment, pre-empt the right to dissolve this legal relationship without affording all citizens access to the means it has prescribed for doing so. . . .

NOTES AND QUESTIONS

1. *Exclusion from Courts.* Imagine, as in the foundational case of Goldberg v. Kelly, that a party is deprived of public assistance without a pre-termination hearing.[92] The Court in *Goldberg* found that the absence of procedural protection for defendants in that context violates the procedural due process principles of the Fourteenth Amendment. How did the idea of due process influence the analysis in *Boddie*? In an unexcerpted portion, the Court drew upon Mullane v. Central Hanover Trust Co., which held that "the statutory provision for notice by publication in a local newspaper, although sufficient as to beneficiaries of a trust whose interests or addresses were unknown to the trustee, was not sufficient notice under the Due Process Clause for known beneficiaries."[93] How is *Mullane*'s focus on the opportunity to be heard instructive in the context of the constitutional claim in *Boddie*?

2. *Boddie's Reach.* Consider the state's imposition of fees to file a petition for bankruptcy. Imagine that a group of plaintiffs is unable to pay the fees to commence such an action. They argue that *Boddie* means that their actions should not be barred by the filing fee requirements. In United States v. Kras, the Court found that the bankruptcy fee was constitutional despite *Boddie* because the right at stake did not merit the same level of protection as the right to seek a divorce.[94] While the holding in *Kras* was eventually superseded by the 1978 Bankruptcy Code, other courts have adopted the same rationale when evaluating constitutional claims against filing fees.[95] What is the difference between access to courts for divorce as opposed to for bankruptcy or other legal claims?

NOTE ON ACCESS TO JUSTICE

Access to courts in the United States is closely tied to the broader issue of inclusive access to the legal system, including income-based legal assistance. As Professor Suzanne Kim has observed, the gap in access to civil legal assistance in the U.S. affects the family law system particularly acutely.[96] According to a 2017 study, 86 percent of civil legal problems that low-income Americans reported received

---

92. 397 U.S. 254 (1970).

93. 339 U.S. 306, 307 (1950).

94. 409 U.S. 434, 446–47 (1973); see also In re Garland, 428 F.2d 1185, 1188 (1st Cir. 1970).

95. *See* In re South, 689 F.2d 162, 166 (10th Cir. 1982); In re Bradford, 14 B.R. 722, 726–27 (Bankr. N.D. Ill. 1981).

96. Suzanne A. Kim, Transitional Equality, 53 U. Rich. L. Rev. 1149, 1185–86 (2019).

insufficient or no legal assistance.[97] Immigrants, communities of color, women, the elderly, LGBTQ individuals, and rural communities disproportionately require income-based legal assistance.[98] As Kim highlights, this gap is especially pronounced for family law matters, with such cases comprising the biggest percentage of income-based legal assistance provided by organizations funded by the federal Legal Services Corporation, the largest funder of civil legal aid.[99] Seventeen percent of low-income families face civil legal problems pertaining to family matters, including domestic violence, sexual assault, divorce, separation, or harm to vulnerable adults.[100] Those seeking domestic violence protection orders are disproportionately self-represented, and more than half of those leaving domestic violence shelters have unmet legal needs.[101]

Cost is one reason for this gap. Individuals who do not seek outside assistance for their civil legal issues report that cost is a factor in 17 percent of cases.[102] The costs of divorce, especially given the relative low asset holdings of average American families, can be prohibitive.[103] Divorce attorney fees can range from $100 to $450 per hour, with an average of $275.[104] Getting divorced costs an estimated $20,000 on average, with more complicated divorces, including contested ones involving trial, costing well over $100,000.[105] Litigation also demands time, requiring individuals to miss work and incur the costs of childcare and travel expenses.[106]

Factors like immigration status, economic dependency, and isolation also shape access to the legal system. Deborah Weissman, Jacqueline Hagan, Ricardo Martinez Schuldt, and Alyssa Peavey have observed:

> Immigrant households experience many of the same family law problems as citizens: domestic violence, divorce, custody and child support, and child

---

97. Legal Servs. Corp., The Justice Gap: Measuring the Unmet Civil Legal Needs of Low-Income Americans 6 (2017) [hereinafter Justice Gap].

98. Kim, supra note 96, at 1185; Rebecca Buckwalter-Poza, Ctr. for Am. Progress, Making Justice Equal (2016); Robin Runge, Addressing the Access to Justice Crisis in Rural America (2014).

99. Kim, supra note 96, at 1185; Justice Gap, supra note 97, at 39.

100. Justice Gap, supra note 97, at 24.

101. Ctr. for Court Innovation, Access to Justice in Domestic Violence & Sexual Assault Cases, https://www.courtinnovation.org/access-justice-domestic-violence; Nicole E. Allen, et al., Battered Women's Multitude of Needs: Evidence Supporting the Need for Comprehensive Advocacy, 10 Violence Against Women 1015, 1023 (2004); see also Laura K. Abel & Susan Vignola, Economic & Other Benefits Associated with the Provision of Civil Legal Aid, 9 Seattle J. for Soc. Just. 139, 147 (2010); Vivek S. Sankaran, Ctr. for Study Soc. Pol'y, Case Closed: Addressing Unmet Legal Needs & Stabilizing Families 1 (2014).

102. Rebecca L. Sandefur, Am. Bar Found., Accessing Justice in the Contemporary USA: Findings from the Community Needs and Services Study 3 (2014).

103. For discussion of the financial position of American families, see Chapter 5.

104. Danielle Braff, DIY Divorce, 105 ABA J. 31 (2019).

105. Michele N. Struffolino, Taking Limited Representation to the Limits: The Efficacy of Using Unbundled Legal Services in Domestic-Relations Matters Involving Litigation, 2 St. Mary's J. Legal Malpractice & Ethics 166, 200–01 (2012); Joshua T. Pierson, The Economics of Marriage Contracts 88 (2018) (on file with ProQuest Dissertations Publishing) ("[E]ven a couple with few assets reaching a negotiated settlement will usually pay a fee of around $15,000, a fee that will skyrocket if some issues are litigated before a court."); Braff, supra note 104, at 31.

106. Struffolino, supra note 105, at 200–01.

protection proceedings. However, these issues often affect immigrants differently. Although the overall incidence of domestic violence is not higher among immigrants than within the population at large, unauthorized status and the precarious position of immigrant women in the labor market, together with related economic dependency, isolation, and mixed status households, affect their ability to seek relief. In custody matters, judges often consider parents who are in the United States without authorization as inherently unsuitable for an award of custody. Child custody issues are further complicated when one parent is deported and thus separated from the family. Mixed-status households are now commonplace; seventeen million people are in families with at least one unauthorized immigrant.[107]

Limited English proficiency and lack of qualified interpreters can also hinder access to courts, either leading individuals to forego the judicial process or resulting in long and repeated adjournments.[108] These barriers are exacerbated by the fact that individuals with limited English proficiency are twice as likely as the general community to live in poverty, making access to legal assistance all the more difficult.[109] Federal immigration policy also shapes the ability to access legal assistance and courts. The past three years have seen dramatic increases in immigration-related arrests of individuals appearing in family court and other civil and criminal courts by agents of Immigration and Customs Enforcement (ICE). According to one study, ICE courthouse arrests or attempted arrests in New York state increased by 1700 percent from 2016 to 2019.[110] These ICE actions have persisted even after some states acted to restrict courthouse arrests.[111] Such arrests have been sharply criticized for interfering with immigrants' willingness or ability to access judicial process in child welfare, domestic violence, and other civil and criminal matters.[112]

Geography also plays an important role in access to justice in family law cases. As observed by Lisa Pruitt and Bradley Showman, while 20 percent of the U.S. population lives in rural areas, only 2 percent of small law practices are located there.[113]

---

107. Deborah M. Weissman et al., The Politics of Immigrant Rights: Between Political Geography and Transnational Interventions, 2018 Mich. St. L. Rev. 117, 172–73 (2018).

108. Christine Clarke & Veronica Cook, Legal Servs. NYC Civil Rights Justice Initiative, Interpreting Justice: Language Access in the New York Courts 5 (2016).

109. Id. In some cities, limited English proficiency is pervasive. Almost one sixth of households in New York City contain no English-proficient individuals over the age of 14. Id.

110. Immigrant Defense Project, Denied, Disappeared, and Deported: The Toll of ICE Operations at New York's Courts in 2019 2–3 (2020); Immigrant Defense Project, ICE Out of Courts.

111. Id.; see also Abené Clayton, 'Courts Must Be Safe Spaces': ICE Arrests Undo Long-held Migrant Protections, Lawyers Warn, Guardian (Mar. 13, 2020).

112. Angela Irvine et al., Ceres Policy Research, The Chilling Effect of ICE Courthouse Arrests: How Immigration and Customs Enforcement Raids Deter Immigrants from Attending Child Welfare, Domestic Violence, Adult Criminal, and Youth Court Hearings 8 (Oct. 2019).

113. Lisa R. Pruitt & Bradley Showman, Law Stretched Thin: Access to Justice in Rural America 59 S.D. L. Rev. 466, 469 (2014); Lisa R. Pruitt et. al., Legal Deserts: A Multi-State Perspective on Rural Access to Justice, 13 Harv. L. & Pol'y Rev. 15, 22 (2018).

These "legal deserts" also feature higher levels of poverty. Ten million people living in rural areas have family incomes below 125 percent of the federal poverty level.[114] Family law figures prominently in rural residents' legal needs. In assessing needs in rural Georgia, Pruitt, along with Amanda Kool, Lauren Sudeall, Michele Statz, Danielle Conway, and Hannah Haksgaard, found that housing and family law issues were among the most common, with consumer needs closely following.[115] Of those surveyed, nearly 75 percent sought to resolve their legal issues on their own, and only 9.1 percent were able to obtain attorney assistance.[116] Even when rural residents can find attorneys, they must often travel far distances to reach attorneys and courts (often without sufficient public transportation).[117] In an effort to address the lawyer shortage, South Dakota became the first state to offer subsidies to lawyers to practice in rural areas.[118]

Some states have sought to make legal services more accessible by licensing non-lawyers. In 2015, Washington became the first state to authorize non-lawyers to provide limited legal services in family law matters. Ordinarily, non-lawyers are not permitted to provide legal services without running afoul of state laws prohibiting the unauthorized practice of law. In a 2012 order, the Washington Supreme Court acknowledged the concerns that prohibitions on unauthorized practice of law address, but nonetheless explained that "there are people who need only limited levels of assistance that can be provided by non-lawyers."[119]

Washington Supreme Court just ended this program: https://www.abajournal .com/news/article/washington-supreme-court-decides-to-sunset-pioneering-limited-license-program must gain 3,000 hours of experience under the supervision of a licensed attorney, complete an approved curriculum, and pass exams covering a core curriculum and professional responsibility.[120] To be certified in family law, LLLTs must complete family law courses and pass a family law exam. LLLTs may do only specific types of legal work, such as drafting and filing certain documents; they are not authorized to take depositions or initiate or respond to an appeal.[121] Although initially prohibited, LLLTs are now permitted in limited circumstances to make court appearances and negotiate on behalf of clients.[122] What kinds of clients would you expect to retain

---

114. See Justice Gap, supra note 97, at 19.

115. Pruitt et al., Legal Deserts, supra note 113, at 15, 68.

116. Id.

117. Id., supra note 113, at 22.

118. Pruitt & Showman, supra note 113, at 467.

119. Order at 2, In re Adoption of New APR 28 — Limited Practice Rule for Limited License Legal Technicians, No. 25700-A-1005 (Wash. June 15, 2012).

120. Wash. Admis. Prac. R. 28 (2019) [hereinafter APR 28] Regs. 3, 9.

121. APR 28(F), (H); APR 28 Regs. 3(B), IO(B).

122. See APR 28(H)(5); APR 28 Reg. 2(B)(2)(h); APR 28(F)(13). See also Stephen R. Crossland & Paula C. Littlewood, Washington's Limited License Legal Technician Rule and Pathway to Expanded Access for Consumers, 122 Dick. L. Rev. 859, 873 (2018) (describing the rationales behind the changes to the initial prohibition on court appearances and negotiations).

LLLTs in divorce cases? What other kinds of family law matters would you expect LLLTs to commonly take on?[123]

The Washington Supreme Court voted in 2020 to "sunset" the LLLT program due to cost, but will permit those already licensed to continue practicing. Other states, however, as well as the American Bar Association (ABA), also have pursued similar kinds of programs.[124] In 2016, the ABA Commission on the Future of Legal Services made recommendations for state programs to license limited practice by non-lawyers.[125] In 2019, the Utah Supreme Court approved recommendations to pursue non-lawyer services in areas such as family law.[126] In 2020, the Arizona Supreme Court approved pilot programs that allow non-lawyers to provide limited legal support to domestic violence victims.[127] Are programs of this kind a good solution to the problem of pro se representation in family law matters? Is there a problem with a two-tiered system in which individuals with resources have lawyer representation and those with less have non-lawyer representation? How else might we address the gaps in representation in the family law system?

NOTE ON UNIFIED FAMILY COURTS

As discussed, access to legal systems and representation is particularly important given the prevalence of family law issues. In some states, family law filings comprise 40 to 50 percent or more of all state trial court filings.[128] According to the most recent national survey of family court structures, three-quarters of states had

---

123. APR 28 Reg. 2(B)(1) allows LLLTs to engage in matters related to "(a) divorce and dissolution, (b) parenting and support, (c) parentage or paternity, (d) child support modification, (e) parenting plan modification, (f) domestic violence protection orders, (g) committed intimate relationships only as they pertain to parenting and support issues, (h) legal separation, (i) nonparental and third party custody, (j) other protection or restraining orders arising from a domestic relations case, and (k) relocation." For a full list of limitations, see APR 28 Reg. 2(B)(2)-(3).

124. Letter from Chief Justice Debra Stephens, Washington Supreme Court, to Stephen Crossland et al. (June 5, 2020).

125. ABA Comm'n on the Future of Legal Serv., Report on the Future of Legal Services in the United States 40–41 (2016).

126. Standing Order No. 14 (Utah Sept. 9, 2019); Annie Knox, How a New Program Connects Utahns to Lower-Cost Legal Advice, Deseret News (Feb. 17, 2020); Utah Supreme Court Adopts Groundbreaking Changes to Legal Service Regulation, Utah Ct. (Aug. 29, 2019); Utah Work Group on Reg. Reform, Narrowing the Access-to-Justice Gap by Reimagining Regulation (Aug. 2019).

127. See In re Authorizing a Legal Document Preparer Pilot Program for Domestic Violence Cases and Related Matters, No. 2020-25 (Ariz. Jan. 29, 2020); see also Stephanie Francis Ward, Training for Nonlawyers to Provide Legal Advice Will Start in Arizona in the Fall, ABA J. (Feb. 6, 2020).

128. Barbara A. Babb, Reevaluating Where We Stand: A Comprehensive Survey of America's Family Justice Systems, 46 Fam. Ct. Rev. 230, 230 (2008) ("In Maryland, nearly forty-six percent (127,974) of the 278,511 total filings in the trial court of general jurisdiction involve family and juvenile cases. In New Jersey, these cases account for forty-one percent (437,216) of the state's 1,071,071 total trial court filings. In Nebraska, family law cases amount to fifty-eight percent of the state's total trial court caseload. In Nevada, forty-nine percent of the statewide trial court caseload involves family-related cases.").

specially designated family courts that are either separate courts or distinct parts of general jurisdiction state courts.[129] These courts have jurisdiction over a wide range of matters pertaining to children and families.[130] Other states handle family law matters within their state general civil trial courts.[131] (In some states, probate courts, which are not courts of general jurisdiction, also handle some family law matters. For example, in Connecticut, petitions to terminate parental rights and adoption petitions are filed in probate court.[132])

Many family courts today are known as "unified" or "integrated" family courts. Matters can be decided by a single court, rather than parceled out across different types of family courts for different types of cases (e.g., divorce, juvenile, nonsupport). Unified family courts are typically intended to have "(1) comprehensive jurisdiction; (2) efficient, modern administration designed to support the concept of 'one family, one team'; (3) multidisciplinary training for all court personnel, from intake staff to judges; and (4) ability to ensure that family members receive the services they need."[133] In a unified family court system, "[o]ne specially-trained and interested judge addresses the legal and accompanying emotional and social issues challenging each family."[134] Under this judge's authority, informal court processes and social service agencies and resources are coordinated to address the individual family's "legal, personal, emotional, and social needs."[135]

Court reform aimed at creating unified family courts gained significant momentum nationally in the 1990s, focused on addressing harms from court systems in which the same family might have legal issues subject to the jurisdiction of different judges.[136]

> The fragmented court system that has overlapping jurisdiction over family cases in most jurisdictions evolved neither from a set of jurisprudential principles nor a theory of judicial administration. With the exception of the juvenile court that handles cases involving unruly and delinquent behavior, the family justice system emerged on an ad hoc basis. . . . As federal district

---

129. Id.

130. Judith Moran, Judicial Independence in Family Courts: Beyond the Election-Appointment Dichotomy, 37 Fam. L. Q. 361, 366–67 (2003).

131. Babb, supra note 128, at 233 (as of the end of 2006, the latest date for which a comprehensive survey is available, these states were Alaska, Arkansas, Idaho, Iowa, Mississippi, Montana, Nebraska, Oklahoma, South Dakota, Tennessee, Utah, Virginia, and Wyoming, which included some states that had piloted but eliminated them).

132. Conn. Gen. Stat. § 45a-8a (2020); see also Mass. Gen. Laws Ann. ch. 215, § 4 (2020); Vt. Stat. Ann. tit. 15A, § 3-101 (2020).

133. Catherine J. Ross, Unified Family Courts: Good Sense, Good Justice, 35 Trial 30, 31 (1999); see also Paul A. Williams, A Unified Family Court for Missouri, 63 UMKC L. Rev. 383, 383–84 (1995).

134. Williams, supra note 133, at 383–8; see also Anne H. Geraghty & Wallace J. Mlyniec, Unified Family Courts: Tempering Enthusiasm with Caution, 40 Fam. Ct. Rev. 435, 436 n.7 (2002).

135. Williams, supra note 133, at 383–84.

136. For a history of family court reform efforts, see Babb supra note 128. For discussion of juvenile court reform, see Geraghty & Mlyniec, supra note 134.

courts declined to hear domestic relations matters, states pieced together courts that all too often had overlapping jurisdiction over different legal questions involving the same family, creating an opportunity for fragmentation and such resulting plagues as expressly conflicting orders. For example, one judge may order visitation in a matrimonial proceeding, while another judge finds evidence of abuse in a child protection proceeding and issues an order precluding unsupervised contact with the same adult.[137]

In addition to pointing to negative safety and welfare effects from inconsistent rulings, advocates for unified family courts critiqued traditional courts for inefficiently dispensing "assembly-line justice."[138] Instead, courts were envisioned as a "one stop shopping center" to meet families' needs based on a therapeutic model.[139] The American Bar Association and the Council of Juvenile and Family Court Judges endorsed unified family courts in the 1980s and 1990s.[140]

The unified family court movement had some detractors. Based on past experiences in the U.S. with juvenile court reform earlier in the twentieth century that resulted in punitive treatment of children under the guise of problem solving, Anne Geraghty and Professor Wallace Mlyniec critique the "solve everything" model:

> A court is, at its core, an instrument of social control. What it does best is resolve disputed factual issues at a point when the litigants cannot resolve them by themselves. Courts gain control over these acrimonious situations only through the threat or reality of coercion. Thus, courts are generally seen as an option of last resort, somewhere for people to go to resolve serious disputes without resort to violence, and a place where society can assert its control over behavior that it considers too egregious to go unpunished. Most people who appear before a court do not wish to be there, and would have chosen another form of dispute resolution had it been possible.[141]

Proponents of unified family courts must face the fact that "sanctions given out by the court, whether or not called 'therapeutic,' are inherently coercive" and that the "focus on therapy may divert the court from its fundamental role as a forum for dispute resolution."[142] Drawing from the family court reform experience to evaluate newer problem-solving courts in other contexts, like drug treatment and mental health courts, Professor Jane Spinak contends that judges fall short of the "idealized

---

137. Catherine J. Ross, The Failure of Fragmentation: The Promise of A System of Unified Family Courts, 33 Rev. Jur. U.I.P.R. 311, 314 (1999).

138. Ross, supra note 133, at 30–31.

139. Geraghty & Mlyniec, supra note 134, at 436–37.

140. See ABA Joint Commission of Juvenile Justice Standards (Standard 1.1, Part 1) (1980); see also Sanford N. Katz & Jeffrey A. Kuhn, Nat'l Council of Juvenile and Family Court Judges, Recommendations for a Model Family Court: A Report from the National Family Court Symposium (1991).

141. Geraghty & Mlyniec, supra note 134, at 440–41.

142. Id. at 441.

conception" of problem-solvers, and that courts are ill-equipped to address the magnitude of social issues through highly interventionist court-based models.[143] Professor Elizabeth MacDowell has also criticized some courts' unification of civil and criminal jurisdiction (in domestic violence and child support enforcement contexts), diminished procedural formality, and greater reliance on non-legal entities like social service actors to fulfill courts' "problem solving" objectives.[144] Such court features, she argues, "expand the operation of the state" and result in families' greater vulnerability.[145]

Do you think families are better served by courts in which judges are intended to play the role of problem-solvers, or should judges and courts be focused more narrowly on dispute resolution? Should judges play a different role in family law cases than in other legal contexts? More generally, what gains are made by a unified family court approach? What disadvantages can you identify?

B. Divorce Jurisdiction

Cost is not the only barrier to divorce. Many litigants face barriers due to jurisdictional requirements that constrain their ability to obtain a divorce. As in any case, an action for divorce must meet subject matter and personal jurisdiction requirements.

1. Subject Matter Jurisdiction

As courts of limited subject matter jurisdiction, federal courts may only hear those actions that fit within its federal question jurisdiction,[146] or diversity jurisdiction.[147] State courts, in contrast, are courts of general jurisdiction.

a. The Domestic Relations Exception to Federal Court Diversity Jurisdiction

Even if a divorce action otherwise satisfies subject matter jurisdiction requirements for federal court, a longstanding "domestic relations exception" means that federal courts may refuse to hear the action if it is premised on diversity rather than subject matter jurisdiction. In the next case, the Supreme Court sets forth the limits of this exception.

---

143. Jane M. Spinak, Romancing the Court, 46 Fam. Ct. Rev. 258, 258 (2008). See Jane M. Spinak, Judicial Leadership in Family Court: A Cautionary Tale, 10 Tenn. J.L. & Pol'y 47, 47, 51–52 (2014).

144. Elizabeth L. MacDowell, Vulnerability, Access to Justice, and the Fragmented State, 23 Mich. J. Race & L. 52, 52–53 (2017).

145. Elizabeth L. MacDowell, Reimagining Access to Justice in the Poor People's Courts, 22 Geo. J. Poverty L. & Pol'y 473, 487 (2015).

146. 28 U.S.C. § 1331 (2018).

147. 28 U.S.C. § 1332 (2018).

ANKENBRANDT V. RICHARDS

504 U.S. 689 (1992)

MR. JUSTICE WHITE delivered the opinion of the Court.

This case presents the issue whether the federal courts have jurisdiction or should abstain in a case involving alleged torts committed by the former husband of petitioner and his female companion against petitioner's children, when the sole basis for federal jurisdiction is the diversity-of-citizenship provision of 28 U.S.C. § 1332.

I

Petitioner Carol Ankenbrandt, a citizen of Missouri, brought this lawsuit on September 26, 1989, on behalf of her daughters L.R. and S.R. against respondents Jon A. Richards and Debra Kesler, citizens of Louisiana, in the United States District Court for the Eastern District of Louisiana. Alleging federal jurisdiction based on the diversity-of-citizenship provision of § 1332, Ankenbrandt's complaint sought monetary damages for alleged sexual and physical abuse of the children committed by Richards and Kesler. Richards is the divorced father of the children and Kesler his female companion. On December 10, 1990, the District Court granted respondents' motion to dismiss this lawsuit. Citing *In re Burrus*, 136 U.S. 586, 593–594 (1890), for the proposition that "[t]he whole subject of the domestic relations of husband and wife, parent and child, belongs to the laws of the States and not to the laws of the United States," the court concluded that this case fell within what has become known as the "domestic relations" exception to diversity jurisdiction, and that it lacked jurisdiction over the case. . . . The Court of Appeals affirmed. . . .

We granted certiorari limited to the following questions: "(1) Is there a domestic relations exception to federal jurisdiction? (2) If so, does it permit a district court to abstain from exercising diversity jurisdiction over a tort action for damages?"

II

The domestic relations exception upon which the courts below relied to decline jurisdiction has been invoked often by the lower federal courts. The seeming authority for doing so originally stemmed from the announcement in *Barber v. Barber*, 16 L. Ed. 226 (1859), that the federal courts have no jurisdiction over suits for divorce or the allowance of alimony. . . .

The statements disclaiming jurisdiction over divorce and alimony decree suits, though technically dicta, formed the basis for excluding "domestic relations" cases from the jurisdiction of the lower federal courts, a jurisdictional limitation those courts have recognized ever since. The *Barber* Court, however, cited no authority and did not discuss the foundation for its announcement. Since that time, the Court has dealt only occasionally with the domestic relations limitation on federal-court jurisdiction, and it has never addressed the basis for such a limitation. Because we are unwilling to cast aside an understood rule that has been recognized for nearly a century and a half, we feel compelled to explain why we will continue to recognize this limitation on federal jurisdiction.

A

Counsel argued in *Barber* that the Constitution prohibited federal courts from exercising jurisdiction over domestic relations cases. An examination of Article III, *Barber* itself, and our cases since *Barber* makes clear that the Constitution does not exclude domestic relations cases from the jurisdiction otherwise granted by statute to the federal courts. . . .

Article III, § 2, of the Constitution provides in pertinent part:

> Section 2. The judicial Power shall extend to all Cases, in Law and Equity, arising under this Constitution, the Laws of the United States, and Treaties made, or which shall be made, under their Authority; — to all Cases affecting Ambassadors, other public Ministers and Consuls; — to all Cases of admiralty and maritime Jurisdiction; — to Controversies to which the United States shall be a Party; — to Controversies between two or more States; — between a State and Citizens of another State; — between Citizens of different States; — between Citizens of the same State claiming Land under Grants of different States, and between a State, or the Citizens thereof, and foreign States, Citizens or Subjects.

This section delineates the absolute limits on the federal courts' jurisdiction. But in articulating three different terms to define jurisdiction — "Cases, in Law and Equity," "Cases," and "Controversies" — this provision contains no limitation on subjects of a domestic relations nature. Nor did *Barber* purport to ground the domestic relations exception in these constitutional limits on federal jurisdiction. The Court's discussion of federal judicial power to hear suits of a domestic relations nature contains no mention of the Constitution, and it is logical to presume that the Court based its statement limiting such power on narrower statutory, rather than broader constitutional, grounds.

Subsequent decisions confirm that *Barber* was not relying on constitutional limits in justifying the exception. In one such case, for instance, the Court stated the "long established rule" that federal courts lack jurisdiction over certain domestic relations matters as having been based on the assumptions that "husband and wife cannot usually be citizens of different States, so long as the marriage relation continues (a rule which has been somewhat relaxed in recent cases), and for the further reason that a suit for divorce in itself involves no pecuniary value." *De la Rama v. De la Rama*, 201 U.S. 303, 307 (1906). Since Article III contains no monetary limit on suits brought pursuant to federal diversity jurisdiction, *De la Rama*'s articulation of the "rule" in terms of the statutory requirements for diversity jurisdiction further supports the view that the exception is not grounded in the Constitution.

Moreover, even while citing with approval the *Barber* language purporting to limit the jurisdiction of the federal courts over domestic relations matters, the Court has heard appeals from territorial courts involving divorce and has upheld the exercise of original jurisdiction by federal courts in the District of Columbia to decide divorce actions. Thus, even were the statements in *De la Rama* referring to the statutory prerequisites of diversity jurisdiction alone not persuasive testament to the statutory origins of the rule, by hearing appeals from legislative, or Article I, courts, this Court implicitly has made clear its understanding that the source of the constraint on jurisdiction from *Barber* was *not* Article III; otherwise the Court itself would have lacked jurisdiction over appeals from these legislative courts. We therefore have no difficulty concluding that when the *Barber* Court "disclaim[ed] altogether any jurisdiction in the courts of the United States upon the subject of divorce," it was not basing its statement on the Constitution.

B

That Article III, § 2, does not mandate the exclusion of domestic relations cases from federal-court jurisdiction, however, does not mean that such courts necessarily must retain and exercise jurisdiction over such cases. . . .

III

In the more than 100 years since this Court laid the seeds for the development of the domestic relations exception, the lower federal courts have applied it in a variety of circumstances. Many of these applications go well beyond the circumscribed situations posed by *Barber* and its progeny. *Barber* itself disclaimed federal jurisdiction over a narrow range of domestic relations issues involving the granting of a divorce and a decree of alimony. . . .

The *Barber* Court thus did not intend to strip the federal courts of authority to hear cases arising from the domestic relations of persons unless they seek the granting or modification of a divorce or alimony decree. The holding of the case itself sanctioned the exercise of federal jurisdiction over the enforcement of an alimony decree that had been properly obtained in a state court of competent jurisdiction. Contrary to the *Barber* dissenters' position, the enforcement of such validly obtained orders does not "regulate the domestic relations of society" and produce an "inquisitorial authority" in which federal tribunals "enter the habitations and even into the chambers and nurseries of private families, and inquire into and pronounce upon the morals and habits and affections or antipathies of the members of every household." And from the conclusion that the federal courts lacked jurisdiction to issue divorce and alimony decrees, there was no dissent.

Subsequently, this Court expanded the domestic relations exception to include decrees in child custody cases. In a child custody case brought pursuant to a writ of habeas corpus, for instance, the Court held void a writ issued by a Federal District Court to restore a child to the custody of the father. "As to the right to the control and possession of this child, as it is contested by its father and its grandfather, it is one in regard to which neither the Congress of the United States nor any authority of the United States has any special jurisdiction." *In re Burrus,* 136 U.S. at 594.

Although *In re Burrus* technically did not involve a construction of the diversity statute, as we understand *Barber* to have done, its statement that "[t]he whole subject of the domestic relations of husband and wife, parent and child, belongs to the laws of the States and not to the laws of the United States," has been interpreted by the federal courts to apply with equal vigor in suits brought pursuant to diversity jurisdiction. This application is consistent with *Barber*'s directive to limit federal courts' exercise of diversity jurisdiction over suits for divorce and alimony decrees. We conclude, therefore, that the domestic relations exception, as articulated by this Court since *Barber,* divests the federal courts of power to issue divorce, alimony, and child custody decrees. Given the long passage of time without any expression of congressional dissatisfaction, we have no trouble today reaffirming the validity of the exception as it pertains to divorce and alimony decrees and child custody orders. . . .

[O]ur conclusion . . . is also supported by sound policy considerations. Issuance of decrees of this type not infrequently involves retention of jurisdiction by the court and deployment of social workers to monitor compliance. As a matter of judicial economy, state courts are more eminently suited to work of this type than are federal courts, which lack the close association with state and local government organizations dedicated to handling issues that arise out of conflicts over divorce, alimony, and child custody decrees. Moreover, as a matter of judicial expertise, it makes far more sense to retain the rule that federal courts lack power to issue these types of decrees because of the special proficiency developed by state tribunals over the past century and a half in handling issues that arise in the granting of such decrees.

By concluding, as we do, that the domestic relations exception encompasses only cases involving the issuance of a divorce, alimony, or child custody decree, we necessarily find that the Court of Appeals erred by affirming the District Court's invocation of this exception. This lawsuit in no way seeks such a decree; rather, it alleges that respondents Richards and Kesler committed torts against L.R. and S.R., Ankenbrandt's children by Richards. Federal subject-matter jurisdiction pursuant to § 1332 thus is proper in this case. . . .

NOTES AND QUESTIONS

1.   *Family Law Exceptionalism?* The domestic relations exception to federal court jurisdiction has been explained in terms of federal court deference to state courts on matters over which the latter are presumed to have more competence and experience.[148] Why do we presume state courts are better suited to handle domestic relations cases? Family law "exceptionalism," or the idea that family law is special and can or should be exempted from standard rules — e.g., relegated to state courts when virtually any other type of case could end up in federal court based on diversity jurisdiction — has been the subject of fierce criticism.[149] Does the domestic relations exception reflect assumptions about family law that are bound up in ideas of gender?[150] How might the split between federal and state courts reflect the "separate spheres" concept that subordinates women to men and views women as belonging in the home and men in the market?[151] Considering the large volume of family law cases on state court dockets, are the interests of family law litigants best met by assuming that state courts are better suited to hear such cases?

2.   *State Versus Federal Family Law.* Although, historically, family law has been considered to be the domain of the states and its courts, the federal government, federal courts, and the U.S. Supreme Court also shape family law and policy. For instance, as we have seen, state action drawing lines of access to marriage implicate federal constitutional issues.[152] Family law in turn shapes constitutional understandings of the family relationships that merit protection.[153]

b. Durational Residency and Domicile

In addition to general jurisdictional requirements for divorce, most states also impose durational residency requirements.[154] Under most applicable statutes, one party to the divorce must be a resident of the state in which the divorce is being pursued for a specified period of time before commencement of the divorce action. Durational residency requirements vary across states and can range from six weeks

---

148. Homer H. Clark, Jr., The Law of Domestic Relations in the United States 415 (2d ed. 1988); Crouch v. Crouch, 566 F.2d 486, 487 (5th Cir. 1978); Solomon v. Solomon, 516 F.2d 1018, 1025 (3rd Cir. 1975).

149. See, e.g., Jill Elaine Hasday, Federalism and the Family Reconstructed, 45 UCLA L. Rev. 1297, 1297–1310 (1998).

150. See Naomi R. Cahn, Family Law, Federalism, and the Federal Courts, 79 Iowa L. Rev. 1073, 1098–1101 (1994).

151. See Reva B. Siegel, She The People: The Nineteenth Amendment, Sex Equality, Federalism, and the Family, 115 Harv. L. Rev. 947 (2002); Judith Resnik, Gender Bias: From Classes to Courts, 45 Stan. L. Rev. 2195 (1993).

152. See, e.g., Loving v. Virginia, 388 U.S. 1 (1967); Obergefell v. Hodges, 135 S. Ct. 2584 (2015).

153. See Douglas NeJaime, The Family's Constitution, 32 Const. Comm. 413 (2017).

154. Alaska, however, has no durational residency requirement. Alaska Stat. Ann. § 25.24.080 (West 2020).

to two years.[155] Some states do not apply durational residency requirements if certain conditions are met, like the spouses were married in the state, the marital breakdown occurred in the state, or if the grounds for divorce arose in the state.[156] The next case addresses the constitutionality of durational residency requirements.

Sosna v. Iowa
419 U.S. 393 (1975)

Mr. Justice Rehnquist delivered the opinion of the Court.

Appellant Carol Sosna married Michael Sosna on September 5, 1964, in Michigan. They lived together in New York between October 1967 and August 1971, after which date they separated but continued to live in New York. In August 1972, appellant moved to Iowa with her three children, and the following month she petitioned the District Court of Jackson County, Iowa, for a dissolution of her marriage. Michael Sosna, who had been personally served with notice of the action when he came to Iowa to visit his children, made a special appearance to contest the jurisdiction of the Iowa court. The Iowa court dismissed the petition for lack of jurisdiction, finding that Michael Sosna was not a resident of Iowa and appellant had not been a resident of the State of Iowa for one year preceding the filing of her petition. In so doing the Iowa court applied the provisions of Iowa Code s 598.6 (1973) requiring that the petitioner in such an action be "for the last year a resident of the state." . . .

The durational residency requirement under attack in this case is a part of Iowa's comprehensive statutory regulation of domestic relations, an area that has long been regarded as a virtually exclusive province of the States. Cases decided by this Court over a period of more than a century bear witness to this historical fact. . . . In *Pennoyer v. Neff*, 95 U.S. 714, 734–735 (1878), the Court said: "The State . . . has absolute right to prescribe the conditions upon which the marriage relation between its own citizens shall be created, and the causes for which it may be dissolved," and the same view was reaffirmed in *Simms v. Simms*, 175 U.S. 162 (1899). . . .

---

155. Emilie F. Short, What constitutes residence or domicile within state by citizen of another country for purposes of jurisdiction in divorce, 51 A.L.R.3d 223 (1973); L.S. Tellier, What constitutes residence or domicile within state for purpose of jurisdiction in divorce, 159 A.L.R. 496 (1946). See, e.g., Idaho Code Ann. § 32-701 (West 2020) (residency requirement of 6 weeks); N.Y. Dom. Rel. Law § 230 (McKinney 2020) (imposing two-year requirement unless one or both spouses live in state, marriage occurred in state, or cause of action occurred in state — then imposing lesser or no requirement).

156. See, e.g., Me. Rev. Stat. Ann. tit. 19-A, § 901 (2020) (no in-state minimum if either (1) the spouses were married in state or (2) the breakdown of the marriage occurred in state. If neither conditions are met, there is a 180-day residency requirement); Md. Code Ann., § 7-101 (West 2020) (six-month residence required unless breakdown of the marriage occurred in state); Mass. Gen. Laws Ann. ch. 208, § 5 (West 2020) (365-day residency requirement unless breakdown of the marriage happened in state); Neb. Rev. Stat. Ann. § 42-349 (West 2020) (no residency requirement if the spouses were married in Nebraska and one spouse still resides there, or a 365-day requirement if married outside the state); Tenn. Code Ann. § 36-4-104 (West 2020) (no minimum requirement if grounds for divorce happened in state).

Jurisdiction over a petition for dissolution is established by statute in "the county where either party resides," Iowa Code § 598.2 (1973), and the Iowa courts have construed the term "resident" to have much the same meaning as is ordinarily associated with the concept of domicile. . . .

The imposition of a durational residency requirement for divorce is scarcely unique to Iowa, since 48 States impose such a requirement as a condition for maintaining an action for divorce. . . .

Appellant contends that the Iowa requirement of one year's residence is unconstitutional for two separate reasons: first, because it establishes two classes of persons and discriminates against those who have recently exercised their right to travel to Iowa, thereby contravening the Court's [prior] holdings; and, second, because it denies a litigant the opportunity to make an individualized showing of bona fide residence and therefore denies such residents access to the only method of legally dissolving their marriage.

State statutes imposing durational residency requirements were, of course, invalidated when imposed by States as a qualification for welfare payments; for voting; and for medical care. What those cases had in common was that the durational residency requirements they struck down were justified on the basis of budgetary or recordkeeping considerations which were held insufficient to outweigh the constitutional claims of the individuals. But Iowa's divorce residency requirement is of a different stripe. Appellant was not irretrievably foreclosed from obtaining some part of what she sought. . . . She would eventually qualify for the same sort of adjudication which she demanded virtually upon her arrival in the State. Iowa's requirement delayed her access to the courts, but, by fulfilling it, she could ultimately have obtained the same opportunity for adjudication which she asserts ought to have been hers at an earlier point in time. . . .

A decree of divorce is not a matter in which the only interested parties are the State as a sort of "grantor," and a divorce petitioner such as appellant in the role of "grantee." Both spouses are obviously interested in the proceedings, since it will affect their marital status and very likely their property rights. Where a married couple has minor children, a decree of divorce would usually include provisions for their custody and support. With consequences of such moment riding on a divorce decree issued by its courts, Iowa may insist that one seeking to initiate such a proceeding have the modicum of attachment to the State required here.

Such a requirement additionally furthers the State's parallel interests both in avoiding officious intermeddling in matters in which another State has a paramount interest, and in minimizing the susceptibility of its own divorce decrees to collateral attack. A State such as Iowa may quite reasonably decide that it does not wish to become a divorce mill for unhappy spouses who have lived there as short a time as appellant had when she commenced her action in the state court after having long resided elsewhere. Until such time as Iowa is convinced that appellant intends to remain in the State, it lacks the "nexus between person and place of such permanence as to control the creation of legal relations and responsibilities of the utmost significance." *Williams v. North Carolina*, 325 U.S. 226, 229 (1945). Perhaps even more important, Iowa's interests extend beyond its borders and include the recognition of its divorce decrees by other States under the Full Faith and Credit Clause of the Constitution, Art. IV, § 1. For that purpose, this Court has often stated that "judicial power to grant a divorce — jurisdiction, strictly speaking — is founded on domicile." *Williams, supra.* Where a divorce decree is entered after a finding of domicile in *ex parte* proceedings, this Court has held that the finding of domicile is not binding upon another State and may be disregarded in the face of "cogent evidence" to the contrary. For that reason, the State asked to enter such a decree is entitled to insist that the putative divorce petitioner satisfy something more than the bare minimum of constitutional requirements before a divorce may be granted. The State's decision to exact a one-year residency requirement as a matter of policy is therefore buttressed by a quite permissible inference that this requirement not only effectuates state substantive policy but likewise provides a greater safeguard against successful collateral attack than would a requirement of bona fide residence alone. This is precisely the sort of determination that a State in the exercise of its domestic relations jurisdiction is entitled to make.

We therefore hold that the state interest in requiring that those who seek a divorce from its courts be genuinely attached to the State, as well as a desire to insulate divorce decrees from the likelihood of collateral attack, requires a different resolution of the constitutional issue presented than was the case in [other contexts].

Nor are we of the view that the failure to provide an individualized determination of residency violates the Due Process Clause of the Fourteenth Amendment. . . . An individualized determination of physical presence plus the intent to remain, which appellant apparently seeks, would not entitle her to a divorce even if she could have made such a showing. For Iowa requires not merely "domicile" in that sense, but residence in the State for a year in order for its courts to exercise their divorce jurisdiction.

In *Boddie v. Connecticut*, this Court held that Connecticut might not deny access to divorce courts to those persons who could not afford to pay the required fee. Because of the exclusive role played by the State in the termination of marriages, it was held that indigents could not be denied an opportunity to be heard "absent a countervailing state interest of overriding significance." 401 U.S. 371, 377 (1971). But the gravamen of appellant Sosna's claim is not total deprivation, as in *Boddie*, but only delay. The operation of the filing fee in *Boddie* served to exclude forever a certain segment of the population from obtaining a divorce in the courts of Connecticut. No similar total deprivation is present in appellant's case, and the delay which attends the enforcement of the one-year durational residency requirement is, for the reasons previously stated, consistent with the provisions of the United States Constitution. . . .

NOTES AND QUESTIONS

1. *Origin of Durational Residency Requirements.* The Court in *Sosna* deemed "reasonable" the state of Iowa's desire to avoid becoming a "divorce mill for unhappy spouses." Residency requirements played a central role in the era of fault-based divorce, as states lengthened and shortened them in order to deter or attract migratory divorce. Nevada was the chief "offender," attracting divorcing couples from all over the country with its six-week residency requirement. In 1929, 1930, and 1931, Nevada had ten times as many divorces per 1,000 residents as the state with the second highest number.[157] But after the shift to no-fault divorce, there was little reason for couples to leave their home state to divorce elsewhere.[158] Why, then, do states still impose a residency requirement on divorce litigants? What is the state interest in presiding only over dissolution of residents' marriages?

2. *Same-Sex Marriage and Divorce* Before the Supreme Court gave the green light to marriages by same-sex couples nationwide in Obergefell v. Hodges,[159] same-sex couples who had validly married or formed civil unions in one state faced barriers to dissolution in other states, even where they were residents.[160] Courts in states that did not permit same-sex couples to marry often refused to dissolve such marriages on grounds that they would have to recognize them in order to dissolve them.[161] *Obergefell* paved the way not only for same-sex couples to marry, but also for them to divorce in any jurisdiction where they could meet the residency requirements.[162]

3. *Domestic Divorce Involving Foreign Residents.* For cases where one or both parties reside or used to reside in a foreign country and are now seeking a divorce within the United States, courts attempt to establish an equitable result even if the parties might not necessarily be domiciled in the state.[163] In situations in which a couple is validly married in the U.S. but living abroad where they are unable to obtain a divorce, as in the case of same-sex couples barred by marriage

---

157. See Grossman & Friedman, supra note 40, at 204.

158. Herma Hill Kay, Equality and Difference: A Perspective on No-Fault Divorce and Its Aftermath, 56 U. Cin. L. Rev. 1, 5 (1987). On the history of divorce mills, see Lawrence M. Friedman, A Dead Language: Divorce Law and Practice Before No-Fault, 86 Va. L. Rev. 1497, 1502–03 (2000).

159. 135 S. Ct. 2584 (2015).

160. See Courtney G. Joslin, Modernizing Divorce Jurisdiction: Same-Sex Couples and Minimum Contacts, 91 B.U. L. Rev. 1669, 1669 (2011); Mary Patricia Byrn & Morgan L. Holcomb, Wedlocked, 67 U. Miami L. Rev. 1, 2 (2012).

161. See, e.g., Rosengarten v. Downes, 806 A.2d 1066 (Conn. 2002); In re Marriage of J.B. and H.B., 326 S.W.3d 654 (Tex. App. 2010).

162. See Czekala-Chatham v. State, 195 So. 3d 187, 187 (Miss. 2015) (finding that the court, in a state that previously prohibited same-sex marriage, now had subject matter jurisdiction over a divorce decree of a same-sex couple as a result of *Obergefell*); see also M.S. v. D.S., 454 S.W.3d 900, 901 (Mo. 2015) (same).

163. See, e.g., In re Marriage of Thornton, 185 Cal. Rptr. 388, 396 (Cal. Ct. App. 1982).

recognition in some countries, a court may rely on equitable principles to determine the scope of jurisdiction.[164]

4. *Nonimmigrant Aliens and Domicile.* Courts have found that nonimmigrant aliens are not precluded from establishing domicile for the purposes of divorce decrees. The factors to consider whether the nonimmigrant alien has established domicile are the same as for any person attempting to establish domicile.[165]

5. *Jurisdictional Limits.* In some jurisdictions, the durational residency requirement is described as jurisdictional.[166] In others, it is construed as part of the elements of the divorce cause of action.[167] Generally, lack of subject matter jurisdiction can be raised at any time and would invalidate a divorce judgment even on collateral attack. Despite this general rule, some states allow a party to cure a jurisdictional defect.[168] Why would courts allow such a cure in the context of divorce?

2. Personal Jurisdiction in Divorce Actions

Even where subject matter jurisdiction exists, a court must also have personal jurisdiction over a defendant in any case. Traditionally, a court cannot exercise jurisdiction over a person who is not domiciled in the forum state unless the person has minimum contacts with the state or the person otherwise subjects themselves to the court's territorial jurisdiction.[169] Actions for divorce, however, fall within the "status" exception to traditional personal jurisdiction; dissolving a marriage is an adjustment to status that does not require personal jurisdiction over a non-resident spouse.[170]

The status exception to ordinary personal jurisdiction requirements is limited to actions to adjust marital status. When a divorce suit extends beyond the dissolution to a marriage to issues regarding division of property or support, the traditional analysis of minimum contacts is required under the doctrine of "divisible divorce," pursuant to which a divorce is divided between the issue of adjustment of legal status (from married to not married) and the separate questions of property division or spousal support.[171] Why is the status exception limited only to actions

---

164. See, e.g., Gruszczynski v. Twarkowski, 62 N.Y.S.3d 780, 783 (N.Y. Sup. Ct. 2017).

165. See In re Marriage of Dick, 18 Cal. Rptr. 2d 743, 747, 749 (Cal. Ct. App. 1993).

166. 24 Am. Jur. 2d Divorce and Separation § 177 (2019) (citing Ex Parte Ferguson, 15 So. 3d 520 (Ala. Civ. App. 2008); Fernandez v. Fernandez, 648 So. 2d 712 (Fla. 1995); Abernathy v. Abernathy, 482 S.E.2d 265 (Ga. 1997); Skiles v. Skiles, 646 N.E.2d 353 (Ind. Ct. App. 1995); Lewis v. Lewis, 930 S.W.2d 475 (Mo. Ct. App. 1996)).

167. Id. (citing Jones v. Jones, 402 N.W.2d 146 (Minn. Ct. App. 1987); Cook v. Mayfield, 886 S.W.2d 840 (Tex. App. 1994); Waite v. Waite, 959 So. 2d 610 (Ala. 2006)).

168. Id. (citing Buck v. Buck, 340 P.3d 546 (Mont. 2014)).

169. Int'l Shoe Co. v. Washington, 326 U.S. 310, 316 (1945).

170. See Pennoyer v. Neff, 95 U.S. 714, 734–35 (1877); see also Dawson-Austin v. Austin, 968 S.W.2d 319, 324 (Tex. 1998).

171. See Estin v. Estin, 334 U.S. 541, 549 (1948); see also Dawson-Austin v. Austin, 968 S.W.2d 319, 324, 328 (Tex. 1998); Puckett v. Puckett, 16 P.3d 876, 877 (Haw. Ct. App. 2000).

to adjust marital status? Should they extend more broadly to include legal claims concerning property or support? Wouldn't it make more sense, and be fairer, to exclude all of these related claims from personal jurisdiction rules?

Sometimes a divorce decree will have been issued by a state pursuant to the status exception from ordinary personal jurisdiction rules. These decrees would involve situations when one party in the marriage is a non-resident or does not otherwise consent to personal jurisdiction. What happens if another state is asked to enforce one of these divorce decrees? A sister state's obligation to enforce this decree would implicate the Constitution's Full Faith and Credit Clause.[172] In Williams v. State of North Carolina (*Williams I*), the Supreme Court was asked to consider the validity of a couple's convictions on bigamy charges. Whether they had committed bigamy turned on whether divorce decrees they had previously obtained in Nevada against their respective spouses were valid. They were each deemed by the Nevada courts to be domiciled in the state for purposes of issuing divorce decrees against their non-resident spouses. Having one spouse legally domiciled in the state issuing the divorce decree was deemed sufficient to establish jurisdiction for the divorce — thus seeming to support the validity of the divorce decrees at issue.[173] Yet, subsequently in the same case, in Williams v. State of North Carolina (*Williams II*), the U.S. Supreme Court concluded that the state being asked to enforce a divorce decree by a sister state is entitled to make its own determination as to whether that sister state's court had jurisdiction originally — thus putting into question the validity of the divorce decrees at issue.[174]

---

172. U.S. Const. art. IV, § 1.
173. 317 U.S. 287 (1942).
174. 325 U.S. 226 (1945).

CHAPTER 5

The Economics
of Dissolution

When a relationship ends, the parties need to resolve their economic entanglements as much as their social and emotional ones. The universal availability of no-fault divorce pushes economic issues to the fore; couples have less need to argue about why they are getting divorced but are still left to apportion assets, allocate debts, and determine if they will have ongoing financial obligations to one another after their relationship ends.[1] This chapter considers the economic aspects of relationship dissolution as between adults. (Child support is considered in Chapter 11.)

During the past half-century, the law's treatment of the economic aspects of relationship dissolution has changed dramatically. No-fault divorce laws reflect not only a retreat from some of the moral judgments that shaped marriages, but also an embrace of formal sex equality. These shifts were significant for a system once based largely on a husband's role as property-owner and provider, as explored in Chapter 3. The modern view of marriage as an equal partnership shapes the rules of economic disentanglement, particularly in the law's increasing willingness to recognize non-economic contributions. Approaches to dissolution have shifted with respect to not only marital but also non-marital relationships. Although courts traditionally would not have intervened in the dissolution of a non-marital relationship—once deemed immoral or even illegal—they now recognize the possibility of property sharing between cohabitants.

The economic unwinding of a relationship encompasses two different types of value: current property and future labor. The law apportions these two types of value under the headings of property distribution on one hand, and spousal support on the other. Property division is authorized in both community property and common law property states. Both systems are designed to divide property along principles

---

1. See Jill Schachner Chanen, Collaborative Counselors: Newest ADR Option Wins Converts, While Suffering Some Growing Pains, 92 A.B.A. J. 52 (2006); Honey Hastings, Dispute Resolution Options in Divorce and Custody Cases, 46 N.H. Bus. J. 48, 48 (2005).

of fairness, although the particulars vary among jurisdictions. Spousal support stat-utes contemplate the payment of ongoing support to one spouse from the future income of the other. While these are distinct concepts as a matter of law, they are deeply intertwined as a practical matter. Both are responses to the same underlying challenge: how to allocate the economic gains and losses of the couple's relationship.[2]

Most decisions about how to unwind the parties' economic relationship are not made by courts. Rather, they are made by the partners themselves and approved by courts. Private ordering in this setting can take many forms, to which courts have been increasingly receptive. Many couples enter formal finan-cial agreements—before marriage, during marriage, or in anticipation of divorce. But however extensive such private ordering, judicial decision-making remains fundamentally important. Parties, and their lawyers, develop agreements in the shadow of the standards and principles supplied by judicial decisions.[3]

In this chapter, we cover the rules of property distribution—both equitable dis-tribution and community property approaches—and the fairness principles that underlie them; the rules of spousal support, with attention to the modern shift away from long-term support; the use of alternative dispute resolution in winding up the economic affairs of a marriage; the role of pre- and post-marriage contracts; and, finally, the economic rights and obligations of unmarried cohabitants.

As you read this extensive set of materials, consider whether the modern regime—governing both marital and non-marital couples—equitably apportions the gains and losses of relationships.

I. Property Division at Divorce

Most state laws contemplate property division as the primary means through which couples will settle their financial affairs.[4] Statutes provide the basis for how prop-erty should be divided, but sometimes leave broad discretion to the courts.[5] While divorce cases involving wealthy celebrities often attract the most public attention, most families do not have large assets to divide: the median net worth of American

---

2. See, e.g., Marsha Kline Pruett et al., The Collaborative Divorce Project: A Court-Based Intervention for Separating Parents with Young Children, 43 Fam. Ct. Rev. 38 (2005); Robert E. Emery et al., Divorce Mediation: Research and Reflections, 43 Fam. Ct. Rev. 22 (2005); Nancy Ver Steegh, Family Court Reform and ADR: Shifting Values and Expectations Transform the Divorce Process, 42 Fam. L.Q. 659 (2008).

3. Robert H. Mnookin & Lewis Kornhauser, Bargaining in the Shadow of the Law: The Case of Divorce, 88 Yale L.J. 950 (1979).

4. Unif. Marriage and Divorce Act § 307, 9A ULA 249 (1998) [hereinafter UMDA]; Sanford N. Katz, Family Law in America 86 (2003).

5. See, e.g., N.J. Rev. Stat. Ann. § 2A:34-23.1(p) (West 2020) ("[T]he court shall consider, but not be lim-ited to, the following factors . . . [a]ny other factors which the court may deem relevant"); see also N.C. Gen. Stat. § 50-20(c)(12) (2020); Fla. Stat. § 61.075(1)(j) (2020); Ohio Rev. Code Ann. § 3105.171(F)(10) (West 2020); Homer H. Clark, Jr., 1 The Law on Domestic Relations § 8.1, 591 (2d ed. 1988).

families in 2016 was $97,300.[6] Net worth of families rises with the age of the head of the household; divorces are most likely to occur early in marriage, which coincides with lower net worth numbers.[7] The median length of a first marriage that ends in divorce is about eight years; and the median age of a spouse upon dissolution of a first marriage is late thirties.[8] In 2016, the median net worth of a household led by someone aged seventy-five and older was $264,800, while that led by someone younger than thirty-five was $11,100.[9] Indeed, couples often have more debt than assets. The average debt in 2015 of a married-couple household was $145,400.[10] Factors like immigrant status and race and ethnicity also shape the economic resources of families in the United States.[11] For example, as of 2016, white non-Hispanic households had a median net worth of $171,000, while black households had a median net worth of $17,600.[12] The impact of the COVID-19 pandemic on the economic position of American households is unclear. As of spring 2020, 43 percent of U.S. adults reported that "they or someone in their household ha[d] lost a job or taken a cut in pay due to the outbreak."[13]

Financial consequences of marriage and divorce do not occur in a vacuum but rather connect with broader economic patterns. As discussed in Chapter 3, while women's labor force participation has increased over the past several decades, it has recently begun to level off. Economists attribute women's stalled labor force participation in the U.S. to the absence of robust family leave policies available in other developed countries.[14] Moreover, while women participate in the workforce more than they did 50 years ago, they experience wage declines with the birth of each child, exacerbating existing gender-based wage gaps. How do you think gender pay gaps influence overall resources for women in same-sex

---

6. Jesse Bricker et al., Changes in U.S. Family Finances from 2013 to 2016: Evidence from the Survey of Consumer Finances, 103 Fed. Res. Bull. 1, 12 (2017). The average net worth is higher, because families at the highest end of the income scale push the average numbers up. Id.

7. Id. at 13.

8. Rose M. Kreider & Renee Ellis, U.S. Census Bureau, Number, Timing, and Duration of Marriages and Divorces: 2009, at 15 (2011). The median length (as well as the age of the parties) may be rising. See Ashley Spangler & Krista K. Payne, Nat'l Ctr. for Marriage & Family Research, Marital Duration at Divorce, 2012 (FP-14-11).

9. Bricker, supra note 6, at 13.

10. U.S. Census Bureau, Wealth, Asset Ownership, & Debt of Households Detailed Tables: 2015 tbl. 4 (2019).

11. U.S. Census Bureau, Median Household Income and Percentage Change by Selected Characteristics (2019); Pew Research Ctr., Demographic Trends and Economic Well-Being (June 27, 2016).

12. Bricker, supra note 6, at 13.

13. Kim Parker et al., Pew Research Ctr., About Half of Lower-Income Americans Report Household Job or Wage Loss Due to Covid-19 (Apr. 21, 2020).

14. Eleni X. Karageorge, Bureau of Lab. Stats., Dep't of Labor, Want More Workers? Improve Parental Leave Policies, Monthly Labor Rev. (March 2019) (largely attributing contrast between Canadian women's strong workforce participation and American women's dropping participation to childcare subsidies and parental leave in Canada).

marriages?[15] Moreover, in the home, among different-sex couples, women continue to assume more of the domestic burden. What light do these dynamics shed on financial allocation post-marriage?

Recall our discussion in Chapter 3 of how marital partners may handle property *during* marriage. In common-law states, title will often dictate who has the power to manage and control property during marriage. Prior to the advent of no-fault divorce, this title-based approach also shaped property distribution *at divorce* in separate property states.[16] This system created harsh effects, especially for women, given their inability to obtain property during marriage under coverture. Even after passage of the Married Women's Property Acts, women remained unlikely to have the means to own property apart from marriage. Strong social and legal norms also shaped women's roles as caregivers and homemakers, occupying the domestic sphere, separate from the public sphere of paid labor and civic life occupied by men.[17]

By providing some economic redistribution at divorce, the system of "equitable distribution" that took hold in the 1970s and predominates today provided a remedy for the harmful effects of a title-based system. This section discusses the concept of equitable distribution, before examining how to identify, characterize, and allocate property subject to distribution. The section also addresses issues raised by special kinds of property.

A. What Is Equitable?

As states shifted to no-fault divorce, a system of "equitable distribution" was adopted in separate property states to guide the division of property at divorce. This system was devised as a way to remedy longstanding economic disadvantages that resulted from the vestiges of coverture and the continuation of gendered family roles.

Traditionally, spousal support was supposed to provide economic protection for women during the era of fault-based divorce. As Professor Marsha Garrison explains, when husbands were not willing or able to pay alimony, courts might look to property as a remedy to make up for the deficit: "From this beginning the modern concept of equitable property distribution developed."[18] Still, alimony was

---

15. Alyssa Schneebaum & M. V. Lee Badgett, Poverty in U.S. Lesbian and Gay Couple Households, 25 Feminist Econ. 1, 3 (2019) (discussing suppressed income of female sex-sex couples due to gender wage gap).

16. See Joanna L. Grossman & Lawrence M. Friedman, Inside the Castle: Law and the Family in 20th Century America 239 (2011); see also Ferguson v. Ferguson, 639 So. 2d 921, 926 (Miss. 1994).

17. For discussion of women's property rights and the effect of Married Women's Property Acts, see, e.g., Norma Basch, In the Eyes of the Law: Women, Marriage, and Property in Nineteenth-Century New York 17, 51–55 (1982); Richard H. Chused, Married Women's Property Law: 1800-1850, 71 Geo. L.J. 1359, 1365–68 (1983).

18. Marsha Garrison, Good Intentions Gone Awry: The Impact of New York's Equitable Distribution Law on Divorce Outcomes, 57 Brook. L. Rev. 621, 627 (1991).

viewed as the primary means to address women's economic disadvantage when a marriage ended.[19]

Alimony was not a reliable remedy, however, with the size and length of alimony left to the discretion of judges, who awarded it only sparingly.[20] Determinations of fault shaped alimony's availability; it was available in some states only for "innocent" spouses.[21] As Professors Joanna Grossman and Lawrence Friedman observe, "In general, alimony never served as an effective financial backstop for women."[22]

Beginning in the 1970s, separate property states began to focus on property distribution as the means to address economic claims at divorce and to account for the financial harms from the traditional title-based system.[23] Equitable property distribution served as "the 'modern' answer to the unfairness of the traditional system of allocating property at divorce."[24] By the mid-1980s, no state relied on the title-based system of property distribution.

Equitable distribution empowered courts to reallocate property to fairly apportion the losses or gains of marriage based on a partnership theory of marriage. Both spouses were assumed to have contributed to "marital property" — the property earned by either spouse during marriage. This approach better recognized domestic or other non-economic contributions during a marriage, often made by women.

As we saw in Chapter 3, nine states have a community property, rather than separate property, system, following rules influenced by Spanish, Mexican, and French law.[25] Community property principles provide that each spouse acquires a present, one-half interest in property acquired through the labor of either spouse, regardless of who "earned" it. Property earned or acquired with earnings is designated "community property." While only community property is shared between spouses, as opposed to separate property (for example, premarital property, gifts, or inheritance), the line between separate property and community property is not always clear. Moreover, the characterization of property has the potential to change based on the spouses' behavior and handling of it.

---

19. Id. at 628-29.

20. Grossman & Friedman, supra 16, at 238-39.

21. Id.

22. Id. at 239.

23. Garrison, supra note 18, at 629. Some states had equitable distribution as early as the 1930s, but the statutes were vague and determinations were left entirely to judicial discretion. Grossman & Friedman, supra note 16, at 239.

24. Grossman & Friedman, supra note 16, at 239.

25. The nine states are Arizona, California, Idaho, Louisiana, Nevada, New Mexico, Texas, Washington, and Wisconsin. Note that Wisconsin uses community property principles during marriage, but, at divorce, courts can divide otherwise separate property "if the court finds that refusal to divide the property will create a hardship on the other party or on the children of the marriage. If the court makes such a finding, the court may divest the party of the property in a fair and equitable manner." Wis. Stat. Ann. § 767.61 (2)(b); Kuhlman v. Kuhlman, 432 N.W.2d 295, 296 (Wis. Ct. App. 1988); Rasmussen v. Rasmussen, 816 N.W.2d 352 n.3 (Wis. Ct. App. 2012). Alaska is a separate property state but allows couples to elect to hold their property as community property. Alaska Stat. Ann. § 34.77.030 (West 2020).

The general principle underlying the community property system is that both parties labor on behalf of the community and are entitled to share in its fruits. This principle guides the organization of property during marriage but also the division at divorce. Community property is shared, while separate property remains with its owner. While in some regimes, community property is divided evenly upon dissolution, in others, it is subject to equitable distribution.

What do courts and legislatures mean by "equitable" distribution? What is fair or just in allocating the property of the marriage? Factors vary by state, but generally reflect two main principles: that "[p]roperty should be allocated in proportion to the spousal contributions to its acquisition, and property should be allocated according to relative spousal need."[26] As you read the next case regarding a common-law state's shift from a title-based approach to equitable distribution, consider how best to implement these principles.

FERGUSON V. FERGUSON
639 So. 2d 921 (Miss. 1994)

PRATHER, PRESIDING JUSTICE, for the Court:

States have devised various methods to divide marital assets at divorce, and approaches have usually followed one of three systems: the separate property system, the equitable distribution system, and a system of fixed rules (community property) are the three systems reflected in American jurisprudence. . . . [T]he separate property system . . . was a system that merely determined title to the assets and returned that property to the title-holding spouse.

Our separate property system at times resulted in unjust distributions, especially involving cases of a traditional family where most property was titled in the husband, leaving a traditional housewife and mother with nothing but a claim for alimony, which often proved unenforceable. In a family where both spouses worked, but the husband's resources were devoted to investments while the wife's earnings were devoted to paying the family expenses or vice versa, the same unfair results ensued.

"The flaw of the separate property system, however, is not merely that it will occasionally ignore the financial contributions of the non-titleholding spouse. The system . . . is also unable to take account of a spouse's non-financial contribution. In the case of many traditional housewives such non-financial contributions are often considerable. . . ." Stephen J. Brake, Equitable Distribution vs. Fixed Rules, 23 B.C. L. Rev. 761, 765 (1982).

[T]hrough an evolution of case law, this Court has abandoned the title theory method of distribution of marital assets and evolved into an equitable distribution system. . . .

---

26. Principles of the Law of Family Dissolution: Analysis and Recommendations § 4.09 cmt. a (Am. Law Inst. 2002).

"It is well-established by this Court that the chancery court has the authority to order an equitable division of property that was accumulated through the joint efforts and contributions of the parties. However, there is no automatic right to an equal division of jointly-accumulated property, but rather, the division is left to the discretion of the court...." Draper v. Draper, 627 So. 2d 302, 305 (Miss. 1993).

Although this listing is not exclusive, this Court suggests the chancery courts consider the following guidelines, where applicable, when attempting to effect an equitable division of marital property:

1. Substantial contribution to the accumulation of the property. Factors to be considered in determining contribution are as follows:
   a. Direct or indirect economic contribution to the acquisition of the property;
   b. Contribution to the stability and harmony of the marital and family relationships as measured by quality, quantity of time spent on family duties and duration of the marriage; and
   c. Contribution to the education, training or other accomplishment bearing on the earning power of the spouse accumulating the assets.
2. The degree to which each spouse has expended, withdrawn or otherwise disposed of marital assets and any prior distribution of such assets by agreement, decree or otherwise.
3. The market value and the emotional value of the assets subject to distribution.
4. The value of assets not ordinarily, absent equitable factors to the contrary, subject to such distribution, such as property brought to the marriage by the parties and property acquired by inheritance or inter vivos gift by or to an individual spouse;
5. Tax and other economic consequences, and contractual or legal consequences to third parties, of the proposed distribution;
6. The extent to which property division may, with equity to both parties, be utilized to eliminate periodic payments and other potential sources of future friction between the parties;
7. The needs of the parties for financial security with due regard to the combination of assets, income and earning capacity; and,
8. Any other factor which in equity should be considered....

Property division should be based upon a determination of fair market value of the assets, and these valuations should be the initial step before determining division....

Linda Ferguson, age 44, and Billy Cleveland Ferguson, Sr., age 48, were married on April 15, 1967, and separated on May 13, 1991. Two children were born of this marriage. When the complaint for divorce was filed on May 21, 1991, the parties' daughter, Tamatha Ferguson, was 23 years of age and emancipated. Their son, Billy Cleveland Ferguson, Jr. (Bubba), was 14 years old and resided in the home with his parents in Chunky, Newton County, Mississippi.

During their 24 years of marriage, Linda worked both as a homemaker and as a cosmetologist/beautician. Billy, employed by South Central Bell as a cable repair technician for 24 years, installed and maintained local telephone service in the Chunky, Mississippi, area.

On May 21, 1991, Linda filed for divorce on the grounds of adultery and requested permanent custody of Bubba. Billy denied the adultery charge and counterclaimed for divorce based on habitual cruel and inhuman treatment. Billy also sought custody of his son, alleging that Bubba had expressed a desire to live with his father, and arguing that the court should respect the wishes of the child. No allegations were made that Linda was not a fit, suitable or proper parent to have custody of the child.

The chancellor denied Billy's request for divorce and awarded Linda (1) a divorce on the ground of adultery; (2) custody of Bubba and $300.00 a month in child support; (3) the marital home and its contents together with four acres of land comprising the homestead, title to the marital home to be divested from Billy and vested in Linda, debt free; (4) one-half interest in Billy's pension plan, stock ownership plan, and savings and security plan; (5) periodic alimony in the amount of $400.00 per month and lump sum alimony in the sum of $30,000.00 to be paid at the rate of $10,000.00 annually beginning on January 1, 1992; (6) attorney fees in the amount of $5,000.00; (7) health insurance through Bell South for as long "as the law allows," and (8) a lien on any and all property owned by Billy to secure the payments ordered by the chancellor. . . .

In her complaint, Linda requested an adjudication that she was entitled to "one-half of all retirement benefits, profit sharing plan or other deferred compensation or stocks or bonds and pension plans to which the Defendant may be entitled, including, but not limited to, Bell South Corporation's Savings and Security Plan."

Billy Ferguson had a vested pension with Bell South, the total value of which was $800.45 as of October 24, 1991. . . .

Billy also owned approximately 85 shares of stock in Bell South Corporation valued at $34,120.90. . . .

Finally, Billy participated in a Bell South Savings and Security Plan which in 1989 contained $32,843.00. Billy admitted during his testimony that he had withdrawn $15,000.00 from the savings plan in September of 1990 and another $15,000.00 in the first part of 1991, and had spent all of it. The paramour testified that Billy told her that Billy had placed this money where it could not be found. The chancellor found her testimony to be trustworthy. As of August 31, 1991, there was a balance of only $677.89 remaining in Billy's Bell South Savings and Security Plan. . . .

Billy claims that the chancellor erred in awarding Linda one-half interest in his Bell South vested pension plan, one-half interest in his Bell South employee stock ownership plan, and one-half interest in his Bell South Corporation Savings and Security Plan. Billy contends that he owned all the interest in the pension plan, stock, and savings, and that it was his separate property. On appeal, Billy claims

Linda in no way contributed to the acquisition of this property, and nothing was ever issued in her name. . . .

This Court concludes that the chancellor had the authority to order a fair division of the Bell South benefits because they were marital assets accumulated through the joint contributions and efforts of the parties during the duration of this twenty-four year marriage. A spouse who has made a material contribution toward the acquisition of an asset titled in the name of the other spouse may claim an equitable interest in such jointly accumulated property.

Although contributions of domestic services are not made directly to a retirement fund, they are nonetheless valid material contributions which indirectly contribute to any number of marital assets, thereby making such assets jointly acquired. And, it must be remembered, the goal of the chancellor in a divorce case is to do equity.

When a couple has been married for twenty-four years, yet the only retirement benefits accumulated throughout the marriage are titled in the name of only one spouse, is it equitable to find only one spouse entitled to financial security upon retirement when both have benefitted from the employer funded plan along the way? When one spouse has contributed directly to the fund, by virtue of his/her labor, while the other has contributed indirectly, by virtue of domestic services and/or earned income which both parties have enjoyed rather than invested, the spouse without retirement funds in his/her own name could instead have been working outside the home and/or investing his/her wages in preparation for his/her own retirement. When separate plans for each spouse are not in existence, it is only equitable to allow both parties to reap the benefits of the one existing retirement plan, to which both parties have materially contributed in some fashion.

Since Linda made material contributions as both a homemaker and a wage earner, she is equitably entitled to some portion of the couple's jointly acquired retirement funds. . . .

Linda, we note, was divested of her undivided one-half interest in the adjoining 33 acres of jointly owned and accumulated real property, which was awarded to Billy. It is noted that Billy was also granted ownership of all farm equipment, a leasehold interest on farm property, a cattle operation, and his 100 shares of stock in a mobile home park. . . .

The equitable distribution system rests on the concept of marriage as a partnership or shared enterprise during which both spouses contribute to the marriage as a whole and to the acquisition of property through their labor. With *Ferguson*, Mississippi joined all other common-law states, which had shifted to dividing marital property at divorce through equitable distribution. The Mississippi Supreme Court recognized the "unjust distributions" and neglect of "non-monetary contributions of a traditional housewife" that could result from a title-based system. How do the factors that the court set forth account for non-monetary types of contributions? Did the court appropriately weigh them in *Ferguson*? In other states, the shift occurred in the legislature rather than the courts. Which institution is better suited to crafting the factors to guide equitable distribution? Consider how the factors the court used in *Ferguson* compare with the approaches in the following excerpts from the Uniform Marriage and Divorce Act (UMDA). The Uniform Law Commission promulgated the UMDA in 1970 to promote consistency across jurisdictions, and it approved an amended version of the Act in 1973. Section 307 sets forth two alternative approaches to equitable distribution.

UNIFORM MARRIAGE AND DIVORCE ACT (1973)

§ 307. Disposition of Property
Alternative A

(a) In a proceeding for dissolution of a marriage, legal separation, or disposition of property following a decree of dissolution of marriage or legal separation by a court which lacked personal jurisdiction over the absent spouse or lacked jurisdiction to dispose of the property, the court, without regard to marital misconduct, shall, and in a proceeding for legal separation may, finally equitably apportion between the parties the property and assets belonging to either or both however and whenever acquired, and whether the title thereto is in the name of the husband or wife or both. In making apportionment the court shall consider the duration of the marriage, and prior marriage of either party, antenuptial agreement of the parties, the age, health, station, occupation, amount and sources of income, vocational skills, employability, estate, liabilities, and needs of each of the parties, custodial provisions, whether the apportionment is in lieu of or in addition to maintenance, and the opportunity of each for future acquisition of capital assets and income. The court shall also consider the contribution or dissipation of each party in the acquisition, preservation, depreciation, or appreciation in value of the respective estates, and the contribution of a spouse as a homemaker or to the family unit.

Alternative B

In a proceeding for dissolution of the marriage, legal separation, or disposition of property following a decree of dissolution of the marriage or legal separation by a court which lacked personal jurisdiction over the absent spouse or lacked jurisdiction to dispose of the property, the court shall assign each spouse's separate property to that spouse. It also shall divide community property, without regard to marital misconduct, in just proportions after considering all relevant factors including:

(1) contribution of each spouse to acquisition of the marital property, including contribution of a spouse as homemaker;

(2) value of the property set apart to each spouse;

(3) duration of the marriage; and

(4) economic circumstances of each spouse when the division of property is to become effective, including the desirability of awarding the family home or the right to live therein for a reasonable period to the spouse having custody of any children.

NOTES AND QUESTIONS

1. *"All-Property" Equitable Distribution.* Alternative A indicates that courts should "equitably apportion" all property, "however or whenever acquired." This "all-property" approach (sometimes called "hotchpot" or "kitchen sink") represents the approach in a minority of common-law states.[27] The Comment to UMDA § 307 Alternative A points out that this alternative "proceeds upon the principle that all the property of the spouses, however acquired, should be regarded as assets of the married couple, available for distribution among them, upon consideration of the various factors enumerated in subsection (a)."[28]

Even when courts are authorized to divide all types of property, they may still exercise discretion to draw distinctions between different kinds of property based on the timing and source of acquisition.[29] What advantages and disadvantages do you see in an all-property approach? How is it likely to affect divorcing parties in their negotiations?

2. *Dual Classification Equitable Distribution.* Alternative B corresponds with the majority approach in common-law states, in which courts will only divide "marital property," leaving separate property with its owner. This means that the distinction between separate and marital property is critical. While Alternative B was originally drafted for use by community property states — urging a shift from equal to equitable division — it aligns with the approach taken by a majority of separate property states.[30] How does Alternative B seek to create a fair outcome in property division?

---

27. Brett R. Turner, Equitable Distribution of Property § 2:8 (4th ed. 2019) (listing Alabama, Connecticut, Indiana, Iowa, Kansas, Massachusetts, Montana, New Hampshire, North Dakota, Oregon, South Dakota, Vermont, Washington, and Wyoming); see also J. Thomas Oldham, Divorce, Separation, and the Distribution of Property § 3.02[2] (2000). For an example of a state statute, see Mass. Gen. Laws Ann. ch. 208, § 34 (2020).

28. UMDA § 307 cmt.

29. Principles of the Law of Family Dissolution § 4.03 (citing Fraase v. Fraase, 315 N.W.2d 271, 274 (N.D. 1982), and Bonelli v. Bonelli, 576 A.2d 587 (Conn. App. Ct. 1990) (awarding property to husband where inherited by him)); see also Turner, supra note 27, § 2:8.

30. UMDA § 307 cmt.

Alternative B lists factors to consider in equitable distribution: "(1) contribution of each spouse to acquisition of the marital property, including contribution of a spouse as homemaker; (2) value of the property set apart to each spouse; (3) duration of the marriage; and (4) economic circumstances of each spouse when the division of property is to become effective." As discussed above, factors in equitable distribution statutes are designed to apportion property based on contributions to their acquisition and also address need.[31] Do the factors in the UMDA support these objectives? What other factors might you add? We discuss allocation of property below.

3.   *Marital Misconduct.* Notice how the UMDA excludes considerations of fault in both alternatives. With the widespread adoption of no-fault divorce, courts and legislatures reconsidered the role of marital fault in financial determinations. Why should fault be relevant to economic issues if irrelevant to whether the marriage should be dissolved? It is important to distinguish between fault as it relates specifically to the property and fault in the more traditional sense with respect to divorce? All states permit consideration of "economic" fault, when one spouse's behavior has reduced the amount of property available to allocate.[32] States also consider misconduct, such as spousal violence, that leads to a spouse's increased financial need because of diminished earning capacity or increased medical costs.[33]But many states also permit consideration of ordinary fault — the fault-based grounds we addressed in the last chapter — whether or not it affected the size of the pie for distribution. Some permit consideration of fault in property division, some permit it in determinations of spousal support, and some permit it for both.[34] In contrast, twenty states do not consider non-economic fault in determinations of property division or spousal support.[35]

B. Identifying and Characterizing Property

In making equitable distributions, courts must determine what property is subject to allocation. In all states, courts must determine whether property exists to apportion and the value of any such property. The concept of marriage as an economic partnership underlies the idea of marital property. As Professor Shari

---

31. Principles of the Law of Family Dissolution § 4.09 cmt. a. For discussion of common factors, see John Tingley & Nicholas B. Svalina, 2 Marital Property Law § 42:19 (2d ed. 2019).

32. See, e.g., Lowrey v. Lowrey, 25 So. 3d 274 (Miss. 2009).

33. Turner, supra note 27, § 8:24; Ira Mark Ellman, The Place of Fault in a Modern Divorce Law, 28 Ariz. St. L.J. 773, 776–77 (1996).

34. Principles of the Law of Family Dissolution § 117.

35. These are Alaska, Arizona, California, Colorado, Delaware, Florida, Hawaii, Illinois, Indiana, Iowa, Maine, Minnesota, Montana, Nebraska, New Mexico, Nevada, Oklahoma, Oregon, Washington, and Wisconsin.

Motro has observed, "[e]arnings from labor are marital property because marriage is considered a joint venture to which each spouse contributes a combination of effort, sacrifice, and mutual support."[36] Courts must determine the source of the asset, including when it was acquired (i.e., before or during marriage), and then apply the legal rules to label it as separate or marital (or, in community property states, "community property"). This excerpt, from the American Law Institute's Principles of the Law of Family Dissolution, sets forth rules for characterizing property.

PRINCIPLES OF THE LAW OF FAMILY DISSOLUTION: ANALYSIS AND RECOMMENDATIONS (2002)

§ 4.03

(1) Property acquired during marriage is marital property, except as otherwise expressly provided in this Chapter.

(2) Inheritances, including bequests and devises, and gifts from third parties, are the separate property of the acquiring spouse even if acquired during marriage.

(3) Property received in exchange for separate property is separate property even if acquired during marriage.

(4) Property acquired during marriage but after the parties have commenced living apart pursuant to either a written separation agreement or a judicial decree, is the separate property of the acquiring spouse unless the agreement or decree specifies otherwise.

(5) For the purpose of this section "during marriage" means after the commencement of marriage and before the filing and service of a petition for dissolution (if that petition ultimately results in a decree dissolving the marriage), unless there are facts, set forth in written findings of the trial court (§ 1.02), establishing that use of another date is necessary to avoid a substantial injustice.

(6) Property acquired during a relationship between the spouses that immediately preceded their marriage, and which was a domestic-partner relationship as defined by § 6.03,[37] is treated as if it were acquired during the marriage.

---

36. Shari Motro, Labor, Luck, and Love: Reconsidering the Sanctity of Separate Property, 102 Nw. U. L. Rev. 1623, 1624 (2008).

37. Principles of the Law of Family Dissolution § 6.03.

NOTES AND QUESTIONS

1. *Characterization.* The definitions for marital and separate property set forth in the ALI Principles correspond with those used in the majority of common-law equitable distribution states and in community property states (with the substitution of the term "community property" for "marital property").[38] Under this scheme, title does not control how property gained during marriage is characterized for purposes of distribution. As illustrated by the ALI Principles, property acquired during marriage by either spouse is presumed to be marital property. The concept of marital property reflects the underlying idea of marriage as an economic partnership, and the labor performed during marriage as part of that partnership. The characterization of property as "separate" is critically important in states in which courts are not authorized to allocate one spouse's separate property to the other spouse.[39]

2. *Timing.* As a general rule, only property acquired *during marriage* can be "marital property," subject to specific exceptions. When does the marriage "begin" and "end"? Under the ALI's approach, "during marriage" means after the marriage begins and before the filing and service of a petition for dissolution. (Courts may value property as of a different date, however.) States overwhelmingly use the date of marriage to mark the time after which assets acquired are marital property.[40] What about property purchased in contemplation of marriage? A very small number of states make an exception to the rule that marital property acquisition starts with the marriage date and will permit property purchased shortly before marriage at a time when a couple was contemplating marriage to be treated as marital property.[41]

When does the marriage end for property classification purposes? What happens when one spouse wins the lottery after the other one has commenced a divorce action?[42] What about if one spouse receives an inheritance while the divorce is being appealed?[43] Can these assets be treated as marital property subject to distribution? States vary in their approach to when a marriage ends for property classification purposes. Statutes may include the earliest of various options, like the date of filing of the divorce action, the date of the divorce hearing, the date of separation, the date of a legal

---

38. Id. § 4.03 cmt. b.

39. Linda D. Elrod & Timothy B. Walker, Family Law in the Fifty States: An Overview, 27 Fam. L.Q. 515, 695 (1994).

40. Ohio courts will sometimes use a date prior to the date of formal marriage. Compare Bryan v. Bryan, No. 97817, 2012 WL 3527120, at *4 (Ohio Ct. App. Aug. 16, 2012), with Klausman v. Klausman, No. 21718, 2004 WL 1461356, at *11 (Ohio Ct. App. June 30, 2004).

41. See, e.g., Stallings v. Stallings, 393 N.E.2d 1065 (Ill. App. Ct. 1979).

42. Questel v. Questel, 960 N.Y.S.2d 860 (N.Y. Sup. Ct. 2013) (not marital property).

43. In re Eckroate-Breagy, 168 A.3d 1148 (N.H. 2017) (not marital property).

separation decree, or the date of a separation agreement.[44] The ALI Principles rely on the date of the filing and service of a petition for dissolution. Instead of any of these options, what about using the date when the relationship, practically speaking, broke down? Given the partnership theory animating equitable distribution, wouldn't this be a more principled approach?

3. *Appreciation of Separate Property.* How should the court treat increases in the value of separate property that occur during marriage? Consider a house purchased by one spouse prior to marriage, which clearly qualifies as separate property. What happens if this home appreciates in value at least in part because of the other spouse's efforts to improve it? Treating this appreciation also as separate property could be unfair to the contributing spouse.[45]

Some courts have addressed this type of unfairness by holding that if marital funds, the other spouse's labor, or other in-kind contributions were used to increase the value of the separate property, this "active appreciation" is classified as marital property.[46] In contrast, "passive appreciation," such as an increase in market value that occurs without any significant effort, would be treated as separate property.[47] Community property jurisdictions seek to recognize community contributions through a doctrine of "equitable reimbursement," which allows the other spouse to recoup contributions that increased the value of separate property.[48]

4. *Converting Property.* Property can be converted by express or implied acts from one category of property to another, for instance, from separate to marital property during marriage by "transmutation."[49] Transmutation by commingling can occur when marital (or community) property and separate property are "mixed together so that it is impossible to discern the marital (or community) and separate components."[50] In these situations, the entire property is then considered marital (or community) property.[51] Intent of the property holder alone will not overcome the failure to be able to trace the separate property.[52]

---

44. Turner, supra note 27, § 5:28. See, e.g., N.Y. Dom. Rel. Law § 236(B)(1)(c) (McKinney 2020) ("before the execution of separation agreement or the commencement of a matrimonial action"); Tenn. Code Ann. §36-4-121(b)(1)(A) (2020) ("date of the final divorce hearing").

45. Turner, supra note 27, § 5.55.

46. Suzanne Reynolds, Increases in Separate Property and the Evolving Marital Partnership, 24 Wake Forest L. Rev. 239, 247 (1989); see also In re Marriage of Jenks, 656 P.2d 286 (Or. 1982).

47. See, e.g., Middendorf v. Middendorf, 696 N.E.2d 575, 578 (Ohio 1998); White v. White, 937 N.W.2d 838, 846 (Neb. 2020).

48. See, e.g., In re Estate of Capps, 173 Wash. App. 1037 (Wash. Ct. App. 2013).

49. Laura W. Morgan & Edward S. Snyder, When Title Matters: Transmutation and the Joint Title Gift Presumption, 18 J. Am. Acad. Matrim. L. 335, 340 (2003).

50. Id.; see, e.g., Kemp v. Kemp, 485 N.E.2d 663 (Ind. Ct. App. 1985); Stahl v. Stahl, 430 P.2d 685 (Idaho 1967).

51. Morgan & Snyder, supra note 49, at 341–42.

52. Turner, supra note 27, § 5:65.

PROBLEMS

1. Declan proposes marriage to Ryder and gives Ryder an engagement ring. During the couple's later divorce proceeding, Declan argues that the ring is marital property subject to distribution. Is the ring separate or marital property?

2. Prior to marriage, Hyae-Jin was looking for a piece of property to purchase. One month after she married Leonard, Hyae-Jin closed on the purchase of 5.25 acres of property. The mortgage, note, and title on the property were all signed by Hyae-Jin using her given name, not the married name she adopted upon marriage. Hyae-Jin testified that she paid the down payment on the property using money from her mother's mutual funds. Some of the monthly payments on the property came from a bank account that Hyae-Jin maintained with her son; other payments were made from an account Hyae-Jin shared with her mother. Still other payments were made from money derived from the sale of her mother's house. Hyae-Jin paid the taxes on the property from her separate account. Leonard testified that he had written the contract leading to the sale of the property. Although Leonard claimed he had made a $1,000.00 down payment on the property, on cross-examination he admitted that the $1,000.00 came from Hyae-Jin's account. Is the property marital or separate property?

3. Prior to marriage, Terry held two bank accounts, one at Apple City Bank and another at Windy City Bank. During the marriage, Terry continuously deposited money from these accounts into the joint checking account she had with her spouse, Dylan. During the marriage, Terry and Dylan continuously deposited funds they each earned and withdrew unspecified sums for their use as a couple from the joint checking account. During the marriage, Terry and Dylan withdrew funds from the joint checking account to acquire an investment account. Terry and Dylan are now divorcing. Terry argues that the investment account is separate property. Unfortunately, Terry has no account balances, deposit slips, cancelled checks, or any other documentation pertaining to specific transactions between the Apple City and Windy City Bank account and the joint checking account. Dylan argues that it is marital property. How should the court characterize the account?

POSTSCRIPT

Problem 3 is based on Nack v. Edwards, in which a Virginia appellate court affirmed a trial court's determination that the investment account was marital property.[53] In the case, the court determined that even if the funds from the bank accounts Terry

---

53. Nos. 2219-06-3, 2288-06-3, 2007 WL 2592902 (Va. Ct. App. Sept. 11, 2007).

held prior to marriage were separate property, the identity of funds of the husband in the actual case "had been lost in countless unspecified transactions involving marital funds, resulting in the irreversible transmutation of separate into marital property." Based on the relevant state statute, it was possible for the property to be construed as "hybrid," a combination of marital and separate property. In order to trace the separate portion of the hybrid property, "a party must prove that the claimed separate portion is identifiably derived from a separate asset. Whether a transmuted asset can be traced back to a separate property interest is determined by the circumstances of each case." However, "if a party 'chooses to commingle marital and non-marital funds to the point that direct tracing is impossible,' the claimed separate property loses its separate status." This is also true if a party can prove that some part is separate but is unable to prove the amount that is separate. The "unknown amount contributed from the separate source transmutes by commingling and becomes marital property." As the husband claiming the investment account was separate property had "no account balances, deposit slips, cancelled checks, or any other documentation" enabling the court to trace the separate funds, it was appropriate for the trial court to determine that the investment account was marital property.

4. Wendi and Alyce are seeking to dissolve their civil union. The applicable state civil union statute grants "civil union couples all of the same benefits, protections and responsibilities under law, whether they derive from statute, administrative or court rule, public policy, common law or any other source of civil law, as are granted to spouses in a marriage." During their civil union, they bought a new home. Alyce claims that the house is hers because it was purchased with money she earned. Is Wendi entitled to an interest in the house?

POSTSCRIPT

For states recognizing civil unions, granting the same rights and obligations of marriage includes those pertaining to dissolution.[54] For instance, the Vermont Supreme Court has held that civil unions are subject to the same property division rules as those for marriage.[55] With the advent of same-sex marriage, a few states that previously granted civil unions converted existing civil unions to marriages, unless the couple dissolved their civil union before the conversion date. Several states, though, continue to recognize civil unions, and a few continue to allow

---

54. See, e.g., Neyman v. Buckley, 153 A.3d 1010 (Pa. Super. Ct. 2016); Vt. Stat. Ann. tit. 15, § 751 (2020).

55. DeLeonardis v. Page, 998 A.2d 1072, 1076 (Vt. 2010).

couples to enter civil unions.[56] (Some state domestic partnership statutes also provide all of the state-law rights and obligations of marriage, including property distribution at dissolution.[57])

C. Allocating Property

This section discusses approaches toward allocating property in the equitable distribution system. As discussed below, these include different approaches within common-law states, some of which presume a 50/50 split for property division, while others take a more discretionary approach. Within these states, courts will consider a variety of factors to reach an equitable distribution; these may include economic needs of the parties, contributions to the acquisition of the property, duration of the marriage, and fault (discussed above).

ARNEAULT V. ARNEAULT
639 S.E.2d 720 (W. Va. 2006)

DAVIS, CHIEF JUSTICE.

A brief synopsis of the relevant facts shows that the parties were married on July 12, 1969, and now have two adult children. The parties had been married for thirty-three years when [Edson R.] Arneault filed for divorce on March 22, 2002. By agreement of the parties, they denominated December 20, 2002, as their date of separation. By order of the family court, the parties were granted a divorce on July 22, 2004. The parties' marital home was located in Grand Rapids, Michigan. During the marriage, [Margaret Beth] Arneault stayed home with the children until 1990, when she returned to work on a part-time basis as a teacher. In 1995, Mrs. Arneault started her own business as a counselor providing college placement and career consulting services to high school students. While there is discord as to the effort Mrs. Arneault applied to her business, there is no dispute that Mrs. Arneault's business did not generate great income.

Mr. Arneault currently holds the same job position as he did at the time of the divorce. Mr. Arneault is Chairman, President, and Chief Executive Officer of MTR

---

56. See Courtney Joslin et al., Lesbian, Gay, Bisexual and Transgender Family Law § 8:3 (2019). Colorado, Hawaii, and Illinois allow same-sex and different-sex couples to enter into civil unions, and New Jersey allows same-sex couples to do so. Id.; see Colo. Rev. Stat. § 14-15-107 (2020); Haw. Rev. Stat. §§ 572B-1 et seq. (2020); 750 Ill. Comp. Stat. Ann. 75/20 (West 2020); N.J. Stat. Ann. §§ 37:1-28 et seq. (West 2020). Rhode Island and Vermont recognize existing civil unions entered into before the state permitted same-sex couples to marry. 15 R.I. Gen. Laws § 15-3.1-12 (2020); Vt. Stat. Ann. tit. 15, § 1204 (2020).

57. See, e.g., Cal. Fam. Code § 297.5 (West 2020).

Gaming Group, Inc., which owns and controls Mountaineer Park, Inc., and operates video lottery terminals. Since 1995, Mr. Arneault has worked in Chester, West Virginia, away from the marital home. Prior to the divorce, he returned to Michigan on most weekends. There is no dispute that Mr. Arneault has been responsible for MTR's great success. In return for his achievements, Mr. Arneault has received a lucrative income from MTR, as well as MTR stock. . . . All parties concede that this stock was acquired during the parties' marriage and is properly the subject of equitable distribution.

In the bifurcated case below, the family court determined that because Mr. Arneault had contributed significantly to the marital estate, a 50/50 split of the estate would be inequitable. Thus, the family court ordered that the parties' marital estate be divided 35/65, with Mr. Arneault receiving the larger share. . . . Mrs. Arneault appealed these adverse rulings to the circuit court. By order entered April 13, 2005, the circuit court affirmed the family court's decisions. Mrs. Arneault now appeals to this Court. . . .

In response, Mr. Arneault argues . . . that the statute prescribes an equitable split, not an equal one, and because of his tremendous contributions, a 50/50 split would be inequitable. . . .

First, we will address the issue of the equitable distribution of the marital estate and, more specifically, the appropriate percentage split to be applied to the estate. . . .

In a divorce proceeding, subject to some limitations, all property is considered marital property . . . .

The parties do not contest the lower courts' classification of the estate as marital or separate; thus, we now address the appropriate percentage of the property to be afforded to each party. . . .

[W]e must presume that the parties' marital estate will be divided equally, subject to the limitations and considerations set forth in W. Va. Code § 48–7–103 (2001), which provides as follows:

> In the absence of a valid agreement, the court shall presume that all marital property is to be divided equally between the parties, but may alter this distribution, without regard to any attribution of fault to either party which may be alleged or proved in the course of the action, after a consideration of the following:
>
> (1) The extent to which each party has contributed to the acquisition, preservation and maintenance, or increase in value of marital property by monetary contributions, including, but not limited to:
>   (A) Employment income and other earnings; and
>   (B) Funds which are separate property.
> (2) The extent to which each party has contributed to the acquisition, preservation and maintenance or increase in value of marital property by monetary contributions, including, but not limited to:

(A) Homemaker services;

(B) Child care services;

(C) Labor performed without compensation, or for less than adequate compensation, in a family business or other business entity in which one or both of the parties has an interest;

(D) Labor performed in the actual maintenance or improvement of tangible marital property; and

(E) Labor performed in the management or investment of assets which are marital property.

(3) The extent to which each party expended his or her efforts during the marriage in a manner which limited or decreased such party's income-earning ability or increased the income-earning ability of the other party, including, but not limited to:

(A) Direct or indirect contributions by either party to the education or training of the other party which has increased the income-earning ability of such other party; and

(B) Foregoing by either party of employment or other income-earning activity through an understanding of the parties or at the insistence of the other party.

(4) The extent to which each party, during the marriage, may have conducted himself or herself so as to dissipate or depreciate the value of the marital property of the parties: Provided, That except for a consideration of the economic consequences of conduct as provided for in this subdivision, fault or marital misconduct shall not be considered by the court in determining the proper distribution of marital property. . . .

[T]he family court judge . . . explained the rationale for the unequal distribution by finding that . . . Mr. Arneault's contributions to the marital estate overwhelmed the contributions made by Mrs. Arneault. Specifically, the family court reasoned as follows: . . .

Were subsections 103(2)(E) and (1)(A) the only factors to be considered, the petitioner would be receiving virtually all of the marital estate. However, . . . the respondent engaged in service contributions which gave the petitioner the freedom to focus on his business pursuits. Those contributions and the other factors in § 103 create the respondent's entitlement to a portion of the estate. This Court believes her contributions were substantial, but not as overwhelming as the petitioner's contributions. . . . It is proper that the petitioner must receive an adequate award for his accomplishments, and, at the same time, the respondent be properly rewarded for her contributions to the environment which permitted him to use his personal talents to amass this fortune.

In that same order, the family court further explained that:

> [t]he petitioner's intelligence and ability are unique to him and the development of these attributes can not [sic] be attributed equally to the petitioner and respondent, regardless of the environment which the respondent created in order to allow the petitioner to achieve the estate that has been amassed. . . . This Court looks at these personal attributes as substantial service contributions to the marital estate. There are many persons who have obtained an MBA and become a CPA during their marriage, but they have not accomplished nearly the achievements of the petitioner. These achievements go beyond the acquisition of degrees or experience, and must be given additional consideration in equitable distribution.

In essence, it appears that the family court judge believed Mr. Arneault's intelligence and ability led to his great financial success, and while Mrs. Arneault's homemaking and child-rearing duties were substantial, they did not compare to Mr. Arneault's contribution to the marital estate. To reach this conclusion, the family court apparently found that Mr. Arneault's personal goodwill was sufficient to overcome the presumption of an equal division of the marital estate. We do not agree.

The value of " '[p]ersonal goodwill' . . . [is] a personal asset that depends on the continued presence of a particular individual and may be attributed to the individual owner's personal skill, training or reputation." While we agree that Mr. Arneault may possess substantial personal goodwill, it is not an appropriate consideration in comparing the contributions of Mr. and Mrs. Arneault to the marriage. Rather, Mr. Arneault's personal goodwill would be relevant if we were asked to value MTR, the company for which Mr. Arneault worked during the parties' marriage and by whom he continues to be employed, and to determine its net value for division. . . .

Significantly, we disagree with the family court's undervaluement of the contributions made to the marital estate by Mrs. Arneault. In essence, the family court found that because Mrs. Arneault's contributions were not monetary in nature, they did not count as substantially as Mr. Arneault's contributions to the marital estate. This idea is contrary to West Virginia jurisprudence. We previously have held:

> Under equitable distribution, the contributions of time and effort to the married life of the couple — at home and in the workplace — are valued equally regardless of whether the parties' respective earnings have been equal. Equitable distribution contemplates that parties make their respective contributions to the married life of the parties in that expectation.

We likewise have stated that "general contributions, rather than economic contributions [a]re to be the basis for a distribution" of a marital estate. . . .

The facts of the present case highlight how important the contributions of both parties were to the marital estate. It was conceded that Mr. Arneault and Mrs. Arneault did not have any unusual fortune at the time of their marriage. Mrs. Arneault had recently received an undergraduate degree, and Mr. Arneault earned his undergraduate degree soon after they married. Mrs. Arneault then earned a masters degree, while Mr. Arneault went on to obtain his CPA license and a masters degree in business administration. The family court found that Mr. Arneault's innate abilities led to the financial wealth of the marital estate. However, the facts illustrate that the opposite is more probable. Mr. Arneault and Mrs. Arneault entered the marriage on fairly equal levels. Mr. Arneault earned a professional license and a graduate degree after the marriage commenced. It is very conceivable that this accumulation of knowledge, after the commencement of the marriage, led to the development of Mr. Arneault's innate abilities.

Even though Mrs. Arneault also had an advanced degree, she abandoned her own career in order to stay home with the couple's children. She also was responsible for the majority of the housework and the maintenance of the marital residence. Her responsibilities were manifestly increased by the fact that Mr. Arneault was completely absent from the marital home during the work week, leaving Mrs. Arneault with even greater responsibilities and household duties than is normally encountered in like circumstances. Rather than the conclusion made by the family court, the facts of this case show it is more likely that Mrs. Arneault's contributions to the marriage are precisely the reason that Mr. Arneault was able to succeed in his work. . . .

In the present case, there is no allegation that Mrs. Arneault did anything to detract from the value of the marital estate, and no suggestion that she did anything to frivolously dispose of marital money or assets. Thus, we conclude that the family court abused its discretion in fixing a 35/65 split of the marital estate. Mr. Arneault's intelligence and financial prowess is not sufficient justification for straying from the presumption of a 50/50 split. This conclusion is especially true under facts such as these where it is clear that Mr. Arneault's success was due in large part to the contributions made to the marriage by Mrs. Arneault. Accordingly, we find that the marital estate should be split 50/50 and reverse the circuit court's contrary ruling. . . .

STARCHER, J., dissenting.

This marriage was *not* a standard fifty/fifty marital partnership, where Mrs. Arneault was the homemaker/support mechanism and Mr. Arneault was the income earner outside the home. Although the couple lived together prior to Mr. Arneault's success . . . , the Arneaults have lived and worked in separate states for more than a decade.

Since 1995, Mrs. Arneault lived in Michigan and Mr. Arneault spent the bulk of his time in West Virginia. He returned to Michigan a few days a week, being actively involved in various activities with his children . . . . Mrs. Arneault only visited West Virginia perhaps three times in ten years. The couple's children are now both emancipated adults and Mrs. Arneault, who received her masters' degree in 1971, works in her consulting business, which she has maintained on a full-time basis since 1995. There was no evidence that Mrs. Arneault's choices regarding work were compelled by Mr. Arneault or the couple's circumstances. Rather, since 1995, the couple pursued separate lives in separate states.

There is no evidence to support Mrs. Arneault's assertions that she provided substantial assistance in Mr. Arneault's success with MTR Gaming. For example, there is no evidence of record that Mrs. Arneault was a host for her husband's business functions. . . . Other than residing in the couple's Michigan home while Mr. Arneault toiled in West Virginia, Mrs. Arneault had nothing to do with MTR Gaming, even long after the children had gone to college.

The record is also undisputed that much of MTR's success was due to Mr. Arneault's considerable efforts. . . . The family court found that Mr. Arneault nearly single-handedly created the gaming industry in West Virginia. . . .

Essentially, Mrs. Arneault makes a "community property" argument, contending that because she was Mr. Arneault's long-time wife, she is automatically entitled to one-half of the stock of a corporation that Mr. Arneault built irrespective of their relative contributions to the corporation.

West Virginia, however, is *not* a "community property" state. Rather, West Virginia is an "equitable distribution" state in which its legislature has prescribed various factors to be considered in making, not an "equal" distribution of marital property, but an "equitable" distribution, based primarily upon the parties' relative contributions. . . .

No details are provided about Mrs. Arneault's contributions to MTR Gaming because Mrs. Arneault made no contributions to MTR Gaming. Few details are provided about Mrs. Arneault's contributions to the marital home and child rearing because third parties provided many housekeeping and childcare services, and despite Mr. Arneault's business travel, he shared the parenting duties. There is no evidence that Mrs. Arneault ever sacrificed her career for Mr. Arneault's. Instead, as was noted, Mr. Arneault's career involved great sacrifice on his part in leaving the marital residence to earn a living which allowed Mrs. Arneault to enjoy a comfortable lifestyle and to pursue her far less lucrative business interests. In contrast to the overwhelming evidence of Mr. Arneault's sacrifices, there was *no* evidence of Mrs. Arneault's sacrifices. . . .

Once a litigant, like Mr. Arneault, rebuts the presumption of equal division by demonstrating that the evidence satisfies the statutory criteria for an unequal division, the burden shifts to the other party to adduce evidence that the statutory criteria support an equal division. In this case, rather than presenting any evidence, Mrs. Arneault essentially argued and continues to argue for "judicial nullification" of the equitable distribution statute in favor of fifty/fifty presumption that can never be rebutted. Mrs. Arneault likens a marriage to a law partnership whereby both parties are entitled to share in the good fortune of the other. Law partnerships, however, are governed by written partnership agreements that force whatever division of good or bad fortune the parties decide or other under governing statutory law.

The West Virginia Legislature, however, has not created a "marital partnership" in which each partner, whatever their relative contributions, is always entitled to share equally in the good fortune of the other. Rather, as this Court stated in Burnside v. Burnside, 460 S.E.2d 264 (W. Va. 1995), "Thus to be equitable, the division need not be equal, but as a starting point, equality is presumptively equitable."...

In considering the merits of Mrs. Arneault's appeal, this Court should consider the following factors, used by courts in cases around the country in similar circumstances:

(1) Mrs. Arneault failed to introduce any evidence that she made major contributions to the marital estate as a result of her efforts as a "corporate spouse;"

(2) She failed to introduce any evidence that she was a full-time homemaker;

(3) She failed to introduce any evidence that she routinely accompanied Mr. Arneault to conventions and social gatherings of MTR;

(4) She failed to introduce any evidence that she was so involved in the dealings of MTR that for all intents and purposes she was considered an employee;

(5) She failed to introduce any evidence that she entertained MTR customers and other business associates in social and business settings;

(6) She failed to introduce any evidence that she suffered an increased workload and extensive social duties as a result of Mr. Arneault's work at MTR;

(7) She failed to introduce any evidence that she hosted events related to the business of MTR;

(8) She failed to introduce any evidence that her entertainment duties expanded with Mr. Arneault's corporate responsibilities;

(9) She failed to introduce any evidence that she traveled extensively with Mr. Arneault to numerous cities for business purposes;

(10) She failed to introduce any evidence that she in any way was a sounding board for Mr. Arneault, giving advice and guidance to him;

(11) She failed to introduce evidence that during the course of the marriage Mr. Arneault frequently shared information with her about business dealings, daily experiences, and/or asked for advice in a wide variety of circumstances;

(12) She failed to introduce any evidence that she played any role (significant or otherwise) in the financial aspects of MTR or Mountaineer Park, in addition to serving as a "homemaker;"

(13) She failed to introduce any evidence that she performed all the typical duties of a wife, parent, and homemaker and still demonstrate that she made an actual economic contribution to the marital estate; and

(14) She failed to introduce any evidence that there is a direct link between her business efforts and the ultimate value of the MTR stock....

What the legislature has instructed is that when the efforts of one spouse are disproportionate to the efforts of another spouse with respect to the acquisition of marital assets, the efforts of the first spouse are *not to be ignored* in the *equitable* distribution of the marital assets; otherwise, slough and neglect would prevail over industry and diligence....

In most cases, in the ordinary circumstances of divorce — which is that neither party can afford it — a relatively strict application of the presumption of equal distribution may be more appropriate. "Let both parties suffer equally" is not an unreasonable principle. But when the "super rich" start dividing things up, and even a person with the shorter end of the stick will be "rich" after a divorce, then it is less harmful to let the equities have their way. The majority opinion is therefore additionally deficient in its discussion of equitable distribution because it pretends that the enormous wealth that Mr. Arneault has amassed through his work is just like the "house and pension and savings" that ninety-nine percent of us have. . . .

NOTES AND QUESTIONS

1. *Does Equitable Mean Equal?* Notice how the West Virginia statute sets forth a presumption that all marital property is to be divided equally. A small number of common-law states rely on a presumption that a 50/50 split of property is equitable.[58] Indiana has a rebuttable presumption that an equal division is "just and reasonable."[59] Evidence to rebut the presumption can include "[t]he contribution of each spouse to the acquisition of property," "[t]he extent to which the property was acquired by each spouse," "[t]he economic circumstances of each spouse at the time of the disposition of the property," "[t]he conduct of the parties during the marriage," and "[t]he earnings or earning ability of the parties."[60] While equitable distribution can result in an equal split, "equitable" does not dictate an equal division. In reaching an equitable distribution, courts have broad discretion to reach overall fairness.[61] For instance, considerations of relative contribution or of need can justify wide departures from an equal division.[62]

In community property jurisdictions, some states, such as California, Louisiana, and New Mexico, mandate a strict 50/50 distribution of community property at divorce.[63]

---

58. See, e.g., Ark. Code Ann. § 9-12-315 (a)(1)(A) (2020) ("All marital property shall be distributed one-half (½) to each party unless the court finds such a division to be inequitable."); see also Lundquist v. Lundquist, 923 P.2d 42, 53 (Alaska 1996) ("The law presumes that a 50-50 split of marital property is equitable"); In re Marriage of Minear, 679 N.E.2d 856, 864 (Ill. App. Ct. 1997) ("Equal distribution of marital property is generally favored").

59. Ind. Code § 31-15-7-5 (2020).

60. Id.; c.f. Horn v. Horn, No. 25A03-0904-CV-155, 2009 WL 4059806, at *4 (Ind. Ct. App. Nov. 24, 2009) ("If the trial court deviates from this presumption, it must state why it did so.").

61. See, e.g., Mathis v. Mathis, 642 S.E.2d 832 (Ga. 2007).

62. See James R. Ratner, Distribution of Material Assets in Community Property Jurisdictions: Equitable Doesn't Equal Equal, 72 La. L. Rev. 21, 23–24 (2011); Robertson v. Robertson, 76 S.W.3d 337 (Tenn. 2002).

63. Principles of the Law of Family Dissolution, supra note 26, at 22 n.31; Grossman & Friedman, supra note 16, at 194; Cal. Fam. Code § 2550 (West 2020); La. Stat. Ann. § 9:2801(A)(4)(b); N.M. Stat. Ann. § 40-4-7(A) (2020).

Other states, such as Arizona, Idaho, Nevada, Texas, and Washington, allow a court to depart from a 50/50 split to achieve an equitable distribution.[64]

2. *Equitable Factors.* The applicable equitable distribution statute in *Arneault* instructs the trial court to reach an equitable allocation based on a presumption of equal division, taking into account a range of factors. Do you think these are the most appropriate factors? What would you add? In seeking to make equitable distributions, courts will engage in balancing instead of following a formula of how much weight to give in each case.[65] Trial courts have broad discretion in making a determination about what is equitable.

While the West Virginia Supreme Court recognized Mr. Arneault's "intelligence and financial prowess" in building MTR gaming, this was not enough to overcome the presumption that an equal division was equitable based on consideration of Mrs. Arneault's contributions.[66] Others have argued, without success, that special ability should be viewed as a type of "super-contribution" that should guide property allocation. In deCastro v. deCastro, a husband argued that his "'genius' alone engendered the considerable estate."[67] The appellate court determined, however, that the trial judge's division of the marital property was supported by "findings that both parties contributed to the marriage, one focusing on work outside the home and the other focusing on work within the home and with the children . . . that the marriage had been a partnership."[68]

3. *Contribution.* Notice how in *Arneault*, the court relied on the idea of contribution, a common factor, to reach a result on what is equitable.[69] The idea of contribution resonates with the concept of marriage as a shared enterprise.[70] In considering non-economic contributions, courts will factor in domestic labor and caregiving.[71] The West Virginia equitable distribution statute explicitly includes domestic activity like housework and childcare as part of the consideration of contributions to the "acquisition, preservation and maintenance or increase in value of marital property." This recognition of domestic work was the result of reform efforts in the 1970s to remedy the economic disparities wrought by title theory, disproportionately suffered

---

64. See, e.g., Idaho Code § 32-712(1)(a)-(b) (2020). For a summary, see Doris Jonas Freed & Timothy B. Walker, Family Law in the Fifty States: An Overview, 19 Fam. L.Q. 331, 353–67 (1986); see also Ariz. Rev. Stat. Ann. § 25-318(A) (2020); Nev. Rev. Stat. § 125.150(1)(b) (2020); Tex. Fam. Code Ann. § 7.001 (West 2020); Wash. Rev. Code § 26.09.080 (2020).

65. Cofer v. Price-Cofer, 825 S.W.2d 369, 375 (Mo. Ct. App. 1992).

66. 639 S.E.2d 720, 729 (W. Va. 2006).

67. 616 N.E.2d 52, 56 (Mass. 1993).

68. Id.; see also Barbara Freedman Wand & Ilana Hurwitz, The "Genius Factor" and Equitable Distribution of Property at Divorce, Boston Bar J., Jan.-Feb. 1994, at 10, 26–27.

69. 639 S.E.2d 720.

70. Mickey v. Mickey, 974 A.2d 641, 657 (Conn. 2009).

71. For instance, in Adams v. Adams, the Massachusetts high court affirmed an equal division based on such contributions by one spouse. 945 N.E.2d 844 (Mass. 2011) (wife was a homemaker and the primary caregiver for the parties' children during a twelve-year marriage).

by women.[72] By the end of the 1970s, most states either explicitly considered domestic contributions or indirectly did so through broad factors that permitted consideration of such contributions.[73] Do you agree with how the court applied the equitable distribution factors in *Arneault*? Where did the majority and dissent part ways? The dissent stated that this was not a "standard fifty/fifty marital partnership." What would that have looked like?

A concurring opinion in *Arneault* faulted the dissent for devaluing nonmonetary contributions in the home and did so in ways that raised the gendered stakes of the decision:

> It has been said that "[w]e honor motherhood with glowing sentimentality, but we don't rate it highly on the scale of creative occupations." Truer words could not be spoken of the view expressed by the dissenters. In dissenting from the majority opinion in this case, I fear my colleagues perpetuate the disdain to which mothers who do not work outside the home are all too often subjected. Rather than dismissing such nonmonetary contributions as being insignificant or less important than those occupations which receive a paycheck, however, the West Virginia Legislature and this Court both have acknowledged that a parent's work inside the home *is* a substantial contribution to the marital estate which a husband and wife have amassed. In fact, such nonmonetary contributions are highly valued and appreciated both for children and as supporting and fostering an environment that permits the work-outside-the-home spouse to do so. Such a result is indeed equitable, particularly in light of the never-ending demands faced by the mother (or father) who works inside the home:
>
> "No ordinary work done by a man is either as hard or as responsible as the work of a woman who is bringing up a family of small children; for upon her time and strength demands are made not only every hour of the day but often every hour of the night. She may have to get up night after night to take care of a sick child, and yet must by day continue to do all her household duties as well. . . . Theodore Roosevelt, Speech, On American Motherhood (Mar. 13, 1905)."[74]

4. *Need.* Many states also permit consideration of the parties' future financial needs in making allocations. Again, formulations will vary across states, but the general view is that "more marital property should go to the party who has the most need for it."[75] This is based on the underlying idea that property division should not only recognize marriage as a partnership but also serve as a means of "providing future

---

72. For discussion of history of this family law reform, see, e.g., Mary Ziegler, An Incomplete Revolution: Feminists and the Legacy of Marital-Property Reform, 19 Mich. J. Gender & L. 259, 261 (2013).

73. Doris Jonas Freed & Henry H. Foster, Jr., Divorce in the Fifty States: An Overview as of 1978, 13 Fam. L.Q. 105, 114 (1979).

74. *Arneault*, 639 S.E.2d at 746 (Benjamin, J., concurring).

75. Turner, supra note 27, § 8:15.

support for an economically dependent spouse."[76] Consider this example. A couple is divorcing in a common-law state. One spouse has been primarily a homemaker, has only recently obtained a four-year college degree, and is working as an unpaid intern. The other spouse has an annual salary three times as much as what the newly graduated spouse is expected to make. In Robertson v. Robertson, the Tennessee court instructed that in a case like this, "a trial court should consider awarding more assets to an economically disadvantaged spouse to provide future support," noting that an equitable distribution does not require an equal division of property.[77] Statutes might guide courts to consider parties' "economic circumstances" more generally or specific factors like "age, health, station, occupation, amount and sources of income, vocational skills, employability, estate, liabilities and needs of each of the parties."[78]

5. *Duration.* Courts will commonly consider duration of marriage as a factor in equitable distribution. Duration can affect how courts weigh other factors, like domestic contributions.[79] It can also give rise to greater financial need.[80] A longer marriage will justify a more equal division, with less regard for actual financial contributions to acquisition of property and more emphasis on domestic contributions.[81] With a shorter marriage, in contrast, courts are more likely to view financial contributions as more important.[82] In some jurisdictions, courts will seek, after a shorter marriage, to restore parties to the positions they would have been in had the marriage not occurred.[83] What should happen if a couple was married only for a relatively short period preceded by a longer cohabitation?

PROBLEM

Deborah and Coralee met in 1992. The following year, they began living together. Approximately fifteen years later, on October 8, 2008, the parties entered into a civil union, and, on January 1, 2011, their civil union converted to a marriage by operation of state law. On March 28, 2012, Deborah filed a petition for divorce.

---

76. Id. (quoting Goller v. Goller, 758 S.W.2d 505, 508 (Mo. Ct. App. 1988)).

77. 76 S.W.3d 337, 341 (Tenn. 2002) (noting that a court should consider awarding more assets to the economically disadvantaged spouse).

78. Turner, supra note 27, § 8:15 (quoting Colo. Rev. Stat. § 14-10-113(1)(c) (2020) and 750 Ill. Comp. Stat. 5/503(d)(8) (2020)).

79. Id. § 8:14.

80. Id.

81. Id.; see, e.g., Repetti v. Repetti, 47 N.Y.S.3d 447, 452 (N.Y. App. Div. 2017).

82. Turner, supra note 27, § 8:14; see, e.g., Hoverson v. Hoverson, 828 N.W.2d 510, 516 (N.D. 2013).

83. Turner, supra note 27, § 8:14 (describing a "rescission" theory in small number of states); see also Rose v. Rose, 755 P.2d 1121, 1123–24 (Alaska 1988).

At trial, Deborah took the position that the parties' marriage was a short-term marriage. Coralee argued, on the other hand, the trial court must consider the couples' lengthy twenty-year relationship in making a property distribution. She argued that prior to the legalization of same-sex marriage, she and Deborah did everything that was available to them to provide for one another, including executing estate plans that left respective estates to the other, Deborah providing life and health insurance for Coralee's benefit, having joint accounts, commingling bank and credit card accounts, sharing duties within the home, and finally joining together in a civil union and then legal marriage.

Under the applicable state equitable distribution statute, the trial court was to "presume that an equal division is an equitable distribution of property." However, the court was also permitted to find "that an equal division would not be appropriate or equitable after considering one or more of a number of factors, which include "the length of the marriage, the ability of the parties to provide for their own needs, the needs of [a] custodial parent, the contribution of each party during the marriage and the value of property contributed by each party." The statute also permits the court to "consider any other factor it deems relevant in equitably distributing the parties' assets." The trial court deemed the marriage a short-term one, which justified a departure from an equal division. Is this the appropriate result?

POSTSCRIPT

In the case upon which this problem is based, the trial court had found that the marriage of Deborah Munson and Coralee Beal was "short-term" and granted Munson eighty-eight percent of the value of the marital estate and Beal the remaining twelve percent and alimony.[84] The trial court determined that the date of the civil union, later automatically converted to marriage, marked the start of Beal's and Munson's marriage, for property division purposes. The New Hampshire Supreme Court noted that, although not dispositive, relative duration of a marriage could justify different treatment for property division purposes. The court rejected Beal's assertion that the "parties' lengthy cohabitation and commingling of assets . . . compel a finding that their relationship was in effect a long-term marriage." Yet, the court reasoned that while the cohabitation period was not part of the marriage, it could be considered, per the statute, as "[a]ny other factor that [the trial court] deems relevant":

---

84. In re Munson, 146 A.3d 153 (N.H. 2016).

> [P]remarital cohabitation may be relevant to the distribution of marital property. For instance, a couple living together may commingle their finances or jointly acquire property in anticipation of marriage. Their marriage may not occur for several years, and after it occurs, it may be short in duration. Still, the couple may have become dependent upon the assets that they shared prior to marriage, such that it may not be just for a court in divorce proceedings to ignore their cohabitation period when determining what constitutes an equitable property division.[85]

The court deemed it appropriate to consider the premarital cohabitation as a factor in determining whether to depart from the presumption of equal division.

LGBT rights groups argued as amici curiae that if the case featured a different-sex couple, the trial court would have taken their premarital cohabitation and economic interdependence into account when dividing property.[86] Do you agree? The New Hampshire Supreme Court in *Munson* clarified that its holding that "the court may consider premarital cohabitation applies to all divorce proceedings."[87]

Munson asserted that Beal's argument that the court should take premarital cohabitation into account because the couple would have gotten married if they could was misplaced because the couple could have gotten a civil union or gotten married in a neighboring state prior to being able to do so in New Hampshire.[88] Does factoring in the cohabitation period assume the couple's intent about their relationship? This case involved whether the premarital period could be considered as an equitable factor. But sometimes the question arises as to when the marriage itself began for purposes of what counts as part of marital property. Professor Katherine Franke worries that backdating might contravene the intentions of the parties.[89] How clear are those intentions? Professor Allison Tait argues for using formal "legal markers," like "[c]ivil unions, registered domestic partnerships, designated beneficiary relationships, and relationship contracts," which "all enable couples to signal a clear legal intent," as opposed to a functional indicator like cohabitation.[90] Does it make more sense to count the time period in a formal legal status for purposes of marital property than cohabitation?[91]

---

85. Id. at 158.

86. Brief for Amici Curiae Gay & Lesbian Advocates & Defenders and the American Civil Liberties Union of New Hampshire, In Matter of Munson, 146 A.3d 153 (N.H. 2016) (No. 2015-0253).

87. *Munson*, 146 A.3d at 159.

88. Id.

89. Katherine Franke, Wedlocked: The Perils of Marriage Equality (2015).

90. Allison Anna Tait, Divorce Equality, 90 Wash. L. Rev. 1245, 1306 (2015).

91. For discussion of retroactivity in the context of Obergefell v. Hodges, see Lee-ford Tritt, Moving Forward by Looking Back: The Retroactive Application of *Obergefell*, 2016 Wis. L. Rev. 873, 874–75 (2016).

Wendt v. Wendt

No. FA96 0149562 S, 1998 WL 161165

(Conn. Super. Ct. Mar. 31, 1998)

Tierney. . . .

The plaintiff wife, whose maiden name was Lorna Jorgenson, and the defendant husband, Gary C. Wendt, were married July 31, 1965, in Rio, Wisconsin. Both parties have resided in Connecticut for more than one year prior to the date of institution of this dissolution of marriage action. The complaint is dated December 19, 1995. There are two daughters born of this marriage. Both daughters have long since completed college. They no longer reside in the family house and are self supporting.

The defendant is the Chairman, President and Chief Executive Officer of GE Capital Services, Inc. with principal offices in Stamford, Connecticut. . . . Early in the marriage the plaintiff earned modest wages as a public school music teacher. Throughout the entire marriage she has been a mother, homemaker and corporate wife entertaining GE customers and other business associates in various social and business settings. . . .

The parties were raised in a small midwestern town near Rio, in central Wisconsin. When they started dating in high school, the plaintiff was a freshman, and the defendant was a sophomore. They attended the same high school. . . .

The defendant attended the University of Wisconsin, and the plaintiff would visit the defendant every weekend during her senior year in high school. The following year the plaintiff attended the University. The parties became engaged when the plaintiff was a junior in college. . . .

The plaintiff received a Bachelor of Music Degree from the University of Wisconsin and is qualified to teach public school music. Upon the plaintiff's graduation, the parties married and moved to Cambridge, Massachusetts where the defendant attended Harvard Business School. For a portion of the first year the plaintiff worked part-time at M.I.T in the industrial relations department. During the second year the plaintiff taught music in the Sudbury public school system at an annual salary of no more than $6,000. The plaintiff also gave private music lessons. The defendant's Harvard tuition was paid by his parents. During the summers the defendant worked full time for a Concord, Massachusetts land developer. The earnings from both parties and a portion of the defendant's $2,500 savings from prior employment supported the household for the two years in Cambridge. The defendant also worked part time during his second MBA year.

The parties believed that they were two little kids from a small town in Wisconsin and that it was exciting to move to a big eastern city. The parties had virtually no money. There was little social life other than seeing other students at their houses. The plaintiff did the shopping and cooking. The defendant was given assignments on Friday for completion on Monday. The plaintiff assisted the defendant by typing his papers. This required extensive weekend work for both parties.

The defendant received an MBA from Harvard after two years. At graduation all the spouses (then wives since there were no women MBA candidates) received PhTs (Putting Hubby Through). . . .

The plaintiff stopped working as a public school music teacher shortly after the birth of their first daughter in December of 1968. This was her last job. The plaintiff continued as a part time piano teacher and church organist. The parties spent four years in Texas. [Every time the parties moved for defendant's career, the plaintiff stayed behind to sell the house and coordinate the move.]

From 1975 through 1986 a large percentage of their social and personal life revolved around family. The plaintiff was a wife, mother, homemaker and a great supporter of her husband in his life. The children were educated in the public elementary system. The plaintiff had household help once a week and no live-in help. . . .

The court concludes that up until 1986, the parties lived modestly. . . .

Much of the trial was devoted to various witnesses testifying about the contributions made by the parties to the marriage and GE from 1986 to date. . . . All the witnesses do agree that the wife spent considerable efforts as a wife, mother, homemaker and "GE wife" and that the husband was highly successful as the CEO of GECS. . . .

On cross-examination the plaintiff testified as to the amount of time that she spent on her duties. She said her job was a mother, housemaid, cook, child care provider, corporate wife and homemaker. The plaintiff described the time spent on her job as "twenty-four hours a day." . . .

A summation of the testimony of the witnesses as to the plaintiff's nonmonetary contributions is as follows: She was an excellent representative of motherhood, very organized, a very good cook and a piano teacher for years. She did house cleaning, and "she even did windows." She paid the household bills, arranged for auto repairs and maintenance. She was a good role model for the children. Her duties included clothing, feeding, driving, music, school, conferences, church activities, clubs, lessons, kids' concerts and recitals, after school activities, car pools, doctors, being present in the house regularly, housecleaning, grocery shopping, kids' needs, kids' questions, games and school homework. She was extremely hospitable and sociable. She talked to people, remembered details about people's lives and mixed with people. She was always pleasant during home entertainment. She related to men and women alike and was a cheerleader on a number of GE trips.

She was extremely neat. The children were neat, their clothes had no stains and the house was immaculate. She ironed her husband's shirts, raised two young children, entertained, sewed clothing, took the children to the doctor, attended Girl Scouts, went to school events, saw children's friends, used organizational skills and polished social skills. Guests were made to feel welcome in her house. She was a good cook. She was a member of the Lutheran Church, and both parties regularly attended with the children. She covered for her husband, i.e., gave reasons why her husband was not present at certain social events. . . .

[T]his court concludes that the plaintiff was not involved in the day-to-day activities of the defendant at his office. Essentially the plaintiff's direct GE contributions were: (1) discussing GE matters with the defendant at home and on trips, (2) providing support to him, (3) entertaining GE customers, associates and business guests away from home, (4) an annual home Christmas party for GE, (5) business travel with the defendant, and (6) participating in GE Pinnacle Club reward trips for GE high executives. . . .

In discussing her Claims for Relief on direct examination, the plaintiff justified her claim for half of all the assets of the marriage on the following basis: "Marriage is a partnership, and I should be entitled to 50%. I gave thirty-one years of my life. I loved the defendant. I worked hard and I was very loyal." The plaintiff breaks down this claim into the following categories:

1. Length of marriage
2. Length of relationship
3. Emotional support
4. Abandonment of plaintiff's career
5. Her career as a GE wife
6. Marriage is a partnership
7. Raising the children
8. Providing a household . . .

Connecticut is an equitable distribution state. . . . By case law Connecticut has been determined to have an "all-property equitable distribution scheme," [which] permits a court to divide all assets and all liabilities. . . . This is sometimes referred to as a "hotchpot" system. . . .

The criteria in the division of property under General Statutes § 46b-81(c) are "contribution of each of the parties in the acquisition, preservation or appreciation in value of their respective estates." . . .

> A property division ought to accord value to those non-monetary contributions of one spouse which enable the other spouse to devote substantial effort to paid employment which, in turn, enables the family to acquire tangible marital assets. The investment of human capital in homemaking has worth and should be evaluated in a property division incident to a dissolution of marriage. We hold, accordingly, that an equitable distribution of property should take into consideration the plaintiff's contributions to the marriage, including homemaking activities and primary caretaking responsibilities. . . .

"[W]e find the statutory mandate to consider the contribution of each spouse to the acquisition of the marital property, including the contribution of the homemaker, is a recognition by the legislature that the homemaking endeavors of both spouses in a marriage have a marital value which contributes to the acquisition of marital property. There is no justification for limiting this factor exclusively to a non-wage earner, primary homemaking spouse. Rather, both functions, homemaking and wage earning, are considerations." . . .

The nonmonetary contributions criterion is spouse and gender neutral and should be wage earner neutral. The trial court, therefore, must consider the nonmonetary contributions of the wage earner spouse as a criterion. . . .

Historically, work in the family has not been treated as comparable with work in the marketplace. . . .

> The distinction between market and nonmarket production is a heavily gendered one; work done predominantly by women remains invisible to economic policy makers. Both the statistical indicators and the policies based upon these indicators privilege market production and the types of economic activity most characteristic of modern, industrialized societies over household production and more traditional economies. . . .

Dr. Myra H. Strober, a Stanford University professor of education, testified on behalf of the plaintiff. . . . She is qualified to testify on the quantification of nonmonetary contributions. . . .

For many years general economic theory stated, "if it does not go through the market, it has no value." Professor Strober indicated that there is a value to nonmarket work performed by women in the house. . . .

The "human capital" theory . . . considers that nonmonetary contributions can be made by a nonworking spouse by putting food on the table, paying for tuition for the husband's going to school and general support of the husband. Human capital may be augmented by education, training, experience and medical care, or it can deteriorate from such causes as lack of current work experience or substance addiction. . . .

Dr. Strober indicated that the "human capital" theory was the best approach for evaluating the plaintiff's nonmonetary contribution to this family. . . .

Underlying the human capital theory, is the phrase "equal efforts and equal sacrifice." This means that both parties expend equal efforts in their areas of expertise and equally sacrificed certain benefits. Dr. Strober referred to the Wendts as a "two person career," i.e., that it required two people to perform the high powered corporate career successfully. Therefore, each of those contributions is valued equally regardless of the underlying economic market value of those efforts. . . .

Dr. Strober's opinion was that both parties made equal efforts and equal sacrifice. . . . Therefore a fifty-fifty division of the assets is appropriate as well as a fifty-fifty division of all earnings. . . .

This court concludes that . . . no reasonable quantification can be made of the nonmonetary contributions of the plaintiff. . . .

[A]n economic approach to establishing a definite value of a spouse's nonmonetary contributions is fraught with danger.

(1) The human capital approach to the financial remedies in marriage defines the entitlements of marriage based on norms of investment, exchange, and maximization. The institution of marriage is changed by this definition because the "intangible benefits" of marriage — sharing and sacrifice, love and obligation, "for better and for worse" — have all been pushed to the periphery. Instead, marriage is held to an economic standard of rationality.

(2) The effort to quantify changes in human capital also alters our view of the individuals within a marriage, requiring that we define and distinguish the components of their income-earning potential. . . .

(3) There are two aspects to the commodification problem created by human capital assets in marriage. The first arises from treating personal capacities as if they could be purchased and sold.

(4) The second arises from thinking about marital interactions as exchanges between husband and wife. One recurring theme in the case law and commentary on career assets is that it is difficult to distinguish the results of education and career development from the results of personal qualities such as talent, intelligence, ambition, and hard work. . . .

(5) Another consistent thread is the concern not to commercialize marriage by treating it as a business or financial venture. . . .

(6) As with the complex formulas for valuation of homemakers in tort, these issues cast doubt on whether the legal system can or should attempt to structure remedies that require such precise measurement.

(7) Judges express the concern that the routine use of experts adds significant expense to the divorce process.

From an economic viewpoint, precise valuation of many "career assets" create large additional transaction costs in the divorce process. . .

(8) Another risk of these methods is that the attempt to value investments in human capital pushes the institution of marriage from a relationship based on love and obligation toward one based on self-interest. . . . In a widely quoted passage, the New Jersey Supreme Court commented that "[m]arriage is not a business arrangement in which the parties keep track of debits and credits, their accounts to be settled upon divorce." . . . .

The plaintiff argues that the assets and income in this case should be divided on an equitable basis: i.e., an equal division. She claims that the marital assets are $90,000,000 as of the last day of trial, and she is entitled to half, i.e., $45,000,000, by reason of her nonmonetary contributions . . . and the theory that a marriage is an equal partnership.

The defendant on the other hand claims that a transfer to the plaintiff of $8,300,000 of property along with the payment of $250,000 a year alimony is more than enough to keep the plaintiff in the lifestyle to which she is accustomed. . . .

The evidence presented indicates that the marriage has broken down irretrievably, and, therefore, judgment may enter dissolving the marriage on those grounds. . . .

The following orders may enter:

1. The defendant will transfer to the plaintiff all his right, title and interest in and to the marital residence . . . and the adjoining lots. . . .
2. The defendant will transfer to the plaintiff all his right, title and interest in and to the real property located [in] Florida. . . .
3. The defendant shall pay to the plaintiff as periodic alimony the sum of $252,000 per year payable in equal monthly installments of $21,000.00 on the first day of each month. Said periodic alimony is to terminate upon the occurrence of the first of the following events: the death of the plaintiff, the plaintiff's remarriage or a court finding under General Statutes § 46b–86(b) as amended. . . .
4. The defendant shall retain as his own property, free and clear of any claim by the plaintiff, the [listed] real property whether held in his name or jointly. . . .
5. The parties shall divide equally all of the currently available cash, stocks, bonds and mutual fund assets of the parties regardless of the registered title, . . . including, but not limited, to [specific funds and accounts]. . . .
16. The General Electric Qualified Pension Plan, currently vested, will be divided by the parties equally. . . .
17. The defendant is awarded all the right, title and interest in and to the General Electric Supplementary Pension Plan (nonqualified plan) including whatever "retirement allowance" payment that may be paid to the defendant by General Electric Corporation. . . .
18. . . . The plaintiff is awarded one-half of the "dividend equivalent" and/or dividends on the entire 199,000 shares of GE restricted stock to be paid if and when received by the defendant. . . .
19. The plaintiff is awarded one-half of 17/30th (i.e. 17/60th to plaintiff, 43/60th to defendant) of the $6,650,000 deferred portion of the defendant's General Electric Long Term Performance Award ("special bonus") to be paid out by GE, upon the defendant's retirement, over a twenty year period. . . .
20. The defendant shall be awarded all the right, title and interest in the General Electric Savings and Security Program (401K plan). . . .
21. The defendant shall be awarded all the right, title and interest in the General Electric Deferred Incentive Compensation Plan. . . .
22. The defendant shall be awarded all the right, title and interest in the General Electric Executive Deferred Salary Plan. . . .
23. The defendant shall pay to the plaintiff the sum of $2,000,000 as property distribution to be paid by January 6, 1998.

24. [T]he defendant owns 175,000 shares of General Electric Vested Stock Options and Appreciation Rights. . . . One half of said sum ought to be distributed to the plaintiff. . . . Therefore, the defendant shall pay to the plaintiff the sum of $1,700,000 as property. . . .

25. The defendant holds 420,000 stock options and appreciation rights in General Electric common stock. . . .

One half of said sum ought to be distributed to the plaintiff. . . .

Therefore, the defendant shall pay to the plaintiff the sum of $1,107,000 as property. . . .

33. The parties have been ordered to divide equally the joint checking accounts. . . .

NOTES AND QUESTIONS

1. *What Did Lorna Wendt Get?* Lorna Wendt's legal battle attracted national attention.[92] In the end, the trial court awarded Lorna property and assets worth about $20 million — less than she sought but much more than Gary offered.[93] Does this seem like a fair result?

2. *"He Who Earns It?"* Do courts treat high-asset couples differently than more modest-income couples? As Professor Joan Williams points out: "Typically, courts treat property as jointly owned when dealing with modest estates, where splitting the property 50/50 often forces the sale of the family home in order to allow the husband to 'get his equity out.'"[94] The offer by the husband in *Wendt* reflected the prevailing view that, "where the estate is large, . . . 'he who earns it, owns it,'"[95] resulting in lower percentages of property being awarded to spouses like Lorna Wendt.[96] Should it matter if the property subject to distribution is very substantial? Did Lorna Wendt "need" the $45,000,000 she sought? Is that the relevant question? She ultimately received $20 million. Was this an equitable result?

3. *Family Work and Market Work.* Williams argues against drawing a distinction between the property distribution in high-asset cases and lower-asset cases: "The joint property theory begins from the principle that ideal workers who are parents are supported by a flow of family work from the primary caregiver of their children. If the ideal worker's performance depends on a flow of family work from his wife, then 'his'

---

92. See Betsy Morris, It's Her Job, Too: Lorna Wendt's $20 Million Divorce Case is the Shot Heard 'Round the Water Cooler, Fortune, Feb. 2, 1998, at 65.

93. Id.; Grossman & Friedman, supra note 26, at 245.

94. Joan Williams, Do Wives Own Half? Winning for Wives After *Wendt*, 32 Conn. L. Rev. 249, 250 (1999).

95. Id.

96. Mary Moers Wenig, The Marital Property Law of Connecticut: Past, Present and Future 1990 Wis. L. Rev. 807, 873.

wage is the product of two adults: his market work, and her family work. If an asset is produced by two family members, it makes no sense to award ownership to only one of them."[97] According to Williams, the "he who earns it, owns it" rule is an "outdated expression of coverture," and spouses like Lorna Wendt should be awarded "half the accumulated family wealth based on her family work, without which that wealth would not have been created."[98]

PROBLEMS

1. Ericka has been a highly-paid executive for a Fortune 500 company. As a result of her earnings, at the time of her divorce from Carl, the couple has $50 million of assets. Carl never worked for pay during the marriage, but he managed the household and did the majority of childrearing for their one child, who is now 30 years old. Under what principle should the parties' assets be divided?

2. Ben has been an highly-paid executive, and Janet did not work for pay during the marriage but managed the household and did the majority of childrearing for their three children now ages 13, 15, and 18. During times when the children were in grade school and middle school, the family relied on a paid caregiver as well. How should the assets be divided at divorce?

D. Special Issues in Property

Any type of traditional property interest can be classified as marital or community and divided — money, cars, houses, jewelry, stocks and bonds, and so on. But what about property that is held in forms that are not easy to value or easy to divide? Courts have grappled with the divisibility of pensions and retirement benefits, professional licenses and degrees, business partnership interests, and personal injury damages awards.

1. Pensions and Retirement Benefits

Courts routinely recognize pension or retirement benefits as divisible marital property or as an asset relevant in the context of property division upon divorce.[99] But are all pensions alike?

---

97. Williams, supra note 94, at 265.
98. Id. at 266.
99. See, e.g., In re Marriage of Brown, 544 P.2d 561 (Cal. 1976).

LAING V. LAING

741 P.2d 649 (Alaska 1987)

COMPTON, JUSTICE. . . .

Kenneth and Marla Laing were married on November 16, 1964. At the time of the marriage, Marla lived in her own furnished home, the equity in which was approximately $15,000. She also had benefits from her first husband's death which amounted to approximately $10,000 and a two-year old car worth approximately $500. Throughout their twenty-year marriage, Marla was responsible for most of the housework and child care, even during approximately ten years she was employed outside the home.

Kenneth apparently had no substantial assets at the time of the marriage. He was employed all but a few months during the marriage.

At the time of divorce, Marla was 49 years old and employed as a dental office receptionist/clerk. She earned $18,750 gross income the year before trial. Kenneth was 50 years old and had been employed at Union Chemicals (now UNOCAL) for seven and a half years. The trial court found that he had earned approximately $40,000 by August 1985; his income in 1984 was $61,471.43. . . .

With the exception of Kenneth's retirement plan, the parties in this case stipulated to the characterization of the divided assets as marital property. . . .

We . . . address the issue whether the trial court properly characterized Kenneth's nonvested pension as marital property. . . .

This court has considered pensions in the equitable division of marital assets.

Alaska thus follows the majority rule that "vested" pension and retirement benefits are subject to division by a divorce court. Whether the majority rule can also be applied with regard to Kenneth's *nonvested*[8] pension rights is a question of first impression in Alaska. Jurisdictions are split on this issue. Those in which nonvested pensions are held not to be divisible marital property rely primarily on the notion that such interests are too speculative and cannot be said to constitute a property right.

The trend, however, is to consider pensions as marital property regardless of whether they have vested.

Supporting this trend is the reasoning that the contingent nature of a nonvested pension presents simply a valuation problem, not bearing on the non-employee spouse's entitlement to a just share of the marital assets. Pension benefits are

---

8. The term "nonvested" is used here to mean that if Kenneth's employment were to terminate immediately he would be entitled to no future retirement or pension benefits. The term is not used, as some courts have done, to indicate merely that the pension rights have not matured. When a pension or retirement benefits plan is vested but not matured, an employee is absolutely entitled to benefits, though he is not entitled to actual payments until some future date. See Copeland v. Copeland, 575 P.2d 99, 101–02 (N.M. 1978); Charles C. Marvel, Annotation, Pension or Retirement Benefits as Subject to Award Division by Court in Settlement of Property Rights Between Spouses, 94 A.L.R.3d 176 (1979).

generally viewed as deferred compensation for services rendered and the employee spouse's right thereto is a contractual right. "The fact that a contractual right is contingent upon future events does not degrade that right to an expectancy."

One commentator provides another persuasive reason for characterizing even nonvested pensions as divisible marital assets:

> The non-employee spouse's contribution to the pension asset is exactly the same whether the pension be labeled a mere *expectancy,* or a *contingent future interest.*

We are persuaded that the contingencies that may prevent the employee spouse from ever collecting his or her nonvested pension should not bar the non-employee spouse from recovering a share if the pension is in fact paid out. Indeed, a contrary rule would frustrate the statutory command that Alaska courts effect a "just division of the marital assets." This obviously requires that the trial court consider the financial circumstances of each party. It would be wholly inconsistent with this policy to ignore the existence of so substantial an asset as a party's pension rights. In this regard, we adopt the rule representing the current trend and recognize nonvested pension rights as a marital asset. . . .

NOTES AND QUESTIONS

1.   *Retirement and Pension Benefits.* Retirement accounts are an important asset; 66.9 percent of married couples have one.[100] The approach in *Laing* follows a trend in common law states to deem retirement and pension benefits divisible. In community property states, courts also have held that retirement or pension benefits are subject to division at divorce.[101] A small number of courts, however, have chosen not to divide unvested (or nonvested) retirement and pension benefits.[102] What is the reason why courts might draw a distinction between vested and unvested benefits or pensions? Even if divisible, a pension might not actually be divided, but it will be included in the accounting of the couple's assets and can be offset by another divisible asset.[103]

---

100. U.S. Census Bureau, Wealth and Asset Ownership for Households, by Type of Asset and Selected Characteristics: 2016 tbl. 2 (2016).

101. Charles C. Marvel, Annotation, Pension or Retirement Benefits as Subject to Award Division by Court in Settlement of Property Rights Between Spouses, 94 A.L.R.3d 176 § 2[a] (1979) (current through 2020). Disability retirement pay also may be subject to equitable distribution. See, e.g., Poullard v. Poullard, 780 So. 2d 498 (La. Ct. App. 2001); Asgari v. Asgari, 533 S.E.2d 643 (Va. Ct. App. 2000).

102. See, e.g., Everson v. Everson, 537 P.2d 624 (Ariz. Ct. App. 1975); Tucker v. Tucker, 298 A.2d 91 (N.J. Super. Ct. 1972).

103. Marvel, supra note 101, § 2[a].

2.   *How and When to Divide Pensions.* Even as pensions are treated as clearly divisible, the process of dividing is often complicated and states handle it differently. The first question is timing: should the pension benefits be shared only when both spouses have reached retirement age? One possibility is to "share" benefits through an immediate offset award that gives the non-employee spouse a piece of property equivalent in value to his or her share of the employee's pension.[104] This has the advantage of giving the spouses a clean break without the prospect of fighting over issues that may not arise until decades in the future. The difficulty with the present offset approach is valuation. Depending on the type of pension (discussed in more detail below), it may be more or less difficult and speculative to assign a net present value to the benefit in order to determine the non-employee spouse's share. A second possibility is for the court to determine the percentage of the pension due the non-employee spouse, but then reserve jurisdiction until the employee spouse reaches retirement age, at which point the court can order compensation of the non-employee spouse with more concrete information about available pension funds.[105] A third possibility is to determine the appropriate share for the non-employee spouse during the divorce proceeding but to defer distribution until the employee reaches retirement age. As explained in the next note, this requires compliance with federal law in many situations, but can be the easiest and fairest way to divide a pension.

3.   *Pension-Sharing, Retirement, and Federal Law.* Although most marital property questions are left to state legislatures and courts, federal law plays an important role. The Employment Retirement Income Security Act (ERISA), which was enacted in 1974, imposes a variety of requirements on pensions designed to ensure the benefits are available to support workers after they retire.[106] ERISA contains an anti-alienation and anti-assignment provision that, in its original form, was interpreted by some courts to preempt state marital and community property laws. Given that ERISA expressly preempts state law, courts reasonably concluded that ERISA-regulated pensions could not be divided upon divorce.[107] Congress changed this through the Retirement Equity Act of 1984, in which it created an exception for the division of pension assets upon

---

104. See, e.g., Berrington v. Berrington, 598 A.2d 31, 35 (Pa. Super. Ct. 1991).

105. See, e.g., In re Marriage of Richardson, 884 N.E.2d 1246, 1252–53 (Ill. App. Ct. 2008) ("[This] approach is used in cases where it is difficult to place a present value on a pension due to uncertainties regarding vesting or maturation or when the present value can be ascertained but lack of marital property makes an offset impractical or impossible.").

106. Employee Retirement Income Security Act of 1974, Pub. L. No. 93-406, 88 Stat. 832 (codified as amended at 29 U.S.C. §§ 1001-1461 (2018)).

107. Compare, e.g., Francis v. United Technol. Corp., 458 F. Supp. 84, 85–86 (N.D. Cal. 1978) (concluding that ERISA preempted California's community property law to the extent it authorized awarding a share of employee's pension to non-employee spouse), with AT&T Co. v. Merry, 592 F.2d 119 (2d Cir. 1979) (finding implied exception to ERISA's anti-assignment provision to permit enforcement of state alimony award). See also 29 U.S.C. § 1144(a) (2018) (the law preempts "any and all State laws insofar as they . . . relate to any employee benefit plan").

divorce through a "qualified domestic relations order" (QDRO).[108] This type of order can be used to facilitate property-sharing (equitable distribution or community property rights), spousal support, or child support. A QDRO must be issued by a court (a marital or separation agreement is not sufficient), and it allows a pension administrator to pay an "alternate payee" instead of the wage earner. QDROs can facilitate property-sharing in different ways. One method is called "shared payment," in which the administrator is ordered to pay the ex-spouse (or noncustodial parent) a percentage (or a fixed dollar amount) of each payment to the wage earner. Another method is called "separate interest" and it separates out the interests of the wage earner and the alternate payee such that each may elect from the different payment structures that are otherwise available under the pension agreement.

The specifics of a QDRO will vary based on the type of pension, among other variables. In "defined benefit" plans, the wage earner is entitled to a particular dollar amount every month based on years of service, salary level, age, or other factors. Defined benefit pensions often do not vest until a certain number of years of service have been completed. In "defined contribution" plans, the wage earner makes contributions to an individual account, and the employer may or may not also make contributions to the account. A 401(k) is the most common type of defined contribution pension, but simplified employee pension plans (SEP) and employee stock ownership plans (ESOP) also qualify. Under ERISA, every dollar contributed by the employee to a defined contribution account and interest earned on that money is immediately vested, while employer contributions can have delayed vesting.[109] Defined contribution plans can present complicated valuation questions, particularly if any portion of the account was earned before marriage or after divorce and the distribution will not occur until the wage earner's retirement. States use one of two methods to determine the ex-spouse's share. With the coverture fraction, the ex-spouse's percentage share is multiplied by the number of months the wage earner worked for the employer while married divided by the number of total months worked. An alternative "accrual of benefits" method subtracts the value of the account at the end of the marriage from the value at the wage earner's retirement to determine the dollar amount that is divisible.

Federal employment pensions are not governed by ERISA. The Supreme Court ruled in separate cases that the pension rules governing railroad employees and

---

108. 29 U.S.C. § 1056(d)(3)(B) (2018).

109. See generally U.S. Dep't of Labor, FAQs about Retirement Plans and ERISA, https://www.dol.gov/sites/dolgov/files/EBSA/about-ebsa/our-activities/resource-center/faqs/retirement-plans-and-erisa-compliance.pdf. ERISA permits employers that make contributions to a defined contribution plan to use either "cliff vesting," which means all employer contributions vest after three years of service, or "graduated vesting," which means 20% vests after 2 years, 40% after 3 years, 60% after four years, 80% after five years, and 100% after six years. For a defined benefit plan, employers must provide cliff vesting after five years or graduated vesting, with 20% vesting from years three through seven.

military personnel broadly preempted state law and did not permit judges to award a share to the non-employee spouse under state law rules of marital or community property.[110] In response, Congress enacted new statutes to permit exempt retirement benefits under both systems from the preemption rules and thus to permit state courts to divide them in divorce proceedings. Under the Uniformed Services Former Spouses Protection Act, a military pension can be divided as long as the court has personal jurisdiction over the servicemember.[111] Railroad retirement benefits can be shared as long as certain conditions are met, including that the non-employee spouse was married to the employee for at least ten years.[112] Benefits under the more general Federal Employees' Retirement System are also divisible pursuant to a divorce decree.[113]

Social Security benefits provide another important source of support during retirement. With those benefits, 9.5 percent of seniors live in poverty; without them, nearly 40 percent would qualify as poor.[114] Moreover, Social Security payments comprise more than half of the income for 50 percent of seniors, while they provide 90 percent of the income for almost a quarter of them.[115] These benefits, however, are not divisible in divorce proceedings under the anti-alienation provision of the Social Security Act.[116] Many courts have considered whether Social Security benefits can nonetheless be considered when dividing other assets. Most have concluded that courts cannot order a direct offset (i.e., property of equivalent value given to the spouse without the benefits), but some permit consideration as one factor in the overall assessment of equity. In Marriage of Zahm, for example, the Washington Supreme Court held that the anti-assignment clause of the Social Security Act did not prevent the court from taking that income into account "within the more elastic parameters of the court's power to formulate a just and equitable division of the parties' marital property."[117] The Social Security Act provides some protection for ex-spouses, as long as the marriage lasted at least ten years, which is discussed at greater length in Chapter 11.[118]

---

110. See Hisquierdo v. Hisquierdo, 439 U.S. 572 (1979) (holding that Railroad Retirement Act benefits are not community property subject to division); McCarty v. McCarty, 453 U.S. 210 (1981) (holding that military nondisability retirement benefits are not community property subject to division). In Howell v. Howell, the Supreme Court refused to allow a state court to indemnify an ex-spouse for the loss in benefits caused by the servicemember's decision to waive a portion of retirement pay in favor of disability pay. 137 S. Ct. 1400, 1402 (2017).

111. 10 U.S.C. § 1408(c)(4) (2018).

112. 45 U.S.C. § 231a(c)(4) (2018).

113. 5 U.S.C. § 8445 (2018).

114. Ctr. Budget & Pol'y Priorities, Top Ten Facts About Social Security (Aug. 14, 2019), https://www.cbpp.org/research/policy-basics-top-ten-facts-about-social-security.

115. Id.

116. 42 U.S.C. § 407 (2018).

117. 978 P.2d 498, 502 (Wash. 1999). But see Webster v. Webster, 716 N.W.2d 47, 54–56 (Neb. 2006).

118. See 20 C.F.R. § 404.331 (2020).

Federal law also protects spouses from the sudden loss of health insurance because of divorce. The Consolidated Omnibus Budget Reconciliation Act (COBRA), enacted in 1985, added a provision to ERISA to permit a non-employee spouse to continue participating in an employer-based group health insurance plan for 36 months after divorce or separation.[119] Because the non-employee spouse must pay the full cost of the premiums, this is not always a feasible option. The increased availability of individual health insurance under the Affordable Care Act has diminished the importance of COBRA protection for divorced spouses.

4.   *Income or Property?* Whether a retirement benefit under a deferred compensation plan is property or income affects whether the court equitably distributes it, or instead merely considers it in relation to spousal support. Consider the reasoning of the New Hampshire Supreme Court in Matter of Cohen:[120]

> In 1996, [employer] and the petitioner entered into a "Deferred Compensation Agreement," by which the petitioner will receive a "retirement benefit" or, alternatively, a "death benefit," upon meeting certain conditions. Pursuant to this agreement, the petitioner became eligible to receive deferred compensation payments of $100,000 a year, in the form of monthly payments, for a period of ten years upon reaching his 21st employment anniversary with [employer] in 2015. However, these payments are conditioned upon the petitioner's continued employment by [employer] until his age of retirement, which is defined as the first day of the month following the petitioner's 65th birthday. Alternatively, if the petitioner dies before he reaches retirement age, his named beneficiary will receive the 10-year payment of $100,000 on a monthly basis or in a lump sum. . . .
>
> Under RSA 458:16-a, I, intangible marital property "includes, but is not limited to, employment benefits, vested and non-vested pension or other retirement benefits, or savings plans." Based upon this broad statutory language, we have previously adopted the "mechanistic approach" to determine whether an item constitutes marital property. Under this approach, property subject to equitable distribution includes any property acquired before the decree of legal separation or divorce. Thus, "future earnings of a spouse from employment are not considered to be property at the time of the divorce."
>
> On this basis, the petitioner argues that the trial court correctly considered payments under both agreements as income because the petitioner did not acquire the payments or meet the conditions that would entitle him to the payments prior to the divorce. Therefore, the petitioner asserts that these payments were a mere "expectancy" at the time of the divorce, and, accordingly, "represent future income" that will be "paid in exchange for future services." . . .

---

119. 29 U.S.C. §§ 1161-1168 (2018).
120. 207 A.3d 729, 734–39 (N.H. 2019).

By including "non-vested pension or other retirement benefits," the statute demonstrates that, at the time of the divorce, a spouse need not acquire either a right to or a specified interest in, a pension or retirement benefit itself, or the eligibility to receive the benefit, for it to constitute marital property subject to equitable division. Rather, the spouse need only have acquired a sufficient interest in receiving the retirement benefit at the time of the divorce based upon the express terms of the benefit plan. . . .

The "retirement benefit" under the deferred compensation agreement here contractually binds [employer] to commence monthly payments of the benefit once the petitioner attained his 21st employment anniversary, provided he remains in [employer]'s employ as of his retirement. . . . [W]e see no relevant distinction between the conditional status of the retirement benefit required by the deferred compensation agreement and the conditional status of a non-vested pension or other retirement benefit enumerated within RSA 458:16-a, I. Accordingly, we conclude that the benefit provided by the petitioner's deferred compensation plan is similar in nature to a non-vested pension benefit and therefore constitutes intangible marital property subject to equitable distribution. . . .

5. *Disability Insurance Benefits.* Parties may seek distribution of disability benefits, which courts generally treat as marital property. Notice the distinction between retirement and disability benefits drawn by West Virginia's high court in Conrad v. Conrad:

This Court is presented with the question of whether long term disability benefits based upon the disability of one spouse are separate or marital property. The lower court ruled that such benefits should be treated as separate property belonging to the disabled spouse. As Mrs. Conrad emphasizes in the case sub judice, however, the premiums to purchase such policy, in the amount of $40.00 monthly for almost thirty years, were paid from marital funds. Mrs. Conrad therefore contends that the benefits derived from such purchase should be shared equally by the divorcing spouses. . . .

Many states have held that disability benefits are to be considered marital property unless a statutory provision specifically excludes such benefits from the marital estate. . . .

The majority of courts contemplating the proper classification of disability benefits have adopted an approach which focuses on the underlying purpose of the specific disability benefits at issue. Thus, benefits which actually compensate for disability are classified as separate property because they are personal to the spouse who receives them. However, where justified by the particular facts of the case, courts adopting this approach have separated the benefits into a retirement component and a true disability component, classifying the retirement component as marital property and the disability component as separate property. . . .

While we refrain from stating a definite rule to be applied in all disability policy questions in divorce cases, we find that the circumstances of the present case indicate that treatment of the disability benefits as marital property most accurately reflects the intent of the parties at the time the disability policy was purchased. The evidence indicated that the parties discussed the issue of disability benefits and decided that marital funds of $40.00 per month for almost thirty years should be invested to secure their future. Furthermore, the disability benefits payable in this case are the major source of funds available to the parties. . . .

The present value of such disability benefits should have been determined as of the date of the parties' separation, and that value should have been divided equally between the parties.[121]

2. Professional Licenses, Degrees, and Enhanced Earning Capacity

Courts have followed a variety of approaches in determining how to treat professional licenses or degrees. For decades, New York was alone in permitting the value of an educational degree acquired during a marriage to be equitably distributed. The state's highest court ruled in O'Brien v. O'Brien that the medical license a husband acquired during marriage was a marital asset subject to equitable distribution.[122] How would a court value the license? Is the determination simply too speculative?[123] Thirty years after O'Brien, the legislature passed a statute to overrule the decision. The law now instructs courts not to treat a "license, degree, celebrity goodwill, or career enhancement" as marital property, but it allows the court to "consider the direct or indirect contributions to the development during the marriage of the enhanced earning capacity of the other spouse."[124]

Some courts, like those in New York, may indirectly treat the degree as marital property by permitting the division of the enhanced earning capacity that comes from a degree or license if the other spouse made substantial contributions to its acquisition.[125] Courts might also consider an equitable claim to be compensated, as a form of reimbursement or restitution, for the contributions to the acquisition of a degree or enhanced earning capacity. For instance, in Postema v. Postema, while the appellate court rejected dividing up an advanced degree, the court observed that "*fairness* dictates that a spouse who did not earn an advanced degree be compensated

---

121. 612 S.E.2d 772, 775–77 (W. Va. 2005).

122. 489 N.E.2d 712 (N.Y. 1985).

123. See Berger v. Berger, 747 N.W.2d 336, 350 (Mich. Ct. App. 2008).

124. N.Y. Dom. Rel. Law § 236 (McKinney 2020).

125. See, e.g., Belilos v. Rivera, 84 N.Y.S.3d 536 (N.Y. App. Div. 2018) (awarding share of enhanced earning capacity where non-degree holding spouse demonstrated substantial contribution to acquisition).

whenever the advanced degree is the end product of a *concerted family effort* involving mutual sacrifice and effort by both spouses."[126] This concerted family effort will not necessarily be assumed. In determining whether an equitable claim existed regarding a college degree and a master of fine arts degree, the court in Berger v. Berger observed "that the plaintiff pursued her dancing education to fulfill her dreams but simultaneously maintained her role as primary caregiver to the children and secondary financial supporter of the family."[127] Further, the court concluded that "[a]t best, defendant tolerated plaintiff's educational pursuits; he did not sacrifice his own business or employment opportunities to support plaintiff's education."[128] Even if degrees are not treated directly as property subject to distribution, the income they produce may serve as a basis for a higher spousal support award.

Despite the attention often devoted to this topic, the majority of states do not treat professional licenses, degrees, or enhanced earning capacity as property subject to distribution.[129] The degree or license — and the earning capacity that derives from it — belong to the spouse to whom it was awarded. Do you agree with this approach?

3. Damages Awards

Damages awards from personal injury claims are treated differently across jurisdictions for purposes of property distribution. A majority of courts follow an "analytic" approach to "classifying a settlement or recovery for a spouse's personal injury claim that accrued during the marriage as marital property or the separate property of the injured spouse. Such an approach requires an examination of the components of the settlement or recovery to determine the purpose of each component."[130] In examining each component, this approach looks to whether it is "compensation for loss experienced by the marriage or loss experienced by the individual and classifies each component of the award as marital or separate property accordingly."[131] If the payment compensates for earnings, which would have belonged to the marriage, then they can be divided upon divorce.

For instance, the Georgia Supreme Court described its rationale as follows: "The property which we have found to be outside the marital estate is property which is very personal to the party to whom it belongs and property which was in no sense

---

126. 471 N.W.2d 912, 915 (Mich. Ct. App. 1991).

127. *Berger*, 747 N.W.2d at 350.

128. Id.

129. See, e.g., Joachim v. Joachim, 942 So. 2d 3 (Fla. Dist. Ct. App. 2006); Wilson v. Wilson, 741 S.W.2d 640 (Ark. 1987); Nelson v. Nelson, 736 P.2d 1145 (Alaska 1987).

130. Kurtis A. Kemper, Divorce and Separation: Determination of Whether Proceeds from Personal Injury Settlement or Recovery Constitute Marital Property, 109 A.L.R. 5th 1 (2003).

131. Amanda Wine, Comment, Treatment of Personal Injury Awards During Dissolution of Marriage, 20 J. Am. Acad. Matrim. L. 155, 155–56 (2006); see Newborn v. Newborn, 754 A.2d 476 (Md. Ct. Spec. App. 2000); Haupt v. Haupt, C9-95-583, 1995 WL 479614 (Minn. Ct. App. Aug. 15, 1995).

generated by the marriage."[132] In parsing the components of the personal injury award at issue before it, the court described the "compensation for pain and suffering and loss of capacity" as "peculiarly personal to the party who receives it."[133] In that light, "[f]or the other party to benefit from the misfortune of the injured party would be unfair. However, to the extent that the settlement amount represents compensation for medical expenses or lost wages during the marriage, the settlement may be considered an asset of the marriage. Any amount which is attributable to loss of consortium is not an asset of the marriage but is the estate of the spouse who suffered the loss of consortium.[134]

In contrast, "[a] minority of jurisdictions, . . . still apply the mechanistic approach that classifies personal injury awards as entirely marital property because they are not included in the statutory definition of separate property."[135] Rarely, courts use a "unitary approach" that treats personal injury awards as entirely separate property.[136]

4. Debts

Courts also face the question of how to treat debt as part of property division in divorce. The average debt of a married couple household in 2015 was $145,400.[137] In most states, marital debt is any debt incurred during the marriage for the parties' joint benefit.[138]

FITZGERALD V. FITZGERALD

914 So. 2d 193 (Miss. Ct. App. 2005)

GRIFFIS, J., for the Court.

Phyllis [Fitzgerald] argues the chancellor failed to equitably divide the assets and debts of the parties' marriage. . . .

Once a determination of marital and non-marital property is made, the chancellor must equitably divide all marital property pursuant to the guidelines listed in Ferguson v. Ferguson, 639 So. 2d 921, 928 (Miss. 1994). . . .

---

132. Campbell v. Campbell, 339 S.E.2d 591, 593 (Ga. 1986).

133. Id.

134. Id.

135. Wine, supra note 131, at 156.

136. Turner, supra note 27, § 6:57.

137. U.S. Census Bureau, Wealth, Asset Ownership, & Debt of Households Detailed Tables: 2015 tbl. 4 (2019).

138. Turner, supra note 27, § 6:97. The minority approach will treat as "[m]arital liabilities" all debts "acquired and incurred by a husband and wife during their marriage." In re Marriage of Jorgenson, 143 P.3d 1169, 1172 (Colo. App. 2006); see also Leis v. Hustad, 22 P.3d 885 (Alaska 2001).

Phyllis . . . argues the chancellor failed to consider the $64,274 the parties borrowed to pay off a pre-marital debt owed by Michael [Fitzgerald]. Michael testified that he and his first wife owed $100,000 in back income taxes to the IRS due to a failed business venture. He further stated that he and Phyllis borrowed $64,274 from People's Bank in order to satisfy this IRS debt. Phyllis asserts that the chancellor erred in failing to classify the $64,274 as a non-marital debt. We agree.

Although the $64,274 was borrowed while the Fitzgerald's [sic] were married, not all debts incurred during a marriage are marital debts. Whether a debt is classified as marital or separate depends on who benefitted from the debt. The $64,274 was used to pay off a debt incurred by Michael before he was married to Phyllis. Phyllis did not benefit from the loan and thus the $64,274 debt should have been classified as non-marital.

In the property distribution, the chancellor failed to classify the $64,274 as a non-marital debt. Instead, he allocated this debt to Phyllis who had no interest in either the failed business venture which led to the debt or the debt itself. As a result of allocating this debt to Phyllis, Michael was unjustly enriched as he had a non-marital debt reduced with the use of marital funds. Upon review, we find the chancellor erred in his distribution of marital assets and debts. Therefore, we reverse and remand for the chancellor to further consider the proper equitable division of the parties' property. . . .

GILLIAM V. MCGRADY
691 S.E.2d 797 (Va. 2010)

SENIOR JUSTICE CHARLES S. RUSSELL . . .

Facts and Proceedings

Louise B. Gilliam (wife) and Arthur L. McGrady (husband) were married in 1990 and separated in 2005. Both were employed when they married, but the husband lost his job in 1999 and, with his wife's agreement, decided to open his own business as a painting contractor. In 2000, he formed Premier Painting, LLC, which he operated until 2004. The husband was solely responsible for the operation of the business and had the sole authority to sign checks. He refused to discuss business affairs with his wife, telling her that she had no business sense.

In the first year of Premier Painting's operation, the wife became aware that the husband owed the Internal Revenue Service unpaid payroll taxes. She told him repeatedly that he must pay the taxes, but he responded that he could not afford to pay them and that she had no business sense. Although the wife raised this question with him at least monthly, the taxes remained unpaid.

The husband decided to close Premier Painting in 2004. During the years of its operation, the business produced net revenue of approximately $214,000. From this revenue, the husband transferred approximately $53,350 to the wife's checking account to be used for household expenses. The husband testified that he had also paid some household expenses directly from his business account.

Both parties were aware that they were living beyond their means and each considered the primary cause of their financial problem to be unnecessary expenses incurred by the other party. By October 2006, the husband owed the IRS $118,287.69 in unpaid trust fund taxes, penalties and interest. . . .

In October 2006, the wife filed a complaint for divorce and equitable distribution of the couple's property in the Circuit Court of Albemarle County, based on a one-year separation. At the trial, the principal issue was the wife's liability, if any, for the unpaid trust fund taxes, including penalties and interest, incurred by Premier Painting during its years of operation. The circuit court ruled that although there was no specific evidence of where the money saved from non-payment of the trust fund taxes went, the court found that both parties had benefited from the non-payment, and that the wife had the burden of showing how and why the debt was incurred and the "purpose of the expenditure [of the proceeds] of the debt." The court ruled that the trust fund taxes, including penalties and interest, were marital debt.[4]

The wife appealed. . . . A panel of the Court of Appeals, in a unanimous published opinion, held that the circuit court did not err in placing the burden of proof on the wife, further ruling that debt should be treated like property, subject to a statutory presumption that it is marital unless one party carries the burden of proving that the debt is separate. . . .

[T]he Court of Appeals . . . reversed the case in part, holding that the circuit court had erred in failing to properly consider the statutory factors required to classify the trust fund tax debt. The Court remanded the case to the circuit court "to consider the purpose of the trust fund tax debt, as well as who benefited from it, in order to classify that debt as marital or separate. . . ." We awarded the wife an appeal.

Analysis

The wife assigns no error to that part of the opinion of the Court of Appeals that reverses the circuit court's judgment for failure to give proper consideration to the statutory factors required to classify the debt. We agree with the reasoning of the Court of Appeals explaining that ruling and, for the reasons stated in the opinion of the Court of Appeals, we will affirm that part of its order remanding the case to the circuit court for proper consideration of those factors. Accordingly, we will confine our consideration to the questions of presumptions and burden of proof. . . .

---

4. Because the wife had made efforts to secure payment of the trust fund taxes as early as 2001, the court ordered the husband to pay 65% of the penalties and interest due; the wife to pay 35%. The principal amount of the taxes due was to be divided equally between the parties.

The equitable distribution statute, Code § 20-107.3, provides for the classification, in matrimonial causes, of assets and debts differently. Code § 20-107.3(A) empowers the circuit courts to determine the legal title to property between spouses, to determine its ownership and value, and to classify property as marital or separate property in accordance with the detailed rules set forth in subsection (A)(3) of that statute. Subsection (A)(2) of the statute expressly creates a presumption that all property acquired by either spouse during marriage is marital property and places the burden of proving otherwise on the party claiming that it is separate property.

There is a marked contrast between that treatment of assets and the legislative prescription, in the same statute, for the apportionment of debts in an equitable distribution proceeding. Code § 20-107.3(C) provides in pertinent part:

> The court shall also have the authority to apportion and order the payment of the debts of the parties, or either of them, that are incurred prior to the dissolution of the marriage, based upon the factors listed in subsection E.

Subsection (E) provides, in pertinent part:

> [T]he apportionment of marital debts, and the method of payment shall be determined by the court after consideration of the following factors: . . .
>   7. The debts and liabilities of each spouse, the basis for such debts and liabilities, and the property which may serve as security for such debts and liabilities; . . .
>   11. Such other factors as the court deems necessary or appropriate to consider in order to arrive at a fair and equitable monetary award.

The equitable distribution statute contains no provisions creating a presumption or allocating a burden of proof with regard to the apportionment of debts between spouses. . . .

We conclude that no presumption exists with respect to the classification of debts incurred by spouses during marriage, individually or jointly. . . . In making its decision, the court will be guided by the factors set forth in Code § 20-107.3(E) "in order to arrive at a fair and equitable monetary award."

Conclusion

Because the circuit court and the Court of Appeals erred by applying a presumption that the debt to the IRS individually incurred by the husband for unpaid trust fund taxes was a marital debt and in placing the burden on the wife to prove otherwise, we will reverse the judgment of the Court of Appeals to that extent. We will affirm the judgment of the Court of Appeals insofar as it reversed the circuit court's decision for its failure to properly consider the statutory factors for classifying and apportioning the debt. We will remand the case to the Court of Appeals with direction to remand the same to the circuit court for further proceedings consistent with this opinion.

NOTES AND QUESTIONS

---

1.   *Debt as Marital Property.* According to the U.S. Census Bureau, debt is common among married couples in the United States.[139] Fifty-two percent of married couples have home debt, 44.8 percent have vehicle debt, 49.5 percent have credit card debt, and 22 percent have student loans.[140] Notice how the court in *Fitzgerald* uses the concept of "benefit" to determine whether a debt is marital or not. Does this approach capture rationales underlying the concept of marital property? How does this analysis contrast with the court's approach in *Gilliam*? Which approach better vindicates the objectives of equitable distribution?

2.   *Educational Debt.* Whether the benefit of educational debt has been felt by the married couple matters for purposes of determining whether the debt is marital or separate property. "The educational component of a student loan is a debt incurred for the purpose of increasing the student spouse's future earning capacity. Where the parties enjoyed the student spouse's increased earnings for a significant period of time after graduation, the educational component is clearly a marital debt."[141] This may be the case even when the loans were incurred prior to marriage. For instance, in Osdoba v. Kelley-Osdoba, the South Dakota Supreme Court held that a trial court did not err in treating the wife's premarital student loans as a marital debt, where parties deliberately decided to refrain from repaying loans in order to spend the wife's income for other purposes.[142]

3.   *Medical Debt.* Generally, debts incurred to pay medical expenses are considered marital property if the event causing the medical services occurred during the marriage.[143] In Miner v. Miner, the appellate court instructed the trial court to determine when the injury causing expenses occurred. If the cause for medical expenses occurred during the time the parties lived together and expenses actually became due before the divorce petition was filed, the fact that the expenses were not incurred until

---

139. U.S. Census Bureau, Wealth, Asset Ownership, & Debt of Households Detailed Tables: 2016 debt tbl. 2 (2019).

140. Id.

141. Turner, supra note 27, § 6:9.

142. 913 N.W.2d 496 (S.D. 2018). Where spouse has an increased earning capacity, student loan debt is treated as marital property even if incurred prior to the marriage. See, e.g., McLaren v. McLaren, 665 N.W.2d 405 (Wis. Ct. App. 2003). Some courts, however, will consider when the loan was incurred. See, e.g., Fox v. Fox, 44 A.D.3d 998, 1000 (N.Y. App. Div. 2007) (finding error in allocating half of husband's student loan to wife, "as the plaintiff earned his medical license prior to the marriage").

143. Turner, supra note 27, § 6:97.

after separation would not justify finding that such expenses were not marital obligations subject to distribution upon divorce.[144]

II. Spousal Support

A. The Modernization of Divorce Law

Historically, marriage in the United States and England was envisioned as a life-long contract, governed by men's primacy through coverture, and women's civil invisibility and economic dependency. In this context, wives were to obey and serve their husbands and were legally entitled to life-long economic support from their husbands. Prior to the advent of full divorce, husbands' economic obligations to their wives continued even if the wife was granted a divorce from bed and board. The husband would maintain control of the property and the wife would remain economically dependent even after the couple was given the right to live separate and apart.

Once full divorce through the judicial process became available, the fault-based system preserved the old arrangement. Husbands were obligated to support their wives during marriage, and that obligation continued after divorce, provided that the court deemed the wife the innocent and injured party and the husband the wrongdoer. If the wife was adjudged at fault in the divorce, she would forfeit her entitlement to continued support.[145] This system was replete with blame, moral judgment, and sex discrimination. It assigned men and women to distinct roles based on misguided assumptions and beliefs about inherent or essential sex-based characteristics.

But as we have seen, no-fault divorce dramatically changed divorce practices over the latter third of the twentieth century. Shifts in the legal, social, and economic status of women also altered the meaning of marriage and divorce. Courts rejected the view that the husband is the master of the home and that the wife is inevitably and inherently dependent. Women's participation in higher education and the paid workforce grew dramatically. A more gender-egalitarian understanding of marriage emerged, in which both husbands and wives enjoy financial rights and assume financial obligations.

These changes have shaped approaches to spousal support. As divorce law modernized, property division became favored over spousal support as the mechanism for settling financial affairs between divorcing parties. That approach would give

---

144. 727 So. 2d 1080 (Fla. Dist. Ct. App. 1999).
145. See Chester G. Vernier, 2 American Family Laws 261 (1936) (all but seven states barred at-fault wives from receiving alimony).

couples a clean break as they moved to the next phase of their lives. Still, the law of every state in the nation allows a court to award spousal support upon divorce, at least in some circumstances. Yet, with the demise of the old view that gender roles dictate the husband's obligation to support and the wife's need for support, there is no consensus as to the contemporary justification for spousal support. If both spouses are expected to work and earn their own income after divorce, and if the couple's property is to be divided fairly between them, why, precisely, should the law grant anyone a claim on the future income of their former spouse?

This question pervades the following cases and materials, which explore a mix of rationales for spousal support — some old, some new.

ORR V. ORR
440 U.S. 268 (1979)

MR. JUSTICE BRENNAN delivered the opinion of the Court.

The question presented is the constitutionality of Alabama alimony statutes which provide that husbands, but not wives, may be required to pay alimony upon divorce.

On February 26, 1974, a final decree of divorce was entered, dissolving the marriage of William and Lillian Orr. That decree directed appellant, Mr. Orr, to pay appellee, Mrs. Orr, $1,240 per month in alimony. . . .

In authorizing the imposition of alimony obligations on husbands, but not on wives, the Alabama statutory scheme "provides that different treatment be accorded . . . on the basis of . . . sex; it thus establishes a classification subject to scrutiny under the Equal Protection Clause," Reed v. Reed, 404 U.S. 71 (1971). The fact that the classification expressly discriminates against men rather than women does not protect it from scrutiny. Craig v. Boren, 429 U.S. 190 (1976). "To withstand scrutiny" under the Equal Protection Clause, 'classifications by gender must serve important governmental objectives and must be substantially related to achievement of those objectives.' Califano v. Webster, 430 U.S. 313 (1977). We shall, therefore, examine the three governmental objectives that might arguably be served by Alabama's statutory scheme.

Appellant views the Alabama alimony statutes as effectively announcing the State's preference for an allocation of family responsibilities under which the wife plays a dependent role, and as seeking for their objective the reinforcement of that model among the State's citizens. We agree, as he urges, that prior cases settle that this purpose cannot sustain the statutes. Stanton v. Stanton, 421 U.S. 7 (1975), held that the "old notio[n]" that "generally it is the man's primary responsibility to provide a home and its essentials," can no longer justify a statute that discriminates on the basis of gender. "No longer is the female destined solely for the home and the rearing of the family, and only the male for the marketplace and the world of ideas."

If the statute is to survive constitutional attack, therefore, it must be validated on some other basis.

The opinion of the Alabama Court of Civil Appeals suggests other purposes that the statute may serve. Its opinion states that the Alabama statutes were "designed" for "the wife of a broken marriage who needs financial assistance." This may be read as asserting either of two legislative objectives. One is a legislative purpose to provide help for needy spouses, using sex as a proxy for need. The other is a goal of compensating women for past discrimination during marriage, which assertedly has left them unprepared to fend for themselves in the working world following divorce. We concede, of course, that assisting needy spouses is a legitimate and important governmental objective. We have also recognized "[r]eduction of the disparity in economic condition between men and women caused by the long history of discrimination against women . . . as . . . an important governmental objective," Califano v. Webster. It only remains, therefore, to determine whether the classification at issue here is "substantially related to achievement of those objectives."

Ordinarily, we would begin the analysis of the "needy spouse" objective by considering whether sex is a sufficiently "accurate proxy," Craig v. Boren, for dependency to establish that the gender classification rests 'upon some ground of difference having a fair and substantial relation to the object of the legislation,' Reed v. Reed. Similarly, we would initially approach the "compensation" rationale by asking whether women had in fact been significantly discriminated against in the sphere to which the statute applied a sex-based classification, leaving the sexes "*not* similarly situated with respect to opportunities" in that sphere.

But in this case, even if sex were a reliable proxy for need, and even if the institution of marriage did discriminate against women, these factors still would "not adequately justify the salient features of" Alabama's statutory scheme, Craig v. Boren. Under the statute, individualized hearings at which the parties' relative financial circumstances are considered already occur. There is no reason, therefore, to use sex as a proxy for need. Needy males could be helped along with needy females with little if any additional burden on the State. In such circumstances, not even an administrative-convenience rationale exists to justify operating by generalization or proxy. Similarly, since individualized hearings can determine which women were in fact discriminated against vis-à-vis their husbands, as well as which family units defied the stereotype and left the husband dependent on the wife, Alabama's alleged compensatory purpose may be effectuated without placing burdens solely on husbands. Progress toward fulfilling such a purpose would not be hampered, and it would cost the State nothing more, if it were to treat men and women equally by making alimony burdens independent of sex. "Thus, the gender-based distinction is gratuitous; without it, the statutory scheme would only provide benefits to those men who are in fact similarly situated to the women the statute aids," and the effort to help those women would not in any way be compromised.

Moreover, use of a gender classification actually produces perverse results in this case. As compared to a gender-neutral law placing alimony obligations on the spouse able to pay, the present Alabama statutes give an advantage only to the financially secure wife whose husband is in need. Although such a wife might have to pay alimony under a gender-neutral statute, the present statutes exempt her from that obligation. Thus, "[t]he [wives] who benefit from the disparate treatment are those who were . . . nondependent on their husbands." They are precisely those who are not "needy spouses" and who are "least likely to have been victims of . . . discrimination," by the institution of marriage. A gender-based classification which, as compared to a gender-neutral one, generates additional benefits only for those it has no reason to prefer cannot survive equal protection scrutiny.

Legislative classifications which distribute benefits and burdens on the basis of gender carry the inherent risk of reinforcing stereotypes about the "proper place" of women and their need for special protection. Thus, even statutes purportedly designed to compensate for and ameliorate the effects of past discrimination must be carefully tailored. Where, as here, the State's compensatory and ameliorative purposes are as well served by a gender-neutral classification as one that gender classifies and therefore carries with it the baggage of sexual stereotypes, the State cannot be permitted to classify on the basis of sex. And this is doubly so where the choice made by the State appears to redound — if only indirectly — to the benefit of those without need for special solicitude. . . .

Reversed and remanded.

NOTES AND QUESTIONS

1. *Sex Classification.* The *Orr* decision was part of the Supreme Court's repudiation of sex discrimination. In Reed v. Reed, the first decision to invalidate a sex-based classification on constitutional grounds, the Supreme Court ruled that state law could not prefer men over women as administrators of estates.[146] A number of subsequent cases over the next few decades struck down federal and state laws that discriminated based on sex.[147]

2. *Women's Rights?* While *Orr* was one of many that invalidated sex-based classifications, it is noteworthy that the claim was filed by a man, who alleged that the system was unfair to him. Should we think of *Orr*, then, as vindicating the rights of men? Or does the Court's decision promote equality for women?[148]

---

146. 404 U.S. 71 (1971).

147. For discussion of constitutional change concerning sex equality, see Chapter 3.

148. For a discussion of litigation strategy, see Ruth Bader Ginsburg, Sexual Equality Under the Fourteenth and Equal Rights Amendments, 1979 Wash. U. L. Rev. 161; see also Cary Franklin, The Anti-Stereotyping Principle in Constitutional Sex Discrimination Law, 85 N.Y.U. L. Rev. 83 (2010).

3. *What Remedy?* States could have complied with the Court's decision in *Orr* by eliminating alimony. Instead, every jurisdiction continued to allow for alimony, making it available to men as well as women. Today, alimony awards (now also referred to as spousal support or maintenance) are relatively uncommon.[149] Spousal support is much more likely to be paid by men to women, than vice versa. Only 3 percent of roughly 400,000 spousal support recipients are male, according to the 2010 census, an asymmetry that stems, at least in part, from the fact that women are more likely than men to forego paid work and to earn less than men when they do work outside the home.[150]

4. *Determining Spousal Support.* State statutes typically list a wide array of factors that courts must consider in adjudicating claims for spousal support.[151] These factors often include the age, physical condition, financial condition, and earning potential of the parties, the length of the marriage, the standard of living during the marriage, and the contribution of either party as homemaker or to the education or earning potential of the other party.[152] In addition, some statutes direct courts to consider marital misconduct and any history of domestic violence.[153] In providing such a wide array of factors for judges to consider but without any determinate standard or rationale, the statutes accord judges broad discretion to decide cases as they see fit. Indeed, in some states, the relevant statutes identify few if any mandatory considerations and simply empower judges to grant spousal support that is "just or necessary under the circumstances."[154] Spousal support law has thus been criticized as leading to unjustifiably disparate outcomes both across and within jurisdictions.[155]

5. *Support Guidelines.* As a means of constraining judicial discretion so as to make spousal support orders more uniform and predictable, some jurisdictions have created spousal support guidelines.[156] Akin to child support guidelines (which are discussed in detail in Chapter 11), spousal support guidelines entail mathematical formulas to determine the duration and amount of support awards.[157] Statewide guidelines have been adopted in Colorado, Illinois, New York, Pennsylvania,

---

149. J. Thomas Oldham, An Overview of the Rules in the USA Regarding the Award of Post-Divorce Spousal Support in 2019, 41 Hous. J. Int'l L. 525, 529 (2019).

150. See Beth Pinsker, Breadwinning Women Are Driving Alimony Reform, Money (Nov. 17, 2015).

151. Charts, 2017: Family Law in the Fifty States, D.C., and Puerto Rico, 51 Fam. L.Q. 543, 544–47 (2018).

152. See, e.g., Ohio Rev. Code Ann. § 3105.18(C) (2020).

153. See Tex. Fam. Code Ann. § 8.052(10)-(11) (2020); Charts, supra note 151, at 544–47.

154. Jennifer L. McCoy, Spousal Support Disorder: An Overview of Problems in Current Alimony Law, 33 Fla. St. U. L. Rev. 501, 514 n.112 (2005).

155. See, e.g., Marshall S. Willick, A Universal Approach to Alimony: How Alimony Should Be Calculated and Why, 27 J. Am. Acad. Matrim. Law. 153, 160 (2014–15).

156. See, e.g., Twila B. Larkin, Guidelines for Alimony: The New Mexico Experiment, 38 Fam. L.Q. 29, 29 (2004); Virginia R. Dugan & Jon A. Feder, Alimony Guidelines: Do They Work?, 25 Fam. Advoc. 20 (2003).

157. Mary Kay Kisthardt, Re-thinking Alimony: The AAML's Considerations for Calculating Alimony, Spousal Support or Maintenance, 21 J. Am. Acad. Matrim. Law 61, 73 (2008).

Massachusetts, and Vermont.[158] In no jurisdiction are the guideline determinations mandatory. They either create a presumption or constitute a factor that the court must consider.[159] As a result, courts operating with guidelines maintain considerable discretion. Under all the state guidelines, the award amount is determined by a formula that turns on the parties' relative incomes.[160] Guidelines differ as to whether the award amount is influenced by the length of the marriage. In Vermont, for example, the extent of post-divorce income sharing increases as the length of the marriage increases. In Colorado, Illinois, and New York, in contrast, the award amount is unrelated to marital duration.[161] Spousal support guidelines typically link the permissible length of an award to the duration of the marriage.[162] The award duration is a percentage of the marriage's duration, with the percentage increasing with longer-term marriages. For example, under the New York guidelines, for marriages lasting less than 15 years, the award duration should be between 15 percent and 30 percent of the length of the marriage. For marriages between 15 and 20 years, the award may be between 30 percent and 40 percent of the length of the marriage, and for marriages longer than 20 years, the award duration may be between 35 percent and 50 percent of the length of the marriage.[163]

6. *Statutory Restrictions.* Some states have substantially constrained judicial discretion to award spousal support. Texas, for example, has among the most restrictive spousal support laws.[164] Under the Texas statute, a spousal maintenance award is only permitted if the payee spouse lacks the property to support the spouse's "minimum reasonable needs" and can prove at least one of four other circumstances: i) the payor spouse was guilty of domestic violence, ii) the payee spouse cannot earn sufficient income to provide for her minimum reasonable needs due to "an incapacitating physical or mental disability," iii) the marriage lasted longer than 10 years and the payee spouse cannot earn sufficient income to provide for her minimum reasonable needs; or iv) the payee spouse cares for a child of the marriage who has sufficiently severe special needs that the payee spouse cannot earn enough income to meet the spouse's

---

158. Oldham, An Overview of the Rules, supra note 149, at 536.

159. In Pennsylvania and Massachusetts, for example, the guideline amount is presumptive (at least in some cases), but the court may deviate from the guideline amount if the court makes written findings as to why deviation is necessary. See Pa. R. Civ. P. 1910.16-1; Mass. Gen. Laws ch. 208, § 53(e) (2020). In Vermont, the guidelines constitute a factor that the court must consider. Oldham, An Overview of the Rules, supra note 149, at 537.

160. Oldham, supra note 149, at 538.

161. Id. Colo. Rev. Stat. § 140-10-114(3)(b)(I)(A) (2020); 750 Ill. Comp. Stat. Ann. 5/504(b-1)(A) (2020).

162. Oldham, supra note 149, at 538. Colorado, Illinois, and Massachusetts guidelines link duration of spousal support to marriage duration only marriages that last 20 years or less. See Colo. Rev. Stat. § 14-10-114 (2020); 750 Ill. Comp. Stat. 5/504(b-1)(1)(B) (2020); Mass. Gen. Laws ch. 208, § 49 (2020). With marriages that lasted longer than 20 years, spousal support may be indefinite.

163. Oldham, supra note 149, at 538.

164. Tex. Fam. Code Ann. § 8.051 (2020).

minimum reasonable needs.[165] And when spousal support is permissible under Texas law, state statutes cap both the duration and amount of any award.[166] In Indiana, another restrictive state, the court may order spousal support only in one of three specific circumstances: i) the payee spouse is physically or mentally incapacitated and as a result cannot support herself, ii) the payee spouse is the custodian of a child whose special needs require the spouse to forgo employment, and the spouse lacks sufficient property to provide for the spouse's needs, or iii) short term rehabilitative maintenance is necessary.[167]

B. Different Types of Alimony

The following case describes the different types of spousal support and the factors that courts are to consider, including the long-standing rationale of spousal need.

GNALL V. GNALL

119 A.3d 891 (N.J. 2015)

JUSTICE FERNADEZ-VINA delivered the opinion of the Court. . . .

This case stems from a divorce, that ended an almost fifteen-year marriage. Litigation proceedings focused on the amount and type of spousal support plaintiff Elizabeth Gnall would receive from defendant James Gnall. James was the sole wage earner of the family, making over $1,000,000.00 annually, while Elizabeth stayed home to raise their three children. . . .

James and Elizabeth Gnall met in 1985 while they were both pursuing bachelor's degrees at the State University of New York in Buffalo. The couple was engaged eight years later, and married on June 5, 1993. The couple began to experience marital differences in October 2007, and on March 10, 2008, Elizabeth filed a complaint for divorce.

At the time of their marriage, Elizabeth had obtained a bachelor's degree in electrical engineering and a master's degree in computer science. Initially, Elizabeth worked as a computer programmer on the foreign exchange sales desk at Goldman Sachs in New York City. Following that job, Elizabeth worked in a similar position at Banker's Trust through 1999.

James obtained an accounting degree in 1989, and then earned his Certified Public Accountant license. In June 2003, he obtained a job at Deutsche Bank, where

---

165. Id.

166. Tex. Fam. Code Ann. §§ 8.054-55 (West 2020).

167. Ind. Code § 31-15-7-2 (2020); Eads v. Eads, 114 N.E.3d 868 (Ind. Ct. App. 2018).

he is currently employed as Chief Financial Officer of the bank's Finance Division in America.

After the birth of their first child, the Gnalls hired a nanny, and Elizabeth continued to work full-time. However, in 1999, the parties decided it would be best if Elizabeth stopped working in order to remain at home to care for the children full-time.

James and Elizabeth have three children, who, at the time the judgment of divorce was entered, were twelve, eleven, and eight years old. Pursuant to their custody agreement, Elizabeth is the primary caretaker of the children. James has parenting time every other weekend, and sees the children occasionally on Wednesday nights for dinner.

After 1999, James was the sole wage earner. James's total compensation was . . . $1,800,000 in 2008. The parties owned several vehicles throughout the course of their marriage. . . . James and Elizabeth frequently vacationed, both with and without their children. Those vacations included trips to Disneyworld and renting oceanfront mansions in North Carolina.

In 2006, Elizabeth faced serious health issues and underwent brain surgery. She has since been able to resume a normal life with only some minor facial paralysis. . . .

Elizabeth sought employment as a math teacher following the divorce. She began to take online courses to obtain her teaching license in New Jersey, reasoning that the online program gave her flexibility to take care of her children. . . .

In determining the alimony award, the court first reviewed the general summary of the parties' marriage. The court then addressed each of the thirteen factors set forth in N.J.S.A. 2A:34–23(b). The trial court found that although the marriage lasted fifteen years, the case was not a permanent alimony case, but rather one requiring limited duration alimony. The court reasoned that the parties were relatively young with at least twenty-three career years before them, both were well educated, in good health, and were either employed or employable at good salaries that could support excellent lifestyles for themselves and their children. . . .

In a published opinion, the Appellate Division reversed the trial court's award of limited duration alimony and remanded the case for an award of permanent alimony. . . .

In making its determination, the Appellate Division stated:

> We do not intend to draw specific lines delineating "short-term" and "long-term" marriages in an effort to define those cases warranting only limited duration rather than permanent alimony. . . . Nevertheless, *we do not hesitate to declare a fifteen-year marriage is not short-term, a conclusion which precludes consideration of an award of limited duration alimony.* . . .

Defendant James Gnall asks this Court to reverse the Appellate Division's judgment and affirm the trial court's award of limited duration alimony. . . .

Alimony relates to support and standard of living; it involves the quality of economic life to which one spouse is entitled, which then becomes the obligation of the other. . . .

New Jersey recognizes four separate types of "final award" alimony that may be ordered in the final judgment of divorce. They are permanent alimony, rehabilitative alimony, limited duration alimony, and reimbursement alimony. . . .

The first type of alimony to be considered is permanent alimony. The concept of permanent alimony stems from the well-established common law principle that a husband has a duty to support his wife after a divorce or separation. . . . The purpose of this type of alimony is to allow the dependent spouse to live the same lifestyle to which he or she grew accustomed during the marriage.

When awarding permanent alimony, courts have great judicial discretion, because "no two cases are alike." When determining the amount of alimony to be awarded, courts are instructed to evaluate the actual needs of the wife and the actual means of the husband, along with "the physical condition and social position of the parties, the husband's property and income (including what he could derive from personal attention to business), and also the separate property and income of the wife. Considering all these, and any other factors bearing upon the question, the sum is to be fixed at what the wife would have [expected] as support, if [she were still] living with her husband." . . .

The second type is limited duration alimony. This type of alimony was created as a remedy in order to address a dependent spouse's post-divorce needs following "shorter-term marriage where permanent or rehabilitative alimony would be inappropriate or inapplicable but where, nonetheless, economic assistance for a limited period of time would be just."

Limited duration alimony is not to be awarded in circumstances where permanent alimony is warranted. "All other statutory factors being in equipoise, the duration of the marriage marks the defining distinction between whether permanent or limited duration alimony is warranted and awarded."

The third type of alimony is rehabilitative alimony. Rehabilitative alimony is a short-term award for the purpose of financially supporting a spouse while he or she prepares to reenter the workforce through training or education. It is an award "from one party in a divorce [to] enable [the] former spouse to complete the preparation necessary for economic self-sufficiency." . . . The objective of rehabilitative alimony is to assist the dependent spouse in obtaining gainful employment so as to "enhance and improve the earning capacity of the economically dependent spouse."

An award of rehabilitative alimony is appropriate where "a spouse who gave up or postponed her own education to support the household requires a lump sum or a short-term award to achieve economic self-sufficiency." Rehabilitative alimony is not an exclusive remedy, and may, in the appropriate circumstance, be awarded in addition to permanent alimony.

iv. Finally, courts may consider a fourth type of alimony, reimbursement alimony. Reimbursement alimony was created to help combat the concept that professional degrees and licenses are "property" subject to equitable distribution at the termination of a marriage. Reimbursement alimony is awarded appropriately to a spouse who has made financial sacrifices, resulting in a temporarily reduced standard of living, in order to allow the other spouse to secure an advanced degree or professional license to enhance the parties' future standard of living.

Reimbursement alimony is limited to "monetary contributions made with the mutual and shared expectation that both parties to the marriage will derive increased income and material benefits." Like rehabilitative alimony, reimbursement alimony can be awarded on its own or in combination with another type of alimony. . . .

While the trial court identified the marriage as "not short-term," it ultimately concluded that consideration of an award of permanent alimony was obviated by the parties' relatively young ages and the fact that they were not married for twenty-five or thirty years. The trial court therefore, in effect, determined that permanent alimony awards are reserved solely for long-term marriages of twenty-five years or more, excluding consideration of the other factors. No per se rule exists indicating that permanent alimony is unwarranted unless the twenty-fifth year anniversary has been reached. Therefore, we find that the trial court improperly weighed duration over the other statutorily defined factors in determining a long-term marriage must be twenty-five years or more.

We further conclude that in its disposition of this appeal the Appellate Division inadvertently created a bright-line rule for distinguishing between a short-term and long-term marriage as it pertains to an award of permanent alimony. Although the Appellate Division stated "we do not intend to draw specific lines delineating 'short-term' and 'long-term' marriages in an effort to define those cases warranting only limited duration rather than permanent alimony," a fair reading of the opinion may lead to such a conclusion. By not clarifying that the statement reflected only the fifteen-year marriage in this particular case, the Appellate Division made a generally applicable declaration.

Moreover, we note that the final clause of the sentence affirms that the "not short-term" nature of a fifteen-year marriage mandates that it cannot be considered for limited duration alimony. Such a holding removes the other twelve factors from consideration for alimony awards once a marriage reaches the fifteen-year mark. Our cases have consistently held that all thirteen factors must be considered and given due weight, and the duration of marriage is only one factor to be considered.

For the reasons set forth above, the judgment of the Appellate Division is reversed, and the case is remanded to the trial court for new findings of fact and a new determination of alimony. . . .

NOTES AND QUESTIONS

1.   *Types of Alimony. Gnall* provides an overview of the various types of spousal support.[168] How does a court decide which type of alimony is appropriate in a specific case? Might a court award more than one type of alimony in a single case?

2.   *Alimony Pendente Lite.* In addition to the types of alimony discussed in *Gnall*, jurisdictions also provide for alimony *pendente lite*, which refers to support awarded while the divorce case is pending. The purpose of alimony *pendente lite* is to allow the dependent spouse to maintain living expenses or pay for divorce-related costs during the process of dissolution. Similarly, some jurisdictions refer to short-term alimony as transitional or "bridge the gap" support.[169] This sort of support is intended to address short-term needs related to the transition to post-marital life.[170]

3.   *Lump-Sum Spousal Support.* Periodic spousal support payments are the most common type of spousal support that courts award, with one spouse usually paying the other monthly benefits. However, in the exercise of its discretion, a court may award a lump-sum amount—a fixed and irrevocable amount that can be paid either at once or in a specified number of installments.[171] Lump-sum spousal support is not subject to subsequent modification.[172] A lump-sum award may be appropriate in unusual circumstances, for example, if the costs of rehabilitation are all due at once or if the payor spouse cannot be relied on to make periodic payments.[173]

4.   *Permanent Alimony.* The *Gnall* court considered the propriety of an award of permanent alimony (also termed indefinite or traditional alimony) after a marriage of 15 years. How did the court direct lower courts to incorporate the length of the marriage into the permanent alimony inquiry? Should a long-term marriage be necessary for an award of indefinite alimony? Should long-term marriages create a presumption of indefinite alimony?

5.   *Marriage Duration.* Many states, either by statute or judicial decision, link the type and duration of alimony to the duration of the marriage.[174] Some statutes limit a judge's discretion to grant alimony based on the length of the marriage, while others provide a presumption of alimony based on the length of the marriage.[175] Based on the *Gnall* court's opinion, what justifies linking marriage duration to spousal support duration?

---

168. Charts, supra note 151, at 544–47.

169. Borchard v. Borchard, 730 So. 2d 748 (Fl. Dist. Ct. App. 1999); Green v. Green, 672 So. 2d 49, 51 (Fl. Dist. Ct. App. 1996).

170. *Borchard*, 730 So. 2d at 748.

171. Lowrey v. Simmons, 186 So. 3d 907 (Miss. Ct. App. 2015).

172. Rivera v. Rivera, 661 S.E.2d 541, 549 (Ga. 2008); *Borchard*, 730 So. 2d at 751.

173. Brett R. Turner, Spousal Support in Chaos, 25 Fam. Advocate 14 (2003).

174. See, e.g., Boemio v. Boemio, 994 A.2d 911 (Md. 2010).

175. See, e.g., Tex. Fam. Code Ann., § 8.052(1) (West 2020); Sommers v. Sommers, 660 N.W.2d 586 (N.D. 2003); Clapp v. Clapp, 653 A.2d 72 (Vt. 1994).

6. *Maintaining the Marital Lifestyle.* The *Gnall* court referred to permanent alimony as providing the payee spouse the lifestyle they would have had if the marriage had continued. Is that a sensible approach? How can there be any expectation of continuing the lifestyle of the marriage if, in light of no-fault divorce, there is no legally enforceable expectation regarding the continuation of the marriage itself?

7. *Rationales for Spousal Support.* There are a variety of rationales that might justify or inform spousal support law. In practice, statutes and judges draw upon a mix of these rationales:

a. The first approach is grounded in the Uniform Marriage and Divorce Act (UMDA), which formally rejected fault-based divorce and women's economic dependency as grounds for alimony.[176] Instead, the UMDA implicitly embraced an ethos of self-sufficiency.[177] Under the UMDA, a maintenance award would only be appropriate if the payee spouse does not have sufficient property to satisfy their reasonable needs and the payee spouse is either custodian of a child whose condition justifies not working outside of the home or the payee spouse cannot earn enough money to provide for their reasonable needs.[178]

b. The rehabilitative rationale casts spousal support as a means of enabling a dependent spouse to pursue education or develop the marketable skills necessary to achieve self-sufficiency. This approach acknowledges that in a role-divided marriage, the spouse who invested in the home and family and did not develop marketable skills in the external labor market, will be unable to support themselves immediately upon divorce. As one court noted:

> Rehabilitative alimony has been awarded to supplement means already available in an amount reasonably required during the post-marriage period to maintain a spouse until he or she in the exercise of reasonable efforts and endeavors is in a position of self support.[179]

c. A third approach focuses on the contribution of the spouse seeking support to the marriage and earning capacity of the payor spouse. As in the equitable distribution context discussed earlier in this chapter, the contribution rationale recognizes the value of the childrearing and domestic efforts that women typically undertake and which traditionally have not been recognized as an economically valuable contribution to the family. This remains a central rationale for spousal support. The reimbursement rationale for spousal support can be

---

176. UMDA § 308(a).

177. Danielle Morone, A Short History of Alimony in England and the United States, 20 J. Contemp. Legal Issues 3, 7 (2011-2012).

178. UMDA § 308(a).

179. Pfohl v. Pfohl, 345 So. 2d 371 (Fla. Dist. Ct. App. 1977).

understood as a variant of the contribution approach. Whereas the contribution approach typically focuses on the value of services provided to the other spouse, the reimbursement approach, as discussed in *Gnall*, applies to financial sacrifices or contributions made by one spouse for the benefit of the other.

d. A fourth approach views spousal support as compensation for *losses* incurred as a result of the marriage. The American Law Institute has promoted this rationale, advocating compensation for two distinct types of losses: the loss of the marital standard of living, and the loss of earning capacity as a result of childcare responsibilities during the marriage.[180]

PROBLEMS

With these different rationales for spousal support in mind, consider the following hypotheticals and whether spousal support is warranted in each of them. Assume that in none of these cases does the family have significant assets to be divided upon divorce:

1. Bill and Jennifer started the marriage with different economic prospects, and these persisted during the marriage. Bill works as a lawyer, and Jennifer is an artist. They dated while Bill was in law school and Jennifer was completing her Master's degree in Fine Arts. They married after both graduated. Bill's income increased substantially and Jennifer's did not. Bill now earns approximately three times as much as Jennifer. They have no children and both work full-time, Jennifer at her studio and Bill at his law office. Jennifer files for divorce after ten years of marriage and seeks spousal support. Should the result in this case be different if the couple had children for whom Jennifer was the primary caretaker?

2. Stacey and Damon are both lawyers. After graduating law school the same year, they married and began working for large law firms. Two years in, both began to feel worn down by their work. Stacey left her firm to join the ACLU, and Damon left his to go to an in-house legal job at a client company. A year later, they had the first of two children. Because Stacey's work was more flexible, she handled most of the childcare duties. Now, after eleven years of marriage, Damon files for divorce, and Stacey seeks spousal support. Would your analysis be different if the couple had no children?

---

180. Principles of the Law of Family Dissolution, supra note 26, §§ 5.04-5.05; Ira Mark Ellman, The Theory of Alimony, 77 Calif. L. Rev. 1 (1989); James Herbie DiFonzo, Toward a Unified Field Theory of the Family: The American Law Institute's Principles of the Law of Family Dissolution, 2001 BYU L. Rev. 923, 926.

3. Josh and Daniel met at work. Both were young lawyers at the same large law firm; they married during their fourth year at the firm. A few years later, Josh made partner. Daniel, in contrast, began to suffer bouts of depression and was diagnosed with bipolar disorder. He left the firm to work part-time at a much smaller firm. He found gardening and cooking to be therapeutic and so began to do a lot of both. Now, after ten years of marriage, Josh files for divorce, and Daniel seeks spousal support. Again, how, if at all, would the analysis differ if the couple had a small child for whom Daniel cared? What if they had a child, and Josh managed the child's caretaking by hiring a nanny and arranging daycare? What if Daniel became unable to work at all?

C. Determining the Length of the Marriage

CONNOR V. BENEDICT

118 N.E.3d 96 (Mass. 2019)

LENK, J.

Layne C. Connor (wife) filed a complaint for divorce in June 2014 against William P. Benedict (husband), to whom she had been married for a little more than two years, and with whom she had lived for much of the prior twelve years. Following a trial, a judge of the Probate and Family Court issued a judgment of divorce nisi that awarded general term alimony to the wife and, among other things, divided the marital estate such that fifty-five percent of the over-all assets were awarded to the husband and forty-five percent to the wife. Although the legal marriage lasted 2.25 years, for purposes of determining the amount of alimony pursuant to the Alimony Reform Act of 2011, the judge considered the marriage to have been of slightly more than eight years' duration. In doing so, the judge took into account an approximately six-year period from 2005 to 2011, during which he found that the parties had lived together and had engaged in an economic marital partnership. The husband appealed, and we transferred the case to this court on our own motion.

The husband challenges the alimony award on two grounds. First, he claims that, as a matter of law, the wife was precluded from entering an economic marital partnership with him during much of the six-year period because she received alimony payments from her former spouse during that time. In the alternative, the husband claims that, even if the wife could have entered into an economic marital partnership, the judge did not make sufficient findings to support a determination that she had done so. . . . We affirm.

1. . . .

a. *Early years (2000 to 2004)*. When the parties met in August 2000, the wife owned a single-family house. In July 2001, she sold that property and used the proceeds to make a down payment on a house in Maynard. The parties began living together in the Maynard house in August 2001, along with the wife's minor son. At the time, the husband recently had filed for bankruptcy; his name did not appear on the deed or mortgage. Nonetheless, the parties shared the mortgage payments, as well as the costs of utilities, groceries, and other household expenses. At some point in 2001, the wife became disabled and unable to work. In 2003, she began receiving disability payments.

b. *Australia (2004 to 2005)*. From March 2004 to September 2005, the wife relocated to Australia with her son in order to receive medical treatment. The parties arranged for the husband to live in the house in Maynard while he coordinated with a realtor to sell it. In September 2004, after the house had been sold, the husband moved to a rental townhouse in Shirley. Some of the proceeds from the sale were used to pay the wife's medical bills; $5,000 went to the husband for improvements he had made to the house while the wife was away; the wife received the remainder.

c. *Reunification (2005 to 2012)*. The wife returned to the United States in October 2005, when her Australian medical visa expired. In November 2005, the wife moved into the townhouse in Shirley and the parties resumed living together, sharing rent and utility expenses. The husband provided for the wife's health insurance through his employer's "domestic partner benefits program." In November 2006, the parties jointly purchased a house in Townsend (marital home). . . . Throughout the time they lived in the marital home, they shared the costs of the mortgage, utilities, and other household expenses. . . . The wife's minor son lived with the parties in the marital home and became close to the husband. . . .

d. *Receipt of alimony from prior spouse*. The wife and her prior spouse had divorced in 2001. After that divorce, the wife received regular child support and alimony payments. By 2006, the husband was "at least somewhat aware" of the alimony payments, which ceased in 2011.

e. *Marriage and separation (2012 to 2014)*. The parties were married on February 18, 2012. Thereafter, the wife again received health insurance through the husband's employer, at that point as his spouse. . . .

[T]hroughout the course of the marriage (including at least the 6.33-year period in which they lived together immediately prior to their legal marriage), the parties enjoyed an "upper-middle-income lifestyle." . . .

During 2013, however, the parties had a series of disagreements. The wife testified to incidents of abuse and harassment by the husband, and both parties suggested that the other had used intoxicating substances to excess. Ultimately, the judge found that the parties suffered from "a great deal of marital discord." The wife and her minor son left the marital home on May 25, 2014, and began renting an apartment, while the husband and his adult son lived in the marital home.

f. *Divorce.* The wife filed a complaint for divorce in the Probate and Family Court on June 2, 2014. . . .

A judgment of divorce nisi issued on August 25, 2016. . . .

2.

The husband contends that the judge erred in calculating the duration of the marriage for purposes of awarding alimony. . . .

a. *Payment of alimony.* In determining the length of alimony payments to be awarded, the judge found that the parties had been legally married for 2.25 years. A judge, however, may "increase the length of the marriage if there is evidence that the parties' economic marital partnership began during their cohabitation period prior to the marriage." Here, the judge determined that the parties had cohabited and engaged in an economic marital partnership for approximately 6.33 years, from November 2005, when they lived together in Shirley, to the date of their marriage in February 2012. The judge therefore increased the duration of the marriage to include that period and ordered payment of alimony for 5.148 years. . . .

i. *Durational limits on alimony.* Alimony is "the payment of support from a spouse, who has the ability to pay, to a spouse in need of support for a reasonable length of time." "The purpose of alimony is to provide adequate support for a spouse who needs it." General term alimony, in particular, aims to support one spouse who has become "economically dependent" on the other.

"A judge has broad discretion when awarding alimony under the statute." Nonetheless, the "reasonable length of time" for which alimony payments may be ordered is constrained by the Alimony Reform Act of 2011, which sets presumptive durational limits on general term alimony. The limits are premised on the length of the parties' marriage; the longer the marriage, the longer the maximum permissible duration of alimony, up to a maximum cap. . . .

General Law c. 208, § 48, defines the "[l]ength of the marriage" as "the number of months from the date of legal marriage to the date of service of a complaint or petition for divorce . . . duly filed in a court." The parties were married on February 18, 2012, and the husband accepted service of the complaint for divorce on June 13, 2014. There was no error in the judge's calculation that the parties had been married for 2.25 years.

As stated, the statute also provides that "the court may increase the length of the marriage if there is evidence that the parties' economic marital partnership began during their cohabitation period prior to the marriage." A period of "cohabitation" and "economic marital partnership" "resembles, but is not equivalent to, a legal marriage." During such a period, the parties act like a married couple, and form the financial dependencies, crystalized in marriage, for which alimony later may compensate.

"[I]n order to ascertain whether the parties were participating in an economic marital partnership," "a judge must consider the factors set forth in G. L. c. 208, § 49(d)(1)." These factors include, but are not limited to, economic dependence or interdependence, collaborative conduct in furtherance of a shared life, benefits derived, and representations made or reputations acquired regarding the relationship. Here, the judge determined that the period from November 2005 to February 2012 constituted an economic marital partnership.

iii. The husband contends that the evidence is insufficient to support a determination that the parties cohabited and entered an economic marital partnership. We do not agree.

The judge found that the parties cohabited between October 2005 and February 2012; during that time, they lived together in Shirley and Townsend. As to their economic marital partnership, the judge properly considered the factors set forth in G. L. c. 208, § 49(d)(1). With respect to economic interdependence, the judge found that the wife had become disabled and relied on the husband's health insurance during this period. The wife also relied, at least in part, on the husband's salary, as she was unable to work. In furtherance of building a life together, the parties shared in the purchase of a house in 2006, the cost of the mortgage, and the work required to perform renovations. During the same period, the husband repeatedly represented his wife to his employer as his "domestic partner." Moreover, the husband held out the wife's son as his own in a 2011 obituary. The judge determined that "[t]he parties acted as a married couple in all respects."

The judge's factual findings, supported by the record, also support his conclusion that the parties engaged in an economic marital partnership from November 2005 to February 2012. Accordingly, the judge did not abuse his discretion in including the entire seventy-six month period in his calculation of the duration of the marriage. . . .

NOTES AND QUESTIONS

---

1. *Premarital Cohabitation.* The court in *Connor* considered the couple's premarital cohabitation in determining the length of the marriage. Today, the vast majority of married couples have had at least one cohabitation before marriage,[181] and more adults between the ages of 18 to 44 have lived with an unmarried partner

---

181. Colleen N. Nugent & Jill Daugherty, A Demographic, Attitudinal, and Behavioral of Cohabiting Adults in the United States, 2011–2015, 111 Nat'l Health Stats. Reps. 1, 9 tbl. 3 (2018).

than have been married.[182] With this increase in the number of unmarried intimate partners, many of whom eventually marry, the issue of whether premarital cohabitation should be included in calculating the duration of the marriage has arisen in many states. The issue arises as well in the equitable distribution context, as discussed earlier in this chapter. Massachusetts's support statute expressly permits the court to consider the existence of a premarital economic partnership when determining the length of the marriage.[183] Why did the *Connor* court believe that premarital cohabitation should be included in determining the length of marriage?

2.   *Ups and Downs.* In Sprouse v. Sprouse, a couple established a common-law marriage over the span of a decade, divorced, resumed cohabitation, remarried, and eventually sought a divorce again.[184] The Georgia court held that a court may consider the entire relationship of the divorcing parties, including premarital cohabitation, even though not directed to do so by a state statute. Is it legitimate for the court to consider cohabitation in determining the length of the marriage in the absence of any explicit statutory authorization to do so? If so, then should the court also take into account the parties' prior common-law marriage?

3.   *Alimony During Premarital Cohabitation.* The husband in *Connor* argued that the couple's premarital cohabitation should not be considered in computing length of the marriage because the wife received alimony from her former husband during that time. Should the fact that she was receiving alimony matter? The husband described forming a marriage-like economic partnership while receiving alimony as a form of "financial infidelity." What's the logic of that claim, and do you find it persuasive?

4.   *The Economic Partnership.* According to the *Connor* court, when precisely did the couple begin their economic partnership? How did and should the court determine when the partnership began?

D. Need and Standard of Living

RULE v. RULE
402 P.3d 153 (Utah Ct. App. 2017)

ROTH, JUDGE:
Richelle Rule appeals from the district court's final order on its supplemental findings and conclusions regarding her alimony award. . . .

---

182. Pew Research Ctr., Marriage and Cohabitation in the U.S. (Nov. 6, 2019).

183. Alimony Reform Act of 2011, Ch. 208, §48 (2020) (defining length of marriage); Charles P. Kindregan, Jr., Reforming Alimony: Massachusetts Reconsiders Postdivorce Spousal Support, 46 Suffolk U. L. Rev. 13, 29 (2013).

184. 678 S.E.2d 328, 329–30 (Ga. 2009).

Geoffrey S. Rule and Richelle Rule married in March 1997. They divorced by bifurcated decree in March 2014, reserving for trial several issues, including alimony. . . .

Both parties were employed during the marriage. Geoffrey continued to work full time as a scientist and indicated that he earned a gross income of approximately $5,900 a month. Richelle had held various jobs during the marriage — most of them part time — but at the time of trial was unemployed and had been since late summer the year before. Richelle indicated in her updated financial declaration that her only income at the time was a temporary alimony and child support award of $1,500 a month. At trial she presented a report and testimony from a vocational expert regarding her employment potential. The report noted that Richelle had most recently been employed as a customer service agent in the insurance industry with an hourly wage of $17.00, but it also noted that there were ongoing concerns that significantly impacted her ability to be successful at work. . . .

As to Richelle's needs and Geoffrey's ability to support her, the court expressly declined to make any finding regarding the standard of living established during the marriage because it found that "neither party [could] maintain the standard of living established during the marriage, given the divorce." Instead, the court determined each party's reasonable monthly expenses by "review[ing] both Financial Declarations of the parties and . . . discount[ing] anything that was voluntary and discretionary." . . . Ultimately, the court awarded Richelle alimony in the amount of $814, to continue for the term of the marriage — seventeen years. . . .

Richelle argued that the court erred by declining to "make a finding of the parties' monthly needs consistent with the standard of living established during the marriage." . . . Ultimately, the court increased Richelle's alimony award from $814 to $874 per month. . . .

Richelle contends that the court abused its discretion by failing to determine the marital standard of living and evaluate alimony in light of that standard, and by failing to equalize the parties' post-divorce standards of living. She also argues that the district court's findings inadequately support the budgetary reductions it made to arrive at its determination of her reasonable monthly needs. Geoffrey, in contrast, argues that we should affirm the district court's alimony award, because the court was within its discretion to base alimony on actual expenses at the time of trial; the court considered the required alimony factors and the marital living standard and supported its decision with adequate findings; and the ultimate result is equitable under the circumstances of the case. We agree with Richelle.

I. Alimony Standards and Policies

In setting an alimony award, district courts must consider the statutory factors set forth in Utah Code section 30-3-5(8)(a), and failure to do so constitutes reversible error. These factors include "(i) the financial condition and needs of the recipient spouse; (ii) the recipient's earning capacity or ability to produce income; [and] (iii) the ability of the payor spouse to provide support."

An alimony award should also "advance, as much as possible," the primary purposes of alimony, which are: "(1) to get the parties as close as possible to the same standard of living that existed during the marriage; (2) to equalize the standards of living of each party; and (3) to prevent the recipient spouse from becoming a public charge." Indeed, we have explained that alimony is not limited "to provid[ing] for only basic needs" but should be fashioned in consideration of "the recipient spouse's station in life" in light of the parties' "customary or proper status or circumstances," with the goal being an alimony award calculated "to approximate the parties' standard of living during the marriage as closely as possible."

Our precedent thus reflects and reinforces the general rule that alimony should be based upon the standard of living the parties established during the marriage rather than the standard of living at the time of trial. This requires a court to determine the parties' needs and expenses as an initial matter in light of the marital standard of living rather than, for example, actual costs being incurred at the time of trial. The needs of each party, determined according to the marital standard of living, then provide a baseline from which to craft an alimony award that best fulfills the purposes of alimony — i.e., to allow the parties to go forward in their separate lives with a standard of living as close as possible to the marital standard and "with relatively equal odds."

There are several considerations that support this general rule. First, in many cases, the level of expenses and the standard of living of the separated parties at the time of trial will not be representative of the parties' "customary or proper status or circumstances." We have therefore cautioned against determining alimony based upon actual expenses at the time of trial because, as Richelle asserts to be true in her case, "[a] party's current, actual expenses 'may be necessarily lower than needed to maintain an appropriate standard of living for various reasons, including, possibly, lack of income.'" A party's circumstances and living standard at the time of trial may also necessarily be "significantly more straitened than during the marriage" "due to the [parties'] separation" and the exigencies inherent in building and establishing a separate life apart from his or her spouse.

Second, assessing the parties' needs based upon the marital standard in the first instance makes sense in terms of a court's continuing jurisdiction over divorce cases, particularly in marriages of long duration, as this one was. The receiving spouse's needs ultimately set the bounds for the maximum permissible alimony award. And while a court has continuing jurisdiction over the alimony award, it may exercise that jurisdiction only to "make substantive changes and new orders regarding alimony *based on a substantial material change in circumstances not foreseeable at the time of the divorce.*" As a result, if the court considers the receiving spouse's needs based only upon a reduced standard of living at the time of trial, the resulting needs determination could prevent the receiving spouse from having her alimony increased to a level consistent with the marital standard should economic circumstances materially change — if, for example, the payor spouse's income substantially increases during the alimony period. And while it would not necessarily be impossible to determine the marital standard of living at a later modification hearing, certainly the potential limitations on the availability of evidence due to the passage of time could make establishing the marital standard much more difficult.

Also, as a practical matter, it seems inherently problematic for a trial court to attempt to design an alimony award that advances the overall goal of allowing the parties to go forward with their lives "as nearly as possible at the standard of living enjoyed during marriage" without first determining what that standard was in the first instance. . . .

With these principles in mind, we have established a process to be followed by courts considering an award of alimony that is applicable generally, including to cases ultimately involving shortfall situations. First, the court should "assess the needs of the parties, in light of their marital standard of living." This means that the court must determine the parties' needs "reasonably incurred, calculated upon the standard of living . . . enjoyed during the marriage." Next, the court should determine the extent to which the receiving spouse is able to meet her own needs with her own income. If the court determines that the receiving spouse is able to meet all her needs with her own income, "then it should not award alimony."

If the court finds, however, that the receiving spouse is not able to meet her own needs, it should then "assess whether [the payor spouse's] income, after meeting his needs, is sufficient to make up some or all of the shortfall between [the receiving spouse's] needs and income." This step should be undertaken "with an eye towards equalizing the parties' standards of living only if there is not enough combined ability to maintain both parties at the standard of living they enjoyed during the marriage." Too often, this is the dilemma that a divorce court must confront — the parties' combined resources do not stretch far enough to meet the legitimate needs of what are now two households rather than one. Although we have referred to this approach as "equalization of income," it is best described as the "equalization of poverty," and its goal "is to ensure that when the parties are unable to maintain the standard of living to which they were accustomed during marriage, the shortfall is equitably shared."

Once a court has properly determined that a shortfall exists between the parties' resources and needs, we accord trial courts broad discretion in dividing the shortfall and apportioning that burden, so long as the award is equitable and supported by the findings. . . . For example, if one party legitimately has greater needs than the other party, or there are other circumstances that bear upon how the shortfall should be divided, . . . such circumstances should be taken into account during the equalization process and reflected in the ultimate alimony award. . . .

II. The Court's Alimony Determination

Here, the district court did not follow the process we have established. Instead, it appears to have skipped over the traditional needs analysis and moved directly to address what it perceived to be insufficient resources. . . .

Thus, the district court . . . determined Richelle's needs in the first instance based on the straitened circumstances in which she found herself as a result of the divorce. The court's only stated justification for refusing to first assess the parties' needs in light of their historical living standard was insufficient resources. We conclude that in these circumstances, the court exceeded its discretion. . . .

Certainly, a court is not obligated to assess the parties' needs in light of the marital standard if evidence is not provided to allow the court to do so. But as Richelle points out, her financial declaration included both her current expenses at the time of trial and expenditures that she claimed reflected the parties' standard of living during the marriage. . . . While Geoffrey did not include both his current and his marital standard for some expense categories, the majority of the expenses in his financial declaration are identical in amount to those identified as marital expenses in Richelle's financial declaration, implying that his expenses were based on a marital standard as well. . . .

The explanation the court gave for declining to determine the marital standard of living as part of the alimony determination was its conclusion that the parties' combined resources were insufficient to sustain the marital standard. But under our well-established precedent, that alone is not enough to justify bypassing the traditional needs analysis. . . . The equitable division of the shortfall begins with a determination of the marital living standard: "The purpose of equalization is to ensure that *when parties are unable to maintain the standard of living to which they were accustomed during marriage*, the shortfall is equitably shared." In other words, our precedent has established that the shortfall that justifies an "equalization of income" determination relates to the difference between the parties' historical living standard and the parties' present combined ability to meet that standard. The parties' historical living standard is therefore a baseline for determining that a shortfall exists at all as well as a necessary reference point in the determination of how to equitably allocate the shortfall. . . .

As a result, we cannot be confident that under the circumstances the court's alimony award is equitable or actually advances one of alimony's "chief functions" — "to permit [both] parties to maintain as much as possible the same standards after the dissolution of the marriage as those enjoyed during the marriage."

Moreover, the court's needs determination represents Richelle's maximum permissible alimony award, and, as she points out, the court's reduced needs determination may well impair her ability in the future to invoke the court's continuing jurisdiction to increase her alimony to a level commensurate with the marital standard, should Geoffrey's income — and commensurate ability to meet her needs — materially change in the future. Such a change in circumstances is certainly possible in the context of a long-term alimony award, such as this one, given the seventeen-year length of the parties' marriage. And such a change is made more difficult to establish if the marital baseline is not established in the original alimony determination when evidence is fresher and more readily obtainable and verifiable. . . .

We vacate the district court's alimony award and remand for the district court to reassess its alimony award in accordance with this opinion.

NOTES AND QUESTIONS

1.   *Determining Need.* The court in *Rule* defined "need" not in an absolute sense (e.g., the avoidance of poverty), but instead based on the standard of living during the marriage. This is the dominant approach in every state, often based on case law.[185] For example, in Clapp v. Clapp,[186] the Vermont court noted: "[W]e have held that reasonable need is not to be judged in relation to subsistence. We have emphasized, on the other hand, that reasonable needs are to be determined 'in light of the standard of living established during the marriage.'"[187]

2.   *The Goals of Alimony Awards.* The *Rule* court identified three primary purposes of an alimony award: to get the parties as close as possible to the marital standard of living; to equalize the parties' standards of living; and to prevent the recipient spouse from becoming a public charge. Were these appropriate goals in the context of the couple's divorce? Are they appropriate goals more generally in the context of divorce after a long-term marriage?

3.   *Standard of Living.* Given the impossibility of maintaining the couple's marital standard of living post-divorce, why did the court insist that the trial court undertake a marital standard of living analysis?

4.   *Which Standard of Living?* For many couples, their standard of living will change during the course of the relationship. How should a court respond if the couple's standard of living just prior to the divorce is, for example, much higher (or lower) than the average standard of living during the course of the marriage?

5.   *What Counts?* The marital standard of living determines reasonable needs and thereby constitutes the basis for any spousal support award. But what are the components of the standard of living?

---

185. See, e.g., Bond v. Bond, 916 P.2d 272 (Okla. Civ. App. 1996); see also Sommers v. Sommers, 660 N.W.2d 586 (N.D. 2003); Magee v. Magee, 553 N.W.2d 363 (Mich. Ct. App. 1996).

186. 653 A.2d 72 (Vt. 1994).

187. Id. at 74.

a. *Charitable Contributions.* In In re Marriage of Stenzel, the divorcing couple had regularly made substantial charitable contributions during the marriage.[188] The court held that "charitable donations . . . in a reasonable sum may be a part of the needs analysis in fixing spousal support."[189] Nonetheless, the court found the wife's stated "level of charitable donations significantly higher than the standard set for the parties as a married couple."[190] The court thus reduced the allotment for charitable contributions to "a more proper sum in light of past standard of living."[191] What is the rationale for including or excluding expenditures in the standard of living calculus? Should charitable expenses be included in the calculus if they were part of the couple's past practice?

b. *Savings.* The court in Lombardi v. Lombardi addressed the calculation of alimony where the parties relied on only a fraction of their household income to pay their monthly expenses and regularly saved the balance during the course of their marriage.[192] The court reasoned: "Because it is the manner in which the parties use their income that is determinative when establishing a marital lifestyle, . . . there is no demonstrable difference between one family's habitual use of its income to fund savings and another family's use of its income to regularly purchase luxury cars or enjoy extravagant vacations."[193] Do you agree? Should standard of living be interpreted to refer only to the material aspects of the family's life such as housing, transportation, and vacations, or to any uses of money?

E. Health and Disability

IN RE MARRIAGE OF ANLIKER
694 N.W.2d 535 (Iowa 2005)

LAVORATO, CHIEF JUSTICE.

In this dissolution of marriage proceeding, Scott Anliker appealed from the district court's award of spousal support in the form of traditional alimony to his spouse Donna Anliker. . . . [The appeals court] reversed the award of spousal support in the form of traditional alimony and awarded her, in lieu of this form of support, rehabilitative alimony. . . .

---

188. 908 N.W.2d 524 (Iowa Ct. App. 2018).
189. Id. at 536.
190. Id.
191. Id.
192. 145 A.3d 709 (N.J. Super. Ct. App. Div. 2016).
193. Id. at 717.

I. Background Facts.

Donna and Scott were married on December 27, 1984. At the time he was twenty-one and she was thirty-three. Donna had three children from a previous marriage, two of whom lived with Donna and Scott and the other child lived with his father.

The parties decided that Donna should stay home and care for the children rather than look for outside employment and incur transportation and child care expenses. Donna, however, did work at a variety of jobs from 1984 through 1996, but never full time.

In 1996 while working at a gas station, Donna fell and injured her left knee. She had multiple surgeries on her knee as a result of the fall, including knee replacement. She has never fully recovered from the injury. . . . In addition to her knee condition, Donna has other health problems. . . . Although Donna can drive, she sometimes suffers from leg cramps. She can dress and groom herself, although putting on shoes, socks, and bottoms can be challenging so that she sometimes needs help tying her shoes. She has great difficulty standing for two to three hours at a time. . . .

In 2001 Donna was employed as a seasonal employee at a toy store where she earned $8 per hour. Because she could not lift, she was told she would not be hired back. Over the year and a half preceding trial, Donna was hospitalized overnight two to three times for severe pain.

Donna currently receives $363.50 per month social security disability benefits because of her knee injury. . . .

In the early 1990s, Donna was injured in an automobile accident and received a settlement of between $7000 and $10,000. The parties applied that money toward the purchase of a home. . . .

Scott has a high school diploma; Donna earned a GED. At the time of trial, Scott was in good health. Since August of 2000, Scott has worked for Golden Furrow Fertilizer where he earns a gross salary of $1026.04 per week. Scott's job is secure, and he does not intend to change jobs in the immediate future. Donna's supplemental medical insurance of $109 per month and life insurance of $14 per month are deducted from Scott's wages.

II. Proceedings. . . .

[T]he court awarded Donna spousal support in the form of traditional alimony in the amount of $1250 per month. . . .

V. Spousal Support. . .

Scott . . . asserted that spousal support in the form of rehabilitative alimony was more appropriate, a contention with which the court of appeals agreed. . . .

When deciding to award alimony, the district court must consider the factors in Iowa Code section 598.21(3). Although our review of the district court's award of alimony is de novo, we give that court considerable latitude in making this determination based on the criteria in section 598.21(3). . . .

The factors in section 598.21(3) pertinent to this case include (1) the length of the marriage; (2) the age and physical and emotional health of the parties; (3) the property distribution; (4) the educational level of each party at the time of the marriage and at the time the action is commenced; (5) the earning capacity of the party seeking alimony, including educational background, training, employment skills, work experience, length of absence from the job market; (6) the feasibility of the party seeking alimony becoming self-supporting at a standard of living reasonably comparable to that enjoyed during the marriage, and the length of time necessary to achieve this goal; and (7) other factors the court may determine to be relevant in an individual case.

We recognize three different types of alimony as an appropriate award of spousal support: traditional, rehabilitative, and reimbursement. . . . Rehabilitative alimony was conceived as a way of supporting an economically dependent spouse through a limited period of re-education or retraining following divorce, thereby creating incentive and opportunity for that spouse to become self-supporting.

Because self-sufficiency is the goal of rehabilitative alimony, the duration of such an award may be limited or extended depending on the realistic needs of the economically dependent spouse, tempered by the goal of facilitating the economic independence of the ex-spouses.

Reimbursement alimony "is predicated upon economic sacrifices made by one spouse during the marriage that directly enhance the future earning capacity of the other." And "[s]imilar to a property award, but based on future earning capacity rather than a division of tangible assets, it should be fixed at the time of the decree." . . .

While Donna is only 51 years of age, the record supports a finding that her health has deteriorated since 1996 and is not likely to improve. . . . Although Scott feels that any alimony award should be for rehabilitative purposes only, the record does not support such a conclusion. Due to her physical infirmities, Donna is an unlikely candidate for further education or training. . . . The Court does not find it to be realistic to think that Donna is employable in her current condition. . . .

This is a long-term marriage of nearly 20 years. Scott has a substantially better earning capacity than Donna, who is permanently disabled. Donna's earning capacity appears limited to her social security disability benefits. Scott continues to have an earning capacity of $50,000 annually or more. . . . While Scott is to be commended for his support of Donna's children, which has been ongoing even after they became adults, the Court takes note that the settlements she received for injuries and future disabilities were invested in the marriage and are no longer available to Donna at the very time she needs the money.

In view of these findings, which are fully supported in the record and which we adopt, we think the spousal support award of $1250 per month in traditional alimony until Donna attains the age of sixty-five or either party dies was equitable and should not be disturbed. . . .

PROBLEMS

1. Bill and Nancy married in 2015. It was the second marriage for both of them. Bill was 37 years old and Nancy 35 years old, and neither had children. They were both delighted and thankful to have found each other. Bill worked as a software engineer, earning approximately $150,000/year, and Nancy worked as a personal trainer at a popular health club, earning $50,000/year. They spent nearly all of their non-working hours together. They ate out a lot, including at fancy restaurants, and traveled extensively, taking two international trips in 2015 and two more in 2016. In 2017, Nancy was diagnosed with sudden onset multiple sclerosis. Within two months, she could barely walk. She had to leave her job, which provided no severance pay. Her illness has made her irritable. Bill has been less than understanding, and in January 2020, he filed for divorce. Because neither party owned any property, and because they had no children together, the divorce was fairly straightforward, except that Nancy wanted permanent alimony. She will never again be able to work as a personal trainer, and her disability payments amount to only $20,000/year. Should she receive permanent alimony? What about if they had married in 2005 instead of 2015? What if they had married in 2005, had two children, and Nancy began to work as a personal trainer because it allowed her the flexibility necessary to care for the children, while Bill worked long hours?

2. Lillian and William married in 2007. In 2012, Lillian slipped as she walked across a patch of ice and broke her hip. She has not been able to work since the accident. They obtained a legal separation in 2014, and divorced in 2016. The couple had no property. Lillian was awarded temporary spousal support for three years. At the end of the three-year period, she petitioned for a continuation of the support, which William opposed. The court ordered that the support be discontinued. William acknowledged that without the spousal support payment, Lillian would have no means of support, other than a minimal government benefits payment. Was the court justified in discontinuing the spousal support award? Why? What if William and Lillian had been married 27 years, instead of 7 years, before they separated?

F. Fault and Support

GARDNER V. GARDNER
452 P.3d 1134 (Utah 2019)

CHIEF JUSTICE DURRANT, opinion of the Court . . .

Nelson Gardner and Christina Gardner were married for twenty-two years before divorcing in 2017. During the course of the marriage, Mr. Gardner worked full-time, and Ms. Gardner stayed home with their five children. Although the couple had agreed to this arrangement, after their youngest child turned five, Mr. Gardner frequently encouraged Ms. Gardner to work outside the home or to obtain additional education.

At the time of the divorce, Mr. Gardner worked as a "global director of business development," making roughly $200,000 per year. Ms. Gardner, on the other hand, did not have consistent employment but "occasionally worked part-time, earning $11 or $12 per hour." Ms. Gardner does not have a college degree or any professional license, but she has earned money teaching swimming, piano, sewing, and art classes. Also, she has earned sizeable commissions for her artwork. . . .

The couple's relationship had a lot of "ups and downs" throughout the marriage. Mr. Gardner testified that the key factor in the couple's marital discord was Ms. Gardner's "multiple episodes of infidelity." In 2007 and 2009, Ms. Gardner had extramarital sexual affairs. . . . And . . . the "final nail" was in 2016 when he discovered that Ms. Gardner had developed an "inappropriate relationship" with another man. He made this discovery after Ms. Gardner was injured in an accident while allegedly spending time with that man. Mr. Gardner filed for divorce shortly thereafter.

Although both parties also testified to the existence of other marital problems, including "mutual verbal abuse" . . . , the district court found that it was Ms. Gardner's "sexual relationships with persons other than [Mr. Gardner that] substantially caused the breakup of the marriage relationship." The district court determined that this constituted "fault" under Utah Code section 30-3-5, and so could be considered as part of the court's alimony determination.

The court factored fault into its alimony determination in two ways. . . .

The court departed from the goal of equalization by calculating Ms. Gardner's alimony award based on "reasonable monthly expenses" rather than on the expected monthly expenses she incurred while living at the lifestyle she enjoyed before the divorce. . . .

The court also factored fault into its alimony calculation by deciding that Ms. Gardner was "not entitled to receive alimony for the maximum allowed duration under the statute, which is the length of the marriage." So the court ordered Mr. Gardner to pay alimony for a ten-year period, rather than the maximum allowed period of twenty-two years.

Ms. Gardner now appeals the terms and the length of the alimony award. . . .

I. We Affirm the District Court's Determination That Ms. Gardner's Affairs Substantially Contributed to the Divorce

First, we consider whether the district court abused its discretion by determining, under Utah Code section 30-3-5(8)(c), that Ms. Gardner was at fault in causing the divorce. We hold that it did not. . . .

In this case, the district court held that Ms. Gardner's "infidelity substantially contributed to the breakup of the marriage relationship." . . .

Ms. Gardner argues the court clearly erred for two reasons. First, she asserts the court clearly erred in concluding that other causes "did not substantially contribute to the breakup of the marriage relationship," because "'irreconcilable differences' provided not only '[an]other reasonable explanation,' but the most 'reasonable explanation' for the divorce." Second, . . . the extramarital affairs played a "relatively minor role in the divorce." . . .

As evidence of irreconcilable differences, Ms. Gardner points to "multiple disputes unrelated to the infidelity," including disputes over their level of religious involvement, their division of labor in the home, and finances, as well as to episodes of mutual verbal abuse, and one episode in which she hit Mr. Gardner. But . . . the evidence of other sources of contention does not foreclose the possibility that Ms. Gardner's multiple episodes of infidelity substantially contributed to the divorce. . . .

In fact, the record evidence suggests that Ms. Gardner's extramarital affairs were a significant, if not the primary, impetus for the demise of the marriage. . . .

[I]t was only after explaining how Ms. Gardner's infidelities affected their marriage that [the husband] explained that there were other sources of "discontent" between them, such as disputes regarding their religion, income, and the division of responsibility within the marriage. This testimony suggests that the extramarital affairs were a significant cause of the divorce, even though there were other areas of contention in their marriage. Accordingly, the evidence supports the district court's conclusion that Ms. Gardner's extramarital affairs substantially contributed to the breakup of the marriage. . . .

The closest Ms. Gardner comes to contradicting Mr. Gardner's testimony is when she discusses his attempts to stay in the marriage from the time he learned of the infidelities until 2016. . . .

The fact that he considered divorce after the first affair in 2007 and sought to find her "help" indicates that Mr. Gardner viewed his wife's infidelity as having significantly damaged their marriage. And this conclusion is not undermined by the fact that he agreed to remain in the marriage once she agreed to go through a formal repentance process through their church. . . .

In sum, the phrase "substantially contributed" in section 30-3-5(8) should be interpreted as referring to conduct that was a significant or important cause of the breakup of the marriage. Under this interpretation, the conduct need not be the only significant cause, or the first significant cause; instead, it need only be significant enough that a reasonable person would conclude that it was an important factor in the divorce. Because evidence supports the conclusion that Ms. Gardner's extramarital sexual relationships in 2007 and 2009 were significant factors in the ultimate demise of the couple's marriage, we cannot say that the district court clearly erred when it found that the affairs substantially contributed to the breakup of the marriage.

II. We Affirm the District Court's Determination of the Terms of the Alimony Award . . .

[U]nder the plain language of section 30-3-5(8), courts have discretion to depart from the default economic rules where one party's fault makes it appropriate to do so. Because the district court determined that Ms. Gardner's conduct qualified as fault under the statute, the court was authorized to depart from the default alimony rules by reducing Ms. Gardner's alimony award by some amount.

B. The district court's reduction of Ms. Gardner's alimony award did not constitute an abuse of discretion

Although we conclude that the district court's fault determination authorized it to consider fault as part of its alimony determination, we must also determine whether the *manner* in which the court factored Ms. Gardner's fault into the alimony award constituted an abuse of discretion in this case. . . .

[W]e hold that before a court considers fault as part of its determination, it must make a threshold determination, under section 30-3-5(8)(c), that the conduct qualifies as fault. It should then make detailed findings regarding the gravity of the harm caused by the fault. In making these findings, the court should focus on the harm the at-fault conduct caused to the marriage and the other party, along with other equitable factors. The court should then articulate the extent to which these findings justify a departure from the default rules of alimony. . . .

Although it is conceivable that the court could have made more detailed factual findings regarding the relative gravity of the fault at issue in this case, there is sufficient support in the record to conclude that her extramarital affairs were severely damaging. . . .

And when we consider the effect of the specific alimony reductions, we also cannot say that they resulted in such serious inequity as to manifest a clear abuse of discretion. Ms. Gardner argues that the court abused its discretion in four ways: (1) by reducing her need by "nearly one-third," (2) by "shorten[ing] the alimony award from the statutory length of the marriage (here, 22 years) to only ten," (3) by providing for a gradual decrease in the alimony amount over the final years of the award, and (4) by imputing to her an income of $1,300. . . .

The district court's reduction of Ms. Gardner's expected monthly expenses did not result in such serious inequity as to manifest a clear abuse of discretion . . .

The court reduced Ms. Gardner's expected monthly expenses "to reflect reasonable and necessary expenses for a person in her circumstances" because it did not believe it was fair to obligate Mr. Gardner to maintain Ms. Gardner at the standard of living she enjoyed during her marriage. . . .

Although Ms. Gardner attempts to portray these adjustments in drastic terms, she fails to persuade us that the court acted unreasonably or that she has suffered a serious inequity. . . . [O]nce a court decides to base a party's alimony award on a lower standard of living than he or she enjoyed during marriage, it will inevitably have to reduce that party's expected monthly expenses. In practice, this will require the court to reduce the costs of specific line items in that person's budget. That is what the court did in this case. . . .

[W]e have previously held that it is an abuse of discretion to award alimony for a shortened period when it is unlikely the receiving spouse would be able to maintain the same standard of living after the alimony period ended. . . .

In this case, the court ordered the alimony to terminate in ten years and then stated it "want[ed] to give [Ms. Gardner] some incentive to start working and be able to be self sufficient." The court explained that "at that point [Ms. Gardner is] going to need to be in a position to be able to take care of herself and so it's important that she start getting some education or work experience." Because ten years provides Ms. Gardner a reasonable amount of time to pursue an education or work experience that would allow her to close the gap between expenses and actual income, the court did not err by ordering a ten-year alimony award.

Additionally, there is evidence on the record to suggest that Ms. Gardner should share some of the responsibility for her lack of work experience and marketable skills. Mr. Gardner testified that he frequently encouraged Ms. Gardner to gain work experience or obtain more education. But Ms. Gardner declined to do so. In *Warren*, we refused to place the burden of a wife's lack of work experience or marketable skills fully on a husband who had "encouraged [his wife] to finish work on her baccalaureate degree and to find a job, [even though the wife] had not done so." . . . So this reason also supports the court's reduction. . . .

In this case, the district court expressly tied the shortened alimony duration to its finding of fault. . . . Because it is reasonable to conclude that imposing an alimony award for twenty-two years upon Mr. Gardner, where it was Ms. Gardner's conduct that caused the divorce, would not be "fair, just, and equitable," we conclude that the court did not abuse its discretion in shortening the duration of the alimony period, even were we to assume that the duration is not justified solely by economic factors. . . .

Because the district court did not abuse its discretion in determining Ms. Gardner's conduct constituted fault or in establishing the terms of her alimony award, we affirm the district court's alimony determination. . . .

NOTES AND QUESTIONS

1. *Is Fault Relevant?* The court in *Gardner* permitted the wife's infidelity to warrant a reduction in the alimony to which she would otherwise have been entitled. This approach represents the incomplete overthrow of the fault-based regime. As of 2017, 27 states still allow consideration of marital fault as part of the determination of spousal support.[194] Yet, states have taken different approaches to allowing such consideration. In Louisiana, for example, only fault on the part of the party seeking alimony is relevant.[195] As we saw with property division, some states consider fault only when it has economic consequences.[196]

2. *Domestic Violence.* Many states have enacted statutes that explicitly address the determination of alimony in the context of domestic violence, by either the higher- or lower-earning spouse. In Texas, for example, a conviction for domestic violence is one of the few permissible bases for an award of alimony against the perpetrator.[197] Louisiana has gone even further, with a statutory mandate to presume permanent spousal support for victims of domestic violence.[198] Other states, though, do not mandate that abusers pay; a handful of states instead require that courts consider any history of domestic violence when deciding whether to award permanent spousal support.[199]

What about the abuser's claim to support? In California, there is a statutory rebuttable presumption against an award of spousal support in favor of a convicted perpetrator of misdemeanor domestic violence.[200] If the criminal conviction was for a violent sexual felony, then any award of spousal support to the convicted spouse is flatly prohibited.[201] Most states' statutes, however, do not have prohibit spousal support in favor of a perpetrator of domestic violence.[202] Is domestic violence an appropriate consideration in the spousal support calculus?

3. *What Kind of Fault?* Did the *Gardner* court give any indication of the types of misconduct that might justify a reduction in alimony? Is it only misconduct sufficient to warrant a fault-based divorce? Or might conduct justify a reduction in alimony even if it is not egregious enough to warrant divorce? For example, should the wife have

---

194. See Charts, supra note 151, at 544–47.
195. Id. at 546.
196. Id. at 547.
197. Tex. Fam. Code Ann. § 8.051(1) (2020).
198. La. Civ. Code Ann. art. 112(C) (2020).
199. Andrea B. Carroll, Family Law and Female Empowerment, 24 UCLA Women's L.J. 1, 27 (2017).
200. Cal. Fam. Code § 4325 (West 2020).
201. Id. § 4324.5.
202. Maria Stamatelatos, Note, Spousal Support and Domestic Violence: What Happens when the Dependent Spouse is the Abuser? 32 J. Civ. Rts. & Econ. Dev. 439, 441 (2019).

been penalized for not gaining more work experience when her husband urged her to do so?

4. *Infidelity.* The *Gardner* court justified the consideration of the wife's infidelity by concluding that it was a substantial factor in the break-up of the marriage. In conducting this inquiry, did the court give greater weight to adultery than to the other types of discord identified by the wife? If so, was the court justified in doing so? Is a court equipped to accurately determine why a marriage ended?

5. *Morality.* Was the inquiry undertaken by the trial court causal, as the court says, or moral? In other words, did the court make a judgment about who caused the divorce or who was to blame for the divorce? If the wife had proven that they would have divorced even if she hadn't committed adultery, would the trial court still have been justified in reducing her alimony award?

G. Modification of Support Orders

PIMM V. PIMM
601 So. 2d 534 (Fla. 1992)

HARDING, JUSTICE.

We . . . certified the following question as a matter of great public importance:

Is the postjudgment retirement of a spouse who is obligated to make support or alimony payments pursuant to a judgment of dissolution of marriage a change of circumstance that *may* be considered together with other relevant factors and applicable law upon a petition to modify such alimony or support payments?

We . . . answer the question in the affirmative.

On July 21, 1975, a final judgment dissolved the twenty-nine-year marriage of petitioner Maurice C. Pimm (husband) and respondent Carolyn M. Pimm (wife). The final judgment incorporated a property settlement agreement of the parties providing that the husband would pay the wife weekly alimony installments which would cease in the event of the wife's remarriage. In 1988, shortly before the husband turned sixty-five years of age, he filed a petition for modification of the final judgment seeking to terminate the alimony obligation upon his retirement at the age of sixty-five. The wife counterpetitioned for an increase in alimony. The trial court denied both petitions. . . . [T]he Second District Court of Appeal . . . reversed the trial court and certified the question to this Court.

At the time of the dissolution of marriage, the husband was a civil engineer and president of his own surveying company. The husband subsequently became a salaried employee of the firm that purchased his company, and it was from this position that the husband contemplated retirement when he filed his petition for modification of the alimony payments.

The wife was a full-time mother and homemaker and was never employed outside the home, either during or after the marriage. However, the record reflects that through inheritance and the sale of jointly-owned property the wife had accumulated considerable liquid assets since the time of the dissolution.

The wife contends that the husband's voluntary act of retirement should not be considered a change of circumstance which would support a modification of alimony. The wife points out that in petitioning to modify alimony, the moving party must show three fundamental prerequisites. First, there must be a substantial change in circumstances. Second, the change was not contemplated at the time of final judgment of dissolution. Third, the change is sufficient, material, involuntary, and permanent in nature. As measured by this standard, the wife argues that the husband's voluntary retirement may be a substantial change, but it is not involuntary; that his retirement was or should have been contemplated at the time of final judgment; and that such a voluntary retirement is not sufficiently permanent in nature.

The husband claims that section Fla. Stat. § 61.14(1) expresses a public policy favoring modification of support in accordance with changed circumstances of the parties. He also asserts that if the reduced income of a payor spouse who retires at "normal" retirement age is not a factor that may be considered in proving a change in circumstances, then the payor spouse is put in the untenable position of being unable to retire at any age. The husband insists that if this Court disapproves the opinion of the district court, then it will be setting separate standards for self-employed payor spouses and non-self-employed payor spouses, whose retirement is generally mandated at a specific age.

Consequently, the husband urges that voluntary retirement is a part of the "total circumstances" which the "court can and should take into consideration" when modification is requested. The husband reasons that if the trial court is permitted to consider the payor spouse's retirement as part of the total circumstances, then the court can inquire into the motivation and facts surrounding the retirement.

The district court held "that unless there is such a "true" or "pure" property settlement agreement that forecloses modification or a showing that a spouse's future retirement was contemplated and considered in establishing the alimony payments, a supporting or payor spouse's retirement is a factor that *may* be considered along with all other relevant factors and applicable law in determining whether the payor spouse is entitled to a modification of alimony or support payments."

In reaching that conclusion, the court rejected the bright line rule, . . . which would not permit "*any* consideration of 'voluntary' retirement as a change of circumstance sufficient to support a modification of alimony or support payments." . . .

The wife argues that the agreement's silence on the issue of retirement combined with its provision that alimony would terminate upon her remarriage indicates that the husband chose to pay her, regardless of retirement, until such time as she remarried. We do not agree with this argument. Although it would be a better practice to incorporate consideration of retirement and what will happen in the event of retirement in an agreement or final judgment, we find that silence in that regard should not preclude consideration of a reasonable retirement as part of the total circumstances in determining if sufficient changed circumstances exist to warrant a modification of alimony.

In determining whether a voluntary retirement is reasonable, the court must consider the payor's age, health, and motivation for retirement, as well as the type of work the payor performs and the age at which others engaged in that line of work normally retire. The age of sixty-five years has become the traditional and presumptive age of retirement for American workers. . . . Based upon this widespread acceptance of sixty-five as the normal retirement age, we find that one would have a significant burden to show that a voluntary retirement before the age of sixty-five is reasonable. Even at the age of sixty-five or later, a payor spouse should not be permitted to unilaterally choose voluntary retirement if this choice places the receiving spouse in peril of poverty. Thus, the court should consider the needs of the receiving spouse and the impact a termination or reduction of alimony would have on him or her. In assessing those needs, the court should consider any assets which the receiving spouse has accumulated or received since the final judgment as well as any income generated by those assets. . . .

Accordingly, we . . . approve the decision below. . . .

NOTES AND QUESTIONS

1. *Modification.* Unlike equitable distribution judgments, which are final, spousal support awards are subject to modification. Modification entails a two-step process. The court first determines whether a sufficient change in circumstances has occurred relating to either the payor's ability to pay or the payee's needs, and then evaluates whether the new circumstances warrant any modification of the support award.[203]

2. *Changed Circumstances.* States differ in the stringency of their changed circumstances standard. Some jurisdictions merely require a "significant and material change in the circumstances of the parties."[204] Others, with statutes modeled on the Uniform Marriage and Divorce Act, require "a showing of changed circumstances so substantial and continuing as to make the terms [of the original support decree] unconscionable."[205]

---

203. See Ex Parte Wilson, 262 So. 3d 1202 (Ala. 2018).
204. Williams v. Williams, 541 S.W.3d 477, 485 (Ark. Ct. App. 2018).
205. Mont. Code Ann. § 40-4-208(2)(b)(i) (2019).

3. *The Ability to Pay (More).* While most modification cases concern whether spousal support should be reduced, courts may also consider whether to increase support. Consider the reasoning of a District of Columbia court:[206]

> A modification of alimony "must reflect changed needs or changed financial resources" (as opposed to "offensive" conduct on the part of the receiving spouse). While it may deter marriage, or divorce, or both, to contemplate that the increase in the income of one divorced spouse, standing alone, will provide justification for an increase in support payments to the receiving spouse, a blanket rule precluding spouses from sharing in the increased resources of their former partners would be unacceptable. It may be, for example, that the spouse receiving support has contributed during the marriage so as to be partly or wholly responsible for the other spouse's subsequent income. Or, at the time of the divorce, there may have been insufficient resources for both spouses to maintain their previous standard of living, and the subsequent increase in the income of the spouse paying support might be used to meet the pre-existing, though previously unmet, financial needs of the other spouse. In short, there may be circumstances, though unusual, in which it may be appropriate for the trial court to award increased alimony where only the income of the paying spouse, and not the needs of the receiving spouse, have increased.[207]

Do you agree with the court that an increase in the payor's ability to pay may on its own, under certain circumstances, justify modifying a spousal support award?

4. *Payor Retirement.* Modification disputes often arise in the context of the voluntary retirement of the payor, like the one in *Pimm*. States take a variety of approaches to such disputes. Consider the range of approaches described by a New Jersey court:

> [In t]he first [category] . . . , the voluntariness of the change in circumstances, in itself, is viewed as barring an application for modification. . . . This rule has the virtue of simplicity, but little else. Indeed, it has been revisited in Florida, and rejected as "too severe."
>
> In the second category, voluntary retirement cases are evaluated solely based upon the motives of the party seeking to make the change. If the change is made in good faith, the application for modification is approved. . . .
>
> A variation on the good faith theme is found in the "sole purpose" category of cases[, where] . . . if the "sole" motivation for the change is to avoid support obligations, good faith is absent. The problem with the sole purpose standard . . . [is] that it is likely that a party moving for modification will always be able to advance at least one legitimate reason for retirement. . . .

---

206. Graham v. Graham, 597 A.2d 355 (D.C. 1991).
207. Id. at 358–59.

The final category includes cases in which any negative impact on the payee spouse is considered sufficient to bar modification based upon voluntary retirement. . . .

Regardless of the ultimate outcome, all of these courts have focused to one extent or another on two issues: the motive of the payor spouse and the effect on the payee. . . .[208]

Which approach seems best?

DACE V. DOSS
530 S.W.3d 893 (Ark. Ct. App. 2017)

DAVID M. GLOVER, JUDGE . . .

Dace and Doss divorced in 2012 after a seventeen-year marriage. . . . Doss remarried on November 7, 2015; after her remarriage, Dace unilaterally terminated his alimony payments to her.

In April 2016, Doss filed a motion for contempt against Dace . . . for terminating her alimony payments in violation of the terms of the divorce decree. . . . [The court found for Doss.] . . .

Court-ordered alimony is always subject to modification. Modification of an alimony award must be based on a significant and material change in the circumstances of the parties, and the burden of showing such a change in circumstances is on the party seeking the modification. . . .

Arkansas Code Annotated section 9–12–312(a)(2)(A) (Repl. 2015) provides, "Unless otherwise ordered by the court or agreed to by the parties, the liability for alimony shall automatically cease upon . . . the date of the remarriage of the person who was awarded the alimony." Dace . . . contends that while the circuit court originally ordered alimony to be paid for the remainder of Doss's life, the new order, entered in October 2016, does not "order otherwise," merely stating that Dace "shall have an ongoing duty to pay alimony in the amount of $234.00 per month."

Arkansas Code Annotated section 9–12–312(a)(2)(A) does not require the circuit court to terminate Dace's alimony obligation to Doss. . . . Dace was originally ordered to pay Doss alimony for the remainder of her life; Doss was forced to file a motion for contempt against Dace when he unilaterally stopped paying alimony after she remarried. . . . [T]he circuit court, fully aware of Doss's remarriage, found Dace "shall have an ongoing duty to pay alimony," although it was reduced from $619 per month to $234 per month . . . , finding Dace's alimony obligation should continue, even in light of Doss's remarriage.

---

208. Deegan v. Deegan, 603 A.2d 542, 545–46 (N.J. Super. Ct. App. Div. 1992).

Dace further contends his alimony obligation should have terminated at the time of Doss's remarriage because she no longer had a need for alimony after that date. . . .

Doss testified that she remarried in November 2015 and moved to Fayetteville, where her new husband was living. She stated she is a hairdresser and had worked at a salon in Vilonia for twenty years; after her remarriage, she continued to commute to Vilonia for two or three days every other week. She said she was now making less money because she was working fewer days and had lost some clients when she moved to Fayetteville; she explained that she did not cut hair in Fayetteville because she could not afford the booth rental and because, at fifty-four, starting a new business with no clientele would be difficult because people do not want to go to the "old girl." . . .

Doss agreed her new husband paid the rent and utilities, and she no longer had those expenses. However, she testified she still had monthly expenses for which she was responsible — [such as] her car payment . . . her cell-phone bill ($130), her gasoline ($400), booth rental at the salon ($250), . . . her credit-card bill, and other expenses, such as occasionally eating out. . . . She testified her new husband made less than Dace.

Doss's new husband, West Doss, testified . . . alimony was necessary for Doss because she was falling short every month in covering her bills. . . .

We hold the circuit court did not abuse its discretion in finding Doss still had a need for alimony. . . . Clearly, the circuit court took into consideration the fact that Doss's remarriage allowed her not to incur certain expenses, i.e., rent and utilities, and reduced Dace's alimony obligation. . . . However, as expressed by the circuit court at the hearing, the reduction of expenses did not automatically translate into a finding that Doss had no need for continuation of alimony in some amount. Doss was still falling short of her monthly expenses, and Dace had the ability to pay the reduced amount of alimony. . . .

NOTES AND QUESTIONS

---

1.   *The Remarriage Rule.* The traditional rule is that alimony terminates on the remarriage of the payee, without any inquiry into the economic effects of the remarriage.[209] What do you think were the original rationales for the rule?

The traditional approach continues to be reflected in current law. Most states, by case law or by statute, provide that a recipient's remarriage either automatically terminates spousal support or creates a prima facie case for termination.[210] The Uniform

---

209. Cynthia Lee Starnes, One More Time: Alimony, Intuition, and the Remarriage-Termination Rule, 81 Ind. L. J. 971 (2006); see also Cynthia Lee Starnes, The Marriage Buyout: The Troubled Trajectory of U.S. Alimony Law (2014).

210. Starnes, One More Time, supra note 209, at 973, 977.

Marriage and Divorce Act provides: "Unless otherwise agreed in writing or expressly provided in the decree, the obligation to pay future maintenance is terminated upon . . . the remarriage of the party receiving maintenance."[211] Are there any persuasive justifications for maintaining the traditional rule today?

2.   *The Arkansas Statute.* The Arkansas statute at issue in *Dace* states that "alimony shall automatically cease" upon the recipient's remarriage. How did the court nonetheless justify not automatically terminating alimony upon the recipient's remarriage?

3.   *The Cohabitation Rule.* Roughly a dozen states have expanded the remarriage rule to encompass cohabitation by the payee spouse, so that alimony terminates if the payee cohabits, regardless of the economic impact of the cohabitation.[212] Most states grant courts discretion to terminate or modify alimony based on the specific circumstances and effects of the payees's cohabitation.[213] Some states do not treat the mere fact of cohabitation as a change in circumstances sufficient to warrant reconsideration of the spousal support award.[214] Which, if any, of these approaches seems sensible? Should cohabitation per se constitute a basis for terminating alimony? Alternatively, should the fact of cohabitation be viewed as a changed circumstance sufficient to reconsider the award in light of the economic effects of the cohabitation?

4.   *Defining Cohabitation.* States with a cohabitation rule confront the challenge of defining cohabitation. One approach in some states is to define cohabitation as a marriage-like relationship.[215] Other states define cohabitation with reference to a list of factors indicative of a committed, conjugal relationship.[216] Whatever the state's approach, questions arise as to how long and how often a couple must be together in the same home. Arkansas requires living together on a full-time basis.[217] New Jersey, in contrast, does not require that the couple live together full-time to be considered in a cohabiting relationship sufficient to trigger a change in spousal support.[218]

5.   *Proving Cohabitation.* Efforts to prove cohabitation can sometimes entail detailed inquiries into personal affairs. In one South Carolina case, the court attempted to determine whether the payee wife lived with her boyfriend long enough to satisfy

---

211. UMDA § 316(b).

212. Cynthia Lee Starnes, I'll Be Watching You: Alimony and the Cohabitation Rule, 50 Fam. L.Q. 261, 264 (2016).

213. Id. at 267.

214. Myers v. Myers. 560 N.E.2d 39, 43 (Ind. 1990); Lyon v. Lyon, 728 A.2d 1273, 1275 (Me. 1999); Cherpelis v. Cherpelis, 914 P.2d 637, 638 (N.M. Ct. App. 1996); Goldman v. Goldman, 543 A.2d 1304, 1306–07 (R.I. 1988).

215. Starnes, supra note 212, at 278–279.

216. Id. at 280–288.

217. Id. at 284.

218. Id.

the state's 90-day cohabitation rule. (There was some evidence she had intentionally separated from her cohabiting partner in order to avoid the 90-day rule.)

> [T]he parties' daughter, Stephanie Brown, testified she thought Wife lived with Erickson because when she went to Wife's house, there was furniture that belonged to Erickson, a different television, his clothes and shoes were in a closet upstairs, a lot of Erickson's other belongings were in the house, he sometimes parked his car in her garage with the garage door closed, and Wife and Erickson were picking out paint colors for the house. She also testified Erickson moved bedroom furniture and a television with a video game system into a spare room for Erickson's son to play with when he was at the house.[219]

Does such an invasive investigation violate the family's right to privacy under Supreme Court precedent? Is it desirable to have a rule that invites courts to undertake this sort of inquiry?

6. *Economic Effects.* A common contemporary justification for decreasing spousal support upon remarriage or cohabitation is that the payee spouse's needs have diminished. But if the payee spouse has been able to reduce expenditures, why should that thriftiness inure to the benefit of the payor spouse? Is there any reason for treating cohabitation differently than if the payee spouse, say, moved in with other family or friends?

7. *Marital Settlement Agreements.* Statutory provisions providing for the termination of spousal support upon the remarriage or cohabitation of the payee spouse must often be construed in light of the parties' marital settlement agreement. As discussed later in this chapter, the parties often craft marital settlement agreements, which are ordinarily incorporated into the divorce decree. Parties might, of course, include in their agreement provisions contrary to the rules that would otherwise govern under the statute. Courts then are confronted with the task of reconciling the parties' agreement with statutory directives.

NOTE ON SPOUSAL SUPPORT JURISDICTION

As discussed in Chapter 4, the Supreme Court has allowed states to assert jurisdiction to grant a divorce even when the state lacks personal jurisdiction over one of the parties.[220] The Court has declined, however, to extend this approach to the resolution of economic obligations arising out of the marriage, including spousal support.[221] The court waived the usual requirement of personal jurisdiction because a divorce constituted only an adjustment of "status," not a "personal claim

---

219. Moore v. Moore, 828 S.E.2d 224, 226–27 (S.C. Ct. App. 2019).
220. Williams v. North Carolina, 317 U.S. 287 (1942); Williams v. North Carolina, 325 U.S. 226 (1945).
221. Estin v. Estin, 334 U.S. 541 (1948); Vanderbilt v. Vanderbilt, 354 U.S. 416 (1957).

or obligation," the determination of which would require personal jurisdiction.[222] In order to settle claims of property and support upon divorce, then, the court must have personal jurisdiction over the defendant.[223] The concept of "divisible divorce" refers to this sort of split jurisdiction, in which a court with authority to grant a divorce may lack authority to resolve matters of spousal support or property division. As a result of the divisible divorce doctrine, a spouse's petition for divorce may result in the ending of the marriage, but, if the other spouse has left the state (or never lived there), not in the resolution of the couple's economic entanglement.

One of the cases that developed the doctrine of divisible divorce was that of Cornelius Vanderbilt, Jr., scion of one of the richest families in American history. After living with his fifth wife Patricia in California, he left for Nevada, and she went to New York. He filed for divorce in Nevada, where his divorce petition was granted on grounds of mental cruelty after an appearance in court that lasted all of twenty minutes.[224] Meanwhile, his wife had filed a complaint in New York that he had failed to support her and that she was likely to become a public charge, an allegation that resulted in a warrant being issued for his arrest.[225] Patricia sought the economic support to which her marriage had entitled her, and Cornelius argued that his Nevada divorce (in which Patricia neither appeared nor filed an answer) eliminated any economic obligations he might have otherwise had to her. The stakes of such a jurisdictional battle are clear: on one side are states' interest in granting divorces that resolve the petitioner's economic claims or obligations, and on the other side are states' interest in protecting the economic claims of their own residents.

States have responded to this jurisdictional predicament through the enactment of long-arm jurisdictional provisions that apply specifically to marriage and divorce and that allow the state to assert jurisdiction over an absent spouse.[226] Thus, the spouse seeking the divorce can have support and property issues adjudicated despite the absentee spouse.[227] In order for the long-arm statute to successfully confer jurisdiction, the defendant must have minimum contacts with the forum state sufficient to satisfy constitutional requirements.[228] These statutes generally enable jurisdiction provided that the defendant has previously resided within the state for

---

222. *Vanderbilt*, 354 U.S. at 418–19.
223. Id.
224. Vanderbilt Wins Divorce, N.Y. Times, July 1, 1953, at 31.
225. Id.
226. See, e.g., Va. Code Ann. § 8.01-328.1(A)(9) (2020) (prior matrimonial domicile); Wis. Stat. § 801.05(11) (2020) (prior residence sufficient).
227. See Soule v. Soule, 14 Cal. Rptr. 417 (Cal. Ct. App. 1961).
228. Int'l Shoe Co. v. Washington, 326 U.S. 310 (1945).

a specified period of time prior to the filing of the action or been domiciled in the state while married.[229] (Domicile refers to one's permanent place of residence.)

The Uniform Interstate Family Support Act (UIFSA) governs the procedures for establishing, enforcing, and modifying spousal support orders.[230] Intended primarily to increase the effectiveness of child support enforcement, UIFSA was promulgated by the Uniform Law Commission in 1992, and amended in 1996, 2001, and 2008. UIFSA has been adopted verbatim in every state, largely because the Personal Responsibility and Work Opportunity Act of 1996 (the welfare reform law passed during the Clinton Administration) required each state's adoption as a condition for receiving certain federal funds.[231] Although concerned primarily with child support, UIFSA encompasses spousal support orders as well. The provisions relating to spousal support provide as follows:

SECTION 201. BASES FOR JURISDICTION OVER NONRESIDENT.
(a) In a proceeding to establish or enforce a support order . . . a tribunal of this state may exercise personal jurisdiction over a nonresident individual [or the individual's guardian or conservator] if:
    (1) the individual is personally served with [citation, summons, notice] within this state;
    (2) the individual submits to the jurisdiction of this state by consent in a record, by entering a general appearance, or by filing a responsive document having the effect of waiving any contest to personal jurisdiction; . . .
    (8) there is any other basis consistent with the constitutions of this state and the United States for the exercise of personal jurisdiction. . . .

SECTION 202. DURATION OF PERSONAL JURISDICTION.
Personal jurisdiction acquired by a tribunal of this state in a proceeding under this [act] or other law of this state relating to a support order continues as long as a tribunal of this state has continuing, exclusive jurisdiction to modify its order or continuing jurisdiction to enforce its order as provided by Section [ ] . . . 211.

SECTION 211. CONTINUING, EXCLUSIVE JURISDICTION TO MODIFY
(a) A tribunal of this state issuing a spousal-support order consistent with the law of this state has continuing, exclusive jurisdiction to modify the spousal-support order throughout the existence of the support obligation.
(b) A tribunal of this state may not modify a spousal-support order issued by a tribunal of another state or a foreign country having continuing,

---

229. See, e.g., Va. Code Ann. § 8.01-328.1(A)(9) (2020); Wis. Stat. § 801.05(11) (2020).
230. Unif. Interstate Family Support Act (Unif. Law Comm'n 2008).
231. 42 U.S.C. § 666(f) (2020).

exclusive jurisdiction over that order under the law of that state or foreign country.

    (c) A tribunal of this state that has continuing, exclusive jurisdiction over a spousal-support order may serve as either of the following:

        (1) An initiating tribunal to request a tribunal of another state to enforce the spousal-support order issued in this state;

        (2) A responding tribunal to enforce or modify its own spousal-support order.

One goal of UIFSA is to establish clear authority for the enforcement and modification of support orders. Once a state establishes personal jurisdiction, UIFSA provides that it lasts for as long as the state maintains continuing, exclusive jurisdiction. And the state maintains continuing, exclusive jurisdiction so long as the support obligation exists. The state may request, as an initiating tribunal, that another state enforce the support order, as would be necessary when the obligor has moved to another state. And the state may also accept requests from outside the state to modify or enforce its support order.

These provisions raise many questions, and courts have interpreted the Act mostly within the context of child support. Why, for example, should a jurisdiction maintain continuing, exclusive jurisdiction to enforce or modify an order even if all the parties have moved away from the state?

We return to UIFSA in Chapter 11 when we discuss child support.

NOTE ON ALTERNATIVES TO ADVERSARIAL LITIGATION

For all the emphasis that we place in this casebook on judicial decision-making, it is important to note that most decisions about how to unwind a couple's relationship are not made by courts after a contested trial. Most dissolution and custody matters do not culminate in a trial at all. They are instead the result of a settlement between the parties that is then approved by a court, often with little substantive review.

Yet, the law remains critically important, as couples settle their family controversies in its shadow.[232] The substantive rules that would apply if they did go to trial constitute the backdrop against which they negotiate. These background rules influence negotiating behavior, inform the parties' vision of a just and reasonable outcome, and help the parties decide whether an expensive and protracted fight is worth it.[233]

Negotiation and settlement have long been part of the litigation process, in all areas of law. The image of lawyers settling their case on the courthouse steps on

---

232. See generally Mnookin & Kornhauser, supra note 3.
233. Id.

the eve trial is not far from the truth. Taking a case to trial is expensive and time-consuming, and the outcomes are unpredictable.

For parties to a family law case, there are even more reasons to avoid litigation. Many people who find themselves within the family law court system cannot afford a lawyer, as discussed in Chapter 4. According to a study by the National Center for State Courts, in more than 7 in 10 cases in family court, at least one of the parties is not represented by a lawyer.[234] Even if the parties do have lawyers, litigation adds stress at a time that is already emotionally wrenching. And, of course, family law disputes implicate such uniquely personal values, preferences, and priorities that, all things considered, may be better resolved by the parties than by an impersonal judge who understands comparatively little about the family. The parties have the best information about their own lives and the lives of their children and are likely in the best position to decide how to resolve issues associated with the relationship.

Courts have responded by establishing an array of supportive services for families who enter the system. Because so many parties are unrepresented, courts maintain self-help centers, allow parties to complete court-provided forms rather than formal pleadings, and engage social-work professionals to help with the non-legal aspects of a family dispute. Many jurisdictions now offer parent-education programs that aim to help parents navigate the myriad challenges associated with divorce and child custody.[235] Parent Coordinators also have become widely available.[236] These professionals work with high-conflict couples and help them quickly resolve post-decree disagreements about their children, so that they do not have to return repeatedly to court.[237]

Courts also have begun to embrace methods of alternative dispute resolution that aim to enable parties to resolve their disputes without going to trial. In addition to programs connected to the courts, parties sometimes employ alternative dispute approaches on their own. These approaches may enable couples to resolve their dispute more quickly, less expensively, and with less acrimony, leaving the couple better able to move on with life. The potential benefits don't accrue only to couples; their children benefit as well. Research has shown that children's post-divorce adjustment depends very much on the level of conflict to which they are exposed during the dissolution process.[238] And parents who carry less resentment toward each other are more likely to become effective co-parents even after their

---

234. Nat'l Ctr. for State Cts., Family Justice Initiative: The Landscape of Domestic Relations Cases in State Courts ii (2018).

235. Nancy Ver Steegh, Family Court Reform and ADR: Shifting Values and Expectations Transform the Divorce Process, 42 Fam. L.Q. 659, 661–62 (2008).

236. See, e.g., In re Marriage of Rozzi, 190 P.3d 815 (Colo. App. 2008).

237. Debra K. Carter & Douglas N. Frenkel, Parenting Coordination and Confidentiality: A (Not-So) Delicate Balance, 58 Fam. Ct. Rev. 68 (2020).

238. Robert E. Emery, Renegotiating Family Relationships: Divorce, Child Custody, and Mediation (2d. ed. 2011).

own intimate relationship has ended. Importantly, alternative dispute resolution methods benefit courts as well, preserving scarce resources and freeing judges from protracted trials.

We now consider major forms of alternative dispute resolution in the family law context:

1. *Mediation.* Mediation is the most widely adopted program of alternative dispute resolution. Mediation is defined by the Model Standards of Practice for Family and Divorce mediation as a:

> process in which a mediator, an impartial third party, facilitates the resolution of family disputes by promoting the participants' voluntary agreement. The family mediator assists communication, encourages understanding, and focuses the participants on their individual and common interests. The family mediator works with the participants to explore options and make decisions and reach their own agreements.[239]

Rather than appear before a judge who issues a ruling, the parties to a mediation work with a facilitator to reach their own agreement. Lawyers may be part of the process, in the sense of either representing a party in the actual mediation or acting as consultants and conferring with their client outside of the mediation.[240] Mediation can also occur without any involvement of lawyers. The mediation can encompass all the parties' disputed issues or it can be limited by agreement to only some of the disputed issues.

Most states mandate that couples try to mediate contested custody and visitation issues.[241] In some states, courts have discretion to order mediation of custody and visitation disputes.[242] There are more than 200 court-annexed mediation programs, and all states offer some form of mediation.[243] States cannot, of course, require that the parties reach agreement, merely that they give the process a try.

Empirical evidence suggests that mediation is effective. In one classic study, Eleanor Maccoby and Robert Mnookin randomly selected divorcing couples with children for mediation and found that those couples were more likely to settle their dispute.[244] In another random assignment study, Robert Emery found

---

239. Ass'n of Family & Conciliation Courts, Model Standards of Practice for Family and Divorce Mediation (2001).

240. Forrest S. Mosten, Lawyer as Peacemaker: Building a Successful Law Practice Without Ever Going to Court, 43 Fam. L.Q. 489 (2009).

241. Linda D. Elrod, Alternative Dispute Resolution, Child Custody Prac. and Proc. § 1:12 (2020); see, e.g., Cal. Fam. Code § 3170 (West 2020); Wis. Stat. § 767.405(5)(a) (2020).

242. See, e.g., Iowa Code § 598.41(2)(d) (2020); Va. Code Ann § 20-124.2 (2020).

243. Elrod, supra note 241, § 1:12.

244. Eleanor E. Maccoby & Robert H. Mnookin, Dividing the Child: Social and Legal Dilemmas of Custody (1998).

that mediation not only reduced rates of litigation, it increased the likelihood of positive familial, and in particular parent-child, relationships more than a decade later.[245]

2. *Arbitration.* Arbitration is the form of alternative dispute resolution that is most similar to the conventional adversarial litigation approach. Arbitration is a process whereby the parties select and pay a neutral third party (the arbitrator or panel of arbitrators) to decide their dispute. The arbitrator conducts a hearing, but without the extensive discovery process, evidentiary rules, and complicated procedural requirements that apply to litigation (unless the parties agree to impose such rules). Many arbitrators are lawyers or retired judges. Each party to an arbitration is typically represented by counsel who presents the party's case to the arbitrator.

To be enforceable, an arbitration award must be submitted to a court to be confirmed and converted into a judicially enforceable judgment. Arbitration awards are subject to very limited judicial review. They can be overturned if they were procured by fraud or resulted from egregious misconduct by the arbitrator, but not because the arbitrator misapplied the law.

Long a mainstay of the resolution of labor and commercial disputes, arbitration has become much more common in the family law context. Arbitrations occur pursuant to a formal agreement to arbitrate, and couples may include an agreement to arbitrate in their separation agreement or premarital agreement. Arbitration is usually faster than litigation, affords a degree of confidentiality not available in a judicial proceeding, and allows a couple to select an arbitrator who reflects their own values, a feature that may be particularly important to members of certain religious communities.[246]

Inasmuch as arbitration awards are subject to limited judicial review, courts historically have limited the types of matters that can be subjected to binding arbitration in the family law context. While courts have long been inclined to allow property and spousal support issues to be arbitrated,[247] they have been less receptive to arbitration agreements purporting to resolve issues related to children. State laws do not permit an arbitration agreement to divest the court of its public responsibility to assert its *parens patriae* power to protect the welfare of children. Accordingly, the Ohio Supreme Court ruled in 2001 that an "agreement to arbitrate custody and visitation disputes impermissibly interferes with the court's ability to carry out [its] responsibility" to protect the best interests

---

245. Robert Emery et al., Child Custody Mediation and Litigation: Custody, Contact and Coparenting 12 Years After Initial Dispute Resolution, 69 J. Consult. & Clin. Psych. 323 (2001); Robert E. Emery et al., Divorce Mediation: Research and Reflections, 43 Fam. Ct. Rev. 22 (2005).

246. See, e.g., Ayelet Shachar, Privatizing Diversity: A Cautionary Tale from Religious Arbitration in Family Law, 9 Theoretical Inquiries L. 573 (2008); Michael A. Helfand, Arbitration's Counter-Narrative: The Religious Arbitration Paradigm, 124 Yale L.J. 2994 (2015).

247. See, e.g., Spencer v. Spencer, 494 A.2d 1279 (D.C. 1985).

of the child.[248] (The Court had previously determined that spousal support and child support could be subjected to arbitration.[249]) Under this traditional view, provisions of premarital agreements or separation agreements that purport to subject child custody or visitation to arbitration are unenforceable, even if, in the case of separation agreements, the agreement was incorporated into a prior court judgment without objection by either party.[250] Some states, including New York, continue to adhere to the traditional view disfavoring arbitration of child custody matters.[251]

Yet states have become increasingly receptive to the arbitration of child custody and visitation matters, and now most states permit them to be submitted to binding arbitration.[252] The New Jersey Supreme Court even declared that "the constitutionally protected right to parental autonomy includes the right to submit any family controversy, including one regarding child custody and parenting time, to a decision maker chosen by the parents."[253] The Court reasoned that "just as parents 'choose' to decide issues of custody and parenting time among themselves without court intervention, they may opt to sidestep the judicial process and submit their dispute to an arbitrator whom they have chosen."[254]

States typically require a more meaningful form of judicial review of arbitration awards concerning child custody issues than would be applied to other types of arbitration awards. In New Jersey, for example, the Supreme Court held that if there is a showing of a "threat of harm" to the child, the court may set aside the arbitration award.[255] Other jurisdictions subject arbitration awards concerning child custody to judicial review based on the best interests of the child standard.[256] Arbitration of family matters is governed by state laws, many modeled on the Uniform Arbitration Act or the Revised Uniform Arbitration Act.[257] Only recently, in 2016, did the Uniform Law Commission adopt a model arbitration law, the Uniform Family Law Arbitration Act (UFLAA), which includes special standards pertaining to the arbitration of family disputes.[258] The UFLAA has been adopted in three states — Arizona, Hawaii, and North Dakota.[259] One aim of the Act is to provide guidelines that will promote the welfare of children

---

248. Kelm v. Kelm, 749 N.E.2d 299, 304 (Ohio 2001).

249. Kelm v. Kelm, 623 N.E.2d 39 (Ohio 1993).

250. *Kelm*, 749 N.E.2d at 304.

251. See, e.g., Conn. Gen. Stat. § 46b-66 (2020); Weisz v. Weisz, 999 N.Y.S.2d 133 (N.Y. App. Div. 2014); Goldberg v. Goldberg, 1 N.Y.S.3d 360 (N.Y. 2015).

252. See, e.g., Colo. Rev. Stat. § 14-10-128.5 (2020); N.M. Stat. Ann. § 40-4-7.2 (2020); Ga. Code Ann. § 19-9-1.1 (2020); Tex. Fam. Code Ann. § 153.0071 (West 2020); Wis. Stat. § 802.12(3)(d) (2020).

253. Fawzy v. Fawzy, 973 A.2d 347, 360 (N.J. 2009).

254. Id.

255. Id. at 361.

256. See, e.g., Miller v. Miller, 620 A.2d 1161 (Pa. Super. Ct. 1993)

257. See, e.g., N.C. Gen. Stat. §§ 50-41 to 50-62 (2020).

258. Unif. Family Law Arbitration Act (Unif. Law Comm'n 2016).

259. Elrod, supra note 241, § 1:12.

by providing for meaningful judicial review. The Act requires proceedings to be recorded and the arbitrator to issue a written decision. Arbitration awards, under the Act, are only to be confirmed if they comply with the applicable law and are consistent with the best interests of the child.

3. *Collaborative Law.* Collaborative law practice began in the early 1990s and is an important alternative to the typical adversarial practice of divorce litigation.[260] While it is difficult to obtain precise estimates of the number of lawyers practicing collaborative law, more than 20,000 lawyers have been trained in the method.[261] The goal of collaborative law practice is to resolve the divorce process without resorting to litigation.[262] More substantively, the goal is to enable parties to achieve outcomes that are fair, more collaborative, and less destructive to the relationships that parents and children will need to have as they move beyond the divorce.

The hallmark of the collaborative process is that while the parties are represented by lawyers throughout, at the outset the lawyers and clients sign a "Participation Agreement" that obligates the lawyers to resign if the collaborative process fails and the matter proceeds to litigation.[263] The disqualification requirement may profoundly change the nature of the process for all parties involved,[264] both by focusing the parties on their common interests and desire for settlement and increasing the cost of ultimately pursuing litigation. (The Participation Agreement also raises professional responsibility concerns. If the lawyer is a party to the agreement, she may be assuming duties to another party, who may have interests that conflict with the client's.[265])

The Participation Agreement includes other stipulations that promote joint problem solving. Parties are required to commit to early and voluntary disclosure of all relevant information and to search for solutions that genuinely work for everyone.[266] The parties will often select and engage professionals from other disciplines, including financial consultants, psychologists, and counselors.[267] Those parties are hired jointly so that they also are invested in working toward the resolution of the conflict rather than representing one party or the other in

---

260. Pauline H. Telser, Collaborative Law: A New Paradigm for Divorce Lawyers, 5 Psychol. Pub. Pol'y & L. 967, 983–84 (1999).

261. Judges Love Collaborative Law; Here's Why, A.B.A. J. (July 2018); Christopher M. Fairman, A Proposed Model Rule for Collaborative Law, 21 Ohio St. J. on Disp. Resol., 73, 83 (2005).

262. Pauline H. Tesler, Collaborative Law: Achieving Effective Resolution in Divorce without Litigation (2d ed. 2008).

263. Id.

264. Id.

265. Christopher M. Fairman, Growing Pains: Changes in Collaborative Law and the Challenge of Legal Ethics, 30 Campbell L. Rev. 237 (2008); Scott R. Peppet, The Ethics of Collaborative Law, 2008 J. Disp. Resol. 131.

266. Tesler, supra note 262, at 10.

267. Id.

an adversarial fashion. If, despite these efforts, the parties cannot come to an agreement, the lawyers will withdraw and be disqualified from further involvement in the case; new counsel will have to be hired.[268]

In 2009, the Uniform Law Commission adopted the Uniform Collaborative Law Act (subsequently renamed the Uniform Collaborative Law Rules and Act), which provides a framework for regulating collaborative law through either court rules or legislation.[269] The Uniform Act also addresses ethical concerns that have been raised about collaborative law by, for example, not requiring that the lawyers be parties to a participation agreement and instead allowing agreements that simply "contain a statement by each collaborative lawyer confirming the lawyer's representation of a party in the collaborative law process."[270] As of 2020, the Uniform Act had been enacted in nearly twenty states.[271]

* * *

For all the promise of these methods of alternative dispute resolution, they are not for everyone and have been subject to extensive criticism. Even processes that work for most couples won't necessarily work well for all types of couples. One significant concern is domestic violence.[272] The very informality that is otherwise a strength of some alternative approaches might create the opportunity for coercion and expose victims to further mistreatment. In recognition of these possibilities, most states provide special rules that apply in cases of domestic violence. They either categorically provide that relationships where there has been domestic violence are not subject to mediation (even if it would otherwise be required),[273] or they allow the domestic violence victim to decide whether to undertake mediation.[274] To further these goals, some jurisdictions provide mediators guidance about how to recognize the signs of domestic violence and to screen out cases that are inappropriate for that reason.[275]

The case of domestic violence highlights a broader issue:

> Whenever there is significant or persistent domestic violence and significant issues of mental health on the part of one or both parties, or

---

268. Id.

269. Uniform Collaborative Law Rules and Uniform Collaborative Law Act (Unif. Law Comm'n 2010).

270. Id., Rule 4(a)(6).

271. According to the Uniform Law Commission's website, the following jurisdictions have enacted the Act: Utah, Texas, Nevada, Hawaii, District of Columbia, Ohio, Alabama, Washington, Maryland, Michigan, New Jersey, Montana, Arizona, Florida, North Dakota, Illinois, New Mexico, Pennsylvania, and Tennessee.

272. Ver Steegh, supra note 260.

273. See, e.g., Del. Code Ann. tit. 13, § 711A (2020).

274. See, e.g., Haw. Rev. Stat. § 580-41.5 (2020).

275. Elrod, supra 241, § 1:12; see also Susan D. Landrum, The On-Going Debate about Mediation in the Context of Domestic Violence: A Call for Empirical Studies of Mediation Effectiveness, 12 Cardozo J. Conflict Resol. 425 (2011).

significant levels of chemical abuse, generally the adversarial model is preferable because of procedural and other safeguards it provides to the victim or less capable party. Essentially, nonadversarial decision-making models presuppose rational actors, that is, parties who are generally capable of accurately perceiving their self-interest and acting upon it.[276]

There have also been criticisms of methods of alternative dispute resolution as systematically disadvantaging women in different-sex relationships. The worry is that differences in power and preferences might result in such women faring less well than they would have in the conventional adversarial system with its formal rules and procedural protections.[277] For example, if women are more committed to maintaining custody of the children, they may trade off financial support in exchange for custody, even when a court proceeding likely would have entitled them to both.[278]

III. Contracting for Dissolution

Today, as a general matter, couples may enter into contracts — before, during, or in anticipation of the end of marriage — about their financial obligations toward one another. This marks a change from historical resistance to many forms of contracting between current or soon-to-be spouses. Such resistance derived in part from the influence of coverture, as discussed in Chapter 3. A husband and wife were treated as "one person in law," such that "a man cannot grant anything to his wife, or enter into covenant with her: for the grant would be to suppose her separate existence; and to covenant with her, would be only to covenant with himself."[279]

Historically, a public policy view of "marriage as a lifelong status" generally made contracts that addressed financial terms in contemplation of divorce void.[280] Moreover, the law conceived of marriage as primarily a status consisting of immutable rights and obligations, defined by the state, as opposed to a relationship subject to personal choice and private ordering.[281] (Recall Graham v. Graham

---

276. William J. Howe & Hugh McIsaac, Finding the Balance: Ethical Challenges and Best Practices for Lawyers Representing Parents When the Interests of Children Are at Stake, 46 Fam. Ct. Rev. 78, 84 (2008).

277. See, e.g., Trina Grillo, The Mediation Alternative: Process Dangers for Women, 100 Yale L.J. 1545 (1991).

278. See Mnookin & Kornhauser, supra note 3.

279. 1 Ehrlich's Blackstone 83–84 (J. W. Ehrlich ed., 1959).

280. Barbara A. Atwood, Marital Contracts and the Meaning of Marriage, 54 Ariz. L. Rev. 11, 22 (2012); see also Margaret F. Brinig & Steven M. Crafton, Marriage and Opportunism, 23 J. Legal Stud. 869, 873 (1994); Herma Hill Kay, From the Second Sex to the Joint Venture: An Overview of Women's Rights and Family Law in the United States During the Twentieth Century, 88 Calif. L. Rev. 2017 (2000).

281. Atwood, supra note 280, at 23; see also Brian H. Bix, Private Ordering and Family Law, 23 J. Am. Acad. Matrim. Law 249 (2010).

from Chapter 3.) For their part, courts were reluctant to intervene in marriages and refused to enforce agreements between spouses, as well as recognized legal duties that spouses owed one another.[282]

Legal and social perspectives on marriage and divorce have shaped legislatures' and courts' willingness to enforce contracts about financial affairs at divorce. Until the 1970s, the law generally tolerated (and enforced) such contracts made in contemplation of death but not those made in contemplation of divorce, on the theory that the latter contracts encouraged divorce.[283] This made a certain amount of sense in that era, when divorce was only permitted on grounds of marital fault and was the subject of widespread social disapproval.[284] But as divorce grew more accessible and less stigmatized, the law evolved toward greater acceptance of premarital, marital, and separation agreements. Since the 1970s, premarital, marital, and separation agreements have also become more common.

Premarital (also called prenuptial or antenuptial) agreements are those made between individuals intending to marry who seek to alter or affirm rights or obligations related to marriage, separation, or divorce. Marital (also called postnuptial or postmarital) agreements are made between spouses who intend to stay married but wish to modify or clarify their rights or obligations during marriage or upon separation, divorce, or death. Separation (or marital settlement) agreements are made in anticipation of imminent separation or dissolution, and enforcement is only possible if the agreement is followed close in time by separation or dissolution of the marriage.[285] While courts typically enforce premarital, marital, and separation agreements as they pertain to financial terms, they do not enforce agreements relating to child custody or support, conduct during marriage, or grounds for divorce.[286] Nonetheless, separation agreements may include provisions governing child custody and support that courts then incorporate into an enforceable judicial decree.

States have taken different approaches toward enforcement of each of these three kinds of agreements, reflecting varying perspectives on the appropriate balance between general contract principles that vindicate individual autonomy and special rules that account for the unique dynamics that exist in the marital context.

Here, we are focused on agreements regulating *marital* dissolution. While nonmarital couples may also contract about dissolution, they are governed by separate rules—a topic we cover later in this chapter. Nonetheless, as you read the

---

282. McGuire v. McGuire, 59 N.W.2d 336, 342 (Neb. 1953).

283. Clark, supra note 5, at 6.

284. See Grossman & Friedman, supra note 26, at 164.

285. Uniform Premarital and Marital Agreement Act § 2 (Unif. Law Comm'n 2012) [hereinafter UPMAA].

286. See Barbara A. Atwood & Brian H. Bix, A New Uniform Law for Premarital and Marital Agreements, 46 Fam. L.Q. 313, 319 (2012); Model Marriage and Divorce Act § 3.06, 9A U.L.A. 169, 248–49 (1973); Delamielleure v. Belote, 704 N.W.2d 746 (Mich. Ct. App. 2005); State v. Bachmann, 521 N.W.2d 886, 888 (Minn. Ct. App. 1994); Hughes v. Lord, 602 P.2d 1030, 1031 (N.M. 1979).

materials below, consider the assumptions about marital and non-marital relationships embedded in the approaches of courts and legislatures.

A. Premarital Agreements

When a couple plans for marriage, they might want to determine in advance the financial consequences of divorce — whether and how their property should be shared and whether either spouse should have a responsibility to pay support to the other. In the second half of the twentieth century, courts shifted from a non-enforcement stance to a more tolerant one. Posner v. Posner is considered a landmark case. In 1970, the Florida Supreme Court enforced a premarital agreement that limited spousal support payments in spite of the state's longstanding view that such contracts "promote the procurement of a divorce" and are thus "illegal as contrary to public policy."[287] Noting the increasing prevalence of divorce and the advent of no-fault divorce, the court observed the "clearly discernible" trend toward recognizing premarital agreements and eliminated the distinction between the legal treatment of contracts resolving financial affairs upon death and those upon divorce.[288]

Instead of worrying that premarital agreements caused divorce, courts began to take the view that a "premarital agreement gave marriage stability because it forced a couple to review financial issues before marriage, taking any uncertainty out of the marriage's finances and reducing the disparity in expectations that the two parties to a marriage might have at the outset."[289] The Uniform Premarital Agreement Act (UPAA), promulgated by the Uniform Law Commission in 1983, reflected this shift, setting a default of enforcement except in limited circumstances pertaining to extreme procedural or substantive unfairness.[290]

Over the past several decades, premarital agreements have reportedly increased in popularity. While they are used most often by couples who are previously divorced or marrying later in life (especially if they have significant assets),[291] practitioners report increasing numbers of younger couples entering into premarital agreements as well.[292] Professor Brian Bix has pointed out, however, that we still have relatively

---

287. Posner v. Posner, 233 So. 2d 381, 382 (Fla. 1970).

288. Id. at 384.

289. Katharine B. Silbaugh, Marriage Contracts and the Family Economy, 93 Nw. U. L. Rev. 65, 73 (1998).

290. Unif. Premarital Agreement Act, 9 B U.L.A. 373 § 6(a) (Unif. Law Comm'n 1983) [hereinafter UPAA].

291. J. Thomas Oldham, With All My Worldly Goods I Thee Endow, or Maybe Not: A Reevaluation of the Uniform Premarital Agreement Act After Three Decades, 19 Duke J. Gender L. & Pol'y 83, 83 (2011); Jeffery G. Sherman, Prenuptial Agreements: A New Reason to Revive an Old Rule, 53 Clev. St. L. Rev. 359, 373 (2005–06).

292. Susan Shain, The Rise in the Millennial Prenup, N.Y. Times, July 6, 2018, at A3; Jessica Dickler, How Millennials are Getting Smarter About Marriage, CNBC (July 2, 2018).

little data about "how many couples sign premarital agreements or the economic situation of the people who enter such agreements."[293]

While all states now accept that premarital agreements can be enforced,[294] there is still much disagreement about the specifics — including the procedural requirements for entering a valid agreement, the content that can be included in an agreement, and the substantive review that courts should undertake in enforcement actions.

SIMEONE V. SIMEONE
581 A.2d 162 (Pa. 1990)

FLAHERTY, JUSTICE.

At issue in this appeal is the validity of a prenuptial agreement executed between the appellant, Catherine E. Walsh Simeone, and the appellee, Frederick A. Simeone. At the time of their marriage, in 1975, appellant was a twenty-three year old nurse and appellee was a thirty-nine year old neurosurgeon. Appellee had an income of approximately $90,000 per year, and appellant was unemployed. Appellee also had assets worth approximately $300,000. On the eve of the parties' wedding, appellee's attorney presented appellant with a prenuptial agreement to be signed. Appellant, without the benefit of counsel, signed the agreement. Appellee's attorney had not advised appellant regarding any legal rights that the agreement surrendered. The parties are in disagreement as to whether appellant knew in advance of that date that such an agreement would be presented for signature. Appellant denies having had such knowledge and claims to have signed under adverse circumstances, which, she contends, provide a basis for declaring it void.

The agreement limited appellant to support payments of $200 per week in the event of separation or divorce, subject to a maximum total payment of $25,000. The parties separated in 1982, and, in 1984, divorce proceedings were commenced. Between 1982 and 1984 appellee made payments which satisfied the $25,000 limit. In 1985, appellant filed a claim for alimony pendente lite. A master's report upheld the validity of the prenuptial agreement and denied this claim. Exceptions to the master's report were dismissed by the Court of Common Pleas of Philadelphia County. The Superior Court affirmed.

We granted allowance of appeal because uncertainty was expressed by the Superior Court regarding the meaning of our plurality decision in *Estate of Geyer*, 533 A.2d 423 (Pa. 1987). The Superior Court viewed *Geyer* as permitting a prenuptial agreement to be upheld if it either made a reasonable provision for the spouse

---

293. Brian H. Bix, Premarital Agreements in the ALI Principles of Family Dissolution, 8 Duke J. Gender L. & Pol'y 231, 232 (2001).

294. Oldham, supra note 291, at 83.

or was entered after a full and fair disclosure of the general financial positions of the parties and the statutory rights being relinquished. Appellant contends that this interpretation of *Geyer* is in error insofar as it requires disclosure of statutory rights only in cases where there has not been made a reasonable provision for the spouse. Inasmuch as the courts below held that the provision made for appellant was a reasonable one, appellant's efforts to overturn the agreement have focused upon an assertion that there was an inadequate disclosure of statutory rights. Appellant continues to assert, however, that the payments provided in the agreement were less than reasonable.

The statutory rights in question are those relating to alimony pendente lite. Other statutory rights, such as those pertaining to alimony and equitable distribution of marital property, did not exist in 1975. Those rights arose under the Divorce Code of 1980, and the Code expressly provides that marital agreements executed prior to its effective date are not affected thereby. Certainly, at the time the present agreement was executed, no disclosure was required with respect to rights which were not then in existence. The present agreement did expressly state, however, that alimony pendente lite was being relinquished. It also recited that appellant "has been informed and understands" that, were it not for the agreement, appellant's obligation to pay alimony pendente lite "might, as a matter of law, exceed the amount provided." Hence, appellant's claim is not that the agreement failed to disclose the particular right affected, but rather that she was not adequately informed with respect to the nature of alimony pendente lite. . . .

While the decision of the Superior Court reflects, perhaps, a reasonable interpretation of *Geyer*, we do not view this case as a vehicle to affirm that interpretation. Rather, there is need for a reexamination of the foundations upon which *Geyer* and earlier decisions rested, and a need for clarification of the standards by which the validity of prenuptial agreements will be judged.

There is no longer validity in the implicit presumption that supplied the basis for *Geyer* and similar earlier decisions. Such decisions rested upon a belief that spouses are of unequal status and that women are not knowledgeable enough to understand the nature of contracts that they enter. Society has advanced, however, to the point where women are no longer regarded as the "weaker" party in marriage, or in society generally. Indeed, the stereotype that women serve as homemakers while men work as breadwinners is no longer viable. Quite often today both spouses are income earners. Nor is there viability in the presumption that women are uninformed, uneducated, and readily subjected to unfair advantage in marital agreements. Indeed, women nowadays quite often have substantial education, financial awareness, income, and assets.

Accordingly, the law has advanced to recognize the equal status of men and women in our society. Paternalistic presumptions and protections that arose to shelter women from the inferiorities and incapacities which they were perceived as having in earlier times have, appropriately, been discarded. It would be inconsistent, therefore, to perpetuate the standards governing prenuptial agreements that were described in *Geyer* and similar decisions, as these reflected a paternalistic approach that is now insupportable.

Further, *Geyer* and its predecessors embodied substantial departures from traditional rules of contract law, to the extent that they allowed consideration of the knowledge of the contracting parties and reasonableness of their bargain as factors governing whether to uphold an agreement. Traditional principles of contract law provide perfectly adequate remedies where contracts are procured through fraud, misrepresentation, or duress. Consideration of other factors, such as the knowledge of the parties and the reasonableness of their bargain, is inappropriate. Prenuptial agreements are contracts, and, as such, should be evaluated under the same criteria as are applicable to other types of contracts. Absent fraud, misrepresentation, or duress, spouses should be bound by the terms of their agreements.

Contracting parties are normally bound by their agreements, without regard to whether the terms thereof were read and fully understood and irrespective of whether the agreements embodied reasonable or good bargains. Based upon these principles, the terms of the present prenuptial agreement must be regarded as binding, without regard to whether the terms were fully understood by appellant. Ignorantia non excusat.

Accordingly, we find no merit in a contention raised by appellant that the agreement should be declared void on the ground that she did not consult with independent legal counsel. To impose a per se requirement that parties entering a prenuptial agreement must obtain independent legal counsel would be contrary to traditional principles of contract law, and would constitute a paternalistic and unwarranted interference with the parties' freedom to enter contracts.

Further, the reasonableness of a prenuptial bargain is not a proper subject for judicial review. *Geyer* and earlier decisions required that, at least where there had been an inadequate disclosure made by the parties, the bargain must have been reasonable at its inception. Some have even suggested that prenuptial agreements should be examined with regard to whether their terms remain reasonable at the time of dissolution of the parties' marriage.

By invoking inquiries into reasonableness, however, the functioning and reliability of prenuptial agreements is severely undermined. Parties would not have entered such agreements, and, indeed, might not have entered their marriages, if they did not expect their agreements to be strictly enforced. If parties viewed an agreement as reasonable at the time of its inception, as evidenced by their having signed the agreement, they should be foreclosed from later trying to evade its terms by asserting that it was not in fact reasonable. Pertinently, the present agreement contained a clause reciting that "each of the parties considers this agreement fair, just and reasonable. . . ."

Further, everyone who enters a long-term agreement knows that circumstances can change during its term, so that what initially appeared desirable might prove to be an unfavorable bargain. Such are the risks that contracting parties routinely assume. Certainly, the possibilities of illness, birth of children, reliance upon a spouse, career change, financial gain or loss, and numerous other events that can occur in the course of a marriage cannot be regarded as unforeseeable. If parties choose not to address such matters in their prenuptial agreements, they must be regarded as having contracted to bear the risk of events that alter the value of their bargains.

We are reluctant to interfere with the power of persons contemplating marriage to agree upon, and to act in reliance upon, what they regard as an acceptable distribution scheme for their property. A court should not ignore the parties' expressed intent by proceeding to determine whether a prenuptial agreement was, in the court's view, reasonable at the time of its inception or the time of divorce. These are exactly the sorts of judicial determinations that such agreements are designed to avoid. Rare indeed is the agreement that is beyond possible challenge when reasonableness is placed at issue. Parties can routinely assert some lack of fairness relating to the inception of the agreement, thereby placing the validity of the agreement at risk. And if reasonableness at the time of divorce were to be taken into account an additional problem would arise. Virtually nonexistent is the marriage in which there has been absolutely no change in the circumstances of either spouse during the course of the marriage. Every change in circumstance, foreseeable or not, and substantial or not, might be asserted as a basis for finding that an agreement is no longer reasonable.

In discarding the approach of *Geyer* that permitted examination of the reasonableness of prenuptial agreements and allowed inquiries into whether parties had attained informed understandings of the rights they were surrendering, we do not depart from the longstanding principle that a full and fair disclosure of the financial positions of the parties is required. Absent this disclosure, a material misrepresentation in the inducement for entering a prenuptial agreement may be asserted. Parties to these agreements do not quite deal at arm's length, but rather at the time the contract is entered into stand in a relation of mutual confidence and trust that calls for disclosure of their financial resources. It is well settled that this disclosure need not be exact, so long as it is "full and fair." In essence therefore, the duty of disclosure under these circumstances is consistent with traditional principles of contract law.

If an agreement provides that full disclosure has been made, a presumption of full disclosure arises. If a spouse attempts to rebut this presumption through an assertion of fraud or misrepresentation then this presumption can be rebutted if it is proven by clear and convincing evidence.

The present agreement recited that full disclosure had been made, and included a list of appellee's assets totalling approximately $300,000. Appellant contends that this list understated by roughly $183,000 the value of a classic car collection which appellee had included at a value of $200,000. The master, reviewing the parties' conflicting testimony regarding the value of the car collection, found that appellant failed to prove by clear and convincing evidence that the value of the collection had been understated. The courts below affirmed that finding. We have examined the record and find ample basis for concluding that the value of the car collection was fully disclosed. Appellee offered expert witnesses who testified to a value of approximately $200,000. Further, appellee's disclosure included numerous cars that appellee did not even own but which he merely hoped to inherit from his mother at some time in the future. Appellant's contention is plainly without merit.

Appellant's final contention is that the agreement was executed under conditions of duress in that it was presented to her at 5 p.m. on the eve of her wedding, a time when she could not seek counsel without the trauma, expense, and embarrassment of postponing the wedding. The master found this claim not credible. The courts below affirmed that finding, upon an ample evidentiary basis.

Although appellant testified that she did not discover until the eve of her wedding that there was going to be a prenuptial agreement, testimony from a number of other witnesses was to the contrary. Appellee testified that, although the final version of the agreement was indeed presented to appellant on the eve of the wedding, he had engaged in several discussions with appellant regarding the contents of the agreement during the six month period preceding that date. Another witness testified that appellant mentioned, approximately two or three weeks before the wedding, that she was going to enter a prenuptial agreement. Yet another witness confirmed that, during the months preceding the wedding, appellant participated in several discussions of prenuptial agreements. And the legal counsel who prepared the agreement for appellee testified that, prior to the eve of the wedding, changes were made in the agreement to increase the sums payable to appellant in the event of separation or divorce. He also stated that he was present when the agreement was signed and that appellant expressed absolutely no reluctance about signing. It should be noted, too, that during the months when the agreement was being discussed appellant had more than sufficient time to consult with independent legal counsel if she had so desired. Under these circumstances, there was plainly no error in finding that appellant failed to prove duress.

Hence, the courts below properly held that the present agreement is valid and enforceable. Appellant is barred, therefore, from receiving alimony pendente lite. . . .

NOTES AND QUESTIONS

---

1. *Standard for Enforceability.* What standard does the court adopt for enforceability? How does the court justify its decision to turn from the prior approach in *Geyer*, which examined reasonableness and informed understanding? What is wrong, in the court's view, with making these inquiries? Do you agree? How does the court suggest addressing any unfairness that may result from applying general contract principles in this context?

2. *Freedom of Contract and* Simeone. What is the role of freedom of contract in the court's analysis? Are contracts between premarital parties the same as others? Should they be treated similarly or differently? Why and how? In contrast to the approach in *Simeone*, in most jurisdictions premarital agreements are not on an "equal footing with other contracts," as courts apply "unique fairness criteria" as they assess premarital agreements in both "substantive and procedural" ways.[295]

As Professor Katharine Silbaugh observes, *Simeone* represents "the maximum freedom to contract of any state" for premarital agreements.[296] The court "require[s] at a minimum that the parties disclose the value of their assets to one another before signing."[297] What does *Simeone*'s "full and fair disclosure of the financial positions of the parties" assume about the relationship between the parties? Are they at "arm's length"?

3. *Uniform Premarital Agreement Act.* *Simeone*'s freedom of contract approach resonates with the general thrust of the UPAA, which is decidedly pro-enforcement. The UPAA allows for courts to reject a premarital agreement only if it: (1) was not voluntary; or (2) was unconscionable at the time of execution, and the individual challenging the agreement was not given sufficient financial disclosure and did expressly waive in writing the right to financial disclosure.[298] This heightened test for contractual invalidation has been criticized as more stringent than general contract law.[299] Still, the Act has been adopted at least in part by 26 states,[300] half without major revisions.[301] Does the UPAA provide adequate protection for the party in the weaker economic position?[302] Should the law be more concerned with protecting the party with less bargaining power in this context than in the ordinary commercial context? Or should all contracts be treated the same?

4. *Uniform Premarital and Marital Agreements Act.* The Uniform Premarital and Marital Agreements Act (UPMAA), promulgated by the Uniform Law Commission in 2012, sought to unify the law on premarital agreements and to create consistency with the law of marital agreements, long treated as a separate category by courts. Compared to the UPAA, the UPMAA takes a less pro-enforcement position and instead provides greater protections to the party in the weaker financial position. The drafters of the UPMAA expressed the approach as follows: "[P]arties should be free, within broad limits, to choose the financial terms of their marriage. The limits are those of due

---

295. Silbaugh, supra note 289, at 74.

296. Id. at 74 n.25.

297. Id.

298. UPAA § 6(a).

299. Atwood & Bix, supra note 286, at 315; J. Thomas Oldham, Would Enactment of the Uniform Premarital and Marital Agreements Act in All Fifty States Change U.S. Law Regarding Premarital Agreements?, 46 Fam. L.Q. 367, 369 (2012).

300. UPMAA, Prefatory Note.

301. Oldham, supra note 291, at 84; see, e.g., 750 Ill. Comp. Stat. 40/2601 et seq. (2020).

302. See, e.g., Oldham, supra note 299, at 369; Gail Frommer Brod, Premarital Agreements and Gender Justice, 9 Yale J.L. & Feminism 229 (1994); Barbara Ann Atwood, Ten Years Later: Lingering Concerns About the Uniform Premarital Agreement Act, 19 J. Legis. 127 (1993).

process in formation, on the one hand, and certain minimal standards of substantive fairness, on the other."[303]

a. Procedural Requirements: Under the UPMAA, an agreement is unenforceable if (1) the party seeking to avoid enforcement proves that consent to the agreement was involuntary or the result of duress; (2) the party didn't have access to independent legal representation; (3) unless the party had independent legal representation, the agreement didn't include a waiver of rights or an explanation in plain language of the rights or obligations modified or waived by the agreement; *or* (4) the party didn't receive adequate financial disclosure before signing the agreement.[304] A party has access to independent legal representation if, before signing, "the party has a reasonable time to: (A) decide whether to retain a lawyer . . . and (B) locate a lawyer . . . , obtain the lawyer's advice, and consider the advice provided."[305] This only applies if the other party is represented by counsel.[306] Accordingly, if the party who seeks to enforce the agreement did not have legal representation, there is no requirement that the party resisting enforcement had "access to independent legal representation."

b. Substantive Requirements: Under the UPMAA, a court can refuse to enforce a term of the agreement if "the term was unconscionable at the time of signing."[307] In a bracketed provision — meaning that the provision can be adopted or omitted without creating inconsistencies with other provisions — the Act also provides that a court may refuse to enforce a term if such enforcement "would result in substantial hardship for a party because of a material change in circumstances arising after the agreement was signed."[308] If you were a state lawmaker, would you advocate for adoption of the bracketed provision? Do you think it's appropriate to assess the substance of the agreement *at the time of enforcement*, as opposed to only at the time of execution? What is the justification for providing this "second look" in the context of marital dissolution? Do you think "substantial hardship" is a good standard?

Thus far, only two states have adopted the UPMAA.[309] Do you think the approach of the UPMAA strikes an appropriate balance between contractual autonomy and the need to protect the weaker party? How does it compare to the approach in *Simeone*?

---

303. UPMAA, Prefatory Note.
304. Id. § 9(a).
305. Id. § 9(b).
306. Id.
307. Id. § 9(f).
308. Id.
309. Colo. Rev. Stat. § 14-2-301 (2020); N.D. Cent. Code § 14-03.2-01 (2020).

5.   *Spousal Support.* Both the UPAA and the UPMAA provide that even if an agreement modifies or eliminates spousal support, a court can order support to avoid the spouse seeking support becoming eligible for public assistance.[310] Why should courts be permitted to invalidate the parties' agreement in this situation? What is the view of marriage embedded in this limit on spousal support agreements?

6.   *Child Custody and Support.* Under both the UPAA and the UPMAA, an agreement may not adversely affect child support.[311] What is the rationale for this limitation? The UPMAA also makes clear that an agreement cannot bind the court regarding child custody.[312] If this provision were not in the Act, could the parties bind the court regarding custody? (We address child custody in Chapter 10 and child support in Chapter 11.)

7.   *The ALI's Approach.* The American Law Institute's Principles of the Law of Family Dissolution, promulgated in 2002, sought to guard against unfairness that might arise in the premarital context.[313] The ALI approach permits a premarital or marital agreement to be invalidated if it works a "substantial injustice" at the time of execution *or* enforcement.[314]

PROBLEMS

1. Margot and Richard entered into a premarital agreement pursuant to which Margot was required to pay Richard $1,000 per month during their marriage, and Richard was to follow Margot on her travels. Richard seeks to enforce the contract during the marriage.[315] Can he do so?

POSTSCRIPT

The problem is based on Graham v. Graham, discussed in Chapter 3.[316] The court declined to enforce the contract on the grounds that it altered the "essentials obligation of the marriage contract," whereby (at the time) a husband was obligated to support his wife, and she was to follow his choice of domicile.[317] Would a court reach the same conclusion today despite the shift toward greater enforcement of premarital agreements? Is there something different about obligations

---

310. UPMAA § 9(e); UPAA § 6(b).
311. UPMAA § 10(b); UPAA § 3(b).
312. UPMAA § 10(c).
313. Bix, supra note 293, at 235.
314. Principles of the Law of Family Dissolution, supra note 26, § 7.05, cmt. a, reporter's notes.
315. Id.
316. 33 F. Supp. 936 (E.D. Mich. 1940).
317. Id. at 940.

during marriage than upon its dissolution? What if the agreement had followed traditional gender roles? Would the court still have refused to enforce it?[318]

2. Philip and Antipas, a same-sex couple in California, planned to enter into a domestic partnership—a formal relationship status that furnishes the rights and obligations of marriage under state law—before California legally recognized marriages by same-sex couples. Before registering with the state, the couple entered into an agreement waiving any rights, claims, or interests they each might otherwise have in the future property, income, or estate of the other. In 2006, they became registered domestic partners. After state law changed to permit same-sex couples to legally marry, Philip and Antipas entered into a marriage. They did not dissolve their domestic partnership. Eventually, the couple seeks a divorce. Is the pre-domestic partnership agreement still valid?

POSTSCRIPT

In Estate of Wilson, a California appellate court held that an agreement of this kind would still be valid to determine the extent of the parties' financial rights.[319] In the actual case, the relationship ended not with divorce, but with the death of Philip Timothy Wilson. Prior to his relationship with Antipas Johnlang Konou, Wilson had made a will. California law protects spouses from unintentional disinheritance, but proof of a valid agreement could waive those and other rights. When Konou sought financial rights as a surviving spouse, the probate court rejected his claim on the grounds that the domestic partnership agreement remained valid after the marriage, and Konou waived his rights to any interest in Wilson's estate in this agreement. Konou did not contest that the domestic partnership agreement would constitute a valid waiver of his inheritance rights, but argued that "the marriage license constituted a contract providing him with particular rights different from those of a domestic partnership, and that this marriage license, signed by both parties, terminated the property arrangement set forth in the domestic partnership agreement."[320] Rejecting his argument, the court reasoned:

> When Wilson and Konou married in 2008, their domestic partnership remained in effect. They never dissolved their domestic partnership. . . . Wilson and Konou did not sign a new agreement regarding their property disposition when they married.

---

318. See Faith H. Spencer, Comment, Expanding Marital Options: Enforcement of Premarital Contracts During Marriage, 1989 U. Chi. Legal F. 281, 290.

319. 150 Cal. Rptr. 3d 699 (Cal. Ct. App. 2012).

320. Id. at 709.

The law is well settled that a marriage license does not invalidate a prenuptial agreement. Parties contemplating marriage may validly contract as to their property rights, both as to property then owned and as to property and earnings that may be acquired during the marriage. Similarly, a domestic partnership agreement remains valid after the parties register as domestic partners. The fact that one agreement is named a domestic partnership agreement and another is named a prenuptial agreement is insignificant as the purpose of both is to permit the parties to enter into a contract that reflects their wishes regarding the property they own and will acquire in the future. . . .

The status of marriage, as well as the status of a domestic partnership, entitles people to statutory rights but they are free to contract and change these rights. Here, the domestic partnership agreement set forth the parties' intent regarding their property and no writing expressly terminated or amended this enforceable agreement. . . .

The domestic partnership agreement did not specify that it would become null if the law changed to permit same-sex marriage. . . .

In 2006, when they entered into the agreement, they had separate legal counsel and their attorneys advised them about their property rights under the law. Thus, we can presume their counsel explained to them that their property rights under the Domestic Partner Act were essentially the same as the state property rights they would have enjoyed were they legally married. Furthermore, we can presume that the parties were well aware that both the marriage laws and domestic partner laws for same-sex couples might change in the future as the City and County of San Francisco — the place where Konou and Wilson were residing — was issuing marriage licenses to same-sex couples in February 2004, and the legality of these marriages was being litigated at the time of the agreement signed by Wilson and Konou. . . .

The state property rights and obligations of spouses and domestic partners do not differ significantly. Thus, a preregistration domestic partnership agreement that . . . [is] enforceable under the Uniform Prenuptial Agreement Act is not automatically invalidated by a marriage license. . . . The waiver in the agreement unambiguously waived Konou's rights to Wilson's estate. . . .

B. Marital Agreements

A couple who is already married — and intends to stay married or seeks to reconcile — may decide to enter an agreement to avoid the default rules of property ownership that would otherwise govern the ongoing marriage or its dissolution.[321]

---

321. See, e.g., In re Hall, 27 N.E.3d 281 (Ind. Ct. App. 2015); Simmons v. Simmons, 249 S.W.3d 843, 846 (Ark. Ct. App. 2007); Vaccarello v. Vaccarello, 757 A.2d 909 (Pa. 2000).

Such an agreement may clarify existing property rights or address property or spousal support rights in the event of any future divorce or contracts that effectuate property transfers.[322] States pursue different approaches to marital agreements, though this body of law is less developed than that for premarital agreements.[323]

In enforcement actions, should courts hold marital agreements to a higher standard than other contracts or premarital agreements? Consider the following case.

ANSIN V. CRAVEN-ANSIN
929 N.E.2d 955 (Mass. 2010)

MARSHALL, C.J.

We granted direct appellate review in this divorce proceeding to determine whether so-called "postnuptial" or "marital" agreements are contrary to public policy and, if not, whether the marital agreement at issue is enforceable. The dispute is between Kenneth S. Ansin (husband) and Cheryl A. Craven–Ansin (wife) concerning the validity of their 2004 written agreement "settling all rights and obligations arising from their marital relationship" in the event of a divorce. Two years after the agreement was executed, in November, 2006, the husband filed a complaint for divorce and sought to enforce the terms of the agreement. At the time of the complaint, the parties had been married for twenty-one years and had two sons.

A judge in the Probate and Family Court upheld the agreement, finding that it was negotiated by independent counsel for each party, was not the product of fraud or duress, and was based on full financial disclosures by the husband, and that the terms of the agreement were fair and reasonable at the time of execution and at the time of divorce. Judgment entered enforcing the marital agreement. The wife appealed, and we granted both parties' applications for direct appellate review. We now affirm.

1. *Facts. . . .*

a. The marital assets

At the time of the execution of the marital agreement in 2004, the value of the combined assets of the husband and wife was approximately $19 million. One of the assets, now at issue, is the husband's interest in certain trusts and business entities established by his grandfather, currently managed by his uncle. The assets of these various entities are substantial real estate holdings in Florida. . . . During the course

---

322. See Linda J. Ravdin, Postmarital Agreements: Validity and Enforceablility, 52 Fam. L.Q. 245, 246–47 (2018); see also In re Estate of Harber, 449 P.2d 7 (Ariz. 1969).

323. UPMAA. For discussion of postmarital agreements, see Ravdin, supra note 322, at 245; Principles of the Law of Family Dissolution, supra note 26, § 7.01(1)(b).

of the marriage, the husband received, and the wife was aware of, distributions from his interest in the Florida real estate. The timing and amount of the distributions was unpredictable, and varied widely, as the wife knew.

During the course of their marriage the couple retained RINET Company LLC (RINET) to provide financial advice to them and to prepare their joint tax returns. The parties' primary financial planner from RINET met with the couple on a quarterly basis, and RINET prepared "periodic summary reports" to permit the couple to monitor their financial affairs . . . [O]n the reports prepared by RINET, the husband's interest in the Florida real estate was given a "placeholder" value of $4 million to $5 million (the amount varied from time to time), of which the wife was well aware. The wife understood that the husband's principal objective in executing a marital agreement was to protect his interest in the Florida real estate in the event of a divorce.

b. The marital agreement

The parties were married in July, 1985. The execution of their marital agreement nineteen years later was precipitated by marital problems that began toward the end of 2003. At the time the couple sought the assistance of a marriage counsellor. In early 2004, the husband informed his wife that he "needed" her to sign an agreement if their marriage was to continue. He testified that his "uncertainty" about the wife's commitment to their relationship was the reason for this request. It caused the wife a "great deal of stress"; she told her husband that she would not sign any such agreement, and that discussion of the issue made her "physically ill." The parties separated, as it turned out for some six weeks. While the parties were separated, the husband promised his wife that he would recommit to the marriage if she would sign a marital agreement. She agreed to do so, she said, in an attempt to preserve the marriage and the family. The parties resumed living together, and went on a "second honeymoon."

In April, 2004, they began negotiating the terms of the agreement, which we describe below. Each retained counsel. The judge's detailed description of the negotiations depicts back-and-forth discussions between counsel for the wife and counsel for the husband, during which the wife negotiated terms more favorable to her. Several draft agreements were exchanged. The judge found that in the course of the negotiations the wife was "fully informed" of the marital assets, and that she was "satisfied" with the disclosures made by the husband with respect to the Florida real estate, which included the financial summaries prepared by RINET that used the "placeholder" values. Finally, with the assistance of their respective counsel, the parties reached an agreement; it was signed in July, 2004.

We briefly summarize key provisions of the marital agreement. The agreement sets forth the parties' intent that, in the event of a divorce, the terms of the agreement are to be "valid and enforceable" against them, and "limit the rights" that "otherwise arise by reason of their marriage." The agreement recites that the parties are aware of the rights to which they may be entitled under Massachusetts law, that each has retained independent legal counsel, and that each executed the agreement "freely and voluntarily." The agreement states that the parties are "aware of the other's income," warrants that each has been provided with "all information requested by the other," and affirms that each "waives his or her rights to further inquiry, discovery and investigation." The agreement further recites that each is "fully satisfied" that the agreement "will promote marital harmony" and "will ensure the treatment of Husband's property to which the parties agreed before their marriage and since their separation."

As for the distribution of property in the event of a divorce, the agreement states that the wife "disclaims any and all interest she now has or ever may have" in the husband's interest in the Florida real estate and other marital assets. The husband agreed to pay the wife $5 million, and thirty per cent of the appreciation of all marital property held by the couple from the time of the agreement to the time of the divorce. The agreement provides that the wife could remain in the marital home for one year after any divorce, with the husband paying all reasonable expenses of that household. The husband agreed to pay for the wife's medical insurance until her death or remarriage, and he agreed to maintain a life insurance policy to the exclusive benefit of the wife in the amount of $2.5 million while the parties remained married.

c. Events following execution of marital agreement

On execution of the marital agreement, the relationship between the husband and wife took on, in the judge's words, a "light and optimistic tone" and both were "looking forward to strengthening their marriage." . . . However, in August, 2004, the parties had a discussion that "led the [w]ife to believe that their marriage was over." The husband had not decided to divorce his wife, and the judge credited his testimony that he was "unwilling" to abandon the marriage at that time.

In response to their marital difficulties, the parties again considered separating, but decided not to do so at least until their younger son graduated from high school. . . . During this time, they purchased a new home for $790,000, and paid $500,000 for its renovations. . . .

In June, 2005, at the wife's request, the husband moved out of the house. He did not file for divorce at that time, believing that while things looked "grim," filing for divorce would have been the "ultimate declaration" that his marriage was over. After separating from her husband, the wife maintained contact with their RINET financial advisor, inquiring on multiple occasions what the value of any payment to her would be under the terms of the marital agreement. In 2006 the wife became involved in a serious relationship with another man. In February of that year, the wife informed the husband that "one of us has to be strong enough to take the steps to bring closure to our relationship." She did not commence divorce proceedings. In November, 2006, the husband filed a petition for divorce.

2. Validity of marital agreement...

Consistent with the majority of States to address the issue, we conclude that [marital] agreements may be enforced. Our decision is consistent with our established recognition that a marital relationship need not vitiate contractual rights between the parties. We have, for example, recognized the validity of premarital agreements, and separation agreements, reasoning that it was important to respect the parties' "freedom to contract" and that such agreements may serve a "useful function" in permitting the parties to arrange their financial affairs "as they best see fit."

The wife argues that marital agreements are different in kind and should be declared void against public policy because they are "innately coercive," "usually" arise when the marriage is already failing, and may "encourage" divorce.... Marital contracts are not the product of classic arm's-length bargaining, but that does not make them necessarily coercive. Such contracts may inhibit the dissolution of a marriage, or may protect the interests of third parties such as children from a prior relationship.

3. Judicial review of a marital agreement

A marital agreement stands on a different footing from both a premarital and a separation agreement. Before marriage, the parties have greater freedom to reject an unsatisfactory premarital contract.

A separation agreement, in turn, is negotiated when a marriage has failed and the spouses "intend a permanent separation or marital dissolution." The family unit will no longer be kept intact, and the parties may look to their own future economic interests. The circumstances surrounding marital agreements in contrast are "pregnant with the opportunity for one party to use the threat of dissolution 'to bargain themselves into positions of advantage.'"

For these reasons, we join many other States in concluding that marital agreements must be carefully scrutinized.

Before a marital agreement is sanctioned by a court, careful scrutiny by the judge should determine at a minimum whether (1) each party has had an opportunity to obtain separate legal counsel of each party's own choosing; (2) there was fraud or coercion in obtaining the agreement; (3) all assets were fully disclosed by both parties before the agreement was executed; (4) each spouse knowingly and explicitly agreed in writing to waive the right to a judicial equitable division of assets and all marital rights in the event of a divorce; and (5) the terms of the agreement are fair and reasonable at the time of execution and at the time of divorce. Where one spouse challenges the enforceability of the agreement, the spouse seeking to enforce the agreement shall bear the burden of satisfying these criteria.

We now elaborate on those points as they apply to the marital agreement here.

a. Fraud and coercion . . .

[W]e see no reason to question [the trial judge's] ultimate finding that the marital agreement was not the product of coercion or fraud. The agreement was the product of lengthy negotiations between the parties, each represented by separate, experienced counsel. . . . The evidence is clear that the wife made an informed, voluntary choice to sign the agreement.

As to fraud, the wife argues that the husband misrepresented his intention to stay in the marriage in order to induce her to sign the agreement. The judge found to the contrary, and her findings are fully supported by the evidence. For example, after the agreement had been signed, the husband worked "hard" in the areas the wife "felt needed improvement." The couple traveled together extensively. They purchased and substantially renovated a new house together. It was not until over two years later, after the wife had asked the husband to leave the marital home and after she had become involved with another man, that the husband filed for divorce. . . .

b. Disclosure of assets

We have explained with respect to premarital agreements that "[f]ull and fair" disclosure of each party's financial circumstances is a "significant aspect" of the parties' obligation to deal with each other fairly "because they stand in a confidential relationship with each other" and must have such information in order to make an informed decision about the terms of the agreement. The obligation is greater with respect to marital agreements because each spouse owes a duty of absolute fidelity to the other. . . . [E]nforcement of a marital agreement can occur only when a judge finds that there was a full disclosure of all assets of both spouses, whether jointly or separately held. The requirement of full disclosure may be satisfied if "prior to signing the agreement the party seeking to enforce it provided the other party with a written statement accurately listing (i) his or her significant assets, and their total approximate market value; (ii) his or her approximate annual income . . . and (iii) any significant future acquisitions, or changes in income, to which the party has a current legal entitlement, or which the party reasonably expects to realize" in the near future. The disclosure need not be exact, but must approximate the value of the assets.

We agree with the judge that the disclosures here were sufficient to meet this rigorous standard. . . .

The wife acknowledged when she executed the marital agreement that she had "been provided with all information requested," that she was "afforded sufficient opportunity to inquire and investigate further financial circumstances" of her husband, and that she waived her "rights to further inquiry." . . .

c. Waiver

By the terms of their agreement, the husband and wife agreed that they intended the marital agreement to limit their rights in the event of divorce, and that the agreement should govern "in lieu of and in full discharge and satisfaction of the rights which otherwise arise by reason of their marriage." . . . In determining whether there was a meaningful waiver of rights, a judge should consider "whether each party was represented by independent counsel, the adequacy of the time to review the agreement, the parties' understanding of the terms of the agreement and their effect, and a party's understanding of his or her rights in the absence of an agreement." Here, the wife was represented by independent counsel, who represented her over the course of several weeks as the terms of the agreement were negotiated. The wife affirmed in writing that she understood the rights she was waiving, and she does not claim that she did not understand any terms of the agreement. The evidence supports the conclusion that the wife's waiver was meaningful.

d. Fair and reasonable terms

We turn finally to the requirement that a marital agreement contain terms that are "fair and reasonable" at the time of execution and at the time of divorce. We do not accept the husband's suggestion that the standard applicable to marital agreements should be the same as the one applicable to premarital agreements. As the wife points out, a marital agreement more closely resembles a separation agreement. The statutory rights and obligations conferred by marriage are not potential benefits for a divorcing spouse but an integral aspect of the marriage itself. . . . [P]arties to a marital agreement do not bargain as freely as separating spouses may do. Because a marital agreement is executed when the parties do not contemplate divorce and when they owe absolute fidelity to each other, . . . heightened scrutiny . . . applies in this context. . . .

In evaluating whether a marital agreement is fair and reasonable at the time of execution, a judge should accordingly consider the entire context in which the agreement was reached, allowing greater latitude for agreements reached where each party is represented by separate counsel of their own choosing. A judge may consider "the magnitude of the disparity between the outcome under the agreement and the outcome under otherwise prevailing legal principles," whether "the purpose of the agreement was to benefit or protect the interests of third parties (such as the children from a prior relationship)," and "the impact of the agreement's enforcement upon the children of the parties."[324] Other factors may include the length of the marriage, the motives of the contracting spouses, their respective bargaining positions, the circumstances giving rise to the marital agreement, the degree of the pressure, if any, experienced by the contesting spouse, and other circumstances the judge finds relevant. . . .

[W]e agree with the judge that the marital agreement at issue here was fair and reasonable. [T]he wife was represented by experienced, independent counsel

---

324. Principles of the Law of Family Dissolution, supra note X, § 7.05(3)(a), (c), (d).

throughout the negotiations. In the event of a divorce, the wife was to receive a substantial fixed sum payment from her husband. If the marital estate appreciated in value after execution of the agreement, she would receive, in addition, a percentage of the increase in value; she did not forgo the fixed payment if the marital assets, including the husband's interest in the Florida real estate, declined substantially. . . .

In determining whether a marital agreement is fair and reasonable at the time of divorce, a judge will be able to satisfy the searching inquiry we require by examining the same factors employed for evaluating a separation agreement. Thus, a judge may consider, among other factors, "(1) the nature and substance of the objecting party's complaint; (2) the financial and property division provisions of the agreement as a whole; (3) the context in which the negotiations took place; (4) the complexity of the issues involved; (5) the background and knowledge of the parties; (6) the experience and ability of counsel; (7) the need for and availability of experts to assist the parties and counsel; and (8) the mandatory and, if the judge deems it appropriate, the discretionary factors set forth in G.L. c. 208, § 34" [addressing factors to be considered for alimony and property division at divorce]. As with a judge's evaluation of separation agreements, . . . the judge . . . considers only whether the agreement is "fair and reasonable" when considered in light of the factors we have identified and any other relevant circumstances. . . . .

A marital agreement need not provide for an equal distribution of assets. . . .

We agree with the judge in the Probate and Family Court that the marital agreement in this case should be specifically enforced.

NOTES AND QUESTIONS

1. *Enforceability as a Matter of Public Policy.* The court in *Ansin* observed that "[m]arital contracts are not the product of classic arm's-length bargaining, but that does not make them necessarily coercive." Do you agree with the court's general view on coercion in marital agreements? What public policy goals are furthered by enforcing marital agreements in general?

2. *Marital Versus Premarital Agreements.* The court in *Ansin* distinguished marital agreements from premarital or separation agreements. Is the court right that parties have less freedom to reject a proposed agreement during marriage than before it? The *Ansin* court relied heavily on the ALI Principles of Family Dissolution, yet did not adopt the recommendation to apply the same principles to premarital and marital agreements.

Consider the following observation by the court in Pacelli v. Pacelli in evaluating the enforceability of a marital agreement introduced by a husband who "informed [his wife] that he would divorce her unless she agreed to certain terms regarding their economic relationship":[325]

> [T]he mid-marriage agreement in the present case differs from pre-nuptial agreements and property settlement agreements made at a marriage's termination. It was entered into before the marriage lost all of its vitality and when at least one of the parties, without reservation, wanted the marriage to survive. [The husband] also wanted to continue the marriage, but only on his terms.
>
> Here, unlike the pre-nuptial bride, [the wife] had entered into the legal relationship of marriage when her husband presented her with his ultimatum. Moreover, the marriage had produced two children. Thus, defendant faced a more difficult choice than the bride who is presented with a demand for a pre-nuptial agreement. The cost to [the wife] would have been the destruction of a family and the stigma of a failed marriage.[326]

The justification for treating premarital and marital agreements differently stems from assumptions about the different bargaining dynamics in the two contexts. According to the ALI's Principles of the Law of Family Dissolution, "opportunities for hard dealing may be greater" with marital contracts than with premarital contracts.[327] Professor Sean Williams contests the assumption that marital partners are worse off than premarital ones in terms of bargaining power:

> Before a marriage, the couple may have limited information about how much the other person wants to get married. This could lead to stalled negotiations. These issues are significantly less likely to affect postnuptial bargaining. Couples presumably get to know one another better the longer they remain together. . . . They are likely to have fairly accurate information about how much their spouses value the marriage, how devastated their spouses would be if the marriage ended, and how valuable they are on the remarriage market.[328]

Do you agree? What implications does this raise for how you would analyze the facts in *Ansin*?

3. *UPMAA and Marital Agreements.* The UPMAA, discussed above, deliberately attempted to bridge the gap between premarital and marital agreements; it sought "to bring clarity and consistency across a range of agreements between spouses and those who are about to become spouses" with the "focus [] on agreements that purport to modify or waive rights that would otherwise arise at the time

---

325. 725 A.2d 56, 58 (N.J. Super. Ct. App. Div. 1999).

326. Id. at 59. The court also distinguished separation agreements from marital agreements: "The mid-marriage agreement in this case also differs from a property settlement agreement made when the marriage has died. In that case, as . . . each party, recognizing that the marriage is over, can look to his or her economic rights; the relationship is adversarial." Id.

327. Principles of the Law of Family Dissolution, supra note 26, § 7.01 cmt. e.

328. Sean Hannon Williams, Postnuptial Agreements, 2007 Wis. L. Rev. 827, 855.

of the dissolution of the marriage or the death of one of the spouses."[329] Notably, the UPMAA, like the ALI's Principles of the Law of Family Dissolution, treats premarital and marital agreements under the same set of standards.[330] What benefits are gained by the UPMAA approach uniting legal treatment of premarital and marital agreements? How does the approach toward marital agreements in the UPMAA compare to that in *Ansin*? Which approach best vindicates the underlying purposes and competing values implicated by marital agreements? What visions of marriage do these approaches demonstrate?

    4. *A Confidential Relationship.* What does it mean for spouses to have a "confidential relationship"? What bearing should this have on enforcing marital agreements? Does the "confidential relationship" between spouses justify closer scrutiny of marital agreements? Could we achieve the same result through basic contract principles? In imposing disclosure requirements, the court in *Ansin* treated marital partners as fiduciaries. In Bedrick v. Bedrick, the Connecticut Supreme Court distinguished marital partners from those in a "fiduciary" relationship, but did emphasize the importance of the special relationship between parties imposing requirements for full and frank disclosure.[331]

    5. *Legal Awareness and Over-Optimism.* Is there a reason to require disclosure of statutory rights in the context of marital agreements? Consider the findings by Professors Lynn Baker and Robert Emery that people's legal understanding of marriage and divorce is sparse and inaccurate.[332] Moreover, Baker and Emery found that even though people believe that half of marriages end in divorce (overestimating the actual rate), they are highly optimistic regarding their own marriages.[333] How could people's over-optimism about whether they will divorce affect how they negotiate their premarital or marital agreements? Should standards for enforcement take into account these effects on marital bargaining?

    6. *Comparing Approaches.* Most states that expressly address marital agreements treat them as generally enforceable, provided that the agreement is "free from fraud, coercion or undue influence, that the parties acted with full knowledge of the property involved and their rights therein, and that the settlement was fair and equitable."[334]

---

329. UPMAA, Prefatory Note.

330. Id.

331. 17 A.3d 17, 27 (Conn. 2011).

332. Lynn A. Baker & Robert E. Emery, When Every Relationship Is Above Average: Perceptions and Expectations of Divorce at the Time of Marriage, 17 Law & Hum. Behav. 439, 443 (1993).

333. Id.

334. See, e.g., Bratton v. Bratton, 136 S.W.3d 595, 599–600 (Tenn. 2004) (explaining majority view); In re Estate of Harber, 449 P.2d 7 (Ariz. 1969); Casto v. Casto, 508 So. 2d 330, 333 (Fla. 1987); Lipic v. Lipic, 103 S.W.3d 144, 149 (Mo. Ct. App. 2003); In re Estate of Gab, 364 N.W.2d 924, 925 (S.D. 1985); Tibbs v. Anderson, 580 So. 2d 1337, 1339 (Ala. 1991); Boudreaux v. Boudreaux, 745 So. 2d 61, 63 (La. Ct. App. 1999); Button v. Button, 388 N.W.2d 546, 547 (Wis. 1986). But see Ohio Rev. Code Ann. § 3103.06 (West 2020) ("A husband and wife cannot, by any contract with each other, alter their legal relations, except that they may agree to an immediate separation and make provisions for the support of either of them and their children during the separation").

Some apply the same standards for enforceability to premarital and marital agreements.[335] Others apply a higher standard for marital agreements than for premarital agreements.[336] Still others designate certain subjects as off-limits for marital agreements, such as changes to spousal support.[337]

PROBLEM

Liza and Jeff are married and have one child, Max. Max has developmental disabilities. Jeff tells Liza five years into marriage that he would like to divorce, but that he will stay and continue to pursue the relationship if they enter into a marital agreement that settles the economic terms of their relationship. Liza is concerned about the impact of a divorce on Max. She thinks that financial and emotional stability is necessary to Max's wellbeing. In light of these concerns, Liza signs the agreement. How should the court evaluate the marital agreement between Jeff and Liza?

C. Separation Agreements

As with premarital and marital agreements, courts have moved toward enforcement of separation agreements. These agreements are the most common of the three covered in this chapter. Rather than eyeing them with suspicion, courts see them as helpful, even essential.[338] Courts encourage private settlement of divorce for economies of time, money, and judicial resources.[339] They worry less about hard-dealing, given that the parties have already given up on the marriage. Separation agreements concerning property and spousal support are treated as presumptively enforceable except when unconscionable or the result of fraud or duress.[340] Although

---

335. See, e.g., *Lipic*, 103 S.W.3d 144; Stoner v. Stoner, 819 A.2d 529 (Pa. 2003).

336. See, e.g., Ansin v. Craven-Ansin, 929 N.E.2d 955 (Mass. 2010).

337. See, e.g., Mont. Code Ann. § 40-2-303 (2020) (barring contracts between spouses that alter legal relations except as to property or for separation); Nev. Rev. Stat. § 123.080 (2020) (same); N.M. Stat. Ann. § 40-2-8 (2020) (same).

338. To guard against a spouse's representation that they intend to stay in the marriage, Minnesota treats a marital agreement as presumptively unenforceable if one of the parties seeks separation or divorce within two years. Minn. Stat. § 519.11 (2020). See Sally Burnett Sharp, Fairness Standards and Separation Agreements: A Word of Caution on Contractual Freedom, 132 U. Pa. L. Rev. 1399 (1984).

339. Mnookin & Kornhauser, supra note 3, at 951, 956; In re Marriage of Patterson, 255 P.3d 634, 645 (Or. Ct. App. 2011); Billington v. Billington, 595 A.2d 1377, 1381 (Conn. 1991); In re Marriage of McDonnal, 652 P.2d 1247, 1250 (Or. 1982).

340. See Mnookin & Kornhauser, supra note 3, at 954–55; see also Shraberg v. Shraberg, 939 S.W.2d 330 (Ky. 1997). But see *Ansin*, 929 N.E.2d at 968–69 (applying same standard to marital and separation agreements and examining for fairness and reasonableness).

doctrinally speaking, terms that affect children fall within the judge's purview and require careful review to ensure they accord with the best interests of the child, courts frequently endorse these with minimal scrutiny.[341]

GARDELLA V. REMIZOV
42 N.Y.S.3d 225 (N.Y. App. Div. 2016)

LEVENTHAL, J.P., MILLER, LaSALLE AND BRATHWAITE NELSON, JJ. . . .

The parties to this matrimonial action were married in 2000. In October 2002, the parties entered into a postnuptial agreement, which provided, among other things, that the marital residence and the plaintiff's private medical practice were the plaintiff's separate property. In 2006, the parties entered into a second post-nuptial agreement, which provided that four parcels of real property in Florida acquired by the parties during the marriage had been purchased with the plaintiff's separate property, and further addressed the distribution of those four parcels in the event of a divorce. In 2010, the parties entered into a separation agreement, which addressed, inter alia, issues of maintenance and equitable distribution of the parties' respective assets. At the time, the plaintiff, a neurologist, was earning approximately $600,000 per year, and the defendant, a wine salesman, was earning approximately $40,000. The separation agreement provided, among other things, that the defendant would have no interest in any of the assets acquired during the parties' marriage, including six parcels of real property, the plaintiff's partnership interest in a neurological practice, and the plaintiff's bank and brokerage accounts, and that he waived his right to spousal maintenance. The defendant was not represented by counsel when he executed the separation agreement.

In November 2011, the plaintiff . . . asked the Supreme Court for a judgment of divorce which incorporated but did not merge the terms of the separation agreement. In his answer, the defendant asserted counterclaims seeking to vacate the separation agreement . . . as unconscionable and the product of fraud, duress, and the plaintiff's overreaching. . . . [T]he court granted the plaintiff's motion for summary judgment. . . [and] dissolved the parties' marriage. The defendant appeals from the judgment.

"Marital settlement agreements are judicially favored and are not to be easily set aside." "A separation agreement or stipulation of settlement which is fair on its face will be enforced according to its terms unless there is proof of fraud, duress, overreaching, or unconscionability." "Although judicial review of such agreements is to be exercised sparingly, with the goal of encouraging parties to settle their differences by themselves . . . 'courts have thrown their cloak of protection' over

---

341. Mnookin & Kornhauser, supra note 3, at 954–55.

postnuptial agreements, 'and made it their business, when confronted, to see to it that they are arrived at fairly and equitably, in a manner so as to be free from the taint of fraud and duress, and to set aside or refuse to enforce those born of and subsisting in inequity.'" "Thus, '[i]n view of the fiduciary relationship existing between the spouses, separation agreements are more closely scrutinized than ordinary contracts.'"

"An agreement is unconscionable if it 'is one which no person in his or her senses and not under delusion would make on the one hand, and no honest and fair person would accept on the other, the inequality being so strong and manifest as to shock the conscience and confound the judgment of any person of common sense.'" In addition, "[a]lthough courts may examine the terms of the agreement as well as the surrounding circumstances to ascertain whether there has been overreaching, the general rule is that if the execution of the agreement is fair, no further inquiry will be made." . . .

The plaintiff demonstrated her prima facie entitlement to judgment as a matter of law dismissing the defendant's first and second counterclaims, which sought to vacate the separation agreement. The separation agreement recited that each party entered into the agreement of his or her own "volition and free will," without the use of "coercion, force, pressure or undue influence," and that each of them either had been afforded an opportunity to obtain counsel or had waived the right to do so. The separation agreement contained a clause stating that both parties had a "full awareness" of the assets and financial condition of the other, or had waived discovery of the same. The plaintiff also submitted a separate affidavit executed by the defendant contemporaneously with the separation agreement in which he stated that he had read the separation agreement "word for word," that he understood its contents, that it was executed voluntarily and of his own free will, and that he chose not to seek the advice of counsel.

In opposition to the plaintiff's prima facie showing, the defendant's submissions were sufficient to raise triable issues of fact as to the validity of the separation agreement. Under the terms of the separation agreement, the defendant relinquished all of the property rights that he acquired during the marriage, including any interest that he may have had in the plaintiff's partnership interest in a neurological practice and the parties' four properties in Florida, as well as any spousal maintenance. Given the vast disparity in the parties' earnings, the evidence that the defendant had no assets of value, and the defendant's documented medical condition which inhibits his future earning capacity, the defendant's submissions were sufficient to create an inference that the separation agreement was unconscionable. In addition, the defendant's evidence indicating that the plaintiff sold almost $1 million in securities in the months preceding his execution of the separation agreement, the value of which were not accounted for in the list of her bank and brokerage accounts therein, raises a triable issue of fact as to whether the plaintiff concealed assets. Under these circumstances, the Supreme Court should have exercised its equitable powers and directed further financial disclosure, to be followed by a hearing to test the validity of the separation agreement. Accordingly, upon remittal, the court should direct financial disclosure and thereafter conduct such a hearing. . . .

NOTES AND QUESTIONS

1. *Standard for Unconscionability.* The Uniform Marriage and Divorce Act, Section 306, treats the terms of the separation agreement, "except those providing for the support, custody, and visitation of children," as "binding upon the court unless it finds, after considering the economic circumstances of the parties and any other relevant evidence produced by the parties, on their own motion or on request of the court, that the separation agreement is unconscionable."[342] The UMDA represents the dominant approach.

2. *Differences in Dealing?* Differences in legal treatment of premarital, marital, and separation agreements reflect varying views of the risks to parties in negotiating such contracts. Is a pro-enforcement policy in favor of separation agreements justified? Are contract principles like unconscionability, fraud, and duress sufficiently protective of the parties? How do the incentives for contractual freedom compare in the separation agreement context to those in the premarital and marital agreement contexts?

In contrast to the UMDA § 306, the ALI Principles advise less deference, raising concerns about "overreaching and unfair bargaining practices" resulting in "oppressive" separation agreements.[343] Under the ALI's approach, the "terms of a separation agreement providing for the disposition of property or for compensatory payments are unenforceable if they substantially limit or augment property rights or compensatory payments otherwise due under law, and enforcement of those terms would substantially impair the economic well-being of a party who has or will have (a) primary or dual residential responsibility for a child or (b) substantially fewer economic resources than the other party."[344]

When people bargain, they theoretically "bargain in the shadow of the law," meaning they bargain in the context of what they would likely be awarded if the case were to go to trial.[345] How can the parties know what these outcomes will be? If courts rely on standards, rather than clearly defined rules, does this make a difference to parties' estimation of their bargaining power?

3. *Incorporation.* A separation agreement is a contract and ordinarily would be enforceable as a contract — meaning only contract remedies would be available. But

---

342. UMDA § 306(b).
343. Principles of the Law of Family Dissolution, supra note 26, §7.09 cmt.
344. Id. §7.09(2).
345. Mnookin & Kornhauser, supra note 3, at 954–55, 968.

with incorporation (or merger), the settlement agreement is incorporated into the judicial decree of divorce. The terms therefore become enforceable as a judgment — meaning that remedies for noncompliance include contempt. Also, unlike a private contract, courts can modify provisions that are part of a decree. (Nonetheless, parties can ordinarily make spousal support nonmodifiable even when such terms are incorporated into the decree.) The UMDA provides that, "unless the separation agreement provides to the contrary, its terms shall be set forth in the decree of dissolution."[346] Terms regarding child support and custody must be part of the decree, as the court retains ongoing jurisdiction over both.

IV. Non-Marital Relationships

Traditionally, courts disfavored economic claims between unmarried intimate partners. As discussed in Chapter 2, such relationships were themselves illegal because they involved non-marital sex. An agreement predicated on such a relationship to share money or property made them akin to prostitution in the view of many courts.

Courts became more receptive to claims between unmarried intimate partners in the 1970s. This development partly reflected the cultural and legal relaxation of the strictures that had confined legitimate and non-criminal sexual relationships to marriage. The availability of birth control and abortion made it possible for women to better control their reproductive and sexual lives within and apart from marriage.[347] The women's rights movement emphasized women's independence and resistance to the confining role of the conventional wife.[348] These changes, in turn, contributed to an increase in the number of couples choosing to live together without being married.

In recent decades, rates of cohabitation have risen steadily.[349] As of 2019, about 18.5 million individuals were living in a non-marital cohabiting relationship.[350] Of those, approximately 469,000 were same-sex couples.[351] In the population of unmarried cohabitants, about 67 percent identify as white, 16 percent as Hispanic, 11 percent as black, and 6 percent as other (including multiracial, Asian, and American

---

346. UMDA § 306(d).

347. See Roe v. Wade, 410 U.S. 113 (1973); Griswold v. Connecticut, 381 U.S. 479 (1965).

348. See, e.g., Flora Davis, Moving the Mountain: The Women's Movement in America Since 1960 (1999).

349. Marriage and Cohabitation in the U.S., supra note 182.

350. U.S. Census Bureau, Table AD-3, Living Arrangements of Adults 18 and Over, 1967 to Present (2019).

351. U.S. Census Bureau Releases CPS Estimates of Same-Sex Households, U.S. Census Bureau (November 19, 2019).

Indian).[352] As compared to the married population, black and Hispanic individuals constitute a larger percentage of unmarried cohabitants.[353] About 10 percent of all non-marital cohabiting relationships are interracial.[354] About 2.5 million cohabiting couples are raising children together.[355]

Research shows that non-marital cohabiting relationships are shorter in duration than marital relationships. A longitudinal study of individuals in their first non-marital cohabiting relationship found that after a year and a half, about half of cohabitating couples had either married each other or broken up, with only 10 percent of cohabitating couples remaining in their current living situation five years after the start of their cohabitation.[356] A CDC study of women in their first different-sex cohabiting relationship found that, after three years, 40 percent of the women had married their partner, 32 percent remained in the non-marital cohabiting relationship, and 27 percent had ended their relationship.[357]

How, if at all, should data on the prevalence and length of non-marital cohabiting relationships influence the legal regime governing relationship dissolution? As is apparent in the materials that follow, states have taken different approaches to adjudicating the claims of unmarried partners who have not otherwise formalized their relationship through arrangements such as civil unions or domestic partnerships.

A. The Contractual Approach to the Economic Rights of Non-Marital Partners

We begin with the groundbreaking California case that has shaped many states' approach to the economic rights of non-marital partners. The defendant was a well-known actor, Lee Marvin, and the plaintiff was his cohabiting partner, Michelle Triola Marvin (who had legally changed her last name).

---

352. Benjamin Gurrentz, Cohabiting Partners Older, More Racially Diverse, More Educated, Higher Earners, U.S. Census Bureau (Sept. 23, 2019).

353. U.S. Census Bureau, America's Families and Living Arrangements: 2017, Table FG3, Married Couple Family Groups, By Presence of Own Children Under 18, And Age, Earnings, Education, And Race and Hispanic Origin of Both Spouses: 2017.

354. Gurrentz, supra note 352. This mirrors the married population. See Brittany Rico, et al., U.S. Census Bureau, Growth in Interracial and Interethnic Married-Couple Households (July 9, 2018).

355. U.S. Census Bureau, America's Families and Living Arrangements: 2017, Table A3, Parents with Coresident Children Under 18, by Living Arrangement, Sex, and Selected Characteristics: 2017.

356. Lawrence W. Waggoner, Marriage is on the Decline and Cohabitation is on the Rise: At What Point, if Ever, Should Unmarried Partners Acquire Marital Rights?, 50 Fam. L.Q. 215, 231 (2016).

357. Ctrs. for Disease Control & Prevention, National Survey of Family Growth: Key Statistics from the National Survey of Family Growth - C Listing (2019).

Marvin v. Marvin
557 P.2d 106 (Cal. 1976)

Tobriner, Justice.

During the past 15 years, there has been a substantial increase in the number of couples living together without marrying. Such nonmarital relationships lead to legal controversy when one partner dies or the couple separates. . . .

Plaintiff avers that in October of 1964 she and defendant "entered into an oral agreement" that while "the parties lived together they would combine their efforts and earnings and would share equally any and all property accumulated as a result of their efforts whether individual or combined." Furthermore, they agreed to "hold themselves out to the general public as husband and wife" and that "plaintiff would further render her services as a companion, homemaker, housekeeper and cook to . . . defendant."

Shortly thereafter plaintiff agreed to "give up her lucrative career as an entertainer (and) singer" in order to "devote her full time to defendant . . . as a companion, homemaker, housekeeper and cook;" in return defendant agreed to "provide for all of plaintiff's financial support and needs for the rest of her life."

Plaintiff alleges that she lived with defendant from October of 1964 through May of 1970 and fulfilled her obligations under the agreement. During this period the parties as a result of their efforts and earnings acquired in defendant's name substantial real and personal property, including motion picture rights worth over $1 million. In May of 1970, however, defendant compelled plaintiff to leave his household. He continued to support plaintiff until November of 1971, but thereafter refused to provide further support.

On the basis of these allegations plaintiff asserts two causes of action. The first, for declaratory relief, asks the court to determine her contract and property rights; the second seeks to impose a constructive trust upon one half of the property acquired during the course of the relationship. . . . [The lower court had granted defendant's motion for judgment on the pleadings.]

Defendant first and principally relies on the contention that the alleged contract is so closely related to the supposed "immoral" character of the relationship between plaintiff and himself that the enforcement of the contract would violate public policy. He points to cases asserting that a contract between nonmarital partners is unenforceable if it is "involved in" an illicit relationship. . . . A review of the numerous California decisions concerning contracts between nonmarital partners, however, reveals that the courts have not employed such broad and uncertain standards to strike down contracts. The decisions instead disclose a narrower and more precise standard: a contract between nonmarital partners is unenforceable only *to the extent* that it *explicitly* rests upon the immoral and illicit consideration of meretricious sexual services. . . .

Although the past decisions hover over the issue in the somewhat wispy form of the figures of a Chagall painting, we can abstract from those decisions a clear and simple rule. The fact that a man and woman live together without marriage, and engage in a sexual relationship, does not in itself invalidate agreements between them relating to their earnings, property, or expenses. Neither is such an agreement invalid merely because the parties may have contemplated the creation or continuation of a nonmarital relationship when they entered into it. Agreements between nonmarital partners fail only to the extent that they rest upon a consideration of meretricious sexual services. Thus the rule asserted by defendant, that a contract fails if it is "involved in" or made "in contemplation" of a nonmarital relationship, cannot be reconciled with the decisions.

The three cases cited by defendant which have *declined* to enforce contracts between nonmarital partners involved consideration that *was expressly founded upon . . . illicit sexual services.* In Hill v. Estate of Westbrook, 213 P.2d 727 (Cal. 1950), the woman promised to keep house for the man, to live with him as man and wife, and to bear his children; the man promised to provide for her in his will, but died without doing so. . . .

In . . . Updeck v. Samuel, 266 P.2d 822 (Cal. Ct. App. 1964), the contract "was based on the consideration that the parties live together as husband and wife." Viewing the contract as calling for adultery, the court held it illegal.

The decisions in the *Hill* and *Updeck* cases thus demonstrate that a contract between nonmarital partners, even if expressly made in contemplation of a common living arrangement, is invalid only if sexual acts form an inseparable part of the consideration for the agreement. In sum, a court will not enforce a contract for the pooling of property and earnings if it is explicitly and inseparably based upon services as a paramour. The Court of Appeal opinion in *Hill*, however, indicates that even if sexual services are part of the contractual consideration, any *severable* portion of the contract supported by independent consideration will still be enforced.

The principle that a contract between nonmarital partners will be enforced unless expressly and inseparably based upon an illicit consideration of sexual services not only represents the distillation of the decisional law, but also offers a far more precise and workable standard than that advocated by defendant. . . .

[I]n the present case a standard which inquires whether an agreement is "involved" in or "contemplates" a nonmarital relationship is vague and unworkable. Virtually all agreements between nonmarital partners can be said to be "involved" in some sense in the fact of their mutual sexual relationship, or to "contemplate" the existence of that relationship. Thus defendant's proposed standards, if taken literally, might invalidate all agreements between nonmarital partners, a result no one favors. Moreover, those standards offer no basis to distinguish between valid and invalid agreements. By looking not to such uncertain tests, but only to the consideration underlying the agreement, we provide the parties and the courts with a practical guide to determine when an agreement between nonmarital partners should be enforced. . . .

In summary, we base our opinion on the principle that adults who voluntarily live together and engage in sexual relations are nonetheless as competent as any other persons to contract respecting their earnings and property rights. Of course, they cannot lawfully contract to pay for the performance of sexual services, for such a contract is, in essence, an agreement for prostitution and unlawful for that reason. But they may agree to pool their earnings and to hold all property acquired during the relationship in accord with the law governing community property; conversely they may agree that each partner's earnings and the property acquired from those earnings remains the separate property of the earning partner. So long as the agreement does not rest upon illicit meretricious consideration, the parties may order their economic affairs as they choose, and no policy precludes the courts from enforcing such agreements.

In the present instance, plaintiff alleges that the parties agreed to pool their earnings, that they contracted to share equally in all property acquired, and that defendant agreed to support plaintiff. The terms of the contract as alleged do not rest upon any unlawful consideration. We therefore conclude that the complaint furnishes a suitable basis upon which the trial court can render declaratory relief. The trial court consequently erred in granting defendant's motion for judgment on the pleadings. . . .

Although our conclusion that plaintiff's complaint states a cause of action based on an express contract alone compels us to reverse the judgment for defendant, resolution of the. . . issue [of an action independent of any express contract] will serve both to guide the parties upon retrial and to resolve a conflict presently manifest in published Court of Appeal decisions. . . .

[P]rior [cases] exhibited a schizophrenic inconsistency. By enforcing an express contract between nonmarital partners unless it rested upon an unlawful consideration, the courts applied a common law principle as to contracts. Yet the courts disregarded the common law principle that holds that implied contracts can arise from the conduct of the parties. Refusing to enforce such contracts, the courts spoke of leaving the parties "in the position in which they had placed themselves." . . .

Still another inconsistency in the prior cases arises from their treatment of property accumulated through joint effort. To the extent that a partner had contributed *funds or property*, the cases held that the partner obtains a proportionate share in the acquisition, despite the lack of legal standing of the relationship. Yet courts have refused to recognize just such an interest based upon the contribution of Services. As Justice Curtis points out "Unless it can be argued that a woman's services as cook, housekeeper, and homemaker are valueless, it would seem logical that if, when she contributes money to the purchase of property, her interest will be protected, then when she contributes her services in the home, her interest in property accumulated should be protected." Vallera v. Vallera, 134 P.2d 761, 764 (Cal. 1943) (diss. opn.). . . .

The principal reason why [earlier] decisions result[ed] in an unfair distribution of property inheres in the court's refusal to permit a nonmarital partner to assert rights based upon accepted principles of implied contract or equity. We have examined the reasons advanced to justify this denial of relief, and find that none have merit.

First, we note that the cases denying relief do not rest their refusal upon any theory of "punishing" a "guilty" partner. Indeed, to the extent that denial of relief "punishes" one partner, it necessarily rewards the other by permitting him to retain a disproportionate amount of the property. Concepts of "guilt" thus cannot justify an unequal division of property between two equally "guilty" persons.

Other reasons advanced in the decisions fare no better. The principal argument seems to be that "(e)quitable considerations arising from the reasonable expectation of . . . benefits attending the status of marriage . . . are not present (in a nonmarital relationship)." But, although parties to a nonmarital relationship obviously cannot have based any expectations upon the belief that they were married, other expectations and equitable considerations remain. The parties may well expect that property will be divided in accord with the parties' own tacit understanding and that in the absence of such understanding the courts will fairly apportion property accumulated through mutual effort. We need not treat nonmarital partners as putatively married persons in order to apply principles of implied contract, or extend equitable remedies; we need to treat them only as we do any other unmarried persons.

The remaining arguments advanced from time to time to deny remedies to the nonmarital partners are of less moment. There is no more reason to presume that services are contributed as a gift than to presume that funds are contributed as a gift; in any event the better approach is to presume . . . "that the parties intend to deal fairly with each other."

The argument that granting remedies to the nonmarital partners would discourage marriage must fail. . . . Although we recognize the well-established public policy to foster and promote the institution of marriage, perpetuation of judicial rules which result in an inequitable distribution of property accumulated during a nonmarital relationship is neither a just nor an effective way of carrying out that policy.

In summary, we believe that the prevalence of nonmarital relationships in modern society and the social acceptance of them, marks this as a time when our courts should by no means apply the doctrine of the unlawfulness of the so-called meretricious relationship to the instant case. . . . [T]he nonenforceability of agreements expressly providing for meretricious conduct rested upon the fact that such conduct, as the word suggests, pertained to and encompassed prostitution. To equate the nonmarital relationship of today to such a subject matter is to do violence to an accepted and wholly different practice.

We are aware that many young couples live together without the solemnization of marriage, in order to make sure that they can successfully later undertake marriage. This trial period, preliminary to marriage, serves as some assurance that the marriage will not subsequently end in dissolution to the harm of both parties. We are aware, as we have stated, of the pervasiveness of nonmarital relationships in other situations.

The mores of the society have indeed changed so radically in regard to cohabitation that we cannot impose a standard based on alleged moral considerations that have apparently been so widely abandoned by so many. Lest we be misunderstood, however, we take this occasion to point out that the structure of society itself largely depends upon the institution of marriage, and nothing we have said in this opinion should be taken to derogate from that institution. The joining of the man and woman in marriage is at once the most socially productive and individually fulfilling relationship that one can enjoy in the course of a lifetime.

We conclude that the judicial barriers that may stand in the way of a policy based upon the fulfillment of the reasonable expectations of the parties to a nonmarital relationship should be removed. As we have explained, the courts now hold that express agreements will be enforced unless they rest on an unlawful meretricious consideration. We add that in the absence of an express agreement, the courts may look to a variety of other remedies in order to protect the parties' lawful expectations.[24]

The courts may inquire into the conduct of the parties to determine whether that conduct demonstrates an implied contract or implied agreement of partnership or joint venture, or some other tacit understanding between the parties. The courts may, when appropriate, employ principles of constructive trust or resulting trust. Finally, a nonmarital partner may recover in quantum meruit for the reasonable value of household services rendered less the reasonable value of support received if he can show that he rendered services with the expectation of monetary reward. . . .

CLARK, JUSTICE (concurring and dissenting). . . .

When the parties to a meretricious relationship show by express or implied in fact agreement they intend to create mutual obligations, the courts should enforce the agreement. However, in the absence of agreement, we should stop and consider the ramifications before creating economic obligations which may violate legislative intent, contravene the intention of the parties, and surely generate undue burdens on our trial courts.

By judicial overreach, the majority perform a nunc pro tunc marriage, dissolve it, and distribute its property on terms never contemplated by the parties, case law or the Legislature.

---

24. We do not seek to resurrect the doctrine of common law marriage, which was abolished in California by statute in 1895. Thus we do not hold that plaintiff and defendant were "married," nor do we extend to plaintiff the rights which the Family Law Act grants valid or putative spouses; we hold only that she has the same rights to enforce contracts and to assert her equitable interest in property acquired through her effort as does any other unmarried person.

NOTES AND QUESTIONS

1. *The Traditional Approach.* As the *Marvin* court noted, the law traditionally disfavored contracts between unmarried cohabitants; courts viewed such contracts as being founded upon sexual services, which may not serve as consideration for an agreement. The *Marvin* court distinguished two categories of cases: those in which sexual services are consideration for the agreement, and those in which the consideration consists of non-sexual aspects of the couple's relationship. In the *Marvin* court's view, the latter agreements are enforceable, and the former are not. Would you distinguish agreements for prostitution from cohabitation agreements in this way? Is it likely that the cohabiting couple's sexual relationship is not an aspect of their agreement?

2. *Trial Evidence.* The evidence produced at trial in *Marvin* left little doubt that Lee Marvin did not want to marry Michelle and that she did want to marry him. But there was conflicting testimony about the nature and extent of any agreement regarding economic obligations between the parties. Should persuasive evidence of his unwillingness to marry her conclusively resolve the case in his favor? Or might she be able to prevail on such facts?

3. *Theories of Recovery.* The *Marvin* court endorsed three theories of recovery: express contract, implied contract, and equitable remedies.

a. *Express Contract.* Michelle asserted that Lee had told her, while on vacation in Hawaii, "I love you. What I have is yours and what you have is mine." She further alleged that on other occasions he told her, "I'll take care of you always." If proven that Lee did make those statements, should such evidence be sufficient for Michelle to prevail? What are the difficulties likely to arise in proving this sort of express contract claim? How would you expect someone in Lee's position to defend against such a claim?

b. *Implied Contract.* The implied contract claim roots the contract not in explicit promises but instead in the behavior of the parties. The court would look to the couple's behavior as evidence of the "parties' own tacit understanding" of their agreement. For example, Michelle asserted that she had given up her career as a singer to support Lee and provide homemaking services to him. How much weight should that fact be accorded in determining the tacit understanding of the parties?

c. *Equitable Remedies.* Even in the absence of an agreement, either express or implied, courts might rely on equitable principles to impose a remedy, if necessary to avoid unjust enrichment.[358] Quantum meruit, for example, is an equitable remedy by which one may be entitled to compensation for the reasonable value of services provided, even when there is no legally enforceable contract.

---

358. See, e.g., Eaton v. Johnston, 681 P.2d 606 (Kan. 1984)

4. *On Remand.* On remand, the trial court denied Michelle recovery under the express contract, implied contract, and quantum meruit claims, yet awarded her $104,000 for rehabilitation purposes.[359] That judgment, itself a fraction of what she originally sought, was overturned on appeal.[360]

5. Marvin's *Progeny. Marvin* represented a watershed in the economic rights of unmarried couples. But in its aftermath, as Professor Marsha Garrison reports, California courts have interpreted the requirements for economic claims in ways that make it difficult to prevail.[361] For example, courts have rejected claims when the partners had not cohabited.[362] And courts have required plaintiffs in some circumstances to meet a clear-and-convincing evidence standard.[363]

6. *A Writing Requirement?* A recurring problem in these cases concerns the difficulties of proof of the existence and terms of any contract. One response to that challenge is to require the parties to reduce any agreement to writing. For example, Minnesota law provides:

> If sexual relations between the parties are contemplated, a contract between a man and a woman who are living together in this state out of wedlock, or who are about to commence living together in this state out of wedlock, is enforceable as to terms concerning the property and financial relations of the parties only if: (1) the contract is written and signed by the parties, and (2) enforcement is sought after termination of the relationship.[364]

Texas likewise provides:

> A promise or agreement [made on consideration of marriage or on consideration of non-marital conjugal cohabitation] is not enforceable unless the promise or agreement, or a memorandum of it, is (1) in writing; and (2) signed by the person to be charged with the promise or agreement or by someone lawfully authorized to sign for him.[365]

7. *Homemaking Services.* The *Marvin* court noted that prior decisions had allowed recovery for contributions of property between intimate partners and extended that approach to contributions of services. The recognition of the value of services within the home reflects changes in divorce law during the period, as discussed earlier in this chapter. But in the context of claims between unmarried cohabitants, is there a reason to accord differential significance to contributions of property versus contributions of

---

359. 5 Fam. L. Rep. (BNA) 3079 (Apr. 24, 1979).

360. Marvin v. Marvin, 176 Cal. Rptr. 555 (Cal. Ct. App. 1981).

361. See Marsha Garrison, Nonmarital Cohabitation: Social Revolution and Legal Regulation, 42 Fam. L.Q. 309, 317 (2008).

362. See Taylor v. Fields, 224 Cal. Rptr. 186 (Ct. App. 1986); Bergen v. Wood, 18 Cal. Rptr. 2d 75 (Ct. App. 1993).

363. See Tannehill v. Finch, 232 Cal. Rptr. 749 (Ct. App. 1986).

364. Minn. Stat. § 513.075 (2020).

365. Tex. Bus. & Com. Code Ann. § 26.01 (West 2020); see also N.J. Stat. Ann. § 25:1-5(h) (West 2020).

services? Or should that distinction be collapsed with respect to unmarried cohabitants just as it has with respect to married couples who divorce?

8. *Expectations.* The *Marvin* court repeatedly referred to the need to avoid unfairness by validating the reasonable expectations of the parties. But what are they? Could Lee Marvin reasonably have expected that when their relationship ended he would have absolutely no financial obligation to Michelle and that all the property titled in his name (which is to say all the property the couple had accumulated) would remain his alone? Could Michelle Marvin reasonably have expected that she would have an equal share in all the property accumulated during the relationship and/or that Lee would support her for the rest of her life?

9. *Valuation of Contributions.* Application of equitable remedies typically involves an assessment of fairness, which in turn entails some evaluation of the contributions of the parties. In a case like *Marvin*, how could a court go about identifying the value of what each party contributed to the relationship? Should the court evaluate Michelle's contribution simply as if she were a household manager, cleaner, and cook? Or should it also attempt to place a value on the opportunities that Michelle forsook in order to be Lee's companion? Given Lee's undisputed financial contributions, could he plausibly argue that Michelle had already been sufficiently compensated during the course of their relationship for any services she provided and any opportunities she sacrificed in order to be with him? If you were the judge, how would you approach the task of valuation?

10. *Cohabitation.* Should courts limit economic remedies to situations in which the couple has cohabited? After all, married couples are not required to live together. Today, many couples maintain long-term intimate relationships without ever marrying or living together. Such relationships have been termed "LATs" ("living apart together").[366]

In 2008, the New Jersey Supreme Court considered whether cohabitation was required for a couple to have the "marital-type relationship" necessary for a palimony claim (a term used to describe a claim for property or support by an unmarried partner):

> [W]hether the parties cohabited is a relevant factor in the analysis of whether a marital-type relationship exists, and in most successful palimony cases, cohabitation will be present. We recognize, however, that palimony cases present highly personal arrangements and the facts surrounding the relationship will determine whether it is a marital-type relationship that is essential to support a cause of action for palimony. There may be circumstances where a couple may hold themselves out to others as if they were married and yet not cohabit (i.e., couples who are separated due to employment,

---

366. See Charles Q. Strohm et al., "Living Apart Together" Relationships in the United States, 21 Demography Res. 177 (2009).

> military, or educational opportunities and who do not cohabit). . . . [I]n addressing a cause of action for palimony, the trial judge should consider the entirety of the relationship and, if a marital-type relationship is otherwise proven, it should not be rejected solely because cohabitation is not present.[367]

In that case, the couple had not spent many nights together. In fact, the man lived with his wife while his unmarried partner lived in a condominium that he had bought for her.[368] The court's decision has since been superseded by a statute requiring that palimony agreements be in writing.[369]

Should courts require at least some cohabitation? In a case involving the famous lawyer Johnnie Cochran, a California appeals court held that "evidence that [the parties] lived together two to four days a week" was enough to constitute cohabitation sufficient to support a *Marvin* claim.[370] The court reasoned that "[t]o require nothing short of full-time cohabitation before enforcing an agreement would defeat the reasonable expectations of persons who may clearly enjoy a significant and stable relationship arising from cohabitation, albeit less than a full-time living arrangement."[371] Is there any reason to require some cohabitation? Should it matter if one of the parties is living with another partner — perhaps a spouse — most of the time?

11. *The Community Property Remedy.* Rather than attempt to value the various contributions of each party, some courts instead have recognized the possibility of applying community property principles to unmarried cohabitants who would otherwise assert *Marvin* claims.[372] Does this seem sensible? (This approach, adopted in Washington state, will be discussed in more detail later in this section.)

12. *The Doctrinal Split. Marvin* signaled a sea change in the law of non-marital relationships. Following *Marvin*, almost all states permit economic claims by unmarried partners — but they differ significantly in how broad or narrow an approach they take.[373] Still, not every state has liberalized its approach.[374] We turn now to the leading example — Illinois.

---

367. Devaney v. L'Esperance, 949 A.2d 743, 750 (N.J. 2008).

368. Id. at 745.

369. N.J. Stat. Ann. § 25:1-5(h) (West 2020).

370. Cochran v. Cochran, 106 Cal. Rptr. 2d 899, 906 (Cal. Ct. App. 2001).

371. Id.

372. W. States Constr. Inc. v. Michoff, 840 P.2d 1220 (Nev. 1992).

373. For recent scholarship on the legal rights and obligations of unmarried couples, see Albertina Antognini, The Law of Nonmarriage, 58 B.C. L. Rev. 1 (2017); Courtney G. Joslin, Autonomy in the Family, 66 UCLA L. Rev. 912 (2019); and Kaiponanea T. Matsumura, Consent to Intimate Regulation, 96 N.C. L. Rev. 1013 (2018).

374. See Margaret Ryznar & Anna Stępień-Sporek, Cohabitation Worldwide Today, 35 Ga. St. U. L. Rev. 299, 303–15 (2019).

B. The Traditional Approach to the Economic Rights of Non-Marital Partners

HEWITT V. HEWITT
394 N.E.2d 1204 (Ill. 1979)

UNDERWOOD, JUSTICE:

The issue in this case is whether plaintiff Victoria Hewitt, whose complaint alleges she lived with defendant Robert Hewitt from 1960 to 1975 in an unmarried, family-like relationship to which three children have been born, may recover from him "an equal share of the profits and properties accumulated by the parties" during that period. . . .

Plaintiff . . . alleg[ed] the following bases for her claim: (1) that because defendant promised he would "share his life, his future, his earnings and his property" with her and all of defendant's property resulted from the parties' joint endeavors, plaintiff is entitled in equity to a one-half share; (2) that the conduct of the parties evinced an implied contract entitling plaintiff to one-half the property accumulated during their "family relationship"; (3) that because defendant fraudulently assured plaintiff she was his wife in order to secure her services, although he knew they were not legally married, defendant's property should be impressed with a trust for plaintiff's benefit; (4) that because plaintiff has relied to her detriment on defendant's promises and devoted her entire life to him, defendant has been unjustly enriched.

The factual background alleged or testified to is that in June 1960, when she and defendant were students at Grinnell College in Iowa, plaintiff became pregnant; that defendant thereafter told her that they were husband and wife and would live as such, no formal ceremony being necessary, and that he would "share his life, his future, his earnings and his property" with her; that the parties immediately announced to their respective parents that they were married and thereafter held themselves out as husband and wife; that in reliance on defendant's promises she devoted her efforts to his professional education and his establishment in the practice of pedodontia, obtaining financial assistance from her parents for this purpose; that she assisted defendant in his career with her own special skills and although she was given payroll checks for these services she placed them in a common fund; that defendant, who was without funds at the time of the marriage, as a result of her efforts now earns over $80,000 a year and has accumulated large amounts of property, owned either jointly with her or separately; that she has given him every assistance a wife and mother could give, including social activities designed to enhance his social and professional reputation. . . .

Plaintiff argues that because her action is founded on an express contract, her recovery would in no way imply that unmarried cohabitants acquire property rights merely by cohabitation and subsequent separation. However, the *Marvin* court expressly recognized and the appellate court here seems to agree that if common law principles of express contract govern express agreements between unmarried cohabitants, common law principles of implied contract, equitable relief and constructive trust must govern the parties' relations in the absence of such an agreement. In all probability the latter case will be much the more common, since it is unlikely that most couples who live together will enter into express agreements regulating their property rights. . . .

The issue of unmarried cohabitants' mutual property rights . . . cannot appropriately be characterized solely in terms of contract law, nor is it limited to considerations of equity or fairness as between the parties to such relationships. There are major public policy questions involved in determining whether, under what circumstances, and to what extent it is desirable to accord some type of legal status to claims arising from such relationships. Of substantially greater importance than the rights of the immediate parties is the impact of such recognition upon our society and the institution of marriage. Will the fact that legal rights closely resembling those arising from conventional marriages can be acquired by those who deliberately choose to enter into what have heretofore been commonly referred to as "illicit" or "meretricious" relationships encourage formation of such relationships and weaken marriage as the foundation of our family-based society? In the event of death shall the survivor have the status of a surviving spouse for purposes of inheritance, wrongful death actions, workmen's compensation, etc.? And still more importantly: what of the children born of such relationships? What are their support and inheritance rights and by what standards are custody questions resolved? What of the sociological and psychological effects upon them of that type of environment? Does not the recognition of legally enforceable property and custody rights emanating from nonmarital cohabitation in practical effect equate with the legalization of common law marriage at least in the circumstances of this case . . . which our legislature outlawed in 1905?

Illinois' public policy regarding agreements such as the one alleged here was implemented long ago [when] this court said: "An agreement in consideration of future illicit cohabitation between the plaintiffs is void." This is the traditional rule, in force until recent years in all jurisdictions. . . .

It is true, of course, that cohabitation by the parties may not prevent them from forming valid contracts about independent matters, for which it is said the sexual relations do not form part of the consideration. Those courts which allow recovery generally have relied on this principle to reduce the scope of the rule of illegality. . . .

The real thrust of plaintiff's argument here is that we should abandon the rule of illegality because of certain changes in societal norms and attitudes. It is urged that social mores have changed radically in recent years, rendering this principle of law archaic. It is said that because there are so many unmarried cohabitants today the courts must confer a legal status on such relationships. . . . If this is to be the result, however, it would seem more candid to acknowledge the return of varying forms of common law marriage than to continue displaying the naivete we believe involved in the assertion that there are involved in these relationships contracts separate and independent from the sexual activity, and the assumption that those contracts would have been entered into or would continue without that activity.

Even if we were to assume some modification of the rule of illegality is appropriate, we return to the fundamental question earlier alluded to: If resolution of this issue rests ultimately on grounds of public policy, by what body should that policy be determined? *Marvin*, viewing the issue as governed solely by contract law, found judicial policy-making appropriate. Its decision was facilitated by California precedent and that State's no-fault divorce law. In our view, however, the situation alleged here was not the kind of arm's length bargain envisioned by traditional contract principles, but an intimate arrangement of a fundamentally different kind. The issue, realistically, is whether it is appropriate for this court to grant a legal status to a private arrangement substituting for the institution of marriage sanctioned by the State. The question whether change is needed in the law governing the rights of parties in this delicate area of marriage-like relationships involves evaluations of sociological data and alternatives we believe best suited to the superior investigative and fact-finding facilities of the legislative branch in the exercise of its traditional authority to declare public policy in the domestic relations field. That belief is reinforced by the fact that judicial recognition of mutual property rights between unmarried cohabitants would, in our opinion, clearly violate the policy of our recently enacted Illinois Marriage and Dissolution of Marriage Act. Although the Act does not specifically address the subject of nonmarital cohabitation, we think the legislative policy quite evident from the statutory scheme. . . .

The Act also provides: "Common law marriages contracted in this State after June 30, 1905 are invalid." The doctrine of common law marriage was a judicially sanctioned alternative to formal marriage. . . . [A common law marriage would exist] if the parties declared their present intent to take each other as husband and wife and thereafter did so. Such marriages were legislatively abolished in 1905. . . .

[Recognizing plaintiff's claim would inappropriately revive common law marriage.]

Further, in enacting the Illinois Marriage and Dissolution of Marriage Act, our legislature considered and rejected the "no-fault" divorce concept that has been adopted in many other jurisdictions, including California. . . . Certainly a significantly stronger pro-marriage policy is manifest in that action, which appears to us to reaffirm the traditional doctrine that marriage is a civil contract between three parties — the husband, the wife and the State. The policy of the Act gives the State a strong continuing interest in the institution of marriage and prevents the marriage relation from becoming in effect a private contract terminable at will. This seems to us another indication that public policy disfavors private contractual alternatives to marriage.

Lastly, in enacting the Illinois Marriage and Dissolution of Marriage Act, the legislature adopted for the first time the civil law concept of the putative spouse. The

Act provides that an unmarried person may acquire the rights of a legal spouse only if he goes through a marriage ceremony and cohabits with another in the good-faith belief that he is validly married. . . .

These circumstances in our opinion constitute a recent and unmistakeable legislative judgment disfavoring the grant of mutual property rights to knowingly unmarried cohabitants. . . .

We accordingly hold that plaintiff's claims are unenforceable for the reason that they contravene the public policy, implicit in the statutory scheme of the Illinois Marriage and Dissolution of Marriage Act, disfavoring the grant of mutually enforceable property rights to knowingly unmarried cohabitants. . . .

PROBLEM

Consider the following scenario: Berta and Carlos, a different-sex couple, live together. They consider purchasing a house together, but don't because Carlos has bad credit. Instead, Berta purchases the house in her name, and Carlos provides the down payment. They move in together. Berta works long hours and earns a substantial salary. Carlos works part-time; he likes to cook, and so he prepares dinner most nights. Berta pays the mortgage and property taxes and for any maintenance related to the house; Carlos pays for groceries and entertainment expenses. They never discuss what would happen if they break up; after all, they don't expect to. Ten years later, Berta and Carlos split up, and Carlos wants 50 percent of the equity in the house, which has appreciated substantially. How would this case be handled by a court following *Marvin*? By a court following *Hewitt*?

Despite the fact that rates of cohabitation have increased substantially in recent decades and societal attitudes toward nonmarital relationships have continued to liberalize, the Illinois Supreme Court has adhered to its ruling in *Hewitt*, as the following case indicates.

BLUMENTHAL V. BREWER
69 N.E.3d 834 (Ill. 2016)

JUSTICE KARMEIER . . .

In this case we are called on to consider the continued viability and applicability of our decision in *Hewitt v. Hewitt*, (1979), which held that Illinois public policy, as set forth in this State's statutory prohibition against common-law marriage, precludes unmarried cohabitants from bringing claims against one another to enforce mutual property rights where the rights asserted are rooted in a marriage-like relationship between the parties.

The issue has arisen here in the context of an action brought by Dr. Jane E. Blumenthal for partition of the family home she shared and jointly owned with Judge Eileen M. Brewer. The couple had maintained a long-term, domestic relationship and raised a family together but had never married. . . . [Brewer claimed an interest in Blumenthal's medical partnership, GSN. The appellate court had upheld Brewer's claim.]

One thing is certain as argued in the briefs: Illinois's statutory prohibition of common-law marriage and this court's prior decision in *Hewitt* are imperative to resolving the issue before this court. . . .

The facts of the present case are almost indistinguishable from *Hewitt*, except, in this case, the parties were in a same-sex relationship. During the course of their long-term, domestic relationship, Brewer alleges that she and Blumenthal had a relationship that was "identical in every essential way to that of a married couple." Although the parties were not legally married, they acted like a married couple and held themselves out as such. For example, the former domestic partners exchanged rings as a symbol of their commitment to each other, executed wills and trusts, each naming the other as the sole beneficiary of her assets, and appointed each other as fiduciary for financial and medical decision making. Blumenthal and Brewer also began to commingle their personal and financial assets, which allowed them to purchase investment property as well as the Chicago home where they raised their three children. Much like in *Hewitt*, Brewer alleges that she contributed to Blumenthal's purchase of an ownership interest in the medical group GSN, helping Blumenthal earn the majority of income for the parties and "thereby guaranteeing the family's financial security." Because Blumenthal was able to earn a high income, Brewer was able to devote more time to raising the couple's children and to attend to other domestic duties. Once Blumenthal's and Brewer's relationship ended, Brewer, like Victoria Hewitt, brought suit seeking various common-law remedies to equalize their assets and receive an interest in Blumenthal's business.

As explained *supra*, our decision in *Hewitt* did no more than follow the statutory provision abolishing common-law marriage, which embodied the public policy of Illinois that individuals acting privately by themselves, without the involvement of the State, cannot create marriage-like benefits. *Hewitt* clearly declared the law on the very issue in this case. Yet, the appellate court in this case declined to follow our ruling, despite the facts being almost identical to *Hewitt*. This was improper. . . . The appellate court had no authority to depart from our decision. It could question *Hewitt* and recommend that we revisit our holding in the case, but it could not overrule it.

The appellate court was also ill-advised to adopt the reasoning in *Marvin* given that in *Hewitt* we unquestionably rejected *Marvin*. . . .

When considering the property rights of unmarried cohabitants, our view of *Hewitt*'s holding has not changed. As in *Hewitt*, the issue before this court cannot appropriately be characterized solely in terms of contract law, nor is it limited to considerations of equity or fairness as between the parties in such marriage-like relationships. These questions undoubtedly involve some of the most fundamental policy concerns in our society. Permitting such claims, as sought by Brewer, would not only impact the institution of marriage but also raise questions pertaining to other family-related issues. Moreover, Brewer's argument that her relationship with Blumenthal should not be viewed differently from others who cohabit, like roommates or siblings living together, ignores the fact that their relationship — which lasted almost three decades and involved raising three children — *was* different from other forms of cohabitation. Brewer herself identified in her counterclaim that her relationship with Blumenthal was not that of roommates or siblings living together but was "identical in every essential way to that of a married couple." . . .

[W]e reject Brewer's invitation to overrule *Hewitt* and hold that it remains good law. . . .

[O]ne of the ways Blumenthal and Brewer's domestic relationship was identical to that of a married couple was, among other things, their decision to "commingle[ ] their personal property and their finances." Beginning around the year 2000, Blumenthal and Brewer . . . pooled their assets and finances, which were used to make purchases including the arrangement to purchase an ownership interest in GSN. According to Brewer, these purchases were made for the benefit of providing the "family's financial security" and to allow Brewer to devote a substantial amount of her time raising the couple's children. The decision between Blumenthal and Brewer to commingle their finances and use those joint funds to make property and financial investments demonstrates that the funds were economically dependent on the parties' marriage-like relationship.

For about eight years, Brewer never objected to the arrangement, nor does the counterclaim allege that she tried to earmark or record which funds of hers were going specifically toward the purchase of GSN, as if she were a business partner. This was unquestionably because Blumenthal and Brewer wanted to live like a married couple. Both parties voluntarily contributed to the joint account because that is typical of a married couple. The parties' arrangement was made possible because Brewer . . . agreed to forgo advancing her own legal career in order for Blumenthal to pursue entrepreneurial endeavors including the purchase of an ownership interest in GSN. Indeed, Brewer is correct in labeling Blumenthal's and her purchase of GSN as an investment. But it was an investment for the family, which included Blumenthal, Brewer, and their children. It was not an investment between business partners. Nor was it the kind of arm's-length bargain envisioned by traditional contract principles. Rather, the arrangement to use the parties' commingled funds was an arrangement of a fundamentally different kind, which . . . is intimately related and dependent on Brewer's marriage-like relationship with Blumenthal.

Additionally, . . . Brewer does not allege that she contributed substantially all of the funds for the purchase of GSN. In fact, Brewer's counterclaim does not provide a specific amount of funds she contributed to Blumenthal's ownership interest in GSN, nor does Brewer allege that she and Blumenthal somehow attempted to keep their contributions separate. Rather, the purchase came after many years of the former domestic partners living together, raising a family, and depositing funds in their joint account as well as making certain family purchases out of the joint account. It is undeniable that the purchase of Blumenthal's ownership interest in GSN was dependent on the parties' relationship, because the purchase was made for the family's financial security. . . .

While we acknowledge that restitution may be a remedy available to a party who has cohabited with another . . . that is not the circumstance concerning Brewer's restitution claim. . . . The joint account used by Blumenthal and Brewer to purchase an ownership interest in GSN was dependent on their desire to live in a marriage-like relationship and make purchases out of this account to better their family situation. Therefore, the purchase of Blumenthal's ownership interest in GSN from the joint account is intimately related to the parties' relationship. Our decision in *Hewitt* bars such relief if the claim is not independent from the parties' living in a marriage-like relationship for the reason it contravenes the public policy, implicit in the statutory scheme of the Marriage and Dissolution Act, disfavoring the grant of mutually enforceable property rights to knowingly unmarried cohabitants. . . .

Central to Brewer's argument are various post-*Hewitt* legislative enactments in Illinois, which she claims indicate that the state's public policy has shifted dramatically in regards to unmarried couples and their children. . . . We disagree.

Since this court's decision in *Hewitt*, the General Assembly has enacted, repealed, and amended numerous family-related statutes. In 1984, the legislature adopted a no-fault ground of divorce based on irreconcilable differences to the Illinois Marriage and Dissolution of Marriage Act. Then in 1985, the Illinois Parentage Act of 1984 provided that "[t]he parent and child relationship, including support obligations, extends equally to every child and to every parent, regardless of the marital status of the parents." Additionally, since *Hewitt*, there has been an amendment to the Probate Act of 1975 extending intestate inheritance rights to children of unmarried parents and a similar amendment to the Illinois Pension Code, which indicates that children born to unmarried parents are entitled to the same survivor's benefits as other children. Further, Illinois also recognizes the rights of unmarried couples (and individuals) to adopt children. . . .

These post-*Hewitt* amendments demonstrate that the legislature knows how to alter family-related statutes and does not hesitate to do so when and if it believes public policy so requires. Nothing in these post-*Hewitt* changes, however, can be interpreted as evincing an intention by the legislature to change the public policy concerning the situation presently before this court. To the contrary, the claim that our legislature is moving toward granting additional property rights to unmarried cohabitants in derogation of the prohibition against common-law marriage is flatly contradicted by the undeniable fact that for almost four decades since *Hewitt*, and despite all of these numerous changes to other family-related statutes, the statutory prohibition against common-law marriage set forth in section 214 of the Marriage and Dissolution Act has remained completely untouched and unqualified. That is so even though this court in *Hewitt* explicitly deferred any policy change to the legislature.

It is well-understood that when the legislature chooses not to amend a statute to reverse a judicial construction, it is presumed that the legislature has acquiesced in the court's statement of the legislative intent. Based on this principle, we can presume that the legislature has acquiesced in *Hewitt*'s judicial interpretation of the statute prohibiting marriage-like rights to those outside of marriage. If this court were to recognize the legal status desired by Brewer, we would infringe on the duty of the legislature to set policy in the area of domestic relations. As mentioned in *Hewitt*, the legislative branch is far better suited to declare public policy in the domestic relations field due to its superior investigative and fact-finding facilities, as declaring public policy requires evaluation of sociological data and alternatives. . . .

Brewer's argument that we should recognize new public policy justifications to support her counterclaim is further undermined by the fact that all of the public policy changes to which she cites resulted not from judicial action but from the legislature. . . .

We also reject Brewer's argument that changes in law since *Hewitt* demonstrate that the "legislature no longer considers withholding protection from nonmarital families to be a legitimate means of advancing the state's interest in marriage." To the contrary, this court finds that the current legislative and judicial trend is to uphold the institution of marriage. Most notably, within the past year, the United States Supreme Court in *Obergefell v. Hodges*, held that same-sex couples cannot be denied the right to marry. . . .

While the United States Supreme Court has made clear that "[t]he Constitution . . . does not permit the State to bar same-sex couples from marriage on the same terms as accorded to couples of the opposite sex", nothing in that holding can fairly be construed as requiring states to confer on non-married, same-sex couples common-law rights or remedies not shared by similarly situated non-married couples of the opposite sex. Legislatures may, of course, decide that matters of public policy do warrant special consideration for non-married, same-sex couples under certain circumstances, notwithstanding the fact that the institution of marriage is available to all couples equally. What is important for the purposes of this discussion is that the balancing of the relevant public policy considerations is for the legislature, not the courts. Indeed, now that the centrality of the marriage has been recognized as a fundamental right for all, it is perhaps more imperative than before that we leave it to the legislative branch to determine whether and under what circumstances a change in the public policy governing the rights of parties in nonmarital relationships is necessary. . . .

Brewer claims that *Hewitt's* rule preventing unmarried domestic partners the ability to bring common-law claims available to all other persons, solely because they are in a marriage-like relationship, does not rationally advance a legitimate governmental purpose and that it deliberately seeks to penalize unmarried partners for exercising their constitutionally protected right to enter into an intimate relationship.... [Yet] *Hewitt's* holding does not prevent or penalize unmarried partners from entering into intimate relationships. Rather, it acknowledges the legislative intent to provide certain rights and benefits to those who participate in the institution of marriage....

Since marriage is a legal relationship that all individuals may or may not enter into, Illinois does not act irrationally or discriminatorily in refusing to grant benefits and protections under the Marriage and Dissolution Act to those who do not participate in the institution of marriage. As noted in *Hewitt* and the line of cases that follow its holding, unmarried individuals may make express or implied contracts with one another, and such contracts will be enforceable if they are not based on a relationship indistinguishable from marriage. Indeed, *Hewitt* did nothing more than effectuate the policy established by the legislature to prevent knowingly unmarried cohabitants from evading the statutory abolition of common-law marriage under section 214 of the Marriage and Dissolution Act by employing theories of implied contract to achieve the same result that would occur if common-law marriage were recognized....

NOTES AND QUESTIONS

1. *Claims of Same-Sex Couples.* The facts in *Blumenthal* are stark. The couple lived together for 26 years and raised three children. They intertwined their lives and finances as many married couples do. As a same-sex couple, though, they were not permitted to marry during their relationship. Much of their property was held in common, but the valuable medical practice was titled solely to Blumenthal, the doctor, even though joint funds enabled its purchase. Yet, the court denied Brewer's claim because it arose out of their familial relationship. During the course of their relationship, what could Brewer have done differently to increase the likelihood she would be granted an interest in the medical practice?

2. *Reviving Common-Law Marriage.* The *Blumenthal* court expressed concern that granting property rights to unmarried cohabitants would recreate common law marriage, which Illinois law prohibits. Does that seem like a justifiable concern? How did the *Marvin* court address that concern?

3. *The State Interest in Marriage.* The *Hewitt* court framed the issue of economic rights of unmarried partners as a major public policy question implicating the state's interest in marriage. The *Blumenthal* court cited *Obergefell v. Hodges*, the Supreme Court decision opening marriage to same-sex couples, to support its statement that

the "current legislative and judicial trend is to uphold the institution of marriage." How is the recognition of economic rights of non-marital partners in tension with the state policy regarding marriage? It is easy to see the governmental interests served by providing marriage to people who want it, but what state interests, if any, are served by denying economic rights to people who don't marry?

4. *Law and Policy on Non-Marital Families.* Even though the *Blumenthal* court referred to the interest in upholding marriage, the state's approach to nonmarital families had changed dramatically since the time the court decided *Hewitt*. After the criticism of its reasoning by the state supreme court, the state appeals court used another case as an opportunity to defend the approach it took in *Blumenthal*:

> [W]e did not believe *Hewitt* was controlling on the question of whether same-sex domestic partners could bring common law claims regarding property they accumulated together. Throughout the entirety of their relationship, Blumenthal and Brewer had been precluded from marrying in Illinois. We focused on public policy and observed an unmistakable and overwhelming trend of recognizing the legitimacy of same-sex domestic partnerships. . . . [I]n the 35 years since *Hewitt*, the Illinois legislature repealed the criminal prohibition on nonmarital cohabitation, prohibited differential treatment of marital and nonmarital children, adopted no-fault divorce in place of the undignified system which had required the court to assign blame or fault to a specific spouse, established civil unions for both opposite-sex and same-sex partners which provided for them to receive all the rights and burdens available to married persons, and extended other protections to nonmarital families [including the right of children to support, inheritance, and survivor benefits irrespective of whether their parents were married]. Thus, there were significant indications after *Hewitt*'s publication that Illinois' legislators no longer disfavored unmarried cohabitation or same-sex relationships in general. . . . In contrast to the parties in *Hewitt*, Blumenthal and Brewer did not have the right to marry in Illinois and our recognition of property claims between them in 2014 was consistent with the public policy and legislative changes acknowledging same-sex rights that we detailed in our opinion. The couples' relationship ended in 2008, which was before Illinois established civil unions as of June 1, 2011 and legally recognized same-sex marriage in a law that took effect on June 1, 2014. We rejected the contention that Brewer was attempting to retroactively define the parties' relationship as a marriage or create a common law marriage in violation of this jurisdiction's express ban on such relationships. We addressed only whether a woman who had been prohibited from marrying her domestic partner should also be prohibited from bringing common law property claims against that person.[375]

---

375. In re Marriage of Allen, 62 N.E.3d 312, 316–17 (Ill. App. Ct. 2016).

5. *Unmarried Partners and the Constitution.* Brewer filed a petition for rehearing in *Blumenthal*, which asked the court to consider her constitutional claims as well. Is it unconstitutional to disallow claims between cohabitants because they were unmarried when the law in effect prohibited them from marrying? Is it unconstitutional to deny a claim based on a sexually intimate and familial relationship that would be permitted if they were simply roommates, friends, or siblings?[376]

6. *Consideration.* A party to an intimate relationship seeking enforcement of a contract claim needs to show valid consideration. Consider Williams v. Ormsby, in which a woman filed suit against her former boyfriend to enforce a written agreement that purportedly made them equal partners in the house where they lived and provided for property disposition if the relationship ended.[377] The woman initially owned the house. In advance of their planned marriage, she transferred the house to her boyfriend after she encountered financial difficulties (perhaps to avoid creditors); he paid the property taxes and eventually paid off the mortgage. After a serious disagreement that fractured their relationship, she moved out of the house; they then drafted but did not sign a document agreeing to sell the house and share the proceeds. Later, as a condition of her moving back into the house and resuming their relationship, they signed the agreement designating them equal partners in the house. The Ohio Supreme Court declined to enforce that agreement, holding that it amounted to a gratuitous promise by the boyfriend to give the girlfriend an interest in the property in exchange for her love and affection, which could not be valid consideration. Thus, the girlfriend's claim failed. How should a court think about consideration with respect to transfers of property in the context of an intimate relationship?

After *Williams*, the Ohio Court of Appeals in Maddali v. Haverkamp permitted a claim on the following facts:

> After dating for some time, Maddali and Haverkamp decided to move in together. They lived with Haverkamp's parents for awhile, and then decided that they wanted to buy a home. . . . After deciding on a potential home, Maddali and Haverkamp agreed that the home would be purchased solely in Haverkamp's name. The two also agreed to divide the household expenses, and that Maddali would be responsible for paying the monthly mortgage payment, which included insurance and real-estate taxes. Haverkamp would be responsible for paying other monthly expenses related to maintaining the household. Maddali and Haverkamp agreed that if the home sold in the future, they would split any profits.
>
> Haverkamp secured the mortgage for the property and bought the home. Maddali and Haverkamp moved in together, and they abided by their division

---

376. On the constitutional dimensions of nonmarriage, see Courtney G. Joslin, The Gay Rights Canon and the Right to Nonmarriage, 97 B.U. L. Rev. 425 (2017); Kaiponanea T. Matsumura, A Right Not to Marry, 84 Fordham L. Rev. 1509 (2016); and Melissa Murray, Rights and Regulation: Lawrence v. Texas and the Evolution of Sexual Regulation, 116 Colum. L. Rev. 573 (2016).

377. 966 N.E.2d 255 (Ohio 2012).

of the financial responsibilities. In addition to paying the mortgage, Maddali also paid for some renovations to the home. Three years after moving in, the couple broke up and Maddali moved out. Haverkamp performed some additional renovations to the property in preparation to sell it. The home sold, and Haverkamp received . . . [the proceeds of] the sale. Haverkamp did not return any of the money to Maddali.[378]

Williams was precedent for the *Maddali* court. How would you square the court's decision to uphold the claim in *Maddali* with the decision of the Ohio Supreme Court to deny the claim in *Williams*?

C. The Status-Based Approach to the Economic Rights of Non-Marital Partners

Yet a third approach to adjudicating the economic rights of non-marital partners is to dispense with the contractual framework entirely, and instead treat economic obligations as arising by operation of law based on the couple having lived together in an intimate committed relationship. Although endorsed by the American Law Institute, this status-based approach has not been widely adopted. Washington is the leading example of this approach, though a few other states have invoked similar reasoning.[379] (The Washington Supreme Court in the following case refers to the "meretricious relationship" doctrine, but that term has a pejorative connotation. More recent Washington decisions refer instead to the "committed intimate relationship" doctrine.[380])

IN RE MARRIAGE OF PENNINGTON
14 P.3d 764 (Wash. 2000)

JOHNSON, J.

In these consolidated cases, we must determine whether the legal requirements to establish a meretricious relationship were satisfied so as to allow for equitable relief. . . .

FACTS

Pennington v. Pennington

Respondent Clark Pennington met petitioner Evelyn Van Pevenage (aka Sammi Pennington) in March 1983. At this time, both Pennington and Van Pevenage were married to other people. Van Pevenage's divorce was finalized in December 1983.

---

378. No. C-180360, 2019 WL 1849302, at *1 (Ohio Ct. App. Apr. 24, 2019).

379. See, e.g., Boulds v. Nielsen, 323 P.3d 58 (Alaska 2014); Shuraleff v. Donnelly, 817 P.2d 764 (Or. Ct. App. 1991).

380. Olver v. Fowler, 168 P.3d 348 (Wash. 2007).

Pennington separated from his wife in October 1983, but remained married until 1990. Pennington and Van Pevenage began dating each other and, in August 1985, moved in together at Pennington's residence in Kapowsin, Washington. The parties also commenced a sexual relationship.

The Kapowsin residence was an airplane hangar with an unfinished apartment upstairs. Clark Pennington and his wife, Jane Pennington, paid the utilities and mortgage payments. Van Pevenage paid for groceries as well as some home furnishings; her income derived from her work as a bartender and lounge manager at various restaurants. Pennington's income derived from his proprietorship of Exacto, Inc., a corporation manufacturing aircraft and machine parts.

Van Pevenage testified at trial that towards the end of 1986 Pennington proposed marriage to her and gave her an engagement ring. Pennington denied ever proposing marriage and characterized the gift as a "cocktail ring."

In 1987, Pennington purchased a lot in Yelm, Washington.... Pennington made the contract payments from his wages and from rent paid to him by Exacto, Inc. The deed to the property conveyed the land to "Clark M. Pennington, a married man dealing with his separate estate." Pennington's wife, Jane Pennington, quitclaimed her interest in the Yelm property to him in 1988. Pennington then took out a loan solely in his name to pay off the real estate contract and finance construction of a hangar and a new home on the property. Van Pevenage testified she participated in the interior design of the home, although the housing contractor testified he did not take instructions from her. Pennington and Van Pevenage moved into the Yelm home in December 1988. The home loan payments were made from Pennington's Exacto, Inc. wages and from the sale of the Kapowsin residence.

During the course of their relationship, Pennington provided vehicles for Van Pevenage to drive and placed her on his automobile insurance policy. He also named Van Pevenage as the beneficiary of a $50,000 life insurance policy. Van Pevenage acquired credit cards in the name of "Sammi Pennington," and registered Clark and herself in the Yelm telephone book as "Pennington Clark & Sammi." Pennington and Van Pevenage also held joint checking accounts. Pennington denied authorizing Van Pevenage to use his last name for either the telephone book or the credit cards, and testified he had no knowledge she had done so until after the relationship terminated.

Van Pevenage lived with Pennington in the Yelm home continuously until 1991. In April 1991, she moved into an apartment, but returned to the Yelm residence shortly thereafter. Several months later, Pennington suffered a stroke and was hospitalized. Van Pevenage temporarily quit her job to help Pennington around the house, but Pennington returned to work only one week after his release from the hospital. After the stroke, Exacto, Inc. provided Van Pevenage with medical insurance coverage and paid her a salary of approximately $1,000 per month, although Van Pevenage did not have an "active role" in the corporation's business. The salary continued intermittently until 1996. After his stroke, Pennington also gave Van Pevenage signing privileges on the corporate account.

Van Pevenage moved out of the Yelm residence from March 1993 until October 1994. In May 1994, Van Pevenage commenced a sexual relationship with another man, whom she resided with in September of that year. Pennington dated another woman during this time period. Van Pevenage eventually returned to the Yelm residence for one more year, before leaving again in October 1995. Her relationship with Pennington was not sexual during this last year. . . .

Chesterfield v. Nash

Petitioner James Nash and respondent Diana Chesterfield began a casual dating relationship in August 1986. A few months later the relationship became sexually intimate. Chesterfield worked as a salesperson at Nordstrom, and Nash operated a dental practice he had purchased in 1985. Chesterfield was married, although separated, at the time she began dating Nash. Chesterfield filed for divorce in November 1987. The parties dated from 1986 until 1989, although Nash dated other women during this time period. In July 1989, Nash and Chesterfield moved into a home purchased the previous year by Chesterfield.

While living together, Nash and Chesterfield opened a joint checking account to which they both contributed funds. . . . Contributions to the account were initially equal, but over time Nash contributed more than Chesterfield. Nash testified he also paid nearly all expenses for their numerous vacations, and a disproportionate amount of their dining out expenses. . . . Chesterfield also testified she would not invest in a house with Nash until they were married. . . .

Nash and Chesterfield periodically assisted each other professionally. . . . Nash offered to compensate Chesterfield for her help, but she refused.

Nash and Chesterfield ceased living together in October 1993. Chesterfield closed the joint account and made a mortgage payment with the remaining funds. In 1994, Nash and Chesterfield briefly reconciled and began dating again, although they did not resume living together. They discussed marriage and Nash purchased a diamond for Chesterfield, but in November 1995 they permanently ended their relationship. . . .

ANALYSIS

Our Legislature requires a solemnized "civil contract" in order for a marriage to be valid. Common-law marriage is not recognized under Washington law. Wholly unrelated to either kind of marriage, courts have recognized the existence of meretricious relationships, which this court has determined to be stable, cohabiting relationships. For nearly a century, Washington law presumed all property acquired by unmarried cohabitants belonged to the holder of the legal title. . . .

In 1984, this court discarded this presumption. [In re Marriage of Lindsey, 678 P.2d 328 (Wash. 1984)] involved a couple who commenced an intimate relationship in 1974, legally married in 1976, and divorced in 1982. The court declined to presume that property acquired before the legal marriage belonged to the holder of title, instead holding "that courts must 'examine the [meretricious] relationship and the property accumulations and make a just and equitable disposition of the property.'" . . .

This court again considered the issue of meretricious relationships in [Connell v. Francisco, 898 P.2d 831 (Wash. 1995)]. *Connell*, like *Lindsey*, involved an uncontested meretricious relationship. . . . We characterized a meretricious relationship as a "stable, marital-like relationship where both parties cohabit with knowledge that a lawful marriage between them does not exist." . . . Accordingly, we listed five relevant factors to analyze when a meretricious relationship exists: "continuous cohabitation, duration of the relationship, purpose of the relationship, pooling of resources and services for joint projects, and the intent of the parties." . . .

Under *Connell*, we further established a three-prong analysis for disposing of property when a meretricious relationship terminates. First, the trial court must determine whether a meretricious relationship exists. Second, if such a relationship exists, the trial court evaluates the interest each party has in the property acquired during the relationship. Third, the trial court then makes a just and equitable distribution of such property.

While property acquired during the meretricious relationship is presumed to belong to both parties, this presumption may be rebutted. . . . If the presumption of joint ownership is not rebutted, the courts may look for guidance to the dissolution statute, RCW 26.09.080, for the fair and equitable distribution of property acquired during the meretricious relationship.

In the present cases, we must review and decide whether the trial courts erred in concluding the facts gave rise to meretricious relationships at all. . . .

We now apply the *Connell* analytic framework, first . . . to the trial court's findings regarding Pennington and Van Pevenage.

Continuous Cohabitation: The trial court found Pennington and Van Pevenage began living together in August 1985. Pennington was married to another person until 1990. The parties continued to cohabit until March or April 1991, when Van Pevenage moved out for a period of time. She resumed cohabiting with Pennington until March 1993. Between March 1993 and October 1994, the court found both parties dated other people. The uncontested evidence also establishes Van Pevenage lived with another man during her separation from Pennington. Van Pevenage then moved back in with Pennington for a period of one year. We conclude the continuous cohabitation factor as contemplated by *Connell* has not been established. . . . These facts suggest while Pennington and Van Pevenage did cohabit, their cohabitation was sporadic and not continuous enough to evidence a stable cohabiting relationship.

Duration of the Relationship: The trial court found the Pennington/Van Pevenage relationship began in October 1983 when the parties began exclusively dating each other. They began living together in August 1985. The trial court also found the parties separated for a short time in 1991, reconciled, separated again in

1993 through 1994, and reconciled again in October 1994. Thus, their relationship, while not continuous, spanned 12 years. While we agree with the trial court this factor was satisfied, a long-term relationship alone does not require the equitable division of property. . . .

Intent of the Parties: The trial court found Van Pevenage intended to be in a long-term relationship with the expectation of marriage. Naturally, Pennington presented testimony denying his intent to be in a meretricious relationship. Pennington was married to a different woman for the first five years of his relationship with Van Pevenage. More importantly, after his divorce in 1990, Pennington refused to marry Van Pevenage. . . . Pennington's refusal, coupled with Van Pevenage's insistence on marrying, belies the existence of the parties' mutual intent to live in a meretricious relationship. Furthermore, Van Pevenage's intent to live in a stable, long-term, cohabiting relationship is also negated by her own actions, particularly her repeated absences from the Yelm home and her relationship with another man. . . .

Pooling of Resources: The trial court found Van Pevenage spent money for food, household furnishings, carpeting and tile, and some kitchen utensils. The court also found she cooked meals, cleaned house, and helped with interior decoration. . . . Van Pevenage has no evidence to suggest she made constant or continuous payments jointly or substantially invested her time and effort into any specific asset so as to create any inequities. Given the evidence presented at trial, we cannot conclude the parties jointly invested their time, effort, or financial resources in any specific asset to justify the equitable division of the parties' property acquired during the course of their relationship.

Purpose of the Relationship: The trial court found the purpose of the Pennington/Van Pevenage relationship included companionship, friendship, love, sex, and mutual support and caring. Although this was significantly disputed by the testimony offered during the trial, we agree with the trial court's conclusion.

One *Connell* factor is not more important than another. However, when the factors and evidence are taken as a whole, the equitable principles recognized in *Connell* are not satisfied in this case. . . .

We next apply the *Connell* factors to the trial court's findings regarding Chesterfield and Nash. . . .

Continuous Cohabitation: The trial court found Chesterfield and Nash moved in together in July 1989 and ceased living together in October 1993. The parties briefly reconciled in 1994 through 1995, when they made plans to marry. However, the parties never married as intended and terminated their relationship in November 1995. . . . [W]hen taken as a whole, the parties' cohabitation was not continuous from 1989 through 1995, but was marked by separation and failed reconciliation.

Duration of the Relationship: The trial court found Chesterfield and Nash had a relationship lasting four years and three months. Additionally, the parties dated from 1986 until 1989, when they moved in together. However, during the first three years of their relationship, Nash dated other women. Similarly, Chesterfield was married, although separated, at the time she began dating Nash. She did not file for divorce until November 1987. The duration of their relationship could help support a conclusion that a meretricious relationship existed between Chesterfield and Nash.

Intent of the Parties: . . . The trial court found they functioned as one would expect a married couple to function, although the parties did not hold themselves out as spouses. However, the evidence also established Chesterfield was married to another man during her relationship with Nash. These facts are too equivocal to conclusively establish that the parties mutually intended to be in a meretricious relationship.

Pooling of Resources: The trial court found Chesterfield and Nash had a joint checking account for living expenses, into which they both deposited money. During their period of continuous cohabitation, Nash assisted Chesterfield with some work-related travel logs. Chesterfield assisted Nash with his office emergencies, his accounts payable, his role as secretary for his study club, and his office correspondence. . . . However, the parties maintained separate bank accounts. They also purchased no property jointly. Each maintained his or her own career and financial independence, contributing separately to their respective retirement accounts. When these facts are examined as a whole, the trial court's findings do not fully establish the parties jointly pooled their time, effort, or financial resources enough to require an equitable distribution of property, as contemplated by *Connell*.

Purpose of the Relationship: The trial court made no findings as to the purpose of the relationship between Chesterfield and Nash. When the factors and evidence are balanced as a whole, the equitable principles recognized in *Connell* are not satisfied by the trial court's findings. While the parties' continuous cohabitation and duration of their relationship do evidence a meretricious relationship, the evidence supporting the mutual intent of the parties to be in such a relationship is too equivocal to support such a conclusion. Similarly, the parties maintained separate accounts, purchased no significant assets together, and did not significantly or substantially pool their time and effort to justify the equitable division of property acquired during the course of their relationship. Therefore, we conclude the relationship between Chesterfield and Nash did not constitute a meretricious relationship and the equitable principles recognized in *Connell* are not triggered by these facts. . . .

NOTES AND QUESTIONS

1. *The Analytical Steps.* The *Pennington* court highlighted three steps in the analysis of economic claims arising under committed intimate relationships: whether a requisite relationship existed sufficient to give rise to economic claims; the determination of the interest each party has in the property acquired during the relationship;

and the determination of a just and equitable distribution of the community-like property.

2. *The Relevant Test.* The dispute in *Pennington* centers on the threshold question of whether a "meretricious" relationship exists. The court identified five factors to be analyzed to determine whether such a relationship exists. Does the court's test require that each factor be satisfied? Or rather that every factor be included in an "all things considered" sort of way? Is the underlying question whether these relationships are marriage-like enough? Or is there some other unstated principle?

The court determined that neither relationship satisfied the test for committed intimate relationships. Do you think the test the court used is: (i) too stringent, (ii) not stringent enough, or (iii) about right? What ideas about marriage, if any, underlie the approach of the court?

3. *The Role of Intent.* Determination of the parties' intent is one element of the meretricious relationship test. How does intent figure differently in the status-based approach as opposed to the contract-based approach of *Marvin*?

4. *The ALI Alternative.* The status-based approach has been endorsed by the American Law Institute, in its 2002 Principles of the Law of Family Dissolution. The ALI approach has influenced policy debate but has not been widely adopted. Under the ALI proposal, principles similar to equitable distribution are presumed to apply when a couple for the requisite number of years "share[s] a primary residence only with each other and family members; or when, if they share a household with other unrelated persons, they act jointly, rather than as individuals, with respect to management of the household."[381]

If the couple did not maintain the common household for the requisite number of years, the claimant has "the burden of proving that for a significant period of time the parties shared a primary residence and a life together as a couple." The provisions provide a long list of factors to be considered in determining whether that standard is met:

(a) the oral or written statements or promises made to one another, or representations jointly made to third parties, regarding their relationship;
(b) the extent to which the parties intermingled their finances;
(c) the extent to which their relationship fostered the parties' economic interdependence, or the economic dependence of one party upon the other;
(d) the extent to which the parties engaged in conduct and assumed specialized or collaborative roles in furtherance of their life together;
(e) the extent to which the relationship wrought change in the life of either or both parties;

---

381. Michael R. Clisham & Robin Fretwell Wilson, American Law Institute's Principles of the Law of Family Dissolution, Eight Years After Adoption: Guiding Principles or Obligatory Footnote?, 42 Fam. L.Q. 573 (2008); Principles of the Law of Family Dissolution, supra note 26.

(f) the extent to which the parties acknowledged responsibilities to each other, as by naming the other the beneficiary of life insurance or of a testamentary instrument, or as eligible to receive benefits under an employee benefit plan;

(g) the extent to which the parties' relationship was treated by the parties as qualitatively distinct from the relationship either party had with any other person;

(h) the emotional or physical intimacy of the parties' relationship;

(i) the parties' community reputation as a couple;

(j) the parties' participation in a commitment ceremony or registration as a domestic partnership;

(k) the parties' participation in a void or voidable marriage that, under applicable law, does not give rise to the economic incidents of marriage;

(l) the parties' procreation of, adoption of, or joint assumption of parental functions toward a child.

Does the ALI approach seem better or worse than the Washington approach? Would it be better for the determination to operate through a (i) presumption, (ii) an "all things considered" balancing test, or (iii) a mix of the two as with the ALI proposal? If a presumption is appropriate, which way should it operate? Should the law presume that unmarried couples who decide to live together and not marry have decided to share assets? Or should the law presume no sharing, and thus require unmarried couples to opt in to a sharing regime?

5. *A Uniform Act?* In 2018, the Uniform Law Commission appointed a committee to draft a Uniform Law on the Economic Rights of Unmarried Cohabitants. At the time of this writing in mid-2020, the draft allows contractual claims and equitable remedies as between cohabitants in committed relationships.[382] "Cohabitant" is defined as "one of two individuals who live together as a couple in an intimate, committed relationship and function as an economic, social, and domestic unit."[383]

6. *Compared to* Marvin. Does the status-based approach seem more or less hospitable to economic claims by unmarried cohabitants, compared to *Marvin*'s contractual approach? In other words, if you thought you might want to bring a claim for property distribution against an intimate partner with whom you have cohabitated without being married, in which jurisdiction would you prefer to file—a contract-based jurisdiction like California or a status-based jurisdiction like Washington?

7. *Identifying the Relevant Property.* While the Washington courts apply an approach comparable to equitable distribution in the case of committed intimate relationships, there is one important distinction: At the dissolution of a marriage, under state law, the court's "just and equitable" distribution encompasses both community

---

382. See Economic Rights of Unmarried Cohabitants Act (draft) (Unif. Law Comm'n Apr. 7, 2020). The draft does not include a status-based remedy but does offer an equitable claim under which a court can award a "fair and equitable division" of the accumulated property and liabilities. Id. § 111.

383. Id. § 102(1).

property and separate property. With the dissolution of a committed intimate relationship, in contrast, the court is only to consider the property that would be community property if the couple had been married, which the courts refer to as "community-like property." The Washington Supreme Court articulated this principle in Connell v. Francisco, the case repeatedly cited in *Pennington*:

> A meretricious relationship is not the same as a marriage. As such, the laws involving the distribution of marital property do not directly apply to the division of property following a meretricious relationship. . . .
>
> Until the Legislature, as a matter of public policy, concludes meretricious relationships are the legal equivalent to marriages, we limit the distribution of property following a meretricious relationship to property that would have been characterized as community property had the parties been married. . . . Any other interpretation equates cohabitation with marriage; ignores the conscious decision by many couples not to marry; confers benefits when few, if any, economic risks or legal obligations are assumed; and disregards the explicit intent of the Legislature. . . .[384]

What is the justification for defining the property subject to distribution more narrowly in the committed intimate relationship context than in the divorce context? How significant is that limitation? A dissenting opinion in *Conell* expressed concern: "In many cases, it will be impossible to carry out the requirement . . . that there be 'a just and equitable distribution of the property' while limiting distribution to only that property that would be characterized as community property had the parties been married."[385] How does that observation relate to questions of property distribution addressed earlier in this chapter?

PROBLEM

Kenneth and Patricia began dating in relationship in 1983 and began living together in Kenneth's house in 1992. Kenneth did not charge Patricia rent. They broke up in 2001. Kenneth owned a car dealership in Spokane, Washington. In 1986, Patricia left her job at a bank to work at Kenneth's car dealership and was paid $18,000 a year. Kenneth took a salary of only $42,000 a year, but he was compensated in other ways and possessed equity in the business. Kenneth gave Patricia $400 a month for household expenses. In 1996, Kenneth bought a vacation home, which Patricia decorated. At both homes that Kenneth owned, Patricia did the housework and cooked the meals.

---

384. Connell v. Francisco, 898 P.2d 831, 835–36 (Wash. 1995).
385. Id. at 838 (Utter, J., dissenting).

During their relationship, Kenneth bought additional car dealerships. His net worth increased from $1.5 million at the time Patricia moved into the house to $4.5 million when they broke up. Patricia owns no property and does not have significant savings or assets.

Patricia sues for an equitable distribution. Should she prevail? If so, what property is subject to distribution and how much of it should she be awarded?

POSTSCRIPT

This problem is based on Soltero v. Wimer, a 2007 Washington Supreme Court case.[386] There was no debate about whether the parties had a committed intimate relationship. Instead, the dispute revolved around property. The trial court had determined that all of the properties and businesses, as well as all the rents, income, and profits, were separate property and thus not subject to distribution.[387] Yet, the trial court also held: "The value of [Patricia's] other services provided as a cohabitating, committed, long-term companion, including the obligations of running the household and business/social matters, net (meaning after consideration for board and room), is: $15,000 a year x nine years or $135,000.00."[388] The Washington Supreme Court reversed, reasoning that "the trial court erred by treating the 'domestic services' provided by [Patricia] as community-like property."[389] Because the trial court "specifically concluded that the increase in [Kenneth's] estate was due to his separate, not community efforts," there were "no community-like assets to distribute."[390] The award to Patricia of $135,000 "could only come from [Kenneth's] separate assets, which are not reachable in a meretricious relationship dissolution."[391] Accordingly, Patricia's domestic services could not provide a basis for an equitable distribution. Do you agree with this result? Why would the assets accumulated during the relationship not be community-like property subject to distribution? Why was it inappropriate for the trial court to consider Patricia's contributions? Should her contributions to the businesses be treated differently than her contributions to the homes?

---

386. 150 P.3d 552 (Wash. 2007).
387. Id. at 554.
388. Id.
389. Id. at 555.
390. Id. at 555–56.
391. Id. at 556.

CHAPTER 6

Parents, Children, and the State

The preceding chapters addressed adult relationships—marital and non-marital, different-sex and same-sex, intact and dissolving. The next several chapters address parent-child relationships—biological and nonbiological, in marital and non-marital families, of different-sex and same-sex couples, in single-parent and multi-parent families, formed through sexual procreation, assisted reproduction, and adoption. In this chapter, we consider the authority that legal parents wield against state intervention, children's authority to make their own decisions, and conflicts among parents, children, and the state.

I. Parental Rights and Responsibilities

Legal parents possess constitutionally protected rights to direct the upbringing of their children. This authority extends to decisions regarding education, religion, medical care, and relationships with third parties. As we will see below, the foundational cases recognizing this constitutional interest date from the 1920s. While parenthood did not emerge as a matter of constitutional concern until the twentieth century, the common law protected parenthood. But this protection reflected understandings of the family that the law has since repudiated. First, only parents who had children within marriage enjoyed protected rights to the parent-child relationship. Non-marital parents did not have legally protected relationships with their children, even though mothers were routinely expected to exercise custodial responsibility over such children. Second, inside marriage, the law enforced gender hierarchy that subordinated women and children to men. Third, the law reflected a natural-law and property-based understanding of children. Fathers had superior custody rights to mothers, and fathers had a recognized economic interest in their children.[1] As we will see, much has changed. The legal understanding of parental authority has become less gendered and less tethered to marriage, and the law has largely rejected a property-based understanding of parent-child relations.[2]

Nonetheless, when the Supreme Court first approached parental rights as a constitutional matter, it did so in the context of a legal regime that privileged marital over non-marital parents and fathers over mothers. And it acted on a property-based understanding of parenthood. As Professor Barbara Woodhouse, a scholar of children and the law, explains — in the view of Justice McReynolds, who authored the Court's first two opinions vindicating parental rights — "parental control of the child, like private ownership of property, was not a feature of social organization that might be tampered with in the name of reform."[3] Of course, even at the time, these views were contested. Across a range of cases, Justice Holmes resisted the natural-law account that animated some of his colleagues.[4] Specifically with respect to parental rights, progressive reformers organized around a more community-based account of children.

A. Care, Custody, and Control

The Constitution does not explicitly identify parental rights. Not until the early twentieth century did parenthood fully enter the constitutional lexicon. In 1923, the Supreme Court deemed parental rights protected as part of the liberty protected by the Fourteenth Amendment's Due Process Clause. In Meyer v. Nebraska, the Court struck down a Nebraska law prohibiting foreign-language instruction in schools.[5] While the case primarily presented the claim of a teacher asserting his right to teach German, the Court viewed his "right to teach" as related to "the right of parents to engage him so to instruct their children" — both protected "within the liberty of the [Fourteenth] Amendment."[6] The Court emphasized a "right of control" and a corresponding "natural duty of the parent to give his children education suitable to their station in life."[7] The state's interest in trying to "foster a homogeneous people with American ideals" was not compelling enough to override the parent's rights.[8] Two years later, the Court affirmed the constitutional status of parental rights in the following case.

---

1. On the history of parental rights, see Mary Ann Mason, From Father's Property to Children's Rights: The History of Child Custody in the United States (1994); Michael Grossberg, Governing the Hearth: Law and the Family in Nineteenth_Century America (1985).

2. For discussion of this change in the context of child custody law, see Chapter 10.

3. Barbara Bennett Woodhouse, "Who Owns the Child?": Meyer and Pierce and the Child as Property, 33 Wm. & Mary L. Rev. 995, 1091 (1992).

4. See, e.g., Oliver Wendell Holmes, Natural Law, 32 Harv. L. Rev. 40, 41 (1918).

5. 262 U.S. 390 (1923).

6. Id. at 400.

7. Id.

8. Id. at 402.

PIERCE V. SOCIETY OF SISTERS
268 U.S. 510 (1925)

MR. JUSTICE MCREYNOLDS delivered the opinion of the Court. . . .

[T]he Compulsory Education Act . . . requires every parent, guardian or other person having control or charge or custody of a child between eight and sixteen years to send him "to a public school for the period of time a public school shall be held during the current year" in the district where the child resides; and failure so to do is declared a misdemeanor. . . .

Appellee, the Society of Sisters, is an Oregon corporation. . . . In its primary schools many children between those ages are taught the subjects usually pursued in Oregon public schools during the first eight years. Systematic religious instruction and moral training according to the tenets of the Roman Catholic Church are also regularly provided. . . .

[T]he bill alleges that the enactment conflicts with the right of parents to choose schools where their children will receive appropriate mental and religious training, the right of the child to influence the parents' choice of a school, the right of schools and teachers therein to engage in a useful business or profession, and is accordingly repugnant to the Constitution and void. And, further, that unless enforcement of the measure is enjoined the corporation's business and property will suffer irreparable injury. . . .

No question is raised concerning the power of the State reasonably to regulate all schools, to inspect, supervise and examine them, their teachers and pupils; to require that all children of proper age attend some school, that teachers shall be of good moral character and patriotic disposition, that certain studies plainly essential to good citizenship must be taught, and that nothing be taught which is manifestly inimical to the public welfare.

The inevitable practical result of enforcing the Act under consideration would be destruction of . . . private primary schools for normal children within the State of Oregon. These parties are engaged in a kind of undertaking not inherently harmful, but long regarded as useful and meritorious. Certainly there is nothing in the present records to indicate that they have failed to discharge their obligations to patrons, students or the State. And there are no peculiar circumstances or present emergencies which demand extraordinary measures relative to primary education.

Under the doctrine of Meyer v. Nebraska, 262 U.S. 390 (1923), we think it entirely plain that the Act of 1922 unreasonably interferes with the liberty of parents and guardians to direct the upbringing and education of children under their control. As often heretofore pointed out, rights guaranteed by the Constitution may not be abridged by legislation which has no reasonable relation to some purpose within the competency of the State. The fundamental theory of liberty upon which all governments in this Union repose excludes any general power of the State to standardize its children by forcing them to accept instruction from public teachers only. The child is not the mere creature of the State; those who nurture him and direct his destiny have the right, coupled with the high duty, to recognize and prepare him for additional obligations. . . .

By the late 1930s, the Court repudiated the constitutional logic that animated the period in which *Meyer* and *Pierce* were decided — the *Lochner* era. The Court rejected key precedents that understood the Due Process Clause to protect economic rights relating to contract and property. Instead, the Court would subject ordinary economic and social legislation to less rigorous constitutional review. Yet, the Court's decisions on parental rights survived. In its 1944 decision in Prince v. Massachusetts, excerpted below, the Court reaffirmed the constitutional status of parental rights by citing *Meyer* and *Pierce*.

Prince v. Commonwealth of Massachusetts
321 U.S. 158 (1944)

Mr. Justice Rutledge delivered the opinion of the Court.

The case brings for review another episode in the conflict between Jehovah's Witnesses and state authority. This time Sarah Prince appeals from convictions for violating Massachusetts' child labor laws, by acts said to be a rightful exercise of her religious convictions. . . .

Mrs. Prince, living in Brockton, is the mother of two young sons. She also has legal custody of Betty Simmons, who lives with them. The children too are Jehovah's Witnesses and both Mrs. Prince and Betty testified they were ordained ministers. The former was accustomed to go each week on the streets of Brockton to distribute "Watchtower" and "Consolation," according to the usual plan. She had permitted the children to engage in this activity previously, and had been warned against doing so by the school attendance officer, Mr. Perkins. But, until December 18, 1941, she generally did not take them with her at night.

That evening, as Mrs. Prince was preparing to leave her home, the children asked to go. She at first refused. Childlike, they resorted to tears and, mother-like, she yielded. Arriving downtown, Mrs. Prince permitted the children "to engage in the preaching work with her upon the sidewalks." That is, with specific reference to Betty, she and Mrs. Prince took positions about twenty feet apart near a street intersection. Betty held up in her hand, for passersby to see, copies of "Watch Tower" and "Consolation." From her shoulder hung the usual canvas magazine bag, on which was printed "Watchtower and Consolation 5¢ per copy." No one accepted a copy from Betty that evening and she received no money. Nor did her aunt. But on other occasions, Betty had received funds and given out copies.

Mrs. Prince and Betty remained until 8:45 p.m. A few minutes before this Mr. Perkins approached Mrs. Prince. A discussion ensued. He inquired and she refused to give Betty's name. However, she stated the child attended the Shaw School. Mr. Perkins referred to his previous warnings and said he would allow five minutes for them to get off the street. Mrs. Prince admitted she supplied Betty with the magazines and said, "[N]either you nor anybody else can stop me. . . . This child is exercising her God-given right and her constitutional right to preach the gospel, and no creature has a right to interfere with God's commands." However, Mrs. Prince and Betty departed. She remarked as she went, "I'm not going through this anymore. We've been through it time and time again. I'm going home and put the little girl to bed." It may be added that testimony, by Betty, her aunt and others, was offered at the trials, and was excluded, to show that Betty believed it was her religious duty to perform this work and failure would bring condemnation "to everlasting destruction at Armageddon." . . .

Appellant . . . rests squarely on freedom of religion under the First Amendment, applied by the Fourteenth to the states. She buttresses this foundation, however, with a claim of parental right as secured by the due process clause of the latter Amendment. These guaranties, she thinks, guard alike herself and the child in what they have done. Thus, two claimed liberties are at stake. One is the parent's, to bring up the child in the way he should go, which for appellant means to teach him the tenets and the practices of their faith. The other freedom is the child's, to observe these; and among them is "to preach the gospel . . . by public distribution" of "Watchtower" and "Consolation," in conformity with the scripture: "A little shall lead them." . . .

To make accommodation between these freedoms and an exercise of state authority always is delicate. It hardly could be more so than in such a clash as this case presents. On one side is the obviously earnest claim for freedom of conscience and religious practice. With it is allied the parent's claim to authority in her own household and in the rearing of her children. The parent's conflict with the state over control of the child and his training is serious enough when only secular matters are concerned. It becomes the more so when an element of religious conviction enters. Against these sacred private interests, basic in a democracy, stand the interests of society to protect the welfare of children, and the state's assertion of authority to that end, made here in a manner conceded valid if only secular things were involved. The last is no mere corporate concern of official authority. It is the interest of youth itself, and of the whole community, that children be both safeguarded from abuses and given opportunities for growth into free and independent well-developed men and citizens. Between contrary pulls of such weight, the safest and most objective recourse is to the lines already marked out, not precisely but for guides, in narrowing the no man's land where this battle has gone on. . . .

It is cardinal with us that the custody, care and nurture of the child reside first in the parents, whose primary function and freedom include preparation for obligations the state can neither supply nor hinder. And it is in recognition of this that [our prior] decisions have respected the private realm of family life which the state cannot enter.

But the family itself is not beyond regulation in the public interest, as against a claim of religious liberty. And neither rights of religion nor rights of parenthood are beyond limitation. Acting to guard the general interest in youth's well-being, the state as *parens patriae* may restrict the parent's control by requiring school attendance, regulating or prohibiting the child's labor, and in many other ways. Its authority is not nullified merely because the parent grounds his claim to control the child's course of conduct on religion or conscience. Thus, he cannot claim freedom from compulsory vaccination for the child more than for himself on religious grounds. The right to practice religion freely does not include liberty to expose the community or the child to communicable disease or the latter to ill health or death. The catalogue need not be lengthened. It is sufficient to show what indeed appellant hardly disputes, that the state has a wide range of power for limiting parental freedom and authority in things affecting the child's welfare; and that this includes, to some extent, matters of conscience and religious conviction. . . .

The state's authority over children's activities is broader than over like actions of adults. This is peculiarly true of public activities and in matters of employment. A democratic society rests, for its continuance, upon the healthy, well-rounded growth of young people into full maturity as citizens, with all that implies. It may secure this against impeding restraints and dangers, within a broad range of selection. Among evils most appropriate for such action are the crippling effects of child employment, more especially in public places, and the possible harms arising from other activities subject to all the diverse influences of the street. It is too late now to doubt that legislation appropriately designed to reach such evils is within the state's police power, whether against the parents claim to control of the child or one that religious scruples dictate contrary action.

It is true children have rights, in common with older people, in the primary use of highways. But even in such use streets afford dangers for them not affecting adults. And in other uses, whether in work or in other things, this difference may be magnified. This is so not only when children are unaccompanied but certainly to some extent when they are with their parents. What may be wholly permissible for adults therefore may not be so for children, either with or without their parents' presence. . . .

The zealous though lawful exercise of the right to engage in propagandizing the community, whether in religious, political or other matters, may and at times does create situations difficult enough for adults to cope with and wholly inappropriate for children, especially of tender years, to face. Other harmful possibilities could be stated, of emotional excitement and psychological or physical injury. Parents may be free to become martyrs themselves. But it does not follow they are free, in identical circumstances, to make martyrs of their children before they have reached the age of full and legal discretion when they can make that choice for themselves. Massachusetts has determined that an absolute prohibition, though one limited to streets and public places and to the incidental uses proscribed, is necessary to accomplish its legitimate objectives. Its power to attain them is broad enough to reach these peripheral instances in which the parent's supervision may reduce but cannot eliminate entirely the ill effects of the prohibited conduct. We think that with reference to the public proclaiming of religion, upon the streets and in other similar public places, the power of the state to control the conduct of children reaches beyond the scope of its authority over adults, as is true in the case of other freedoms, and the rightful boundary of its power has not been crossed in this case. . . .

Our ruling does not extend beyond the facts the case presents. . . . The religious training and indoctrination of children may be accomplished in many ways, some of which, as we have noted, have received constitutional protection through decisions of this Court. These and all others except the public proclaiming of religion on the streets, if this may be taken as either training or indoctrination of the proclaimer, remain unaffected by the decision. . . .

NOTES AND QUESTIONS

1. *Parens Patriae.* In *Prince*, the state interest in the welfare of the child justified the restriction on the guardian's decision with respect to the child. The state exerts *parens patriae* authority, acting as "parent of the nation," in a way that allows it to intervene to protect children. The Supreme Court has described this doctrine as "inherent in the supreme power of every state, . . . a most beneficent function, and often necessary to be exercised in the interests of humanity, and for the prevention of injury to those who cannot protect themselves."[9] From what exactly was the government protecting the child in *Prince*? Does the government's interest justify the intervention that the Court allowed?

2. *Parental Rights and Free Exercise of Religion.* Cases on parental rights often implicate religious liberty as well. In *Prince*, free exercise claims were more central than parental rights claims. Indeed, the case is one of many in which Jehovah's Witnesses challenged government action that restricted their religious practice. *Pierce* also raised free exercise concerns, as the challenged law restricted Catholic schools from operating and prevented parents from sending their children to such schools. Indeed, anti-Catholic sentiment was a significant feature in the conflict over the Oregon law.[10] How, if at all, do the religious discrimination dimensions of *Pierce* and *Prince* affect the strength of the parental rights claims in each case? Are parental rights claims more

---

9. Late Corp. of the Church of Jesus Christ of Latter-Day Saints v. U.S., 136 U.S. 1, 57 (1890). On the doctrine generally, see Developments in the Law — The Constitution and the Family, 93 Harv. L. Rev. 1156, 1221 (1980); George B. Curtis, The Checkered Career of Parens Patriae: The State as Parent or Tyrant?, 25 DePaul L. Rev. 895, 896-98 (1976).

10. See Woodhouse, supra note 3, at 1017-21.

compelling when asserted by religious minorities against laws that reflect the majority's religious views and practices?

––––––––––––––

As *Meyer*, *Pierce*, and *Prince* show, parents have strong, but not unlimited, rights to the "care, custody, and control" of children. The state has a competing power in its role as super-parent. Children also sometimes have rights that are in tension with either the rights of their parents or the power of the state, or both. But among the three, parents have the greatest say in childrearing. Why? What do we assume about parental conduct or motivations that leads to this allocation of power?

In the following article, Professor Elizabeth Scott, the Chief Reporter on the American Law Institute's Restatement of Children and the Law, and Professor Clare Huntington, also a Reporter on the Restatement, present what they term a "child wellbeing" framework as a descriptive and normative account of the legal regulation of children. In the excerpt below, they draw on case law and scholarship to explain how "child wellbeing" relates to and justifies a strong parental rights doctrine.

Clare Huntington & Elizabeth S. Scott, *Conceptualizing Legal Childhood in the Twenty-First Century*
118 Mich. L. Rev. 1371 (2020)

[P]arental rights usually promote child wellbeing and expanding state authority does not. First, deference to parental authority protects the stability of the parent-child relationship. To be sure, some indeterminacy exists about how to define and promote child wellbeing, given the complexity of children's lives and empirical uncertainty about the impact of different childrearing approaches. But there is no controversy about the importance of the child's relationship with her parent. Based on a large body of research, it is clear that a strong, stable parent-child relationship is critical for healthy child development, and the disruption and destabilization of this relationship threatens serious harm to the child. A regime of robust parental rights is likely the best means of satisfying this fundamental need of children because it restricts state intervention in the family and thus reduces the child's exposure to the accompanying risks, particularly removal of the child from the home. Protection from state intervention is especially important for children of color and low-income families in light of racial disproportionality and disparities in the child welfare system. Parental rights provide an essential shield against excessive state intrusion driven by bias.

Second, deference to parental decisionmaking also promotes child wellbeing because parents are generally better positioned than state actors, such as judges, social workers, or other third parties, to understand their child's needs and make decisions that will further that child's interests. This advantage is rooted in the parent's superior knowledge of and association with the child as compared with outsiders to the family. Moreover, the legal system is not well equipped to determine what will promote the wellbeing of a particular child. Deference is further justified by the well-founded assumption that parents are intrinsically motivated to care for their children due to powerful affective bonds. . . .

In addition to promoting child wellbeing, robust protection of parental rights also advances society's interests. In a country in which family-state relations are governed by libertarian principles, parents are burdened with the weighty responsibility of raising the next generation of citizens. Having placed this burden on parents, with only limited support from the state, society has an interest in ensuring that parents discharge their obligations adequately. Strong protection of parental rights shows respect for and deference to parents for the important job they undertake. This deference reinforces parental commitment to undertake the duties of parenthood and facilitates their ability to do so without excessive interference. Society then benefits when parents perform their duties satisfactorily and children mature to healthy adulthood; otherwise the state itself must assume responsibility at substantial cost. Even in a society in which the state provided greater support for families, respect for parental authority would further social welfare because parents would be even better equipped to provide for their children's needs. Given the current allocation of responsibility, enhancing parents' role satisfaction and facilitating adequate performance of their child-rearing duties takes on a special urgency.

Analysis in the [Child Wellbeing] framework justifies strong protection of parental rights, but the framework also provides a more compelling rationale for restricting parental authority than the traditional justification. The constitutional grounding of parental rights in liberal principles, supporting family privacy and parental freedom, provides no defined boundaries. With child wellbeing as the pole star, our framework clarifies that parents are not free to inflict serious harm on their children or to create a serious risk of such harm. Such actions do not further child wellbeing and thus are not protected under this rationale for parental authority. This is true even if the parent's decision is motivated by deeply held values or religious beliefs. When a parent's action seriously threatens the child's welfare, state intervention overriding parental authority is justified. In this way, the child-wellbeing justification for parental rights is self-limiting. . . .

[D]octrinal examples illustrate the descriptive and normative power of the framework we identify. . . .

We begin with an example that is perhaps counterintuitive, showing that the modern privilege to use reasonable corporal punishment is consistent with the Child Wellbeing framework. The law has long recognized a parental privilege to use reasonable corporal punishment, but the justification rested on deference to parental rights, together with the notion that physical punishment benefitted the child. By contrast, the modern privilege, which applies in both criminal and civil proceedings, does not endorse corporal punishment as beneficial to children and instead is justified as a limit on state power in light of the dangers that accompany state intervention. Further, the modern privilege restricts the understanding of reasonable corporal punishment: a parent's use of corporal punishment is not privileged if, in the criminal context, the punishment inflicts serious harm or grossly degrades the child, or, in the child-protection context, the punishment inflicts physical harm beyond minor pain or transient marks. . . .

By maintaining the privilege and tailoring the reasonableness requirement to the form of state action, the privilege recognizes the trade-off between protecting children from harm inflicted by parents and protecting children from harm inflicted by state intervention. The privilege thus promotes the child's interest in the stability of the parent-child relationship and shields the child from the risks that accompany state intervention by limiting it to truly necessary circumstances. . . .

NOTES AND QUESTIONS

1.   *Harm.* Huntington and Scott justify the protection of parental authority on child-centered grounds. Do you agree? Child-centered concerns also animate limits on parental authority. In *Prince*, the state expressed its concern that the child could be harmed by the activity at issue, and it cited its child labor regulations as evidence of the state's interest. Would the child be physically harmed by proselytizing in public in the evening? When should the potential for physical harm justify the state's intrusion into parental authority? Should emotional or psychological harm provide a basis on which the state could limit parental rights?

2.   *Discipline.* Huntington and Scott point to the parental privilege to use corporal punishment as an illustration of how child wellbeing justifies strong parental authority. Should we allow parents to hit or spank a child as a form of discipline? What is the line between legitimate discipline and abuse? In Willis v. State, a mother was convicted of battery on her 11-year-old son.[11] In response to her son's lying, the mother ordered her son to remove his pants and lean against a bed while she hit him with either a belt or an extension cord. A school nurse reported the mother to child protective services after observing bruises on the child. The Indiana Supreme Court reversed the mother's conviction, holding that the exercise of parental privilege to use physical force in disciplining her son was a complete defense to a charge for battery on a child. The court reasoned that the fundamental right of parents to direct

---

11. 888 N.E.2d 177 (Ind. 2008).

the upbringing of their children includes "the use of reasonable or moderate physical force to control behavior."[12] The "difficult task" of prosecutors and courts, then, "is to determine when parental use of physical force in disciplining children turns an otherwise law-abiding citizen into a criminal."[13] The court adopted principles outlined in the Restatement (Second) of Torts, holding that in determining the reasonableness of punishment, a number of factors should be considered, including the age of the child, the nature of the child's offense, whether force is reasonably necessary, and "whether it is disproportionate to the offense, unnecessarily degrading, or likely to cause serious or permanent harm."[14] Do you think parents have a constitutional right to use physical discipline? Many states make prospective adoptive parents agree that they will not use physical discipline as a condition to being certified as eligible to adopt. Does this seem like a reasonable requirement? Is it constitutional? We will return to questions of physical discipline in the next chapter when we examine the child welfare system.

B. The Right to Exclude — Parents and Non-Parents

The ability to exclude third parties is a central aspect of the parental rights protected by the Constitution. Parents wield authority to decide who has contact with their children and to determine the type and amount of that contact. The law generally presumes that fit parents act in the best interests of their children, and therefore the government should not second-guess their judgment or allow others to override it. The important question, then, becomes when the government can permit a third party to seek contact with a child against the wishes of the child's parent or parents. In this context, "third party" is generally synonymous with "non-parent." Third parties include relatives, friends, romantic partners, teachers, and childcare providers. In the following materials, we first consider the circumstances in which the state can order visitation with a third party even when the child's parent objects. Of course, the line between parent and non-parent is not always clear. Accordingly, we then consider when an individual who is not the child's existing legal parent might in fact qualify as a legal parent.

1. Grandparent Visitation

The paradigmatic case of third-party visitation involves grandparents. A grandparents' rights campaign in the late twentieth century succeeded in convincing legislators in all fifty states to enact laws that allow grandparents to petition a court for

---

12. Id. at 180.
13. Id.
14. Id. at 182 (quoting Restatement (Second) of Torts § 150 (1965)).

visitation with their grandchildren. Some of these laws authorized such petitions in relatively narrow circumstances — after the death of the grandparents' child (the grandchildren's mother or father), or during the course of a divorce action between the parents. But others applied more broadly — allowing a petition at any time and including not only grandparents but other non-parents. Eventually, in the following case, the U.S. Supreme Court considered application of this type of broader statute.

TROXEL V. GRANVILLE
530 U.S. 57 (2000)

JUSTICE O'CONNOR announced the judgment of the Court and delivered an opinion, in which THE CHIEF JUSTICE, JUSTICE GINSBURG, and JUSTICE BREYER join. . . .

Tommie Granville and Brad Troxel shared a relationship that ended in June 1991. The two never married, but they had two daughters, Isabelle and Natalie. Jenifer and Gary Troxel are Brad's parents, and thus the paternal grandparents of Isabelle and Natalie. After Tommie and Brad separated in 1991, Brad lived with his parents and regularly brought his daughters to his parents' home for weekend visitation. Brad committed suicide in May 1993. Although the Troxels at first continued to see Isabelle and Natalie on a regular basis after their son's death, Tommie Granville informed the Troxels in October 1993 that she wished to limit their visitation with her daughters to one short visit per month.

In December 1993, the Troxels commenced the present action by filing, in the Washington Superior Court for Skagit County, a petition to obtain visitation rights with Isabelle and Natalie. . . . Section 26.10.160(3) [of the Washington Code] provides: "Any person may petition the court for visitation rights at any time including, but not limited to, custody proceedings. The court may order visitation rights for any person when visitation may serve the best interest of the child whether or not there has been any change of circumstances." At trial, the Troxels requested two weekends of overnight visitation per month and two weeks of visitation each summer. Granville did not oppose visitation altogether, but instead asked the court to order one day of visitation per month with no overnight stay. In 1995, the Superior Court issued an oral ruling and entered a visitation decree ordering visitation one weekend per month, one week during the summer, and four hours on both of the petitioning grandparents' birthdays.

Granville appealed, during which time she married Kelly Wynn. . . .

[The Washington Supreme Court invalidated the statute as violative of the United States Constitution, insofar as it did not require a showing of harm to the child, and allowed "any person" to petition for visitation at "any time."]

II

The demographic changes of the past century make it difficult to speak of an average American family. The composition of families varies greatly from household to household. While many children may have two married parents and grandparents who visit regularly, many other children are raised in single-parent households. In 1996, children living with only one parent accounted for 28 percent of all children under age 18 in the United States. U.S. Dept. of Commerce, Bureau of Census, Current Population Reports, 1997 Population Profile of the United States 27 (1998). Understandably, in these single-parent households, persons outside the nuclear family are called upon with increasing frequency to assist in the everyday tasks of child rearing. In many cases, grandparents play an important role. For example, in 1998, approximately 4 million children — or 5.6 percent of all children under age 18 — lived in the household of their grandparents.

The nationwide enactment of nonparental visitation statutes is assuredly due, in some part, to the States' recognition of these changing realities of the American family. Because grandparents and other relatives undertake duties of a parental nature in many households, States have sought to ensure the welfare of the children therein by protecting the relationships those children form with such third parties. The States' nonparental visitation statutes are further supported by a recognition, which varies from State to State, that children should have the opportunity to benefit from relationships with statutorily specified persons — for example, their grandparents. The extension of statutory rights in this area to persons other than a child's parents, however, comes with an obvious cost. For example, the State's recognition of an independent third-party interest in a child can place a substantial burden on the traditional parent-child relationship. . . .

The liberty interest at issue in this case — the interest of parents in the care, custody, and control of their children — is perhaps the oldest of the fundamental liberty interests recognized by this Court. . . .

Section 26.10.160(3), as applied to Granville and her family in this case, unconstitutionally infringes on that fundamental parental right. The Washington nonparental visitation statute is breathtakingly broad. According to the statute's text, "*any person* may petition the court for visitation rights *at any time*," and the court may grant such visitation rights whenever "visitation may serve *the best interest of the child*." § 26.10.160(3) (emphases added). That language effectively permits any third party seeking visitation to subject any decision by a parent concerning visitation of the parent's children to state-court review. Once the visitation petition has been filed in court and the matter is placed before a judge, a parent's decision that visitation would not be in the child's best interest is accorded no deference. Section 26.10.160(3) contains no requirement that a court accord the parent's decision any presumption of validity or any weight whatsoever. Instead, the Washington statute places the best-interest determination solely in the hands of the judge. Should the judge disagree with the parent's estimation of the child's best interests, the judge's view necessarily prevails. Thus, in practical effect, in the State of Washington a court can disregard and overturn *any* decision by a fit custodial parent concerning visitation whenever a third party affected by the decision files a visitation petition, based solely on the judge's determination of the child's best interests. The Washington Supreme Court had the opportunity to give § 26.10.160(3) a narrower reading, but it declined to do so.

Turning to the facts of this case, the record reveals that the Superior Court's order was based on precisely the type of mere disagreement we have just described and nothing more. The Superior Court's order was not founded on any special factors that might justify the State's interference with Granville's fundamental right to make decisions concerning the rearing of her two daughters. To be sure, this case involves a visitation petition filed by grandparents soon after the death of their son — the father of Isabelle and Natalie — but the combination of several factors here compels our conclusion that § 26.10.160(3), as applied, exceeded the bounds of the Due Process Clause.

First, the Troxels did not allege, and no court has found, that Granville was an unfit parent. That aspect of the case is important, for there is a presumption that fit parents act in the best interests of their children. As this Court explained in *Parham v. J.R.*:

> Our constitutional system long ago rejected any notion that a child is the mere creature of the State and, on the contrary, asserted that parents generally have the right, coupled with the high duty, to recognize and prepare [their children] for additional obligations. . . . The law's concept of the family rests on a presumption that parents possess what a child lacks in maturity, experience, and capacity for judgment required for making life's difficult decisions. More important, historically it has recognized that natural bonds of affection lead parents to act in the best interests of their children. 442 U.S. 584, 602 (1979).

Accordingly, so long as a parent adequately cares for his or her children (*i.e.*, is fit), there will normally be no reason for the State to inject itself into the private realm of the family to further question the ability of that parent to make the best decisions concerning the rearing of that parent's children.

The problem here is not that the Washington Superior Court intervened, but that when it did so, it gave no special weight at all to Granville's determination of her daughters' best interests. More importantly, it appears that the Superior Court applied exactly the opposite presumption. In reciting its oral ruling after the conclusion of closing arguments, the Superior Court judge explained:

> The burden is to show that it is in the best interest of the children to have some visitation and some quality time with their grandparents. I think in

> most situations a commonsensical approach [is that] it is normally in the best
> interest of the children to spend quality time with the grandparent, unless
> the grandparent, [sic] there are some issues or problems involved wherein
> the grandparents, their lifestyles are going to impact adversely upon the chil-
> dren. That certainly isn't the case here from what I can tell.

The judge's comments suggest that he presumed the grandparents' request
should be granted unless the children would be "impacted adversely." In effect, the
judge placed on Granville, the fit custodial parent, the burden of *disproving* that visitation would be in the best interest of her daughters. The judge reiterated moments
later: "I think [visitation with the Troxels] would be in the best interest of the children and I haven't been shown it is not in [the] best interest of the children."

The decisional framework employed by the Superior Court directly contravened the traditional presumption that a fit parent will act in the best interest of
his or her child. In that respect, the court's presumption failed to provide any protection for Granville's fundamental constitutional right to make decisions concerning the rearing of her own daughters. In an ideal world, parents might always seek
to cultivate the bonds between grandparents and their grandchildren. Needless to
say, however, our world is far from perfect, and in it the decision whether such an
intergenerational relationship would be beneficial in any specific case is for the parent to make in the first instance. And, if a fit parent's decision of the kind at issue
here becomes subject to judicial review, the court must accord at least some special
weight to the parent's own determination.

Finally, we note that there is no allegation that Granville ever sought to cut off
visitation entirely. . . . [Yet] [t]he Washington Superior Court failed to accord the
determination of Granville, a fit custodial parent, any material weight. In fact, the
Superior Court made only two formal findings in support of its visitation order.
First, the Troxels "are part of a large, central, loving family, all located in this area,
and the [Troxels] can provide opportunities for the children in the areas of cousins and music." Second, "the children would be benefitted from spending quality
time with the [Troxels], provided that that time is balanced with time with the
childrens' [sic] nuclear family." These slender findings, in combination with
the court's announced presumption in favor of grandparent visitation and its failure to accord significant weight to Granville's already having offered meaningful
visitation to the Troxels, show that this case involves nothing more than a simple
disagreement between the Washington Superior Court and Granville concerning
her children's best interests. The Superior Court's announced reason for ordering
one week of visitation in the summer demonstrates our conclusion well: "I look
back on some personal experiences . . . . We always spent as kids a week with one
set of grandparents and another set of grandparents, [and] it happened to work out
in our family that [it] turned out to be an enjoyable experience. Maybe that can,
in this family, if that is how it works out." As we have explained, the Due Process
Clause does not permit a State to infringe on the fundamental right of parents to

make childrearing decisions simply because a state judge believes a "better" decision could be made. . . .

JUSTICE SOUTER, concurring in the judgment. . . .

The Supreme Court of Washington invalidated its state statute based on the text of the statute alone, not its application to any particular case. Its ruling rested on two independently sufficient grounds: the failure of the statute to require harm to the child to justify a disputed visitation order, and the statute's authorization of "any person" at "any time" to petition and to receive visitation rights subject only to a free-ranging best-interests-of-the-child standard. I see no error in the second reason, that because the state statute authorizes any person at any time to request (and a judge to award) visitation rights, subject only to the State's particular best-interests standard, the state statute sweeps too broadly and is unconstitutional on its face. Consequently, there is no need to decide whether harm is required or to consider the precise scope of the parent's right or its necessary protections. . . .

JUSTICE KENNEDY, dissenting. . . .

As our case law has developed, the custodial parent has a constitutional right to determine, without undue interference by the state, how best to raise, nurture, and educate the child. The parental right stems from the liberty protected by the Due Process Clause of the Fourteenth Amendment. *Pierce v. Society of Sisters*, 268 U.S. 510 (1925), and *Meyer v. Nebraska*, 262 U.S. 390 (1923), had they been decided in recent times, may well have been grounded upon First Amendment principles protecting freedom of speech, belief, and religion. Their formulation and subsequent interpretation have been quite different, of course; and they long have been interpreted to have found in Fourteenth Amendment concepts of liberty an independent right of the parent in the "custody, care and nurture of the child," free from state intervention. *Prince v. Massachusetts*, 321 U.S. 158, 166 (1944). The principle exists, then, in broad formulation; yet courts must use considerable restraint, including careful adherence to the incremental instruction given by the precise facts of particular cases, as they seek to give further and more precise definition to the right.

The State Supreme Court sought to give content to the parent's right by announcing a categorical rule that third parties who seek visitation must always prove the denial of visitation would harm the child. . . .

To say that third parties have had no historical right to petition for visitation does not necessarily imply, as the Supreme Court of Washington concluded, that a parent has a constitutional right to prevent visitation in all cases not involving harm. . . . The State Supreme Court's conclusion that the Constitution forbids the application of the best interests of the child standard in any visitation proceeding . . . appears to rest upon assumptions the Constitution does not require.

My principal concern is that the holding seems to proceed from the assumption that the parent or parents who resist visitation have always been the child's primary caregivers and that the third parties who seek visitation have no legitimate and established relationship with the child. That idea, in turn, appears influenced by the concept that the conventional nuclear family ought to establish the visitation standard for every domestic relations case. As we all know, this is simply not the structure or prevailing condition in many households. For many boys and girls a traditional family with two or even one permanent and caring parent is simply not the reality of their childhood. This may be so whether their childhood has been marked by tragedy or filled with considerable happiness and fulfillment.

Cases are sure to arise — perhaps a substantial number of cases — in which a third party, by acting in a caregiving role over a significant period of time, has developed a relationship with a child which is not necessarily subject to absolute parental veto. Some pre-existing relationships, then, serve to identify persons who have a strong attachment to the child with the concomitant motivation to act in a responsible way to ensure the child's welfare. As the State Supreme Court was correct to acknowledge, those relationships can be so enduring that "in certain circumstances where a child has enjoyed a substantial relationship with a third person, arbitrarily depriving the child of the relationship could cause severe psychological harm to the child," and harm to the adult may also ensue. In the design and elaboration of their visitation laws, States may be entitled to consider that certain relationships are such that to avoid the risk of harm, a best interests standard can be employed by their domestic relations courts in some circumstances.

Indeed, contemporary practice should give us some pause before rejecting the best interests of the child standard in all third-party visitation cases, as the Washington court has done. The standard has been recognized for many years as a basic tool of domestic relations law in visitation proceedings. Since 1965 all 50 States have enacted a third-party visitation statute of some sort. Each of these statutes, save one, permits a court order to issue in certain cases if visitation is found to be in the best interests of the child. While it is unnecessary for us to consider the constitutionality of any particular provision in the case now before us, it can be noted that the statutes also include a variety of methods for limiting parents' exposure to third-party visitation petitions and for ensuring parental decisions are given respect. . . .

It must be recognized, of course, that a domestic relations proceeding in and of itself can constitute state intervention that is so disruptive of the parent-child relationship that the constitutional right of a custodial parent to make certain basic determinations for the child's welfare becomes implicated. The best interests of the child standard has at times been criticized as indeterminate, leading to unpredictable results. . . . I do not discount the possibility that in some instances the best interests of the child standard may provide insufficient protection to the parent-child relationship. We owe it to the Nation's domestic relations legal structure, however, to proceed with caution.

It should suffice in this case to reverse the holding of the State Supreme Court that the application of the best interests of the child standard is always unconstitutional in third-party visitation cases. Whether, under the circumstances of this case, the order requiring visitation over the objection of this fit parent violated the Constitution ought to be reserved for further proceedings. Because of its sweeping ruling requiring the harm to the child standard, the Supreme Court of Washington did not have the occasion to address the specific visitation order the Troxels obtained. . . .[15]

NOTES AND QUESTIONS

1.   *The Fate of the Washington Visitation Statute.* In *Troxel*, the U.S. Supreme Court held that the Washington third-party visitation statute was unconstitutional *as applied* to Granville. In a subsequent case, In re Parentage of C.A.M.A., the Washington Supreme Court struck down the same statute as unconstitutional on its face.[16] The court reasoned that the statute's presumption that grandparent visitation was in a child's best interest upon a showing of a substantial relationship between the grandparent and child violated parents' due process rights. Finding that this provision was not severable, the court struck down the entire statute.

2.   *Post-*Troxel *Litigation Across the Country.* The plurality opinion in *Troxel* affirmed the fundamental right of parents to make decisions regarding the "care and control" of their children, including the right to exclude other adults from the child's life. But parental rights are not absolute, and the plurality left many unanswered questions regarding when non-parent visitation or custody could be granted. While *Troxel* held that parental decisions must be accorded "special weight" in visitation disputes, the Court neither instructed states on how to operationalize the requirement of "special weight" nor specified when a court would be authorized to contravene a parent's wishes.[17] Why would the Court have held back from giving clearer guidance? This ambiguity has led to a lack of uniformity across state third-party visitation and custody statutes.[18] After *Troxel*, courts have struggled with cases where a third party — such as a stepparent, grandparent, or other relative — seeks visitation with, or custody of, a child with whom they have established a significant relationship. The central questions post-*Troxel* can be thought of as: *Who* can seek visitation with a child? *When* can such individuals seek visitation? And *what standard* applies to their requests for visitation?

---

15. Justice Stevens' dissent is excerpted in the next section.
16. 109 P.3d 405 (Wash. 2005).
17. 530 U.S. 57, 69 (2000).
18. See Jeff Atkinson, Shifts in the Law Regarding the Rights of Third Parties to Seek Visitation and Custody of Children, 47 Fam. L.Q. 1 (2013); Daniel R. Victor & Keri L. Middleditch, Grandparent Visitation: A Survey of History, Jurisprudence, and Legislative Trends Across the United States in the Past Decade, 22 J. Am. Acad. Matrimonial L. 391 (2009).

a. *Who?* Even the threshold question of who can file suit for third-party custody or visitation varies across jurisdictions. Some states have broad standing provisions. Virginia, for example, grants standing to petition for visitation to any "person with a legitimate interest" in the child's care, instructing courts to "broadly" construe the term to "accommodate the best interest of the child."[19] Some states, however, limit standing to specific relatives, such as stepparents or grandparents.[20] Other states grant standing to a wider range of relatives.[21] Washington's grant of standing to "any person" was one factor that led the plurality to describe the statute as "breathtakingly broad" and to determine it was unconstitutional as applied to Tommie Granville.[22]

Do foster parents qualify as third parties who can petition for custody or visitation? Foster parents generally are not entitled to visitation once the foster placement has ended. Some state statutes explicitly exclude foster parents from third-party visitation statutes.[23] Oregon's statute, on the other hand, expressly allows former foster parents to seek visitation where a "child-parent" relationship has been established.[24] How should the law treat a former foster parent? Why?

b. *When?* Washington's statute allowed an individual to seek visitation "at any time." In contrast, many state statutes restrict standing to cases where the family is not "intact" — for example, because the parents are divorced or one or both parents are deceased.[25] Why might parental rights be treated differently in such situations? In these states, a non-parent cannot petition for custody or visitation if a child's parents are married. Some statutes specify other circumstances in which a non-parent is authorized to petition for custody or visitation. For example, some permit third-party standing when the parents are absent.[26] Louisiana's visitation statute specifies that "parents of . . . [an] incarcerated party may have

---

19. Va. Code Ann. § 20-124.1 (West 2020).

20. See, e.g., N.H. Rev. Stat. Ann. § 461-A:6(V) (2020) ("If the court determines that it is in the best interest of the children, it shall in its decree grant reasonable visitation privileges to a party who is a stepparent of the children or to the grandparents. . . ."); Tex. Fam. Code Ann. § 153.432 (West 2020) (allowing a "biological or adoptive grandparent" to request visitation with a grandchild).

21. See, e.g., Ga. Code Ann. § 19-7-1 (West 2020) (authorizing a "grandparent, great-grandparent, aunt, uncle, great aunt, great uncle, sibling, or adoptive parent" to seek custody).

22. *Troxel*, 530 U.S. at 67.

23. See, e.g., Minn. Stat. § 257C.08(3) (2020) ("If an unmarried minor has resided in a household with a person, other than a foster parent, . . . the person may petition the district court for an order granting the person reasonable visitation rights. . . .").

24. Or. Rev. Stat. § 109.119 (2020).

25. See Neb. Rev. Stat. § 43-1802 (2020) (granting standing in grandparent visitation cases if the "child's parent or parents are deceased" or "[t]he marriage of the child's parents has been dissolved"); Wis. Stat. § 54.56(2) (2020) ("If one or both parents of a minor are deceased and the minor is in the custody of the surviving parent or any other person, a grandparent or stepparent of the minor may petition for visitation privileges with respect to the minor. . . .").

26. See, e.g., Ariz. Rev. Stat. Ann. § 25-409(C)(1) (2020) (establishing third-party standing when one of the parents is deceased or has been missing at least three months).

reasonable visitation rights to the child" provided that it is in the child's best interest.[27] Some states grant standing to third parties who have resided with a child for a specified period of time.[28] A few states grant special standing for siblings who have been separated.[29] (The law's treatment of sibling relationships is considered more fully in Chapter 10.)

c. *What standard?* Standing simply determines whether a party can seek visitation in court. Once there, what substantive legal standard must be met in order to obtain an order for custody or visitation? Because the *Troxel* Court rested its decision on the statute's "sweeping breadth" and its application to the grandparents in the case, it did not consider the broader issue addressed by the Washington Supreme Court. In *Troxel's* wake, litigants were left without a clear answer to whether the Due Process Clause required all non-parent visitation statutes to include a showing of harm (or potential harm) to the child as a condition for granting visitation.

Since *Troxel*, many state courts have considered how to balance the constitutional rights of the legal parent, the interests of the child, and the non-parent's interest in continued contact. The results have been mixed, and we are left with a range of standards across states.

Troxel appears to suggest that an order of third-party visitation that turns merely on the child's best interests, with no special weight accorded to the legal parent's decision, is constitutionally suspect. Some states, however, continue to maintain statutes that require that custody or visitation simply be in the "best interest of the child." Such a statute might still be constitutional if courts apply it in a manner that demonstrates due consideration of the fit parent's decision. In determining the child's best interests, courts are ordinarily instructed to consider a number of factors, including the parent's wishes, the child's wishes, and the child's relationships with her parents and other relatives or non-parents.[30] Some states account for the parent's superior rights through procedural rules, even though the substantive standard remains "best interests" of the child. For example, some states provide a rebuttable presumption that the parent's decision is in the child's best interest.[31] Others raise the burden of proof — more than twenty jurisdictions require third parties to prove by

---

27. La. Stat. Ann. § 9:344(B) (2020).

28. See, e.g., Minn. Stat. § 257C.08(3) (2020) (granting grandparents standing to seek visitation if they have resided with a child "for a period of 12 months").

29. See, e.g., N.Y. Dom. Rel. Law § 71 (McKinney 2020); N.J. Stat. Ann. § 9:2-7.1 (West 2020). Without a special statute granting them standing, siblings are likely to be regarded like any other third party. See, e.g. In re Victoria C., 88 A.3d 749 (Md. 2014).

30. Del. Code Ann. tit. 13, § 722 (2020).

31. See, e.g., S.D. Codified Laws § 25-5-29 (2020); Or. Rev. Stat. § 109.119(4)(b) (2020).

clear-and-convincing evidence that visitation or custody is in the child's best interests.[32]

Many states require more than a showing of best interests. At least ten state supreme courts have held that a non-parent must show that the denial of visitation or custody would result in harm to the child, even though the plurality in *Troxel* did not require such an exacting standard.[33] Under Tennessee's law, for example, grandparents must show there would be "substantial harm" to the child if visitation is denied.[34] Some states draw a distinction between custody and visitation, requiring a showing of harm for the former but not the latter.[35]

In some states, courts have read a higher standard into the statute in order to preserve its constitutionality. For example, while New Jersey's grandparent visitation statute required only that the applicant prove "by a preponderance of the evidence that the granting of visitation is in the best interests of the child,"[36] the New Jersey Supreme Court held that "harm to a child" must be proven in order to meet the heightened requirements of *Troxel*.[37] In other states, courts have simply struck down the statute as constitutionally inadequate.[38]

Some states go beyond the harm standard and require a showing of parental unfitness — that is, the non-parent can prevail only by showing that the legal parent is unfit. This standard is more common in proceedings in which the third party seeks custody rather than visitation.[39]

---

32. See Ala. Code § 30-3-4.2 (2020); Ct. Gen. Stat. § 46b-59(b) (2020); D.C. Code § 16-831.03(b) (2020); Ga. Code Ann. § 19-7-3(c) (2020); Idaho Code § 32-1704(6) (2020); Ind. Code 31-17-2-8.5(a) (2020); Iowa Code § 600C.1 (2020); Ky. Rev. Stat. Ann. §§ 403.270, 403.280 (West 2020); Me. Stat. tit. 19-A, § 1891(3) (2020); Mich. Comp. Laws § 722.25(1) (2020); Minn. Stat. § 257C.03 (2020); Mont. Code Ann. § 40-4-228(2) (2020); Nev. Rev. Stat. § 125C.050(4) (2020); N.H. Rev. Stat. Ann. 461-A:6(II) (2020); Neb. Rev. Stat. § 43-1802(2) (2020); Okla. Stat. tit. 43, § 109.4 (2020); Or. Rev. Stat. § 109.119 (2020); 23 Pa. Cons. Stat. § 5327(b) (2020); 15 R.I. Gen. Laws § 15-5-24.3(a)(2)(v) (2020); S.C. Code Ann. § 63-15-60 (2020); Utah Code Ann. § 30-5a-103(2) (West 2020); Va. Code Ann. § 20-124.2(B) (2020); W. Va. Code § 48-10-702(b) (2020).

33. See Crockett v. Pastore, 789 A.2d 453 (Conn. 2002); Sullivan v. Sapp, 866 So. 2d 28 (Fla. 2004); Doe v. Doe, 172 P.3d 1067 (Haw. 2007); In re Marriage of Howard, 661 N.W.2d 183 (Iowa 2003); Blixt v. Blixt, 774 N.E.2d 1052 (Mass. 2002); Moriarty v. Bradt, 827 A.2d 203 (N.J. 2003); Craig v. Craig, 253 P.3d 57 (Okla. 2011); Smallwood v. Mann, 205 S.W.3d 358 (Tenn. 2006); Jones v. Jones, 359 P.3d 603 (Utah 2015); In re Parentage of C.A.M.A., 109 P.3d 405 (Wash. 2005). In addition, statutes in nine states explicitly require "harm," "detriment," or similar proof before visitation can be granted. See, e.g., Ala. Code § 30-3-4.2 (2020); Ark. Code Ann. § 9-13-103(e) (2020); Conn. Gen. Stat. § 46b-59(b) (2020); Utah Code Ann. § 30-5a-103(2)(f) (West 2020).

34. See Tenn. Code § 36-6-306 (2020) ("In considering a petition for grandparent visitation, the court shall first determine the presence of a danger of substantial harm to the child.").

35. See, e.g., In re Marriage of Friedman and Roels, 418 P.3d 884 (Ariz. 2018).

36. N.J. Stat. Ann. § 9:2-7.1 (West 2020).

37. See Moriarty v. Bradt, 827 A.2d 203 (N.J. 2003).

38. See, e.g., *Doe*, 172 P.3d 1067.

39. See, e.g., In re Blake, 786 N.E.2d 78, 80 (Ohio Ct. App. 2003) ("Ohio law clearly does not permit a nonparent to obtain custody of a child without showing the parents to be unsuitable."). But see Iowa Code § 600C.1 (2020) (requiring parental unfitness for visitation).

3. *Harm from Denying Grandparent Contact?* Regardless of the particular substantive standard applied, the importance of grandparent relationships — and the potential harm to a child of being deprived of them — is always lurking in these cases. The issue of "grandparents' rights" has arisen at a time when an increasing number of children are being raised by non-parents. According to the most recent version of the U.S. Census, 7.8 million children are raised at least in part by their grandparents.[40] When harm is expressly part of the legal standard, what sets of facts tend to show evidence of harm or potential harm to the child if visitation was denied? Courts generally have held that the grandparents' claim that they have a positive relationship with the grandchild is not sufficient to justify an order of visitation over the objection of a parent.[41] Where a grandparent has raised a child for a significant period of time, however, courts have recognized a basis for granting visitation to the grandparent. For example, the Maine Supreme Court granted visitation where the grandparents had raised the grandchildren for extended periods of time, including raising one grandchild for the first seven years of her life.[42] The court explained that even though "something more than the best interest of the child must be at stake in order to establish a compelling state interest," "harm consisting of a threat to physical safety or imminent danger is not a *sine qua non* for the existence of a compelling state interest."[43]

Should legislatures or courts take more account of the ways in which children might benefit from grandparent involvement when the grandparent has not taken on a quasi-parent status? Research suggests that there is scientific support for the idea that "it takes a village to raise a child;" children benefit from an "alloparenting" system in which people other than parents contribute to a child's care.[44] Studies show that adults who are close to a grandparent have lower rates of depression than those who are not.[45] Can lawmakers or judges constitutionally consider these studies? In what manner? Do children have a right to benefit from relationships with their grandparents?[46] Why do fit parents sometimes sever these ties?

---

40. AARP, GrandFacts: National Fact Sheet for Grandparents and Other Relatives Raising Children, https://www.aarp.org/content/dam/aarp/relationships/friends-family/grandfacts/grandfacts-national.pdf.

41. See, e.g., Dorr v. Woodard, 140 A.3d 467 (Me. 2016); Neal v. Lee, 14 P.3d 547 (Okla. 2000); Flynn v. Henkel, 880 N.E.2d 166 (Ill. 2007).

42. See Rideout v. Riendeau, 761 A.2d 291 (Me. 2000).

43. Id. at 300-01.

44. See Sarah Blaffer Hrdy, Mothers and Others (2011); cf. Brooke C. Feeney & Nancy L. Collins, A New Look at Social Support: A Theoretical Perspective on Thriving Through Relationships, 19 Personality & Social Psychol. Rev. 113, 121 (2015) (explaining how individual well-being is linked to care and support that derive from multiple relationships, beyond the primary parent-child relationship).

45. Sara M. Moorman & Jeffrey E. Stokes, Solidarity in the Grandparent-Adult Grandchild Relationship and Trajectories of Depressive Symptoms, 56 Gerontologist 408 (2014).

46. See Anne C. Dailey, Children's Constitutional Rights, 95 Minn. L. Rev. 2099 (2011); James G. Dwyer, The Relationship Rights of Children (2006).

4. *The Uniform Nonparent Custody and Visitation Act.* Recognizing that many state statutes "do not . . . provide a reliable indicator of whether nonparent visitation (or custody) should be allowed," in 2018 the Uniform Law Commission approved a Uniform Nonparent Custody and Visitation Act (UNCVA) intended to serve as a model for state legislatures.[47] The UNCVA provides two bases for non-parents to seek custody and visitation: (1) non-parents who have consistently served as caretakers of a child, without expectation of compensation, and (2) those who have a "substantial relationship with the child" and can demonstrate that the denial of custody or visitation would result in harm to the child. There is no fixed number of persons who may seek custody or visitation. Additionally, the UNCVA includes an optional provision that state legislators could adopt to exclude foster parents from the state's non-parent visitation statute.

The UNCVA includes a rebuttable presumption that a parent's decision regarding custody or visitation is in the child's best interest. Non-parents seeking custody or visitation must prove by clear-and-convincing evidence that the parent's decision is *not* in the child's best interest. In keeping with the general factors used by many states, the UNCVA considers factors such as "the nature and extent" of the relationship between the non-parent and child, as well as that between the parent and child, when determining the "best interests" of the child. As of June 2020, North Dakota was the only state to adopt the UNCVA.[48]

PROBLEMS

1. Mark and Teddy, a same-sex couple, had a child through a gestational surrogacy arrangement using a donor egg. Both Mark and Teddy were recognized as the legal parents of the child, Lily. Because both Mark and Teddy work full-time, they hired Bridget as a nanny. Bridget was twenty-four at the time, and it was her first job as a nanny. Bridget lived in Mark and Teddy's home, woke with Lily during the night, and fed and cared for Lily during the day. In the evening, when Mark and Teddy were home, they would feed Lily, give her a bath, and put her to bed. Bridget would help Mark and Teddy care for Lily in the evenings, but she usually had a few hours for herself. Bridget received room and board and an annual salary of $48,000. This arrangement continued until Lily was five, at which time she began to attend kindergarten. Bridget would bring Lily to school in the morning and pick her up in the early afternoon. She would do some household tasks while Lily was in school, but otherwise had the time for herself. After school, Bridget would look after Lily until Mark and Teddy came home around 5:00 p.m. and

---

47. See Unif. Nonparent Custody and Visitation Act 3 (Unif. Law Comm'n 2018).
48. N.D. Cent. Code § 14-09.4 (2020).

6:00 p.m., respectively. She received the same benefits and salary. Once Lily began first grade and thus would be in school longer, Mark and Teddy let Bridget go. They decided to hire a childcare provider on a part-time basis.

Bridget was devastated by her loss of the nanny position with Mark and Teddy. She had developed a strong bond with Lily. Bridget lives in a state with a third-party visitation statute that allows an individual who "consistently cared" for the child and developed a "substantial relationship" to seek visitation "in the best interest of the child." Should Bridget be able to obtain visitation with Lily, over the objection of Mark and Teddy? Is there any additional information you would like to have to help make a decision? Is the third-party visitation statute in Bridget's state constitutional? Could it be applied constitutionally in a way that grants Bridget visitation with Lily?

2. Imagine you are a lawmaker in a state where the courts have not considered the constitutionality of third-party custody and visitation and where lawmakers are interested in replacing the existing statute. You are a member of the legislature's judiciary committee. You are considering whether to introduce the text of the UNCVA as a bill that would become the state's third-party custody and visitation statute. You are focusing on two of the most critical sections of the UNCVA.

Section 4. Requirements for Order of Custody or Visitation.
  (a) A court may order custody or visitation to a nonparent if the nonparent proves that:
    (1) the nonparent:
        (A) is a consistent caretaker; or
        (B) has a substantial relationship with the child and the denial of custody or visitation would result in harm to the child; and
    (2) an order of custody or visitation to the nonparent is in the best interest of the child.
  (b) A nonparent is a consistent caretaker if the nonparent without expectation of compensation:
    (1) lived with the child for not less than 12 months, unless the court finds good cause to accept a shorter period;
    (2) regularly exercised care of the child;
    (3) made day-to-day decisions regarding the child solely or in cooperation with an individual having physical custody of the child; and
    (4) established a bonded and dependent relationship with the child with the express or implied consent of a parent of the child, or without the consent of a parent if no parent has been able or willing to perform parenting functions.

(c) A nonparent has a substantial relationship with the child if:
   (1) the nonparent:
      (A) is an individual with a familial relationship with the child by blood or law; or
      (B) formed a relationship with the child without expectation of compensation; and
   (2) a significant emotional bond exists between the nonparent and the child.

Section 5. Presumption for Parental Decision.
(a) In an initial proceeding under this [act], a decision by a parent regarding a request for custody or visitation by a nonparent is presumed to be in the best interest of the child.
(b) . . . [A] nonparent has the burden to rebut the presumption under subsection (a) by clear-and-convincing evidence of the facts required by Section 4(a). Proof of unfitness of a parent is not required to rebut the presumption under subsection (a).

You bring together your legislative aides, legislative counsel, and some colleagues on the judiciary committee to discuss the following:

(1) Are the provisions likely to survive constitutional review? Are there any revisions you think would improve the provisions?
(2) What are your strongest policy arguments in favor of the bill? What objections to the bill do you expect to hear?
(3) Why does the UNCVA specify that consistent caretakers provide care "without expectation of compensation"? Why does it distinguish between relatives and non-relatives on this front, permitting relatives to seek visitation on the basis of a substantial relationship with the child, even if the relative was compensated for the childcare provided?[49]

2. Third Parties or Parents?

Up to this point, we have considered custody and visitation rights for third parties who openly acknowledge that they are *not* parents of the child. But what if the adult claims to be a parent? The next case considers the status of an individual who has "parented" the child, but is not the biological parent, has not adopted the child, and is not married to the child's parent. May this individual nonetheless be granted

---

49. See Unif. Nonparent Custody and Visitation Act, supra note 47, at 13 ("If a grandparent or other relative received compensation for caring for the child, that would not preclude the grandparent or other relative from seeking custody or visitation.").

parental recognition? Does the existing parent no longer have a right to exclude this individual from the child's life?

IN RE PARENTAGE OF L.B.
122 P.3d 161 (Wash. 2005)

BRIDGE, J.

In 1989, after dating for several months, Page Britain and Sue Ellen ("Mian") Carvin began living together as intimates. Five years later, they decided to add a child to their relationship and together artificially inseminated Britain with semen donated by a male friend. On May 10, 1995, Britain gave birth to a baby girl, L.B., and the partners began actively co-parenting her, both taking a committed, active, and loving role in her nurturing and upbringing. Then, when L.B. was six years old, Britain and Carvin ended their relationship and an acrimonious spate of litigation over access to L.B. ensued. . . .

The equitable power of the courts to adjudicate relationships between children and families is well recognized, and our legislature has evinced no intent to preclude the application of an equitable remedy in circumstances such as these. Accordingly, we now hold, as did the Court of Appeals, that Washington's common law recognizes the status of *de facto* parents and grants them standing to petition for a determination of the rights and responsibilities that accompany legal parentage in this state. Therefore, Carvin should have the opportunity to present evidence to the court sufficient to establish her status as a *de facto* parent of L.B. and if successful to obtain the rights and responsibilities attendant to parentage. However, because we have previously held Washington's third party visitation statutes to be unconstitutional and thereby inoperative, we reverse the Court of Appeals' alternative holding that Carvin may petition for visitation pursuant to RCW 26.10.160(3).

I. Facts and Procedural History . . .

For the first six years of L.B.'s life, Carvin, Britain, and L.B. lived together as a family unit and held themselves out to the public as a family. Carvin and Britain shared parenting responsibilities, with Carvin actively involved in L.B.'s parenting, including discipline decisions, day care and schooling decisions, and medical care decisions. Both parties were named as "parents" on L.B.'s kindergarten and first grade records. While the parties now dispute the nature of their relationship and the extent of Carvin's role as a "mother," as the Court of Appeals notes, "the record reflects that Carvin provided much of the child's 'mothering' during the first six years of her life." This conclusion is supported by the fact that L.B., in her interactions with the two women, referred to Carvin as "'mama'" and Britain as "'mommy.'"

L.B. was nearly six years old when the parties ended their relationship. After initially sharing custody and parenting responsibilities, Britain eventually took measures to limit Carvin's contact with L.B. and in the spring of 2002, unilaterally terminated all of Carvin's contact with L.B. L.B. was then seven years old.

Seeking to continue her relationship with L.B., on November 15, 2002, Carvin filed a petition for the establishment of parentage in King County Superior Court. In it she sought, in relevant part, (1) that she be declared the legal parent of L.B. pursuant to the Uniform Parentage Act (UPA), chapter 26.26 RCW, (2) that she be declared a parent by equitable estoppel or that she be recognized as a *de facto* parent, and finally (3) that she be allowed statutory third party visitation rights. . . .

II. Analysis

In the face of advancing technologies and evolving notions of what comprises a family unit, this case causes us to confront the manner in which our state, through its statutory scheme and common law principles, defines the terms "parents" and "families." During the first half of Washington's statehood, determinations of the conflicting rights of persons in family relationships were made by courts acting in equity. But over the past half-century, our legislature has established statutory schemes intended to govern various aspects of parentage, child custody disputes, visitation privileges, and child support obligations. Yet, inevitably, in the field of familial relations, factual scenarios arise, which even after a strict statutory analysis remain unresolved, leaving deserving parties without any appropriate remedy, often where demonstrated public policy is in favor of redress.

And so we turn to the question before us: whether our state's common law recognizes *de facto* parents and, if so, what rights and obligations accompany such recognition. Specifically, we are asked to discern whether, in the absence of a statutory remedy, the equitable power of our courts in domestic matters permits a remedy *outside* of the statutory scheme, or conversely, whether our state's relevant statutes provide the exclusive means of obtaining parental rights and responsibilities. . . .

C. Recognition of Common Law *De Facto* Parentage

Persuasive Authority for De facto *Parents:* In recent years, numerous other jurisdictions have faced issues similar to those presented here, often in the face of a statutory scheme which failed to contemplate the scenario presented. As this remains a case of first impression in this state, a review of decisions of other jurisdictions is instructive.

In 1995, the Wisconsin Supreme Court was presented with a situation factually analogous to the one presented here. *See In re Custody of H.S.H.-K.,* 533 N.W.2d 419, 421-23 (Wis. 1995). In that case, two women "shared a close, committed relationship for more than ten years" and jointly decided to raise a child. One partner was artificially inseminated with sperm from an anonymous donor, became pregnant, and in December 1988 a child was born. The women gave the child names honoring the families of both partners, held themselves out to the public as a family unit, and actively co-parented the child until their relationship ended in 1993. Three months after the parties separated, the biological mother terminated her former partner's relationship with the child and filed a restraining order seeking to prohibit all contact. In response, the biological mother's former partner filed a petition for visitation and custody.

The Wisconsin Supreme Court determined that under the Wisconsin statutory scheme, the biological mother's former female partner lacked standing to petition for custody or visitation. The relevant custody statute, Wis. Stat. § 767.24 (1991-1992), provided that a nonparent may petition for custody only if a parent is " 'unfit or unable to care for the child' " or other compelling reasons exist. *H.S.H.-K.*, 533 N.W.2d at 423. The former partner was unable to meet this standard and thus lacked standing. In addition, the court rejected the former partner's statutory visitation claim because the court determined that the "legislature enacted the ch. 767 visitation statute with the dissolution of marriage in mind." Because the parties' dispute did not arise in the context of dissolution of a marriage, a legal impossibility because of their lesbian relationship, statutory visitation was unavailable.

In spite of this determination, the court held that the legislature had not intended to preempt the equitable power of the court in domestic matters so as to preclude a remedy *outside* of the statutory scheme. It then examined the history of that state's visitation law and the relevant legislative enactments to discern whether the statutory scheme was intended as the exclusive means of obtaining visitation rights and concluded that "[i]t is reasonable to infer that the legislature did not intend the visitation statutes to bar the courts from exercising their equitable power to order visitation in circumstances not included within the statutes but in conformity with the policy directions set forth in the statutes." The court thus concluded that courts have equitable power to hear a visitation petition if it finds that the nonparent has a "parent-like relationship with the child" and that "a significant triggering event justifies state intervention." . . .

Numerous other jurisdictions have recognized common law rights on behalf of *de facto* parents. These cases provide a well reasoned and just template for the recognition of *de facto* parent status in Washington.

Conclusion: Our state's current statutory scheme reflects the unsurprising fact that statutes often fail to contemplate all potential scenarios which may arise in the ever changing and evolving notion of familial relations.

Yet, simply because a statute fails to speak to a specific situation should not, and does not in our common law system, operate to preclude the availability of potential redress. This is especially true when the rights and interests of those least able to speak for themselves are concerned. We cannot read the legislature's pronouncements on this subject to preclude any potential redress to Carvin or L.B. In fact, to do so would be antagonistic to the clear legislative intent that permeates this field of law — to effectuate the best interests of the child in the face of differing notions of family and to provide certain and needed economical and psychological support and nurturing to the children of our state. While the legislature may eventually choose to enact differing standards than those recognized here today, and to do so would be within its province, until that time, it is the duty of this court to "endeavor to administer justice according to the promptings of reason and common sense."

Reason and common sense support recognizing the existence of *de facto* parents and according them the rights and responsibilities which attach to parents in this state. We adapt our common law today to fill the interstices that our current legislative enactment fails to cover in a manner consistent with our laws and stated legislative policy. As Justice O'Connor noted, "[t]he demographic changes of the past century make it difficult to speak of an average American family," *Troxel v. Granville*, 530 U.S. 57, 63 (2000) (plurality opinion).

Recognition of a *de facto* parent is supported primarily by our legislature's pronouncements on the subject, our courts' historic common law role with respect to visitation, child custody, and support obligations. . . . As such, the common law grants Carvin standing to prove she is a *de facto* parent and if so determined, to petition for the corresponding rights and obligations of parenthood.

To establish standing as a *de facto* parent we adopt the following criteria, delineated by the Wisconsin Supreme Court and set forth in the Court of Appeals opinion below: (1) the natural or legal parent consented to and fostered the parent-like relationship, (2) the petitioner and the child lived together in the same household, (3) the petitioner assumed obligations of parenthood without expectation of financial compensation, and (4) the petitioner has been in a parental role for a length of time sufficient to have established with the child a bonded, dependent relationship, parental in nature. In addition, recognition of a *de facto* parent is "limited to those adults who have fully and completely undertaken a permanent, unequivocal, committed, and responsible parental role in the child's life."

We thus hold that henceforth in Washington, a *de facto* parent stands in legal parity with an otherwise legal parent, whether biological, adoptive, or otherwise. As such, recognition of a person as a child's *de facto* parent necessarily "authorizes [a] court to consider an award of parental rights and responsibilities . . . based on its determination of the best interest of the child." . . .

D. Fundamental Parental Liberty Interest

Britain asserts the recognition of Carvin as a *de facto* parent, and granting her rights akin to a biological or adoptive parent violates Britain's constitutionality protected liberty interest to care for and control her child without unwarranted state intervention, in contravention of United States Supreme Court precedent. *See Prince v. Massachusetts*, 321 U.S. 158 (1944). She notes that "the law presumes that biological parents are not only fit, but will act in the best interest of their children," and there is no indication that she is in anyway [sic] unfit as a parent. Carvin counters that common law recognition of *de facto* parents does not implicate the constitutional infirmities recognized in *Troxel* and that the first of the four *de facto* parent standards, that the "natural or legal parent consented to and fostered the parent-like relationship," "incorporates the constitutionally requisite deference to the legal parent."

It is well recognized that "[t]he liberty interest . . . of parents in the care, custody, and control of their children [ ] is perhaps the oldest of the fundamental liberty interests recognized by [the United States Supreme] Court." *Troxel*, 530 U.S. at 65 (plurality opinion). Additionally, in *In re Custody of Smith*, this court applied a strict scrutiny analysis in discerning whether a grandparent's invocation of the visitation statute infringed on the biological parent's "fundamental 'liberty' interest." 969 P.2d 21, 27 (Wash. 1998). In doing so, this court stated that "state interference is justified only if the state can show that it has a compelling interest and such interference is narrowly drawn to meet only the compelling state interest involved."

[*In re Parentage of C.A.M.A.*, 109 P.3d 405 (Wash. 2005)] reaffirmed *Smith's* holding establishing strict scrutiny analysis as the appropriate analytic framework in reviewing the State's infringement on a parent's fundamental liberty interest. However, like *Smith*, *C.A.M.A.* dealt with the competing interests of biological parents and *third parties*, in both cases grandparents. No case has ever applied a strict scrutiny analysis in cases weighing the competing interests of *two parents*. Rather, in Washington, courts attempt to discern the best interests of the child. Given the now equivalent parental positions of the parties, no heightened scrutiny is warranted.

Significantly, our holding today regarding the common law status of *de facto* parents renders the crux of Britain's constitutional arguments moot. Britain's primary argument is that the State, through judicial action, cannot infringe on or materially interfere with her rights as a biological parent in favor of Carvin's rights as a nonparent third party. However, today we hold that our common law recognizes the status of *de facto* parents and places them in parity with biological and adoptive parents in our state. Thus, if, on remand, Carvin can establish standing as a *de facto* parent, Britain and Carvin would *both* have a "fundamental liberty interest[ ]" in the "care, custody, and control" of L.B. *Troxel*, 530 U.S. at 65.

Additionally, contrary to Britain's assertions, *Troxel* does not establish that recognition of a *de facto* parentage right infringes on the liberty interests of a biological or adoptive parent. First, *Troxel* did not address the issue of state law determinations of "parents" and "families," rather simply disapproved of the grant of visitation in that case, narrowly holding that "[t]he problem . . . is not that the [trial court] intervened" but that, when it did so, "it gave no special weight at all" to the *parents'* determination regarding the *grandparents'* visitation. *Troxel*, 530 U.S. at 69. . . . *Troxel* does not imply any constitutional infirmity in our holding today, and importantly, nor does it place any constitutional limitations on the ability of states to legislatively, or through their common law, define a parent or family. Neither the United States Supreme Court nor this court has ever held that "family" or "parents" are terms limited in their definition by a strict biological prerequisite. Our common law recognition of another class of "parents" eradicates the parent/nonparent dichotomy that was the crux of both the *Smith* and *Troxel* opinions.

Finally, in contrast to Britain's fears that "teachers, nannies, parents of best friends, . . . adult siblings, aunts, [ ] grandparents," and every "third-party . . . caregiver" will now become *de facto* parents, attaining such recognition should be no easy task. Critical to our constitutional analysis here, a threshold requirement for the status of the *de facto* parent is a showing that the legal parent "consented to and fostered" the parent-child relationship. The State is not interfering on behalf of a third party in an insular family unit but is enforcing the rights and obligations of parenthood that attach to *de facto* parents; a status that can be achieved only through the active encouragement of the biological or adoptive parent by affirmatively establishing a family unit with the *de facto* parent and child or children that accompany the family. In sum, we find that the rights and responsibilities which we recognize as attaching to *de facto* parents do not infringe on the fundamental liberty interests of the other legal parent in the family unit.

Finding no constitutional infirmities in recognizing *de facto* parents, we accordingly affirm the Court of Appeals on this issue and remand to the trial court for a determination of whether Carvin is L.B.'s *de facto* parent and any further appropriate proceedings in accord with this opinion. . . .

NOTES AND QUESTIONS

---

1. *Parental Status?* For the Washington court, an individual who satisfies the de facto parent standard is a full legal parent and thus stands in parity with the existing legal parent. Accordingly, the de facto parent can exercise parental authority over the child and seek custody of the child. While the clear modern trend is to treat de facto parents as legal parents, some courts have granted de facto parents only rights to visitation, rather than parental status. For example, the Wisconsin Supreme Court's 1995 decision in In re Custody of H.S.H.-K., which the Washington Supreme Court relied on in articulating its test for de facto parenthood, held that a de facto parent may merely petition for visitation.[50]

2. *The Constitutional Stakes.* In his dissent in *Troxel*, Justice Kennedy observed that "a fit parent's right vis-à-vis a complete stranger is one thing; her right vis-à-vis another parent or a *de facto* parent may be another."[51] Consistent with this distinction, the *L.B.* court rejected the argument that recognition of a de facto parent would unconstitutionally dilute the parental rights of a biological mother, in part because

---

50. 533 N.W.2d 419 (Wis. 1995).
51. Troxel, 530 U.S. at 100-01 (Kennedy, J., dissenting).

the doctrine only applies when the legal parent has actively fostered the creation of a parent-child relationship. As a constitutional matter, why does it matter that the existing legal parent fostered or consented to the de facto parent's relationship with the child? What types of conduct might support or undermine a claim of "active fostering" of the relationship?

3. *The Rise of De Facto Parentage.* Although they have used different terms to define the concept, courts in an increasing number of states have adopted de facto parent standards as a matter of common law or equitable authority.[52] More recently, legislatures in some states have enacted de facto parent provisions.[53] We return to these cases and statutes in Chapter 9.

4. *Guardianship.* Some individuals may seek guardianship, not parental status, with respect to a child they are raising.[54] A legal guardian has authority to make decisions on behalf of the child, known as the guardian's "ward." If a child's parents are deceased, courts typically will appoint a guardian named in the parents' will. If no guardian had been designated by the parents, courts generally will appoint the "nearest ascendant" or next-of-kin who comes forward to petition for guardianship. By statute, though, minors in most states may nominate their own guardians starting at the age of twelve to fourteen, subject to judicial approval and suitability review.[55] By contrast, if one or both parents are still living, they may consent to guardianship. But in the absence of such consent, those seeking guardianship face a high burden: a required showing by "clear and convincing evidence" of parental unfitness and that guardianship is in the child's best interest.[56] In these circumstances, courts require potential guardians to submit substantial proof to the court that continued parental custody threatens the child's physical or psychological safety.[57]

While the appointment of a guardian may have the practical (if not legal) effect of terminating parental rights, it usually is not a "final and complete" severance of the relationship, as guardians generally are subject to removal at the discretion of the court.[58] Nonetheless, where children have been placed with guardians for multiple

---

52. See, e.g., Bethany v. Jones, 378 S.W.3d 731 (Ark. 2011) (in loco parentis); E.N.O. v. L.M.M., 711 N.E.2d 886 (Mass. 1999) (de facto parent); V.C. v. M.J.B., 748 A.2d 539 (N.J. 2000) (psychological parent); Boseman v. Jarrell, 704 S.E.2d 494 (N.C. 2010) (equity); J.A.L. v. E.P.H., 682 A.2d 1314 (Pa. Super Ct. 1996) (in loco parentis); In re Clifford K., 619 S.E.2d 138 (W. Va. 2005) (psychological parent).

53. See, e.g., Del. Code Ann. tit. 13, § 8-201 (2020); Me. Rev. Stat. Ann. tit. 19-A, § 1891 (2020).

54. See Guardianship of Z.C.W., 84 Cal. Rptr. 2d 48 (Cal. Ct. App. 1999) (rejecting guardianship claim).

55. See, e.g., Cal. Prob. Code § 1510 (West 2020); W. Va. Code § 44-10-4 (2020).

56. See In re Lakota Z., 804 N.W.2d 174, 181 (Neb. 2011) (noting that in guardianship proceedings, constitutional due process "demands some showing of parental unfitness if parents are to be deprived of their interest in the care, custody, and control of their children").

57. See, e.g., N.Y. Soc. Serv. Law § 384-b (McKinney 2020).

58. See In re Guardianship of Nicholas P., 27 A.3d 653 (N.H. 2011) (noting that guardianship appointments are not de facto termination of parental rights).

years, courts have declined to grant parental custody, as displacement would be against the child's best interest.[59]

PROBLEM

Sara met Mark when she was five months pregnant. They began dating, and were living together by the time Sara gave birth. The child, Owen, was given Mark's last name, and Sara and Mark were listed as parents on Owen's birth certificate. Mark, Sara, and Owen lived together in Laramie, Wyoming for almost two years. Mark says that he paid most of the family's expenses during this time, but Sara characterizes Mark's financial support as sporadic and minimal.

Eventually, Mark and Sara decided to "take a break from each other." While Mark assumed this would only be temporary, Sara left Laramie with Owen and did not tell Mark where she was. Sara and Owen stayed in two "safe houses" designed to help women escape domestic violence. Sara eventually moved with Owen to Cheyenne, Wyoming, where she rented an apartment.

Mark found Sara in Cheyenne and rented an apartment across the street. Owen would spend time with both Sara and Mark. While Mark contends that he supported Sara and Owen financially during this time, Sara says that Mark "helped some, but not a lot."

Eventually, Sara filed a "Petition to Disprove Father-Child Relationship." Mark counter-petitioned by seeking to legally establish a father-child relationship with Owen. Is Mark Owen's father?

POSTSCRIPT

In *LP v. LF*, the case on which the problem above is based, the Wyoming Supreme Court found that a man in Mark's position is not a legal father of the child.[60] The court concluded that because genetic testing showed a 0.00 percent probability that LP, the man claiming parenthood, was the biological father, his paternity had been conclusively rebutted. The court "decline[d] to adopt de facto parentage . . . , instead leaving that important policy decision to the Wyoming Legislature.[61] The Wyoming court extensively discussed the Washington Supreme Court's reasoning in *L.B.* and

---

59. See Guardianship of Zachary H., 86 Cal. Rptr. 2d 7 (Cal. Ct. App. 1999) (finding that a 4-year-old child's "fundamental interest" in remaining with his permanent guardian superseded his biological father's constitutional right to parent).

60. 338 P.3d 908 (Wyo. 2014).

61. Id. at 921.

ultimately found such reasoning unpersuasive. While the court recognized that the child might be harmed by severing his relationship with the man he viewed as his father, it worried that "practical problems" would arise if it were to adopt a de facto parent standard.[62] For example, the court expressed concern about "how recognizing de facto parentage would affect a noncustodial biological parent's rights" — for instance, the biological father of the child in the case. The court also cited *Troxel* as it noted the concern that de facto parentage would interfere with "the fundamental nature of the rights of a biological parent."[63]

Ultimately, while courts in many states have adopted de facto parenthood or a similar concept, courts in some states have rejected such common law or equitable approaches.[64] The Wyoming court's reasoning is representative of the latter approach. (We return to de facto parenthood in the parentage materials in Chapter 9.)

II. Children's Rights?

Up to this point, we have focused on the rights of parents, and have seen that the American legal system ordinarily presumes that parents act in the best interest of their children. Why not look at things from the perspective of children? Why not assume that children have rights that can be asserted against the state or in ways that contravene their parents?

In many jurisdictions outside the U.S., analysis begins with the interests of the child rather than the rights of the parent. In this sense, parental authority is limited by children's interests. Rather than assume that fit parents act in their children's best interest in every aspect of life, the government exerts a greater role in ordering the parent-child relationship and in protecting the rights of the child. For example, some countries prohibit home schooling on the assumption that a child has a right to education that prepares her for citizenship. The parent, in that case, has no right to direct the child's upbringing and education through home schooling. Consistent

---

62. Id. at 919.

63. Id. at 919-20.

64. See, e.g., Jones v. Barlow, 154 P.3d 808, 811 (Utah 2007) (rejecting de facto parentage because it "would abrogate a portion of the [biological mother's] parental rights"); Titchenal v. Dexter, 693 A.2d 682 (Vt. 1997); Black v. Simms, 12 So. 3d 1140, 1143 (La. Ct. App. 2009) (rejecting doctrine because the "paramount right of a parent in the care, custody, and control of his or her child" can only be abrogated in "rare circumstances"). Two state high courts have overturned earlier decisions rejecting the doctrine. See Conover v. Conover, 146 A.3d 433, 447 (Md. 2016); Brooke S.B. v. Elizabeth A.C.C., 61 N.E.3d 488, 499. 499-500 (N.Y. 2016). On the constitutional issues raised by de facto parentage, see Joanna L. Grossman, Constitutional Parentage, 32 Constit. Comment. 307, 333-39 (2017). On the constitutional status of de facto parents, see Douglas NeJaime, The Constitution of Parenthood, 72 Stan. L. Rev. 261 (2020).

with this approach to parental authority, many countries recognize children's rights much more extensively than under U.S. law. While children's rights are certainly not coterminous with adults' rights, children have cognizable legal interests that their parents are not assumed to represent.

As we will see, there are pockets of U.S. law in which children wield rights against the state, and such rights can trump parental authority. But these areas are limited in number and scope. Ultimately, the U.S. legal system has generally been reluctant to extend "rights" to children, and instead largely reasons in terms of children's "interests." The following materials consider children's rights in American law by focusing on the relationship between the child and the state. When can the child assert a right that restricts state action? And when can the child assert a right that requires state action? First, we focus on children's rights to relationships, including parental and non-parental relationships. Second, we consider children's rights to protection and safety. We conclude by contemplating more robust accounts of children's rights observable in scholarly work and international human rights frameworks. This section's focus on children's rights provides important background before we address conflicts that arise when parental authority, children's interests, and state power point in different directions.

A. Relationship Rights

We have already seen that parents have constitutionally protected relationships with their children. But does that mean that children also have constitutionally protected relationships with their parents? The following case considers the status of non-marital children, or what the law long called "illegitimate" children. The common law for centuries did not recognize such children as having legally protected relationships with their parents, such that they could not claim the same rights that marital children could claim with respect to their parents. That changed in the second half of the twentieth century, when, in the wake of state-level reform efforts, the Supreme Court subjected laws that discriminated against non-marital children to heightened constitutional scrutiny. The following case is one of two landmark cases that the Court decided in 1968.

1. Parental Relationships

LEVY v. LOUISIANA
391 U.S. 68 (1968)

MR. JUSTICE DOUGLAS delivered the opinion of the Court.

Appellant sued on behalf of five illegitimate children to recover, under a Louisiana statute (La. Civ. Code Ann. Art. 2315 (Supp. 1967)) for two kinds of damages as a result of the wrongful death of their mother: (1) the damages to them for the loss of their mother; and (2) those based on the survival of a cause of action which the mother had at the time of her death for pain and suffering. Appellees are the doctor who treated her and the insurance company.

We assume in the present state of the pleadings that the mother, Louise Levy, gave birth to these five illegitimate children and that they lived with her; that she treated them as a parent would treat any other child; that she worked as a domestic servant to support them, taking them to church every Sunday and enrolling them, at her own expense, in a parochial school. The Louisiana District Court dismissed the suit. The Court of Appeal affirmed, holding that "child" in Article 2315 means "legitimate child," the denial to illegitimate children of "the right to recover" being "based on morals and general welfare because it discourages bringing children into the world out of wedlock."

The case is here on appeal. . . .

While a State has broad power when it comes to making classifications, it may not draw a line which constitutes an invidious discrimination against a particular class. Though the test has been variously stated, the end result is whether the line drawn is a rational one.

In applying the Equal Protection Clause to social and economic legislation, we give great latitude to the legislature in making classifications.

Even so, would a corporation, which is a "person," for certain purposes, within the meaning of the Equal Protection Clause be required to forgo recovery for wrongs done its interests because its incorporators were all bastards? However that might be, we have been extremely sensitive when it comes to basic civil rights and have not hesitated to strike down an invidious classification even though it had history and tradition on its side.

The rights asserted here involve the intimate, familial relationship between a child and his own mother. When the child's claim of damage for loss of his mother is in issue, why, in terms of "equal protection," should the tortfeasors go free merely because the child is illegitimate? Why should the illegitimate child be denied rights merely because of his birth out of wedlock? He certainly is subject to all the responsibilities of a citizen, including the payment of taxes and conscription under the Selective Service Act. How under our constitutional regime can he be denied correlative rights which other citizens enjoy?

Legitimacy or illegitimacy of birth has no relation to the nature of the wrong allegedly inflicted on the mother. These children, though illegitimate, were dependent on her; she cared for them and nurtured them; they were indeed hers in the biological and in the spiritual sense; in her death they suffered wrong in the sense that any dependent would.

We conclude that it is invidious to discriminate against them when no action, conduct, or demeanor of theirs is possibly relevant to the harm that was done the mother.

NOTES AND QUESTIONS

1. *"Illegitimacy" Laws. Levy* represented the beginning of a long line of cases addressing penalties against non-marital, parent-child relationships. The Court decided *Levy* at the same time it decided Glona v. American Guarantee & Liability Insurance Company.[65] Rather than featuring claims by children based on the death of their mother, *Glona* featured a claim by a mother based on the death of her son. Louisiana's wrongful death statute did not permit the parent of an "illegitimate" child to recover. Consistent with its reasoning in *Levy*, the Court held that the law violated the guarantee of equal protection.

In the years after *Levy* and *Glona*, the Court struck down laws that discriminated against non-marital children.[66] But the Court also upheld laws that disadvantaged "illegitimate" children — so long as the law did not create "an insurmountable barrier" to the non-marital child.[67] The Court ultimately settled on "intermediate scrutiny" as the proper level of review for "illegitimacy" laws, requiring that the challenged provision be "substantially related to . . . important state interests the statute is intended to promote."[68] Even under this rigorous standard, the Court allowed laws that distinguished between marital and non-marital children. For example, in Lalli v. Lalli, the Court upheld a New York statute that required "that the paternity of the father be declared in a judicial proceeding sometime before his death" in order for the child to inherit from the father.[69] The Court concluded that problems with "[p]roof of paternity . . . when the father is not part of a formal family unit" justified the additional requirement placed on nonmarital fathers.[70]

2. *A Right to Support?* As part of its "illegitimacy" jurisprudence, the Court ruled that non-marital children have a right to parental, and specifically paternal, support.[71] In a series of decisions, the Court struck down statutes of limitations that prevented non-marital children from seeking support from their fathers while they

---

65. 391 U.S. 73 (1968).

66. See, e.g., Trimble v. Gordon, 430 U.S. 762 (1977) (striking down statute that permitted marital children to inherit from both parents but allowed non-marital children to inherit only from their mothers); Jimenez v. Weinberger, 417 U.S. 628 (1974) (rejecting discrimination against nonmarital children in Social Security Act); Weber v. Aetna Cas. & Sur. Co., 406 U.S. 164 (1972) (striking down statute that prevented non-marital children from recovering worker's compensation benefits after their father's death).

67. See Labine v. Vincent, 401 U.S. 532, 539 (1971) (upholding Louisiana law barring "illegitimate" child from sharing equally in father's estate when father dies intestate).

68. Lalli v. Lalli, 439 U.S. 259, 275 (1978).

69. Id. at 267.

70. Id. at 269.

71. See Gomez v. Perez, 409 U.S. 535 (1973).

were minors.[72] Applying intermediate scrutiny, the Court in Clark v. Jeter found that the "6-year statute of limitations is not substantially related to Pennsylvania's interest in avoiding the litigation of stale or fraudulent claims."[73] The Court noted that a similar statute of limitations did not apply to paternity claims — that is, claims brought by a man seeking to establish his paternity.[74] And it explained that Pennsylvania had, during the course of the litigation, enacted an 18-year statute of limitations for paternity and support actions.[75] Of course, that development emerged in light of Congressional action that threatened states with loss of federal funding if they did not adopt statutes of limitations that ran through a child's minority.[76] Nonetheless, the Court read Pennsylvania's new statute as "a tacit concession that proof problems are not overwhelming."[77] We examine the issue of paternal support for non-marital children in Chapter 11.

3.   *"Illegitimacy" Discrimination Today.* Given that the Court first repudiated the discriminatory "illegitimacy" regime in the 1960s, one might assume that such discrimination no longer exists. But, in fact, laws continue to disadvantage non-marital children, vis-à-vis their marital counterparts. As Professor Solangel Maldonado describes:

> [D]espite statements to the contrary, the law continues to discriminate against nonmarital children, imposing economic, social, and psychic harms. First, federal and state laws still treat nonmarital children differently in a number of areas, including support for postsecondary education and rules of intestacy and citizenship. These laws place heavier economic burdens on nonmarital children than on their marital counterparts. These laws also signal to society that there is a material distinction between marital and nonmarital childbirth. Moreover, lawmakers and courts continue to express disapproval of nonmarital families, thereby reinforcing societal biases against nonmarital children.[78]

4.   *Unmarried Fathers.* As the Court's reasoning in Clark v. Jeter suggests, the non-marital child's right to support from her father corresponds with rights of the unmarried father to be recognized as a legal parent. Only a few years after the Court repudiated "illegitimacy" in *Levy* and *Glona*, it ruled in Stanley v. Illinois that the

---

72. See, e.g., Clark v. Jeter, 486 U.S. 456 (1988) (striking down six-year statute of limitations); Pickett v. Brown, 462 U.S. 1 (1983) (striking down two-year statute of limitations); Mills v. Habluetzel, 456 U.S. 91 (1982) (rejecting one-year statute of limitations).

73. 486 U.S. at 464.

74. Id.

75. Id. at 465.

76. Id.

77. Id.

78. Solangel Maldonado, Illegitimate Harm: Law, Stigma, and Discrimination against Nonmarital Children, 63 Fla. L. Rev. 345, 349 (2011).

government could not exclude unmarried fathers who had formed parent-child relationships from the legal definition of "parent."[79] We explore *Stanley* and other cases on the rights of unmarried fathers in Chapter 9.

5.   *A Right to Terminate a Parental Relationship? — Emancipation.* We have been focused on children's rights to legally protected relationships with their parents and to financial support from their parents. But what about children who seek not to cement, but instead to terminate, the relationship with their parents? Emancipation is the legal process by which children gain freedom from the care, custody, and control of their parents before the age of majority. Some of the rights commonly granted to a fully emancipated minor include the rights to enter into binding contracts, buy and sell property, give informed consent for medical care, and retain one's own earnings. However, emancipation also typically ends the child's right to parental support. In many cases, it is parents seeking to avoid financial responsibilities who claim that their minor child is emancipated.

Consider Nicholason v. Follweiler, a case in which a divorced, non custodial father sought to terminate his child support obligations for his 16-year-old son based on the argument that the son was emancipated.[80] The father relied on the fact that the child had dropped out of high school and did not seek approval from his mother, with whom he lived, to go out. After the trial court granted the father's petition, the mother appealed. The court faulted the lower court for "relying on the misplaced notion that a minor who quits high school is 'assumed' to be emancipated."[81] Instead, the court explained that "the touchstone of emancipation refers to the minor's establishment as a self-supporting individual independent of parental control. When a minor still has a need for care, custody and maintenance, the minor is not emancipated and the duty of support continues."[82] Because the child did not financially support himself and continued to live with his mother, the court observed that the trial court's order "ostensibly relieved both parents of their duty of support, but in actuality shifted the full support obligation to the Mother."[83] Accordingly, the court ruled that "the Father's support obligation should have continued."[84]

While laws vary by state, children can generally obtain emancipated status by getting married, joining the military, or securing a court order. In some states, minors may file their own petitions, while in others, they must ask a parent or "next friend" to file the petition. The majority of states have set sixteen as the minimum age for a minor to commence emancipation proceedings, although a few states have no minimum age

---

79. See 405 U.S. 645 (1972).
80. 735 A.2d 1275 (Pa. Super. Ct. 1999).
81. Id. at 1279.
82. Id. at 1278.
83. Id. at 1279.
84. Id.

requirement.[85] California has the lowest minimum age requirement in the country at fourteen years of age.[86]

Emancipation law in many states is controlled by statute.[87] Emancipation statutes often use the "best interests of the child" standard — the standard that appears throughout family law.[88] Modern emancipation statutes require minors to demonstrate an ability to support themselves financially for necessities such as food, clothing, and housing.[89] Many statutes also require that minors live apart from their parents to become emancipated.[90] In some states, emancipation law is governed by common law rather than statute. In New Jersey, for instance, courts look to all of the facts to determine whether the child has moved "beyond the sphere of influence and responsibility exercised by a parent and obtains an independent status on his or her own."[91] In doing so, courts examine similar factors as those codified by statutes, such as age, financial self-sufficiency, and the desire to live independently of parents.[92] Of course, an emancipated minor is still a minor for all purposes other than the parent-child relationship. For example, an emancipated minor still cannot vote before eighteen years of age or consume alcoholic beverages before turning twenty-one.

Parental notification is required in emancipation cases. But only some states require parental consent. Is a child's emancipation the equivalent of termination of the rights of the child's parents? If so, should emancipation require the parent's consent? If not, should it turn merely on a determination of a child's best interest? Or should a stronger showing — such as the parent's unfitness — be required? We address termination of parental rights in the next chapter.

What if a minor is seeking emancipation not for the purpose of independence but to be adopted by someone else? Consider the famous case of Shawn Russ (formerly known as Gregory Kingsley). Rachel Kingsley gave birth to Gregory when she was eighteen. At four, Gregory went to live with his father. Claiming that his father was abusive and an alcoholic, Gregory went back to live with his mother at eight. Eventually, she placed him in foster care. Eleven-year-old Gregory sued to terminate the parental rights of his biological parents and be adopted by George and Lizabeth Russ, the foster parents with whom he had lived for almost a year. In a high-profile ruling, a Florida court granted his

---

85. See, e.g., Kan. Stat. Ann. § 38-109 (2020).

86. Cal. Fam. Code § 7120(b)(1) (West 2020).

87. See, e.g., Cal. Fam. Code § 7120 (2020).

88. See, e.g., Cal. Fam. Code § 7122(a) (2020); Conn. Gen. Stat. Ann. § 46b-150b (2020).

89. See, e.g., Alaska Stat. § 09.55.590(a) (2020); Cal. Fam. Code § 7120(b)(3) (2020); Conn. Gen. Stat. Ann. § 46b-150b(3) (2020).

90. See, e.g., Alaska Stat. § 09.55.590(a) (2020).

91. Bishop v. Bishop, 671 A.2d 644, 646 (N.J. Super. Ct. Ch. Div. 1995).

92. Berks Cty. Children & Youth Servs. v. Rowan, 631 A.2d 615, 619 (Pa. Super. Ct. 1993).

petition.[93] Should children have standing to initiate abuse and neglect proceedings against their parents? The Florida Court of Appeal held that Gregory, as a minor, did not have the capacity to bring a termination of parental rights proceeding.[94] Nonetheless, the court concluded that the trial court's decision to allow Gregory to bring such a proceeding was harmless error since other parties, including the foster parents and the guardian ad litem, properly filed termination petitions on Gregory's behalf.[95]

When a media outlet caught up with Russ in 2012, he discussed the difficulties he experienced in dealing with both his relationship with his biological mother and his unexpected fame because of the case. "It took 28 years to come to terms with feeling abandoned by my mother," Russ admitted. After Rachel Kingsley's 2006 death, Russ dealt with regret over not connecting with her after the case. "She loved me," Russ realized. "My mother was human and she made mistakes." Even through his difficulties, Russ explained that the Russ family "never turned their back on me." That experience, he reported, "developed my understanding of what a family is."[96]

2. Non-Parental Relationships

Levy and its progeny were decided on equal protection, rather than due process, grounds. The Court did not rule that children have a liberty interest — a fundamental right protected as a matter of due process — with respect to the parental relationship. Should children have such a right? And might such rights extend beyond parents to other important figures in a child's life? While the "illegitimacy" cases focus on children's relationships with their parents, we have already seen that courts and legislatures have been asked to address children's relationships with individuals who are not their parents — grandparents, for example. As we saw in *Troxel*, parents have authority to prevent grandparents and other third parties from forming or maintaining relationships with their children. In that case, the Court found that Washington's third-party visitation statute violated the constitutional rights of the parent in the suit. What would it look like to approach this issue from the perspective of the child? When might a child have a right to a relationship with an adult? Justice Stevens contemplated children's liberty interests in his dissenting opinion in *Troxel*.

---

93. In re Kingsley, No. JU90-5245, 1992 WL 551484 (Fla. Cir. Ct. Oct. 21, 1992). See also Boy Is Granted 'Divorce' From Natural Parents, L.A. Times, Sept. 26, 1992, at A1.

94. Kingsley v. Kingsley, 623 So. 2d 780 (Fla. Dist. Ct. App. 1993).

95. Id. at 785.

96. See Lydia Warren, The Boy Who Divorced His Parents, Daily Mail (Dec. 13, 2012).

TROXEL V. GRANVILLE

530 U.S. 57 (2000)

JUSTICE STEVENS, dissenting. . . .

[T]he Washington Supreme Court's holding . . . that the Federal Constitution requires a showing of actual or potential "harm" to the child before a court may order visitation continued over a parent's objections . . . finds no support in this Court's case law. While, as the Court recognizes, the Federal Constitution certainly protects the parent-child relationship from arbitrary impairment by the State, we have never held that the parent's liberty interest in this relationship is so inflexible as to establish a rigid constitutional shield, protecting every arbitrary parental decision from any challenge absent a threshold finding of harm. The presumption that parental decisions generally serve the best interests of their children is sound, and clearly in the normal case the parent's interest is paramount. But even a fit parent is capable of treating a child like a mere possession.

Cases like this do not present a bipolar struggle between the parents and the State over who has final authority to determine what is in a child's best interests. There is at a minimum a third individual, whose interests are implicated in every case to which the statute applies — the child.

It has become standard practice in our substantive due process jurisprudence to begin our analysis with an identification of the "fundamental" liberty interests implicated by the challenged state action. My colleagues are of course correct to recognize that the right of a parent to maintain a relationship with his or her child is among the interests included most often in the constellation of liberties protected through the Fourteenth Amendment. . . .

[T]hese interests have never been seen to be without limits. . . .

A parent's rights with respect to her child . . . are limited by the existence of an actual, developed relationship with a child, and are tied to the presence or absence of some embodiment of family. These limitations have arisen, not simply out of the definition of parenthood itself, but because of this Court's assumption that a parent's interests in a child must be balanced against the State's long-recognized interests as *parens patriae*, and, critically, the child's own complementary interest in preserving relationships that serve her welfare and protection.

While this Court has not yet had occasion to elucidate the nature of a child's liberty interests in preserving established familial or family-like bonds, it seems to me extremely likely that, to the extent parents and families have fundamental liberty interests in preserving such intimate relationships, so, too, do children have these interests, and so, too, must their interests be balanced in the equation. At a minimum, our prior cases recognizing that children are, generally speaking, constitutionally protected actors require that this Court reject any suggestion that when it comes to parental rights, children are so much chattel. The constitutional protection against arbitrary state interference with parental rights should not be extended to prevent the States from protecting children against the arbitrary exercise of parental authority that is not in fact motivated by an interest in the welfare of the child.

This is not, of course, to suggest that a child's liberty interest in maintaining contact with a particular individual is to be treated invariably as on a par with that child's parents' contrary interests. . . .

[W]e should recognize that there may be circumstances in which a child has a stronger interest at stake than mere protection from serious harm caused by the termination of visitation by a "person" other than a parent. The almost infinite variety of family relationships that pervade our ever-changing society strongly counsel against the creation by this Court of a constitutional rule that treats a biological parent's liberty interest in the care and supervision of her child as an isolated right that may be exercised arbitrarily. It is indisputably the business of the States, rather than a federal court employing a national standard, to assess in the first instance the relative importance of the conflicting interests that give rise to disputes such as this. Far from guaranteeing that parents' interests will be trammeled in the sweep of cases arising under the statute, the Washington law merely gives an individual — with whom a child may have an established relationship — the procedural right to ask the State to act as arbiter, through the entirely well-known best-interests standard, between the parent's protected interests and the child's. . . .

NOTES AND QUESTIONS

1. *Children as Property.* Justice Stevens worries that the *Troxel* Court's decision may be understood to grow out of a view of children as "chattel." Do you agree? Did Justice O'Connor appropriately consider the children's interests?

2. *Children's Liberty Interests.* Justice Stevens explains that the Court "has not yet had occasion to elucidate the nature of a child's liberty interests in preserving established familial or family-like bonds," but he assumes that some such interest must exist — clearly with respect to the parent-child relationship and also with respect to some non-parental relationships. What would lead him to such a conclusion? From where does the liberty interest he imagines derive? Does *Levy* support his view?

3. *Children's Relationship Rights.* Family law scholars have urged courts and legislatures to recognize children's rights to certain relationships. For example, Professors Anne Dailey and Laura Rosenbury argue that "taking children's broader interests seriously . . . supports giving children greater access to important adults in

their lives."[97] The situations they contemplate go well beyond the grandparent scenario in *Troxel*:

> Children's relationships with paid caregivers might be recognized in certain contexts, for example. The [existing legal] framework treats such relationships as mere employment relationships, ignoring the close bonds that children may form with their caregivers. Our framework instead seeks to foster those bonds, although not necessarily by bestowing legally enforceable rights on paid caregivers. Instead, courts might take into account children's interests in continued access to former caregivers when making custody and visitation decisions.
>
> Our approach also better promotes children's interests in their relationships with foster parents. Under current law, foster parents — even where there are kinship ties or placement has been since infancy — have few rights. The Supreme Court has indicated that any interest a foster parent might have is inferior to the interests of biological parents. Yet these relationships are quite important from the perspective of the child. When a child is placed in foster care at birth, or has resided with foster care parents for an extended period of time, the attachment to a foster parent from the child's point of view may be indistinguishable from the attachment to any other parental figure. In such circumstances, efforts can and should be made to maintain a child's primary attachment, while at the same time recognizing the child's interest in maintaining ties to his or her biological parents. Foster parents are not a homogenous group; each case will present different issues depending on the type of proceeding, the kinship relationship, the duration of the foster care, and other factors. Our framework's child-centric approach does not guarantee that a child will always have access to a former foster parent, but rather that children's broader interests in these relationships will be taken into account when a court is determining custody or visitation issues.[98]

Dailey and Rosenbury's focus on the child's perspective leads them to view some relationships as protected in ways that current law rejects.

Professors Clare Huntington and Elizabeth Scott, in contrast, see child-centered rationales for authorizing parents to limit children's relationships with others.

> [C]ourt-ordered contact with a third party overrides the decision of the adult who bears full child-rearing responsibility, with little reason to believe that the court will make a better decision. A parent is better positioned than a judge to assess what third-party contact, if any, is best for the child. In the typical case, a parent's knowledge of the child and affective bonds of attachment will lead to a decision in the child's interest. Further,

---

97. Anne C. Dailey & Laura A. Rosenbury, The New Law of the Child, 127 Yale L.J. 1448, 1487 (2018).
98. Id. at 1513–14.

allowing ongoing contact over the parent's objection likely will strain the parent-child relationship, the stability of which is central to healthy child development. Separate from the substantive outcome, the deferential standard protects the child from the predictable stress of a protracted and high-conflict legal dispute. Finally, if the intrusion allows contact with a third party (who lacks any responsibility for the child's care) over the parent's objections, the parent may understandably feel resentment, potentially affecting the parent's enthusiasm for fulfilling those obligations that society has imposed on her . . . .

This analysis makes clear that child wellbeing is served by the deferential standard, which overrides the parent's objection only when the decision threatens serious harm to the child.[99]

What do you think? Should children have a right to maintain a relationship with a non-parental caregiver? Over the parent's objection? Does it depend on the child's age? What if the caregiver is paid? This takes us back to the materials on non-parental visitation, but from the perspective of the child rather than the adult.

PROBLEM

Lisa, a single mother, works full-time and has to depend on her sister, Monica, for help. Every weekday morning at 8:00 a.m., Lisa drops her 3-year-old daughter, Elle, at Monica's house. Monica watches Elle all day. Lisa picks up Elle around 5:30 p.m. each day. Monica also cares for her own children — 18-month-old Lucy and 3-year-old Lucas. Monica has been watching Elle during the day, Monday through Friday, since Elle was two months old. Lisa pays her sister $200 per week — much less than she would otherwise pay for childcare. She also buys Monica's groceries periodically, and she takes Monica and the kids out for a meal every month.

A few weeks before Elle's fourth birthday, Lisa and Monica have a huge fight. They stop speaking, and Lisa stops bringing Elle to Monica's house. Instead, Lisa finds another family member to watch Elle three days per week and pays for daycare the other two days. After a month of this situation, Monica files a petition in superior court seeking visitation with Elle. Lisa opposes the petition. The relevant statute allows an individual who has formed a "significant relationship with a child" to seek visitation and authorizes a court to grant such visitation when not doing so would be "detrimental to the child." The state also maintains a statute authorizing a judge to appoint an attorney for the child in any case where the judge finds that the child's interests are not otherwise adequately represented.

---

99. Clare Huntington & Elizabeth S. Scott, Conceptualizing Legal Childhood in the Twenty-First Century, 118 Mich. L. Rev. 1371, 1423-24 (2020).

You are the judge assigned to the case. What is your instinct regarding whether Monica should have visitation with Elle over Lisa's objection? Which way do you think Elle's interests point? What questions would you ask the parties at a hearing? Would you appoint an attorney to represent Elle?

B. A Right to Protection?

Up to this point, we have focused on children's interests in relationships of care and support. The children in *Levy*, according to the Court, "were dependent on [their mother]; she cared for them and nurtured them." And in his *Troxel* dissent, Justice Stevens focused on a child's interest "in preserving relationships that serve her welfare and protection." But what about a parental relationship that undermines a child's welfare and protection? With *Prince*, we considered when the state may have authority to intervene to protect a child. Now we ask when the state may not simply have authority but an affirmative obligation to intervene on a child's behalf. This issue raises specific questions of children's rights and more general questions of constitutional law. It also implicates the child welfare system, which we address in the next chapter.

DeShaney v. Winnebago County Department of Social Services
489 U.S. 189 (1989)

Chief Justice Rehnquist delivered the opinion of the Court.

Petitioner is a boy who was beaten and permanently injured by his father, with whom he lived. Respondents are social workers and other local officials who received complaints that petitioner was being abused by his father and had reason to believe that this was the case, but nonetheless did not act to remove petitioner from his father's custody. Petitioner sued respondents claiming that their failure to act deprived him of his liberty in violation of the Due Process Clause of the Fourteenth Amendment to the United States Constitution. We hold that it did not.

I

The facts of this case are undeniably tragic. Petitioner Joshua DeShaney was born in 1979. In 1980, a Wyoming court granted his parents a divorce and awarded custody of Joshua to his father, Randy DeShaney. The father shortly thereafter moved to Neenah, a city located in Winnebago County, Wisconsin, taking the infant Joshua with him. There he entered into a second marriage, which also ended in divorce.

The Winnebago County authorities first learned that Joshua DeShaney might be a victim of child abuse in January 1982, when his father's second wife complained to the police, at the time of their divorce, that he had previously "hit the boy causing marks and [was] a prime case for child abuse." The Winnebago County Department of Social Services (DSS) interviewed the father, but he denied the accusations, and DSS did not pursue them further. In January 1983, Joshua was admitted to a local hospital with multiple bruises and abrasions. The examining physician suspected child abuse and notified DSS, which immediately obtained an order from a Wisconsin juvenile court placing Joshua in the temporary custody of the hospital. Three days later, the county convened an ad hoc "Child Protection Team" — consisting of a pediatrician, a psychologist, a police detective, the county's lawyer, several DSS caseworkers, and various hospital personnel — to consider Joshua's situation. At this meeting, the Team decided that there was insufficient evidence of child abuse to retain Joshua in the custody of the court. The Team did, however, decide to recommend several measures to protect Joshua, including enrolling him in a preschool program, providing his father with certain counselling services, and encouraging his father's girlfriend to move out of the home. Randy DeShaney entered into a voluntary agreement with DSS in which he promised to cooperate with them in accomplishing these goals.

Based on the recommendation of the Child Protection Team, the juvenile court dismissed the child protection case and returned Joshua to the custody of his father. A month later, emergency room personnel called the DSS caseworker handling Joshua's case to report that he had once again been treated for suspicious injuries. The caseworker concluded that there was no basis for action. For the next six months, the caseworker made monthly visits to the DeShaney home, during which she observed a number of suspicious injuries on Joshua's head; she also noticed that he had not been enrolled in school, and that the girlfriend had not moved out. The caseworker dutifully recorded these incidents in her files, along with her continuing suspicions that someone in the DeShaney household was physically abusing Joshua, but she did nothing more. In November 1983, the emergency room notified DSS that Joshua had been treated once again for injuries that they believed to be caused by child abuse. On the caseworker's next two visits to the DeShaney home, she was told that Joshua was too ill to see her. Still DSS took no action.

In March 1984, Randy DeShaney beat 4-year-old Joshua so severely that he fell into a life-threatening coma. Emergency brain surgery revealed a series of hemorrhages caused by traumatic injuries to the head inflicted over a long period of time. Joshua did not die, but he suffered brain damage so severe that he is expected to spend the rest of his life confined to an institution for the profoundly retarded. Randy DeShaney was subsequently tried and convicted of child abuse.

Joshua and his mother brought this action under 42 U.S.C. § 1983 in the United States District Court for the Eastern District of Wisconsin against respondents Winnebago County, DSS, and various individual employees of DSS. The complaint alleged that respondents had deprived Joshua of his liberty without due process of law, in violation of his rights under the Fourteenth Amendment, by failing to intervene to protect him against a risk of violence at his father's hands of which they knew or should have known. The District Court granted summary judgment for respondents.

The Court of Appeals for the Seventh Circuit affirmed . . . .

II

The Due Process Clause of the Fourteenth Amendment provides that "[n]o State shall . . . deprive any person of life, liberty, or property, without due process of law." Petitioners contend that the State deprived Joshua of his liberty interest in "free[dom] from . . . unjustified intrusions on personal security," by failing to provide him with adequate protection against his father's violence. The claim is one invoking the substantive rather than the procedural component of the Due Process Clause; petitioners do not claim that the State denied Joshua protection without according him appropriate procedural safeguards, but that it was categorically obligated to protect him in these circumstances.

But nothing in the language of the Due Process Clause itself requires the State to protect the life, liberty, and property of its citizens against invasion by private actors. The Clause is phrased as a limitation on the State's power to act, not as a guarantee of certain minimal levels of safety and security. It forbids the State itself to deprive individuals of life, liberty, or property without "due process of law," but its language cannot fairly be extended to impose an affirmative obligation on the State to ensure that those interests do not come to harm through other means. Nor does history support such an expansive reading of the constitutional text. Like its counterpart in the Fifth Amendment, the Due Process Clause of the Fourteenth Amendment was intended to prevent government "from abusing [its] power, or employing it as an instrument of oppression[.]" Its purpose was to protect the people from the State, not to ensure that the State protected them from each other. The Framers were content to leave the extent of governmental obligation in the latter area to the democratic political processes.

Consistent with these principles, our cases have recognized that the Due Process Clauses generally confer no affirmative right to governmental aid, even where such aid may be necessary to secure life, liberty, or property interests of which the government itself may not deprive the individual. . . . If the Due Process Clause does not require the State to provide its citizens with particular protective services, it follows that the State cannot be held liable under the Clause for injuries that could have been averted had it chosen to provide them. As a general matter, then, we conclude that a State's failure to protect an individual against private violence simply does not constitute a violation of the Due Process Clause.

Petitioners contend, however, that even if the Due Process Clause imposes no affirmative obligation on the State to provide the general public with adequate protective services, such a duty may arise out of certain "special relationships" created or assumed by the State with respect to particular individuals. Petitioners argue that such a "special relationship" existed here because the State knew that Joshua faced a special danger of abuse at his father's hands, and specifically proclaimed, by word and by deed, its intention to protect him against that danger. Having actually undertaken to protect Joshua from this danger — which petitioners concede the State played no part in creating — the State acquired an affirmative "duty," enforceable through the Due Process Clause, to do so in a reasonably competent fashion. Its failure to discharge that duty, so the argument goes, was an abuse of governmental power that so "shocks the conscience" as to constitute a substantive due process violation.

We reject this argument. It is true that in certain limited circumstances the Constitution imposes upon the State affirmative duties of care and protection with respect to particular individuals. . . . [T]he Eighth Amendment's prohibition against cruel and unusual punishment, made applicable to the States through the Fourteenth Amendment's Due Process Clause, requires the State to provide adequate medical care to incarcerated prisoners. . . . [B]ecause the prisoner is unable " 'by reason of the deprivation of his liberty [to] care for himself,' " it is only " 'just' " that the State be required to care for him.

In *Youngberg v. Romeo*, 457 U.S. 307 (1982), we extended this analysis beyond the Eighth Amendment setting, holding that the substantive component of the Fourteenth Amendment's Due Process Clause requires the State to provide involuntarily committed mental patients with such services as are necessary to ensure their "reasonable safety" from themselves and others. . . .

But these cases afford petitioners no help. Taken together, they stand only for the proposition that when the State takes a person into its custody and holds him there against his will, the Constitution imposes upon it a corresponding duty to assume some responsibility for his safety and general well-being. The rationale for this principle is simple enough: when the State by the affirmative exercise of its power so restrains an individual's liberty that it renders him unable to care for himself, and at the same time fails to provide for his basic human needs — *e.g.*, food, clothing, shelter, medical care, and reasonable safety — it transgresses the substantive limits on state action set by the Eighth Amendment and the Due Process Clause. The affirmative duty to protect arises not from the State's knowledge of the individual's predicament or from its expressions of intent to help him, but from the limitation which it has imposed on his freedom to act on his own behalf. In the substantive due process analysis, it is the State's affirmative act of restraining the individual's freedom to act on his own behalf — through incarceration, institutionalization, or other similar restraint of personal liberty — which is the "deprivation of liberty" triggering the protections of the Due Process Clause, not its failure to act to protect his liberty interests against harms inflicted by other means. . . .

Petitioners concede that the harms Joshua suffered occurred not while he was in the State's custody, but while he was in the custody of his natural father, who was in no sense a state actor. While the State may have been aware of the dangers that Joshua faced in the free world, it played no part in their creation, nor did it do anything to render him any more vulnerable to them. That the State once took temporary custody of Joshua does not alter the analysis, for when it returned him to his father's custody, it placed him in no worse position than that in which he would have been had it not acted at all; the State does not become the permanent guarantor of an individual's safety by having once offered him shelter. Under these circumstances, the State had no constitutional duty to protect Joshua.

It may well be that, by voluntarily undertaking to protect Joshua against a danger it concededly played no part in creating, the State acquired a duty under state tort law to provide him with adequate protection against that danger. But the claim here is based on the Due Process Clause of the Fourteenth Amendment, which, as we have said many times, does not transform every tort committed by a state actor into a constitutional violation. A State may, through its courts and legislatures, impose such affirmative duties of care and protection upon its agents as it wishes. But not "all common-law duties owed by government actors were . . . constitutionalized by the Fourteenth Amendment." Because . . . the State had no constitutional duty to protect Joshua against his father's violence, its failure to do so — though calamitous in hindsight — simply does not constitute a violation of the Due Process Clause.

Judges and lawyers, like other humans, are moved by natural sympathy in a case like this to find a way for Joshua and his mother to receive adequate compensation for the grievous harm inflicted upon them. But before yielding to that impulse, it is well to remember once again that the harm was inflicted not by the State of Wisconsin, but by Joshua's father. The most that can be said of the state functionaries in this case is that they stood by and did nothing when suspicious circumstances dictated a more active role for them. In defense of them it must also be said that had they moved too soon to take custody of the son away from the father, they would likely have been met with charges of improperly intruding into the parent-child relationship, charges based on the same Due Process Clause that forms the basis for the present charge of failure to provide adequate protection.

The people of Wisconsin may well prefer a system of liability which would place upon the State and its officials the responsibility for failure to act in situations such as the present one. They may create such a system . . . by changing the tort law of the State in accordance with the regular lawmaking process. But they should not have it thrust upon them by this Court's expansion of the Due Process Clause of the Fourteenth Amendment.

Affirmed.

JUSTICE BRENNAN, with whom JUSTICE MARSHALL and JUSTICE BLACKMUN join, dissenting.

"The most that can be said of the state functionaries in this case," the Court today concludes, "is that they stood by and did nothing when suspicious circumstances dictated a more active role for them." Because I believe that this description of respondents' conduct tells only part of the story and that, accordingly, the Constitution itself "dictated a more active role" for respondents in the circumstances presented here, I cannot agree that respondents had no constitutional duty to help Joshua DeShaney.

It may well be, as the Court decides, that the Due Process Clause as construed by our prior cases creates no general right to basic governmental services. That, however, is not the question presented here; indeed, that question was not raised in the complaint, urged on appeal, presented in the petition for certiorari, or addressed in the briefs on the merits. No one, in short, has asked the Court to proclaim that, as a general matter, the Constitution safeguards positive as well as negative liberties.

This is more than a quibble over dicta; it is a point about perspective, having substantive ramifications. In a constitutional setting that distinguishes sharply between action and inaction, one's characterization of the misconduct alleged under § 1983 may effectively decide the case. . . .

The Court's baseline is the absence of positive rights in the Constitution and a concomitant suspicion of any claim that seems to depend on such rights. From this perspective, the DeShaneys' claim is first and foremost about inaction (the failure, here, of respondents to take steps to protect Joshua), and only tangentially about action (the establishment of a state program specifically designed to help children like Joshua). And from this perspective, holding these Wisconsin officials liable — where the only difference between this case and one involving a general claim to protective services is Wisconsin's establishment and operation of a program to protect children — would seem to punish an effort that we should seek to promote.

I would begin from the opposite direction. I would focus first on the action that Wisconsin *has* taken with respect to Joshua and children like him, rather than on the actions that the State failed to take. . . .

[T]o the Court, the only fact that seems to count as an "affirmative act of restraining the individual's freedom to act on his own behalf" is direct physical control. I would not, however, give *Youngberg* . . . such a stingy scope. I would recognize, as the Court apparently cannot, that "the State's knowledge of [an] individual's predicament [and] its expressions of intent to help him" can amount to a "limitation . . . on his freedom to act on his own behalf" or to obtain help from others. Thus, I would read *Youngberg* . . . to stand for the much more generous proposition that, if a State cuts off private sources of aid and then refuses aid itself, it cannot wash its hands of the harm that results from its inaction. . . .

Wisconsin has established a child-welfare system specifically designed to help children like Joshua. Wisconsin law places upon the local departments of social services such as respondent (DSS or Department) a duty to investigate reported instances of child abuse. See Wis. Stat. § 48.981(3) (1987-1988). While other governmental bodies and private persons are largely responsible for the reporting of possible cases of child abuse, see § 48.981(2), Wisconsin law channels all such reports to the local departments of social services for evaluation and, if necessary, further action. § 48.981(3). Even when it is the sheriff's office or police department that receives a report of suspected child abuse, that report is referred to local social services departments for action, see § 48.981(3)(a); the only exception to this occurs when the reporter fears for the child's *immediate* safety. § 48.981(3)(b). In this way, Wisconsin law invites — indeed, directs — citizens and other governmental entities to depend on local departments of social services such as respondent to protect children from abuse.

The specific facts before us bear out this view of Wisconsin's system of protecting children. Each time someone voiced a suspicion that Joshua was being abused, that information was relayed to the Department for investigation and possible action. . . .

Even more telling than these examples is the Department's control over the decision whether to take steps to protect a particular child from suspected abuse. While many different people contributed information and advice to this decision, it was up to the people at DSS to make the ultimate decision (subject to the approval of the local government's corporation counsel) whether to disturb the family's current arrangements. When Joshua first appeared at a local hospital with injuries signaling physical abuse, for example, it was DSS that made the decision to take him into temporary custody for the purpose of studying his situation — and it was DSS, acting in conjunction with the corporation counsel, that returned him to his father. Unfortunately for Joshua DeShaney, the buck effectively stopped with the Department.

In these circumstances, a private citizen, or even a person working in a government agency other than DSS, would doubtless feel that her job was done as soon as she had reported her suspicions of child abuse to DSS. Through its child-welfare program, in other words, the State of Wisconsin has relieved ordinary citizens and governmental bodies other than the Department of any sense of obligation to do anything more than report their suspicions of child abuse to DSS. If DSS ignores or dismisses these suspicions, no one will step in to fill the gap. Wisconsin's child-protection program thus effectively confined Joshua DeShaney within the walls of Randy DeShaney's violent home until such time as DSS took action to remove him. Conceivably, then, children like Joshua are made worse off by the existence of this program when the persons and entities charged with carrying it out fail to do their jobs.

It simply belies reality, therefore, to contend that the State "stood by and did nothing" with respect to Joshua. Through its child-protection program, the State actively intervened in Joshua's life and, by virtue of this intervention, acquired ever more certain knowledge that Joshua was in grave danger. . . .

As the Court today reminds us, "the Due Process Clause of the Fourteenth Amendment was intended to prevent government 'from abusing [its] power, or employing it as an instrument of oppression.'" My disagreement with the Court arises from its failure to see that inaction can be every bit as abusive of power as action, that oppression can result when a State undertakes a vital duty and then ignores it. Today's opinion construes the Due Process Clause to permit a State to displace private sources of protection and then, at the critical moment, to shrug its shoulders and turn away from the harm that it has promised to try to prevent. Because I cannot agree that our Constitution is indifferent to such indifference, I respectfully dissent.

JUSTICE BLACKMUN, dissenting.

Today, the Court purports to be the dispassionate oracle of the law, unmoved by "natural sympathy." But, in this pretense, the Court itself retreats into a sterile formalism which prevents it from recognizing either the facts of the case before it or the legal norms that should apply to those facts. . . . [T]he facts here involve not mere passivity, but active state intervention in the life of Joshua DeShaney — intervention that triggered a fundamental duty to aid the boy once the State learned of the severe danger to which he was exposed.

The Court fails to recognize this duty because it attempts to draw a sharp and rigid line between action and inaction. But such formalistic reasoning has no place in the interpretation of the broad and stirring Clauses of the Fourteenth Amendment. . . .

Poor Joshua! Victim of repeated attacks by an irresponsible, bullying, cowardly, and intemperate father, and abandoned by respondents who placed him in a dangerous predicament and who knew or learned what was going on, and yet did essentially nothing except, as the Court revealingly observes, "dutifully recorded these incidents in [their] files." It is a sad commentary upon American life, and constitutional principles — so full of late of patriotic fervor and proud proclamations about "liberty and justice for all" — that this child, Joshua DeShaney, now is assigned to live out the remainder of his life profoundly retarded. Joshua and his mother, as petitioners here, deserve — but now are denied by this Court — the opportunity to have the facts of their case considered in the light of the constitutional protection that 42 U.S.C. § 1983 is meant to provide.

NOTES AND QUESTIONS

---

1. *Action Versus Inaction.* The dissenting justices see action where the majority sees inaction. Justice Brennan asserts that if the state creates a system in which private actors are instructed to report to government officials so that those actors can intervene on behalf of the abused child, then the state has assumed authority over the child's welfare and thus has obligations to the child. On this view, Joshua DeShaney is more analogous to the individual in state custody than the majority admits. Do you agree?

2. *Positive Rights.* The Court rejects Joshua DeShaney's claim on the assumption that the Constitution confers only negative rights. Do the dissenting justices believe the Constitution furnishes positive rights? Even if adults do not enjoy positive rights under the Constitution, should we approach the rights of children differently? Does the government have an affirmative obligation to ensure children's safety? Support? Health? Education? If so, what is the basis of that obligation? If not, why not? Note that some state constitutions provide affirmative rights, including rights that apply to children.[100] For example, in a provision adopted in 1938, the New York constitution requires the government to provide "aid, care and support [to] the needy."[101] The New Jersey constitution requires the government to "provide for the maintenance and support of a thorough and efficient system of free public schools for the instruction of all the children of the State between the ages of five and eighteen years."[102]

Is the distinction between negative and positive rights clear? Scholars not only have criticized understandings of the Constitution that foreclose affirmative rights, but also have questioned the stability and coherence of the very distinction between negative and positive rights. Professors Stephen Holmes and Cass Sunstein show that many rights that are considered "negative" rights "presuppose taxpayer funding of effective supervisory machinery for monitoring and enforcement."[103] On this view, because rights frequently require affirmative state support and resources, it is not clear that positive rights are in tension with existing constitutional understandings.

3. *A Scholarly Perspective.* Family law scholars have long criticized U.S. law for failing to adequately recognize and protect children's rights. Consider again the perspective of Professors Anne Dailey and Laura Rosenbury, who urge a "new law of the child" more attuned to children's perspective:

> [O]ur approach highlights that children's lives are more than lesser versions of adult lives or way stations on the road to autonomous adulthood. Our focus on children's interests beyond dependency and autonomy takes account of the unique strengths and capacities of children, as well as the special vulnerabilities that distinguish human experience in this early stage of life. By focusing on children's lives in the here and now, we aim to free the field of children and law from the ideal of the autonomous, freely acting adult individual. Our approach takes seriously the idea of children as individuals in their own right, worthy of respect, even as they are dependent in varying ways upon the adults in their lives. . . .

---

100. See Emily J. Zackin, Looking for Rights in All the Wrong Places: Why State Constitutions Contain America's Positive Rights (2013).

101. N.Y. Const., art. XVII, § 1.

102. N.J. Const., art. VIII, § IV, ¶ 1.

103. Stephen Holmes & Cass R. Sunstein, The Cost of Rights: Why Liberty Depends on Taxes 44 (2000).

[O]ur approach supports the recognition and enforcement of children's affirmative rights rooted in their broader interests in the here and now. The new law of the child rejects the Supreme Court's decision in *DeShaney v. Winnebago County Department of Social Services*, which . . . ignor[ed] the shared responsibilities of both parents and the state to further children's interest in protection from harm at the hands of custodial caregivers. . . . [We] would recognize children's affirmative rights as children to certain goods and services essential to furthering their broader interests. . . .

Our approach also . . . emphasize[s] that children often have the capacity to make decisions for themselves at the same time that they are dependent upon adults. . . .

The new law of the child . . . lays the foundation for revising or overruling many foundational Supreme Court decisions. . . . In *Prince* . . . , our approach would consider the child's broad interests in her relationship with her guardian, in expressing her religious identity, and in engaging in the world beyond home and school. . . . [I]n *Troxel* . . . , our framework would make children's interests in maintaining relationships with nonparental figures the centerpiece of the analysis. . . .[104]

4.   *Reforming State Policy.* Imagine that the Court decided the case differently and held the state responsible for Joshua's injuries. How might the state change its practices and policies in light of such a ruling? What actions can the state take to prevent future cases like Joshua's? Would state actors do more to intervene in families where a child may be harmed? That is, would the state be more likely to remove children? Or would the state do much less, given that its obligations would arise only if it established a child welfare system that purported to protect children from abuse?

5.   *DeShaney's Implications.* Even though *DeShaney* arose in the child abuse context, its effects have been felt in other areas, including most prominently in cases of intimate partner violence. In Town of Castle Rock v. Gonzales, which is excerpted in Chapter 3, the Supreme Court considered a civil rights action that Jessica Gonzales filed after police failed to enforce a restraining order against her husband during the time that he kidnapped and killed their three daughters.[105] In *DeShaney*, the Court had not decided whether the Wisconsin child protective statutes conferred on Joshua an entitlement to protective services that enjoyed due process protections.[106] But in *Town of Castle Rock*, the Court reached the analogous question, concluding that Colorado law did not confer on recipients of domestic abuse restraining orders an entitlement to enforcement. Even though Colorado maintained a statute requiring police to "use every reasonable means to enforce a restraining order," the Court, in an opinion by Justice Scalia, reasoned that, given the "well-established tradition of police discretion,"

---

104. Dailey & Rosenbury, supra note 97, at 1451-55.
105. 545 U.S. 748 (2005).
106. 489 U.S. at 195 n.2.

"[w]e do not believe that . . . Colorado law truly made enforcement of restraining orders *mandatory*."[107] Going further, the Court concluded that even if Jessica enjoyed an entitlement created by state law, "it is by no means clear that an individual entitlement of a restraining order could constitute a 'property' interest for purposes of the Due Process Clause."[108]

What is the value of a restraining order if there is no guarantee of enforcement? How would the policies and practices of police departments change if the Court had found that Jessica possessed an entitlement that gave rise to due process protections?

C. An International Perspective on Children's Rights

In many ways, the American approach to children's rights is distinctive. Other countries more extensively and explicitly protect children's rights. So too do international human rights frameworks. The leading international treaty on children's rights, the United Nations Convention on the Rights of the Child, sets out rights that nations must guarantee to children.[109] It includes provisions that are familiar from an American perspective. For example, the Convention identifies "the best interests of the child" as "the primary consideration" in "actions concerning children," and it requires that nations "respect the rights and duties of the parents . . . to provide direction to the child in the exercise of his or her right in a manner consistent with the evolving capacities of the child."[110]

The Convention also includes a number of negative rights for children. For instance, nations must "respect the right of the child to freedom of thought, conscience and religion."[111] And they must "ensure that a child shall not be separated from his or her parents against their will, except when competent authorities subject to judicial review determine . . . that such separation is necessary for the best interests of the child."[112]

The Convention also includes positive rights, such as rights to healthcare, education, and "a standard of living adequate for the child's physical, mental, spiritual, moral and social development."[113] In contrast to the logic of *DeShaney*, the Convention requires the government to "take all appropriate legislative, administrative, social and educational measures to protect the child from all forms of physical

---

107. 545 U.S. at 760.
108. Id. at 766.
109. United Nations Convention on the Rights of the Child, Nov. 20, 1989, 1577 U.N.T.S. 3.
110. Id. arts. 3, 14.
111. Id. art. 14.
112. Id. art. 9.
113. Id. arts. 24, 27, 28.

or mental violence, injury or abuse, neglect or negligent treatment, maltreatment or exploitation, including sexual abuse, while in the care of parent(s), legal guardian(s) or any other person who has the care of the child."[114] The Convention also contemplates support that must be provided to families, requiring nations to "take all appropriate measures to ensure that children of working parents have the right to benefit from child-care services and facilities for which they are eligible."[115] As a general matter, the Convention places on nations an obligation to implement "economic, social and cultural rights . . . to the maximum extent of their available resources."[116]

Almost 200 countries are parties to the Convention on the Rights of the Child. This includes every member state of the United Nations except the U.S. While the U.S. helped draft the Convention and the U.S. Ambassador to the United Nations signed the Convention, the U.S. has not ratified the Convention. Conservative opposition to the Convention has focused both on general resistance to the U.N. (as an elite, international organization) and on concerns about parental rights. Why would parental rights advocates oppose U.S. ratification of the Convention?

III. Conflicts Among Child, Parent, and State

Up to this point, we have devoted significant attention to parental rights — which, generally, U.S. law robustly protects — and children's rights — which, generally, U.S. law does much less to protect. We also have seen that the state has an interest as a super-parent of sorts, grounded in its *parens patriae* power. Often the interests of the parent, the child, and the state align. But what happens when they do not? The following cases present concrete settings in which conflicts among parents, children, and the state have occurred and raise the question of how to weigh parental rights, children's interests, and state prerogatives.

A. Education

WISCONSIN V. YODER
406 U.S. 205 (1972)

Mr. Chief Justice Burger delivered the opinion of the Court.

On petition of the State of Wisconsin, we granted the writ of certiorari in this case to review a decision of the Wisconsin Supreme Court holding that respondents'

---

114. Id. art. 19.
115. Id. art. 18.
116. Id. art. 4.

convictions for violating the State's compulsory school-attendance law were invalid under the Free Exercise Clause of the First Amendment. . . . For the reasons hereafter stated we affirm the judgment of the Supreme Court of Wisconsin.

Respondents Jonas Yoder and Wallace Miller are members of the Old Order Amish religion, and respondent Adin Yutzy is a member of the Conservative Amish Mennonite Church. . . . Wisconsin's compulsory school-attendance law required them to cause their children to attend public or private school until reaching age 16 but the respondents declined to send their children, ages 14 and 15, to public school after they complete the eighth grade. The children were not enrolled in any private school, or within any recognized exception to the compulsory-attendance law, and they are conceded to be subject to the Wisconsin statute.

On complaint of the school district administrator for the public schools, respondents were charged, tried, and convicted of violating the compulsory-attendance law . . . and were fined the sum of $5 each. Respondents defended on the ground that the application of the compulsory-attendance law violated their rights under the First and Fourteenth Amendments. The trial testimony showed that respondents believed, in accordance with the tenets of Old Order Amish communities generally, that their children's attendance at high school, public or private, was contrary to the Amish religion and way of life. They believed that by sending their children to high school, they would not only expose themselves to the danger of the censure of the church community, but, as found by the county court, also endanger their own salvation and that of their children. The State stipulated that respondents' religious beliefs were sincere. . . .

[Respondents] object to the high school, and higher education generally, because the values they teach are in marked variance with Amish values and the Amish way of life; they view secondary school education as an impermissible exposure of their children to a "worldly" influence in conflict with their beliefs. The high school tends to emphasize intellectual and scientific accomplishments, self-distinction, competitiveness, worldly success, and social life with other students. Amish society emphasizes informal learning-through-doing; a life of "goodness," rather than a life of intellect; wisdom, rather than technical knowledge; community welfare, rather than competition; and separation from, rather than integration with, contemporary worldly society.

Formal high school education beyond the eighth grade is contrary to Amish beliefs, not only because it places Amish children in an environment hostile to Amish beliefs with increasing emphasis on competition in class work and sports and with pressure to conform to the styles, manners, and ways of the peer group, but also because it takes them away from their community, physically and emotionally, during the crucial and formative adolescent period of life. During this period, the children must acquire Amish attitudes favoring manual work and self-reliance and the specific skills needed to perform the adult role of an Amish farmer or housewife. They must learn to enjoy physical labor. Once a child has learned basic reading, writing, and elementary mathematics, these traits, skills, and attitudes admittedly fall within the category of those best learned through example and "doing" rather than in a classroom. And, at this time in life, the Amish child must also grow in his faith and his relationship to the Amish community if he is to be prepared to accept the heavy obligations imposed by adult baptism. In short, high school attendance with teachers who are not of the Amish faith — and may even be hostile to it — interposes a serious barrier to the integration of the Amish child into the Amish religious community. . . .

The Amish do not object to elementary education through the first eight grades as a general proposition because they agree that their children must have basic skills in the "three R's" in order to read the Bible, to be good farmers and citizens, and to be able to deal with non-Amish people when necessary in the course of daily affairs. They view such a basic education as acceptable because it does not significantly expose their children to worldly values or interfere with their development in the Amish community during the crucial adolescent period. While Amish accept compulsory elementary education generally, wherever possible they have established their own elementary schools in many respects like the small local schools of the past. In the Amish belief higher learning tends to develop values they reject as influences that alienate man from God. . . .

I . . .

[A] State's interest in universal education, however highly we rank it, is not totally free from a balancing process when it impinges on fundamental rights and interests, such as those specifically protected by the Free Exercise Clause of the First Amendment, and the traditional interest of parents with respect to the religious upbringing of their children so long as they, in the words of *Pierce*, "prepare (them) for additional obligations." . . .

[I]n order for Wisconsin to compel school attendance beyond the eighth grade against a claim that such attendance interferes with the practice of a legitimate religious belief, it must appear either that the State does not deny the free exercise of religious belief by its requirement, or that there is a state interest of sufficient magnitude to override the interest claiming protection under the Free Exercise Clause. . . .

II . . .

As the society around the Amish has become more populous, urban, industrialized, and complex, particularly in this century, government regulation of human affairs has correspondingly become more detailed and pervasive. The Amish mode of life has thus come into conflict increasingly with requirements of contemporary society exerting a hydraulic insistence on conformity to majoritarian standards. So long as compulsory education laws were confined to eight grades of elementary basic education imparted in a nearby rural schoolhouse, with a large proportion of students of the Amish faith, the Old Order Amish had little basis to fear that school attendance would expose their children to the worldly influence they reject. But modern compulsory secondary education in rural areas is now largely carried on in a consolidated school, often remote from the student's home and alien to his daily home life. As the record so strongly shows, the values and programs of the modern secondary school are in sharp conflict with the fundamental mode of life mandated by the Amish religion; modern laws requiring compulsory secondary education have accordingly engendered great concern and conflict. The conclusion is inescapable that secondary schooling, by exposing Amish children to worldly influences in terms of attitudes, goals, and values contrary to beliefs, and by substantially interfering with the religious development of the Amish child and his integration into the way of life of the Amish faith community at the crucial adolescent stage of development, contravenes the basic religious tenets and practice of the Amish faith, both as to the parent and the child. . . .

III . . .

The State advances two primary arguments in support of its system of compulsory education. It notes . . . that some degree of education is necessary to prepare citizens to participate effectively and intelligently in our open political system if we are to preserve freedom and independence. Further, education prepares individuals to be self-reliant and self-sufficient participants in society. We accept these propositions.

However, the evidence adduced by the Amish in this case is persuasively to the effect that an additional one or two years of formal high school for Amish children in place of their long-established program of informal vocational education would do little to serve those interests. Respondents' experts testified at trial, without challenge, that the value of all education must be assessed in terms of its capacity to prepare the child for life. It is one thing to say that compulsory education for a year or two beyond the eighth grade may be necessary when its goal is the preparation of the child for life in modern society as the majority live, but it is quite another if the goal of education be viewed as the preparation of the child for life in the separated agrarian community that is the keystone of the Amish faith.

The State attacks respondents' position as one fostering "ignorance" from which the child must be protected by the State. No one can question the State's duty to protect children from ignorance but this argument does not square with the facts disclosed in the record. Whatever their idiosyncrasies as seen by the majority, this record strongly shows that the Amish community has been a highly successful social unit within our society, even if apart from the conventional "mainstream." Its members are productive and very law-abiding members of society; they reject public welfare in any of its usual modern forms. The Congress itself recognized their self-sufficiency by authorizing exemption of such groups as the Amish from the obligation to pay social security taxes. . . .

The State, however, supports its interest in providing an additional one or two years of compulsory high school education to Amish children because of the possibility that some such children will choose to leave the Amish community, and that if this occurs they will be ill-equipped for life. The State argues that if Amish children leave their church they should not be in the position of making their way in the world without the education available in the one or two additional years the State requires. However, on this record, that argument is highly speculative. There is no specific evidence of the loss of Amish adherents by attrition, nor is there any showing that upon leaving the Amish community Amish children, with their practical agricultural training and habits of industry and self-reliance, would become burdens on society because of educational shortcomings. Indeed, this argument of the State appears to rest primarily on the State's mistaken assumption, already noted, that the Amish do not provide any education for their children beyond the eighth grade, but allow them to grow in "ignorance." To the contrary, not only do the Amish accept the necessity for formal schooling through the eighth grade level, but continue to provide what has been characterized by the undisputed testimony of expert educators as an "ideal" vocational education for their children in the adolescent years.

There is nothing in this record to suggest that the Amish qualities of reliability, self-reliance, and dedication to work would fail to find ready markets in today's society. Absent some contrary evidence supporting the State's position, we are unwilling to assume that persons possessing such valuable vocational skills and habits are doomed to become burdens on society should they determine to leave the Amish faith, nor is there any basis in the record to warrant a finding that an additional one or two years of formal school education beyond the eighth grade would serve to eliminate any such problem that might exist. . . .

IV

Finally, the State, on authority of *Prince v. Massachusetts*, 321 U.S. 158 (1944), argues that a decision exempting Amish children from the State's requirement fails to recognize the substantive right of the Amish child to a secondary education, and fails to give due regard to the power of the State as *parens patriae* to extend the benefit of secondary education to children regardless of the wishes of their parents. Taken at its broadest sweep, the Court's language in *Prince* might be read to give support to the State's position. However, the Court was not confronted in *Prince* with a situation comparable to that of the Amish as revealed in this record; this is shown by the Court's severe characterization of the evils that it thought the legislature could legitimately associate with child labor, even when performed in the company of an adult. . . .

This case, of course, is not one in which any harm to the physical or mental health of the child or to the public safety, peace, order, or welfare has been demonstrated or may be properly inferred. The record is to the contrary, and any reliance on that theory would find no support in the evidence. . . .

Our holding in no way determines the proper resolution of possible competing interests of parents, children, and the State in an appropriate state court proceeding in which the power of the State is asserted on the theory that Amish parents are preventing their minor children from attending high school despite their expressed desires to the contrary. Recognition of the claim of the State in such a proceeding would, of course, call into question traditional concepts of parental control over the religious upbringing and education of their minor children recognized in this Court's past decisions. It is clear that such an intrusion by a State into family decisions in the area of religious training would give rise to grave questions of religious freedom comparable to those raised here and those presented in *Pierce*. On this record we neither reach nor decide those issues.

The State's argument proceeds without reliance on any actual conflict between the wishes of parents and children. It appears to rest on the potential that exemption of Amish parents from the requirements of the compulsory-education law might allow some parents to act contrary to the best interests of their children by foreclosing their opportunity to make an intelligent choice between the Amish way of life and that of the outside world. The same argument could, of course, be made with respect to all church schools short of college. There is nothing in the record or in the ordinary course of human experience to suggest that non-Amish parents generally consult with children of ages 14-16 if they are placed in a church school of the parents' faith.

Indeed it seems clear that if the State is empowered, as *parens patriae*, to "save" a child from himself or his Amish parents by requiring an additional two years of compulsory formal high school education, the State will in large measure influence, if not determine, the religious future of the child. Even more markedly than in *Prince*, therefore, this case involves the fundamental interest of parents, as contrasted with that of the State, to guide the religious future and education of their children. The history and culture of Western civilization reflect a strong tradition of parental concern for the nurture and upbringing of their children. This primary role of the parents in the upbringing of their children is now established beyond debate as an enduring American tradition. . . .

The duty to prepare the child for "additional obligations," referred to by the Court [in *Pierce v. Society of Sisters*], must be read to include the inculcation of moral standards, religious beliefs, and elements of good citizenship. *Pierce*, of course, recognized that where nothing more than the general interest of the parent in the nurture and education of his children is involved, it is beyond dispute that the State acts "reasonably" and constitutionally in requiring education to age 16 in some public or private school meeting the standards prescribed by the State.

However read, the Court's holding in *Pierce* stands as a charter of the rights of parents to direct the religious upbringing of their children. And, when the interests of parenthood are combined with a free exercise claim of the nature revealed by this record, more than merely a "reasonable relation to some purpose within the competency of the State" is required to sustain the validity of the State's requirement under the First Amendment. To be sure, the power of the parent, even when linked to a free exercise claim, may be subject to limitation under *Prince* if it appears that parental decisions will jeopardize the health or safety of the child, or have a potential for significant social burdens. But in this case, the Amish have introduced persuasive evidence undermining the arguments the State has advanced to support its claims in terms of the welfare of the child and society as a whole. The record strongly indicates that accommodating the religious objections of the Amish by forgoing one, or at most two, additional years of compulsory education will not impair the physical or mental health of the child, or result in an inability to be self-supporting or to discharge the duties and responsibilities of citizenship, or in any other way materially detract from the welfare of society. . . .

V

For the reasons stated we hold, with the Supreme Court of Wisconsin, that the First and Fourteenth Amendments prevent the State from compelling respondents to cause their children to attend formal high school to age 16. . . .

Mr. Justice Douglas, dissenting in part.

I . . .

The Court's analysis assumes that the only interests at stake in the case are those of the Amish parents on the one hand, and those of the State on the other. The difficulty with this approach is that, despite the Court's claim, the parents are seeking to vindicate not only their own free exercise claims, but also those of their high-school-age children. . . .

If the parents in this case are allowed a religious exemption, the inevitable effect is to impose the parents' notions of religious duty upon their children. Where the child is mature enough to express potentially conflicting desires, it would be an invasion of the child's rights to permit such an imposition without canvassing his views. . . . As the child has no other effective forum, it is in this litigation that his rights should be considered. And, if an Amish child desires to attend high school, and is mature enough to have that desire respected, the State may well be able to override the parents' religiously motivated objections. . . .

II . . .

On this important and vital matter of education, I think the children should be entitled to be heard. While the parents, absent dissent, normally speak for the entire family, the education of the child is a matter on which the child will often have decided views. He may want to be a pianist or an astronaut or an oceanographer. To do so he will have to break from the Amish tradition.

It is the future of the student, not the future of the parents, that is imperiled by today's decision. If a parent keeps his child out of school beyond the grade school, then the child will be forever barred from entry into the new and amazing world of diversity that we have today. The child may decide that that is the preferred course, or he may rebel. It is the student's judgment, not his parents', that is essential if we are to give full meaning to what we have said about the Bill of Rights and of the right of students to be masters of their own destiny. If he is harnessed to the Amish way of life by those in authority over him and if his education is truncated, his entire life may be stunted and deformed. The child, therefore, should be given an opportunity to be heard before the State gives the exemption which we honor today. . . .

NOTES AND QUESTIONS

1.   *An Amish Exception?* Courts and commentators largely have viewed *Yoder* as a case confined to its facts.[117] The *Yoder* Court stressed the exceptional situation of the Amish in ways that seemed to foreclose extension of the holding to other claimants. The Court seemed almost enamored with the Amish way of life. Should other parents be able to exempt their children from compulsory education laws? Under what circumstances?

2.   *Hybrid Rights?* As we saw in Pierce v. Society of Sisters and Prince v. Massachusetts, with which we began this chapter, claims of parental rights are often entangled with claims of religious free exercise. Was the free exercise claim, standing alone, sufficient to justify the result in *Yoder*? In Employment Division v. Smith, the Supreme Court pulled back on the judicial scrutiny that would be given to free exercise challenges to neutral and generally applicable laws.[118] Members of the Native American Church had been denied unemployment benefits after being fired from their jobs for using peyote as part of a religious ritual. Rejecting their claim for an exemption from the criminal drug laws, the Court decided that searching scrutiny would be applied only when the government targets religion. Rather than expressly overrule free exercise precedents, the Court characterized those precedents as involving either unemployment compensation or what it termed "hybrid" rights. The *Smith* Court pointed to *Yoder* to illustrate hybrid rights claims, given that the free exercise claim was paired with the parental rights claim. After *Smith*, courts

---

117. See, e.g., Duro v. Dist. Attorney, 712 F.2d 96, 98 (4th Cir. 1983) (rejecting Pentecostalist objection to compulsory education law and finding *Yoder* distinguishable "because it arose in an entirely different factual context").

118. 494 U.S. 872 (1990).

have struggled to apply the hybrid rights concept and have interpreted the concept in different ways.[119] Nonetheless, courts have rarely found a viable claim based on the theory of hybrid rights.[120]

3. *Children's Rights?* In his dissent in *Yoder*, Justice Douglas raised the perspective of Amish children. Some children may decide to leave the Amish faith and may not have the education necessary to give them an equal opportunity to participate in mainstream society. What role do you think the interest of Amish children should have played in resolution of the case? Would the outcome have changed if one of the children at issue had asserted an interest in additional education in a public school? In San Antonio Independent School District v. Rodriguez,[121] the Supreme Court rejected the idea that children have a fundamental right to education — a decision that largely insulated school funding schemes based on local property taxes from federal constitutional scrutiny. Almost a decade after *Rodriguez*, in Board of Education, Island Trees Union Free School District No. 26 v. Pico,[122] the Court considered the constitutionality of a school district's decision to remove materials from the school library. In a plurality opinion, the Court found that the government's action violated the students' First Amendment right to receive information.[123] Could such a right ever extend to children who are not enrolled in public school?

PROBLEMS

1. The Board of Education in Hawkins County, Tennessee adopted the Holt, Rinehart, and Winston basic reading series as part of the curriculum in the county public schools. First- through fourth-graders receive reading instruction throughout the day in conjunction with other subjects, as opposed to in separate reading sessions. Fifth- through eighth-graders, in contrast, cover reading as a separate subject at designated times each day. Still, the schools use an integrated curriculum such that themes raised in the reading program arise in other subjects. The public schools in Hawkins County do not include reading simply to teach word and sound recognition, but instead to teach "critical reading" — that is, to teach the development of cognitive skills so that students can evaluate material, contrast ideas presented, and understand complex characters.

---

119. Compare Miller v. Reed, 176 F.3d 1202, 1207 (9th Cir. 1999) (requiring "colorable claim" of an additional constitutional violation), with Kissinger v. Bd. of Trs. of Ohio St. Univ., 5 F.3d 177, 180 (6th Cir. 1993) (finding the concept "completely illogical").

120. See, e.g., Parker v. Hurley, 514 F.3d 87, 99 (1st Cir. 2008); Leebaert v. Harrington, 332 F.3d 134, 143 (2d Cir. 2003).

121. 411 U.S. 1 (1973).

122. 457 U.S. 853 (1982).

123. See id. at 866-67, 870-71.

Vicki Frost is the mother of three children who are students in public schools in Hawkins County — a second-grader, a fourth-grader, and a sixth-grader. In reviewing a story in the sixth-grader's reading program, Frost observed that it involved "mental telepathy." Frost, who describes herself as a "born again Christian," objects on religious grounds to any instruction about mental telepathy. Frost found additional themes, not only in the sixth-grade reading program but also in the second- and fourth-grade reading programs, that she objected to as inconsistent with her religious beliefs and the religious instruction she provided her children. More concretely, she believed the readings taught tolerance of views and ways of being that she rejected on Biblical grounds. Indeed, she objected to her children learning "tolerance" to the extent such tolerance meant "accepting other religious views on an equal basis with her own."

After discussing her objections with other parents, Frost talked with the principals of the elementary school and middle school that her children attend. She asked each school to create an alternative reading program for students whose parents objected to the assigned reader. In the alternative program, students would leave their classrooms during the reading sessions and work on reading assignments approved by their parents.

You are the school principal of the middle school that the sixth-grade student attends. Would you grant Frost's request for an alternative reading program? Would Frost have a constitutional right to remove her children from the school's reading program? Would she have a right to an alternative reading program for her children?

POSTSCRIPT

This problem is based on Mozert v. Hawkins County Board of Education.[124] In that case, the Sixth Circuit Court of Appeals rejected the constitutional challenge of Frost and other parents. The court noted the breadth of the plaintiffs' challenge: "Because the plaintiffs perceive every teaching that goes beyond the 'three Rs' as inculcating religious ideas, they admit that any value-laden reading curriculum that did not affirm the truth of their beliefs would offend their religious convictions."[125] Ultimately, the court found that the reading program did not create an "unconstitutional burden" on the objecting parents.[126]

The court distinguished *Yoder.* First, it limited the case to its facts, reasoning that "*Yoder* rested on such a singular set of facts that we do not believe it can be held

---

124. 827 F.2d 1058 (6th Cir. 1987).
125. Id. at 1069.
126. Id. at 1070.

to announce a general rule that exposure without compulsion to act, believe, affirm or deny creates an unconstitutional burden."[127] Second, the court drew a distinction between rejecting public school completely — as in *Yoder* — and rejecting elements of it — as in the case before it:

> The parents in *Yoder* were required to send their children to some school that prepared them for life in the outside world, or face official sanctions. The parents in the present case want their children to acquire all the skills required to live in modern society. They also want to have them excused from exposure to some ideas they find offensive. Tennessee offers two options to accommodate this latter desire. The plaintiff parents can either send their children to church schools or private schools, as many of them have done, or teach them at home.[128]

In other words, the parents could remove their children from public school completely. But once they decided to send their children to public school, they could not dictate the curriculum or remove their children from general instruction.

The *Mozert* court acknowledged that public schools have an "assimilative force."[129] Is assimilation a form of indoctrination? Is it appropriate for the government to instill the values of secular liberalism in its citizens? Consider Professor Nomi Stolzenberg's analysis of *Mozert* and the issues at stake:

> *Mozert* raises the fundamental question of what, if anything, is wrong with assimilation. If liberalism condemns indoctrination but refuses to acknowledge its own reliance upon it, and communitarianism condemns the effect of liberalism's alleged indoctrination, a third strand of legal thought [civic republicanism] both recognizes and offers to justify "indoctrination in tolerance" as necessary to democracy and individual self-fulfillment. . . . [A] series of precedents that draw on this civic republican approach may be taken to refute the claim that assimilative exposure is necessarily bad.
>
> However, an answer to the fundamentalists' complaint is not supplied by relying on any one of these three philosophies. From the vantage point of the *Mozert* complaint, the asserted distinctions among liberalism, communitarianism, and republicanism seem overstated, if not illusory. Confronted with the question whether to treat assimilation as a harm or a good, each of these philosophies can be manipulated to support either result. As *Mozert* demonstrates . . . , this is because all three philosophies take beliefs and values to be subjective — and such subjectivism is paradoxically and unavoidably assimilationist.[130]

---

127. Id. at 1067.

128. Id.

129. Id. at 1068.

130. Nomi Maya Stolzenberg, "He Drew a Circle that Shut Me Out": Assimilation, Indoctrination, and the Paradox of Liberal Education, 106 Harv. L. Rev. 581, 586-87 (1993).

Do you agree with Professor Stolzenberg? What is the purpose of public education in a liberal society?

2. A public elementary school in Palmdale, California distributed a survey to students in first, third, and fifth grades. Parents were notified in advance and asked to give parental consent to their child's participation. The consent form identified the survey as focused on "early trauma" and explained that there would be "sensitive questions." The survey included questions about sex and sexuality. When a group of parents later learned about these questions, they filed a lawsuit in federal court alleging that the school district had violated their substantive due process right to direct their children's upbringing. You are the judge assigned to the case. At a hearing, what questions would you ask the parties to help you reach a decision? How do you think you would rule?

POSTSCRIPT

The federal Court of Appeals for the Ninth Circuit ultimately rejected the parents' claims. In Fields v. Palmdale School District,[131] the court held that parents had no fundamental right to exclusively provide their children with information regarding sexual matters. Because no fundamental right was implicated, the court applied rational basis review and found that the survey questions were justified by the government's legitimate interest in effective education and its concern for the mental welfare of students.

   The court used the case as an occasion to comment more broadly on the relationship between public school education and parental rights:

> [T]he *Meyer-Pierce* right does not extend beyond the threshold of the school door. The parents' asserted right "to control the upbringing of their children by introducing them to matters of and relating to sex in accordance with their personal and religious values and beliefs," by which they mean the right to limit what public schools or other state actors may tell their children regarding sexual matters, is not encompassed within the *Meyer-Pierce* right to control their children's upbringing and education. Accordingly, *Meyer-Pierce* provides no basis for finding a substantive due process right that could have been violated by defendants' authorization and administration of the survey.[132]

The court worried about the consequences of a parental rights doctrine that would reach the survey at issue:

> If all parents had a fundamental constitutional right to dictate individually what the schools teach their children, the schools would be forced to cater a curriculum for each student whose parents had genuine moral disagreements with the school's choice of subject matter. We cannot see that

---

131. 427 F.3d 1197 (9th Cir. 2005).
132. Id. at 1207.

the Constitution imposes such a burden on state educational systems, and accordingly find that the rights of parents . . . do not encompass a broad-based right to restrict the flow of information in the public schools.[133]

The court relied on a similar 1995 decision from the federal Court of Appeals for the First Circuit.[134] The First Circuit had rejected the claims of parents who objected to sexually explicit AIDS education programming for high school students. As these cases suggest, courts routinely deny parental rights claims in the context of public school programming. In 2008, the First Circuit again rejected claims by parents who opposed curricular material — this time, an elementary-school family diversity curriculum that included materials encouraging "respect for gay persons and couples." The court determined that the parents' substantive due process rights do not provide "the degree of control over their children's education that their requested relief seeks."[135] More recently, courts have rejected claims by parents who object to public school policies that allow transgender students to use restrooms and locker rooms that match their gender identity.[136]

Of course, after *Pierce*, parents have a right to withdraw their children from public school and instead seek instruction in a private or parochial school. Parents can also homeschool their children, provided they meet minimum requirements. But once parents send their children to public school, they can rarely invoke parental rights to object to the school's decisions. As one court put it, "While parents may have a fundamental right to decide *whether* to send their child to a public school, they do not have a fundamental right generally to direct *how* a public school teaches their child."[137]

3. In recent years, homeschooling has gained in popularity — among both conservative religious parents and secular progressive parents. Some object to homeschooling because they believe children should be exposed to the civic education that public schools purport to provide. Others worry that children being homeschooled are not receiving the kind of substantive instruction that they need to develop into successful adults. Still others object because they fear that abuse and neglect will go undetected if children are not interacting with teachers and other professionals outside the home. In response to these objections, the state legislature is considering a bill to ban homeschooling. If the bill becomes law, parents would not have to send their children to public school, but they would have to send their children to an educational institution that meets the minimum standards prescribed by the state.

   (1) You are a legislator in the state. What do you think of the bill as a policy matter?
   (2) You are legal counsel to the legislative committee in charge of the bill. Is the bill constitutional?

---

133. Id. at 1205 (quoting Brown v. Hot, Sexy & Safer Prods., Inc., 68 F.3d 525, 533–34 (1st Cir. 1995)).
134. Brown v. Hot, Sexy & Safer Prods., Inc., 68 F.3d 525 (1st Cir. 1995).
135. Parker v. Hurley, 514 F.3d 87, 103 (1st Cir. 2008).
136. See, e.g., Parents for Privacy v. Dallas School District No. 2, 326 F. Supp. 3d 1075 (D. Or. 2018).
137. Blau v. Fort Thomas Pub. Sch. Dist., 401 F.3d 381, 395 (6th Cir. 2005).

B. Healthcare

Parental consent is required for children to do many things. This includes receiving medical care. Generally, the requirement of parental consent will not pose a problem. Indeed, ordinarily parents carefully oversee their children's medical care and make decisions in the best interest of their children. But are there some situations where parents who make healthcare decisions fail to act in their child's best interest? How do we know? Who decides? Are there some healthcare decisions that children should be able to make for themselves? Are the consequences of some decisions so serious that the individual has a liberty interest in deciding for herself, even if she is not an adult?

In the following materials, we first consider what constitutional limits exist on a parent's authority to make healthcare decisions for the child. We then assess the authority of the child to make her own healthcare decisions. In doing so, we consider specific settings in which children may have particularly strong autonomy interests in healthcare decision-making. As you read the materials, consider whether and when the state should be able to override a parent's decision regarding a child's healthcare, and whether and when the child should be able to override her parent's decision.

PARHAM V. J.R.
442 U.S. 584 (1979)

Mr. Chief Justice Burger delivered the opinion of the Court.

The question presented in this appeal is what process is constitutionally due a minor child whose parents or guardian seek state administered institutional mental health care for the child and specifically whether an adversary proceeding is required prior to or after the commitment.

I

Appellee[s] . . . sought a declaratory judgment that Georgia's voluntary commitment procedures for children under the age of 18, Ga. Code §§ 88-503.1, 88-503.2 (1975), violated the Due Process Clause of the Fourteenth Amendment and requested an injunction against their future enforcement. . . .

J. L., a plaintiff before the District Court who is now deceased, was admitted in 1970 at the age of 6 years to Central State Regional Hospital in Milledgeville, Ga. Prior to his admission, J. L. had received outpatient treatment at the hospital for over two months. J. L.'s mother then requested the hospital to admit him indefinitely.

The admitting physician interviewed J. L. and his parents. He learned that J. L.'s natural parents had divorced and his mother had remarried. He also learned that

J. L. had been expelled from school because he was uncontrollable. He accepted the parents' representation that the boy had been extremely aggressive and diagnosed the child as having a "hyperkinetic reaction of childhood."

J. L's mother and stepfather agreed to participate in family therapy during the time their son was hospitalized. Under this program, J. L. was permitted to go home for short stays. Apparently his behavior during these visits was erratic. After several months, the parents requested discontinuance of the program.

In 1972, the child was returned to his mother and stepfather on a furlough basis, *i.e.*, he would live at home but go to school at the hospital. The parents found they were unable to control J. L. to their satisfaction, and this created family stress. Within two months, they requested his readmission to Central State. J. L's parents relinquished their parental rights to the county in 1974.

Although several hospital employees recommended that J. L. should be placed in a special foster home with "a warm, supported, truly involved couple," the Department of Family and Children Services was unable to place him in such a setting. On October 24, 1975, J. L. (with J. R.) filed this suit requesting an order of the court placing him in a less drastic environment suitable to his needs.

Appellee J. R. was declared a neglected child by the county and removed from his natural parents when he was 3 months old. He was placed in seven different foster homes in succession prior to his admission to Central State Hospital at the age of 7.

Immediately preceding his hospitalization, J. R. received outpatient treatment at a county mental health center for several months. He then began attending school where he was so disruptive and incorrigible that he could not conform to normal behavior patterns. Because of his abnormal behavior, J. R's seventh set of foster parents requested his removal from their home. The Department of Family and Children Services then sought his admission at Central State. The agency provided the hospital with a complete sociomedical history at the time of his admission. In addition, three separate interviews were conducted with J. R. by the admission team of the hospital.

It was determined that he was borderline retarded, and suffered an "unsocialized, aggressive reaction of childhood." It was recommended unanimously that he would "benefit from the structured environment" of the hospital and would "enjoy living and playing with boys of the same age."

J. R's progress was re-examined periodically. In addition, unsuccessful efforts were made by the Department of Family and Children Services during his stay at the hospital to place J. R. in various foster homes. On October 24, 1975, J. R. (with J. L.) filed this suit requesting an order of the court placing him in a less drastic environment suitable to his needs.

Georgia Code § 88-503.1 (1975) provides for the voluntary admission to a state regional hospital of children such as J. L. and J. R. Under that provision, admission begins with an application for hospitalization signed by a "parent or guardian." Upon application, the superintendent of each hospital is given the power to admit temporarily any child for "observation and diagnosis." If, after observation, the superintendent finds "evidence of mental illness" and that the child is "suitable for treatment" in the hospital, then the child may be admitted "for such period and under such conditions as may be authorized by law."

Georgia's mental health statute also provides for the discharge of voluntary patients. Any child who has been hospitalized for more than five days may be discharged at the request of a parent or guardian. Even without a request for discharge, however, the superintendent of each regional hospital has an affirmative duty to release any child "who has recovered from his mental illness or who has sufficiently improved that the superintendent determines that hospitalization of the patient is no longer desirable."

Georgia's Mental Health Director has not published any statewide regulations defining what specific procedures each superintendent must employ when admitting a child under 18. Instead, each regional hospital's superintendent is responsible for the procedures in his or her facility. There is substantial variation among the institutions with regard to their admission procedures and their procedures for review of patients after they have been admitted. . . .

III

In an earlier day, the problems inherent in coping with children afflicted with mental or emotional abnormalities were dealt with largely within the family. Sometimes parents were aided by teachers or a family doctor. While some parents no doubt were able to deal with their disturbed children without specialized assistance, others, especially those of limited means and education, were not. Increasingly, they turned for assistance to local, public sources or private charities. Until recently, most of the states did little more than provide custodial institutions for the confinement of persons who were considered dangerous.

As medical knowledge about the mentally ill and public concern for their condition expanded, the states, aided substantially by federal grants, have sought to ameliorate the human tragedies of seriously disturbed children. Ironically, as most states have expanded their efforts to assist the mentally ill, their actions have been subjected to increasing litigation and heightened constitutional scrutiny. Courts have been required to resolve the thorny constitutional attacks on state programs and procedures with limited precedential guidance. In this case, appellees have challenged Georgia's procedural and substantive balance of the individual, family, and social interests at stake in the voluntary commitment of a child to one of its regional mental hospitals.

The parties agree that our prior holdings have set out a general approach for testing challenged state procedures under a due process claim. Assuming the existence of a protectable property or liberty interest, the Court has required a balancing of a number of factors:

First, the private interest that will be affected by the official action; second, the risk of an erroneous deprivation of such interest through the procedures used, and the probable value, if any, of additional or substitute procedural safeguards; and finally, the Government's interest, including the function involved and the fiscal and administrative burdens that the additional or substitute procedural requirement would entail. . . .

In applying these criteria, we must consider first the child's interest in not being committed. Normally, however, since this interest is inextricably linked with the parents' interest in and obligation for the welfare and health of the child, the private interest at stake is a combination of the child's and parents' concerns. Next, we must examine the State's interest in the procedures it has adopted for commitment and treatment of children. Finally, we must consider how well Georgia's procedures protect against arbitrariness in the decision to commit a child to a state mental hospital.

It is not disputed that a child, in common with adults, has a substantial liberty interest in not being confined unnecessarily for medical treatment and that the state's involvement in the commitment decision constitutes state action under the Fourteenth Amendment. . . . We also recognize that commitment sometimes produces adverse social consequences for the child because of the reaction of some to the discovery that the child has received psychiatric care. . . .

This reaction, however, need not be equated with the community response resulting from being labeled by the state as delinquent, criminal, or mentally ill and possibly dangerous. . . . The state through its voluntary commitment procedures does not "label" the child; it provides a diagnosis and treatment that medical specialists conclude the child requires. In terms of public reaction, the child who exhibits abnormal behavior may be seriously injured by an erroneous decision not to commit. Appellees overlook a significant source of the public reaction to the mentally ill, for what is truly "stigmatizing" is the symptomatology of a mental or emotional illness. . . . The pattern of untreated, abnormal behavior — even if non-dangerous — arouses at least as much negative reaction as treatment that becomes public knowledge. A person needing, but not receiving, appropriate medical care may well face even greater social ostracism resulting from the observable symptoms of an untreated disorder.

However, we need not decide what effect these factors might have in a different case. For purposes of this decision, we assume that a child has a protectable interest not only in being free of unnecessary bodily restraints but also in not being labeled erroneously by some persons because of an improper decision by the state hospital superintendent.

We next deal with the interests of the parents who have decided, on the basis of their observations and independent professional recommendations, that their child needs institutional care. Appellees argue that the constitutional rights of the child are of such magnitude and the likelihood of parental abuse is so great that the parents' traditional interests in and responsibility for the upbringing of their child must be subordinated at least to the extent of providing a formal adversary hearing prior to a voluntary commitment.

Our jurisprudence historically has reflected Western civilization concepts of the family as a unit with broad parental authority over minor children. Our cases have consistently followed that course; our constitutional system long ago rejected any notion that a child is "the mere creature of the State" and, on the contrary, asserted that parents generally "have the right, coupled with the high duty, to recognize and prepare [their children] for additional obligations." Pierce v. Society of Sisters, 268 U.S. 510, 535 (1925). Surely, this includes a "*high duty*" to recognize symptoms of illness and to seek and follow medical advice. The law's concept of the family rests on a presumption that parents possess what a child lacks in maturity, experience, and capacity for judgment required for making life's difficult decisions. More important, historically it has recognized that natural bonds of affection lead parents to act in the best interests of their children. . . .

As with so many other legal presumptions, experience and reality may rebut what the law accepts as a starting point; the incidence of child neglect and abuse cases attests to this. That some parents "may at times be acting against the interests of their children" . . . creates a basis for caution, but is hardly a reason to discard wholesale those pages of human experience that teach that parents generally do act in the child's best interests. . . . The statist notion that governmental power should supersede parental authority in *all* cases because *some* parents abuse and neglect children is repugnant to American tradition.

Nonetheless, we have recognized that a state is not without constitutional control over parental discretion in dealing with children when their physical or mental health is jeopardized. Moreover, the Court recently declared unconstitutional a state statute that granted parents an absolute veto over a minor child's decision to have an abortion. Appellees urge that these precedents limiting the traditional rights of parents, if viewed in the context of the liberty interest of the child and the likelihood of parental abuse, require us to hold that the parents' decision to have a child admitted to a mental hospital must be subjected to an exacting constitutional scrutiny, including a formal, adversary, pre-admission hearing.

Appellees' argument, however, sweeps too broadly. Simply because the decision of a parent is not agreeable to a child or because it involves risks does not automatically transfer the power to make that decision from the parents to some agency or officer of the state. The same characterizations can be made for a tonsillectomy, appendectomy, or other medical procedure. Most children, even in adolescence, simply are not able to make sound judgments concerning many decisions, including their need for medical care or treatment. Parents can and must make those judgments. Here, there is no finding by the District Court of even a single instance of bad faith by any parent of any member of appellees' class. We cannot assume that the result in *Meyer v. Nebraska*, 262 U.S. 390 (1923), and *Pierce v. Society of Sisters, supra*, would have been different if the children there had announced a preference to learn only English or a preference to go to a public, rather than a church, school. The fact that a child may balk at hospitalization or complain about a parental refusal to provide cosmetic surgery does not diminish the parents' authority to decide what is best for the child. . . . Neither state officials nor federal courts are equipped to review such parental decisions. . . .

In defining the respective rights and prerogatives of the child and parent in the voluntary commitment setting, we conclude that our precedents permit the parents to retain a substantial, if not the dominant, role in the decision, absent a finding of neglect or abuse, and that the traditional presumption that the parents act in the best interests of their child should apply. We also conclude, however, that the child's rights and the nature of the commitment decision are such that parents cannot always have absolute and unreviewable discretion to decide whether to have a child institutionalized. They, of course, retain plenary authority to seek such care for their children, subject to a physician's independent examination and medical judgment.

The State obviously has a significant interest in confining the use of its costly mental health facilities to cases of genuine need. The Georgia program seeks first to determine whether the patient seeking admission has an illness that calls for inpatient treatment. To accomplish this purpose, the State has charged the superintendents of each regional hospital with the responsibility for determining, before authorizing an admission, whether a prospective patient is mentally ill and whether the patient will likely benefit from hospital care. In addition, the State has imposed a continuing duty on hospital superintendents to release any patient who has recovered to the point where hospitalization is no longer needed.

The State in performing its voluntarily assumed mission also has a significant interest in not imposing unnecessary procedural obstacles that may discourage the mentally ill or their families from seeking needed psychiatric assistance. The *parens patriae* interest in helping parents care for the mental health of their children cannot be fulfilled if the parents are unwilling to take advantage of the opportunities because the admission process is too onerous, too embarrassing, or too contentious. It is surely not idle to speculate as to how many parents who believe they are acting in good faith would forgo state-provided hospital care if such care is contingent on participation in an adversary proceeding designed to probe their motives and other private family matters in seeking the voluntary admission.

The State also has a genuine interest in allocating priority to the diagnosis and treatment of patients as soon as they are admitted to a hospital rather than to time-consuming procedural minutes before the admission. One factor that must be considered is the utilization of the time of psychiatrists, psychologists, and other behavioral specialists in preparing for and participating in hearings rather than performing the task for which their special training has fitted them. Behavioral experts in courtrooms and hearings are of little help to patients. . . .

We now turn to consideration of what process protects adequately the child's constitutional rights by reducing risks of error without unduly trenching on traditional parental authority and without undercutting "efforts to further the legitimate interests of both the state and the patient that are served by" voluntary commitments. We conclude that the risk of error inherent in the parental decision to have a child institutionalized for mental health care is sufficiently great that some kind of inquiry should be made by a "neutral factfinder" to determine whether the statutory requirements for admission are satisfied. That inquiry must carefully probe the child's background using all available sources, including, but not limited to, parents, schools, and other social agencies. Of course, the review must also include an interview with the child. It is necessary that the decision maker have the authority to refuse to admit any child who does not satisfy the medical standards for admission. Finally, it is necessary that the child's continuing need for commitment be reviewed periodically by a similarly independent procedure.

We are satisfied that such procedures will protect the child from an erroneous admission decision in a way that neither unduly burdens the states nor inhibits parental decisions to seek state help.

Due process has never been thought to require that the neutral and detached trier of fact be law trained or a judicial or administrative officer. Surely, this is the case as to medical decisions. . . . [A] staff physician will suffice, so long as he or she is free to evaluate independently the child's mental and emotional condition and need for treatment.

It is not necessary that the deciding physician conduct a formal or quasi-formal hearing. . . . [D]ue process is not violated by use of informal, traditional medical investigative techniques. . . .

Although we acknowledge the fallibility of medical and psychiatric diagnosis, we do not accept the notion that the shortcomings of specialists can always be avoided by shifting the decision from a trained specialist using the traditional tools of medical science to an untrained judge or administrative hearing officer after a judicial-type hearing. . . .

Another problem with requiring a formalized, fact-finding hearing lies in the danger it poses for significant intrusion into the parent-child relationship. Pitting the parents and child as adversaries often will be at odds with the presumption that parents act in the best interests of their child. . . .

Surely, there is a risk that [a formal hearing] would exacerbate whatever tensions already exist between the child and the parents. . . . [T]here is a serious risk that an adversary confrontation will adversely affect the ability of the parents to assist the child while in the hospital. Moreover, it will make his subsequent return home more difficult. These unfortunate results are especially critical with an emotionally disturbed child; they seem likely to occur in the context of an adversary hearing in which the parents testify. . . .

By expressing some confidence in the medical decision-making process, we are by no means suggesting it is error free. On occasion, parents may initially mislead an admitting physician or a physician may erroneously diagnose the child as needing institutional care either because of negligence or an overabundance of caution. That there may be risks of error in the process affords no rational predicate for holding unconstitutional an entire statutory and administrative scheme that is generally followed in more than 30 states. . . . In general, we are satisfied that an independent medical decision-making process, which includes the thorough psychiatric investigation described earlier, followed by additional periodic review of a child's condition, will protect children who should not be admitted; we do not believe the risks of error in that process would be significantly reduced by a more formal, judicial-type hearing. . . . [T]he Georgia practices, as described in the record before us, comport with these minimum due process requirements. . . .

IV

Our discussion in Part III was directed at the situation where a child's natural parents request his admission to a state mental hospital. Some members of appellees' class, including J. R., were wards of the State of Georgia at the time of their admission. Obviously their situation differs from those members of the class who have natural parents. While the determination of what process is due varies somewhat when the state, rather than a natural parent, makes the request for commitment, we conclude that the differences in the two situations do not justify requiring different procedures at the time of the child's initial admission to the hospital.

For a ward of the state, there may well be no adult who knows him thoroughly and who cares for him deeply. Unlike with natural parents where there is a presumed natural affection to guide their action, . . . the presumption that the state will protect a child's general welfare stems from a specific state statute. . . . [W]e cannot assume that when the State of Georgia has custody of a child it acts so differently from a natural parent in seeking medical assistance for the child. No one has questioned the validity of the statutory presumption that the State acts in the child's best interest. Nor could such a challenge be mounted on the record before us. There is no evidence that the State, acting as guardian, attempted to admit any child for reasons unrelated to the child's need for treatment. . . .

The absence of an adult who cares deeply for a child has little effect on the reliability of the initial admission decision, but it may have some effect on how long a child will remain in the hospital. . . . "[T]he concern of family and friends generally will provide continuous opportunities for an erroneous commitment to be corrected." For a child without natural parents, we must acknowledge the risk of being "lost in the shuffle." Moreover, there is at least some indication that J. R.'s commitment was prolonged because the Department of Family and Children Services had difficulty finding a foster home for him. Whether wards of the State generally have received less protection than children with natural parents, and, if so, what should be done about it, however, are matters that must be decided in the first instance by the District Court on remand, if the court concludes the issue is still alive.

V

It is important that we remember the purpose of Georgia's comprehensive mental health program. It seeks substantively and at great cost to provide care for those who cannot afford to obtain private treatment and procedurally to screen carefully all applicants to assure that institutional care is suited to the particular patient. . . .

On this record, we are satisfied that Georgia's medical fact-finding processes are reasonable and consistent with constitutional guarantees. . . .

Reversed and remanded.

Mr. Justice Stewart, concurring in the judgment. . . .

This is not an easy case. Issues involving the family and issues concerning mental illness are among the most difficult that courts have to face, involving as they often do serious problems of policy disguised as questions of constitutional law. But when a state legislature makes a reasonable definition of the age of minority, and creates a rebuttable presumption that in invoking the statutory procedures for voluntary commitment a parent is acting in the best interests of his minor child, I cannot believe that the Fourteenth Amendment is violated. This is not to say that in this area the Constitution compels a State to respect the traditional authority of a parent, as in the *Meyer* and *Pierce* cases. I believe, as in *Prince* . . ., that the Constitution would tolerate intervention by the State. But that is a far cry from holding that such intervention is constitutionally compelled. . . .

For these reasons I concur in the judgment.

Mr. Justice Brennan, with whom Mr. Justice Marshall and Mr. Justice Stevens join, concurring in part and dissenting in part.

I agree with the Court that the commitment of juveniles to state mental hospitals by their parents or by state officials acting *in loco parentis* involves state action that impacts upon constitutionally protected interests and therefore must be accomplished through procedures consistent with the constitutional mandate of due process of law. I agree also that the District Court erred in interpreting the Due Process Clause to require preconfinement commitment hearings in all cases in which parents wish to hospitalize their children. I disagree, however, with the Court's decision to pretermit questions concerning the post admission procedures due Georgia's institutionalized juveniles. While the question of the frequency of post admission review hearings may properly be deferred, the right to at least one post admission hearing can and should be affirmed now. I also disagree with the Court's conclusion concerning the procedures due juvenile wards of the State of

Georgia. I believe that the Georgia statute is unconstitutional in that it fails to accord preconfinement hearings to juvenile wards of the State committed by the State acting *in loco parentis*.

Parham concerned parental authority and the potentially countervailing liberty interest of the child. When should the government override a parent's decision regarding her child's healthcare? Should it do so only in situations where the child opposes the parent's decision? Or when the child *might* have countervailing interests?

Are there situations in which the government should override the child's decision — a decision supported by the parent? Why would it be appropriate for the state to second-guess both the parent and the child? Consider the following case.

In re E.G.
549 N.E.2d 322 (Ill. 1990)

Justice Ryan delivered the opinion of the court:

Appellee, E.G., a 17-year-old woman, contracted leukemia and needed blood transfusions in the treatment of the disease. E.G. and her mother, Rosie Denton, refused to consent to the transfusions, contending that acceptance of blood would violate personal religious convictions rooted in their membership in the Jehovah's Witness faith. Appellant, the State of Illinois, filed a neglect petition in juvenile court in the circuit court of Cook County. The trial court entered an order finding E.G. to be neglected, and appointed a guardian to consent to the transfusions on E.G.'s behalf. . . .

In February of 1987, E.G. was diagnosed as having acute nonlymphatic leukemia, a malignant disease of the white blood cells. When E.G. and her mother, Rosie Denton, were informed that treatment of the disease would involve blood transfusions, they refused to consent to this medical procedure on the basis of their religious beliefs. As Jehovah's Witnesses, both E.G. and her mother desired to observe their religion's prohibition against the "eating" of blood. Mrs. Denton did authorize any other treatment and signed a waiver absolving the medical providers of liability for failure to administer transfusions.

As a result of Denton's and E.G.'s refusal to assent to blood transfusions, the State filed a neglect petition in juvenile court. At the initial hearing on February 25, 1987, Dr. Stanley Yachnin testified that E.G. had approximately one-fifth to one-sixth the normal oxygen-carrying capacity of her blood and consequently was excessively fatigued and incoherent. He stated that without blood transfusions, E.G. would likely die within a month. Dr. Yachnin testified that the transfusions, along with chemotherapy, achieve remission of the disease in about 80% of all patients so afflicted. Continued treatment, according to Dr. Yachnin, would involve the utilization of drugs and more transfusions. The long-term prognosis is not optimistic, as the survival rate for patients such as E.G. is 20 to 25%.

Dr. Yachnin stated that he discussed the proposed course of treatment with E.G. He testified that E.G. was competent to understand the consequences of accepting or rejecting treatment, and he was impressed with her maturity and the sincerity of her beliefs. Dr. Yachnin's observations regarding E.G.'s competency were corroborated by the testimony of Jane McAtee, the associate general counsel for the University of Chicago Hospital. At the conclusion of this hearing, the trial judge entered an order appointing McAtee temporary guardian, and authorizing her to consent to transfusions on E.G.'s behalf.

On April 8, 1987, further hearings were held on this matter. E.G., having received several blood transfusions, was strong enough to take the stand. She testified that the decision to refuse blood transfusions was her own and that she fully understood the nature of her disease and the consequences of her decision. She indicated that her decision was not based on any wish to die, but instead was grounded in her religious convictions. E.G. further stated that when informed that she would undergo transfusions, she asked to be sedated prior to the administration of the blood. She testified that the court's decision upset her, and said: "[I]t seems as if everything that I wanted or believe in was just being disregarded."

Several other witnesses gave their opinions extolling E.G.'s maturity and the sincerity of her religious beliefs. One witness was Dr. Littner, a psychiatrist who has special expertise in evaluating the maturity and competency of minors. Based on interviews with E.G. and her family, Dr. Littner expressed his opinion that E.G. had the maturity level of an 18 to 21 year old. He further concluded that E.G. had the competency to make an informed decision to refuse the blood transfusions, even if this choice was fatal. . . .

This case presents several issues for our consideration: (1) whether this appeal should be dismissed as moot, since E.G. turned 18 on November 25, 1987, and is no longer a minor; (2) whether a minor has a right to refuse medical treatment and if so, how this right may be exercised; and (3) whether the trial court's finding of neglect against Denton should stand. . . .

The paramount issue raised by this appeal is whether a minor like E.G. has a right to refuse medical treatment. In Illinois, an adult has a common law right to refuse medical treatment, even if it is of a life-sustaining nature. This court has also held that an adult may refuse life-saving blood transfusions on first amendment free exercise of religion grounds. An infant child, however, can be compelled to accept life-saving medical treatment over the objections of her parents. In the matter before us, E.G. was a minor, but one who was just months shy of her eighteenth birthday, and an individual that the record indicates was mature for her age. Although the age of majority in Illinois is 18, that age is not an impenetrable barrier that magically precludes a minor from possessing and exercising certain rights normally associated with adulthood. Numerous exceptions are found in this juris-diction and others which treat minors as adults under specific circumstances.

In Illinois, our legislature enacted "An Act in relation to the performance of medical, dental or surgical procedures on and counseling for minors", which grants minors the legal capacity to consent to medical treatment in certain situations. For example, a minor 12 years or older may seek medical attention on her own if she believes she has venereal disease or is an alcoholic or drug addict. Similarly, an individual under 18 who is married or pregnant may validly consent to treatment. Thus, if E.G. would have been married she could have consented to or, presumably, refused treatment. Also, a minor 16 or older may be declared emancipated under the Emancipation of Mature Minors Act, and thereby control his or her own health care decisions. These two acts, when read together in a complementary fashion, indicate that the legislature did not intend that there be an absolute 18-year-old age barrier prohibiting minors from consenting to medical treatment. . . .

Another area of the law where minors are treated as adults is constitutional law, including the constitutional right of abortion. . . . While we find the language from the cases cited [] instructive, we do not feel, as the appellate court did, that an extension of the constitutional mature minor doctrine to the case at bar is "inev-itable." These cases do show, however, that no "bright line" age restriction of 18 is tenable in restricting the rights of mature minors, whether the rights be based on constitutional or other grounds. Accordingly, we hold that in addition to these constitutionally based rights expressly delineated by the Supreme Court, mature minors may possess and exercise rights regarding medical care that are rooted in this State's common law. . . .

We note that in other jurisdictions, courts have ordered health care for minors over the objections of the minors' parents. These cases, however, involve minors who were younger than E.G. . . . Moreover, the issue in [those] cases was not whether a minor could assert a right to control medical treatment decisions, but whether the minor's parents could refuse treatment on behalf of their child. Here, E.G. contends she was mature enough to have controlled her own health care. We find that she may have done so if indeed she would have been adjudged mature.

The trial judge must determine whether a minor is mature enough to make health care choices on her own. . . . We feel the intervention of a judge is appropriate for two reasons.

First, Illinois public policy values the sanctity of life. When a minor's health and life are at stake, this policy becomes a critical consideration. A minor may have a long and fruitful life ahead that an immature, foolish decision could jeopardize. Consequently, when the trial judge weighs the evidence in making a determination of whether a minor is mature enough to handle a health care decision, he must find proof of this maturity by clear and convincing evidence.

Second, the State has a *parens patriae* power to protect those incompetent to pro-tect themselves. "[I]t is well-settled that the State as *parens patriae* has a special duty to protect minors and, if necessary, make vital decisions as to whether to submit a minor to necessary treatment where the condition is life threatening, as wrenching and distasteful as such actions may be." The State's *parens patriae* power pertaining to minors is strongest when the minor is immature and thus incompetent (lacking in capacity) to make these decisions on her own. The *parens patriae* authority fades, however, as the minor gets older and disappears upon her reaching adulthood. The State interest in protecting a mature minor in these situations will vary depending upon the nature of the medical treatment involved. Where the health care issues are potentially life threatening, the State's *parens patriae* interest is greater than if the health care matter is less consequential.

Therefore, the trial judge must weigh these two principles against the evidence he receives of a minor's maturity. If the evidence is clear and convincing that the minor is mature enough to appreciate the consequences of her actions, and that the minor is mature enough to exercise the judgment of an adult, then the mature minor doctrine affords her the common law right to consent to or refuse medical treatment. . . . [H]owever, this common law right is not absolute. The right must be balanced against four State interests: (1) the preservation of life; (2) protecting the interests of third parties; (3) prevention of suicide; and (4) maintaining the ethical integrity of the medical profession. Of these four concerns, protecting the interests of third parties is clearly the most significant here. The principal third parties in these cases would be parents, guardians, adult siblings, and other relatives. If a parent or guardian opposes an unemancipated mature minor's refusal to consent to treatment for a life-threatening health problem, this opposition would weigh heavily against the minor's right to refuse. In this case, for example, had E.G. refused the transfusions *against* the wishes of her mother, then the court would have given serious consideration to her mother's desires.

Nevertheless, in this case both E.G. and her mother agreed that E.G. should turn down the blood transfusions. They based this refusal primarily on religious grounds, contending that the first amendment free exercise clause entitles a mature minor to decline medical care when it contravenes sincerely held religious beliefs. Because we find that a mature minor may exercise a common law right to consent to or refuse medical care, we decline to address the constitutional issue.

The final issue we must address is whether the finding of neglect entered against Rosie Denton, E.G.'s mother, should stand. If the trial judge had ruled that E.G. was a mature minor, then no finding of neglect would be proper. Although the trial judge was impressed with E.G.'s maturity and sincerity, the judge did not explicitly hold that E.G. was a mature minor. The trial judge, guided only by the law as it existed prior to this opinion, rightly felt that he must protect the minor's health and well-being. This case is one of first impression with this court. Therefore, the trial judge had no precedent upon which to base a mature minor finding. Because E.G. is no longer a minor, nothing would be gained by remanding this case back to the trial court for an explicit determination of E.G.'s maturity. Nevertheless, since the trial judge did not have any clear guidance on the mature minor doctrine, we believe that the finding of neglect should not stand. Accordingly, we affirm the appellate court in part and reverse in part, and remand this case to the circuit court of Cook County for the sole purpose of expunging the finding of neglect against Denton.

JUSTICE WARD, dissenting:

I must respectfully dissent. I consider the majority has made an unfortunate choice of situations to announce, in what it calls a case of first impression, that a minor may with judicial approval reject medical treatment, even if the minor's death will be a medically certain consequence. The majority cites decisions where a minor was permitted to exercise what was called a common law right to consent to medical treatment. The safeguarding of health and the preservation of life are obviously different conditions from one in which a minor will be held to have a common law right, as the majority puts it, to refuse medical treatment and sometimes in effect take his own life. That violates the ancient responsibility of the State as *parens patriae* to protect minors and to decide for them, as the majority describes, vital questions, including whether to consent to or refuse necessary medical treatment. . . .

Unless the legislature for specific purposes provides for a different age, a minor is one who has not attained legal age. It is not disputed that E.G. has not attained legal age. It is fundamental that where language is clear there is no need to seek to interpret or depart from the plain language and meaning and read into what is clear exceptions or limitations. . . .

I am sure that in a host of matters of far lesser importance it would not be held that a minor however mature could satisfy a requirement of being of legal age. It would not be held that a minor was eligible to vote, to obtain a driver's or a pilot's license, or to enlist in one of the armed services before attaining enlistment age.

The trial court appointed a guardian to consent to transfusions for the minor. The appellate court reversed as to this, stating the minor was a mature minor. This court affirms the appellate court in this regard but does not attempt to state a standard by which "mature" is to be measured by judges in making these important findings.

NOTES AND QUESTIONS

---

1. *Parental Authority.* As we have seen throughout this chapter, parents are given broad authority to make decisions regarding their children. This includes healthcare decisions. Parental authority is not unlimited, though. As Professors Clare Huntington and Elizabeth Scott explain, "contemporary law defers to parental authority but limits that authority if the parent's decision poses a risk of serious harm to the child or, in some instances, to public health."[138]

---

138. Huntington & Scott, supra note 99, at 1426.

But what constitutes "serious harm"? Some courts have permitted parental decisions that many would view as seriously harmful. For example, in In re Green, a boy was unable to stand or move because of "paralytic scoliosis (94% Curvature of the spine)."[139] A spinal fusion was recommended, but his mother, a Jehovah's Witness, refused on religious grounds to consent to the blood transfusions that would be necessary for the surgery. The Pennsylvania Supreme Court determined that the mother had not engaged in medical neglect of the child. The court observed that, "where an adult refuses to consent to blood transfusions necessary to save the life of his infant son or daughter, other jurisdictions have uniformly held that the state can order such blood transfusions over the parents' religious objections."[140] But in the case before it, the child's life was not in danger. The court reasoned that, "as between a parent and the state, the state does not have an interest of sufficient magnitude outweighing a parent's religious beliefs when the child's life is not *immediately imperiled* by his physical condition."[141] The conflict involved the parent and the state; it was not clear what the child's wishes were. Since the record did not indicate the child's religious beliefs, the court "reserve[d] any decision regarding a possible parent-child conflict and remand[ed] the matter for an evidentiary hearing."[142] Would evidence about the child's religious beliefs really be necessary? Shouldn't the parent be able to dictate the child's religion? The child in the case was sixteen. Should that matter?

In *Green*, the fact that the parent's decision was grounded in religious beliefs mattered significantly. What if the mother refused to consent to the spinal fusion for non-religious reasons? In In re Hofbauer, the court considered "whether a child suffering from Hodgkin's disease whose parents failed to follow the recommendation of an attending physician to have their child treated by radiation and chemotherapy, but, rather, placed their child under the care of physicians advocating nutritional or metabolic therapy, including injections of laetrile, is a 'neglected child.'"[143] In finding that the child was not "neglected," the court emphasized that the controversial treatment was undertaken at the direction of a physician and that both the physician and the parents expressed an openness to more conventional treatments if the metabolic therapy did not work.[144] Do you think the parents neglected their child's medical needs? Does the fact that a parent can find a doctor who recommends a treatment that is widely considered controversial and ineffective mean that the parent's decision should not be questioned? What if the parents rejected all medical advice and decided

---

139. 292 A.2d 387, 388 (Pa. 1972).
140. Id. at 390.
141. Id. at 392.
142. Id.
143. 393 N.E.2d 1009, 1011 (N.Y. 1979).
144. Id. at 1012, 1014.

on metabolic therapy after reading an article by a layperson? Would the child then be a "neglected child"?

2. *Vaccination.* Should parents be able to refuse to vaccinate their children? Every state has laws requiring parents to vaccinate their children against certain diseases. The Supreme Court has upheld the constitutionality of compulsory vaccination laws as a proper exercise of the state's general police power.[145] Presumably, if the state can require everyone to receive a particular vaccine, it can require parents to have their children vaccinated. But most states have provided an exemption for parents with religious, or sometimes ethical, objections to vaccination. Why? At what point should parental prerogatives give way to public health concerns? Recent outbreaks of measles around the country have led to calls to repeal existing exemptions — a step some states have taken.[146] If a vaccine is developed to prevent coronavirus infections, but must be received annually, could the government make it mandatory for children? What if the virus causes more harm to adults but can be transmitted by children?

3. *Age.* In re E.G. essentially asks whether the state can intervene in ways that override the healthcare decisions of parent and child. How much does it matter that E.G. was seventeen at the time? How much should it matter?

4. *Parent Versus Child.* In *E.G.*, the wishes of the parent and the child aligned. What if the child wanted to make a decision that contravened the parent's wishes? Should children be empowered to make decisions over the objections of their parents? Should parents always be informed when children seek to make healthcare decisions for themselves?

The authority of a minor to make healthcare decisions generally has turned on application of the mature minor doctrine. Dissenting in *E.G.*, Judge Ward questioned the meaningfulness of the mature minor concept. How would a court determine whether a minor is sufficiently mature to make a particular healthcare decision? Are there some decisions for which no level of maturity would justify the decision?

In line with the mature minor doctrine, several states have statutes that allow minors to access medical care. A few state statutes permit children in their mid-teenage years to consent to general medical care absent parental consent.[147] Other states permit minors to make such decisions only in certain circumstances, such as when life-sustaining treatment is at issue or when the delay caused by obtaining parental consent would endanger the patient's health.[148]

---

145. Jacobson v. Massachusetts, 197 U.S. 11 (1905).

146. See, e.g., Cal. Health & Safety Code § 120365 (West 2020); Vt. Stat. Ann. tit. 18, § 1122 (2020) (removing philosophical exemptions).

147. See, e.g., Ala. Code § 22-8-4 (2020); Ark. Code Ann. § 20-9-602 (2020); Nev. Rev. Stat. § 129.030 (2020).

148. See Mont. Code Ann. § 41-1-405(2) (2020); N.M. Stat. Ann. § 24-7A-6.1 (2020).

5. *Is Maturity the Right Question?* Scholars pressing a more robust children's rights doctrine would recast the inquiry away from maturity and toward children's interests. Consider the perspective of Professors Dailey and Rosenbury, who would "put an end to seemingly futile debates over children's 'maturity.'"

> The concept of maturity has emerged in recent years as a focal point of legal decision making about children. Children who are deemed mature have access to adult rights and responsibilities, while those who are deemed immature remain subject to more paternalistic regulations. Yet focusing exclusively on maturity risks masking the real interests at stake in any given situation. . . interests in sexuality, reproductive agency, expression of identity, and civic engagement. While maturity is not irrelevant to identifying and weighing these interests, it should not be the endpoint of the analysis.[149]

As Dailey and Rosenbury suggest, many healthcare decisions affect individuals in significant ways that relate to identity formation, reproductive autonomy, and sexuality. Minors seek to make healthcare decisions that implicate these interests, but may be prevented from doing so by the need for parental consent. What kinds of decisions should minors be able to make without parental oversight? What principles should shape judicial and legislative determinations as to the kinds of decisions that fall into this category? In the materials that follow, we consider decisions regarding abortion and contraception.

BELLOTTI V. BAIRD
443 U.S. 622 (1979)

MR. JUSTICE POWELL announced the judgment of the Court and delivered an opinion, in which THE CHIEF JUSTICE, MR. JUSTICE STEWART, and MR. JUSTICE REHNQUIST joined.

These appeals present a challenge to the constitutionality of a state statute regulating the access of minors to abortions. . . .

I

A

On August 2, 1974, the Legislature of the Commonwealth of Massachusetts passed, over the Governor's veto, an Act pertaining to abortions performed within

---

149. Dailey & Rosenbury, supra note 97, at 1454.

the State. 1974 Mass. Acts, ch. 706. . . Mass. Gen. Laws Ann., ch. 112, § 12S (West Supp. 1979) . . . provides in part:

> If the mother is less than eighteen years of age and has not married, the consent of both the mother and her parents [to an abortion to be performed on the mother] is required. If one or both of the mother's parents refuse such consent, consent may be obtained by order of a judge of the superior court for good cause shown, after such hearing as he deems necessary. Such a hearing will not require the appointment of a guardian for the mother. If one of the parents has died or has deserted his or her family, consent by the remaining parent is sufficient. If both parents have died or have deserted their family, consent of the mother's guardian or other person having duties similar to a guardian, or any person who had assumed the care and custody of the mother is sufficient. The commissioner of public health shall prescribe a written form for such consent. Such form shall be signed by the proper person or persons and given to the physician performing the abortion who shall maintain it in his permanent files.

Physicians performing abortions in the absence of the consent required by § 12S are subject to injunctions and criminal penalties. . . .

II . . .

[T]he tradition of parental authority is not inconsistent with our tradition of individual liberty; rather, the former is one of the basic presuppositions of the latter. Legal restrictions on minors, especially those supportive of the parental role, may be important to the child's chances for the full growth and maturity that make eventual participation in a free society meaningful and rewarding. . . .

III . . .

Massachusetts has attempted to reconcile the constitutional right of a woman, in consultation with her physician, to choose to terminate her pregnancy . . . with the special interest of the State in encouraging an unmarried pregnant minor to seek the advice of her parents in making the important decision whether or not to bear a child. . . .

A

The pregnant minor's options are much different from those facing a minor in other situations, such as deciding whether to marry. A minor not permitted to marry before the age of majority is required simply to postpone her decision. She and her intended spouse may preserve the opportunity for later marriage should they continue to desire it. A pregnant adolescent, however, cannot preserve for long the possibility of aborting, which effectively expires in a matter of weeks from the onset of pregnancy.

Moreover, the potentially severe detriment facing a pregnant woman is not mitigated by her minority. Indeed, considering her probable education, employment skills, financial resources, and emotional maturity, unwanted motherhood may be exceptionally burdensome for a minor. In addition, the fact of having a child brings with it adult legal responsibility, for parenthood, like attainment of the age of majority, is one of the traditional criteria for the termination of the legal disabilities of minority. In sum, there are few situations in which denying a minor the right to make an important decision will have consequences so grave and indelible.

Yet, an abortion may not be the best choice for the minor. The circumstances in which this issue arises will vary widely. In a given case, alternatives to abortion, such as marriage to the father of the child, arranging for its adoption, or assuming the responsibilities of motherhood with the assured support of family, may be feasible and relevant to the minor's best interests. Nonetheless, the abortion decision is one that simply cannot be postponed, or it will be made by default with far-reaching consequences.

For these reasons, as we held in *Planned Parenthood of Central Missouri v. Danforth*, 428 U.S. 52, 74 (1976), "the State may not impose a blanket provision . . . requiring the consent of a parent or person *in loco parentis* as a condition for abortion of an unmarried minor during the first 12 weeks of her pregnancy." . . . [T]he unique nature and consequences of the abortion decision make it inappropriate "to give a third party an absolute, and possibly arbitrary, veto over the decision of the physician and his patient to terminate the patient's pregnancy, regardless of the reason for withholding the consent." 428 U.S. at 74. We therefore conclude that if the State decides to require a pregnant minor to obtain one or both parents' consent to an abortion, it also must provide an alternative procedure whereby authorization for the abortion can be obtained.

A pregnant minor is entitled in such a proceeding to show either: (1) that she is mature enough and well enough informed to make her abortion decision, in consultation with her physician, independently of her parents' wishes; or (2) that even if she is not able to make this decision independently, the desired abortion would be in her best interests. The proceeding in which this showing is made must assure that a resolution of the issue, and any appeals that may follow, will be completed with anonymity and sufficient expedition to provide an effective opportunity for an abortion to be obtained. In sum, the procedure must ensure that the provision requiring parental consent does not in fact amount to the "absolute, and possibly arbitrary, veto" that was found impermissible in *Danforth*.

B

It is against these requirements that § 12S must be tested. We observe initially that . . . the statute satisfies some of the concerns that require special treatment of a minor's abortion decision. It provides that if parental consent is refused, authorization may be "obtained by order of a judge of the superior court for good cause shown, after such hearing as he deems necessary." A superior court judge presiding over a § 12S proceeding "must disregard all parental objections, and other considerations, which are not based exclusively on what would serve the minor's best interests." . . .

Despite these safeguards, which avoid much of what was objectionable in the statute successfully challenged in *Danforth*, § 12S falls short of constitutional standards in certain respects. We now consider these.

(1)

[The state supreme court had construed the statute such that] . . . an available parent must be given notice of any judicial proceedings brought by a minor to obtain consent for an abortion.

We think that, construed in this manner, § 12S would impose an undue burden upon the exercise by minors of the right to seek an abortion. . . . "[T]here are parents who would obstruct, and perhaps altogether prevent, the minor's right to go to court." There is no reason to believe that this would be so in the majority of cases where consent is withheld. But many parents hold strong views on the subject of abortion, and young pregnant minors, especially those living at home, are particularly vulnerable to their parents' efforts to obstruct both an abortion and their access to court. It would be unrealistic, therefore, to assume that the mere existence of a legal right to seek relief in superior court provides an effective avenue of relief for some of those who need it the most. . . .

There is, however, an important state interest in encouraging a family rather than a judicial resolution of a minor's abortion decision. Also, as we have observed above, parents naturally take an interest in the welfare of their children — an interest that is particularly strong where a normal family relationship exists and where the child is living with one or both parents. These factors properly may be taken into account by a court called upon to determine whether an abortion in fact is in a minor's best interests. If, all things considered, the court determines that an abortion is in the minor's best interests, she is entitled to court authorization without any parental involvement. On the other hand, the court may deny the abortion request of an immature minor in the absence of parental consultation if it concludes that her best interests would be served thereby, or the court may in such a case defer decision until there is parental consultation in which the court may participate. But this is the full extent to which parental involvement may be required. For the reasons stated above, the constitutional right to seek an abortion may not be unduly burdened by state-imposed conditions upon initial access to court.

(2)

Section 12S requires that both parents consent to a minor's abortion. . . .

We are not persuaded that, as a general rule, the requirement of obtaining both parents' consent unconstitutionally burdens a minor's right to seek an abortion. . . . At least when the parents are together and the pregnant minor is living at home, both the father and mother have an interest — one normally supportive — in helping to determine the course that is in the best interests of a daughter. Consent and involvement by parents in important decisions by minors long have been recognized as protective of their immaturity. . . . As every pregnant minor is entitled in the first instance to go directly to the court for a judicial determination without prior parental notice, consultation, or consent, the general rule with respect to parental consent does not unduly burden the constitutional right. . . .

(3)

[The state supreme court had explained:]

> [W]e do not view the judge's role as limited to a determination that the minor is capable of making, and has made, an informed and reasonable decision to have an abortion. Certainly the judge must make a determination of those circumstances, but, if the statutory role of the judge to determine the best interests of the minor is to be carried out, he must make a finding on the basis of all relevant views presented to him. We suspect that the judge will give great weight to the minor's determination, if informed and reasonable, but in circumstances where he determines that the best interests of the minor will not be served by an abortion, the judge's determination should prevail, assuming that his conclusion is supported by the evidence and adequate findings of fact.

The Supreme Judicial Court's statement reflects the general rule that a State may require a minor to wait until the age of majority before being permitted to exercise legal rights independently. But we are concerned here with the exercise of a constitutional right of unique character. . . . [I]f the minor satisfies a court that she has attained sufficient maturity to make a fully informed decision, she then is entitled to make her abortion decision independently. We therefore agree with the District Court that § 12S cannot constitutionally permit judicial disregard of the abortion decision of a minor who has been determined to be mature and fully competent to assess the implications of the choice she has made.

IV

Although it satisfies constitutional standards in large part, § 12S falls short of them in two respects: First, it permits judicial authorization for an abortion to be withheld from a minor who is found by the superior court to be mature and fully competent to make this decision independently. Second, it requires parental consultation or notification in every instance, without affording the pregnant minor an opportunity to receive an independent judicial determination that she is mature enough to consent or that an abortion would be in her best interests. . . .

NOTES AND QUESTIONS

1. *Judicial Bypass in Practice.* In practice, minors' ability to access abortion through the judicial bypass mechanism varies considerably based on geography, demographics, and even the disposition of the particular judge. One study of parental consent and judicial bypass in Arkansas found that minors who obtained an abortion through the judicial bypass process were older and terminated the pregnancy earlier than those who obtained an abortion with parental consent.[150] A study of minors who sought a judicial bypass in Texas found that the process was burdensome, unpredictable, and traumatic.[151] Although several studies suggest that, in practice, minors face great difficulty using the judicial bypass process, these studies are relatively small-scale, due in part to the difficulty of empirically studying this issue.

There is evidence suggesting that courts may not be fully equipped to guide minors through the judicial bypass process. One study found that, of the sixty counties in Pennsylvania, only eight courts were able to provide complete and accurate information regarding minor's rights under the state's parental involvement law.[152] In states such as Tennessee, Alabama, Pennsylvania, and Minnesota, judges in a number of counties have refused to hear bypass petitions, at times citing moral or religious objections to abortion that would compromise their impartiality.[153]

2. *Minors in State Custody.* Do minors in the custody of the government have a right to abortion? Can the government attempt to prevent such minors from accessing abortion services? In Garza v. Hargan, the federal Court of Appeals for the D.C. Circuit confronted the question of whether an unaccompanied immigrant minor held in state custody had a right to access abortion.[154] The minor, J.D., had gone through the judicial bypass process and obtained an order giving her the legal right to consent to abortion, but the government nonetheless refused to allow her to access an abortion while in state custody. The district court granted a temporary restraining order, which required the government to permit J.D. to obtain an abortion while in state custody. A panel of the D.C. Circuit stayed the injunction. In an en banc decision, the D.C. Circuit vacated the stay, thereby permitting J.D. to access an abortion, which she did the following day. The government filed a petition for certiorari. In a per curiam

---

150. See Ted Joyce, Parental Consent for Abortion and the Judicial Bypass Option in Arkansas: Effects and Correlates, 42 Persp. on Sexual & Repro. Health 168, 172 (2010).

151. See Kate Coleman-Minahan et al., Young Women's Experiences Obtaining Judicial Bypass for Abortion in Texas, 64 J. Adolescent Health 20 (2019).

152. See Helena Silverstein, Road Closed: Evaluating the Judicial Bypass Provision of the Pennsylvania Abortion Control Act, 24 Law & Soc. Inquiry 73, 81 (1999).

153. See Adam Liptak, On Moral Grounds, Some Judges are Opting Out of Abortion Cases, N.Y. Times, Sept. 4, 2005; see also Hodgson v. Minnesota, 497 U.S. 417, 440 (1990).

154. 874 F.3d 735 (D.C. Cir. 2017), vacated as moot sub nom., Azar v. Garza, 138 S. Ct. 1790 (2018).

opinion, the Supreme Court vacated the D.C. Circuit's en banc order and remanded the case to the D.C. Circuit with instructions to direct the district court to dismiss the case as moot.

Writing in concurrence to the D.C. Circuit's en banc order, Judge Millett asserted that the Fifth Amendment's Due Process Clause protected J.D.'s right to an abortion, regardless of the fact that she was an undocumented minor in government custody. Judge Millett rejected the government's position that J.D. had the burden of extracting herself from government custody if she wanted to get an abortion. Instead, Judge Millett argued that the government's position constituted an undue burden that imposed substantial and unjustified obstacles on J.D.'s ability to access an abortion. First, she rejected the government's argument that waiting for J.D. to obtain a sponsor did not impose an undue burden. Pointing to the already-seven-week-long delay in finding a sponsor for J.D., as well as the extensive screening required in order for someone to become a sponsor, Judge Millett explained that delay caused by this process constituted an undue burden. Second, Judge Millett rejected the government's argument that permitting J.D. to get an abortion amounted to the government's *facilitating* her abortion. Instead, given the support of J.D.'s guardian ad litem, the only requirement on the government would be not to interfere with the abortion or make things more difficult.

Judge Henderson, dissenting, argued that J.D. had no constitutional right to an abortion because she was not a U.S. citizen. Judge (now Justice) Kavanaugh also wrote a separate dissent, expressing concern that the majority opinion would "allow unlawful immigrant minors to have an immediate abortion on demand."[155] He argued that this order created new law, instead of applying existing law. Heavily emphasizing the differences between minors and adults, Judge Kavanaugh argued that placing J.D. with a sponsor would help her in deciding whether to have an abortion.

CAREY V. POPULATION SERVICES INTERNATIONAL
431 U.S. 678 (1977)

MR. JUSTICE BRENNAN delivered the opinion of the Court (Parts I, II, III, and V), together with an opinion (Part IV), in which MR. JUSTICE STEWART, MR. JUSTICE MARSHALL, and MR. JUSTICE BLACKMUN joined.

Under New York Educ. Law § 6811(8) (McKinney 1972) it is a crime . . . for any person to sell or distribute any contraceptive of any kind to a minor under the age of 16 years. . . .

---

155. Garza, 874 F.3d at 755 (Kavanaugh, J., dissenting).

The District Court . . . held unconstitutional, as applied to nonprescription contraceptives, the provision of § 6811(8) prohibiting the distribution of contraceptives to those under 16 years of age. Appellants contend that this provision of the statute is constitutionally permissible as a regulation of the morality of minors, in furtherance of the State's policy against promiscuous sexual intercourse among the young.

The question of the extent of state power to regulate conduct of minors not constitutionally regulable when committed by adults is a vexing one, perhaps not susceptible of precise answer. We have been reluctant to attempt to define "the totality of the relationship of the juvenile and the state." Certain principles, however, have been recognized. "Minors, as well as adults, are protected by the Constitution and possess constitutional rights." *Planned Parenthood of Central Missouri v. Danforth*, 428 U.S. 52, 74 (1976). . . . On the other hand, we have held in a variety of contexts that "the power of the state to control the conduct of children reaches beyond the scope of its authority over adults." *Prince v. Massachusetts*, 321 U.S. 158, 170 (1944).

Of particular significance to the decision of this case, the right to privacy in connection with decisions affecting procreation extends to minors as well as to adults. . . .

Since the State may not impose a blanket prohibition, or even a blanket requirement of parental consent, on the choice of a minor to terminate her pregnancy, the constitutionality of a blanket prohibition of the distribution of contraceptives to minors is a fortiori foreclosed. The State's interests in protection of the mental and physical health of the pregnant minor, and in protection of potential life are clearly more implicated by the abortion decision than by the decision to use a nonhazardous contraceptive.

Appellants argue, however, that significant state interests are served by restricting minors' access to contraceptives, because free availability to minors of contraceptives would lead to increased sexual activity among the young, in violation of the policy of New York to discourage such behavior. The argument is that minors' sexual activity may be deterred by increasing the hazards attendant on it. The same argument, however, would support a ban on abortions for minors, or indeed support a prohibition on abortions, or access to contraceptives, for the unmarried, whose sexual activity is also against the public policy of many States. Yet, in each of these areas, the Court has rejected the argument. . . . The reason for this unanimous rejection was stated in *Eisenstadt v. Baird*: "It would be plainly unreasonable to assume that [the State] has prescribed pregnancy and the birth of an unwanted child [or the physical and psychological dangers of an abortion] as punishment for fornication." 405 U.S. 438, 448 (1972). . . .

Moreover, there is substantial reason for doubt whether limiting access to contraceptives will in fact substantially discourage early sexual behavior. Appellants themselves conceded in the District Court that "there is no evidence that teenage extramarital sexual activity increases in proportion to the availability of contraceptives," and accordingly offered none, in the District Court or here. Appellees, on the other hand, cite a considerable body of evidence and opinion indicating that there is no such deterrent effect. Although we take judicial notice, as did the District Court, that with or without access to contraceptives, the incidence of sexual activity among minors is high, and the consequences of such activity are frequently devastating, the studies cited by appellees play no part in our decision. It is enough that we again confirm the principle that when a State, as here, burdens the exercise of a fundamental right, its attempt to justify that burden as a rational means for the accomplishment of some significant state policy requires more than a bare assertion, based on a conceded complete absence of supporting evidence, that the burden is connected to such a policy. . . .

MR. JUSTICE POWELL, concurring in part and concurring in the judgment. . . .

Although I concur in the judgment of the Court, I am not persuaded that the Constitution requires the severe constraints that the Court's opinion places upon legislative efforts to regulate the distribution of contraceptives, particularly to the young. . . .

There is . . . no justification for subjecting restrictions on the sexual activity of the young to heightened judicial review. Under our prior cases, the States have broad latitude to legislate with respect to adolescents. . . . Restraints on the freedom of minors may be justified "even though comparable restraints on adults would be constitutionally impermissible."

New York has exercised its responsibility over minors in areas falling within the "cluster of constitutionally protected choices" relating to sex and marriage. It has set an age limitation below which persons cannot marry without parental consent, and has established by statute the age at which a minor is legally recognized as having the capacity to consent to sexual activity. These provisions highlight the State's concern that its juvenile citizens generally lack the maturity and understanding necessary to make decisions concerning marriage and sexual relationships.

Until today, I would not have thought it was even arguably necessary to review state regulation of this sort under a standard that for all practical purposes approaches the "compelling state interest" standard. . . .

New York has made it a crime for anyone other than a physician to sell or distribute contraceptives to minors under the age of 16 years. This element of New York's program of regulation for the protection of its minor citizens is said to evidence the State's judgment that the health and well-being of minors would be better assured if they are not encouraged to engage in sexual intercourse without guidance. Although I have no doubt that properly framed legislation serving this purpose would meet constitutional standards, the New York provision is defective in two respects. First, it infringes the privacy interests of married females between the ages of 14 and 16, in that it prohibits the distribution of contraceptives to such females except by a physician. In authorizing marriage at that age, the State also sanctions sexual intercourse between the partners and expressly recognizes that once the marriage relationship exists the husband and wife are presumed to possess the requisite understanding and maturity to make decisions concerning sex and procreation. Consequently, the state interest that justifies a requirement of prior counseling with respect to minors in general simply is inapplicable with respect to minors for whom the State has affirmatively approved marriage.

Second, this provision prohibits parents from distributing contraceptives to their children, a restriction that unjustifiably interferes with parental interests in rearing their children. "[C]onstitutional interpretation has consistently recognized that the parents' claim to authority in their own household to direct the rearing of their children is basic in the structure of our society. 'It is cardinal with us that the custody, care and nurture of the child reside first in the parents, whose primary function and freedom include preparation for obligations the state can neither supply nor hinder.'" Moreover, this statute would allow the State "to enquire into, prove, and punish," Poe v. Ullman, 367 U.S. 497, 548 (1961) (Harlan, J., dissenting), the exercise of this parental responsibility. The State points to no interest of sufficient magnitude to justify this direct interference with the parental guidance that is especially appropriate in this sensitive area of child development....

I therefore agree with the Court that the entire provision must be invalidated.

But in my view there is considerably more room for state regulation in this area than would be permissible under the plurality's opinion. It seems clear to me, for example, that the State would further a constitutionally permissible end if it encouraged adolescents to seek the advice and guidance of their parents before deciding whether to engage in sexual intercourse. The State justifiably may take note of the psychological pressures that might influence children at a time in their lives when they generally do not possess the maturity necessary to understand and control their responses. Participation in sexual intercourse at an early age may have both physical and psychological consequences. These include the risks of venereal disease and pregnancy, and the less obvious mental and emotional problems that may result from sexual activity by children. Moreover, society has long adhered to the view that sexual intercourse should not be engaged in promiscuously, a judgment that an adolescent may be less likely to heed than an adult.

Requiring minors to seek parental guidance would be consistent with our prior cases....

A requirement of prior parental consultation is merely one illustration of permissible regulation in this area. As long as parental distribution is permitted, a State should have substantial latitude in regulating the distribution of contraceptives to minors....

Mr. Justice Rehnquist, dissenting.

Those who valiantly but vainly defended the heights of Bunker Hill in 1775 made it possible that men such as James Madison might later sit in the first Congress and draft the Bill of Rights to the Constitution. The post-Civil War Congresses which drafted the Civil War Amendments to the Constitution could not have accomplished their task without the blood of brave men on both sides which was shed at Shiloh, Gettysburg, and Cold Harbor. If those responsible for these Amendments, by feats of valor or efforts of draftsmanship, could have lived to know that their efforts had enshrined in the Constitution the right of commercial vendors of contraceptives to peddle them to unmarried minors through such means as window displays and vending machines located in the men's room of truck stops, notwithstanding the considered judgment of the New York Legislature to the contrary, it is not difficult to imagine their reaction. . . .

NOTES AND QUESTIONS

1. *Contraception.* Roughly half of all states allow all minors to access contraception without parental consent.[156] Several other states allow some minors to access contraceptive services if they fall into certain categories: for example, if they are married or have been pregnant in the past.[157] Under federal law, clinics that are funded by Title X family planning funds cannot require parental consent for birth control, even in states that otherwise require it.[158] Minors also have over-the-counter access without parental consent to the "morning after" pill, which is used within forty-eight hours of unprotected sex to prevent conception.[159] Should minors have access to contraception without parental consent? Why might parents object to their children's access to or use of contraception? Under what circumstances, if any, should the law recognize such objections? Does the government have a public health interest that justifies providing access to contraception to minors? If teenage pregnancy rates are higher in states where contraceptive access requires parental consent, would the government have sufficient reason to limit parental authority in this context?[160] Should the question of contraceptive access be approached as one of children's rights, rather than state limits on parental authority? Are there also equality interests at stake? Scholars and advocates have long argued that access to contraception is critical to women's equality.[161] Control over reproduction allows women to pursue educational and career opportunities. Does the same argument apply to girls?

---

156. See Guttmacher Inst., Minors' Access to Contraceptive Services (June 1, 2020). See, e.g., Cal. Fam. Code § 6925(a) (West 2020); Tenn. Code Ann. § 68-34-107 (2020); Va. Code Ann. § 54.1-2969(E)(2) (2020).

157. See Minors' Access to Contraceptive Services, supra note 156. See, e.g., Colo. Rev. Stat. § 13-22-105 (2020).

158. See 42 U.S.C. § 300(a) (2018); 42 C.F.R. §§ 59.5(a)(4), (14) (2020).

159. See Gardiner Harris, F.D.A. Easing Access to 'Morning After' Pill, N.Y. Times, Apr. 22, 2009, at A14; Michael D. Shear & Pam Belluck, U.S. Drops Bid to Limit Sales of Morning-After Pill, N.Y. Times, June 10, 2013, at A1.

160. Carol A. Ford & Abigail English, Limiting Confidentiality of Adolescent Health Services: What Are the Risks?, 288 JAMA 752 (2002).

161. See, e.g., Neil S. Siegel & Reva B. Siegel, Compelling Interests and Contraception, 47 Conn. L. Rev. 1025 (2015).

2. *HIV/AIDS and STD/STI Testing and Treatment.* States generally allow min access to testing and treatment for sexually transmitted disease and infection without parental consent, and many states allow minors to access preventative care without parental consent.[162] Thirty-two states have laws that explicitly include HIV testing and treatment, while others refer to STD testing more generally.

Of the states that allow minors to access diagnosis and treatment without parental consent, most have no age requirement; a few require that the consenting minor be at least twelve; a few require the minor to be at least fourteen; and one state—South Carolina—requires the minor to be at least sixteen.[163] In general, states allow for both diagnosis and treatment under the same circumstances. However, there are some exceptions. For example, in Alabama, a minor of any age may seek a diagnosis for an STD, but must be twelve years or older to unilaterally consent to treatment.[164]

What is the right approach? Should minors have access to testing and treatment without parental consent? Why might a state permit minors to access STD/STI testing and treatment, but not contraception?

While the conversation around HIV has focused on testing and treatment, preventative drug therapies, termed pre-exposure prophylaxis (PrEP), are now available. Should minors have access to PrEP without parental consent? As the Centers for Disease Control explains, PrEP is recommended for individuals who are at high risk of HIV infection, including men who have sex with men (MSM) and injection drug users.[165] Does a parent have a right to know the information that renders the child high-risk? Are there other interests at stake, such as the child's privacy interests in sex and sexuality?

3. *Substance Abuse.* The vast majority of states allow minors to access substance abuse treatment without parental consent. Forty states allow minors to receive inpatient treatment without parental consent, and forty-seven states allow minors to receive outpatient treatment without parental consent.[166] Nevertheless, these statutes may have limited use in practice. Because of the nature of addiction, very few minors seek treatment on their own initiative.[167]

---

162. See Ctrs. for Disease Control and Prevention, Minors' Consent Laws for HIV and STD Services (2018); see also, e.g., Fla. Stat. § 384.30 (2020); Minn. Stat. § 144.343(1) (2020); Wash. Rev. Code § 70.24.110 (2020).

163. See Minors' Consent Laws for HIV and STD Services, supra note 162.

164. See Ala. Code §§ 22-8-6, 22-11A-19 (2020).

165. See Ctrs. for Disease Control and Prevention, Pre-Exposure Prophylaxis (PrEP), https://www .cdc.gov/hiv/risk/prep/index.html.

166. See, e.g., Conn. Gen. Stat. § 17a-688(d) (2020); Del Code Ann. tit. 16, § 2201(b) (2020); 71 Pa. Cons. Stat. § 1690.112 (2020).

167. See generally Mary Louise E. Kerwin et al., What Can Parents Do? A Review of State Laws Regarding Decision Making for Adolescent Drug Abuse and Mental Health Treatment, 24 J. Child Adolescent Substance Abuse 166 (2015).

alth Treatment. Twenty-seven states permit minors to access men-
~~it~~ without parental consent.[168] However, the majority of these states
~~ge~~ requirements, most of which are higher than the age require-
~~s~~ to access STD/STI services without parental consent.[169] Should such
~~.~~ in light of rising rates of depression and anxiety among young peo-
~~~ut the fact of rising suicide rates?[171] Could data of this kind justify government ~~~ that limits parental authority over children's access to mental health
services?

5. *Sexual Orientation and "Conversion Therapy"*. In recent years, many states have
banned mental health providers from offering to minors "sexual orientation change efforts"
(also commonly called "conversion" or "reparative" therapy). Parents challenged bans of
this kind as a violation of their constitutional rights to direct their children's upbringing.
In Pickup v. Brown, the Ninth Circuit Court of Appeals rejected these claims, finding that
parental rights do not include a "right to choose a specific mental health treatment that
the state has reasonably deemed harmful to minors."[172] In that case, children were named
as plaintiffs along with their parents. With decisions like *Pickup*, the government is authorized to withhold the therapy from parents and children in order to prevent harm. It is
less clear whether, in states that do not prohibit therapy of this kind, children's interest in
rejecting such therapy can override their parents' decision to subject them to it.

6. *Intersex Children*. Some children are born with ambiguous genitalia or
other intersex conditions.[173] For many years, medical professionals and parents have
sought to "confirm" the sex of intersex children through surgical interventions. But
procedures of this kind can have devastating consequences, as the child's assigned
sex may not match their gender identity. That is, an intersex child who has the identity female surgically imposed shortly after birth may have a male gender identity.
Accordingly, advocacy groups have demanded that doctors stop this practice and
instead wait until the child is old enough to make a decision about any medical
intervention. According to these groups, the harm to the child is so grave that parents should not be allowed to demand surgical intervention, and doctors should not
be allowed to offer or perform it. In 2018, California became the first state to move
in this direction. The state senate passed Resolution 110, which "recognizes that
intersex children should be free to choose whether to undergo life-altering surgeries that irreversibly — and sometimes irreparably — cause harm," and therefore "calls

---

168. See, e.g., Colo. Rev. Stat. § 27-65-103 (2020); Me. Rev. Stat. Ann. tit. 22, § 1502 (2020); Va. Code
Ann. § 54.1-2969 (2020).

169. See, e.g., Haw. Rev. Stat. § 334-60.1 (2020); Md. Code Ann., Health-Gen § 20-104 (West 2020);
Or. Rev. Stat. § 109.675 (2020).

170. See Jean M. Twenge et al., Age, Period, and Cohort Trends in Mood Disorder Indicators and
Suicide-Related Outcomes in a Nationally Representative Dataset, 2005-2017, 128 J. Abnormal Psych. 185
(2019).

171. See id.

172. 740 F.3d 1208, 1225 (9th Cir. 2014)

173. See Julie Greenberg, Intersexuality and the Law: Why Sex Matters (2012).

upon stakeholders in the health professions to foster the well-being of children born with variations of sex characteristics, and the adults they will become, through the enactment of policies and procedures that ensure individualized, multidisciplinary care that respects the rights of the patient to participate in decisions, [and] defers medical or surgical intervention . . . until the child is able to participate in decision-making."[174] Is there a justification for crafting a special rule for this medical procedure? Should parents be permitted to make other irreversible medical decisions such as the decision to circumcise a male infant?

7. *Distinguishing Among Minors.* Generally, we have been considering the rights of children who remain in parental custody. For children in state custody, the state may generally make medical decisions for the minor or authorize foster parents to make such decisions.[175] For homeless youth who are neither in state nor parental custody, the issue is more complicated. The vast majority of states are silent on the question of when homeless youth may consent to medical treatment. However, Arizona and Florida both permit homeless minors to consent to medical care without parental consent.[176] Other states allow minors to consent to healthcare if they are living apart from their parents and managing their own affairs, even if they are not formally emancipated.[177]

PROBLEM

A growing number of transgender children are receiving gender-related treatment. Many of these children receive care with — indeed, because of — parental support. But Alex, a 12-year-old transgender boy, does not enjoy such parental support. When Alex informed his parents after years of struggle that he identifies as a boy, even though he was assigned female at birth, his parents resisted. They refuse to use male pronouns and refer to Alex as Alexandra, the name they gave their child at birth. Alex wants to consult a therapist and a physician about gender-related care. Alex would like to learn more about a diagnosis of gender dysphoria, which may assist Alex in seeking medical care, and would like to learn about hormone blockers. Alex's parents refuse to allow Alex to access these healthcare services. You are an attorney at a statewide LGBT legal organization, and Alex calls you to discuss his options. Do you believe Alex has any claim to gender-related healthcare over his parents' objections? On what grounds might Alex be able to obtain such care? How likely is Alex to prevail if he were to petition a court?

---

174. S. Res. 110, 2017-2018 Leg., Reg. Sess. (Cal. 2018).

175. See, e.g., Conn. Gen. Stat. § 46b-132a (2020); Tex. Fam. Code Ann. § 266.004(b) (West 2020).

176. See Ariz. Rev. Stat. Ann. § 44-132(a), (c) (2020); Fla. Stat. § 743.067(3)(b) (2020).

177. See, e.g., Cal. Fam. Code § 6922(a) (West 2020); Colo. Rev. Stat. § 13-22-103(1) (2020); Wyo. Stat. Ann. § 14-1-101(b)(iv) (2020).

The Child Welfare System

In Chapter 6, we saw that the United States has a strong parental rights tradition. Parents generally are trusted — and expected — to raise their children as they see fit, without government intervention or second-guessing. This parental authority may end, though, when the parent is causing the child harm. The state, exercising its *parens patriae* power, may intervene in the family to protect the child. This power justifies federal child welfare law as well as states' child welfare systems, which are tasked with responding to reports of suspected child abuse or neglect and arranging temporary or permanent care for children without parents or guardians. Unlike many of the other areas of family law we address, child welfare law is a place where the federal government exerts significant influence. A vast body of federal laws and regulations governs how states structure and operate their child welfare systems. Throughout this chapter, we draw on federal and state law, seeing how the two interact.

This chapter's sequence of topics reflects the sequence of stages in the child welfare system: after addressing the role of the federal government, we examine abuse and neglect, intervention and removal, foster care, and termination of parental rights. In the middle of the chapter, we explore critiques of the system, with a focus on questions of race and class. As you read, consider the following questions: Is the child welfare system a positive force in society? How does it help children? How does it help parents? Or is the child welfare system a state function to be viewed with suspicion? What should be the primary goal of the child welfare system? Child safety? Family preservation? Stable placements for children who have been abused or neglected? How well does the current system achieve any of these goals? How might it do better?

I. The Federal Government's Role in the Child Welfare System

Although state agencies are responsible for the child welfare system, the federal government exerts substantial control by requiring states to meet certain conditions in order to receive federal funds. Between 2013 and 2017, the federal government spent between $7.5 and $8.9 billion annually on child welfare programs.[1] Because of this substantial funding, state child welfare programs comply with federal requirements.

Federal law governing child welfare has vacillated between a focus on child safety and a focus on family preservation. Before the 1960s, the federal government played a limited role in the child welfare system. It primarily provided federal assistance to states, often by paying for cash assistance for low-income families. In the first half of the twenty-first century, this federally subsidized system focused on family preservation, causing the foster care population to drop substantially.[2]

This trend reversed in the 1960s for two reasons. First, academic research increased public awareness about child abuse, which ultimately led Congress to pass the Child Abuse Prevention and Treatment Act (CAPTA) of 1974.[3] CAPTA mandated that states use particular definitions of abuse and neglect and that they impose mandatory reporting requirements in cases of suspected child abuse; in exchange, states received federal funds for their child welfare systems. Second, Congress began to structure funding for foster care in a way that ended the de facto preference for family preservation. Beginning in 1961, a series of amendments to the federal welfare program permitted federal funding to be used for cash payments to foster children whose parents would have been eligible to receive welfare benefits.[4] The laws that governed federal funds in the child welfare system changed over time but continued to deprioritize family preservation, which increased the number of children in foster care. By 1980, there were approximately 500,000 children in foster care, and children stayed in foster care for an average of 2.5 years.[5]

In response to the large number of children in foster care, Congress passed the Adoption Assistance and Child Welfare Act of 1980 (AACWA), which emphasized family preservation and reunification.[6] AACWA required that state agencies make "reasonable efforts" to avoid removing children from their families and to prioritize

---

1. See Emilie Stoltzfus, Cong. Research Serv., R43458, Child Welfare: An Overview of Federal Programs and Their Current Funding 2 (2017).

2. See Brenda G. McGowan, Historical Evolution of Child Welfare Services, in Child Welfare for the 21st Century: A Handbook of Practices, Policies & Programs 26–27 (Gerald P. Mallon & Peg McCartt Hess, eds., 2005).

3. Pub. L. No. 93-247 (codified at 42 U.S.C. §§ 5101 et seq.). The landmark article is C. Henry Kempe et al., The Battered-Child Syndrome, 181 J. Am. Med. Ass'n 17 (1962).

4. See Pub. L. No. 87–31 § 2 (codified at 42 U.S.C. § 608); Pub. L. No. 87-543 § 135 (codified as amended at 42 U.S.C. § 608); Pub. L. No. 90-248, tit. II, § 208(a) (codified as amended at 42 U.S.C. § 602(a)(20)).

5. Stephanie Jill Gendell, In Search of Permanency: A Reflection on the First Three Years of the Adoption and Safe Families Act Implementation, 39 Fam. & Conciliation Cts. Rev. 25, 27 (2001).

6. Pub. L. No. 96-272 (codified as amended in scattered sections of 42 U.S.C.).

family reunification for children who had been removed. In large part due to these efforts at family preservation, the number of children removed dropped dramatically and the foster care population was cut in half by the mid-1980s. But by the late 1990s, the population had risen to approximately 500,000 again.[7] During this time, the emphasis on family preservation and reunification began to draw criticism. One commentator suggests that the efforts at family preservation "came to symbolize for its critics a lack of attention to the safety needs of children, and a willingness to put concern about parents ahead of concern about children."[8]

The Adoption and Safe Families Act of 1997 (ASFA) was passed amidst this backlash to family reunification,[9] and sought to promote permanency by expediting removal and termination. It clarified that "the child's health and safety shall be paramount" in the requirement that states make "reasonable efforts" to reunify families.[10] ASFA requires that child protective services commence "concurrent planning" after a child has been removed, mandating that the state contemporaneously make plans to secure a successful adoption for the child in the event that reunification does not occur.[11] While concurrent planning reflects the belief that permanent placement is in the child's best interests, some argue that strict statutory deadlines — combined with overworked agencies and prejudice against parents of lower socioeconomic status — result in families unduly being separated.[12]

ASFA requires states to file a petition to terminate parental rights of any child who has been in state custody for fifteen of the past twenty-two months unless the child is being cared for by a relative, the agency has documented a compelling reason why filing a petition is not in the child's best interests, or the state has failed to provide the family with needed services.[13] Similarly, agencies are required to file petitions to terminate parental rights if a court determines that the child has been abandoned or that the parent has committed certain violent crimes. ASFA also created financial incentives for states that increased the number of children adopted out of foster care each year. Advocates of ASFA assert that expediting terminations and adoptions has helped more children to achieve permanency, but critics argue that this increased intervention is traumatic for many children and point to disproportionate rates of removal and termination in families of color.[14]

---

7. See Kathleen S. Bean, Reasonable Efforts: What State Courts Think, 36 U. Tol. L. Rev. 321, 325–26 (2005).

8. Frank Farrow, The Shifting Policy Impact of Intensive Family Preservation Services 9 (Chapin Hall Ctr. for Children 2001).

9. Pub. L. No. 105-89 (codified in scattered sections of 42 U.S.C.).

10. Id. § 101(a) (codified at 42 U.S.C. § 671(a)(15)).

11. 42 U.S.C. § 671(a)(15)(F) (2018).

12. See, e.g., Lisa R. Pruitt, Judging Parents, Judging Place: Poverty, Rurality, and Termination of Parental Rights, 77 Mo. L. Rev. 95, 148 (2012).

13. Pub. L. No. 105-89 § 103(3) (codified at 42 U.S.C. § 675(5)).

14. See generally Jessica Dixon, The African-American Child Welfare Act: A Legal Redress for African American Disproportionality in Child Protection Cases, 10 Berkeley J. Afr.-Am. L. & Pol'y 109, 114–117 (2008); Susan L. Brooks & Dorothy E. Roberts, Social Justice and Family Court Reform, 40 Fam. Ct. Rev. 453, 454 (2002).

As part of a bipartisan budget deal, Congress enacted the Family First Prevention Services Act of 2018 (FFPSA).[15] In enacting FFPSA, Congress shifted back toward a more preventative approach. FFPSA permits states to use federal funds for up to twelve months of preventative services, including mental health services and substance abuse treatment, for families in which children are at risk of entering foster care. Although FFPSA prioritizes family maintenance and reunification, it leaves many of ASFA's measures in place that hasten termination, such as states' obligations to file a termination petition if the child has been in state custody for fifteen of the past twenty-two months.

II. Abuse and Neglect

Attempts to address child abuse and neglect originally came from private charities in the late nineteenth century.[16] Eventually, state and local governments responded as well. By the late 1960s, every state had laws regulating the reporting of child abuse to public agencies.[17] But reporting itself would not solve the problem. Concerned with the inadequacy of efforts at the state level, Congress enacted CAPTA in 1974.[18] CAPTA set out federal requirements for child abuse reporting and prevention and supplied federal funding to state child welfare programs.[19] While some criticized CAPTA as too modest to address the pressing and complex problem of child abuse and neglect, the legislation nonetheless represented the federal government's first widescale effort to address the issue.

The funding authorized by CAPTA was conditioned on states' adoption of uniform statutory definitions of child abuse and neglect.[20] Most state statutory schemes separately recognize four categories of child "maltreatment": physical abuse, sexual abuse, emotional abuse, and neglect.[21] Some states have also codified parental substance abuse and abandonment as distinct categories.[22] Despite the more uniform definitions mandated by federal law, states vary in how they operationalize these definitions — with some speaking in general terms and others offering more specific criteria.

---

15. Pub. L. No. 115-123.

16. On this history, see Jill Elaine Hasday, Parenthood Divided: A Legal History of the Bifurcated Law of Parental Relations, 90 Geo. L.J. 299 (2002).

17. See Children's Bureau, Nat'l Child Abuse and Neglect Training Publ'ns Project, The Child Abuse Prevention and Treatment Act: 40 Years of Safeguarding America's Children 4 (2014); see also McGowan, supra note 2, at 10–44.

18. 42 U.S.C. § 5101 (2018).

19. Id.

20. Id.

21. Children's Bureau, Child Welfare Info. Gateway, Definitions of Child Abuse and Neglect: State Statutes 2 (2019).

22. Id.

California, for example, lays out highly particularized, specific standards for physical abuse that render a child "dependent" and subject to the supervision of the Department of Social Services. Physical abuse is defined as the child's guardian or parent subjecting a child to "serious physical harm," which includes permanent physical trauma, a single act of sexual abuse, and willful starvation.[23] By contrast, New Hampshire does not distinguish its standards in the same way, defining an "abused child" more generally as "any child who has been sexually abused, intentionally physically injured, or physically injured by other than accidental means."[24]

The definition of child neglect likewise varies across states. In New York, neglect is specifically indicated by evidence that a caregiver has failed to "exercise a minimum degree of care" with respect to supplying "the child with proper supervision or guardianship;" "by unreasonably inflicting or allowing harm to be inflicted, or a substantial risk thereof, including the infliction of excessive corporal punishment;" "by misusing drugs or alcoholic beverages that he or she loses self-control of his or her actions;" or "by any other acts of a similarly serious nature requiring the aid of the court."[25] Alaska, on the other hand, defines neglect generally as "the failure by a person responsible for the child's welfare to provide necessary food, care, clothing, shelter, or medical attention."[26]

Some states also have codified exceptions from their definitions of child abuse and neglect. Financial inability to care for a child is exempted from the definition of neglect in many states.[27] What about physical discipline? As long as it is reasonable and causes no serious bodily injury to a child, physical discipline is omitted from the definition of abuse in many states.[28] As we saw in the previous chapter, the legality of corporal punishment is controversial. How should a judge in an abuse and neglect proceeding distinguish between the use of legally reasonable force to discipline and force that is cruel or excessive?[29]

As you read the cases that follow, ask yourself whether you would find that the parents engaged in abuse or neglect. And consider what course of action you think is in the best interests of the children — staying with their parents, being removed with the possibility of reunification, or being removed with the prospect of finding a permanent placement. A warning: the second case involves child sexual abuse.

---

23. Cal. Welf. & Inst. Code § 300 (West 2020).

24. N.H. Rev. Stat. § 169-C:3 (2020).

25. N.Y. Fam. Ct. Act § 1012 (2020).

26. Alaska Stat. § 47.17.2 (2020).

27. Definitions of Child Abuse and Neglect: State Statutes, supra note 21, at 4.

28. Id.

29. Compare Gonzalez v. Santa Clara Cty. Dep't of Soc. Servs., 223 Cal. App. 4th 72, 75 (2014) (holding that the "parental privilege to impose reasonable physical discipline" could include spanking a child with a wooden spoon with enough force to produce bruising), with G.A.C. v. State ex rel. Juvenile Dep't of Polk Cty., 182 P.3d 223 (Or. Ct. App. 2008) (holding that disciplining a child with a wooden spoon constituted child abuse since it caused substantial physical injury via bruising).

In Interest of W.P.

534 So. 2d 905 (Fla. Dist. Ct. App. 1988)

PARKER, JUDGE.

The parents of W.P. appeal the trial court's order adjudicating W.P. to be a dependent child. We reverse.

The Department of Health and Rehabilitative Services (HRS) filed a petition for dependency on behalf of W.P., alleging that W.P. was an abused child. The petition specifically alleged that W.P.'s father slapped the daughter on the side of the face with his hand and that the mother pulled W.P.'s hair. The trial court, finding physical abuse, entered an order of dependency requiring protective service supervision by HRS.

HRS is required to establish the status of dependency, as alleged in its petition, by the preponderance of the evidence. We have examined the record and find insufficient evidence to establish that W.P.'s parents "abused" her. Abuse is defined in the statute as "any willful act that results in any physical, mental, or sexual injury that causes or is likely to cause the child's physical, mental, or emotional health to be significantly impaired." Here, the facts adduced at the adjudicatory hearing are undisputed. The father admitted slapping W.P. on the side of her face with his open hand when W.P. used vulgar language toward her mother. Then W.P. pushed her father against the wall which caused the mother to pull W.P.'s hair. The father's hand left a mark on W.P.'s face; however, she required no medical attention. Further, there was no testimony from any witness that the slap or hair pulling significantly impaired W.P.'s physical, mental, or emotional health. Accordingly, the trial court's order granting the petition for dependency on the ground of abuse must be reversed.

In re Mariah T.

71 Cal. Rptr. 3d 542 (Cal. Ct. App. 2008)

RUBIN, J. . . .

In February 2007, respondent Los Angeles County Department of Children and Family Services (DCFS) took custody of eight-year-old Mariah T. and her three-year-old brother Bryce T. after their father, Anthony T., reported that Mariah told him she had been sexually fondled by mother Monique B.'s live-in boyfriend Jason. Mariah told a DCFS social worker that for two nights in a row Jason came into her room while she was sleeping, lay down next to her, and fondled her thigh near the crotch area. When she awoke and asked what was happening, Jason put his finger to his lips as a signal that she should keep quiet. Mariah told mother what happened, but mother accused her of lying and dismissed her claims. Mariah and Bryce also reported that mother had whipped them with a belt. According to father, Mariah told him that mother warned Mariah not to tell anyone what Jason had done and that, if she did, she would never see father again.

Based on this, DCFS filed a petition seeking to have the children declared dependents of the court under Welfare and Institutions Code section 300. The petition alleged that the children suffered or were at risk of serious physical harm from mother's corporal punishment methods, and that Mariah had been sexually abused by a household member. The sexual abuse claims were also the basis of allegations that mother failed to protect the children from sexual abuse and that mother's conduct placed Bryce at risk of sexual abuse. . . .

Mariah testified that mother hit her in the back with a belt five times, once because she had lost her jacket. According to Mariah, one of those beatings left her with a red line on her back. Mariah testified that mother also used a belt on Bryce's stomach and hands on three occasions, once because he would not write out the letter 'B' and once because he sprayed mother's perfume in his own eye. Mariah recalled that one of those incidents left Bryce with marks on his hands that turned from yellow to purple or red. Mother also hit both children with her open hand several times. The court also considered a DCFS report where father stated he once found a large bruise on Bryce's forearm that was changing from purple to dark yellow.

As for the incidents with Jason, Mariah testified that on two nights in a row she woke up to find Jason in bed with her, touching her thigh through her clothes. She described Jason's hand as being near her crotch and said she felt uncomfortable and cried when these incidents happened because she believed Jason was trying to put his hand on her crotch. When Mariah told mother what happened, mother told her to stop lying. Father testified that when Mariah was finally able to tell him what had happened with Jason, she was hyperventilating and was so upset that she urinated on herself.

Mother admitted to hitting Mariah once on the buttocks with a belt and to once hitting Bryce's buttocks with a belt because he "was defying direct orders." Mother minimized the nature of her punishment methods and claimed father had engineered the accusations. In a pre-hearing DCFS report, mother told a social worker that Mariah was a compulsive liar, and at the hearing, mother denied that Mariah ever told her about the incidents with Jason.

The court said it believed Mariah and disbelieved mother and sustained the petition. At the later dispositional hearing, the court placed the children with father and ordered both visitation and reunification services for mother. Mother appeals. . . .

Mother contends there is insufficient evidence to support the . . . allegations that were based on physical injuries to the children because there is no evidence that she ever inflicted serious physical harm when she punished them. According to mother, evidence that she once left a red line on Mariah's back and once left purple and yellow marks on Bryce after hitting them with a belt does not show that the children suffered serious physical harm. Conceding for discussion's sake only that the line on Mariah's back did not amount to serious physical harm, we believe there was sufficient evidence that Bryce suffered serious physical harm. . . .

[I]t appears that mother used a belt on a three-year-old child as punishment, striking him not on the buttocks, but on the stomach and forearms. On at least one occasion, this left Bryce with deep, purple bruises. In the context of a three year old, we hold that Bryce's injuries were serious enough for the court to assume jurisdiction. . . .

The dependency court believed Mariah's claims that Jason had twice come to her bed and fondled her thigh and that mother accused her of lying about it. Based on that evidence, the court assumed jurisdiction of Mariah under section 300, subdivision (d) [child was sexually abused . . . by household member and parent did not take reasonable steps to protect the child] and assumed jurisdiction of Bryce under section 300, subdivision (j) [child's sibling was abused as defined by other subdivisions, including (d), and there is substantial risk the child will be so abused as well]. . . .

Penal Code section 288 makes it a felony to commit lewd or lascivious acts on the body of a child under 14 "with the intent of arousing, appealing to, or gratifying the lust, passions, or sexual desires of that person or the child. . . ."

Mother attacks the court's sex abuse findings on one ground only: there was no evidence that Jason touched Mariah with the specific intent of arousing or sexually gratifying either himself or Mariah. . . . Because intent for purposes of Penal Code section 288 can seldom be proven by direct evidence, it may be inferred from the circumstances. . . . [W]e conclude there was sufficient evidence from the circumstances to infer that Jason acted with the requisite sexual intent. . . .

According to Mariah, she was clothed and asleep when Jason lay down next to her and fondled her thigh up high near her crotch. When she awoke, he signaled for her to remain quiet, from which an inference of guilty intent could be drawn. She felt uncomfortable and cried because she believed Jason was trying to touch her crotch. Jason came back the next night and repeated his conduct. Based on this, we believe it would be quite easy for a reasonable trier of fact to conclude that Jason acted with the requisite sexual intent. . . .

The dependency court placed the children with father after finding by clear and convincing evidence that leaving them with mother created a substantial danger to their physical and emotional well-being and that there were no reasonable means to protect the children short of removing them from mother's custody. Mother [contends that] the court should have pursued other alternatives, such as providing family maintenance services, prohibiting contact with Jason, or strictly supervising a "no corporal punishment" order. . . .

Before the children were detained, mother was given the option of having Jason move out so the children could remain with her, or having them placed outside the home. She chose the latter. Mother continued to deny that Jason had done anything wrong. A DCFS report prepared for the jurisdiction hearing showed that Jason continued to live in mother's home and at that hearing mother referred to Jason as her fiancé. Although a DCFS report prepared for the disposition hearing reported mother's claim that Jason had moved out on March 10, the report quoted mother as making the unlikely claim that she did not know Jason's new address and phone number. Mother also told the DCFS social worker that even though she was unsure whether she and Jason would continue their relationship, "*we're* going to appeal" the court's jurisdictional ruling. On this record, we hold that the dependency court could reasonably have concluded that Jason would remain in mother's home, thus placing the children at continued risk of sexual abuse. As a result, no reasonable alternatives to removal of custody from the mother were available. . . .

As to the allegations based on mother's use of a belt to punish the children, there was also sufficient evidence that lesser measures would not have worked. Mother had denied or minimized what she had done, refused to believe that Jason had fondled Mariah, and threatened to keep father away if Mariah told anyone what Jason did. The court was therefore free to reject mother's claim that she would no longer use corporal punishment, and could therefore find that removing the children from mother's custody was necessary on that ground as well. . . .

NOTES AND QUESTIONS

1. *Serious Physical Harm?* The California court emphasized the marks that the mother's physical discipline left as well as the age of the child. What if the mother committed the same acts but left no marks? What if Bryce was sixteen, instead of three?

2. *Failure to Protect.* Should Monique, the mother in *Mariah T.*, be held responsible for the sexual abuse that her boyfriend, Jason, committed? Would the fact of the sexual abuse be enough to find abuse or neglect? What if Monique had kicked Jason out of the house when Mariah told her what happened? Is the important thing that Monique did not believe her daughter?

3. *The Conduct of Partners.* When, if ever, should the conduct of a parent's cohabiting partner constitute a basis on which to find that a child is abused or neglected? In In re C.E., the mother, Brandy, had a boyfriend, Jeremy, who was a registered sex offender.[30] After being jailed for removing his monitoring ankle bracelet, Jeremy returned to Brandy's home, even though she had agreed that he would not have contact with the children. Brandy and Jeremy married, with the children present. The court found "clear and convincing evidence . . . that the children cannot be returned to Brandy's care," reasoning that "Brandy has chosen to gamble with her children's safety to continue having Jeremy in her life."[31] The court worried that the "young children are defenseless should Jeremy perpetrate abuse upon them."[32] Should the fact that a

---

30. 808 N.W.2d 756, 2011 WL 5868231 (Iowa Ct. App. 2011).
31. Id. at *4.
32. Id.

partner is a registered sex offender constitute a basis on which to remove a
om the home? What if the previous offense involved sexual abuse of a child?

hat if the parent's partner commits domestic violence? In In re K.P., the mother's boyfriend physically abused her. At one point, the police were called and found the mother with her eye "bruised and swollen shut," "a chipped tooth," and bruises and lacerations.[33] The children were removed from the mother's home "once it became clear the mother was accepting phone calls from the boyfriend in jail and intended to maintain a relationship with him."[34] In finding that the state "established by clear and convincing evidence that the children could not be returned to the mother's care," the court emphasized that the mother "continued to show a lack of insight into why she should not have contact with the boyfriend."[35] When the mother said that "she no longer intended to pursue a relationship with the boyfriend," the court countered that "even if she does not continue her relationship with the boyfriend, the mother has a history of dating violent men and failing to appreciate the danger of doing so."[36] Is the mother being punished as a parent for someone else's conduct? Is the court blaming the victim? Why does domestic violence justify removal of the children? Should the court require evidence that the boyfriend abused the children as well, or do the children necessarily suffer when their mother is abused? Are there services that the state could provide that would mitigate the concerns presented by the mother's relationship with an abusive partner?

4. *Child Protection and Criminal Law.* Criminal statutes play a significant role in abuse and neglect proceedings. The relevant question may involve whether the parent engaged in criminal conduct that justifies child welfare intervention. For example, in *Mariah T.*, the court was considering whether the boyfriend's conduct constituted sexual assault as defined in the penal code. Such conduct furnished a basis on which the court could exercise jurisdiction under the state's child welfare law. In other cases, courts are considering whether a parent's conduct constitutes criminal assault. If a parent's conduct does not rise to the level of a criminal act, does that mean they should not be found to have abused or neglected their child?

PROBLEMS

1. Tamara and her 4-year-old son, Henry, live in a home with Tamara's mother and stepfather (Henry's grandparents). Tamara and Henry live downstairs, and Tamara's mother and stepfather live upstairs. Henry is permitted to move freely

---

33. 896 N.W.2d 785, 2017 WL 362009, at *1 (Iowa Ct. App. 2017).
34. Id. at *2.
35. Id. at *5.
36. Id.

between his room and the part of the house occupied by his grandparents. The grandparents assist Tamara with childcare three or four nights a week and, at times, on weekends. Tamara's mother works during the day, and her stepfather works at night.

One Sunday, Tamara and Henry had spent the day at her sister's house. They returned home around 7 p.m. Henry had fallen asleep in the car. Tamara saw her mother's car in the driveway; as her mother had been ill, Tamara assumed she was upstairs asleep (and that her stepfather had gone to work). But in fact, they had gone out of town for the night. Tamara put Henry to bed and went out to have dinner with a friend. Henry woke up and found himself alone in the dark house. He walked across the street to a neighbor's house. Tamara's residence is located on a corner intersection, where the speed limit is twenty-five miles per hour. The police were called, and Henry told the officers that he went to the neighbor's house because he could not find his mother.

Around 9:30 or 10:00 p.m., Tamara returned home with her friend. When Tamara learned that Henry had walked across the street to the neighbor's house, she became very upset and began to cry. Henry was reunited with his mother. He was happy to see her, and stated, "Where were you? I thought you went to heaven."

After the police reported the incident to the state's department of youth and family services, Tamara was charged with "gross and wanton neglect." To sustain this charge, the department has to prove that Tamara acted in reckless disregard for Henry's safety. Did she? Is it appropriate to place her name on a registry of parents who have committed child abuse or neglect?

2. On May 24, 2010, Artemio arrived home at approximately 4:30 p.m. Over the previous year, he had repeatedly told his 14–year–old daughter, Penelope, that he didn't want her friends coming to the house. He told her that he didn't want her to hang out with them because they were a bad influence. Penelope testified that her father told her every day not to have her friends to the house. Even so, Penelope's friends were usually there when he came home from work. Artemio had told Penelope that if she violated the house rules, which included the prohibition on her friends coming to the house, he would spank her with a belt. Nevertheless, according to Penelope's testimony, she deliberately brought her friends home every day.

On the day in question, Artemio heard Penelope and her friends in the house and a girl was crying. Three friends were with Penelope in her room. Artemio called Penelope out of her room and asked what happened to Lee (the friend who was crying). He got no satisfactory answer. He told Penelope's friends to go home, but they refused. At this point, Artemio hit Penelope from six to ten times, with a crisscross motion, on her stretch pants, above the knees, with a 36–inch–long belt, folded in two. The belt was one and one-half inch wide. Penelope testified that she felt a little pain, that the spanking stung her, and that the pain lasted an hour and a half. She had bruises for about a week. She cried for half an hour. About 10 to 15 minutes after the spanking, Artemio cut Penelope's waist-long hair to about level with her neck. Penelope's friends called the police; she was crying when they came, but was not bleeding and did not require any medical attention.

State law permits a parent to use force toward a child as long as: "(a) The force is used for the purpose of safeguarding or promoting the welfare of the minor, including the prevention or punishment of his misconduct; and (b) The force used is not designed to cause or known to create a substantial risk of causing death, serious bodily injury, disfigurement, extreme pain or mental distress, or gross degradation." Are Artemio's actions justifiable under this standard?

III. State Intervention and Removal

State and local child protection agencies investigate allegations of child abuse, maltreatment, and neglect by parents and other caregivers and may intervene when they deem it necessary. Such interventions can take the form of family assessments, formal investigations, mandatory in-home services, removal of the child, and — in extreme cases — termination of parental rights. We will return to termination later in this chapter.

A significant number of children face child protective services investigations every year: according to the most recent data from the National Child Abuse and Neglect Data System, 3,534,000 children were subject to an investigation in 2018, and around 678,000 children were found to be victims of abuse and neglect. Of those, around 60 percent were found to be subject only to neglect, while 10 percent suffered only physical abuse.[37] In 2018, an estimated 1,770 children died as a result of parental abuse or neglect.[38] As you read the following materials, think about what it would be like to be a child welfare official making determinations about whether a particular child has been abused or neglected — and what to do about it. At the same time, think about what it would be like to be a parent who is confronted with the intervention of state actors and the potential removal of their child. Also, think about what it would be like to be a child who is removed from their parents and placed in someone else's custody.

A. Referrals and Reports

A state's child protective services (CPS) agency usually becomes involved with a family after a "referral" or "report" of alleged maltreatment. Not all cases come via

---

37. U.S. Dep't of Health and Human Servs., Admin. for Children & Families, Child Maltreatment ii, 19, 21 (2018).

38. Id. at 46.

referral: sometimes a family seeks assistance and services of its own volition or a case comes to the attention of the child welfare agency from the juvenile or family court system. In the latter set of cases, a child is not necessarily referred due to maltreatment but in an attempt to access resources to help the child with school, mental illness, or substance abuse.

Certain professionals who frequently interact with children — such as teachers, social workers, doctors, nurses, and therapists — are classified by state statute as "mandatory reporters." They must report a reasonable suspicion of child abuse or neglect to CPS. In 2017, about 65 percent of referrals came from mandatory reporters.[39] Other reports come from neighbors, extended family members, and others who interact with the family, such as landlords. While referrals are ordinarily made to protect the child, some individuals may make referrals as a form of leverage over the parents.

Once a report has been made, most CPS agencies govern intervention by a two-step process: (1) screening, and (2) investigation and alternative response. Referrals may be screened-out if they plainly do not concern child abuse or neglect, they contain insufficient information, or intervention by another agency is deemed more fitting for the particular circumstances. Once a referral is screened-in, it is formally called a "report" and is subject to investigation according to state law and policy.

B. Investigations

For screened-in cases, the state normally commences an investigation within three days (or within twenty-four hours if serious abuse is alleged). If the child is not immediately removed, the caseworker develops a "safety plan" with the family to ensure the child's safety in the present. Increasingly, in an effort to prioritize family preservation, reports of low to moderate risk of maltreatment are assigned to a new track, known as "differential response." In these cases, a family will agree to a "family assessment" by a caseworker of what would be required to ensure a child's safety and well-being. If the child remains at home, the family may be provided with "in-home" services. These services can include: "minimal services" (including education about parenting, child discipline, grocery shopping, and budgeting); "intermediate services" (including therapy, outpatient treatment for substance abuse or mental health problems for the parent and/or child); and "intensive services" (including "intensive family intervention by a caseworker for a short period of time to resolve issues contributing to maltreatment").[40] If parents actively engage

---

39. Id. at 8.

40. Remain in the Home, Child & Family Servs. Reviews, U.S. Dep't of Health and Human Servs., https://training.cfsrportal.acf.hhs.gov/section-2-understanding-child-welfare-system/3017.

these services, the case will be closed; if not, the case may be moved back to the investigatory path.[41]

According to the U.S. Department of Health and Human Services, the "primary purpose of the investigation is to determine, within a set timeframe, if children in the home are safe, if abuse or neglect has occurred, and if there is risk of child maltreatment occurring in the future."[42] CPS focuses on the alleged maltreatment, facts about the particular child (age, health, behavior, etc.), facts about the parent or caregiver (mental health, history of violence, substance abuse, etc.), and the overall family functioning. Depending on the state, statutes require investigations to be completed within thirty to ninety days. Through the investigation, the agency determines whether the allegation is substantiated ("founded") or unsubstantiated ("unfounded").

If the case is substantiated, the case may still be closed if the mistreatment is found to be a one-off incident or if the family could receive in-home services. If the parent refuses services and the child is deemed unsafe, the agency can seek a court order to require that the family adopt the in-home services. Otherwise — if the agency determines the child's safety is still in danger — the child will be removed.

If you were a social worker handling an investigation and deciding how to proceed, what factors would influence your decision? Would you be more concerned about leaving children in potentially unsafe conditions, or about removing children from the only parents they have known? If you are focused on ensuring that no child dies or is severely hurt, you may be more likely to prefer removal. You then may remove children in cases in which removal is unnecessary to protect the child. If you are focused on keeping children with their parents, you may be more reluctant to recommend removal. You then may fail to remove in cases where the child will be exposed to serious harm. Which type of error do you think you would be more likely to tolerate? What other factors may shape your assessment: reputational consequences? employer expectations? stress?

C. Removal

Removal is broadly governed by a "best interests" determination, guided by various factors depending on state law — including family integrity and a general resistance to removal, the health and safety of the child, the importance of timely permanent placement, and an assurance that the removed child will be given the care needed.[43] The implementation of child welfare systems, however, can vary greatly

---

41. Differential Response, Child & Family Servs. Reviews, U.S. Dep't of Health and Human Servs., https://training.cfsrportal.acf.hhs.gov/section-2-understanding-child-welfare-system/3011.

42. Investigation, Child & Family Servs. Reviews, U.S. Dep't of Health and Human Servs., https://training.cfsrportal.acf.hhs.gov/section-2-understanding-child-welfare-system/3012.

43. Children's Bureau, Child Welfare Info. Gateway, Determining the Best Interests of the Child 2 (2016).

from locality to locality, with the nuances of interpreting state policies or creating local guidelines often left to the discretion of individual cities and counties.[44] Excessive local variation concerns both advocates and government officials, who fear that parents and children in different parts of the state receive different levels of protection and resources.[45]

If an agency concludes that a child must be removed, it is required to seek and receive a court order to remove the child. However, in cases of serious harm (or risk of such harm), the agency can immediately remove the child and seek an order retroactively. In most states, matters involving children subject to child welfare investigations are handled by a juvenile (or dependency) court, rather than a family court.[46] The requirements of the initial pleading vary by state, but the court generally possesses the authority to order one of three outcomes: (1) grant *ex parte* custody to the agency; (2) schedule an initial hearing before removal; or (3) deny the petition.[47] In the majority of cases, the agency is granted *ex parte* custody.

In cases where CPS has substantiated a report of serious abuse and neglect for one child in a household and elected for removal, CPS will also likely remove that child's underage siblings on the assumption that there is a substantial risk of harm. California, for example, notes in its definition of child abuse that "a history of repeated inflictions of injury . . . on the child's siblings" connotes a substantial risk of physical abuse warranting state intervention.[48]

In some states, as we will see when we read Santosky v. Kramer later in this chapter, CPS will remove children or newborns under an "anticipatory neglect" theory, seeking to protect "not only children who are the direct victims, but also those who have a probability to be subject to neglect or abuse because they reside. . . . with an individual who has been found to have abused or neglected another child."[49] New York state courts describe the "anticipatory neglect" doctrine as "derivative neglect," but caution that "there is no *per se* rule that a finding of neglect of one sibling requires a finding of derivative neglect with respect to the other siblings."[50] Courts thus must focus their inquiry on "whether the evidence of abuse or neglect of one child indicates a fundamental defect in the parent's understandings of the duties of parenthood."[51]

---

44. See Rob Green & Karen C. Tumlin, Urban Inst., State Efforts to Remake Child Welfare: Responses to New Challenges and Increased Scrutiny 6 (1999).

45. Id. at 6–7.

46. See, e.g., Conn. Gen. Stat. § 46b-121 (2020); Cal. Welf. & Inst. Code § 300 (West 2020).

47. Initial Pleading, Child & Family Servs. Reviews, U.S. Dep't of Health and Human Servs., https://training.cfsrportal.acf.hhs.gov/section-2-understanding-child-welfare-system/3020.

48. Cal. Welf. & Inst. Code § 300 (West 2020).

49. In re Arthur H., 819 N.E.2d 734 (Ill. App. Ct. 2004).

50. In re Andrew B.-L., 844 N.Y.S.2d 337, 339 (N.Y. App. Div. 2017).

51. Matter of Dutchess Cty. Dep't of Soc. Servs. v. Douglas E., 191 A.D.2d 694, 694 (N.Y. App. Div. 1993).

After the child is removed from the household, parties will generally have an *initial hearing* to assess, via a best-interests determination, whether the child should be placed in foster care or returned to the family during the pendency of the process.[52] In child abuse and neglect proceedings, the court often assigns the child a guardian ad litem (GAL) or a court appointed special advocate (CASA), an attorney or trained layperson whose role is to represent the best interests of the child; this person's duties may include conducting an independent investigation, attending all hearings, and making recommendations to the court.[53]

If the child remains out of the home and the case is not resolved through mediation between the parents and the agency, a court will hold an *adjudication hearing* (also called a fact-finding or jurisdictional hearing) to determine whether the agency can support its findings that removal is warranted. If the judge rules in favor of the agency, the child's removal will continue and the judge will enter an order finding facts about the maltreatment that must be resolved, whether the agency has made reasonable efforts to avoid placement in foster care and achieve reunification, and whether the child's placement is appropriate given the child's needs. During these hearings, children are often placed with a foster care provider, either formally through a licensed nonrelative foster parent or with a "kinship provider," meaning a relative caregiver. (We address foster care later in the chapter.)

If a judge decides that removal is necessary for the time being, there may be a *disposition hearing* to determine which additional services are to be ordered, including a case plan and options for reunification. A case plan must include: a description of where the child is to be placed; a plan for ensuring that the child receives safe and proper care, and that the parents, child, and foster parents are receiving appropriate services; a plan to improve conditions in the parental home; a plan to facilitate reunification; and a plan to address the child's needs while in foster care, including ensuring educational stability.[54]

Federal law requires states to make "reasonable efforts" to reunify families — but ASFA excuses this requirement if "aggravated circumstances" are present. In practice, the meaning and implications of "reasonable efforts" vary across states as well as across cases. What do you think "reasonable efforts" would require of the state? What kind of support must the parent be given: parenting classes? therapy? job training? childcare options? monetary assistance?

---

52. Initial Hearing, Child & Family Servs. Reviews, U.S. Dep't of Health and Human Servs., https://training.cfsrportal.acf.hhs.gov/section-2-understanding-child-welfare-system/3021.

53. Children's Bureau, Child Welfare Info. Gateway, Representation of Children in Child Abuse and Neglect Proceedings (2017).

54. 42 U.S.C. § 675(1) (2018).

Federal law also requires that a *review hearing* be held at least every six months, though some states require more frequent hearings.[55] The case plan can be revised at these hearings.

Finally, federal law requires a *permanency hearing* within twelve months after the child has entered foster care, to be repeated every twelve months thereafter.[56] This hearing will establish a permanency plan that could include reunification, adoption, legal guardianship, or another planned permanent living arrangement (APPLA) (all of which are discussed more when we address foster care). Generally, reunification is considered the preferred goal.[57]

PROBLEM

You are a trial judge in Iowa considering a petition seeking to terminate the parental rights of a single mother. The mother, Jenny, was seventeen when she gave birth to her daughter, and her son was born two years later. The Department of Health Services (DHS) launched an investigation and removed the children from Jenny's care after her daughter was twice found unsupervised by the highway near the family apartment. The state commenced services and supervised visits with Jenny. While the social workers testified that the visits went well, they also expressed concerns about Jenny's level of engagement with the children. During one visit, Jenny's son fell and got a black eye — an incident the social workers cited as further evidence of Jenny's poor parenting skills. The social workers also criticized Jenny's limited budget and perceived hostility to their suggestions regarding her relationships with men. The foster mother with whom the children had been placed testified that she was willing to adopt both children.

Under Iowa law, DHS must make reasonable efforts, including facilitating visitation, to return children to their home as quickly as possible, consistent with their best interests. Citing safety concerns, the State has filed a petition for termination. Jenny has requested more liberal visitation moving toward reunification with her children. You are now considering how to rule in the matter.

(1) Has DHS made "reasonable efforts" to reunite Jenny with her children? What additional information would you like to know in making this determination?
(2) Should more liberal visitation be ordered?

---

55. 42 U.S.C. § 675(5)(B) (2018).

56. Id.

57. Achieving Permanency, Child & Family Servs. Reviews, U.S. Dep't of Health and Human Servs., https://training.cfsrportal.acf.hhs.gov/section-2-understanding-child-welfare-system/3030.

POSTSCRIPT

This problem is based on In re E.C.-N., in which an Iowa appellate court overturned the family court's decision to grant the termination petition.[58] The court determined that "the testimony from the social workers offered by the State at the termination hearing was too vague to support a finding of reasonable efforts."[59] A "six-month extension" with "semisupervised or unsupervised visitation" was ordered.[60]

IV. Inequality and the Child Welfare System

A. Race, Class, and Child Welfare

The well-being of every child should matter equally. Yet, as we have seen throughout the casebook, troubling race, gender, sexual orientation, and class disparities persist throughout family law. These disparities similarly pervade the child welfare system. Studies have shown that racial disparities appear at every stage of the child welfare system, including reporting, investigation, and removal. In New York, 93 percent of the 11,500 youth in the city's child welfare system are black and Hispanic.[61] In Cook County, Illinois, which encompasses Chicago, black and Hispanic children composed 85 percent of the children in the child welfare system.[62] Nationwide, black children are represented in foster care at almost twice their rate in the general population.[63]

A national study of child protective services by the U.S. Department of Health and Human Services reported that "[m]inority children, and in particular African American children, are more likely to be in foster care placement than receive in-home services, even when they have the same problems and characteristics as white children."[64] The state also terminates the parental rights of black parents at higher rates than that of white parents.[65]

---

58. 815 N.W.2d 410, 2012 WL 1066883 (Iowa Ct. App. 2012).

59. Id. at *4.

60. Id.

61. Collier Meyerson, For Women of Color, the Child-Welfare System Functions Like the Criminal-Justice System, Nation (May 24, 2018).

62. Ill. Dep't of Children & Family Servs, Number of Children in Foster Care by Demographics (2019).

63. See Children's Bureau, Child Welfare Info. Gateway, Racial Disproportionality and Disparity in Child Welfare (2016).

64. Children's Bureau, U.S. Dep't of Health & Human Servs., National Study of Protective, Preventive and Reunification Services Delivered to Children and Their Families xi (1997).

65. See Dorothy Roberts & Lisa Sangoi, Black Families Matter: How the Child Welfare System Punishes Poor Families of Color, Appeal (May 26, 2018).

Racial disparities clearly exist. But there is significant debate about what causes these disparities and what to do about them. Might these differences be attributed to different rates of abuse and neglect? Or may mandatory reporters — for example, doctors who treat children or pregnant women — be more likely to report black parents to child welfare authorities?[66] Are racial disparities the result of biased social workers? Institutional racism? Some critics see a significant civil rights issue in the child welfare system, evoking comparisons to racial disparities in mass incarceration.[67] Lawyers have even developed a name for the contemporary practice of removing children from predominantly poor women of color: "Jane Crow." Does it matter whether government actors have engaged in intentional discrimination?

Are racial disparities explained by the relationship between race and poverty? According to the Pew Research Center, in 2013, black children were significantly more likely to be living in poverty than Hispanic children and four times as likely as white or Asian children to be living in poverty. For the first time since the U.S. Census began collecting this data, the number of poor black children (4.2 million) may have eclipsed the number of poor white children (4.1 million), even though black children constitute a much smaller percentage of the population.[68] What is the relationship between poverty and the child welfare system?

PROBLEM

In 2016, Allegheny County, Pennsylvania, which includes Pittsburgh, began to use a predictive-analysis software to aid child welfare agencies in identifying children at risk. This type of software can sift through the information on record about a particular family and make an assessment about the need for intervention. The software can scour vast databases in a matter of seconds, which would otherwise take human screeners hours.

You are the head of a child welfare agency in another state. You are in charge of a county that includes a major city. You are considering whether to adopt the predictive-analysis software that your colleagues in Pittsburgh are using. What questions would you want to ask officials in Pittsburgh? What other individuals would you like to consult? What data would you like to view in making a decision? What empirical considerations would matter most to your decision whether to adopt the software? What normative considerations would matter most?

---

66. See id.

67. See Dorothy Roberts, Child Welfare and Civil Rights, 2003 U. Ill. L. Rev. 171, 178.

68. Eileen Patten & Jens Manuel Krogstad, Black Child Poverty Rate Holds Steady, Even as Other Groups See Declines, Pew Research Ctr. (July 14, 2015).

POSTSCRIPT

Proponents of algorithmic software argue that it helps to screen out human error and bias by giving equal weight to a number of different factors and consequently a more balanced and accurate assessment of the likelihood of risk to the child. Critics argue that there is little transparency in how the algorithm actually reaches a decision. The software is usually conceived and developed at private tech firms and then sold to public agencies. Critics also question the "objectivity" of algorithms, worrying that they simply reflect and reproduce existing racial and class biases. Algorithms are also solely reliant on the data they are fed, which encompass information (such as substance abuse or addiction counseling) about those who are on federal assistance programs such as Medicaid, but not those who have private health insurance — meaning that poor parents are captured in ways that others are not. As one critic argues, "[M]ore information exists on those who use the services than on those who don't. Families who don't have enough information in the system are excluded from being scored."[69] How would you weigh all of these considerations?[70]

The following excerpts are from leading child welfare scholars. The first two come from Professors Martin Guggenheim and Dorothy Roberts, two of the nation's most prominent and forceful critics of the child welfare system. The third comes from Professor Elizabeth Bartholet, an influential scholar who sees problems in the child welfare system but not the ones that Guggenheim and Roberts identify. As you read, consider what the child welfare system would look like and what aims it would pursue if Guggenheim and Roberts were in charge, or if Bartholet were in charge. Which system do you prefer? Is either of these systems better than what we have now? What are the costs of changing the system in the ways these scholars envision?

Martin Guggenheim, Somebody's Children: Sustaining the Family's Place in Child Welfare Policy
113 Harv. L. Rev. 1716 (2000)

[S]tudies have consistently found that the great majority of children in foster care could remain safely at home. Professor Duncan Lindsey, a leading child

---

69. Elizabeth Brico, New Algorithms Perpetuate Old Biases in the Child Welfare Cases, Undark (Sept. 20, 2018).

70. For discussions of this issue, see Dan Hurley, Can an Algorithm Tell When Kids Are in Danger?, N.Y. Times Mag., Jan. 2 2018, at 30; Christopher E. Church & Amanda J. Fairchild, In Search of a Silver Bullet: Child Welfare's Embrace of Predictive Analytics, 68 Juv. & Fam. Ct. J. 67 (2017).

welfare researcher, concluded that "studies clearly demonstrate that child abuse is not the major reason children are removed from their parents"; he found instead that "inadequacy of income, more than any other factor, constitutes the reason that children are removed." In fact, when Lindsey evaluated placements of children in foster care, he found that 48% of the children did not require placement.

A study of Boston placement decisions led one team of researchers to conclude that:

> [A]mong a group of children referred for suspected abuse in the emergency and surgical units of a hospital, the best predictor of removal of the child from the family was not severity of abuse, but Medicaid eligibility, which we might interpret as a proxy variable for the income status of the family.

Likewise, Lindsey found that "inadequacy of income increased the odds for placement by more than 120 times." The evidence also clearly suggests that many children regularly remain in foster care merely because their parents are unable to secure adequate housing without assistance from the state. This seems to be a regular practice in Chicago and New York City. The court-appointed administrator of the District of Columbia's foster care system also found that between one-third and one-half of the children in foster care could have been returned immediately to their parents but for a lack of adequate housing. . . .

Since the 1970s, the concept of "child welfare" has been artificially narrowed to mean little more than protecting children from parental harm. During this same period, child welfare agencies have been transformed from programs that attempt to serve needy families to investigative bodies that follow up on often spurious allegations of maltreatment. . . .

As we look to the near future, we can predict that child welfare personnel will be able to provide even less for poor families as changes in government policies require that they interact with increasing numbers of families. We need to change this predictable path if we are to improve the lives of poor children. To accomplish this, it is critical that we restructure child welfare to include, for example, early intervention services for health care, child care, and education. Paradoxically, this vision requires that we find a way to narrow what now overwhelms the child welfare system — the investigative function of child welfare personnel. . . .

There has been considerable ferment in the field during the past few years surrounding initiatives that would advance this specific and important agenda. . . . [A] number of communities have experimented with "community partnerships" that seek to change the function of child welfare from policing to helping. In these initiatives, the focus is on helping families rather than assessing blame.

The simple fact is that government agencies alone cannot protect children. Thus, efforts to organize networks of neighborhood and community support that reach out to families at risk provide great hope for the future. The goals are to reach these families before a crisis occurs and to expand the scope of those who receive services well beyond the category of "unfit families". . . .

The narrow picture of child welfare policy that is currently accepted primarily focuses on children harmed by their own families and the apparatus and policies of state action that aim to find and protect those children. However important the issue of children being harmed by their parents, it is far from the most pressing issue in child welfare. Those of us who care most about children need to develop strategies that broaden the lens of problems facing children so that states with the will to ameliorate or avoid these problems can do so. Most important, this strategy must find a way to maximize the chance that children will be raised by their own willing families.

There will, of course, be occasions when it is necessary to separate children from their families and even to sever permanently all legal ties between children and their families to protect them from harm and to permit them to be raised by new families who will love and guide them. But a child-friendly child welfare policy certainly will regard the forcible removal of children from their families, and particularly the permanent banishment of birth relatives from their lives, as a necessary failure, rather than an outcome worthy of celebration.

Dorothy E. Roberts, Child Welfare and Civil Rights
2003 U. Ill. L. Rev. 171

Child welfare is not usually viewed as a civil rights issue. If child welfare is discussed as a matter of rights at all, it is usually framed as a contest between children's rights and parents' rights. Most books by legal scholars and activists about the child welfare system paint a battle between bad government and innocent parents, or bad parents and innocent children. . . .

Strangely, criticisms of the child welfare system are not placed among the burning violations of civil rights on the basis of race. I say "strangely" because anyone who is familiar with the child welfare system in the nation's large cities knows that it is basically an apartheid institution. . . .

The disproportionate number of black children in America's child welfare system is staggering. Black children make up more than two-fifths of the foster care population, although they represent less than one-fifth of the nation's children. In Chicago, ninety-five percent of children in foster care are black. The racial imbalance in New York City's foster care population is truly mind-boggling: out of 42,000 children in the system at the end of 1997, only 1,300 were white.

The worst part of the child welfare system's treatment of black children is that it unnecessarily separates them from their parents. Child protective agencies are far more likely to place black children in foster care instead of offering their families less traumatic assistance. According to federal statistics, fifty-six percent of black children in the child welfare system have been placed in foster care, twice the percentage for white children. . . .

White children who are abused or neglected are twice as likely as black children to receive services in their own homes, avoiding the emotional damage and physical risks of foster care placement. Put another way, most white children who enter the system are permitted to stay with their families, while most black children are taken away from theirs. Foster care is the main "service" state agencies provide to black children brought to their attention.

Think for a moment what it means to rip children from their parents and their siblings to be placed in the care of strangers. Removing children from their homes is perhaps the most severe government intrusion into the lives of citizens. It is also one of the most terrifying experiences a child can have. Because parents involved with child protective services are so often portrayed as brutal monsters, the public usually ignores the trauma of taking their children. But many children in foster care, who typically have been removed because of neglect, have close and loving relationships with their parents, and it is indescribably painful to be separated from them.

Of course, these harms of removal may be outweighed by the harm of leaving children with violent or very neglectful parents. But just as we should pay attention to the risks of child maltreatment, we should not minimize the very real pain caused by separating children from their families. The damage caused by disrupting these ties may be far greater than the harm agencies are trying to avoid.

Once removed from their homes, black children remain in foster care longer, are moved more often, receive fewer services, and are less likely to be either returned home or adopted than any other children. . . .

The color of America's child welfare system undeniably shows that race matters to state interventions in families. But in what sense does race matter? What are the reasons for the striking racial disparity in every aspect of child protective services, and why should we be concerned about it? Can we describe it as a civil rights violation? . . .

The child welfare system is designed to address mainly the problems of poor families. Because black children are disproportionately poor, we would expect a corresponding racial disparity in the child welfare caseload. The Illinois Department of Children and Family Services prepares a multicolored map that shows the distribution of abuse and neglect cases in Chicago. Neighborhoods with the highest concentration of cases form an L-shaped pattern colored in red. There is another map of Chicago with the same color coding that shows levels of poverty across the city. The poorest neighborhoods in the city form an identical red L-shaped pattern. A third map shows the distribution of ethnic groups in Chicago. The red-colored section marking the city's segregated black neighborhoods is virtually a perfect match. In Chicago, there is a geographical overlap of child maltreatment cases, poverty, and black families.

There is a persistent and striking gap in the economic status of blacks and whites that exists in unemployment, poverty, and income. The strength of the economy has not erased the racial gap in child poverty nor improved the situation of black children at the very bottom. Black children are still more than three times as likely as whites to live in extreme poverty. Despite several years of decline, the U.S. child poverty rate is still exceptionally high by international standards. Extreme poverty is actually growing, and black children still lag far behind.

Race also influences child welfare decision making through strong and deeply embedded stereotypes about black family dysfunction. In *Killing the Black Body: Race, Reproduction, and the Meaning of Liberty*, I described a popular mythology that portrays black women as unfit to have children. The purpose of that book was to expose the explosion of rhetoric and policies that degrade black women's reproductive decisions. The same set of stereotypes also supports the removal of black women's children. Some case workers and judges view black parents as less reformable than white parents, and less willing and able to respond to the treatment that child protection agencies prescribe.

So far I have discussed the systemic factors outside the child welfare system that make black families more vulnerable to state intrusion, as well as racial bias on the part of actors in the system. The racial disparity is also caused by a fundamental flaw in the system's very conception. The child welfare system is designed not as a way for government to assist parents in taking care of their children, but as a means to punish parents for their failures by threatening to take their children away. The child welfare system, then, is a misnomer. The primary mission of state agencies is not to promote children's welfare. Rather, their purpose has become child protection: they try to protect children from the effects of society's colossal failure to care enough about children's welfare. The system is activated only after children have already experienced harm and puts all the blame on parents for their children's problems. This punitive function falls heaviest on African American parents because they are most likely to suffer from poverty and institutional discrimination, and to be blamed for the effects on their children.

Under current civil rights jurisprudence, the racial disparity in the child welfare system may not constitute racial discrimination without a showing of racial motivation. The system is racist only if black children are pulled out of their homes by bigoted caseworkers or as part of a deliberate government scheme to subjugate black people. Any other explanation, such as higher rates of black poverty, negates the significance of race. . . .

Even if the racial disparity could be explained entirely by higher black poverty rates and not intentional discrimination, this would not negate the racist impact of the system or the racist reasons for its inequities. State disruption of families is one symptom of this institutionalized discrimination. It reflects the persistent gulf between the material welfare of black and white children in America. The racial disparity in the child welfare system — even if related directly to economic inequality — ultimately results from racial injustice.

The reasons for the racial disparity can be attributed to racial inequality, but does the child welfare system itself violate the civil rights of families on the basis of race? Understanding the nature of this harm is crucial to taking the correct steps to redress the racial disparity. . . .

Both aspects of the child welfare system's racial disparity — the State's intrusion in families and its racial bias — are essential to explaining its injustice. First, the overrepresentation of black children in the child welfare system, especially foster care, represents massive state supervision and dissolution of families. Second, this interference with families helps to maintain the disadvantaged status of black people in the United States. The child welfare system not only inflicts general harms disproportionately on black families, it also inflicts a particular harm — a racial harm — on black people as a group.

Family disruption has historically served as a chief tool of group oppression. The racial bias in state interventions in the family clarifies the reasons for safeguarding family autonomy. Parents' freedom to raise their children is important not only to individuals but also to the welfare or even survival of ethnic, cultural, and religious groups. Weakening the parent-child bond and disintegrating families within a group is a means of subordinating the entire group. The individualized focus on preserving personal choice in the private sphere of family life fails to recognize the family's political role. Families are not only expressions of individual choices, they are social institutions serving political ends.

Elizabeth Bartholet, The Racial Disproportionality Movement in Child Welfare: False Facts and Dangerous Directions
51 Ariz. L. Rev. 871 (2009)

"Racial Disproportionality" is the new war cry of a powerful group of players in the child welfare policy arena. . . . [T]hey characterize as overrepresentation the fact that black children are represented in the foster care system at a higher rate than white children as compared to their general population percentages. They claim that this overrepresentation is caused by systemic biases in child welfare system decision-making. They call for solutions which would reduce the rate at which black children are removed from their parents for maltreatment and increase the rate at which those removed to foster care are reunified with their parents. Their goal is to achieve what they term racial equity — the removal of black and white children to foster care at rates equal to their general population percentages.

The players include powerful foundations, non-profit organizations, and academics. Many of them have fought for years for policies that put a high priority on keeping children in their birth families and in their racial communities of origin. . . .

The Movement's reliance on statistics as evidence of discrimination calls upon a valuable tradition in our nation's discrimination law. Demonstration of disparate racial impact has been an important tool in proving intentional discrimination in many areas of law. Disparate impact theory, which enables courts to find discrimination even in the absence of discriminatory intent, has been helpful in the employment area to strike down racially exclusionary practices that could not be justified as job-related.

But, in considering whether statistical impact warrants a conclusion of discrimination, it is important to determine whether non-discriminatory factors explain and justify the impact. . . .

It is particularly important to be careful with the use of statistics in assessing whether the child welfare system is guilty of discrimination in removing children because of alleged harmful maltreatment by their parents. Black parents are disproportionately characterized by risk factors for maltreatment, such as extreme poverty, serious substance abuse, and single parenting; therefore, there is good reason to believe that black parents actually commit maltreatment at higher rates than whites. If black children are in fact subject to serious maltreatment by their parents at higher rates than white children, it is in their interest to be removed at higher rates than white children. If the child welfare system is wrongfully found discriminatory, and, as a result, stops removing black children at serious risk for ongoing maltreatment, the children will suffer immediate and dangerous consequences. . . .

Obviously, black parents are neither inherently more likely to abuse and neglect their children than whites, nor inherently more likely to be associated with poverty, single parenting, substance abuse, and other risk factors associated with child maltreatment. They are victims of historic and ongoing racial and economic injustice that has put them in a seriously disadvantaged position in our society.

The raw racial statistics that the Movement relies on in the child welfare area do represent a very real problem, both for black children and for the larger black community. Children removed from their parents for maltreatment, and placed in foster care for significant periods of time, generally do not fare well in later life. Appallingly high numbers end up in homeless shelters, unemployed, on drugs, and in prisons. They often end up continuing the cycle of child maltreatment into the next generation. This represents an ongoing problem for the black community, as does the fact that that community is disproportionately plagued by the risk factors that are so linked to child maltreatment.

But the question is what kind of problem these statistics represent, because that will determine what corrective action is appropriate. Black children are removed and placed in foster care because the social workers and judges involved in the child protective system conclude that the parents have been guilty of serious child maltreatment and are not capable of avoiding such maltreatment if the children remain in their care. There are many reasons to think that the social workers and judges are getting it right in terms of needed child protection by removing black children at higher rates than white children compared to their population percentages.

If actual child maltreatment rates for black children are in fact disproportionately high, then the racial problems we should focus on are the disproportionate maltreatment of black children, and the disproportionate victimization of the black community by severe poverty, unemployment, substance abuse, and other risk factors that are associated with maltreatment. Appropriate reform should be directed toward reducing black maltreatment rates by, for example, expanding programs to support fragile families at risk of maltreatment, and programs to address the substance abuse so strongly associated with maltreatment. There is little mention, however, of such prevention programs in the Racial Disproportionality Movement literature. Instead the focus is almost entirely on preventing the removal of black children from their parents, and on addressing the discrimination alleged to occur at various points in the child welfare decision-making process.

Appropriate reform should also include the fundamental social changes that would address the poverty, unemployment, and related social ills characterizing the lives of so many poor and black people in our society. Recognition of the racially disparate breakup of black families can usefully focus attention on finally taking more effective action to solve some of the results of our societal legacy of slavery and of racial and economic injustice.

NOTES AND QUESTIONS

1. *The Least Detrimental Alternative.* Bartholet argues that removal is necessary to serve the interests of children who are maltreated. Are you convinced that the child will be better off in the post-removal situation? In a highly influential collaboration, Yale law professor Joseph Goldstein, psychoanalyst Anna Freud, and Yale Child Study Center professor Albert Solnit argued that decisionmakers should ensure that children are placed in the least detrimental alternative.[71] This would suggest that removal would be appropriate only if the government can show that there is a less detrimental *available* alternative. What if children removed from their homes are placed in a series of foster homes? Or in congregate care?

2. *Poverty and Public Lives.* Despite their different perspectives, Guggenheim, Roberts, and Bartholet draw attention to poverty as a factor in the child welfare system. How does poverty interact with government oversight? Consider Professor Annette Appell's perspective:

> Poor families are more susceptible to state intervention because they lack power and resources and because they are more directly involved with governmental agencies. . . . [P]oor families lead more public lives than their

---

71. Joseph Goldstein et al., The Best Interests of the Child: The Least Detrimental Alternative (1996).

middle-class counterparts: rather than visiting private doctors, poor families are likely to attend public clinics and emergency rooms for routine medical care; rather than hiring contractors to fix their homes, poor families encounter public building inspectors; rather than using their cars to run errands, poor mothers use public transportation.[72]

What is the relationship between more public lives and the child welfare system? Is it that more third parties, including mandatory reporters, observe one's family? Might racial disparities be explained by differential reporting of families of color by mandatory reporters? By private citizens, like neighbors? What role do government actors play? If a mother receives government benefits or services, should that constitute consent to government oversight?

Consider the work of Professor Khiara Bridges, who shows how poor pregnant women are subjected to a range of government interventions by virtue of needing government support. As Bridges writes:

> [I]f a state or the federal government compelled all pregnant women — poor and non-poor alike — to be counseled about smoking and drinking alcohol, to undergo "treatment and intervention directed toward helping [them] understand the importance of . . . good nutrition during pregnancy," and to discuss with a state actor their "goals for [themselves] in this pregnancy" and their "general emotional status," one would expect an uproar about the privacy invasions visited upon pregnant women by a paternalistic and overreaching state. Nevertheless, courts have routinely upheld the constitutionality of the privacy invasions that Medicaid programs force upon poor women.[73]

Appell and Bridges suggest concrete ways in which poverty renders families more susceptible to the intervention of child welfare authorities. But is the role of poverty more deep-seated? Bridges also argues that the state presumes poor parents unfit because of its moral construction of poverty — "the idea that people are poor because they are lazy, irresponsible, averse to work, promiscuous, and so on . . . the simple idea that people are poor because there is something wrong with them."[74]

3. *Reforms.* Bartholet draws a contrast between the kinds of interventions she advocates and those that she sees scholars like Roberts and Guggenheim advocating. Even if they disagree about immediate questions of family preservation and child removal, is there some common ground? Each author urges us to place the child welfare system in broader context. How could the government support families so that they do not come into contact with child protective services? Are anti-poverty programs the

---

72. Annette R. Appell, Protecting Children or Punishing Mothers: Gender, Race, and Class in the Child Protection System, 48 S.C. L. Rev. 577, 584 (1997).

73. Khiara M. Bridges, The Poverty of Privacy Rights 5–6 (2017).

74. Id. at 7.

answer? What if quality childcare and generous parental leave were available to all families? Should the government intervene in ways that focus on parent-child bonds? For example, the government could provide instruction and therapy to support healthy attachment between parents and children.

4. *Ending the Child Welfare System as We Know It?* What if we ended current practices and instead created a child welfare system that was entirely voluntary? That is, protective services could only be accessed on the request of the parent or caregiver. What would be the advantages and disadvantages of that approach?

B. The Indian Child Welfare Act

The preceding discussion focused on the contemporary child welfare system and the disproportionate impact on poor families of color. But questions of race and poverty in the child welfare system are not new. Beginning in the second half of the nineteenth century, Indian children were forcibly removed from their parents and placed in residential boarding schools aimed at "assimilation."[75] Child welfare authorities also placed Indian children in foster homes or with adoptive families who were usually non-Indian. As the Supreme Court observed:

> Studies undertaken by the Association on American Indian Affairs in 1969 and 1974 . . . showed that 25 to 35% of all Indian children had been separated from their families and placed in adoptive families, foster care, or institutions. Adoptive placements counted significantly in this total: in the State of Minnesota, for example, one in eight Indian children under the age of 18 was in an adoptive home, and during the year 1971–1972 nearly one in every four infants under one year of age was placed for adoption. The adoption rate of Indian children was eight times that of non-Indian children. Approximately 90% of the Indian placements were in non-Indian homes.[76]

Not until 1978 with the passage of the Indian Child Welfare Act (ICWA) did parents gain a legal right to refuse such removal.[77] ICWA sought to address not only the individualized harms to parents and children inflicted by U.S. policy up to that point but also the devastating impact such policy had on Indian culture.

ICWA sets out "a dual jurisdiction scheme,"[78] whereby tribal courts exercise exclusive jurisdiction over proceedings involving an Indian child "who resides or is

---

75. We use the term "Indian" in this section to track the language of the Indian Child Welfare Act and judicial decisions applying it.

76. Mississippi Band of Choctaw Indians v. Holyfield, 490 U.S. 30, 32 (1989).

77. 25 U.S.C. § 1901 et seq. (2018).

78. *Holyfield*, 490 U.S. at 36.

domiciled within the reservation of such tribe."[79] For a child not domiciled on a reservation, there is "concurrent but presumptively tribal jurisdiction,"[80] such that the child's parent or the tribe may seek, and generally be granted, transfer to a tribal court of a state-court action involving foster care placement or termination of parental rights.[81]

ICWA also has more substantive provisions aimed at protecting Indian families and preserving tribal identity. It requires caseworkers to engage in active efforts to support the family at risk of removal. Further, it establishes a set of placement preferences to govern the selection of adoptive or foster parents for Indian children in state court proceedings. Absent good cause to the contrary, ICWA directs that adoptive placements be made preferentially to: (1) a member of the child's extended family, (2) other members of the same tribe, or (3) other Indian families.[82] A similar preference scheme applies for foster care placements.[83]

The Supreme Court has only heard two cases under ICWA. The first case, Mississippi Band of Choctaw Indians v Holyfield,[84] concerned the jurisdictional provision of the statute. The Court held that children, whose parents were members of the Choctaw Indian Tribe and residents of the reservation, were "domiciled" on the reservation for purposes of granting exclusive jurisdiction to the tribal courts, even if the children never had been physically present on the reservation.[85] The Court's decision had the effect of undoing the adoption decrees that had been issued by a state court and instead sending the determination about custody of the children to the tribal courts.[86]

As Professor Solangel Maldonado notes, the Choctaw Tribe litigated the case to the Supreme Court in part because of the fear that its very survival was at risk:

> The Tribe was . . . concerned that allowing the twins to be adopted by a non-Choctaw family could compromise its ability to sustain itself. The Tribe's requirements for tribal membership are stricter than those of most tribes. Tribal members must have at least fifty percent Mississippi Choctaw blood; indeed, most enrolled members are full-blooded Choctaws. As a result of its stringent enrollment requirements, the Tribe's membership is relatively small (less than 5000 members). . . . [T]he loss of two full-blooded Choctaws to a non-Indian family would have had a greater impact on the Choctaw Tribe than a similar loss to nations without a minimum blood quantum, since those nations are open to a significantly larger potential membership.[87]

---

79. 25 U.S.C. § 1911(a) (2018).
80. *Holyfield*, 490 U.S. at 36.
81. 25 U.S.C. § 1911(b) (2018).
82. Id. § 1915(b).
83. Id.
84. 490 U.S. 30.
85. Id. at 48–49.
86. Id. at 53–54.
87. Solangel Maldonado, Race, Culture, and Adoption: Lessons from Mississippi Band of Choctaw Indians v. Holyfield, 17 Colum. J. Gender & L. 1, 13–14 (2008).

The only other ICWA case to be decided by the Supreme Cour[t] adoption by a non-Indian couple and the rights of the child's biologica[l] examine that case, Adoptive Couple v. Baby Girl,[88] in Chapter 8.

V. Foster Care

Foster care is intended to be a temporary placement for children who have been removed from their homes. The ultimate goal is either reunification with the child's parents or adoption (including by the foster parent). This section examines the foster care system. As you read, consider whether the system is serving its intended purpose.

A. Origins of the Foster Care System

The immediate predecessor to foster care was developed in the mid-nineteenth century by Charles Loring Brace and the New York Children's Aid Society. This system — known as "placing out" — placed New York children in the homes of rural midwestern families. Driven by an anti-urban and anti-immigrant ideology, advocates of "placing out" believed that they could protect children by removing them from an urban environment that was seen as corrupting and from parents who were seen as unable to properly raise them. Organizations that engaged in placing out in this period were usually religious and often Protestant. Often, children were removed from their families temporarily, when their parents fell on hard economic times, and the children returned home after a few years.[89]

By the 1880s, some state agencies paid foster parents to house children. This boarding-out system increased government involvement in children's welfare and eventually evolved into the modern foster system. Between 1900 and 1930, states began to develop juvenile court systems that handled issues related to children, including adjudicating claims to mother's pensions (cash payments to widows raising young children). In these cases, courts often would conduct investigations of families and could order children to be removed from their homes. The government's role in foster care gradually expanded and became increasingly bureaucratized and professionalized.

In 1912, at the behest of Jane Addams and other activists, the federal government created a Children's Bureau, which eventually became a part of the Department of Health & Human Services. Today, the Children's Bureau monitors

---

88. 570 U.S. 637 (2013).

89. See generally McGowan, supra note 2; Tim Hacsi, From Indenture to Family Foster Care: A Brief History of Child Placing, 74 Child Welfare 162 (1995).

state compliance with federal law and collects data to share with states, localities, and the general public.

B. Federal Regulation of Foster Care

As we have seen, in 1980 there were approximately 500,000 children in foster care, who stayed in care for an average of 2.5 years.[90] In response, Congress legislated in ways that emphasized family preservation and reunification.[91] Further, Title IV-E of the Social Security Act, where the regulation of foster care was located, was amended to require states to "giv[e] preference to an adult relative over a non-related caregiver when determining a placement for a child."[92] (As we saw, ICWA already included a placement preference for "a member of the Indian child's extended family."[93]) The foster care population was cut in half by the mid-1980s, but by the late 1990s had grown again to approximately 500,000.[94] ASFA represented a response, expediting removal and emphasizing permanency (generally with the aim of adoption).[95] Then, in 2018, Congress shifted again to a more preventative approach with FFPSA.[96] That law extends the time period for which children who exit foster care can receive services; previously, federal law only permitted reunification services for up to fifteen months after a child had returned from foster care, and FFPSA removed this fifteen-month limit. FFPSA also limits funding for foster placements that occur outside family settings, thereby seeking to reduce the number of foster children living in group homes.

C. How Placement Decisions Are Made

In addition to affecting when children enter and leave foster care, federal and state laws also regulate the living situations of children in foster care and the children who leave foster care. This section discusses the regulation of foster care placements. It also addresses permanency options, or what happens to children after they leave foster care. In both of these areas, there is some disconnect between the legal framework that governs placement options and the demographic reality of the situation. While federal law gives preference to children in kinship care placements

90. Gendell, supra note 5, at 27.

91. Pub. L. No. 96-272 (codified as amended in scattered sections of 42 U.S.C.).

92. Personal Responsibility and Work Opportunity Reconciliation Act of 1996, Pub. L. No. 104-193 (codified at 42 U.S.C. § 671(a)(19)).

93. 25 U.S.C. § 1915(b) (2018).

94. See Bean, supra note 7, at 325–26.

95. Pub. L. No. 105-89 (codified in scattered sections of 42 U.S.C.).

96. Pub. L. No. 115-123.

and single-family homes, the majority of children in foster care do not live with a relative, and a substantial minority live in congregate care, which includes group homes and other institutions. Similarly, while federal law prioritizes family reunification or adoption for children who enter foster care, many children do not receive these placements and remain in foster care, often until they age out.

1. Foster Care Placements

Both federal and state laws impose requirements on who may provide foster care. Federal law prohibits adults from becoming foster parents if they have been convicted of certain felonies, such as child abuse, spousal abuse, or other violent crimes.[97] States also maintain separate laws that require background checks for foster parents and identify convictions that disqualify individuals from being foster parents.

Federal law requires that states give preference to kinship care placements, in which foster children are placed with relatives.[98] As of 2017, approximately one-third of foster children are placed with relatives, and nearly half of foster children are placed with non-relative foster parents. One in eight foster children is in an institution or group home. The remainder of children are in trial home visits, pre-adoptive homes, supervised independent living, or have run away.[99]

States prioritize kinship care for a number of reasons. Children may have a more stable transition if they are placed with a relative with whom they already have a preexisting relationship. Children in kinship care may also maintain closer relationships with birth parents and siblings. Kinship placements may also reduce the burden on states, which usually have a shortage of licensed foster parents. States may provide kinship caregivers with less training and instructional support than non-kinship caregivers.[100] (Before a 1979 Supreme Court decision required states to provide payments to kinship caregivers at the same rate as other foster parents, many states would not provide foster care assistance when children were placed with relatives.[101])

In contrast to kinship care, agencies generally seek to avoid placing children in group homes unless other options are unavailable. Group homes usually contain six to nine adolescents who live together. Group homes are associated with worse outcomes than other foster care options, including increased involvement in the criminal justice system and lower educational attainment.[102] In addition to group

---

97. See 42 U.S.C. § 671(a)(20) (2018).

98. 42 U.S.C. § 671(a)(19), (29).

99. See Children's Bureau, Child Welfare Info. Gateway, Foster Care Statistics 2017, at 4 (2018).

100. For a discussion of outcomes of foster children in kinship care, see U.S. Dep't of Health & Human Servs., Admin. for Children & Families, Report to the Congress on Kinship Foster Care (1999).

101. See Miller v. Youakim, 440 U.S. 125 (1979).

102. See generally Joseph Ryan et al., Juvenile Delinquency in Child Welfare: Investigating Group Home Effects, 30 Child. & Youth Servs. Rev. 1088 (2008).

homes, states also run institutions that are designed for children with specialized needs, such as severe mental or behavioral issues or disabilities. Yet in 2015, nearly 30 percent of children in congregate care had no clinical diagnosis of any mental or behavioral disorder.[103] FFPSA, enacted in 2018, limits the amount of time that children can spend in group homes and institutional settings and requires that group care providers adopt a number of best practices.

2. Planning for Permanency

Foster care is intended to be temporary. As we have seen, federal law requires state agencies to develop permanency plans for children within twelve months of the time that the child enters foster care. Permanency options may include: reunification with a child's parent, adoption following the termination of parental rights, guardianship with a permanent guardian, guardianship with a fit and willing relative while remaining in the state's legal custody, or another planned permanent living arrangement (APPLA).[104]

In determining a child's permanency plan, the agency must weigh several factors. Federal law requires that the states, first, make an effort to reunify the family, or, second, place the child with a fit and willing relative. If the child is fourteen years or older, the permanency plan must be developed in consultation with the child.[105] In making determinations, state agencies must consider the best interests of the child. Federal law also requires that states make reasonable efforts to place siblings together or, if that is not possible, to allow ongoing visitation between siblings.[106]

Reunification. Reunification is both the preferred and most common outcome for foster children. States provide services to parents in order to promote reunification, such as therapy, parenting classes, drug and alcohol treatment, and home visiting programs. However, states do not provide direct financial assistance to parents, as they do for foster parents. Before reunification may occur, states generally arrange home trial visits to ensure that the parent is able to provide a safe home for the child.

Adoption. For a child to be available for adoption, the state must first terminate the rights of the existing parent or parents — a topic we discuss later in this chapter. As with other placements, agencies must give priority to the child's relatives when finding an adoptive placement for the child.[107]

Guardianship. Guardianship allows a non-parent to assume legal custody without terminating the existing parent's rights. Guardianship may be chosen when relative caregivers wish to avoid triggering the termination of parental rights or when

---

103. See Children's Bureau, A National Look at the Use of Congregate Care in Child Welfare 1 (2015).
104. 42 U.S.C. §§ 675, 675a (2018).
105. Id. § 675(1)(C).
106. Id. § 671(a)(31).
107. Id. § 671(a)(19).

older children do not want their parents' rights to be terminated but want to remain with their current caregiver. Guardianship permits the caregiver to exercise custody and control over education and other legal decisions.[108] Guardians generally must meet the same criteria as foster parents, and a court must approve legal guardianship after a hearing.

APPLA. Although the option is disfavored, states may also choose another planned permanent living arrangement (APPLA) for the child, which includes permanent foster care, independent living, and residential psychiatric care.[109] Many states require the agency to explain compelling reasons why other options were not selected in order to include APPLA in the child's permanency plan.[110]

Aging Out. If children do not have a permanent placement, they will age out of the foster care system. In approximately half of the states, children age out at eighteen. In other states, aging out does not occur until twenty-one, although some states only authorize this extension if the child meets certain criteria, such as remaining in school or working a minimum number of hours.[111] Although the government may provide financial support and other services to children who age out of foster care, these children often have only a minimal support system as they transition into adulthood.

NOTES AND QUESTIONS

1. *Demographics.*

a. *Age.* In 2018, there were more than 437,000 children in foster care. Almost one-third of foster children were three years old or younger, and around a quarter of foster children were teenagers.[112]

b. *Race.* Nationally, 44 percent of foster children were white, 23 percent were black, 21 percent were Hispanic, 8 percent were multiracial, and 2 percent were Native American.[113] Black and Native American children are overrepresented in the foster care system. Although black and Native American children respectively make up just 14 percent and 0.9 percent of children in the general population, they represent 23 percent and 2 percent of foster children, respectively.[114]

---

108. Id. § 675(7).

109. Id. § 675(5)(C).

110. See, e.g., Ala. Code § 12-15-315 (2020); Conn. Gen. Stat. § 46b-129 (2020).

111. See, e.g., Ill. Rev. Stat. ch. 20 § 505/5(a)(1) (2020); Tex. Fam. Code § 264.101(a-1) (2020).

112. See U.S. Dep't of Health & Human Servs., Admin. for Children & Families, AFCARS Report 1 (2018).

113. See id. at 2.

114. See Steve Wood & Alice Summers, Nat'l Council of Juvenile & Family Ct. Court Judges, Disproportionality Rates for Children of Color in Foster Care (2014).

c. *Sexual Orientation and Gender Identity.* LGBT youth are disproportionately represented in the foster care system and, once they enter foster care, are more likely to be placed in multiple foster homes or in group homes, as compared to non-LGBT youth.[115]

2. *Reasons for Foster Care Placement.* Most children enter foster care based on an agency determination of neglect (62 percent). Other major reasons that children enter foster care include parental drug abuse (36 percent), caretaker inability to cope (14 percent), physical abuse (12 percent), housing issues (10 percent), child behavior problems (9 percent), and parental incarceration (7 percent). In many families, a combination of these factors is present.

3. *Drug Use, Removal, and Race.* The number of children who have entered foster care due to parental drug use has increased amidst the opioid crisis.[116] As Professor Khiara Bridges observes, "[a]n important element of the opioid crisis is its whiteness."[117] Yet, women of color remain disproportionately vulnerable to child removal based on drug use.[118] Even when rates of drug use are comparable, women of color are brought to the attention of child welfare authorities at higher rates.[119] This may partly be due to racial disparities in test-and-report practices. Hospitals that serve low-income mothers and their newborns routinely conduct drug tests, while private hospitals in wealthier neighborhoods rarely do so.[120] And even within the same hospital, women of color are tested at higher rates.[121] As we have seen before, the relationship between race and class matters. Laws in many states require drug screening or testing of welfare recipients.[122]

Should criminal drug laws be enforced against pregnant women? Should healthcare providers help criminal authorities enforce such laws against pregnant women? In Ferguson v. City of Charleston, the Supreme Court found that the Medical University of South Carolina's policy of performing drug tests on pregnant women, without their

---

115. See Bianca D.M. Wilson et al., Williams Inst. Sexual and Gender Minority Youth in Foster Care: Assessing Disproportionality and Disparities in Los Angeles (2014); Jill Jacobs & Madelyn Freundlich, Achieving Permanency for LGBTQ Youth, 85 Child Welfare 299 (2006).

116. See AFCARS Report , supra note 112.

117. Khiara M. Bridges, Race, Pregnancy, and the Opioid Epidemic: White Privilege and the Criminalization of Opioid Use During Pregnancy, 133 Harv. L. Rev. 770 (2020). See also U.S. Dep't of Health & Human Servs., Office on Women's Health, Final Report: Opioid Use, Misuse, and Overdose in Women 12 (2017).

118. Douglas Waite et al., Putting Families First: How the Opioid Epidemic Is Affecting Children and Families, and the Child Welfare Policy Options to Address It, 9 J. Applied Res. on Child. 1, 4 (2018).

119. Id.

120. Oren Yaniv, Weed Out: More than a Dozen City Maternity Wards Regularly Test New Moms for Marijuana and Other Drugs, N.Y. Daily News (Dec. 29, 2012).

121. Marc A. Ellsworth, Infant Race Affects Application of Clinical Guidelines when Screening for Drugs of Abuse in Newborns, 125 Pediatrics 1379 (2010); see also Brenda Warner Rotzoll, Black Newborns Likelier to be Drug-Tested: Study, Chi. Sun-Times (Mar. 16, 2001); Troy Anderson, Race Tilt in Foster Care Hit; Hospital Staff More Likely to Screen Minority Mothers, L.A. Daily News (June 30, 2008).

122. Nat'l Conference of State Legislatures, Drug Testing for Welfare Recipients and Public Assistance (2017).

consent, for the purpose of providing evidence of criminal conduct to law enforcement constituted an unreasonable search under the Fourth Amendment.[123] Deterring drug use by pregnant women did not provide a sufficient justification for the warrantless searches. Why would the hospital have started its drug testing program? How might such a program shape the behavior of pregnant women?

The potential harm caused by substance use and abuse during pregnancy raises complicated legal and policy questions. According to the Department of Health and Human Services, 9.9 percent of pregnant women use alcohol during pregnancy, and 11.6 percent use tobacco — more than twice as many the number of pregnant women who use illegal drugs (including marijuana) (5.4 percent).[124] These substances all enhance certain risks to an unborn child, though not as significantly as once believed and not necessarily more than other, unregulated sources of harm. What is the role for the criminal or civil law in addressing this issue?

Prosecutors in virtually every state have charged drug-addicted pregnant women under laws prohibiting child abuse or endangerment or the delivery of a controlled substance to a minor. A disproportionate number of these defendants are women of color.[125] Many charges have been reversed on appeal on the theory that the laws were not intended to protect fetuses.[126] The Kentucky Supreme Court, for example, reversed a criminal conviction of a woman whose baby tested positive for cocaine at birth, concluding that substance abuse by pregnant women should be treated as a public health, rather than a legal, issue.[127] Still, other states have upheld the criminalization of prenatal substance use.[128] And in 2014, Tennessee became the first state to expressly criminalize drug use by a pregnant woman.[129] By 2017, about 100 women had been charged under the law, "mostly in rural eastern Tennessee, an area severely lacking in drug treatment facilities, and in Memphis, a majority African-American city."[130]

State child abuse and neglect statutes have also been used during pregnancy in cases of prenatal substance use, but only where they clearly apply to prenatal conduct.[131] Abuse and neglect laws also have the potential to be used just after birth, if a newborn tests positive for an illegal drug. In a 2013 case, however, the New Jersey Supreme Court held that a court cannot make a finding of abuse or neglect based on

---

123. 532 U.S. 67 (2001).

124. Elinore F. McCance-Katz, Substance Abuse and Mental Health Servs. Admin. Nat'l Survey on Drug Use and Health: 2018, at 30.

125. Lynn M. Paltrow & Jeanne Flavin, Arrests of and Forced Interventions on Pregnant Women in the United States, 1973–2005, 38 J. Health Pols., Pol'y & L. 299, 311 (2013).

126. Editorial Bd., The Mothers Society Condemns, N.Y. Times (Jan. 30, 2019); see also Paltrow & Flavin, supra note 125, at 309.

127. Cochran v. Commonwealth, 315 S.W.3d 325 (Ky. 2010).

128. Courts in South Carolina and Alabama have upheld convictions in similar circumstances. See Whitner v. State, 492 S.E.2d 777 (S.C. 1997); see also Ex Parte Ankrom, 152 So. 3d 397 (Ala. 2013).

129. Tenn. Code Ann. § 39-13-107 (2020).

130. Amnesty Int'l, Criminalizing Pregnancy, 7–8 (2017).

131. See, e.g., Fla. Stat. Ann. § 415.503(9)(g)(1), repealed by Laws 1998, ch. 98-403, § 173; 705 Ill. Comp. Stat. Ann. § 405/2-18(2)(c)(d) (2020); Nev. Rev. Stat. Ann. § 432B.330(1)(b) (2020).

mother's drug use during pregnancy unless there is evidence of actual harm when the baby is born, and a positive drug test at birth alone is ~idence of such harm.[132]

... prenatal exposure to a controlled substance constitute neglect? If so, what legal responses are most appropriate? Removal of the child from the parent and in some cases termination of parental rights are the most likely options, but is that a good option for the child?

4. *Exiting Foster Care.* In 2017, 51 percent of children who exited foster care were reunified with their parents or primary caretakers;[133] 23 percent were adopted; 10 percent went to live with guardians; 8 percent were emancipated; and 7 percent lived with other relatives. Younger children and white children were disproportionately likely to be adopted, whereas older children and black children were less likely to be adopted. The majority of adoptions were by a child's foster parents.[134]

5. *Aging Out of Foster Care.* Between 20,000 and 30,000 children per year will "age out" of the foster care system without having been reunified with their parents or placed in other permanent homes. This is an extremely vulnerable population with higher rates of homelessness, substance abuse, unwanted pregnancy, and poverty than their peers. A study of aged-out youth in Texas found that, by the age of 21, 25 percent had experienced homelessness, 30 percent had had a child, 25 percent had been incarcerated, and less than half had been employed.[135] What is the appropriate role for the state with respect to these young people? While in the foster care system, the state served as their legal guardian. Should that continue past the age of 18? Until what age? Some states offer extended foster care programs that permit youth to apply to receive housing support, continued case management, or other services, but many youth do not meet the educational or work requirements necessary to enroll. Others offer group-housing programs that give aged-out youth support as they transition to independent living, though enrollment in such programs is low. What practical problems might you expect aged-out youth to face? In what ways do young adults who grew up in parental care continue to benefit from family support as they navigate young adulthood?[136]

6. *Suits by Foster Children.* While children are often removed from their homes because of abuse or neglect, they may encounter harmful circumstances in the child welfare system as well. Foster children have sued state officials and agencies for abuse

---

132. New Jersey Dep't of Children & Families, Div. of Youth & Family Servs. v. A.L, 59 A.3d 576 (N.J. 2013).

133. While many assume that reunification is an optimal outcome, for some children — for example, LGBTQ youth — reunification may return them to an environment hostile to their identity. See Jordan Blair Woods, Unaccompanied Youth and Private-Public Order Failures, 103 Iowa L. Rev. 1639 (2018).

134. See AFCARS Report, supra note 112.

135. Child Trends, Transition-Age Youth in Foster Care in Texas (2015); TexProtects, Texas Foster Care System Analysis and Recommendation (Jan. 2017).

136. See Richard Fry, For First Time in Modern Era, Living with Parents Edges Out Other Living Arrangements for 18-34-Year-Olds, Pew Research Ctr. (May 24, 2016); Nat'l Poverty Ctr., Family Support During the Transition to Adulthood (Aug. 2004); Jim Casey Youth Opportunities Initiative, The Adolescent Brain: New Research and Its Implications for Young People Transitioning from Foster Care (2011).

and neglect, and have been successful with respect to the denial of medical care and excessive caseloads of caseworkers.[137] Other suits have challenged excessive removals from children's homes; the lack of needed support services, healthcare, and mental health treatment; overuse of congregate care; the sedation of and use of physical restraints on foster children; mistreatment of children with disabilities; the lack of transition planning for children aging out of the foster care system; and improper housing conditions, including abusive or neglectful homes, homeless shelters, and juvenile detention facilities.[138]

D. The Foster Family and the Constitution

Foster parents also have brought several challenges to foster care policies and to actions taken by child welfare officials. But foster parents' suits have met with little success. In its 1977 decision in Smith v. OFFER,[139] the Supreme Court held that New York's procedure for removing children from foster homes was permissible under the Fourteenth Amendment. The Court declined to decide whether foster parents had a protected liberty interest in the relationship with their foster children. The court held that even if such an interest existed, the process for removing children from foster homes was constitutionally permissible. Courts have routinely ruled against foster parents' constitutional claims since *OFFER*.[140] Still, a closer look at the Court's opinion reveals a more uncertain constitutional status for the foster parent-child relationship.

Smith v. Organization of Foster Families for Equality and Reform (OFFER)
431 U.S. 816 (1977)

Justice Brennan delivered the opinion of the Court. . . .

The appellees' basic contention is that when a child has lived in a foster home for a year or more, a psychological tie is created between the child and the foster parents which constitutes the foster family the true "psychological family" of the child. See J. Goldstein, A. Freud, & A. Solnit, Beyond the Best Interests of the Child (1973). That family, they argue, has a "liberty interest" in its survival as a family

---

137. See Tinsley v. McKay, 156 F. Supp. 3d. 1024, 1026 (D. Ariz. 2015); M.D. v. Abbott, 152 F. Supp. 3d 684, 694 (S.D. Tex. 2015).

138. See, e.g., B.L. by next friend Tinsley v. Snyder, 922 F.3d 957 (9th Cir. 2019) (affirming class certification in challenge to Arizona foster care system); Complaint, Ashley W. v. Holcomb, No. 3:19-cv-00129-RLY-MPB (S.D. Ind. June 25, 2019) (alleging that Indiana child welfare system violated children's rights under the First, Ninth, and Fourteenth Amendments); Complaint, Wyatt B. v. Brown, No. 6:19-cv-00556-aA (D. Or. Apr. 16, 2019) (alleging multiple constitutional violations in the Oregon foster care system).

139. 431 U.S. 816 (1977).

140. See, e.g., Rodriguez v. McLoughlin, 214 F.3d 328 (2d Cir. 2000); Procopio v. Johnson, 994 F.2d 325 (7th Cir. 1993).

protected by the Fourteenth Amendment. Upon this premise they conclude that the foster child cannot be removed without a prior hearing satisfying due process. Appointed counsel for the children, . . . however, disagrees, and has consistently argued that the foster parents have no such liberty interest independent of the interests of the foster children, and that the best interests of the children would not be served by procedural protections beyond those already provided by New York law. The intervening natural parents of children in foster care . . . also oppose the foster parents, arguing that recognition of the procedural right claimed would undercut both the substantive family law of New York, which favors the return of children to their natural parents as expeditiously as possible, and their constitutionally protected right of family privacy, by forcing them to submit to a hearing and defend their rights to their children before the children could be returned to them.

It is, of course, true that "freedom of personal choice in matters of . . . family life is one of the liberties protected by the Due Process Clause of the Fourteenth Amendment." There does exist a "private realm of family life which the state cannot enter," that has been afforded both substantive and procedural protection. But is the relation of foster parent to foster child sufficiently akin to the concept of "family" recognized in our precedents to merit similar protection? Although considerable difficulty has attended the task of defining "family" for purposes of the Due Process Clause, we are not without guides to some of the elements that define the concept of "family" and contribute to its place in our society.

First, the usual understanding of "family" implies biological relationships, and most decisions treating the relation between parent and child have stressed this element. *Stanley v. Illinois*, 405 U.S. 645, 651 (1972), for example, spoke of "(t)he rights to conceive and to raise one's children" as essential rights. And *Prince v. Massachusetts*, stated:

> It is cardinal with us that the custody, care and nurture of the child reside first in the parents, whose primary function and freedom include preparation for obligations the state can neither supply nor hinder. 321 U.S. 158, 166 (1944).

A biological relationship is not present in the case of the usual foster family. But biological relationships are not exclusive determination of the existence of a family. The basic foundation of the family in our society, the marriage relationship, is of course not a matter of blood relation. Yet its importance has been strongly emphasized in our cases:

> We deal with a right of privacy older than the Bill of Rights — older than our political parties, older than our school system. Marriage is a coming together for better or for worse, hopefully enduring, and intimate to the degree of being sacred. It is an association that promotes a way of life, not causes; a harmony in living, not political faiths; a bilateral loyalty, not commercial or social projects. Yet it is an association for as noble a purpose as any involved in our prior decisions. *Griswold v. Connecticut*, 381 U.S. 479, 486 (1965).

Thus the importance of the familial relationship, to the individuals involved and to the society, stems from the emotional attachments that derive from the intimacy of daily association, and from the role it plays in "promot(ing) a way of life" through the instruction of children, *Wisconsin v. Yoder*, 406 U.S. 205, 231–33 (1972), as well as from the fact of blood relationship. No one would seriously dispute that a deeply loving and interdependent relationship between an adult and a child in his or her care may exist even in the absence of blood relationship. At least where a child has been placed in foster care as an infant, has never known his natural parents, and has remained continuously for several years in the care of the same foster parents, it is natural that the foster family should hold the same place in the emotional life of the foster child, and fulfill the same socializing functions, as a natural family. For this reason, we cannot dismiss the foster family as a mere collection of unrelated individuals.

But there are also important distinctions between the foster family and the natural family. First, unlike the earlier cases recognizing a right to family privacy, the State here seeks to interfere, not with a relationship having its origins entirely apart from the power of the State, but rather with a foster family which has its source in state law and contractual arrangements. The individual's freedom to marry and reproduce is "older than the Bill of Rights." Accordingly, unlike the property interests that are also protected by the Fourteenth Amendment, the liberty interest in family privacy has its source, and its contours are ordinarily to be sought, not in state law, but in intrinsic human rights, as they have been understood in "this Nation's history and tradition." Here, however, whatever emotional ties may develop between foster parent and foster child have their origins in an arrangement in which the State has been a partner from the outset. While the Court has recognized that liberty interests may in some cases arise from positive-law sources, . . . where, as here, the claimed interest derives from a knowingly assumed contractual relation with the State, it is appropriate to ascertain from state law the expectations and entitlements of the parties. In this case, the limited recognition accorded to the foster family by the New York statutes and the contracts executed by the foster parents argue against any but the most limited constitutional "liberty" in the foster family.

A second consideration related to this is that ordinarily procedural protection may be afforded to a liberty interest of one person without derogating from the substantive liberty of another. Here, however, such a tension is virtually unavoidable. Under New York law, the natural parent of a foster child in voluntary placement has an absolute right to the return of his child in the absence of a court order obtainable only upon compliance with rigorous substantive and procedural standards, which reflect the constitutional protection accorded the natural family. Moreover, the natural parent initially gave up his child to the State only on the express understanding that the child would be returned in those circumstances. These rights are difficult to reconcile with the liberty interest in the foster family relationship claimed by appellees. It is one thing to say that individuals may acquire a liberty interest against arbitrary governmental interference in the family-like associations into which they have freely entered, even in the absence of biological connection or state-law recognition of the relationship. It is quite another to say that one may acquire such an interest in the face of another's constitutionally recognized liberty interest that derives from blood relationship, state-law sanction, and basic human right an interest the foster parent has recognized by contract from the outset. Whatever liberty interest might otherwise exist in the foster family as an institution, that interest must be substantially attenuated where the proposed removal from the foster family is to return the child to his natural parents.

As this discussion suggests, appellees' claim to a constitutionally protected liberty interest raises complex and novel questions. It is unnecessary for us to resolve those questions definitively in this case, however, for . . . we conclude that "narrower grounds exist to support" our reversal. We are persuaded that, even on the assumption that appellees have a protected "liberty interest," the District Court erred in holding that the preremoval procedures presently employed by the State are constitutionally defective. . . .

PROBLEM

Ann and Greg Elwell were foster parents of multiple children, including Travis, who had lived with the Elwells since he was three months old. The rights of Travis's biological parents had been terminated by the state. The Elwells bonded with Travis and began the process of adopting him. An adoption plan was put in place and a final adoption date was set for fifteen months after Travis first came to live with the Elwells.

A month before Travis's adoption was set to become final, the Kansas Department of Social and Rehabilitative Services (SRS) received a report that Sophia, another child in the Elwells's care, had been emotionally abused by Ann. Although SRS initially designated the report regarding Sophia as unsubstantiated, it subsequently classified the report as substantiated and decided to terminate the Elwells's foster care license and remove both Sophia and Travis from the Elwells's home. It did not notify the Elwells that it was considering removing Travis until the day he was removed.

At the time, Kansas law stated that if a child had the same foster home for more than six months, SRS shall provide written notice no less than 30 days before removing the child, unless the move is to a preadoptive home. The Elwells sued SRS, arguing that Kansas law gave them a right to be notified before Travis was removed and further alleging that the agency violated their procedural and substantive due process rights when it did not provide them with notice before removing Travis from their home.

You are considering the Elwells' constitutional claims. Do foster parents have constitutionally protected liberty interests that are implicated when foster children are removed from their homes? If so, are those rights implicated here? If they are, what is the appropriate remedy?

POSTSCRIPT

While most cases after the Supreme Court's decision in Smith v. OFFER have rejected the due process claims of foster parents, the Tenth Circuit in Elwell v. Byers held that foster parents may, under certain circumstances, claim a protected liberty interest in the relationship with their foster children.[141] The court observed that while "the typical foster care arrangement generally does not create a liberty interest in familial association,"[142] the *OFFER* "Court indicated that the liberty interest in family association may extend to foster parents in certain circumstances."[143]

The court found a number of factors weighed in favor of the Elwells. First, "the parental rights of [the child] T.S.'s biological parents had been terminated," and so the competing rights of biological parents were not at issue.[144] Second, "the Elwells had cared for T.S. for an extended period of time; they were essentially the only parents T.S. had ever known when the events at issue occurred."[145] Third, "[t]he Elwells were very close to becoming adoptive parents, although some steps remained in that process."[146] On the court's view, "preadoptive parents" have a more significant claim than ordinary foster parents "'because of the possibility of developing a permanent adoptive relationship.'"[147]

Ultimately, the court explained: "we do not need to define precisely where the liberty interest threshold falls on the spectrum but conclude that the Elwells fall on the protected side of that line."[148] Ordinarily, this would mean that foster parents would be entitled to notice and a hearing before foster children were removed from their home. Nonetheless, the court concluded that state officials were protected by qualified immunity, because the foster parents' rights were not clearly established. At the time of the conduct in question, "no court had answered whether preadoptive parents in the Elwells' position possessed a liberty interest in familial association."[149]

---

141. 699 F.3d 1208 (10th Cir. 2012).
142. Id. at 1217.
143. Id. at 1216.
144. Id.
145. Id. at 1216–17.
146. Id. at 1217.
147. Id. at 1216 (quoting Spielman v. Hildebrand, 873 F.2d 1377 (10th Cir. 1989)).
148. Id. at 1217.
149. Id. at 1219.

VI. Termination of Parental Rights

While child welfare authorities often seek reunification after a child is removed from her parents, they may determine that reunification is inappropriate. In such cases, they may seek termination of the parents' rights — a step that would also free the child for adoption. When is termination of parental rights appropriate? What must the state show to terminate parental rights? How should we account for the interests of the child? Does termination serve or undermine the interests of the child? How do we know? This section addresses termination of parental rights from the perspective of parents, children, and the state.

A. Parental Unfitness and Best Interests of the Child

While the grounds and procedures governing termination of parental rights vary by state, most states require two separate determinations: first, that the parent is unfit; and second, that termination is in the child's best interests.[150] Other states require courts to consider the child's best interests as part of a broader determination, which also includes unfitness.[151] A few states base termination determinations exclusively on whether a statutory ground of unfitness has been proved, without additional consideration of the child's best interests.[152]

Why should a state consider both parental unfitness and the child's best interests? The first question is centrally concerned with the status of the parent — whether the parent is meeting some minimal level of competence imposed by the state. The second question is centrally concerned with the status of the child — whether the child's interest will be promoted if her parent's rights are extinguished. Is it appropriate to consider both? When would the answers to those two questions point in different directions?

Consider Georgia's statute on termination of parental rights, which includes a section on unfitness and a section on best interests.

Georgia Code Annotated § 15-11-310 (2020)

(a) In considering the termination of parental rights, the court shall first determine whether one of the following statutory grounds for termination of parental rights has been met:

---

150. See, e.g., Conn. Gen. Stat. § 17a-112(j) (2020); Ga. Code § 15-11-310 (2020); Ohio Rev. Code § 2151.414(A) (2020).

151. See, e.g., Ariz Rev. Stat. § 8-533 (2020); Minn. Stat. § 260C.301 (2020); 23 Pa. Cons. Stat. § 2511 (2020).

152. See, e.g., Fla. Stat. § 39.806 (2020); La. Child. Code art. 1015 (2020); N.H. Rev. Stat. § 170-C:5 (2020).

(1) The parent has given written consent to termination which has been acknowledged by the court or has voluntarily surrendered his or her child for adoption;

(2) The parent has subjected his or her child to aggravated circumstances;

(3) The parent has wantonly and willfully failed to comply for a period of 12 months or longer with a decree to support his or her child that has been entered by a court of competent jurisdiction of this or any other state;

(4) A child is abandoned by his or her parent; or

(5) A child is a dependent child due to lack of proper parental care or control by his or her parent, reasonable efforts to remedy the circumstances have been unsuccessful or were not required, such cause of dependency is likely to continue or will not likely be remedied in the reasonably foreseeable future, and:

    (A) Returning such child to his or her parent is likely to cause serious physical, mental, moral, or emotional harm to such child or threaten the physical safety or well-being of such child; or

    (B) Continuation of the parent and child relationship will cause or is likely to cause serious physical, mental, moral, or emotional harm to such child.

(b) If any of the statutory grounds for termination has been met, the court shall then consider whether termination is in a child's best interests after considering the following factors:

    (1) Such child's sense of attachments, including his or her sense of security and familiarity, and the continuity of affection for such child;

    (2) Such child's wishes and long-term goals;

    (3) Such child's need for permanence, including his or her need for stability and continuity of relationships with a parent, siblings, and other relatives;

    (4) Any benefit to such child of being integrated into a stable and permanent home and the likely effect of delaying such integration into such stable and permanent home environment;

    (5) The detrimental impact of the lack of a stable and permanent home environment on such child's safety, well-being, or physical, mental, or emotional health;

    (6) Such child's future physical, mental, moral, or emotional well-being; and

    (7) Any other factors . . . considered by the court to be relevant and proper to its determination.

(c) If the court determines that a parent has subjected his or her child to aggravated circumstances because such parent has committed the murder of the other parent of such child, the court shall presume that termination of parental rights is in the best interests of the child.

As you can see from Georgia's statute, there are many potential grounds on which a court can find parental unfitness. One such ground is abandonment. What does it mean to abandon one's child? Has a parent who is incarcerated abandoned her child?

The federal government reports that, as of 2007, more than 800,000 state and federal prisoners were parents of children under the age of eighteen. Given the gender disparity in the prison population, it is not surprising that more than 90 percent of these parents were men.[153] Yet, women's incarceration has grown dramatically in the past few decades, and more than half of incarcerated women are mothers.[154] A 2016 study of federal and state prisoners found that 3.8 percent of women were pregnant when newly admitted to prison.[155] For many children, parental incarceration removes them from their primary caregivers. More than three-quarters of mothers who lived with their children prior to incarceration provided all or most of their children's daily care.[156] Communities of color are disproportionately affected. While 8 percent of children have lived with a parent or guardian who has been incarcerated, that figure jumps to 16 and 14 percent for black and Native American children, respectively.[157]

Many incarcerated parents struggle to maintain contact with their children. Geographical distance and prison policies can make it difficult to maintain relationships. Federal law now requires that prisoners be placed within 500 miles from family — though this of course is still too far for most families to make routine visits.[158] Some states have developed programs that allow incarcerated mothers to live with their young children.

Still, incarcerated parents are at particular risk of having their parental rights terminated. In every jurisdiction, a court may consider whether a parent is incarcerated in terminating parental rights. In one-third of the states, the mere fact of parental incarceration can be a sufficient ground for termination. For instance, under Tennessee law, a court may terminate parental rights if the parent is sentenced to ten or more years and the child is under eight years of age at the time the parent is sentenced.[159] In the remaining jurisdictions, the fact of a parent's incarceration can be a factor in support of, but not the sole basis for, termination. However, these states vary widely in the

153. See Lauren E. Glaze & Laura M. Maruschak, Bureau of Justice Stats., NCJ 222984, Parents in Prison and Their Minor Children 2 (2010).

154. See Wendy Sawyer, The Gender Divide: Tracking Women's State Prison Growth (2018); Spencer K. Beall, "Lock Her Up!: How Women Have Become the Fastest-Growing Population in the American Carceral State, 23 Berkeley J. Crim. L. 1, 6 (2018).

155. See Carolyn Sufrin et al., Pregnancy Outcomes in U.S. Prisons, 2016–2017, 109 Am. J. Pub. Health 799 (2019).

156. See Glaze & Maruschak, supra note 153, at 5.

157. See Kids Count, Annie E. Casey Found. Children Who Had a Parent Who Was Ever Incarcerated (2017).

158. See First Step Act, S. 2795, 115th Cong. (2018).

159. Tenn. Code § 36-1-113(g)(6) (2020).

degree to which they scrutinize incarceration and its direct consequences in issuing termination orders. What role do you think incarceration should play in determinations of parental unfitness? When might it be in a child's best interest to terminate the parental rights of an incarcerated parent?

Although the two stages of termination of parental rights — parental unfitness and the child's best interests — often go hand in hand, there are circumstances in which courts have found that the determination of the child's best interests does *not* support termination, despite a finding of parental unfitness. Indeed, research suggests that even where parents are unfit, the termination of parental rights may cause substantial psychological harm to the child.[160]

The Georgia statute excerpted above instructs the court to consider the child's interest in "a stable and permanent home environment." How much should it matter what alternatives are available for the child? That is, does the child's interest figure differently if a prospective adoptive parent is willing and able to adopt the child, as opposed to a situation in which foster parents are not willing to adopt the child and no other adoptive placement has been identified? In the latter situation, might it be in the child's best interest to maintain the parental rights of a parent who is unfit?

Consider the perspective of an Arizona court, which refused to terminate parental rights of a father unable to meet his parental responsibilities because of mental health issues.[161] A state statute lowered the standard by which parental rights could be terminated in cases where the child had been in an "out-of-home placement," including foster care, for more than two years. The statute sought to allow children who have spent significant time in foster care to be adopted — or, as the court explained, "to enable children to have a permanent family through adoption."[162] But in addressing the father's two older children who had been in long-term, out-of-home placements but were "not in a fost-adopt home (a potential adoptive home)" and were "at best, questionable candidates for adoption,"[163] the court denied the petition to terminate parental rights.[164] It explained:

> The rule of law that prevents the best interest of the child from being the sole factor supporting termination does not however mandate that the child's interests may not be a factor at all. In this case, due to his mental illness, we have a father incapable of parenting full time adequately, but, a father nevertheless, who has maintained contact with his children. We have older children who have adjusted to long term foster care and whose chances for adoption are described as "slim." Moreover, we have expert testimony that

---

160. See generally Ferol E. Mennen et al., Do Maltreated Children Who Remain at Home Function Better than Those Who Are Placed?, 32 Child & Youth Serv. Rev. 1675 (2010).

161. Appeal of Maricopa Cty. Juvenile Action No. JS-6520, 756 P.2d 335 (Ariz. Ct. App. 1988).

162. Id. at 340.

163. Id. at 340–41.

164. Id. at 343.

suggests the children should be evaluated before terminating the parent-child relationship. And finally, we have a record devoid of any reference to the benefit of severance for the children or the detriment should severance be denied.[165]

Do you agree with the Arizona court? Are there other circumstances in which maintaining the parental rights of an "unfit" parent would serve the child's best interests?

B. Termination Proceedings

Termination of parental rights is a drastic remedy in which the government deprives a parent of rights that the Supreme Court has long treated as fundamental. What protections must the parent be afforded when the state seeks to exercise this power? Does the parent have a right to an attorney provided by the state if they cannot afford one? Does the state need to meet a higher burden of proof than would ordinarily apply in a civil proceeding? What conduct by the parent constitutes grounds to terminate their rights? What efforts does the government need to take in an attempt to avoid termination? The following materials first consider the procedural protections afforded to parents faced with termination, including evidentiary standards and right to counsel. The materials then address the kinds of showings that would allow the state to terminate parental rights, including the types of actions that are sufficient to find the requisite parental fault, the types of facts that demonstrate that termination would be in the child's best interests, and the types of efforts the government must pursue before seeking termination.

1. Procedural Protections

SANTOSKY V. KRAMER
455 U.S. 745 (1982)

JUSTICE BLACKMUN delivered the opinion of the Court.

Under New York law, the State may terminate, over parental objection, the rights of parents in their natural child upon a finding that the child is "permanently neglected." The New York Family Court Act § 622 requires that only a "fair preponderance of the evidence" support that finding. Thus, in New York, the factual certainty required to extinguish the parent-child relationship is no greater than that necessary to award money damages in an ordinary civil action.

Today we hold that the Due Process Clause of the Fourteenth Amendment demands more than this. Before a State may sever completely and irrevocably the

---

165. Id.

rights of parents in their natural child, due process requires that the State support its allegations by at least clear and convincing evidence.

I

A

New York authorizes its officials to remove a child temporarily from his or her home if the child appears "neglected." . . . Once removed, a child under the age of 18 customarily is placed "in the care of an authorized agency," usually a state institution or a foster home. At that point, "the state's first obligation is to help the family with services to . . . reunite it. . . ." But if convinced that "positive, nurturing parent-child relationships no longer exist," the State may initiate "permanent neglect" proceedings to free the child for adoption.

The State bifurcates its permanent neglect proceeding into "fact-finding" and "dispositional" hearings. At the factfinding stage, the State must prove that the child has been "permanently neglected." The Family Court judge then determines at a subsequent dispositional hearing what placement would serve the child's best interests.

At the factfinding hearing, the State must establish, among other things, that for more than a year after the child entered state custody, the agency "made diligent efforts to encourage and strengthen the parental relationship." The State must further prove that during that same period, the child's natural parents failed "substantially and continuously or repeatedly to maintain contact with or plan for the future of the child although physically and financially able to do so." Should the State support its allegations by "a fair preponderance of the evidence," the child may be declared permanently neglected. That declaration empowers the Family Court judge to terminate permanently the natural parents' rights in the child. Termination denies the natural parents physical custody, as well as the rights ever to visit, communicate with, or regain custody of the child. . . .

New York permits its officials to establish "permanent neglect" with less proof than most States require. Thirty-five States, the District of Columbia, and the Virgin Islands currently specify a higher standard of proof, in parental rights termination proceedings, than a "fair preponderance of the evidence." . . . The question here is whether New York's "fair preponderance of the evidence" standard is constitutionally sufficient.

B

Petitioners John Santosky II and Annie Santosky are the natural parents of Tina and John III. In November 1973, after incidents reflecting parental neglect, respondent Kramer, Commissioner of the Ulster County Department of Social Services, initiated a neglect proceeding and removed Tina from her natural home. About 10 months later, he removed John III and placed him with foster parents. On the day John was taken, Annie Santosky gave birth to a third child, Jed. When Jed was only three days old, respondent transferred him to a foster home on the ground that immediate removal was necessary to avoid imminent danger to his life or health.

In October 1978, respondent petitioned the Ulster County Family Court to terminate petitioners' parental rights in the three children. Petitioners challenged the constitutionality of the "fair preponderance of the evidence" standard specified in Fam. Ct. Act § 622. . . .

II . . .

The fundamental liberty interest of natural parents in the care, custody, and management of their child does not evaporate simply because they have not been model parents or have lost temporary custody of their child to the State. Even when blood relationships are strained, parents retain a vital interest in preventing the irretrievable destruction of their family life. If anything, persons faced with forced dissolution of their parental rights have a more critical need for procedural protections than do those resisting state intervention into ongoing family affairs. When the State moves to destroy weakened familial bonds, it must provide the parents with fundamentally fair procedures. . . .

[T]he nature of the process due in parental rights termination proceedings turns on a balancing of the "three distinct factors" specified in *Mathews v. Eldridge*, 424 U.S. 319 (1976): the private interests affected by the proceeding; the risk of error created by the State's chosen procedure; and the countervailing governmental interest supporting use of the challenged procedure. . . .

In *Addington v. Texas*, 441 U.S. 418 (1979), the Court, by a unanimous vote of the participating Justices, declared: "The function of a standard of proof, as that concept is embodied in the Due Process Clause and in the realm of factfinding, is to 'instruct the factfinder concerning the degree of confidence our society thinks he should have in the correctness of factual conclusions for a particular type of adjudication.'" *Id.* at 423. *Addington* teaches that, in any given proceeding, the minimum standard of proof tolerated by the due process requirement reflects not only the weight of the private and public interests affected, but also a societal judgment about how the risk of error should be distributed between the litigants. . . .

This Court has mandated an intermediate standard of proof — "clear and convincing evidence" — when the individual interests at stake in a state proceeding are both "particularly important" and "more substantial than mere loss of money." *Addington v. Texas*, 441 U.S. at 424. Notwithstanding "the state's 'civil labels and good intentions,'" *id.* at 427, the Court has deemed this level of certainty necessary to preserve fundamental fairness in a variety of government-initiated proceedings that threaten the individual involved with "a significant deprivation of liberty" or "stigma." *Id.* at 425, 426. . . .

III

In parental rights termination proceedings, the private interest affected is commanding; the risk of error from using a preponderance standard is substantial; and the countervailing governmental interest favoring that standard is comparatively slight. Evaluation of the three *Eldridge* factors compels the conclusion that use of a "fair preponderance of the evidence" standard in such proceedings is inconsistent with due process.

A

"The extent to which procedural due process must be afforded the recipient is influenced by the extent to which he may be 'condemned to suffer grievous loss.'" *Goldberg v. Kelly*, 397 U.S. 254, 262–263 (1970). . . .

When the State initiates a parental rights termination proceeding, it seeks not merely to infringe that fundamental liberty interest, but to end it. "If the State prevails, it will have worked a unique kind of deprivation. . . . A parent's interest in the accuracy and justice of the decision to terminate his or her parental status is, therefore, a commanding one." *Lassiter v. Department of Social Services*, 452 U.S. 18, 27 (1981). . . .

Thus, the first *Eldridge* factor — the private interest affected — weighs heavily against use of the preponderance standard at a state-initiated permanent neglect proceeding. We do not deny that the child and his foster parents are also deeply interested in the outcome of that contest. But at the factfinding stage of the New York proceeding, the focus emphatically is not on them.

The factfinding does not purport — and is not intended — to balance the child's interest in a normal family home against the parents' interest in raising the child. Nor does it purport to determine whether the natural parents or the foster parents would provide the better home. Rather, the factfinding hearing pits the State directly against the parents. The State alleges that the natural parents are at fault. The questions disputed and decided are what the State did — "made diligent efforts" — and what the natural parents did not do — "maintain contact with or plan for the future of the child." The State marshals an array of public resources to prove its case and disprove the parents' case. Victory by the State not only makes termination of parental rights possible; it entails a judicial determination that the parents are unfit to raise their own children.

At the factfinding, the State cannot presume that a child and his parents are adversaries. After the State has established parental unfitness at that initial proceeding, the court may assume at the *dispositional* stage that the interests of the child and the natural parents do diverge. But until the State proves parental unfitness, the child and his parents share a vital interest in preventing erroneous termination of their natural relationship. Thus, at the factfinding, the interests of the child and his natural parents coincide to favor use of error-reducing procedures.

However substantial the foster parents' interests may be, they are not implicated directly in the factfinding stage of a state-initiated permanent neglect proceeding against the natural parents. . . .

B

Under *Mathews v. Eldridge*, we next must consider both the risk of erroneous deprivation of private interests resulting from use of a "fair preponderance" standard and the likelihood that a higher evidentiary standard would reduce that risk. Since the factfinding phase of a permanent neglect proceeding is an adversary contest between the State and the natural parents, the relevant question is whether a preponderance standard fairly allocates the risk of an erroneous factfinding between these two parties.

In New York, the factfinding stage of a state-initiated permanent neglect proceeding bears many of the indicia of a criminal trial. The Commissioner of Social Services charges the parents with permanent neglect. They are served by summons. The factfinding hearing is conducted pursuant to formal rules of evidence. The State, the parents, and the child are all represented by counsel. The State seeks to establish a series of historical facts about the intensity of its agency's efforts to reunite the family, the infrequency and insubstantiality of the parents' contacts with their child, and the parents' inability or unwillingness to formulate a plan for the child's future. The attorneys submit documentary evidence, and call witnesses who are subject to cross-examination. Based on all the evidence, the judge then determines whether the State has proved the statutory elements of permanent neglect by a fair preponderance of the evidence.

At such a proceeding, numerous factors combine to magnify the risk of erroneous factfinding. Permanent neglect proceedings employ imprecise substantive standards that leave determinations unusually open to the subjective values of the judge. In appraising the nature and quality of a complex series of encounters among the agency, the parents, and the child, the court possesses unusual discretion to underweigh probative facts that might favor the parent. Because parents subject to termination proceedings are often poor, uneducated, or members of minority groups, such proceedings are often vulnerable to judgments based on cultural or class bias.

The State's ability to assemble its case almost inevitably dwarfs the parents' ability to mount a defense. No predetermined limits restrict the sums an agency may spend in prosecuting a given termination proceeding. The State's attorney usually will be expert on the issues contested and the procedures employed at the factfinding hearing, and enjoys full access to all public records concerning the family. The State may call on experts in family relations, psychology, and medicine to bolster its case. Furthermore, the primary witnesses at the hearing will be the agency's own professional caseworkers whom the State has empowered both to investigate the family situation and to testify against the parents. Indeed, because the child is already in agency custody, the State even has the power to shape the historical events that form the basis for termination.

The disparity between the adversaries' litigation resources is matched by a striking asymmetry in their litigation options. Unlike criminal defendants, natural parents have no "double jeopardy" defense against repeated state termination efforts. If the State initially fails to win termination, as New York did here, it always can try once again to cut off the parents' rights after gathering more or better evidence. Yet even when the parents have attained the level of fitness required by the State, they have no similar means by which they can forestall future termination efforts.

Coupled with a "fair preponderance of the evidence" standard, these factors create a significant prospect of erroneous termination. A standard of proof that by its very terms demands consideration of the quantity, rather than the quality, of the evidence may misdirect the factfinder in the marginal case. Given the weight of the private interests at stake, the social cost of even occasional error is sizable.

Raising the standard of proof would have both practical and symbolic consequences. The Court has long considered the heightened standard of proof used in criminal prosecutions to be "a prime instrument for reducing the risk of convictions resting on factual error." An elevated standard of proof in a parental rights termination proceeding would alleviate "the possible risk that a factfinder might decide to [deprive] an individual based solely on a few isolated instances of unusual conduct [or] . . . idiosyncratic behavior." "Increasing the burden of proof is one way to impress the factfinder with the importance of the decision and thereby perhaps to reduce the chances that inappropriate" terminations will be ordered.

The Appellate Division approved New York's preponderance standard on the ground that it properly "balanced rights possessed by the child . . . with those of the natural parents. . . ." By so saying, the court suggested that a preponderance standard properly allocates the risk of error *between* the parents and the child. That view is fundamentally mistaken.

The court's theory assumes that termination of the natural parents' rights invariably will benefit the child. Yet we have noted above that the parents and the child share an interest in avoiding erroneous termination. Even accepting the court's assumption, we cannot agree with its conclusion that a preponderance standard fairly distributes the risk of error between parent and child. Use of that standard reflects the judgment that society is nearly neutral between erroneous termination of parental rights and erroneous failure to terminate those rights. For the child, the likely consequence of an erroneous failure to terminate is preservation of an uneasy status quo. For the natural parents, however, the consequence of an erroneous termination is the unnecessary destruction of their natural family. A standard that allocates the risk of error nearly equally between those two outcomes does not reflect properly their relative severity.

C

Two state interests are at stake in parental rights termination proceedings — a *parens patriae* interest in preserving and promoting the welfare of the child and a fiscal and administrative interest in reducing the cost and burden of such proceedings. A standard of proof more strict than preponderance of the evidence is consistent with both interests. . . .

[W]hile there is still reason to believe that positive, nurturing parent-child relationships exist, the *parens patriae* interest favors preservation, not severance, of natural familial bonds. . . .

The State's interest in finding the child an alternative permanent home arises only "when it is *clear* that the natural parent cannot or will not provide a normal family home for the child." At the factfinding, that goal is served by procedures that promote an accurate determination of whether the natural parents can and will provide a normal home.

Unlike a constitutional requirement of hearings or court-appointed counsel, a stricter standard of proof would reduce factual error without imposing substantial fiscal burdens upon the State. As we have observed, 35 States already have adopted a higher standard by statute or court decision without apparent effect on the speed, form, or cost of their factfinding proceedings.

Nor would an elevated standard of proof create any real administrative burdens for the State's factfinders. New York Family Court judges already are familiar with a higher evidentiary standard in other parental rights termination proceedings not involving permanent neglect. New York also demands at least clear and convincing evidence in proceedings of far less moment than parental rights termination proceedings. We cannot believe that it would burden the State unduly to require that its factfinders have the same factual certainty when terminating the parent-child relationship as they must have to suspend a driver's license.

IV

The logical conclusion of this balancing process is that the "fair preponderance of the evidence" standard prescribed by Fam. Ct. Act § 622 violates the Due Process Clause of the Fourteenth Amendment. . . . The next question, then, is whether a "beyond a reasonable doubt" or a "clear and convincing" standard is constitutionally mandated. . . .

[T]ermination proceedings often require the factfinder to evaluate medical and psychiatric testimony, and to decide issues difficult to prove to a level of absolute certainty, such as lack of parental motive, absence of affection between parent and child, and failure of parental foresight and progress. The substantive standards applied vary from State to State. . . .

A majority of the States have concluded that a "clear and convincing evidence" standard of proof strikes a fair balance between the rights of the natural parents and the State's legitimate concerns. We hold that such a standard adequately conveys to the factfinder the level of subjective certainty about his factual conclusions necessary to satisfy due process. We further hold that determination of the precise burden equal to or greater than that standard is a matter of state law properly left to state legislatures and state courts. . . .

JUSTICE REHNQUIST, with whom THE CHIEF JUSTICE, JUSTICE WHITE, and JUSTICE O'CONNOR join, dissenting.

I believe that few of us would care to live in a society where every aspect of life was regulated by a single source of law, whether that source be this Court or some other organ of our complex body politic. But today's decision certainly moves us in that direction. By parsing the New York scheme and holding one narrow provision unconstitutional, the majority invites further federal-court intrusion into every facet of state family law. If ever there were an area in which federal courts should heed the admonition of Justice Holmes that "a page of history is worth a volume of logic," it is in the area of domestic relations. This area has been left to the States from time immemorial, and not without good reason.

Equally as troubling is the majority's due process analysis. The Fourteenth Amendment guarantees that a State will treat individuals with "fundamental fairness" whenever its actions infringe their protected liberty or property interests. By adoption of the procedures relevant to this case, New York has created an exhaustive program to assist parents in regaining the custody of their children and to protect parents from the unfair deprivation of their parental rights. And yet the majority's myopic scrutiny of the standard of proof blinds it to the very considerations and procedures which make the New York scheme "fundamentally fair."

I

State intervention in domestic relations has always been an unhappy but necessary feature of life in our organized society. For all of our experience in this area, we have found no fully satisfactory solutions to the painful problem of child abuse and neglect. We have found, however, that leaving the States free to experiment with various remedies has produced novel approaches and promising progress. . . .

II

A

[T]he State's extraordinary 4-year effort to reunite petitioners' family was not just unsuccessful, it was altogether rebuffed by parents unwilling to improve their circumstances sufficiently to permit a return of their children. At every step of this protracted process petitioners were accorded those procedures and protections which traditionally have been required by due process of law. Moreover, from the beginning to the end of this sad story all judicial determinations were made by one

Family Court Judge. After four and one-half years of involvement with petitioners, more than seven complete hearings, and additional periodic supervision of the State's rehabilitative efforts, the judge no doubt was intimately familiar with this case and the prospects for petitioners' rehabilitation.

It is inconceivable to me that these procedures were "fundamentally unfair" to petitioners. Only by its obsessive focus on the standard of proof and its almost complete disregard of the facts of this case does the majority find otherwise. . . . [S]uch a focus does not comport with the flexible standard of fundamental fairness embodied in the Due Process Clause of the Fourteenth Amendment.

B . . .

The interests at stake in this case demonstrate that New York has selected a constitutionally permissible standard of proof.

On one side is the interest of parents in a continuation of the family unit and the raising of their own children. The importance of this interest cannot easily be overstated. Few consequences of judicial action are so grave as the severance of natural family ties. . . .

On the other side of the termination proceeding are the often countervailing interests of the child. A stable, loving home life is essential to a child's physical, emotional, and spiritual well-being. It requires no citation of authority to assert that children who are abused in their youth generally face extraordinary problems developing into responsible, productive citizens. The same can be said of children who, though not physically or emotionally abused, are passed from one foster home to another with no constancy of love, trust, or discipline. If the Family Court makes an incorrect factual determination resulting in a failure to terminate a parent-child relationship which rightfully should be ended, the child involved must return either to an abusive home or to the often unstable world of foster care. The reality of these risks is magnified by the fact that the only families faced with termination actions are those which have voluntarily surrendered custody of their child to the State, or, as in this case, those from which the child has been removed by judicial action because of threatened irreparable injury through abuse or neglect. . . .

In addition to the child's interest in a normal homelife, "the State has an urgent interest in the welfare of the child." . . . "[T]he whole community" has an interest "that children be both safeguarded from abuses and given opportunities for growth into free and independent well-developed . . . citizens."

When, in the context of a permanent neglect termination proceeding, the interests of the child and the State in a stable, nurturing homelife are balanced against the interests of the parents in the rearing of their child, it cannot be said that either set of interests is so clearly paramount as to require that the risk of error be allocated to one side or the other. Accordingly, a State constitutionally may conclude that the risk of error should be borne in roughly equal fashion by use of the preponderance-of-the-evidence standard of proof. This is precisely the balance which has been struck by the New York Legislature. . . .

III . . .

The Court finds a constitutional violation only by a tunnel-vision application of due process principles that altogether loses sight of the unmistakable fairness of the New York procedure.

Even more worrisome, today's decision cavalierly rejects the considered judgment of the New York Legislature in an area traditionally entrusted to state care. The Court thereby begins, I fear, a trend of federal intervention in state family law matters which surely will stifle creative responses to vexing problems. Accordingly, I dissent.

NOTES AND QUESTIONS

1. *Parental Unfitness Versus Best Interests of the Child.* The *Santosky* Court held that states could not apply a "preponderance of the evidence" standard to determinations of unfitness in termination proceedings. The parental unfitness part of New York's process is what the Court describes as the "fact-finding" stage. The Court appears to allow a less rigorous standard to the best interests determination, which the Court describes as the "dispositional" stage. What is the rationale for permitting a less rigorous evidentiary standard in the best interests determination? At the unfitness stage, the Court explains, "the child and his parents share a vital interest in preventing erroneous termination of their natural relationship." Accordingly, "the interests of the child and his natural parents coincide to favor use of error-reducing procedures." But, the best interests stage considers the child's interest in light of a determination of parental unfitness. In other words, if the parent has been deemed unfit (for instance, because the parent neglected or abused the child), the child's interest no longer necessarily coincides with the parent's interest. On this reasoning, states may apply different evidentiary standards to the unfitness and best interests determinations.

2. *State Responses.* The vast majority of states explicitly incorporate the "clear and convincing" standard into their statutes defining grounds for the termination of parental rights.[166] Several other states have adopted the "clear and convincing" standard through judicial decisions. Notably, New Hampshire has adopted a higher standard for the termination of parental rights, holding that a court must find that a parent is unfit "beyond a reasonable doubt."[167]

---

166. See, e.g., 15 R.I. Gen. Laws § 15-7-7 (2020); Tex. Fam. Code § 161.001(b) (2020); Wyo. Stat. § 14-2-309 (2020).

167. See N.H. Rev. Stat. Ann. § 170-C:10 (2020) ("The court's finding with respect to grounds for termination shall be based upon proof beyond a reasonable doubt. . . ."); In re S.T., 151 A.3d 522, 528 (N.H. 2016) ("Before a court may order the termination of parental rights, the petitioning party must prove a statutory ground for termination beyond a reasonable doubt.").

For states that require a separate determination of the child's best interests, some adopt the "preponderance of the evidence" standard.[168] Others require the court to determine by "clear and convincing evidence" that termination is in the child's best interests.[169]

3. *A Right to Counsel?* In *Santosky*, the Court cited its decision in Lassiter v. Department of Social Services, issued the year before, holding that parents are not guaranteed the right to counsel in termination of parental rights proceedings.[170] Why would indigent parents threatened with termination be entitled to a "clear and convincing" evidentiary standard but not appointed counsel?

After beginning from "the presumption that an indigent litigant has a right to appointed counsel only when, if he loses, he may be deprived of his physical liberty,"[171] the Court in *Lassiter* applied the same Mathews v. Eldridge factors it applied in *Santosky*:

> The dispositive question . . . is whether the three *Eldridge* factors, when weighed against the presumption that there is no right to appointed counsel in the absence of at least a potential deprivation of physical liberty, suffice to rebut that presumption and thus to lead to the conclusion that the Due Process Clause requires the appointment of counsel when a State seeks to terminate an indigent's parental status. To summarize the above discussion of the *Eldridge* factors: the parent's interest is an extremely important one (and may be supplemented by the dangers of criminal liability inherent in some termination proceedings); the State shares with the parent an interest in a correct decision, has a relatively weak pecuniary interest, and, in some but not all cases, has a possibly stronger interest in informal procedures; and the complexity of the proceeding and the incapacity of the uncounseled parent could be, but would not always be, great enough to make the risk of an erroneous deprivation of the parent's rights insupportably high.
>
> If, in a given case, the parent's interests were at their strongest, the State's interests were at their weakest, and the risks of error were at their peak, it could not be said that the *Eldridge* factors did not overcome the presumption against the right to appointed counsel, and that due process did not therefore require the appointment of counsel. But since the *Eldridge* factors will not always be so distributed, and since "due process is not so rigid as to require that the significant interests in informality, flexibility and economy must always be sacrificed," neither can we say that the Constitution requires the appointment of counsel in every parental termination proceeding. We therefore . . . leave the decision whether due process calls for the appointment of counsel for indigent parents in

---

168. See, e.g., Chloe W. v. State, Dep't of Health & Soc. Servs., 336 P.3d 1258, 1264 (Alaska 2014); Kent K. v. Bobby M., 110 P.3d 1013, 1022 (Ariz. 2005); In re D.T., 818 N.E.2d 1214, 1227 (Ill. 2004).

169. See, e.g., Conn. Gen. Stat. § 17a-112(j) (2020); Ky. Rev. Stat. Ann. § 625.090(1) (West 2020); Me. Stat. tit. 22 § 4055(B)(2) (2020).

170. 452 U.S. 18 (1981).

171. Id. at 26–27.

termination proceedings to be answered in the first instance by the trial court, subject, of course, to appellate review.[172]

Even as the *Lassiter* Court did not rule that Due Process requires appointed counsel in termination of parental rights proceedings, it suggested that "[a] wise public policy . . . may require that higher standards be adopted than those minimally tolerable under the Constitution."[173] At the time, thirty-three states and the District of Columbia had statutes that provided for the appointment of counsel in termination proceedings.[174] Since *Lassiter*, additional states have passed statutes providing for guaranteed counsel in these cases; now, all but a handful of states statutorily provide a right to counsel to indigent parents in termination proceedings.[175] Additionally, the Indian Child Welfare Act guarantees the right to counsel in termination proceedings governed by the statute.[176]

2. Applying Law to Facts

Many states have laws that require the state to commence a termination proceeding under certain circumstances. These provisions largely track federal law, which conditions federal funding upon the states requiring termination proceedings in various situations: when a child has been out of parental custody (usually in foster care) for fifteen of the last twenty-two months; or when the state finds that the parent has committed murder, manslaughter, or felony assault of another child, or attempted to do so.[177] Nonetheless, there are exceptions to this obligation to commence proceedings: when another relative is caring for the child; when the state has documented a compelling reason that filing such a petition would not be in the child's best interest; or when the state has failed to provide the family reasonable services that are required by law.[178]

---

172. Id. at 31–32.

173. Id. at 33.

174. Id. at 34.

175. See, e.g., Ala. Code § 12-15-305(b) (2020); Minn. Stat. § 260C.163(3)(a) (2020); Or. Rev. Stat. § 419B.518 (2020). Delaware and Wyoming give courts discretion to appoint counsel in certain proceedings, but do not require it. Wyo. Stat. Ann. § 14-3-211 (2020); Moore v. Hall, 62 A.3d 1203 (Del. 2013). New Mexico provides for the appointment of counsel at the beginning of abuse and neglect proceedings, but not specifically in parental rights termination proceedings. N.M. Stat. Ann. § 32A-4-10(B) (2020). Finally, Mississippi has no statute requiring appointment of counsel, and the state courts have not required it. See, e.g., K.D.G.L.B.P. v. Hinds Cty. Dep't of Human Servs., 771 So. 2d 907 (Miss. 2000) (holding that the mother's due process rights were not violated when the chancery court did not appoint counsel to represent her in the termination of parental rights proceeding).

176. 25 U.S.C. § 1912(b).

177. See 42 U.S.C. § 675(5)(E); see also, e.g., Conn. Gen. Stat. § 17a-111a(a) (2020); Iowa Code § 232.111(2) (2020); N.J. Stat. Ann. § 30:4C-15(f) (West 2020).

178. See 42 U.S.C. § 675(5)(E) (2018).

Just as there are exceptions to state obligations to commence termination proceedings, there are also exceptions to judicial determinations to terminate parental rights. For example, several states provide that parental rights shall not be terminated if the child is of a minimum age and objects to termination.[179] A few states explicitly provide that poverty may not be the sole reason for the termination of parental rights.[180] And, as we saw with the commencement of proceedings, many states provide that the court need not terminate parental rights when a relative has custody of the child, termination is not in the child's best interests, or the state has failed to provide the family with adequate services.[181]

The vast majority of state statutes provide only that the court *may* order the termination of parental rights if a parent meets the statutory criteria.[182] A small minority of states provide that the court *shall* terminate parental rights if the court finds that the statutory criteria have been satisfied.[183]

The following cases represent appellate courts reviewing decisions to terminate parental rights. As you read, consider how the court's standard of review affects the ultimate result. In your view, does the parent's conduct rise to the level that justifies termination? Is termination in the child's best interest? Did the state meet its obligation to attempt to reunify the family before seeking termination? A warning: the second case involves sexual assault of a minor and the exposure of children to sexual abuse.

IN RE PARENTAL RIGHTS AS TO A.J.G. AND A.C.W.
148 P.3d 759 (Nev. 2006)

BECKER, J.

In this appeal, we consider two issues. First, we consider whether the State must prove the existence of an adoptive placement for a child before a court can terminate a parent's rights to that child. Second, we decide which party has the burden to present evidence of a child's desires, under NRS 128.107(2), in a parental rights termination case when the State has established the presumption under NRS 128.109(2) that it is in the child's best interest for the parent's rights to be terminated. . . .

---

179. See, e.g., Cal. Welf. & Inst. Code § 366.26(c)(1)(B) (West 2020); Colo. Rev. Stat. § 19-3-702(4)(e)(II) (2020); Va. Code § 16.1-283(G) (2020).

180. See, e.g., Fla. Stat. § 39.806(1)(e) (2020); N.C. Gen. Stat. § 7B-1111(a)(2) (2020); 23 Pa. Cons. Stat. § 2511(b) (2020).

181. See, e.g., Ind. Code § 31-35-2-4.5(d)(2) (2020); Iowa Code § 232.116(3) (2020); Miss. Code § 93-15-123 (2020).

182. See, e.g., D.C. Code § 16-2353 (2020); Haw. Rev. Stat. § 571-61(b) (2020); Iowa Code § 232.116 (2020).

183. See, e.g., N.M. Stat. § 32A-4-28(B) (2020); 15 R.I. Gen. Laws § 15-7-7(a) (2020).

In May 2002, Child Protective Services (CPS) removed A.J.G., then twelve years old, and A.C.W., then eleven years old, from the home of their mother, appellant Tammila G. and her boyfriend, George L. CPS received a referral that the children were being bound with duct tape, slapped, and kicked by friends of Tammila and George while they were away from home. According to the children, such incidents occurred repeatedly. Although the children informed Tammila about the incidents, she did not take steps to prevent the abuse from recurring.

Following the children's removal from the home, a CPS specialist and a probation officer conducted a home visit at Tammila and George's residence. Tammila admitted to recently using methamphetamine, and officers arrested George for violation of his probation after finding methamphetamine and other drug paraphernalia at the house. The juvenile division of the district court ordered that the children remain in protective custody pending further proceedings.

The Children's Resource Bureau (CRB) of the Division of Child and Family Services (DCFS) conducted a clinical assessment of the children and their family. Reports from family members indicated that Tammila exhibited auditory and visual hallucinations and erratic behavior. Because Tammila did not participate in a CRB assessment, however, CRB was unable to determine the impact of Tammila's mental state on the children and whether her behavior was caused by drug use or a naturally occurring psychosis. CRB recommended that the children be placed in foster care and that they have regular visitation with Tammila.

Upon the filing of an appropriate petition by the State, the district court found that it would be contrary to the children's welfare to reside with Tammila and George. Accordingly, the district court ordered that the children be made wards of the State and placed in foster care.

Subsequently, DCFS devised a case plan for Tammila with the ultimate goal of reunifying her and the children. From November 2002 to May 2005, DCFS filed six reports with the district court on a biannual basis updating the court on Tammila's progress in completing her case plan and on the children's situation in their foster home. Each report indicated that Tammila was not fulfilling the objectives of her case plan. Specifically, she failed to (1) submit to drug tests, (2) submit to a psychiatric evaluation, (3) enroll in and complete a parenting class, (4) provide proof of economic and residential stability, and (5) submit to a CRB assessment. Tammila attempted to comply with the mental-health objective of her case plan, but the facility denied her treatment because she refused to see a psychiatrist or take medication if necessary. To Tammila's credit, she did attend visitations with her children regularly, only missing one visit.

Following the third DCFS report, the district court concluded that Tammila had made only token efforts in her attempt to reunify with the children. DCFS, with the district court's approval, changed the children's permanency plan from reunification to "Other Permanent Planned Arrangement." Under this new permanency plan, the children would reside in foster care until reaching the age of majority.

Alternatively, they could be adopted. If adoption became a viable option, DCFS would seek termination of Tammila's parental rights.

At some point, the children's maternal aunt and uncle, in Louisiana, expressed an interest in and willingness to accept placement of the children with them in Louisiana. The aunt and uncle were open to either foster placement or adoption. Based on the aunt and uncle's interest in caring for the children, DCFS, with the district court's approval, changed the children's permanency plan to "relative adoption by the maternal aunt and uncle in Louisiana." DCFS, along with the aunt and uncle, began the process necessary for the children's adoption. In 2004, DCFS placed the children with their aunt and uncle in Louisiana. According to DCFS, at that time, the children adjusted well to their new environment, and DCFS would continue to monitor their progress.

In April 2005, the State petitioned the district court to terminate Tammila's parental rights. At a hearing, the State presented the district court with evidence of Tammila's failure to fulfill substantially the objectives of her case plan. The district court also heard testimony from the children's aunt, with whom they were living. The aunt testified that the children were doing well in their home in Louisiana and that they were or would be receiving some counseling. The aunt also testified that Tammila had not visited the children in Louisiana and offered them no support beyond sending some nonmonetary gifts. Tammila did telephone the children frequently, but she would not keep to a specific schedule, and the children were often upset after talking to her, which led DCFS to terminate Tammila's telephone privileges with the children.

The district court also heard testimony from Tammila, who expressed her desire to be reunited with her children but also acknowledged her failure to comply with her case plan. Tammila testified that she had been sober for two years but that she had not submitted proof of her sobriety to DCFS. She further testified that she was economically stable and in a stable residence, but she admitted that she never submitted proof of such stability to DCFS.

George, Tammila's boyfriend, also testified. He stated that he dealt with the friends who had abused the children by telling them never to do it again and by making them move off his property where they were living. He also admitted to not fulfilling his own case plan, stating that he would only work on his plan when Tammila worked on her plan.

Following the hearing, the district court granted the State's petition. The district court found that the State had established by clear and convincing evidence that it was in the children's best interest to terminate Tammila's parental rights and that parental fault existed. Specifically, the district court found that the presumption under NRS 128.109(2) applied, which established that it was in the children's best interest to terminate Tammila's parental rights. Additionally, the district court found that the presumptions under NRS 128.109(1)(a) and (b) applied, which established parental fault.

The district court also found that Tammila did not rebut these presumptions. Rather, the district court found that Tammila had failed within a reasonable time to remedy the conditions that led to the children's removal from her home, even though DCFS made reasonable efforts to reunite Tammila with her children, and that Tammila had failed to comply substantially with her case plan for over three-and-a-half years.

On appeal, Tammila argues that the evidence does not support terminating her parental rights because the State failed to prove that an adoptive placement existed for A.J.G. and A.C.W. She further argues that the State had the burden to, but did not, assert evidence of the children's desires to the district court. We conclude that Tammila's contentions lack merit for two reasons. . . .

A party petitioning to terminate parental rights must establish by clear and convincing evidence that (1) termination is in the child's best interest, and (2) parental fault exists. As we have stated previously, terminating parental rights is "'an exercise of awesome power'" that is "'tantamount to imposition of a civil death penalty.'" Therefore, we "closely scrutinize[ ] whether the district court properly preserved or terminated the parental rights at issue." On appeal, we review the district court's factual findings in its order terminating parental rights for substantial evidence, and we will not substitute our own judgment for that of the district court.

Tammila contends that under the Federal Adoption and Safe Families Act of 1997 (ASFA or the Act), permanency for children is the primary focus in adoption and parental rights termination cases. Based on that primary focus, Tammila argues that, under federal law, a party seeking to terminate parental rights must prove the existence of an adoptive placement. Additionally, because Nevada complies with the ASFA in order to receive federal funding for child welfare services, Tammila contends that state law also places a burden on the State to prove an adoptive placement for the child before the district court can terminate parental rights.

With the adoption of Assembly Bill 158 in 1999, Nevada amended much of its law on the placement of children in foster care, adoption, and termination of parental rights to comply with the ASFA. Under the ASFA, a state wishing to receive federal funds for child welfare services must create a system in accordance with the Act. To that end, a state shall either initiate a petition to terminate parental rights or join an existing petition if certain criteria are met, while concurrently "identify[ing], recruit[ing], process[ing], and approv[ing] a qualified family for adoption." Contrary to Tammila's argument, this provision does not place a burden on the State to prove that an adoptive placement exists. Rather, a plain reading of 42 U.S.C. § 675(5)(E) indicates that state agencies must begin seeking an adoptive placement for the child concurrently with seeking termination of parental rights. The statute even permits a state to forgo seeking an adoptive placement concurrently with a petition to terminate parental rights, when "the child is being cared for by a relative," as is the case here.

Nevada law also does not contemplate a burden on the State to prove an adoptive placement when seeking to terminate parental rights. Under NRS 128.110(1), upon termination of parental rights, the child is to be placed in the custody and control of "some person or agency qualified by the laws of this State to provide services and care to children." That person or agency may thereafter seek further placement with a relative. Nowhere in Nevada's statutes is there a requirement that the State prove an adoptive placement for the child before parental rights can be terminated. . . .

Based on the above analysis, we conclude that, in the present matter, neither federal nor state law required the State to prove the existence of an adoptive placement for A.J.G. and A.C.W. before the district court could terminate Tammila's parental rights.

Next, Tammila argues that the State had a burden to produce evidence, under NRS 128.107(2), of the children's desires with regard to termination of Tammila's parental rights. The State contends, however, that because it established the presumption under NRS 128.109(2), that it is in the children's best interests to terminate Tammila's parental rights, the burden of evidencing A.J.G.'s and A.C.W.'s desires rested with Tammila. We agree with the State's analysis.

In a parental rights termination case, when the child is not in the physical custody of the parent, the district court shall consider "[t]he physical, mental or emotional condition and needs of the child and *his desires regarding termination,* if the court determines he is of sufficient capacity to express his desires." The statute does not specify whether a particular party has a burden to offer evidence of the child's desires.

Under NRS 128.109(2), termination of parental rights is presumed to be in the child's best interest when the "child has been placed outside of his home pursuant to chapter 432B of NRS and has resided outside of his home pursuant to that placement for 14 months of any 20 consecutive months." Once the presumption applies, the parent has the burden to offer evidence to overcome the presumption that termination of his or her rights is in the child's best interest. . . .

A parent's evidence that the child does not wish his or her parent's rights to be terminated would be a consideration for the district court in determining whether the parent has overcome the presumption. . . .

Tammila . . . did not offer such evidence. A CASA [Court Appointed Special Advocate] report written approximately two years before Tammila's hearing indicated that the children did not wish to be adopted. The report was also written before the children began living with their aunt and uncle — the prospective adoptive parents. The district court considered this information when deciding to terminate Tammila's parental rights and terminated them nonetheless.

The district court found that the State established by clear and convincing evidence that (1) it was in A.J.G.'s and A.C.W.'s best interests to terminate Tammila's parental rights, and (2) Tammila exhibited parental fault. Substantial evidence supports these findings. . . .

In an attempt to rebut the presumption [that termination was in the children's best interests], Tammila testified that she had not used drugs in over two years. However, she presented no independent evidence of her sobriety such as submitting to drug counseling as required by her case plan. Tammila did present evidence that she has a relationship with her children in that she spoke to them frequently until her telephone-call privileges were terminated and that she visited them regularly when they were in Nevada. The appellate record, however, also indicates that she did not attempt to support her children while they lived outside her home. Tammila testified that if the children were with her now and a domestic violence situation arose, she would take the children and leave. But she offered no evidence that her home situation is any different from the one in which the children were abused. She still lives with her boyfriend in the same house, and although her boyfriend allegedly dealt with the friends who abused the children, the record does not indicate that the threat no longer exists. Finally, Tammila did not present evidence of the children's desires with regard to termination.

Conversely, the record indicates that the children are flourishing while living with their aunt and uncle in Louisiana. They have become well integrated into that family. Their performance in school has improved as have their behaviors, resulting from structured parenting by their aunt and uncle.

We therefore conclude that substantial evidence supports the district court's finding that it is in the children's best interests to terminate Tammila's parental rights. . . .

The presumption under NRS 128.109(1)(b) provides that if the parent fails to substantially comply with the terms and conditions of the reunification plan within six months after the date on which the child was removed from the home or the case plan commenced, that failure evidences a failure of parental adjustment under NRS 128.105(2)(d). Substantial evidence also supports application of this presumption.

Tammila's case plan began on July 24, 2002. As evidenced by the first two DCFS reports, Tammila did not substantially comply with the plan's terms within the first six months. She did not submit to drug testing, a psychiatric evaluation, a CRB assessment, or a domestic violence assessment. She failed to enroll in parenting classes, and she failed to provide DCFS with proof of economic or residential stability. Although she did visit her children regularly while they were in Nevada, her attempts to otherwise comply with her case plan were minimal. Tammila's noncompliance with her case plan continued during the three years until the hearing to terminate her parental rights.

According to Tammila, her failure to obtain proper drug counseling was because of a mistake at the drug counseling agency, but she presented no independent evidence to support this assertion. Likewise, she claimed that her failure to obtain a domestic violence assessment was because of a mistake, but again she presented no supporting evidence. We therefore conclude that the district court did not err in finding that Tammila did not present ample evidence to overcome the presumption of failure of parental adjustment under NRS 128.109(1)(b). . . .

Based on the foregoing, we conclude that (1) a party seeking termination of parental rights does not have a burden to demonstrate that an adoptive placement for a child exists; (2) when the presumption under NRS 128.109(2) applies, it is the parent's burden to adduce evidence of the child's desires regarding termination of parental rights under NRS 128.107(2) as a consideration for the district court in rebutting the presumption; and (3) substantial evidence supports the district court's termination of Tammila's parental rights. Accordingly, we affirm the district court's order.

IN RE M.B. AND N.B.
709 N.W.2d 11 (N.D. 2006)

SANDSTROM, JUSTICE. . . .

I.B. and K.S. . . . had two children. They married in 2000, after the children were born, and divorced roughly four years later. The children have been diagnosed with attention deficit hyperactivity disorder and oppositional defiant disorder. They have witnessed episodes of domestic violence between their parents. Their mother testified the children were abused by I.B. K.S. and Cathy Hjelle, the children's therapist, testified the children were exposed to pornographic and horror movies and sexual activities. In April 2002, the juvenile court found the children were deprived and placed them in social services' care. They were reunified with their parents in the summer of 2002, after some family counseling. Marlene Sorum, the petitioner and a social worker with Cass County Social Services, testified at the trial that any involvement in therapy ceased after reunification. The parents separated again in 2003, and custody of the children was given to the mother. In July and October 2003, the juvenile court found the children were deprived and placed them in social services' care.

In July 2004, Sorum petitioned to terminate the parents' rights. After receiving notice by publication, the father appeared to defend against the petition, declaring that he wanted to provide for the children. The mother submitted an affidavit consenting to her termination. The children's guardian ad litem recommended a reunification plan for the father and the termination of the mother's rights.

A three-day trial was held in October 2004. . . . The district judge adopted the referee's order terminating the father's parental rights and adopted the referee's order denying visitation. On appeal, I.B. argues . . . there is insufficient evidence to terminate his rights or to conclude any deprivation will continue, and he should be afforded an opportunity for reunification. . . .

To terminate parental rights, N.D.C.C. § 27–20–44(1)(b) requires the petitioner to prove three elements by clear and convincing evidence: (1) "The child is a deprived child," (2) "The conditions and causes of the deprivation are likely to continue or will not be remedied," and (3) "that by reason thereof the child is suffering or will probably suffer serious physical, mental, moral, or emotional harm." "Clear and convincing evidence means evidence that leads to a firm belief or conviction the allegations are true." A lower court's decision to terminate parental rights is a question of fact that will not be overturned unless the decision is clearly erroneous. "A finding of fact is clearly erroneous if it is induced by an erroneous view of the law, if no evidence exists to support the finding, or if, on the entire record, we are left with a definite and firm conviction a mistake has been made."

A "deprived child" is a child who:

> Is without proper parental care or control, subsistence, education as required by law, or other care or control necessary for the child's physical, mental, or emotional health, or morals, and the deprivation is not due primarily to the lack of financial means of the child's parents, guardian, or other custodian[.]

N.D.C.C. § 27–20–02(8)(a). . . .

Ginny Leon, a parent aide with Cass County Social Services, testified the children's home was very unkempt, as were the parents and children. The children's mother testified that she and I.B. were abusive toward each other in the children's presence and that I.B. was also abusive toward the children. She also testified I.B. would threaten to burn one of the children with a lighter if they did not recite the alphabet. The children's mother claimed that one of the boys was sexually assaulted by I.B.'s brother. She further testified the children were exposed to horror and pornographic films and were obsessed with sexual matters. Cathy Hjelle, the children's therapist, testified one of the boys told her that they had watched pornographic films and watched their father engage in sexual intercourse in front of them. K.S. testified I.B. moved out of a trailer home so K.S. and the children would have someplace to live after she was evicted from her apartment. When the mother and the children first moved in, the trailer had no electricity. Hjelle also testified the children told her there was often a shortage of food and they were hungry. This conduct falls well below the minimum standards of care for a parent and meets the circumstances necessary to find a child is deprived. . . .

Before parental rights may be terminated, the State must prove that the deprivation is "likely to continue or will not be remedied." To show this, the State cannot rely on past deprivation alone, but must provide prognostic evidence, demonstrating the deprivation will continue. A parent's lack of cooperation is probative. The juvenile court may also examine the parent's background. . . .

Leon testified I.B. saw himself only as the financial provider. She testified he expressed no desire to change the nature of their home. The children's mother testified that I.B. did not think the children needed therapy and that, despite the children's "special needs," he did not help maintain their therapy. She testified I.B. expressed no interest in having the boys around when the parents were together or when they were separated. Georgia Holt, a therapist with Lutheran Social Services who worked with the family starting in 2003, testified I.B. had no involvement with their aid sessions before or after the parents separated. Sorum testified that between September 2003 and June 2004, I.B. stated he wished to terminate his parental rights. She testified that when the boys were being placed in foster care in 2002 and 2003, I.B. did not want to take custody and thought they should be placed with someone who could provide and care for them because he could not. Sorum testified that in August 2004, after the petition to terminate rights was filed, I.B. expressed an interest in being a parent to the children. She believed after meeting with him, however, that I.B. did not understand the children's needs or the effort required to provide for the children. Although I.B. was dating someone who appeared willing to be the children's mother, I.B. believed, according to Sorum's testimony, he would always be able to find another mother for the boys if his current girlfriend was no longer with him. Finally, Hjelle testified that the children were afraid of I.B. She testified that when the boys were first placed in foster care, they were often violent and angry. Since being in foster care, their behavior has improved, and a more normal caregiver-child relationship has evolved with their foster parents. She testified a continued positive environment is needed to ensure their progress. Hjelle testified that the boys "would act up after visitation" with their parents. Her conclusion about I.B., based on the information available to her, was that I.B. would not take responsibility for what has happened and that he may revert to acting as he did when the children's mother and he were together if the boys were returned to him. The conclusions of a social worker, a parent aide, two therapists, and the children's mother provided clear and convincing evidence to the referee that the children would continue to be deprived if returned to their father. . . .

The final element of the three-part test is "the child is suffering or will probably suffer serious physical, mental, moral, or emotional harm." The risk of harm may also be shown by prognostic evidence.

The children's mother testified that when the children were in the care of their parents, they were exposed to mental and physical abuse, possibly exposed to sexual abuse, and viewed violent and pornographic films. Hjelle testified the boys were diagnosed with ADHD and ODD, and she believed they suffered from post-traumatic stress disorder. She testified that when the parents first visited the children, they "would act up. . . ." Given this evidence, the referee could conclude, by clear and convincing evidence, that the children continue to suffer from some harm and could suffer additional harm if returned to I.B. . . . The record supports the juvenile court's conclusion that I.B.'s parental rights should be terminated.

I.B. argues the court erred by terminating his parental rights without a showing from Cass County Social Services that it used "reasonable efforts" to reunify him with his children. . . . Section 27–20–32.2, N.D.C.C., provides, in part:

1. As used in this section, "reasonable efforts" means the exercise of due diligence, by the agency granted authority over the child under this chapter, to use appropriate and available services to meet the needs of the child and the

child's family in order to prevent removal of the child from the child's family or, after removal, to use appropriate and available services to eliminate the need for removal and to reunite the child and the child's family. In determining reasonable efforts to be made with respect to a child under this section, and in making reasonable efforts, the child's health and safety must be the paramount concern.

2. Except as provided in subsection 4, reasonable efforts must be made to preserve and reunify families:

   a. Prior to the placement of a child in foster care, to prevent or eliminate the need for removing the child from the child's home; and

   b. To make it possible for a child to return safely to the child's home.

3. If the court or the child's custodian determined that continuation of reasonable efforts, as described in subsection 2, is inconsistent with the permanency plan for the child, reasonable efforts must be made to place the child in a timely manner in accordance with the permanency plan and to complete whatever steps are necessary to finalize the permanent placement of the child. . . .

Beginning in 2002 after the children's first placement in foster care, Cass County Social Services provided parenting aid to the parents. Leon testified I.B. took little interest in the parenting sessions. He was either not home or was sleeping during the day because he worked at night. Although their household was in need of improvement, Leon testified I.B. expressed no interest in changing it. The children's mother testified I.B. did not believe the children needed therapy or medication and did not help in the children's treatment. Sorum testified that . . . I.B.'s involvement in the family therapy was poor despite efforts to include him. Sorum also testified that although I.B. loves his children and now wants to be a father for them, he did not understand the efforts it would take to support the children and their needs. . . . Sorum also testified that after the children were placed in foster care in 2003, I.B. made it clear that he was not a resource for the children and his parental rights should be terminated. Finally, Hjelle testified I.B. visited the children, but when he did, they "would act up. . . ." . . . The evidence before the referee was sufficient to conclude Cass County Social Services made reasonable efforts to keep this family intact, but the father chose not to participate in them. . . .

NOTES AND QUESTIONS

1. *Appellate Review.* Is it appropriate for the North Dakota Supreme Court to review the findings below only for "clear error"? Who is in the best position to assess whether a particular parent's rights should be terminated with respect to a particular child? A social worker? A juvenile court judge? An appellate judge? Someone else?

2.   *The Role of Professional Authority.* Note the role that social workers, therapists, and guardians ad litem or court appointed special advocates play in termination proceedings. How confident are you that these professionals are in a position to assess the parent's actions or the child's best interests? Should the social worker or therapist charged with helping the family reunify also be allowed to testify against the parent in a subsequent termination proceeding? Do you think there are trust issues that would lead the parents to be skeptical of the social worker and therapist? If so, in In re M.B. and N.B., should I.B.'s reluctance to engage in therapy be used against him?

3.   *Parental Responses to Removal.* Removal of children from their parents is traumatic and can have devastating effects on both parents and children. Should a parent's psychological problems triggered by a child's removal be used against the parent in subsequent termination proceedings? In In re M.J.B. & M.W.S., "[t]he forced loss of her children was a serious psychological blow to" the mother such that "she was admitted to the intensive care unit" at a hospital "after taking an overdose of anti-anxiety medication."[184] Can such hospitalization be used to show unfitness? The mother also had "chronic psychological difficulties which impair[ed] her ability to keep and hold a job."[185] Is that relevant to termination? The mother also "failed to take her medications consistently without good reason."[186] Why is that relevant? The court concluded that the state had met its burden to terminate the mother's parental rights.

4.   *Financial Support.* We have already seen that poverty may play a role in child welfare authorities intervening in a family. Parents have a legal duty to financially support their minor children. But does that obligation continue after the children are removed from the home by the state? Does a parent have an obligation to provide financial support to the child once the child is in state custody? Could the failure to provide such support constitute a basis on which to terminate the parent's rights? Even though the court affirmed the termination in *M.J.B. & M.W.S.*, discussed in the previous Note, it rejected the lack of post-removal financial support as a justification. The court explained that "when parents no longer have custody of their children, the nature and extent of their duty may be defined and controlled by external factors other than the parents' ability to support."[187] That is, it may be defined by court order or as part of the permanency plan. In the case before it, "[t]he permanency plans . . . required [the mother] to support her children financially only if ordered by the court," and no such court order had been issued.[188] The court also emphasized that the mother had attempted to support her children "as

---

184. 140 S.W.3d 643, 646 (Tenn. Ct. App. 2004).
185. Id. at 658.
186. Id. at 657.
187. Id. at 655.
188. Id.

best she could prior to their removal," including "by selling [her] plasma twice a week."[189]

5.   *After Termination.* How much should questions about what happens to the child if termination is granted affect the termination decision? Isn't post-termination placement relevant to whether termination is in the child's best interest? Should the government have to show that an adoptive placement is available in order to terminate parental rights? Even though the Nevada Supreme Court held that the government has no such obligation, did the fact that the maternal aunt and uncle appeared willing to adopt affect the court's conclusion about best interests? What if the children were to be placed in a group home for foster children? Would termination have been in their best interests?

6.   *Reinstatement of Parental Rights.* Since 2005, many states have enacted laws allowing parental rights to be reinstated in certain circumstances.[190] These statutes generally require that the child has not been adopted, and several states require that the child be a minimum age or that a minimum amount of time has passed since parental rights have been terminated. Why would a court reinstate parental rights? Data on the number of reinstatements are largely unavailable, but the limited evidence suggests that reinstatement petitions are quite rare.[191]

---

189. Id.

190. See, e.g., Cal. Welf. & Inst. Code § 366.26(h)(3)(C)(i)(3) (West 2020); Del. Code Ann. tit. 13 § 1116 (2020); Nev. Rev. Stat. § 128.170 (2020).

191. See generally Meredith L. Schalick, The Sky is Not Falling: Lessons and Recommendations from Ten Years of Reinstating Parental Rights, 51 Fam. L.Q. 219, 230 (2017).

CHAPTER 8

Adoption

Historian Michael Grossberg describes adoption as "the most far-reaching innovation of nineteenth-century custody law" in America.[1] In 1851, Massachusetts enacted an adoption statute that became a model for other states: "The act made adoption a legal procedure, and charged the courts with making sure that the new parents were of 'sufficient ability to bring up the child, and furnish suitable nurture and education, having reference to the degree and condition of its parents, and that it is fit and proper such adoption should take place.'"[2] Other states quickly followed the lead of Massachusetts, authorizing adoptions if courts found that, as Pennsylvania's statute provided, the "welfare of such child will be promoted by such adoption."[3] Before the enactment of adoption statutes, there was no way to create a legal parent-child relationship that did not arise at birth. People often raised children who had been born into different families, but they did so without the legal structure of formal adoption. With adoption, "natural family ties were dissolved, and replaced by relations with the adopted parents."[4] Still, through the early decades of the twentieth century, adoptions were not confidential or anonymous, and children generally retained inheritance ties to their biological families. They were also not full members of their adoptive families in many situations. Many states, for example, followed a "stranger to the adoption" rule, which denied an inheritance relationship between the adopted child and the adoptive parents' relatives on the theory that the parents did not have the power to "impose" kinship on others.[5] Thus, in a variety of respects, adoption began as a narrow legal relationship between

---

1. Michael Grossberg, Governing the Hearth: Law and the Family in Nineteenth-Century America 268 (1985).

2. Id. at 271–72.

3. Id.; see also Chris Guthrie & Joanna L. Grossman, Adoption in the Progressive Era: Preserving, Creating, and Re-Creating Families, 43 J. Am. Leg. Hist. 235 (1999).

4. Grossberg, supra note 1, at 272.

5. See, e.g., In re Uihlein's Estate, 68 N.W.2d 816, 820 (Wis. 1955).

the child and the adoptive parents. But over time, adoption evolved into a complete substitution of a new family expected to mimic, and supplant, the biological family. An adopted child's ties to the birth family were severed and replaced with ties to the adoptive family that were the same as a child born into that family.

Adoption represents yet another context where courts and other policymakers confront the difficult question of how to define children's best interests, and also how to balance children's interests against those of birth parents and prospective adoptive parents. In the past, adoption has been grossly misused under the guise of promoting children's interests. Adoption was at the heart of the controversial "child-saving movement," which led to the removal of many poor and minority children from their parents, often without their consent.[6] As discussed later in the chapter and more extensively in Chapter 7, beginning in the latter half of the nineteenth century, many Indian children were removed from their families and placed either with non-Indian families or in institutional settings.[7] This fate befell as many as one in four Indian children.[8] As we will see later in this chapter, controversies about the relationship between race, identity, and children's best interests continue to arise in conflicts over adoption.

I. Types of Adoption

Once shrouded in secrecy and shame, adoption has become a widely accepted method of family formation. The high-water mark for U.S. adoptions occurred many decades ago, with roughly 175,000 adoptions in 1970.[9] As abortion and birth control became available, the total number of adoptions in the U.S. decreased, recently declining from 133,737 in 2007 to 110,373 in 2014.[10] These adoptions arise in a variety of situations.

As the child welfare materials in Chapter 7 make clear, many children become eligible for adoption after entering the state's custody by virtue of the government removing them from their parents' care. In these situations, adoptions occur through a public agency. We saw that while state agencies may in many cases aim to reunify a parent and child, they may also seek to facilitate a child's placement with an adoptive family. While parents may voluntarily consent to their child's adoption in this setting, the more common scenario features the state's terminating the parent's rights over the parent's objections.

---

6. Walter I. Trattner, From Poor Law to Welfare State: A History of Social Welfare in America 111 (5th ed. 1994).

7. As in Chapter 7, we use the term "Indian" to reflect the language of the Indian Child Welfare Act and judicial decisions applying the statute.

8. See Mississippi Band of Choctaw Indians v. Holyfield, 490 U.S. 30, 32 (1989).

9. Adoption Factbook IV, National Council for Adoption (2007).

10. Jo Jones & Paul Placek, Nat'l Council for Adoption, Adoption: By the Numbers ii, 2 (2017).

When adoptions occur through the child welfare system, the child may be adopted by a relative or by an unrelated individual. Federal legislation encourages states to prefer relative care,[11] and state statutes prioritize kinship adoptions. For example, California provides that adoptive placement with a relative should be considered before other placement options.[12] States also treat relative adoption more favorably by exempting grandparents and other relatives from certain requirements during the adoption process, such as pre-adoption investigation and certification.[13] Still, the preference for relative placement is not absolute. Generally, the "best interest of the child" supersedes any preference for relatives.[14] Accordingly, for children who have resided with an unrelated foster family for some time, strong emotional ties with that family may outweigh a statutory preference for placement with a relative.[15]

Many individuals who adopt through a state agency begin by fostering the child. In 2017, 59,430 foster placements resulted in adoption through the involvement of a government agency. This represents 24 percent of the total foster care exits that year (247,631).[16] Because public adoptions generally arise out of removal by child welfare authorities, the children who are adopted through this avenue range in age — but older children are less likely to be adopted than their younger counterparts.

In contrast to public adoptions coordinated by the state's child welfare authorities, many adoptions occur through private channels. When children are adopted by unrelated individuals (what is often referred to as stranger adoption), the adoption may be arranged by a private adoption agency or otherwise by private individuals (e.g., an attorney or simply the adoptive parents and the birth parents). Private agencies handle about a quarter of unrelated adoptions in the U.S.[17] These agencies work with birth mothers to match them with prospective adoptive parents. Because of this, most private agencies are placing newborn babies. The private agency must be licensed by the state, and the home study process that the adoptive parents must pass is prescribed by the state and requires clearances from state and federal government agencies.

There are over 2000 licensed private agencies in the U.S.[18] It is estimated that private agency adoptions cost anywhere from $20,000 to more than $45,000.[19] Costs

---

11. See, e.g., 42 U.S.C. § 671(a)(19) (2018).

12. Cal. Fam. Code § 8710(a) (West 2020).

13. See, e.g., Ariz. Rev. Stat. § 8-105(N) (2020).

14. See Kan. Stat. Ann. § 38-2270 (2020) ("[T]he court shall give preference, to the extent that the court finds it is in the best interests of the child, first to granting such custody for adoption to a relative of the child and second to granting such custody to a person with whom the child has close emotional ties").

15. See, e.g., In re K.E., 809 S.E.2d 531 (W. Va. 2018).

16. U.S. Dep't of Health & Human Servs., Admin. for Children & Families, AFCARS Report 1 (2018).

17. Jones & Placek, supra note 10, at 8.

18. Children's Bureau, Child Welfare Info. Gateway, How to Assess the Reputation of Licensed, Private Adoption Agencies (2004).

19. Children's Bureau, Child Welfare Info. Gateway, Planning for Adoption: Knowing the Costs and Resources 3 (Nov. 2016).

(which are paid by the prospective adoptive parents) include fees to the agency for a home study, a match with a birth mother, and placement. Costs also include expenses for the birth mother and fees to the attorney who finalizes the adoption.

While most private agency adoptions are domestic, some are international. Of the more than 75,000 unrelated adoptions in the U.S. in 2014, 69,350 were domestic and 5,987 were international.[20] The percentage of international adoptions has dropped significantly in recent years, from more than 20 percent of total adoptions in 2007 to less than 8 percent in 2014.[21] This is due in large part to restrictions imposed by other countries, such as China, Russia, and South Korea, on intercountry adoptions.[22]

In both the public and private adoption settings considered up to this point, when the child is adopted, the birth parents' rights are extinguished. But another very common form of adoption — stepparent adoption — does not require that both birth parents' rights be terminated or relinquished. The child can be adopted by the stepparent with only the consent of the spouse-parent, who does not relinquish rights to the child.[23] In some states, stepparent adoption emerged as a common-law innovation, as courts reasoned that such adoption would further children's best interests.[24] In other states, stepparent adoption emerged solely through statutory law, as legislatures provided specific carve-outs from relinquishment requirements that otherwise applied to adoption.[25] Stepparent adoption is generally more straightforward than ordinary adoption. Certain procedural requirements, such as home studies, can be waived.[26] And pre- or post-placement reports may not be required.[27]

Even though the custodial parent (the stepparent's spouse) need not relinquish parental rights, the other parent (the one not married to the stepparent seeking to adopt) must. That is, if there is another existing parent, that person's rights ordinarily must either be terminated or relinquished for the child to be adopted by the stepparent. Why? Do you think this is an impediment to stepparent adoption? Why can't the child have three parents if the stepparent seeks to adopt? This is a question to which we return in Chapter 9. While the parent not married to the stepparent

---

20. Jones & Placek, supra note 10, at 4.

21. Id.

22. See, e.g., As China's Economy Improves, Adoptions of Foreign Children by US Parents Continues to Plunge, South China News, Mar. 15, 2019; Maggie Jones, The Returned, N.Y. Times Mag., Jan. 18, 2015, at 29; Clifford J. Levy, Russia Seeks Ways to Keep Its Children, N.Y. Times, Apr. 15, 2010, at A4.

23. See, e.g., Ind. Code Ann. § 31-19-15-2 (2020) ("If the adoptive parent of a child is married to a biological parent of the child, the parent-child relationship of the biological parent is not affected by the adoption.").

24. For a foundational case, see Marshall v. Marshall, 239 P. 36 (Cal. 1925).

25. For an example of one of these early statutes, see Ala. Code § 27-6 (1940).

26. See, e.g., Ala. Code § 26-10A-27 (2020); Utah Code Ann. § 78B-6-128 (West 2020).

27. See, e.g., Wash. Rev. Code § 26.33.220 (2020).

no longer enjoys parental rights with respect to the child who is adopted by the stepparent, in many jurisdictions the child is still able to inherit from that parent.[28] Why would this be the case?

What if the person seeking to adopt is not married to the existing parent but nonetheless is raising the child with that parent? This type of adoption — termed second-parent or co-parent adoption — gained traction in the 1980s and 1990s, particularly with respect to families formed by same-sex couples. Only one individual was the biological parent and thus had legal status. The other partner was neither biologically related to the child nor married to the biological parent, given the exclusion of same-sex couples from marriage. That individual would then attempt to adopt the child. The first such adoptions were granted by state trial court judges in the mid-1980s.[29] Eventually, appellate courts were asked to consider the propriety of second-parent adoption. A number of courts found that second-parent adoption was consistent with the animating principle of the adoption statutes — the best interests of the child.[30] Some courts, in contrast, concluded that that the statutory adoption framework did not permit a child to be adopted by an unmarried person without the existing parents' rights being terminated.[31] Courts on both sides of this question were addressing second-parent adoption in the absence of explicit statutory guidance. A legislature, as the Connecticut legislature did, could simply allow such adoptions.[32] Nonetheless, in most states, there is neither an appellate decision nor a statute expressly authorizing second-parent adoption. Now that same-sex couples can marry across the country, reform on second-parent adoption has slowed significantly — even though second-parent adoption is not limited to intimate couples, and parents may seek to have a relative or friend engage in a co-parent adoption.

---

28. See, e.g., Alaska Stat. § 13.12.114(2) (2020) (preserving child's ability to inherit from or through the non-spouse parent, consistent with the approach taken in the Uniform Probate Code); but see Or. Rev. Stat. § 112.175 (2020) (preserving child's right to inherit through the non-spouse parent only if that parent died before the adoption); Wyo. Stat. 2-4-107 (2020) (failing to preserve child's inheritance relationship with non-spouse parent).

29. See Douglas NeJaime, Marriage Equality and the New Parenthood, 129 Harv. L. Rev. 1185, 1201 & n.75 (2016).

30. See In re Adoption of Tammy, 619 N.E.2d 315 (Mass. 1993); Sharon S. v. Superior Court, 73 P.3d 554 (Cal. 2003); Matter of Jacob, 660 N.E.2d 397 (N.Y. 1995); In re Adoption of Doe, 326 P.3d 347 (Idaho 2014); Adoption of R.B.F. & R.C.F., 803 A.2d 1195 (Pa. 2002); In re Adoption of B.L.V.B., 628 A.2d 1271 (Vt. 1993).

31. See In re Adoption of Luke, 640 N.W.2d 374 (Neb. 2002); Boseman v. Jarrell, 704 S.E.2d 494 (N.C. 2010); In re Adoption of Doe, 719 N.E.2d 1071 (Ohio 1998); In Interest of Angel Lace M., 516 N.W.2d 678 (Wis. 1994).

32. In response to In re Adoption of Baby Z, 724 A.2d 1035 (Conn. 1999), which rejected second-parent adoption, the legislature adopted a statute to provide that "any parent of a minor child may agree in writing with one other person who shares parental responsibility for the child with such parent that the other person shall adopt or join in the adoption of the child." Conn. Gen. Stat. § 45a-724(a)(3) (2020).

II. Procedural Requirements

In order for an individual to adopt a child, the child must be available for adoption. Except with respect to stepparent or second-parent adoption, a child becomes available for adoption because both parents' rights have been terminated by the state — a topic we explored in Chapter 7 — or because the parents have consented to the adoption and voluntarily relinquished their rights. The cases that follow address consent to relinquishment of parental rights and termination of parental rights as necessary steps for an adoption. They also raise topics that we will consider more extensively later in the chapter — open adoption and the rights of unmarried fathers.

VELA V. MARYWOOD

17 S.W.3d 750 (Tex. App. 2000)

LEE YEAKEL, JUSTICE.

This case presents the question of how forthright a licensed child-placing agency must be with an unmarried, expectant mother who seeks its counsel prior to the birth of her child. The child's mother, Corina Vela, is an exemplary young woman who made a mistake. The district court held that the law compels the compounding of her error, terminated her parental rights, and appointed appellee Marywood managing conservator of her child. Corina appeals the district-court judgment.

FACTUAL BACKGROUND

In September 1997, Corina, then nineteen years of age and unmarried, learned she was pregnant. At the time of the district-court trial, Corina, still living with her parents, had completed two years at Austin Community College where she had earned high grades and was planning to attend Southwest Texas State University. Corina is a member of a strong, stable, and supportive family. . . .

In February 1998, this pregnant young woman sought counseling services from Marywood, a licensed child-placing agency. Corina had seen a Marywood advertisement and requested information; Marywood mailed her an "admission assessment form" that inquired about her and her family, why she sought services from Marywood, and her views about adoption. Corina completed and returned the form. She met with a Marywood counselor, Aundra Moore, several times in early March. During these meetings, Corina informed Moore that she wanted to place her child for adoption. In Moore's view, Corina was adamant that her child have a future, be in a two-parent family, be safe, and have the security of a family. Moore observed that Corina wanted "the best for her child" and felt that adoption "was the place to go with that." Corina indicated to Moore that her parents could help but she didn't want to burden them. Moore told Corina that "the adoption process is very much at [Corina's] discretion" and that Corina's "wishes and requests" as to what type of family she would place her child with and what type of relationship she would have with her child after adoption would be "considered." At a meeting on March 16, Corina reported to Moore that she had bonded with her unborn child, and Moore noted that Corina "may be grasping the difficulty of her decision."

On March 25, Corina and Moore discussed what Marywood terms an "open adoption," a process by which the birth mother expresses her criteria for adoptive parents. Corina requested a Mexican-American, Catholic couple who had no other children. She also told Moore that "she wanted to visit with the child after the adoption." Moore informed Corina that "her relationship with the adoptive family would establish what type of ongoing relationship [with her child] she would have."

Moore first showed Corina an "Affidavit of Voluntary Relinquishment of Parental Rights" (the "relinquishment affidavit") on March 30. Moore did not discuss the relinquishment affidavit with Corina and did not explain the meaning of the term "irrevocable"; rather, Moore simply "showed her the form" but did not give her a copy to take with her to study. At the March 30 meeting, Corina signed only an "Affidavit of Status" concerning the identity of the father.

Corina selected an adoptive couple at her next counseling session with Moore and had a face-to-face meeting with them on April 8. The meeting lasted about an hour. The prospective adoptive parents met all of Corina's criteria and indicated their willingness to comply with post-adoption visits. Throughout Corina's counseling sessions, she and Moore discussed a "sharing plan," a standard practice of Marywood. A sharing plan ostensibly allows the birth mother to select the adoptive family, visit her child on a regular basis after the adoption, and exchange letters and pictures. The adoptive parents are aware of the plan prior to placement and agree in writing with Marywood to conform to this arrangement. Significantly, the birth mother does not sign this agreement; thus, neither Marywood nor the adoptive parents enter into any agreement with the birth mother. Marywood admits that aside from advocating that the adoptive parents abide by the plan, Marywood can do nothing if the adoptive parents decide, post-adoption, to disregard it. In fact, the executive director of Marywood admits that the sharing plan is an "empty promise." Clearly, the birth mother has no power to enforce such an agreement. Marywood never discussed the unenforceability of the sharing plan with Corina.

At Corina's last meeting with Moore before her child's birth, they discussed the procedures at the hospital and the various documents Corina would have to sign at the hospital, including a temporary foster-care request. Moore also discussed the relinquishment affidavit with Corina. Moore read the affidavit to Corina and "talk[ed] about each paragraph, what each paragraph means, what it is saying." Moore also asked Corina if she had any questions. Although Moore did not first explain the word "irrevocable," she asked Corina if she knew what it meant. Corina replied that once the relinquishment is signed, it cannot be undone. Moore confirmed that meaning and also told Corina that once she signed the affidavit, she could not "take it back, undo it, or change it."

Corina gave birth to a son on April 24. Moore met with Corina at the hospital on April 26, and Corina signed a temporary foster-care request. Moore told Corina that she "would always be able to visit her baby" and that her baby would always know that Corina was his mother. Corina cried throughout the one-and-one-half-hour visit. Moore scheduled a subsequent meeting with Corina to complete the adoption process. The child was placed in foster care on April 27.

On April 28, Corina and her parents visited Marywood. Before the meeting, Corina was not aware that she was to sign the relinquishment affidavit then and was undecided as to whether she wanted to sign it. During the two-hour meeting, Corina, her parents, and Moore read and discussed the relinquishment affidavit in detail. Eventually, Corina signed the affidavit. During the meeting, and before Corina signed the relinquishment affidavit, Moore told Corina that she would "always be that child's birth mother and that with her sharing plan that she had with the adoptive family that she would have an opportunity to be in that child's life forever"; that she would "always have a relationship with [the adoptive] family and with [her] child"; that requests she made of the adoptive family would be "respect[ed]"; that the baby would have "two mothers," "both of whom would have input into his life"; that Corina "would be able to see her son grow up"; and that the birth family would be like the child's extended family. Corina specifically asked what the agency could do to guarantee that she would have continual, post-adoptive visits with the child. Moore responded by "assur[ing] her that the adoptive family has an adoption worker working with them and that they would encourage them to respect what she wished for in terms of sharing and visits. And during their face-to-face visit and even after that, they said that they would respect her wishes in having that sharing plan." Moore repeated to Corina that she would always be a part of the baby's life. According to Corina and her mother, these promises are what convinced Corina to sign the relinquishment affidavit; the promises were "the only reason she signed."

Before the April 28 meeting, Corina did not have a copy of the relinquishment affidavit and did not review it with her parents. Corina was crying when she signed the affidavit, but Moore testified that "it's very common to have tears." Moore asked Corina if signing the relinquishment affidavit "was what she wanted to do" and informed Corina that once she signed it, she "couldn't undo or take it back." Moore never told Corina that signing the relinquishment affidavit meant that she would "never have any legal rights to see [her] child." According to Corina, Moore told her that she would only be "giving up [her] guardianship of [the child]." Corina understood this to mean that she would not be the one "taking care of him and raising him." Corina was not aware and no one informed her that she could have signed a second foster-care agreement to allow herself more time to make the final decision. Moore was the only person who explained the relinquishment affidavit to Corina, and she never told Corina that she could seek legal counsel or another person's opinion. Marywood never revealed to Corina that the relinquishment affidavit could nullify the sharing plan that she believed would allow her a continuing role in her child's life. It is significant that the relinquishment affidavit was never mentioned to Corina until after she and Marywood had devised a sharing plan satisfactory to her. From that point forward, all of Corina's actions and decisions were founded on her belief in and reliance on the sharing plan.

The following day, April 29, Corina asked to visit her child. The same day Marywood filed a petition to terminate Corina's parental rights. On May 1, Corina was allowed to visit her son for one hour at Marywood. Later that day, Corina called Marywood. Exactly what was said in that phone call is disputed. Moore claims that although Corina was crying, in emotional pain, and "having a hard time," Corina never indicated that she wanted to terminate the adoption process. Corina claims that she told Moore that she "wanted [her] baby back" and that she "changed [her] mind." She asked if there was anything she could do, including hiring an attorney. Moore responded that there was nothing that could be done. Corina's mother also called on the afternoon of May 1 and according to Moore, asked if they "could undo the papers" because her daughter was in so much pain. Moore told Corina's mother that the relinquishment was "irrevocable and that it is signed and that there is no way to undo the document." Moore stated that there was nothing "in her conversation with Corina's mother on May 1st that would [have led her] to believe that Corina wanted the baby back" and that the conversation was "about documents." Yet Moore testified at trial that had Marywood known before the child was placed with the adoptive parents that Corina wanted to keep him, Marywood would have returned the child to Corina.

On May 12, an associate judge recommended termination of Corina's parental rights. Although Corina had that day retained counsel to contest the termination and adoption, the termination occurred before she could intervene. In spite of the earlier conversations between Marywood, Corina, and Corina's mother, Marywood placed Corina's child with the prospective adoptive parents the day after the associate judge's decision. Corina immediately gave notice that she was appealing the associate judge's termination recommendation to the district court. Even in the face of this clear and immediate assertion that Corina did not want to give up her child, Marywood continued its efforts to terminate Corina's parental rights. . . .

[T]he district court terminated Corina's parental rights. . . .

Corina brings this appeal, arguing that (1) there was not clear and convincing evidence that she knowingly and voluntarily executed the relinquishment affidavit, and in fact evidence showing that she did not execute it voluntary; and (2) there was not clear and convincing evidence that termination of Corina's parental rights was in the best interest of the child. Marywood also appeals, asserting that the district court erred in requiring it to prove by clear and convincing evidence that Corina knowingly and voluntarily executed the relinquishment affidavit.

DISCUSSION . . .

Termination of Parental Rights

The Family Code provides that the:

> court may order termination of the parent-child relationship if the court finds by clear and convincing evidence: (1) that the parent has: . . . (K) executed before or after the suit is filed an unrevoked or irrevocable affidavit of relinquishment of parental rights as provided in this chapter; . . . and (2) that termination is in the best interest of the child.

Tex. Fam. Code Ann. § 161.001. . . .

The natural right existing between parents and their children is one of constitutional dimension. . . . Termination proceedings must be strictly scrutinized, and termination statutes are strictly construed in favor of the parent. . . .

1. Whether the Relinquishment Affidavit was Executed Voluntarily

It is undisputed that Marywood proved by clear and convincing evidence that the relinquishment affidavit was executed in conformity with section 161.001 of the Family Code. However, . . . [t]he Family Code implicitly recognizes that an affidavit of relinquishment must be executed voluntarily. Since an affidavit of relinquishment waives rights of constitutional magnitude, it must be made voluntarily, knowingly, intelligently, and with full awareness of the legal consequences. . . .

2. Marywood's Duty to Corina

Corina argues that Marywood affirmatively misrepresented to her facts that induced her to sign the relinquishment affidavit. Specifically, Corina claims that the only reason she signed the relinquishment affidavit was that Marywood led her to believe that she had the right and would continue to play a significant role in her child's life after the adoption, would continue to have contact with her child, and was only giving up guardianship of her child. At the time they were made, these representations were either false or misleading because Marywood knew that Corina would have no legal right to enforce the sharing plan against the adoptive parents. And, because Marywood was in a close relationship with Corina as her counselor, it had a duty to fully disclose that the open-adoption arrangement had no legal effect. Corina also emphasizes that she was never given a copy of the relinquishment affidavit to bring home with her; Marywood never suggested she seek legal advice; and Moore was the only person who ever explained the relinquishment affidavit to her. Thus, Corina insists that she did not voluntarily and knowingly execute the relinquishment affidavit and that she signed only as the result of coercion, misrepresentation, fraud, and over-reaching.

In general, coercion is "[c]ompulsion by physical force or threat," or "the improper use of economic power." Black's Law Dictionary 106 (7th ed. 1999). Misrepresentation is a falsehood or untruth with the intent and purpose to deceive.

In the context of fraud, courts have stated that misrepresentation is making a false statement of fact or a false expression of opinion by one claiming or implying special knowledge. Silence can constitute a misrepresentation: "When the particular circumstances impose on a person a duty to speak and he deliberately remains silent, his silence is equivalent to a false representation."

Fraud "is an elusive and shadowy term which has been defined in some cases as any cunning or artifice used to cheat or deceive another." Fraud may consist of both active misrepresentation and passive silence. At common law, the word "fraud" refers to an act, omission, or concealment in breach of a legal duty, trust, or confidence justly imposed, when the breach causes injury to another or the taking of an undue and unconscientious advantage. The "legal duty" may arise from several sources.

Marywood, by its own admission, is more than an adoption agency. It provides extensive parental-counseling services and advertises these services to the public. Moore testified that she is given the discretion to counsel "openly, objectively, and honestly." Corina, in seeking counseling from Marywood, was reasonably entitled to rely fully and unconditionally on Marywood's representations. We hold that Marywood owed Corina a duty of complete disclosure when discussing adoption procedures, including any proposed post-adoption plan. Complete disclosure encompassed the obligation to tell Corina the entire truth about the ramifications of the sharing plan she had chosen with Marywood's help and to make her fully aware that it lacked legally binding effect. Marywood's duty springs from two sources. First, when Marywood made a partial disclosure to Corina about the post-adoption plan, it assumed the duty to tell the whole truth. Second, the evidence conclusively establishes that Corina placed special confidence in Moore, who by virtue of the counseling relationship occupied a position of superiority and influence on behalf of Marywood; thus, Moore and Marywood became bound, in equity and good conscience, to act in good faith and with due regard to Corina's interests. This Court has recognized that a "higher obligation is owed to certain groups because of their vulnerabilities." A young unmarried mother considering placement of her child for adoption is clearly vulnerable and is owed that "higher obligation" when she confides in a maternity counselor.

3. Whether There Is Any Evidence that Corina Voluntarily Signed the Relinquishment Affidavit . . .

Marywood argues that it discharged any duty it owed Corina and that there is ample evidence that Corina fully understood the relinquishment affidavit and wanted to proceed with the adoption. Marywood points out that Moore read and explained the relinquishment affidavit to Corina on three separate occasions; that Corina and her mother both testified that Corina fully understood the relinquishment affidavit when she signed it; that the relinquishment affidavit itself says it was voluntary; and that after Marywood discussed with Corina her option to parent, Corina still wanted to place the child for adoption.

Although the face of the affidavit reflects it was signed knowingly and voluntarily, we must consider the surrounding circumstances to determine if Corina's signature on the document was procured by misrepresentation, fraud, or the like. Corina neither signed nor understood the relinquishment affidavit in a vacuum. She signed and understood it in the context of and in reliance on the post-adoption plan that she and Marywood created, a plan that Marywood now admits is an "empty promise." The evidence conclusively establishes that Corina wanted to proceed with the adoption *only* if she could have post-adoption visits with her child; there is no evidence to the contrary.

Marywood submits that the record shows that Corina understood the post-adoption plan and that if anyone breached the plan, it was Corina. Marywood states that it "did not make any guarantees about the [post-adoption] plan." Instead, Marywood merely told Corina that her wishes for post-adoption visits would be "respected" and that Marywood would " 'encourage' the adoptive parents to follow through with the planned relationship with [Corina]."

There is no evidence in the record, however, that Corina was ever told that the post-adoption plan could not be legally enforced. Marywood's words to Corina were at worst deceptive and at best vague. According to Moore, Corina asked her during the April 28 signing of the relinquishment affidavit what Marywood could do to guarantee continual, post-adoptive visits with her child. . . . Marywood was obligated to answer Corina's question directly and tell her that the agency could not guarantee post-adoption visits. Instead, in counseling Corina, Moore carefully selected her words and minced her explanation of the sharing plan with the result that Corina understood one thing while Moore meant another. Whether the incomplete disclosure was deliberate or inadvertent, it does not satisfy the duty of full disclosure that Marywood owed Corina. . . .

4. Whether Corina Established as a Matter of Law that the Relinquishment Affidavit was Wrongfully Procured . . .

[W]e find conclusive evidence in the record that the relinquishment affidavit was wrongfully procured. Considering only Marywood's version of events, we conclude as a matter of law that its statements and omissions to Corina constituted misrepresentation, fraud, or overreaching. . . . Marywood's statements are misleading and stop short of complete disclosure. They are half-truths that would lead a reasonable person in Corina's circumstance to believe that she had a continuing right to see her child according to the terms of the sharing plan. . . .

CONCLUSION

In conclusion, we hold that once a child-placing agency undertakes to counsel an expectant mother with regard to her alternatives upon the birth of her child, the agency must provide her with complete information regarding those alternatives. It may not leave the mother to speculate on the consequences of the action upon which she and the agency have agreed. In this particular case, our decision is made difficult because the child is now two years of age and has spent almost his entire life with the prospective adoptive parents. However, any fault lies with the pace of the legal system and not with the mother. . . .

NOTES AND QUESTIONS

---

1. *Duties of Adoption Agencies.* To whom does the adoption agency owe duties? The court found that Marywood is "more than an adoption agency. It provides extensive parental-counseling services and advertises these services to the public." But that is true of many adoption agencies. They employ social workers who counsel birth mothers through the process. The agency is paid by the prospective adoptive parents, who give the agency fees to complete the home study, advertise them to birth parents, and facilitate the match. Does the agency have a conflict? Can the agency adequately serve the interests of both the birth parents and the adoptive parents? Does *Vela* suggest that they cannot? What should the agency representative in *Vela* have done differently? Is full disclosure sufficient to resolve the potential conflict?

2. *The Child's Best Interests.* The litigation over the validity of Corina's relinquishment dragged on for several months. The child had been living with the prospective adoptive parents, but was ordered to be returned to the birth mother. Is this a good result? Was it possible for the court to find that Corina's rights had been violated but nonetheless have left the child with the prospective adoptive parents? Does the fact that "any fault lies . . . not with the mother" justify the decision to return the child to the mother when she has not had a role in raising the child? How would you decide the case if you were looking at it from the perspective of the child? Is that how the case should be decided? Are there any other solutions to this dilemma?

IN RE B.G.C.

496 N.W.2d 239 (Iowa 1992)

LARSON, J.

This case is, we observe thankfully, an unusual one. It involves the future of a baby girl, B.G.C., who was born on February 8, 1991. Her mother, Cara, who was not married, decided to give up the baby for adoption and signed a release of parental rights as provided by Iowa Code section 600A.4 (1991). She named "Scott" as the father of the baby, and Scott also signed a release of parental rights. Later, both Cara and Scott signed waivers of notice of the termination hearing. After the hearing, the court ordered the termination of the parental rights of both Cara and Scott. Custody of the child was given to the potential adoptive parents, R.D. and J.D.

Cara moved to set aside the termination, asserting that her release was defective for several reasons. She also asserted, for the first time, that the real father was "Daniel," not Scott. She informed Daniel that he was the father of her child, and Daniel intervened in the adoption proceeding to assert his parental rights. . . .

In the meantime, the adoption case proceeded. The district court found that Daniel was in fact the real father, that he had not released his parental rights, and that he had not abandoned the baby. The court denied the adoption and ordered the baby to be surrendered to Daniel. R.D. and J.D. appealed and obtained a stay of the district court's order transferring custody. The baby has remained in the custody of R.D. and J.D. virtually from the time of her birth. . . .

We agree with the district court in the adoption case that Daniel proved he was the father, that he had not abandoned the baby, and that the adoption proceeding was therefore fatally flawed. Custody of the baby is ordered to be transferred to Daniel.

As tempting as it is to resolve this highly emotional issue with one's heart, we do not have the unbridled discretion of a Solomon. Ours is a system of law, and adoptions are solely creatures of statute. As the district court noted, without established procedures to guide courts in such matters, they would "be engaged in uncontrolled social engineering." This is not permitted under our law; "courts are not free to take children from parents simply by deciding another home appears more advantageous."[1] We point out that this case does not invalidate an adoption decree. Adoption of the baby was denied by the district court because the father's rights were not terminated.

Iowa Code § 600A.8 requires that abandonment be shown by clear and convincing evidence. To hold that Daniel's action was required immediately on knowledge of the pregnancy, at the risk of losing his parental rights, would fly in the face of that standard. These facts would fall far short of clear and convincing evidence. More important, a finding of abandonment under these circumstances would deprive a father of a meaningful right, protected by the constitution, to develop a parent-child relationship. . . .

The argument that the best interests of the baby are best served by allowing her to stay with R.D. and J.D. is a very alluring argument. Daniel has had a poor performance record as a parent. He fathered two children prior to this child, a son, age fourteen, and a daughter born out of wedlock, now age twelve. The record shows

---

1. It has been urged that the court should uphold this proposed adoption on the ground that the father had abandoned his rights by failing to protect them, beginning at the time the pregnancy became known. In other words, it is suggested that this father should have acted to protect his parental rights immediately when the pregnancy became known, even though he had no indication from her that he was the father and even though she was dating another man at the time. This, of course, is totally unrealistic; it would require a potential father to become involved in the pregnancy on the mere speculation that he might be the father because he was one of the men having sexual relations with her at the time in question.

that Daniel has largely failed to support these children financially and has failed to maintain meaningful contact with either of them.

In contrast, as the district court found, R.D. and J.D. "have provided exemplary care for the child [and] view themselves as the parents of this child in every respect."

What R.D. and J.D. ask us to do, however, is to . . . order the granting of the adoption without establishment of any of the grounds for termination . . . because it would be in the baby's best interest.

Their argument is that, although Daniel was not a party to the original termination hearing . . . , his rights could, and should, have been terminated by the court. . . . [T]hey argue, specific grounds for termination need not be established; the best interest of the child determines the issue of termination in an adoption case. We do not believe that our law is capable of this interpretation. . . .

The general rule is that:

> the state cannot interfere with the rights of natural parents simply to better the moral and temporal welfare of the child as against an unoffending parent, and, as a general rule, the court may not consider whether the adoption will be for the welfare and best interests of the child where the parents have not consented to an adoption or the conditions which obviate the necessity of their consent do not exist. However, where a parent by his conduct forfeits the right to withhold consent, but nevertheless contests the adoption, the welfare of the child is the paramount issue.

2 C.J.S. Adoption of Persons § 67, at 491 (1972).

Our case law is in accord with this view; statutory grounds for termination must be established in addition to establishing the child's best interests in order to terminate. . . .

Daniel's parental rights had not been terminated, and the adoption proceedings were therefore fatally flawed. . . .

R.D. and J.D. contend that the court should have terminated the parental rights of Daniel on the ground that he had abandoned the child. . . .

While it is true that Daniel has not shared in any of the expenses in connection with the birth, he was never requested to do so. Nor was there any need to pay the expenses until he learned that the child was his. Abandonment is defined as the relinquishment or surrendering of parental rights and includes both the intention to abandon and the acts by which the intention is evidenced. Abandonment is said to be a relinquishment of parental rights and responsibilities with an intent to forego them. . . .

In this case, the mother informed Daniel on February 27, 1991, that she suspected that Daniel was the father. Daniel, a truck driver, was due to leave town the next day with his truck and asked the mother to see what she could do to "retrieve" the baby. Daniel testified that the mother called him while he was on the road trip and told him that she had located an attorney who would take the case. The next

Saturday, ten days after he learned that the mother thought he was the father, Daniel met with the attorney to discuss how he might assert his parental rights. He still did not know for sure that he was the father, because the blood tests that ultimately confirmed that fact came later. Nevertheless, he immediately filed a request to vacate the termination order on March 12, 1991, and an affidavit on March 18, 1991. He then filed his petition to intervene in the adoption case on March 27, 1991, one month after he first learned that he might be the father.

We agree with the district court that abandonment was not established by clear and convincing evidence. In fact, virtually all of the evidence regarding Daniel's intent regarding this baby suggests just the opposite: Daniel did everything he could reasonably do to assert his parental rights, beginning even before he actually knew that he was the father.

We empathize with the district court, which observed that:

> The court had an opportunity to observe [R.D. and J.D.] at the time of hearing and the court is under no illusion that this tragic case is other than an unbelievably traumatic event. . . . While cognizant of the heartache which this decision will ultimately cause, this court is presented with no other option than that dictated by the law in this state. Purely equitable principles cannot be substituted for well-established principles of law.

The parental rights of this father may not be dismissed without compliance with our termination statute, and the court correctly ordered that the petition for adoption be dismissed. . . .

SNELL, dissenting

I respectfully dissent.

The evidence is sufficient to show abandonment of the baby by Daniel. The record shows he has previously failed to raise or support his other two children. He quit supporting his son, born in 1976, after two years. From 1978 to 1990 he saw him three times. He has another daughter whom he has never seen and has failed to support. He stated he just never took any interest in her. In every meaningful way, he abandoned them.

Daniel knew that Cara was pregnant in December 1990. He saw her in the building where they worked for the same employer. The child was born in February 1991. Having knowledge of the facts that support the likelihood that he was the biological father, nevertheless, he did nothing to protect his rights. The mother, Cara, who knew better than anyone who the father was, named Scott as the father. The legal proceedings logically and reasonably were based on these representations. The termination of parental rights as known to exist at the time were legally completed and an adoption process was commenced.

Daniel's sudden desire to assume parental responsibilities is a late claim to assume rights that he forfeited by his indifferent conduct to the fate of Cara and her child. The specter of newly named genetic fathers, upsetting adoptions, perhaps years later, is an unconscionable result. Such a consequence is not driven by the language of our statutes, due process concerns or the facts of this case. . . .

NOTES AND QUESTIONS

---

1. *Consent to Adoption.* In a part of the case that was omitted, Cara, the birth mother, asserted that her relinquishment was invalid because it came before the 72-hour waiting period prescribed by state law had passed. While some states allow a consent form to be signed any time after the child's birth, most states provide waiting periods before a birth mother can consent to adoption. Is this a good idea? How long would you make the waiting period if you were a state legislator? Many states impose 48- to 72-hour waiting periods.[33]

Even after the initial consent is signed, it may be revoked. As we saw in Vela v. Marywood, fraud, duress, coercion, or misrepresentation constitute grounds for revocation.[34] Some states also allow revocation for any reason. While some permit such revocation up to the point at which a court enters an order terminating parental rights, others require that such revocation occur within a shorter time period — for example, within ten days.[35] In all states, once a court issues a final decree of adoption, consent becomes irrevocable.[36] (Notice that the *B.G.C.* court emphasized that "this case does not invalidate an adoption decree.")

2. *The Rights of Unmarried Fathers.* The court found that Daniel's parental rights were protected as a constitutional matter. On what basis did he have a constitutional right? Should the rights of the mother and of the father be the same? Or should the mother have rights that the father doesn't automatically have because she alone gestated and birthed the baby? In Chapter 9, we examine the rights of unmarried fathers — an issue that clearly affects adoption. At this point, though, consider what, if anything biological fathers should have to do to gain or preserve their rights in this context? Should, as the dissent suggested, Daniel have done something earlier? Should he have suspected that Cara was pregnant with his biological child? If he had known, should he be required to pay some of the expenses associated with the pregnancy in order to

---

33. See, e.g., Conn. Gen. Stat. § 45a-715(d) (2020) (48 hours); Fla. Stat. § 63.082 (2020) (the earlier of 48 hours or notification that birth mother can be discharged from hospital); Iowa Code § 600A.4(2)(g) (2020) (72 hours).

34. See, e.g., S.C. Code Ann. § 63-9-330(A)(7) (2020); Or. Rev. Stat. § 109.312 (2020).

35. See, e.g., D.C. Code § 4-1406(c) (2020) (10 days); Iowa Code § 600A.4(4) (2020) (96 hours after signing of consent); N.Y. Dom. Rel. Law § 115-b(3) (2020) (45 days after execution when consent not signed in court); Wash. Rev. Code § 26.33.160 (2020) (at any point before consent approved by court such that parental rights are terminated).

36. In general, state rules of civil procedure govern courts' consideration of motions to set aside adoption decrees. See, e.g., Matter of Adoption of J.H.G., 869 P.2d 648, 650 (Kan. 1994). Some states, though, maintain specific rules governing motions to set aside adoption decrees. See, e.g., R.I. R. Juv. Proc. Rule 40.

preserve his rights to contest an adoption? What should constitute "abandonment"? Should his treatment of his previous children be relevant to his rights with respect to the new child?

3. *The Child's Interests.* The court recognized that the child's removal from the adoptive parents and placement with the biological father — a man she has never known — is a "traumatic event." Yet the court ordered that result, explaining that "[p]urely equitable principles cannot be substituted for well-established principles of law." What role should the child's interest play in cases of this kind? The dissent worried that the rights of biological fathers are being used in ways that harm children's interests in secure adoptive placements. Is there a way to recognize that the biological father suffered a harm and yet not order that the child be removed from her home? Does the child have any right to maintain a relationship with her adoptive parents? Why was there no discussion of the child's rights? Think back to Chapter 6, where we examined parents' rights and children's rights. Why did the prospective adoptive parents not have a right to maintain their parental relationship with the child?

PROBLEM

Joe and Cathy were high school sweethearts. When Cathy got pregnant, she didn't want to tell Joe. When she did tell him, she said that she would probably have an abortion and wanted to know whether he would pay for it. Joe said he would not pay for an abortion because he didn't want her to have one. Angered by Joe's refusal to help pay for an abortion, Cathy stopped talking to him and didn't return his calls. Joe, in response, became angry at Cathy, and stopped calling her.

Soon Cathy moved in with her cousin in a neighboring town. While with her cousin, Cathy had a change of heart. She had been raised as a Catholic, and she decided on the basis of her religious beliefs that she didn't want to have an abortion. But she dreaded the prospect of raising the child alone (which she thought she would have to do now that her relationship with Joe had ended).

Accordingly, Cathy decided to place the child for adoption. She contacted an agency and chose as adoptive parents a married couple in another part of the state. When the adoptive couple's lawyer contacted her, Cathy told him that she did not know who the father was. After she gave birth, the lawyer brought the forms Cathy would need to sign to relinquish her parental rights and consent to the adoption. Cathy started to have second thoughts. She wondered whether she could actually release the baby to someone else, and she began to fantasize that she and Joe could get back together and raise the child.

After she began to express doubts about going through with the adoption, the lawyer told her that placing the child for adoption would be in the best interest of the child. He also assured her that she could not financially support herself and the child, and that the state Department of Children and Family Services might then have to take the child away from her anyway. At least if she did this now, she would know that the child was in good hands. In tears, Cathy signed the necessary forms. Eventually, the adoption was finalized.

Ten months after the birth of the child (and several weeks after the adoption was finalized), Cathy moved back to her hometown. One day, she saw Joe at the grocery store. They began talking, and soon they started to see each other again. A few weeks into dating, Cathy explained that she had not had an abortion and instead had carried the baby to term and placed the child for adoption. At that point, Cathy and Joe jointly decided that they would like to raise the child together.

What arguments might they make? What would be their likelihood of success in their quest to raise the child? How would you rule if you were a judge in the case?

III. Open Adoption

Open adoption refers to arrangements in which the prospective adoptive parents and the birth parents (or birth mother) know each other's identities, form a relationship, and often arrange for post-adoption contact, through in-person visits, phone calls, emails, or social media. In *Vela v. Marywood*, Corina placed her child for adoption on the assumption that she would have a significant relationship with the child after the adoption. But the agreement was unenforceable and thus Corina would have no way to ensure post-adoption contact. The following case revisits the question of the validity of post-adoption contact agreements and considers the court's role in enforcing them.

GROVES V. CLARK
982 P.2d 446 (Mont. 1999)

JUSTICE HUNT.

Lon and Loralee Clark (the Clarks), adoptive parents of L.C., appeal from the Findings of Fact, Conclusions of Law, and Judgment entered by the Eighth Judicial District Court, Cascade County, allowing Debbie Groves (Groves), L.C.'s birth mother, monthly weekend visitation and weekly telephone contact with L.C. . . .

BACKGROUND . . .

[I]n January 1994, when L.C. was three years old, Groves signed a document terminating her parental rights to L.C., relinquishing custody of L.C. to Lutheran Social Services (LSS), and consenting to adoption. Groves and the Clarks signed a written visitation agreement which provided the following: Groves would have unrestricted visitation with L.C. so long as she gave the Clarks two days' notice; Groves would have unrestricted telephone contact with L.C.; and Groves would have the right to take L.C. out of school in the event she had to "go to Butte for some emergency." This agreement was drafted by the LSS and neither party consulted an attorney before signing it. In February 1994, the District Court entered an order terminating Groves' parental rights to L.C. and awarding custody of L.C. to LSS. In September 1994, the Clarks legally adopted L.C.

Groves and the Clarks abided by the terms of the visitation agreement until June 5, 1995, when Groves notified the Clarks that she wanted to take L.C. to Butte for the weekend and the Clarks refused. The Clarks told Groves that she was welcome to visit L.C. in their home, but could not take L.C. on extended out-of-town trips. Several weeks later, Groves filed a petition requesting specific performance of the visitation agreement. . . .

In December 1995, the District Court denied Groves' petition for specific performance of the visitation agreement. The court concluded that . . . the document whereby Groves terminated her parental rights and relinquished custody of L.C. to LSS constituted the final, controlling agreement concerning relations between Groves and L.C. Because that document did not reserve any visitation, the court concluded that Groves was not entitled to post-adoption visitation. Based on these conclusions, the court held that the post-adoption visitation agreement was void and unenforceable. Groves appealed to this Court.

This Court reversed the District Court concluding that . . . Groves and the Clarks specifically bargained for the right of visitation and voluntarily signed a written notarized agreement which provided the terms of the visitation arrangement. We further noted that . . . the Montana Legislature enacted § 40-8-136, MCA (1995), which we interpreted as providing for the recognition of agreements for post-adoption contact and visitation. On this basis, we held:

> [B]irth parents and prospective adoptive parents are free to contract for post-adoption visitation and . . . trial courts must give effect to such contracts when continued visitation is in the best interest of the child.

We remanded the case to the District Court for a hearing on whether enforcement of the parties' visitation agreement would be in the best interest of L.C.

The District Court . . . found that a bond existed between Groves and L.C. and that it was highly likely L.C. would suffer from issues of abandonment, identity, and grieving unless appropriate visitation with Groves was granted. Ultimately, the court found that continued visitation between Groves and L.C. was in L.C.'s best interest. The court ordered continued visitation and telephone contact between Groves and L.C. but not in accordance with the terms of the parties' liberal visitation agreement. Rather, the court found that a more structured visitation arrangement was in the best interest of L.C. Specifically, the court granted Groves unsupervised monthly weekend visitation with L.C. and required the parties to share equally in the transportation costs. Additionally, the court granted Groves telephone contact with L.C. at least once per week. The court recommended that the parties seek adoption counseling and attempt to agree upon future visitation modifications that may be appropriate as L.C. matures. . . .

DISCUSSION

Issue 1 — Did the District Court err in finding that post-adoption visitation with Groves was in the best interest of L.C.? . . .

[T]he Clarks assert that the adoptive parents' wishes are paramount in deciding whether a post-adoption visitation agreement should be enforced. The Clarks cite several cases from other jurisdictions purportedly holding that adoptive parents have the right to determine whether it is in the best interest of the adopted child to maintain contact with the birth mother. The Clarks also cite cases from other jurisdictions purportedly holding that the mere fact that the adoptive parents oppose visitation provides a sufficient basis for finding that visitation is not in the best interest of the child.

We reject the Clarks' assertions that the adoptive parents have sole discretion, or that the adoptive parents' wishes are paramount, in deciding whether a post-adoption visitation agreement should be enforced. The law in Montana, which also happens to be the law of this case, is clear: whether a post-adoption visitation agreement is enforceable shall be decided by the District Court pursuant to a "best interests" analysis. The adoptive parents' wishes is but one factor among many to be considered by the District Court. . . .

We . . . reject the Clarks' assertion that the evidence did not support a finding that a bond existed between Groves and L.C. The record demonstrates that L.C. and Groves were together for the first three years of L.C.'s life. The court heard testimony from Debbie O'Brien, a marriage and family counselor who had been counseling Groves since August 1996. Ms. O'Brien testified that in her opinion, a bond existed between L.C. and Groves. Although the majority of post-adoption visitation sessions between L.C. and Groves were short and infrequent, this does not necessarily mean that no bond existed between L.C. and Groves. We note that several of Groves' attempts to have visitation with L.C. were frustrated by the Clarks' own actions. The Clarks often refused to talk to Groves. At trial, Mrs. Clark admitted that when Groves called her about attending L.C.'s birthday party, she pretended she could not hear who was calling. The record also shows that the Clarks outright refused visitation. We hold that substantial evidence existed to support the finding that a bond existed between L.C. and Groves. . . .

[T]he court's finding that visitation between Groves and L.C. was in the best interest of L.C. was not clearly erroneous. . . .

Issue 2 — Did the District Court err in modifying *sua sponte* the parties'
post-adoption visitation agreement? . . .

[T]he original agreement contemplated that Groves could have visitation with
L.C. whenever she wanted so long as she gave the Clarks two days' notice. No time
restriction on visitation was incorporated into the agreement. The court found that
a more structured visitation arrangement, monthly weekend visitation, was in the
best interests of L.C. . . . . [T]he court held that modification of the parties' original
visitation agreement was within its discretion in accordance with determining the
best interests of L.C.

The Clarks argue that the court erred in modifying *sua sponte* the terms of
the original visitation agreement because no statute or other legal authority exists
granting the court this power. The Clarks argue that when the court found that visitation was in the best interests of L.C., the court was bound to enforce the parties'
visitation agreement as written.

We agree with the District Court that modification of the parties' original visitation agreement was within its discretion in accordance with determining the best
interests of L.C. The policy of this state is that "[i]n matters relating to children, the
best interests of the children are paramount." It is a well-established rule that parties
cannot make binding agreements concerning the support, custody, or visitation of
children. Although this rule has been expressed in the context of separation agreements made between spouses, we believe it applies equally to post-adoption agreements made between an adopted child's birth parents and adoptive parents. . . .

NOTES AND QUESTIONS

1.   *Open Adoption and Post-Adoption Contact Agreements.* As *Vela* illustrates,
post-adoption contracts or post-adoption contact agreements may not be enforceable.
But as *Groves* demonstrates, some states have determined that agreements of this kind
are enforceable. As post-adoption contact has become more prevalent over the past
few decades, states have significantly revised their statutory schemes to reflect this
trend. Over half of the states in the U.S. now have statutes that permit enforceable post-
adoption contact agreements — a number that continues to grow.[37] Although details
differ from state to state, these statutes generally uphold the legality of post-adoption
contact agreements so long as the agreement is in writing and approved by the court,
meaning that the court finds enforcement to be in the adoptee's best interests. While
many states simply do not address the legal enforceability of these contracts, a few
states explicitly render them unenforceable.[38]

---

37. See, e.g., N.Y. Dom. Rel. Law § 112-b (2020); Cal. Fam. Code § 8616.5 (West 2020); Md. Code
Ann., Fam. Law § 5-308 (West 2020).
38. See, e.g., Del. Code tit. 13 § 929(a)(2)(c) (2020); N.C. Gen. Stat. § 48-3-610 (2020); Tenn. Code
Ann. § 36-1-121(f) (2020). See generally Carol Sanger, Bargaining for Motherhood: Postadoption Visitation
Agreements, 41 Hofstra L. Rev. 309 (2012).

How do you square the enforcement of such agreements with the parental rights doctrine we examined in Chapter 6? If a legal parent has the authority to decide who the child spends time with and when, how can a court force an adoptive parent to allow the child to spend time with the birth mother? After all, the birth mother is a non-parent after termination of parental rights. Is this an unconstitutional incursion on the rights of the adoptive parents? Is the fact that there is an agreement enough to overcome any constitutional objection? Is the child's best interest sufficient to justify forced visitation? Should the law treat birth parents who place a child for adoption differently than other non-parents?

Most adoptions now incorporate some level of openness between birth parents and adoptive parents. Several factors have contributed to the increasing openness of adoption. In the early 1970s, society began to accept more diverse family forms and the stigma surrounding non-marital births started to decrease. In addition, with the growing acceptance of single parenting and the increasing availability of contraception and abortion, the number of babies available for adoption declined. To stay in business, some adoption agencies began offering birth mothers the option of selecting the child's adoptive parents from a preapproved list, a practice considered quite controversial when first introduced. As more birth parents and adult adoptees returned to adoption agencies over the years to seek information about each other, more agencies set up infrastructures to facilitate open adoption.

2. *Closed Adoptions.* For decades, adoptions generally were closed. Now, only a small percentage of birth mothers request closed adoptions. With closed adoptions, the adoptive parents do not know who the birth mother is, and the birth mother does not know who the adoptive parents are. Why might adoptive parents prefer closed adoptions? Would such adoptions ever be in children's best interests?

For children who were adopted in closed arrangements, should they have a right to know who their birth parents are? When adoption laws were first passed, the proceedings were open and a matter of public record. But beginning in the early twentieth century, states moved first to make adoption records confidential (not available to third parties) and later also anonymous so that one party had no right to know the identity of the other. Adoption secrecy became the norm.[39] By the 1950s, virtually all states treated the "true" parents and the circumstances of birth as deep, dark secrets. The strong social norm was for adoption law to create "as if" families — matching children with parents of the same race and ethnicity and the right age such that outsiders might plausibly infer a biological connection.[40] Attitudes around adoption secrecy changed dramatically toward the end of the twentieth century. But this created a tension, as adoptees asserted increasingly compelling claims to information that had been made

---

39. E. Wayne Carp, Family Matters: Secrecy and Disclosure in the History of Adoption (1998); Elizabeth J. Samuels, The Idea of Adoption: An Inquiry into the History of Adult Adoptee Access to Birth Records, 53 Rutgers L. Rev. 367 (2001).

40. Mary Lyndon Shanley, Making Babies, Making Families: What Matters Most in an Age of Reproductive Technologies, Surrogacy, Adoption, and Same-sex and Unwed Parents (2001).

secret pursuant to agreements entered in an earlier era. Do children have the right to the information their biological and adoptive parents agreed to keep secret? Can the government force agencies to disclose that information? Over the objection of the adoptive parents? Over the objection of the birth parents? Just as the U.S. has moved towards open adoptions and greater transparency surrounding parental origins, the same has occurred with respect to adoption records. Adoptee rights groups have led a national movement to improve access to adoption records over the past several years. In litigation, adoptees generally were unsuccessful in obtaining access to their birth records.[41] But today, more than half of U.S. states offer adoptees at least some form of access to their original birth certificate. In some states — Alabama, Alaska, Colorado, Hawaii, Kansas, Maine, New Hampshire, New York, Rhode Island, and Oregon — adult adoptees have unrestricted access to their birth records.[42] Other states restrict access to adult adoptees born during certain years or only allow access if the birth parent has not filed a request for nondisclosure. For states that still seal birth certificate records, such as California, an adoptee must obtain a court order to unseal records.[43]

IV. Adoption, Identity, and Race

Just as miscegenation statutes once did, adoption laws also reinforced the monoracial family. In the middle of the twentieth century, policymakers generally thought that the adoptive family should mimic the biological family. Thus, black children in need of adoption were placed only with black families, and white children were placed only with white families. Biracial children were placed with mixed-race couples. In some states, cross-racial adoptions were precluded, either by statute, judicial decision, or social work practice. As adoption became less stigmatized, so too did race matching become less pervasive. Through the 1960s, increasing numbers of black children were placed with white couples.

Race matching typically refers to state policy or practice that results in children being placed with families of the same race. But same-race adoptive families can also result from the operation of the preferences of prospective adoptive parents or of birth parents. (Adoptive and birth parents might express other sorts of preferences as well.)

The pool of children available for adoption from the foster care system has long included disproportionately more children of color than the general population,[44]

---

41. See, e.g., Mills v. Atlantic City Dep't of Vital Statistics, 372 A.2d 646 (N.J. 1977).

42. See, e.g., Ala. Code § 22-9A-12(c)-(d) (2020); N.H. Rev. Stat. Ann. § 5-C:9 (2020).

43. See, e.g., Cal. Health & Safety Code § 102705 (West 2020) (requiring "good and compelling cause" for court order).

44. See Child Trends, United States Adoption from Foster Care Factsheet Federal Fiscal Year 2015 (2016).

while the pool of adoptive parents has more closely resembled the general population.[45] As adoption agencies began to pursue transracial adoptions in the second half of the twentieth century, some civil rights advocates objected, as reflected in this 1972 statement of the National Association of Black Social Workers (NABSW):

> The National Association of Black Social Workers has taken a vehement stand against the placement of black children in white homes for any reason. We affirm the inviolable position of black children in black families where they belong physically, psychologically, and culturally in order that they receive the total sense of themselves and develop a sound projection of their future.
>
> In our society, the developmental needs of Black children are significantly different from those of white children. Black children are taught, from an early age, highly sophisticated coping techniques to deal with racist practices perpetrated by individuals and institutions. These coping techniques become successfully integrated into ego functions and can be incorporated only through the process of developing positive identification with significant black others. Only a black family can transmit the emotional and sensitive subtleties of perception and reaction essential for a black child's survival in a racist society.

The impact of this position was substantial, resulting in a significant decrease in the number of black children adopted by white families.[46] While the NABSW released its statement in 1972, the issues it raised have remained important and divisive. The following case considers the adoptive placement of children across racial lines.

DeWees v. Stevenson
779 F. Supp. 25 (E.D. Pa. 1991)

Waldman, District Judge.

Plaintiffs seek to enjoin defendants from refusing to consider plaintiffs as adoptive parents for their foster child, Dante Kirby, and from taking him from the foster home on November 23, 1991 to participate in a National Adoption Center event to attempt to find prospective adoptive parents. Plaintiffs allege that defendants have refused to consider plaintiffs' request to adopt Dante because of their race and in so doing have violated the equal protection [clause] . . .

---

45. See Sharon Vandivere et al., U.S. Dep't of Health & Human Servs., Adoption USA: A Chartbook Based on the 2007 National Survey of Adoptive Parents 9 (2009).

46. See Dawn Day, The Adoption of Black Children: Counteracting Institutional Discrimination 93 tbl. 6–1 (1979); Elizabeth Bartholet, Where Do Black Children Belong? The Politics of Race Matching in Adoption, 139 U. Pa. L. Rev. 1163, 1180 (1991); Douglas R. Esten, Transracial Adoption and the Multiethnic Placement Act of 1994, 68 Temple L. Rev. 1941, 1947–48 (1995).

The court provided an opportunity for hearing and argument on November 20, 1991 [and] . . . makes the following findings of fact and conclusions of law.

I. FINDINGS

Plaintiffs are a white couple who have been married for 27 years and who reside in Royersford, Pennsylvania in an almost exclusively white area.

Mrs. DeWees is a high school graduate and housewife.

Mr. DeWees is the maintenance manager for a trucking company.

Plaintiffs have three natural children, ages 26, 23 and 21 years, and five grand-children for whom they have cared.

Defendants are the Chester County, Pennsylvania Children and Youth Services Agency (CCCYS), its director and its adoption supervisor, Kay Thalheimer.

In January of 1988, plaintiffs applied to CCCYS to be foster parents.

During the ensuing review and evaluation process, Mrs. DeWees stated that she did not want to take any black foster children because "[she] did not want people to think that [she] or her daughter were sleeping with a black man." According to Mrs. DeWees, she gave this reason because she was reluctant to give her real reason which was her concern that she would not know how to take care of a black child. . . .

CCCYS variously placed seven foster children with plaintiffs. They were from two to twenty months in age. Three were black and two were bi-racial.

Plaintiffs never received any complaints from CCCYS about their care of any foster child. Plaintiffs' attitude about black children changed and they came "to accept them as any other child."

On November 10, 1989, CCCYS placed Dante Kirby, then two months old, with plaintiffs. Since August 20, 1991, Dante is plaintiffs' only remaining foster child. . . .

Dante's mother is white and his father is black. On November 12, 1991, with their consent, their parental rights were terminated by the Chester County Court of Common Pleas.

Plaintiffs have cared well for Dante. They provide him with his own room and interact frequently with him. He plays and interacts well with plaintiffs' grand-children. They have supplemented the amounts provided by CCCYS for clothing and toys, and have provided Dante with medical care for his respiratory problems. There clearly is a bond of mutual affection between plaintiffs and Dante.

On June 13, 1991, after being advised by Dante's caseworker that Dante's mother and father intended to relinquish their parental rights, plaintiffs wrote to defendant Thalheimer to express an interest in adopting Dante.

On July 18, 1991, defendant Thalheimer met with and interviewed plaintiffs for an hour and a half, and then referred them to Dr. Joseph Crumbley for further evaluation of their request to adopt Dante.

On August 22, 1991, Dr. Crumbley interviewed plaintiffs at his office in Philadelphia for approximately two hours. Dante was present.

In assessing plaintiffs' ability to raise and socialize a bi-racial child, Dr. Crumbley utilized the Workers' Assessment Guide for Families Adopting Cross-Racially and Cross-Culturally of the U.S. Department of Health and Human Services.

Ms. Thalheimer is a social worker with 20 years of experience in the field of adoption. She has experience with trans-racial adoptions. She has placed bi-racial children with white, black and bi-racial adoptive parents respectively. She is white.

Dr. Crumbley is a family therapist and consultant with a Ph.D. in social work. He is a consultant to three adoption agencies and among his areas of specialization are child abuse, foster care and adoption. He has experience with trans-racial adoptions. He is black.

Dr. Crumbley forwarded an evaluation and recommendation to Ms. Thalheimer on September 11, 1991. He concluded that although Dante was emotionally attached to plaintiffs, they would not be appropriate adoptive parents.

That a foster child has bonded with his foster parents is viewed by professionals as strong evidence that he would bond with new adoptive parents as well.

Dr. Crumbley was concerned about plaintiffs' responses that race had "no impact" on developing a child's identity and self-esteem, that addressing racial issues was not important in raising a minority child; and, that they would not prepare Dante to deal with racial discrimination but rather would address the problem if and when it occurred. He was also concerned about plaintiffs' lack of friends in and contact with the minority community, and Mrs. DeWees' statement that she would "not manufacture black friends."

Dr. Crumbley concluded that plaintiffs lacked the ability to: be sufficiently sensitive to the needs of a bi-racial child during the critical period of socialization, self-identification and personality development of age two through six years; educate a minority child about prejudice and provide him with the skills effectively to respond to it; and, provide positive bi-racial and minority role models through interaction with the minority community.

Based on her interview and Dr. Crumbley's report, Ms. Thalheimer concluded that plaintiffs lacked the sensitivity to racial issues and inter-racial network of community resources needed properly to raise Dante. She decided not to grant plaintiffs' request to adopt Dante, and so advised them by letter of September 26, 1991.

Since receiving this letter, plaintiffs have a greater realization of the importance of the issues identified by Dr. Crumbley and are willing to undertake any course of action recommended by defendants to prepare to address the needs of a bi-racial child. They are willing to "grow and learn." They have located and are prepared to participate in a support group of trans-racial adoptive families.

In Dr. Crumbley's opinion, the only evidence adduced on the point, plaintiffs could learn to address Dante's race-related psychological and social needs with appropriate counseling, education and training but this would take a substantial period of time and Dante is now at a "critical" point.

The court has no expertise in the area of cross-racial adoption. Nevertheless, the court cannot accept Dr. Crumbley's view that generally only whites with extensive specialized training or who have experienced discrimination themselves will be able adequately to address the needs of a minority child in his or her formative years.

The court does find that particular sensitivity, awareness and skills are necessary for a successful trans-racial adoption of a young child, and that Dr. Crumbley based his recommendation on his conclusion that plaintiffs had not demonstrated those qualities and could acquire them only over a long period.

Ms. Thalheimer did not refuse to consider plaintiffs as adoptive parents because of race or any other reason. Rather, she did consider plaintiffs' request to adopt Dante and decided not to grant it. Ms. Thalheimer is currently prepared to place Dante for adoption with any suitable couple, regardless of race, who appear to her to have the awareness, sensitivity and skills to address adequately the needs of a bi-racial child in his formative years. Her decision was based on the perceived best interests of the child, and not on the color of plaintiffs' skins.

II. CONCLUSIONS OF LAW . . .

The essence of the equal protection clause is a requirement that similarly situated people be treated alike. . . .

The state's responsibility to protect the best interests of a child in its custody is a compelling interest for purposes of the equal protection clause.

Because of the potential difficulties inherent in a trans-racial adoption, a state agency may consider race and racial attitudes in assessing prospective adoptive parents.

While the degree of plaintiffs' sensitivity and attitudes about racial issues may be related to their race and experience as whites in a white majority society, defendants refused their request to adopt a minority child because of perceptions about their attitudes and not their race. To the extent that perceived attitudes about race and coping with race-related problems motivated defendants' decision, this was Constitutionally permissible in determining the best interests of a young child eligible for adoption. . . .

II. CONCLUSION . . .

This court is not empowered to sit as a super adoption agency review board. The court thus is not passing upon the wisdom of defendants' actions but only on whether they were motivated by Constitutionally impermissible considerations of race. The court has found that defendants made a considered judgment based on professional input and Constitutionally permissible factors.

This finding turns on the importance of awareness of and sensitivity to issues of race in the context of a trans-racial adoption. These factors, in turn, are important largely because of the realities of the larger society in which we live.

As the court stated at the hearing on November 20, 1991, it is concerned that the very problems which give rise to race-related concerns may unintentionally be exacerbated by overemphasizing them. It is difficult to make race irrelevant, as it should be, if adoption and other social decisions are driven by racial considerations, however benign.

In making adoption decisions, state agencies cannot ignore the realities of the society in which children entrusted to them for placement will be raised, or the [e]ffect on children of those realities as documented by professional studies. The court would hope, however, that these agencies also will be mindful of the possibility that an overemphasis on racial issues may retard efforts to achieve a color blind society, and of the need to avoid even the appearance that an adoption decision may have been based on race *per se*. . . .

NOTES AND QUESTIONS

1. *The Constitutional Standard.* Despite controversy about the role of race in adoptive placements, the Supreme Court has never clarified the constitutional standard. Not since Palmore v. Sidoti, a 1984 child custody decision excerpted in Chapter 10, has the Court issued any opinion concerning the constitutionality of considering race in child placement.[47] In *Palmore*, the Court overturned the trial court's consideration of race in a custody dispute between divorced parents, but left open the question of how, or whether, its analysis would extend to adoption. Many courts thus construed *Palmore* narrowly and accorded courts discretion to consider race as a factor in the best interests of the child calculus. Should social workers placing a child for adoption be permitted to consider a prospective parent's race as a factor in the best interests analysis?

2. *Racial Attitudes.* The *DeWees* court permitted the consideration of the racial attitudes of the prospective adoptive parents. Is it possible, or desirable, to consider adoptive parents' racial attitudes without considering their race? What is the rationale for distinguishing between the consideration of race per se and the consideration of racial attitudes? Should the latter be any more constitutionally permissible than the former?

3. *Transracial Adoption Training.* The *DeWees* court referred to the possibility of "counseling, education and training" to increase the racial sensitivity and awareness of the white prospective adoptive parents. Would it be permissible for a social work agency to require that white parents adopting black children attend such a "counseling,

---

47. 466 U.S. 429 (1984).

education and training" program (for example, weekly sessions for two months), when it would not require black parents adopting black children to do so? What if black parents adopting white children were subject to the same sort of program?

4. *Race Matching.* The arguments typically offered in support of race matching in adoption relate to i) identity, ii) coping skills, iii) culture, and iv) stigma. The coping skills argument is that black parents are better able than white parents to teach a black child how to thrive in a racist society. Race-matching proponents further contend that being raised in a black family enables a black child to develop a strong sense of racial identity and a cultural rootedness that is less likely if the child is adopted by white parents. Finally, a black child raised by white parents might feel a sense of stigma, arising from the visible difference between the child and other family members. To what extent do each of these arguments weigh in favor of race matching? To argue against race matching, how would you respond to these claims?

5. *The Multi-Ethnic Placement Act.* To counter race-matching policies that were believed to impede the adoptive placement of black children and thereby contribute to their disproportionate representation in the foster care system,[48] Congress in 1994 passed the Multi-Ethnic Placement Act (known as MEPA).[49] MEPA was amended in 1996 by the Interethnic Placement Act.[50] The law declares:

> [N]either the State nor any other entity in the State that receives funds from the Federal Government and is involved in adoption or foster care placements may —
>
> (A) deny to any person the opportunity to become an adoptive or a foster parent, on the basis of the race, color, or national origin of the person, or of the child, involved; or
>
> (B) delay or deny the placement of a child for adoption or into foster care, on the basis of the race, color, or national origin of the adoptive or foster parent, or the child, involved.[51]

In order to increase the pool of minority foster and adoptive parents, MEPA also requires states receiving federal funding for child welfare programs to engage in diligent efforts to recruit a more diverse pool of foster and adoptive parents.[52]

---

48. Policy Guidance on the Use of Race, Color or National Origin as Considerations in Adoption and Foster Care Placements, 60 Fed. Reg. 20,272, 20,273 (Apr. 25, 1995) (stating that MEPA "focuses on the possibility that policies with respect to matching children with families of the same race, culture, or ethnicity may result in delaying, or even preventing, the adoption of children by qualified families").

49. Howard M. Metzenbaum Multiethnic Placement Act of 1994, Pub. L. No. 103–382, 108 Stat. 4056, codified as amended at 42 U.S.C. § 622 (2018).

50. Interethnic Placement Act of 1996, Pub. L. No. 104–188, 110 Stat. 1904 (2018), codified at 42 U.S.C. § 622 (2018).

51. 42 U.S.C. § 671(a)(18) (2018).

52. 42 U.S.C. § 622b(3)(9) (2018) (requiring diligent recruitment of "potential foster and adoptive families that reflect the ethnic and racial diversity of children in the state for whom foster and adoptive homes are needed").

DeWees was decided prior to the enactment of MEPA. But would the approach endorsed by the court conform to, or violate, MEPA?

6. *The Enforcement of MEPA.* Although MEPA unquestionably was intended to restrict race matching, some social work professionals—from frontline case workers to administrators who set policy—continue to believe that minority children benefit from being placed with families from their own racial or ethnic group. Because there are very few litigated challenges brought by private plaintiffs, the enforcement of MEPA has fallen to the Office of Civil Rights (OCR) in the Department of Health and Human Services. OCR has interpreted MEPA's nondiscrimination mandate in an expansive manner that would prohibit i) requiring white parents adopting a black child to attend any sort of racial sensitivity training if black parents would not be required to attend the same sort of training, ii) using race as a tiebreaker even if it would not delay a particular child's placement, iii) only considering a transracial placement if no same-race placement is immediately available, iv) declining to place a black child with white parents because they had few black friends and lived in a predominantly white area with predominantly white schools, or v) according the adoptive child's racial preferences greater weight than other sorts of preferences about the type of family with which the child would like to be placed.[53] In which, if any, of these situations did OCR go too far? For each scenario, consider whether you think the practice: i) furthers the best interests of the child, and ii) whether, on balance, the practice should be prohibited as a matter of policy.

7. *MEPA and Personal Preferences.* Adoption policies typically defer to prospective adoptive parents' preferences as to the type of child they want to adopt.[54] Yet, in one widely noted enforcement action, the Department of Health and Human Services concluded that the South Carolina Department of Social Services had violated MEPA by granting prospective adoptive parents' preference to adopt a same-race child greater deference than other sorts of preferences (e.g., preferences related to the age or sex of the child). Viewing South Carolina's approach as an indirect yet intentional form of race matching, the Department of Health and Human Services made clear that such subtle forms of race matching are no more permissible than more overt practices.[55]

8. *Evaluating MEPA.* The empirical evidence about MEPA's effects is equivocal. After the passage of MEPA, adoption rates of black children from foster care increased, but black children remained less likely than white children to be adopted.[56] According

---

53. See Ralph Richard Banks, The Multiethnic Placement Act and the Troubling Persistence of Race Matching, 38 Cap. U. L. Rev. 271 (2010).

54. For an examination of adoption agencies' facilitation of adoptive parents' racial preferences, see R. Richard Banks, The Color of Desire: Fulfilling Adoptive Parents' Racial Preferences Through Discriminatory State Action, 107 Yale L.J. 875 (1998).

55. See Banks, supra note 53.

56. U.S. Gov't Accountability Office, GAO-07-816, African American Children in Foster Care: Additional HHS Assistance Needed to Help States Reduce the Proportion in Care 8, 26 (2007).

to data from 2006 (ten years after the Interethnic Placement Act's amendments to MEPA), black children represented 35 percent of those awaiting adoption, yet only 27 percent of those adopted.[57] But of the children adopted from foster care, a greater percentage of black children were adopted by a different-race family—an increase from 14 percent in 1998 to 26 percent in 2004.[58] According to a report by the Evan B. Donaldson Adoption Institute, some of the states that most increased the adoption rates of black children also had relatively low rates of transracial adoption. Increased adoption rates may have been spurred by other policy changes that prompted states to move children more quickly from foster care to adoption, such as the Adoption and Safe Families Act of 1997 (discussed in Chapter 7). Whether MEPA has contributed significantly to the increased adoption of black children is thus unclear. Is MEPA's aim of ending racial discrimination in adoption sufficient justification for the law, or must it also improve the actual placement of black children? Assuming the law doesn't substantially influence placement rates, does it nonetheless produce a benefit?

PROBLEM

You are a social worker charged with placing children for adoption. You are trying to decide how to place an infant whose parents are both African American. The parents, who want the child to go to a "good family," have relinquished the child to your agency for placement.

There are three families who would like to adopt the child. They are all married couples. They all have college degrees and household incomes above the national median. The first family is a white, different-sex couple with no children. They live in a racially diverse neighborhood in a large city. The wife believes that "people are people" and stated that she would teach the child that race does not matter. The second family is a white, same-sex couple who live in a predominantly white neighborhood in a large city. They previously adopted a child, who is African American. They state that they would teach any African American child to be proud of their racial heritage. The third family is an African American, different-sex couple with one biological child. They live in a racially diverse neighborhood in a small city. The husband stated that he would teach the child to be an individual and not to think of himself primarily in terms of race.

You now must recommend a family with which the child should be placed. Which family will you choose? Why?

---

57. See Donaldson Institute Report, Finding Families for African American Children: The Role of Race and Law in Adoption from Foster Families (May 2008).

58. David D. Meyer, *Palmore* Comes of Age: The Place of Race in the Placement of Children, 18 U. Fla. J.L. & Publ. Pol'y 183, 192 (2007).

In Chapter 7, we introduced the Indian Child Welfare Act (ICWA), which regulates the obligations of child welfare authorities with respect to Indian children and prioritizes adoptive placements with Indian families. MEPA expressly provides that it has no effect on ICWA.[59] Why not? The basis for treating ICWA's classification as nonracial is that Indian tribes are semi-sovereign political entities with an interest in self-government and regulating their internal affairs. Thus, in Morton v. Mancari, the Supreme Court rejected the claim that hiring preferences for tribal Indians at the Bureau of Indian Affairs (BIA) constituted a racial classification.[60] Not only were the preferences limited to the BIA, which itself promotes self-government among the tribes, but, the Court reasoned, "[t]he preference, as applied, is granted to Indians not as a discrete racial group, but, rather, as members of quasi-sovereign tribal entities whose lives and activities are governed by the BIA in a unique fashion."[61] The Court also observed that "[t]he preference is not directed towards a 'racial' group consisting of 'Indians'; instead, it applies only to members of 'federally recognized' tribes. This operates to exclude many individuals who are racially to be classified as 'Indians.' In this sense, the preference is political rather than racial in nature."[62]

This distinction between a political classification and a racial classification has persisted as a basis for exempting ICWA from the heightened scrutiny applicable to racial classifications. Yet, in the context of ICWA, the two types of classifications are intertwined rather than neatly separable. ICWA defines "Indian child" with reference to eligibility for tribal membership, yet tribes define eligibility with reference to descent from a tribal member or a specified percentage of Indian "blood."

While most courts have declined to treat ICWA as creating a racial classification, some state courts have held ICWA unconstitutional as applied to cases in which neither the parents nor the child have any connection to the tribe other than genetically. For example, in In re Santos Y., a California appellate court reasoned:

> The ICWA unquestionably requires Indian children who are dependents of the juvenile court to be treated differently from court dependents who are not Indian children. . . .
>
> Absent social, cultural, and political relationships, or where the relationships are very attenuated, the only basis for applying ICWA rather than state law in dependency proceedings is the child's genetic heritage . . .
>
> "[A]ny application of ICWA which is triggered by an Indian child's genetic heritage, without substantial social, cultural or political affiliations between the child's family and a tribal community, is an application based solely, or

---

59. 42 U.S.C. § 1996b(3) (2018).
60. 417 U.S. 535 (1974).
61. Id. at 554.
62. Id. at 553 n.24.

at least predominantly, upon race and is subject to strict scrutiny under the equal protection clause." . . .

[A] determination based on "blood," on its face invokes strict scrutiny to determine whether the classification serves a compelling governmental interest and is narrowly tailored to achieve that interest. We find that it does not.[63]

In 2013, the Supreme Court considered ICWA's application to a conflict between a biological father and a non-Indian adoptive couple. As you read the case, consider whether the application of ICWA amounts to a racial classification. Consider also how the case raises and resolves issues that we already confronted in this chapter regarding termination of parental rights and the status of unmarried fathers.

ADOPTIVE COUPLE v. BABY GIRL
570 U.S. 637 (2013)

JUSTICE ALITO delivered the opinion of the Court.

This case is about a little girl (Baby Girl) who is classified as an Indian because she is 1.2% (3/256) Cherokee. Because Baby Girl is classified in this way, the South Carolina Supreme Court held that certain provisions of the federal Indian Child Welfare Act of 1978 required her to be taken, at the age of 27 months, from the only parents she had ever known and handed over to her biological father, who had attempted to relinquish his parental rights and who had no prior contact with the child. The provisions of the federal statute at issue here do not demand this result. . . .

I . . .

Three provisions of the ICWA are especially relevant to this case. *First*, "[a]ny party seeking" an involuntary termination of parental rights to an Indian child under state law must demonstrate that "active efforts have been made to provide remedial services and rehabilitative programs designed to prevent the breakup of the Indian family and that these efforts have proved unsuccessful." 25 U.S.C. § 1912(d). *Second*, a state court may not involuntarily terminate parental rights to an Indian child "in the absence of a determination, supported by evidence beyond a reasonable doubt, including testimony of qualified expert witnesses, that the continued custody of the child by the parent or Indian custodian is likely to result in serious emotional or physical damage to the child." § 1912(f). *Third*, with respect to adoptive placements for an Indian child under state law, "a preference shall be

---

63. 112 Cal. Rptr. 2d 692, 727–30 (Cal. Ct. App. 2001).

given, in the absence of good cause to the contrary, to a placement with (1) a member of the child's extended family; (2) other members of the Indian child's tribe; or (3) other Indian families." § 1915(a).

II

In this case, Birth Mother (who is predominantly Hispanic) and Biological Father (who is a member of the Cherokee Nation) became engaged in December 2008. One month later, Birth Mother informed Biological Father, who lived about four hours away, that she was pregnant. After learning of the pregnancy, Biological Father asked Birth Mother to move up the date of the wedding. He also refused to provide any financial support until after the two had married. The couple's relationship deteriorated, and Birth Mother broke off the engagement in May 2009. In June, Birth Mother sent Biological Father a text message asking if he would rather pay child support or relinquish his parental rights. Biological Father responded via text message that he relinquished his rights.

Birth Mother then decided to put Baby Girl up for adoption. Because Birth Mother believed that Biological Father had Cherokee Indian heritage, her attorney contacted the Cherokee Nation to determine whether Biological Father was formally enrolled. The inquiry letter misspelled Biological Father's first name and incorrectly stated his birthday, and the Cherokee Nation responded that, based on the information provided, it could not verify Biological Father's membership in the tribal records.

Working through a private adoption agency, Birth Mother selected Adoptive Couple, non-Indians living in South Carolina, to adopt Baby Girl. Adoptive Couple supported Birth Mother both emotionally and financially throughout her pregnancy. Adoptive Couple was present at Baby Girl's birth in Oklahoma on September 15, 2009, and Adoptive Father even cut the umbilical cord. The next morning, Birth Mother signed forms relinquishing her parental rights and consenting to the adoption. Adoptive Couple initiated adoption proceedings in South Carolina a few days later, and returned there with Baby Girl. After returning to South Carolina, Adoptive Couple allowed Birth Mother to visit and communicate with Baby Girl.

It is undisputed that, for the duration of the pregnancy and the first four months after Baby Girl's birth, Biological Father provided no financial assistance to Birth Mother or Baby Girl, even though he had the ability to do so. Indeed, Biological Father "made no meaningful attempts to assume his responsibility of parenthood" during this period.

Approximately four months after Baby Girl's birth, Adoptive Couple served Biological Father with notice of the pending adoption. (This was the first notification that they had provided to Biological Father regarding the adoption proceeding.) Biological Father signed papers stating that he accepted service and that he was "not contesting the adoption." But Biological Father later testified that, at the time he signed the papers, he thought that he was relinquishing his rights to Birth Mother, not to Adoptive Couple.

Biological Father contacted a lawyer the day after signing the papers, and subsequently requested a stay of the adoption proceedings. In the adoption proceedings, Biological Father sought custody and stated that he did not consent to Baby Girl's adoption. Moreover, Biological Father took a paternity test, which verified that he was Baby Girl's biological father.

A trial took place in the South Carolina Family Court in September 2011, by which time Baby Girl was two years old. The Family Court concluded that Adoptive Couple had not carried the heightened burden under § 1912(f) of proving that Baby Girl would suffer serious emotional or physical damage if Biological Father had custody. The Family Court therefore denied Adoptive Couple's petition for adoption and awarded custody to Biological Father. On December 31, 2011, at the age of 27 months, Baby Girl was handed over to Biological Father, whom she had never met.

The South Carolina Supreme Court affirmed the Family Court's denial of the adoption and the award of custody to Biological Father. The State Supreme Court first determined that the ICWA applied because the case involved a child custody proceeding relating to an Indian child. It also concluded that Biological Father fell within the ICWA's definition of a "'parent.'" The court then held that two separate provisions of the ICWA barred the termination of Biological Father's parental rights. *First,* the court held that Adoptive Couple had not shown that "active efforts ha[d] been made to provide remedial services and rehabilitative programs designed to prevent the breakup of the Indian family." *Second,* the court concluded that Adoptive Couple had not shown that Biological Father's "custody of Baby Girl would result in serious emotional or physical harm to her beyond a reasonable doubt." Finally, the court stated that, even if it had decided to terminate Biological Father's parental rights, § 1915(a)'s adoption-placement preferences would have applied. We granted certiorari.

III

It is undisputed that, had Baby Girl not been 3/256 Cherokee, Biological Father would have had no right to object to her adoption under South Carolina law. The South Carolina Supreme Court held, however, that Biological Father is a "parent" under the ICWA and that two statutory provisions—namely, § 1912(f) and § 1912(d)—bar the termination of his parental rights. In this Court, Adoptive Couple contends that Biological Father is not a "parent" and that § 1912(f) and § 1912(d) are inapplicable. We need not—and therefore do not—decide whether Biological Father is a "parent." Rather, assuming for the sake of argument that he is a "parent," we hold that neither § 1912(f) nor § 1912(d) bars the termination of his parental rights.

A

Section 1912(f) addresses the involuntary termination of parental rights with respect to an Indian child. Specifically, § 1912(f) provides that "[n]o termination of parental rights may be ordered in such proceeding in the absence of a determination, supported by evidence beyond a reasonable doubt, . . . that the *continued custody* of the child by the parent or Indian custodian is likely to result in serious emotional or physical damage to the child." . . .

Section 1912(f) conditions the involuntary termination of parental rights on a showing regarding the merits of "*continued* custody of the child by the parent." The adjective "continued" plainly refers to a pre-existing state. . . . The phrase "continued custody" therefore refers to custody that a parent already has (or at least had at some point in the past). As a result, § 1912(f) does not apply in cases where the Indian parent *never* had custody of the Indian child. . . .

Our reading of § 1912(f) comports with the statutory text demonstrating that the primary mischief the ICWA was designed to counteract was the unwarranted *removal* of Indian children from Indian families due to the cultural insensitivity and biases of social workers and state courts. . . . [W]hen, as here, the adoption of an Indian child is voluntarily and lawfully initiated by a non-Indian parent with sole custodial rights, the ICWA's primary goal of preventing the unwarranted removal of Indian children and the dissolution of Indian families is not implicated. . . .

B

Section 1912(d) provides that "[a]ny party" seeking to terminate parental rights to an Indian child under state law "shall satisfy the court that active efforts have been made to provide remedial services and rehabilitative programs designed *to prevent the breakup of the Indian family* and that these efforts have proved unsuccessful." . . .

Consistent with the statutory text, we hold that § 1912(d) applies only in cases where an Indian family's "breakup" would be precipitated by the termination of the parent's rights. The term "breakup" refers in this context to "[t]he discontinuance of a relationship," American Heritage Dictionary 235 (3d ed. 1992). . . . But when an Indian parent abandons an Indian child prior to birth and that child has never been in the Indian parent's legal or physical custody, there is no "relationship" that would be "discontinu[ed]" . . . by the termination of the Indian parent's rights. In such a situation, the "breakup of the Indian family" has long since occurred, and § 1912(d) is inapplicable.

Our interpretation of § 1912(d) is, like our interpretation of § 1912(f), consistent with the explicit congressional purpose of providing certain "standards for the *removal* of Indian children from their families." . . .

IV

In the decision below, the South Carolina Supreme Court suggested that if it had terminated Biological Father's rights, then § 1915(a)'s preferences for the adoptive placement of an Indian child would have been applicable. In so doing, however, the court failed to recognize a critical limitation on the scope of § 1915(a).

Section 1915(a) provides that "[i]n any adoptive placement of an Indian child under State law, a preference shall be given, in the absence of good cause to the contrary, to a placement with (1) a member of the child's extended family; (2) other members of the Indian child's tribe; or (3) other Indian families." Contrary to the South Carolina Supreme Court's suggestion, § 1915(a)'s preferences are inapplicable in cases where no alternative party has formally sought to adopt the child. This is because there simply is no "preference" to apply if no alternative party that is eligible to be preferred under § 1915(a) has come forward.

In this case, Adoptive Couple was the only party that sought to adopt Baby Girl in the Family Court or the South Carolina Supreme Court. Biological Father is not covered by § 1915(a) because he did not seek to *adopt* Baby Girl; instead, he argued that his parental rights should not be terminated in the first place. Moreover, Baby Girl's paternal grandparents never sought custody of Baby Girl. Nor did other members of the Cherokee Nation or "other Indian families" seek to adopt Baby Girl, even though the Cherokee Nation had notice of — and intervened in — the adoption proceedings.

The Indian Child Welfare Act was enacted to help preserve the cultural identity and heritage of Indian tribes, but under the State Supreme Court's reading, the Act would put certain vulnerable children at a great disadvantage solely because an ancestor — even a remote one — was an Indian. As the State Supreme Court read §§ 1912(d) and (f), a biological Indian father could abandon his child *in utero* and refuse any support for the birth mother — perhaps contributing to the mother's decision to put the child up for adoption — and then could play his ICWA trump card at the eleventh hour to override the mother's decision and the child's best interests. If this were possible, many prospective adoptive parents would surely pause before adopting any child who might possibly qualify as an Indian under the ICWA. Such an interpretation would raise equal protection concerns, but the plain text of §§ 1912(f) and (d) makes clear that neither provision applies in the present context. Nor do § 1915(a)'s rebuttable adoption preferences apply when no alternative party has formally sought to adopt the child. We therefore reverse the judgment of the South Carolina Supreme Court and remand the case for further proceedings not inconsistent with this opinion.

JUSTICE SCALIA, dissenting. . . .

The Court's opinion, it seems to me, needlessly demeans the rights of parenthood. It has been the constant practice of the common law to respect the entitlement of those who bring a child into the world to raise that child. We do not inquire whether leaving a child with his parents is "in the best interest of the child." It sometimes is not; he would be better off raised by someone else. But parents have their rights, no less than children do. This father wants to raise his daughter, and the statute amply protects his right to do so. There is no reason in law or policy to dilute that protection.

JUSTICE SOTOMAYOR, with whom JUSTICE GINSBURG and JUSTICE KAGAN join, and with whom JUSTICE SCALIA joins in part, dissenting.

A casual reader of the Court's opinion could be forgiven for thinking this an easy case, one in which the text of the applicable statute clearly points the way to the only sensible result. In truth, however, the path from the text of the Indian Child Welfare Act of 1978 (ICWA) to the result the Court reaches is anything but clear, and its result anything but right. . . .

I

Beginning its reading with the last clause of § 1912(f), the majority concludes that a single phrase appearing there — "continued custody" — means that the entirety of the subsection is inapplicable to any parent, however committed, who has not previously had physical or legal custody of his child. Working back to front, the majority then concludes that § 1912(d), tainted by its association with § 1912(f), is also inapplicable; in the majority's view, a family bond that does not take custodial form is not a family bond worth preserving from "breakup." . . .

A . . .

ICWA commences with express findings. Congress recognized that "there is no resource that is more vital to the continued existence and integrity of Indian tribes than their children," 25 U.S.C. §1901(3), and it found that this resource was threatened. State authorities insufficiently sensitive to "the essential tribal relations of Indian people and the cultural and social standards prevailing in Indian communities and families" were breaking up Indian families and moving Indian children to non-Indian homes and institutions.

Consistent with these findings, Congress declared its purpose "to protect the best interests of Indian children and to promote the stability and security of Indian tribes and families by the establishment of minimum Federal standards" applicable to child custody proceedings involving Indian children. . . .

The majority . . . asserts baldly that "when an Indian parent abandons an Indian child prior to birth and that child has never been in the Indian parent's legal or physical custody, there is no 'relationship' that would be 'discontinu[ed]' . . . by the termination of the Indian parent's rights." Says who? Certainly not the statute. Section 1903 recognizes Birth Father as Baby Girl's "parent," and, in conjunction with ICWA's other provisions, it further establishes that their "parent-child relationship" is protected under federal law. In the face of these broad definitions, the majority has no warrant to substitute its own policy views for Congress' by saying that "no 'relationship'" exists between Birth Father and Baby Girl simply because, based on the hotly contested facts of this case, it views their family bond as insufficiently substantial to deserve protection. . . .

II

The majority's textually strained and illogical reading of the statute might be explicable, if not justified, if there were reason to believe that it avoided anomalous results or furthered a clear congressional policy. But neither of these conditions is present here.

A

With respect to §1912(d), the majority states that it would be "unusual" to apply a rehabilitation requirement where a natural parent has never had custody of his child. The majority does not support this bare assertion, and in fact state child welfare authorities can and do provide reunification services for biological fathers who have not previously had custody of their children. . . .

B

On a more general level, the majority intimates that ICWA grants Birth Father an undeserved windfall: in the majority's words, an "ICWA trump card" he can "play . . . at the eleventh hour to override the mother's decision and the child's best interests." The implicit argument is that Congress could not possibly have intended to recognize a parent-child relationship between Birth Father and Baby Girl that would have to be legally terminated (either by valid consent or involuntary termination) before the adoption could proceed.

But this supposed anomaly is illusory. In fact, the law of at least 15 States did precisely that at the time ICWA was passed. And the law of a number of States still does so. . . .

Without doubt, laws protecting biological fathers' parental rights can lead — even outside the context of ICWA — to outcomes that are painful and distressing for both would-be adoptive families, who lose a much wanted child, and children who must make a difficult transition. On the other hand, these rules recognize that biological fathers have a valid interest in a relationship with their child. And children have a reciprocal interest in knowing their biological parents. These rules also reflect the understanding that the biological bond between a parent and a child is a strong foundation on which a stable and caring relationship may be built. Many jurisdictions apply a custodial preference for a fit natural parent over a party lacking this biological link. . . .

Balancing the legitimate interests of unwed biological fathers against the need for stability in a child's family situation is difficult, to be sure, and States have, over the years, taken different approaches to the problem. Some States, like South Carolina, have opted to hew to the constitutional baseline established by this Court's precedents and do not require a biological father's consent to adoption unless he has provided financial support during pregnancy. Other States, however, have decided to give the rights of biological fathers more robust protection and to afford them consent rights on the basis of their biological link to the child. . . .

ICWA, on a straightforward reading of the statute, is consistent with the law of those States that protected, and protect, birth fathers' rights more vigorously. This reading can hardly be said to generate an anomaly. ICWA, as all acknowledge, was "the product of rising concern . . . [about] abusive child welfare practices that resulted in the separation of large numbers of Indian children from their families." It stands to reason that the Act would not render the legal status of an Indian father's relationship with his biological child fragile, but would instead grant it a degree of protection commensurate with the more robust state-law standards. . . .

C

The majority also protests that a contrary result to the one it reaches would interfere with the adoption of Indian children. This claim is the most perplexing of all. A central purpose of ICWA is to "promote the stability and security of Indian . . . families," 25 U.S.C. §1902, in part by countering the trend of placing "an alarmingly high percentage of [Indian] children . . . in non-Indian foster and adoptive homes and institutions." §1901(4). The Act accomplishes this goal by, first, protecting the familial bonds of Indian parents and children; and, second, establishing placement preferences should an adoption take place, see §1915(a). ICWA does not interfere with the adoption of Indian children except to the extent that it attempts to avert the necessity of adoptive placement and makes adoptions of Indian children by non-Indian families less likely.

The majority may consider this scheme unwise. But no principle of construction licenses a court to interpret a statute with a view to averting the very consequences Congress expressly stated it was trying to bring about. Instead, it is the "'judicial duty to give faithful meaning to the language Congress adopted in the light of the evident legislative purpose in enacting the law in question.'"

The majority further claims that its reading is consistent with the "primary" purpose of the Act, which in the majority's view was to prevent the dissolution of "intact" Indian families. We may not, however, give effect only to congressional goals we designate "primary" while casting aside others classed as "secondary"; we must apply the entire statute Congress has written. While there are indications that central among Congress' concerns in enacting ICWA was the removal of Indian children from homes in which Indian parents or other guardians had custody of them, Congress also recognized that "there is no resource that is more vital to the continued existence and integrity of Indian tribes than their children," §1901(3). A tribe's interest in its next generation of citizens is adversely affected by the placement of Indian children in homes with no connection to the tribe, whether or not those children were initially in the custody of an Indian parent.

Moreover, the majority's focus on "intact" families, begs the question of what Congress set out to accomplish with ICWA. In an ideal world, perhaps all parents would be perfect. They would live up to their parental responsibilities by providing the fullest possible financial and emotional support to their children. They would never suffer mental health problems, lose their jobs, struggle with substance dependency, or encounter any of the other multitudinous personal crises that can make it difficult to meet these responsibilities. In an ideal world parents would never become estranged and leave their children caught in the middle. But we do not live in such a world. Even happy families do not always fit the custodial-parent mold for which the majority would reserve IWCA's substantive protections; unhappy families all too often do not. They are families nonetheless. Congress understood as much. ICWA's definitions of "parent" and "termination of parental rights" provided in §1903 sweep broadly. They should be honored. . . .

* * *

The majority opinion turns § 1912 upside down, reading it from bottom to top in order to reach a conclusion that is manifestly contrary to Congress' express purpose in enacting ICWA: preserving the familial bonds between Indian parents and their children and, more broadly, Indian tribes' relationships with the future citizens who are "vital to [their] continued existence and integrity." § 1901(3).

The majority casts Birth Father as responsible for the painful circumstances in this case, suggesting that he intervened "at the eleventh hour to override the mother's decision and the child's best interests." I have no wish to minimize the trauma of removing a 27-month-old child from her adoptive family. It bears remembering, however, that Birth Father took action to assert his parental rights when Baby Girl was four months old, as soon as he learned of the impending adoption. . . .

Baby Girl has now resided with her father for 18 months. However difficult it must have been for her to leave Adoptive Couple's home when she was just over 2 years old, it will be equally devastating now if, at the age of 3½, she is again removed from her home and sent to live halfway across the country. Such a fate is not foreordained, of course. But it can be said with certainty that the anguish this case has caused will only be compounded by today's decision. . . .

NOTES AND QUESTIONS

1. *A Racial Classification?* The *Baby Girl* Court did not explicitly address the question of whether ICWA constitutes a racial or political classification. But the issue surfaced more obliquely. The majority began its opinion by observing: "This case is about a little girl (Baby Girl) who is classified as an Indian because she is 1.2% (3/256) Cherokee." Although the Court did not invoke equal protection analysis, it repeatedly mentioned the classification of the child as 1.2% Cherokee, as if to emphasize the

irrationality of applying the statute in that circumstance. The Court noted, for example, that "under the State Supreme Court's reading, the Act would put certain vulnerable children at a great disadvantage solely because an ancestor — even a remote one — was an Indian." Justice Sotomayor, in dissent, took issue with "[t]he majority's repeated, analytically unnecessary references to the fact that Baby Girl is 3/256 Cherokee by ancestry [which] do nothing to elucidate its intimation that the statute may violate the Equal Protection Clause as applied here."

In the *Baby Girl* case, the guardian ad litem for the child had asserted that treating her as an Indian child would amount to a racial classification, arguing:

> The key to whether legislation involving Indians triggers the relaxed review of *Mancari*, or the exacting scrutiny traditionally demanded of classifications based on race, is whether the challenged legislation "relates to Indian land, tribal status, self-government or culture." . . . [W]hen tribal preferences are untethered from tribal land or tribal self-government and simply provide a naked preference based on race, strict scrutiny is imperative. . . . Conferring special privileges on the biological father — or more to the point, special disabilities on a child — simply because of race serves no purpose relating to "Indian self-government[.]"[64]

The Court did not address the issue raised by the guardian ad litem.

In 2018, in Brackeen v. Zinke, a federal district court, for the first time, struck down ICWA as unconstitutional.[65] The court concluded that "ICWA relies on racial classifications" and that the statute's "blanket classification of Indian children is not narrowly tailored to a compelling governmental interest and thus fails to survive strict scrutiny review."[66]

2. *Anti-Commandeering.* The *Brackeen* court struck down ICWA not only on equal protection grounds but also on anti-commandeering grounds.[67] The Supreme Court has held that, under the Tenth Amendment, Congress may not "commandee[r] the legislative processes of the States by directly compelling them to enact and enforce a federal regulatory program."[68] Does ICWA require state legislatures to enact and enforce a federal regulatory program? What if it only requires state agencies to act? Or only state courts? The *Brackeen* court took issue with ICWA's requirement that state courts enact a federal placement preference scheme in adoption, pre-adoption, and foster care proceedings involving Indian children. In addition, the court objected to ICWA's requirement that state agencies abide by the law's provisions (e.g., verifying a child's

---

64. Brief for Respondent Guardian Ad Litem at 11–12, Baby Girl v. Adoptive Couple, 570 U.S. 637 (2013) (No. 12–399).

65. 338 F. Supp. 3d 514 (N.D. Tex. 2018), rev'd sub nom. Brackeen v. Bernhardt, 937 F.3d 406 (5th Cir. 2020).

66. Id. at 536.

67. Id. at 540.

68. New York v. United States, 505 U.S. 144 (1992); see also Printz v. United States, 521 U.S. 898 (1997).

tribal status before proceeding with an adoptive or foster care placement). On appeal, a three-judge panel of the Fifth Circuit reversed, upholding ICWA's constitutionality.[69] But in partial dissent, Judge Owen maintained that ICWA unconstitutionally violates the anti-commandeering principle.[70] The Fifth Circuit then granted rehearing en banc.[71]

3.   *Parental Rights.* A central issue in *Baby Girl* concerned the legal rights of the unmarried father. As the dissent noted, states vary in the protection they accord an unmarried father who never has fulfilled any of the duties of a parent. In the majority's view, the biological father did not possess rights protected by ICWA and thus was entitled only to the protections furnished by state law. (Under state law, the biological father's consent to the adoption would not have been required.) In the dissent's view, the biological father should have received the greater protections ICWA affords. Which is the more justifiable interpretation of ICWA? Which is the better policy? Justice Scalia suggested that the father's parental rights should be respected even if doing so is not in the best interest of the child. Do you agree?

4.   *Community Interests and Children's Interests.* The majority's approach — in emphasizing that no existing Indian family was disrupted — is consistent with another way that courts have limited the reach of ICWA: the Existing Indian Family Exception. As we saw with the *Santos Y.* decision discussed before the *Baby Girl* excerpt, some courts use this judicially created doctrine to justify not applying ICWA to parents and children who do not have cultural links to a tribe. Is it appropriate for judges to create this exception to the reach of ICWA? Professor Solangel Maldonado argues against the exception, asserting that:

> [T]he exception undermines the law's explicit purpose of keeping Indian children in Indian communities[,] . . . infringe[s] on tribes' exclusive authority to decide who has satisfied the requirements for tribal membership[,] . . . [and] perpetuates stereotypes about who is authentically Indian.[72]

The dissent in *Baby Girl* gave great weight to the goal of keeping Indian children with Indian parents, while the majority was disinclined to create rules that would discourage families from adopting Indian children. Which interpretation of ICWA is more justifiable? Which would you embrace? Does the effort to keep children within the Indian community further the interests of those individual children? Or does it conscript them into service of the tribe? Consider this view from Terry Cross, the executive director of the National Indian Children Welfare Association:

> The long term benefits of keeping Indian families together are well-documented. Security, pride in heritage, and connection to many caring

---

69. See Brackeen v. Bernhardt, 937 F.3d 406 (5th Cir. 2019).
70. See id. at 441 (Owen, J., concurring in part and dissenting in part).
71. Brackeen v. Bernhardt, 942 F.3d 287 (5th Cir. 2019).
72. Solangel Maldonado, Op-Ed., The Problem with Allowing the Courts to Decide Who Is Indian, N.Y. Times (Jan. 24, 2013).

adults within the tribe are just some of the protective cultural factors demonstrated to keep Indian youth from at-risk behavior. As these children grow into adults, they become strong parents and are more likely to be healthy members of a tribal community. Such outcomes are not shared by many raised outside of their culture and communities.[73]

NOTE ON INTERNATIONAL ADOPTION

Two international adoption treaties establish the rights of children eligible for adoption and set standards for governments to follow to protect these rights. As we explored in Chapter 6, the Convention on the Rights of the Child was adopted by the United Nations in 1989 and has been ratified by almost 200 countries.[74] The United States is the only signatory that has failed to ratify the Convention.[75] The Convention recognizes the right to "identity" and creates obligations for the government to protect a child's cultural background, mandating that "when considering [placement] solutions, due regard shall be paid to the desirability of continuity in a child's upbringing and to the child's ethnic, religious, cultural and linguistic background."[76]

The second major international adoption treaty is the Hague Convention on Protection of Children and Co-operation in Respect of Intercountry Adoption.[77] Adopted in 1993, the treaty has been ratified by more than 100 countries, including the United States.[78] The Hague Convention is intended to protect the rights of children, birth parents, and adoptive parents through the regulation of international adoptions.[79] It acknowledges the importance of a child's identity, requiring a child's birth country to "give due consideration to the child's upbringing and to his or her ethnic, religious and cultural background" and "determine, on the basis in particular of the reports relating to the child and the prospective adoptive parents, whether the envisaged placement is in the best interest of the child."[80]

---

73. Terry Cross, Op-Ed., The Indian Child Welfare Act Provides Necessary Protection, N.Y. Times (Jan. 24, 2013).

74. United Nations Convention on the Rights of the Child (adopted Nov. 20, 1989 and effective Sept. 2, 1990).

75. Status of Ratification Interactive Dashboard, United Nations Human Rights Office of the High Commissioner (May 21, 2020).

76. U.N. Convention on the Rights of the Child, supra note 74, at art. 8, 20.

77. Hague Conference on Private Int'l Law, Convention on the Protection of Children and Co-operation in Respect of Intercountry Adoption (May 29, 1993).

78. Status Table, Hague Conference on Private International Law, Convention of 29 May 1993 on Protection of Children and Co-operation in Respect of Intercountry Adoption (Dec. 19, 2019).

79. Convention on Protection of Children and Co-operation in Respect of Intercountry Adoption, supra note 77, at art. 1.

80. Id. at art. 16.

In order to bring the United States into compliance with the Hague Convention standards, Congress enacted the Intercountry Adoption Act of 2000.[81] Regulations issued by the State Department, as the designated authority for international adoptions, require that prospective adoptive parents receive ten hours of pre-adoption training on the long-term implications of cross-cultural adoptions, as well as counseling from service providers about their child's cultural, racial, religious, and linguistic background.[82] As we mentioned at the outset of this chapter, the number of international adoptions has fallen dramatically in recent years.[83]

---

81. Intercountry Adoption Act, 42 U.S.C. §§ 14901-54 (2018).

82. 22 C.F.R. § 96.48 (2020).

83. See Jones & Placek, supra note 20.

CHAPTER 9

Who Is a Parent?

Parenthood is often regarded as a biological fact—a reality that preexists legal determinations, political judgments, and even social consensus. But in reality, parenthood does not precede law and politics; rather, it is a consequence of them. Parenthood is an effect of legal rules and political judgments, which in turn are shaped by prevailing social practices and understandings. This chapter considers how law determines who is a parent of a particular child. In doing so, it examines various pathways to parentage (the legal determination of who is a parent) and shows how those pathways have changed and grown over time. As we will see, parentage is not always clear and simple; disagreement exists not only about whether a particular person is a parent of a particular child but also about the criteria that give rise to a legal parent-child relationship. What makes someone a parent? Giving birth? Genetics? Marriage? Intent to parent? Parental conduct? These criteria may matter differently in different circumstances. Often, an individual's parental status and the ground on which parentage turns depend on whether there are other candidates for parentage. For example, the government may routinely render biological fathers of nonmarital children legal fathers; but courts may refuse to do so when the biological father is competing for parentage against another man, such as the mother's husband. Accordingly, at times genetics may form a sufficient basis for parentage, and at other times it may not. Before turning to the question of how one becomes a parent, we consider in what circumstances one has control over the decision whether or not to become a parent.

I. Reproductive Autonomy and the Right Not to Be a Parent

For some, reproductive rights primarily implicate a right to bodily autonomy. But reproductive rights also relate to parenthood. The ability to use contraception or to terminate a pregnancy allows an individual to avoid parenthood. We have already seen that parental rights hold a prominent and longstanding place in our constitutional tradition. But what exactly does the right to parent include? Does it entail a right *not* to parent? Does it entail an *affirmative* right to the resources and support necessary to parent?

A. Abortion

ROE v. WADE
410 U.S. 113 (1973)

MR. JUSTICE BLACKMUN delivered the opinion of the Court. . . .

Three reasons have been advanced to explain historically the enactment of criminal abortion laws in the 19th century and to justify their continued existence.

It has been argued occasionally that these laws were the product of a Victorian social concern to discourage illicit sexual conduct. Texas, however, does not advance this justification in the present case, and it appears that no court or commentator has taken the argument seriously. . . .

A second reason is concerned with abortion as a medical procedure. When most criminal abortion laws were first enacted, the procedure was a hazardous one for the woman. This was particularly true prior to the development of antisepsis. . . . Abortion mortality was high. Even after 1900, and perhaps until as late as the development of antibiotics in the 1940's, standard modern techniques such as dilation and curettage were not nearly so safe as they are today. Thus, it has been argued that a State's real concern in enacting a criminal abortion law was to protect the pregnant woman, that is, to restrain her from submitting to a procedure that placed her life in serious jeopardy.

Modern medical techniques have altered this situation. . . . Of course, important state interests in the areas of health and medical standards do remain. The State has a legitimate interest in seeing to it that abortion, like any other medical procedure, is performed under circumstances that insure maximum safety for the patient. . . . Thus, the State retains a definite interest in protecting the woman's own health and safety when an abortion is proposed at a late stage of pregnancy,

The third reason is the State's interest — some phrase it in terms of duty — in protecting prenatal life. Some of the argument for this justification rests on the theory that a new human life is present from the moment of conception. . . . In assessing the State's interest, recognition may be given to the less rigid claim that as long as at least *potential* life is involved, the State may assert interests beyond the protection of the pregnant woman alone. . . .

The Constitution does not explicitly mention any right of privacy. In a line of decisions, however, . . . the Court has recognized that a right of personal privacy, or a guarantee of certain areas or zones of privacy, does exist under the Constitution. . . . These decisions make it clear that only personal rights that can be deemed "fundamental" or "implicit in the concept of ordered liberty," are included in this guarantee of personal privacy. They also make it clear that the right has some extension to activities relating to marriage; procreation; contraception; family relationships; and child rearing and education.

This right of privacy . . . is broad enough to encompass a woman's decision whether or not to terminate her pregnancy. The detriment that the State would impose upon the pregnant woman by denying this choice altogether is apparent. Specific and direct harm medically diagnosable even in early pregnancy may be involved. Maternity, or additional offspring, may force upon the woman a distressful life and future. Psychological harm may be imminent. Mental and physical health may be taxed by child care. There is also the distress, for all concerned, associated with the unwanted child, and there is the problem of bringing a child into a family already unable, psychologically and otherwise, to care for it. In other cases, as in this one, the additional difficulties and continuing stigma of unwed motherhood may be involved. All these are factors the woman and her responsible physician necessarily will consider in consultation. . . .

The Court's decisions recognizing a right of privacy also acknowledge that some state regulation in areas protected by that right is appropriate. . . .

With respect to the State's important and legitimate interest in potential life, the "compelling" point is at viability. This is so because the fetus then presumably has the capability of meaningful life outside the mother's womb. State regulation protective of fetal life after viability thus has both logical and biological justifications. If the State is interested in protecting fetal life after viability, it may go so far as to proscribe abortion during that period, except when it is necessary to preserve the life or health of the mother.

NOTES AND QUESTIONS

1. *Planned Parenthood of Southeastern Pennsylvania v. Casey.* In its 1992 decision in *Casey*, which is excerpted in Chapter 3, the Court affirmed "the essential holding of *Roe v. Wade*."[1] Yet, in a joint opinion by Justices O'Connor, Kennedy, and Souter, the Court articulated a new standard — the "undue burden" standard — by which to judge restrictions on abortion:

> Only where state regulation imposes an undue burden on a woman's ability to make this decision does the power of the State reach into the heart of the liberty protected by the Due Process Clause. . . .

---

1. 505 U.S. 833, 846 (1992).

The very notion that the State has a substantial interest in potential life leads to the conclusion that not all regulations must be deemed unwarranted. Not all burdens on the right to decide whether to terminate a pregnancy will be undue. In our view, the undue burden standard is the appropriate means of reconciling the State's interest with the woman's constitutionally protected liberty. . . .

A finding of an undue burden is a shorthand for the conclusion that a state regulation has the purpose or effect of placing a substantial obstacle in the path of a woman seeking an abortion of a nonviable fetus. A statute with this purpose is invalid because the means chosen by the State to further the interest in potential life must be calculated to inform the woman's free choice, not hinder it. And a statute which, while furthering the interest in potential life or some other valid state interest, has the effect of placing a substantial obstacle in the path of a woman's choice cannot be considered a permissible means of serving its legitimate ends.[2]

As you saw in Chapter 3, the Court struck down the spousal notification statute that Pennsylvania had enacted by concluding that it constituted an "undue burden" on a woman's right to abortion. Still, the Court upheld other provisions that the state had enacted, including a 24-hour waiting period (except in cases of medical emergency) and a parental consent law (that included a judicial bypass mechanism).

2.   *More Recent Developments.* In a 5-to-4 decision in 2007, the Supreme Court ruled that a federal law, known as the Partial-Birth Abortion Ban Act of 2003, did not place an undue burden on a woman's right to terminate a pregnancy.[3] The law prohibited one of the primary methods used to terminate a pregnancy in the second trimester, which is known as "intact dilation and evacuation." The Court reasoned that a woman might come to regret her choice to terminate because of the method used. Does the state have an interest in ensuring adults carefully consider whether to avoid parenthood through this or other means?

In 2016, in Whole Woman's Health v. Hellerstedt, the Supreme Court struck down restrictions that Texas had enacted in 2013.[4] Like other states, Texas adopted so-called TRAP laws (targeted regulation of abortion providers) that would make it difficult for providers to stay in operation. The state required doctors who performed abortions to hold admitting privileges at nearby hospitals and required clinics that provided abortion services to meet the standards mandated for ambulatory surgical centers. Texas justified the laws not on grounds of protecting fetal life but rather on the basis of protecting women's health. In a 5-to-3 ruling, the Court struck down the law's two requirements, concluding: "[N]either of these provisions confers medical benefits sufficient to justify the burdens upon access that each imposes.

---

2. Id. at 874, 874–77.

3. Gonzales v. Carhart, 550 U.S. 124 (2007); see generally Mary Ziegler, After *Roe*: The Lost History of the Abortion Debate (2015).

4. 136 S. Ct. 2292 (2016).

Each places a substantial obstacle in the path of women seeking a previability abortion, each constitutes an undue burden on abortion access, and each violates the Federal Constitution."[5] The facts on the ground made it difficult to see how the law was intended to protect women's health, as opposed to simply restrict access to abortion. As the Court observed, "before the act's passage, abortion in Texas was extremely safe with particularly low rates of serious complications and virtually no deaths occurring on account of the procedure."[6] The law reduced the number of abortion providers in the state: "[T]he admitting-privileges requirement led to the closure of half of Texas' clinics, or thereabouts," and the surgical-center requirement "would further reduce the number of abortion facilities available to seven or eight facilities" from a total of about forty.[7] Moreover, Texas did not regulate other medical procedures, including those much more likely to lead to complications or death, in the way it regulated abortion. Why are these facts relevant? The Court concluded that "[t]hese facts indicate that the surgical-center provision imposes a requirement that simply is not based on differences between abortion and other surgical procedures that are reasonably related to preserving women's health, the asserted purpose of the Act in which it is found."[8]

In 2020, the Court struck down a Louisiana admitting-privileges law nearly identical to the one at issue in *Whole Woman's Health*. Justice Breyer announced the Court's judgment in June Medical Services L.L.C. v. Russo and issued a plurality opinion upholding the district court's conclusion that the law "poses a 'substantial obstacle' to women seeking an abortion; . . . offers no significant health-related benefits; and . . . consequently imposes an 'undue burden' on a woman's constitutional right to choose to have an abortion."[9] In a concurring opinion, Chief Justice Roberts rested on *stare decisis* grounds, reasoning that, because "[t]he Louisiana law imposes a burden on access to abortion just as severe as that imposed by the Texas law, . . . Louisiana's law cannot stand under our precedents."[10]

3. *The Future of the Abortion Right.* Given that the Supreme Court has become more conservative in recent years, many believe the constitutional right to abortion is under deep threat. Notwithstanding the decision in *June Medical Services*, some predict the Court will tolerate greater restrictions on abortion, while not expressly overturning *Roe*. Others believe the Court will rule that the Constitution does not protect a woman's right to abortion. A number of recent state laws starkly pose the question of whether the Constitution protects a right to abortion — including

---

5. Id. at 2300.
6. Id. at 2302.
7. Id. at 2313, 2316.
8. Id. at 2315.
9. June Medical Services, LLC v. Russo, 591 U.S. ___ (2020) (slip op. at 38).
10. Id. (Roberts, C.J., concurring) (slip op. at 2).

outright bans on abortion within the first weeks of pregnancy.[11] What would happen if the Court were to overturn *Roe*? How might states respond? Already, a number of states provide stronger protection for abortion rights under state law.[12] Yet many states have sought to dramatically limit access to abortion.[13]

4. *Abortion Restrictions, Race, and Class.* Do abortion restrictions affect women equally? As more abortion providers have closed in the face of TRAP laws, the cost of traveling (including missing work) to obtain an abortion has significantly limited access for low-income women.[14] This impact is particularly felt by women living in rural areas and in the South where abortion providers are concentrated in urban areas.[15] Abortion restrictions also have a disparate racial impact. For example, given that women of color are disproportionately likely to have public health insurance, restrictions on government funding for abortion services disproportionately burden women of color.[16]

5. *Conceptualizing the Abortion Right.* The abortion right is often conceptualized as a right to bodily autonomy. A pregnant woman has what the *Casey* Court described as "the ultimate control over her destiny and her body."[17] Is this the way you think about the right to abortion? Are there alternative ways that the Court conceptualizes the right at stake? In *Roe*, the Court discussed the woman's interest in avoiding "[m]aternity, or additional offspring." Is that a cognizable interest protected by a right to abortion? The pregnant woman can decide to place the child for adoption. Does that mitigate the harm that the Court identifies? Or is there nonetheless an interest in avoiding having a child even if one does not parent that child? The Court also credited the state's interest in potential life. Yet in the same passage where the *Roe* Court discussed avoiding maternity, it also talked about "the unwanted child." Which way do children's interests point in considering a right to abortion?

6. *Abortion and Equality.* Restrictions on abortion clearly regulate women more than men. Should the right to abortion be understood more as an equality

---

11. In 2019 alone, twenty-five new abortion bans were signed into law. See, e.g., H.B. 314, 31st Leg., 1st Reg. Sess. (Ala. 2019) (enacting a total ban on abortion at any point in pregnancy, exempting only medical emergencies); H.B. 126, 100th Gen. Assemb., 1st Reg. Sess. (Mo. 2019) (banning abortions at eight weeks of pregnancy, exempting only medical emergencies).

12. This has occurred through state constitutional interpretation as well as legislative measures. See, e.g., Planned Parenthood of Middle Tenn. v. Sundquist, 38 S.W.3d 1 (Tenn. 2000) (mandatory waiting period requirement failed to meet strict scrutiny required under privacy protections of the Tennessee constitution); Joanna L. Grossman, On the Anniversary of Roe v. Wade, New York Moves to Shore Up Reproductive Rights, Justia's Verdict (Jan. 29, 2019).

13. See Susan Milligan, A Guide to Abortion Laws by State, U.S. News (June 27, 2019).

14. See Jonathan Bearak et al., Disparities and Change Over Time in Distance Women Would Need to Travel to Have an Abortion in the USA: A Spatial Analysis, 2 Lancet Pub. Health 493 (2017).

15. Id.

16. See Megan K. Donovan, Guttmacher Inst., In Real Life: Federal Restrictions on Abortion Coverage and the Women They Impact (Jan. 5, 2017); see also Harris v. McRae, 448 U.S. 297, 322 (1980) (rejecting constitutional challenge to the Hyde Amendment, which withdrew federal funding even for "medically necessary abortions").

17. 505 U.S. at 869.

right than a privacy or liberty right? Even though it did not rule on equal protection grounds, the *Casey* Court related reliance on the abortion right to women's status:

> [F]or two decades . . . , people have organized intimate relationships and made choices that define their views of themselves and their places in society, in reliance on the availability of abortion in the event that contraception should fail. The ability of women to participate equally in the economic and social life of the Nation has been facilitated by their ability to control their reproductive lives. The Constitution serves human values, and while the effect of reliance on *Roe* cannot be exactly measured, neither can the certain cost of overruling *Roe* for people who have ordered their thinking and living around that case be dismissed.[18]

Do restrictions on abortion reflect judgments about the proper role of women in society? Professor Reva Siegel argues that abortion regulation — historically and in contemporary society — draws on and perpetuates views about women's destiny as mothers and reflects beliefs that women's proper domain is the family.

> [L]egislators may view abortion as repellant because it betrays a lack of maternal solicitude in women, or otherwise violates expectations of appropriately nurturing female conduct. If legislators assume that women are "child-rearers," they will take for granted the work women give to motherhood and ignore what it takes from them, and so will view women's efforts to avoid some two decades of life-consuming work as an act of casual expedience or unseemly egoism. Thus, they will condemn women for seeking abortion "on demand," or as a mere "convenience," judging women to be unnaturally egocentric because they do not give their lives over to the work of bearing and nurturing children — that is, because they fail to act like mothers, like normal women should.[19]

7. *Reproductive Justice.* While reproductive rights traditionally have been understood to encompass contraception and abortion, the field of reproductive justice has attempted to broaden the lens as to both the choices covered and the axes of identity contemplated. As Loretta Ross and Rickie Solinger explain:

> Reproductive justice is . . . a political movement that splices *reproductive rights* with *social justice* to achieve *reproductive justice*. The definition of reproductive justice goes beyond the pro-choice/pro-life debate and has three primary principles: (1) the right *not* to have a child; (2) the right to *have* a child; and (3) the right to *parent* children in safe and healthy environments. In addition, reproductive justice demands sexual autonomy and gender freedom for every human being.

---

18. 505 U.S. at 856.

19. See Reva B. Siegel, Reasoning from the Body: An Historical Perspective on Abortion Regulation and Questions of Equal Protection, 44 Stan. L. Rev. 261, 361–62 (1992).

> At the heart of reproductive justice is this claim: all fertile persons and persons who reproduce and become parents require a safe and dignified context for these most fundamental human experiences. Achieving this goal depends on access to specific, community-based resources including high-quality health care, housing and education, a living wage, a healthy environment, and a safety net for times when these resources fail. Safe and dignified fertility management, childbirth, and parenting are impossible without these resources.[20]

As authors of a recent volume put it: "The framework of 'reproductive justice' highlights the intersecting relations of race, class, sexuality, and sex that shape the regulation of reproduction. It examines the many ways law shapes the choice to have, as well as to avoid having, children."[21] The reproductive justice movement expands the traditional focus on abortion and contraception to include other dimensions of reproductive control such as coercive sterilization, welfare caps, the prosecution of pregnant women, access to prenatal care for incarcerated women, and the treatment of pregnant immigrant women.[22] Would a reproductive justice lens view the abortion right in terms of the right to avoid parenthood? Would it mandate government funding for abortion?

8. *Involuntary Sterilization.* Sterilization is currently the second-most widely used birth control technique, but it has a troubling history in this country due to the involuntary sterilization of poor women, minorities, and those with intellectual disabilities. In a 1927 case permitting such sterilization, Justice Oliver Wendell Holmes infamously declared: "Three generations of imbeciles is enough."[23] The view of the Supreme Court toward compulsory sterilization ultimately changed; the Court held in Skinner v. Oklahoma that the right to procreate is fundamental and protected under the Fourteenth Amendment.[24] Some states continue to authorize sterilization as punishment, however, for certain offenses such as child sexual abuse.[25] Due to a disturbing record of requiring poor and minority women to undergo sterilization as a condition of receiving welfare benefits, the federal and state governments have imposed regulations designed to prevent such coercion. These regulations have made it more difficult for parents or guardians to consent to sterilization of developmentally disabled women, even with evidence that sterilization might enhance the woman's autonomy in other respects. State approaches vary, but one approach allows

---

20. Loretta J. Ross & Rickie Solinger, Reproductive Justice: An Introduction 9 (2017).

21. Melissa Murray et al., Reproductive Rights and Justice Stories 1 (2019).

22. See Lisa C. Ikemoto, Reproductive Rights and Justice: A Multiple Feminist Theories Account, in Research Handbook on Feminist Jurisprudence 249 (Robin West & Cynthia Bowman eds., 2019).

23. Buck v. Bell, 274 U.S. 200, 207 (1927).

24. See Skinner v. Oklahoma, 316 U.S. 535 (1942).

25. See, e.g., Cal. Penal Code § 645 (West 2020) (authorizing hormone suppression treatment for parolees convicted of certain sexual offenses); Wash. Rev. Code § 9.92.100 (2020) (authorizing sterilization for persons convicted of sex with female under age ten).

courts to authorize sterilization if presented with clear and convincing evidence that it is in the best interests of the individual or that the individual would choose it for herself if able.[26] Does that offer sufficient protection for the ward's right to procreate?

9. *Assisted Reproduction.* Does the right to procreation extend to the right to procreation through assisted reproduction? With donor gametes? Through surrogacy? When the Court in Eisenstadt v. Baird struck down a law that prohibited use of contraception by unmarried individuals, it reasoned about the right "to be free from unwarranted governmental intrusion into matters so fundamentally affecting a person as the decision whether to bear or beget a child."[27] Many scholars have argued that such a right reaches the use of assisted reproduction,[28] but courts have yet to elaborate procreative rights that include assisted reproduction.[29]

B. Surrogacy

We explore surrogacy later in this chapter primarily from the perspective of the intended parents. What about the woman who serves as the surrogate? How does surrogacy implicate her reproductive rights? A woman who serves as a surrogate is carrying a child she does not intend to raise. Yet in many states that woman is the presumptive mother of the child. Her name goes on the birth certificate as the parent. To avoid parenthood, she must relinquish her rights to the child and consent to the child's adoption by the intended parent or parents. In most cases, she has signed a contract in advance promising relinquishment, usually in exchange for compensation.

Does this treatment violate her right not to be a parent? In Arizona, a court concluded that the state's ban on commercial surrogacy was unconstitutional to the extent it precluded an intended mother, who was also the child's genetic mother, from being treated as the child's legal mother.[30] A concurring opinion looked at the issue from the perspective of the woman who served as the surrogate for the intended mother:

> I agree with the trial court's reason for holding the statute unconstitutional, namely that it imposes the burden of motherhood on a surrogate mother who almost certainly does not wish it and did not contract for it. Her contract is to carry the child, not to nurture and raise it. The statute thrusts these burdens on her as a duty well beyond her contract.[31]

Do you agree?

---

26. Conn. Gen. Stat. § 45a-699(b) (2020).

27. 405 U.S. 438, 453 (1972).

28. See John A. Robertson, Children of Choice: Freedom and the New Reproductive Technologies (1994); Kimberly M. Mutcherson, Procreative Pluralism, 30 Berkeley J. Gender L. & Just. 22 (2015). But see Radhika Rao, Constitutional Misconceptions, 93 Mich. L. Rev. 1473 (1995).

29. But see Lifchez v. Hartigan, 735 F. Supp. 1361, 1377 (N.D. Ill. 1990).

30. Soos v. Super. Ct., 897 P.2d 1356 (Ariz. Ct. App. 1994).

31. Id. at 1361 (Gerber, J., specially concurring).

Some see reproductive rights cutting the other way. They view surrogacy as a harmful practice that undermines women's reproductive autonomy. In 2019, feminist icon Gloria Steinem opposed a bill to allow commercial surrogacy in New York:

> The danger here is . . . the state legalizing the commercial and profit-driven reproductive surrogacy industry. As has been seen here and in other countries, this harms and endangers women in the process, especially those who feel that they have few or no economic alternatives.
>
> Under this bill, women in economic need become commercialized vessels for rent, and the fetuses they carry become the property of others. The surrogate mother's rights over the fetus she is carrying are greatly curtailed and she loses all rights to the baby she delivers.[32]

Are women exploited by surrogacy arrangements? Is consent meaningful when given under conditions of unequal economic conditions? Consider the California Supreme Court's perspective:

> Although common sense suggests that women of lesser means serve as surrogate mothers more often than do wealthy women, there has been no proof that surrogacy contracts exploit poor women to any greater degree than economic necessity in general exploits them by inducing them to accept lower-paid or otherwise undesirable employment.[33]

Who are the women who serve as surrogates? As one review of the empirical literature concludes:

> The profile of surrogate mothers from the empirical research in the United States and Britain does not support the stereotype of poor, single, young, ethnic minority women whose family, financial difficulties, or other circumstances pressure her into a surrogacy arrangement. Nor does it support the view that surrogate mothers are naively taking on a task unaware of the emotional and physical risks it might entail. Rather, the empirical research establishes that surrogate mothers are mature, experienced, stable, self-aware, and extroverted non-conformists who make the initial decision that surrogacy is something they want to do.[34]

Moreover, "the vast majority of surrogacy arrangements are successfully executed and consented to by women who are financially and psychologically stable."[35] Many women also report significant satisfaction with having served as a surrogate.[36]

---

32. Letter from Gloria Steinem (June 11, 2019), reprinted at http://www.cbc-network.org/2019/06/gloria-steinem-calls-to-not-legalize-commercial-surrogacy/.

33. Johnson v. Calvert, 851 P.2d 776, 785 (Cal. 1993).

34. Karen Busby & Delaney Vun, Revisiting The Handmaid's Tale: Feminist Theory Meets Empirical Research on Surrogate Mothers, 26 Can. J. Fam. L. 13, 51–52 (2010).

35. Lina Peng, Surrogate Mothers: An Exploration of the Empirical and the Normative, 21 Am. U. J. Gender Soc. Pol'y & L. 555, 559–60 (2013).

36. See Hazel Baslington, The Social Organization of Surrogacy: Relinquishing the Baby and the Role of Payment in the Psychological Detachment Process, 7 J. Health Psychol. 57 (2002); Vasanti Jadva et al., Surrogacy: The Experiences of Surrogate Mothers, 18 Hum. Reprod. 2196 (2003).

Steinem's position seems to suggest that a woman serving as a surrogate has a *parental* interest in the child. What is the relationship between surrogacy and motherhood? Other critics of the New York bill focused on this question:

> [C]ommercial surrogacy is baby selling, baby buying, reproductive prostitution, and the commodification of women. It is also matricidal. Surrogacy has now become a way of slicing and dicing biological motherhood into three parts: an egg donor, who undergoes painful and dangerous IVF procedures; a "gestational" mother who faces all the risks of pregnancy and childbirth, and an adoptive mother or father.[37]

Who is the "real" mother? Does the fact of pregnancy mean that a mother-child bond develops? Empirical studies show that women who serve as surrogates report relinquishment of the baby as a happy occasion in which they are giving the intended parents *their* child.[38] Should the woman who serves as a surrogate have the right to parent the child if she wishes? Some feminist critics argue that a surrogate possesses parental rights that can be terminated only with her *post-birth* consent. Surrogacy contracts, therefore, would be unenforceable.[39]

Some feminist objections find common ground with social conservative opposition to surrogacy. As Harold Cassidy, a leading opponent of both surrogacy and abortion rights asks, "Will we use [state power] to take a child from the arms of her mother when the mother is perfectly fit . . .?"[40] Represented by Cassidy, a pregnant woman in California filed suit in 2016 to invalidate an agreement she had made to serve as a surrogate for a single man in Georgia. In her complaint, she referred to herself as a mother "as a matter of biologic fact" and cited studies on the physiological and emotional aspects of pregnancy. The court rejected the argument that the state's surrogacy law violated her constitutional right to be recognized as the legal mother of the triplets she was carrying.[41]

While feminist opposition to surrogacy enjoyed strong support in the late twentieth century, today it is viewed more skeptically — in part because of the commonality between anti-surrogacy and anti-abortion arguments. As Professor Elizabeth Scott explains:

> The feminist position on surrogacy [in the late 1980s and early 1990s] always seemed to be in tension with the commitment to preserving women's autonomy in other reproductive contexts — particularly abortion. The claim that

---

37. Susan L. Bender & Phyllis Chesler, Handmaids for Hire: Should Commercial Surrogacy Be Legalized in NYS?, N.Y.L.J. (Online) (Feb. 22, 2019).

38. See Olga B.A. van den Akker, Psychological Aspects of Surrogate Motherhood, 13 Hum. Reprod. Update 53 (2007).

39. See Martha A. Field, Surrogate Motherhood: The Legal and Human Issues (1988).

40. Harold Cassidy, The Surrogate Uterus: The AGR Case and Melissa Brisman, Pub. Discourse (Sept. 7, 2012).

41. C.M. v. M.C., 213 Cal. Rptr. 3d 351 (Cal. Ct. App. 2017).

women lacked agency because of coercive circumstances was unsettling, but even more discordant with feminist values was the assertion that women needed protection because they could not anticipate their response to pregnancy. Such an assertion suggested views about the power of female biology that historically contributed to women's subordination—views that feminists have challenged in fighting for gender equality. The prediction that women were likely to regret their surrogacy decision on the basis of "natural" biological or physiological urges embodied essentialist assumptions about the role of motherhood in women's lives.[42]

Given this shift, Steinem's position is now seen as an outlier in debates over commercial surrogacy in the U.S. Indeed, in 2020, over the objections of Steinem and others, New York enacted a law allowing compensated gestational surrogacy.[43]

Where do you come out on the question of surrogacy? Does a woman have a right to serve as a surrogate? Or does the practice of surrogacy violate women's rights? How would you look at surrogacy from a reproductive justice perspective?

Even if you believe that the woman serving as a surrogate is not a parent and should have no standing to assert parental rights, do you believe she has a right to terminate a pregnancy that occurs pursuant to the surrogacy arrangement? What are the rights of the intended parents before the child is born? Some surrogacy contracts include provisions that restrict the decision-making authority of the woman serving as the surrogate during the pregnancy. These contracts may not only seek to prohibit the woman from smoking or drinking; they may also seek to prohibit her from making a decision about termination or selective reduction (reducing the number of embryos after implantation) that contravenes the wishes of the intended parents. Can a woman prospectively waive her constitutional right to abortion? Do you think a court would enforce such a provision? Professor Deborah Forman observes:

> Although contracts often contain abortion and selective reduction provisions . . . , practitioners routinely describe these as unenforceable, even while advocating their inclusion in the contract. A closer look reveals a somewhat more nuanced perspective: consensus that specific performance of such provisions would never occur but disagreement about whether a surrogate could be liable in damages for breach of contract.[44]

If you were a lawyer for intended parents, would you include a clause governing termination or selective reduction? What if you were representing the woman serving as the surrogate?

---

42. Elizabeth S. Scott, Surrogacy and the Politics of Commodification, 72 L. & Contemp. Probs. 109, 142 (2009).

43. S. 7506-B, 243d Leg. (N.Y. 2020). See also Elizabeth Chuck, New York State, Long a Holdout Against Legalizing Surrogacy, Overturns Ban, NBC News (Apr. 3, 2020).

44. Deborah L. Forman, Abortion Clauses in Surrogacy Contracts: Insights from a Case Study, 49 Fam. L.Q. 29, 34–35 (2015).

Some states that recently have enacted legislation regulating surrogacy prohibit such provisions. For example, the surrogacy law that New York enacted in 2020 contains a Surrogates' Bill of Rights, which includes "the right to make health and welfare decisions regarding themselves and their pregnancy."[45] Washington's recent parentage reform, which is based on the 2017 Uniform Parentage Act, provides: "The agreement must permit the woman acting as a surrogate to make all health and welfare decisions regarding herself and her pregnancy and . . . provisions in the agreement to the contrary are void and unenforceable."[46] The statute makes clear that the surrogacy law "does not diminish the right of the woman acting as a surrogate to terminate her pregnancy."[47] Nonetheless, as Professor Courtney Joslin explains, "many permissive regimes, including some recently enacted ones, omit protections regarding the bodily autonomy and integrity interests of people acting as surrogates. Indeed, some schemes expressly allow for the curtailment of autonomy rights in this regard, and others do implicitly."[48]

Some states have enacted other protections for a woman who acts as a surrogate. For example, the Surrogates' Bill of Rights in the New York law includes the requirement that she be represented by independent counsel paid for by the intended parents.[49] As Joslin points out, many recent surrogacy laws include this requirement.[50]

C. Embryo Disposition

With *in vitro* fertilization (IVF), an egg is fertilized outside the woman's body. The resulting embryo can then be implanted in the uterus of either the intended mother or a woman serving as a gestational surrogate. According to the Centers for Disease Control and Prevention, in 2015, more than 70,000 children were born in the U.S. as a result of IVF.[51] Twenty percent of the egg-retrieval or IVF procedures performed in 2015 were undertaken with the intent to cryopreserve and store the resulting eggs or embryos.[52] Many of these embryos remain in storage.

---

45. N.Y. Fam. Ct. Act §§ 581-602 (2020).

46. Wash. Rev. Code § 26.26A.715 (2020).

47. Id.

48. Courtney G. Joslin, (Not) Just Surrogacy, 109 Calif. L. Rev. __ (forthcoming 2021). See, e.g., Okla. Stat. tit. 10 § 557.6(D) (2020) (allowing contract clauses requiring the woman acting as surrogate to "undergo all medical examinations, treatments and fetal monitoring procedures recommended for the success of the pregnancy by the physician providing care to the gestational carrier during the pregnancy").

49. See N.Y. Fam. Ct. Act §§ 581-602 (2020); see also Wash. Rev. Code § 26.26A.710 ("The woman acting as a surrogate . . . must have independent legal representation" and "[t]he intended parent or parents must pay for independent legal representation for the woman acting as a surrogate").

50. Joslin, supra note 48, at (manuscript app. C at 67–69) (listing eight jurisdictions in addition to New York).

51. See Ctrs. for Disease Control & Prevention, 2015 Assisted Reproductive Technology National Summary Report 3 (2017).

52. See id.

What should happen to them? This issue of embryo disposition has come up most frequently in the context of disputes between divorcing spouses.

In 1992, the Tennessee Supreme Court became one of the first to resolve an embryo dispute.[53] In Davis v. Davis, a couple divorced before using the embryos they had created and frozen. At divorce, the wife sought to keep the embryos for future use, while the husband sought to prevent such use. The trial court granted the embryos to the wife, reasoning that they are "human beings" whose interests the wife sought to protect. The Tennessee Court of Appeals reversed, based in part on its conclusion that the husband had a constitutionally protected right not to have a child. On appeal to the Tennessee Supreme Court, the wife shifted positions; she no longer sought to use the embryos herself but instead wanted to donate them for someone else's use.

The Tennessee Supreme Court did not adopt the position of either of the lower courts. Instead, it reasoned that "preembryos are not, strictly speaking, either 'persons' or 'property,' but occupy an interim category that entitles them to special respect because of their potential for human life."[54] The court urged parties to enter agreements addressing disposition before creating embryos. In the absence of an agreement, the court felt it necessary to balance the competing interests. The husband possessed an interest in avoiding "unwanted parenthood . . ., with all of its possible financial and psychological consequences."[55] For the wife, "[r]efusal to permit donation of the preembryos would impose on her the burden of knowing that the lengthy IVF procedures she underwent were futile, and that the preembryos to which she contributed genetic material would never become children."[56] Weighing these interests against each other, the court concluded:

> While this is not an insubstantial emotional burden, we can only conclude that [wife's] interest in donation is not as significant as the interest [husband] has in avoiding parenthood. If she were allowed to donate these preembryos, he would face a lifetime of either wondering about his parental status or knowing about his parental status but having no control over it. He testified quite clearly that if the preembryos were brought to term he would fight for custody of his child or children. Donation, if a child came of it, would rob him twice — his procreational autonomy would be defeated and his relationship with his offspring would be prohibited.[57]

What if the wife had stuck to her attempt to use, rather than donate, the embryos? The court explained that "[t]he case would be closer . . ., but only if she could not

---

53. Davis v. Davis, 842 S.W.2d 588 (Tenn. 1992).

54. Id. at 597.

55. Id. at 603.

56. Id. at 604.

57. Id.

achieve parenthood by any other reasonable means."[58] What would a woman have to show to meet this standard? The wife, the court observed, still "would have a reasonable opportunity, through IVF, to try once again to achieve parenthood in all its aspects — genetic, gestation, bearing, and rearing."[59] And, even if she "were unable to undergo another round of IVF, or opted not to try, she could still achieve the child-rearing aspects of parenthood through adoption."[60] Is adoption an adequate remedy?

Since *Davis*, courts in other states have confronted the issue. In many cases, as the *Davis* court hoped, divorcing spouses have preexisting contracts or other advance agreements to determine the disposition of the embryos. Courts generally have enforced agreements when they provide that the embryos be disposed or donated for research. For example, in Kass v. Kass, the New York Court of Appeals affirmed the decision to enforce the disposition agreement and ordered that the embryos be donated to research because "the informed consents signed by the parties unequivocally manifest their mutual intention" regarding disposition.[61] Courts in Texas, Oregon, and elsewhere have reached similar conclusions regarding the enforceability of these agreements[62] — though a few courts have declined to treat such agreements as enforceable.[63]

Courts generally have declined to enforce agreements when they would allow one party to implant the embryo over the other's objection. That is, courts have favored the objecting party's right not to be a parent over the other party's right to be a parent. For example, the Massachusetts Supreme Judicial Court explained that it "would not enforce an agreement that would compel one [party] to become a parent against his or her will."[64] The New Jersey Supreme Court reached a similar conclusion, explaining that a person's "fundamental right not to procreate is irrevocably extinguished" if the embryo is used to create a child.[65]

As in *Davis*, in the absence of an existing agreement, courts generally apply a balancing test to determine the disposition of the embryos. For example, the New Jersey Supreme Court held that the right *not* to become a parent outweighed the right to become a parent.[66] In applying a balancing test to embryo disputes,

---

58. Id.

59. Id.

60. Id.

61. 696 N.E. 2d 174, 181 (N.Y. 1998).

62. Roman v. Roman, 193 S.W.3d 40 (Tex. App. 2006); In re Marriage of Dahl, 194 P.3d 834 (Or. Ct. App. 2008); Bilbao v. Goodwin, 217 A.3d 977 (Conn. 2019); In re Litowitz, 48 P.3d 261 (Wash. 2002).

63. See, e.g., In re Marriage of Witten, 672 N.W.2d 768 (Iowa 2003) (rejecting a contractual approach but nonetheless holding that the wife could not use the embryos without her husband's consent). In at least one case, a court has declined to apply a consent form determining the disposition of the embryos in the event of divorce to a situation in which an unmarried couple splits up. See Szafranski v. Dunston, 34 N.E.3d 1132 (Ill. Ct. App. 2015).

64. A.Z. v. B.Z., 725 N.E.2d 1051, 1057 (Mass. 2000).

65. J.B. v. M.B., 783 A.2d 707, 717 (N.J. 2001).

66. Id.

courts typically consider a number of factors, such as the intended use of the party seeking to preserve the embryos, the ability or inability of the party seeking to implant the embryo to have genetically-related children through other means, the original reason for pursuing IVF, the hardship to the person seeking to avoid becoming a genetic parent, and any bad faith use of the embryos as leverage during the divorce proceeding by either party.[67] The *Davis* court had suggested that the outcome might have been different if the wife could not have a child another way. In Reiber v. Reiss, the Superior Court of Pennsylvania held that the embryos should go to the wife, who wished to implant them, because the embryos were created to enable the wife to have a genetically-related child after she completed her cancer treatment.[68] How should courts balance an individual's only opportunity at genetic parenthood against another individual's wish to avoid parenthood? Does the sex of the individual who wants to use the embryos matter? Is the claim of a woman more compelling than the claim of a man?

Is the right to be a genetic parent the same as the right to be a parent? Professor Glenn Cohen has disaggregated the right at stake: "a right not to be a gestational parent, a right not to be a genetic parent, and a right not to be a legal parent."[69] The embryo cases, Cohen shows, feature "a 'naked' right not to be a genetic parent, unbundled from unwanted gestational or legal parenthood."[70] Is the right not to be a genetic parent sufficient to overcome the competing claim of the individual who seeks to use the embryos? If the husband in *Davis* could be treated as a sperm donor, rather than as a legal parent, he would have no legal responsibilities for the resulting child. Would that address his concerns? Is that a position lawmakers should adopt?

A number of state legislatures have weighed in on embryo disposition. Laws in some states place an obligation on healthcare providers to inform parties undergoing IVF about options for unused embryos and require the parties to decide the disposition of any unused embryos in advance.[71] In contrast, other states have sought to preserve the likelihood that the embryo will be implanted. For example, Louisiana law expressly prohibits the intentional destruction of viable embryos and mandates that courts apply a "best interest" standard to embryo disputes.[72] In other words, the law treats embryos more like children over whom a custody decision must be made.

---

67. See, e.g., In re Marriage of Rooks, 429 P.3d 579, 593–94 (Colo. 2018).

68. 42 A.2d 1131 (Pa. Super. Ct. 2012).

69. I. Glenn Cohen, The Right Not to be a Genetic Parent?, 81 S. Cal. L. Rev. 1115, 1121–22 (2008).

70. Id. at 1124.

71. See, e.g., Cal. Health & Safety Code § 125315(b) (West 2020); Mass. Gen. Laws ch. 111L, § 4 (2020); N.J. Stat. Ann. § 26:2Z-2 (West 2020).

72. La. Rev. Stat. §§ 9:129, 131 (2020).

PROBLEM

You are a state lawmaker sitting on your legislature's Children's Committee. Another lawmaker on the committee has proposed a bill to address embryo disputes. It would require courts to "award the human embryos to the spouse who intends to allow the human embryos to develop to birth," regardless of any preexisting contract. Would you support the bill? What do you think of the bill as a policy matter? Do you think the bill poses any constitutional problems?

POSTSCRIPT

The hypothetical bill is based on a law that Arizona enacted in 2018.[73] That law not only provides for the award of embryos to the spouse who intends to use them to have a child; it also provides that if the spouse who is not awarded the embryos does not consent to parenthood, that spouse has no parental rights or responsibilities with respect to any resulting child.[74] Does this mitigate concerns you had with the bill? In a 2020 case involving an embryo dispute, the Arizona Supreme Court expressly declined to consider the statute, instead determining that it does not apply retroactively.[75]

II. Parenthood Based on Marriage

Now that we have considered the status of *not being a parent*, we turn in the remainder of this chapter to the status of *being a parent*. For most of this nation's history, marriage defined and limited legal parenthood. In the absence of adoption, only a married woman and her husband had a legally enforceable parent-child relationship. Even if unmarried parents assumed custodial or financial responsibilities for their biological children, they did not ordinarily enjoy the status of legal parents. This was most important for purposes of inheritance, ensuring that marital children inherited from their fathers but non-marital children did not. The materials that follow focus on the significance of marriage for parentage in contemporary times.

---

73. Ariz. Rev. Stat. Ann. § 25-318.03 (2020).
74. Id. § 25-318.03(C)-(D).
75. In re Terrell v. Torres, 456 P.3d 13, 15 n.1 (Ariz. 2020).

A. The Marital Presumption

At common law, when a married woman gave birth to a child, she was treated as the child's legal mother. Under the marital presumption — also called the presumption of legitimacy — her husband was treated as the child's legal father. The marital presumption reflected the intuition that the husband was the biological father. But the law also operated to hide biological facts that departed from the legal presumption. In fact, traditionally neither spouse was allowed to testify to the husband's "non-access," such that the presumption remained intact even when both knew that the husband was not the biological father. And courts sometimes ignored compelling evidence of non-paternity in favor of preserving marital "harmony."[76]

Over time, the marital presumption loosened. As non-marital parents and children gained legal protections and scientific advances made determinations of biological paternity possible, states began to entertain more challenges to the presumption's operation. Consider the approach of the Massachusetts Supreme Judicial Court in balancing the competing interests at stake. As you do, ask yourself what interests are at stake when another man is the biological father of a married woman's child? Where do the child's interests fall?

C.C. v. A.B.
550 N.E.2d 365 (Mass. 1990)

NOLAN, J.

This case involves the question whether a man, who alleges that he is the father of a child, may bring an action to establish his paternity when the mother of the child is, and was at the time of the child's conception and birth, married to another man.

The plaintiff, C.C., filed a complaint in which he alleged that he is the father of a certain child. The plaintiff sought an adjudication of his paternity and a right of visitation with the child. The defendant, A.B., is admittedly the mother of the child.

The mother moved to dismiss the plaintiff's complaint. She alleged that she was married to a man other than the plaintiff when the child was born and argued that G. L. c. 209C, Section 5(a), precluded the plaintiff's action. The plaintiff opposed the mother's motion on the ground that G. L. c. 209C, Section 5(a), to the extent that it denied him standing to bring a paternity action, was unconstitutional. . . .

The parties stipulate that . . . [a]t the time of the child's conception and birth the mother lived with the plaintiff and had sexual relations with the plaintiff. During the entire time that the mother lived with the plaintiff, including the time during

---

76. See, e.g., Prochnow v. Prochnow, 80 N.W.2d 278 (Wis. 1957) (finding paternity despite blood typing evidence that made it biologically impossible).

which the child was born, the mother was married to another man. The mother and her husband have since reconciled, and they now live together. . . .

According to the mother, Section 5(a) bars the plaintiff from bringing suit to establish the paternity of her child. . . . The purpose of the statute is to deal with actions to establish paternity in the context of children born out of wedlock. Not surprisingly then, Section 5(a) contains the following exclusion from the list of persons who may bring an action under the statute: "provided, however, that if the mother of the child was or is married and the child's birth occurs during the marriage or within three hundred days of its termination by death, annulment or divorce, complaints under this chapter may not be filed by a person presumed to be or alleging himself to be the father unless he is or was the mother's husband at the time of the child's birth or conception." It is this exclusion which the plaintiff claims is unconstitutional.

Prior to the enactment of G. L. c. 209C, a putative father could seek an adjudication of paternity under the general equity jurisdiction of the Probate Court. The putative father's argument in this case assumes that the Legislature's enactment of c. 209C precludes him from bringing such an action. We disagree with that assumption.

General Laws c. 209C, Section 5(a), expressly bars a putative father in the plaintiff's position from bringing an action "under this chapter." In light of this clear declaration, . . . "nothing in [G. L. c. 209C] . . . limits (or was intended to limit) the scope of the preexisting general equity jurisdiction of the Probate Court under G. L. c. 215, Section 6." In our view, G. L. c. 209C, Section 5(a), does not abrogate or modify a putative father's right, as established by prior cases of this court, to bring a complaint to establish paternity under the general equity jurisdiction of the Probate Court.

The critical question in this case is whether the plaintiff may bring an action to establish paternity. It is not enough to conclude, as we do, that the enactment of G. L. c. 209C places no limit on the Probate Court's general equity jurisdiction. We must address the nature of an action to establish paternity.

The law has always drawn a distinction between legitimate and illegitimate children. A child who was not legitimate was, at common law, "filius nullius" (the son of no one). The status of illegitimacy brought with it a host of social and legal disabilities. The English common law placed no obligation on the parents of an illegitimate child to support that child. The American courts adopted that view as well. An illegitimate child, being filius nullius, could inherit from neither parent under the common law. Until 1987, use of the word "issue," in the absence of anything indicating a contrary intent, was presumed to mean only legitimate children.

The common law severely burdened the illegitimate child, imposing harsh results on the child as punishment of the parents' actions. In recognition of the sad lot of illegitimate children, the common law generated a presumption of legitimacy. "The legal presumption always is, that a child born in lawful wedlock is legitimate."

Phillips v. Allen, 2 Allen 453, 454 (1861). While the law has always recognized that a child born to a married woman could nonetheless be an illegitimate child, it created a strong presumption to avoid that result. In England, the presumption could only be overcome by proof that the husband was "extra quatuor maria (beyond the four seas), for above nine months," or if "there is an apparent impossibility of procreation on the part of the husband, as if he be only eight years old, or the like." The application of the presumption has changed somewhat, and it has become rebuttable. But the presumption may only be rebutted by "facts which prove, beyond all reasonable doubt, that the husband could not have been the father." Phillips v. Allen, supra at 454. Accordingly, "it must be shown, 'beyond all reasonable doubt,' either that: (1) the husband had no access to the wife during the time of possible conception; (2) the husband was impotent; or (3) a properly conducted blood grouping test, administered by a qualified expert, definitively excludes the husband as a father." . . .

Society has come to recognize that discrimination against illegitimate children is not justified. As noted, statutes were enacted at an early date to alleviate some of the hardships thrust on illegitimate children by the common law. The United States Supreme Court has invoked the equal protection clause of the Fourteenth Amendment to the United States Constitution to strike down statutes discriminating against illegitimate children. This court has noted that numerous Federal statutes reflect the principle that adverse treatment of illegitimate children does not comport with current notions of justice. As we noted, "[o]urs is an era in which logic and compassion have impelled the law toward unburdening children from the stigma and the disadvantages heretofore attendant upon the status of illegitimacy." The enactment of G. L. c. 209C is another step in that direction. In Section 1, the Legislature proclaims that "[c]hildren born to parents who are not married to each other shall be entitled to the same rights and protections of the law as all other children." Thus, the trend of the law has been to remove the disadvantages placed on illegitimate children. It was the avoidance of those disadvantages which gave rise to the strict application of the presumption of legitimacy.

At the same time, the law has come to recognize an interest with which it had not historically dealt. The fathers of illegitimate children have certain rights, under the due process clause of the United States Constitution, to maintain a relationship with those children. See Stanley v. Illinois, 405 U.S. 645, 651–652 (1972). In the constitutional sense, the father's interest is not one of a biological nature alone. Rather, the protected interest arises when there is a substantial relationship between a putative father and an illegitimate child. . . .

The case sub judice involves a clash of the interests of the plaintiff, an unwed putative father, and the interest in preserving the legitimacy of the child that the plaintiff claims to have sired. We continue to adhere to the common law principle that motivated the presumption of legitimacy — that there is a strong interest in not bastardizing children. We are no longer convinced, however, that that interest can be protected only by requiring the rebuttal of a presumption by proof beyond a reasonable doubt. In view of the gradual betterment of the illegitimate child's legal position, which weakens the purpose behind the presumption, coupled with the corresponding recognition of the interests of unwed putative fathers, we think that there is no longer any need for a presumption of legitimacy. The interests involved can be adequately protected by requiring that a putative father in the plaintiff's position be required to prove paternity by clear and convincing evidence.

The function of a standard of proof is to "instruct the factfinder concerning the degree of confidence our society thinks he should have in the correctness of factual conclusions for a particular type of adjudication." Proof beyond a reasonable doubt was required to rebut the presumption of legitimacy because of the enormous importance of avoiding the conclusion that a child was illegitimate. Under that framework, the interests of the unwed father who claimed to have sired a child by a married woman were, by necessity, considered of little importance. The entire risk of an erroneous judgment was placed on the unwed father who sought to pursue a relationship with his child. We think that the father's interest warrants greater recognition. The requirement that the putative father prove paternity by clear and convincing evidence better allocates the risks of error involved in cases such as this one and gives better recognition to the competing interests involved.

Proof of paternity must rest in the evidence. The effect of the common law presumption of legitimacy was, in many instances, to prevent the fact finder from reaching the true issue in the case. The advances of modern science make determinations and exclusions of paternity much more accurate than was ever historically possible. In this context we think it preferable that a putative father in the plaintiff's position be able to produce the evidence he has on the issue of paternity. Placing a barrier between the plaintiff and the fact finder by requiring that the plaintiff first prove, beyond a reasonable doubt, non-access, impotency, or scientific exclusion of the husband, is no longer warranted. To be sure, those issues are still relevant, but they should not be dispositive on the issue whether the plaintiff is indeed the father of the child. . . .

In altering the nature of the common law action to establish paternity, we are not acting without guidance. Modern trends in the law, combined with changes in social attitudes, have brought into question the continuing validity of archaic rules which obfuscate the truth-seeking principles our system of jurisprudence strives to achieve. The Legislature, in G. L. c. 209C, has effectively eliminated the presumption of legitimacy. Under c. 209C, a married woman may bring an action against a man other than her husband to establish paternity. The only requirement is that she prove paternity by clear and convincing evidence. The Department of Public Welfare (department) may similarly bring a paternity action against a man other than the husband if the child is or was a recipient of public assistance. The department must prove paternity by clear and convincing evidence. . . . [W]e think the common law should move forward. The common law is "designed to meet and be susceptible of being adapted 'to new institutions and conditions of society . . . new usages and practices, as the progress of society in the advancement of civilization may require.'" Our decision today fairly balances the interests present in modern society.

We now proceed to the dispositive issue — whether a man in the plaintiff's position is entitled to bring an action to establish paternity pursuant to G. L. c. 215, Section 6. In P.B.C. v. D.H., 396 Mass. 68 (1985), we held that a man other than the husband has no common law right, in all circumstances, to be heard on the question of paternity. In the circumstances of this case, we think that the putative father has such a right. The parties' statement of agreed facts indicates, as already noted, that the mother, although married to another man, lived with the plaintiff at the time that the minor child was conceived and when the child was born. The plaintiff's name is listed as "father" on the child's birth certificate and on the child's baptismal record. The child bears the plaintiff's name. The mother has admitted that the plaintiff may be the father of the child. After the child's birth, the plaintiff, the mother, and the child lived together. The plaintiff has indicated, both by his actions and his words that he has an interest in continuing his relationship with the child. On this record, there is sufficient evidence of a substantial parent-child relationship between the plaintiff and the child to allow the plaintiff to proceed with his paternity action.

The existence of a substantial parent-child relationship is, in our view, the controlling factor in determining whether this plaintiff may pursue his claim. The United States Supreme Court has indicated that, "[w]hen an unwed father demonstrates a full commitment to the responsibilities of parenthood by 'com[ing] forward to participate in the rearing of his child,' . . . his interest in personal contact with his child acquires substantial protection under the Due Process Clause." Lehr v. Robertson, 463 U.S. 248, 261 (1983), quoting Caban v. Mohammed, 441 U.S. 380, 392 (1979). Quite apart from the constitutional implications, we think that the existence of a substantial relationship between a putative father and the child is an appropriate prerequisite for the commencement of an action such as this. "[T]he existence or nonexistence of a substantial relationship between the putative father and child is relevant in evaluating both the rights of the parent and the best interests of the child." It is the developed parent-child relationship of which both the plaintiff and the child were suddenly deprived, that the plaintiff seeks to renew. Accordingly, in cases such as this, the Probate Court must hold a preliminary hearing to determine the extent of the relationship between the putative father and the child. This is, in its nature, a fact-based question. The court must look at the relationship as a whole and consider emotional bonds, economic support, custody of the child, the extent of personal association, the commitment of the putative father to attending to the child's needs, the consistency of the putative father's expressed interest, the child's name, the names listed on the birth certificate, and any other factors which bear on the nature of the alleged parent-child relationship.

The requirement of showing a substantial parent-child relationship serves another important interest as well. In cases where the mother of a child is married and living with her husband, there is admittedly an extant marital relationship on which the plaintiff's action will intrude. The traditional family unit is at the core of our society. Despite a vast array of recent challenges to the traditional concept of the family, our civilization still places inestimable value on the importance of family life. Without regard to the outcome of a paternity case, even the very trial of such a case might place great strain on a unitary family. Where, however, the plaintiff has exhibited that he has had a substantial parent-child relationship with the child, it will certainly come as no surprise to the marital family that there is a question as to paternity. If the plaintiff cannot come forward with clear and convincing evidence of such a relationship, he will not be able to proceed beyond the preliminary stages of the action. The family will be protected against significant intrusion. If, on the other hand, the putative father can demonstrate that he has enjoyed a substantial relationship with the child, then his interest warrants protection and the interest in protecting a family which, by necessary implication, has already suffered substantial interference (by the acts of one of the marital partners) is greatly decreased. In these circumstances, the putative father should be allowed to proceed with his action.

In view of our conclusion that the plaintiff has a viable cause of action at common law, we need not address his contention that G. L. c. 209C, Section 5(a), denies him due process of law. We do not address the issue of what rights this plaintiff may have if he succeeds in establishing paternity. The overriding principle in determining those rights must be the best interest of the child. We limit our decision to the conclusion that the defendant's motion to dismiss should be denied and that the plaintiff should be given the opportunity to prove paternity. The case is remanded to the Probate Court.

O'CONNOR, J., with whom LYNCH, J., joins, dissenting.

The issue presented by this case is whether the plaintiff has standing to invoke the jurisdiction of the Probate Court to inquire into and decide whether he is the father of a child born to a woman who (1) was married to another man when the child was conceived and born, and (2) now lives with that husband, who accepts the child as his own. Stated another way, the issue is whether, in those circumstances, the husband is conclusively presumed to be the father. If he is, evidence to the contrary is legally irrelevant. . . .

The policy question has been addressed by the Legislature and for that reason is not open to the court. When the elected representatives of the people have declared the Commonwealth's policy on a matter within their jurisdiction, the court exceeds its lawful powers by announcing an inconsistent policy. General Laws c. 209C (1988 ed.) provides for the rights of children born to parents who are not married to each other. Section 5(a) provides with respect to complaints to establish paternity that such a complaint may be commenced by, among other persons, the putative father, "provided, however, that if the mother of the child was or is married and the child's birth occurs during the marriage or within three hundred days of its termination by death, annulment or divorce, complaints under [c. 209C] may not be filed by a person . . . alleging himself to be the father unless he is or was the mother's husband at the time of the child's birth or conception." It is true, as the court asserts, that G. L. c. 209C, Section 5(a), expressly bars a putative father in the situation of this plaintiff only from bringing an action "under this chapter"; that is, under c. 209C. But the social policy that motivated that enactment is quite clear: namely, that the unitary family traditionally respected by society and sought to be protected by the Legislature includes the family of the mother, her husband, and the child, and does not include the mother, child, and the mother's lover. The Legislature has made clear that the policy of this Commonwealth is to withhold from a plaintiff a judicial forum in which to launch an attack on the legitimacy of a child and to otherwise disrupt family harmony. . . .

NOTES AND QUESTIONS

1. *Rebutting the Marital Presumption.* In recent decades, states have made it easier to rebut the marital presumption: husbands can seek to disestablish paternity; wives can challenge the parental status of their husband; and biological fathers can attempt to establish paternity. As *C.C.* illustrates, biological evidence is used to rebut the presumption. Even as biological evidence is clearly relevant, states have diverged on questions of when such evidence can be introduced and whether it should be treated as determinative of the question of parentage. Some states require that a challenge to the marital presumption be brought within the first two years of the child's life, regardless of when a party discovers there may be a reason to question paternity. For instance, California's statute provides that the husband or wife who seeks to challenge the presumption file a "notice of motion for blood tests . . . not later than two years from the child's date of birth."[77] Why have such a time limit? Judges also may have discretion in determining whether to allow rebuttal and accordingly may refuse to admit biological evidence.[78] In some states, judges are authorized to make a decision that contravenes the results of genetic testing in order to vindicate the best interest of the child. For example, Washington's code provides that, "[i]f the presumed parent is not identified . . . as a genetic parent of the child and the presumed parent or the woman who gave birth to the child challenges the presumed parent's parentage of the child, the court shall adjudicate the parentage of the child

---

77. Cal. Fam. Code § 7541 (West 2020).

78. Id., § 7512 ("a rebuttable presumption . . . *may* be rebutted in an *appropriate* action") (emphasis added).

in the best interest of the child."[79] When might disallowing rebuttal of the marital presumption serve the child's best interest? The Massachusetts court required not only that the putative father prove his biological paternity, but also that he prove a "substantial relationship" with the child. In other words, a man who can merely show that he is the biological father would not be authorized to rebut the marital presumption and thus establish parentage over the mother's husband. Other courts have reasoned similarly.[80] Courts also have found that the presumption should not be rebutted if doing so would legally sever a parent-child relationship that already has formed between the husband and the child. For example, in a situation in which there was an "established and continuing emotional and financial father-daughter relationship" between the husband and the child, the California Supreme Court held that the alleged genetic father had no right to "establish[] a biological relationship in a court of law."[81] Some states, in contrast, have allowed biological evidence to rebut the marital presumption even in the face of an established relationship between the husband and child.[82] How would you design the system of rebuttal if you were a state lawmaker?

2. *Rights of Unmarried Fathers.* The Massachusetts court did not reach the constitutional question that the biological father raised. Unmarried biological fathers consistently have asserted that state statutory regimes that prevent them from establishing a parental relationship with their biological child violate their constitutional rights. As we will see later in the chapter, the Supreme Court has ruled that unmarried biological fathers possess a constitutional liberty interest in the parent-child relationship only if they demonstrate a sufficient commitment to parenting the child. Further, the Court has limited the rights of such a father if he seeks to challenge the parental status of a husband who established parentage by virtue of the marital presumption. This means that the question at issue in C.C. v. A.B. is largely left to state courts and legislatures to decide.

B. Marital Children Conceived with Donor Sperm

The marital presumption assumes, but does not require, that the mother's husband is the biological father. In many circumstances, the husband will remain the legal father even if the biological father comes forward seeking to establish paternity. This suggests that the marital presumption operates in ways that do not simply treat biological connection as the basis of parenthood, but rather prioritize family form

---

79. Wash. Rev. Code § 26.26A.435(3)(c) (2020).

80. See, e.g., Dawn D. v. Super. Ct., 952 P.2d 1139, 1144 (Cal. 1998) (rejecting biological father's attempt to rebut marital presumption because he "has never had any personal relationship with [the] child").

81. Michelle W. v. Ronald W., 703 P.2d 88, 92–93 (Cal. 1985).

82. See, e.g., Gantt v. Gantt, 716 So. 2d 846 (Fla. Dist. Ct. App. 1998).

(marriage). Why would marriage be an appropriate basis on which to rest parentage? Can we assume that the married couple will parent the child together?

What if we know from the outset that the mother's husband is not the biological father — because the couple used donor sperm to conceive a child? (This is often called artificial insemination, alternative insemination, or insemination by donor.) In early cases regarding the status of the husband in such circumstances, some courts found that he was not the legal father. A few even suggested that the insemination might qualify as a form of adultery.[83] That changed when the California Supreme Court ruled that a husband who consented to his wife's insemination with donor sperm was financially responsible for the child.[84] His consent operated as a substitute for a biological tie that the marital presumption would otherwise assume to exist.

Eventually, many states simply applied the general marital presumption to situations involving donor insemination. Of course, it would be important that biological evidence not be allowed to rebut the presumption in such situations. Rather than relying solely on the marital presumption, many states adopted specific statutes regulating donor insemination. The Uniform Parentage Act of 1973, promulgated by the Uniform Law Commission, was adopted by nearly 20 states.

UNIFORM PARENTAGE ACT (1973)

§ 5. [Artificial Insemination]
    (a) If, under the supervision of a licensed physician and with the consent of her husband, a wife is inseminated artificially with semen donated by a man not her husband, the husband is treated in law as if he were the natural father of a child thereby conceived. The husband's consent must be in writing and signed by him and his wife. . . .
    (b) The donor of semen provided to a licensed physician for use in artificial insemination of a married woman other than the donor's wife is treated in law as if he were not the natural father of a child thereby conceived.

PROBLEM

The Utah Uniform Parentage Act, enacted in 2008, provides that a man is the legal father of a child born to his wife through assisted reproduction, so long as he "consents to the assisted reproduction by his wife," and such consent is "in a record signed by the woman and her husband."

---

83. See, e.g., Doornbos v. Doornbos, 23 U.S.L.W. 2308 (Ill. Super. Ct. 1954).
84. See People v. Sorensen, 437 P.2d 495 (Cal. 1968).

Angie and Kami are a married same-sex couple in Utah. With Angie's consent, Kami conceived through intrauterine insemination at the hospital at the University of Utah. Both women signed a "Donor Semen Agreement," which explained that donor semen was being used for insemination of Kami and identified Angie as Kami's wife.

Kami gave birth to a boy, Lucas. Relying on the parentage statute, the Utah Department of Health will not issue a birth certificate listing Angie as a parent and instead asserts that Angie must adopt Lucas through a stepparent adoption — a process that requires fees, a background check, and a judicial hearing. Kami and Angie challenge the Utah parentage statute and the state's application of it. If you were representing Kami and Angie, what constitutional arguments would you make on their behalf? If you were representing the Utah Department of Public Health, what arguments would you make to justify the statute and the refusal to apply it to Kami and Angie?

POSTSCRIPT

In 2015, a federal district court ruled in favor of Angie and Kami, enjoining the state "from enforcing [the statute] in a way that differentiates between male spouses of women who give birth through assisted reproduction with donor sperm and similarly situated female spouses of women who give birth through assisted reproduction with donor sperm."[85] The state attempted to justify the statute by citing "a concern over accuracy of vital statistics records for researchers" and "a concern for making parentage clear."[86] The court, though, faulted the state for failing to explain "how recognizing a female spouse as a parent and listing her as a parent on a birth certificate undermined the clarity of parentage" or had "any tangible effect . . . on the accuracy of [vital statistics] records."[87] Finding it unnecessary to determine "the applicable level of scrutiny for an Equal Protection analysis," the court found no rational basis for the state's treatment of same-sex couples.[88] Do you think the state also violated the Due Process Clause?

---

85. Roe v. Patton, No. 2:15-cv-00253-DB, 2015 WL 4476734, at *4 (D. Utah July 22, 2015).
86. Id. at *3.
87. Id.
88. Id.

NOTES AND QUESTIONS

1. *What Does the Statute Cover?* Statutes enacted more recently, like Utah's, cover "assisted reproduction." But older statutes contemplate only "artificial insemination." Should an older statute necessarily reach newer forms of assisted reproduction, or must the legislature amend the statute to identify additional procedures that are covered? For example, should a court read a statute that specifies only "artificial insemination" to include IVF, such that when a married different-sex couple creates an embryo using donor sperm, the husband is treated as the legal father by operation of the artificial insemination statute? Courts that have confronted this question have resolved it differently.[89]

2. *Donor Insemination and Marital Status.* Notice that both the 1973 UPA and the 2008 Utah law are limited to married couples. What happens when an unmarried woman gives birth to a child conceived with donor sperm? Ordinarily, when an unmarried woman gives birth, the state can treat the biological father as a legal father who owes financial support to the child. In many states, the statutes regulating donor insemination apply only to married couples, thus leaving the default treatment of biological fathers in place when an unmarried woman gives birth.[90] Even if the mother and the sperm donor agreed otherwise, the sperm donor may have parental rights and obligations.[91] Of course, an unmarried woman can avoid this result by using sperm from an anonymous donor. If the mother plans to raise the child with another individual — perhaps a man or woman with whom she is in a relationship — that individual is not treated as a legal parent under the law of most states. Instead, that individual must ordinarily adopt the child — provided second-parent adoption is available in the state — to gain parental status.

3. *The Uniform Parentage Act of 2017.* To address disparities between married and unmarried individuals, the most recent Uniform Parentage Act — UPA (2017) — promulgated by the Uniform Law Commission applies to individuals regardless of marital status. Section 703 provides: "An individual who consents . . . to assisted reproduction by a woman with the intent to be a parent of a child conceived by the assisted reproduction is a parent of the child."[92] The provision does not apply to surrogacy. We will return to the 2017 UPA's regulation of assisted reproduction later in the chapter.

---

89. Compare Sieglein v. Schmidt, 120 A.3d 790 (Md. Ct. Spec. App. 2015) (holding that the statute applies to IVF), with Patton v. Vanterpool, 806 S.E.2d 493 (Ga. 2017) (holding that the legislature must revise the statute in order for it to apply to a procedure other than donor insemination).

90. See, e.g., Alaska Stat. § 25.20.045 (2020); Ga. Code Ann. § 19-7-21 (2020); Mo. Ann. Stat. § 257.56 (West 2020); Okla. Stat. Ann. tit 10, § 552 (West 2020).

91. See In re Paternity of M.F., 938 N.E.2d 1256 (Ind. Ct. App. 2010).

92. Unif. Parentage Act § 703 (Unif. Law Comm'n 2017) [hereinafter UPA (2017)].

C. Same-Sex Couples and the Marital Presumption

We have seen that the marital presumption generally applies to husbands who are biological fathers but that it also applies to husbands who are not biological fathers. The children may have been conceived through the wife's extramarital relationship or with donor sperm. We also have seen that some states have adopted statutes specifically treating husbands as fathers in situations of donor insemination, and these statutes now apply to married same-sex couples. But what about the general marital presumption? Should that also apply to same-sex couples who are married? Does it matter that such couples necessarily include a non-genetic parent? Consider the approach that the Iowa Supreme Court took in 2013, four years after it ruled that same-sex couples must be allowed to marry in the state.

GARTNER V. IOWA DEPARTMENT OF PUBLIC HEALTH
830 N.W.2d 335 (Iowa 2013)

WIGGINS, JUSTICE.

In this appeal, we must decide whether Iowa Code section 144.13(2) (2011) requires the Iowa Department of Public Health to list as a parent on a child's birth certificate the non-birthing spouse in a lesbian marriage when the child was born to one of the spouses during the couple's marriage. . . .

Background Facts and Proceedings

Melissa and Heather Gartner are a lesbian couple. They have been in a loving, committed relationship since December 2003. . . . Heather conceived their first child by anonymous donor insemination. Melissa participated in every step of Heather's pregnancy, which included choosing the anonymous sperm donor. Melissa was present for the birth of the couple's first child.

Because Melissa and Heather were not legally married at the time of the first child's birth, the couple went through formal adoption procedures to ensure Melissa's name was on the child's birth certificate. The Gartners successfully navigated the adoption process after both Melissa and Heather underwent background checks for criminal misconduct and sexual abuse. Heather characterized the adoption process as expensive, intrusive, and laborious. Once the couple finalized the adoption, the Department issued the child's birth certificate, which named both Heather and Melissa as parents.

Two years later, in April 2009, we decided *Varnum v. Brien*, 763 N.W.2d 862 (Iowa 2009), which held Iowa's Defense of Marriage Act unconstitutional. Thereafter, the state began solemnizing same-sex marriages. Melissa and Heather Gartner subsequently married in Des Moines on June 13. Heather was approximately six months pregnant with the couple's second child, Mackenzie Jean Gartner, at the time of their marriage.

Three months later, on September 19, Heather gave birth to Mackenzie. Heather conceived Mackenzie using the same anonymous donor as for their first child. The day after Mackenzie's birth, Heather and Melissa completed a form at the hospital to obtain Mackenzie's birth certificate. The Department provided the form. On the form, the Gartners indicated that both Heather and Melissa are Mackenzie's parents and that they are legally married. The Department issued Mackenzie's birth certificate on approximately November 19. The certificate only listed Heather as Mackenzie's parent. The space for the second parent's name was blank.

After receiving Mackenzie's birth certificate naming only Heather, the Gartners sent a letter to the Department requesting a birth certificate recognizing both Heather and Melissa as Mackenzie's parents. The Department denied the request. The Department refused to place the name of the non-birthing spouse in a lesbian marriage on the birth certificate without the spouse first adopting the child, pursuant to Iowa Code section 144.23(1). The Department indicated: "The system for registration of births in Iowa currently recognizes the biological and 'gendered' roles of 'mother' and 'father,' grounded in the biological fact that a child has one biological mother and one biological father. . . ." . . .

We must decide if we can interpret Iowa Code section 144.13(2), otherwise known as Iowa's presumption of parentage statute, to require the Department to list as a parent on a child's birth certificate the non-birthing lesbian spouse, when the other spouse conceived the child during the marriage using an anonymous sperm donor. If we cannot adopt such an interpretation of the statute, we then must determine whether the Department's refusal to list the non-birthing lesbian spouse on the child's birth certificate violates the equal protection clauses in article I, sections 1 and 6 of the Iowa Constitution.

Iowa's Presumption of Parentage Statute . . .

For purposes of preparing a birth certificate, [Iowa Code § 144.13(2)] includes a presumption of parentage. The legislature articulated the following procedure for preparing a child's birth certificate, based upon the presumption of parentage:

> If the mother was married at the time of conception, birth, or at any time during the period between conception and birth, the name of the husband shall be entered on the certificate as the father of the child unless paternity has been determined otherwise by a court of competent jurisdiction, in which case the name of the father as determined by the court shall be entered by the department. . . .

Statutory Interpretation of Iowa Code Section 144.13(2) . . .

A specific rule of construction found in Iowa Code section 4.1 applies to statutes containing gendered terms and assists us in ascertaining the legislature's intent. Section 4.1 provides: "Words of one gender include the other genders." This is not, however, a blanket rule applicable to all types of statutes. Instead, courts construing statutes can only utilize this rule when the statute uses a specific type of gendered language. . . .

[W]hen the statute employs both masculine and feminine words, . . . [r]eading such a statute in a gender-neutral manner "would destroy or change" the plain and unambiguous language, and would "nullif[y] the intent of the Legislature."

Iowa's presumption of parentage statute expressly uses *both* masculine and feminine words by referring to a mother, father, and husband. . . . If we . . . imposed a gender-neutral interpretation of the presumption, we would destroy the legislature's intent to *unambiguously* differentiate between the roles assigned to the two sexes. Only a male can be a husband or father. Only a female can be a wife or mother. The legislature used plain and unambiguous language to convey its intent. Thus, we cannot nullify the intent of the legislature by finding otherwise through statutory construction. . . .

Constitutional Analysis . . .

[T]he refusal to list the non-birthing lesbian spouse on the child's birth certificate "differentiates implicitly on the basis of sexual orientation." . . . Under *Varnum*, a sexual-orientation-based classification is subject to a heightened level of scrutiny under the Iowa Constitution. . . . Heightened scrutiny requires the State to show the statutory classification is substantially related to an important governmental objective. Accordingly, we must evaluate whether the governmental objectives proffered by the State are important and whether the statutory classification substantially relates to those objectives. . . .

The plain language of the statute requires the Department to put a husband's name on the birth certificate if a married opposite-sex couple has a child born during the marriage and if the couple used an anonymous sperm donor to conceive the child. Thus, the statute treats married lesbian couples who conceive through artificial insemination using an anonymous sperm donor differently than married opposite-sex couples who conceive a child in the same manner. We must analyze this differential treatment to determine if it is substantially related to an important governmental objective. . . .

The Department enumerates three objectives supporting section 144.13(2)'s differing treatment of married, lesbian and opposite-sex couples. Specifically, the Department argues the government has an interest in the accuracy of birth certificates, the efficiency and effectiveness of government administration, and the determination of paternity.

First, we understand that ensuring the accuracy of birth records for identification of biological parents is a laudable goal. However, the present system does not always accurately identify the biological father. When a married opposite-sex couple conceives a child using an anonymous sperm donor, the child's birth certificate reflects the male spouse as the father, not the biological father who donated the sperm. In that situation, the Department is not aware the couple conceived the child by an anonymous sperm donor.

Furthermore, the Department claims that the only way a married lesbian couple, who uses an anonymous sperm donor to conceive the child, can list the non-birthing spouse as the parent on the birth certificate is to go through an adoption proceeding. This will not make the birth certificate any more accurate than applying the presumption of parentage for married lesbian couples, because the birth certificate still will not identify the biological father. The birth records of this state do not contain a statistical database listing the children conceived using anonymous sperm donors. Thus, the classification is not substantially related to the asserted governmental purpose of accuracy.

The Department next asserts the refusal to apply the presumption of parentage to non-birthing spouses in lesbian marriages serves administrative efficiency and effectiveness. The Department argues that it takes valuable resources to reissue a birth certificate when a challenger successfully rebuts the presumption of parentage. However, when couples use an anonymous sperm donor, there will be no rebuttal of paternity. . . .

It is *more* efficient for the Department to list, presumptively, the non-birthing spouse as the parent on the birth certificate when the child is born, rather than to require the Department to issue a birth certificate with only one spouse's name on the certificate and then later, after an adoption is complete, reissue the certificate. These realities demonstrate that the disparate treatment of married lesbian couples is less effective and efficient, and that some other unarticulated reason, such as stereotype or prejudice, may explain the real objective of the State.

The third proffered reason for the Department's action is the government's interest in establishing paternity to ensure financial support of the child and the fundamental legal rights of the father. When a lesbian couple is married, it is just as important to establish who is financially responsible for the child and the legal rights of the non-birthing spouse. . . .

It is important for our laws to recognize that married lesbian couples who have children enjoy the same benefits and burdens as married opposite-sex couples who have children. By naming the non-birthing spouse on the birth certificate of a married lesbian couple's child, the child is ensured support from that parent and the parent establishes fundamental legal rights at the moment of birth. Therefore, the only explanation for not listing the non-birthing lesbian spouse on the birth certificate is stereotype or prejudice. The exclusion of the non-birthing spouse on the birth certificate of a child born to a married lesbian couple is not substantially related to the objective of establishing parentage. . . .

We find the presumption of parentage statute violates equal protection under the Iowa Constitution as applied to married lesbian couples. However, we are not required to strike down the statute because our obligation is to preserve as much of a statute as possible, within constitutional restraints. Accordingly, instead of striking section 144.13(2) from the Code, we will preserve it as to married opposite-sex couples and require the Department to apply the statute to married lesbian couples. Therefore, we affirm the district court and order the Department to issue a birth certificate naming Melissa Gartner as the parent of the child, Mackenzie Jean Gartner. . . .

Douglas NeJaime, Marriage Equality and the New Parenthood
129 Harv. L. Rev. 1185 (2016)

While the marital presumption always had the capacity to embody functional parenthood, it often did so by masking, rather than owning, biological reality. Even when the mother's husband was not the biological father, the law could act on the fiction that he was. But with same-sex couples, where there can be no mistake about biological fact, the marital presumption is detached from notions of biology on a wholesale basis. With same-sex marriage, the presumption makes sense only because it provides an indication of intent and "holding out." . . .

[T]he conceptual underpinnings of donor-insemination regulation, which premises marital parentage on intent and conduct, may become generalizable through marriage equality. Previously, donor insemination constituted an exception to the normal operation of presumptions. Many states . . . maintain a separate provision setting out intent-based rules for married couples using donor insemination. The assumption, of course, is that donor insemination makes the biological reality explicit in ways that complicate application of the marital presumption and point toward a competing claim by the sperm donor. For those states that nonetheless route donor insemination through the general marital presumption, the biological reality for most different-sex couples can remain hidden. With same-sex marriage, however, the logic of alternative insemination informs the logic of the marital presumption more generally, such that the presumption effectively becomes a de facto donor-insemination statute. . . .

[T]he refusal to apply the marital presumption to same-sex couples can be understood not merely as continuing resistance to LGBT equality, but also as an attempt to recenter biology as a dominant marker of parentage and to maintain the primacy of gendered notions of parenting. . . .

Applying the marital presumption to same-sex couples is important not only from a sexual-orientation-equality perspective, but also from a more general family law perspective. The push and pull between biology and function continues to play out in disputes involving different-sex parents. In fact, in some states, biology has gained prominence in the context of married different-sex couples in which the husband seeks to disestablish paternity. Even when a man has served as a father for a substantial period of time, some courts have allowed the introduction of genetic evidence to terminate his parental obligations. These types of disputes arise at divorce, when, at a particularly unsettling time for children, courts may terminate an established parent-child relationship.

Paternity disestablishment is troubling from the perspective of a model of parenthood that values functional relationships and children's best interests, and it should be seen as connected to conflicts over the application of the marital presumption to same-sex couples. If the marital presumption applies to lesbian mothers in a way that is relatively insulated from rebuttal by genetic evidence, then it may similarly apply to husbands who have been serving as (nonbiological) fathers. Of course, competing claims by biological fathers present an additional consideration. Still, it is important to see that part of what is at stake in paternity disestablishment is a model of parenthood that values parent-child relationships regardless of biology. . . .

PAVAN V. SMITH
137 S. Ct. 2075 (2017)

PER CURIAM. . . .

The petitioners here are two married same-sex couples who conceived children through anonymous sperm donation. Leigh and Jana Jacobs were married in Iowa in 2010, and Terrah and Marisa Pavan were married in New Hampshire in 2011. Leigh and Terrah each gave birth to a child in Arkansas in 2015. When it came time to secure birth certificates for the newborns, each couple filled out paperwork listing both spouses as parents — Leigh and Jana in one case, Terrah and Marisa in the other. Both times, however, the Arkansas Department of Health issued certificates bearing only the birth mother's name.

The department's decision rested on a provision of Arkansas law, Ark. Code § 20-18-401 (2014), that specifies which individuals will appear as parents on a child's state-issued birth certificate. "For the purposes of birth registration," that statute says, "the mother is deemed to be the woman who gives birth to the child." And "[i]f the mother was married at the time of either conception or birth," the statute instructs that "the name of [her] husband shall be entered on the certificate as the father of the child." There are some limited exceptions to the latter rule — for example, another man may appear on the birth certificate if the "mother" and "husband" and "putative father" all file affidavits vouching for the putative father's paternity. But as all parties agree, the requirement that a married woman's husband appear on her child's birth certificate applies in cases where the couple conceived by means of artificial insemination with the help of an anonymous sperm donor.

The Jacobses and Pavans brought this suit in Arkansas state court against the director of the Arkansas Department of Health — seeking, among other things, a declaration that the State's birth-certificate law violates the Constitution. . . . [A] divided Arkansas Supreme Court . . . conclude[ed] that the statute "pass[es] constitutional muster." In that court's view, "the statute centers on the relationship of the biological mother and the biological father to the child, not on the marital relationship of husband and wife," and so it "does not run afoul of *Obergefell*." . . .

The Arkansas Supreme Court's decision, we conclude, denied married same-sex couples access to the "constellation of benefits that the Stat[e] ha[s] linked to marriage." *Obergefell v. Hodges*, 135 S.Ct. 2584, 2601 (2015). . . .

Obergefell proscribes such disparate treatment. As we explained there, a State may not "exclude same-sex couples from civil marriage on the same terms and conditions as opposite-sex couples." Indeed, in listing those terms and conditions — the "rights, benefits, and responsibilities" to which same-sex couples, no less than opposite-sex couples, must have access — we expressly identified "birth and death certificates."

Echoing the court below, the State defends its birth-certificate law on the ground that being named on a child's birth certificate is not a benefit that attends marriage. Instead, the State insists, a birth certificate is simply a device for recording biological parentage — regardless of whether the child's parents are married. But Arkansas law makes birth certificates about more than just genetics. . . . [W]hen an opposite-sex couple conceives a child by way of anonymous sperm donation — just as the petitioners did here — state law requires the placement of the birth mother's husband on the child's birth certificate. And that is so even though (as the State concedes) the husband "is definitively not the biological father" in those circumstances. Arkansas has thus chosen to make its birth certificates more than a mere marker of biological relationships: The State uses those certificates to give married parents a form of legal recognition that is not available to unmarried parents. Having made that choice, Arkansas may not, consistent with *Obergefell*, deny married same-sex couples that recognition. . . .

JUSTICE GORSUCH, with whom JUSTICE THOMAS and JUSTICE ALITO join, dissenting. . . .

To be sure, *Obergefell* addressed the question whether a State must recognize same-sex marriages. But nothing in *Obergefell* spoke (let alone clearly) to the question whether § 20-18-401 of the Arkansas Code, or a state supreme court decision upholding it, must go. The statute in question establishes a set of rules designed to ensure that the biological parents of a child are listed on the child's birth certificate. Before the state supreme court, the State argued that rational reasons exist for a biology based birth registration regime, reasons that in no way offend *Obergefell* — like ensuring government officials can identify public health trends and helping individuals determine their biological lineage, citizenship, or susceptibility to genetic disorders. In an opinion that did not in any way seek to defy but rather earnestly engage *Obergefell*, the state supreme court agreed. And it is very hard to see what is wrong with this conclusion for, just as the state court recognized, nothing in *Obergefell* indicates that a birth registration regime based on biology, one no doubt with many analogues across the country and throughout history, offends the Constitution. . . .

NOTES AND QUESTIONS

1.   *Post-*Pavan *Cases. Pavan* involved birth certificates, which generally do not establish parentage but are simply evidence of parentage. Nonetheless, *Pavan* clearly has consequences for the law of parentage. After *Pavan*, the Arizona Supreme Court resolved conflicting decisions of the state appellate courts by holding that the state's marital presumption applies to married female same-sex couples.[93] Like the Court in *Pavan*, the Arizona court reasoned that, "[b]ecause the marital paternity presumption does more than just identify biological fathers, Arizona cannot deny same-sex spouses the benefit the presumption affords."[94] More recently, the federal Court of Appeals for the Seventh Circuit rejected Indiana's refusal to apply its marital presumption to same-sex couples, holding that "after *Obergefell* and *Pavan*, a state cannot presume that a husband is the father of a child born in wedlock, while denying an equivalent presumption to parents in same-sex marriages."[95] Nonetheless, not all states have applied the marital presumption to married female same-sex couples, and conflict over this issue persists.[96]

2.   *Legislative Reform.* Many states have codified a gender-neutral marital presumption such that it applies to a man or a woman married to a woman who gives birth.[97] The 2017 Uniform Parentage Act, which the drafters described as reforming the law in light of *Obergefell* and *Pavan*, also includes a presumption of this kind. Section 204 provides: "An individual is presumed to be a parent of a child if . . . the individual and the woman who gave birth to the child are married to each other and the child is born during the marriage."[98]

---

93. See McLaughlin v. Jones, 401 P.3d 492 (Ariz. 2017).
94. Id. at 498.
95. See Henderson v. Box, 947 F.3d 482, 487 (7th Cir. 2020).
96. See, e.g., In re A.E., No. 09-16-00019-CV, 2017 WL 1535101 (Tex. App. Apr. 27, 2017).
97. See, e.g., Cal. Fam. Code § 7611 (West 2020); D.C. Code § 16-909 (2020); Me. Rev. Stat. Ann. tit. 19-A, § 1881 (2020).
98. UPA (2017), supra note 93, § 204.

3.   *Gender Neutrality?* In states that have moved toward a gender-neutral marital presumption, the presumption applies to the individual married to the biological *mother*, and not to the individual married to the biological *father*. As Professor Douglas NeJaime explains, this affects both same-sex and different-sex couples:

> Much follows simply from the determination that a child is "a child of the marriage." Parties to the marriage, even if not biologically related to the child, have standing to assert parental rights, including rights to custody.
>
> Yet, without a biological mother in the marriage, male same-sex couples do not technically have marital children. Parentage presumptions applicable to same-sex couples replicate the gender-differentiated rules applicable to different-sex couples. Presumptions of parentage for the second parent, even when they apply to both women and men, relate to that person's marriage to "the woman giving birth" or the "natural mother." Accordingly, a woman can derive parentage by virtue of her marriage to the biological mother . . . But a man can only derive parentage by virtue of marriage to the biological mother, not the biological father. Without biological ties, men in same-sex couples and women in different-sex couples find themselves in the same position: neither can [ordinarily] establish parentage without adoption.[99]

Courts have found that this regime does not offend equal protection principles. Consider this reasoning from a California court in Amy G. v. M.W., in which a woman who had been raising her husband's biological child asserted claims to parentage when the biological mother attempted to establish a parent-child relationship:

> While a biological father's genetic contribution to his child may arise from nothing more than a fleeting encounter, the biological mother carries the child for the nine-month gestational period. Because of this inherent difference between men and women with respect to reproduction, the wife of a man who fathered a child with another woman is not similarly situated to a man whose wife was impregnated by another man.[100]

Why do reproductive differences between men and women justify the differential treatment of nonbiological mothers and fathers? NeJaime questions the California court's logic:

> Of course, men and women are not similarly situated with respect to reproductive biology. But . . . the court translated biological differences between women and men into social and legal differences between mothers and fathers. The point here is not to suggest that the birth mother should not have prevailed. Rather, it is that the court relied on biological differences to justify a system that denies standing to assert parentage to a woman who had formed a parent-child relationship on social grounds.

---

99. Douglas NeJaime, The Nature of Parenthood, 126 Yale L.J. 2260, 2312 (2017).
100. 47 Cal. Rptr. 3d 297, 308 (Cal. Ct. App. 2006).

In contrast, an [alternative] approach . . . would have asked whether, notwithstanding biological differences between women and men, the gender-differentiated parentage law is substantially related to an important governmental objective. Parentage laws, as many courts have recognized, are driven by the state's interests in identifying those individuals responsible for the support of the child, protecting the integrity of the family, and safeguarding the child's interest in continuity of care. The differentiation between men and women who step forward to parent children — that is, the recognition of nonbiological fathers but not mothers — may not advance those interests but instead may undermine them. A sex-neutral alternative could promote the government's interests as effectively. . . .

[C]ourts . . . might focus the constitutional inquiry not simply on means-ends analysis but also on the law's social meaning. . . . A court might ask whether the parentage law reflects views that tie women to child rearing as a matter of biology. . . . [T]he non-recognition of nonbiological mothers . . . perpetuates the notion that the social role of motherhood flows inevitably from the biological fact of maternity. Guided by an equality-inflected approach, the *Amy G.* court, for instance, might have repudiated the trial court's reasoning, which suggested that the nonbiological mother was "[no] different from a live-in nanny" — presumably also a woman who cares for a child not biologically her own.[101]

III. Parenthood Based on Biology

We have seen that marriage historically defined parentage. The marital presumption operated in ways that led nonbiological fathers to be treated as legal fathers. This meant that the actual biological father was not treated as a legal father of the child. The law sought to maintain the child's legitimacy, given that "illegitimate" children did not have legally enforceable rights with respect to their biological parents.

Still, mothers ordinarily assumed custodial responsibility for their non-marital children. Eventually, courts and legislatures, in historian Michael Grossberg's description, began to treat the relationships between mothers and their non-marital children as one entailing "a web of reciprocal legal rights and duties."[102] Fathers of non-marital children often had financial obligations forced on them by local authorities seeking to ensure the child's support with nonpublic funds. Despite these

---

101. NeJaime, supra note 100, at 2357–58. For notable exceptions applying the marital presumption to the woman or man married to the biological father, see In re S.N.V., 284 P.3d 147 (Colo. App. 2011) (after biological father's wife had been raising the child, the court held that she could "bring an action to establish legal maternity" based on the marital presumption); In re Maria-Irene D., 61 N.Y.S.3d 221 (N.Y. App. Div. 2017) (assuming that when a married male same-sex couple has a child through a surrogacy arrangement, a presumption arises "that the child is the legitimate child of both [men]").

102. Michael Grossberg, Governing the Hearth: Law and the Family in Nineteenth-Century America 207 (1985).

developments, the relevance of legitimacy persisted well into the twentieth century. Law recognized mothers of non-marital children as legal parents but generally withheld such recognition from fathers. In some states, unmarried fathers had to adopt their biological children to have a legally protected relationship. As we saw in Chapter 6, in the late 1960s, the U.S. Supreme Court repudiated the discriminatory treatment of "illegitimate" children. As the next case demonstrates, soon after the Court protected non-marital children, it protected the rights of unmarried fathers.

A. The Constitutional Rights of Unmarried Fathers

STANLEY V. ILLINOIS
405 U.S. 645 (1972)

MR. JUSTICE WHITE delivered the opinion of the Court.

Joan Stanley lived with Peter Stanley intermittently for 18 years, during which time they had three children. When Joan Stanley died, Peter Stanley lost not only her but also his children. Under Illinois law, the children of unwed fathers become wards of the State upon the death of the mother. Accordingly, upon Joan Stanley's death, in a dependency proceeding instituted by the State of Illinois, Stanley's children were declared wards of the State and placed with court-appointed guardians. Stanley appealed, claiming that he had never been shown to be an unfit parent and that since married fathers and unwed mothers could not be deprived of their children without such a showing, he had been deprived of the equal protection of the laws guaranteed him by the Fourteenth Amendment. The Illinois Supreme Court accepted the fact that Stanley's own unfitness had not been established but rejected the equal protection claim, holding that Stanley could properly be separated from his children upon proof of the single fact that he and the dead mother had not been married. Stanley's actual fitness as a father was irrelevant.

Stanley presses his equal protection claim here. The State continues to respond that unwed fathers are presumed unfit to raise their children and that it is unnecessary to hold individualized hearings to determine whether particular fathers are in fact unfit parents before they are separated from their children. We granted certiorari to determine whether this method of procedure by presumption could be allowed to stand in light of the fact that Illinois allows married fathers — whether divorced, widowed, or separated — and mothers — even if unwed — the benefit of the presumption that they are fit to raise their children.

I

At the outset we reject any suggestion that we need not consider the propriety of the dependency proceeding that separated the Stanleys because Stanley might be able to regain custody of his children as a guardian or through adoption proceedings. . . . This Court has not, however, embraced the general proposition that a wrong may be done if it can be undone. . . .

It is first urged that Stanley could act to adopt his children. But under Illinois law, Stanley is treated not as a parent but as a stranger to his children, and the dependency proceeding has gone forward on the presumption that he is unfit to exercise parental rights. Insofar as we are informed, Illinois law affords him no priority in adoption proceedings. It would be his burden to establish not only that he would be a suitable parent but also that he would be the most suitable of all who might want custody of the children. Neither can we ignore that in the proceedings from which this action developed, the "probation officer," the assistant state's attorney, and the judge charged with the case, made it apparent that Stanley, unmarried and impecunious as he is, could not now expect to profit from adoption proceedings. . . .

Before us, the State focuses on Stanley's failure to petition for "custody and control"—the second route by which, it is urged, he might regain authority for his children. Passing the obvious issue whether it would be futile or burdensome for an unmarried father—without funds and already once presumed unfit—to petition for custody, this suggestion overlooks the fact that legal custody is not parenthood or adoption. A person appointed guardian in an action for custody and control is subject to removal at any time without such cause as must be shown in a neglect proceeding against a parent. He may not take the children out of the jurisdiction without the court's approval. He may be required to report to the court as to his disposition of the children's affairs. Obviously then, even if Stanley were a mere step away from "custody and control," to give an unwed father only "custody and control" would still be to leave him seriously prejudiced by reason of his status.

We must therefore examine the question that Illinois would have us avoid: Is a presumption that distinguishes and burdens all unwed fathers constitutionally repugnant? We conclude that, as a matter of due process of law, Stanley was entitled to a hearing on his fitness as a parent before his children were taken from him and that, by denying him a hearing and extending it to all other parents whose custody of their children is challenged, the State denied Stanley the equal protection of the laws guaranteed by the Fourteenth Amendment.

II

Illinois has two principal methods of removing non-delinquent children from the homes of their parents. In a dependency proceeding it may demonstrate that the children are wards of the State because they have no surviving parent or guardian. In a neglect proceeding it may show that children should be wards of the State because the present parent(s) or guardian does not provide suitable care.

The State's right—indeed, duty—to protect minor children through a judicial determination of their interests in a neglect proceeding is not challenged here. Rather, we are faced with a dependency statute that empowers state officials to circumvent neglect proceedings on the theory that an unwed father is not a "parent" whose existing relationship with his children must be considered. "Parents," says the State, "means the father and mother of a legitimate child, or the survivor of them, or the natural mother of an illegitimate child, and includes any adoptive parent," but the term does not include unwed fathers.

Under Illinois law, therefore, while the children of all parents can be taken from them in neglect proceedings, that is only after notice, hearing, and proof of such unfitness as a parent as amounts to neglect, an unwed father is uniquely subject to the more simplistic dependency proceeding. By use of this proceeding, the State, on showing that the father was not married to the mother, need not prove unfitness in fact, because it is presumed at law. Thus, the unwed father's claim of parental qualification is avoided as "irrelevant."

The private interest here, that of a man in the children he has sired and raised, undeniably warrants deference and, absent a powerful countervailing interest, protection. . . . The Court has frequently emphasized the importance of the family.

Nor has the law refused to recognize those family relationships unlegitimized by a marriage ceremony. The Court has declared unconstitutional a state statute denying natural, but illegitimate, children a wrongful-death action for the death of their mother, emphasizing that such children cannot be denied the right of other children because familial bonds in such cases were often as warm, enduring, and important as those arising within a more formally organized family unit. . . .

[A]t the least, Stanley's interest in retaining custody of his children is cognizable and substantial.

For its part, the State has made its interest quite plain: Illinois has declared that the aim of the Juvenile Court Act is to protect "the moral, emotional, mental, and physical welfare of the minor and the best interests of the community" and to "strengthen the minor's family ties whenever possible, removing him from the custody of his parents only when his welfare or safety or the protection of the public cannot be adequately safeguarded without removal. . . ." These are legitimate interests, well within the power of the State to implement. We do not question the assertion that neglectful parents may be separated from their children.

But we are here not asked to evaluate the legitimacy of the state ends, rather, to determine whether the means used to achieve these ends are constitutionally defensible. What is the state interest in separating children from fathers without a hearing designed to determine whether the father is unfit in a particular disputed case? We observe that the State registers no gain towards its declared goals when it separates children from the custody of fit parents. Indeed, if Stanley is a fit father, the State spites its own articulated goals when it needlessly separates him from his family.

It may be, as the State insists, that most unmarried fathers are unsuitable and neglectful parents. It may also be that Stanley is such a parent and that his children should be placed in other hands. But all unmarried fathers are not in this category; some are wholly suited to have custody of their children. . . . Given the opportunity to make his case, Stanley may have been seen to be deserving of custody of his off-spring. Had this been so, the State's statutory policy would have been furthered by leaving custody in him.

It may be argued that unmarried fathers are so seldom fit that Illinois need not undergo the administrative inconvenience of inquiry in any case, including Stanley's. The establishment of prompt efficacious procedures to achieve legitimate state ends is a proper state interest worthy of cognizance in constitutional adjudication. But the Constitution recognizes higher values than speed and efficiency. Indeed, one might fairly say of the Bill of Rights in general, and the Due Process Clause in particular, that they were designed to protect the fragile values of a vulnerable citizenry from the overbearing concern for efficiency and efficacy that may characterize praiseworthy government officials no less, and perhaps more, than mediocre ones.

Procedure by presumption is always cheaper and easier than individualized determination. But when, as here, the procedure forecloses the determinative issues of competence and care, when it explicitly disdains present realities in deference to past formalities, it needlessly risks running roughshod over the important interests of both parent and child. It therefore cannot stand.

The State's interest in caring for Stanley's children is *de minimis* if Stanley is shown to be a fit father. It insists on presuming rather than proving Stanley's unfitness solely because it is more convenient to presume than to prove. Under the Due Process Clause that advantage is insufficient to justify refusing a father a hearing when the issue at stake is the dismemberment of his family.

III

The State of Illinois assumes custody of the children of married parents, divorced parents, and unmarried mothers only after a hearing and proof of neglect. The children of unmarried fathers, however, are declared dependent children without a hearing on parental fitness and without proof of neglect. Stanley's claim in the state courts and here is that failure to afford him a hearing on his parental qualifications while extending it to other parents denied him equal protection of the laws. We have concluded that all Illinois parents are constitutionally entitled to a hearing on their fitness before their children are removed from their custody. It follows that denying such a hearing to Stanley and those like him while granting it to other Illinois parents is inescapably contrary to the Equal Protection Clause.

Mr. Chief Justice Burger, with whom Mr. Justice Blackmun concurs, dissenting. . . .

When explaining at oral argument why Illinois does not recognize the unwed father, counsel for the State presented two basic justifications for the statutory definition of "parents" here at issue. First, counsel noted that in the case of a married couple to whom a legitimate child is born, the two biological parents have already "signified their willingness to work together" in caring for the child by entering into the marriage contract; it is manifestly reasonable, therefore, that both of them be recognized as legal parents with rights and responsibilities in connection with the child. There has been no legally cognizable signification of such willingness on the part of unwed parents, however, and "the male and female . . . may or may not be willing to work together towards the common end of child rearing." To provide legal recognition to both of them as "parents" would often be "to create two conflicting parties competing for legal control of the child."

The second basic justification urged upon us by counsel for the State was that, in order to provide for the child's welfare, "it is necessary to impose upon at least one of the parties legal responsibility for the welfare of [the child], and since necessarily the female is present at the birth of the child and identifiable as the mother," the State has selected the unwed mother, rather than the unwed father, as the biological parent with that legal responsibility. . . .

I agree with the State's argument that the Equal Protection Clause is not violated when Illinois gives full recognition only to those father-child relationships that arise in the context of family units bound together by legal obligations arising from marriage or from adoption proceedings. . . .

Where there is a valid contract of marriage, the law of Illinois presumes that the husband is the father of any child born to the wife during the marriage; as the father, he has legally enforceable rights and duties with respect to that child. When a child is born to an unmarried woman, Illinois recognizes the readily identifiable mother, but makes no presumption as to the identity of the biological father. . . .

Illinois' different treatment of [unwed mothers and unwed fathers] is part of that State's statutory scheme for protecting the welfare of illegitimate children. . . .

[A] State is fully justified in concluding, on the basis of common human experience, that the biological role of the mother in carrying and nursing an infant creates stronger bonds between her and the child than the bonds resulting from the male's often casual encounter. This view is reinforced by the observable fact that most unwed mothers exhibit a concern for their offspring either permanently or at least until they are safely placed for adoption, while unwed fathers rarely burden either the mother or the child with their attentions or loyalties. Centuries of human experience buttress this view of the realities of human conditions and suggest that unwed mothers of illegitimate children are generally more dependable protectors of their children than are unwed fathers. While these, like most generalizations, are not without exceptions, they nevertheless provide a sufficient basis to sustain a statutory classification whose objective is not to penalize unwed parents but to further the welfare of illegitimate children in fulfillment of the State's obligations as *parens patriae*.

Stanley depicts himself as a somewhat unusual unwed father, namely, as one who has always acknowledged and never doubted his fatherhood of these children.

He alleges that he loved, cared for, and supported these children from the time of their birth until the death of their mother. He contends that he consequently must be treated the same as a married father of legitimate children. Even assuming the truth of Stanley's allegations, I am unable to construe the Equal Protection Clause as requiring Illinois to tailor its statutory definition of "parents" so meticulously as to include such unusual unwed fathers, while at the same time excluding those unwed, and generally unidentified, biological fathers who in no way share Stanley's professed desires.

Indeed, the nature of Stanley's own desires is less than absolutely clear from the record in this case. Shortly after the death of the mother, Stanley turned these two children over to the care of a Mr. and Mrs. Ness; he took no action to gain recognition of himself as a father, through adoption, or as a legal custodian, through a guardianship proceeding. Eventually it came to the attention of the State that there was no living adult who had any legally enforceable obligation for the care and support of the children; it was only then that the dependency proceeding here under review took place and that Stanley made himself known to the juvenile court in connection with these two children. Even then, however, Stanley did not ask to be charged with the legal responsibility for the children. He asked only that such legal responsibility be given to no one else. He seemed, in particular, to be concerned with the loss of the welfare payments he would suffer as a result of the designation of others as guardians of the children.

Not only, then, do I see no ground for holding that Illinois' statutory definition of "parents" on its face violates the Equal Protection Clause; I see no ground for holding that any constitutional right of Stanley has been denied in the application of that statutory definition in the case at bar.

NOTES AND QUESTIONS

1.   *The "Illegitimacy" Cases.* Just a few years before *Stanley*, the Court had invalidated laws penalizing non-marital children — a topic we covered in Chapter 6.[103] When the Court recognized constitutional rights for unmarried fathers in *Stanley*, it drew on these precedents to support the idea that non-marital families were worthy of constitutional protection.

2.   Stanley *and Substantive Due Process.* The Court decided *Stanley* on equal protection and procedural due process grounds, holding that the state impermissibly denied Stanley a hearing that would be provided "to all other parents whose custody of their children is challenged." Despite the technical grounds on which the decision

---

103. See Levy v. Louisiana, 391 U.S. 68 (1968); Glona v. Am. Guar. & Liab. Ins. Co., 391 U.S. 73 (1968).

rested, the Court's decision came to represent a right rooted in substantive due process, one that built on the early twentieth century cases (*Meyer* and *Pierce*, which we covered in Chapter 6) recognizing the constitutional dimension of parental rights. Yet, while those earlier cases involved rights against government interference in the parent-child relation, *Stanley* involved a right to have the state affirmatively recognize a parent-child relationship. After *Stanley*, at least some unmarried fathers were understood to possess a liberty interest in parental recognition.

3. *Post-*Stanley *Legislative Reform.* Even before the Court intervened to invalidate "illegitimacy" laws and protect unmarried fathers on constitutional grounds, reformers were seeking to change state laws. Professor Harry Krause, one of the leaders of these efforts, had drafted model legislation before the Court's decision.[104] After *Stanley*, Krause served as the reporter-draftsman for the Uniform Parentage Act, which was promulgated by the Uniform Law Commission in 1973. Nearly twenty states adopted the UPA.[105]

States that adopted the UPA, as well as states that did not, provided paths for unmarried fathers to establish their parentage. States did not treat unmarried fathers as automatically entitled to legal recognition. Rather, they required unmarried fathers to take some action to "legitimate" the child. For instance, a man might have to acknowledge paternity in writing, receive the child into his home and openly hold out the child as his child, or obtain a judgment of paternity.[106] In some states, men had to sign up with the state's "paternity registry" in order to be a party who would receive notice regarding the child's adoption.[107] Do you think men in these states would know that they have to register in order to preserve their rights? Would you expect men to register with respect to every sexual encounter that may have unknowingly produced a child? Men who failed to take the necessary steps challenged their states' statutory schemes, and some of these cases made their way to the U.S. Supreme Court.

4. *Parenting, Marriage, and Gender.* The Court in *Stanley* observed — and the dissent explicitly credited — the state's view "that most unmarried fathers are unsuitable and neglectful parents." Why might the state assume that unmarried fathers are less suitable than either married fathers or unmarried mothers? Would the same assumption be invoked today? Why or why not?

---

104. Harry D. Krause, Bringing the Bastard into the Great Society — A Proposed Uniform Act on Illegitimacy, 44 Tex. L. Rev. 829 (1966).

105. Harry D. Krause, The Uniform Parentage Act, 8 Fam. L.Q. 1 (1974).

106. See, e.g., Unif. Parentage Act § 5 (Unif. Law. Comm'n 1973); Ga. Code Ann. § 74-103 (1977); N.Y. Dom. Rel. Law § 111 (McKinney 1977).

107. See N.Y. Soc. Serv. Law § 372-c (McKinney 1978) ("The department shall establish a putative father registry which shall record the names and addresses of . . . any person who has filed with the registry before or after the birth of a child out of wedlock, a notice of intent to claim paternity of the child."); see also Ark. Code Ann. § 9-9-210 (1987); Idaho Code § 16-1513 (1992); Okla. Stat. Ann. tit. 10, § 55.1 (West 1987).

The Illinois scheme that the Court struck down in *Stanley* required an unmarried father in Stanley's position to essentially adopt his own children. This was not the only way in which adoption featured in the case. Adoption advocates argued that granting rights to unmarried fathers would jeopardize adoption. Individuals would be less likely to pursue adoption if they knew that the child's biological father might be able to block the adoption even if the birth mother consented.[108] As our coverage of adoption in Chapter 8 demonstrated, conflicts between adoptive parents and the rights of unmarried fathers persisted. The following case provides a famous example.

PETITION OF DOE
638 N.E.2d 181 (Ill. 1994)

JUSTICE HEIPLE delivered the opinion of the court:

John and Jane Doe filed a petition to adopt a newborn baby boy. The baby's biological mother, Daniella Janikova, executed a consent to have the baby adopted four days after his birth without informing his biological father, Otakar Kirchner, to whom she was not yet married.

The mother told the father that the baby had died, and he did not find out otherwise until 57 days after the birth. The trial court ruled that the father's consent was unnecessary because he did not show sufficient interest in the child during the first 30 days of the child's life. The appellate court affirmed. . . .

Otakar and Daniella began living together in the fall of 1989, and Daniella became pregnant in June of 1990. For the first eight months of her pregnancy, Otakar provided for all of her expenses.

In late January 1991, Otakar went to his native Czechoslovakia to attend to his gravely ill grandmother for two weeks. During this time, Daniella received a phone call from Otakar's aunt saying that Otakar had resumed a former romantic relationship with another woman.

Because of this unsettling news, Daniella left their shared apartment, refused to talk with Otakar on his return, and gave birth to the child at a different hospital than where they had originally planned. She gave her consent to the adoption of the child by the Does, telling them and their attorney that she knew who the father was but would not furnish his name. Daniella and her uncle warded off Otakar's persistent inquiries about the child by telling him that the child had died shortly after birth.

Otakar found out that the child was alive and had been placed for adoption 57 days after the child was born. He then began the instant proceedings by filing

---

108. See Serena Mayeri, Foundling Fathers: (Non-)Marriage and Parental Rights in the Age of Equality, 125 Yale L.J. 2292 (2016).

an appearance contesting the Does' adoption of his son. As already noted, the trial court ruled that Otakar was an unfit parent under section 1 of the Adoption Act (the Act) because he had not shown a reasonable degree of interest in the child within the first 30 days of his life. Therefore, the father's consent was unnecessary under section 8 of the Act.

The finding that the father had not shown a reasonable degree of interest in the child is not supported by the evidence. In fact, he made various attempts to locate the child, all of which were either frustrated or blocked by the actions of the mother. Further, the mother was aided by the attorney for the adoptive parents, who failed to make any effort to ascertain the name or address of the father despite the fact that the mother indicated she knew who he was. Under the circumstances, the father had no opportunity to discharge any familial duty.

In the opinion below, the appellate court, wholly missing the threshold issue in this case, dwelt on the best interests of the child. Since, however, the father's parental interest was improperly terminated, there was no occasion to reach the factor of the child's best interests. That point should never have been reached and need never have been discussed.

Unfortunately, over three years have elapsed since the birth of the baby who is the subject of these proceedings. To the extent that it is relevant to assign fault in this case, the fault here lies initially with the mother, who fraudulently tried to deprive the father of his rights, and secondly, with the adoptive parents and their attorney, who proceeded with the adoption when they knew that a real father was out there who had been denied knowledge of his baby's existence. When the father entered his appearance in the adoption proceedings 57 days after the baby's birth and demanded his rights as a father, the petitioners should have relinquished the baby at that time. It was their decision to prolong this litigation through a lengthy, and ultimately fruitless, appeal.

The adoption laws of Illinois are neither complex nor difficult of application. Those laws intentionally place the burden of proof on the adoptive parents in establishing both the relinquishment and/or unfitness of the natural parents and, coincidentally, the fitness and the right to adopt of the adoptive parents. In addition, Illinois law requires a good-faith effort to notify the natural parents of the adoption proceedings. These laws are designed to protect natural parents in their preemptive rights to their own children wholly apart from any consideration of the so-called best interests of the child. If it were otherwise, few parents would be secure in the custody of their own children. If best interests of the child were a sufficient qualification to determine child custody, anyone with superior income, intelligence, education, etc., might challenge and deprive the parents of their right to their own children. The law is otherwise and was not complied with in this case.

Accordingly, we reverse.

NOTES AND QUESTIONS

1. *Best Interest of the Child?* In their seminal treatment of the case, Yale law professor Joseph Goldstein, psychoanalyst Anna Freud, and Yale Child Study Center professor Albert Solnit vehemently object to the outcome and argue that the court should have done what was in the best interest of the child.[109] Why didn't the court reason in this way?

2. *Timing.* Is part of the problem that litigation takes too long? Should there be a requirement that challenges to adoptions be conducted on an expedited basis? Would that have mitigated the consequences of the court's decision for the child?

3. *Remedies.* Once a court determines that the biological father's constitutional rights were insufficiently protected, it awards him custody of the child. This shift in custody may be traumatic for the child. Is there some other way that a court might recognize the injury to the father and yet protect the interests of the child in remaining with his adoptive parents? Would money damages provide adequate redress?

4. *The Supreme Court.* In the 1970s and 1980s, the Court decided a number of cases involving unmarried fathers challenging their child's adoption by the mother's husband. But the Court did not decide a case featuring an unmarried father challenging the mother's decision to relinquish her rights and place the child for adoption. Cases involving stranger adoption confronted the Court during this time, but the Court never reached the merits.[110]

5. *State Laws.* Even though the Court did not weigh in on the rights of unmarried fathers to challenge a mother's decision to place the child for adoption, state legislatures amended their laws in ways that sought to avoid conflicts of the kind raised in Petition of Doe (popularly referred to as the Baby Richard case).[111] Parties seeking to adopt must take specific affirmative steps to locate the biological father and seek his consent to the adoption or otherwise allow him to contest the adoption.[112] Still, some states place especially high burdens on biological fathers seeking to assert rights to the child when the mother has decided to place the child for adoption. For instance, men in Utah must register in the state's putative father registry and file an affidavit promising to provide financial support to the child and assume custody.[113] Clearly, states differ in how they strike the balance between the rights of biological fathers and the desire to promote adoption.

---

109. Joseph Goldstein et al., The Best Interests of the Child: The Least Detrimental Alternative 51–61 (1996).

110. See Kirkpatrick v. Christian Homes of Abilene, 460 U.S. 1074 (1983); McNamara v. San Diego Dep't of Soc. Servs., 488 U.S. 152 (1988).

111. Joanna L. Grossman & Lawrence M. Friedman, Inside the Castle: Law and the Family in 20th Century America 294–97 (2011).

112. See, e.g., D.C. Code Ann. § 16-304 (West 2020).

113. In re Adoption of J.S., 358 P.3d 1009, 1011–12 (Utah 2014) (upholding these requirements against constitutional challenges).

PROBLEM

You are an attorney at the ACLU Women's Rights Project (WRP). You are considering a Florida case in which an unmarried biological father is challenging the state's regulation of adoption and the rights of unmarried fathers. In order to protect his rights, the man must register with the Florida Putative Father Registry. According to the state, "The purpose of the registry is to permit a man alleging to be the unmarried biological father of a child to preserve his right to notice and consent in the event of an adoption."[114] Once he obtains notice, the unmarried father's ability to successfully contest the adoption depends on whether he "demonstrate[d] a timely and full commitment to the responsibilities of parenthood, both during the pregnancy and after the child's birth" by "providing appropriate medical care and financial support."[115] Many unmarried fathers do not know of these requirements. According to one article, the Florida registry in the year 2004 had "just 47 registrants for the [state's] 89,436 out-of-wedlock births."[116] The director of the WRP has explained that the ACLU has filed amicus briefs in the past in cases involving unmarried fathers and adoption. She has asked you to come to a meeting prepared to discuss what position, if any, the WRP should take in the case. What position would you advocate? Why?

As you can see, questions about the rights of unmarried fathers are complicated. They implicate other critical areas, like adoption, the welfare of children, and gender equality. As Professor Serena Mayeri has shown, feminists were divided over whether more rights for unmarried fathers would further, or instead undermine, the rights of women. More precisely, would recognizing unmarried fathers as legal fathers break down stereotypes that saw women, and not men, as caretakers? Or would such recognition harm women, who continued to assume the vast majority of responsibility for children, by allowing men to second-guess their decisions, such as the decision to place the child for adoption? The conflicts over stranger adoption and unmarried fathers crystallized much of this "feminist dilemma." Consider Mayeri's discussion of Kirkpatrick v. Christian Homes of Abilene, a case that raised sex equality questions but which the Court ultimately remanded for resolution of a state law question.

---

114. Putative Father Registry, Fla. Dep't of Health, http://www.floridahealth.gov/certificates/ certificates/birth/Putative_Father/index.html.

115. Fla. Stat. § 63.022(e) (2020).

116. Tamar Lewin, Unwed Fathers Fight for Babies Placed for Adoption by Mothers, N.Y. Times, Mar. 19, 2006, at A1. See generally Laura Oren, Thwarted Fathers or Pop-Up Pops?: How to Determine When Putative Fathers Can Block the Adoption of Their Newborn Children, 40 Fam. L.Q. 153 (2006).

Serena Mayeri, Foundling Fathers: (Non-)Marriage and Parental Rights in the Age of Equality
125 Yale L.J. 2292 (2016)

Kirkpatrick was the first case to present the Court with a feminist argument against sex neutrality in non-marital parental rights. In a small Nebraska town, Donald Kirkpatrick and Laura S. began an intimate relationship when he was 22 and she was 14. At 15, Laura became pregnant, and decided, in consultation with her parents, to place the child for adoption. An adoptee herself, Laura "had great concern for the stigma attached to a child born out of wedlock in a small town." . . .

When Laura informed [Kirkpatrick] of the pregnancy, Kirkpatrick proposed marriage, but Laura declined. In Texas, biological fathers were entitled to receive notice of adoption proceedings, but could not veto an adoption and take custody of an unlegitimated child unless a court agreed that legitimation was in the child's best interests. The trial court denied Kirkpatrick's legitimation petition and placed the infant in foster care pending appeal. The state appellate court affirmed. . . .

Supporters said Kirkpatrick was a responsible, upstanding young man devoted to his daughter and eager to marry her mother; detractors claimed he was an irreligious statutory rapist with inconstant paternal instincts who planned to turn the child over to the care of his female relatives. Both characterizations enjoyed some support in the record. . . .

[T]he national ACLU agreed to represent Kirkpatrick before the U.S. Supreme Court. The ACLU argued that substantive due process and equal protection required that unmarried fathers be permitted to legitimate their children over the mother's objection, veto an adoption, and obtain custody unless they were proven unfit. The Court should, the ACLU argued, declare the best-interests standard unconstitutionally vague, at least with respect to terminations of parental rights. And the Texas statute was "freighted with the 'baggage of sexual stereotypes' so often condemned by this Court." The injury to "caring fathers" was "patent." "Less obvious but equally invidious" was "the harm done to women," who were "inevitably locked into the childcare role, unable to share childrearing responsibilities equally with men." . . .

Feminist attorney Nancy Erickson authored an amicus brief on behalf of "unwed mothers" who opposed unmarried fathers' asserted right to veto an adoption and obtain custody for themselves. She quoted unmarried mothers who said they would not have pursued adoption if it meant that the father might gain custody. Instead, these mothers might have felt pressured to have an abortion or to raise an unwanted child, Erickson asserted, violating their right to privacy and decisional autonomy and flouting the child's best interests. Mothers should also have the right to give up their children for adoption anonymously, Erickson argued, and men should not be allowed to use their sexual partners as involuntary surrogate mothers.

Erickson denied that the Texas statutory scheme reflected "an impermissible gender bias" or promoted "sexual stereotypes that portray men as incapable of good parenting." . . . Kirkpatrick had married a "full-time homemaker" who allegedly was eager to raise the child, leading Erickson to observe that awarding custody to a man who did not intend to assume a caregiving role hardly served feminist objectives. Feminists like Erickson embraced the goal of greater paternal involvement in the care of children, but they worried about the effects of formal equality on unequal social circumstances. . . .

Stanley clearly led to greater protections for unmarried biological fathers. But state laws generally required some affirmative action in order for unmarried men to secure their parent-child relationships. Until the next case, the Court had never considered how those rights could be secured with an infant — or how difficult a state could make it for an unmarried biological father to establish a relationship without running afoul of the Due Process Clause.

Lehr v. Robertson
463 U.S. 248 (1983)

Justice Stevens delivered the opinion of the Court.

The question presented is whether New York has sufficiently protected an unmarried father's inchoate relationship with a child whom he has never supported and rarely seen in the two years since her birth. The appellant, Jonathan Lehr, claims that the Due Process and Equal Protection Clauses of the Fourteenth Amendment, give him an absolute right to notice and an opportunity to be heard before the child may be adopted. We disagree.

Jessica M. was born out of wedlock on November 9, 1976. Her mother, Lorraine Robertson, married Richard Robertson eight months after Jessica's birth. On December 21, 1978, when Jessica was over two years old, the Robertsons filed an adoption petition in the Family Court of Ulster County, New York. The court heard their testimony and received a favorable report from the Ulster County Department of Social Services. On March 7, 1979, the court entered an order of adoption. In this proceeding, appellant contends that the adoption order is invalid because he, Jessica's putative father, was not given advance notice of the adoption proceeding.

The State of New York maintains a "putative father registry." A man who files with that registry demonstrates his intent to claim paternity of a child born out of wedlock and is therefore entitled to receive notice of any proceeding to adopt that child. Before entering Jessica's adoption order, the Ulster County Family Court had the putative father registry examined. Although appellant claims to be Jessica's natural father, he had not entered his name in the registry.

In addition to the persons whose names are listed on the putative father registry, New York law requires that notice of an adoption proceeding be given to several other classes of possible fathers of children born out of wedlock — those who have been adjudicated to be the father, those who have been identified as the father on the child's birth certificate, those who live openly with the child and the child's mother and who hold themselves out to be the father, those who have been identified as the father by the mother in a sworn written statement, and those who were married to the child's mother before the child was six months old. Appellant admittedly was not a member of any of those classes. He had lived with appellee prior to Jessica's birth and visited her in the hospital when Jessica was born, but his name does not appear on Jessica's birth certificate. He did not live with appellee or Jessica after Jessica's birth, he has never provided them with any financial support, and he has never offered to marry appellee. Nevertheless, he contends that the following special circumstances gave him a constitutional right to notice and a hearing before Jessica was adopted.

On January 30, 1979, one month after the adoption proceeding was commenced in Ulster County, appellant filed a "visitation and paternity petition" in the Westchester County Family Court. In that petition, he asked for a determination of paternity, an order of support, and reasonable visitation privileges with Jessica. Notice of that proceeding was served on appellee on February 22, 1979. Four days later appellee's attorney informed the Ulster County Court that appellant had commenced a paternity proceeding in Westchester County; the Ulster County judge then entered an order staying appellant's paternity proceeding until he could rule on a motion to change the venue of that proceeding to Ulster County. On March 3, 1979, appellant received notice of the change of venue motion and, for the first time, learned that an adoption proceeding was pending in Ulster County.

On March 7, 1979, appellant's attorney telephoned the Ulster County judge to inform him that he planned to seek a stay of the adoption proceeding pending the determination of the paternity petition. In that telephone conversation, the judge advised the lawyer that he had already signed the adoption order earlier that day. According to appellant's attorney, the judge stated that he was aware of the pending paternity petition but did not believe he was required to give notice to appellant prior to the entry of the order of adoption.

Thereafter, the Family Court in Westchester County granted appellee's motion to dismiss the paternity petition, holding that the putative father's right to seek paternity "must be deemed severed so long as an order of adoption exists." . . . On June 22, 1979, appellant filed a petition to vacate the order of adoption on the ground that it was obtained by fraud and in violation of his constitutional rights. The Ulster County Family Court . . . denied the petition. . . .

Appellant has now invoked our appellate jurisdiction. He offers two alternative grounds for holding the New York statutory scheme unconstitutional. First, he contends that a putative father's actual or potential relationship with a child born out of wedlock is an interest in liberty which may not be destroyed without due process of law; he argues therefore that he had a constitutional right to prior notice and an opportunity to be heard before he was deprived of that interest. Second, he contends that the gender-based classification in the statute, which both denied him the right to consent to Jessica's adoption and accorded him fewer procedural rights than her mother, violated the Equal Protection Clause.

The Due Process Claim. . . .

When an unwed father demonstrates a full commitment to the responsibilities of parenthood by "[coming] forward to participate in the rearing of his child," his interest in personal contact with his child acquires substantial protection under the Due Process Clause. At that point it may be said that he "[acts] as a father toward his children." But the mere existence of a biological link does not merit equivalent constitutional protection. . . . "[The] importance of the familial relationship, to the individuals involved and to the society, stems from the emotional attachments that derive from the intimacy of daily association, and from the role it plays in '[promoting] a way of life' through the instruction of children . . . as well as from the fact of blood relationship."

The significance of the biological connection is that it offers the natural father an opportunity that no other male possesses to develop a relationship with his offspring. If he grasps that opportunity and accepts some measure of responsibility for the child's future, he may enjoy the blessings of the parent-child relationship and make uniquely valuable contributions to the child's development. If he fails to do so, the Federal Constitution will not automatically compel a State to listen to his opinion of where the child's best interests lie.

In this case, we are not assessing the constitutional adequacy of New York's procedures for terminating a developed relationship. Appellant has never had any significant custodial, personal, or financial relationship with Jessica, and he did not seek to establish a legal tie until after she was two years old. We are concerned only with whether New York has adequately protected his opportunity to form such a relationship.

The most effective protection of the putative father's opportunity to develop a relationship with his child is provided by the laws that authorize formal marriage and govern its consequences. But the availability of that protection is, of course, dependent on the will of both parents of the child. Thus, New York has adopted a special statutory scheme to protect the unmarried father's interest in assuming a responsible role in the future of his child.

After this Court's decision in *Stanley*, the New York Legislature appointed a special commission to recommend legislation that would accommodate both the interests of biological fathers in their children and the children's interest in prompt and certain adoption procedures. The commission recommended, and the legislature enacted, a statutory adoption scheme that automatically provides notice to seven categories of putative fathers who are likely to have assumed some responsibility for the care of their natural children. [In addition,] as all of the New York courts that reviewed this matter observed, the right to receive notice was completely within appellant's control. By mailing a postcard to the putative father registry, he could have guaranteed that he would receive notice of any proceedings to adopt Jessica. The possibility that he may have failed to do so because of his ignorance of the law cannot be a sufficient reason for criticizing the law itself. The New York Legislature concluded that a more open-ended notice requirement would merely complicate the adoption process, threaten the privacy interests of unwed mothers, create the risk of unnecessary controversy, and impair the desired finality of adoption decrees. Regardless of whether we would have done likewise if we were legislators instead of judges, we surely cannot characterize the State's conclusion as arbitrary.

Appellant argues, however, that even if the putative father's opportunity to establish a relationship with an illegitimate child is adequately protected by the New York statutory scheme in the normal case, he was nevertheless entitled to special notice because the court and the mother knew that he had filed an affiliation proceeding in another court. This argument amounts to nothing more than an indirect attack on the notice provisions of the New York statute. The legitimate state interests in facilitating the adoption of young children and having the adoption proceeding completed expeditiously that underlie the entire statutory scheme also justify a trial judge's determination to require all interested parties to adhere precisely to the procedural requirements of the statute. The Constitution does not require either a trial judge or a litigant to give special notice to nonparties who are presumptively capable of asserting and protecting their own rights. . . . [W]e find no merit in the claim that his constitutional rights were offended because the Family Court strictly complied with the notice provisions of the statute.

The Equal Protection Claim.

The legislation at issue in this case is intended to establish procedures for adoptions. Those procedures are designed to promote the best interests of the child, to protect the rights of interested third parties, and to ensure promptness and finality. To serve those ends, the legislation guarantees to certain people the right to veto an adoption and the right to prior notice of any adoption proceeding. The mother of an illegitimate child is always within that favored class, but only certain putative fathers are included. Appellant contends that the gender-based distinction is invidious.

As we have already explained, the existence or nonexistence of a substantial relationship between parent and child is a relevant criterion in evaluating both the rights of the parent and the best interests of the child. We have held that these statutes [which grant mothers but not fathers the right to veto an adoption] may not constitutionally be applied in that class of cases where the mother and father are in fact similarly situated with regard to their relationship with the child.

Whereas appellee had a continuous custodial responsibility for Jessica, appellant never established any custodial, personal, or financial relationship with her. If one parent has an established custodial relationship with the child and the other parent has either abandoned or never established a relationship, the Equal Protection Clause does not prevent a State from according the two parents different legal rights.

Justice White, with whom Justice Marshall and Justice Blackmun join, dissenting.

The question in this case is whether the State may, consistent with the Due Process Clause, deny notice and an opportunity to be heard in an adoption proceeding to a putative father when the State has actual notice of his existence, whereabouts, and interest in the child.

According to Lehr, he and Jessica's mother met in 1971 and began living together in 1974. The couple cohabited for approximately two years, until Jessica's birth in 1976. Throughout the pregnancy and after the birth, Lorraine acknowledged to friends and relatives that Lehr was Jessica's father; Lorraine told Lehr that she had reported to the New York State Department of Social Services that he was the father. Lehr visited Lorraine and Jessica in the hospital every day during Lorraine's confinement. According to Lehr, from the time Lorraine was discharged from the hospital until August 1978, she concealed her whereabouts from him. During this time Lehr never ceased his efforts to locate Lorraine and Jessica and achieved sporadic success until August 1977, after which time he was unable to locate them at all. On those occasions when he did determine Lorraine's location, he visited with her and her children to the extent she was willing to permit it. When Lehr, with the aid of a detective agency, located Lorraine and Jessica in August 1978, Lorraine was already married to Mr. Robertson. Lehr asserts that at this time he offered to provide financial assistance and to set up a trust fund for Jessica, but that Lorraine refused. Lorraine threatened Lehr with arrest unless he stayed away and refused to permit him to see Jessica. Thereafter Lehr retained counsel who wrote to Lorraine in early December 1978, requesting that she permit Lehr to visit Jessica and threatening legal action on Lehr's behalf. On December 21, 1978, perhaps as a response to Lehr's threatened legal action, appellees commenced the adoption action at issue here. . . .

Lehr's version of the "facts" paints a far different picture than that portrayed by the majority. The majority's recitation, that "[appellant] has never had any significant custodial, personal, or financial relationship with Jessica, and he did not seek to establish a legal tie until after she was two years old," obviously does not tell the whole story. Appellant has never been afforded an opportunity to present his case. The legitimation proceeding he instituted was first stayed, and then dismissed, on appellees' motions. Nor could appellant establish his interest during the adoption proceedings, for it is the failure to provide Lehr notice and an opportunity to be heard there that is at issue here. We cannot fairly make a judgment based on the quality or substance of a relationship without a complete and developed factual record. This case requires us to assume that Lehr's allegations are true — that but for the actions of the child's mother there would have been the kind of significant relationship that the majority concedes is entitled to the full panoply of procedural due process protections.

I reject the peculiar notion that the only significance of the biological connection between father and child is that "it offers the natural father an opportunity that no other male possesses to develop a relationship with his offspring." A "mere biological relationship" is not as unimportant in determining the nature of liberty interests as the majority suggests. . . .

The "biological connection" is itself a relationship that creates a protected interest. Thus the "nature" of the interest is the parent-child relationship; how well developed that relationship has become goes to its "weight," not its "nature." Whether Lehr's interest is entitled to constitutional protection does not entail a searching inquiry into the quality of the relationship but a simple determination of the *fact* that the relationship exists — a fact that even the majority agrees must be assumed to be established.

Beyond that, however, because there is no established factual basis on which to proceed, it is quite untenable to conclude that a putative father's interest in his child is lacking in substance, that the father in effect has abandoned the child, or ultimately that the father's interest is not entitled to the same minimum procedural protections as the interests of other putative fathers. Any analysis of the adequacy of the notice in this case must be conducted on the assumption that the interest involved here is as strong as that of *any* putative father. That is not to say that due process requires actual notice to every putative father or that adoptive parents or the State must conduct an exhaustive search of records or an intensive investigation before a final adoption order may be entered. The procedures adopted by the State, however, must at least represent a reasonable effort to determine the identity of the putative father and to give him adequate notice.

II

In this case, of course, there was no question about either the identity or the location of the putative father. The mother knew exactly who he was and both she and the court entering the order of adoption knew precisely where he was and how to give him actual notice that his parental rights were about to be terminated by an adoption order. . . .

Absent special circumstances, there is no bar to requiring the mother of an illegitimate child to divulge the name of the father when the proceedings at issue involve the permanent termination of the father's rights. Likewise, there is no reason not to require such identification when it is the spouse of the custodial parent who seeks to adopt the child. . . .

Even assuming that Lehr would have been foreclosed if his failure to utilize the register had somehow disadvantaged the State, he effectively made himself known by other means, and it is the sheerest formalism to deny him a hearing because he informed the State in the wrong manner.

No state interest is substantially served by denying Lehr adequate notice and a hearing. The State no doubt has an interest in expediting adoption proceedings to prevent a child from remaining unduly long in the custody of the State or foster parents. But this is not an adoption involving a child in the custody of an authorized state agency. Here the child is in the custody of the mother and will remain in her custody. Moreover, had Lehr utilized the putative fathers' register, he would have been granted a prompt hearing, and there was no justifiable reason, in terms of delay, to refuse him a hearing in the circumstances of this case.

The State's undoubted interest in the finality of adoption orders likewise is not well served by a procedure that will deny notice and a hearing to a father whose identity and location are known. As this case well illustrates, denying notice and a hearing to such a father may result in years of additional litigation and threaten the reopening of adoption proceedings and the vacation of the adoption. . . .

[I]n my view the failure to provide Lehr with notice and an opportunity to be heard violated rights guaranteed him by the Due Process Clause. . . .

NOTES AND QUESTIONS

1. *Biology-Plus.* The Court's decision in *Lehr* is credited with articulating the "biology-plus" standard for the constitutional rights of unmarried fathers. The biological connection standing alone does not give rise to a constitutionally protected interest in parental recognition. Instead, the unmarried father must have "grasp[ed] the opportunity" to form a parent-child relationship.

This standard purported to harmonize the Court's earlier decisions. In Quilloin v. Wolcott, a 1978 decision, the Court unanimously rejected a biological father's attempt to block his child's adoption by the mother's husband, reasoning that he had not taken "steps to support or legitimate the child over a period of more than 11 years."[117] Distinguishing *Stanley*, the Court explained that Quilloin "had never been a *de facto* member of the child's family unit."[118] A year later in Caban v. Mohammed, the biological father challenged a state law requiring consent to adoption from unmarried mothers but not unmarried fathers.[119] The mother sought to have her new husband

---

117. 434 U.S. 246, 253 (1978).
118. Id.
119. 441 U.S. 380 (1979).

adopt the children, over the wishes of the biological father, who previously had lived with the mother and children. Seeing *Caban* much differently than *Quilloin*, the Court emphasized that "both mother and father participated in the care and support of their children."[120] The Court did not rule on due process grounds but instead held that the law violated equal protection because it constituted a "broad, gender-based distinction" impermissibly based on the belief that there was a "universal difference between maternal and paternal relations at every phase of a child's development."[121]

Notice that in both *Quilloin* and *Caban*, the unmarried biological father was one of two men seeking legal parental status. In those cases, a decision favoring the biological father would preclude the mother's husband from becoming the child's legal parent. Ordinarily, a biological father can establish his parentage at any point. But when another man has stepped forward to parent the child, courts may refuse to accord the biological father priority. Instead, the parental status of the biological father may turn on whether he can satisfy the more demanding constitutional standard. What facts do you think should be relevant in determining whether a biological father has "grasped" his opportunity to be a father?

2.   *Thwarted Fathers?* In *Lehr*, the biological father claimed that the mother deliberately hid the child from him so that he could not form a relationship with her. Should it matter if the mother frustrates the father's attempt to form the relationship that would lead to constitutional protection? It seemed to matter to the Illinois Supreme Court in Petition of Doe, the case we read before *Lehr*, in which the court protected the rights of an unmarried father who had been told that the baby had died. State courts have been more sympathetic than the U.S. Supreme Court to men who claim to have been thwarted in their attempts to form a parental relationship. In Adoption of Kelsey S., the California Supreme Court found the state statutory scheme violated the rights of unmarried fathers "*to the extent that the statutes allow a mother to unilaterally preclude her child's biological father from becoming a presumed father and thereby allowing the state to terminate his parental rights on nothing more than a showing of the child's best interest.*"[122] The court found support in *Lehr*, which it explained "can fairly be read to mean that a father need only make a reasonable and meaningful attempt to establish a relationship, not that he must be successful against all obstacles."[123]

3.   *The Child's Interest.* Where does the interest of the child fit in *Lehr*? Is it best for the child to be adopted by her stepfather? To have a relationship with her biological father? To have both men in her life?

4.   *Knowledge of the Law.* Is there a putative father registry in your state? How would you find it? What information does it ask of a putative father, and at what point

---

120. Id. at 389.
121. Id.
122. 823 P.2d 1216, 1226 (Cal. 1992) (emphasis in original).
123. Id. at 1228.

is the putative father supposed to sign up for the registry? What specific rights does the law grant to men on the registry?

5. *Parenthood and Gender.* According to the Court, unmarried fathers, but not unmarried mothers, must take post-birth steps to establish a legally protected relationship with the child. The Court explained: "The mother carries and bears the child, and in this sense her parental relationship is clear. The validity of the father's parental claims must be gauged by other measures."[124] Do the reproductive differences between women and men justify this differential treatment of mothers and fathers?[125] Why or why not?

6. *Unmarried Parents, Gender, and Derivative Citizenship.* The status of unmarried mothers and fathers also arose in the citizenship context. In Nguyen v. INS, the Court upheld a federal scheme that distinguished between non-marital mother-child and father-child relationships.[126] Under the law, a non-marital child born abroad acquires U.S. citizenship at birth if the citizen parent is the mother. But if the father is the citizen parent, the child acquires U.S. citizenship only if the father legitimated the child, signed a written acknowledgment of paternity, or obtained an adjudication of paternity during the child's minority. Nguyen, who had been born abroad to a Vietnamese mother and American father, had been raised by his father in the U.S. Yet his father had not taken the necessary steps, and thus Nguyen was not entitled to U.S. citizenship and could be deported. In upholding the citizenship scheme against an equal protection challenge, the Court rested largely on reproductive differences between women and men: "Given the proof of motherhood that is inherent in birth itself, it is unremarkable that Congress did not require the same affirmative steps of mothers."[127] The Court viewed biological differences as relevant to the social relationships between parents and children: "The mother knows that the child is in being and is hers and has an initial point of contact with him. There is at least an opportunity for mother and child to develop a real, meaningful relationship."[128] In contrast, for fathers, "[t]he same opportunity does not result from the event of birth, as a matter of biological inevitability."[129]

While the Court has not revisited its decision in *Nguyen*, more recently it invalidated a law that distinguished between the children of unmarried mothers and

---

124. 463 U.S. at 260 n.16.

125. For scholarly commentary supporting the Court's reasoning on feminist grounds, see Jennifer S. Hendricks, Essentially a Mother, 13 Wm. & Mary J. Women & L. 429 (2007); E. Gary Spitko, The Constitutional Function of Biological Paternity: Evidence of the Biological Mother's Consent to the Biological Father's Co-parenting of Her Child, 48 Ariz. L. Rev. 97 (2006). For commentary critical of the Court's logic on feminist grounds, see Dara Purvis, The Origin of Parental Rights: Labor, Intent, and Fathers, 41 Fla. St. L. Rev. 645 (2014); Albertina Antognini, From Citizenship to Custody: Unwed Fathers Abroad and at Home, 36 Harv. J.L. & Gender 405 (2013).

126. 533 U.S. 53 (2001).

127. Id. at 64.

128. Id. at 65.

129. Id.

fathers with respect to residency requirements for derivative citizenship. A non-marital child born abroad to a citizen mother attained U.S. citizenship at birth, as long as the mother resided in the U.S. for at least one year at any point before the child was born. If the father was the citizen parent, the child attained citizenship at birth if the father resided in the U.S. for ten years, at least five of which had to be before age fourteen. In Sessions v. Morales-Santana, the Court struck down the distinction on equal protection grounds.[130] Quoting Caban v. Mohammed, discussed above, the Court explained that "no 'important [governmental] interest' is served by laws grounded . . . in the obsolescing view that 'unwed fathers [are] invariably less qualified and entitled than mothers' to take responsibility for non-marital children."[131] The Court worried that laws based on such "[o]verbroad generalizations" "creat[e] a self-fulfilling cycle of discrimination that force[s] women to continue to assume the role of primary family caregiver."[132] Laws of this kind, the Court continued, also "disserve men who exercise responsibility for raising their children."[133] Accordingly, the Court rejected the differential durational residency requirements for "unwed mothers and fathers who have accepted parental responsibility [as] stunningly anachronistic."[134]

In the materials on marriage, we considered whether and under what circumstances biological fathers should be allowed to challenge the marital presumption. The materials in that section focused on family law's treatment of the marital presumption but suggested that constitutional questions were also relevant. Now we delve into those constitutional questions. What rights does an unmarried biological father possess when the child is born to a married woman and the husband wants to raise the child?

MICHAEL H. v. GERALD D.
491 U.S. 110 (1989)

JUSTICE SCALIA announced the judgment of the Court and delivered an opinion, in which THE CHIEF JUSTICE, joined, and in all but footnote 6 of which JUSTICE O'CONNOR and JUSTICE KENNEDY, J.J., joined.

---

130. 137 S. Ct. 1678 (2017).

131. Id. at 1692.

132. Id. at 1693.

133. Id. at 1693.

134. Id. Nonetheless, the Court did not order that the residency requirement for men be lowered to that of women. Instead, it left Congress to determine the durational requirement that should apply to both men and women Id. at 1701.

Under California law, a child born to a married woman living with her husband is presumed to be a child of the marriage. The presumption of legitimacy may be rebutted only by the husband or wife, and then only in limited circumstances. The instant appeal presents the claim that this presumption infringes upon the due process rights of a man who wishes to establish his paternity of a child born to the wife of another man, and the claim that it infringes upon the constitutional right of the child to maintain a relationship with her natural father.

I

The facts of this case are, we must hope, extraordinary. On May 9, 1976, in Las Vegas, Nevada, Carole D., an international model, and Gerald D., a top executive in a French oil company, were married. The couple established a home in Playa del Rey, California, in which they resided as husband and wife when one or the other was not out of the country on business. In the summer of 1978, Carole became involved in an adulterous affair with a neighbor, Michael H. In September 1980, she conceived a child, Victoria D., who was born on May 11, 1981. Gerald was listed as father on the birth certificate and has always held Victoria out to the world as his daughter. Soon after delivery of the child, however, Carole informed Michael that she believed he might be the father.

In the first three years of her life, Victoria remained always with Carole, but found herself within a variety of quasi-family units. In October 1981, Gerald moved to New York City to pursue his business interests, but Carole chose to remain in California. At the end of that month, Carole and Michael had blood tests of themselves and Victoria, which showed a 98.07% probability that Michael was Victoria's father. In January 1982, Carole visited Michael in St. Thomas, where his primary business interests were based. There Michael held Victoria out as his child. In March, however, Carole left Michael and returned to California, where she took up residence with yet another man, Scott K. Later that spring, and again in the summer, Carole and Victoria spent time with Gerald in New York City, as well as on vacation in Europe. In the fall, they returned to Scott in California.

In November 1982, rebuffed in his attempts to visit Victoria, Michael filed a filiation action in California Superior Court to establish his paternity and right to visitation. In March 1983, the court appointed an attorney and guardian ad litem to represent Victoria's interests. Victoria then filed a cross-complaint asserting that if she had more than one psychological or *de facto* father, she was entitled to maintain her filial relationship, with all of the attendant rights, duties, and obligations, with both. In May 1983, Carole filed a motion for summary judgment. During this period, from March through July 1983, Carole was again living with Gerald in New York. In August, however, she returned to California, became involved once again with Michael, and instructed her attorneys to remove the summary judgment motion from the calendar.

For the ensuing eight months, when Michael was not in St. Thomas he lived with Carole and Victoria in Carole's apartment in Los Angeles and held Victoria out as his daughter. In April 1984, Carole and Michael signed a stipulation that Michael was Victoria's natural father. Carole left Michael the next month, however, and instructed her attorneys not to file the stipulation. In June 1984, Carole reconciled with Gerald and joined him in New York, where they now live with Victoria and two other children since born into the marriage.

In May 1984, Michael and Victoria, through her guardian ad litem, sought visitation rights for Michael *pendente lite*. To assist in determining whether visitation would be in Victoria's best interests, the Superior Court appointed a psychologist to evaluate Victoria, Gerald, Michael, and Carole. The psychologist recommended that Carole retain sole custody, but that Michael be allowed continued contact with Victoria pursuant to a restricted visitation schedule. The court concurred and ordered that Michael be provided with limited visitation privileges *pendente lite*.

On October 19, 1984, Gerald, who had intervened in the action, moved for summary judgment on the ground that under Cal. Evid. Code § 621 there were no triable issues of fact as to Victoria's paternity. This law provides that "the issue of a wife cohabiting with her husband, who is not impotent or sterile, is conclusively presumed to be a child of the marriage." The presumption may be rebutted by blood tests, but only if a motion for such tests is made, within two years from the date of the child's birth, either by the husband or, if the natural father has filed an affidavit acknowledging paternity, by the wife.

On January 28, 1985, having found that affidavits submitted by Carole and Gerald sufficed to demonstrate that the two were cohabiting at conception and birth and that Gerald was neither sterile nor impotent, the Superior Court granted Gerald's motion for summary judgment, rejecting Michael's and Victoria's challenges to the constitutionality of § 621. The court also denied their motions for continued visitation pending the appeal.

II

The California statute that is the subject of this litigation is, in substance, more than a century old. In their present form, the substantive provisions of the statute are as follows:

§ 621. Child of the marriage; notice of motion for blood tests

(a) Except as provided in subdivision (b), the issue of a wife cohabiting with her husband, who is not impotent or sterile, is conclusively presumed to be a child of the marriage.

(b) Notwithstanding the provisions of subdivision (a), if the court finds that the conclusions of all the experts, as disclosed by the evidence based upon blood tests performed pursuant to Chapter 2 (commencing with Section

890) of Division 7 are that the husband is not the father of the child, the question of paternity of the husband shall be resolved accordingly.

(c) The notice of motion for blood tests under subdivision (b) may be raised by the husband not later than two years from the child's date of birth.

(d) The notice of motion for blood tests under subdivision (b) may be raised by the mother of the child not later than two years from the child's date of birth if the child's biological father has filed an affidavit with the court acknowledging paternity of the child.

(e) The provisions of subdivision (b) shall not apply to any case coming within the provisions of Section 7005 of the Civil Code [dealing with artificial insemination] or to any case in which the wife, with the consent of the husband, conceived by means of a surgical procedure.

III . . .

Michael raises two related challenges to the constitutionality of § 621. First, he asserts that requirements of procedural due process prevent the State from terminating his liberty interest in his relationship with his child without affording him an opportunity to demonstrate his paternity in an evidentiary hearing. We believe this claim derives from a fundamental misconception of the nature of the California statute. While § 621 is phrased in terms of a presumption, that rule of evidence is the implementation of a substantive rule of law. California declares it to be, except in limited circumstances, *irrelevant* for paternity purposes whether a child conceived during, and born into, an existing marriage was begotten by someone other than the husband and had a prior relationship with him. . . . Of course the conclusive presumption not only expresses the State's substantive policy but also furthers it, excluding inquiries into the child's paternity that would be destructive of family integrity and privacy. . . .

Michael contends as a matter of substantive due process that, because he has established a parental relationship with Victoria, protection of Gerald's and Carole's marital union is an insufficient state interest to support termination of that relationship. This argument is, of course, predicated on the assertion that Michael has a constitutionally protected liberty interest in his relationship with Victoria. . . .

In an attempt to limit and guide interpretation of the Clause, we have insisted not merely that the interest denominated as a "liberty" be "fundamental" (a concept that, in isolation, is hard to objectify), but also that it be an interest traditionally protected by our society. . . .

The legal issue in the present case reduces to whether the relationship between persons in the situation of Michael and Victoria has been treated as a protected family unit under the historic practices of our society, or whether on any other basis it has been accorded special protection. We think it impossible to find that it has. In fact, quite to the contrary, our traditions have protected the marital family (Gerald, Carole, and the child they acknowledge to be theirs) against the sort of claim Michael asserts. . . .

What counts is whether the States in fact award substantive parental rights to the natural father of a child conceived within, and born into, an extant marital union that wishes to embrace the child. We are not aware of a single case, old or new, that has done so. This is not the stuff of which fundamental rights qualifying as liberty interests are made.[6] . . .

It is a question of legislative policy and not constitutional law whether California will allow the presumed parenthood of a couple desiring to retain a child conceived within and born into their marriage to be rebutted. . . .

IV . . .

Victoria . . . claims a due process right to maintain filial relationships with both Michael and Gerald. . . . [T]he claim that a State must recognize multiple father-hood has no support in the history or traditions of this country. Moreover, even if we were to construe Victoria's argument as forwarding the lesser proposition that, whatever her status vis-a-vis Gerald, she has a liberty interest in maintaining a filial relationship with her natural father, Michael, we find that, at best, her claim is the obverse of Michael's and fails for the same reasons.

O'CONNOR, J., with whom Justice KENNEDY joins, concurring in part.

I concur in all but footnote 6 of Justice Scalia's opinion. This footnote sketches a mode of historical analysis to be used when identifying liberty interests protected by the Due Process Clause of the Fourteenth Amendment that may be somewhat inconsistent with our past decisions in this area. See *Griswold v. Connecticut*, 381 U.S. 479 (1965); *Eisenstadt v. Baird*, 405 U.S. 438 (1972). On occasion the Court has characterized relevant traditions protecting asserted rights at levels of generality that might not be "the most specific level" available. See *Loving v. Virginia*, 388 U.S.

---

6. Justice Brennan criticizes our methodology in using historical traditions specifically relating to the rights of an adulterous natural father, rather than inquiring more generally "whether parenthood is an interest that historically has received our attention and protection." . . .

We do not understand why, having rejected our focus upon the societal tradition regarding the natural father's rights vis-à-vis a child whose mother is married to another man, Justice Brennan would choose to focus instead upon "parenthood." Why should the relevant category not be even more general — perhaps "family relationships"; or "personal relationships"; or even "emotional attachments in general"? Though the dissent has no basis for the level of generality it would select, we do: We refer to the most specific level at which a relevant tradition protecting, or denying protection to, the asserted right can be identified. If, for example, there were no societal tradition, either way, regarding the rights of the natural father of a child adulterously conceived, we would have to consult, and (if possible) reason from, the traditions regarding natural fathers in general. But there is such a more specific tradition, and it unqualifiedly denies protection to such a parent. . . .

1, 12 (1967); *Turner v. Safley*, 482 U.S. 78, 94 (1987). I would not foreclose the unanticipated by the prior imposition of a single mode of historical analysis.

BRENNAN, J., with whom Justices MARSHALL and BLACKMUN, join, dissenting....

[O]nly one other Member of the Court fully endorses Justice Scalia's view of the proper method of analyzing questions arising under the Due Process Clause. Nevertheless, because the plurality opinion's exclusively historical analysis portends a significant and unfortunate departure from our prior cases and from sound constitutional decision-making, I devote a substantial portion of my discussion to it.

I...

[T]he plurality pretends that tradition places a discernible border around the Constitution. The pretense is seductive; it would be comforting to believe that a search for "tradition" involves nothing more idiosyncratic or complicated than poring through dusty volumes on American history.... [W]herever I would begin to look for an interest "deeply rooted in the country's traditions," one thing is certain: I would not stop (as does the plurality) at Bracton, or Blackstone, or Kent, or even the American Law Reports in conducting my search. Because reasonable people can disagree about the content of particular traditions, and because they can disagree even about which traditions are relevant to the definition of "liberty," the plurality has not found the objective boundary that it seeks.

Even if we could agree, moreover, on the content and significance of particular traditions, we still would be forced to identify the point at which a tradition becomes firm enough to be relevant to our definition of liberty and the moment at which it becomes too obsolete to be relevant any longer. The plurality supplies no objective means by which we might make these determinations. Indeed, as soon as the plurality sees signs that the tradition upon which it bases its decision (the laws denying putative fathers like Michael standing to assert paternity) is crumbling, it shifts ground and says that the case has nothing to do with that tradition, after all....

It is ironic that an approach so utterly dependent on tradition is so indifferent to our precedents. Citing barely a handful of this Court's numerous decisions defining the scope of the liberty protected by the Due Process Clause to support its reliance on tradition, the plurality acts as though English legal treatises and the American Law Reports always have provided the sole source for our constitutional principles. They have not....

It is not that tradition has been irrelevant to our prior decisions. Throughout our decision-making in this important area runs the theme that certain interests and practices — freedom from physical restraint, marriage, childbearing, childrearing, and others — form the core of our definition of "liberty." Our solicitude for these interests is partly the result of the fact that the Due Process Clause would seem an empty promise if it did not protect them, and partly the result of the historical and traditional importance of these interests in our society. In deciding cases arising under the Due Process Clause, therefore, we have considered whether the concrete limitation under consideration impermissibly impinges upon one of these more generalized interests.

Today's plurality, however, does not ask whether parenthood is an interest that historically has received our attention and protection; the answer to that question is too clear for dispute. Instead, the plurality asks whether the specific variety of parenthood under consideration — a natural father's relationship with a child whose mother is married to another man — has enjoyed such protection.

If we had looked to tradition with such specificity in past cases, many a decision would have reached a different result. Surely the use of contraceptives by unmarried couples, or even by married couples, . . . and even the right to raise one's natural but illegitimate children were not "interest[s] traditionally protected by our society" at the time of their consideration by this Court. If we had asked, therefore, in *Eisenstadt*, *Griswold*, . . . or *Stanley* itself whether the specific interest under consideration had been traditionally protected, the answer would have been a resounding "no." That we did not ask this question in those cases highlights the novelty of the interpretive method that the plurality opinion employs today.

The plurality's interpretive method is more than novel; it is misguided. It ignores the good reasons for limiting the role of "tradition" in interpreting the Constitution's deliberately capacious language. In the plurality's constitutional universe, we may not take notice of the fact that the original reasons for the conclusive presumption of paternity are out of place in a world in which blood tests can prove virtually beyond a shadow of a doubt who sired a particular child and in which the fact of illegitimacy no longer plays the burdensome and stigmatizing role it once did. . . .

In construing the Fourteenth Amendment to offer shelter only to those interests specifically protected by historical practice, moreover, the plurality ignores the kind of society in which our Constitution exists. We are not an assimilative, homogeneous society, but a facilitative, pluralistic one, in which we must be willing to abide someone else's unfamiliar or even repellent practice because the same tolerant impulse protects our own idiosyncrasies. Even if we can agree, therefore, that "family" and "parenthood" are part of the good life, it is absurd to assume that we can agree on the content of those terms and destructive to pretend that we do. In a community such as ours, "liberty" must include the freedom not to conform. The plurality today squashes this freedom by requiring specific approval from history before protecting anything in the name of liberty.

The document that the plurality construes today is unfamiliar to me. It is not the living charter that I have taken to be our Constitution; it is instead a stagnant, archaic, hidebound document steeped in the prejudices and superstitions of a time long past. *This* Constitution does not recognize that times change, does not see that sometimes a practice or rule outlives its foundations. I cannot accept an interpretive method that does such violence to the charter that I am bound by oath to uphold.

II

The plurality's reworking of our interpretive approach is all the more troubling because it is unnecessary. This is not a case in which we face a "new" kind of interest, one that requires us to consider for the first time whether the Constitution protects it. On the contrary, we confront an interest — that of a parent and child in their relationship with each other — that was among the first that this Court acknowledged in its cases defining the "liberty" protected by the Constitution. . . . Where the interest under consideration is a parent-child relationship, we need not ask, over and over again, whether that interest is one that society traditionally protects.

Thus, to describe the issue in this case as whether the relationship existing between Michael and Victoria "has been treated as a protected family unit under the historic practices of our society, or whether on any other basis it has been accorded special protection," is to reinvent the wheel. The better approach — indeed, the one commanded by our prior cases and by common sense — is to ask whether the specific parent-child relationship under consideration is close enough to the interests that we already have protected to be deemed an aspect of "liberty" as well. On the facts before us, therefore, the question is not what "level of generality" should be used to describe the relationship between Michael and Victoria, but whether the relationship under consideration is sufficiently substantial to qualify as a liberty interest under our prior cases.

On four prior occasions, we have considered whether unwed fathers have a constitutionally protected interest in their relationships with their children. Though different in factual and legal circumstances, these cases have produced a unifying theme: although an unwed father's biological link to his child does not, in and of itself, guarantee him a constitutional stake in his relationship with that child, such a link combined with a substantial parent-child relationship will do so. "When an unwed father demonstrates a full commitment to the responsibilities of parenthood by 'com[ing] forward to participate in the rearing of his child,' . . . his interest in personal contact with his child acquires substantial protection under the Due Process Clause. At that point it may be said that he 'act[s] as a father toward his children.'" This commitment is why Mr. Stanley and Mr. Caban won; why Mr. Quilloin and Mr. Lehr lost; and why Michael H. should prevail today. Michael H. is almost certainly Victoria D.'s natural father, has lived with her as her father, has contributed to her support, and has from the beginning sought to strengthen and maintain his relationship with her.

Claiming that the intent of these cases was to protect the "unitary family," the plurality waves *Stanley*, *Quilloin*, *Caban*, and *Lehr* aside. In evaluating the plurality's dismissal of these precedents, it is essential to identify its conception of the "unitary family." If, by acknowledging that *Stanley* et al. sought to protect "the relationships that develop within the unitary family," the plurality meant only to describe the kinds of relationships that develop when parents and children live together (formally or informally) as a family, then the plurality's vision of these cases would be correct. But that is not the plurality's message. Though it pays lip service to the idea that marriage is not the crucial fact in denying constitutional protection to the relationship between Michael and Victoria, the plurality cannot mean what it says.

The evidence is undisputed that Michael, Victoria, and Carole did live together as a family; that is, they shared the same household, Victoria called Michael "Daddy," Michael contributed to Victoria's support, and he is eager to continue his relationship with her. Yet they are not, in the plurality's view, a "unitary family," whereas Gerald, Carole, and Victoria do compose such a family. The only difference between these two sets of relationships, however, is the fact of marriage. The plurality, indeed, expressly recognizes that marriage is the critical fact in denying Michael a constitutionally protected stake in his relationship with Victoria: no fewer than six times, the plurality refers to Michael as the "*adulterous* natural father" (emphasis added) or the like. However, the very premise of *Stanley* and the cases following it is that marriage is not decisive in answering the question whether the Constitution protects the parental relationship under consideration. These cases are, after all, important precisely because they involve the rights of *unwed* fathers. . . .

The plurality's exclusive rather than inclusive definition of the "unitary family" is out of step with other decisions as well. This pinched conception of "the family," crucial as it is in rejecting Michael's and Victoria's claims of a liberty interest, is jarring in light of our many cases preventing the States from denying important interests or statuses to those whose situations do not fit the government's narrow view of the family. From *Loving v. Virginia*, 388 U.S. 1 (1967), to *Levy v. Louisiana*, 391 U.S. 68 (1968), and *Glona v. American Guarantee & Liability Ins. Co.*, 391 U.S. 73 (1968), and from *Gomez v. Perez*, 409 U.S. 535 (1973), to *Moore v. East Cleveland*, 431 U.S. 494 (1977), we have declined to respect a State's notion, as manifested in its allocation of privileges and burdens, of what the family should be. Today's rhapsody on the "unitary family" is out of tune with such decisions. . . .

NOTES AND QUESTIONS

1. *California Law Post*-Michael H. California's conclusive marital presumption at the time that Michael H. sought to challenge it permitted only the husband or wife to move for blood tests to rebut it. After *Michael H.*, California revised its law to allow a "presumed father" to file a motion for blood tests within two years of the child's birth.[135] In other words, a man seeking to challenge the marital presumption

---

135. Cal. Fam. Code § 7541(a) (West 2020).

contained in § 7540 could do so within the time limit if he satisfied a presumption of parentage under the parentage act. One such presumption, modeled on the 1973 UPA, applied to a man who "welcomes the child into his home and holds the child out as his natural child."[136] Would Michael H. have satisfied that presumption?

2. *State Cases.* The situation that arose in *Michael H.* has recurred across cases in various states. Indeed, California has seen many more cases involving conflicts between husbands and biological fathers. (We will read one later in the chapter.) As we saw in our examination of the marital presumption, some states limit the circumstances under which the presumption can be challenged and thus favor the marital father over the biological father. Other states allow the biological father, either on policy grounds (as we saw in Massachusetts) or constitutional grounds, to challenge the presumption. Still, most of these cases are fact-specific. They often depend on whether the biological father formed a relationship with the child, and they frequently turn on what the court finds to be in the best interest of the particular child.[137] Now, in some jurisdictions, a court can recognize both the marital father and the biological father as legal fathers, as we will explore in the last section of this chapter.

B. The Obligations of Unmarried Fathers

We have been focusing on unmarried men seeking the *rights* of fatherhood. But with parental rights come parental *responsibilities*. Now we look at the status of unmarried fathers from the perspective of obligations, rather than rights.

In 1975, Congress enacted the Child Support Enforcement (CSE) program as a federal-state system intended to secure financial support for children from non-custodial parents, and to ensure that families remained self-sufficient and off public assistance.[138] We discuss child support more fully in Chapter 11. But it is important to see how child support relates to parentage establishment. The effort to secure child support payments developed into a federal mandate that states meet certain Paternity Establishment Percentages (PEP).[139] In time, the streamlined process for families to attain legal recognition of paternity for a child's father at birth became part and parcel of Congressional efforts to collect child support and reshape the nation's welfare system. With the Personal Responsibility and Work Opportunity Reconciliation Act of 1996 (PRWORA), the federal government conditioned the receipt of federal child support enforcement funds on state adoption of a voluntary acknowledgement of paternity (VAP) process (termed "acknowledgement of

---

136. Cal. Fam. Code § 7611(d) (West 1994).

137. Compare Michelle W. v. Ronald W., 703 P.2d 88 (Cal. 1985) (upholding marital presumption where mother's former husband had established a parental relationship with the child), with Brian C. v. Ginger K., 92 Cal. Rptr. 2d 294 (Cal. Ct. App. 2000) (ruling in favor of biological father who had established relationship with the child, while husband had not).

138. Social Services Amendments, Pub. L. No. 93-647 (1975) (codified at 42 U.S.C. §§ 1397(a)-1397(h)).

139. Family Support Act of 1988, 88 Stat. 2337, Pub. L. No. 100-485, 102 Stat. 2344 (codified at 42 U.S.C. § 666 (2018)).

paternity," or AOP, in some states), and state enactment of laws that strengthened the effect of such acknowledgements so that they would be treated as equivalent to a judicial determination of paternity.[140]

As Professor Leslie Harris explains:

> Federal law imposes additional rules to govern [VAPs]. . . . The law must treat a VAP as if it resolves a legal dispute; when a VAP is filed with the state office of vital statistics, it has the legal effect of a judicial determination of paternity. The state cannot condition the validity of the acknowledgment on any kind of proceeding. States must give full faith and credit to acknowledgments signed in other states if they contain the information required by federal standards and have been executed in compliance with the procedures required by the state in which they were signed.[141]

Today, VAPs are the most common way that unmarried fathers establish parentage in the United States. Federal law conditions state funding on states creating and maintaining hospital-based programs so that VAPs are signed immediately after a child's birth.[142] If not done in the hospital, VAPs can also be completed through government offices that handle vital records.

Empirical studies suggest that VAPs have meaning beyond merely paternity establishment:

> [U]nmarried parents are using VAPs . . . to identify themselves as a child's co-parents and to memorialize that relationship. The most complete, recent evidence about unmarried parents and their children comes from the Fragile Families and Child Wellbeing study, a longitudinal study of about 5,000 children and their parents that is generalizable to all urban areas with a population of over 200,000. Researchers using this data found that at the time of birth, the great majority of unmarried parents are strongly connected to each other and to their children, and that they regard themselves as families. At the time of birth, fifty-one percent of unmarried parents are living together, and thirty-one percent are dating each other. Most of these parents sign VAP forms soon after birth. The Fragile Families researchers found that in urban areas, the paternity establishment rate is sixty-nine percent and that eighty-one percent of the paternity establishments are in the hospital or birthing center. While the paternity establishment rate for couples not living together is lower, it is still fifty-eight percent, although only forty-two percent of these establishments occur in the hospital.[143]

---

140. Personal Responsibility and Work Opportunity Reconciliation Act of 1996, Pub. L. No. 104–193, 110 Stat. 2105 (1996) (codified as amended in sections of 8 U.S.C. and 42 U.S.C.).

141. Leslie Joan Harris, Voluntary Acknowledgments of Parentage for Same-Sex Couples, 20 J. Gender, Soc. Pol'y & Law 467, 476 (2012).

142. 42 U.S.C. § 666(a)(5)(C)(ii) (2018).

143. Harris, supra note 141, at 477.

What, exactly, does a VAP form look like? Consider the form used in Illinois:

Illinois Voluntary Acknowledgment of Paternity

PLEASE READ ALL PARTS OF THIS FORM INCLUDING YOUR RIGHTS AND RESPONSIBILITIES AND INSTRUCTIONS ON THE OTHER SIDE BEFORE COMPLETING THE FOLLOWING INFORMATION.

File Date for ACU use only

ALL ITEMS MUST BE ANSWERED

Child's Information as shown or will be shown on Birth Certificate   Print all requested information

Child's Name (First)	Middle (if any)	Last (same as on birth certificate)	Suffix (Jr, II, III)
Date of Birth (mm/dd/yy)	Gender ☐ M ☐ F	Name of Hospital or Address of Place of Birth	City, County, and State of Birth

Biological Father's Name (first)	Middle (if any)	Last		Suffix (Jr, II, III)
Place of Birth (city, state or foreign country address)		Date of Birth (mm/dd/yy)	SSN/TIN	
Address (street address and/or PO box)	City, State, and Zip		Daytime Phone (include area code)	

Biological Mother's Name (First)	Middle (if any)	Current Last Name	Maiden Name (before 1ˢᵗ marriage)
Place of Birth (city, state or foreign country address)		Date of Birth (mm/dd/yy)	SSN/TIN
Address (street address and/or PO box)	City, State, and Zip		Daytime Phone (include area code)

Were you married to or in a civil union with a person **other than** the above named father when this child was born or within 300 days before this child was born?   Yes☐   No ☐
If yes, that person is presumed to be the father (presumed parent) of this child and you are required to provide the presumed parent's name (first/middle/last) _____. A Denial of Parentage must also be completed by the biological mother and presumed parent to place the biological father's name on this child's birth certificate.

By signing I acknowledge that I have read the rights and responsibilities and instructions on the other side of this form. I have been provided an oral explanation about the VAP and understand my rights and responsibilities created and waived by signing this form.
I UNDERSTAND THAT I CAN REQUEST A GENETIC TEST REGARDING THE CHILD'S PATERNITY. BY SIGNING THIS FORM I GIVE UP MY RIGHT TO A GENETIC TEST.

Each parent must sign and date this form in the presence of a witness age 18 or older. The witness must not be a parent or child named on the VAP.

BIOLOGICAL FATHER: Under the penalties of perjury provided by Section 1-109 of the Illinois Code of Civil Procedure, I certify that my statements in this document are true and correct. I acknowledge that I am the biological father of the above named child and I give my permission to enter my name as the legal father on the birth certificate. I understand that the acknowledgment is the same as a court order for parentage of the child and that a challenge to the acknowledgment is allowed only under limited circumstances and is generally not allowed after 2 years.	**BIOLOGICAL MOTHER**: Under the penalties of perjury provided by Section 1-109 of the Illinois Code of Civil Procedure, I certify that my statements in this document are true and correct. I am the birth mother of the above named child and I give my permission to enter the biological father's name as the legal father on the birth certificate. I understand that the acknowledgment is the same as a court order for parentage of the child and that a challenge to the acknowledgment is allowed only under limited circumstances and is generally not allowed after 2 years.
Biological Father's Signature _____	Biological Mother's Signature _____
Witness Information	**Witness Information**
Printed Name_____	Printed Name_____
Signature_____	Signature_____
Address_____	Address_____
Phone Number_____	Phone Number _____
Date Parties Signed_____	Date Parties Signed_____

HFS 3416B (R-4-17) To request a certified copy of the VAP go to www.childsupport.illinois.gov and complete and follow instructions on HFS 3416H, Request for a Certified copy of the Voluntary Acknowledgment of Paternity and/or Denial of Parentage.

For Official Use Only_____
          Case #   Docket #   CP RIN   NCP RIN

**Instructions for Completing the
Illinois Voluntary Acknowledgment of Paternity**

PURPOSE: The Voluntary Acknowledgment of Paternity (hereafter called VAP) legally establishes the biological father and child relationship **(when the biological father is not married to the child's biological mother)** and allows the biological father's name to be placed on the birth certificate. The biological father becomes the legal father of the child when the VAP is properly signed, witnessed and filed with the Illinois Department of Healthcare and Family Services (hereafter called HFS), creating certain legal rights and responsibilities for the child and the parents. The VAP may be completed before your child is born, but is not valid until the child is born and the VAP is filed with HFS. A VAP (and Denial, if necessary) may be completed after you leave the hospital, and the VAP (and Denial, if necessary) may also be completed for a child born in another state. **Forms that contain errors will be rejected. As a result, paternity is not established and the biological father's name will not be placed on the birth certificate.**

If the biological mother is or was married to or in a civil union with a person who is not the biological father when the child was born or within 300 days before this child was born, a Denial of Parentage (hereafter called Denial) must be signed, witnessed and filed in conjunction with the completion of the VAP by the biological mother and biological father.

YOUR RIGHTS AND RESPONSIBILITIES
I understand that:
1.   the VAP is a legal document, and when signed, witnessed and filed with HFS, is the same as a court order determining the legal relationship between a biological father and child.
2.   if I am a minor, I have the right to sign and have this form witnessed without my guardian's permission.
3.   it is my responsibility to provide financial support for the child that may include child support and medical support starting from the child's birth until the child is at least 18 years old.
4.   this VAP does not give parental responsibility allocation or parenting time to the biological father; however, it gives him the right to ask for parental responsibility allocation and parenting time.
5.   either the biological mother or biological father may rescind the action by signing a Rescission of VAP. The Rescission must be signed, witnessed and filed with HFS within 60 days from the effective date of the VAP or the date of a proceeding relating to the child, whichever occurs earlier.

INSTRUCTIONS – USE BLACK OR BLUE INK
1.   The biological mother must indicate "yes" or "no" if she is or was married to or in a civil union with a person other than the biological father when this child was born or within 300 days before this child was born. If "yes", the biological mother must provide the name of that person (referred to as the presumed parent). The presumed parent and biological mother must sign the Denial and the biological mother and biological father must sign the VAP to establish legal paternity and place the biological father's name on the birth certificate. **If the presumed parent and the biological mother do not sign the Denial, the presumed parent is considered to be the parent of the child and that person's name, by law, must be placed on the birth certificate.**
2.   Each person must sign and date all forms in front of a witness. A witness must be an adult age 18 or older but cannot be the parents or child named on the VAP.
3   If the VAP (and Denial, if necessary) is completed at the hospital when the child is born, hospital staff will add the biological father's name to the birth certificate and send the VAP to HFS for filing.
4.   If the VAP (and Denial, if necessary) is not completed at the hospital, each person must sign and date the form(s) in front of a witness, age 18 or older but not the parents or child named on the VAP, and submit the original documents to HFS.
5.   Send only the original document. Do not send a photocopy (must be original signatures)

Mail original document to: Administrative Coordination Unit (ACU)
(copies will be rejected)   110 West Lawrence Avenue
                                                    Springfield, Illinois 62704

The Administrative Coordination Unit (ACU) will file the original VAP and send a copy of the completed VAP (and Denial, if necessary) to either the: 1. Illinois Department of Public Health, Division of Vital Records (for Illinois births); or 2. Vital Records Office in affected state (for out of state births)

For more information about the VAP, ask hospital staff for the HFS 3416A, "Two Parents…Give Your Child Hope" flyer. You may also obtain a copy from state and local registrars, county clerks, Department of Human Services offices, Child Support Services offices or by going to the Forms and Brochures section of the Child Support Services website.

This form is available in English and Spanish upon request and on the HFS website (www.childsupport.illinois.gov). The Spanish version may be used for translation purposes only. The **Spanish version is not acceptable as a legal document**. Only the English version of this document may be signed, witnessed and filed with HFS.

SI LAS PIDE, TENEMOS VERSIONES EN ESPAÑOL DISPONIBLES Y EN EL SITIO DEL DEPARTAMENTO EN EL INTERNET EN (WWW.CHILDSUPPORT.ILLINOIS.GOV), PERO SÓLO SE PUEDEN USAR PARA PROPÓSITOS DE TRADUCCIÓN. **LAS VERSIONES EN ESPAÑOL NO SON DOCUMENTOS LEGALES ACEPTABLES**. SÓLO LA VERSIÓN EN INGLES DEL DOCUMENTO SE PUEDE FIRMAR Y ATESTIGUAR.

If you have any questions relating to the child's birth certificate, contact the Department of Public Health's Division of Vital Records at www.idph.state.il.us/vitalrecords or 217-782-6554.

Get oral explanation and answers to questions relating to the completion of this form by calling the Child Support Customer Service Call Center at 1-800-447-4278.

HFS 3416B (R-4-17)   IOCI17-0532

Several aspects of the form stand out. First, VAPs must be signed by the mother as well as the putative father. Neither party can unilaterally use a VAP to insist on paternity of the putative father. Second, the form notifies the signatories that they are making the acknowledgement under "penalty of perjury." Third, the form is being signed by the man who purports to be the "biological father." Finally, the form makes clear that the man is waiving his right to genetic testing.

The man can decline to sign the VAP at that time and instead request genetic testing to determine paternity. Do you think most men would request such testing? Consider the perspective of a recent Michigan study, which found that:

> [E]ven when free genetic testing was offered to anyone who requested it before signing a VAP, only a tiny fraction asked for the test. Of the 1,660 non-marital births examined, a VAP was signed in seventy-eight and a half percent, and only in 112 cases was a genetic test requested. Parents who establish paternity by signing VAPs, like married parents, generally do not want to challenge the integrity of their relationships by requesting genetic testing at the time of birth.[144]

What if a man requests genetic testing? Although some states still authorize blood-grouping tests or Human Leukocyte Antigen (HLA) tests, DNA testing is the most common means of paternity testing. In general, DNA testing is initiated by swabbing the inside of a person's cheek in order to collect buccal cells, which are analyzed by a laboratory and compared to another sample (i.e., a child's buccal cells are compared to the cells of a parent or alleged parent). States usually contract with laboratories or certify which laboratories are approved to do paternity testing for legal purposes. The laboratories calculate the probability that a person is the genetic parent of a child. In order to establish parentage, many states require that genetic tests determine that the probability of paternity be at least 99 percent.[145]

What if a man does not request genetic testing and later discovers that he is not the biological father? Should he be able to undo the VAP? Who else should be able to challenge the VAP? And on what grounds? Signatories are allowed to rescind the VAP within sixty days. After that initial period, the VAP has the force of a judgment and, as provided by federal law, can only be challenged on the basis of fraud, duress, or material mistake of fact.[146] What constitutes fraud or material mistake of fact?

---

144. Id. at 477–78.

145. See, e.g., Mich. Comp. Laws Ann. § 722.1497 (West 2020); 23 Pa. Cons. Stat. § 4343 (2020). The 2017 Uniform Parentage Act also sets forth a 99% parentage threshold. But in Montana, the threshold is 95%. Mont. Code Ann. § 40-5-234 (2020). In Maryland, the results of blood or genetic tests can be received in evidence if the probability of the alleged father's paternity is at least 97.3%, while a rebuttable presumption of paternity requires a 99% probability of paternity. Md. Code Ann., Fam. Law §5-1029 (West 2020).

146. 42 U.S.C. § 666(a)(5)(D)(iii) (2018).

DAVIS V. WICOMICO COUNTY BUREAU

135 A.3d 419 (Md.)

BATTAGLIA, JUSTICE.

Justin Davis, Petitioner, twice sought to secure a paternity test years after he had executed an Affidavit of Parentage, in which he attested, shortly following the birth of twin boys in 2009, that he was their father. The Wicomico County Bureau of Support Enforcement, in 2011, had filed a Complaint for Child Support against Mr. Davis, in which it alleged that Mr. Davis was responsible for support, because he had attested that he was the father of the twins; Mr. Davis, in turn, requested a paternity test and denied parentage of the children, alleging that his signature on the affidavit had been obtained through fraud or misrepresentation. Judge David B. Mitchell . . . ordered Mr. Davis to pay child support; he also denied the request for a paternity test, because Mr. Davis had executed the affidavits of parentage and there was "nothing in this record and before this Court today that would even broach the subject of fraud, duress, or material mistake of fact." . . .

Judge Mitchell specifically responded to Mr. Davis's repeated requests for a paternity test when he denied the existence of fraud at the time Mr. Davis executed the affidavit:

> . . . [F]or a period of 60 days after you sign the affidavit, you have the right to rescind it. You can rescind it in writing, or you can rescind it in a judicial proceeding. . . . Beyond that 60-day period of time, the statute provides that you may rescind the Affidavit of Paternity and its contents only upon a showing of fraud, duress, or a material mistake of fact.
>
> The issue in this case is not the fatherhood of the child. The issue in this case is whether there is the presence of fraud, mistake, or duress that would justify the rescission of an Affidavit signed by you and acknowledged to be signed by the defendant wherein he confesses to the paternity of these two children.
>
> There is no dispute that the mother and the defendant executed these documents. There is no suggestion of the presence of any fraud or any duress at the time they executed the document.
>
> There is testimony from the mother before the Court that she advised the defendant prior, seven months actually, prior to the birth of the children that he was not the biological father. That's interesting but irrelevant. It's irrelevant because the defendant armed with whatever knowledge he had chose to voluntarily execute an affidavit establishing him as the father of these children. We have heard nothing in this record and before this Court today that would even broach the subject of fraud, duress or material mistake of fact. . . .
>
> You were clearly — you meaning, both mother and father, were clearly advised, don't sign if you have a doubt. You can get assistance if you want because you don't understand what you're about to sign. But the moment you affix your pen to that paper and sign your name, you have obligated yourself to these children. And it is the finding of this Court that there is no

fraud, duress, or mistake of material fact that would justify the rescission of the Affidavits of Parentage properly executed. These are your children by law, and that's the end of the story. . . .

When Mr. Davis executed the Affidavit of Parentage, Section 5-1028 of the Family Law Article of the Maryland Code governed and provided then, as it does now, that: . . .

> The legal finding of paternity established by completion of the Affidavit, can be reversed only if:
>   a. Within 60 days of signing, either party named in the Affidavit signs a written rescission . . . ;
>   b. Within 60 days of signing, either party named in the Affidavit appears in court in a proceeding related to the child and informs the court of his or her decision to rescind; or
>   c. After expiration of the 60 day period, a court orders a rescission after the party challenging the Affidavit proves fraud, duress or material mistake of fact. . . .

To permit Mr. Davis to pursue blood or genetic testing in the face of the self-limiting language [of the acknowledgment statute] totally eviscerates the word "only." . . .

Our conclusion . . . comports with the decision of the Supreme Court of Illinois when that court, interpreting the same language as our [statute], ruled out a challenge when a father, who had executed an affidavit of paternity, actually found out that he was not the father; the court was emphatic that "a man who voluntarily acknowledges paternity can later challenge the voluntariness of the acknowledgment if he can show that it was procured by fraud, duress, or material mistake of fact, but the Parentage Act does not allow him to challenge the conclusive presumption of paternity with contrary evidence." . . .

Mr. Davis now is not entitled to a blood or genetic test to contest the parentage he established after execution of his Affidavit of Parentage.

NOTES AND QUESTIONS

1. *Biological Evidence and VAPs.* Courts in many states have refused to set aside VAPs based on the fact that the man who signed is not the biological father.[147] Yet courts in some states have found that a man can prove fraud if he signed the

---

147. See, e.g., Burden v. Burden, 945 A.2d 656 (Md. Ct. Spec. App. 2008); In re S.R.B., 262 S.W.3d 428 (Tex. App. 2008); People ex rel. Dep. of Public Aid v. Smith, 818 N.E.2d 1204 (Ill. 2004).

VAP knowing he was not the biological father.[148] What explains this difference? Many courts have interpreted fraud to require that one of the parties committed fraud with respect to the other — for example, the mother mispresented to the man who signed the VAP that he was the biological father and was the only man with whom she was having sex around the time the child was conceived. In contrast, other courts have interpreted fraud to encompass fraud with respect to some other party, like the government or the court. Accordingly, on the first interpretation, a VAP cannot be undone if both signatories knew at the time it was signed that the man was not the biological father; but on the second interpretation, it may be undone. Which interpretation do you think is more persuasive?

Why might courts be more or less open to challenges to VAPs? What are the competing policies at stake? The federal government has made the burden especially high for challenges to VAPs because it seeks to hold men to the obligations they voluntarily undertake. As the *Davis* case demonstrates, the state has a strong interest in collecting child support and therefore favors a policy that makes VAPs difficult to challenge. Judges, on the other hand, may be reluctant to hold men accountable for children who are the biological children of another man. In this sense, the child support order that can follow from a VAP should align with the individual who owes responsibility for the child. Of course, this relies on a view that responsibility follows from biological paternity. There may also be an interest in preserving developed parent-child relationships, regardless of a biological connection. A judge may be reluctant to allow a VAP to be challenged by a man who finds out years down the road that he is not the child's biological father. From this perspective, a policy that makes challenges to VAPs difficult may promote children's interests in parental attachments. Indeed, in some states, even when a challenger has met his burden by showing fraud, duress, or material mistake of fact, the court is instructed to set aside the VAP only if doing so is in the best interest of the child.[149]

2. *Ordering Genetic Testing.* In *Davis*, the acknowledged father sought blood tests to prove he was not the child's biological father. The court refused to order such tests since the VAP constituted a judgment of paternity. But if Davis had not signed a VAP and paternity was to be adjudicated, the court could order genetic testing in light of Davis's denial of paternity. A court order of genetic testing may require not only the alleged father but also the child to submit to testing. In some states, when a party in a paternity action fails to comply with an order for genetic testing, a judge can issue a warrant for their arrest and compel them to appear for genetic testing.[150]

---

148. See, e.g., Alvarado v. Thomson, 240 P.3d 77 (Ariz. Ct. App. 2016); McGee v. Gonyo, 140 A.3d 162 (Vt. 2016); Clark v. Kreamer, 405 P.3d 1123 (Ariz. Ct. App. 2017).
149. See, e.g., Wash. Rev. Code §§ 26.26A.445, 460 (2020).
150. See, e.g., Mich. Comp. Laws Ann. § 722.1497 (West 2020).

Is there anything wrong with forcing an individual to hand over genetic material to the state for purposes of establishing paternity? Where does the DNA go, and who owns it? Are there privacy or other constitutional concerns raised by DNA testing in parentage cases? Some states maintain laws punishing the misuse of genetic material obtained for purposes of paternity establishment.[151] Is that a sufficient response? As voluntary, at-home tests gain in popularity, individuals may be gaining access to their genetic history and relationships without any court orders. What implications might these tests have in the parentage context, even if they are not permitted as probative evidence of a person's parentage in court?

3. *Paternity Establishment and Child Support.* In *Davis*, the state was trying to collect child support from the acknowledged father. As we have seen, the federal regulations that have produced VAP programs at the state level are part of a broader federal effort to establish paternity and collect child support.[152] More specifically, the government seeks to ensure that the support of children comes from private, rather than public, sources. Accordingly, when a custodial parent seeks government benefits, state and local governments attempt to identify the child's other parent and hold that individual accountable for child support. The state may threaten to withhold benefits from the custodial parent — usually the mother — unless she reveals the identity of the other parent — usually the father. The state thus has authority to file a paternity action. Instead of going to the custodial parent, any support obtained from the noncustodial parent may be used to reimburse the government for benefits that have been distributed.

PROBLEM

You are a state legislator considering a bill regarding challenges to VAPs. The bill would require that a challenge be brought within two years from when the VAP was signed. Such challenges would be allowed based only on fraud, duress, or material mistake of fact. The two-year limit would apply to challenges by the woman and man who signed the VAP, as well as to challenges by a man who did not sign the VAP but is alleging that he is the child's biological father. Do you plan to support the bill? Who do you expect will support it, and who do you expect will oppose it? Would you offer any amendments to the bill?

---

151. See, e.g., Wash. Rev. Code § 26.26A.355 (2020) (making it a misdemeanor to "intentionally release" a specimen collected for parentage purposes).

152. See 42 U.S.C. § 666 (2018).

C. Assisted Reproduction: Donors or Fathers?

As the law around unmarried fathers demonstrates, biological connection generally forms the basis for parental rights and obligations in non-marital families. A man may establish his parentage by attesting to his status as the child's biological father. And the mother or the state may hold a man accountable for child support by establishing the man's paternity through genetic evidence. The paradigm situation of paternity establishment involves a man who fathered a child through sexual intercourse.

But what if the child was conceived through assisted reproduction? Is the man a legal father or a sperm donor? As we have seen, in all states, when a married woman gives birth to a child conceived with donor sperm, her husband is treated as the legal father. The sperm donor is not a parent. Yet in some states, when an unmarried woman gives birth to a child conceived with donor sperm, there is no statute absolving the sperm donor of parental responsibility.[153] In these states, unmarried women can use anonymous donors to avoid any potential claim by the man. In many other states, sperm donors are not legal fathers, regardless of whether their semen is donated to a married or unmarried woman.[154] Still, some of these statutes apply only if the semen is given to a licensed physician, rather than directly to the woman.[155] Why do you think states would enact statutes with this physician requirement? The trend among states is to remove such a requirement.

PROBLEM

Nadia and Tammy, an unmarried same-sex couple, decide to have a child together. They post an ad online seeking a sperm donor. Marcus responds to the ad. After corresponding with Marcus and meeting him in person, Nadia and Tammy sign an agreement with Marcus in which he agrees to donate sperm for use by Nadia. In the agreement, Marcus relinquishes all rights to the resulting child and is relieved of all responsibility for the resulting child. Marcus delivers his semen to the home of Nadia and Tammy, and Nadia inseminates herself and eventually becomes pregnant. After Nadia gives birth, she and Tammy raise the child for eighteen months before splitting up. Eventually, Nadia applies for welfare benefits. The state obtains a copy of the agreement and files a paternity action against Marcus. Tammy intervenes in the action, seeking to be declared a parent. You are the judge in the case. What legal questions would you want to research to help you make a decision? What result do you think you are likely to reach?

---

153. See, e.g., Ala. Code §§ 26-17-702 to -703 (2020); Ark. Code Ann. § 9-10-201 (2020); Mo. Ann. Stat. § 210.824 (West 2020); Tenn. Code. Ann. § 68-3-306 (2020).

154. See, e.g., Cal. Fam. Code § 7613 (West 2020); Tex. Fam. Code Ann. § 160.702-703 (West 2020); Va. Code. Ann. § 20-158 (2020).

155. See, e.g., Idaho Code § 39-5405 (2020); Wis. Stat. Ann. § 891.40 (West 2020).

POSTSCRIPT

This problem is based on the high-profile Kansas case of "the Craigslist sperm donor."[156] Under Kansas law, a "donor of semen provided to a licensed physician for use in artificial insemination of a woman other than the donor's wife is treated in law as if he were not the birth father of a child thereby conceived, unless agreed to in writing by the donor and the woman."[157] Because the parties had not used a licensed physician in the process, the sperm donor was treated as a legal father who owed child support. The fact that Marcus had entered an agreement with Nadia making clear that he had no parental responsibilities did not matter, because, as the court explained, a parent may not terminate parental rights by contract. The court did not decide whether the nonbiological parent in the same-sex couple was a parent. But given the ruling that the sperm donor was a father, it seemed that under existing Kansas law, the nonbiological parent could not attain parental status.[158]

A sperm donor ordinarily is not a legal father of the resulting child, provided the individuals complied with the relevant regulations. The problem above suggests that in the absence of compliance, sperm donors may be obligated to pay child support. What about a sperm donor who affirmatively seeks to be recognized as a legal father? When might that man be a father and not a donor, even if the statute regulating assisted reproduction divests donors of parental rights?

L.F. v. BREIT
736 S.E.2d 711 (Va. 2013)

Opinion by JUSTICE WILLIAM C. MIMS.

In these appeals, we consider whether Code §§ 20-158(A)(3) and 32.1-257(D) bar an unmarried, biological father from establishing legal parentage of his child conceived through assisted conception, pursuant to a voluntary written agreement as authorized by Code § 20-49.1(B) (2).

I. Background and Material Proceedings Below

Beverley Mason and William D. Breit had a long-term relationship and lived together as an unmarried couple for several years. They wished to have a child

---

156. See State ex rel. Secretary Dept. for Children and Families v. W.M., No. 2012DM2686, 2016 WL 8293872 (Kan. Dist. Ct. Nov. 22, 2016).

157. Kan. Stat. Ann. § 23-2208(f) (West 2020).

158. For a summary of the case, see Joanna L. Grossman, Why a Craigslist Sperm Donor Owes Child Support, Justia's Verdict (Jan. 27, 2014).

together. Unable to conceive naturally, they sought reproductive assistance from Dr. Jill Flood, a board-certified fertility doctor.

Dr. Flood performed two cycles of in vitro fertilization ("assisted conception"). Each time, she retrieved eggs from Mason, fertilized them outside her body using Breit's sperm, and transferred the resulting embryos into Mason's body. Breit was present for all stages of the in vitro fertilization process and continued to live with Mason throughout the resulting pregnancy.

Prior to the child's birth, Mason and Breit entered into a written custody and visitation agreement providing Breit with reasonable visitation rights and agreeing that such visitation was in the child's best interests.

On July 13, 2009, Mason gave birth to L.F. Breit was present for L.F.'s birth and is listed as the father on her birth certificate. The couple named her after Mason's paternal grandmother and Breit's maternal grandmother, and her last name is a hyphenated combination of their surnames.

On the day after L.F.'s birth, Mason and Breit jointly executed a written agreement, identified as an "Acknowledgement of Paternity," stating that Breit is L.F.'s legal and biological father. The couple jointly mailed birth announcements naming Mason and Breit as L.F.'s parents. They stated to friends and family that Breit was L.F.'s father, and continued to live together for four months following L.F.'s birth.

After the couple separated, Breit continued to provide for L.F. financially. He maintained her as his child on his health insurance policy and continued to provide child support. He consistently visited L.F. on weekends and holidays, thereby beginning to establish an ongoing parent-child relationship with her. Breit took an active role in L.F.'s life until August 2010, when Mason unilaterally terminated all contact between Breit and L.F. . . .

Breit filed a petition to determine parentage and establish custody and visitation. . . . He filed a motion for summary judgment, arguing that the acknowledgement of paternity that he and Mason voluntarily executed created a final and binding parent-child legal status between Breit and L.F. Mason filed pleas . . . asserting that . . . Breit was barred from being L.F.'s legal parent because he and Mason were never married and L.F. was conceived through assisted conception. . . .

II. Legislative History and Policy . . .

Code § 20-49.1 *et seq.* is the statutory scheme designed to establish the legal parentage of children born to unmarried parents. . . .

Since its enactment in 1988, Code § 20-49.1 has provided for the establishment of paternity by a voluntary written agreement of the biological father and mother, made under oath, acknowledging paternity. In 1992, it was expanded to permit the establishment of paternity through the use of scientifically reliable genetic testing. There is no limitation in Chapter 3.1 barring parents who conceive through assisted conception from *voluntarily* establishing paternity by such a written agreement.

Consequently, Code § 20-49.1 *et seq.*, read without referencing other statutes, would control the determination of paternity in all cases concerning children of unwed biological parents who enter into such voluntary written agreements.

Code § 20-156 *et seq.* (the "assisted conception statute") is intended to establish legal parentage of children born as a result of assisted conception. Unlike Code § 20-49.1 *et seq.*, it was enacted specifically to protect the interests of married parents.

The assisted conception statute was enacted in response to *Welborn v. Doe*, 394 S.E.2d 732 (Va. Ct. App. 1990), a case involving a married couple and a third-party sperm donor. In *Welborn*, the Court of Appeals held that the only sure way for the husband of a gestational mother to secure parental rights, thereby divesting any rights of a third-party donor, was for the husband to adopt the child. The court noted the General Assembly's failure to enact legislation terminating the rights of such sperm donors, stating: "[u]ntil such time as the Code is amended to terminate possible parental rights of a sperm donor, only through adoption may the rights of the sperm donor be divested and only through adoption may the rights of Mr. Welborn and the twins born to his wife be as secure as their rights would be in a natural father-child relationship."

In 1991, at the next legislative session following *Welborn*, the General Assembly enacted the assisted conception statute, stating: "[t]he husband of the gestational mother of a child is the child's father" and "[a] donor is not the parent of a child conceived through assisted conception." The statute clearly was enacted to ensure that infertile married couples such as the Welborns, referred to as "intended parents" under the statute, were not threatened by parentage claims from third-party donors. The policy goal was to ensure that a married couple could obtain sperm from an outside donor without fear that the donor would claim parental rights.

Code § 20-158(A)(3) was amended in 1997 to embody its current language: "[a] donor is not the parent of a child conceived through assisted conception, *unless the donor is the husband of the gestational mother.*" (Emphasis added.) The amendment addressed situations in which the "donor" is also the husband of the gestational mother and therefore is permitted to establish parentage. In such cases, there is no possibility of interference from outside, third-party donors.

III. ANALYSIS . . .

Mason . . . claims that the assisted conception statute prevents all unmarried sperm donors from asserting parental rights with respect to children conceived by assisted conception, whether the mother is married or unmarried and without regard to her relationship with the donor. She argues that when a statute is unambiguous, we must apply the plain meaning of that language without reference to related statutes.

We disagree with Mason's interpretation of this statute, because her argument ignores a significant provision of the assisted conception statute. Code § 20-164 states:

> A child whose status as a child is declared or negated by this chapter [chapter 9] is the child only of his parent or parents as determined under this chapter, Title 64.1, *and, when applicable, Chapter 3.1 (§ 20-49.1 et seq.) of this title* for all purposes. . . .

(Emphasis added.) This explicit cross reference to Chapter 3.1 (Code § 20-49.1 *et seq.*) requires that the assisted conception statute be read in conjunction with Code § 20-49.1 in the circumstances presented in this case.

Mason's argument is grounded in two provisions of the assisted conception statute, Code §§ 20-157 and 20-158(A)(3). We will consider these provisions in reverse order.

Code § 20-158(A)(3) provides that "[a] donor is not the parent of a child conceived through assisted conception, unless the donor is the husband of the gestational mother." It is undisputed that Breit was a "donor" in an assisted conception, and that Breit was never married to Mason. Thus, Mason contends that the statute bars Breit from establishing legal parentage of L.F., regardless of their voluntary written agreement.

Mason argues that Code § 20-49.1, despite being specifically referenced in the assisted conception statute, is not applicable in the present context and therefore their voluntary written agreement is a nullity. First, she contends that Code § 20-49.1 is merely a procedural vehicle by which existing parent-child relationships can be recognized, and that the statute cannot be used to *create* new parentage rights. We disagree. Code § 20-49.1(B) expressly provides that a parent-child relationship "may be established by" genetic testing or an acknowledgement of paternity:

The parent and child relationship between a child and a man may be established by:

> 1. Scientifically reliable genetic tests, including blood tests, which affirm at least a ninety-eight percent probability of paternity. Such genetic test results shall have the same legal effect as a judgment entered pursuant to § 20-49.8.
>
> 2. A voluntary written statement of the father and mother made under oath acknowledging paternity. . . . The acknowledgement may be rescinded by either party within sixty days from the date on which it was signed. . . . A written statement shall have the same legal effect as a judgment entered pursuant to § 20-49.8 and shall be binding and conclusive unless, in a subsequent judicial proceeding, the person challenging the statement establishes that the statement resulted from fraud, duress or a material mistake of fact.

Code § 20-49.1 has been amended four times since its enactment, including three times since the enactment of the assisted conception statute. Yet it has consistently been titled "[h]ow parent and child relationship *established.*" (Emphasis added.) Black's Law Dictionary defines "establish" as "[t]o make or form; to bring about or into existence," a definition that clearly contemplates the creation rather than the mere recognition of parentage rights.

Mason next argues that allowing unmarried sperm donors such as Breit to establish parentage pursuant to Code § 20-49.1(B) directly conflicts with Code § 20-158(A)(3). Code § 20-49.1(B) contains two independent and disparate provisions: (B)(1) allows paternity to be established unilaterally by scientifically reliable genetic testing, and (B)(2) allows paternity to be established by a voluntary written statement of both biological parents acknowledging paternity. We must examine these two independent sections separately. . . .

Mason argues that, under Code § 20-49.1(B)(1), donors could manufacture parent-child relationships over the gestational mother's objection through the use of genetic testing. Similarly, a gestational mother who became impregnated by a sperm donor could use Code § 20-49.1(B)(1) to force parental responsibilities on the donor, including the obligation of child support, solely by establishing a biological link. Mason asserts that the General Assembly intended to foreclose such scenarios when it enacted the assisted conception statute. We agree.

Code § 20-49.1(B)(1) directly conflicts with Code § 20-158(A)(3), since it allows paternity to be established solely on the basis of biological ties, which circumvents Code § 20-158(A)(3)'s instruction that mere donors cannot establish parentage. Consequently, a sperm donor aided only by the results of genetic testing may not establish parentage.

Code § 20-49.1(B)(2) does not present such a conflict. Executing an acknowledgement of paternity involves an assumption of rights and responsibilities well beyond biological ties. It is a voluntary agreement to establish an actual parent-child relationship that more closely approximates the status of a gestational mother's husband rather than a third-party donor. The assisted conception statute simply did not contemplate situations where, as here, unmarried donors have long-term relationships as well as biological ties that have been voluntarily acknowledged in writing pursuant to Code § 20-49.1(B)(2), and have voluntarily assumed responsibilities to their children.

As previously discussed, the assisted conception statute was written specifically with married couples in mind. The statute's primary purpose is to protect cohesive family units from claims of third-party intruders who served as mere donors. But Breit is not an intruder. He is the person whom Mason originally intended to be L.F.'s parent, whom she treated as L.F.'s parent for an extended period, and whom she voluntarily acknowledged as L.F.'s parent in a writing that she intended to be legally binding. Until Mason terminated Breit's visitation, Breit cared for, supported, and had begun to establish a parent-child relationship with L.F. Mason and Breit represented the closest thing L.F. had to a "family unit." . . .

[T]he General Assembly did not intend to divest individuals of the ability to establish parentage solely due to marital status, where, as here, the biological mother and sperm donor were known to each other, lived together as a couple, jointly assumed rights and responsibilities, and voluntarily executed a statutorily prescribed acknowledgement of paternity.

Having determined that Code § 20-49.1(B)(2) would apply in this context notwithstanding Code § 20-158(A)(3), we turn to Mason's next argument. Mason asserts that Code § 20-157 forecloses a conclusion that Code § 20-49.1(B)(2) applies. Code § 20-157 expressly states that the provisions of Chapter 9 control, without exception, in any related litigation:

> The provisions of this chapter [chapter 9] shall control, without exception, in any action brought in the courts of this Commonwealth to enforce or adjudicate any rights or responsibilities arising under this chapter.

This provision requires this Court to give precedence to Code §§ 20-158(A)(3) and 20-164 when confronted with contrary arguments. However, we must also harmonize Code § 20-49.1, when applicable, due to its explicit inclusion in Code § 20-164. Read in isolation, Code § 20-157 could support Mason's argument. But we do not read statutes in isolation. As stated above, we must construe statutes "to avoid repugnance and conflict between them." Likewise, we are bound to construe statutes in a manner that "avoid[s] any conflict with the Constitution." . . . Breit contends that accepting Mason's argument would render the assisted conception statute unconstitutional. That we cannot do, if there is any reasonable interpretation that conforms to the Constitution. Consequently, we must address Mason's argument regarding Code § 20-157 in the light of two constitutional imperatives. . . .

The relationship between a parent and child is a constitutionally protected liberty interest under the Due Process Clause of the Fourteenth Amendment. . . . Any statute that seeks to interfere with a parent's fundamental rights survives constitutional scrutiny only if it is narrowly tailored to serve a compelling state interest.

Significantly, in *Lehr v. Robertson*, 463 U.S. 248 (1983), the Supreme Court . . . recognized that parental rights do not arise solely from the biological connection between a parent and child. . . .

Prior to his visitation being terminated, Breit demonstrated a full commitment to the responsibilities of parenthood. . . . [T]he Due Process Clause protects Breit's fundamental right to make decisions concerning L.F.'s care, custody and control, despite his status as an unmarried donor. . . .

NOTES AND QUESTIONS

---

1. *Sperm Donors and the Constitution.* While courts have held that statutes divesting sperm donors of parental rights are constitutional as a general matter, courts in some jurisdictions have, as in *L.F.*, held that the statute would be

unconstitutional as applied to a known donor who agrees with the mother that he will be the father of the child.[159]

2. *Sperm Donors and Legal Parentage.* Might a sperm donor be able to attain legal parentage even if the sperm donor statute divests him of parental rights? In Jason P. v. Danielle S., actor Jason Patric claimed parentage under California law. Jason and Danielle were an on-again, off-again couple who at one point unsuccessfully tried to have a child together.[160] But when Danielle was single, she tried to have a child on her own, and eventually used Jason's sperm with the agreement that no one would know and he would not be the father. Jason and Danielle complied with the California statutes regulating donor insemination. But once the child, Gus, was born and Jason and Danielle got back together, Jason formed a relationship with the child. Gus viewed Jason as his father, and Danielle and Gus would regularly spend time with Jason and fly to see him when he was away from Los Angeles. Eventually, Jason and Danielle broke up, and Danielle sought to prevent Jason from spending time with Gus. Jason claimed parentage, and also asserted that application of the sperm donor statute would violate his constitutional parental rights. The California Court of Appeal did not reach the constitutional issue. Instead, the court held that under the sperm donor statute, Jason was not a father of Gus. But the court also held that Jason's lack of parentage under the sperm donor statute did not preclude him from proving parentage through another route — one that did not turn on his biological connection to the child. Accordingly, the court found that Jason qualified as a legal father because he welcomed Gus into his home and held Gus out as his child.[161] (Years earlier, the California Supreme Court had concluded that this "holding out" presumption could apply to an unmarried man who forms a parent-child relationship even though he is not the child's biological father. We will read this case, In re Nicholas H., later in the chapter.[162]) Does this seem like the right result? Should Danielle have been able to allow Jason to form a relationship with Gus without worry that he would have a legal claim to parentage — given that she complied with the sperm donor statute? What if you looked at the issue from Gus's perspective? Does that change your evaluation?

3. *Egg and Embryo Donors.* The first generation of statutes regulating donors involved sperm. But many states now have statutes that make clear that egg and

---

159. See, e.g., McIntyre v. Crouch, 780 P.2d 239, 245 (Or. Ct. App. 1989) ("The constitutionality of [the sperm donor statute], as applied to petitioner, turns on whether he can establish" that he and the mother agreed he would have the rights and obligations of fatherhood.); cf. In re K.M.H., 169 P.3d 1025 (Kan. 2007) (holding that statute barring sperm donor's paternity in the absence of a written agreement does not violate due process).

160. 171 Cal. Rptr. 3d 789 (Cal. Ct. App. 2014).

161. Id. at 796.

162. 46 P.3d 932 (Cal. 2002).

embryo donors are not legal parents (regardless of the marital status of the individual who uses the donor egg or embryo).[163]

PROBLEM

Concerned that Congress has failed to regulate assisted reproduction sufficiently, your state legislature has passed a new law addressing sperm donation. The law has a few central provisions:

(1) It would allow an individual to purchase donor sperm only after a doctor certifies that the individual has been unable to get pregnant through sexual intercourse.

(2) It would prohibit anonymous sperm donation and instead require that donors consent to their identities being disclosed to the would-be parents.

(3) It would limit the number of times a man may sell sperm and the number of times that a particular man's sperm can be used for insemination.

(4) It would grant to children conceived with donor sperm the "right to know" the personal identity and medical history of the sperm donor. The child would be able to attain this information at age sixteen, or at an earlier point with parental consent.

Do you support the new law, or at least some of it? What concerns do you have about the law? Is the law, or any part of it, susceptible to constitutional challenge?

POSTSCRIPT

Sperm donation is less regulated in the U.S. than in other countries. In the U.S., licensed banks collect and sell sperm. But informal markets for sperm also exist, and some websites facilitate matches between sperm donors and women seeking sperm.[164] In contrast, governments in other countries tightly regulate access to donor sperm.[165] In the U.S., individuals can engage in donor insemination regardless

---

163. See, e.g., Ala. Code § 26-17-702 (2020); Colo. Rev. Stat. Ann. § 19-4-106 (West 2020); Tenn. Code Ann. § 36-2-403 (2020); Va. Code Ann. § 20-158 (2020).

164. See Joanna L. Grossman, Men Who Give It Away: The Potential Perils of Free and Non-Anonymous Sperm Donation, Justia's Verdict (Jan. 24, 2012).

165. See Nikos Kalampalikis, Marjolaine Doumergue & Sophie Zadeh, Sperm Donor Regulation and Disclosure Intentions: Results from a Nationwide Multi-Centre Study in France, 5 Reprod. Biomed. & Soc'y Online 38, 39 (2018) ("Since 1973, French fertility centres have been organized in a national network embedded within public healthcare provision [French Federation of CECOS (FFC)], and regulated by French bioethics law. . . ."); Soo Youn, America's Hottest Export? Sperm, Guardian (Aug. 15, 2018) (explaining how in France, "a state-run, national sperm bank" oversees the number of donors, donations, and resultant births).

of marital status or sexual orientation, whereas some other countries have limited access to married, different-sex couples.[166] Nonetheless, health insurance providers in the U.S. frequently have limited coverage to cases of "infertility," which conventionally has been defined as heterosexual intercourse without pregnancy.[167] This limitation has been changing in light of same-sex couples' family formation efforts.[168] In the U.S., anonymous sperm donation is allowed and is common practice, while in other countries it is prohibited.[169] Unlike some other countries, the U.S. puts no legal limit on the number of sperm donations that a particular man can make or that can be used for insemination.[170] Still, professional organizations in the U.S. recommend limits.[171] In the U.S., a child conceived through donor insemination does not have a right to know the donor's identity, whereas non-U.S. authorities are more sympathetic to such a claim.[172] (Can clinics guarantee anonymity to the donor, given the rise of at-home genetic testing?) Recently, some states have legislated in ways that provide children with greater access to medical information about donors, even if these mandates stop short of personal information.[173]

IV. Parenthood Based on Intent

Intent has become an important concept in the law of parental recognition, at least with respect to assisted reproduction. As we saw in L.F. v. Breit, an individual's status as a legal parent may turn on whether that individual intended to be the parent of the child conceived through assisted reproduction. In this section, we consider the circumstances under which intent is relevant to parentage, showing the distinction

---

166. See Isabel Kaplan, France Debates Single Women's and Lesbians' Access to IVF, The Nation (Nov. 28, 2019).

167. See Stephanie Fairyington, Should Same-Sex Couples Receive Fertility Benefits?, N.Y. Times (Nov. 2, 2015).

168. Id.

169. See I. Glenn Cohen et al., Sperm Donor Anonymity and Compensation: An Experiment with American Sperm Donors, 3 J. L. & Biosciences 468, 469 (2016).

170. See Human Fertilisation & Embryology Authority, Donating Your Sperm, https://www.hfea.gov.uk/donation/donors/donating-your-sperm/ ("Donated sperm cannot be used to create more than 10 families, with no limits on the number of children born within each family.").

171. See American Society for Reproductive Medicine, Recommendations for Gamete and Embryo Donation: A Committee Opinion, 99 Fertility & Sterility 47, 53 (2013) ("It has been suggested that in a population of 800,000, limiting a single donor to no more than 25 births would avoid any significant increased risk of inadvertent consanguineous conception.").

172. See Maud de Boer-Buquicchio (Special Rapporteur on the Sale and Sexual Exploitation of Children), Report of the Special Rapporteur on the Sale and Sexual Exploitation of Children, Including Child Prostitution, Child Pornography and Other Child Sexual Abuse Material, ¶ 38, U.N. Doc. A/74/92 (July 15, 2019) ("blanket enforcement of anonymity for gamete donors . . . will prevent the child . . . from having access to his or her origins" and is a "violation of the rights of the child."). See also Cohen et al., supra note 168, at 469.

173. See, e.g., Wash. Rev. Code §§ 26.26A.800-825 (2020); see also UPA (2017), supra note 93, art. 9.

that the law has drawn between sexual procreation and assisted reproduction. We address how intent might be demonstrated in cases of assisted reproduction — most clearly, through an agreement. We focus on how intent may be invoked by biological as well as nonbiological parents.

A. Sex Versus Assisted Reproduction

As we have seen, in many situations, a man can avoid legal fatherhood when his sperm is used in assisted reproduction. Why can't the same man avoid legal fatherhood when the child results from sexual intercourse? What if he and the mother agreed that he would not be a legal parent? It doesn't matter. He can be held responsible as the legal father, regardless of the parties' intent and regardless of any agreement. Why does law recognize a donor in one situation but not in the other? Professor Courtney Cahill calls "the belief that sexual and alternative reproduction are essentially different in fact and therefore deserve different treatment in law" "reproductive binarism."

Courtney Megan Cahill, Reproduction Reconceived
101 Minn. L. Rev. 617 (2016)

A sex/non-sex binary drives paternity determinations in American jurisdictions where the question has been addressed. States vary significantly with respect to who constitutes a donor or a father when individuals or couples use either known or anonymous donors to conceive children through alternative reproductive means. States vary not at all, however, with respect to the legal status of donors who help unmarried women to conceive through a sexual act: in all states, that donor is a father, regardless of the intentions of the parties and regardless of whether or not a written non-paternity contract existed between them. . . .

No court has ever recognized a waiver of paternity where an unmarried woman intentionally conceives a child with a man through sexual intercourse. For instance, in *Straub v. B.M.T.*, the Indiana Supreme Court refused to uphold a written pre-conception contract between a man and a woman who agreed to conceive a child through sexual intercourse rather than through alternative insemination. In addition to rejecting the legal possibility of "artificial insemination by intercourse," the court reasoned that pre-conception contracts predicated on sex violated public policy because "sexual intercourse as consideration is itself against public policy." . . .

Other courts have similarly drawn an explicit sex/non-sex distinction when discussing when a donor becomes a father, reasoning that where "conception [takes] place by intercourse, there [is] no question that the 'donor' [is] the father." For these courts, the notion that sexual intercourse results in paternity is so obvious as to defy explanation. As the Supreme Court of Pennsylvania recently remarked, the "distinction between reproduction via sexual intercourse and the non-sexual clinical options for conception" — two "extremes of an increasingly complicated continuum," in the court's words — is a matter of simple "commonsense." . . .

The law's treatment of the status of men who sexually conceive with unmarried women by *design* tracks its treatment of the status of men who sexually conceive with unmarried women by *accident*: the latter cohort, as the law in every state makes clear, cannot avoid the obligations of fatherhood, even if the legal mother agrees to a waiver of paternity. In addition, the law's treatment of "insemination by intercourse" tracks its treatment of men who become fathers as the result of an underlying sexual act to which they never consented, as when a pregnancy results from statutory rape of a male by a female or from non-consensual sex between two adults. It also tracks the law's treatment of men whose sperm is "misappropriated" by women and used by them to self-inseminate (without the men's consent) following an act of consensual oral sex or who were misled about the woman's use of contraception or ability to conceive. Conception between men and unmarried women that is the product of some sexual act, it turns out, whether consensual or not and whether by design or not, results in paternity. As one court put it, "some sort of sexual contact" between unmarried women and unwilling men that results in conception is enough to justify the imposition of paternity on those men. . . .

NOTES AND QUESTIONS

---

1. *Sex versus Assisted Reproduction.* Why do we distinguish between these two forms of reproduction in the way that Cahill identifies? Is it justified? Are we concerned with child support? If so, then why allow single women to have children with donor sperm? Are we only concerned with those who have not planned for the child? If so, then why not distinguish between accidental and deliberate procreation?

2. *Fraud.* Should a man be obligated to pay child support if he had sex based on the woman's statement that she was infertile? That she had a hysterectomy? That she was using contraception? Should a teenage boy be obligated to pay child support when the sex that produced the child constituted statutory rape? What if the boy was 17 and the woman was 21? What if the boy was 14 and the woman was 36?

B. Parenting Agreements

Should the law allow individuals to privately decide who will be a parent of a child? Should courts enforce agreements regarding parentage? We have just seen that an agreement that the man will not be a father of a child conceived through sexual intercourse cannot be enforced. What about agreements formed in the context of assisted reproduction? Should we treat these arrangements like ordinary contracts? Or is there something special about agreements regarding parentage? Consider the role that the parties' agreement plays in the following case.

St. Mary v. Damon
309 P.3d 1027 (Nev. 2013)

Saitta, J.

This appeal concerns the establishment of custodial rights over a minor child born to former female partners, appellant Sha'Kayla St. Mary and respondent Veronica Lynn Damon. The couple became romantically involved and decided to have a child. They drafted a co-parenting agreement, and eventually, St. Mary gave birth to a child through in vitro fertilization, using Damon's egg and an anonymous donor's sperm. Thereafter, their relationship ended, leading to the underlying dispute concerning the parties' custodial rights over the child. . . .

Approximately one year after entering into a romantic relationship with each other, St. Mary and Damon moved in together. They planned to have a child, deciding that Damon would have her egg fertilized by a sperm donor, and St. Mary would carry the fertilized egg and give birth to the child. In October 2007, Damon's eggs were implanted into St. Mary. Around the same time, Damon drafted a co-parenting agreement, which she and St. Mary signed. The agreement indicated that Damon and St. Mary sought to "jointly and equally share parental responsibility, with both of [them] providing support and guidance." In it, they stated that they would "make every effort to jointly share the responsibilities of raising [their] child," including paying for expenses and making major child-related decisions. The agreement provided that if their relationship ended, they would each work to ensure that the other maintained a close relationship with the child, share the duties of raising the child, and make a "good-faith effort to jointly make all major decisions affecting" the child.

St. Mary gave birth to a child in June 2008. The hospital birth confirmation report and certificate of live birth listed only St. Mary as the child's mother. The child was given both parties' last names, however, in the hyphenated form of St. Mary-Damon.

For several months, St. Mary primarily stayed home caring for the child during the day while Damon worked. But, nearly one year after the child's birth, their romantic relationship ended, St. Mary moved out of the home, and St. Mary and Damon disagreed about how to share their time with the child. St. Mary signed an affidavit declaring that Damon was the biological mother of the child, and in 2009, Damon filed an ex parte petition with the district court to establish maternity, seeking to have the child's birth certificate amended to add Damon as a mother. The district court issued an order stating that St. Mary gave birth to the child and that Damon "is the biological and legal mother of said child." The 2009 order also directed that the birth certificate be amended to add Damon's name as a mother.

Thereafter, St. Mary instituted the underlying case by filing a complaint and motion, in a separate district court case, to establish custody, visitation, and child support. In response, Damon contended that, due to her biological connection, she was entitled to sole custody of the child. Damon attached the 2009 order to her opposition.

[In a 2011 order, the district court treated St. Mary as a surrogate rather than as a legal parent, and did so by relying on the 2009 order adjudicating Damon's parentage.] . . . [T]he court also concluded that the co-parenting agreement was null and void because . . . "a surrogate agreement is only for married couples, which only include one man and one woman." . . .

St. Mary argues that the district court erred in determining that, legally, she was a surrogate and not the child's legal mother and in deeming the co-parenting agreement unenforceable as a matter of law. . . .

St. Mary may be the child's legal mother . . .

In Nevada, all of the "rights, privileges, duties and obligations" accompanying parenthood are conferred on those persons who are deemed to have a parent-child relationship with the child, regardless of the parents' marital status. Surrogates who bear a child conceived through assisted conception for another, on the other hand, are often not entitled to claim parental rights. . . .

The multiple ways to prove maternity

Given the medical advances and changing family dynamics of the age, determining a child's parents today can be more complicated than it was in the past. To this end, although perhaps not encompassing every possibility, the Nevada Parentage Act provides several ways to determine a child's legal mother. . . . [A] woman's status as a legal mother can be established by "proof of her having given birth to the child." In maternity actions . . . , the statutes under which paternity may be determined apply "[i]nsofar as practicable." Paternity may be established in a variety of ways, including through presumptions based on marriage and cohabitation, presumptions based on receiving the child into the home and openly holding oneself out as a parent, genetic testing, and voluntary acknowledgment. Hence, a determination of parentage rests upon a wide array of considerations rather than genetics alone.

This case presents a situation where two women proffered evidence that could establish or generate a conclusive presumption of maternity to either woman. St. Mary testified that she gave birth to the child, thereby offering proof to establish that she is the child's legal mother. Damon showed that her egg was used to produce the child, demonstrating a genetic relationship to the child that may be a basis for concluding that she is the child's legal mother. By dividing the reproductive roles of conceiving a child, St. Mary and Damon each assumed functions traditionally used to evidence a legal maternal relationship. Hence, this matter raises the issue of whether the Nevada Parentage Act and its policies preclude a child from having two legal mothers where two women split the genetic and physical functions of creating a child.

The law does not preclude a child from having two legal mothers . . .

[T]he district court determined that St. Mary was not the child's legal mother. The court appears to have grounded this conclusion on the 2009 order, which provided that Damon was the child's legal mother and required Damon's name to be added to the child's birth certificate. But while that order stated that Damon was "the biological and legal mother" of the child, it in no way purported to undo or deny St. Mary's parent-child relationship with the child. . . . [W]hether St. Mary had rights to the child was not an issue that Damon's 2009 petition sought to resolve because it requested that "maternity be established" and "[t]hat the birth certificate be amended to add the biological mother's name of . . . D[amon]."

Further, . . . the district court erred in refusing to consider the parentage issue and limiting the scope of [its review] based on its conclusion that St. Mary was a surrogate — which was a conclusion that was made without an evidentiary hearing on that issue. . . .

Although St. Mary's parentage can be established by virtue of her having given birth to the child, the parties dispute whether they intended for St. Mary to be the child's parent or simply a surrogate or gestational carrier who lacked a legal parent-child relationship to the child. Therefore, upon remand, the district court must hold an evidentiary hearing to determine whether St. Mary is the child's legal mother or if she is someone without a legal relationship to the child, during which the court may consider any relevant evidence for establishing maternity under the Nevada Parentage Act.

The co-parenting agreement was not a surrogacy agreement and was consistent with Nevada's public policy

St. Mary asserts that the co-parenting agreement demonstrates the parties' intent regarding parentage and custody of the child and that the district court erred in determining that the co-parenting agreement was an unenforceable surrogacy agreement. . . . Damon responds that, because the agreement was between an unmarried intended parent and a surrogate and purported to resolve issues of parentage and child custody, the district court correctly deemed that the co-parenting agreement was prohibited. . . .

At the time of the district court's determinations, . . . [the surrogacy statute] required [surrogacy] contracts to specify the parties' rights, including the "[p]arentage of the child," the "[c]ustody of the child in the event of a change of circumstances," and the "respective responsibilities and liabilities of the contracting parties." Additionally, the statute defined a "[s]urrogate" as "an adult woman who enters into an agreement to bear a child conceived through assisted conception for the intended parents," and "[i]ntended parents" were defined as "a man and woman, married to each other," who agree to "be the parents of a child born to a surrogate through assisted conception." Here, St. Mary and Damon's co-parenting agreement was not within the scope of [the statute]. The agreement lacked any language intimating that St. Mary acted as a surrogate, such as language indicating that she surrendered custody of the child or relinquished her rights as a mother to the child. Rather, the agreement expressed that St. Mary would share the parental duties of raising the child and would jointly make major parenting decisions with Damon. . . .

In the event that both parties are determined to be the child's parents, nothing in Nevada law prevents two parents from entering into agreements that demonstrate their intent concerning child custody.

"Parties are free to contract, and the courts will enforce their contracts if they are not unconscionable, illegal, or in violation of public policy." It is presumed that fit parents act in the best interest of their children. Thus, public policy favors fit parents entering agreements to resolve issues pertaining to their minor child's custody, care, and visitation.

When a child has the opportunity to be supported by two loving and fit parents pursuant to a co-parenting agreement, this opportunity is to be given due consideration and must not be foreclosed on account of the parents being of the same sex. . . . To bar the enforceability of a co-parenting agreement on the basis of the parents' genders conflicts with the Nevada Parentage Act's policies of promoting the child's best interest with the support of two parents.

St. Mary and Damon's co-parenting agreement was aligned with Nevada's policy of allowing parents to agree on how to best provide for their child. Within their co-parenting agreement, St. Mary and Damon sought to provide for their child's best interest by agreeing to share the responsibilities of raising the child, even if the relationship between St. Mary and Damon ended. The agreement's language provides the indicia of an effort by St. Mary and Damon to make the child's best interest their priority. Thus, in the event that St. Mary is found to be a legal mother, the district court must consider the parties' co-parenting agreement in making its child custody determination. . . .

[W]e reverse the 2011 order. We remand this matter to the district court for further proceedings to determine the child's parentage, custody, and visitation.

NOTES AND QUESTIONS

---

1. *Co-Maternity (or Ova Sharing).* Some women in same-sex couples have children through IVF by having one woman be the genetic mother and the other be the birth mother. In *St. Mary*, the legal status of the birth mother was challenged. In other cases, the legal status of the genetic mother has been challenged. In California, the state supreme court found that both the birth mother and the genetic mother qualified as legal parents.[174] In Florida, the courts resolved the issue on constitutional grounds. The Florida Supreme Court analyzed a statute that, in divesting gamete donors of parental rights, excluded "the commissioning couple," but defined "commissioning couple" as "the intended mother and father of a child."[175] The statute thus had the effect of treating the genetic mother as a donor rather than an intended parent. The Court found the statute unconstitutional as applied to the genetic mother in a same-sex couple who intended to be the child's parent and then co-parented the child with the birth mother, until the couple separated.[176] It found that the statute violated the genetic mother's fundamental right to be a parent:

> Because T.M.H. accepted responsibility for raising her child from the beginning and did in fact parent and support the child until D.M.T. prevented her from doing so, we hold that T.M.H.'s inchoate interest has developed into a protected fundamental right to be a parent to her child.[177]

The court also found that the statute discriminated based on sexual orientation in violation of equality guarantees:

> Consistent with equal protection, a same-sex couple must be afforded the equivalent chance as a heterosexual couple to establish their intentions in using assisted reproductive technology to conceive a child.[178]

2. *Enforcing Agreements Regarding Children.* Law constrains individuals in many ways from making enforceable agreements with respect to parental rights and responsibilities. This is justified by the state's interest in protecting the welfare of children. We have already seen that individuals cannot waive rights or responsibilities when they have a child through sexual intercourse. And we will see that in some states individuals cannot enforce surrogacy agreements that render the intended parents, and not the surrogate, the legal parents. Outside of parentage, prenuptial agreements cannot bind parties or the court with respect to custody or child support. Similarly, courts must approve provisions relating to custody and

---

174. K.M. v. E.G., 117 P.3d 673 (Cal. 2005).
175. Fla. Stat. § 742.14 (2020).
176. D.M.T. v. T.M.H., 129 So. 3d 320 (Fla. 2013).
177. Id. at 339.
178. Id. at 343.

child support in separation agreements. Does this seem like good policy? Why not assume that parents will do what is best for their children?

Why was the agreement in *St. Mary* consistent with Nevada policy? Does *St. Mary* stand for the proposition that co-parenting agreements are enforceable such that both individuals will be treated as legal parents with rights and responsibilities? What if one of the women did not otherwise "prove maternity"? How is the agreement relevant to determining the parental status of the women? Would the co-parenting agreement still matter if one of the women did not have a gestational or genetic connection to the child?

3. *Reproductive Clinic Forms and Requirements.* The genetic mother, Damon, asserted that "she and St. Mary did not intend to create an enforceable co-parenting agreement but created the agreement to satisfy the fertility clinic's requirements and to seek insurance coverage for the pregnancy." Should agreements required by fertility clinics bind the parties? While the clinic in the case did not appear to require an agreement, why might a clinic require agreements regarding parentage? Should patients be required to seek legal counsel before signing any agreements at the clinic? What if the clinic provides forms that purport to waive or assign rights and responsibilities? Should such forms be enforceable in a later dispute between the parties?

In K.M. v. E.G., the California case referenced in Note 1, the genetic mother signed a "Consent Form for Ovum Donor (Known)" at the clinic.[179] Why would she have signed a form that said she was an egg donor and not a parent of the resulting child? What if she didn't read it? K.M. testified that she saw the form only ten minutes before she signed it and that she only signed it so that "we can have children."[180] The California Supreme Court did not give the form any effect, explaining:

> The superior court in the present case found that K.M. signed a waiver form, thereby "relinquishing and waiving all rights to claim legal parentage of any children who might result." But such a waiver does not affect our determination of parentage. . . . "Regardless of its terms, an agreement between an alleged or presumed father and the mother or child does not bar an action under this chapter." A woman who supplies ova to be used to impregnate her lesbian partner, with the understanding that the resulting child will be raised in their joint home, cannot waive her responsibility to support that child. Nor can such a purported waiver effectively cause that woman to relinquish her parental rights.[181]

In other words, the court simply concluded that agreements to waive parental rights cannot be enforced. But that sounds like the principle applied to sexual procreation.

---

179. 117 P.3d at 676.
180. Id.
181. Id. at 682.

Doesn't the law allow individuals to waive parental rights when they donate gametes for assisted reproduction? Did the result actually depend on the belief that the women understood that "the resulting child will be raised in their joint home"? In other words, does that make the genetic mother in *K.M.* analogous to the sperm donor in *L.F.* who intended to parent the child?

C. Biological Parents and Intent

St. Mary and Damon used *in vitro* fertilization (IVF) to conceive a child. With IVF, a woman undergoes egg retrieval, fertilization occurs outside the body, and the embryo is implanted. Use of IVF has steadily increased. More than 70,000 children were born in the U.S. in 2015 as a result of IVF.[182] Many individuals use IVF along with a gamete donor, while many others do not. St. Mary and Damon used donor sperm. The following case considers the legal status of a woman who gives birth to a child conceived with a donor egg.

1. Giving Birth

In re C.K.G.
173 S.W.3d 714 (Tenn. 2005)

Frank F. Drowota, III, C.J.

This controversy involves a maternity dispute. An unmarried, heterosexual couple had three children by obtaining eggs donated from an anonymous third-party female, fertilizing the eggs *in vitro* with the man's sperm, and implanting the fertilized eggs in the woman's uterus. The couple intended to rear the children together as father and mother. When the couple's relationship deteriorated, the woman filed a parentage action seeking custody and child support. In response, the man claimed that the woman had no standing as a parent because, lacking genetic connection to the children, she failed to qualify as a parent under Tennessee's parentage statutes. On this basis, the man sought sole and exclusive custody.

I. Factual and Procedural Background

Dr. Charles K. G. and Ms. Cindy C. first met in 1993 while working at Vanderbilt University Medical Center in Nashville. Cindy was a nurse practitioner who managed a department through which Charles, then a medical resident, rotated. Charles and Cindy began dating in 1994. After an initial period of closeness, they

---

182. See Ctrs. for Disease Control and Prevention, 2015 Assisted Reproductive Technology National Summary Report, supra note 51, at 3.

maintained for several years an unsteady dating relationship which included an extended period of estrangement.

In 1999, Charles and Cindy not only reunited as an unmarried couple but also soon thereafter began discussing having a child together. By this time Cindy was forty-five years old and Charles was also in his mid-forties. Charles had never had children. He had not grown up in Tennessee, and a December 1999 visit to his birthplace influenced him; he wanted to be a father. Even though Cindy had at least two adult children from prior marriages as well as grandchildren, she was amenable to starting a family with Charles. However, given her age, Cindy was concerned about the viability of her ova, or eggs.

Having decided to have a child, Charles and Cindy pursued *in vitro* fertilization through the Nashville Fertility Center. On May 2, 2000, they jointly executed several agreements with the Fertility Center. Although Charles and Cindy were unmarried, they did not alter the boilerplate language that the Center frequently used in its agreements describing them as "husband" and "wife." Included among these agreements was a "RECIPIENT CONSENT FOR DONATION OF OOCYTES BY ANONYMOUS DONOR" ("Recipient Consent") which describes the fertilization procedure and its risks, waives the right of Charles and Cindy to know the egg donor's identity, and outlines the responsibilities of the parties to the agreement. The Recipient Consent further provides as follows:

> I, Cindy (wife), understand that the child(ren) conceived by this method will not have my genetic material, but will have that of the oocyte [egg] donor and my husband [sic]. However, regardless of the outcome, I will be the mother of any child(ren) born to me as a result of egg donation and hereby accept all the legal responsibilities required of such a parent.

This document was signed by Cindy as "wife" and by Charles as "husband" and was witnessed and signed by a physician who represented that he had fully explained the procedure to Charles and Cindy and had answered all their questions. However, Charles and Cindy executed no other agreements concerning their intentions as to parentage or surrogacy.

Shortly thereafter, Charles paid the Fertility Center $10,000 for the procedure of having two anonymously donated eggs fertilized with Charles's sperm and inserted in Cindy's uterus. Charles intended for them to conceive only one child (presumably two eggs were used to increase the procedure's odds of success). After fertilization, one of the eggs divided, resulting in the development of three embryos. All three embryos flourished; Cindy had become pregnant with triplets.

During Cindy's pregnancy, Charles began residing consistently at Cindy's home. Due to complications with the pregnancy, Cindy took an early leave from her job. When she was placed on bed rest, Charles maintained the household and cooked for her. On February 21, 2001, Cindy gave birth via caesarian section to three children: C.K.G., C.A.G., and C.L.G. Tennessee Department of Health birth certificates for the children identify Charles as the father and Cindy as the mother.

Although Charles had never promised to marry Cindy, he represented that he desired permanence and stability with her. Further, Cindy understood and expected that they would raise the children together as mother and father. In fact, Cindy even sought assurance from Charles that she would not have to rear them by herself. Cindy stayed home with the triplets on maternity leave until June 2001 when she returned to work four days per week. Having set aside money in anticipation of having a child, Charles took a one-year leave of absence (February 2001 to January 2002) from his position as an emergency room physician. For the first several months after the triplets' birth, Charles and Cindy lived together and shared parenting responsibilities. They each provided financially for the children's needs. Further, for some time they had discussed the need for a larger home, and they purchased a house in Brentwood together as tenants in common with the understanding that they would bear the cost equally. Cindy sold her prior residence, and she, Charles, and the triplets moved into the new house in August 2001.

After hiring a nanny, Charles and Cindy's relationship soon deteriorated. Cindy alleged that Charles began cultivating or renewing relationships with several other women; Charles admitted to having sex with another woman during a December 2001 trip to London, England. Cindy further alleged that once their relationship had begun to deteriorate, Charles not only became dramatically less involved with the children, but also began withholding financial support from them. In April 2002, after utility service to their home had been cut off, Cindy filed a petition in the juvenile court of Williamson County to establish parentage and to obtain custody and child support.

II. Analysis

The facts of this case thus present us with a question of first impression in Tennessee: under such circumstances, who as a matter of law is the children's mother? . . .

A. The Question of Maternity . . .

1. The Impact of Modern Reproductive Technology on the Legal Definition of Parenthood

"Historically, gestation proved genetic parentage beyond doubt, so it was unnecessary to distinguish between gestational and genetic mothers." However, recent developments in reproductive technology have caused a tectonic shift in the realities which underlie our legal conceptions of parenthood. . . .

[T]echnological fragmentation of the procreative process, insofar as it includes techniques for egg and sperm donation and preservation, has engendered a bewildering variety of possibilities which are not easily reconciled with our traditional definitions of "mother," "father," and "parent."

We now live in an era where a child may have as many as five different "parents." These include a sperm donor, an egg donor, a surrogate or gestational host, and two non-biologically related individuals who intend to raise the child. . . .

The degree to which current statutory law governs or fails to govern these realities provides the initial framework for our analysis.

2. The Limited Scope of Tennessee's Parentage Statutes

Parentage is an area of law governed primarily by statute. Unfortunately, Tennessee's parentage and related statutes do not contemplate many of the scenarios now made possible by recent developments in reproductive technology. . . .

The parentage statutes define "mother" as "the *biological* mother of a child born out of wedlock." Similarly, "parent" is defined as "the *biological* mother or *biological* father of a child, regardless of the marital status of the mother and father." The parentage statutes do not define "biological mother." . . .

[T]he parentage statutes generally fail to contemplate dispute over maternity. . . . Tennessee's parentage and related statutes do not provide for or control the circumstances of this case. . . .

3. Tests for Legal Maternity in Other Jurisdictions . . .

Among the few jurisdictions which have addressed cases like this one, where a gestational carrier implanted with donated eggs seeks parental status of the resulting children and where legislation does not clearly resolve the matter, two tests for maternity have arisen. Some courts have focused on intent, holding that under such circumstances the intended "mother" is to be deemed the legal mother.

The intent test has developed primarily in California. In *Johnson v. Calvert*, 851 P.2d 776 (Cal. 1993), . . . the California Supreme Court held that when gestation and genetic consanguinity "do not coincide in one woman, she who intended to procreate the child — that is, she who intended to bring about the birth of the child that she intended to raise as her own — is the natural mother under California law." The *Johnson* Court justified its holding in part by strongly affirming the validity of surrogacy contracts.

The genetic test has been set forth most thoroughly by the Ohio Court of Common Pleas in *Belsito v. Clark*, 644 N.E.2d 766 (Ohio Ct. Com. Pl. 1994). In *Belsito*, a married couple wanted children, and the wife could produce eggs but could not sustain a pregnancy. By agreement, one of the wife's eggs was fertilized with the husband's sperm and then implanted in the uterus of a gestational surrogate (the wife's sister). Without objection from the surrogate, the couple sought a declaratory judgment of maternity and paternity. Like California, Ohio had adopted a version of the Uniform Parentage Act which provided that "maternity can be established by identifying the natural mother through the birth process or by other means, including DNA blood tests," as provided by statute. Also declining to recognize two legal mothers, the court applied a two-stage analysis for establishing maternity. First, if the male and female genetic providers have not waived parental rights, they must be declared the legal parents. Second, if the female genetic provider has waived her parental rights, then the gestator is the legal mother. On this basis, the court held that the married couple, as the child's genetic progenitors, were the legal parents.

Significantly, Tennessee's statutory framework for establishing maternity differs markedly from the California and Ohio statutes under consideration in *Johnson* and *Belsito*. Consequently, neither California's intent test nor Ohio's genetic test is strictly apposite to our statutory scheme.

Further, both the intent test and the genetic test suffer from inadequacies. For example, in *Johnson* the California Supreme Court crafted an unnecessarily broad rule which could afford maternal status even to a woman who failed to qualify under either of California's two statutory bases for maternity. According to *Belsito*, the intent formulation of *Johnson* has "discarded both genetics and birth as the primary means of identifying the natural maternal parent," and provides for, "in effect, a private adoption process that is readily subject to all the defects and pressures of such a process." In Tennessee, unlicensed and unregulated adoption is statutorily prohibited and subject to criminal penalties.

However, the genetic test of *Belsito* also has significantly broad implications. In the event that a dispute were to arise between an intended mother who had obtained eggs from a third-party donor and a gestational surrogate in whom the eggs had been implanted, the genetic test would implicitly invalidate any surrogacy agreement. . . . [A]n intended "mother" who employs techniques for assisted reproduction including egg donation would by default have to submit to government-controlled adoption procedures to attain a secure legal status as "mother." Policy-wise, the requirement of such regulation may or may not be sound.

Consequently, we decline to adopt either the intent test or the genetic test as a general rule for resolving this case. . . .

4. Factors for Establishing Legal Maternity

In light of the foregoing analysis, we deem it appropriate to decide this case on particularly narrow grounds. . . . [I]n resolving this case we focus closely on its particular facts. . . .

i. Genetics

Both statute and sound policy support genetics as an important factor in establishing legal maternity. Human reproduction as we now know it cannot take place without the involvement of genetic material. . . . Tennessee's domestic relations statutes provide for the establishment of legal maternity based on genetic consanguinity. . . .

However, . . . [i]n cases such as this one, where a woman has become intimately involved in the procreation process even though she has not contributed genetic material, factors other than genetics take on special significance.

ii. Intent

Before the children's birth, both Cindy and the genetic father, Charles, voluntarily demonstrated the bona fide intent that Cindy would be the children's legal mother, and they agreed that Cindy would accept all the legal responsibility as well as the legal rights of parenthood. We consider the intent to take on both parental rights and responsibilities as one important factor among others for resolving this controversy. . . .

[T]aking intent into consideration as a factor is consistent with policy implicit in Tennessee's domestic relations statutes.

Significantly, the artificial insemination statute . . . supports the consideration of intent as a factor for establishing legal maternity. . . . It provides as follows: "A child born to a married woman as a result of artificial insemination, with consent of such married woman's husband, is deemed to be the legitimate child of the husband and wife." . . . [The statute] confers parental status on a husband even though the child conceived in his wife via artificial insemination is not necessarily genetically related to him. The artificial insemination statute thus reflects a policy which favors taking into account intent in establishing parentage when technological assistance is involved.

iii. Gestation

Cindy became pregnant and gave birth to the children with the intent of raising them as her own. As mentioned above, historically gestation "proved genetic parentage beyond doubt" and thus was conclusive of maternity. The common law thus has presumed that the birth mother is the legal mother of the child. It is only quite recently that modern technology has made it possible to separate and to distribute among multiple persons or environments the genetic and gestational roles. We consider gestation as another important factor in determining legal maternity in this case. . . .

Although giving birth is conspicuously absent from Tennessee's parentage statutes, . . . there is no indication that the General Assembly sought to exclude it as a basis for legal maternity or even sought to decide questions of maternity at all. In this regard, the artificial insemination statute is once again significant. In addition to recognizing paternity where artificial insemination is involved, [it] confers parental status on a wife when she gives birth to a child as the result of artificial insemination. This statute displays a policy which favors recognizing gestation and giving birth as a basis for legal maternity.

Accordingly, we conclude that sound policy and common sense favor recognizing gestation as an important factor for establishing legal maternity. . . .

iv. The Absence of Controversy Between the Gestator and the Genetic "Mother"

Another factor to consider in resolving this case is the nature of the controversy. Here we are not faced with a controversy between a birth "mother" and a genetic "mother" where the genetic and gestational roles have been separated and distributed among two women. In this case, the genetic "mother" has fully waived her parental rights and remains anonymous. Nor is this a case involving a dispute between a traditional or gestational surrogate and a genetically-unrelated intended "mother" who wishes to raise the child as her own. Rather, Cindy became pregnant and gave birth to triplets on her own behalf, and the sole dispute is between her and the genetic father, Charles. The other kinds of conflicts present different questions and ones which would be inappropriate for us to decide here. Instead, we limit our holding today to cases where there is no controversy between the gestator and the genetic "mother."

5. Establishing Legal Maternity in This Case

Deciding this case narrowly based on its particular facts, . . . Cindy is the legal mother. Our holding that Cindy is the legal mother of C.K.G., C.A.G., and C.L.G. with all the legal rights and responsibilities of parenthood is based on the following factors. First, prior to the children's birth, both Cindy, the gestator, and Charles, the genetic father, voluntarily demonstrated the bona fide intent that Cindy would be the children's legal mother and agreed that Cindy would accept the legal responsibility as well as the legal rights of parenthood. Second, Cindy then became pregnant, carried to term, and gave birth to the three children as her own. Third, this case does not involve a controversy between a gestator and a female genetic progenitor where the genetic and gestative roles have been separated and distributed among two women, nor does this case involve a controversy between a traditional or gestational surrogate and a genetically-unrelated intended mother; our holding today is not designed to control such controversies. Even though Cindy lacks genetic connection to the triplets, in light of all the factors considered we determine that Cindy is the children's legal mother. We further conclude that in light of the factors considered, Charles's genetic paternity does not give him a parental status superior to that of Cindy. . . .

6. The Need for Legislative Action

Given the far-reaching, profoundly complex, and competing public policy considerations necessarily implicated by the present controversy, we conclude that crafting a general rule to adjudicate all controversies so implicated is more appropriately accomplished by the Tennessee General Assembly. The General Assembly is better suited than the courts to gather data, to investigate issues not subject to current litigation, and to debate the competing values and the costs involved in such an issue as deciding whether generally to subject procreation via technological assistance to governmental oversight, and if so, to determine what kind of regulation to impose. . . .

ADOLPHO A. BIRCH, JR., dissenting. . . .

My colleagues have cobbled together a resolution which would appear at first glance to be just and reasonable. But in so doing, they have side-stepped a clear legislative mandate: the statutory definition of "parent." . . .

[O]ur statutes expressly define "parent." "Parent" is limited to biological, legal and adoptive parents.

I would resolve this case through genetics. It is scientific, certain, and has found acceptance in several courts that have addressed the issue. Furthermore, it is easier to apply. Moreover, this is the test that our legislature has already ordained by providing that parentage may be established by either biology or adoption. Indeed, "courts have looked at genetics as the primary basis to determine who is the parent" based on the importance of historical precedence and common ancestry.

The plaintiff is, a fortiori, a non-parent, at least as is determined by the statutory definitions of "mother" and "parent" as one who has biological ties to the child(ren). . . .

Tennessee statutes do not use gestation or intent to confer parental status, instead genetics, marriage and adoption are the routes available. Therefore, by reviewing and analyzing the Tennessee statutes which are based on biology, Ms. C. is not the parent nor is she the legal mother of the children for purposes of this case, and she has no legal standing to sue for custody or support as a parent. Adoption, nevertheless, remains an option.

We, as interpreters of the law, not makers of the law, are powerless, in my view, to reach a different resolution. . . .

2. Surrogacy and Genetics

In the late 1980s, a surrogacy dispute from New Jersey, In re Baby M, captured the nation's attention.[183] A married couple, William and Elizabeth Stern, had arranged to have a surrogate, Mary Beth Whitehead, be inseminated with William's sperm and deliver a baby that the Sterns would raise. But when Whitehead changed her mind and refused to surrender the child, the courts got involved. While the trial court found the surrogacy agreement valid, the New Jersey Supreme Court disagreed and ruled that surrogacy agreements were unenforceable as against public policy. Accordingly, William Stern was the legal father and Mary Beth Whitehead was the legal mother, and so each would have claims to custody and visitation. Elizabeth Stern, without a biological connection to the child, would remain a legal stranger — even though she would essentially be parenting the child with the legal father, as the child's stepmother. While the court found that Whitehead was the legal mother, it gave primary custody of the child to the Sterns. The court explained its conclusion:

> We invalidate the surrogacy contract because it conflicts with the law and public policy of this State. While we recognize the depth of the yearning of infertile couples to have their own children, we find the payment of money

---

183. 537 A.2d 1227 (N.J. 1988).

to a "surrogate" mother illegal, perhaps criminal, and potentially degrading to women. Although in this case we grant custody to the natural father, the evidence having clearly proved such custody to be in the best interests of the infant, we void both the termination of the surrogate mother's parental rights and the adoption of the child by the wife/stepparent. We thus restore the "surrogate" as the mother of the child.[184]

While *Baby M* involved traditional (or genetic) surrogacy — in which the surrogate is genetically related to the child — IVF facilitated gestational surrogacy, in which the surrogate is not genetically related to the child. With gestational surrogacy, the intended parents either use their own gametes (egg and sperm) or rely on donors. Accordingly, the gestational surrogate gives birth to a child genetically related to either the intended mother or an egg donor. A few years after *Baby M*, the California Supreme Court addressed a conflict between a surrogate and the intended parents. But unlike *Baby M*, the situation involved gestational surrogacy, and the intended mother was also the genetic mother.

JOHNSON V. CALVERT
851 P.2d 776 (Cal. 1993)

PANELLI, J. . . .

Mark and Crispina Calvert are a married couple who desired to have a child. Crispina was forced to undergo a hysterectomy in 1984. Her ovaries remained capable of producing eggs, however, and the couple eventually considered surrogacy. In 1989 Anna Johnson heard about Crispina's plight from a coworker and offered to serve as a surrogate for the Calverts.

On January 15, 1990, Mark, Crispina, and Anna signed a contract providing that an embryo created by the sperm of Mark and the egg of Crispina would be implanted in Anna and the child born would be taken into Mark and Crispina's home "as their child." Anna agreed she would relinquish "all parental rights" to the child in favor of Mark and Crispina. In return, Mark and Crispina would pay Anna $10,000 in a series of installments, the last to be paid six weeks after the child's birth. Mark and Crispina were also to pay for a $200,000 life insurance policy on Anna's life.

The zygote was implanted on January 19, 1990. Less than a month later, an ultrasound test confirmed Anna was pregnant.

Unfortunately, relations deteriorated between the two sides. Mark learned that Anna had not disclosed she had suffered several stillbirths and miscarriages. Anna felt Mark and Crispina did not do enough to obtain the required insurance policy. She also felt abandoned during an onset of premature labor in June.

---

184. Id. at 1234.

In July 1990, Anna sent Mark and Crispina a letter demanding the balance of the payments due her or else she would refuse to give up the child. The following month, Mark and Crispina responded with a lawsuit, seeking a declaration they were the legal parents of the unborn child. Anna filed her own action to be declared the mother of the child, and the two cases were eventually consolidated. . . .

The child was born on September 19, 1990. . . At trial in October 1990, the parties stipulated that Mark and Crispina were the child's genetic parents. After hearing evidence and arguments, the trial court ruled that Mark and Crispina were the child's "genetic, biological and natural" father and mother, that Anna had no "parental" rights to the child, and that the surrogacy contract was legal and enforceable against Anna's claims. . . .

Passage of the [Uniform Parentage] Act clearly was not motivated by the need to resolve surrogacy disputes, which were virtually unknown in 1975. Yet it facially applies to any parentage determination, including the rare case in which a child's maternity is in issue. We are invited to disregard the Act and decide this case according to other criteria, including constitutional precepts and our sense of the demands of public policy. We feel constrained, however, to decline the invitation. . . . The Act offers a mechanism to resolve this dispute, albeit one not specifically tooled for it. We therefore proceed to analyze the parties' contentions within the Act's framework. . . .

Both women . . . have adduced evidence of a mother and child relationship as contemplated by the Act. Yet for any child California law recognizes only one natural mother, despite advances in reproductive technology rendering a different outcome biologically possible.

We see no clear legislative preference in [the parentage code] as between blood testing evidence and proof of having given birth. . . . Because two women each have presented acceptable proof of maternity, we do not believe this case can be decided without enquiring into the parties' intentions as manifested in the surrogacy agreement. Mark and Crispina are a couple who desired to have a child of their own genes but are physically unable to do so without the help of reproductive technology. They affirmatively intended the birth of the child, and took the steps necessary to effect in vitro fertilization. But for their acted-on intention, the child would not exist. Anna agreed to facilitate the procreation of Mark's and Crispina's child. The parties' aim was to bring Mark's and Crispina's child into the world, not for Mark and Crispina to donate a zygote to Anna. Crispina from the outset intended to be the child's mother. Although the gestative function Anna performed was necessary to bring about the child's birth, it is safe to say that Anna would not have been given the opportunity to gestate or deliver the child had she, prior to implantation of the zygote, manifested her own intent to be the child's mother. No reason appears why Anna's later change of heart should vitiate the determination that Crispina is the child's natural mother.

We conclude that although the Act recognizes both genetic consanguinity and giving birth as means of establishing a mother and child relationship, when the two means do not coincide in one woman, she who intended to procreate the child — that is, she who intended to bring about the birth of a child that she intended to raise as her own — is the natural mother under California law. . . .

In deciding the issue of maternity under the Act we have felt free to take into account the parties' intentions, as expressed in the surrogacy contract, because in our view the agreement is not, on its face, inconsistent with public policy. . . .

Anna urges that surrogacy contracts violate several social policies. [S]he cites the public policy prohibiting the payment for consent to adoption of a child. She argues further that the policies underlying the adoption laws of this state are violated by the surrogacy contract because it in effect constitutes a pre-birth waiver of her parental rights.

We disagree. Gestational surrogacy differs in crucial respects from adoption and so is not subject to the adoption statutes. The parties voluntarily agreed to participate in in vitro fertilization and related medical procedures before the child was conceived; at the time when Anna entered into the contract, therefore, she was not vulnerable to financial inducements to part with her own expected offspring. As discussed above, Anna was not the genetic mother of the child. The payments to Anna under the contract were meant to compensate her for her services in gestating the fetus and undergoing labor, rather than for giving up "parental" rights to the child. Payments were due both during the pregnancy and after the child's birth.

It has been suggested that gestational surrogacy may run afoul of prohibitions on involuntary servitude. Involuntary servitude has been recognized in cases of criminal punishment for refusal to work. We see no potential for that evil in the contract at issue here, and extrinsic evidence of coercion or duress is utterly lacking. We note that although at one point the contract purports to give Mark and Crispina the sole right to determine whether to abort the pregnancy, at another point it acknowledges: "All parties understand that a pregnant woman has the absolute right to abort or not abort any fetus she is carrying. Any promise to the contrary is unenforceable." We therefore need not determine the validity of a surrogacy contract purporting to deprive the gestator of her freedom to terminate the pregnancy.

Finally, Anna and some commentators have expressed concern that surrogacy contracts tend to exploit or dehumanize women, especially women of lower economic status. Anna's objections center around the psychological harm she asserts may result from the gestator's relinquishing the child to whom she has given birth. Some have also cautioned that the practice of surrogacy may encourage society to view children as commodities, subject to trade at their parents' will.

We are all too aware that the proper forum for resolution of this issue is the Legislature, where empirical data, largely lacking from this record, can be studied and rules of general applicability developed. However, in light of our responsibility to decide this case, we have considered as best we can its possible consequences.

We are unpersuaded . . . by the claim that surrogacy will foster the attitude that children are mere commodities; no evidence is offered to support it. The limited data available seem to reflect an absence of significant adverse effects of surrogacy on all participants.

The argument that a woman cannot knowingly and intelligently agree to gestate and deliver a baby for intending parents carries overtones of the reasoning that for centuries prevented women from attaining equal economic rights and professional status under the law. To resurrect this view is both to foreclose a personal and economic choice on the part of the surrogate mother, and to deny intending parents what may be their only means of procreating a child of their own genes. Certainly in the present case it cannot seriously be argued that Anna, a licensed vocational nurse who had done well in school and who had previously borne a child, lacked the intellectual wherewithal or life experience necessary to make an informed decision to enter into the surrogacy contract.

KENNARD, J., dissenting.

When a woman who wants to have a child provides her fertilized ovum to another woman who carries it through pregnancy and gives birth to a child, who is the child's legal mother? Unlike the majority, I do not agree that the determinative consideration should be the intent to have the child that originated with the woman who contributed the ovum. In my view, the woman who provided the fertilized ovum and the woman who gave birth to the child both have substantial claims to legal motherhood. . . .

To determine who is the legal mother of a child born of a gestational surrogacy arrangement, I would apply the standard most protective of child welfare — the best interests of the child. . . .

The majority's approach entirely devalues the substantial claims of motherhood by a gestational mother such as Anna. True, a woman who enters into a surrogacy arrangement intending to raise the child has by her intent manifested an assumption of parental responsibility in addition to her biological contribution of providing the genetic material. But the gestational mother's biological contribution of carrying a child for nine months and giving birth is likewise an assumption of parental responsibility. A pregnant woman's commitment to the unborn child she carries is not just physical; it is psychological and emotional as well. . . . Indeed, a fetus would never develop into a living child absent its nurturing by the pregnant woman. A pregnant woman intending to bring a child into the world is more than a mere container or breeding animal; she is a conscious agent of creation no less than the genetic mother, and her humanity is implicated on a deep level. Her role should not be devalued. . . .

The allocation of parental rights and responsibilities necessarily impacts the welfare of a minor child. . . Consequently, I would apply "the best interests of the child" standard to determine who can best assume the social and legal responsibilities of motherhood for a child born of a gestational surrogacy arrangement.

The determination of a child's best interests does not depend on the parties' relative economic circumstances, which in a gestational surrogacy situation will usually favor the genetic mother and her spouse. As this court has recognized, however, superior wealth does not necessarily equate with good parenting.

Factors that are pertinent to good parenting, and thus that are in a child's best interests, include the ability to nurture the child physically and psychologically and to provide ethical and intellectual guidance. Also crucial to a child's best interests is the "well recognized right" of every child "to stability and continuity." The intent of the genetic mother to procreate a child is certainly relevant to the question of the child's best interests; alone, however, it should not be dispositive. . . .

NOTES AND QUESTIONS

---

1. *Best Interests of the Child?* In her dissenting opinion, Justice Kennard explained that she would have decided the issue based on the best interests of the child. Why did her colleagues not agree? Parentage determinations — who is a parent? — proceed custody determinations. The first-order question of parentage generally does not turn on a best interests determination. Instead, it is simply about an adult's status vis-à-vis a particular child. Once we know who the legal parents are, a dispute between them over custody and visitation is governed by a best interests standard. The court approached *Johnson* as a parentage dispute, not a custody dispute, and thus the best interest analysis would have been inappropriate.

2. *Intentional Parenthood.* The court decided that, as between two individuals who each have valid claims to parentage, the individual who intended to parent the child is the legal parent. Is this the same as enforcing the surrogacy agreement? The court looked to the agreement as evidence of intent, but it did not purport to actually enforce the agreement. That makes sense because the determination of parentage is one governed by family law, not contract law; and nothing in California law at the time authorized parentage through surrogacy arrangements. Now, California has a statutory regime permitting and regulating gestational surrogacy. Provided that individuals comply with the requirements, the intended parents are the legal parents, and the woman serving as the gestational surrogate has no parental rights.

States' approaches to surrogacy have developed quickly over recent years, with more and more jurisdictions enacting laws that authorize at least some forms of surrogacy. Professor Courtney Joslin describes the state of statutory law in 2020:

> Of the 26 jurisdictions with statutory provisions addressing surrogacy, twenty-one (21) permit gestational surrogacy. Of these twenty-one (21), five (5) authorize both gestational and genetic surrogacy, and eighteen (18) permit compensation. In contrast, eight (8) states civilly ban some or all forms of surrogacy. . . .
>
> State law also varies with regard to whether one or both intended parents must be genetically related to the resulting child. A minority of states — Florida, Illinois, Iowa, Louisiana, and North Dakota — include such

requirements. Two of these states — Louisiana and North Dakota — require both intended parents to be genetically related to the resulting child. . . . In contrast, the overwhelming majority of permissive states — 16 of the 21 — do not include such a requirement.

Surrogacy laws vary on the timing of and procedures regarding determinations of parenthood. Half of the permissive jurisdictions . . . clearly provide for automatic determinations that the intended parents are parents of children conceived pursuant to a compliant gestational surrogacy agreement. Four additional states have laws that are not explicit on this point, but may also provide for this result.

This approach, it is argued, provides the parties with certainty and finality. . . .

Laws providing for automatic determinations of parentage also minimize the costs, time, and procedural hurdles associated with having one or more required court appearances. These appearances can be particularly burdensome when the proceedings must occur in states other than the home state of one or more of the parties.

Relatedly, there is a trend in favor of statutes that permit courts to issue parentage orders prior to the birth of the child. . . . Having such an order can provide the parties with a greater degree of certainty and security over their respective statuses regarding the future child. From a practical perspective, the order can facilitate a number of important steps both before and shortly after the birth of the child. For example, it can streamline issues related to securing health insurance for the resulting child. Having the order can also facilitate the completion of the child's original birth certificate.

In some states, these provisions clarify that while such orders can be *issued* prior to birth, they do not become *effective* until the birth of the child. The relevant Washington provision provides, for example, that a pre-birth order can "order[ ] *that parental rights and duties vest immediately on the birth of the child exclusively in each intended parent.*"[185]

3.   *Traditional Versus Gestational Surrogacy.* Not long after *Johnson*, California courts refused to enforce a traditional (or genetic) surrogacy agreement or to recognize the intended mother as the legal mother.[186] Why would that case come out differently as a legal matter, given the reasoning in *Johnson*? The court explained:

In traditional surrogacy the so-called "surrogate" mother is not *only* the woman who gave birth to the child, but the child's *genetic* mother as well. She is, without doubt, the "natural" parent of the child, as is the father. This fact is critical if the "surrogate" changes her mind before she formally consents to an adoption. In such a case, only the initial agreement itself can arguably defeat her claim to parenthood.

---

185. Joslin, supra note 48 (manuscript at 17–26) (emphasis in original).
186. In re Marriage of Moschetta, 30 Cal. Rptr. 2d 893 (Cal. Ct. App. 1994).

In the present case, there has been no formal consent to adoption, so there is only the surrogacy agreement to deprive the "surrogate" of the legal parental tie she would otherwise possess. We decline to enforce the agreement, not for the public policy reasons sometimes advanced by those who oppose surrogacy, but because enforcement of a traditional surrogacy contract *by itself* is incompatible with the parentage and adoption statutes already on the books.[187]

While California's laws now allow and regulate gestational surrogacy, they do not include traditional surrogacy. Does this make sense as a policy matter? Should the law treat women who serve as traditional surrogates as legal parents but withhold such treatment from women who serve as gestational surrogates?

Soos v. Superior Court

897 P.2d 1356 (Ariz. Ct. App. 1994)

Claborne, Presiding Judge. . . .

The Father and his then wife, Pamela J. Soos ("the Mother"), entered into a surrogate parentage contract with Debra Ballas ("the Surrogate") because the Mother was unable to have children because of a partial hysterectomy. Eggs were removed from the Mother and fertilized in vitro (in a test tube) by sperm obtained from the Father. Pursuant to a "Host Uterus Program" at the Arizona Institute of Reproductive Medicine, the fertilized eggs were implanted in the Surrogate. The Surrogate became pregnant with triplets.

During the pregnancy of the Surrogate, the Mother filed a petition for dissolution of marriage requesting shared custody of the unborn triplets. The Father responded to the petition, alleging that he was the biological father of the unborn triplets, and that pursuant to A.R.S. section 25-218 (1991), the Surrogate was the legal mother of the triplets. The Father further alleged that since the Surrogate was the legal mother of the triplets, the Mother had no standing to request custody.

In September of 1993, the Surrogate gave birth to triplets. The Father and the Surrogate filed a request for order of paternity with the Maricopa County Superior Court. An order was entered naming the Father as the natural father of the triplets, and the Father took custody of the triplets.

The Mother responded by . . . attack[ing] the constitutionality of A.R.S. section 25-218(B) declaring the Surrogate to be the legal mother. The trial court in its minute entry said:

---

187. Id. at 894–95.

THE COURT FINDS that there is not a compelling state interest that justifies terminating the substantive due process rights of the genetic mother in such a summary fashion.

The current law could leave a child without any mother, as a gestational mother may have no desire to do more than she was hired to do, which is to carry and give birth to a child. The current law also ignores the important role that generations of genetics may play in the determination of who a child is and becomes. The current law does not consider what is in the best interest of each individual child.

THE COURT FINDS A.R.S. § 25-218(B) to be unconstitutional.

An evidentiary hearing was set to determine which mother could better assume the social and legal responsibilities of motherhood. The trial court also ordered that the Mother have visitation rights with the triplets, and that the triplets would remain in the temporary custody of the Father. Following the denial of a motion for reconsideration, the Father filed this Petition for Special Action. . . .

The Mother responded to the Father's petition alleging that A.R.S. section 25-218(B) violated her due process, equal protection, and privacy rights guaranteed by the United States and Arizona Constitutions. The Surrogate also filed a response to the petition, joining the Father in his petition. We agree with the trial court and the Mother that A.R.S. section 25-218(B) is unconstitutional because it violates the Mother's equal protection rights.

A.R.S. section 25-218 provides in relevant part:

A. No person may enter into, induce, arrange, procure or otherwise assist in the formation of a surrogate parentage contract.
B. A surrogate is the legal mother of a child born as a result of a surrogate parentage contract and is entitled to custody of that child.
C. If the mother of a child born as a result of a surrogate contract is married, her husband is presumed to be the legal father of the child. *This presumption is rebuttable.*

(Emphasis added.) This statute was fashioned after the Michigan statute and enacted for the purpose of prohibiting surrogate parentage contracts. . . . The statute was designed to stop "baby brokers" and to stop the trafficking of human beings.

The question before us is whether the State's reasons for enacting the surrogate parentage contracts statute are sufficient to withstand constitutional scrutiny under the due process, equal protection, and privacy rights guaranteed by the United States and Arizona Constitutions. We must keep in mind that we are dealing with a custody issue between the biological mother and biological father and the constitutional issues surrounding their competing interests. This is *not* a case of the surrogate mother versus the biological mother. We are *not* dealing with the constitutional questions that arise when the surrogate mother wishes to keep the child she bore.

Thus, we limit ourselves to the question of whether the statute withstands constitutional scrutiny when it affords a biological father an opportunity to prove paternity and gain custody, but does not afford a biological mother the same opportunity....

A parent's right to the custody and control of one's child is a fundamental interest guaranteed by the United States and Arizona Constitutions....

A.R.S. section 25-218(C) allows a man to rebut the presumption of legal paternity by proving "fatherhood" but does not provide the same opportunity for a woman. A woman who may be genetically related to a child has no opportunity to prove her maternity and is thereby denied the opportunity to develop the parent-child relationship. She is afforded no procedural process by which to prove her maternity under the statute. The Mother has parental interests not less deserving of protection than those of the Father. "By providing dissimilar treatment for men and women who are thus similarly situated," the statute violates the Equal Protection Clause ... of the United States and Arizona Constitutions....

Elizabeth S. Scott, Surrogacy and the Politics of Commodification
72 Law & Contemp. Probs. 109 (2009)

In 2004, the Illinois legislature passed the Gestational Surrogacy Act, which provides that a child conceived through in vitro fertilization (IVF) and born to a surrogate mother automatically becomes the legal child of the intended parents at birth if certain conditions are met. Under the Act, the woman who bears the child has no parental status. The bill generated modest media attention, but little controversy; it passed unanimously in both houses of the legislature and was signed into law by the governor.

This mundane story of the legislative process in action stands in sharp contrast to the political tale of surrogacy that unfolded in the 1980s and early 1990s as the *Baby M* case left its mark on American law. It was through the lens of *Baby M* that this innovative use of reproductive technology was first scrutinized as an issue of social, political, and legal interest. Over the course of the litigation between the intended parents, William and Elizabeth Stern, and the surrogate mother, Mary Beth Whitehead, hostility toward commercial surrogacy arrangements hardened. Opponents of surrogacy — mostly feminists and religious groups — argued that the contracts were baby-selling arrangements that exploited poor women who either were coerced or did not understand the consequences of their decisions. Opponents argued that surrogacy degraded the female reproductive function and undermined the family. This framing of the transaction as illegitimate commodification was adopted by the New Jersey Supreme Court in *Baby M* and prevailed for several years thereafter, with far-reaching effects on legal regulation. By the early 1990s, many states had enacted laws prohibiting or severely restricting surrogacy agreements. Some observers predicted the end of this particular use of reproductive technology.

But that did not happen. In fact, the politics and social meaning of surrogacy arrangements have slowly changed, and the alarm and hostility that surrounded this issue have diminished substantially. An alternative frame has emerged, in which altruistic surrogates (contractually bound and compensated nonetheless) provide the "gift of life" to deserving couples who otherwise would be unable to have children. News stories about surrogacy arrangements in the past decade have tended to be upbeat, human-interest tales describing warm relationships between surrogates and the couples for whom they bear children — a far cry from the acrimonious battle between Ms. Whitehead and the Sterns over *Baby M*.

The political and judicial response to surrogacy has also changed in recent years. In Illinois and other states, the contemporary legislative approach has been largely pragmatic, driven by a perception that parties will continue to enter these agreements and thus, that it is important to have procedures that establish parental status in intended parents. In the absence of statutory authority, several courts . . . have held that the intended parents can be named on the birth certificate. Although social conservatives continue to speak out against surrogacy in the political arena, most contemporary groups interested in this issue advocate in favor of laws enforcing the arrangements. . . .

[W]hy did the politics and social meaning of surrogacy change, such that a more sanguine view of the practice seems to have emerged in recent years? Why did interest groups, particularly feminists, that played such a key role in advocating restrictive laws after *Baby M*, mobilize during the litigation and then over time seemingly lose interest in this issue? . . .

Several factors have been important: The moral panic has dissipated, as many of the predicted harms have not been realized. Further, advances in IVF have expanded the use of gestational surrogacy, which, because the surrogate is not genetically related to the baby, was less readily framed as commodification and thus was more palatable than traditional surrogacy. Finally, the interest-group dynamic has changed: women's groups have withdrawn their engagement with the issue, perhaps because their arguments against surrogacy were increasingly adopted by anti-abortion advocates. These conditions have contributed to a political climate in which lawmakers have adopted a pragmatic approach, authorizing surrogacy arrangements while seeking to minimize potential tangible harms. . . .

NOTE ON INTERNATIONAL PERSPECTIVES ON SURROGACY

U.S. law has grown increasingly supportive of surrogacy, but many other countries as well as international authorities continue to look skeptically at the practice. For example, the European Court of Human Rights (ECtHR) ruled in 2017 that Italy did not violate the European Convention on Human Rights when it removed a child from intended parents who purportedly had gone to Russia to engage in surrogacy and had no genetic connection to the child.[188] The ECtHR reasoned:

> There is no doubt that recourse to [surrogacy] . . . raises sensitive ethical questions on which no consensus exists among [European nations]. By prohibiting surrogacy arrangements, Italy has taken the view that it is pursuing the public interest of protecting the women and children potentially affected by practices which it regards as highly problematic from an ethical point of view. This policy is considered very important . . . , where, as here, commercial surrogacy arrangements are involved. That underlying public interest is also of relevance in respect of measures taken by a State to discourage its nationals from having recourse abroad to such practices which are forbidden on its own territory.[189]

Even in countries that prohibit the practice, citizens continue to travel abroad to have children through surrogacy. Authorities in the intended parents' home countries have grown increasingly willing to facilitate legal recognition of the resulting parent-child relationships. In fact, after the ECtHR issued its ruling, the Italian Constitutional Court declared that the best interest of the child can be considered when determining the legal relationship between children and intended parents who evaded Italian law to engage in surrogacy abroad.[190] More recently, the ECtHR concluded that, while France may continue to prohibit surrogacy, it must provide "an effective mechanism" — such as adoption — to allow a nonbiological intended parent to establish a legal parent-child relationship when the parent and child return to France.[191]

The evolving positions on surrogacy are also evident in the United Nations. A 2018 report of the U.N. Special Rapporteur on the Sale and Sexual Exploitation of Children declared: "Surrogacy, in particular commercial surrogacy, often involves abusive practices. Furthermore, it involves direct challenges to the legitimacy of human rights norms. . . . [M]any of the arguments provided in support of these legal regimes for commercial surrogacy could, if accepted, legitimate practices in other fields, such as adoption, that are considered illicit."[192] The report also rebuked the role of "permissive" countries in transnational conflicts over surrogacy: "The demand that domestic parentage orders be recognized globally without appropriate restrictions and without consideration of human rights concerns raises the

---

188. Paradiso v. Italy, Eur. Ct. H.R. (Grand Chamber No. 25358/12, 2017).

189. Id. ¶ 203.

190. Corte Cost., 18 dicembre 2017, n. 272, G.U., 2017, Anno 158, n. 51, 115.

191. Advisory Op. Concerning the Recognition in Domestic Law of a Legal Parent-Child Relationship Between a Child Born Through a Gestational Surrogacy Agreement Abroad and the Intended Mother, Eur. Ct. H.R. (Grand Chamber No. P16-2018-001, 2019).

192. Maud de Boer-Buquicchio (Special Rapporteur on the Sale and Sexual Exploitation of Children), Report of the Special Rapporteur on the Sale and Sexual Exploitation of Children, Including Child Prostitution, Child Pornography and Other Child Sexual Abuse Material ¶ 24, U.N. Doc. A/HRC/37/60 (Jan. 15, 2018).

related risk that a minority of jurisdictions with permissive approaches to commercial surrogacy, and with regulations that fail to protect the rights of vulnerable parties against exploitation, could normalize practices globally that violate human rights."[193] Yet, the following year, the Special Rapporteur released a report taking a different and more pragmatic approach, urging countries to establish "a clear decision-making framework . . . to provide clarity and certainty" for children born through transnational surrogacy arrangements.[194] In other words, countries that prohibit surrogacy should provide pathways for children to have legally recognized relationships with their intended parents.

Does the transnational surrogacy industry raise issues that the domestic surrogacy industry in the U.S. does not? What is the problem with couples leaving Italy and France to have children through surrogacy abroad? Does your answer depend on the country in which the surrogacy takes place? What if it is the U.S.? Thailand? Russia?

D. Nonbiological Parents and Intent

1. Surrogacy and Egg Donors

In Johnson v. Calvert, the California Supreme Court recognized the intended mother as a legal parent and ruled that the gestational surrogate was not a parent. In that case, it was critical that the intended mother had a claim to parentage based on her genetic connection to the child. What would have happened if the intended mother had used a donor egg, rather than her own? Is intent standing alone enough to give rise to parentage?

PROBLEM

Actress Sherry Shepherd married Lamar Sally in 2011 and moved from New York to New Jersey. Shepherd and Sally eventually entered an agreement with Reproductive Possibilities, which coordinates gestational surrogacy arrangements. Shephard and Sally then entered an agreement with J.B., a Pennsylvania resident who would serve as the gestational surrogate. The agreement explicitly stated that Shepherd and Sally were the intended parents and were to be treated as the child's parents upon birth, and that J.B. had no parental rights with respect to the child. Sally's sperm and a donor egg were used to create the embryo. Both Shepherd and Sally were parties to

---

193. Id. ¶ 23.
194. Report of the Special Rapporteur on the Sale and Sexual Exploitation of Children, Including Child Prostitution, Child Pornography and Other Child Sexual Abuse Material, supra note 171, ¶ 20.

the egg donation agreement, which released the egg donor of any responsibility for the child and named Shepherd and Sally as the intended parents.

The attorney for Shepherd and Sally began preparing the petition seeking an order of parentage that would allow Shepherd and Sally to be listed on the birth certificate. The petition was to be filed in a Pennsylvania court. But Shepherd refused to sign the petition because she and Sally were fighting and contemplating ending their marriage. In August 2014, J.B. gave birth, and without the necessary paperwork naming Shepherd and Sally as parents, was listed on the child's birth certificate as the mother. Nonetheless, Sally took custody of the baby and moved to another state. Shepherd expressed no interest in the baby.

J.B. filed a parentage petition in Pennsylvania seeking an order declaring her not to be the legal parent of the child. Shepherd responded by claiming the surrogacy agreement was unenforceable as against public policy, and that J.B. was the child's legal mother. Pennsylvania had no statute or court decision regulating surrogacy. But the Pennsylvania Department of Public Health had regulations governing birth certificates in situations involving assisted reproduction, and it had applied those regulations to gestational surrogacy arrangements.

Who is the legal mother of the child?

POSTSCRIPT

These facts come from the actual case involving Sherry Shepherd. Ultimately, the Pennsylvania courts ruled that Shepherd is the child's legal mother, and that J.B. is not. The lack of Pennsylvania statutes or caselaw on the question meant that the state had not articulated any clear public policy for or against surrogacy. Accordingly, the appellate court found no basis on which to treat the agreement as unenforceable. Based on the parties' intent, Shepherd was the child's legal mother and was obligated to financially support the child, even though she and Sally had split, and he was raising the child alone.[195]

In Pennsylvania, Shepherd was deemed a parent of the child even though she did not give birth and was not genetically related to the child. But in many other states, Shepherd would be a legal stranger to the child and would need to adopt the child to create a legal parent-child relationship. The woman who served as the

---

195. In re Baby S., 128 A.3d 296 (Pa. Super. Ct. 2015).

surrogate would be the legal parent unless and until she relinquishes her parental rights. In these states, a male same-sex couple is in the same situation as a different-sex couple who engages both a gestational surrogate and an egg donor. Only one man in the couple can be genetically related to the child.

In a 2009 New Jersey decision, a court addressed a conflict between a male same-sex couple and the woman who served as a gestational surrogate. The couple, D.R. and S.H., sought to have a child, and D.R.'s sister, A.G.R., agreed to be the gestational surrogate. The parties entered into formal agreements regarding the surrogacy and the resolution of parentage. Embryos were created using the sperm of S.H. and a donor egg, and A.G.R. eventually gave birth to twins. When relations between the couple and A.G.R. broke down, a court ultimately had to resolve parentage:

> A legal analysis of the rights involved in this matter unquestionably begins with an understanding of *In the Matter of Baby M*, 109 N.J. 396 (1988). . . . It should be noted that the surrogacy agreement involved in *Baby M* pertained to a surrogate mother whose eggs were indeed utilized, as opposed to the instant matter where the eggs were supplied by an unknown woman then fertilized before being transplanted into plaintiff. The lack of plaintiff's genetic contribution to the makeup of the twins is one of the main arguments raised by [the same-sex couple] in contending that *Baby M* is not applicable to the instant matter. . . .
>
> If the *Baby M* Court felt that its holding was only limited to situations involving a genetically linked birth mother, such concerns were never stated within the opinion. *Baby M* also held that children should remain with and be brought up by both of their natural parents.
>
> It was pointed out in *Baby M* that the Parentage Act was silent as to acknowledging surrogacy agreements and that Court suggested that the silence of the Legislature suggested that the Legislature chose not to recognize surrogacy. If that interpretation of the Legislature's silence is correct, the additional twenty-one years of silence as to surrogacy agreements speaks even louder. . . .
>
> "The surrogacy contract . . . guarantees the separation of a child from its mother; it looks to adoption regardless of suitability; it totally ignores the child; it takes the child from the mother regardless of her wishes and her maternal fitness;" *Baby M, supra*, 109 N.J. at 441, 442. Would it really make any difference if the word "gestational" was substituted for the word "surrogacy" in the above quotation? I think not. . . .
>
> The parties' intent in voluntarily entering into the surrogacy agreement was of no significance under *Baby M*. This clearly suggests that arguments derived from intent . . . would be of no significance either. . . .
>
> [T]he court holds that plaintiff A.G.R. possesses parental rights under New Jersey law with respect to the twins . . . and that the gestational carrier agreement . . . is void and serves as no basis for termination of parental rights

of the plaintiff . . . . The court also finds that defendant S.H. is the legal father of the twins. . . .[196]

D.R., the nonbiological father, was the child's primary caretaker but was treated as a legal stranger by the court. In a subsequent opinion, the court awarded primary custody to S.H., the biological father, which meant the child would reside with the nonbiological father as well. In other words, the nonbiological father could continue to be the child's primary caretaker. A.G.R. was awarded visitation.[197]

Given *Baby M* and its legacy, New Jersey was long considered especially hostile to surrogacy. But in 2018, the state enacted the New Jersey Gestational Carrier Agreement Act, a law permitting gestational surrogacy and recognizing the intended parents as the legal parents.[198] "Intended parents" may be different-sex or same-sex couples, married or unmarried. An "intended parent" can also be a single individual.[199] An intended parent need not have a genetic connection to the child. Provided the parties comply with the statute's requirements — which include psychological evaluations for both the gestational surrogate and the intended parent(s), as well as independent legal representation for both — the intended parents are treated as the legal parents and the gestational surrogate has no claim to parental recognition. New Jersey's parentage law has been amended to provide that the "natural mother may be established by . . . proof of her having given birth to the child unless the child is born in connection with a gestational carrier agreement."

Obviously, the same-sex couple in *A.G.R.* would be able to establish parentage under the 2018 New Jersey law if they engaged in the same arrangement today. But the law in many states continues to reflect the earlier New Jersey approach, lacking a framework regulating parentage in surrogacy arrangements and instead addressing surrogacy through the ordinary rules of parentage. Accordingly, when a same-sex or different-sex couple has a child through gestational surrogacy and uses an egg donor, the woman who serves as the surrogate is treated as the legal mother whose rights must be terminated, and the nonbiological intended parent is treated as a legal stranger who must adopt the child. Do parentage regimes of this kind conform to principles of gender equality? What about LGBT equality? Consider the perspective of Professor Douglas NeJaime.

---

196. A.G.R. v. D.R.H., No. FD-09-001838-07, 2009 N.J. Super. LEXIS 3250, at *3-*6 (N.J. Super. Ct. Ch. Div. Dec. 23, 2009).

197. A.G.R. v. D.R.H., No. FD-09-001838-07 (N.J. Super. Ct. Ch. Div. Dec. 13, 2011).

198. N.J. Stat. Ann. § 26:8-28 (West 2020).

199. As Professor Courtney Joslin observes, among states that recently have enacted laws allowing surrogacy arrangements, "the strong trend is in favor of statutes to permit any intended parents regardless of sex, sexual orientation, or marital status." Joslin, supra note 48 (manuscript at 18).

Douglas NeJaime, The Nature of Parenthood
126 Yale L.J. 2260 (2017)

Nonbiological mothers in different-sex couples are not the only ones who struggle to achieve parentage when they engage in egg-donor gestational surrogacy. Nonbiological fathers in same-sex couples do as well. Gay male couples engaging in gestational surrogacy necessarily include a nonbiological intended parent. . . .

[E]ven in an age of sex and sexual-orientation equality, courts and legislatures continue to treat *biological mothers* as the parents from whom the *legal family* necessarily springs. This treatment is rooted in the marital presumption and is carried forward by the presumption's adaptation to ART (assisted reproductive technologies). Traditionally, the woman giving birth is the legal mother, and, if she is married, her husband is the legal father. Law has adapted this reasoning to different-sex and same-sex couples using donor insemination. And this reasoning has reached different-sex and same-sex couples using donor eggs and embryos when the intended mother is the birth mother.

The gendered, heterosexual legacy of marital parentage — parentage by virtue of marriage to the woman giving birth — is justified by resort to the gendered, heterosexual logic of reproductive biology. But law's accommodation of ART reveals the instability of that very logic. Courts are willing to deviate from the gendered logic of reproductive biology to recognize the genetic mother who engages a gestational surrogate to carry her child. Within a regime that prioritizes biological ties, contemporary courts view the genetic mother like the biological father protected by the [U.S. Supreme] Court in the 1970s. The differential treatment of genetic mothers and fathers poses an equality problem. Yet, in considering the claim of a nonbiological mother who engages in egg-donor gestational surrogacy, reproductive biology persists as a justification to reject her claim to parental recognition. Courts do not see an equality problem when law recognizes a nonbiological father as a legal parent but withholds recognition from a nonbiological mother.

In either of these cases, one could imagine courts invoking reproductive biology to justify the differential treatment of mothers and fathers. In fact, in some of the earliest gestational surrogacy cases, courts rejected the claims of genetic intended mothers based precisely on grounds of reproductive biology; motherhood resulted from the specific act of birth. But today, courts disclaim reproductive biology as a basis to withhold recognition from a genetic mother. Indeed, . . . in accepting gestational surrogacy, the Massachusetts Supreme Judicial Court deemed the children of the genetic intended mother "children of [the] marriage." The mother's genetic — not gestational — connection produced marital children. Yet a father's genetic connection does not produce marital children, and therefore does not offer a route to parentage to a nonbiological mother. Reproductive biology continues to justify treating the claims of nonbiological mothers differently than the claims of nonbiological fathers. . . .

For a man or woman *married to a biological mother*, biological connection is not necessary for legal parenthood; that man or woman is deemed a legal parent by virtue of marriage. But for a man or woman *married to a biological father*, the lack of a biological connection excludes that individual from legal parenthood. . . .

---

2. Traditional (Genetic) Surrogacy

As New Jersey demonstrates, states are increasingly accommodating gestational surrogacy through legislation, and in most of these jurisdictions legal authorization extends to gestational surrogacy with egg donors. Despite the increasing recognition of intended parents in gestational surrogacy arrangements that involve donor eggs, states generally have failed to regulate traditional (or what some call "genetic") surrogacy in the same way. Ordinarily, intended parents who engage in traditional surrogacy must adopt the child (after the rights of the woman who served as the surrogate are terminated). Why treat gestational surrogacy and traditional surrogacy differently?

Nonetheless, a few states have enacted laws that allow both gestational and traditional surrogacy arrangements and treat the intended parents as the legal parents in both types of arrangements.[200] For example, when the District of Columbia repealed its ban on surrogacy in 2017, it authorized both gestational and traditional surrogacy. The law provides that "[i]n the case of a child born by a gestational surrogate" as well as "[i]n the case of a child born by a traditional surrogate," "an intended parent or parents shall be the parent or parents of the child . . . regardless of whether the intended parent or parents has a genetic relationship to the child."[201] And the law makes clear that a "gestational surrogate" and a "traditional surrogate" "shall not be the parent . . . of the child."[202]

The 2017 Uniform Parentage Act also authorizes both forms of surrogacy and treats intended parents as legal parents, but it "imposes additional safeguards or requirements on genetic surrogacy agreements."[203] First, it requires that genetic surrogacy agreements be validated by a court before the assisted reproduction occurs.[204] Why should a court be involved with one form of surrogacy and not the other? Second, the UPA "allows genetic surrogates to withdraw their consent any time up until 72 hours after birth."[205] In other words, the regulation of genetic surrogacy looks like a hybrid of gestational surrogacy and adoption. Do you think

---

200. See id. (manuscript app. A at 62–64) (identifying five jurisdictions that expressly permit both gestational and genetic surrogacy).

201. D.C. Code § 16-407 (2020).

202. Id.

203. UPA (2017), supra note 93, art. 8, cmt.

204. Id. § 813.

205. Id.

the surrogate should have different rights depending on whether she is genetically related to the child? Why would the UPA adopt this approach? The drafters explained that the "differentiation between genetic and gestational surrogacy is intended to reflect both the factual differences between the two types of surrogacy as well as the reality that policy makers view these two forms of surrogacy as being quite different."[206]

3. Other Forms of Assisted Reproduction

As we have seen, parentage is commonly established through marriage, biological connection, or adoption. Adoption is the traditional paradigm for the formation of nonbiological parent-child relationships. Yet, we have seen that many individuals who lack a biological connection to the child have been able to become legal parents without adopting. As our common-law tradition demonstrates — and as the Court's decision in *Michael H.* confirmed — marriage provides a pathway by which a man can be a legal parent of a child to whom he is not genetically related. The regulation of donor insemination replicated this logic on a broader scale. And the onset of marriage for same-sex couples has meant that the marital presumption can identify a nonbiological mother as a legal mother by virtue of her marriage to the birth mother. But what happens to women in same-sex couples who do not marry? Is the nonbiological mother a co-equal legal parent or a legal stranger?

BROOKE S.B. v. ELIZABETH A.C.C.
61 N.E.3d 488 (N.Y. 2016)

ABDUS-SALAAM, J.

[This case] call[s] upon us to assess the continued vitality of the rule promulgated in *Matter of Alison D. v. Virginia M.*, 572 N.E.2d 27 (N.Y. 1991) — namely that, in an unmarried couple, a partner without a biological or adoptive relation to a child is not that child's "parent" for purposes of standing to seek custody or visitation under Domestic Relations Law § 70(a), notwithstanding their "established relationship with the child." Petitioner . . . who similarly lack[s] any biological or adoptive connection to the subject children, argue[s] that [she] should have standing to seek custody and visitation pursuant to Domestic Relations Law § 70(a). We agree that, in light of more recently delineated legal principles, the definition of "parent" established by this Court 25 years ago in *Alison D.* has become unworkable when applied to increasingly varied familial relationships. Accordingly, today, we overrule *Alison D.* and hold that where a partner shows by clear and convincing evidence that the parties agreed to conceive a child and to raise the child together, the

---

206. Id. art. 8, cmt.

non-biological, non-adoptive partner has standing to seek visitation and custody under Domestic Relations Law § 70.

I. . . .

Petitioner and respondent entered into a relationship in 2006 and, one year later, announced their engagement. At the time, however, this was a purely symbolic gesture; same-sex couples could not legally marry in New York. Petitioner and respondent lacked the resources to travel to another jurisdiction to enter into a legal arrangement comparable to marriage, and it was then unclear whether New York would recognize an out-of-state same-sex union.

Shortly thereafter, the couple jointly decided to have a child and agreed that respondent would carry the child. In 2008, respondent became pregnant through artificial insemination. During respondent's pregnancy, petitioner regularly attended prenatal doctor's appointments, remained involved in respondent's care, and joined respondent in the emergency room when she had a complication during the pregnancy. Respondent went into labor in June 2009. Petitioner stayed by her side and, when the subject child, a baby boy, was born, petitioner cut the umbilical cord. The couple gave the child petitioner's last name.

The parties continued to live together with the child and raised him jointly, sharing in all major parental responsibilities. Petitioner stayed at home with the child for a year while respondent returned to work. The child referred to petitioner as "Mama B."

In 2010, the parties ended their relationship. Initially, respondent permitted petitioner regular visits with the child. In late 2012, however, petitioner's relationship with respondent deteriorated and, in or about July 2013, respondent effectively terminated petitioner's contact with the child.

Subsequently, petitioner commenced this proceeding seeking joint custody of the child and regular visitation. Family Court appointed an attorney for the child. That attorney determined that the child's best interests would be served by allowing regular visitation with petitioner.

Respondent moved to dismiss the petition, asserting that petitioner lacked standing to seek visitation or custody under Domestic Relations Law § 70 as interpreted in *Alison D.* because, in the absence of a biological or adoptive connection to the child, petitioner was not a "parent" within the meaning of the statute. Petitioner and the attorney for the child opposed the motion, contending that, in light of the legislature's enactment of the Marriage Equality Act and other changes in the law, *Alison D.* should no longer be followed. . . .

After hearing argument on the motion, Family Court dismissed the petition. While commenting on the "heartbreaking" nature of the case, Family Court noted that petitioner did not adopt the child and therefore granted respondent's motion to dismiss on constraint of *Alison D.* The attorney for the child appealed.

The Appellate Division unanimously affirmed. The Court concluded that, because petitioner had not married respondent, had not adopted the child, and had no biological relationship to the child, *Alison D.* prohibited Family Court from ruling that petitioner had standing to seek custody or visitation. We granted the attorney for the child leave to appeal . . .

II.

Domestic Relations Law § 70 provides:

> Where a minor child is residing within this state, *either parent* may apply to the supreme court for a writ of habeas corpus to have such minor child brought before such court; and on the return thereof, the court, on due consideration, may award the natural guardianship, charge and custody of such child to either parent for such time, under such regulations and restrictions, and with such provisions and directions, as the case may require, and may at any time thereafter vacate or modify such order. In all cases there shall be no prima facie right to the custody of the child in either parent, but the court shall determine solely what is for the *best interest of the child, and what will best promote its welfare and happiness*, and make award accordingly. (Domestic Relations Law § 70[a] [emphases added]).

Only a "parent" may petition for custody or visitation under Domestic Relations Law § 70, yet the statute does not define that critical term, leaving it to be defined by the courts.

In *Alison D.*, we supplied a definition. In that case, Alison D. and Virginia M. were in a long-term relationship and decided to have a child. They agreed that Virginia M. would carry the baby and that they would jointly raise the child, sharing parenting responsibilities. After the child was born, Alison D. acted as a parent in all major respects, providing financial, emotional and practical support. Even after the couple ended their relationship and moved out of their shared home, Alison D. continued to regularly visit the child until he was about six years old, at which point Virginia M. terminated contact between them.

Alison D. petitioned for visitation pursuant to Domestic Relations Law § 70. . . .

We decided that the word "parent" in Domestic Relations Law § 70 should be interpreted to preclude standing for a de facto parent who . . . might otherwise be recognized as the child's parent for visitation purposes. Specifically, we held that "a biological stranger to a child who is properly in the custody of his biological mother" has no "standing to seek visitation with the child under Domestic Relations Law § 70."

We rested our determination principally on the need to preserve the rights of biological parents. Specifically, we reasoned that, "[t]raditionally, in this State it is the child's mother and father who, assuming fitness, have the right to the care and custody of their child." We therefore determined that the statute should not be read to permit a de facto parent to seek visitation of a child in a manner that "would necessarily impair the parents' right to custody and control." . . .

Judge Kaye dissented on the ground that a person who "stands in loco parentis" should have standing to seek visitation under Domestic Relations Law § 70. Observing that the Court's decision would "fall[ ] hardest" on the millions of children raised in nontraditional families — including families headed by same-sex couples, unmarried opposite-sex couples, and stepparents — the dissent argued that the majority had "turn[ed] its back on a tradition of reading section 70 so as to promote the welfare of the children." The dissent asserted that, because Domestic Relations Law § 70 did not define "parent" — and because the statute made express reference to the "best interest of the child" — the Court was free to craft a definition that accommodated the welfare of the child. . . .

In 1991, same-sex partners could not marry in this state. Nor could a biological parent's unmarried partner adopt the child. As a result, a partner in a same-sex relationship not biologically related to a child was entirely precluded from obtaining standing to seek custody or visitation of that child under our definition of "parent" supplied in *Alison D.*

Four years later, in *Matter of Jacob*, 660 N.E.2d 397 (1995), we . . . decide[d] [that] "the unmarried partner of a child's biological mother, whether heterosexual or homosexual, who is raising the child together with the biological parent, can become the child's second parent by means of adoption." . . .

[W]e declined to revisit *Alison D.* when confronted with a nearly identical situation almost 20 years later. *Debra H. v. Janice R.*, 930 N.E.2d 184 (2010), as did *Alison D.*, involved an unmarried same-sex couple. Petitioner alleged that they agreed to have a child, and to that end, Janice R. was artificially inseminated and bore the child. Debra H. never adopted the child. After the couple ended their relationship, Debra H. petitioned for custody and visitation. We declined to expand the definition of "parent" for purposes of Domestic Relations Law § 70, noting that "*Alison D.*, in conjunction with second-parent adoption, creates a bright-line rule that promotes certainty in the wake of domestic breakups."

Nonetheless, in *Debra H.*, we arrived at a different result than in *Alison D.* Ultimately, we invoked the common-law doctrine of comity to rule that, because the couple had entered into a civil union in Vermont prior to the child's birth — and because the union afforded Debra H. parental status under Vermont law — her parental status should be recognized under New York law as well. Seeing no obstacle in New York's public policy or comity doctrine to the recognition of the non-biological mother's standing, we declared that "New York will recognize parentage created by a civil union in Vermont," thereby granting standing to Debra H. to petition for custody and visitation of the subject child.

In a separate discussion, we also "reaffirm[ed] our holding in *Alison D.*" We acknowledged the apparent tension in our decision to authorize parentage by estoppel in the support context and yet deny it in the visitation and custody context, but we decided that this incongruity did not fatally undermine *Alison D.* . . .

III.

We must now decide whether, as respondents claim, the doctrine of stare decisis warrants retention of the rule established in *Alison D.* . . .

Long before our decision in *Alison D.*, New York courts invoked their equitable powers to ensure that matters of custody, visitation and support were resolved in a manner that served the best interests of the child. Consistent with these broad equitable powers, our courts have historically exercised their "inherent equity powers and authority" in order to determine "who is a parent and what will serve a child's best interests."

Domestic Relations Law § 70 evolved in harmony with these equitable practices. The statute expanded in scope from a law narrowly conferring standing in custody and visitation matters upon a legally separated, resident "husband and wife" pair to a broader measure granting standing to "either parent" without regard to separation. The legislature made many of these changes to conform to the courts' preexisting equitable practices. Tellingly, the statute has never mentioned, much less purported to limit, the court's equitable powers, and even after its original enactment, courts continued to employ principles of equity to grant custody, visitation or related extra-statutory relief.

Departing from this tradition of invoking equity, in *Alison D.*, we narrowly defined the term "parent," thereby foreclosing "all inquiry into the child's best interest" in custody and visitation cases involving parental figures who lacked biological or adoptive ties to the child. And, in the years that followed, lower courts applying *Alison D.* were "forced to . . . permanently sever strongly formed bonds between children and adults with whom they have parental relationships." By "limiting their opportunity to maintain bonds that may be crucial to their development," the rule of *Alison D.* has "fall[en] hardest on the children." . . .

Alison D.'s foundational premise of heterosexual parenting and non-recognition of same-sex couples is unsustainable, particularly in light of the enactment of same-sex marriage in New York State, and the United States Supreme Court's holding in *Obergefell v. Hodges*, 135 S.Ct. 2584 (2015), which noted that the right to marry provides benefits not only for same-sex couples, but also the children being raised by those couples.

Under the current legal framework, which emphasizes biology, it is impossible — without marriage or adoption — for both former partners of a same-sex couple to have standing, as only one can be biologically related to the child. By contrast, where both partners in a heterosexual couple are biologically related to the child, both former partners will have standing regardless of marriage or adoption. It is this context that informs the Court's determination of a proper test for standing that ensures equality for same-sex parents and provides the opportunity for their children to have the love and support of two committed parents. . . .

By "fixing biology as the key to visitation rights," the rule of *Alison D.* has inflicted disproportionate hardship on the growing number of nontraditional families across our state. . . . [R]ecent census statistics reflect the large number of same-sex couples residing in New York, and that many of New York's same-sex couples are raising children who are related to only one partner by birth or adoption.

Relatedly, legal commentators have taken issue with *Alison D.* for its negative impact on children. A growing body of social science reveals the trauma children suffer as a result of separation from a primary attachment figure — such as a de facto parent — regardless of that figure's biological or adoptive ties to the children.

We must, however, protect the substantial and fundamental right of biological or adoptive parents to control the upbringing of their children. . . . But here we do not consider whether to allow a third party to contest or infringe on those rights; rather, the issue is who qualifies as a "parent" with coequal rights. Nevertheless, the fundamental nature of those rights mandates caution in expanding the definition of that term and makes the element of consent of the biological or adoptive parent critical.

While "parents and families have fundamental liberty interests in preserving" intimate family-like bonds, "so, too, do children have these interests," which must also inform the definition of "parent," a term so central to the life of a child. The "bright-line" rule of *Alison D.* promotes the laudable goals of certainty and predictability in the wake of domestic disruption. But bright lines cast a harsh light on any injustice and, as predicted by Judge Kaye, there is little doubt by whom that injustice has been most finely felt and most finely perceived. We will no longer engage in the "deft legal maneuvering" necessary to read fairness into an overly-restrictive definition of "parent" that sets too high a bar for reaching a child's best interest and does not take into account equitable principles. Accordingly, we overrule *Alison D.*

IV.

Our holding that Domestic Relations Law § 70 permits a non-biological, non-adoptive parent to achieve standing to petition for custody and visitation requires us to specify the limited circumstances in which such a person has standing as a "parent" under Domestic Relations Law § 70. Because of the fundamental rights to which biological and adoptive parents are undeniably entitled, any encroachment on the rights of such parents and, especially, any test to expand who is a parent, must be . . . appropriately narrow.

Petitioners and some of the amici urge that we endorse a functional test for standing, which has been employed in other jurisdictions that recognize parentage by estoppel in the custody and/or visitation context. The functional test considers a variety of factors, many of which relate to the post-birth relationship between the putative parent and the child. Amicus Sanctuary for Families proposes a different test that hinges on whether petitioner can prove, by clear and convincing evidence, that a couple "jointly planned and explicitly agreed to the conception of a child with the intention of raising the child as co-parents."

Although the parties and amici disagree as to what test should be applied, they generally urge us to adopt a test that will apply in determining standing as a parent for all non-biological, non-adoptive, non-marital "parents" who are raising children. We reject the premise that we must now declare that one test would be appropriate for all situations, or that the proffered tests are the only options that should be considered.

Petitioner . . . alleged that the parties entered into a pre-conception agreement to conceive and raise a child as co-parents. We hold that these allegations, if proved by clear and convincing evidence, are sufficient to establish standing. . . . [I]t would be premature for us to consider adopting a test for situations in which a couple did not enter into a pre-conception agreement. Accordingly, we do not now decide whether, in a case where a biological or adoptive parent consented to the creation of a parent-like relationship between his or her partner and child after conception, the partner can establish standing to seek visitation and custody. . . .

NOTES AND QUESTIONS

1. *On Remand.* Given the court's decision, the case went back to the trial court, giving Brooke the possibility to establish parentage. The trial court found that Brooke was a parent and thus entitled to custody.

2. *A Companion Case.* The *Brooke S.B.* case had been consolidated with *Estrellita A. v. Jennifer L.D.*, another case involving a same-sex couple who had a child through donor insemination.[207] They parented together for the first three years of the child's life, but eventually separated. The biological mother petitioned for child support, and the nonbiological mother petitioned for visitation. The New York court determined that the biological mother was estopped from denying the nonbiological mother's parental status, since she took a contrary position in seeking child support from the woman. The court's decision resolved a tension in New York law. The courts had "authorize[d] parentage by estoppel in the support context and yet den[ied] it in the visitation and custody context."[208] (In 2006, the court had found that a "man who has mistakenly represented himself as a child's father may be estopped from denying paternity and made to pay child support."[209])

---

207. 61 N.E.2d at 491–92.
208. Id. at 496.
209. Shondel J. v. Mark D., 853 N.E.2d 610 (N.Y. 2006).

By recognizing parentage in both the support and custody contexts for a nonbiological, non-adoptive parent, the court rejected this "inconsistency in the rights and obligations attendant to parenthood."[210]

3. *Children's Interests.* The *Brooke S.B.* court repeatedly noted that children had been harmed because unmarried nonbiological parents were denied standing to seek custody or visitation. What role should the child's interest play in determining parentage? Should the attorney for the child have argued that the child has a constitutional right to maintain his relationship with the nonbiological mother? How do you think such an argument would have fared?

4. *Nonbiological Parenthood and Sexual Orientation Equality.* The *Brooke S.B.* court connected nonbiological parentage to equality for same-sex couples. As Professor Douglas NeJaime explains:

> While courts in other states had ruled that unmarried, non-biological co-parents could be recognized as legal parents, the New York court broke new ground by explicitly acknowledging that sexual orientation equality requires parental recognition that does not hinge on biological connection. In a concurring opinion, Judge Pigott agreed with the result because Brooke and Elizabeth could not have gotten married. Going forward, in his view, marriage and second-parent adoption solved the dilemma faced by same-sex couples. But the majority rejected this position, acknowledging that marriage and second-parent adoption did not by themselves furnish genuine equality for same-sex couples. . . . Because different-sex and same-sex couples are differently situated with respect to biological connection, "a proper test for standing that ensures equality for same-sex parents" requires paths to non-biological parentage outside of marriage and adoption.
>
> On this view, to treat same-sex couples as truly belonging, the state must move away from a parentage regime designed around the heterosexual family and thus designed around biological relationships. That was the regime inside which *Alison D.* was decided, and it did not reflect contemporary principles of sexual orientation equality.[211]

5. *Intent Versus Function.* In the next section, we explore functional parenthood — parenthood based on the actual act of parenting and having formed a parent-child relationship. The lawyers representing the child and Brooke both argued that the court should adopt a functional test. Instead, the court adopted an intentional standard. Organizations working on domestic violence filed an amicus brief in the case in support of Brooke but opposing a functional test. Why might such organizations take this position? The brief asserted that a "functional approach, requiring a case-by-case analysis, would empower former abusive partners with no

---

210. *Brooke S.B.,* 61 N.E.2d at 498.

211. Douglas NeJaime, The Story of Brooke S.B. v. Elizabeth A.C.C., in Reproductive Rights and Justice Stories, supra note 21, at 256.

biological or adoptive connection to a child to claim parental rights as a way to continue threatening their victims."[212] The court ultimately adopted the intent-based standard articulated in the brief of domestic violence organizations. But it also did not foreclose the possibility of a functional test in other cases.[213]

The New York court in *Brooke S.B.* articulated an intent-based standard in the absence of any legislative guidance. In 2020, New York effectively codified the *Brooke S.B.* standard by enacting a new parentage law addressing assisted reproduction. The law provides: "An individual . . . who consents to . . . assisted reproduction with the intent to be a parent of the child with the consent of the gestating parent . . . is a parent of the resulting child for all legal purposes."[214] Lawmakers in other states also have enacted legislation that provides for intentional parenthood regardless of gender, sexual orientation, or marital status.[215] Consider the 2017 UPA's treatment of intended parents.

UNIFORM PARENTAGE ACT (2017)

SECTION 301. ACKNOWLEDGMENT OF PARENTAGE.
A woman who gave birth to a child and an alleged genetic father of the child, intended parent under [Article] 7, or presumed parent may sign an acknowledgment of parentage to establish the parentage of the child. . . .

SECTION 305. EFFECT OF ACKNOWLEDGMENT OR DENIAL OF PARENTAGE.
(a) [A]n acknowledgment of parentage that complies with this [article] and is filed with the [state agency maintaining birth records] is equivalent to an adjudication of parentage of the child and confers on the acknowledged parent all rights and duties of a parent. . . .

SECTION 309. CHALLENGE AFTER EXPIRATION OF PERIOD FOR RESCISSION.
(a) After the period for rescission . . . expires, but not later than two years after the effective date . . . of an acknowledgment of parentage or denial of parentage, a signatory of the acknowledgment or denial may commence a proceeding to challenge the acknowledgment or denial . . . only on the basis of fraud, duress, or material mistake of fact. . . .

---

212. Brief for Sanctuary for Families, et al., as Amici Curiae for Petitioner-Respondent at 8, Brooke S.B. v. Elizabeth A.C.C., 61 N.E.3d 488 (N.Y. 2016) (No. APL-2015-00236).

213. *Brooke S.B.*, 61 N.E.2d at 500–01.

214. N.Y. Fam. Ct. Act §§ 581-303 (2020).

215. See, e.g., Me. Stat. tit. 19-A, § 1923 (2020).

SECTION 703. PARENTAGE OF CHILD OF ASSISTED REPRODUCTION.
An individual who consents . . . to assisted reproduction by a woman with
the intent to be a parent of a child conceived by the assisted reproduction
is a parent of the child.

NOTES AND QUESTIONS

---

1. *Consent.* What is needed to show "consent"? Should consent have to be in writing? What if the parties did not commit their agreement to writing? The UPA provides that in the absence of a written agreement, the person seeking to establish parentage may prove "by clear-and-convincing evidence the existence of an express agreement entered into before conception that the individual and the woman [who gave birth] intended they both would be parents of the child."[216]

2. *Surrogacy.* Section 703 applies to forms of assisted reproduction other than surrogacy, which is covered in Article 8. Most states that allow surrogacy also treat it separately from other forms of assisted reproduction. Why?

3. *Acknowledgments of Parentage.* The 2017 UPA changes the Voluntary Acknowledgment of *Paternity* to a Voluntary Acknowledgment of *Parentage.* The VAP can be signed by an intended parent, whether married or unmarried — though again it does not include surrogacy. The UPA also includes a provision calling for a denial of parentage: "A presumed parent or alleged genetic parent may sign a denial of parentage in a record."[217] When do you imagine a denial of parentage would be involved?

V. Parenthood Based on Conduct

This section considers whether courts and legislatures should extend parentage to individuals based on the fact that they function as a child's parent. Think back to In re Parentage of L.B., a case we read after Troxel v. Granville in Chapter 6. There the Washington Supreme Court found that a woman qualified as a de facto parent based on the parent-child relationship she established with the child.

The focus on parental conduct grows out of influential work on child development. In their groundbreaking 1973 text, Beyond the Best Interests of the Child, Yale law professor Joseph Goldstein, psychoanalyst Anna Freud, and Yale Child Study Center psychiatrist Albert Solnit urged decisionmakers to keep children in the custody of their "psychological parent." "Whether a person becomes the

---

216. UPA (2017), supra note 93, § 704(b)(1).
217. Id. § 303.

psychological parent of a child is based on day-to-day interaction, companionship, and shared experiences," and does not depend on a "biological or legal relationship to the child."[218] As Dr. Solnit explained in 1983:

> The mutuality of the parent-child relationship arises not so much from what is originally associated with the blood tie, but more from the hour-to-hour, day-to-day care of the child by the parents and the response of the child to the parents. These interactions establish resonating bonds and affectionate, empathic attachments that constitute the primary psychological relationship between parents and their children. These primary parent-child psychological relationships are the essential ingredients of the family. . . .[219]

A. Common-Law and Equitable Doctrines

What does the concept of psychological parenthood mean for purposes of parental recognition? Should the law recognize an individual as a parent when that individual has been parenting the child, but is not the child's biological parent, is not married to the legal parent, and has not adopted the child? If so, on what basis? Who should decide? Should courts make determinations on a case-by-case basis, or should only legislatures provide avenues for parental recognition of psychological parents?

V.C. v. M.J.B.
748 A.2d 539 (N.J. 2000)

Long, J. . . .

V.C. and M.J.B., who are lesbians, met in 1992 and began dating on July 4, 1993. On July 9, 1993, M.J.B. went to see a fertility specialist to begin artificial insemination procedures. . . . She had been planning to be artificially inseminated since late 1980. According to M.J.B., she made the final decision to become pregnant independently and before beginning her relationship with V.C. . . .

According to V.C., early in their relationship, the two discussed having children. However, V.C. did not become aware of M.J.B.'s visits with the specialist and her decision to have a baby by artificial insemination until September 1993. In fact, the doctor's records of M.J.B.'s first appointment indicate that M.J.B. was single and that she "desires children."

---

218. Joseph Goldstein et al., supra note 110, at 12–13.
219. Albert J. Solnit, Psychological Dimensions in Child Placement Conflicts, 12 N.Y.U. Rev. L. & Soc. Change 495, 497 (1983).

Nonetheless, V.C. claimed that the parties jointly decided to have children and that she and M.J.B. jointly researched and decided which sperm donor they should use. M.J.B. acknowledged that she consulted V.C. on the issue but maintained that she individually made the final choice about which sperm donor to use.

Between November 1993 and February 1994, M.J.B. underwent several insemination procedures. V.C. attended at least two of those sessions. In December 1993, V.C. moved into M.J.B.'s apartment. Two months later, on February 7, 1994, the doctor informed M.J.B. that she was pregnant. M.J.B. called V.C. at work to tell her the good news. Eventually, M.J.B. was informed that she was having twins.

During M.J.B.'s pregnancy, both M.J.B. and V.C. prepared for the birth of the twins by attending pre-natal and Lamaze classes. In April 1994, the parties moved to a larger apartment to accommodate the pending births. V.C. contended that during that time they jointly decided on the children's names. M.J.B. admitted consulting V.C., but maintained that she made the final decision regarding names.

The children were born on September 29, 1994. V.C. took M.J.B. to the hospital and she was present in the delivery room at the birth of the children. At the hospital, the nurses and staff treated V.C. as if she were a mother. Immediately following the birth, the nurses gave one child to M.J.B. to hold and the other to V.C., and took pictures of the four of them together. After the children were born, M.J.B. took a three-month maternity leave and V.C. took a three-week vacation.

The parties opened joint bank accounts for their household expenses, and prepared wills, powers of attorney, and named each other as the beneficiary for their respective life insurance policies. At some point, the parties also opened savings accounts for the children, and named V.C. as custodian for one account and M.J.B. as custodian for the other.

The parties also decided to have the children call M.J.B. "Mommy" and V.C. "Meema." M.J.B. conceded that she referred to V.C. as a "mother" of the children. In addition, M.J.B. supported the notion, both publicly and privately, that during the twenty-three months after the children were born, the parties and the children functioned as a family unit. M.J.B. sent cards and letters to V.C. that referred to V.C. as the children's mother, and indicated that the four of them were a family. The children also gave cards to V.C. that indicated that V.C. was their mother. M.J.B. encouraged a relationship between V.C. and the children and sought to create a "happy, cohesive environment for the children." M.J.B. admitted that, when the parties' relationship was intact, she sometimes thought of the four of them as a family. However, although M.J.B. sometimes considered the children "theirs," other times she considered them "hers".

M.J.B. agreed that both parties cared for the children but insisted that she made substantive decisions regarding their lives. For instance, M.J.B. maintained that she independently researched and made the final decisions regarding the children's pediatrician and day care center. V.C. countered that she was equally involved in all decision-making regarding the children. Specifically, V.C. claimed that she participated in choosing a day care center for the children, and it is clear that M.J.B. brought V.C. to visit the center she selected prior to making a final decision.

M.J.B. acknowledged that V.C. assumed substantial responsibility for the children, but maintained that V.C. was a mere helper and not a co-parent. However, according to V.C., she acted as a co-parent to the children and had equal parenting responsibility. Indeed, M.J.B. listed V.C. as the "other mother" on the children's pediatrician and day care registration forms. M.J.B. also gave V.C. medical power of attorney over the children. . . .

Together the parties purchased a home in February 1995. Later that year, V.C. asked M.J.B. to marry her, and M.J.B. accepted. In July 1995, the parties held a commitment ceremony where they were "married." At the ceremony, V.C., M.J.B. and the twins were blessed as a "family." . . .

[I]n August 1996, M.J.B. ended the relationship. The parties then took turns living in the house with the children until November 1996. In December 1996, V.C. moved out. M.J.B. permitted V.C. to visit with the children until May 1997. During that time, V.C. spent approximately every other weekend with the children, and contributed money toward the household expenses.

In May 1997, M.J.B. went away on business and left the children with V.C. for two weeks. However, later that month, M.J.B. refused to continue V.C.'s visitation with the children, and at some point, M.J.B. stopped accepting V.C.'s money. M.J.B. asserted that she did not want to continue the children's contact with V.C. because she believed that V.C. was not properly caring for the children, and that the children were suffering distress from continued contact with V.C. Both parties became involved with new partners after the dissolution of their relationship. Eventually, V.C. filed this complaint for joint legal custody.

At trial, expert witnesses appeared for both parties. . . . Both experts arrived at similar conclusions. . . . [One expert] concluded that both children view V.C. as a maternal figure and that V.C. regards herself as one of the children's mothers. . . . [The other expert] concluded that V.C. and the children enjoyed a bonded relationship that benefitted both children. . . .

There are no statutes explicitly addressing whether a former unmarried domestic partner has standing to seek custody and visitation with her former partner's biological children. That is not to say, however, that the current statutory scheme dealing with issues of custody and visitation does not provide some guiding principles. N.J.S.A. 9:2-3 prescribes:

> When the parents of a minor child live separately, or are about to do so, the Superior Court, in an action brought by either parent, shall have the same power to make judgments or orders concerning care, custody, education and maintenance as concerning a child whose parents are divorced. . . .

Further, N.J.S.A. 9:2-4 provides, in part, that:

> [t]he Legislature finds and declares that it is in the public policy of this State to assure minor children of frequent and continuing contact with both parents after the parents have separated or dissolved their marriage and that it is in the public interest to encourage parents to share the rights and responsibilities of child rearing in order to effect this policy. In any proceeding involving the custody of a minor child, the rights of both parents shall be equal. . . .

By that scheme, the Legislature has expressed the view that children should not generally be denied continuing contact with parents after the relationship between the parties ends.

N.J.S.A. 9:2-13(f) provides that "[t]he word 'parent,' when not otherwise described by the context, means a natural parent or parent by previous adoption." M.J.B. argues that because V.C. is not a natural or adoptive parent, we lack jurisdiction to consider her claims. That is an incomplete interpretation of the Act. Although the statutory definition of parent focuses on natural and adoptive parents, it also includes the phrase, "when not otherwise described by the context." That language evinces a legislative intent to leave open the possibility that individuals other than natural or adoptive parents may qualify as "parents," depending on the circumstances.

By including the words "when not otherwise described by the context" in the statute, the Legislature obviously envisioned a case where the specific relationship between a child and a person not specifically denominated by the statute would qualify as "parental". . . . Although the Legislature may not have considered the precise case before us, it is hard to imagine what it could have had in mind in adding the "context" language other than a situation such as this, in which a person not related to a child by blood or adoption has stood in a parental role vis-a-vis the child. It is that contention by V.C. that brings this case before the court and affords us jurisdiction over V.C.'s complaint. . . .

At the heart of the psychological parent cases is a recognition that children have a strong interest in maintaining the ties that connect them to adults who love and provide for them. That interest, for constitutional as well as social purposes, lies in the emotional bonds that develop between family members as a result of shared daily life. That point was emphasized in *Lehr v. Robertson*, 463 U.S. 248, 261 (1983), where the Supreme Court held that a stepfather's *actual* relationship with a child was the determining factor when considering the degree of protection that the parent-child link must be afforded. The Court stressed that "the importance of the familial relationship, to the individuals involved and to the society, stems from the emotional attachments that derive from the intimacy of daily association, and from the role it plays in 'promot[ing] a way of life' through the instruction of children as well as from the fact of blood relationship." . . .

The next issue we confront is how a party may establish that he or she has, in fact, become a psychological parent to the child of a fit and involved legal parent. . . .

The most thoughtful and inclusive definition of *de facto* parenthood is the test enunciated in *Custody of H.S.H.-K.*, 533 N.W.2d 419, 421 (Wisc. 1995), and adopted by the Appellate Division majority here. It addresses the main fears and concerns both legislatures and courts have advanced when addressing the notion of psychological parenthood. Under that test,

> [t]o demonstrate the existence of the petitioner's parent-like relationship with the child, the petitioner must prove four elements: (1) that the biological or adoptive parent consented to, and fostered, the petitioner's formation and establishment of a parent-like relationship with the child; (2) that the petitioner and the child lived together in the same household; (3) that the petitioner assumed the obligations of parenthood by taking significant responsibility for the child's care, education and development, including contributing towards the child's support, without expectation of financial compensation [a petitioner's contribution to a child's support need not be monetary]; and (4) that the petitioner has been in a parental role for a length of time sufficient to have established with the child a bonded, dependent relationship parental in nature. . . .

Prong one is critical because it makes the biological or adoptive parent a participant in the creation of the psychological parent's relationship with the child. Without such a requirement, a paid nanny or babysitter could theoretically qualify for parental status. To avoid that result, in order for a third party to be deemed a psychological parent, the legal parent must have fostered the formation of the parental relationship between the third party and the child. By fostered is meant that the legal parent ceded over to the third party a measure of parental authority and autonomy and granted to that third party rights and duties vis-a-vis the child that the third party's status would not otherwise warrant. Ordinarily, a relationship based on payment by the legal parent to the third party will not qualify.

The requirement of cooperation by the legal parent is critical because it places control within his or her hands. That parent has the absolute ability to maintain a zone of autonomous privacy for herself and her child. However, if she wishes to maintain that zone of privacy she cannot invite a third party to function as a parent to her child and cannot cede over to that third party parental authority the exercise of which may create a profound bond with the child.

Two further points concerning the consent requirement need to be clarified. First, a psychological parent-child relationship that is voluntarily created by the legally recognized parent may not be unilaterally terminated after the relationship between the adults ends. Although the intent of the legally recognized parent is critical to the psychological parent analysis, the focus is on that party's intent during the formation and pendency of the parent-child relationship. The reason is that the ending of the relationship between the legal parent and the third party does not end the bond that the legal parent fostered and that actually developed between the child and the psychological parent. Thus, the right of the legal parent "[does] not extend to erasing a relationship between her partner and her child which she voluntarily created and actively fostered simply because after the party's separation she regretted having done so."

In practice, that may mean protecting those relationships despite the later, contrary wishes of the legal parent in order to advance the interests of the child. As long as the legal parent consents to the continuation of the relationship between another adult who is a psychological parent and the child after the termination of the adult parties' relationship, the courts need not be involved. Only when that consent is withdrawn are courts called on to protect the child's relationship with the psychological parent.

The second issue that needs to be clarified is that participation in the decision to have a child is not a prerequisite to a finding that one has become a psychological parent to the child. . . . Although joint participation in the family's decision to have a child is probative evidence of the legally recognized parent's intentions, not having participated in the decision does not preclude a finding of the third party's psychological parenthood. Such circumstances parallel the situation in which a woman, already pregnant or a mother, becomes involved with or marries a man who is not the biological or adoptive father of the child, but thereafter fully functions in every respect as a father. There is nothing about that scenario that would justify precluding the possibility of denominating that person as a psychological parent. It goes without saying that adoption proceedings in these circumstances would eliminate the need for a psychological parent inquiry altogether and would be preferable to court intervention. However, the failure of the parties to pursue that option is not preclusive of a finding of psychological parenthood where all the other indicia of that status are present.

Concerning the remaining prongs of the *H.S.H.-K.* test, we accept Wisconsin's formulation with these additional comments. The third prong, a finding that a third party assumed the obligations of parenthood, is not contingent on financial contributions made by the third party. Financial contribution may be considered but should not be given inordinate weight when determining whether a third party has assumed the obligations of parenthood. Obviously, as we have indicated, the assumption of a parental role is much more complex than mere financial support. It is determined by the nature, quality, and extent of the functions undertaken by the third party and the response of the child to that nurturance. . . .

It bears repeating that the fourth prong is most important because it requires the existence of a parent-child bond. A necessary corollary is that the third party must have functioned as a parent for a long enough time that such a bond has developed. What is crucial here is not the amount of time but the nature of the relationship. How much time is necessary will turn on the facts of each case including an assessment of exactly what functions the putative parent performed, as well as at what period and stage of the child's life and development such actions were taken.

Most importantly, a determination will have to be made about the actuality and strength of the parent-child bond. Generally, that will require expert testimony. . . .

This opinion should not be viewed as an incursion on the general right of a fit legal parent to raise his or her child without outside interference. What we have addressed here is a specific set of circumstances involving the volitional choice of a legal parent to cede a measure of parental authority to a third party; to allow that party to function as a parent in the day-to-day life of the child; and to foster the forging of a parental bond between the third party and the child. In such circumstances, the legal parent has created a family with the third party and the child, and has invited the third party into the otherwise inviolable realm of family privacy. By virtue of her own actions, the legal parent's expectation of autonomous privacy in her relationship with her child is necessarily reduced from that which would have been the case had she never invited the third party into their lives. Most important, where that invitation and its consequences have altered her child's life by essentially giving him or her another parent, the legal parent's options are constrained. It is the child's best interest that is preeminent as it would be if two legal parents were in a conflict over custody and visitation.

Once a third party has been determined to be a psychological parent to a child, under the previously described standards, he or she stands in parity with the legal parent. Custody and visitation issues between them are to be determined on a best interests standard. . . .

That is not to suggest that a person's status as a legal parent does not play a part in custody or visitation proceedings in those circumstances. . . . The legal parent's status is a significant weight in the best interests balance because eventually, in the search for self-knowledge, the child's interest in his or her roots will emerge. Thus, under ordinary circumstances when the evidence concerning the child's best interests (as between a legal parent and psychological parent) is in equipoise, custody will be awarded to the legal parent. . . .

V.C. is a psychological parent to the twins.

That said, the issue is whether V.C. should be granted joint legal custody and visitation. . . .

We note that V.C. is not seeking joint physical custody, but joint legal custody for decision-making. However, due to the pendency of this case, V.C. has not been involved in the decision-making for the twins for nearly four years. To interject her into the decisional realm at this point would be unnecessarily disruptive for all involved. We will not, therefore, order joint legal custody in this case.

Visitation, however, is another matter. V.C. and the twins have been visiting during nearly all of the four years since V.C. parted company from M.J.B. Continued visitation in those circumstances is presumed. Nothing suggests that V.C. should be precluded from continuing to see the children on a regular basis. Indeed, it is clear that continued regular visitation is in the twins' best interests because V.C. is their psychological parent. . . .

NOTES AND QUESTIONS

1.   *Parental Rights.* Remember *Troxel*, the U.S. Supreme Court decision finding the application of Washington's third-party visitation statute unconstitutional. As both *Parentage of L.B.*, which we read in Chapter 6 after *Troxel*, and *V.C.* illustrate, courts that protect individuals as de facto or psychological parents, over the objection of the existing legal parent, have found that *Troxel* does not preclude such protection. First, the existing parent consented to the formation of the other parent-child relationship and thus cannot later wield parental authority so as to exclude the other parent from the child's life. Second, and relatedly, the de facto parent is not a third party and thus does not present the kind of case contemplated by *Troxel*. Parents have rights to exclude non-parents, but they do not have rights to exclude other parents.

2.   *Different Labels.* Approximately half of the states provide some route by which they recognize functional parents.[220] Courts in different jurisdictions have used different labels for this concept: de facto parent, equitable parent, parent by estoppel, psychological parent, and *in loco parentis*. While some jurisdictions do not treat parents of this sort as legal parents and instead accord them only visitation rights, the clear trend is to treat functional parents as legal parents.

3.   *Custody and Visitation.* The *V.C.* court explained that a legal parent and a psychological parent "stand[] in parity," but then observed that the legal parent's status matters because of the child's interest in "self-knowledge." What did the court mean by this? Did the court conflate "legal" with "natural"? The court awarded legal custody to the biological mother and granted visitation to the nonbiological mother. Legal custody refers to decision-making authority for the child. This is different than physical custody, which involves time with the child. Why did the court conclude that even though each parent was equally bonded to the child, the biological mother should have sole legal custody? Do you agree with this conclusion? Is there any way to avoid a result like this in future cases involving psychological parents?

B.   The Codification of De Facto Parenthood

While functional parenthood emerged as a judicial creation through common law and equitable principles, recently states have begun to enact de facto parent statutes.[221] De facto parenthood is simply another statutory path to establishing parentage — though one that requires adjudication. Once adjudicated, the de facto parent is a full legal parent with all of the rights and responsibilities that come with that status.

---

220. See Courtney G. Joslin, De Facto Parentage and the Modern Family, 4 Fam. Advoc. 31, 31 (Spring 2018).

221. See, e.g., Del. Code Ann tit. 13, § 8-201(c) (2020); Vt. Stat. Ann. 15C, § 501 (2020).

Delaware Code Annotated Title 13, § 8-201

... (c) De facto parent status is established if the Family Court determines that the de facto parent:

(1) Has had the support and consent of the child's parent or parents who fostered the formation and establishment of a parent-like relationship between the child and the de facto parent;

(2) Has exercised parental responsibility for the child . . .; and

(3) Has acted in a parental role for a length of time sufficient to have established a bonded and dependent relationship with the child that is parental in nature.

Uniform Parentage Act (2017)

SECTION 609. ADJUDICATING CLAIM OF DE FACTO PARENTAGE OF CHILD. . . .

(d) . . . [T]he court shall adjudicate the individual who claims to be a de facto parent to be a parent of the child if the individual demonstrates by clear-and-convincing evidence that:

(1) the individual resided with the child as a regular member of the child's household for a significant period;

(2) the individual engaged in consistent caretaking of the child;

(3) the individual undertook full and permanent responsibilities of a parent of the child without expectation of financial compensation;

(4) the individual held out the child as the individual's child;

(5) the individual established a bonded and dependent relationship with the child which is parental in nature;

(6) another parent of the child fostered or supported the bonded and dependent relationship required under paragraph (5); and

(7) continuing the relationship between the individual and the child is in the best interest of the child.

NOTES AND QUESTIONS

1. *Evidentiary Standards.* The UPA requires the elements of de facto parentage be proved by clear and convincing evidence. Why have a heightened standard? The UPA also treats de facto parentage differently in other ways: it allows only the person seeking to be adjudicated a de facto parent to initiate a de facto parent proceeding.[222] Why not allow the legal parent to bring a petition seeking to have

---

222. UPA (2017), supra note 93, § 609(a).

another person adjudicated a de facto parent? Why not allow the state to bring such a petition?

2.   *De Facto Parenthood and Domestic Violence.* As we saw in the Notes and Questions after *Brooke S.B.*, organizations that work on domestic violence urged the New York court to adopt an intentional parentage standard, rather than a functional parentage standard. Some fear that de facto parentage and other functional approaches will make domestic violence survivors vulnerable to additional abuse. They worry that an abusive partner or former partner, who is not married to the mother and is not the biological parent of the child, will threaten to file a de facto parent petition or will pursue de facto parentage as a way to control and harass the mother. How significant do you think these concerns should be in considering whether to enact a de facto parentage statute? Is there a way to balance competing interests in this context? In Vermont, legislators codified de facto parentage in 2018 while also permitting a parent to "use evidence of duress, coercion, or threat of harm to contest an allegation that the parent fostered or supported a bonded and dependent relationship" between the person and the child.[223]

C. The "Holding Out" Presumption

Some states have protected functional parents without recognizing de facto parenthood on common law, equitable, or statutory grounds. Instead, these states have interpreted and applied existing statutory presumptions of parentage — which had contemplated biological parents — in ways that reach nonbiological parents.

IN RE NICHOLAS H.
46 P.3d 932 (Cal. 2002)

BROWN, J.

A man who receives a child into his home and openly holds the child out as his natural child is presumed to be the natural father of the child. (Fam. Code, § 7611(d).) The presumption that he is the natural father "is a rebuttable presumption affecting the burden of proof and may be rebutted in an appropriate action only by clear and convincing evidence." (§ 7612(a).) The question presented by this case is whether a presumption arising under section 7611(d) is, under section 7612(a), necessarily rebutted when the presumed father seeks parental rights but admits that he is not the biological father of the child.

---

223. Vt. Stat. Ann. 15C, § 501(a)(2) (2018).

The answer to this question is of the gravest concern to the six-year-old boy involved in this case. While his presumed father is providing a loving home for him, his mother has not done so, and his biological father, whose identity has never been judicially determined, has shown no interest in doing so. Therefore, if, as the Court of Appeal concluded, the juvenile court had no discretion under section 7612(a) but to find that the presumption arising under section 7611(d) was rebutted by the presumed father's admission that he is not the biological father, this child will be rendered fatherless and homeless.

This harsh result, we conclude, is not required by section 7612(a). The Court of Appeal's paraphrase of section 7612(a) reveals the fundamental flaw in its analysis. "[W]e are not free to ignore the statute, which expressly states that the section 7611(d) presumption *is* rebutted by clear and convincing evidence that the presumed father is not the child's natural father." However, that is not what section 7612(a) says. Rather, the section provides that "a presumption under Section 7611 is a rebuttable presumption affecting the burden of proof and *may* be rebutted *in an appropriate action* only by clear and convincing evidence."

The juvenile court acted well within its discretion in concluding that this case, in which no one else was a candidate for the privilege and responsibility of fathering this little boy, was not *an appropriate action* in which to find that the section 7611(d) presumption of fatherhood had been rebutted.

FACTUAL AND PROCEDURAL BACKGROUND

The Alameda County Social Services Agency filed a juvenile dependency petition alleging that Nicholas H. was taken into custody pursuant to section 300, subdivision (b) of the Welfare and Institutions Code because his parents had failed to adequately supervise and protect him. . . .

When Kimberly was pregnant with Nicholas, she moved in with Thomas. Thomas is not Nicholas's biological father, as he admits, but both Kimberly and Thomas wanted Thomas to act as a father to Nicholas, so Thomas participated in Nicholas's birth, was listed on Nicholas's birth certificate as his father, and provided a home for Kimberly and Nicholas for several years.

Thomas has been the constant in Nicholas's life. As the Court of Appeal observed, in concluding the evidence "more than satisfied the requirements of section 7611(d)," Thomas has lived with Nicholas for long periods of time, he has provided Nicholas with significant financial support over the years, and he has consistently referred to and treated Nicholas as his son. "In addition, there is undisputed evidence that Nicholas has a strong emotional bond with Thomas and that Thomas is the only father Nicholas has ever know[n]."

Kimberly, on the other hand, has been a frail reed for Nicholas to lean upon. The investigation report prepared by a family services counselor stated that "information from friends and relatives of the family supported Thomas's allegations of

Kimberly's drug use, transiency, lack of gainful employment and violence towards others." . . .

Jason S., Kimberly claims, is Nicholas's biological father. However, Jason has not come forward to assert any parental rights he may have, and because the Agency has been unable to obtain enough information from Kimberly to locate Jason, his paternity could not be established.

On this record, the juvenile court found that the presumption under 7611(d) that Thomas was Nicholas's natural father had not been rebutted. The court expressly rejected the contention that Thomas's admission that he is not Nicholas's biological father necessarily rebutted the presumption. "If I were to agree with County Counsel that [Thomas's] admission that he is not Nicholas's biological father rebuts the presumption, then what we would be doing is leaving Nicholas fatherless." . . .

DISCUSSION

The Court of Appeal concluded that Thomas qualified as Nicholas's presumed father under section 7611(d), but that, under section 7612(a), his admission that he is not Nicholas's biological father necessarily rebutted that presumption. . . .

The Court of Appeal satisfied itself through an examination of relevant Family Code provisions that "the Legislature has used the term 'natural' to mean 'biological,'" and, through a review of family law decisions, that "courts construing sections 7611 and 7612 have assumed that natural means biological." . . . [T]he Court of Appeal felt it was "not free to ignore the statute, which expressly states that the section 7611(d) presumption is rebutted by clear and convincing evidence that the presumed father is not the child's natural father."

In its misreading of section 7612(a) — "that the section 7611(d) presumption *is* rebutted by clear and convincing evidence that the presumed father is not the child's natural father" — the Court of Appeal appears to have conflated two of the three subdivisions of section 7612. Subdivision (a) provides that "a presumption under Section 7611 is a rebuttable presumption affecting the burden of proof and *may* be rebutted *in an appropriate action* only by clear and convincing evidence." Subdivision (c), on the other hand, provides that "[t]he presumption under Section 7611 *is* rebutted by a judgment establishing paternity of the child by another man." No judgment establishing the paternity of another man has been entered here. Kimberly asserts Jason is Nicholas's biological father, but Jason has not come forward to affirm that claim and, indeed, has not even been located. "A man who may be the father of a child, but whose biological paternity has not been established, or, in the alternative, has not achieved presumed father status, is an 'alleged' father."

Our conclusion — that a man does not lose his status as a presumed father by admitting he is not the biological father — is also supported by subdivision (b) of section 7612. Subdivision (b) provides: "If two or more presumptions arise under section 7611 which conflict with each other, the presumption which on the facts is founded on the weightier considerations of policy and logic controls." As a matter of statutory construction, if the Legislature had intended that a man who is not a biological father cannot be a presumed father under section 7611, it would not have provided for such weighing, for among two competing claims for presumed father status under section 7611, there can be only one biological father.

Moreover, for persons who are presumed fathers under section 7611 by virtue of a voluntary declaration of paternity . . . , the Legislature permits but does not require that blood test evidence may be considered to extinguish such a person's presumed paternity. It is unlikely the Legislature would — without explicitly so stating — adopt a contrary rule that blood test evidence (or an admission) must defeat the claim of a person who claims presumed father status under section 7611(d). . . .

CONCLUSION

To review: Section 7612(a) provides that "a presumption under Section 7611 [that a man is the natural father of a child] is a rebuttable presumption affecting the burden of proof *and may be rebutted in an appropriate action* only by clear and convincing evidence." When it used the limiting phrase *an appropriate action*, the Legislature is unlikely to have had in mind an action like this — an action in which no other man claims parental rights to the child, an action in which rebuttal of the section 7611(d) presumption will render the child fatherless. Rather, we believe the Legislature had in mind an action in which another candidate is vying for parental rights and seeks to rebut a section 7611(d) presumption in order to perfect his claim, or in which a court decides that the legal rights and obligations of parenthood should devolve upon an unwilling candidate. . . .

In this case it is not necessary to reach, and we do not reach, the question . . . whether, under section 7612, subdivision (b), biological paternity by a competing presumptive father necessarily defeats a non-biological father's presumption of paternity. It is also unnecessary to reach the question [of] . . . what constitutional rights are enjoyed by a man who is not a child's biological father but who is seeking to receive a child into his home and to achieve presumed father status. . . .

NOTES AND QUESTIONS

---

1. *"Holding Out" and Nonbiological Parents.* After the California Supreme Court applied the "holding out" presumption of parentage to a nonbiological unmarried father, it also applied the presumption to a nonbiological unmarried mother. In Elisa B. v. Superior Court, the court held that a nonbiological mother in a same-sex couple was a legal parent because she held the children out as her own.[224] In that case, the nonbiological mother had sought to avoid financial obligations for

---

224. 117 P.3d 660 (Cal. 2005).

the children, and the county had sought to hold her responsible for support after the biological mother sought government aid. Courts in other states have reached similar results under their respective "holding out" presumptions.[225]

2. *Second-Generation "Holding Out" Statutes.* Some states now have "holding out" presumptions that are explicitly gender-neutral and apply to nonbiological parents.[226] Some of these states have moved in this direction by adopting the 2017 UPA, which provides:

> An individual is presumed to be a parent of a child if: . . . the individual resided in the same household with the child for the first two years of the life of the child, including any period of temporary absence, and openly held out the child as the individual's child.[227]

3. *Constitutional Objections.* With de facto parenthood, we saw that courts and legislatures address constitutional objections by requiring that the de facto parent show that the existing legal parent fostered or supported the parental relationship between the de facto parent and the child. Do the same types of constitutional concerns exist with respect to "holding out" parents? Does the California court's reasoning do anything to mitigate constitutional concerns? Does the UPA provision?

4. *The Constitutional Status of Nonbiological Parents.* The discussion about the Constitution and nonbiological parents mostly involves the constitutional rights of the biological parent. Yet, in *Nicholas H.*, the court raised a question it did not need to reach: "what constitutional rights are enjoyed by a man who is not a child's biological father but who is seeking to receive a child into his home and to achieve presumed father status"? Does a nonbiological parent — one who has been parenting the child — have a constitutional interest in being treated as a legal parent?[228]

VI. Multiple Parents?

Can a child have more than two parents? If so, when should the law recognize more than two parents? And what is the outer limit on the number of parents? Should we move from two to three? Or more?

---

225. See Partanen v. Gallagher, 59 N.E.3d 1133 (Mass. 2016); In re Guardianship of Madelyn B., 98 A.3d 494 (N.H. 2014); Chatterjee v. King, 280 P.3d 283 (N.M. 2012); In re Parental Responsibilities of A.R.L., 318 P.3d 582 (Colo. App. 2013).

226. See, e.g., Me. Stat. tit. 19-A, § 1881(3) (2020); Vt. Stat. Ann. tit. 15C, § 401(a)(4) (2020); N.H. Rev. Stat. Ann. § 168-B:2(V)(d) (2020).

227. UPA (2017), supra note 93, § 204(a)(2).

228. For arguments that nonbiological parents possess a liberty interest in parental recognition, see Douglas NeJaime, The Constitution of Parenthood, 72 Stan. L. Rev. 261 (2020); Michael J. Higdon, Constitutional Parenthood, 103 Iowa L. Rev. 1483 (2018).

Courts and lawmakers have long faced the possibility of more than two parents. With divorce and remarriage, children may have stepparents that function as parents. Yet, as we saw in Chapter 8, stepparents are ordinarily not treated as legal parents unless they adopt the child, which usually requires that the noncustodial parent relinquishes his rights. In this arrangement, the child still can have only two legal parents.

The possibility of multiple parents has even confronted the Supreme Court. In Michael H. v. Gerald D., which we read earlier in the chapter, the child's attorney argued that Victoria should be able to preserve a parental relationship with both men, since she viewed both men as fathers. But Justice Scalia, writing the plurality opinion for the Court, responded that "California law, like nature itself, makes no provision for dual fatherhood."[229]

Of course, shifts in reproduction and family formation have made multiple parents more thinkable today. Two intended parents, a sperm donor, an egg donor, and a gestational surrogate may contribute to the creation of one child. Same-sex parents may choose a known gamete donor who they intend to have a parental relationship with the child. Polyamorous or polygamous families may raise children together.

Recently, states have begun to expressly endorse the idea that a child can have more than two parents. California was the first state to enact a statute authorizing a court to recognize more than two parents for a child. In 2011, the California Court of Appeal addressed a dispute involving three potential parents: a biological mother, her same-sex spouse, and a biological father with whom the mother had a sexual relationship. In In re M.C.,[230] the biological mother's spouse and the biological father appeared to be more suitable parents than the biological mother, but the court felt constrained by the parentage statutes to choose between the spouse and the biological father. In response, California enacted a law permitting courts to find that a child has more than two parents if not doing so would be detrimental to the child.[231] California courts have begun to apply that law, as in the decision below.

C.A. v. C.P.
240 Cal. Rptr. 3d 38 (Cal. Ct. App. 2018)

Duarte, J.

This case involves a little girl bonded to and loved by each of her three parents.

The wife in a married couple (defendants C.P. and J.P., wife and husband) conceived the child with a coworker (plaintiff C.A.), but hid that fact from wife's employer and—initially—from husband. The marriage remains intact and wife

---

229. 491 U.S. 110, 118 (1989).
230. 123 Cal. Rptr. 3d 856 (Cal. Ct. App. 2011).
231. Cal. Fam. Code § 7612(c) (West 2020).

and husband parent the child. For the first three years of the child's life, the couple allowed plaintiff to act in an alternate parenting role, and the child bonded with him and his close relatives. Defendants excluded plaintiff from the child's life when he filed the instant petition seeking legal confirmation of his paternal rights. The trial court . . . found the child was . . . bonded to all three parents and found this to be a "rare" case where, pursuant to statutory authority, each of three parents should be legally recognized as such, to prevent detriment to their child. Defendants appeal. We shall affirm. . . .

Defendants never questioned plaintiff's status as the child's biological father, a fact each defendant had known before the child was born. Wife led plaintiff to believe she was separated but continued to cohabit with husband without plaintiff's knowledge. Plaintiff and wife were coworkers, and wife wanted to ensure other coworkers did not find out about the affair, which caused plaintiff to refrain from seeking paternity leave from their employer. Plaintiff was involved with the child's early medical evaluations and treatment, openly held her out as his daughter, received her into his home, paid child support, and had regular visitation until defendants cut him off after he filed the instant petition. Plaintiff's close relatives (sister, nieces, and mother) also developed relationships with the child. Plaintiff had thought the child bore his last name until he saw a prescription bottle showing otherwise, when the child was about eight or nine months old.

Plaintiff had regular overnight parenting that increased over time to every other weekend, and saw the child "from time to time" during the week, from when the child was about seven months old until late in 2015, when this petition was filed.

When the child was about 18 months old, all parties participated in autism screening and therapy for her. Neither defendant refused plaintiff's informal child support payments, set in an amount determined by wife. Plaintiff only stopped paying when defendants refused to let him continue to see the child. Plaintiff respected the marriage and wanted to co-exist with husband; in turn, husband was committed to maintaining his marriage and conceded that if the roles were reversed he would want to be recognized as a third parent.

The trial court found "no doubt" the child was "well bonded to [plaintiff] and his extended family" and that "he has established a strong, long and enduring bond with" her that defendants had allowed to form. Plaintiff and husband were each found to be a presumed father of the child. Weighing the two presumptions, the court found it appropriate to recognize all three adults as parents, otherwise the child would suffer detriment. The judgment declares that the child has three parents who shall share custody. . . .

Defendants primarily contend the trial court should not have found plaintiff was a third parent under the relevant statutes, and make the subsidiary claims that such a finding interferes with the state's interest in preserving the institution of marriage and impinges on their parental rights. As we explain, we disagree. . . .

[T]here is no dispute that husband is presumed to be at least a father of the child under section 7540. Plaintiff is also presumed to be a father, under section 7611, subdivision (d), which provides that a person "is presumed to be the natural parent" if the "presumed parent receives the child into his or her home and openly holds out the child as his or her natural child." Defendants do not challenge the sufficiency of the evidence showing that plaintiff has satisfied this statute. Therefore, they cannot deny that plaintiff is a presumed father under this statute. The question is whether he can be deemed a third parent, as the trial court deemed him.

The pertinent bill (Sen. Bill No. 274 (2013-2014 Reg. Sess.)) included a statement of legislative intent as follows:

(a) Most children have two parents, but in rare cases, children have more than two people who are that child's parent in every way. Separating a child from a parent has a devastating psychological and emotional impact on the child, and courts must have the power to protect children from this harm.

(b) The purpose of this bill is to abrogate *In re M.C.* (2011) 195 Cal. App. 4th 197, insofar as it held that where there are more than two people who have a claim to parentage under the Uniform Parentage Act, courts are prohibited from recognizing more than two of these people as the parents of a child, regardless of the circumstances.

(c) This bill does not change any of the requirements for establishing a claim to parentage under the Uniform Parentage Act. It only clarifies that where more than two people have claims to parentage, the court may, if it would otherwise be detrimental to the child, recognize that the child has more than two parents.

(d) It is the intent of the Legislature that this bill will only apply in the rare case where a child truly has more than two parents, and a finding that a child has more than two parents is necessary to protect the child from the detriment of being separated from one of his or her parents. (Stats. 2013, ch. 564, § 1.)

To advance the public policy reflected by these explicit legislative findings, section 7612, subdivision (c) now provides as follows:

> In an appropriate action, a court may find that more than two persons with a claim to parentage under this division are parents if the court finds that recognizing only two parents would be detrimental to the child. In determining detriment to the child, the court shall consider all relevant factors, including, but not limited to, the harm of removing the child from a stable placement with a parent who has fulfilled the child's physical needs and the child's psychological needs for care and affection, and who has assumed that role for a substantial period of time. A finding of detriment to the child does

not require a finding of unfitness of any of the parents or persons with a claim to parentage. . . .

[B]*oth* defendant husband (by virtue of section 7540) and plaintiff (by virtue of section 7611, subd. (d)) have "a claim to parentage under this division" as provided by section 7612, subdivision (c). . . .

Defendants point to statements in part of the legislative history to argue the three-parent statute was not meant to be applied where a stable marriage exists. But the relevant report explains that "cases involving more than two parents are, almost by definition, complicated and will require courts to balance many competing interests" and the bill allows a three-parent result "in very narrow situation when necessary to prevent detriment to the child." . . . If the Legislature wanted to limit the bill's application to cases where no stable marriage existed, it easily could have said so. Instead, it directed courts to consider "all relevant factors." . . .

The trial court discussed all appropriate factors before making the "rare" case finding. The court distinguished this case from others where a married couple *consistently* excluded a biological father, because here defendants allowed plaintiff (and his close relatives) to establish a bond with the child. The court found the child "must be protected from the detriment of being separated from one of her three parents. The court finds it would be detrimental to [her] to recognize only two parents, thus separating her from either [husband or plaintiff]. Moreover, it would be detrimental to [the child] and her progress to not allow [both men] to participate in legal custody decision-making such as health and education. The evidence establishes [she] is a child who would benefit greatly from the continued love, devotion and day to day involvement of three parents."

The trial court gave "significant weight to the strong, long and enduring bond shared by [the child and plaintiff] from the time leading up to her birth and from her birth and following for more than three years. [Plaintiff] was deeply involved in [her] life until he was unilaterally excluded from visits . . . after he filed his petition for custody. It is also established [that husband] has a strong bond with [her] and has been part of her life since she was born. Both [men] provided persuasive and convincing testimony regarding . . . their affection and love for [her. She] is fortunate, to have two devoted Fathers that care deeply for her, love her and are prepared to continue to play an active role in her life." Plaintiff wanted "to respectfully co-exist with" husband, who himself had admitted "that if he stood in [plaintiff's] shoes he would want to be acknowledged as a third parent and have a role as a parent." . . .

[T]he record shows that the trial court carefully and conscientiously conducted the weighing process contemplated by the Legislature before finding that this was one of the "rare" cases permitted by statute, where a child truly has three parents, and depriving her of one of them would be detrimental to her. . . .

[D]efendants contend that if the statutory scheme authorizes the result herein, it violates constitutional norms in two ways. First, they contend it impinges on the state's right to protect marriage. Second, they contend it impinges on their ability to exercise their parental rights. But defendants do not contend the statutory scheme is facially unconstitutional, and their as-applied challenges falter on the facts as found by the trial court. . . .

Defendant's claim that the judgment attacks the institution of marriage fails because the state expresses its will primarily through statutes passed by the Legislature and signed by the Governor. By such means, the state now authorizes three-parent findings in "rare" cases. The trial court, following the text of the relevant statutes, found the child would suffer detriment if she had only two parents. The state's interests in promoting and defending both the institution of marriage and the stability of a given child's life have been protected by the judgment under attack. . . .

[D]efendants provide no authority for the implicit proposition that a *child's* detriment should be subordinated to a *marriage's* detriment. The adult parties to a marriage will either work out any marital challenges they face, or they will not. But generally, even if a marriage fails, the parties thereto will remain lawful parents of any child therefrom. . . .

Defendants paint plaintiff as a would-be homewrecker, and point out that they have other children together who could be impacted by a divorce. But the trial court found wife misled plaintiff, causing him to believe she and husband were separated. Before the child was born, all parties knew plaintiff was the biological father and, with that knowledge, defendants allowed plaintiff to parent the child and she bonded with him and his relatives. For defendants now to claim plaintiff poses such a severe threat to their marriage that he should be excluded despite the finding that his exclusion would be detrimental to the child rings hollow. . . .

[D]efendants contend that by recognizing plaintiff as a father, husband's status as a father was diminished. Within this claim they also assert their joint parental rights are diminished. . . .

Defendants point out that " '[a] parent's right to care, custody and management of a child is a fundamental liberty interest protected by the federal Constitution that will not be disturbed except in extreme cases where a parent acts in a manner incompatible with parenthood.' " We agree. But what defendants overlook is that plaintiff, too, is a parent. He is the biological father of the child, who has consistently supported her both financially and otherwise. As we have explained, the fact defendant husband is conclusively presumed to be the child's father does not exclude the possibility that she may have a second father. . . .

The judgment is affirmed. . . .

NOTES AND QUESTIONS

1. *Multiple Parenthood by Case Law.* Before California enacted its law allowing courts to recognize more than two parents, courts had begun to contemplate three parents.[232] Indeed, Louisiana courts long had permitted a finding of dual paternity when the child's functional father was different than the child's biological father.[233]

2. *Multiple Parenthood by Statute.* Remember that in situations involving multiple parents, each person must have a valid claim to parentage. Only then is the court authorized to adjudicate more than two parents for a child. After California, additional states enacted laws allowing courts to recognize more than two parents for a child.[234] California's law includes a detriment standard, empowering the court to adjudicate a third parent only if not doing so would be detrimental to the child. Other states, in contrast, have adopted a best interest standard, thus lowering the bar for a court to adjudicate more than two parents.[235] Which standard do you support?

The 2017 Uniform Parentage Act gives states two alternatives with respect to numerosity. States can enact a provision limiting parentage to two individuals.[236] Or states can enact a provision allowing a court to adjudicate more than two parents "if the court finds that failure to recognize more than two parents would be detrimental to the child."[237] Even though some states have resisted multiple parenthood and the possibility exists in only a small number of states, the states that first adopted the 2017 UPA enacted Alternative B, rather than Alternative A, and thus authorized multiple parenthood.

3. *Stepparents.* When would a stepparent qualify as a third parent? The person seeking parental status must otherwise be able to establish parentage, so, depending on the state, the stepparent would need to show that he is a "holding out" parent or a de facto parent. In a regime in which a child has only two parents, courts have been reluctant to find that a stepparent qualifies as a de facto parent.[238] But courts might

---

232. See, e.g., Jacob v. Shultz-Jacob, 923 A.2d 473 (Pa. Super. Ct. 2007) (extending rights to biological mother, her former same-sex partner, and the sperm donor with whom the children had a relationship).

233. See, e.g., Smith v. Cole, 553 So. 2d 847 (La. 1989) ("Louisiana law may provide the presumption that the husband of the mother is the legal father of her child while it recognizes a biological father's actual paternity.").

234. See, e.g., Me. Stat. tit. 19-A, § 1853(2) (2020) ("a court may determine that a child has more than 2 parents"); D.C. Code § 16-831.01 (2020) (allowing recognition of a de facto parent if the individual "[h]as held himself or herself out as the child's parent with the agreement of the child's parent or, if there are 2 parents, both parents").

235. See Vt. Stat. Ann. 15C, § 206(b) (2020) ("[A] court may determine that a child has more than two parents if the court finds that it is in the best interests of the child to do so.").

236. UPA (2017), supra note 93, § 613, Alternative A.

237. Id. § 613, Alternative B.

238. See Margaret M. Mahoney, Stepparents as Third Parties in Relation to Their Stepchildren, 40 Fam. L.Q. 81 (2006). For a rare case finding that a stepfather stood in loco parentis and therefore had standing to seek custody, see Bodwell v. Brooks, 686 A.2d 1179 (N.H. 1996).

be more open to the claims of stepparents if they could recognize the stepparent as a de facto parent without terminating the rights of one of the existing parents. What are the advantages and disadvantages of recognizing stepparents as legal parents? Would it be better to provide rights of visitation to a stepparent but not full legal parentage? In California, stepparents for decades have had the right to seek visitation with the stepchild upon divorce from the legal parent.[239]

4. *Multiple Parenthood and Adoption.* In Chapter 8, we explored adoption. What does the possibility of multiple parenthood mean for the law of adoption? Could a court authorize an adoption without requiring that the existing parents relinquish their rights? Or would this run afoul of the adoption statute, which requires relinquishment? Could a court authorize stepparent adoption, which already represents a carve-out from ordinary termination requirements, without extinguishing the rights of the noncustodial parent? California law now provides that "termination of the parental duties and responsibilities of the existing parent or parents . . . may be waived if both the existing parent or parents and the prospective adoptive parent or parents sign a waiver at any time prior to the finalization of the adoption."[240] Is this a good development? Does it change the very nature of adoption?

5. *Children's Interests.* Does multiple parenthood further children's interests? How do we know? Might multiple parenthood undermine children's interests? Under what circumstances? If a child has more than two parents, should the parents share legal custody (i.e., decision-making authority)? Should they share physical custody (i.e., parenting time)? Should they each have support obligations? As Professor Susan Appleton explains:

> The portrait painted by some supporters of multi-parentage is that of the intact family — or the ongoing community. . . . [W]hen three (or more) parents are collaborating and the child is thriving, the case for multi-parentage becomes especially compelling. . . . [H]owever, the prospect of multi-parentage becomes much more controversial upon the community's dissolution. Indeed, all signs indicate that the animosity, possessiveness, factual contests, and willingness to use children as pawns often seen upon the dissolution of traditional marriages arise with equal regularity upon the dissolution of same-sex and other nontraditional relationships. . . . As the parental community expands, moreover, the possibilities for such disputes increase. . . .
>
> [The] prospect of a group of adults, perhaps feeling post-dissolution antagonism, collectively trying to decide how to rear a child justifiably sets off alarms, among multi-parentage's supporters and detractors alike. And group decision-making would logically follow from the current prominence

---

239. Cal. Fam. Code § 3101 (West 2020).
240. Id. § 8617.

in family law of joint legal custody, which generally entails in the bi-parentage case jointly exercised or shared decision-making. . . .[241]

Should legislatures furnish separate standards to govern custody in multi-parent situations?

PROBLEM

Dawn and Michael, a married couple in New York, tried to have a child together but were unsuccessful. They became friends with Audria, who moved into the apartment below them with her boyfriend. After Audria broke up with her boyfriend, she moved in with Dawn and Michael and the three of them began an intimate relationship. They considered themselves a family and decided to have a child together. Audria became pregnant through sexual intercourse with Michael. Michael, Dawn, and Audria agreed to raise the child together, which they did for several months until their relationship soured. Dawn initiated a divorce action against Michael, and Audria and Dawn moved into an apartment together with the child. As part of the divorce action, Dawn sought joint custody of the child. Michael argued that, without a biological tie to the child, Dawn was not a legal parent and thus had no claim to custody. (Because the husband, rather than the wife, was the biological parent, the marital presumption was not relevant and the child was not a "child of the marriage.") Audria intervened in support of Dawn's claim to custody. You are the judge assigned to the case. How would you rule?

POSTSCRIPT

This case is based on Dawn M. v. Michael M., in which a New York court awarded "tri-custody."[242] The court relied heavily on *Brooke S.B.*, which we read earlier in this chapter, in finding that because the three individuals agreed to have a child together and in fact jointly raised the child, the child should maintain a parental relationship with each of them.[243] Does *Brooke S.B.* support this result? New York did not have express statutory authority for multi-parent recognition, yet the court felt empowered to rule as it did in order to vindicate the child's interest.[244]

---

241. Susan Frelich Appleton, Parents By the Numbers, 37 Hofstra L. Rev. 11, 40–42 (2008).
242. 47 N.Y.S.3d 898, 903 (N.Y. Sup. Ct. 2017).
243. Id.
244. Id. But see Tomeka N.H. v. Jesus R., 122 N.Y.S.3d 461 (App. Div. 2020).

In states that maintain statutes authorizing courts to find that a child has more than two parents, should such statutes reach children being raised in multi-partner families? Does it matter whether the child resulted from assisted reproduction or sexual procreation? Does multi-parent recognition mean that polygamous and polyamorous arrangements also should be legally recognized? Or is there a justification for extending parental status to individuals in polygamous or polyamorous families while withholding legal status from the adult relationships?

CHAPTER 10

Custody and Visitation

Custody and visitation issues arise whenever there is a question about where children will live and which adults will have responsibility for their care. Many divorces involve couples with minor children, but custody disputes can arise in other situations as well—between parents who never married, between parents who are separated but not divorced, and, less often, between parents and non-parents.

The scenarios in which custody arises reflect changing patterns of family formation and childrearing. For instance, in 2018, nearly 40 percent of children were born to unmarried mothers,[1] a rate that has increased twenty-fold since 1940.[2] As single-parent households have increased generally, so too have fathers comprised a growing percentage of such households. Single-father households are now 24 percent of all single-parent households, as compared to 14 percent in 1960.[3] Increasing numbers of children are born to non-marital cohabiting couples as well.[4]

Traditionally, custody of children was governed by strong presumptions. Early in our nation's history, children would practically always remain in the custody of their father, provided that he had been married to the mother.[5] A father even had the legal authority to appoint a guardian other than the mother in the event of his

---

1. Joyce A. Martin et al., Births: Final Data for 2018, 68 Nat'l Vital Stat. Rep. 1, 5 (2019).

2. Stephanie J. Ventura, Nat'l Ctr. for Health Stats., Changing Patterns of Nonmarital Childbearing in the United States, Data Brief No. 18, at 2 (2009).

3. Gretchen Livingston, Pew Research Ctr., The Rise of Single Fathers: A Ninefold Increase Since 1960 (July 2, 2013); see also Roberta L. Coles, Single Father Families: A Review of the Literature, 7 J. Fam. Theory & Rev. 144 (2015) (proportion of children living with fathers has increased from 1.3 percent in 1960 to 3.7 percent in 2009).

4. W. Bradford Wilcox & Laurie DeRose, Ties that Bind: Childrearing in the Age of Cohabitation, Foreign Aff. (Feb. 14, 2017); Wendy D. Manning et al., Nat'l Ctr. for Family & Marriage Research, Trends in Births to Single and Cohabiting Mothers, 1980-2013, at 1 (2015).

5. Michael Grossberg, Governing the Hearth: Law and the Family in Nineteenth Century America 235 (1985); see also Sarah Abramowicz, English Child Custody Law, 1660-1839: The Origins of Judicial Intervention in Paternal Custody, 99 Colum. L. Rev. 1344, 1347 (1999).

death.[6] Paternal control reflected a view of the father as head of the household, with a property-like interest in his wife and children.[7] Women's rights activists in the middle of the nineteenth century advocated for custody rights, one of the many demands included in the Declaration of Sentiments from the 1848 convention at Seneca Falls, New York.[8]

By the late nineteenth century, courts had relinquished the model of absolute paternal control in favor of considerations of children's best interests or welfare.[9] As these considerations took hold in American courts, the view of children as fathers' property weakened (coinciding also with the rise of restrictions on child labor), and recognition of women's claims to parental rights grew.[10] Courts began to use a "tender years" rule, according to which children under the age of seven were presumptively placed with the mother unless she was unfit.[11] This approach reflected societal norms of the time, including a gender-based ideology of "separate spheres," in which men participated in public life and paid market work and women tended to the domestic front.[12]

During the last half century, custody law has changed considerably. The child's best interests remain paramount in custodial decision-making. But now, unlike in generations past, the dominant understanding associates the child's best interests with maintaining ongoing relationships with both parents. One expression of this intuition is that custody orders typically are coupled with visitation orders that allow the noncustodial parent to have regular contact with the child.[13] Also reflective of the ethos that children should have contact with both parents is the trend toward joint custody, an arrangement under which parents share authority to make decisions about the child, the obligation to house and care for the child, or both.[14]

---

6. Grossberg, supra note 5, at 235–36; see also Mary Ann Mason, From Father's Property to Children's Rights: The History of Child Custody in the United States (1994).

7. Grossberg, supra note 5, at 235–35, 242; Mason, supra note 6; J. Herbie DiFonzo, From the Rule of One to Shared Parenting: Custody Presumptions in Law and Policy, 52 Fam. Ct. Rev. 213, 214 (2014); Linda D. Elrod, Presumption for Father, Child Custody Prac. & Proc. § 1:5 (2019). For discussion of the origins and implications of male household headship, see Reva B. Siegel, She the People: The Nineteenth Amendment, Sex Equality, Federalism, and the Family, 115 Harv. L. Rev. 947, 981 (2002).

8. Miriam Gurko, The Ladies of Seneca Falls: The Birth of the Woman's Rights Movement 96 (1974).

9. Grossberg, supra note 5, at 238–39. Parens patriae describes the state's obligation and ability to protect those who cannot protect themselves. 1 William Blackstone, Commentaries on the Law of England 463 (1893); Homer H. Clark, The Law of Domestic Relationships in the United States 786–87 (2d ed. 1988).

10. DiFonzo, supra note 7, at 214.

11. Grossberg, supra note 5, at 248. Courts often placed older children with the parent of the same sex as the child. Joanna L. Grossman & Lawrence M. Friedman, Inside the Castle: Law and the Family in 20th Century America 262–63 (2011).

12. Grossman & Friedman, supra note 11, at 263.

13. The California statute, for example, provides that "the court shall grant reasonable visitation rights to a parent when it is shown that the visitation would be in the best interest of the child." Cal. Fam. Code § 3100(a) (West 2020).

14. Julie E. Artis & Andrew V. Krebs, Family Law and Social Change: Judicial Views of Joint Custody, 1998-2011, 40 Law & Soc. Inquiry 723, 725–26 (2015). Concerns about impacts of conflict in divorce on children have also led to exploration of alternative arrangements to create greater stability for children. With "nesting," children stay in the marital home, and parents move in and out for their custodial time. Michael T. Flannery, Is "Bird Nesting" in the Best Interest of Children?, 57 SMU L. Rev. 295, 296–97 (2004).

An important point to ponder as you work through the materials in this chapter is that the nationwide embrace of the best interests of the child standard co-exists with disagreement about its precise meaning in any particular circumstance. Judges and commentators who agree that the best interests of the child standard governs may nonetheless disagree about how to apply it to a concrete controversy. The standard justifiably has been criticized as being frustratingly indeterminate and giving too much authority to judges.[15] Presumptions, in contrast, can constrain judges, lead to predictable outcomes, and, by providing a clear rule around which the parties can bargain, reduce litigation.

Courts may confront custodial decisions, and the complications of the best interests calculus, at either of two times. An initial custody order occurs when parents get divorced or in connection with a parentage adjudication. After the original order is entered, either party may petition to modify custody because of an unanticipated and material change in circumstances. Standards differ across jurisdictions, but the common purpose of the change-in-circumstances requirement is to avoid relitigation simply because one party does not like the initial ruling or wants to harass the other parent.

Finally, it is worth noting that most custody decisions are not made by courts. They are made by parents and approved by courts. Of course, statutory standards and prior judicial decisions provide the parties information about how their dispute would be handled if they go to trial. The parties' bargaining occurs in the shadow of the law and is shaped by it.[16]

I. Evolving Presumptions and Best Interests of the Child

A. Tender Years Presumption

Until the middle of the nineteenth century, marital fathers in the U.S. had an almost absolute right to custody of their minor children. In the following case, the court considers the maternal preference that replaced the paternal one.

---

15. See, e.g., Andrea Charlow, Awarding Custody: The Best Interests of the Child and Other Fictions, 5 Yale L. & Pol'y Rev. 267 (1987); Robert E. Emery, Rule or Rorschach? Approximating Children's Best Interests, 2 Child Dev. Persp. 132 (2007); Raymie H. Wayne, The Best Interests of the Child: A Silent Standard — Will You Know It When You Hear It?, 2 J. Pub. Child Welfare 33 (2008).

16. Robert H. Mnookin & Lewis Kornhauser, Bargaining in the Shadow of the Law: The Case of Divorce, 88 Yale L.J. 950 (1979).

PUSEY v. PUSEY
728 P.2d 117 (Utah 1986)

DURHAM, JUSTICE: . . .

We believe the time has come to discontinue our support, even in dictum, for the notion of gender-based preferences in child custody cases. . . . . [T]he provisions of article IV, section 1 of the Utah Constitution and of the fourteenth amendment of the United States Constitution would preclude us from relying on gender as a determining factor.

Several courts have declared the maternal preference, or "tender years presumption," unconstitutional. . . . Although [one court] used a strict scrutiny test, it is equally doubtful that the maternal preference can be sustained on an intermediate level of review. This is particularly true when the tender years doctrine is used as a "tie-breaker," as it is in Utah, because in that situation the Court is "denying custody to all fathers who . . . *are as capable as the mother.* . . . [W]hile over inclusiveness [sic] is tolerable at the rational basis level of review, it becomes problematic at the heightened level of scrutiny recognized in gender discrimination cases."

Even ignoring the constitutional infirmities of the maternal preference, the rule lacks validity because it is unnecessary and perpetuates outdated stereotypes. The development of the tender years doctrine was perhaps useful in a society in which fathers traditionally worked outside the home and mothers did not; however, since that pattern is no longer prevalent, particularly in post-separation single-parent households, the tender years doctrine is equally anachronistic. Further, "[b]y arbitrarily applying a presumption in favor of the mother and awarding custody to her on that basis, a court is not truly evaluating what is in the child's best interests."

We believe that the choice in competing child custody claims should instead be based on function-related factors. Prominent among these, though not exclusive, is the identity of the primary caretaker during the marriage. Other factors should include the identity of the parent with greater flexibility to provide personal care for the child and the identity of the parent with whom the child has spent most of his or her time pending custody determination if that period has been lengthy. Another important factor should be the stability of the environment provided by each parent.

In accord with those guidelines, we disavow today those cases that continue to approve, even indirectly, an arbitrary maternal preference. . . .

NOTES AND QUESTIONS

1. *Tender Years Doctrine.* The presumption that maternal custody is ordinarily best for young children spread quickly and was "adopted in virtually all jurisdictions by the end of the nineteenth century either by case law . . . or, particularly

[handwritten: old doctrine]

in the frontier states, directly by statute."[17] A typical statute made clear that neither parent had a superior right of custody, "but other things being equal, if the child is of tender years, it should be given to the mother, and if it is of an age to require education and preparation for labor or business, then to the father."[18] The tender years doctrine operated as an evidentiary presumption employed under the more general "best interests" principle.

2. *Arbitrariness.* The court in *Pusey* refers to the tender years presumption as arbitrary. Does the court mean that it is unrelated to the child's best interest or that it is unfair to the other parent? If the tender years presumption is rebuttable and only operates when all other things are equal, how does it disserve the child's interest?

3. *Benefit of Presumptions.* Presumptions reduce litigation and provide parties a more determinate rule around which they can bargain. In contrast, are there benefits to a system that examines various aspects of a child's life before reaching a custody determination?

4. *Tender Years Presumption as a Continuing Factor in Best Interests.* Courts in some jurisdictions, like Mississippi, continue to consider the tender years doctrine as one factor in a best interests of the child analysis while acknowledging that the doctrine has weakened.[19] For instance, in *Ethridge v. Ethridge,* a Mississippi appellate court approved a trial court's award of custody of an 8-month-old child to the mother because the trial court acknowledged that the tender years doctrine "is only one factor out of the numerous [best interests] factors."[20]

5. *Tender Years Rationale.* As Professor J. Herbie DiFonzo observes: "Mothers were seen as the instinctive custodians for both young children and those with disabilities. . . . A mother was 'God's own institution for the rearing and upbringing of the child,' and thus maternal custody placed 'child culture in the hands of an expert.'"[21] To what extent does this perspective still inform ideas about parenting?

B. Best Interests of the Child in the Modern Era

Custody is a process of selecting the placement or arrangement that will be most likely to produce a desired end goal: healthy, happy, well-adjusted, self-sufficient adults. A child's "best interests" are served when the custodial arrangement provides for the child's immediate needs and maximizes the chance of a "successful" childhood. In the best interests of the child calculus, there are two different sources of indeterminacy: empirical and normative. Put simply, decisionmakers might apply

---

17. Ramsay Laing Klaff, The Tender Years Doctrine: A Defense, 70 Calif. L. Rev. 335, 341 (1982).

18. Ferguson v. Ferguson, 202 N.W.2d 760, 764 (N.D. 1972).

19. Passmore v. Passmore, 820 So. 2d 747, 750 (Miss. Ct. App. 2002).

20. 226 So. 3d 1261, 1263–64 (Miss. Ct. App. 2017).

21. DiFonzo, supra note 7, at 214.

the best interests of the child standard differently because they disagree about facts or values. In addition to factual disputes about the current state of affairs, there will also be uncertainty about the future. Whether a particular experience or relationship will influence a child for good or for ill is impossible to forecast with certainty.

PAINTER V. BANNISTER
140 N.W.2d 152 (Iowa 1966)

STUART, JUSTICE. . . .

[T]he custody dispute before us in this habeas corpus action is between the father, Harold Painter, and the maternal grandparents, Dwight and Margaret Bannister. Mark's mother [Jeanne] and younger sister were killed in an automobile accident on December 6, 1962, near Pullman, Washington. The father, after other arrangements for Mark's care had proved unsatisfactory, asked the Bannisters to take care of Mark. . . . Mr. Painter remarried in November 1964 and about that time indicated he wanted to take Mark back. The Bannisters refused to let him leave and this action was filed in June 1965. Since July 1965 he has continued to remain in the Bannister home under an order of this court staying execution of the judgment of the trial court awarding custody to the father until the matter could be determined on appeal. . . .

Mark's parents came from highly contrasting backgrounds. His mother was born, reared and educated in rural Iowa. Her parents are college graduates. . . . The Bannister home is in the Gilbert community and is well kept, roomy and comfortable. The Bannisters are highly respected members of the community. Mr. Bannister has served on the school board and regularly teaches a Sunday school class at the Gilbert Congregational Church. Mark's mother graduated from Grinnell College. She then went to work for a newspaper in Anchorage, Alaska, where she met Harold Painter.

Mark's father was born in California. When he was two and one-half years old, his parents were divorced and he was placed in a foster home. . . . He flunked out of a high school and a trade school because of a lack of interest in academic subjects, rather than any lack of ability. He joined the navy at 17. He did not like it. After receiving an honorable discharge, he took examinations and obtained his high school diploma. He lived with the McNellys and went to college for two and one-half years under the G.I. bill. He quit college to take a job on a small newspaper in Ephrata, Washington, in November 1955. In May 1956 he went to work for the newspaper in Anchorage which employed Jeanne Bannister. . . .

We are not confronted with a situation where one of the contesting parties is not a fit or proper person. There is no criticism of either the Bannisters or their home. There is no suggestion in the record that Mr. Painter is morally unfit. It is obvious the Bannisters did not approve of their daughter's marriage to Harold Painter and do not want their grandchild reared under his guidance. The philosophies of life are entirely different. . . .

The Bannister home provides Mark with a stable, dependable, conventional, middle-class, middlewest background and an opportunity for a college education and profession, if he desires it. It provides a solid foundation and secure atmosphere. In the Painter home, Mark would have more freedom of conduct and thought with an opportunity to develop his individual talents. It would be more exciting and challenging in many respects, but romantic, impractical and unstable. . . .

Our conclusion as to the type of home Mr. Painter would offer is based upon his Bohemian approach to finances and life in general. . . . His main ambition is to be a free-lance writer and photographer. He has had some articles and picture stories published, but the income from these efforts has been negligible. At the time of the accident, Jeanne was willingly working to support the family so Harold could devote more time to his writing and photography. In the ten years since he left college, he has changed jobs seven times. . . .

The psychiatrist classifies him as "a romantic and somewhat of a dreamer." An apt example are the plans he related for himself and Mark in February 1963: "My thought now is to settle Mark and myself in Sausilito, near San Francisco; this is a retreat for wealthy artists, writers, and such aspiring artists and writers as can fork up the rent money. . . ."

The house in which Mr. Painter and his present wife live, compared with the well kept Bannister home, exemplifies the contrasting ways of life. In his words "it is a very old and beat-up and lovely home. . . ." They live in the rear part. The interior is inexpensively but tastefully decorated. The large yard on a hill in the business district of Walnut Creek, California, is of uncut weeds and wild oats. The house "is not painted on the outside because I do not want it painted. I am very fond of the wood on the outside of the house."

The present Mrs. Painter has her master's degree in cinema design and apparently likes and has had considerable contact with children. She is anxious to have Mark in her home. Everything indicates she would provide a leveling influence on Mr. Painter and could ably care for Mark.

Mr. Painter is either an agnostic or atheist and has no concern for formal religious training. . . .

He is a political liberal and got into difficulty in a job at the University of Washington for his support of the activities of the American Civil Liberties Union in the university news bulletin. . . .

These matters are not related as a criticism of Mr. Painter's conduct, way of life or sense of values. . . . They do serve however to support our conclusion as to the kind of life Mark would be exposed to in the Painter household. We believe it would be unstable, unconventional, arty, Bohemian and probably intellectually stimulating.

key F

Were the question simply which household would be the most suitable in which to rear a child, we would have unhesitatingly chosen the Bannister home. We believe security and stability in the home are more important than intellectual stimulation in the proper development of a child. There are, however, several factors which have made us pause.

First, there is the presumption of parental preference, which, though weakened in the past several years, exists by statute. . . . A father should be encouraged to look for help with the children, from those who love them without the risk of thereby losing the custody of the children permanently. This fact must receive consideration in cases of this kind. However, as always, the primary consideration is the best interest of the child and if the return of custody to the father is likely to have a seriously disrupting and disturbing effect upon the child's development, this fact must prevail.

rea for the rule

Second, Jeanne's will named her husband guardian of her children and, if he failed to qualify or ceased to act, named her mother. The parent's wishes are entitled to consideration.

Third, the Bannisters are 60 years old. By the time Mark graduates from high school they will be over 70 years old. . . .

We have considered all of these factors and have concluded that Mark's best interest demands that his custody remain with the Bannisters. Mark was five when he came to their home. The evidence clearly shows he was not well adjusted at that time. . . . He was very aggressive toward smaller children, cruel to animals, not liked by his classmates and did not seem to know what was acceptable conduct. . . . In two years he made a great deal of improvement. He now appears to be well disciplined, happy, relatively secure and popular with his classmates, although still subject to more than normal anxiety.

We place a great deal of reliance on the testimony of Dr. Glenn R. Hawks, a child psychologist. . . .

Doctor Hawks concluded that it was not for Mark's best interest to be removed from the Bannister home. He is criticized for reaching this conclusion without investigating the Painter home or finding out more about Mr. Painter's character. He answered:

> "I was most concerned about the welfare of the child, not the welfare of Mr. Painter, not about the welfare of the Bannisters. In as much as Mark has already made an adjustment and sees the Bannisters as his parental figures in his psychological makeup, to me this is the most critical factor. . . ."

Doctor Hawks stated: "I am appalled at the tremendous task Mr. Painter would have if Mark were to return to him because he has got to build the relationship from scratch. . . . Mark is aware Mr. Painter is his father, but he is not very clear about what this means. In his own mind the father figure is Mr. Bannister." . . .

Mark has established a father-son relationship with Mr. Bannister, which he apparently had never had with his natural father. He is happy, well adjusted and progressing nicely in his development. We do not believe it is for Mark's best interest to take him out of this stable atmosphere in the face of warnings of dire consequences from an eminent child psychologist and send him to an uncertain future in his father's home. Regardless of our appreciation of the father's love for his child and his desire to have him with him, we do not believe we have the moral right to gamble with this child's future. He should be encouraged in every way possible to know his father. We are sure there are many ways in which Mr. Painter can enrich Mark's life.

For the reasons stated, we reverse the trial court and remand the case for judgment in accordance herewith. . . .

NOTES AND QUESTIONS

1. *Expert Testimony.* One factor in the court's decision-making was the expert testimony of Dr. Hawks, a professor in the Department of Child Development at Iowa State University. Was it appropriate for the court to defer to, or at least accord great weight to, the testimony of such an expert? Is there any reason to discount the testimony of this particular expert? Are judges qualified to determine which placement will maximize the child's well-being without input from experts?

2. *The Best Interests Factors.* What factors should and should not be considered in the best interests calculus? The court did not treat the grandparents' age as disqualifying. Should it have? And did the fact that the grandparents were college educated and more financially stable than Mr. Painter weigh in their favor? Was it appropriate to consider the parties' differing "philosophies of life"?

3. *The UMDA's Approach.* The Uniform Marriage and Divorce Act (UMDA) includes a provision on Best Interest of the Child. Section 402 instructs a court to "consider all relevant factors," including:

(1) The wishes of the child's parent or parents as to his custody;
(2) The wishes of the child as to his custodian;
(3) The interaction and interrelationship of the child with his parent or parents, his siblings, and any other person who may significantly affect the child's best interest;
(4) The child's adjustment to his home, school, and community; and
(5) The mental and physical health of all individuals involved.[22]

Many state laws reflect the UMDA's approach, but with important modifications.

4. *Parental Presumptions?* In Chapter 6, we saw that biological or legal parents enjoy a presumption of custody that non-parents, like grandparents, can overcome only with a particularly strong showing. Today, as a constitutional matter, a custody

---

22. Unif. Marriage and Divorce Act § 402, 9A U.L.A. 249 (1998) [hereinafter UMDA].

conflict between a parent and non-parent cannot turn merely on best interests. In *Painter*, the Bannisters were considered non-parents. Would they prevail in a similar contest today? Could they be treated as de facto parents? Should they be recognized as legal parents?

C. Primary Caretaker

While most states shifted directly from the tender years presumption to a best interests standard, an alternative approach featured a presumption in favor of the primary caretaker, as the following case highlights. How does this presumption relate to the best interests of the child analysis?

Garska v. McCoy

278 S.E.2d 357 (W. Va. 1981)

Neely, Justice:

The appellant, Gwendolyn McCoy, appeals from an order of the Circuit Court of Logan County which gave the custody of her son, Jonathan Conway McCoy, to the appellee, Michael Garska, the natural father. . . .

In February, 1978 the appellant moved from her grandparents' house in Logan County, where she had been raised, to Charlotte, North Carolina to live with her mother. At that time appellant was 15 years old and her mother shared a trailer with appellee, Michael Garska. In March, Gwendolyn McCoy became pregnant by Michael Garska and in June, she returned to her grandparents' home in West Virginia.

The appellant received no support from the appellee during her pregnancy, but after she gave birth to baby Jonathan the appellee sent a package of baby food and diapers. In subsequent months the baby developed a chronic respiratory infection which required hospitalization and considerable medical attention. . . .

In October, 1979 Gwendolyn McCoy signed a consent in which she agreed to the adoption of Jonathan by her grandparents, the Altizers. Upon learning of the adoption plan, the appellee visited the baby for the first time and began sending weekly money orders for $15. The Altizers filed a petition for adoption in the Logan County Circuit Court on 9 November 1979 and on 7 January 1980 the appellee filed a petition for a writ of habeas corpus to secure custody of his son. . . .

The circuit court awarded custody of Jonathan McCoy to the appellee based upon the following findings of fact:

(a) The petitioner, Michael Garska, is the natural father of the infant child, Jonathan Conway McCoy;

(b) The petitioner, Michael Garska, is better educated than the natural mother and her alleged fiance;

(c) The petitioner, Michael Garska, is more intelligent than the natural mother;

(d) The petitioner, Michael Garska, is better able to provide financial support and maintenance than the natural mother;

(e) The petitioner, Michael Garska, can provide a better social and economic environment than the natural mother;

(f) The petitioner, Michael Garska, has a somewhat better command of the English language than the natural mother;

(g) The petitioner, Michael Garska, has a better appearance and demeanor than the natural mother;

(h) The petitioner, Michael Garska, is very highly motivated in his desire to have custody of the infant child, and the natural mother had previously executed an adoption consent, for said child. . . .

While the issue of adoption by the Altizers does, indeed, enter into this case, in the final analysis the entire dispute comes down to a custody fight between the natural father and the natural mother. . . . The final order was entered after the operative date of the 1980 Amendment to W. Va. Code, 48-2-15, the relevant part of which provides:

> In making any such order respecting custody of minor children, there shall be no legal presumption that, as between the natural parents, either the father or the mother should be awarded custody of said children, but the court shall make an award of custody solely for the best interest of the children based upon the merits of each case. . . .

This Amendment was enacted in response to *J.B. v. A.B.*, 242 S.E.2d 248 (W. Va. 1978), where we said:

> In a divorce proceeding where custody of a child of tender years is sought by both the mother and father, the Court must determine in the first instance whether the mother is a fit parent, and where the mother achieves the minimum, objective standard of behavior which qualifies her as a fit parent, the trial court must award the child to the mother.

In the case before us the father, by providing fifteen dollars a week child support, probably showed sufficient parental interest to give him standing to object to an adoption. However, there is no evidence before us to indicate that the mother was an unfit parent and, consequently, no justification for the trial court to remove custody from the primary caretaker parent and vest it in a parent who had had no previous emotional interaction with the child.

I

It is now time to address explicitly the effect which the strong presumption in favor of the primary caretaker parent articulated in *J.B. v. A.B.* has upon the equity of divorce and child custody dispositions. . . .

primary
caretaker
genderless

The loss of children is a terrifying specter to concerned and loving parents; however, it is particularly terrifying to the primary caretaker parent who, by virtue of the caretaking function, was closest to the child before the divorce or other proceedings were initiated. While the primary caretaker parent in most cases in West Virginia is still the mother, nonetheless, now that sex roles are becoming more flexible and high-income jobs are opening to women, it is conceivable that the primary caretaker parent may also be the father. . . .

Our experience instructs us that uncertainty about the outcome of custody disputes leads to the irresistible temptation to trade the custody of the child in return for lower alimony and child support payments. . . . While Code, 48-2-15 (1980) speaks in terms of "the best interest of the children" in every case, the one enormously important function of legal rules is to inspire rational and equitable settlements in cases which never reach adversary status in court. . . .

J.B. v. A.B. attempted to remove from most run-of-the-mine divorce cases the entire issue of child custody. . . . While in *J.B. v. A.B.* we expressed ourselves in terms of the traditional maternal preference, . . . we are convinced that the best interests of the children are best served in awarding them to the primary caretaker parent, regardless of sex. . . .

The 1980 Amendment to Code, 48-2-15 was not intended to disturb our determination that in most instances the issue of child custody between two competent parents cannot be litigated effectively. Its intent was merely to correct the inherent unfairness of establishing a gender-based, maternal presumption which would defeat the just claims of a father if he had, in fact, been the primary caretaker parent.

II

In setting the child custody law in domestic relations cases we are concerned with three practical considerations. First, we are concerned to prevent the issue of custody from being used in an abusive way as a coercive weapon to affect the level of support payments and the outcome of other issues in the underlying divorce proceeding. . . . Second, in the average divorce proceeding intelligent determination of relative degrees of fitness requires a precision of measurement which is not possible given the tools available to judges. . . . Third, there is an urgent need in contemporary divorce law for a legal structure upon which a divorcing couple may rely in reaching a settlement.

While recent statutory changes encourage private ordering of divorce upon the "no-fault" ground of "irreconcilable differences," . . . our legal structure has not simultaneously been tightened to provide a reliable framework within which the divorcing couple can bargain intelligently. . . .

This phenomenon may be denominated the "Solomon syndrome", that is that the parent who is most attached to the child will be most willing to accept an inferior bargain. . . . Moreover, it is likely that the primary caretaker will have less financial security than the nonprimary caretaker and, consequently, will be unable to sustain the expense of custody litigation. . . .

Therefore, in the interest of removing the issue of child custody from the type of acrimonious and counter-productive litigation which a procedure inviting exhaustive evidence will inevitably create, we hold today that there is a presumption in favor of the primary caretaker parent, if he or she meets the minimum, objective standard for being a fit parent . . . regardless of sex. . . .

In establishing which natural or adoptive parent is the primary caretaker, the trial court shall determine which parent has taken primary responsibility for, *inter alia*, the performance of the following caring and nurturing duties of a parent: (1) preparing and planning of meals; (2) bathing, grooming and dressing; (3) purchasing, cleaning, and care of clothes; (4) medical care, including nursing and trips to physicians; (5) arranging for social interaction among peers after school, i.e. transporting to friends' houses or, for example, to girl or boy scout meetings; (6) arranging alternative care, i.e. babysitting, day-care, etc.; (7) putting child to bed at night, attending to child in the middle of the night, waking child in the morning; (8) disciplining, i.e. teaching general manners and toilet training; (9) educating, i.e. religious, cultural, social, etc.; and, (10) teaching elementary skills, i.e., reading, writing and arithmetic.

In those custody disputes where the facts demonstrate that child care and custody were shared in an entirely equal way, then indeed no presumption arises and the court must proceed to inquire further into relative degrees of parental competence. . . .

[W]e should point out that the absolute presumption in favor of a fit primary caretaker parent applies only to children of tender years. Where a child is old enough to formulate an opinion about his or her own custody the trial court is entitled to receive such opinion and accord it such weight as he feels appropriate. . . .

III

In the case before us it is obvious that the petitioner was the primary caretaker parent . . . , and there is no finding on the part of the trial court judge that she is an unfit parent. In fact, all of the evidence indicates that she mobilized all of the resources at her command, namely the solicitous regard of her grandparents, in the interest of this child and that she went to extraordinary lengths to provide for him adequate medical attention and financial support. While, as the trial court found, the educational and economic position of the father is superior to that of the mother, nonetheless, those factors alone pale in comparison to love, affection, concern, tolerance, and the willingness to sacrifice — factors about which conclusions can be made for the future most intelligently upon a course of conduct in the past. . . .

NOTES AND QUESTIONS

---

1. *Gender Neutrality?* Did the court adopt the primary caretaker standard as a substitute for the prohibited tender years approach and its maternal preference? If so, should the primary caretaker presumption be any more permissible than a tender years maternal presumption?

2. *Primary Caretaker and Best Interests.* The court awarded custody to the mother, who was the primary caretaker. If the court had applied a best interests standard without a presumption, to which parent should it have awarded custody? Why? Would the best interests calculus lead to the same outcome as the primary caretaker presumption?

The primary caretaker standard is based on two ideas — that the parent who currently provides care is more competent to do so in the future and that children benefit from continuing to be cared for by the same person as in the past. For a brief time, West Virginia as well as Minnesota presumed that the primary caretaker should receive custody. Eventually, though, this approach was superseded legislatively by a best interests approach that makes past caretaking merely one factor.[23] While the primary caretaker presumption did not catch on outright, many state statutes consider past caretaking in the best interests analysis.[24] What are the benefits and drawbacks of a primary caretaker presumption?[25] Does it make more sense to rely on a presumption or to factor caretaking into a broader analysis?

D. Past Allocation of Care

YOUNG V. HECTOR
740 So. 2d 1153 (Fla. Dist. Ct. App. 1999)

GREEN, J.

[T]he simple issue for our consideration is whether the trial court abused its discretion when it determined that the best interests of the two minor children dictated that their mother be designated their primary custodial parent. . . . [B]oth the mother and father are very loving and capable parents. . . . What then tilted the

---

23. Garska v. McCoy, 278 S.E.2d 357, 363 (W. Va. 1981), superseded by statute, W. Va. Code § 48-9-206(a) (2020); Pikula v. Pikula, 374 N.W.2d 705, 712 (Minn. 1985), superseded by statute, Minn. Stat. § 518.17(1)(a)(3) (2020).

24. See, e.g., Iowa Code § 598.41(3)(d) (2020) ("Whether both parents have actively cared for the child before and since the separation.").

25. See, e.g., Katharine T. Bartlett, Prioritizing Past Caretaking in Child-Custody Decisionmaking, 77 Law & Contemp. Probs. 29, 42 (2014) (discussing predictability).

scales in favor of awarding custody to the mother? The father suggests that it was gender bias. The record evidence, however, simply does not support this suggestion.

I

At the time of their marriage in 1982, both the father and mother were successful professionals in New Mexico. He was an architectural designer with his own home design firm as well as an entrepreneur with a publishing company. She was an attorney in private practice at her own firm. Their marriage was a second for both. He had no children from his first marriage. She had custody of her two minor children (now grown) from her first marriage which she successfully reared while simultaneously juggling the demands of her law practice.

Hector and Young became the parents of two daughters born in 1985 and 1988. After the birth of their children, both parents continued to work outside of the home and pursued their respective professional endeavors with the assistance of a live-in nanny. . . . Both contributed to and shared in the household expenditures at all times.

Sometime in late 1987, the father's business ventures began to suffer certain financial reversals and the mother became bored with her practice in New Mexico. Both parties agreed to relocate to Miami. . . .

In June 1989, the mother and her two minor daughters arrived in Miami first. During that summer, she studied for and took the Florida Bar exam and landed a position with a mid-sized law firm. The father stayed behind in New Mexico until October 1989 in order to complete the construction of a new house and to remodel the couple's New Mexico home in order to enhance its resale potential.

After the father's move to Miami in the fall of 1989, he studied for and passed the Florida contractor's examination. Thereafter, during the spring and summer of 1990, the father spent his time repairing the couple's first marital residence in Miami. Thereafter, he renovated the home which ultimately became the couple's second marital residence. . . . [F]rom the time the minor children were brought to Miami in 1989 until the fall of 1993, the needs of the minor children were attended to by a live-in housekeeper when they were not in school during the day and by the mother upon her arrival from work in the evenings. . . .

Although the mother was earning a very decent income as an attorney at the time, it was undisputed that this family was operating with a negative cash flow.

Rather than pursue gainful employment to financially assist the household and his minor children, the father turned his attentions elsewhere. During the remainder of 1990 through 1993, the father left the state and was frequently away from the mother and minor children for months at a time. . . . The father saw his family during this fourteen month period once every five weeks and according to the mother, only at her insistence and pursuant to her arrangements for such family reunions.

When the father finally returned to South Florida, in the fall of 1993, the mother had accepted a partnership position with a large Florida law firm at a salary of approximately $300,000 annually. Even with the mother's salary increase, the family remained steep in debt. . . . The mother engaged in activities with the children on a full-time basis on the weekends. When the children became ill or distressed during the middle of the night, the mother was always the parent they looked to for assistance or solace.

Approximately one month after the father's return to the household in 1993, the mother asked the father for a divorce because of his continued refusal to seek gainful employment and due to his extramarital affair in New Mexico. It must be re-emphasized that at no time did the mother and father have any mutually expressed or tacit agreement for the father to remain unemployed. . . .

Once the mother announced to the father that she wanted a divorce, the father began to spend less of his time away from Miami. Although he steadfastly refused to make any efforts to obtain employment, he did become more involved in the activities of his two daughters, who by that time, were 8 and 5. . . . Upon the mother's arrival at the home, the father generally absented himself.

The father nevertheless maintained that he was the "primary caretaker" or "Mr. Mom" of these two children in the three years preceding this dissolution proceeding. The trial court viewed this contention with some degree of skepticism as it was entitled. The trial court's skepticism or disbelief was not at all unreasonable, given the father's admission that the nanny, Hattie, had taken care of these children in large part during the afternoon hours until their mother's arrival at home. . . .

Given the undisputed large financial indebtedness of this couple, the trial court's inquiry about the need to employ a full-time nanny was both logical and practical under these circumstances and certainly could have also been appropriately posed to the mother if she had been recalcitrant about seeking gainful employment to assist the family's financial situation. . . .

[T]he court also had the report and recommendations of the guardian ad litem upon which to rely. In recommending that the mother be named the primary custodial parent, the guardian ad litem cited three factors. . . . First of all, . . . the mother had been the more economically stable of the two parents throughout the marriage. . . . Given the father's skills and experience, the trial court was certainly entitled to reasonably conclude that the father was employable upon his return to Miami in 1993 — one year after Hurricane Andrew literally destroyed thousands of residences and commercial establishments in South Dade County and building contractors were in heavy demand. Given a choice between the mother, who maintained constant steady employment throughout the marriage to support the children (regardless of the amount of her income), and the father who unilaterally and steadfastly refused to do the same, the trial court's designation of the mother as custodial parent cannot be deemed an abuse of discretion.

The second factor . . . was the fact that the mother had been a constant factor and dominant influence in the children's lives and the father had not. . . . [T]he trial court, in an effort to maintain continuity, could have legitimately determined that the children's best interests dictate that they remain with the parent who had continuously been there to care for their needs throughout their young lives rather than the parent who had devoted a substantial amount of time with them perhaps only when it was convenient and/or opportunistic to do so. . . . The record evidence clearly supports the trial court's conclusion that the mother had been the constant parent throughout the children's lives. . . .

The last factor cited by the guardian ad litem . . . was the mother's superior ability to control her anger around the children. The guardian ad litem testified that he personally witnessed one of the father's outbursts of anger in the presence of the children. . . .

Custody determinations are perhaps the most sensitive and delicate decisions that family court judges make. We recognize that at times, it can be a very difficult and agonizing call for the trial judge to make when both parents are as loving and caring as the mother and father are in this case. Nevertheless, once the trial court makes this decision and the decision is supported by substantial competent evidence, we recognize that the trial court's determination should not be lightly second-guessed and overturned by an appellate court merely reviewing the cold-naked record. . . . As long as the trial court's decision is supported by substantial competent evidence and is not based upon legally impermissible factors such as gender bias, it must be affirmed on appeal. For this reason, we affirm the order awarding primary residential custody of the minor children to the mother. However, on remand, the trial court should grant the father liberal and frequent access to the children. . . .

SCHWARTZ, CHIEF JUDGE (dissenting).

[T]he children's parents, who know and care most about their welfare, had themselves established an arrangement prior to the dissolution as a part of which, upon any fair assessment, the father was the primary caretaker. As everyone agrees, under that regime, if not because of it, their girls have turned out to be well-behaved, well-adjusted, and accomplished young women who love both their parents: just what we all devoutly wish for and from our children. There is simply no reason for a court to tamper with what has worked so well. This is not only because it is almost always better to preserve a known good rather than to risk what the unknown future may bring, but, much more important, because the children are themselves entitled to stability in their lives and routine which would be compromised by any purposeless change in their caregiver. . . .

In my opinion, there is no question whatever that the result below was dictated by the gender of the competing parties. . . .

GODERICH, J. (dissenting):

It is apparent that the trial court abused its discretion by awarding primary residential custody of the minor children to the parent who has been working long hours as a senior litigation partner in one of Miami's top law firms as opposed to the parent who has not worked outside of the home for the three years preceding the filing of the dissolution action.

The majority opinion focuses on the fact that the parties did not mutually agree that the father would stay at home to care for the children. Although it may be true that the mother did not expressly agree, the record demonstrates that the mother nonetheless acquiesced to this arrangement by allowing it to continue for three years. . . . [T]here is no doubt that the mother benefited from this arrangement (and possibly that is why she allowed it to continue). As a result of this caretaking arrangement, the mother was free to dedicate herself to her legal career by working extremely long hours without having to worry about whether the minor children's emotional needs were being met. . . .

The majority opinion also suggests that the father should have obtained gainful employment in order to financially assist the household and minor children in light of the parties' financial condition. The record clearly demonstrates that with the husband's present skills, he did not have the ability to earn a substantial amount of money. . . .

The majority opinion also addresses the three "determinative factors" that the guardian ad litem looked at in recommending that the mother be named the primary residential parent. First, the guardian focused on the fact that the mother has been more economically stable throughout the marriage. Once again, if the roles were reversed, I believe that the guardian ad litem would not have considered economical stability as a "determinative factor." . . .

The second "determinative factor" was that the mother has been "the more constant factor throughout the entire relationship." The guardian ad litem focused on the fact that the father had been "away from the home for substantial periods of time." . . . [T]he reasons for the father's absence from the home were valid. Further, the fact that the father had been away from the family should not be a "determinative factor" when taking into consideration that the father has been the primary caretaker since the fall of 1993.

Finally, the third determinative factor was that the mother "controls her anger better around the kids." . . . However, the father's anger was based on the "financial inequities of the situation". . . .

NOTES AND QUESTIONS

---

1. *Past Division of Care and Time.* What benefits come from relying on a past division of care to determine future care? Why did the court focus on the course of the relationship as the relevant time frame? Why not look at the division of caretaking labor at the time of separation?

2. *Gender Bias.* Would the court have reasoned the same way if the roles had been reversed? What aspects of the court's reasoning would the father point to as evidence of gender bias?

3. *The ALI's "Approximation" Approach.* Under the "approximation" approach taken by the American Law Institute's Principles of the Law of Family Dissolution, custodial time should be based on each parent's caretaking time. Section 2.08, Allocation of Custodial Responsibility, provides:

> Unless otherwise resolved by agreement of the parents . . ., the court should allocate custodial responsibility so that the proportion of custodial time the child spends with each parent approximates the proportion of time each parent spent performing caretaking functions for the child prior to the parents' separation or, if the parents never lived together, before the filing of the action. . . .[26]

Exceptions can be made for various reasons, such as keeping siblings together or accommodating the child's wishes.[27]

II. Joint Custody

As we have seen, the law has developed in ways that recognize the rights of parents more equally and also accord primacy to the best interests of children, the lodestar of child custody decision-making. More recently, the idea of joint custody has gained traction both as a recognition of equal parental status and a mechanism for serving children's best interests.[28] As the name implies, joint custody avoids the need to choose one or the other parent, and instead continues to view both parents as full, active, and engaged parents for their child.

---

26. Principles of the Law of Family Dissolution: Analysis and Recommendations § 2.08(1) (Am. Law Inst. 2002).

27. Id.

28. See, e.g., Artis & Krebs, supra note 14, at 725–26; Linda D. Elrod & Robert G. Spector, A Review of the Year in Family Law: Numbers of Disputes Increase, 45 Fam. L.Q. 443, 468 (2012).

Rivero v. Rivero
216 P.3d 213 (Nev. 2009)

By the Court, Gibbons, J. . . .

Ms. Rivero and Mr. Rivero stipulated to a divorce decree that provided for "joint physical custody" of their minor child, with Ms. Rivero having the child five days each week and Mr. Rivero having the child two days each week. The decree awarded no child support. . . . Ms. Rivero brought a motion to modify child custody and support. The district court . . . ordered the parties to mediation to devise a timeshare plan. . . .

[T]he parties were unable to reach a timeshare agreement. . . .

[T]he court found that the [divorce] decree's order for joint physical custody was inconsistent with the decree's timeshare arrangement because the decree's five-day, two-day timeshare did not constitute joint physical custody. In its order, the district court concluded that the parties intended joint physical custody and ordered an equal timeshare. . . .

The term "custody" is often used as a single legal concept, creating ambiguity. To emphasize the distinctions between these two types of custody and to provide clarity, we separately define legal custody, including joint and sole legal custody, and then we define physical custody, including joint physical and primary physical custody.

I. Legal custody

Legal custody involves having basic legal responsibility for a child and making major decisions regarding the child, including the child's health, education, and religious upbringing. Sole legal custody vests this right with one parent, while joint legal custody vests this right with both parents. Joint legal custody requires that the parents be able to cooperate, communicate, and compromise to act in the best interest of the child. In a joint legal custody situation, the parents must consult with each other to make major decisions regarding the child's upbringing, while the parent with whom the child is residing at that time usually makes minor day-to-day decisions.

Joint legal custody can exist regardless of the physical custody arrangements of the parties. Also, the parents need not have equal decision-making power in a joint legal custody situation. For example, one parent may have decisionmaking authority regarding certain areas or activities of the child's life, such as education or healthcare. If the parents in a joint legal custody situation reach an impasse and are unable to agree on a decision, then the parties may appear before the court "on an equal footing" to have the court decide what is in the best interest of the child.

II. Physical custody

Physical custody involves the time that a child physically spends in the care of a parent. During this time, the child resides with the parent and that parent provides supervision for the child and makes the day-to-day decisions regarding the child. Parents can share joint physical custody, or one parent may have primary physical custody while the other parent may have visitation rights.

The type of physical custody arrangement is particularly important in three situations. First, it determines the standard for modifying physical custody. Second, it requires a specific procedure if a parent wants to move out of state with the child. Third, the type of physical custody arrangement affects the child support award. Because the physical custody arrangement is crucial in making these determinations, the district courts need clear custody definitions in order to evaluate the true nature of parties' agreements. Absent direction from the Legislature, we define joint physical custody and primary physical custody in light of existing Nevada law.

A. Joint physical custody . . .

Although Nevada law suggests that joint physical custody approximates an equal timeshare, to date, neither the Nevada Legislature nor this court have explicitly defined joint physical custody or specified whether a specific timeshare is required for a joint physical custody arrangement. . . .

1. Defining joint physical custody

"In determining custody of a minor child . . . the sole consideration of the court is the best interest of the child." The Legislature created a presumption that joint legal and joint physical custody are in the best interest of the child if the parents so agree. The policy of Nevada is to advance the child's best interest by ensuring that after divorce "minor children have frequent associations and a continuing relationship with both parents . . . and [t]o encourage such parents to share the rights and responsibilities of child rearing." To further this policy, the Legislature adopted the statutes that now comprise NRS Chapter 125 to educate and encourage parents regarding joint custody arrangements, encourage parents to cooperate and work out a custody arrangement before going to court to finalize the divorce, ensure the healthiest psychological arrangement for children, and minimize the adversarial, winner-take-all approach to custody disputes. . . .

Joint physical custody is "[a]warding custody of the minor child or children to BOTH PARENTS and providing that physical custody shall be shared by the parents in such a way to ensure the child or children of frequent associations and a continuing relationship with both parents." This does not include divided or alternating custody, where each parent acts as a sole custodial parent at different times, or split custody, where one parent is awarded sole custody of one or more of the children and the other parent is awarded sole custody of one or more of the children.

2. The timeshare required for joint physical custody . . .

Our law presumes that joint physical custody approximates a 50/50 timeshare. This court has noted that the public policy, as stated in NRS 125.490, is that joint custody is presumably in the best interest of the child if the parents agree to it and that this policy encourages *equally* shared parental responsibilities.

Although joint physical custody must approximate an equal timeshare, given the variations inherent in child rearing, such as school schedules, sports, vacations, and parents' work schedules, to name a few, an exactly equal timeshare is not always possible. Therefore, there must be some flexibility in the timeshare requirement. The question then becomes, when does a timeshare become so unequal that it is no longer joint physical custody? Courts have grappled with this question and come to different conclusions. For example, this court has described a situation where the children live with one parent and the other parent has every-other-weekend visitation as primary physical custody with visitation, even when primary custody was changed for one month out of the year. . . .

Similarly, the California Court of Appeal has held that "[physical] custody one day per week and alternate weekends constitutes liberal visitation, not joint [physical] custody." Likewise, when the mother has temporary custody and the father has visitation for a one-month period, the parties do not have joint physical custody. Rather, the father has a period of visitation, and the mother has sole physical custody thereafter. Just as Nevada has defined joint physical custody as requiring an equal timeshare, the California Court of Appeal noted that joint physical custody includes situations in which the children split their time living with each parent and spend nearly equal time with each parent. Some jurisdictions have adopted bright-line rules regarding the timeshare requirements for joint physical custody so that anything too far removed from a 50/50 timeshare cannot be considered joint physical custody.

We conclude that, consistent with legislative intent and our caselaw, in joint physical custody arrangements, the timeshare must be approximately 50/50. However, absent legislative direction regarding how far removed from 50/50 a timeshare may be and still constitute joint physical custody, the law remains unclear. Therefore, to approximate an equal timeshare but allow for necessary flexibility, we hold that each parent must have physical custody of the child at least 40 percent of the time to constitute joint physical custody. We acknowledge that the Legislature is free to alter the timeshare required for joint physical custody, but we adopt this guideline to provide needed clarity for the district courts. This guideline ensures frequent associations and a continuing relationship with both parents. If a parent does not have physical custody of the child at least 40 percent of the time, then the arrangement is one of primary physical custody with visitation. . . .

3. Calculating the timeshare

The district court should calculate the time during which a party has physical custody of a child over one calendar year. Each parent must have physical custody of the child at least 40 percent of the time, which is 146 days per year. Calculating the timeshare over a one-year period allows the court to consider weekly arrangements as well as any deviations from those arrangements such as emergencies, holidays, and summer vacation. In calculating the time during which a party has physical custody of the child, the district court should look at the number of days during which a party provided supervision of the child, the child resided with the party, and during which the party made the day-to-day decisions regarding the child. The district court should not focus on, for example, the exact number of hours the child was in the care of the parent, whether the child was sleeping, or whether the child was in the care of a third-party caregiver or spent time with a friend or relative during the period of time in question.

Therefore, absent evidence that joint physical custody is not in the best interest of the child, if each parent has physical custody of the child at least 40 percent of the time, then the arrangement is one of joint physical custody.

B. Defining primary physical custody . . .

A parent has primary physical custody when he or she has physical custody of the child subject to the district court's power to award the other parent visitation rights. The focus of primary physical custody is the child's residence. The party with primary physical custody is the party that has the primary responsibility for maintaining a home for the child and providing for the child's basic needs. . . .

III. Custody modification . . .

We conclude that the district court properly disregarded the parties' definition of joint physical custody because the district court must apply Nevada's physical custody definition — not the parties' definition. . . .

PICKERING, J., concurring in part and dissenting in part. . . .

I have a threshold concern with court-mandated formulas, in general, and with the 40-percent joint physical custody formula the majority adopts in this case, in particular, to determine child support and relocation disputes. A legislature has the capacity to debate social policy and to enact, amend, and repeal laws as experience and society dictate. Courts do not. The law courts apply is precedent-driven, or has its origin in statute or constitutional mandate. It is not only that judges tend to be innumerate, or that court-adopted formulas are of suspect provenance — though both are so — it is that laws adopted by judges are difficult to change if they do not work out. . . .

The point is not whether a formulaic approach is good policy, providing helpful bright-line rules; or bad policy, creating a hostile "on the clock" mentality inconsistent with truly cooperative joint parenting. On this, reasonable policymakers differ. . . . The point is that percentage time/support formulas are for the Legislature to evaluate, not for the court to establish by fiat. . . .

Joint physical custody may ideally signify something approaching a 50/50 time-share. However, I am concerned that our judicially mandated 40-percent formula will prove unsatisfactory, especially when used, as intended, to determine support and relocation disputes. Lives change and a child's time is divided, not just between his or her parents, but among friends, school or day care, extended family, sports, and other pursuits. Practical questions seem certain to scuff the bright-line rule — questions like how to count hours the child spends with people besides either parent, or which parent to credit for time the child spends pursuing activities both parents support. Of greater concern, making child support, relocation, and custody determinations depend on parents keeping logs of the number of hours each year a child spends with one parent or the other (leaving aside the calculation and credit questions) detracts from the type of true co-parenting our statutes try to promote. . . .

When parties have agreed to joint physical custody, absent a showing that some other arrangement is in the child's best interest, courts should try to make that agreement succeed. . . .

NOTES AND QUESTIONS

1.   *Joint Custody.* Traditionally, statutory law provided for the placement of a child with one parent or the other, but not both. More recently, though, states have authorized joint custody orders, with some even presuming joint custody to be in the child's best interest under certain circumstances. Now, every state at least grants judges the discretion to order joint custody.[29]

2.   *Physical Versus Legal Custody.* Physical custody refers to where children physically live or spend time. (This is also called residential custody or parenting time.) Legal custody refers to the authority to make decisions for a child, such as where a child would attend school. As *Rivero* makes clear, these two forms of custody need not be in the same form. For example, it is possible for parents to have joint legal custody but not joint physical custody.

3.   *Sole or Joint Custody?* As the facts of *Rivero* indicate, courts are not always clear whether a custody order should be characterized as joint or sole with visitation. Why did that distinction matter in *Rivero*?

4.   *Labels Versus Reality.* What should matter — how the parties define the arrangement or what the arrangement actually means in practice? Consider the Nebraska Supreme Court's approach: "In several cases, we have looked past the labels used by the trial court when describing the physical custody arrangement and have

---

29. For a review of statutes authorizing courts to order joint custody, see Charts, 2017: Family Law in the Fifty States, D.C., and Puerto Rico, 51 Fam. L.Q. 543, 548–55 (2018).

focused instead on the actual terms of the parenting plan adopted by the court."[30] Why would the court take this view?

5. *Joint Custody and Gender.* The rise of joint custody was fueled in part by the fathers' rights movement, which asserted that divorced men who were made to pay child support should have ongoing contact with their children.[31] Some research suggests that joint custody has gendered consequences for parents.[32] Though joint custody results in lower levels of parenting stress for mothers, these mothers report lower satisfaction with their custody arrangements than mothers with sole custody — apparently because they "perceive that their legal role is out of proportion to their caregiving responsibilities."[33] They also report less open communication with their children, in contrast to fathers, who enjoy greater contact and communication but also increased conflict in joint custody arrangements.[34]

BRUEGMAN V. BRUEGMAN

417 P.3d 157 (Wyo. 2018)

LAVERY, DISTRICT JUDGE. . . .

The parties were married July 26, 2008. . . . After the birth of their child in the spring of 2014, Mother stayed at home full-time. Father continued to work full-time. . . .

[T]he couple began experiencing marital difficulties and in September 2014 Mother moved to Torrington, Wyoming and filed for divorce in Goshen County. . . . The parties made efforts to reconcile the marriage and Mother later dismissed the first divorce action in February 2016.

A few months later, on May 27, 2016, Mother filed this case. By that time Father had moved to Wheatland, Wyoming and Mother had moved back to Cheyenne, Wyoming. . . . [T]he district court divorced the parties. . . .

---

30. Kaaden S. v. Jeffery T., 932 N.W.2d 692 (Neb. 2019).

31. For changing trends regarding joint custody and the impact of the fathers' rights movement, see Michael Alison Chandler, Shared-Parenting Bills May Reshape Custody Battles, Wash. Post, Dec. 12, 2017, at A1. For a history of the advocacy for joint custody, see generally Deborah Dinner, The Divorce Bargain: The Fathers' Rights Movement and Family Inequalities, 102 Va. L. Rev. 79 (2016).

32. See Anja Steinbach, Children's and Parents' Well-Being in Joint Physical Custody: A Literature Review, 58 Fam. Process 353, 363 (2019) ("The very few existing results regarding the consequences of joint physical custody for parents suggested different costs and rewards for mothers and fathers.").

33. Marjorie L. Gunnou & Sanford L. Braver, The Effects of Joint Legal Custody on Mothers, Fathers, and Children, Controlling for Factors That Predispose a Sole Maternal versus Joint Legal Award, 25 Law & Hum. Behav. 25, 38 (2001). This may be exacerbated by the fact that joint custody fathers are no more likely than noncustodial fathers to comply with child support orders. See, e.g., Judith Seltzer, Fathers by Law: Effects of Joint Legal Custody on Nonresident Father's Involvement with Children, 35 Demography 135 (1998).

34. An Katrien Sodermans et al., Involved Fathers, Liberated Mothers? Joint Physical Custody and the Subjective Well-being of Divorced Parents, 122 Soc. Indicators Res. 257, 270–71 (2015).

The district court viewed this case as close, with two fit, competent parents willing to accept the responsibilities of parenting. Both parents supported the child's best interests by taking advantage of opportunities to spend time with the child and encouraging the child's relationship with the other parent. The district court found the child had a good relationship with both parents but a very close, special bond with Father, who was probably the child's primary caretaker, with Father taking the child with him while he works around the ranch. . . .

A substantial portion of the evidence was devoted to the level of conflict in the parties' relationship, and the district court carefully weighed this. . . .

At trial, Mother introduced three video recordings she took of fights between her and Father. Father testified he was set up, intentionally angered so that Mother could record his outburst. . . . The court specifically found no evidence of spousal abuse nor evidence that Father lost his temper with his son or any sort of child abuse occurred.

The district court also considered the child's special needs a relevant factor, concluding this factor did not weigh against allowing shared custody for the child because the federally subsidized non-profit centers serving preschool-aged children with special needs in Cheyenne and Wheatland jointly evaluated the child and developed an individualized education program (IEP) for him. Though it might be challenging, both centers are required to follow the IEP and he would receive the same instruction if he were to switch between centers.

The district court ultimately concluded it was in the minor child's best interests to continue to see each parent as much as possible, ordering shared custody with exchanges every two weeks. The court viewed this as the best way to maintain the close relationship with each parent. . . . Mother filed a timely notice of appeal. . . .

I. Shared Custody Standard of Review

Mother claims the district court abused its discretion in ordering shared custody in violation of this Court's clear rule that shared custody arrangements are disfavored. . . .

The thrust of Mother's argument is that the district court never really articulated its reasoning for imposing a joint custody arrangement other than to ensure that both parents have equal time with the child. We have called this "a laudable goal" that "falls well short of the 'good reasons' needed to justify" a disfavored form of custody and said the fact that both parents are good parents is "true in many, if not most, divorces" but is "not sufficient to support a custody arrangement that this Court has noted is not favored and carries the potential for disrupting the child's life." . . .

Many states that formerly recognized a presumption against shared custody have, through legislation or court decision, rejected it. As explained in a thoughtful opinion from the Supreme Court of Iowa:

> [I]n light of the changing nature of the structure of families and challenges to the sweeping application of psychological parent attachment theory, we believe the joint physical care issue must be examined in each case on the unique facts and not subject to cursory rejection based on a nearly irrebuttable presumption found in our prior cases. . . . Any consideration of joint physical care, however, must still be based on Iowa's traditional and statutorily required child custody standard — the best interest of the child. Physical care issues are not to be resolved based upon perceived fairness to the *spouses*, but primarily upon what is best for the *child*. The objective of a physical care determination is to place the children in the environment most likely to bring them to health, both physically and mentally, and to social maturity. . . .

In Wyoming, the fundamental consideration in determining child custody should be "the best interests of the children." We hold there is no presumption that shared custody is contrary to the best interests of the children and shared custody should be considered on an equal footing with other forms of custody.

II. The District Court's Shared Custody Determination

Overall, Mother contends shared custody will not promote stability in the child's life and the parties are unable to communicate or agree on major issues affecting the child well enough to facilitate a shared custody arrangement.

The Child's Developmental Needs

More specifically, Mother argues stability was a major factor to be considered due to their child's developmental delays. . . .

Mother emphasizes the special education coordinator's testimony that receiving specialized instruction is critical to this child being successful as well as her testimony that, in general, young children grow by having a consistent program and fluctuation in schedules is a challenge for young children. Mother's argument that the district court did not address the potential difficulties the child may experience splitting time between two different learning facilities is not correct. . . . The district court undoubtedly considered this evidence as a factor, specifically finding shared custody is appropriate because the child can get the same preschool curriculum regardless of which town he is in at a given time. . . .

Under our abuse of discretion standard of review, we cannot say the district court was required to view stability in the child's schedule or routine as more important to the child's best interests than ensuring he sees each parent as much as possible. . . .

Ability of the Parties to Communicate . . .

Mother testified that she and Father had difficulties communicating due to Father's temper. . . .

While there is no question that the parties fought, the videos predate the temporary custody hearing. . . . [W]e have recognized it is not an abuse of discretion to decline to base a custody decision on past bad behavior no longer occurring. The district court did not abuse its discretion when it declined to base its custody decision on evidence of strife at the end of the marriage. . . .

Mother finally argues the district court failed to address the parties' inability to communicate well enough to make joint decisions regarding the child. . . . Mother cites Father's testimony that the parties do not often make joint decisions regarding the child — specifically, that he does not get to be involved in making many decisions. He testified "I don't necessarily argue with her decisions, but my decisions aren't welcome very often, so . . . I didn't get to decide where he was going to have his birthday party. She did that. . . ." Father went on to testify that Mother chose . . . babysitting providers in Cheyenne without his involvement. Father also testified this was not a problem. "I don't get to make very many decisions. I'm not saying my wife makes bad decisions. I'm not saying she makes decisions counterproductive to my son's development. It's just — I don't get to make decisions. It's up to my wife."

Mother fails to explain why the district court should have considered this problematic when Father apparently did not. . . . Mother does not point to any instance where the parties were unable to resolve a decision concerning the child's welfare or the types of services he should be provided.

Overall, the record is replete with instances of the parties' cooperating and sharing time with the child, including sharing his birthday, caring for him in lieu of a babysitter, spending time with him at each other's homes during each other's custodial weeks, communicating with each other about him frequently, and allowing the other party to take the child to family events. . . .

Under our abuse of discretion standard of review, we cannot say the district court was required to find the difficulties the parties had with communication at times outweighed the child's interest in ensuring he sees each parent as much as possible. . . .

[T]he record and the trial court's findings fully sustain the overall conclusion that the shared custody plan is in the child's best interests.

NOTES AND QUESTIONS

1. *Approaches to Joint Custody.* In a small number of states, joint custody is permissible but not generally considered to be in the child's best interest.[35] In contrast, many states maintain a statutory presumption in favor of joint custody.[36] In

---

35. See, e.g., Peek v. Berning, 622 N.W.2d 186 (N.D. 2001).
36. See, e.g., Wis. Stat. § 767.41(2) (2020).

some states, there is a presumption that joint custody is in the best interest of a child only when the parents agree to joint custody,[37] or when either or both parties requests it.[38] Finally, in many other states, joint custody is permissible but there is no presumption for or against it.[39]

2. *Parents' Rights.* While courts justify joint custody as furthering children's best interests, the policy also can be viewed as vindicating the rights of parents to ongoing and equal involvement with their child. Should the interest of parents play *any* role in a court's deciding whether to award joint custody?

3. *Conflict and Communication.* Divorce does not end, and may exacerbate, patterns of parental conflict for some families. In response, some states have introduced Parenting Coordination interventions, in which a mental health professional or a lawyer assigned by the court manages ongoing issues in high-conflict cases.[40] Technology, such as the mobile app Our Family Wizard, is used in some states to facilitate co-parenting communication. Is conflict a sufficient reason for a court to reject joint custody?

4. *Custody and Domestic Violence.* Courts consider domestic violence, if present, in determining custody. Some state statutes explicitly identify domestic violence as a factor to be considered in analyzing best interests.[41] Some states also identify domestic violence as relevant specifically to considerations of joint custody. Minnesota law, for example, instructs courts to "use a rebuttable presumption that joint legal custody or joint physical custody is not in the best interests of the child if domestic abuse . . . has occurred between the parents."[42] Does this seem appropriate? The statute states: "In determining whether the presumption is rebutted, the court shall consider the nature and context of the domestic abuse and the implications of the domestic abuse for parenting and for the child's safety, well-being, and developmental needs."[43] In what situations, if any, do you imagine that joint custody would be appropriate even if domestic violence is present? What factors would you expect courts to consider? Perhaps whether the child has suffered any abuse; whether the child has witnessed the domestic violence; or whether the child has a close relationship with the abusive parent.[44]

5. *How Common is Joint Physical Custody?* In the mid-2000s, according to a 2014 study of physical custody in Wisconsin, "we reached a significant

---

37. See, e.g., Cal. Fam. Code §§ 3040-3041 (West 2020).

38. See, e.g., Minn. Stat. §§ 518.17, 518.165 (2020).

39. See, e.g., Fla. Stat. §§ 61.13, 61.401 (2020); Ga. Code Ann. § 19-9-3 (2020).

40. See Am. Psychological Ass'n, Guidelines for the Practice of Parenting Coordination, 67 Am. Psychol. 63 (Jan. 2012); Linda Fieldstone et al., Perspectives on Parenting Coordination: Views of Parenting Coordinators, Attorneys, and Judiciary Members, 50 Fam. Ct. Rev. 441 (2012).

41. See, e.g., Cal. Fam. Code § 3011 (West 2020).

42. See, e.g., Minn. Stat. § 518.17(b)(9) (2020).

43. Id.

44. See, e.g., Thornton v. Bosquez, 933 N.W.2d 781 (Minn. 2019).

milestone: there are more divorce judgments without mother-sole custody than with it."[45] Father-sole custody has remained stable (at about 10 percent of cases), while the rise of joint custody has substantially affected the frequency of mother-sole custody.[46] According to the study's authors, from 1988 to 2008, sole custody by mothers declined from about 80 percent of cases to only 42 percent, equal shared custody increased from 5 percent of cases to 27 percent, and unequal shared custody increased from 3 percent of cases to 18 percent.[47] Shared custody is more common among higher-income couples.[48] In more than 80 percent of the unequal shared custody cases, the mother has the child the majority of the time.[49]

6. *(When) Does Joint Custody Serve Children's Best Interests?* A review of research examining child adjustment in joint versus sole custody arrangements found that children in joint physical or legal custody arrangements were better adjusted than children in sole custody settings.[50] This more positive adjustment existed with respect to not only general adjustment, but also family relationships, self-esteem, emotional and behavioral adjustment, and divorce-specific adjustment.[51] These results are attributable to the ongoing positive involvement with both parents that joint custody facilitates.[52]

Some child development researchers, though, have been critical of joint custody, especially joint physical custody.[53] Joseph Goldstein, Anna Freud, and Albert Solnit, authors of the highly influential Beyond the Best Interests of the Child, took the view that custody should be awarded to the child's primary psychological parent, who should then determine the other parent's access to the child.[54] Emphasizing the importance of continuity in parent-child relationships, they argued that joint custody often threatens psychological bonding between children and their parents.[55] Some recent research has corroborated these conclusions; one study found that 43 percent of infants who spent at least one night a week with their nonresident fathers were insecurely attached to their mothers, as compared with 25 percent of infants who only had day, rather than overnight, visits

45. Maria Cancian et al., Who Gets Custody Now? Dramatic Changes in Children's Living Arrangements After Divorce, 51 Demography 1381, 1393 (2014).

46. Id. at 1387.

47. Id.

48. Id. at 1393.

49. Id. at 1387.

50. Robert Bauserman, Child Adjustment in Joint-Custody Versus Sole-Custody Arrangements: A Meta-Analytic Review, 16 J. Fam. Psychol. 91 (2002).

51. Id.

52. Id.

53. See, e.g., Robert E. Emery, Two Homes, One Childhood: A Parenting Plan to Last a Lifetime (2016).

54. See Joseph Goldstein et al., Beyond the Best Interests of the Child (1973).

55. See id. at 38 (asserting that children have difficulty "relating to, profiting from and maintaining contact with two psychological parents who are not in positive contact with each other").

with their fathers.[56] These differences remained statistically significant even when demographic background and measures of mothers' reports of parental conflict, co-parenting quality, and the quality of fathering were considered.[57]

PROBLEM

Sora and Gil are a divorcing couple. They don't agree about any major decisions regarding their ten-year-old son, Jack. Sora wants to send Jack to the local public school, Gil wants him to go to private school. Sora wants Jack to receive Catholic instruction after school, Gil does not want him to receive any religious instruction. Sora wants Jack to attend sleep-away camp in the summer, Gil wants him to remain home. Sora wants Jack to play basketball and baseball, Gil wants him to focus on music instead of sports. At the time of his parents' divorce, Jack was attending public school. He also had been attending Catholic Mass weekly with his mother; Jack had received his First Communion. Jack was also taking violin lessons at the time his parents divorced. You are the judge assigned to the divorce case. What decision would you make about custody over Jack?

POSTSCRIPT

Courts facing couples who struggle to agree on decisions regarding their children take a variety of approaches. Some simply deny joint custody because of the "parents' inability to cooperate."[58] Others allow joint custody but intervene to make decisions—based on the child's best interests—when the parents cannot agree.[59] In a third approach, some courts order joint custody but include "tie-breaking provisions in the [custody] award so one parent would have the last word if they reached an impasse."[60] According to one court, "the tie-breaker parent cannot make the final call until after weighing in good faith the ideas the other parent has expressed regarding their children."[61] Is there any way to enforce this provision? Would enforcement serve the child's interests?

---

56. Samantha L. Tornello et al., Overnight Custody Arrangements, Attachment, and Adjustment Among Very Young Children, 75 J. Marriage & Fam. 871, 882 (2013). The study found similar disparities among toddlers. Id.

57. Id. Children with insecure attachment are more likely to develop anxiety, depression, hostility toward other children, and vulnerability to peer pressure. See Mokhtar Malekpour, Effects of Attachment on Early and Later Development, 53 Brit. J. Developmental Disabilities 81, 86–87 (2007).

58. Hongyang "Brian" Li v. Yi Ding, 519 S.W.3d 738 (Ark. 2017).

59. Arcella v. Arcella, 407 P.3d 341 (Nev. 2017).

60. Santo v. Santo, 141 A.3d 74 (Md. 2016).

61. Id.

III. The Role of the Child

A. Children's Preferences

What weight should be given to a child's preferences in custodial decision-making? How does and should the age of the child matter? How should children's preferences be weighed against interests in other relationships, like relationships with siblings?

Maier v. Maier
874 N.W.2d 725 (Mich. Ct. App. 2015)

Per Curiam.

Plaintiff appeals . . . the trial court's order awarding defendant sole physical and legal custody of the parties' son, JM. We affirm. . . .

Plaintiff . . . argues that the court erred by failing to consider the reasonable preference of the child. . . .

Plaintiff's first claim of error is that the trial court failed to consider JM's reasonable preference because it did not interview him. Plaintiff asks this Court to hold that the recent case of *Kubicki v. Sharpe,* 858 N.W.2d 57 (2014), requires that a trial court conduct an interview of the child in all but the most extraordinary of circumstances. In *Kubicki,* the Court stated, "Regardless whether the parties wished for an interview, the court was affirmatively required to consider the child's preference." In the instant case, the trial court declined to interview the child. In doing so, the court stated: . . .

> [JM] turned nine during these proceedings. Neither party asked that he be interviewed. He suffers from anxiety and adjustment disorder and has been subjected to various evaluations and counseling appointments. There is a concern he struggles with ADHD. He has been exposed to inappropriate and inaccurate information and there are concerns which I will expand on later that [JM] has been coached. It is unlikely even if he were interviewed that he would be able to express a reasonable preference. . . .

Kubicki did not announce a new legal mandate that every child over a certain age be interviewed to ascertain a reasonable preference. Following a long line of cases, *Kubicki* highlighted the standing principle that a court may not abrogate its responsibility to consider each of the enumerated best-interest child custody factors on the basis of a stipulation of the adults in a case. The right to have a reasonable preference considered attaches to the best interests of the child, not to the rights of the contestants in the custody battle. The term "reasonable preference" has been defined by this Court as a standard that "exclude[s] those preferences that are arbitrary or inherently indefensible." The Child Custody Act requires that the court consider the reasonable preference of the child, if one exists. A preliminary question is always whether the child has the capacity to form a reasonable preference and, if so, whether the child has actually formed a preference. A child over the age of six is presumed to be capable of forming a reasonable preference. Undoubtedly, "an expression of preference by an intelligent, unbiased child might be the determining factor in deciding what the 'best interests' of the child are." However, no court has ruled that every child over the age of six actually has the capacity to form a preference. Just as adults may lack the capacity to give competent testimony because of infirmity, disability, or other circumstances, so may a child's presumed capacity be compromised by circumstances peculiar to that child's life. Additionally, an interview is merely one avenue from which to adduce a child's capacity to form a preference and the preference itself, and not the sine qua non from which that determination must be made. Trial judges, learned in the law, are not necessarily the best persons to approach a child on this issue. Just as a protocol has been developed for interviewing child assault victims, this issue might well be best addressed with the development of an evidence-based protocol for interviewers seeking to ascertain a child's preference for custody. Additionally, it is not uncommon for children in the midst of family reorganization to be under the care of trained mental health care professionals from whom the trial court can seek input on many of the best-interest factors, including preference.

In this case the trial court did not interview JM, but did make an implicit fact-finding that this particular child could not formulate or express a reasonable preference, one that was not based on the inherently indefensible basis of coaching and emotional distress. In making this fact-finding, the court had before it a record that included JM's diagnosis of both depressive disorder and ADHD. Additionally, the record contained . . . testimony from therapists who opined that JM was being coached, and a traumatic visitation exchange that JM perceived to be a kidnapping. Additionally, more than one witness also testified that plaintiff voiced concerns and criticisms of defendant in the child's presence. Accordingly, the court found that while JM was of sufficient age to be able to form and express a preference, his fragile emotional state, coupled with significant efforts to influence his preference, rendered him unable at the time to form a reasonable preference. Clearly, the court fulfilled its statutory duty. The court's fact-finding was supported by the record and is affirmed. . . .

NOTES AND QUESTIONS

1. *Who Should Decide?* Many jurisdictions require courts to consider the child's "reasonable preferences" as one factor among many in determining the child's best interests for custody purposes. But the court has discretion to determine whether a child is competent to form and express reasonable preferences. Some

jurisdictions, however, have adopted statutes providing that a child above a certain age has the right to choose the custodial parent. Georgia law, for example, states: "In all custody cases in which the child has reached the age of 14 years, the child shall have the right to select the parent with whom he or she desires to live. The child's selection for purposes of custody shall be presumptive unless the parent so selected is determined not to be in the best interests of the child."[62] What are the advantages and disadvantages of a mandatory approach? What about a discretionary approach?

2.   *When?* The *Maier* court explained that under its state law, a child over six is presumed to be able to express a reasonable preference for custody. Is that too young? At what age should a court consider a child's preference? Most statutes that set a threshold age at which courts must consider a child's preference contemplate older children — such as children twelve and up.[63] Some states do not set a minimum age but require a showing of maturity before a child's preference should be considered.[64]

3.   *Why?* Should a court be inquiring into *why* the child wants to live with a particular parent? Are some reasons legitimate, and others not? What if the child simply wants to live with the more lenient parent? In Yvonne S. v. Wesley H, the Alaska Supreme Court described the trial court's reasoning about the child's preference:[65]

> Allison testified that she was hurt by her mother's excessive criticism of her weight and appearance. Allison also testified that she had a difficult relationship with her stepfather.
>
> The court found that Allison was mature, made good decisions, had a healthy self-image, did not use drugs or alcohol, did well in school, and had not had trouble with the law. The court also found that the criticism Allison perceived from her mother was problematic and that some conflicts existed between Allison and her stepfather. The court found that Allison clearly wanted to live with her father, that she had legitimate reasons for her preference, that she was not being unduly influenced by either parent, and that she was of sufficient capacity and maturity to warrant consideration of her custody preference.[66]

What if Allison did not do well in school and had been arrested? Would these facts have made her reasons any less "legitimate"? Would they have called into question her "capacity and maturity"?

---

62. Ga. Code Ann. § 19-9-3(a)(5) (2020).

63. See, e.g., Cal. Fam. Code § 3042 (West 2020).

64. See, e.g., Tex. Fam. Code Ann. § 153.009 (West 2020) (requiring the court to interview a child 12 or older in custody dispute).

65. 245 P.3d 430 (Alaska 2011).

66. Id. at 431.

4. *Children's Rights?* Do children have a constitutional right to exercise a custodial preference? In Zaubi v. Hoejme, a federal court considered whether the constitutional rights of two children might be infringed by a custody order that allowed their mother to remove them from the United States under circumstances that might cause them to lose their American citizenship.[67] The court acknowledged the children's right to assert a claim to retain citizenship, but abstained from the case because Pennsylvania law afforded the minors a sufficient opportunity to express their custodial preferences or to advocate for themselves through a guardian or "next friend."[68]

5. *Siblings.* Children may want to reside with one parent over the other. They may also want, more than anything, to reside with their siblings. "Siblings can give each other support, love, nurturing, and stability," yet, as Professor Jill Hasday observes:

> [E]xisting law largely fails to safeguard sibling bonds. . . . [P]arental divorce can leave siblings in separate households and threaten the maintenance of functioning ties between siblings, at a time when children often have more need than ever for support and stability in their sibling relationships. . . . Sometimes courts ordering split custody are attempting to resolve custody disputes between two parents who each want custody of all their children. Sometimes courts accept split custody plans that one parent has advocated or that both parents support and perhaps have already implemented upon separating. Split custody can appeal to a parent as a way of distributing the financial burdens and psychological benefits of childrearing. Alternatively or in addition, split custody can appeal to a parent who feels closer ties to some of his children rather than others. . . . Half-siblings are especially likely to be separated at divorce or when their shared parent dies.[69]

Even though custody disputes focus on the parent-child relationship, there is a strong public policy favoring preservation of sibling relationships. Should courts disfavor split custody arrangements, where siblings are placed in different households? Does it matter if the siblings are close in age?

B. Children's Representation

In family law cases involving custody or visitation, the court often assigns the child a representative. While most states grant courts the discretion to appoint such a representative in private custody matters, a few states require such an appointment when custody is contested or when one of the parties requests it.[70] While we cover

---

67. 530 F. Supp. 831 (W.D. Pa. 1980).
68. Id.
69. Jill Elaine Hasday, Siblings in Law, 65 Vand. L. Rev. 897 (2012).
70. See Linda D. Elrod, Child Custody Prac. & Proc. § 12:4 (database updated Feb. 2020).

abuse and neglect in Chapter 7, it is worth noting here that in court proceedings involving abuse or neglect, states must appoint a representative for the child as a condition of receiving federal grant money for state child protective services under the Child Abuse Prevention and Treatment Act (CAPTA).[71] All states currently abide by the requirements set out by CAPTA.[72]

Representation of children in private custody matters generally takes the form of a guardian ad litem (GAL), best interest attorney, child's attorney, or some combination. The statutory provisions governing their respective responsibilities "vary dramatically from state to state."[73] In general, a GAL is an attorney or trained layperson whose mandate is to assist the court in protecting the child's best interests. The GAL's role can involve conducting investigations, mediating, testifying as an expert witness, and making recommendations to the court. In contrast, a child's attorney is tasked with advocating for the child's wishes, just as an attorney would in a traditional attorney-client relationship. A best interest attorney, on the other hand, is a lawyer who advocates for the position that the attorney believes to be in the best interests of the child, whether or not the child herself desires that outcome.

A look at some state approaches reveals important variations across jurisdictions. California, for example, grants courts the discretion to appoint a best interest attorney for a child in private custody matters. In the course of representation, the attorney must present the child's wishes to the court if the child requests it.[74] In deciding whether to appoint counsel, the court is instructed to consider whether the "issues of child custody and visitation are highly contested or protracted," whether knowledgeable counsel is available for appointment, and whether the "best interest of the child appears to require independent representation."[75] In New York, courts are required to assign an attorney for the child in family court proceedings. The attorney must advocate the child's position, except in very limited circumstances such as when there is a substantial risk of imminent, serious harm to the child or when the child is unable to convey her desires.[76] In Arizona, courts have the discretion to appoint a best interest attorney, a child's attorney, or a court-appointed advisor (whose role is similar to a GAL's).[77] In deciding between appointing a best interest attorney and a child's attorney, Arizona courts are more likely to appoint a child's attorney "for an older child who has judgment and maturity."[78]

---

71. 42 U.S.C. § 5106a(b)(2)(B)(xiii) (2018).

72. Children's Bureau, Child Welfare Information Gateway, Representation of Children in Child Abuse and Neglect Proceedings 2 (2018).

73. Barbara Ann Atwood, The Uniform Representation of Children in Abuse, Neglect, and Custody Proceedings Act: Bridging the Divide Between Pragmatism and Idealism, 42 Fam. L.Q. 63, 65 (2008).

74. Cal. Fam. Code §§ 3150-3151 (West 2020).

75. Cal. Ct. R. 5.240 (West 2020).

76. See N.Y. Fam. Ct. Act §§ 241–249-b (2020).

77. See Ariz. Rev. Stat. Ann. § 25-321 (2019); 17B A.R.S. Rules Fam. Law Proc., Rules 10–10.1 (2020).

78. Aksamit v. Krahn, 227 P.3d 475, 479 (Ariz. Ct. App. 2010).

Endeavoring to make the roles of child representatives in custody cases more uniform, three leading organizations have proposed standards: the American Academy of Matrimonial Lawyers (AAML) in 2009, the American Bar Association (ABA) in 2003, and the Uniform Law Commission (ULC) in 2007.[79] The AAML's custody standards eliminate the role of a best interest attorney and instead permit the appointment of only two categories of representatives: (1) a counsel for the child, who represents the child in the traditional attorney-client relationship; and (2) a court-appointed professional, who assists the court otherwise in tasks such as investigations or providing expert testimony. In contrast, the ABA's custody standards envision two distinct attorney roles. An attorney serves either as: (1) the child's attorney (similar to the AAML's counsel for the child); or (2) the best interest attorney. The ABA's best interest attorney is required to advocate independently of the child's wishes but must inform the court of the child's views unless the child requests otherwise. Lastly, the ULC's custody standards build upon the ABA's existing two categories by adding a third: the lay best interest advocate. The lay best interest advocate, as the name suggests, acts not as an attorney but assists the court in determining the best interests of the child. The ULC's custody standards also modify the ABA-type child's attorney role by requiring the child's attorney to request the appointment of a best interest advocate or best interest attorney if the attorney considers the child's wishes to be seriously self-injurious.[80]

These proposed standards illustrate the field's disagreements over what the ideal representation of children should look like. In reality, about half of the states employ a GAL who generally functions as a best interest attorney, eight jurisdictions appoint a child's attorney, and the remaining states appoint a hybrid best interest and child's attorney or some other combination.[81] The hybrid attorney-GAL role in particular has drawn significant criticism, as the duties appear to conflict with the ethical requirements that lawyers maintain client confidentiality, abide by the client's wishes (rather than seek to determine the client's best interests), and avoid serving as a witness in the client's case.[82]

For matters involving custody and visitation disputes with third parties, such as grandparents or other relatives that have cared for the child, some states expressly

---

79. See Am. Ass'n of Matrimonial Lawyers, Representing Children: Standards for Attorneys for Children in Custody or Visitation Proceedings with Commentary, 22 J. Am. Acad. Matrim. Law. 227 (2009); Standards of Practice for Lawyers Representing Children in Custody Cases, 37 Fam. L. Q. 131 (Am. Bar Ass'n 2003); Unif. Representation of Children in Abuse, Neglect, and Custody Proceedings Act (amended 2007), 9C U.L.A. 26 (Supp. 2010).

80. See Elizabeth R. Ellis, Whose Role Is It Anyway? Deciphering the Role, Functions, and Responsibilities of Representing Children in Custody Matters, 31 J. Am. Acad. Matrim. Law. 533, 539–544 (2019).

81. Elrod, Child Custody Prac. & Proc., supra note 70, § 12:4.

82. Barbara Ann Atwood, Representing Children: The Ongoing Search for Clear and Workable Standards, 19 J. Am. Acad. Matrim. Law. 183, 200 (2005).

specify that counsel for the child may be appointed.[83] Likewise, Section 10(1) of the Uniform Nonparent Custody and Visitation Act (discussed in Chapter 6) states that a court may "appoint an attorney, guardian ad litem, or similar representative for the child."

PROBLEM

You are a judge on a state appellate court. You have a case in which a mother is appealing from a trial court order granting sole legal custody and primary physical custody of her child, Isabella, to the father. During the underlying proceedings, the trial court appointed a GAL, who also served as the child's attorney, for Isabella.

The relevant state law states that the trial court has the discretion to appoint a GAL separate from the child's attorney "if the same person cannot properly represent the legal interests of the child as legal counsel and also represent the best interest of the child as guardian ad litem." In a prior case also involving a private custody matter, colleagues on the state appellate court held that a separate attorney should have been appointed to represent the child's wishes given the child's age and maturity. In that case, the child was twelve years old at the time of the proceeding. The court found that the child "was impressive and demonstrated a maturity beyond her years," in part because she recognized her parents' shortcomings.

In this case, Isabella turned eleven during the custody matter. Isabella has had several tantrums in the past few months and seems to struggle when she is not the center of attention. Isabella does not seem to understand that her own issues and behavior likely stem in part from her mother's substance abuse issues. The attorney-GAL explained that he advocated that sole legal custody and primary physical custody to the father was in the child's best interests in part because Isabella did not express any opposition to such an award during a conversation he had with her.

The mother now argues that the attorney-GAL should have bifurcated his role because Isabella preferred a joint custody arrangement, although the mother has not presented any evidence indicating that Isabella felt this way. Do you affirm the award of sole custody? Or do you find that the trial court should have appointed a separate attorney to represent Isabella in this matter? How, if at all, would the standard of review in the case matter to your decision?

---

83. See, e.g., Md. Rule 9-205.1(b)(9) (2020) (stating that, among other situations, appointment of an attorney for a child "may be most appropriate" in cases involving consideration of "awarding custody or visitation to a non-parent"); Wash. Rev. Code § 26.10.070 (2020) (stating that a court may appoint an attorney to represent the interests of a child in nonparental actions for child custody).

POSTSCRIPT

This problem is analogous to a case that arose not in the context of a private custody dispute but rather in the context of a proceeding to terminate parental rights.[84] There, both parents of the child appealed from an order terminating their parental rights, arguing in part that the conflict arising from the attorney-GAL's dual role required reversal and remand for a new hearing. The Iowa Court of Appeals rejected this argument and affirmed the termination of parental rights after finding the child not to be "of sufficient age and maturity to make an informed decision about a potential termination with his parents."[85]

The fictional state law quoted in the problem is based on Iowa Code § 232.89(4), which states: "The same person may serve both as the child's counsel and as guardian ad litem. However, the court may appoint a separate guardian ad litem, if the same person cannot properly represent the legal interests of the child as legal counsel and also represent the best interest of the child as guardian ad litem. . . ." While this statute applies in the context of termination proceedings, a separate statute, § 598.12, governs the court's discretion to make dual-role appointments in private custody matters. In 2017, the Iowa state legislature amended the statute governing private custody matters so that the same person can no longer serve as both a GAL and child's attorney.[86]

IV. Parental Characteristics, Nondiscrimination, and Parental Fitness

Even as the child's best interest has moved to the forefront, the adults' interests remain relevant. Today more than ever, the law strives to treat parents fairly regardless of not only sex but also race, religion, sexual orientation, gender identity, and disability. While the best interests standard unquestionably contemplates treating parents differently based on their conduct (i.e., what they do), the antidiscrimination ethos disfavors treating parents differently based on their status (i.e., who they are). The California custody statute, for example, dictates that "the court shall

---

84. In re D.F., 873 N.W.2d 301 (Iowa Ct. App. 2015).

85. Id.

86. For further discussion of cases addressing the potential attorney-GAL conflict, see Nancy J. Moore, Conflicts of Interests in the Representation of Children, 64 Fordham L. Rev. 1819, 1842–1843 nn.114-18 (1996).

not consider the sex, gender identity, gender expression, or sexual orientation of a parent, legal guardian, or relative in determining the best interests of the child."[87]

A. Race

PALMORE V. SIDOTI
466 U.S. 429 (1984)

CHIEF JUSTICE BURGER delivered the opinion of the Court.

We granted certiorari to review a judgment of a state court divesting a natural mother of the custody of her infant child because of her remarriage to a person of a different race.

When petitioner Linda Sidoti Palmore and respondent Anthony J. Sidoti, both Caucasians, were divorced in May 1980 in Florida, the mother was awarded custody of their 3-year-old daughter.

In September 1981 the father sought custody of the child by filing a petition to modify the prior judgment because of changed conditions. The change was that the child's mother was then cohabiting with a Negro, Clarence Palmore, Jr., whom she married two months later. Additionally, the father made several allegations of instances in which the mother had not properly cared for the child. . . .

The court . . . concluded that the best interests of the child would be served by awarding custody to the father. The court's rationale is contained in the following:

> The father's evident resentment of the mother's choice of a black partner is not sufficient to wrest custody from the mother. It is of some significance, however, that the mother did see fit to bring a man into her home and carry on a sexual relationship with him without being married to him. Such action tended to place gratification of her own desires ahead of her concern for the child's future welfare. This Court feels that despite the strides that have been made in bettering relations between the races in this country, it is inevitable that Melanie will, if allowed to remain in her present situation and attains school age and thus becomes more vulnerable to peer pressures, suffer from the social stigmatization that is sure to come. . . .

The judgment of a state court determining or reviewing a child custody decision is not ordinarily a likely candidate for review by this Court. However, the court's opinion . . . raises important federal concerns arising from the Constitution's commitment to eradicating discrimination based on race.

The Florida court did not focus directly on the parental qualifications of the natural mother or her present husband, or indeed on the father's qualifications to have custody of the child. The court found that "there is no issue as to either party's devotion to the child, adequacy of housing facilities, or respectability of the new

---

87. Cal. Fam. Code § 3011(b) (West 2020).

spouse of either parent." This, taken with the absence of any negative finding as to the quality of the care provided by the mother, constitutes a rejection of any claim of petitioner's unfitness to continue the custody of her child.

The court correctly stated that the child's welfare was the controlling factor. But that court was entirely candid and made no effort to place its holding on any ground other than race. Taking the court's findings and rationale at face value, it is clear that the outcome would have been different had petitioner married a Caucasian male of similar respectability.

A core purpose of the Fourteenth Amendment was to do away with all governmentally imposed discrimination based on race. Classifying persons according to their race is more likely to reflect racial prejudice than legitimate public concerns; the race, not the person, dictates the category. Such classifications are subject to the most exacting scrutiny; to pass constitutional muster, they must be justified by a compelling governmental interest and must be "necessary . . . to the accomplishment" of their legitimate purpose.

The State, of course, has a duty of the highest order to protect the interests of minor children, particularly those of tender years. In common with most states, Florida law mandates that custody determinations be made in the best interests of the children involved. The goal of granting custody based on the best interests of the child is indisputably a substantial governmental interest for purposes of the Equal Protection Clause.

It would ignore reality to suggest that racial and ethnic prejudices do not exist or that all manifestations of those prejudices have been eliminated. There is a risk that a child living with a stepparent of a different race may be subject to a variety of pressures and stresses not present if the child were living with parents of the same racial or ethnic origin.

The question, however, is whether the reality of private biases and the possible injury they might inflict are permissible considerations for removal of an infant child from the custody of its natural mother. We have little difficulty concluding that they are not. The Constitution cannot control such prejudices but neither can it tolerate them. Private biases may be outside the reach of the law, but the law cannot, directly or indirectly, give them effect. . . .

The effects of racial prejudice, however real, cannot justify a racial classification removing an infant child from the custody of its natural mother found to be an appropriate person to have such custody. . . .

NOTES AND QUESTIONS

1.   *What Does* Palmore *Stand For?* Although decided two decades ago, *Palmore* remains the only Supreme Court decision concerning courts' use of race in child custody decisions. Does *Palmore* follow naturally from Loving v. Virginia (discussed in Chapter 2)? How is *Palmore* distinguishable from *Loving*? Was the *Palmore* Court

making a legal determination that race cannot be considered or a factual determination that the trial judge clearly erred in his assessment of the child's best interest? If the latter, what was the Supreme Court's basis for second guessing the trial judge who had considered the testimony of the parents and experts?

2. *A Narrow Interpretation of* Palmore. Does *Palmore* mean judges can't take race into account in custody decisions? Or that race can't be the sole or determinative factor in a custody determination? Many courts have embraced the latter interpretation of *Palmore*. Consider, for example, In re Marriage of Gambla and Woodson, in which a white father and African American mother of a 6-month-old biracial child had an especially acrimonious split.[88] When the couple filed for divorce, each sought sole custody of the child, Kira. Although the trial court found both the father and the mother would be fine parents, it was determined to make a sole custody award due to their inability to co-parent. After finding that the factors enumerated in the custody statute did not favor placement with one parent over the other, the trial court took race into account. It rejected a "broad stroke" approach under which the mother would be awarded custody *solely* because she was African American, but nonetheless found that the mother would be able to provide Kira with a "breadth of cultural knowledge and experience that [the father] will not be able to do." The court granted custody to the mother, and visitation to the father.

The appeals court rejected the father's argument that the trial court decision contravened *Palmore*. In *Palmore*, the court reasoned, "[t]he Supreme Court [had] determined that the custody award was unconstitutional, not because the trial court considered race, but because the trial court considered solely race. Indeed, the Supreme Court was careful to premise its holding with the following statement: 'But that court was entirely candid and made no effort to place its holding on any ground other than race.'"[89] But in the custody determination involving Kira, the *Gambla* court observed, the fact that the trial court "carefully weighed each of the statutory factors," before looking to *other* relevant factors, meant that, though "Kira's racial status did play a role in the trial court's decision to award custody to Kimberly . . . it was not the sole factor." Thus, the trial court did not run afoul of *Palmore*. In its opinion, the court stated that "[v]olumes of cases from other jurisdictions have interpreted *Palmore* as not prohibiting the consideration of race in matters of child custody."

If *Palmore* is read to apply only to cases in which race is the sole consideration, then its application is quite narrow. Statutes that prohibit the placement of children across racial lines would meet that standard. But these are the very sorts of statutes that no longer exist. For a judge to violate *Palmore*, on the sole factor interpretation, he would have to be committed to awarding custody to the father in *Palmore* and the mother in *Gambla* wholly irrespective of the characteristics of the other parent.

---

88. 853 N.E.2d 847 (Ill. 2006).
89. Id. at 869.

Such a circumstance is rather unlikely. Does this interpretation serve or undermine racial equality? Are antidiscrimination principles vindicated by allowing decision-makers to rely on race so long as race is not the sole factor?

3. *Broader Interpretations of* Palmore. A broader interpretation of *Palmore* sees the case as prohibiting considerations of race in custody determinations. The Supreme Court of Montana declared: "Constitutional requirements of equal protection prohibit courts from relying on race to make decisions regarding child custody."[90] Likewise, the Supreme Court of Tennessee held that the "appropriate factors governing child custody . . . exclude race."[91] On this view, the trial judge in *Gambla* erred by taking race into account at all.

Might a better interpretation of *Palmore* be that it prohibits considerations of race that do not further the child's best interest? When might consideration of race further a child's best interest? In Jones v. Jones, the South Dakota Supreme Court asserted: "To say . . . that a court should never consider whether a parent is willing and able to expose to and educate children on their heritage, is to say that society is not interested in whether children ever learn who they are. *Palmore* does not require this, nor do the constitutions of the United States or the State of South Dakota."[92] Should it be considered proper, as the court found, "for a trial court, when determining the best interests of a child in the context of a custody dispute between parents, to consider the matter of race as it relates to a child's ethnic heritage and which parent is more prepared to expose the child to it"?[93]

4. *Harm.* The *Palmore* Court observed that no actual harm to the child had been documented, referring instead to the "possible injury" that might result from private biases. The father in *Palmore* made sweeping generalizations about how the mother's interracial marriage would cause harm to their daughter, but there was no evidence that anything bad happened to the child and there was no specific reason to believe that anything would, other than citing to general racist attitudes in the surrounding community. How does the speculative nature of the asserted harm cast doubt on the contention that the best interest of the child warranted the change in custody?

If there had been uncontroverted evidence that the child was teased and taunted as a result of her mother's interracial relationship, would a judge still have been obligated not to order a change in custody? In Holt v. Chenault,[94] the Supreme Court of Kentucky considered a case in which there was actual harm. Danny Holt and Barbara Chenault—both white—were the parents of Dawn Holt. When Danny and Barbara divorced, custody of Dawn, who was then an infant, was granted to

---

90. In re Marriage of Olson, 190 P.3d 619, 624 (Mont. 2008).
91. Parker v. Parker, 986 S.W.2d 557, 562 (Tenn. 1999).
92. 542 N.W.2d 119, 123 (S.D. 1996).
93. Id. at 123–24.
94. 722 S.W.2d 897 (Ky. 1987).

Barbara. Four years after her separation from Danny, Barbara married an African American man, and following the marriage, Danny sought a change in custody. At the time the suit was filed, Barbara was pregnant. At trial, Dawn testified that she had been taunted by schoolmates when her mother married a black man. Dawn was further taunted about her mother's "black" baby. Dawn complained to her father about her home situation and stated her intent to leave her mother's home. Later, Dawn left school to go to her father's house instead of taking the bus home to her mother's house. Another time, Dawn was left with her stepfather's mother when her mother went to work. While the older woman slept, Dawn left and walked to her father's workplace. Though the trial court specifically found the mother to be a suitable parent, it granted the modification of custody.

The Supreme Court of Kentucky overturned the trial court ruling, holding that the trial court's consideration of the mother's subsequent interracial marriage was impermissible because it "[gave] effect to private racial biases."[95] The Kentucky Supreme Court thus seemed to say that even actual harm does not justify a change of custody, at least when the actual harm is a result of private racial biases. Is this approach to *Palmore*'s nondiscrimination mandate in tension with the best interests of the child?

5. *Nonmarital Cohabitation and Gender.* The trial court in *Palmore* considered not only the race of the mother's partner but also the fact that the mother and her partner had been cohabiting prior to marriage. Why should this matter? Professor Katharine Bartlett focuses on the role of gender in *Palmore*:

> According to the trial court, the mother's "see[ing] fit to bring a man into her home and carry[ing] on a sexual relationship with him without being married to him" showed that she "tended to place gratification of her own desires ahead of her concern for the child's future welfare." Nothing more seems to have been made of this factor, either by the trial court or on review, but some courts have since noticed that mothers who cohabit outside of marriage tend to be penalized in ways fathers who cohabit outside of marriage are not, and have concluded that differential treatment constitutes sex discrimination.[96]

PROBLEM

Rita, a black woman, and Dante, a white man, divorced. They were granted joint legal and physical custody of their two children. Two years later, Rita petitioned for sole legal and physical custody of the children so she could move with them from Lincoln, Nebraska — where Dante also lived — to New York City. Rita claimed that

---

95. Id. at 898.
96. Katharine T. Bartlett, Comparing Race and Sex Discrimination in Custody Cases, 28 Hofstra L. Rev. 877, 881 (2000).

the biracial children would be better off in the more racially diverse population of New York City than the less diverse community of Lincoln. You are the judge hearing Rita's motion to modify custody. Do you think you can consider the effects of community racial diversity on the emotional, physical, and social development of the children? Or is consideration of the children's race and the racial diversity of the relevant communities constitutionally forbidden? Would you want to consider these factors if you could?

B. Sex of Parent and Child

DALIN V. DALIN
512 N.W.2d 685 (N.D. 1994)

LEVINE, JUSTICE. . . .

The Dalins were married on June 9, 1989 in Tioga, North Dakota. They had one child during the marriage, born on December 11, 1989. [The parties divorced.] . . . The trial court awarded custody to Patricia from August 25 to June 5 of each year and to Roland during the summer. . . .

Roland appealed. He argues that the trial court's custody determination was clearly erroneous and a result of gender bias. . . .

The trial court determined that the best interests of the child were met by placing the child in Patricia's custody. The trial court concluded that although "both parents care deeply" for the child and "are fit parents for custody," Patricia "seems best able to give love and affection without jeopardizing the relationship desirable with the non-custodial parent." . . . [T]he trial court was concerned about the future of the child's relationship with Patricia, should Roland receive custody, given his unyielding disapproval of Patricia's parenting style. . . .

Roland also raises the issue of whether the trial court based its custody determination on improper gender bias. Roland points to the trial court's questioning of Roland's mother:

> THE COURT: In the event Rollie were the primary custodian, and in the event there [were] certain things in [the child's] training that might best be done by a woman, would it be your anticipation that you would be the teacher?
> THE WITNESS: No, Rollie is the teacher. And I just help him[.]
> THE COURT: Getting back to my question, in the event there are certain things that a girl should learn that [are] easiest to learn from a woman, would you be anticipating that you would be that woman?
> THE WITNESS: Yes.

Gender bias in judicial proceedings is wholly unacceptable. We agree that if the trial court assumed that fathers, as a group, are incapable of adequately raising their daughters, it would be relying on an improper factor to determine custody. Trial courts should not "perpetuate the damaging stereotype that a mother's role is one of caregiver, and the father's role is that of an apathetic, irresponsible, or unfit parent." *In re Dubreuil*, 629 So. 2d 819, 828 (Fla.1993). However, we do not believe the above exchange evidences that the trial court based its custody determination on the misguided, stereotypical assumption that daughters require female caregivers, as Roland argues. It was Roland himself who introduced the notion that help was available from his mother for tasks he had not performed or was uncertain about performing. The trial court merely followed up Roland's attorney's inquiry as to who did the cooking and Roland's disclosure that he relied on his mother for tasks such as potty training and hair braiding. Because Roland invited the trial court's questioning by introducing the idea that he felt some inability or discomfort in performing certain childcare tasks, he may not complain about the trial court's pursuit of the issue. Under the circumstances, we conclude that the trial court's questions were not motivated by or evidence of gender bias. After finding that both parents were fit and loving, the trial court "fairly weighed the evidence between two fit parents and properly determined custody on appropriate factors." . . .

Affirmed.

SANDSTROM, JUSTICE, dissenting.

I respectfully dissent.

North Dakota law provides: "Between the mother and father, whether natural or adoptive, there is no presumption as to who will better promote the best interests and welfare of the child." N.D.C.C. § 14–09–06.1.

Given the testimony presented . . . , I am convinced that if the gender of the parties had been reversed, the result would have been the opposite. The majority mischaracterizes the evidence; it was the judge, not Roland, who introduced the concept of things "that might best be done by a woman." Roland testified he received help from his mother in learning to care for the child. In response to a question about toilet training, Roland testified:

> I did that before [Patty] went to Colorado.

* * *

> I guess I started early last spring, we kind of worked with her. My mom helped me because my mom has raised kids before. So got a lot of help from my mom.

In response to a question about fixing the child's hair every morning, Roland testified:

> Um, I normally just pull it back and put it in a ponytail. I haven't gotten to the point where I can learn how to braid. So I have my mother assist me in

helping her getting her hair braided. And I comb it. I wash it. And I generally just kind of put it in a pony tail.

The court, on the other hand, specifically assumed because Roland is a man, some tasks of child rearing would be inappropriate for him. . . .

NOTES AND QUESTIONS

1. *Sex and Custody.* Is it permissible for a court to consider the sex of the parent and child in a custody determination? In Mississippi, the best interest factors are identified in a state supreme court decision, rather than in a statute, and include "the age, health and sex of a child."[97] Does consideration of the sex of the child rely on an impermissible gender stereotype? Can this factor be applied in a manner consistent with constitutional sex equality mandates?

2. *Personal Preferences.* Consider the longstanding societal preference for having boy children.[98] Gallup has polled Americans eleven times since 1941 on their gender preferences for children if they were only to have one child.[99] In the latest study, 36 percent of Americans said they would want a boy, and 28 percent said they would want a girl.[100] Over a 27-year trajectory of Gallup's polling on this issue, there has been an average 11-point gap in preferences for boys over girls, "driven by the marked preference among men for a baby boy and the more closely divided preferences among women."[101] The reasons behind this preference for boys are varied, but one common reason cited is that men relate better to males.[102] How does this assumption relate to the role of gender in custody decisions, like in *Dalin*?

C. Sexual Orientation and Gender Identity

Ex Parte J.M.F.
730 So. 2d 1190 (Ala. 1998)

Lyons, Justice. . . .

I.

The parties were divorced in January 1993, after a six-year marriage, and the trial court awarded custody of the parties' minor daughter to the mother. Shortly

---

97. Albright v. Albright, 437 So. 2d 1003 (Miss. 1983).
98. Frank Newport, Slight Preference for Having Boy Children Persists in U.S., Gallup (July 4, 2018).
99. Id.
100. Id.
101. Id.
102. Frank Newport, Americans Continue to Express Slight Preference for Boys, Gallup (July 5, 2007).

thereafter, the mother began a homosexual relationship with G.S., and in April 1992 she and her daughter moved into an apartment with G.S. Although the apartment had three bedrooms, the mother began sharing a bedroom with G.S. The father was aware of the relationship but, according to him, his conversations with the mother led him to believe that the mother and G.S. would maintain a discreet relationship, that they would not share a bedroom, and that they would represent themselves to the child and others as being merely roommates.

The father subsequently remarried, and the child regularly visited him and his new wife in their home. During the course of these visits, the father learned that his former wife and G.S. were sharing a bedroom, that the child occasionally slept with them in their bed, and that they kissed in the presence of the child. The father also noticed one instance where the child, while playing a game with her stepmother, grabbed the stepmother's breast in a way that appeared to him to be inappropriate. During visitation, the child remarked to the father that "girls could marry girls and boys could marry boys."

After the father learned that the mother and G.S. were not conducting a discreet relationship but were, in fact, openly displaying their affair to the child, and after observing the effect that this was having upon the child, he moved to modify the divorce judgment in order to obtain custody of the daughter. . . .

Terry M. Cromer, the child's appointed guardian ad litem[,] . . . confirmed . . . that the child was pretty, well-groomed, intelligent, energetic, healthy, and generally happy. He also confirmed that the child is bonded with both parents and enjoys a loving relationship with both. He recognized that . . . there were studies that had determined that there is generally no significant difference in various factors between a child who has been reared by a heterosexual couple and one who has been reared by a homosexual couple. He also pointed out that there are studies . . . which suggest that a child reared by homosexual parents could suffer exclusion, isolation, a drop in school grades, and other problems. After summarizing the evidence, Cromer recommended to the trial court that it grant the father's motion to change custody.

After considering all the evidence, the trial court entered an order changing custody to the father, finding that the change would materially promote the child's best interests and setting forth the mother's visitation rights. . . .

In reviewing the trial court's judgment, the Court of Civil Appeals pointed out that, in Alabama, evidence of a parent's heterosexual misconduct cannot, in itself, support a change of custody unless the trial court finds that the misconduct has a detrimental effect upon the child. . . . [T]he Court of Civil Appeals determined that the record contained no evidence indicating that the mother's relationship with G.S. has a detrimental effect upon the child, and it thus concluded that the trial court had improperly changed custody based solely upon the mother's homosexuality.

II.

It is, of course, well established that a noncustodial parent seeking a change of custody must show not only that he or she is fit to have custody, but that the change would materially promote the child's best interests. This requires a showing that the positive good brought about by the modification would more than offset the inherently disruptive effect caused by uprooting the child. Where a parent seeks a change of custody based solely upon the heterosexual misconduct of the custodial parent, our law requires that there be an additional showing that the misconduct has a detrimental effect upon the child.

In this case, however, the father has not sought to change the custody of the child based upon the fact that the mother is engaged in a homosexual affair. . . . The father sought custody of the child only after he had remarried and had discovered that the mother and G.S. were not conducting a discreet affair in the guise of "room-mates" but were, instead, presenting themselves openly to the child as affectionate "life partners" with a relationship similar to that of the father and the stepmother. This is, therefore, not a custody case based solely upon the mother's sexual conduct, where the "substantial detrimental effect" element might be applicable. Rather, it is a custody case based upon two distinct changes in the circumstances of the parties: (1) the change in the father's life, from single parenthood to marriage and the creation of a two-parent, heterosexual home environment, and (2) the change in the mother's homosexual relationship, from a discreet affair to the creation of an openly homosexual home environment. The father . . . was required to establish that, based upon the changes in the circumstances of the parties, a change in custody would materially promote the child's best interests and that the positive good brought by this change would more than offset the inherently disruptive effect of uprooting the child.

III. . . .

The mother has testified that she has not had any significant concern about the adverse effect her transformation from a married heterosexual to a committed homosexual could have on the child. The mother has repeatedly denied that the child will suffer any ill effects from the mother's choice of lifestyle; however, the mother has also testified that it will be up to the child to cope with any ridicule or prejudice that the child might suffer as she gets older, because, she said, "all children have to cope with prejudice anyway."

The mother and G.S. have homosexual couples as guests in their home, and the evidence suggests that the child believes that "girls can marry girls." Both the mother and G.S. have testified that they would not discourage the child from adopting a homosexual lifestyle. In short, the mother and G.S. have established a two-parent home environment where their homosexual relationship is openly practiced and presented to the child as the social and moral equivalent of a heterosexual marriage.[3]

The trial court also heard evidence indicating that the father is no longer a single parent, but has now established a happy marriage with a woman who loves the child, assists in her care, and has demonstrated a commitment to sharing the responsibility of rearing the child should the father gain custody of her. The child has consistently expressed love for the stepmother and acceptance of her as a parental figure. The father and the stepmother have a house with ample room for the child, and they are able to provide for her material needs, as well as her emotional and physical needs. In short, the father and the stepmother have established a two-parent home environment where heterosexual marriage is presented as the moral and societal norm.

The trial court had before it a number of scientific studies as to the effect of child-rearing by homosexual couples, and much of the information presented by those studies suggests that a homosexual couple with good parenting skills is just as likely to successfully rear a child as is a heterosexual couple. The trial court was also presented with studies indicating that a child reared by a homosexual couple is more likely to experience isolation, behavioral problems, and depression and that the optimum environment for rearing a child is one where both a male and a female role model are present, living together in a marriage relationship. . . .

After carefully considering all of the evidence, we simply cannot hold that the trial court abused its discretion in determining that the positive good brought about by placing the child in the custody of her father would more than offset the inherent disruption brought about by uprooting the child from her mother's custody. While the evidence shows that the mother loves the child and has provided her with good care, it also shows that she has chosen to expose the child continuously to a lifestyle that is "neither legal in this state, nor moral in the eyes of most of its citizens." *Ex parte D.W.W.,* 717 So. 2d 793, 796 (Ala. 1998).[5] The record contains evidence from which the trial court could have concluded that "[a] child raised by two women or two men is deprived of extremely valuable developmental experience and the opportunity for optimal individual growth and interpersonal

---

3. Act 98-500, Ala. Acts 1998, approved by the Governor on May 1, 1998, forbids the issuance of a marriage license "in the State of Alabama to parties of the same sex" and provides that the State of Alabama "shall not recognize as valid any marriage of parties of the same sex that occurred or was alleged to have occurred" anywhere else.

5. Under Ala. Code 1975, § 13A-6-65, it is a Class A misdemeanor to engage in consensual "deviate sexual intercourse with another person"; this statute was specifically altered by the legislature from the original draft of the "Alabama Criminal Code" proposed to the legislature, so as "to make all homosexual conduct criminal." See Commentary to § 13A-6-65 and § 13A-1-1.

In addition, Alabama has established that "[c]ourse materials and instruction" in the public schools "that relate to [sex] education" shall emphasize, "in a factual manner and from a public health perspective, that homosexuality is not a lifestyle acceptable to the general public and that homosexual conduct is a criminal offense under the laws of the state." Ala. Code 1975, § 16-40A-2(c)(8).

development" and that "the degree of harm to children from the homosexual conduct of a parent is uncertain . . . and the range of potential harm is enormous." Lynn D. Wardle, *The Potential Impact of Homosexual Parenting on Children*, 1997 U. Ill. L. Rev. 833, 895 (1997).

While much study, and even more controversy, continue to center upon the effects of homosexual parenting, the inestimable developmental benefit of a loving home environment that is anchored by a successful marriage is undisputed. The father's circumstances have changed, and he is now able to provide this benefit to the child. The mother's circumstances have also changed, in that she is unable, while choosing to conduct an open cohabitation with her lesbian life partner, to provide this benefit. The trial court's change of custody based upon the changed circumstances of the parties was not an abuse of discretion; thus, the Court of Civil Appeals erred in reversing the trial court's judgment. . . .

NOTES AND QUESTIONS

1.   *"Nexus" Test.* For many years, courts denied custody to lesbian, gay, and bisexual parents who had been married to a different-sex spouse; such parents were deemed "unfit." Eventually, though, courts began to apply a nexus test when considering whether a parent's sexual orientation should play a role in a custody determination. As a Florida appellate court described the test in 2000, the court is to consider parental conduct only if it has a "direct effect or impact upon the children."[103] The nexus test can be applied in ways that are more or less friendly to lesbian, gay, and bisexual parents. For the *J.M.F.* court, the mother's sexual orientation was relevant because the mother was openly gay and in a same-sex relationship. On this view, being out produces a nexus. In contrast, the Florida court in Jacoby v. Jacoby refused to treat the mother's same-sex relationship as necessarily having an effect on the children and dismissed the trial court's findings against the mother as "conclusory or unsupported by the evidence."[104] Citing Palmore v. Sidoti, the *Jacoby* court also refused to allow evidence of anti-gay bias in the community to provide a basis on which a court could deprive a lesbian mother of custody.[105]

Even though the nexus test constituted an improvement over earlier judicial approaches to lesbian, gay, and bisexual parents, it has attracted criticism. As Professor Nancy Polikoff argues, "The nexus test implies that a child might be uniquely harmed because a parent is gay or lesbian. . . ."[106] Echoing this view, the

---

103. Jacoby v. Jacoby, 763 So. 2d 410, 413 (Fla. Dist. Ct. App. 2000).

104. Id.

105. Id.

106. Nancy D. Polikoff, Custody Rights of Lesbian and Gay Parents Redux: The Irrelevance of Constitutional Principles, 60 UCLA L. Rev. Discourse 226 (2013).

American Law Institute's Principles of the Law of Family Dissolution provide that a "court should not consider . . . the sexual orientation of a parent."[107]

2.   *Gender and Sexual Orientation*. Based on an analysis of 200 opinions from 1950 to 2007, Professor Cliff Rosky argues that gender shapes custodial decisions involving lesbian and gay parents:

> [B]oth gay fathers and lesbian mothers are subjected to two stereotypes that are influenced by the child's gender. They are stereotyped as recruiters and role models — people who encourage children to become homosexual. Although recruiting and role modeling stereotypes are applied to both gay and lesbian parents, they are applied more often to the parents of sons than the parents of daughters, and they are rarely applied to the fathers of daughters. This pattern betrays patriarchal concerns about the importance of fathers in the production of masculine, heterosexual boys. Finally, all of these stereotypes are influenced by the judge's gender. Male judges are more likely than female judges to accept gender-influenced stereotypes about gay and lesbian parents.[108]

3.   *Sexual Conduct*. The *J.M.F.* court treated the mother's same-sex relationship as a species of sexual conduct relevant to custody determinations. The issue of parental sexual conduct arises most frequently when women begin a non-marital cohabiting relationship with a man after a divorce — an issue we raised after *Palmore*. What would be the conceivable nexus between a non-marital relationship and the child? Should such non-marital relationships be deemed irrelevant?[109]

4.   *Gender Identity*. More recently, attention has shifted toward the relevance of a parent's transgender status. In Magnuson v. Magnuson, a Washington appellate court viewed the nexus test that applied in the context of sexual orientation as appropriate in the context of gender identity.[110] The court upheld the trial court's ruling against the transgender parent, finding that it had focused on "the children's need for 'environmental and parental stability,'" and not the parent's "transgender status."[111] The dissent charged, however, that "the trial court found a lack of stability based on [the parent's] transgender status," with "no finding that [the parent's] transgender status endangered the physical, mental, or emotional health of the children."[112] In cases involving transgender parents, should a nexus test apply? Is Polikoff's critique of the nexus test with respect to sexual orientation equally

---

107. Principles of the Law of Family Dissolution, supra note 26, § 2.12(1).

108. Clifford J. Rosky, Like Father, Like Son: Homosexuality, Parenthood, and the Gender of Homophobia, 20 Yale J.L. & Feminism 257 (2009).

109. See Suzanne A. Kim, The Neutered Parent, 24 Yale J.L. & Feminism 1 (2012) (discussing legal treatment of non-marital heterosexual mothers and gay and lesbian parents).

110. 170 P.3d 65, 67 (Wash. Ct. App. 2007).

111. Id.

112. Id. (Kulik, J., dissenting).

applicable to gender identity? Should courts be instructed never to consider a parent's gender identity?

Consider the analysis of Professor Sonia Katyal and LGBT rights attorney Ilona Turner:

> We have reviewed every case we could find, published or unpublished, that involved a transgender parent, coming up with thirty cases in total, spanning from 1971 to 2015. We found that at trial, 63 percent of transgender parents lost their cases, and 62 percent of transgender parents lost on appeal, in part due to explicit biases that relate to the transgender status of the parent. . . . Just as the nexus test can serve to suggest an increasing liberalization regarding the rights of lesbian and gay parents, it can also serve to mask the employment of stereotypical, prejudicial viewpoints about transgender parents and have the same result as a per se denial of custody. The only difference here is that the discrimination is harder to spot because it is often couched in indirect observations regarding the transgender parent's behavior. . . . In the first set of cases, the court expresses a fear of harm to the child based on the presumed effect on the child due to the permanence of the gender *transition* of the parent. In a second set of cases, . . . courts express a somewhat opposing fear surrounding exposing the child to what we describe as gender *volition* — that is, that the child will be harmed by witnessing the destabilization of the parent's gender expression in transgressing their state-assigned gender. . . . In these cases, the courts may directly require the parent to restrict their gender expression in front of the child. . . . A third category of cases . . . expresses concern about the harm posed to the child through the lens of gender *contagion* — the idea that normalizing gender transition or variance can introduce a level of instability into the child's own gender identity.[113]

NOTE: CUSTODY OF TRANSGENDER AND GENDER-NONCONFORMING CHILDREN

We have focused on custody in the context of the gender identity of a parent. But courts also encounter custody disputes involving transgender or gender-nonconforming children. What happens when parents disagree about whether and how to affirm a transgender or gender-nonconforming child? These conflicts may surface through custody change petitions. In Kristen L. v. Benjamin W., the Alaska Supreme Court affirmed a trial court's change of custody from a mother to a father, due to the mother's abusive conduct toward the child and lack of support of the

---

113. Sonia K. Katyal & Ilona M. Turner, Transparenthood, 117 Mich. L. Rev. 1593, 1599, 1628, 1630, 1632 (2019).

child's gender expression.[114] The trial court had determined that the change in custody would be "in the best interests of the child."[115] In other, earlier cases, courts have been less supportive of parents who sought to affirm their child's gender identity. For instance, in Smith v. Smith, an Ohio appellate court affirmed a trial court order shifting custody from the mother to the father based on findings that the mother "pushed the boy into believing he was a transgender child" and that she "could not be trusted to obey any court orders concerning the child's gender confusion."[116] Social scientist Katherine Kuvalanka and colleagues have studied mothers who have faced custody battles after affirming their transgender or gender-nonconforming child's identity.[117] These mothers reported similar experiences, including being blamed for causing their child's gender nonconformity, coercion by ex-partners, and bias in courts.[118] They also reported a negative impact on the child from the custody battle and an emotional and financial toll on all parties.[119]

PROBLEMS

1. Imagine that you serve on a committee that the Uniform Law Commission has appointed to revise the Uniform Marriage and Divorce Act (UMDA). This week's meeting is focused on Section 402, which contains the factors to be considered in determining the child's best interests. This section declares: "The court shall not consider conduct of a proposed custodian that does not affect his relationship to the child."[120] Your committee is considering whether to revise this provision on parental conduct. Would you? What would it say? What commentary would you include to explain its meaning and application?

2. Rob and Marcy are divorcing after twelve years of marriage. They have one child, Sam, who is ten. Sam, who was assigned male at birth, has been stating over the past year that she is a girl. She has demanded that her parents use female

---

114. No. S-15302, 2014 WL 2716842 (Alaska June 11, 2014).

115. Id. at *2, *4.

116. No. 05 JE 42, 2007 WL 901599, at *9-10 (Ohio Ct. App. Mar. 23, 2007). See also Williams v. Frymire, 377 S.W.3d 579, 590–91 (Ky. Ct. App. 2012). In *Williams*, the court affirmed the trial court's transfer of mother's sole custody to joint custody with father, who would also have primary residential custody, based on conclusions of experts that child was improperly diagnosed with gender identity disorder and concern that mother would not be "agreeable to what the court might direct her to do with regard to [child's] best interests." Id.

117. Katherine A. Kuvalanka et al., An Exploratory Study of Custody Challenges Experienced by Affirming Mothers of Transgender and Gender-Nonconforming Children, 57 Fam. Ct. Rev. 54, 54–55 (2019).

118. Id.

119. Id.

120. UMDA, supra note 22, § 402.

pronouns and officially change her first name from Samuel to Samantha. Rob has been supportive of Sam's gender identity, has taken Sam to a licensed therapist, and has scheduled an appointment with a doctor who specializes in gender identity in children. Marcy sincerely believes that "Sam is going through a phase and will eventually realize he is a boy." Marcy believes that to treat Sam as a girl will be more confusing and detrimental than helpful. Marcy has refused to take Sam to the therapist, and she is urging Rob to cancel the appointment with the doctor. Over the past several months, Rob and Marcy have fought often about what to do with Sam. They are now fighting over custody. They each seek primary legal and physical custody. You are the judge assigned to the case. What information would you like to obtain to help you make a decision? What decision do you think you're likely to reach?

D. Disability

ARNESON V. ARNESON
670 N.W.2d 904 (S.D. 2003)

KONENKAMP, JUSTICE.

This appeal concerns whether the circuit court improperly considered the father's physical limitations resulting from his cerebral palsy in deciding child custody between the parents. The father challenges . . . the child custody award to the mother. . . .

I. Background

Travis and Teresa Arneson married on March 28, 1998. Their only child, Grace Marie Ann Arneson, was born on September 24, 1998. When Travis was six months old, he was diagnosed with cerebral palsy. At birth, he suffered a lack of oxygen caused by a physician's negligence. From the resulting medical malpractice settlement, Travis now receives monthly personal injury payments for life. He uses a wheel chair and a personal attendant. He does not consider himself "confined" to a wheelchair. He feeds and bathes himself. As he explained to the court in an affidavit, he is independent and capable of caring for himself: "I do hire personal assistants to help me with my day to day routines, not because I need the help but to make my life easier and improve the quality of my life."

Travis suffers no disability of intellect. He graduated with honors from high school and Southeastern Votech. An advocate for people with disabilities on both the local and national level, Travis works as a counselor at the Jaycee Camp for the

Exceptional. He believes he is capable of caring for his child, "without assistance of an aide." On the subject of his daughter, he is passionate:

> I am no different than any other parent. I love my child and I am able to care for her, albeit, not societies [sic] standard idea of care. My daughter gets all of her needs met with me; I love her and I am a positive influence on her emotionally. She loves spending time with me and I love spending time with her; we need each other just like any other parent/child relationship. Grace does not see me as disabled; she sees me as her daddy.

Teresa is equally devoted to her child. She believes that she provided for a greater share of Grace's physical needs when she and Travis lived together. For five months, when Grace was still in diapers, Teresa worked a night shift from 11:00 p.m. to 7:00 a.m., leaving Grace at home alone with Travis. During these absences, Teresa was comfortable with their arrangements for Grace because before Teresa left for work, Grace was already asleep and she slept through the night; Grace was an infant and not able to climb out of her crib; Teresa was only eight blocks away from the residence and had made arrangements with her supervisor to leave if there was an emergency. Moreover, Travis and Teresa had both talked to the neighbors about the situation so that Travis could call on a neighbor for help when needed. In fact, Teresa testified that Travis did call on neighbors to assist with diaper changes on occasions when Teresa ran errands. Teresa made sure before she left that Travis had attendants to assist him and that everything was lined up beforehand. On one other occasion, when the parties were having marital difficulties, Teresa went to stay with her parents. Although she wanted to take Grace with her, Travis would not allow it. She was gone for approximately one week.

In April 2001, Travis sued Teresa for divorce. While the action was pending, the circuit court ordered that they share custody of the child on alternating weeks. Travis's attendant later testified that during and before the time when this interim order was in place, Travis bathed, dressed, and fed his daughter. The attendant thought that any concerns about Travis's inability to react in an emergency situation were unfounded. This attendant had worked in the home for four months while the parties were still living together. She believed that Travis was more active in parenting than Teresa.

Since August 2001, Travis has lived with Edith Krueger. They were married during the pendency of this appeal. Edith and Travis have known each other since 1985, when Edith was a child care worker at the Children's Care Hospital and School. Edith provides day care for six children in Travis's home. Although Grace was at the day care in Travis's home during his alternating weeks, Teresa refused to let Grace stay there on the weeks the child was with her because Travis would not let her take the child each night.

By stipulation, the parties agreed that the court would appoint Judy Zimbelman, MSW CSW-PIP, to perform a formal custody evaluation. Zimbelman filed a report and appeared at trial to give her opinion. In her report, she wrote:

> Although Travis was able to demonstrate how he was able to care for Grace's physical needs, the majority of this time Travis has someone with him to take care of him should he need assistance. This person also cares for Grace when needed. Travis does a good job of being able to respond to Grace as needed. There are concerns for how Travis would be able to respond to Grace in times of sickness or emergency. He is able to move about in his wheelchair but it is unclear if he would be able to respond to an emergency. Travis described being able to place Grace into the bath tub as needed. With his own limitations, it appears Teresa would be able to better respond to Grace at her young age. Because of Grace's young age, it is important that she has supervision and can be responded to quickly.

Zimbelman later repeated these concerns in her testimony. On the other hand, Zimbelman reported that Travis had scored higher on the Parent Awareness Skills Survey. And Teresa had made some poor choices in male companions. Teresa took pains to tell Zimbelman that her latest companion was not around Grace often. Zimbelman recommended that Teresa obtain individual counseling on her relationship decisions.

On the subject of his disability, Zimbelman questioned whether Travis could care for Grace by himself. While acknowledging that he always made sure that Grace had the care she needs, Zimbelman noted that "Travis has care givers in his home for himself the majority of the time." She concluded that Travis's "limitations make him less able to care for Grace than Teresa." On the other hand, Zimbelman believed that at different stages of Grace's development, "there may be a need to change the parenting arrangement." As Grace becomes older, Zimbelman thought, "[I]t may be possible for her to split her time more equally with her parents."

Zimbelman concluded that "Grace is emotionally tied to her mother at this stage and needs to be with her mother on a daily basis." She also felt it important that Grace be in one home or the other: "Because of Grace's young age, it is better for a child to have a primary home. As she grows older, it may be easier for Grace to split her time with her parents." Although Travis preferred that Grace be with him every evening, Zimbleman thought that "at this age Grace needs stability. She is not able to comprehend the change of a home every week." Moreover, because of her emotional tie to her mother, "Grace would suffer by not seeing her mother all week." Zimbelman believed that "[b]y living with Teresa and going to her father's for daycare, Grace's schedule is stable." . . .

The trial court awarded joint legal custody to the parents, naming Teresa as the primary physical custodian. . . .

II. Custody Award

In deciding custody disputes between parents, "the court shall be guided by consideration of what appears to be for the best interests of the child in respect to the child's temporal and mental and moral welfare." . . .

It is a poignant reality that when parents contest the custody of their children, a court must make a choice. That choice is often difficult because between two loving parents there may be little to distinguish one over the other. Choosing between two satisfactory options falls within a judge's discretion. Thus, in our review of an ultimate decision on custody, we decide only whether the court abused its discretion. . . .

[W]e stress that a physical disability is not a per se impediment to custody. This principle is well illustrated in another authority Travis cites: Carney v. Carney, 24 Cal. 3d 725 (Cal. 1979). There, a decision on custody turned on the trial judge's stereotypical perceptions about the father's disability. The father had custody of his two boys for almost five years during which time their mother never once visited them nor made any contribution to their support. After the father became a quadriplegic resulting from an automobile accident, the mother sought a change in custody. Equating disability with parental unfitness, the court transferred custody to her, basing its decision on the father's physical handicap and its presumed adverse effect on his capacity to care for the boys. Rather than considering the deeper contributions the father made to his sons' lives, the judge puzzled over the father's inability to function with the boys in sports activities.

In reversing, the *Carney* court pointed out that the trial judge became fixed on the father's disability and disregarded other important factors in making the decision. The judge allowed assumptions about people with disabilities to control. But the *Carney* court went on to explain:

> We do not mean, of course, that the health or physical condition of the parents may not be taken into account in determining whose custody would best serve the child's interests. In relation to the issues at stake, however, this factor is ordinarily of minor importance; and whenever it is raised whether in awarding custody originally or changing it later it is essential that the court weigh the matter with an informed and open mind. . . .
>
> [I]n all cases the court must view the handicapped person as an individual and the family as a whole.

We agree with the holding in *Carney*. Although the health and physical condition of a parent is a valid factor in determining a child's best interests, a judge must neither presume the existence of limitations nor fail to adequately consider other relevant factors. When faced with a parent's disability in a custody dispute, the judge should consider: (1) the person's actual and potential physical capabilities; (2) how the parent has managed and adapted to the disability; (3) how the other members of the household have adjusted to it; and (4) "the special contributions the person may make to the family despite, or even because of, the handicap." Weighing these and other relevant factors together, the court should then decide what effect, if any, the parent's condition will have on the best interests of the child.

Here, unlike in *Carney*, the trial court took evidence on Travis's disability, but properly centered on the three [ ] elements most relevant in these circumstances: fitness, stability, and primary caretaker. Concerning the fitness factor, the court found that Teresa was more willing to "maturely encourage and provide frequent and meaningful contact between the child and the other parent." In addition, the court noted that Travis was living with a woman to whom he was not married. They eventually married during the pendency of this appeal, but, of course, the court could not have counted on that at the time. As to the stability factor, the court noted that both parents were equal. The court concluded that Teresa was Grace's primary caretaker and then concurred in Zimbelman's observation that at her present age, Grace needs to be with the one she is most emotionally attached to, Teresa.

Travis takes issue with Zimbelman's assessment of his limitations, especially her concerns about his ability "to respond to Grace in times of sickness or emergency." He insists that in so concluding, Zimbelman "let her stereotypical assumptions prevail." The trial court never found that Travis had such limitations. However, the court did find "the opinions and observations of the expert to be reasonable and well grounded and . . . placed great weight upon them." Travis believes that Zimbelman should have tested his response times before coming to her conclusions about his ability to respond. But Zimbelman did observe Travis in his daily activities. As she stated in her report,

> Travis demonstrated how he was able to move around the house and how he was able to care for Grace. He drove his wheel chair to the stairs and slid down the stairs to his bedroom. . . . Travis also demonstrated how he was able to get Grace a drink if she asked for one and how he was able to get something for her to eat or drink.

Only then did she express her concerns about his ability to respond in an emergency. Travis may take exception to her opinion, but this is not a case of discrimination, as Travis contends, by reliance on assumptions about a physical condition as prima facie evidence of parental unfitness. On the contrary, Zimbelman directly observed Travis's mobility in his home. By stipulation of the parties, Zimbelman was appointed by the court to perform a home study on each parent. If Travis felt that Zimbelman's assessment misrepresented his abilities, he could have brought in his own expert to contradict her.

Travis also contends that the court resurrected the "tender years" doctrine. He quotes the court's bench comments: "[B]ecause of the age of the child . . . the mother is the important one now. As the child gets older, as the discipline comes into it, discipline is necessary and so forth and guidance, perhaps things may change." We do not ordinarily probe the court's oral pronouncements. In reviewing decisions, we look to the formal written findings. Nonetheless, although we must base our review on the written findings, we acknowledge that these remarks sound as if the tender year's doctrine were still alive in the trial court's view. Yet, an examination of the entire fact findings does not bear out Travis's complaint. In commenting on tender years, the court was speaking primarily in the context of the child's emotional attachment to her mother, a matter on which Zimbelman gave her expert opinion. As Zimbelman said, small children are more emotionally attached for nurturing and security to their primary caretakers, whether male or female. At the same time, the trial court recognized that children's needs change over time, just as the South Dakota Visitation Guidelines envision. . . . Concluding that Teresa had been Grace's primary caretaker until the separation when Travis became more active, the court followed Zimbelman's recommendation that Grace needed "daily contact with her mother to [meet] her needs." . . .

On the whole, the record does not reveal that the trial court's findings were clearly erroneous. We conclude that the court properly considered the relevant factors in making its custody determination and did not abuse its discretion in awarding primary physical custody to Teresa.

NOTES AND QUESTIONS

1. *Individualized Assessment.* Notice how in *Arneson*, as well as in the *Carney* decision discussed in *Arneson*, the court sought to make an individualized assessment of the custody claim involving a parent with a disability. Does this seem like the right approach? In identifying factors to be considered in the best interest determination, the Uniform Marriage and Divorce Act § 402(5) includes a parent's physical and mental health. Do you favor inclusion of this factor?

Some scholars express concerns that when judges are given discretion to consider disability in the best interests analysis, they may act on harmful assumptions. Consider the view of Professor Nicole Buonocore Porter: "Courts are often worried about children having to be too independent at too young of an age or having to 'parent' the parent with a disability. For instance, one judge insisted that a mother with a physical disability could not be a good parent because of her disability. The judge assumed that the children would function as her caregivers, despite evidence that the home was modified, the mother had a personal assistant, and the children did not have more than normal chores."[121]

2. *Gender and Disability.* Consider the relationship between gender norms and disability in *Arneson* and *Carney*. In *Arneson*, did the trial court revive the tender years presumption? How did gender norms affect perceptions of parenting in *Carney*?

---

121. Nicole Buonocore Porter, Mothers with Disabilities, 33 Berkeley J. Gender L. & Just. 75, 90–91, 92 (2018); see also Robyn M. Powell, Family Law, Parents with Disabilities, and the Americans with Disabilities Act, 57 Fam. Ct. Rev. 37, 41 (2019).

E. Religion

PATER V. PATER
588 N.E.2d 794 (Ohio 1992)

WRIGHT, JUSTICE.

Today we reaffirm that a domestic relations court may consider the religious practices of the parents in order to protect the best interests of a child. However, the United States Constitution flatly prohibits a trial court from ever evaluating the merits of religious doctrine or defining the contents of that doctrine. Furthermore, custody may not be denied to a parent solely because she will not encourage her child to salute the flag, celebrate holidays, or participate in extracurricular activities. We reverse the trial court's custody and visitation orders because these decisions were improperly based on Jennifer Pater's religious beliefs. . . .

A reviewing court will not overturn a custody determination unless the trial court has acted in a manner that is arbitrary, unreasonable, or capricious.

It is against this standard of broad discretion that we must review the scope of a trial court's inquiry into the parents' religious practices. The other starting point for our analysis is that a court may well violate the parent's constitutional rights if its decision is improperly based on religious bias. See *Palmore v. Sidoti*, 466 U.S. 429 (1984) (courts cannot implement private prejudices, even if they are widely held by the population). The United States Constitution and the Ohio Constitution forbid state action which interferes with the religious freedom of its citizens or prefers one religion over another. To the extent that a court refuses to award custody to a parent because of her religious beliefs, the court burdens her choice of a religion in violation of the Free Exercise Clause of the United States Constitution.

In addition to their free exercise rights, parents have a fundamental right to educate their children, including the right to communicate their moral and religious values. *Wisconsin v. Yoder*, 406 U.S. 205 (1972); *Pierce v. Society of Sisters*, 268 U.S. 510 (1925). . . . In a custody dispute, the parents' rights must be balanced against the state's need to determine the best interests of the child. . . .

Courts have repeatedly held that custody cannot be awarded solely on the basis of the parents' religious affiliations and that to do so violates the First Amendment to the United States Constitution.

On the other hand, a parent's actions are not insulated from the domestic relations court's inquiry just because they are based on religious beliefs, especially actions that will harm the child's mental or physical health. In *Birch v. Birch*, 463 N.E.2d 1254, 1257 (Ohio 1984), we held that courts can examine the parent's religious practices to determine the best interests of the child because ". . . the law does not require that a child be actually harmed or that a parent's unsuitability to have custody of her children be disregarded because the parent claims that the bases of her unsuitability are religious practices." The state's compelling interest in protecting children from physical or mental harm clearly allows a court to deny custody to a parent who will not provide for the physical and mental needs of the child.

The facts of this case, however, bear little or no resemblance to those in *Birch*. That case involved a woman who had formerly been hospitalized for schizophrenia and who had neglected her children's physical needs as a result of her religious fanaticism. In contrast, Robert and Jennifer Pater are both loving parents, and no testimony seriously disputed either parent's ability to nurture Bobby. This case requires us to decide whether courts may deny a parent custody based on beliefs that do not pose a direct threat to the child's mental or physical welfare. Given the undisputed fact that both parents would meet Bobby's basic needs, the question is whether the intrusion into Jennifer's rights was justified by appellee's claims that if awarded custody, Jennifer would not allow Bobby to participate in certain extracurricular activities, celebrate holidays, or salute the flag.

Appellee claims that Jennifer will not allow their son to celebrate birthdays and holidays, sing the national anthem, salute the flag, participate in extracurricular activities, socialize with non-Witnesses, or attend college. Appellee is concerned that the child will be socially ostracized and not adequately exposed to ideas other than those endorsed by the Jehovah's Witnesses. We can sympathize with his parental concern for his child, but are concerned that the state not exceed its proper role in resolving what is essentially a dispute between the parents' religious beliefs. Although the listed activities are those that most people may consider important to the socialization of children, we need to separate the value judgments implicit in the so-called norm from any actual harm caused by these practices.

Even if we accept the premise that Jennifer will actively forbid Bobby to celebrate holidays, be involved in extracurricular activities, or salute the flag,[4] these practices do not appear to directly endanger the child's physical or mental health. A showing that a child's mental health will be adversely affected requires more than proof that a child will not share all of the beliefs or social activities of the majority of his or her peers. A child's social adjustment is very difficult to measure, and the relative importance of various social activities is an extremely subjective matter.[5]

---

4. This very well may be an assumption that we are not entitled to make. Jennifer testified that she was willing to allow Bobby to choose his own religion when he reached a suitable age. . . . She further testified that Bobby would be allowed to form friendships with other children so long as they were not a bad influence on him and that he could participate in suitable extracurricular activities. The evidence that she would do otherwise is based on the testimony of other Jehovah's Witnesses and religious publications. . . .

5. Not only is an evaluation of the merits of different social activities subjective, but it is also of limited relevance to the best interests of a child. This can be easily demonstrated by considering plaintiff's claims that the child will be harmed if he does not participate in particular activities. For example, we first consider plaintiff's allegation that the child will suffer socially if he is not permitted to display patriotism, by saluting the flag or singing the national anthem. As important as these activities are personally to those of us who honor our country in these ways, these activities are just that, personal expressions, which a court should not force upon parents or their children. It seems obvious that this sort of personal decision that affects only the expression of political or religious beliefs should not be the basis for a custody decision. . . .

For these reasons, a court must base its decision that a particular religious practice will harm the mental health of a child on more than the fact that the child will not participate in certain social activities. A parent may not be denied custody on the basis of his or her religious practices unless there is probative evidence that those practices will adversely affect the mental or physical health of the child. Evidence that the child will not be permitted to participate in certain social or patriotic activities is not sufficient to prove possible harm.

The evidence offered by appellee to prove that these practices would harm Bobby consisted of two expert witnesses. Dr. Bergman testified, on the basis of a dissertation he had written, that mental illness was more common among Jehovah's Witnesses than among the general population. This testimony was a blatant attempt to stereotype an entire religion. . . .

Dr. Denber testified that generally extracurricular activities are beneficial to a child's socialization. Neither Dr. Denber nor Dr. Bergman had interviewed Bobby. No proof was offered that this particular child was suffering or would suffer any ill effects from being exposed to his mother's religious practices. In the absence of any probative evidence that a child will be harmed by a parent's religious practices regarding social activities, the court may not use those beliefs to disqualify the parent as the custodial parent.

We feel it is appropriate to question a parent about her general philosophy of childrearing. However, the scope of this inquiry into the religious beliefs and practices, not just of the mother, but of an entire religion was improper and an abuse of discretion. . . .

The trial court appears to have awarded custody to Robert because of Jennifer's religious affiliation. There is no dispute that both parents are excellent parents and we must begin from the assumption that both are equally competent to care for this child. However, at the time of the hearing, Jennifer had been Bobby's primary caretaker for the first three years of his life. She also testified that she would have more time during the week to devote to the child because she worked on only one or two weekdays. Jennifer deserves a custody hearing free from religious bias.

The visitation order in this case also indicates that the court's decision was based on Jennifer's religion. The order demands that Jennifer "shall not teach or expose the child to the Jehovah[']s Witnesses' beliefs in any form." This order is so broad that it could be construed as forbidding any discussion of the Bible. It is equally unclear whether Jennifer is permitted to discuss moral values because these values are influenced by religious beliefs.

"The rule appears to be well established that the courts should maintain an attitude of strict impartiality between religions and should not disqualify any applicant for custody or restrain any person having custody or visitation rights from taking the children to a particular church, except where there is a clear and affirmative showing that the conflicting religious beliefs affect the general welfare of the child." This rule has been adopted to protect both parents' right to expose their children to their religious beliefs, a right that does not automatically end when they are divorced. The courts should not interfere with this relationship between parent and child unless a child is exhibiting genuine symptoms of distress that are caused by the differences in the parents' religious beliefs. Today, we adopt the majority rule that a court may not restrict a non-custodial parent's right to expose his or her child to religious beliefs, unless the conflict between the parents' religious beliefs is affecting the child's general welfare. Because a divorce is a stressful event for a child, a court must carefully separate the distress caused by that event from any distress allegedly caused by religious conflict.

Accordingly, the judgment of the court of appeals is reversed, and the cause is remanded to the trial court for further proceedings in accordance with this opinion. . . .

ALICE ROBIE RESNICK, JUSTICE, concurring in part and dissenting in part. . . .

I agree that the trial court's order forbidding Jennifer from exposing Bobby to her religious beliefs was unduly broad . . . . However, I do not agree that the trial judge abused his discretion in awarding custody to Robert. . . .

I question the workability of the standard the majority formulates. . . . I am not sure how a trial judge should apply the standard. It would seem to be difficult for anyone to ever prove that specific religious practices will or will not adversely affect the health of a child in the future.

It is the role of a trial judge at a custody hearing to consider all relevant factors, and then reach a decision. That decision is based primarily on the best interests of the child, with *all* other concerns of secondary importance. Because the trial judge is in the best position to evaluate the child's best interests, a reviewing court should accord great deference to the decision of the trial judge. In this case, the trial judge considered all the relevant factors, and made a decision in a difficult situation involving two "conscientious and loving" parents.

Because I do not think the decision of the trial judge was "unreasonable, arbitrary, or unconscionable," I would affirm the judgment of the court of appeals.

NOTES AND QUESTIONS

1. *Harm to the Child.* How do courts balance parents' religious rights (as a matter of both individual liberty and parental authority) with children's interests? In Kendall v. Kendall, the Massachusetts Supreme Judicial Court observed, " '[P]arents together have freedom of religious expression and practice which enters into their liberty to manage their familial relationships.' Those individual liberties may be restricted where there is a compelling interest. A parent's right to practice religion

may be restricted only where limited exposure to that parent's beliefs is necessary to further the child's best interests."[122]

In *Pater*, what evidence would have made "a clear and affirmative showing that the conflicting religious beliefs affect[ed] the general welfare of the child" sufficient to bar custody or limit exposure to the mother's faith during visitation? What if the mother forbade birthday parties in accordance with her religion, and the psychologist had reported that the child was highly distressed about this?

The court in *Kendall* found an "affirmative showing of harm caused by exposure to the conflicting religious teachings,"[123] where the father observed a Christian fundamentalist faith, and the parents had agreed that the children would be raised Jewish, like their mother. The trial court found that harm rose above "generalized fears" and identified emotional distress among the children.[124] This included distress from exposure to negative messages about those who did not adhere to the father's faith,[125] the feeling of choosing a religion "as choosing between [the] parents," and conflict between wanting approval from the father and wanting to pursue the child's own faith, resulting in "a decline in the child's motivation and academic performance."[126] After observing that "[t]he determinative issue is whether the harm found to exist in this case [is] so substantial so as to warrant a limitation on the defendant's religious freedom," the court upheld the trial court's restrictions on the children's exposure to the father's religious beliefs.[127]

2.   *Religious Upbringing Agreements.* Parents may reach agreements about children's religious upbringing governing custody and visitation. Courts are reluctant to interfere with parents' religious practices or the religious training they give children during custodial time.[128] Even if parents have reached an express understanding in a separation agreement, courts are often reluctant to enforce them,[129] particularly in a way that would appear to dictate parents' particular religious practices. In Weisberger v. Weisberger, a New York appellate court declined to enforce a religious upbringing clause in a separation agreement to "give the children a Hasidic [Jewish] upbringing in all details" in such a way as to require a gay mother to "practice full religious observance in accordance with the Hasidic practices of ultra Orthodoxy during any period in which she has physical custody of the children."[130] The court held that the agreement concerned only the children's religious upbringing and so

---

122. Kendall v. Kendall, 687 N.E.2d 1228, 1232 (Mass. 1997).

123. Id.

124. Id. at 1233.

125. Id. (finding that "the oldest child . . . has drawn . . . the conclusion that [the mother] may go to hell, and that this causes him substantial worry and upset").

126. Id. at 1234.

127. Id. at 1232.

128. Brian H. Bix, Marriage Agreements and Religion, 2016 U. Ill. L. Rev. 1665, 1673–74.

129. Id.

130. Weisberger v. Weisberger, 60 N.Y.S.3d 265, 268 (N.Y. App. Div. 2017).

did not "require the mother to practice any type of religion, to dress in any particular way, or to hide her views or identity from the children. Nor may the courts compel any person to adopt any particular religious lifestyle."[131]

PROBLEM

Sejal and Mahendra divorced one year ago and share legal and physical custody of their 2-year-old daughter. During their marriage, Sejal and Mahendra followed the tenets of their Hindu faith. This included Hindu ceremonies related to their daughter, including a religious baby shower, a naming ceremony, and an ear-piercing ceremony. They attended temple weekly and even had a temple in their home at which they worshipped daily. They both continue to practice their Hindu faith.

Sejal and Mahendra disagree about whether a Hindu religious ritual, Chudakarana, should be performed on their daughter. Chudakarana involves shaving the child's head, placing an auspicious mark on her head, and conferring blessings. The ceremony should be performed before the child turns three. If the ceremony is not performed by this point, a family elder may atone, permitting the ritual to be performed at a later time.

Sejal seeks to have the ritual performed on his daughter. He asserts that Chudakarana is considered a prerequisite for an individual to have a Hindu marriage. Mahendra does not want the ritual performed. She maintains that it is not integral to the Hindu faith. Neither she nor her brother participated in Chudakarana. Sejal did not inquire about this before they married.

You are the judge assigned to their case. What decision would you make concerning the daughter's proposed Chudakarana? What additional information would help you make a decision? How would constitutional concerns affect your reasoning?

V. Custody Modification and Relocation Disputes

Even after a court's initial determination of child custody, parental disagreements may persist notwithstanding the court's efforts to resolve matters. Parents who are unhappy with the court's resolution might try to find their way back into court to

---

131. Id. at 275.

have the custody order modified to suit their preferences. And sometimes circumstances will change to such an extent that the prior order is no longer appropriate and should be modified.

Custody modification disputes arise in a wide variety of circumstances — some of which you saw in the preceding section in cases like *Palmore* and *J.M.F.* One common scenario is when the parent with primary physical custody desires to relocate with the child, and the other parent opposes the relocation. Relocation disputes, like other custody modification controversies, pit two legal principles against each other. On the one hand, judicial determinations are meant to be final and accorded res judicata effect. Parties are not permitted to relitigate issues previously decided. On the other hand, children's best interests and the ability of either parent to serve them may undergo tremendous change after an initial decree is entered. Thus, in the child custody context, courts are authorized to address changes that are significant enough to mean the initial placement is no longer serving the child's best interests. That is why courts maintain continuing jurisdiction in child custody cases, just as they do with child support and spousal support.

Two questions dominate the caselaw: (1) what changes are material enough to justify reopening the custody matter; and (2) once reopened, what standard should be applied to decide whether to modify the existing custody order? To avoid repetitive, frivolous, or otherwise burdensome litigation, the law imposes a threshold requirement for letting the case back into court. Although some jurisdictions will entertain modification petitions more liberally, the general rule is that a party may petition for a modification of the prior custody order only upon a showing of a material change in circumstances. As a Michigan appellate court explained the standard in its state:

> To establish a change of circumstances sufficient for a court to consider modifying a custody order, the movant must prove by a preponderance of the evidence that "since the entry of the last custody order, the conditions surrounding custody of the child, which have or could have a *significant* effect on the child's well-being, have materially changed." "[T]he evidence must demonstrate something more than the normal life changes (both good and bad) that occur during the life of a child, and there must be at least some evidence that the material changes have had or will almost certainly have an effect on the child." . . .
>
> The purpose of this threshold showing "is to minimize unwarranted and disruptive changes of custody orders, except under the most compelling circumstances." . . .[132]

The Michigan court explained that once the moving party makes the necessary showing of changed circumstances, "the court may proceed to an analysis of

---

132. Lieberman v. Orr, 900 N.W.2d 130, 138–39 (Mich. Ct. App. 2017).

whether the requested modification is in the child's best interests."[133] But some juris-dictions, as well as the Uniform Marriage and Divorce Act, apply a higher standard. Section 409 of the UMDA provides: "No motion to modify a custody decree may be made earlier than 2 years after its date, unless the court permits it to be made on the basis of affidavits that there is reason to believe the child's present environment may endanger seriously his physical, mental, moral, or emotional health."[134]

Approaches to modification may also vary depending on the type of change at issue. For example, many states apply a more lenient standard when a parent seeks only a change in parenting time or visitation, as opposed to a change in custody.[135] In fact, in contrast to its approach to custody modification, the UMDA provides that a "court may modify an order granting or denying visitation rights whenever modification would serve the best interest of the child."[136]

Parental relocation is another context in which states might depart from their general approach to modification and instead examine relocation as a distinctive problem. The next case addresses this issue.

ARNOTT V. ARNOTT
293 P.3d 440 (Wyo. 2012)

BURKE, JUSTICE.

[T]he parties were married in 2001 and lived together in Jackson, Wyoming until their divorce in 2010. Their first daughter, AGA, was born on June 6, 2003, and their second daughter, ALA, was born on June 30, 2005. At the time of their divorce, the parties agreed that they would share joint legal custody of the children, and that Mother would have primary physical custody, subject to Father's reason-able visitation. The parties agreed to "consult with each other regarding major deci-sions involving the children, including but not limited to their education, health, and other issues involving the children's welfare." The parties agreed that Father would have visitation every other weekend, as well as on alternating Thursdays. They also agreed to Father's visitation on alternating holidays and during two two-week periods in the summer. The decree of divorce required Mother to provide notice if she intended to relocate.

On July 8, 2011, Mother filed a notice of intent to relocate, indicating that she intended to move with the children to Mechanicsville, Virginia on August 13, 2011....

The district court began the hearing by noting that [our prior decision in] *Watt v. Watt*, 971 P.2d 608 (Wyo. 1999), and its progeny had established a presumption in favor of the custodial parent's right to relocate with the children....

---

133. Id. at 138.
134. UMDA, supra note 22, § 409(b).
135. See, e.g., Lieberman, 900 N.W.2d 130.
136. UMDA, supra note 22, § 407(a).

During the hearing, the court received testimony from several witnesses, including the parties, the children's dual-language immersion teacher, a nurse from their pediatrician's office, Mother's sister, and a close personal friend of Father's. At the conclusion of the hearing, the court issued its ruling from the bench.

The court found that the children had "an outstanding set of parents" and "an incredibly involved father whose life revolves around his relationship with his children." The court noted that both Mother and Father were exemplary parents, that the children were "thriving" in their current environment, and that the "arrangement here in Jackson has worked incredibly well." The court further commented that "If I had my wish it would be that Ms. Arnott would find some way to stay here or nearer so that the extraordinary relationship that Mr. Arnott has with his children could continue to blossom in a similar fashion." But the court again noted that Wyoming precedent had created a "strong presumption in favor of allowing the custodial parent to move with [the] children" and had placed a "difficult burden" on the noncustodial parent to show a material change in circumstances based on the custodial parent's relocation.

Following the criteria set forth in *Watt*, the district court determined that Mother's motives for the relocation were legitimate, sincere, and in good faith. The court also found that Mother's relocation would still permit Father's reasonable visitation if visitation was expanded. The court concluded that Father had not established that Mother's relocation constituted a material change of circumstances sufficient to warrant consideration of a change in custody. . . .

After both parties submitted proposals for a revised visitation schedule, the court ordered a visitation plan for Father that increased his summer visitation to eight weeks, and expanded visitation during school holidays and during a week in February. The visitation plan also allowed Father to visit the children at any time in Virginia with advance notice. Father appeals from the district court's order. . . .

Disputes arising from the relocation of a custodial parent "present some of the knottiest and most disturbing problems that our courts are called upon to resolve." . . .

As a general rule, the provisions of a divorce decree, including those pertaining to child custody, are subject to the doctrine of res judicata, which bars litigation of issues that were or could have been determined in a prior proceeding. Res judicata "is mandated by public necessity; there must be an end to litigation at some point, or else the legal system would become so bogged down that nothing would ever remain decided." This Court has recognized, however, that application of res judicata to a petition for modification of child custody is not appropriate where there has been a "material or substantial change in circumstances" with respect to the initial custody determination. In that instance, res judicata does not apply because "[the] modification proceeding involves new issues framed by facts differing from those existing when the original decree was entered. A new adjudication of the rights of the parties must be made. For all intents and purposes it is a separate and distinct case from the original proceeding." . . .

The district court does not properly acquire jurisdiction to reopen an existing custody order until there has been a showing of "a substantial or material change of circumstances which outweigh society's interest in applying the doctrine of res judicata" to a custody order. In short, unless the district court finds a material change in circumstances, it cannot proceed to the second step — determining whether a modification would be in the best interests of the child. . . .

The present case relates to the threshold inquiry under Wyo. Stat. Ann. § 20-2-204(c): whether relocation of a custodial parent may constitute a material change in circumstances sufficient to warrant consideration of whether modification of custody is in the best interests of the children. Because relocation of a custodial parent is not addressed in [Wyoming statutes] . . . , our analysis is guided by relevant case law. . . .

In [Watt] . . . , mother was granted primary physical custody of the parties' three children. However, the divorce decree provided for an automatic change in custody from mother to father if mother moved more than fifty miles from Upton, Wyoming, where the parties resided. After mother was accepted into the pharmacy program at the University of Wyoming, she sought modification of the divorce decree in order to allow her to pursue her degree in Laramie. Father opposed the modification and requested that custody be awarded to him based on the automatic change in custody provision in the divorce decree. The trial court ruled that it had erred in providing for an automatic change of custody in the decree and refused to invoke it. Nonetheless, the district court found a material change in circumstances based on mother's relocation and found that the children's best interests would be served by remaining with their father in Upton.

On appeal, this Court [emphasized] . . . that "So long as the court is satisfied with the motives of the custodial parent in seeking the move and reasonable visitation is available to the remaining parent, removal should be granted." . . . In determining that the trial court abused its discretion in finding a material change in circumstances based on mother's relocation, Watt held that "a relocation, by itself, is not a substantial or material change in circumstances sufficient to justify a change in custody order." The decision focused heavily on the custodial parent's right to travel, reasoning as follows:

> The constitutional question posed is whether the rights of a parent and the duty of the courts to adjudicate custody serve as a premise for restricting or inhibiting the freedom to travel of a citizen of the State of Wyoming and of the United States of America. We hold this to be impossible. The right of travel enjoyed by a citizen carries with it the right of a custodial parent to have the children move with that parent. This right is not to be denied, impaired, or disparaged unless clear evidence before the court demonstrates another

substantial and material change of circumstance and establishes the detrimental effect of the move upon the children. While relocation certainly may be stressful to a child, the normal anxieties of a change of residence and the inherent difficulties that the increase in geographical distance between parents imposes are not considered to be "detrimental" factors. . . .

Reasonable visitation remains possible, even if that visitation might be less than what Mr. Watt previously enjoyed. Visitation can be resolved by the appropriate exercise of the broad discretion of the trial court to modify orders with respect to contact and visitation in order to minimize the loss of contact and visitation between children and the non-custodial parent. Relocation indeed is a ground for such a modification. It is not a ground for modifying custody. . . .

Father [in this case] claims that our precedent, which establishes a strong presumption in favor of the relocating parent, does not adequately account for his constitutional right to raise his children. Father asserts that "The clear multi-jurisdictional trend in relocation cases is one that favors an approach that balances the fundamental constitutional rights of the parties in order to arrive at a solution that respects the rights of both parents, but holds paramount the best interests of the children." He urges us to follow this trend, and to overrule *Watt*'s holding that a relocation cannot by itself constitute a material change in circumstances sufficient to warrant consideration of the best interests of the children.

Mother . . . contends that we should uphold Wyoming precedent pursuant to the doctrine of *stare decisis*. She asserts that "Father does not have a [c]onstitutional right to raise his children which is superior to Mother's own [c]onstitutional right as the custodial parent," and that "[t]he right of [M]other to associate with her children in their new familial configuration is important and should be respected." Mother does not dispute that most jurisdictions follow the rule recognizing that a relocation may constitute a material change of circumstances sufficient to justify a modification of custody. She notes, however, that "our own legislature has not adopted statutory presumptions for or against relocation, nor has it determined that [] a noncustodial parent's rights trump those of a custodial parent." As a corollary, Mother asserts that this Court "should not adopt a new standard based on the examples of other states and other, differing statutes." . . .

We begin our analysis by identifying the competing rights and interests at stake in a case involving modification of child custody based on the relocation of a custodial parent. First, as this Court properly recognized in *Watt*, the custodial parent has a right of travel worthy of protection. Importantly, however, the custodial parent's right to travel is not the only interest deserving of protection in relocation cases. The minority time parent in a shared custody arrangement has an equally important fundamental right of familial association.

[W]e have repeatedly held that, "'[t]he right to associate with one's immediate family is a fundamental liberty protected by the state and federal constitutions.' . . . Resolution of which parent shall have custody necessarily implicates the fundamental right of family association."

Further, just as parents have a fundamental right to associate with their children, "Children have as fundamental a right to familial association [with their] parents."

Additionally, the state has a compelling interest in promoting the best interests of the children. . . .

Despite this clear Wyoming authority recognizing both the minority time parent's right to parent and the state's compelling interest in promoting the best interests of the children in child custody cases, these interests did not receive attention or consideration in *Watt*. As noted above, this Court's holding in *Watt* was very explicitly, and exclusively, grounded in the custodial parent's right to travel. . . .

In *Watt*, we seemed to marginalize both a parent's and a child's right to familial association, as well as the state's interest in the welfare of children. . . .

On further examination of *Watt*, we find that its exclusive focus on the custodial parent's right to travel is not supported by our earlier precedent, and that the decision, in holding that a relocation, by itself, cannot constitute a material change in circumstances, unjustifiably elevates the custodial parent's right to travel over the competing interests of the minority time parent and the state's concern for the best interests of the child. Although a custodial parent's right to travel is entitled to protection, this interest must be weighed against the minority time parent's right to maintain a close relationship and frequent contact with his or her children. Further, because the goal in custody cases is to reach an arrangement that promotes the best interests of the children, the rights of both parents must be considered only to the extent that they are consistent with that goal. Ultimately, we agree with the conclusion reached in other jurisdictions that presumptions in favor of one parent or another are detrimental to the interests of all parties in cases involving modification of child custody based on relocation of a custodial parent. . . .

In summary, we conclude that *Watt*'s prohibition against considering relocation as a factor contributing to a material change in circumstances does not properly account for the minority time parent's right to associate with his or her family, the child's right to familial association, or the state's "paramount concern" for promoting the best interests of the children. With this decision, we explicitly recognize that a relocation by the primary physical custodian, as well as "factors that are derivative of the relocation" — including "the inherent difficulties that the increase in geographical distance between parents imposes" — may constitute a material change in circumstances sufficient to warrant consideration of the best interests of the children. To the extent this conflicts with this Court's holding in *Watt*, we hereby overrule *Watt*.

Further, based on the facts of the present case, we find that Mother's relocation to Virginia, over 2,000 miles away from Father, constitutes a material change in circumstances. As we have previously noted, however, "a material change of circumstance does not automatically equate with a change in custody." . . . We must emphasize, by this decision, we are not suggesting a particular result. We are only requiring that the determination be made by application of the correct legal standard. . . .

NOTES AND QUESTIONS

---

1. *Post-*Arnott *Elaboration.* According to the court's ruling in *Arnott*, what sort of threshold showing is necessary to show that a proposed relocation constitutes a change in circumstance sufficient to permit the court to consider the modification of its prior custody order? In a case decided after *Arnott*, the Wyoming Supreme Court set forth a multi-factor test to determine whether relocation would constitute a material change in circumstances. The factors include any "change in the ability of the parties to maintain the existing parenting agreement, a change in the ability of the child[] to maintain a close relationship with the remaining parent, factors affecting the quality of life in the new location, the child's geographic preference, and the relative merits of available social and educational opportunities in the new location."[137]

Courts vary considerably in their assessment of what constitutes a sufficient change in circumstances to warrant reconsideration of the custody decree. But in most states, relocation over a considerable distance that would strain the other parent's ability to visit with the child is sufficient to constitute a material change in circumstances.[138]

2. *Constitutional Rights.* The right to travel is a constitutional right that has been recognized by the U.S. Supreme Court.[139] Some state courts have asserted that the right to travel precludes significantly limiting a custodial parent's ability to relocate with the child.[140] Courts in other states, in contrast, do not view limits on relocation of the custodial parent and child as unconstitutionally infringing the right to travel.[141] Note that even when a court denies a relocation motion, the court does not prohibit the custodial parent from moving away from the jurisdiction, just from moving *and* taking the child. Formally, both parents are free to move. The noncustodial parent typically can move even without providing notice to the court. Are the parents' rights to move equal? Or is the custodial parent unfairly burdened by the threat of a change in custody?

---

137. Kappen v. Kappen, 341 P.3d 377 (Wyo. 2015).

138. See, e.g., Schrag v. Spear, 858 N.W.2d 865 (Neb. 2015) (affirming trial court's denial of relocation from Nebraska to New York where mother with custody did not have firm offer of employment or other income-generating activity and concluding that move would adversely affect father's ability to exercise visitation).

139. Shapiro v. Thompson, 394 U.S. 618 (1969).

140. See, e.g., Jaramillo v. Jaramillo, 823 P.2d 299 (N.M. 1991).

141. See, e.g., Braun v. Headley, 750 A.2d 624 (Md. Ct. Spec. App. 2000).

What other constitutional rights are implicated by relocation disputes? How heavily do you weigh the parental rights of each parent? Or the rights of the child?

3.   *Private Ordering and Future Relocation.* Courts typically do not allow prior agreements by the ex-spouses about eventual relocation to dictate the results of custody modification motions, even if the parties' agreement was incorporated into the couple's divorce decree.[142] While courts do not pronounce such provisions invalid, neither do they allow them to control the court's resolution.[143] Should these agreements have more weight?

4.   *Varying Standards.* The law regarding relocation is in flux, with no single standard dominating. As the New Jersey Supreme Court observed in 2017:

> Today, the majority of states, either by statute or by case law, impose a best interests test when considering a relocation application filed by a parent with primary custody or custody for the majority of the child's time;[144] some have recently abandoned a presumption in favor of the parent of primary residence. A minority of jurisdictions apply a standard that expressly or implicitly favors the relocation decision of the parent with primary or majority-time custody;[145] some but not all of those jurisdictions characterize that preference as a "presumption."[146]

Some jurisdictions employ shifting presumptions, requiring the non-relocating parent to show that the move is not in the child's best interests, but only after the relocating parent has made a showing that the move is both in good faith and in the child's best interests.[147]

The relevant sources of law also vary. While in some states the standards governing relocation disputes come solely from case law, in other states statutes address these disputes. A Washington statute, for example, lists eleven factors that a court must consider when adjudicating a dispute about parental relocation, including the noncustodial parent's mobility.[148] A similar statute regarding child relocation came into force in Florida in 2006.[149]

---

142. In re Marriage of Francis, 919 P.2d 776 (Colo. 1996); Zeller v. Zeller, 640 N.W.2d 53 (N.D. 2002); Frauenshuh v. Giese, 599 N.W.2d 153 (Minn. 1999).

143. Lee v. Cox, 790 P.2d 1359 (Alaska 1990).

144. The examples cited by the court include: Ariz. Rev. Stat. Ann. § 25-408(A), (G); Conn. Gen. Stat. § 46b-56d(a); Chesser-Witmer v. Chesser, 117 P.3d 711 (Alaska 2005); and In re Marriage of Ciesluk, 113 P.3d 135 (Colo. 2005).

145. The examples cited by the court include: Okla. Stat. tit. 43, § 112.3(K); Wis. Stat. § 767.481(3)(a); Singletary v. Singletary, 431 S.W.3d 234 (Ark. 2013); In re Marriage of Hoffman, 867 N.W.2d 26 (Iowa 2015).

146. Bisbing v. Bisbing, 166 A.3d 1155, 1167–69 (N.J. 2017).

147. See Linda D. Elrod, States Differ on Relocation: A Panorama of Expanding Case Law, 28 Fam. Advoc. 8 (2005).

148. Child Relocation Act, Wash. Rev. Code §§ 26.09.405–.560. Washington courts considered this factor prior to the 2000 Act. See, e.g., In re Marriage of Littlefield, 940 P.2d 1362, 1365 (Wash. 1997).

149. Fla. Stat. § 61.13001 (2020).

5. *Joint Physical Custody.* Some states apply different standards to relocation disputes depending on whether the parties have joint physical custody. For example, a parent with primary physical custody might have a presumptive right to relocate with the child, while a parent in a joint custody arrangement would not.[150] Why would states distinguish in this way? As the Arkansas Supreme Court explained:

> The rationale behind [a presumption for the primary physical custodian is] to preserve and protect the stability of the relationship between the child and the custodial parent with whom the child spent the majority of his time . . . . However, in a true joint-custody arrangement, both parents share equal time and custody with the child; therefore, there is not one child-parent relationship to take preference over the other.[151]

Other states apply a unitary standard regardless of the custodial arrangement. For example, in Bisbing v. Bisbing, the New Jersey Supreme Court rejected the application of differential standards and held that a best interest standard governs both joint and primary physical custody.[152] The court offered a practical rationale:

> The parties and the court should select the parent of primary residence based on that parent's capacity to meet the needs of the child. If a designation as the parent of primary residence will determine the result of a relocation dispute, parties may be motivated to contest that designation even if one parent is clearly in a better position to serve that primary role. . . . [T]ethering the relocation standard to one party's status as the parent of primary residence . . . may generate unnecessary disputes regarding that designation.[153]

Do you agree? If you were a state legislator, would you adopt a unitary standard?

6. *Empirical Evidence.* The empirical evidence that might inform policy about relocation disputes is mixed and subject to dispute. Some researchers contend, in short, that what benefits the custodial parent benefits the child.[154] Other researchers, in contrast, identify potential adverse effects from the stress of relocation coupled with the potential diminution of the child's relationship with the noncustodial parent.[155] As the New Jersey Supreme Court summarized in *Bisbing*:

> In short, social scientists who have studied the impact of relocation on children following divorce have not reached a consensus. Instead, the vigorous

---

150. See, e.g., *Singletary*, 431 S.W.3d 234.

151. Id. at 240.

152. 166 A.3d 1155.

153. Id. at 1169.

154. See, e.g., Judith Wallerstein & Tony J. Tanke, To Move or Not to Move: Psychological and Legal Considerations in the Relocation of Children Following Divorce, 30 Fam. L.Q. 305 (1996).

155. See, e.g., Joan B Kelly & Michael Lamb, Developmental Issues in Relocation Cases Involving Young Children: When, Whether and How? 17 J. Fam. Psychol. 193 (2003); Sanford L. Braver, Relocation after Divorce and Children's Best Interests: New Evidence and Legal Considerations, 17 J. Fam. Psychol. 206 (2003).

scholarly debate reveals that relocation may affect children in many different ways. The . . . conclusion . . . that in general, "what is good for the custodial parent is good for the child" is no doubt correct with regard to some families following a divorce. As the social science literature reflects, however, that statement is not universally true; a relocation far away from a parent may have a significant adverse effect on a child.[156]

PROBLEMS

1. Marta and Ryan are divorced. Marta has primary residential custody of their sons, ages 11 and 13, and they both have joint legal custody. Marta is an intensive care unit doctor specializing in pulmonary diseases. When the COVID-19 pandemic hit, Marta began treating patients gravely ill with the virus. Ryan files a petition for a custody modification, seeking primary residential custody of the children, due to Marta's job. How should the court rule?

2. Kira and Mandy are divorced. They have joint legal custody of their twin daughters, and Kira is the parent with primary residential custody. Mandy has the children every other weekend and for one weekday visit per week.

   Since their divorce, Kira and Mandy have lived four miles away from each other and have cooperated in the care of their daughters, who are now ten. Mandy's alternate-weekend time with the children often extends until Monday morning. The children also usually stay overnight at Mandy's house after their scheduled weekday visit. Kira has taken primary responsibility for the girls' school and extracurricular activities, but Mandy also has been extensively involved in their daughters' lives. She is their soccer coach and drives them to and from music lessons. Because Kira must leave her New Jersey home early in the morning to get to her job in New York City, Mandy goes to Kira's house several mornings per week to get the children ready for school.

   Several months ago, Kira began dating Ayana, who lives in Missouri but makes frequent trips to New Jersey. Kira recently left her job and is being supported financially by Ayana. Kira and Ayana are planning to marry. Ayana's job makes it impossible for her to leave Missouri permanently.

   Kira files a motion to relocate with the children from New Jersey to Missouri. You are the judge hearing the case. Does Kira's move constitute a substantial change in circumstances? Is it in the children's best interests to move? Would you grant Kira's motion? What other information would you want to help you reach a decision?

3. Nia and Blake had a child, Ry, together in 2015. The couple were never married. Blake established his parentage through a voluntary acknowledgment

---

156. 166 A.3d at 1166-67.

of parentage. Nia has been working toward her Ph.D. in mathematics at UC Berkeley. Blake has been involved with several successful start-up companies in the Bay Area and has a net worth of several million dollars. Pursuant to a court order, Nia and Blake share joint legal custody, and Nia has primary physical custody. Ry spends one night a week at Blake's home in San Francisco and two weekends a month with Blake at his home in Sonoma. Blake takes Ry to and from the Sonoma house on a private jet.

Nia has gone on the academic job market to find a tenure-track position in a mathematics department. The job market in mathematics is very tight, with many more applicants than positions. The vast majority of tenured and tenure-track positions in mathematics are occupied by men. Women historically have been under-represented in the field. No school in the Bay Area, or in California more broadly, has decided to interview Nia. Eventually, Nia is offered a tenure-track position at the University of Washington. This would require her to move to Seattle.

Nia tells Blake about this opportunity. She proposes a plan that includes "virtual visitation," which would allow Blake to interact with Ry on FaceTime or Zoom every day during the school year in lieu of his in-person visits.[157] Blake refuses to consent to Nia's move with Ry. Nia retains you to represent her, and you file a motion to relocate. What arguments would you make on Nia's behalf? What arrangements might you suggest to mitigate the impact of the move on the relationship between Blake and Ry?

NOTE ON CHILD CUSTODY JURISDICTION

Every state but Massachusetts has adopted the Uniform Child Custody Jurisdiction and Enforcement Act (UCCJEA), which the Uniform Law Commission promulgated in 1997.[158] The UCCJEA replaced the 1968 Uniform Child Custody Jurisdiction Act (UCCJA).[159] The UCCJA was the first attempt to bring order to a chaotic area of law in which states were assuming concurrent jurisdiction over custody matters and reopening judgments from other states. There are many areas of law in which states take different approaches. Why is such inconsistency especially concerning in this context? How is the child affected?

---

157. See, e.g., Kime v. Kime, No. 107/00, 2001 WL 1665824 (N.Y. Sup. Ct. Sept. 28, 2001); McCoy v. McCoy, 764 A.2d. 449 (N.J. Super. Ct. App. Div. 2001); see generally Anne LeVasseur, Virtual Visitation: How Will Courts Respond to a New and Emerging Issue?, 17 Quinnipiac Prob. L.J. 362 (2004); Jenna Charlotte Spatz, Note, Scheduled Skyping with Mom or Dad: Communicative Technology's Impact on California Family Law, 31 Loy. L.A. Ent. L. Rev. 143 (2011).

158. Unif. Child Custody Jurisdiction and Enforcement Act (Unif. Law Comm'n 1997) [hereinafter UCCJEA].

159. Unif. Child Custody Jurisdiction Act (Unif. Law Comm'n 1968).

Even though the UCCJA was adopted by every state, variation in legislative enactments and competing judicial interpretations produced inconsistency across jurisdictions. In 1980, by enacting the Parental Kidnapping Prevention Act (PKPA), Congress attempted to address some of the continuing problems with respect to custody jurisdiction.[160] Contrary to popular belief, the majority of child abductions involve not strangers but family members. According to the Department of Justice, over 200,000 parental abductions occur each year.[161] These parental abductions can raise jurisdictional issues when a parent flees to another state with the child. The PKPA requires states to extend Full Faith and Credit to custody determinations from other states when those determinations comply with the PKPA.[162] While some of the PKPA's provisions on jurisdiction mirrored those in the UCCJA, there were important differences. Most critically, the federal legislation granted exclusive jurisdiction for custody modification to the court that rendered the original decree, provided one of the parents or the child remained in the state.[163] The interaction between the UCCJA and the PKPA was, according to leading family law scholar Homer Clark, "technical enough to delight a medieval property lawyer."[164] Inconsistency and uncertainty once again prevailed, which led to adoption of the UCCJEA.

The UCCJEA governs "child-custody determination[s]," which include custody and visitation, initial decrees and subsequent modifications, and temporary and permanent orders.[165] It covers all "child-custody proceeding[s]," whether the custody dispute arises out of an action for divorce, separation, paternity, abuse or neglect, dependency, guardianship, termination of parental rights, or domestic violence protection.[166] The custody dispute in such a proceeding is governed by the UCCJEA's jurisdictional requirements, even though other issues may be governed by different jurisdictional rules. For example, in a divorce action, the rules for divorce jurisdiction would govern whether the court has jurisdiction to dissolve the parties' marriage (explored in Chapter 4), whereas the rules supplied by the UCCJEA would govern whether that same court can determine custody.

The UCCJEA gives priority in custody matters to home state jurisdiction. The "home state" is "the State in which a child lived with a parent or a person acting as a parent for at least six consecutive months immediately before the commencement of a child-custody proceeding."[167] If the child is under six months, the home state is

---

160. 28 U.S.C. § 1738A (2018).

161. U.S. Dep't of Justice, The Crime of Family Abduction: A Child's and Parent's Perspective ix (2010).

162. The PKPA also addresses child abduction. It gives state agencies access to the Federal Parent Locator Service to aid in locating a parent who has abducted a child, and it applies the Fugitive Felon Act, 18 U.S.C. § 1073 (2018), to felony parental kidnapping cases.

163. 28 U.S.C. § 1738A(d) (2018).

164. Homer H. Clark, Domestic Relations § 12.5 at 494 (2d ed. 1988).

165. UCCJEA, supra note 158, § 102(3).

166. Id., § 102(4).

167. Id., § 102(7).

"the State in which the child lived from birth with" a parent or a person acting as a parent.[168]

201. Initial Child-Custody Jurisdiction

(a) ... [A] court of this State has jurisdiction to make an initial child-custody determination only if:

    (1) this State is the home state of the child on the date of the commencement of the proceeding, or was the home State of the child within six months before the commencement of the proceeding and the child is absent from this State but a parent or person acting as a parent continues to live in this State;

    (2) a court of another State does not have jurisdiction under paragraph (1), or a court of the home State of the child has declined to exercise jurisdiction on the ground that this State is the more appropriate forum ... and:

        (A) the child and the child's parents, or the child and at least one parent or a person acting as a parent, have a significant connection with this State other than mere physical presence; and

        (B) substantial evidence is available in this State concerning the child's care, protection, training, and personal relationships;

    (3) all courts having jurisdiction under paragraph (1) or (2) have declined to exercise jurisdiction on the ground that a court of this State is the more appropriate forum to determine the custody of the child ... or

    (4) no court of any other State would have jurisdiction under the criteria specified in paragraph (1), (2), or (3).

(b) Subsection (a) is the exclusive jurisdictional basis for making a child-custody determination by a court of this State.

(c) Physical presence of, or personal jurisdiction over, a party or a child is not necessary or sufficient to make a child-custody determination.[169]

With respect to modification of custody orders, the UCCJEA grants exclusive jurisdiction to the state that rendered the initial custody judgment, provided the parent or child resides in that state.

202. Exclusive, Continuing Jurisdiction

(a) ... [A] court of this State which has made a child-custody determination consistent with Section 201 or 203 has exclusive, continuing jurisdiction over the determination until:

---

168. Id.
169. Id., § 201.

(1) a court of this State determines that neither the child, nor the child and one parent, nor the child and a person acting as a parent have a significant connection with this State and that substantial evidence is no longer available in this State concerning the child's care, protection, training, and personal relationships; or

(2) a court of this State or a court of another State determines that the child, the child's parents, and any person acting as a parent do not presently reside in this State.

(b) A court of this State which has made a child-custody determination and does not have exclusive, continuing jurisdiction under this section may modify that determination only if it has jurisdiction to make an initial determination under Section 201.[170]

203. Jurisdiction To Modify Determination

... [A] court of this State may not modify a child-custody determination made by a court of another State unless a court of this State has jurisdiction to make an initial determination under Section 201(a)(1) or (2) and:

(1) the court of the other State determines it no longer has exclusive, continuing jurisdiction under Section 202 or that a court of this State would be a more convenient forum . . .; or

(2) a court of this State or a court of the other State determines that the child, the child's parents, and any person acting as a parent do not presently reside in the other State.[171]

These sections do not apply in cases in which emergency jurisdiction is necessary. When might that arise? If "the child has been abandoned or it is necessary in an emergency to protect the child because the child, or a sibling or parent of the child, is subjected to or threatened with mistreatment or abuse," a court can exercise what the UCCJEA terms "temporary emergency jurisdiction."[172]

The UCCJEA also governs interstate enforcement of custody determinations. Why is that a problem to be addressed by a uniform law? If a parent left the state that issued the custody order, the other parent would often struggle to enforce the order. The parent might have to pay lawyers in two states and engage in a long, arduous process simply to enforce the order. The parent might also find that a court in the state to which the other parent had moved issues an order inconsistent with the original

---

170. Id., § 202.
171. Id., § 203.
172. Id., § 204.

decree. The UCCJEA addresses this problem, making clear that a court "shall recognize and enforce a child-custody determination of a court of another State if the latter court exercised jurisdiction in substantial conformity with [the UCCJEA] or the determination was made under factual circumstances meeting the jurisdictional standards of [the UCCJEA]."[173] The UCCJEA also aids custodial parents by providing clear and quick paths to enforcing orders.[174]

What if a parent takes a child to another country during a dispute? The 1980 Hague Convention on the Civil Aspects of International Child Abduction, which entered into force in the U.S. in 1988, governs judicial proceedings involving the wrongful retention or removal of a child from her country of habitual residence.[175] The treaty "serves two primary purposes: first, to deter future child abductions; and second, to provide a prompt and efficient process for the return of the child to the status quo that existed before the abduction."[176] In the United States, state and federal courts exercise concurrent original jurisdiction over Hague Convention cases.[177] Even though they are rare, federal courts have appeared to prioritize these cases, taking care to expedite them.[178] Furthermore, since 2010, the Supreme Court has decided four cases concerning this treaty.[179] Note that although the Hague Convention offers a provisional remedy for wrongful removals, the underlying merits of the child custody case are still to be determined by the courts and law of the child's habitual residence.

---

173. Id., § 303.

174. See, e.g., id., § 305 ("Registration of Child-Custody Determination"); § 306 (Enforcement of Registered Determination"); § 308 ("Expedited Enforcement of Child-Custody Determination"); § 311 ("Warrant to Take Physical Custody of Child"); § 315 ("Role of [Prosecutor or Public Official]").

175. Hague Convention on the Civil Aspects of International Child Abduction, Oct. 25, 1980, T. I. A. S. No. 11,670, 1343 U.N.T.S. 89. The United States implements this treaty through the International Child Abduction Remedies Act (ICARA), 22 U.S.C. §§ 9001-9011 (2018). Section 302 of the UCCJEA specifies that state courts may also enforce an order for the return of a child under this Convention.

176. James D. Garbolino, Fed. Jud. Ctr., The 1980 Hague Convention on the Civil Aspects of International Child Abduction: A Guide for Judges ix (2015).

177. 22 U.S.C. § 9003(a) (2018).

178. See Garbolino, supra note 176, at vi, xviii fig.1; Jennifer Baum, Ready, Set, Go to Federal Court: The Hague Child Abduction Treaty, Demystified, Am. Bar Ass'n (July 14, 2014).

179. In the first case in 2010, the Court held that a father's right to consent before the other parent may take the child to another country under Chilean law constituted a right of custody under the Convention. Abbott v. Abbott, 560 U.S. 1, 10 (2010). In 2013, the Court found that a child's removal to her habitual residence outside of the U.S., pursuant to an order of return, does not render a case moot. Chafin v. Chafin, 568 U.S. 165, 180 (2013). A year later, the Court ruled that the American concept of equitable tolling does not apply to the Convention's one-year period for filing a petition for return of a child. Lozano v. Montoya Alvarez, 572 U.S. 1, 18 (2014). Finally, in 2020, the Court held that a determination of a child's "habitual residence," which is left undefined in the treaty, "depends on the totality of the circumstances specific to the case." Monasky v. Taglieri, 140 S. Ct. 719, 723 (2020). Although parental intent is one such factor, the Court rejected a proposed categorical approach that would have required an actual agreement between the parents to raise their child in that country. Id.

PROBLEM

In 2000, Lisa Miller and Janet Jenkins traveled to Vermont from Virginia, where they had been living together, to enter into a civil union. In 2002, Lisa Miller gave birth through donor insemination to Isabella Miller-Jenkins in Virginia. A few months later, Miller and Jenkins moved to Vermont, wanting to raise Isabella in a state that endorsed same-sex relationships. A year later, Miller and Jenkins ended their relationship. Miller moved back to Virginia with Isabella, over Jenkins' objections. Miller filed a petition in a Vermont family court, seeking a dissolution of the civil union along with physical and legal custody of Isabella. The Vermont family court dissolved the union and granted temporary custody to Miller and temporary visitation to Jenkins. However, Miller refused to follow the terms of the order and instead filed a petition in a Virginia trial court seeking a declaration that she was the sole parent of Isabella (based on the fact that Jenkins was not biologically related to the child and Virginia would not recognize the couple's civil union from Vermont and so therefore Jenkins had no path to parental recognition under Virginia law). The Virginia trial court sided with Miller.

Jenkins, meanwhile, sought enforcement of the Vermont custody order by the Vermont court, which issued an order holding that both Miller and Jenkins were parents of Isabella. Jenkins now appeals the Virginia trial court's decision. She argues that the Virginia trial court did not have jurisdiction to enter its order because the dispute was a custody and visitation determination subject to the Parental Kidnapping Prevention Act. Therefore, she argues, Vermont should have been accorded sole jurisdiction over the dispute. Is Jenkins correct?

POSTSCRIPT

The Virginia Court of Appeals agreed with Jenkins.[180] Miller failed to timely appeal the decision to the Virginia Supreme Court, and subsequently lost a related appeal to the Virginia Supreme Court under the "law of the case doctrine," which forbids relitigation of issues in the same case.[181] In 2009, the Vermont family court found that Miller's persistent refusal to allow visitation amounted to a change in circumstances that warranted modifying its previous order by granting Jenkins sole legal and physical custody.[182] But before Jenkins could take custody of Isabella, Miller fled to Nicaragua with their daughter. Miller's flight was aided by a network

---

180. Miller-Jenkins v. Miller-Jenkins, 637 S.E.2d 330 (Va. Ct. App. 2006).
181. Miller-Jenkins v. Miller-Jenkins, 661 S.E.2d 822 (Va. 2008).
182. Miller-Jenkins v. Miller-Jenkins, 12 A.3d 768 (Vt. 2010).

of conservative Christians who supported Miller's desire to protect her child from exposure to a "homosexual lifestyle" after Miller had declared herself a born-again Christian and denounced her previous same-sex relationship.[183] Federal charges were brought against several individuals who helped Miller flee, but as of mid-2020 Miller and Isabella remain at large and are believed to still be hiding in Nicaragua.[184]

VI. Visitation

Parents who are not awarded physical custody of their child are typically entitled to visitation with the child, also known as parenting time.[185] Prior to the advent of joint custody in the 1980s, visitation was the only mechanism for fostering a connection between the child and the noncustodial parent, typically the father.[186]

Now, the law of every state favors an award of visitation for the noncustodial parent, an approach that reflects both respect for the constitutional rights of the parent and the belief that children's best interests generally are served by maintaining relationships with both their parents.[187]

The noncustodial parent's right to visitation, however, is far from absolute. Although visitation is presumed to be in the best interests of the child, visitation can be restricted or even denied if the parent seeking visitation is unfit or if the child would be significantly harmed. Many of the considerations of parental behavior and circumstance that arise in the custody context may also be relevant to visitation. And just as custody orders may be modified, so too may visitation schedules. The standards in most jurisdictions permit courts to more readily modify visitation than custody.

The strong preference in favor of visitation orders is reflected in the Uniform Marriage and Divorce Act. Section 407(a) provides:

> A parent not granted custody of the child is entitled to reasonable visitation rights unless the court finds, after a hearing, that visitation would endanger seriously the child's physical, mental, moral, or emotional health.[188]

---

183. See Erik Eckholm, Which Mother for Isabella? Civil Union Ends in an Abduction and Questions, N.Y. Times, July 28, 2012, at A1.

184. See Erik Eckholm, New Charges in Virginia Kidnapping Over Custody, N.Y. Times, Oct. 8, 2014, at A21.

185. See, e.g., In re Marriage of Hansen, 733 N.W.2d 683 (Iowa 2007).

186. See, e.g., Mason, supra note 6.

187. See, e.g., Sarfati v. DeJesus, 71 N.Y.S.3d 165 (N.Y. App. Div. 2018).

188. UMDA, supra note 22, § 407(a).

A. Denial of Visitation

Some of the cases in this section involve child sexual abuse.

MICHAEL v. SMITH
237 So. 3d 183 (Miss. Ct. App. 2018)

GRIFFIS, P.J., for the Court: . . .

FACTS

E.M.S. was born to [father Daniel W.] Michael and [mother Kelli Michelle] Smith in August 2013. Michael and Smith were never married. . . .

Smith was granted legal and physical custody of E.M.S. . . .

[T]he chancellor granted Michael unsupervised visitation . . . every other weekend from 10 a.m. on Saturday through 5 p.m. on Sunday, and set a standard holiday and summer-visitation schedule. . . .

On appeal, Michael [asserts that] the chancellor abused his discretion in ordering visitation from Saturday through Sunday rather than Friday through Sunday. . . .

"The chancellor has broad discretion when determining appropriate visitation and the limitations thereon." The chancellor's findings of fact will be affirmed when supported by substantial evidence, unless the chancellor abused his discretion or applied an incorrect legal standard, or if the decision was manifestly wrong or clearly erroneous. . . .

In support of his argument, Michael relies on *Fields v. Fields*, 830 So. 2d 1266 (Miss. Ct. App. 2002). In *Fields*, the chancellor awarded the father visitation every other weekend from 5 p.m. on Friday until 6 p.m. on Sunday. However, the chancellor awarded no holiday or summer visitation, and required that the father ensure that the child participated in up to three church activities chosen by the mother during his weekend visitations. . . .

On appeal, this Court found no basis in the record for the chancellor's imposition of these restrictions on visitation. In so finding, this Court first pointed to the chancellor's award of overnight visitation, which created an inference that standard visitation was not detrimental to the child. Further, this Court noted that in the temporary order entered prior to the final judgment, the chancellor "did not hesitate in awarding . . . standard summer and holiday visitation privileges." . . .

Here, as in *Fields*, there is no indication that standard visitation would be detrimental to the child. The chancellor awarded Michael overnight visitation and further awarded standard summer — and holiday — visitation privileges. While the chancellor did not place the same restrictions at issue in *Fields*, he did in fact restrict Michael's visitation, as Michael's weekend visitations did not include Friday.

"Except in unusual circumstances, a noncustodial parent is entitled to unrestricted standard or liberal visitation." Standard visitation includes "two weekends a month until Sunday afternoon and at least five weeks of summer visitation[,] plus some holiday visitation." "Awarding less is an abuse of discretion unless there is concrete proof of actual harm to a child." "Appropriate visitation restrictions often relate to abusive behavior, drug or alcohol abuse, or mental illness."

Here, there is no evidence of actual harm to E.M.S., nor is there evidence of abusive behavior, drug or alcohol abuse, or mental illness by Michael. . . .

"Our courts have adopted a policy of maintaining relationships between parents and their children even though the parent may be non-custodial." . . .

"[A]bsent evidence that the child [would be] harmed by standard visitation, the chancellor may not impose limitations on the visitation privileges of the non[-]custodial parent." Here, as in *Fields*, there is no evidence to support the chancellor's restrictions on Michael's visitation with E.M.S. Moreover, there is no evidence that E.M.S. would be harmed by standard visitation. Accordingly, we find the chancellor abused his discretion in restricting Michael's visitation, and reverse and remand with instructions to award Michael standard visitation with E.M.S., to include Fridays. . . .

GREENLEE, J., concurring in part and dissenting in part:

I disagree with the majority's conclusion that the chancellor abused his discretion in setting visitation every other weekend from Saturday through Sunday. . . .

In *Fields*, the . . . chancellor restricted the father's weekend visitation by ordering that, during his visitation, he "ensure that [the child] participates in [up to three] church[-]related functions as determined by [the child's mother]." . . .

The chancellor here did not place such requirements or restrictions on Michael's visitation. Michael was awarded summer and holiday visitation and visitation every other weekend. There were no requirements or restrictions on the manner of Michael's visitation; rather, the chancellor simply set the days and times he determined appropriate for visitation based on the child's age and relationship with Michael. . . . As explained in *Horn v. Horn*, 909 So. 2d 1151, 1162 (Miss. Ct. App. 2005), while "the *manner* of visitation may not be restricted" without compelling reason, "the *time restraints*" are in the chancellor's discretion. . . .

In *Horn*, the noncustodial parent argued that the Christmas visitation schedule set by the chancellor was impermissibly restrictive. Christmas visitation was set for every other year from 3 p.m. on December 24 through 3 p.m. on December 25. In upholding the chancellor's decision, this Court stated: "While the chancellor may not restrict a non[-]custodial parent's *activities* during visitation without compelling reason, the chancellor has broad discretion to specify *times* for visitation." (emphasis added). . . .

In setting the visitation schedule, the chancellor repeatedly stated that there was a lack of bonding between Michael and E.M.S. — who was two years and nine months old at the time of the amended judgment. It was undisputed that Smith had been E.M.S.'s caretaker since birth. Smith testified that Michael "was involved on a limited basis" after E.M.S. was born, and would come by "maybe a couple times a week." But by the time E.M.S. was three months old, he only visited "maybe once a week" or "once every other week for . . . an hour or two hours at a time. And then after she was three months old, he never asked to see her again." . . .

Michael testified that he visited E.M.S. from her birth in August 2013 through November 2013. But in December 2013, Smith sent him a text message that gave him the "impression that [Smith] . . . was done with [him]" and "didn't want [his] family to ever meet [E.M.S.]." So he stopped visiting. . . .

Both Smith and Michael testified that E.M.S. does not recognize Michael as her father, although Michael stated that he desired to have a father-daughter relationship with her. . . .

I cannot find that the chancellor abused his discretion in setting the visitation schedule. "[T]he chancellor must award visitation based on what is in the best interest of the child." The chancellor has done so here. . . .

TRAN V. NGUYEN

480 S.W.3d 119 (Tex. App. 2015)

MARTHA HILL JAMISON, JUSTICE . . .

[Father] Tran and [mother] Nguyen began holding themselves out as married in October 1998. They have two children together, daughters K.N. and P.T., and Nguyen has one child from a previous relationship, daughter J.T. At the time of trial [for divorce], J.T. was seventeen years old, K.N. was fifteen, and P.T. was thirteen. In 2012, Tran pleaded guilty to sexually assaulting J.T. when she was thirteen years old. Pursuant to a plea bargain agreement, Tran was sentenced to twelve years in prison for the offense. Tran and Nguyen separated in 2010 after his crime was revealed. Nguyen subsequently filed a petition for divorce. . . .

Nguyen testified regarding Tran's conviction, noting that the younger children were aware of the nature of the crime. She said that P.T. does not currently speak or write to Tran, and K.N., although initially maintaining a relationship with him after his incarceration began, recently stopped communicating with Tran. . . .

During his cross-examination of Nguyen . . . Tran additionally questioned Nguyen regarding his virtues as a father. She responded that he had a close relationship with their children prior to his offense but also that he was "doing [his] own thing a lot of the time." She said that she has talked to K.N. and P.T., the children of the marriage, about visiting him in prison but they do not want to go. She acknowledged that, prior to his incarceration, Tran exercised periods of possession with the children. . . .

At the conclusion of trial, the judge granted the divorce on the grounds of Tran's felony conviction. . . . The judge stated that in light of Tran's conviction, it was not in the children's best interest that he be granted other specific rights or duties or specified access [to the children]. . . .

The trial judge subsequently signed a final decree of divorce. . . . In regards to possession or access by Tran, the court stated in the decree "that it is in the best interest of the children to not make any ORDERS granting [Tran] possession of or access to the children due to [his] conviction for family violence." . . .

Tran contends that the trial court abused its discretion in denying him visitation with P.T. and K.N. and in failing to provide specific terms and conditions governing his right to possession or access. "The terms of an order that denies possession of a child to a parent or imposes restrictions or limitations on a parent's right to possession of or access to a child may not exceed those that are required to protect the best interest of the child." . . .

Tran focuses much of his argument on the absence of evidence demonstrating the potential harmful effects on the children of regularly visiting a prison environment and on the evidence suggesting he had a good relationship with his biological daughters prior to his conviction. But the trial court reasonably placed more weight on the fact that Tran pleaded guilty to, and was convicted of, the aggravated sexual assault of his stepdaughter, who, the parties agreed, believed she was Tran's biological daughter until around the time she was ten. Nguyen further testified that Tran's molestation of J.T. occurred over a twelve-month period. The evidence indicating that over a prolonged period of time Tran molested a thirteen year-old girl who viewed him as a father figure was sufficient to support the trial court's decision to deny Tran regular visitation with his biological daughters of around the same age. The trial court did not abuse its discretion. . . .

DESANTIS V. PEGUES
35 A.3d 152 (Vt. 2011)

SKOGLUND, J.

Father appeals the family court's denial of his motion to reinstate parent-child contact following a voluntary suspension of such contact due to an allegation of child sexual abuse. . . .

The parties were married in 1991, adopted their daughter in 1996, and separated in July 2004. Mother and daughter stayed in the marital home, and father sought alternate housing, eventually moving into a two-bedroom condominium. The parties worked out an informal visitation schedule during this time, though there was no overnight contact due to mother's concerns about father's drinking.

The separation affected daughter badly: she had nightmares and emotional outbursts with tears and tantrums. Mother wanted daughter to have counseling to address the issues triggered by the separation and eventual divorce. She was also concerned about father's "physical boundary" issues. Starting when daughter was very young, she and father engaged in lots of physical play. She would climb all over him, and he would tickle her, at times until she fell down laughing and at times to the point of tears. He would grab her ankles, stare into her eyes, and suck her toes, calling them "tasty morsels." He would also kiss her repeatedly, sometimes so much that her cheeks would redden from his beard. Mother believed that, as daughter grew, the kisses became more "soulful" and "passionate." The level of play between the two and its intensity became a source of concern for her. The two played a game where they would kiss one another's bare stomachs, making slurping sounds. Mother explained to daughter that "Daddies and girls don't kiss that way." Toward the end of the marriage, when father was drinking heavily, mother often found him asleep in daughter's room; on one occasion she found him asleep in daughter's bed with his hand on her bare buttocks. Father's condominium had a separate bedroom for daughter that included a long, narrow closet, which he outfitted with a beanbag chair, a sleeping bag, and a place for toys. Mother testified that daughter referred to it as the "secret closet" and said she and father played kissing and tickling games there. At the hearing, daughter testified that she and father played a game called "How naked can you get?" in the closet where father would begin taking his clothes off and then start taking her clothes off. She did not say whether either of them got completely undressed, though she did say it made her feel uncomfortable. . . .

Mother then contacted New York State Child Protective Services (CPS). . . .

The CPS investigation moved forward, and daughter was repeatedly interviewed by multiple investigators, social workers, and psychologists about the nature of father's physical contact with her. She did not report being sexually abused to any of them. In March 2006, mother engaged a licensed clinical social worker, Corey Sorce, and told her about the family's history of visitation conflicts and that daughter had disclosed sexual abuse to mother. Ms. Sorce met with daughter and testified that daughter disclosed sexual abuse by father within the first twenty minutes of their initial session. . . .

On October 19, 2006, father was charged with felony aggravated sexual assault of his daughter. After an eighteen-month investigation, the State dismissed the charges with prejudice. Father moved to dissolve the interim suspension order in July 2008. . . .

The court recognized the evidence presented . . . would not "rise to the criminal 'beyond a reasonable doubt' standard" for a finding of sexual abuse. The court also specifically held that there was not sufficient evidence of abuse to meet the clear and convincing standard required to terminate all parent-child contact, citing *Mullin v. Phelps*, 647 A.2d 714 (Vt. 1994). However, the court concluded that there was sufficient evidence to support a finding of sexual abuse by a preponderance of evidence. . . .

The court then reviewed the best-interests-of-the-child factors . . . . It concluded that . . . "it would be contrary to the child's best interest to force this child to have contact with father at this time." The court stated that its decision not to order visitation was "not a termination of parental rights, but based on the child's needs and situation at this time." . . .

The record evidence of father's actions with daughter was sufficient to support the court's finding by a preponderance standard that father sexually abused daughter....

[In] *Mullin v. Phelps*, ... the mother moved to gain custody of the parties' two sons after the father was accused of abusing the boys. The family court transferred custody, which had been with the father for the previous six years, upon a finding of sexual abuse by a preponderance of the evidence, and the court conditioned father's visitation upon his acknowledgement of the sexual abuse. We affirmed the court's finding of abuse and the resulting transfer of custody, but we reversed the court's visitation order because it "effectively terminated the father's parental rights." In so doing, we adopted the standard that, as a matter of due process, a court must find evidence of sexual abuse by clear and convincing evidence in order to terminate all contact between a parent and child.

The family court here expressly concluded that the evidence presented did not reach the standard required to terminate father's parental rights....

The Legislature has made clear that after separation or divorce, "it is in the best interests of [the parents'] minor child to have the opportunity for maximum continuing physical and emotional contact with both parents, unless direct physical harm or significant emotional harm to the child ... is likely to result from such contact." The family court made no findings that father ever perpetrated abuse on his daughter during supervised, nonovernight visits.... Absent a showing by clear and convincing evidence that any visitation would be detrimental to daughter's best interests, the court erred by halting all contact between father and daughter....

We ... leave it to the parties and the family court to craft a new structure for visitation, one that does not deny father his remaining parental rights.

Johnson, J., concurring...

[D]ecisions by the U.S. Supreme Court and others strongly suggest that preservation of a noncustodial parent's visitation rights in any context is a constitutionally protected liberty interest requiring clear and convincing evidence before it may be terminated in its entirety....

[N]ot one cogent reason has been produced to abandon a precedent grounded in fundamental due process and the compelling state interest in preserving the relational interests between parents and children....

Crawford, Supr. J., Specially Assigned, dissenting....

I disagree with the application of a clear-and-convincing-evidence standard to family court decisions about parent-child contact in divorce and parentage cases. A higher standard of proof is constitutionally mandated in cases in which the state seeks to deprive an individual of a liberty interest so that the possibility of error is borne more heavily by the state. In disputes over custody and visitation between individuals, however, the higher burden simply shifts the possibility of error from one parent to another. . . . [B]ecause the private interests are equally balanced, there is no compelling reason that one individual should more heavily bear the burden of error. . . .

[T]he burden of proof can greatly affect the outcome of a case. The evidence of father's actions, including inappropriate kissing, touching, and partial nudity over the course of many years, supported the trial court's conclusion that it was more likely than not that he had sexually abused his daughter. The trial court was scrupulous in concluding that this evidence, as compelling as it appears in the paper record, fell short of the clear-and-convincing-evidence standard in much the same way that it evidently fell short of the proof-beyond-a-reasonable-doubt threshold in father's related criminal prosecution.

What constitutional principle requires the family court to order continued visitation in a divorce case when the evidence shows that it is more likely than not that one parent has committed sexual abuse? . . .

There is no constitutional basis for deciding that one parent's interest in visitation outweighs the other's interest in safeguarding the child from abuse. . . .

NOTES AND QUESTIONS

1. *Types of Visitation.* The purpose of visitation is to facilitate the relationship between the child and the noncustodial parent. While visitation typically concerns the physical presence and interaction of the child and parent, it can also encompass other forms of interaction. Visitation orders may include provision for telephone contact, mail, email, text messaging, video calling, or social media interaction.[189] These forms of virtual visitation become especially important when the parties are unable, due to distance or some other factor, to visit in person.[190]

2. *The Visitation Determination.* Courts have considerable discretion in crafting orders of visitation. Most statutes provide a long list of factors that judges are to consider. Typical factors include: the wishes of the parents; the wishes of the child; the relationship between each parent and the child; the ability of the parent seeking visitation to supervise and care for the child; the mental and physical health of all individuals involved; the child's needs; the distance between the parents' residences; the cost and difficulty of transporting the child; each parent's and the child's daily schedules; and the ability of the parents to cooperate in the arrangement.[191]

---

189. Haasken v. Haasken, 396 N.W.2d 253 (Minn. Ct. App. 1986); Finch v. Finch, 479 So. 2d 473 (La. Ct. App. 1985); LaGraize v. Filson, 171 So. 3d 1047 (La. Ct. App. 2015).

190. Danti v. Danti, 204 P.3d 1140 (Idaho 2009).

191. See, e.g., Dare v. Frost, 540 S.W.3d 281 (Ark. 2018); 750 Ill. Comp. Stat. 5/602.7 (2020).

3.   *Visitation Duration.* The court in Michael v. Smith described standard visitation as "two weekends a month until Sunday afternoon and at least five weeks of summer visitation[,] plus some holiday visitation." Statutes typically do not specify what constitutes standard or normal visitation, leaving the matter instead to judicial discretion and parent preference. Standards vary. Some courts have affirmed visitation orders for three weekends each month for the noncustodial parent,[192] while other courts have overturned orders for three weekends per month as excessive.[193] In another Mississippi case decided several years before *Michael*, a father's contention that he should have been granted *standard visitation* was met by the appeals court with the rejoinder: "Since there is no standard visitation, it cannot be said that the chancellor abused his discretion by not requiring standard visitation."[194]

4.   *Identifying a Restriction.* The court in *Michael* expressed an unusually strong sense of the noncustodial parent's entitlement to a specific amount of visitation. Many courts would adopt the dissenting judge's view and treat that sort of time limitation as wholly within the discretion of the trial court.[195] Assuming that full weekend visitation was the norm in the jurisdiction, if you were an appeals court judge, would you treat the denial of full weekend visitation as a restriction? In *Michael*, were the child's interests well served by the chancellor's decision not to grant full weekend visitation?

5.   *Denial of Visitation.* As exemplified by *Tran*, courts can deny any visitation to the noncustodial parent based on considerations of the welfare of the child.[196] Complete denial of visitation is the most extreme form of restriction and thus typically requires substantial evidence that any visitation would harm the child. As a New York court has noted, "denial of visitation to a noncustodial parent constitutes such a drastic remedy that it should be ordered only when there are compelling reasons, and there must be substantial evidence that such visitation is detrimental to the [child's] welfare."[197] Did the court in *Tran* find that any visitation would have been detrimental to the children? Should it have been required to do so? Or is the mere fact that Tran sexually abused his stepchild sufficient to deny him visitation with his biological children?

6.   *Sexual Abuse.* Courts often order supervised visitation or deny visitation between a parent and a child who has been sexually abused by that parent. The mere fact of allegations of sexual abuse is not enough to deny visitation. In a nationwide study, Professor Joan Meier analyzed custodial cases involving allegations by

---

192. See, e.g., Thomas v. Thomas, 281 So. 3d 1191 (Miss. 2019).
193. *Sarfati*, 71 N.Y.S.3d 165.
194. Strange v. Strange, 43 So. 3d 1169 (Miss. Ct. App. 2010).
195. In re Marriage of Ross, 824 N.E.2d 1108 (Ill. App. Ct. 2005).
196. See, e.g., Goodson v Bennett, 562 S.W.3d 847 (Ark. Ct. App. 2018).
197. Kleinbach v. Cullerton, 56 N.Y.S.3d 733, 736 (N.Y. App. Div. 2017).

one parent of abuse by the other.[198] A parent might cross-claim that the abuse claim is intended to "alienate" the child from them. A pronounced gender effect exists in such cases. Mothers are more likely to lose custody when they assert claims of abuse against fathers, especially child physical or sexual abuse. The effect doubles when fathers cross-claim alienation. The same does not occur when fathers allege abuse, and mothers assert alienation. Even when abuse is considered proven, mothers lose custody three times more often than fathers when they allege abuse.[199]

7. *Domestic Violence.* Many state statutes now set forth specific provisions that apply when there is evidence of domestic violence between the parents. Arizona law provides that the parent who committed the domestic violence bears the burden of proving that visitation will not seriously endanger the child.[200] California law provides that if a protective order has been entered on account of domestic violence, the court must consider whether any visitation should be supervised.[201] Oklahoma law creates a presumption against unsupervised visitation for a parent proven to have engaged in domestic violence.[202]

8. *Incarceration.* Courts also have considered petitions for visitation by parents who are incarcerated.[203] In *Tran*, how should the fact that the father was incarcerated have informed the court's reasoning?

9. *Denials of Visitation Versus Termination of Parental Rights.* Is the denial of visitation to a noncustodial parent equivalent to a termination of parental rights? Is that how the *Desantis* court saw it? To deny visitation, should the party seeking denial meet a heightened evidentiary standard? Is a heightened evidentiary standard required by Santosky v. Kramer, which we read in Chapter 7? The *Desantis* concurrence took this position. What was the dissent's position? Why might the standard that is constitutionally required when the government seeks to terminate parental rights not be constitutionally required when a court denies visitation?

10. *Parenting Plans.* While these cases all consider visitation denials or restrictions imposed by judges, it is important to keep in mind that in many cases visitation schedules are developed by the parents. In accord with the trend toward private ordering in family law, parents in the midst of a custody or visitation dispute are often encouraged or even required to develop their own parenting plan.[204] Courts

---

198. Joan S. Meier, 42 J. of Soc. Welf. & Fam. L. 92, 92 (2020) (including domestic violence against mother or sexual or physical abuse of child).

199. Id.; see also Naomi Cahn, Why Women Lose Custody, Forbes.com (Jan. 26, 2020).

200. Ariz. Rev. Stat. Ann. § 25-403.03 (2020).

201. Cal. Fam. Code § 3100(b) (West 2020).

202. Okla. Stat. tit. 43, § 112.2 (2020).

203. See, e.g., Baldwin v. Mollette, 527 S.W.3d 830 (Ky. Ct. App. 2017).

204. See, e.g., Michael Boulette, Child Custody and Parenting Time, 14 Minn. Prac., Family Law § 8.17 (3d ed. Nov. 2019); Eric Johnson, Parenting Plan — Filing — Modifications, 2 Utah Prac., Family Law § 30-3-10.8 (2019 ed.).

then incorporate the parenting plan into a judicial decree, so that the court could subsequently modify the plan or enforce it through a contempt order if necessary.[205] Many states now offer mediation services and agreement templates to guide parents through the process of developing a plan.[206] States also offer advice about being partners in parenting and help parents to think and work through details — such as specific recommended visitation schedules, the importance of punctuality in picking up or dropping off children, and the necessity of sending the child for visitation with clean clothes.[207]

11. *Marijuana, Custody, and Visitation.* A growing number of states have legalized marijuana, most commonly for medical use, but marijuana remains illegal under federal law.[208] Moreover, marijuana use is prevalent, and public opinion in the United States reflects greater acceptance of it.[209] Based on a concern about impacts on custody and visitation (and parental rights in the child welfare context), some states have included provisions to bar discrimination against parents for medical marijuana use. Arizona's medical marijuana statute, for instance, states: "No person may be denied custody of or visitation or parenting time with a minor, and there is no presumption of neglect or child endangerment for conduct allowed under [the medical marijuana statute], unless the person's behavior creates an unreasonable danger to the safety of the minor as established by clear and convincing evidence."[210] Is a prohibition like this likely to be effective? How could marijuana use affect custody or visitation in states without such prohibitions?[211]

205. Scott J. Horenstein, Procedure for Determining Permanent Parenting Plan, 20 Wash. Prac., Fam. and Community Prop. L. § 33.11 (Dec. 2019).

206. Indiana Parenting Time Guidelines, Ind. Rules of Ct. (Jan. 1, 2020); see also Fletcher v. Fletcher, No. M2010-01777-COA-R3-CV, 2011 WL 4447903 (Tenn. Ct. App. Sept. 26, 2011); Mason v. Mason, 607 S.E.2d 434 (W. Va. 2004).

207. Indiana Parenting Time Guidelines, Ind. Rules of Ct. (Jan. 1, 2020).

208. Nat'l Conf. of State Legislatures, State Medical Marijuana Laws (Mar. 10, 2020) (33 states have legalized medical use of marijuana); Audrey McNamara, These States Now Have Legal Weed, and Which States Could Follow Suit in 2020, CBS News (Jan. 1, 2020) (11 states have legalized recreational marijuana).

209. Marist College Inst. for Pub. Opinion, Yahoo News/Marist Poll: Weed & The American Family (April 17, 2017) (over 16 million parents with children under the age of 18 use marijuana); McNamara, supra note 208 (according to CBS News Poll, "support for legal pot hit a new high in 2019, with 65% of U.S. adults saying marijuana should be legal").

210. Ariz. Rev. Stat. Ann. § 36-2813 (2020).

211. See Alice Kwak, Medical Marijuana and Child Custody: The Need to Protect Patients and Their Families from Discrimination, 28 Hastings Women's L.J. 119 (2017).

PROBLEM

Mark and Claire met in 2011, married, and had a son, Jeremy, in 2013. Mark is a recovering alcohol and drug addict. In 2016, the parties separated after Claire confronted Mark, who admitted to regularly patronizing prostitutes during their marriage. Shortly after the parties' separation Mark was arrested for driving under the influence. Despite an attempt at reconciliation, the parties divorced in 2019. During the custody hearing, counsel for Claire asked the court to consider a psychological report on Mark submitted by Dr. Finkelstein. The report described Mark as an admitted sex addict. It recommended that if Mark were to have any visitation with Jeremy, it should be supervised and that the court should require Mark to receive treatment for substance abuse and sex addiction as a condition of any visitation with Jeremy. If you were the trial judge, would you adopt Dr. Finkelstein's recommendations? Would you require that Mark's visitation with Jeremey be supervised?

POSTSCRIPT

In the case from which this problem is drawn, the trial court concluded that the father should have unrestricted reasonable visitation with Jeremy, one night during the week, every other weekend, and four weeks during the summer. The appeals court affirmed the trial court's judgment that there was insufficient evidence that the father's sexual issues had or would result in harm to the child. Therefore, his visitation could not be restricted.[212]

B. RESTRICTIONS

CARTER V. ESCOVEDO
175 So. 3d 583 (Miss. Ct. App. 2015)

MAXWELL, J., for the Court: . . .

On November 29, 2010, Carter and Escovedo had a daughter out of wedlock, Kylee Sue Escovedo. Carter appeared on MTV's show "Sixteen and Pregnant," while she was pregnant with Kylee. And she was seventeen years old when Kylee was born. For the first few years of Kylee's life, Carter and Escovedo lived together. The couple then split up and began fighting over Kylee.

---

212. Kraft v. Kraft, 29 A.3d 246 (Del. 2011).

On February 26, 2014, Escovedo filed a complaint for child custody. And an order was entered granting Escovedo sole legal and physical custody, subject to Carter's visitation rights. Carter was awarded visitation every other weekend from Friday night to Sunday night and also received two weeks during the summer. Every year she got Kylee for three hours on her birthday and three hours on Kylee's birthday, and on Mother's Day. Every other year Kylee was to visit her on New Year's Day, Easter, Memorial Day, July 4th, Labor Day, Thanksgiving, and Christmas.

The order also directed that Carter "shall have such other reasonable visitation . . . as can be mutually agreed upon by the parties." But there was one specific restriction that Carter disputes on appeal. The chancellor prohibited "overnight visitors of the opposite sex (or of an intimate nature) unless related by blood or marriage" while Kylee was with Carter or Escovedo.

Carter appealed the chancellor's order. . . .

"Visitation should be set up with the best interests of the children as the paramount consideration, keeping in mind the rights of the non-custodial parent and the objective that parent and child should have as close and loving a relationship as possible, despite the fact that they may not live in the same house." This is why "[v]isitation and restrictions placed upon it are within the discretion of the chancery court."

Our supreme court has held "an extramarital relationship is not, per se, an adverse circumstance." So to restrict visitation of overnight guests of the opposite sex, there must be "something approaching actual danger or *other substantial detriment to the children.*" Indeed, restrictions should be imposed when circumstances present "an appreciable danger of hazard cognizable in our law." If the presence of a lover would be detrimental to a child, restrictions may be appropriate.

The chancellor was concerned Carter was "bringing a lot of different men around [Kylee] or sleeping with men with [Kylee] in the same bed." Carter lived in a one-bedroom apartment and admitted she had allowed men to sleep in the bed with both her and Kylee. Of particular concern was one of Carter's boyfriends, Michael.

Wendy Ward, Kylee's therapist, testified that Kylee suffered from anxiety. And Kylee had confided in Ward that she was scared of Michael. Ward testified that Kylee feared Michael when he "was mean." According to Kylee, Carter and Michael had fought in front of her, and Michael "made her feel scared and mad." Because of Kylee's anxiety over this boyfriend, Ward recommended neither party should have "romantic relationships spending the night when Kylee is present."

While we recognize our supreme court has not condoned per se visitation restrictions of overnight guests of the opposite sex, it is clear that such restrictions are in fact necessary when justified. And here, much of the chancellor's focus honed in on her duty to look out for the best interests of a then three-year-old girl. Based on Carter's admission of sharing her bed with Kylee and overnight romantic guests, and the therapist's testimony that Carter's boyfriend's presence was detrimental to Kylee, we find the chancellor tailored this prohibition to minimize the detriment to Kylee. We thus find the chancellor did not abuse her discretion in prohibiting overnight nonfamilial opposite-sex guests when Kylee is present.

<h1 style="text-align:center">PRATT V. PRATT</h1>

56 So. 3d 638 (Ala. Civ. App. 2010)

MOORE, JUDGE.

Susanne M. Pratt ("the mother") appeals from a judgment of the Montgomery Circuit Court ("the trial court") divorcing her from John W. Pratt ("the father") and awarding her supervised visitation with the parties' three children. . . .

<h3 style="text-align:center">Procedural and Factual Background . . .</h3>

The pertinent evidence at trial . . . indicates that the mother had developed health problems following the birth of the parties' three children that caused her lethargy and other disabling symptoms, which sometimes prevented her from properly caring for the children. The mother used narcotic and other medications to treat those health problems, resulting in what one expert considered a substance-abuse problem, which another expert described as an "iatrogenic addiction." The mother appeared to overcome those problems after the parties separated, which allowed her to start working as a nurse and permitted her to exercise custody of the children uneventfully for a period. However, in early December 2008, the mother experienced a seizure-like episode and lost consciousness late at night while at her home in Montgomery with the children and her father. Following that episode, the father obtained custody of the children while the mother remained hospitalized. Upon her discharge several days later, the mother's treating physicians, who did not definitively diagnose the cause of the episode but suspected it may have arisen from the mother's medically unsupervised attempt to withdraw from all of her medications, recommended that the mother cease using narcotic medications; however, at the time of trial, the mother continued to use narcotic medications prescribed by her pain-management physician. Some evidence suggested that the mother had also obtained prescription medications from other physicians without coordinating with her primary doctor. All the expert testimony on the subject recommended that, due to her unresolved health and prescription-drug-use problems, the mother should have supervised visitation with the children.

The trial court . . . divorced the parties, awarded the parties joint legal custody of the children, awarded the father primary physical custody of the children, and awarded the mother supervised visitation. In reference to the mother's supervised visitation, the judgment stated:

> 3. . . . The [mother] shall have supervised visitation with the children and said visitation shall be supervised by Roger and Gloria Burk. The counselor, Laurie Mattson Shoemaker, shall prepare guidelines to be given to the supervisors for the supervised visitation.
>
> 4. The schedule of supervised visitation may be upon agreement of the parties, however, said visitation shall occur no less than once every two weeks,

beginning June 26, 2009. The location and length of visits are at the discretion of the [father] and the supervising party, however, each visit should last at least two hours and should be held in as "home-like" a setting as possible, so that the children feel comfortable. . . .

Analysis

Supervised Visitation

We initially address the mother's argument that the trial court exceeded its discretion in ordering supervised visitation based on its concern that the mother had developed an addiction to prescription pain medication. From our reading of her brief, the mother does not complain that the trial court did not have sufficient evidence before it to support its concern that the children could be at risk while visiting the mother due to her prescription-drug-use problem. Rather, the mother contends that the trial court should have protected the children by using means other than supervised visitation that would be less intrusive on the parent-child relationship.

"The trial court has broad discretion in determining the visitation rights of a noncustodial parent, and its decision in this regard will not be reversed absent an abuse of discretion." In exercising its discretion over visitation matters, " '[t]he trial court is entrusted to balance the rights of the parents with the child's best interests to fashion a visitation award that is tailored to the specific facts and circumstances of the individual case.' "

A noncustodial parent generally enjoys "reasonable rights of visitation" with his or her children. However, those rights may be restricted in order to protect children from conduct, conditions, or circumstances surrounding their noncustodial parent that endanger the children's health, safety, or well-being. In fashioning the appropriate restrictions, out of respect for the public policy encouraging interaction between noncustodial parents and their children, the trial court may not use an overbroad restriction that does more than necessary to protect the children. . . .

[O]ur supreme court recently endorsed supervised visitation as a reasonable means of protecting the child of a noncustodial parent who was suffering from, among other problems, an unresolved substance-abuse condition when the evidence showed that unsupervised visitation would have subjected the child to an unreasonable risk of harm. The mother argues that, in this case, the trial court could have adequately addressed its safety concern for the children by simply ordering that she refrain from using prescription drugs. . . . The mother in this case uses narcotic and other prescription medications daily, which use has adversely affected her ability to parent the children in the past and the cessation of which may have caused or contributed to her prior "black-out" episode while in her home with the children. . . . [W]e conclude that the trial court in this case could not have merely ordered the mother to refrain from using her prescription medications while visiting with the children.

Because the trial court reasonably could have concluded that supervised visitation was necessary to protect the children from an unreasonable risk of physical or emotional harm emanating from the condition of the mother, and because the trial court reasonably could have rejected as inadequate the less intrusive means of protection advocated by the mother, we find that the trial court did not exceed its discretion in awarding the mother supervised visitation with the children.

The Discretion Over the Mother's Visitation Granted to the Father and the Visitation Supervisors

The mother next contends that the manner in which the trial court structured its award of supervised visitation granted the father so much discretion over her right to visitation that the father, in essence, may effectively veto that right. Although the trial court specified that the mother was to receive, at a minimum, two hours of visitation every two weeks, the trial court did not specify the location or the length of the mother's visits. Rather, the trial court granted the father and the visitation supervisors the exclusive discretion to determine the location of the visitation and whether the mother's visits should be extended beyond the minimum two-hour period. Additionally, although the trial court's judgment did not expressly grant the father the right to dictate the time at which the mother's visits are to be held, the judgment places considerable discretion in the father by requiring his agreement as to the timing of the visitation. Thus, whether the discretion granted to the father and/or the visitation supervisors violates Alabama law is squarely before this court.

Although Alabama law originally found no problem with vesting a custodial parent with complete discretion over the visitation of the noncustodial parent . . . over time our appellate courts began to recognize that divorced parties often disagree regarding visitation matters, and that a custodial parent should not be allowed to unilaterally limit or restrict the noncustodial parent's visitation. This court eventually held that a visitation order awarding "'reasonable visitation with the minor children at the discretion of the [custodial parent]'" generally should not be allowed because it authorizes the custodial parent to deny visitation altogether, which would not be in the best interests of the children. . . .

[T]his court has repeatedly held that a judgment awarding visitation to be supervised by the custodian of the child, without establishing a minimal visitation schedule for the noncustodial parent, impermissibly allows the custodian to control all visitation. . . . [A]n order of visitation granting a custodian so much discretion over a visitation schedule that visitation could be completely avoided if the custodian so desired should be deemed to be an award of no visitation and to be in violation of the rights of the noncustodial parent. . . .

The propriety of the judgment depends on whether the noncustodial parent has a sufficient, specified visitation schedule to rely upon, independent of the custodial parent's discretion. . . .

[W]e agree with the mother that the visitation schedule is unduly vague and that it, in fact, fails to provide her with any schedule at all. . . .

We also reiterate that "'[t]he *trial court* is entrusted to balance the rights of the parents with the child's best interests to fashion a visitation award that is tailored to the specific facts and circumstances of the individual case.'" (emphasis added). That judicial function may not be delegated to a third party. A trial court is not empowered to delegate its judicial functions even to another governmental agency. . . .

By delegating to the children's counselor the authority to specify guidelines governing the mother's visitation, the trial court improperly delegated its judicial function to a third party. . . .

NOTES AND QUESTIONS

1. *Conduct Restrictions.* Traditionally, restrictions on a parent's conduct were explicitly justified by moral judgments. Now courts justify restrictions based on the impact of parental conduct on the child.[213] For example, if the child suffers from asthma or some other respiratory condition, numerous courts have barred parents from smoking when they are with the child or having the child in a location where others smoke.[214] This approach resonates with the Uniform Marriage and Divorce Act. The comment to Section 407 indicates that the child endangerment standard "was chosen to prevent the denial of visitation to the noncustodial parent on the basis of moral judgments about parental behavior which have no relevance to the parent's interest in or capacity to maintain a close and benign relationship to the child."[215] This discussion though begs a larger question: is there any role for moral judgments in visitation determinations?

2. *Identifying Harm.* One challenging aspect of visitation cases is to identify when there is a sufficient likelihood of harm to the child to justify a restriction. In one case, a trial court prohibited a noncustodial father from allowing his current wife to be within 100 yards of his children, reasoning that "even the slightest exposure of the children to [the current wife] will be . . . very significantly harmful to them emotionally."[216] (The father had been having an affair with his current wife when he was married to the children's mother.) The appeals court invalidated the restriction as an abuse of discretion.[217]

---

213. In re Marriage of Miller, 345 P.3d 472 (Or. Ct. App. 2015).

214. See, e.g., Arrowood v. DiBenedetto, No. A-3886-14T3, 2016 WL 3369520 (N.J. Super. Ct. App. Div. June 20, 2016); Rice v. Sobel, No. 27458, 2015 WL 3623646 (Ohio Ct. App. June 10, 2015); Heck v. Reed, 529 N.W.2d 155 (N.D. 1995).

215. UMDA, supra note 22, § 407 cmt.

216. In re Marriage of Martin, 42 P.3d 75 (Colo. App. 2002).

217. Id.

3.   *The Noncustodial Parent's Interest.* Conduct restrictions also raise questions about the interest of the noncustodial parent. How much weight should courts give to the type of burden the noncustodial parent is being asked to bear?

4.   *Delegation to Professionals.* In Clark v. Clark, a Missouri trial court granted the mother's therapist and the children's therapist the right to determine visitation. The appeals court held that the trial court had erred by failing to "specifically detail" the mother's visitation rights as required by statute and by improperly delegating its authority to the therapists.[218] Putting aside the requirements of the statutes, is it sensible to deny the court the option to defer to specially trained professionals, who possess expertise the court may lack?

5.   *Delegation to the Other Parent.* As in *Pratt*, appeals courts typically invalidate visitation orders that, in effect, delegate authority to the custodial parent to determine whether, when, or how much visitation may occur. So too have courts invalidated orders that allow the custodial parent to determine when conditions have occurred so that visitation can be denied.[219] Courts, though, may allow delegation to the custodial parent in limited circumstances. For example, an Alabama court considered the noncustodial father's history of drug use, alcohol abuse, and violence, and upheld an order giving the mother "the right to refuse visitation of the father if, in her judgment, (1) the father appears to be under the influence of drugs or alcohol, or (2) the father appears to be placing the children in an unsafe environment or to be placing them in a place of danger."[220]

6.   *Reconsidering Parental Delegation.* While it is understandable that the noncustodial parent may not want to be subject to the desires of the other parent, how is the child's interest implicated by a court's delegation of authority to the custodial parent? In a famous series of books, Yale law professor Joseph Goldstein, psychoanalyst Anna Freud, and Yale Child Study Center professor Albert Solnit argued that children are best served by vesting significant control in the custodial parent.[221] Why might it be important for the child to see the custodial parent as controlling the child's interactions with others, including the other parent?

7.   *Delegation to the Children.* Courts have considered visitation orders that vest decision-making authority in the children, and have concluded in most cases that children should not be granted authority to decide whether to visit the noncustodial parent.[222] What's the rationale for invalidating these provisions? The visitation right, courts reason, is a right of the noncustodial parent.[223] Is there any harm in a court formally recognizing that visitation should and will happen only if

---

218. Clark v. Clark, 568 S.W.3d 920 (Mo. Ct. App. 2019).
219. See, e.g., Barth v. Barth, 851 N.W.2d 104 (Neb. Ct. App. 2014).
220. Watkins v. Lee, 227 So. 3d 84 (Ala. Civ. App. 2017).
221. Joseph Goldstein et al., The Best Interests of the Child: The Least Detrimental Alternative (1996).
222. See, e.g., Milligan v. Milligan, 149 So. 3d 623 (Ala. Civ. App. 2014); Brown v. Erbstoesser, 928 N.Y.S.2d 92 (N.Y. App. Div. 2011); In re Marriage of Kimball, 119 P.3d 684 (Kan. 2005).
223. Storrie v. Simmons, 693 S.E.2d 70 (W. Va. 2010).

the children want it to? Should the parent's right be secondary to the desires of the child?[224]

8. *Supervised Visitation.* There are a number of ways that supervised visitation can occur. Courts may designate other family members or therapeutic professionals to supervise visitation, or courts may mandate that visitation occur at a visitation center.

9. *Modification of Visitation.* We addressed modification in the previous section. Some courts employ the same standard with visitation as we saw with custody, requiring a significant change in circumstances before revisiting a prior order. For example, Florida statutory law mandates that "[a] determination of parental responsibility, a parenting plan, or a time-sharing schedule may not be modified without a showing of a substantial, material, and unanticipated change in circumstances and a determination that the modification is in the best interests of the child."[225] In most jurisdictions, though, the standard for revisiting a visitation order is less onerous than a significant change in circumstances. In Arkansas, a court "may modify or vacate [visitation] orders at any time when it becomes aware of a change in circumstances or facts not known to it at the time of the initial order."[226] Missouri requires a "substantial change" in circumstances to modify custody, and only a "change" in circumstances to modify visitation.[227] Other courts also say that they require a change in circumstances in order to reconsider a visitation agreement, but not necessarily a substantial change.[228] Some states go further. Mississippi, for example, requires no showing of a change of circumstances, allowing modification of a visitation order based on the child's best interests.[229] Such states follow the Uniform Marriage and Divorce Act in allowing modification simply upon a showing that it would serve the best interests of the child.[230]

10. *Visitation Enforcement.* If the custodial parent sufficiently impedes the noncustodial parent's effort to visit with the child, an action to enforce visitation may be necessary. The primary means of enforcement of visitation is through a contempt order, which typically results in a monetary fine and in extreme cases the possibility of incarceration.[231] Some states have allowed a suspension of child support in the most egregious cases, as a way to enforce visitation if a custodial parent interferes with visitation.[232] While this approach would give the custodial

---

224. Cf. Hendrickson v. Hendrickson, 603 N.W.2d 896 (N.D. 2000).
225. Fla. Stat. § 61.13(3) (2020).
226. Brown v. Brown, 387 S.W.2d 159 (Ark. 2012).
227. Clark v. Clark, 568 S.W.3d 920 (Mo. Ct. App. 2019).
228. Meehan-Greer v. Greer, 415 P.3d 274 (Wyo. 2018).
229. Nurkin v. Nurkin, 171 So. 3d 561 (Miss. Ct. App. 2015).
230. See, e.g., In re Marriage of Parr, 240 P.3d 509 (Colo. App. 2010); UMDA, supra note 22, § 407(b).
231. See, e.g., Carlson v. Carlson, 663 S.E.2d 673 (Ga. 2008).
232. See, e.g., Wuebbeling v. Clark, 502 S.W.3d 676 (Mo. Ct. App. 2016).

parent a potentially strong incentive to allow visitation, it is not an approach that courts typically take.[233]

11. *Unused Visitation.* In some cases, the noncustodial parent is awarded more visitation than that parent actually uses. Should the court have any role to play in that circumstance? Why might the custodial parent care if the other parent does not use all of the legally mandated visitation? Should the unused parenting time matter to child support obligations?

C. VISITATION AND CHILD SUPPORT

PERKINSON V. PERKINSON
989 N.E.2d 758 (Ind. 2013)

DAVID, JUSTICE. . . .

Facts and Procedural History

Michael D. Perkinson (Father) married Kay Char Perkinson (Mother) in October 2004. . . . In August 2005, Mother gave birth to L.P. In September 2005, Father filed a petition for dissolution of the marriage. . . .

A dissolution decree was entered in February 2006. . . . Father and Mother entered into an agreement in which Father agreed to waive his parenting time rights in exchange for Mother assuming sole financial responsibility and waiving enforcement of Father's child support arrearage.

The agreement also set out that if Father sought parenting time in the future, "he shall be obligated to pay any support arrearage through the date of the approval" of the agreement by the trial court. The agreement was approved by the court in March 2006.

In February 2008, Father filed a verified petition for modification of parenting time, seeking to reestablish visitation with L.P. The trial court denied that petition in April 2008. . . .

Discussion . . .

This is ultimately a decision about parenting time, which requires us to "give foremost consideration to the best interests of the child." Parenting time decisions are reviewed for an abuse of discretion. . . .

It is incomprehensible to this Court to imagine that either parent would ever stipulate to give up parenting time in lieu of not paying child support. It has long

_____

233. See Laura W. Morgan, Deviating from Guidelines, in Child Support Guidelines Interpretation and Application § 8.14 (2d ed. 2020-21 Supp.).

been established by this Court that "[a]ny agreement purporting to contract away these [child support] rights is directly contrary to this State's public policy of protecting the welfare of children." . . .

Even if it is not in a child's best interest to visit with a parent, it is still in that child's best interest to be financially supported by that parent. . . .

Furthermore, the clause of the agreement purporting to obligate the Father to pay any support arrearage if he sought parenting time in the future acts to discourage the Father's future involvement with his child. As our Court of Appeals previously held, "[v]isitation rights and child support are separate issues, not to be comingled. A court cannot condition visitation upon the payment of child support if a custodial parent is not entitled to do so."

"Indiana has long recognized that the right of parents to visit their children is a precious privilege that should be enjoyed by noncustodial parents," and thus a noncustodial parent is "generally entitled to reasonable visitation rights." Indiana Code section 31–17–4–2 states that parenting time rights shall not be restricted unless there is a finding "that the parenting time might endanger the child's physical health or significantly impair the child's emotional development." . . .

Indiana is not alone in recognizing a noncustodial parent's right of visitation with his or her own children. . . .

As if the forgoing rationales were not supportive enough to deny effect to the parenting agreement in question here, there is yet another reason to do so. The Indiana Parenting Time Guidelines explicitly declares that "[a] child has the right both to support *and parenting time*. . . ." This is not mere surplusage; Indiana has both long recognized the best interest of the child as being paramount in any custody consideration and has a legislatively-expressed presumption in favor of parenting time with the noncustodial parent. The derivative of these dual declarations is that, not only does a noncustodial parent have a presumed right of parenting time, but the child has the correlative right to receive parenting time from the noncustodial parent because it is presumed to be in the child's best interest. Just as allowing an agreement purporting to contract away a child's right to support must be held void, an agreement to contract away a child's right to parenting time, where the presumption that such parenting time is in the child's best interest has not been defeated, must also be held void as a matter of public policy. . . .

Extraordinary circumstances must exist to deny parenting time to a parent, which necessarily denies the same to the child. If the trial court finds such extraordinary circumstances do exist, then the trial court shall make specific findings regarding its conclusion that parenting time would endanger the child's physical health or significantly impair the child's emotional development. . . .

For two years, Father was not in contact with L.P. However, for the past five years, the record is clear that Father has attempted to reenter L.P.'s life. He has twice petitioned the court for parenting time. He is currently raising a child younger than

L.P. and has parenting time with his first born. These facts do support Father's position that he no longer wants to remain disconnected from L.P. . . .

The trial court in the present case makes a finding that parenting time "would not be in the child's best interest and would create significant emotional harm to her" but provides insufficient facts to support its finding other than its footnote asking "How do you explain to a six (6) year old that her Father exchanged time with her for money?" As horrific as that rhetorical question is, Mother agreed to it. . . .

In this case, Mother did not offer any DCS reports, therapist reports, or expert testimony to show that parenting time between Father and L.P. would not be in the child's best interest. We understand Mother went through significant emotional turmoil in being a single mother while putting herself through college and testified she felt abandoned by Father. However, again, Mother agreed to this arrangement.

The only evidence before the trial court regarding any endangerment to the child was the testimony of the Mother. . . . While under the right circumstances, one parent's testimony alone could be sufficient, here Mother's testimony was only that Father was verbally abusive to Mother and Father's oldest child in 2005, and that he threatened to destroy the relationship between Mother and L.P. . . . There is no evidence to support Mother's belief that it would not be in the best interests of L.P. to spend time with her Father. . . .

The decision of the trial court is reversed and this case is remanded.

NOTES AND QUESTIONS

1. *Private Ordering.* In *Perkinson*, the court held that any agreement to relinquish visitation in exchange for a waiver of child support is unenforceable and cannot be a basis for later denying the noncustodial parent visitation. What precisely is the basis for rejecting an agreement that both parents have voluntarily entered? After all, these agreements will almost certainly occur, irrespective of the legal rule.

2. *Visitation and Child Support.* In most jurisdictions, the failure of the noncustodial parent to pay child support is an insufficient reason, by itself, to deny visitation.[234] However, a noncustodial parent who has the means to pay child support and willfully fails to do so may sacrifice visitation rights.[235] Is such a parent deliberately harming the child?

---

234. See, e.g., Perkinson v. Perkinson, 989 N.E.2d 758 (Ind. 2013).

235. See, e.g., Turner v. Turner, 919 S.W.2d 340 (Tenn. Ct. App. 1995).

CHAPTER 11

Family Support

In this chapter, we address the system for financial support for the dependency that arises within and from family relationships, specifically between parents and children. We first raise — and question — the assumptions underlying our current system of addressing dependency. The bulk of this chapter then addresses child support — who must pay, how much, and why. Finally, we turn to other forms of dependency that may arise within families — for instance, between children and aging parents. As you read, consider how our legal rules and systems differentiate between types of dependency arising from family relationships. Are these distinctions justified?

I. Who Supports Dependency?

What role is the family expected to play in addressing financial, physical, and other forms of dependency? Why? What inequalities does this system reflect and replicate? Consider these questions as you read this section.

Martha Albertson Fineman, The Vulnerable Subject and the Responsive State
60 Emory L.J. 251 (2010)

Recognition of human dependency and vulnerability should present the traditional political and legal theorist with a dilemma. Unfortunately, dependency is not part of many approaches to theory in politics or law. Instead, a structure and set of social orderings have been constructed in which the family has been deemed the primary societal institution responsible for dependency. The family is the mechanism by which we privatize, and thus hide dependency and its implications. This allows simplistic assertions of the attainability, as well as the superiority, of individual independence and self-sufficiency, which are spun out in an ideology of autonomy and personal responsibility that bears little relationship to the human condition. . . .

In one most basic form, dependency should be thought of as unavoidable and inevitable; it is developmental and biological in nature. All of us are dependent on others for care and provision as infants, and many will become dependent as we age, are taken ill, or become disabled. This form of dependency is the type that generally is viewed sympathetically and sparks our charitable impulses, as well as government programs. . . .

There is a second form of dependency that needs to be discussed in relation to, but separate from, inevitable dependency, however. This form of dependency is much less obvious, but when it is noticed it is often stigmatized and condemned. I label[] this form of dependency *derivative* to reflect the very simple but often overlooked fact that those who cared for inevitable dependents were themselves dependent on resources in order to accomplish that care. This form of dependency is *neither* inevitable, *nor* is it universally experienced. Rather, it is socially imposed through our construction of institutions such as the family, with roles and relationships traditionally defined and differentiated along gendered lines. . . .

I argue[] for a more collective and institutionally shared notion approach to dependency: a reallocation of primary responsibility for dependency that would place some obligation on other societal institutions to share in the burdens of dependency, particularly those associated with the market and the state. This reallocation of responsibility seem[s] particularly appropriate, since both state and market institutions reap[] the benefits that care work produce[s] in the form of the reproduction and regeneration of society. . . .

We all benefit from society and its institutions, but some are relatively advantaged and privileged in their relationships, while others are disadvantaged. . . . Under a vulnerability analysis, the state . . . has a responsibility to structure conditions in which individuals can aspire to meaningfully realize their individual capabilities as fully as possible. . . .

Maxine Eichner, The Free-Market Family: How the Market Crushed the American Dream (and How It Can Be Restored) (2019)

The myth to which we Americans have long subscribed is known as the "American Dream." . . . What sets America apart, as this myth has it, is that our society ensures every person, regardless of age, gender, and socio-economic status, the opportunity to develop to their fullest potential. . . .

In the past half-century, though, the American Dream has come to be interpreted as simply guaranteeing the right to compete for wealth in an ever more brutal market. . . .

Some of the subject's most insightful commentators have targeted our country's increasing economic inequality as the source of the problem. . . . Those [critics] do get it right, but only partly so. . . . The problem driving American discontent is . . . broader . . . as economic forces besides inequality play a role. Yet the problem is also narrower in that our discontent stems not generally from the havoc caused by economic forces, but specifically from the damage these forces are wreaking on our family lives. . . .

The result is that market forces, rather than supporting sound family lives, today are strangling the life out of American families. Economic changes in the last decades have made the lot of American families, which was never all that easy, much tougher. For poor and working-class Americans, uncertain job prospects and low wages mean that many won't ever form the stable relationships they badly want. Within this group, the declining few who marry are likely to divorce; rising numbers of children are born to unmarried parents; and most children are at some point raised by unmarried mothers. Low-income families' tight budgets also mean that parents can't prepare their children to go on to bigger and better things. . . . For American families across the economic spectrum, economic hardship, pressure, and insecurity make life a grinding slog to keep it together between long hours of paid work and family responsibilities. All this means that American families are stretched and stressed to their limits, if they haven't broken down altogether.

This matters so much because of the vital role that families play in our individual and collective wellbeing. Children need strong family relationships to build the stable foundation that will enable them to become sound adults. And it's through families that children will (or won't) get the economic support and caretaking they need to fulfill their potential. . . .

The struggles that low-, middle-, and high-income American families are having today look very different, but they are all manifestations of the same problem: the increasingly large toll that market forces have been taking on families during the past several decades. The harm inflicted on families, however, wasn't inevitable, and it wasn't the necessary result of the forces of globalization or technology. Instead, the defeat of American families by market forces was the product of a long-term failure of American public policy. . . .

The result of five decades of policymakers' market-centric decisions is that market forces have crushed Americans' ability to have thriving family lives, as well as to raise strong, solid kids. . . . [I]nstead of helping families get the things they need to thrive, policymakers just keep cheering the market on, telling families that, if they only work a little harder, they can achieve their dreams. . . .

Anne L. Alstott, Neoliberalism in U.S. Family Law: Negative Liberty and Laissez-Faire Markets in the Minimal State
77 Law & Contemp. Probs. 25 (2014)

Neoliberalism permeates U.S. family law. The law protects negative liberty in family life but denies positive rights to the resources that make family life possible. The law endorses laissez-faire market outcomes and portrays the state as overbearing and incompetent.

Even seemingly progressive landmarks in family law remain within the neoliberal frame. *Loving v. Virginia*, *Lawrence v. Texas*, and *United States v. Windsor*, for instance, mark true victories for social progressives, protecting important rights long denied to persecuted groups. And yet, none of them challenges in any deep way the three core ideals of neoliberal family law: negative liberty, laissez-faire market distributions and the minimal state. To take another example, the earned income tax credit (EITC) passes in today's United States for a progressive welfare program, even though it alleviates only modestly the harshness of laissez-faire labor markets. . . .

[N]eoliberalism dominates U.S. family law in three legal arenas. The first is federal constitutional law, where the Supreme Court has adopted a thoroughly neoliberal vision of the family. According to the Court, the Federal Constitution grants individuals wide latitude to assert negative liberty — that is, freedom from state intervention — in family life. But individuals have no constitutional right to claim any distribution of resources other than that produced by the marketplace. So strong is the Court's ideal of negative liberty, and so extreme is its skepticism about state power, that it has insulated the state from any responsibility to protect children — even against vicious and foreseeable parental attacks.

The second legal arena is state family law, which pursues a limited mission shaped by the contours of constitutional law. When individuals have sweeping rights to negative liberty but no rights at all to challenge market distributions, the primary task of subconstitutional law is simply to create legal space for individuals to exercise negative liberty. Accordingly, state family law pursues no broad mandate to foster family life. Rather, it seeks only to authorize private ordering and to adjudicate private disputes. Even in the parent-child relationship, neoliberalism dominates, as state law leaves children's fates to depend on their parents' market earnings. Rich children prosper and poor ones suffer, and neither children nor their parents can seek legal redress.

The third legal arena is federal and state welfare law. One might suppose that welfare would provide a legal vehicle for citizens to challenge market outcomes. However, in the United States today, welfare provision tends to ratify market distributions rather than upend them. Absent constitutional rights to aid, welfare programs exist at the sufferance of political actors, and the programs' terms reflect neoliberal commitments. So, for instance, the major U.S. social insurance programs privilege paid employment by granting benefits that reward high earnings and steady participation in the workforce. And welfare programs often feature time limits, work requirements, and other conditions that ensure that poor individuals and their families subsist primarily on their market earnings. The predictable consequence is that individuals and families can suffer dire poverty without any entitlement to state assistance. . . .

According to the Supreme Court, individual liberty in family life begins and ends with negative liberty — the absence of state intervention in the family. Every major constitutional right in family law that has been recognized by the Supreme Court sounds in negative liberty. . . . *Loving* and *Windsor* . . . invoked individuals' claim to negative liberty in choosing marital partners.

Reproductive rights cases have also reflected the constitutional allegiance to negative liberty. In *Griswold v. Connecticut* . . . [and] *Roe v. Wade*, . . . the Court protected negative liberty, framed as "zones of privacy" in *Griswold* and "rights of personal privacy" in *Roe*. Today, reproductive rights remain contested, with social conservatives scoring some victories limiting access to abortion, but the key rights protected by the Constitution are rights to act free of government interference.

The Supreme Court has extended negative liberty to sexual activity as well. In *Lawrence*, the Court struck down a Texas statute criminalizing sexual acts between persons of the same sex. The Court admonished that "[t]he petitioners are entitled to respect for their private lives. The State cannot demean their existence or control their destiny by making their private sexual conduct a crime."

Despite these negative rights against the state, individuals have no positive rights at all to the resources they need to conduct family life. Families have no constitutional right to cash welfare, to housing, or to education, for instance. In federal constitutional parlance, welfare, taxation, and other distributive policies face only "rational basis" review, meaning that they are essentially beyond constitutional challenge. Poverty is not a suspect classification triggering constitutional scrutiny. Thus, for instance, states can cap welfare benefits regardless of family size, can refuse to build public housing projects, and can fund public schools inadequately (or, apparently, not at all). The United States can constitutionally limit welfare benefits to five years, deny Supplemental Nutrition Assistance Program (SNAP, formerly Food Stamps) benefits to a household if a parent fails to pursue employment, and deny welfare benefits to children based on parental behavior.

The Supreme Court's rejection of a positive right to state support reflects the second neoliberal ideal that dominates U.S. family law: the primacy of resource allocations produced by laissez-faire markets. When the Court denies welfare rights, it endorses market outcomes and rejects the notion that individuals are entitled to basic resources (or any resources at all) other than those earned in the marketplace. . . .

Together, the neoliberal ideals of negative liberty and market distribution create an asymmetric pattern of federal constitutional protections for family life. Individuals have fundamental rights to marry, engage in sexual activity, and otherwise carry on family life, but their legal rights enable them only to fend off state regulation. Individuals have no right to the resources they need to marry, to divorce, or even to remain alive (a rather obvious prerequisite to family life). Every individual is expected to support herself and her spouse on what she can earn in the labor market. And she has no recourse if the market prices of basic necessities are beyond her reach. The absence of positive rights to income or to sustenance impose de facto limits on citizens' access to marriage and family life, but these limitations are invisible in federal constitutional law.

Constitutional cases on parental rights dance the same neoliberal two-step. Parents have near-absolute rights to rear their children as they choose, but the law protects only negative liberties. . . . At the same time, parenthood, like other family activities, confers no positive rights to the resources needed to rear children. Families have no right to welfare and no constitutional hook to challenge the adequacy of their wages or living standard. Even education is optional from a federal constitutional perspective, according to the Supreme Court. . . .

The Federal Constitution, then, paints parenthood in neoliberal colors: parents may rear their children (mostly) as they like but must support them out of their own earnings and have no claim to state support. Indeed, so strong is the Supreme Court's endorsement of market outcomes that the Court has approved draconian measures, including jail time, for parents who fail to support their children out of their own earnings. States routinely impose sanctions for child-support nonpayment, including wage withholding and the denial of state licenses, even when payors are indigent. . . .

The third neoliberal ideal endorses a minimal state, an aspiration that permeates the constitutional canon in family law. Negative-liberty cases often highlight the dangers of the overreaching state. . . . The ideal of the minimal state played a heartbreaking role in the tragedy of Joshua De[S]haney. Four-year-old Joshua was nearly beaten to death by his father, who had a history of abusing the child. But the Supreme Court held that the state had no constitutional obligation to protect the child:

> The [Due Process] Clause is phrased as a limitation on the State's power to act, not as a guarantee of certain minimal levels of safety and security; it forbids the State itself to deprive individuals of life, liberty, and property without "due process of law," but its language cannot fairly be extended to impose an affirmative obligation on the State to ensure that those interests do not come to harm through other means."

The three neoliberal ideals are, of course, intertwined. The minimal state is deeply consistent with negative liberty and distribution via laissez-faire markets. The state's implicit role is to facilitate market transactions by protecting property rights. Beyond that, the state need not take any particular actions to promote family life, protect children, or mitigate the poverty, distress, and isolation produced by free markets.

NOTES AND QUESTIONS

1. *Dependency and the Family.* Professor Martha Fineman argues that our legal and political system fails to take account of "unavoidable and inevitable" dependency—that vulnerability that we all have or will experience at some point in our lives. She critiques our legal and political system for constructing "family" as "the mechanism by which we privatize, and thus hide dependency and its implications." Our system also imposes dependency derivatively, she argues, often along gendered lines, on those who engage in caring for dependents. In what ways do our laws and policies "privatize" dependency to be addressed by the family? What broad reforms would you advocate to pursue Fineman's "reallocation of primary responsibility for dependency that would place some obligation on other societal institutions to share in the burdens of dependency"? What rationales support society taking on some of the burden of addressing dependency, instead of just individual families? If addressing dependency means supporting caregiving, consider the United States compared to other countries with advanced economies. For instance, unlike the United States, Sweden guarantees 480 days of parental leave split between a child's two parents.[1] What impediments do you see for implementing policies like this or achieving other reforms you might suggest? Consider these questions as you the materials in this chapter and reflect on what you have already read.

2. *The Family and the Market.* While many blame growing economic inequality for the struggles of American families, Professor Maxine Eichner argues that the fault also lies with a decidedly "market-centric" approach to economic policy over the past fifty years that has made families, which are vitally important for "our individual and collective wellbeing," more susceptible to market forces. How does a market-centric approach hurt families? Which families? What improvements would you suggest to address the struggles in families' lives and make families less vulnerable to market forces? Fineman critiques the ethic of "autonomy and personal responsibility." How does this ethic make it harder to support families in their ability to thrive in the way that Eichner envisions?

3. *Privatized Care, Race, Class, and Gender.* If our social system leaves care work to families individually, and women disproportionately do this care, what are

---

1. Parental Leave, Official Site of Sweden, https://sweden.se/society/family-friendly-life-the-swedish-way; Mallory Campbell, Family Leave: Comparing the United States' Family and Medical Leave Act with Sweden's Parental Leave Policy, 9 Notre Dame J. Int'l & Comp. L. 116, 136 (2019); Kate Ryan, Gay Fathers Receive Less Parental Leave than Other Couples: Study, Reuters.com (Sept. 5, 2019) (Sweden gives same-sex and different-sex couples the same paid parental leave).

the economic implications for families? Consider this in the context of gender and wages. Women who work full time are paid about 80 cents for every dollar paid to men.[2] That wage gap is exacerbated by the fact that mothers also experience wage penalties.[3] What are the implications financially for those engaging in dependency work when families go through transitions like divorce? In what ways are the economic effects of divorce gender-based?[4] What reforms in the law of divorce could mitigate these effects?

Child support systems are one way in which governments delegate state responsibility for responding to family needs to individuals and families. This system has significant class and race dimensions. Professor Tonya Brito critiques the child support system for constructing the "crushing economic burden" of child support debt "owed by noncustodial fathers to custodial mothers in low-income and predominately Black families."[5] According to Brito, this debt is a "financial bubble," insofar as it is "artificially inflated, largely uncollectible, and potentially destructive," built on "policymakers' 'magical thinking' about what impoverished fathers should earn in the labor market," and "also manufactured by a series of institutional practices — layered one on top of the other — that cause low-wage noncustodial parents to rapidly accrue ever-mounting arrears."[6] Professor Solangel Maldonado, who also faults the child support system for unfairly punishing poor fathers of color, argues that fathers' non-monetary contributions to their children should be recognized as support.[7] As you read the rest of this chapter, consider how the law could, and should, address the gender, race, and class dynamics at stake in the child support system.

4. *Negative Rights, Positive Rights, and the Minimal State.* Professor Alstott critiques a legal order based on the ideal of a "minimal state" unwilling to intervene in family law or to guarantee resources to support family life. Alstott locates this approach in federal constitutional law, state family law, and federal and state welfare law. How could the Court in cases like Loving v. Virginia, Lawrence v. Texas, and United States v. Windsor, discussed in Chapter 2, have "challenge[d] in any deep way the three core ideals of neoliberal family law: negative liberty, laissez-faire market distributions and the minimal state"? What "positive rights" might we develop to support communities in conducting family life?

---

2. Nat'l Women's Law Ctr., Equal Pay & The Wage Gap (Mar. 8, 2020).

3. See, e.g., Michelle J. Budig & Paula England, The Wage Penalty for Motherhood, 66 Am. Soc. Rev. 204 (2001); see also Stephen Benard et al., Cognitive Bias and the Motherhood Penalty, 59 Hastings L.J. 1359 (2008).

4. See, e.g., Thomas Leopold, Gender Differences in the Consequences of Divorce: A Study of Multiple Outcomes, 55 Demography 769 (2018); David de Vaus et al., The Economic Consequences of Divorce in Six OECD Countries, 52 Austl. J. Soc. Issues 180 (2017); Suzanne M. Bianchi et al., The Gender Gap in the Economic Well-Being of Nonresident Fathers and Custodial Mothers, 36 Demography 195 (1999).

5. Tonya L. Brito, The Child Support Debt Bubble, 9 U.C. Irvine L. Rev. 953, 955 (2019).

6. Id.

7. Solangel Maldonado, Deadbeat or Deadbroke: Redefining Child Support for Poor Fathers, 39 U.C. Davis L. Rev. 991 (2006).

II. Child Support

Parents have a legal obligation to support their children. At common law, this duty was understood as a "mere moral obligation creating no civil liability."[8] But as early as the seventeenth century in the United States, "bastardy" laws imposed a duty of support on the parents of illegitimate children. By 1900, every state had imposed a support duty in both civil and criminal codes. The goal was to establish paternity and coerce support, or marriage, from fathers; the admitted purpose of these laws was to prevent the children from becoming a public burden.[9] A child's mother, a third party, or the district attorney could institute "bastardy" proceedings. In Arkansas, for example, in the 1920s, if the mother of a "bastard child" swore that Mr. X was the father, the judge could issue a warrant for his arrest. The judge could also, on his own, bring the woman in and require her, under oath, to give the name of the father, "or give security to indemnify the county; and if she refuses to do either to commit her to jail."[10] Under this law, the father could be charged with expenses for the birth, up to $15, and between $1 and $3 per month for child support.[11] The law "gave no rights to the father, only responsibilities."[12] Unmarried mothers ordinarily assumed responsibility for their children, regardless of whether the law formally imposed an obligation, but many ended up needing public assistance.[13]

As states began to permit judicial divorce, they also gave judges the authority to order support for children upon dissolution of their parents' marriage. This paved the way for the modern child support system in which, typically, a noncustodial parent is ordered to make child support payments to the custodial parent in order to share in the costs of raising the child. Although these laws initially focused on married fathers — and sometimes expressly did not apply to mothers or unmarried fathers — they have evolved to be both gender-neutral and detached from marriage.[14] Today, the general obligation of parents to support their children flows from the determinations of parentage we covered in Chapter 9. Whether a person is

---

8. Chester G. Vernier, 4 American Family Laws 4 (1936); see also Donna Schuele, Origins and Development of the Law of Parental Child Support, 27 J. Fam. L. 807, 825 (1988).

9. Vernier, supra note 8, at 207; Mary Ann Mason, From Father's Property to Children's Rights 25 (1994); Nan D. Hunter, Child Support Law and Policy: The Systematic Imposition of Costs on Women, 6 Harv. Women's L.J. 1, 3 (1983).

10. Ark. Code Ann. § 772-85 (1921), in Vernier, supra note 8, at 222.

11. The Uniform Illegitimacy Act of 1922 tried to provide for more support of "illegitimate" children. The Act was later withdrawn. See Unif. Parentage Act (1973), Prefatory Note, 9B U.L.A. 378 (2001).

12. Mason, supra note 9, at 70.

13. Id. at 99–100 (citing 1914 study of unmarried mothers in Massachusetts, which found that 60 percent of their children ended up wards of the state).

14. See, e.g., Rand v. Rand, 374 A.2d 900 (Md. 1977) (placing disproportionate burden of support on father was inconsistent with state's equal rights amendment). The Maryland legislature amended the child support guidelines to remove all references to parental gender. See Md. Code Ann., Fam. Law § 12-201 (West 2020).

deemed a legal parent by virtue of biology, function, intent, marriage, or any other basis, that parent is legally responsible for supporting their child.

The general obligation of support is also enforced (though loosely) through the abuse and neglect system discussed in Chapter 7. The failure to meet a child's basic needs despite the ability to do so constitutes neglect and can be the basis for state intervention, removal, and termination, if appropriate. This system disproportionately affects poor, non-white, and single-parent families. By and large, parents raising children in marital families and providing support above the minimal level defined by neglect laws seldom face any public enforcement of their obligation to support their children. One parent cannot sue to force the other to spend more money on a child, and a child cannot sue her parents, for example, because she wants them to buy her nicer clothes or pay private school tuition.[15]

The primary mechanism by which the obligation to support children is formally enforced is through child support orders, which can be sought and obtained in a number of different contexts: parentage suits, abuse and neglect proceedings, custody proceedings between unmarried parents, and divorce or annulment proceedings for married parents. The law largely has developed in the context of divorce actions, but the rules governing who must pay and how much are not limited to that context. Although courts had discretion to order child support long ago, courts did not routinely impose child support obligations until the 1970s. Awards were infrequent, inconsistent, and often too low to provide meaningful support to the children of divorced parents. Each state developed its own standards, which typically vested great discretion in the trial judge, to the detriment of many custodial mothers and their children. Discretion tended to be exercised based more on sympathy for noncustodial fathers than on children's needs.[16]

The lack of sufficient child support exacerbated the economic plight of single mothers and their children, who were disproportionately likely to be living in poverty and in need of government assistance. The main cash assistance program, Aid to Families with Dependent Children (AFDC), which eventually was replaced by the Temporary Assistance to Needy Families Act (TANF) in 1996, was designed to provide assistance to children living with a single parent. The size and overall cost of this program had grown dramatically due to a rise in the number of single parents, a result of both accelerating divorce rates and an increase in non marital parenting.[17] The federal government subsidizes most welfare programs, including TANF, and, thus, Congress began to take an interest in the issue of child support. Congressional intervention proceeded from a general view that the government

---

15. See, e.g., Peggy Wright & Michael Izzo, Teen Who Sued Parents for College Funds Denied, USA Today (Mar. 4, 2014).

16. For an overview of the child support system in the 1970s, see Harry Krause, Child Support in America: The Legal Perspective (1981).

17. Hunter, supra note 9, at 15–17.

should not be supporting children through welfare when those children could be supported by a noncustodial parent instead. Does this seem like a reasonable justification for congressional action? Should the government take more of a role in directly supporting families, especially those living, or at risk of living, in poverty?

The current system for awarding child support and enforcing child support orders is a hybrid federal-state system. Although Congress first got involved as a means of controlling welfare spending, it eventually passed rules that would apply to child support in all contexts. In 1975, Congress created the Office of Child Support Enforcement as Part D of the Social Security Act ("the IV-D program"). In 1984, Congress made state AFDC funding contingent on the adoption of methods to enforce child support, which we discuss later in the chapter.[18] In 1988, Congress went further, and conditioned federal funding on states' adoption of mandatory child support guidelines.[19] Judges are permitted to deviate from the guidelines only in narrow circumstances. The law did not mandate any particular formula or set of guidelines, but in order to maintain their welfare subsidies, states had to ensure that awards were generally higher and that they were more consistent across the board. A 1996 study showed that 83 percent of child support orders over a ten-year period were for the guideline amount, suggesting that more consistency was achieved by narrowing judicial discretion.[20]

As you read the materials in this section, consider whether the modern approach to child support appropriately balances the interests of children and parents. The law of child support is critically important not only because children's welfare depends on it, but also because it affects so many people. Thirty percent of adults in the United States have been either the payor or payee with respect to a child support order.[21] Four in ten children today are born to unmarried parents, and two-thirds of divorces are in families with at least one minor child.[22] Who are the winners and losers in this system? Are there ways the system could be reformed to work better for all those affected by it?

The establishment of child support involves three broad issues: (1) the obligation to pay; (2) the amount of payment; and (3) the enforcement of the award. We address these issues in turn.

---

18. See Child Support Enforcement Amendments of 1984, Pub. L. No. 98-378, codified at 42 U.S.C. § 667 (2018).

19. See Family Support Act of 1988, Pub. L. No. 100-485, codified at 42 U.S.C. § 667(b)(2) (1988); see also Laura W. Morgan, Child Support Fifty Years Later, 42 Fam. L.Q. 365, 365–70 (2008).

20. See Maureen A. Pirog et al., Interstate Comparisons of Child Support Orders Using State Guidelines, 47 Fam. Rel. 289 (1998).

21. See Ira Mark Ellman & Tara O'Toole Ellman, The Theory of Child Support, 45 Harv. J. Legis. 107, 108 (2008).

22. Joyce A. Martin et al., Births: Final Data for 2017, Nat'l Vital Stat. Rep. 5 (Nov. 7, 2018); George J. Cohen & Carol C. Weitzman, Helping Children and Families Deal with Divorce and Separation, 138 Pediatrics 1 (2016).

A. Who Must Pay? Proving and Disproving Paternity

Child support is usually tied to a determination of parentage. As you saw in Chapter 9, many disputes about parentage are motivated by the desire to obtain or avoid an order of child support. Do parentage and support laws have common goals? If biology is the basis for the child support obligation, under what circumstances should someone be able to prove or disprove a genetic tie to a child? In Clark v. Jeter, the Supreme Court invalidated a Pennsylvania law that imposed a six-year statute of limitations to prove paternity, running from the child's birth.[23] Like most states, Pennsylvania required proof of paternity before a parent could seek child support for a nonmarital child. The Court held that the statute of limitations ran afoul of the Equal Protection Clause because marital children were permitted to seek support from parents at any point during their minority. The Court had announced in earlier cases that any statute of limitations on paternity suits "must be sufficiently long in duration to present a reasonable opportunity for those with an interest in such children to assert claims on their behalf" and that "any time limitation placed on that opportunity must be substantially related to the State's interest in avoiding the litigation of stale or fraudulent claims."[24] Applying this standard, the Court had previously struck down one- and two-year limitations periods. In Clark, it concluded that the six-year period was also invalid:

> Even six years does not necessarily provide a reasonable opportunity to assert a claim on behalf of an illegitimate child. "The unwillingness of the mother to file a paternity action on behalf of her child, which could stem from her relationship with the natural father or . . . from the emotional strain of having an illegitimate child, or even from the desire to avoid community and family disapproval, may continue years after the child is born. The problem may be exacerbated if, as often happens, the mother herself is a minor." Mills, 456 U.S. 91, 105 (1982). (O'Connor, J., concurring). . . .
>
> We do not rest our decision on this ground, however, for it is not entirely evident that six years would necessarily be an unreasonable limitations period for child support actions involving illegitimate children. We are, however, confident that the 6-year statute of limitations is not substantially related to Pennsylvania's interest in avoiding the litigation of stale or fraudulent claims. In a number of circumstances, Pennsylvania permits the issue of paternity to be litigated more than six years after the birth of an illegitimate child. . . . For example, the intestacy statute, permits a child born out of wedlock to establish paternity as long as "there is clear and convincing evidence that the man was the father of the child." Likewise, no statute of limitations applies to a father's action to establish paternity. . . .

---

23. 486 U.S. 456 (1988).
24. Mills v. Habluetzel, 456 U.S. 91, 99–100 (1982).

> A more recent indication that Pennsylvania does not consider proof problems insurmountable is the enactment by the Pennsylvania Legislature in 1985 of an 18-year statute of limitations for paternity and support actions. To be sure the legislature did not act spontaneously, but rather under the threat of losing some federal funds. Nevertheless, the new statute is a tacit concession that proof problems are not overwhelming. The legislative history of the federal Child Support Enforcement Amendments explains why Congress thought such statutes of limitations are reasonable. Congress adverted to the problem of stale and fraudulent claims, but recognized that increasingly sophisticated tests for genetic markers permit the exclusion of over 99% of those who might be accused of paternity, regardless of the age of the child. . . .

As the Court noted in *Clark*, Congress required states to adopt an 18-year statute of limitations for paternity suits as a condition of receiving child support enforcement funds.[25] What does the federal mandate reveal about the government's conception of parenthood? Consider the role of biology in establishing parental obligation as you read the next two cases.

Hermesmann v. Seyer

847 P.2d 1273 (Kan. 1993)

Holmes, Chief Justice:

Shane Seyer *et al.*, appeal from an order of the district court granting the Kansas Department of Social and Rehabilitation Services (SRS) judgment for amounts paid for the birth and support of Seyer's daughter and ordering Seyer to pay monthly child support reimbursement to SRS. . . .

Colleen Hermesmann routinely provided care for Shane Seyer as a baby sitter or day care provider during 1987 and 1988. The two began a sexual relationship at a time when Colleen was 16 years old and Shane was only 12. The relationship continued over a period of several months and the parties engaged in sexual intercourse on an average of a couple of times a week. As a result, a daughter, Melanie, was born to Colleen on May 30, 1989. At the time of the conception of the child, Shane was 13 years old and Colleen was 17. Colleen applied for and received financial assistance through the Aid to Families with Dependent Children program (ADC) from SRS.

On January 15, 1991, the district attorney's office of Shawnee County filed a petition requesting that Colleen Hermesmann be adjudicated as a juvenile offender for engaging in the act of sexual intercourse with a child under the age of 16, Shanandoah (Shane) Seyer, to whom she was not married. . . . Thereafter, Colleen

---

25. Child Support Enforcement Amendments of 1984, Pub. L. No. 98-378, 98 Stat. 1305 (codified at 42 U.S.C. §§ 666-667 (2018)).

Hermesmann entered into a plea agreement with the district attorney's office, wherein she agreed to stipulate to the lesser offense of contributing to a child's misconduct. On September 11, 1991, the juvenile court accepted the stipulation, and adjudicated Colleen Hermesmann to be a juvenile offender.

On March 8, 1991, SRS filed a petition on behalf of Colleen Hermesmann, alleging that Shane Seyer was the father of Colleen's minor daughter, Melanie. The petition also alleged that SRS had provided benefits through the ADC program to Colleen on behalf of the child and that Colleen had assigned support rights due herself and her child to SRS. The petition requested that the court determine paternity and order Shane to reimburse SRS for all assistance expended by SRS on Melanie's behalf. . . .

The court found that the issue of Shane's consent was irrelevant and ordered Shane to pay child support of $50 per month. The court also granted SRS a joint and several judgment against Shane and Colleen in the amount of $7,068, for assistance provided by the ADC program on behalf of Melanie through February 1992. The judgment included medical and other birthing expenses as well as assistance paid after Melanie's birth. Shane appeals the judgment rendered and the order for continuing support but does not contest the trial court's paternity finding. SRS has not cross-appealed from any of the orders or judgment of the district court. . . .

Shane asserts as his first issue that, because he was a minor under the age of 16 at the time of conception, he was legally incapable of consenting to sexual intercourse and therefore cannot be held legally responsible for the birth of his child. Shane cites no case law to directly support this proposition.

The Kansas Parentage Act specifically contemplates minors as fathers and makes no exception for minor parents regarding their duty to support and educate their child. . . .

If the legislature had wanted to exclude minor parents from responsibility for support, it could easily have done so.

[S]hane does not contest that he is the biological father of the child. As a father, he has a common-law duty, as well as a statutory duty, to support his minor child. This duty applies equally to parents of children born out of wedlock. . . .

We conclude that the issue of consent to sexual activity under the criminal statutes is irrelevant in a civil action to determine paternity and for support of the minor child of such activity. . . .

For Shane's next issue, he asserts that it is not sound public policy for a court to order a youth to pay child support for a child conceived during the crime of indecent liberties with a child when the victim was unable to consent to the sexual intercourse. . . .

This State's interest in requiring minor parents to support their children overrides the State's competing interest in protecting juveniles from improvident acts, even when such acts may include criminal activity on the part of the other parent. Considering the three persons directly involved, Shane, Colleen, and Melanie, the interests of Melanie are superior, as a matter of public policy, to those of either or

both of her parents. This minor child, the only truly innocent party, is
support from both her parents regardless of their ages.

As his third issue, Shane asserts that the district court erred in fin
Colleen were jointly and severally liable for the child support. He argues
Colleen was the perpetrator of the crime of statutory rape, she alone should be held
responsible for the consequences of the act. . . .

Nowhere does the law in this state suggest that the mother's "wrongdoing" can
operate as a setoff or bar to a father's liability for child support. Under the facts as
presented to this court, the district court properly held that Shane owes a duty of
support to Melanie and properly ordered that Shane and Colleen were jointly and
severally liable for the monies previously paid by SRS. . . .

The judgment of the district court is affirmed.

PARKER V. PARKER

916 So. 2d 926 (Fla. Dist. Ct. App. 2005)

TAYLOR, J. . . .

The Facts

The petition filed by appellant alleged that the parties were married on June 26,
1996. A minor child was born of the marriage on June 10, 1998. The former wife
represented to the former husband that he was the biological father, and the former
husband had no reason to suspect otherwise.

On December 5, 2001, when the child was three and a half years old, the parties
entered into a marital settlement agreement which obligated the former husband
to pay $1,200 monthly in child support. This agreement was based on the former
wife's representation that the former husband was the child's biological father. The
marital settlement agreement was incorporated into the final judgment of dissolution dated December 7, 2001. During the dissolution of marriage proceeding, the
former wife represented to the court and the former husband that the former husband was the child's biological father. On or about March 28, 2003, the former wife
filed a motion for contempt and enforcement, alleging that the former husband
owed her certain monies for child support and the child's medical expenses. One
week later, the former husband subjected the child to DNA paternity testing. The
testing excluded the former husband as the child's biological father.

Immediately after the child's fifth birthday, the former husband filed this independent action, alleging that at all material times, the former wife knew that the
former husband was not the child's biological father due to sexual relations she had
with another man. He claims that she purposefully concealed the fact that he was
not the child's biological father to collect child support from him.

Procedural Setting . . .

As a preliminary matter, we note that the husband filed this petition as an action for compensatory damages for past and future child support obligations. . . . Because he has not suggested that there are any additional facts which he seeks to add by amendment, we accept his invitation to treat this as if he had alleged in his petition that this was fraud on the court under [Floria Rule of Civil Procedure] 1.540.

Because we are faced here with an attempt to upset the marital presumption of legitimacy in favor of a conclusion of illegitimacy and adultery, we are in territory "fraught with difficult social issues." *Lefler v. Lefler*, 722 So. 2d 941, 943 (Fla. 4th DCA 1998) (Klein J., concurring). One report states that as many as ten percent of all children born to married women during the 1940's were the product of adultery. There is little reason to suspect that this number has declined.

The advancing technology has made the temptation to DNA test a child even greater:

> While testing at one time involved a blood draw, many laboratories now offer testing with sample collection by mail . . . using cheek swabs. Testing hair and other materials easily collected without the knowledge or cooperation of the subject is increasingly available.

Mary J. Anderlik, Disestablishment Suits: What Hath Science Wrought?, 4 J. Center for Families, Child. & Cts. 3, 4 (2003). Thus, the instant case presents a question which can be expected to recur with increasing frequency.

Florida Paternity Law

In *Daniel v. Daniel*, 695 So. 2d 1253 (Fla. 1997), the trial court had required the former husband to pay child support as part of the marital dissolution decree, despite the fact that the child born during the marriage was not his biological child. The Second District Court of Appeal reversed. The Florida Supreme Court approved that decision, declaring it:

> . . . the well-settled rule of law in this state that "a person has no legal duty to provide support for a minor child who is neither his natural nor his adopted child and for whose care and support he has not contracted."

Id. at 1254. Thus, had the former husband in this case presented the DNA test results at the time of dissolution, *Daniel* would have controlled and he would have no child support obligation. However, because he did not present these test results until more than a year after the dissolution decree, he runs headlong into principles of res judicata.

In *State Department of Health & Rehabilitative Services v. Robinson*, 629 So.2d 1000 (Fla. 3d DCA 1993), the court held that because the dissolution decree discussed "the minor children born of the marriage," the attempted re-determination of the paternity of the children was barred on res judicata grounds.

In *D.F. v. Department of Revenue*, 823 So. 2d 97, 100 (Fla. 2002), the Florida Supreme Court stated bluntly:

> We hold that a final judgment of dissolution of marriage which establishes a child support obligation for a former husband is a final determination of paternity. Any subsequent challenge of paternity must be brought under the provisions of Florida Rule of Civil Procedure 1.540.

Florida Rule of Civil Procedure 1.540(b) permits relief from judgments on grounds of fraud "whether heretofore denominated intrinsic or extrinsic" within one year of the judgment. This claim was brought outside one year, so this main fraud provision does not apply. However, this rule further provides:

> This rule does not limit the power of a court to entertain an independent action to relieve a party from a judgment, decree, order, or proceeding or to set aside a judgment or decree for fraud upon the court.

Fla. R. Civ. P. 1.540(b) (2004). The former husband argues, and we agree, that his action is essentially an attempt to set aside the dissolution decree's paternity and child support obligations for fraud on the court, i.e., extrinsic fraud.

The distinction between intrinsic and extrinsic fraud is "elusive," particularly where the circumstances appear to be somewhat of a "hybrid" nature. "Extrinsic fraud, which constitutes fraud on the court, involves conduct which is collateral to the issues tried in a case." The leading Florida case on extrinsic fraud, *DeClaire v. Yohanan*, 453 So. 2d 375, 377 (Fla. 1984), summed up the concept, stating that extrinsic fraud occurs "where a defendant has somehow been prevented from participating in a cause." It defined intrinsic fraud as "fraudulent conduct that arises within a proceeding and pertains to the issues in the case that have been tried or could have been tried." ...

Presumably, this would apply to the marital settlement agreement in this case. . . . We believe that the basic misrepresentation alleged in this case concerned an issue that could have been raised in the dissolution proceedings, rather than an issue collateral to those proceedings. . . .

Our research discloses numerous cases wherein courts in other jurisdictions have considered this extrinsic fraud question. The prevailing view appears to be that the nondisclosure of true paternity presents a question of intrinsic fraud.

Texas appellate courts have the highest number of reported cases on this issue. They have consistently ruled that concealment or misrepresentation of paternity during divorce proceedings involves intrinsic fraud. . . .

The Vermont Supreme Court's decision in *Godin v. Godin*, 725 A.2d 904 (Vt. 1998), took a slightly different tack in reaching the same result. That court held that the mother's representation in the original divorce proceeding that the child was "born of the marriage" merely signified that the child was born while the parties were legally married, so that it was not a materially false statement. It went on to hold that the mere non-disclosure to an adverse party of facts pertinent to a controversy does not constitute fraud on the court for purposes of vacating the judgment. . . .

In *Miller v. Miller*, 956 P.2d 887, 905 (Okla. 1998), the Oklahoma Supreme Court found that the former wife's misrepresentations during the divorce decree were intrinsic fraud, as perjury is the prototypical example of intrinsic fraud. . . .

In the early 1980s, the Alabama courts ruled that references in a divorce decree to the parties' minor child rendered paternity res judicata and that the former wife's misrepresentations to the court were not extrinsic fraud. These rulings would later be largely superseded by the Alabama legislature's adoption of legislation permitting the challenge of paternity at any time based on DNA testing. Of course, Florida has no such legislation.

We note that Nevada has held that a wife's misrepresentations of paternity are extrinsic fraud which will permit reopening the divorce decree. However, we disagree with this apparent minority view.

Because the effect of our conclusion is to create a one-year window after the divorce to perform any DNA testing or be forever barred, we now discuss whether a time-based limitation is supportable as a matter of policy. There is ample authority that post-dissolution challenges to paternity should not be permitted beyond a "relatively brief passage of time."

We consider it significant that many states have legislatively adopted a "statute of limitations" approach based on the age of the child. The original Uniform Parentage Act (UPA), which has been adopted by 19 states (in whole or in part) mandated a five-year limitations period, so that any petition to disestablish would have to be brought by the child's fifth birthday or be forever barred. Theresa Glennon, Somebody's Child: Evaluating the Erosion of the Marital Presumption of Paternity, 102 W. Va. L. Rev. 547, 566 (2000). Several other states (including California and Oklahoma) and the 2000 version of the UPA (adopted by four states), now provide for a two-year limitations period from the child's birth. Had the minor child in this case lived in any of these states, his legitimacy would be safe from disruption, as he was five years old at the time this petition was filed. . . .

In her dissenting opinion in *Mr. G. v. Mrs. G*, Judge Hearn pointed out a potential policy ramification of refusing a post-dissolution disestablishment suit:

> The holding that the allegations of fraud contained in Mr. G's complaint cannot serve as the basis for attacking a judgment may be interpreted by the Family Court bar to require every male litigant in a domestic proceeding to request and secure a blood test.

465 S.E.2d 101, 106 (S.C. 1995) (Hearn J., dissenting). While this view appears a bit extreme, there may be some merit in telling divorcing fathers who are in doubt to "test now, or forever hold your peace."

Many courts state that there is an overriding special concern for the finality of judgments in this area. . . .

The Vermont Supreme Court agreed that finality is important, taking the view that the public interest primarily derives from the interests of the child:

> Thus, the State retains a strong and direct interest in ensuring that children born of a marriage do not suffer financially or psychologically merely because of a parent's belated and self-serving concern over a child's biological origins. These themes underlie the conclusion, reached by numerous courts, that the public interest in finality of paternity determinations is compelling, and that the doctrine of res judicata therefore bars subsequent attempts to disprove paternity.

Godin, 725 A.2d at 910.

The fundamental choice in these cases is between the interests of the legal father on the one hand and the child on the other. . . .

The main issue affecting the child in a disestablishment suit is the psychological devastation that the child will undoubtedly experience from losing the only father he or she has ever known. As Theresa Glennon pointed out, these children are hit with a "double-whammy." First, they must endure the trauma of divorce, then experience the pain of their parentage in dispute.

We realize that as judges, we cannot order a man to love a child. In *In re Paternity of Cheryl*, 746 N.E.2d 488 (Mass. 2001), the Massachusetts Supreme [Judicial] Court stated that it harbored no illusions about its ability to protect the child fully from the consequences of the former husband's decisions. Still, it felt that relieving the former husband of his financial obligations might itself "unravel the parental ties, as the payment of child support 'is a strand tightly interwoven with other forms of connection between father and child,' and often forms a critical bond between them." Or, as the Iowa Supreme Court more bluntly put it, "We hope that David's heart will follow his money."

Other courts have been less kind. The Vermont Supreme Court in *Godin*, said:

> The fact that plaintiff chose for self-serving purposes to jeopardize his relationship with Christina is beyond our control. We need not, however, award plaintiff a financial windfall for his conduct, or deprive Christina of not only a father's affection, but also the legal rights and financial benefits of the parental relationship.

725 A.2d at 911. By refusing to set aside paternity decrees based on belated requests, courts "will help deter other parents who might otherwise seek, for financial or other self-serving reasons, to dissolve their parental bonds." *Id.*

Stability and continuity of support, both emotional and financial, are essential to a child's welfare. Indeed, one of the factors most important to a child's post-divorce adjustment is the degree of economic hardship.

that the former husband in this case may feel victimized. However, a argues cogently that:

> some individuals are innocent victims of deceptive partners, adults ware of the high incidence of infidelity and only they, not the children, able to act to ensure that the biological ties they may deem essential are resent. . . . The law should discourage adults from treating children they have parented as expendable when their adult relationships fall apart. It is the adults who can and should absorb the pain of betrayal rather than inflict additional betrayal on the involved children.

Theresa Glennon, Expendable Children: Defining Belonging in a Broken World, 8 Duke J. Gender L. & Pol'y 269, 275 (2001). . . .

In sum, we conclude, along with the majority of states, that the issue of paternity misrepresentation in marital dissolution proceedings is a matter of intrinsic fraud. It is not extrinsic fraud, or a fraud upon the court, that can form the basis for relief from judgment more than a year later. Any relevant policy considerations that would compel a different result are best addressed by the legislature.

For the reasons stated above, we affirm the trial court's dismissal of the former husband's petition for relief based on fraud.

NOTES AND QUESTIONS

1. *The Government's Interest in Child Support.* In *Hermesmann*, the state pursued support from Shane because the mother had sought government aid. The state sought reimbursement for benefits it had provided to the mother and child. Does protection of the public fisc justify this approach to child support? What benefit does the child derive from the government's authority being exercised in this way?

2. *Paternity Disestablishment.* We first encountered the question of paternity disestablishment in Chapter 9. How should states handle cases in which a man learns he is not the biological father of a child he has participated in raising? The statutory scheme applicable to Richard Parker's case may seem hyper-technical, but it is a typical legislative compromise between two competing goals: (i) preserving children's emotional and financial ties with the men they believe to be their fathers; and (ii) permitting men to avoid responsibility to support a child conceived through sexual intercourse by another man. Although the precise mechanisms vary, state laws and the Uniform Parentage Act all try to thread this same needle.[26] In general, a man may disestablish paternity, even

---

26. See, e.g., Unif. Parentage Act § 608 (Unif. Law Comm'n 2017) [hereinafter UPA (2017)] ("A presumption of parentage . . . cannot be overcome after the child reaches two years of age unless the court determines . . . the presumed parent is not a genetic parent, never resided with the child, and never held out the child as the presumed parent's child. . . ."); Paula Roberts, Truth and Consequences: Questioning the Paternity of Marital Children, 37 Fam. L.Q. 55 (2003).

for children born during a marriage, but only within short time limits, and only with irrefutable evidence of the lack of a genetic tie. Does Florida take the right approach? Is there any inconsistency between allowing paternity to be established at any time during a child's minority but disestablishing it only within narrow constraints? Whose interests are served or undermined by this approach? Are the mother's interests relevant, or only the child's and the man's?

3. *Involuntary Parenthood.* As a general matter, child support obligations can be imposed regardless of whether parenthood is intended or voluntary. For children conceived through sexual intercourse, the genetic tie is a sufficient basis for the obligation unless it has been severed through adoption or some other formal mechanism. There are many circumstances in which men and women might become parents involuntarily. Women may become pregnant through rape, for example. Men may secretly remove a condom. Men may impregnate a female partner who has misrepresented herself to be infertile or on birth control. Men or women may be the victim of statutory rape. Courts, almost uniformly, assign child support obligations regardless of the circumstances of conception.[27]

As we explored in Chapter 3, the Supreme Court has held that states cannot constitutionally require women to notify or obtain consent from their husbands (or any third party, including a biological father) before obtaining an abortion. Men and women do not have equal rights to decide whether to terminate a pregnancy; they are not similarly situated before the child is born. Should men be permitted to avoid child support obligations if they would have preferred abortion to childbirth?

Matt Dubay challenged a court order requiring him to pay $500 per month in child support because, he argued, he never intended to become a father. His girlfriend represented that she was unable to get pregnant. Funded by the National Center for Men, Dubay argued for his right to a "financial abortion." How would you have responded to his claim? The court held that the constitutional right to privacy "does not encompass a right to decide not to become a parent after conception and birth."[28] There are many cases in which men have sued to recoup child support expenses because of alleged fraud relating to contraception or fertility, but courts have uniformly rejected these claims.[29] Rejecting a similar claim by a father who had offered to pay for an abortion, the Colorado Supreme Court explained its reasoning as follows:

> The statutory presumption of a shared parental obligation of child support
> protects three critical interests: the interest of the child in receiving adequate

---

27. See, e.g., N.E. v. Hedges, 391 F.3d 832 (6th Cir. 2004) (requiring biological father to pay child support despite allegation that mother fraudulently misrepresented her use of birth control).

28. Dubay v. Wells, 506 F.3d 422, 429 (6th Cir. 2007), aff'g 442 F. Supp. 2d 404 (E.D. Mich. 2006); see also Pamela P. v. Frank S., 449 N.E.2d 713 (N.Y. 1983).

29. See generally Anne M. Payne, Sexual Partner's Tort Liability to Other Partner for Fraudulent Misrepresentation Regarding Sterility or Use of Birth Control Resulting in Pregnancy, 2 A.L.R. 5th 301 (1992). Women, however, have sometimes been successful in suing for damages if a pregnancy that resulted from a misrepresentation caused them physical harm.

support, the interest of the state in ensuring that children not become its wards, and the interest of the parents in being free from governmental intrusion into the intimate sphere of family life. In view of these critical functions, the state has no "reasonable alternative means of making the crucial determination" that a nexus exists between conception and child birth. The alternative, which the appellant propounds, is a case-by-case determination of whether the presumed nexus was broken by the father's offer to pay for an abortion, by prior agreement between the parties, by a subsequent "release" of one party's obligation by another, or by any of a multitude of legal theories which ingenious litigants and their lawyers might advance. A judicial inquiry of this nature represents unconscionable governmental interference with privacy rights which the Supreme Court has deemed inviolate.

There are additional untoward consequences which lurk behind the establishment of a rule of law that fathers could avoid the obligation to support their children in the manner suggested by appellant. Once the criteria for proving a firm offer of an abortion had been enunciated, any man could forever escape this duty simply by making the offer in the prescribed manner. Taking this theory to its logical extreme, a woman could similarly avoid her obligation of support by proving that she had made a firm offer to procure an abortion and that the father, by declining it, assumed all responsibility for their child. The statutory presumption that parents who have participated in the conception of a child assume a joint responsibility for that child reflects the well-considered judgment of the legislature as to the only feasible means of achieving legitimate societal goals.[30]

Ordinarily, as we saw in Chapter 9, child support obligations and parental rights constitute two sides of the same coin, such that a man with a support obligation also has the right to custody or visitation. Increasingly, though, the two might be separated when the child is the result of sexual assault. Under the Uniform Parentage Act of 2017, courts are instructed to "adjudicate that the man . . . is not a parent of the child" but "require the man to pay child support . . . unless the woman requests otherwise and the court determines that granting the request is in the best interest of the child."[31] Do you think this is a good approach?

4. *Agreements Regarding Child Support.* Adults sometimes enter into private agreements that purport to waive any potential child support obligation of a genetic parent. This is common, for example, when a woman obtains donor sperm from a friend or through some means other than a cryobank. In exchange for the sperm, she promises not to seek a finding of paternity or a child support award against the donor. In Chapter 9, we saw this arrangement with the Craigslist sperm donor, who

---

30. People in Interest of S.P.B., 651 P.2d 1213 (Colo. 1982).
31. UPA (2017), supra note 26, § 614; see also Anastasia Doherty, Choosing to Raise a Child Conceived Through Rape: The Double-Injustice of Uneven State Protection, 39 Women's Rts. L. Rep. 220 (2018).

was ordered to pay child support despite an agreement releasing him from the obli-gation. In his case, the biological mother sought public assistance and, as a condi-tion of becoming eligible, had to assign her right to collect child support to the State of Kansas, which turned around and successfully sued the donor.[32] But even without involvement of a welfare agency, courts uniformly have held that agreements to waive child support are invalid.[33] Is there any circumstance in which one parent ought to be able to release another genetic parent from the obligation to support a child? In a New York case, a separation agreement provided that the father could stop paying if his teenage son worked full-time. The court refused to accept this arrangement. Parties "cannot contract away the duty of child support"; the contract had to yield to the "welfare of the children."[34] For the same reasons, a prenuptial, postnuptial, or separation agreement that is otherwise enforceable will not bind the parties on the issue of child support.

B. How Child Support Amounts Are Determined

Each state has a set formula for calculating child support. Depending on the approach adopted by a particular state, the formula might rely on different factors, but each is designed to accomplish a set of common goals. According to the federal Advisory Panel on Child Support Guidelines, states should base guidelines on the following principles:

1. Both parents should share legal responsibility for support of their children, with the economic responsibility divided between the parents in proportion to their income;
2. The subsistence needs of each parent should be taken into consideration in set-ting child support, but in virtually no event should the child support obligation be set at zero;
3. Child support must cover a child's basic needs as a first priority, but, to the extent either parent enjoys a higher than subsistence-level standard of living, the child is entitled to share in the benefit of that improved standard;
4. Each child of a given parent has an equal right to share in that parent's income, subject to factors such as age of the child, income of the parent, income of a cur-rent spouse, and the presence of other dependents;

---

32. State v. W.M., No. 12D2686 (Kan. Dist. Ct. Jan. 22, 2014); Steve Fry, Marotta is a Father, Not Merely a Sperm Donor, CJONLINE.com (Jan. 22, 2014). The donor in this case was not protected by Kansas's non-paternity law for sperm donors because the insemination was not conducted by a licensed physician.

33. See, e.g., Ferguson v. McKiernan, 940 A.2d 1236 (Pa. 2007); Brady v. Brady, 592 P.2d 865 (Kan. 1979); Napoleon v. Napoleon, 585 P.2d 1270 (Haw. 1978).

34. Thomas B. v. Lydia D., 886 N.Y.S.2d 22 (N.Y. App. Div. 2009).

itled to determination of support without respect to the marital
rents at the time of the child's birth. Consequently, the guidelines
l equally in cases of paternity, separation, and divorce;
of the guidelines should be sexually nondiscriminatory;
should not create extraneous negative effects on the major life deci-
her parent. In particular, the guideline should avoid creating eco-
incentives for remarriage or labor force participation;

8. A gu. ine should encourage the involvement of both parents in the child's upbringing. A guideline should take into consideration the financial support provided by parents in shared physical custody and extended visitation arrangements.[35]

The ALI Principles on Family Dissolution, which of course do not have the force of law, suggest additional objectives, including one focused on guaranteeing a minimum standard of living that ensures access to "important life opportunities," and another focused on minimizing conflict between parents.[36] Would you advocate that these be added to the federal principles?

Rather than directly shape judges' determinations of support, the federal principles inform the work of legislatures, which develop standard guidelines and then turn them into tables that permit judges (and parties) simply to look up the guideline child support amount appropriate given parental income and number of children. Judges have limited power to deviate from the guidelines. Because of the routinized nature of this process, there is relatively little litigation compared with other aspects of family law, such as distribution of marital property and child custody. Litigation tends to focus on a few common issues, which we address in turn in this section: (i) whether and how much child support should be paid from income that exceeds the guidelines; (ii) whether a parent can or should be ordered to pay post-majority support, specifically for post-secondary education; (iii) how to balance the needs among children in different households, for example, when a parent with a child from a previous marriage has a child in a new marriage; and (iv) how to measure a parent's earning capacity or income, including whether to impute income to a parent. The last two issues raise the question of modification, since they often feature a parent asking that a child support award be modified based on changed circumstances. Before proceeding to these specific topics, we address child support guidelines and their application, as well as methods of calculation.

---

35. See Laura W. Morgan, Child Support Guidelines: Interpretation and Application § 1.04 (2d ed. 2019) (citing Robert Williams, U.S. Dep't of Health & Human Servs., Office of Child Support Enforcement, Development of Guidelines for Child Support Orders: Advisory Panel Recommendations and Final Report (1987)).

36. Principles of the Law of Family Dissolution: Analysis and Recommendations § 3.04 (Am. Law Inst. 2002).

1. Guidelines, Calculations, and Deviations

TURNER V. TURNER
684 S.E.2d 596 (Ga. 2009)

THOMPSON, JUSTICE.

Raymond and Jessica Turner were married in 1999 and had two children. Raymond filed for divorce in January 2008. The parties reached a partial settlement agreement which provided, inter alia, that husband and wife would share joint legal and physical custody of their two minor children, the custody arrangement being structured so husband is to have physical custody of the children from Friday a.m. until Tuesday a.m., and wife is to have physical custody from Tuesday a.m. through Friday a.m., with exceptions for holidays and other special occasions. Husband also agreed to pay wife $11,000 representing her interest in the marital residence. Left unresolved and submitted to the trial court for determination were issues of child support and the division of extracurricular expenses. The parties waived a hearing, and after an in-chambers conference, the court entered a final judgment and divorce decree which incorporated the partial settlement agreement, ordered husband to pay $552.09 in monthly child support, and apportioned the expenses for the children's extracurricular activities two-thirds to husband and one-third to wife. . . .

The trial court's order includes a finding that husband earned gross monthly income of $5,483.56, approximately 65 percent of the parties' combined income. After determining a basic child support obligation of $1,582 for the parties' two minor children, the court calculated husband's pro rata share of the basic child support obligation to be $986.75. As evidenced in Schedule E attached to the court's order, however, the court applied a parenting time deviation of $434.66, reducing husband's monthly child support obligation to $552.09. See OCGA § 19–6–15(i)(2)(K). Husband does not on appeal challenge the court's decision to deviate from the presumptive child support obligation. Instead, he contends the trial court erred by failing to explain how the court calculated the deviation and failing to include express findings that the deviation was in the best interests of the children and would not seriously impair his ability to provide for the children. We agree. . . .

The [current] guidelines permit the factfinder to deviate

> from the presumptive amount of child support when special circumstances make the presumptive amount of child support excessive or inadequate due to extended parenting time as set forth in the order of visitation or when the child resides with both parents equally.

Where a deviation is determined to apply and the factfinder deviates from the presumptive amount of child support, the order must explain the reasons for the deviation, provide the amount of child support that would have been required if no deviation had been applied, and state how application of the presumptive amount of child support would be unjust or inappropriate and how the best interest of the children for whom support is being determined will be served by the deviation. In addition, the order must include a finding that states how the court's . . . application of the child support guidelines would be unjust or inappropriate considering the relative ability of each parent to provide support. Because the court in this case applied a discretionary parenting time deviation from the presumptive amount of child support but failed to make all of the findings required under OCGA § 19–6–15I(2)(E) and (i)(1)(B), we reverse the trial court's final judgment and remand this case to the trial court for further proceedings consistent with this opinion.

We address husband's challenge to the trial court's apportionment of the expenses of the children's extracurricular activities because that issue is likely to recur on remand. The trial court's order requires husband to pay two-thirds of the children's extracurricular activities. Husband contends he is paying twice for the cost of extracurricular activities because such costs are included in the presumptive amount of child support.

The language of OCGA § 19–6–15(i)(2)(J)(ii) makes clear that a portion of the basic child support obligation is intended to cover average amounts of special expenses for raising children, including the cost of extracurricular activities. If a fact-finder determines that the full amount of special expenses described in that division exceeds seven percent of the basic child support obligation, the "additional amount of special expenses shall be considered as a deviation to cover the full amount of the special expenses." Such a deviation must then be included in Schedule E of the Child Support Worksheet and, as with other deviations from the presumptive amount of child support, the factfinder must make the required written findings.

The trial court here made no provision in its Schedule E for a deviation for special expenses. Instead, the court included a provision in the final judgment apportioning among the parties the entire cost of the children's extracurricular expenses using essentially the same ratio as applied to the basic child support obligation. This a court is no longer entitled to do. Under the revised guidelines, a court may only deviate from the presumptive child support amount based on special expenses incurred for child-rearing, including extracurricular expenses, by complying with OCGA § 19–6–15(i)(2)(J)(ii) (defining "special expenses" as certain child-rearing expenses exceeding seven percent of basic child support obligation) and OCGA § 19–6–15(i)(1)(B) (requiring written findings for all deviations). Thus, while the court was free to reject husband's claim for a deviation from the presumptive child support amount based on the cost of the children's extracurricular activities, it was without authority to make a separate child support award, one outside the parameters of the Child Support Worksheet, based on the cost of such activities.

Jane C. Venohr, Child Support Guidelines and Guidelines Reviews: State Differences and Common Issues
47 Fam. L.Q. 327 (2013)

Since 1989, federal regulations require each state to provide presumptive guidelines (formulas) for determining the amount of child support awards and to review their guidelines at least once every four years. Most states developed and adopted their initial guidelines in the late 1980s. States developed their guidelines based on similar premises and guidelines models and relied on a limited number of available economic studies on the cost of child-rearing.

In the past two decades, most states have made some change to their guidelines, but some states have made more substantive changes than others. Most states have extended their guidelines to cover higher incomes, expanded their guidelines to consider medical child support, and have made other changes to their guidelines. . . .

Child support guidelines play an important role in the financial well-being of many children. In 2010, there were twenty million children eligible for child support in the United States. According to U.S. Census data, child support receipts averaged $5,135 per year among families that received child support and represented 16% of their average income in 2009. National research finds that child support contributes to 40% of family income among poor custodial families receiving child support on average, and without child support, child poverty would increase by 4.4%. . . .

Federal regulation does not prescribe which guidelines model a state must use. Instead, federal regulation allows states considerable flexibility in their guidelines. The only requirements imposed on state guidelines are that the guidelines:

- be based on specific descriptive and numeric criteria;
- take into consideration all earnings and income of the non-custodial parent; and
- address how the parents will provide for the child(ren)'s health care needs through health insurance coverage and/or through cash medical support. . . .

When developing guidelines, all states considered the best interest of the child and the appropriateness of the guidelines-determined support awards. Other policy considerations common to states in both the adoption of guidelines and their subsequent revisions are the fairness, equity, comprehensiveness, predictability, transparency, and ease of use of the guidelines.

[A]s of 2013, thirty-nine states base their guidelines on the Income Shares Model, nine states based their guidelines on the Percentage of Obligor Income Model, and three states base their guidelines on the Melson Formula. Researchers classify both the Income Shares Model and the Percentage of Obligor Income Model as a Continuity of Expenditures Model because they both relate to measurements of childrearing costs that consider how much intact families typically spend on their children. The underlying premise of the Continuity of Expenditures Model is that children should continue to receive the same amount of expenditures they would have received had the parents never separated or divorced. . . . Nonetheless, all states relying on the Continuity of Expenditures Model also apply the principle to children whose parents never married or lived together. . . . The underlying premise is that children of never-married parents and children of divorced or separated parents should be treated the same. Several states specify this premise in their guidelines.

Under the Income Shares Model, each party is responsible for his or her prorated share of child-rearing expenditures. The obligated parent's share becomes the base of the support award calculation. The Income Shares Model requires information about each party's income in the calculation of the support award. In contrast, the Percentage of Obligor Income Model considers the obligor's income only. Many Percentage of Obligor Income guidelines, however, assume that the custodial parent's child-rearing expenditures are the same dollar amount or percentage of income as the support award. The key difference between the award amounts under the Income Shares Model and the Percentage of Obligor Income Model is the impact of the custodial parent's income on the support award amount. Under the Income Shares Model, the support award is lowered if the custodial parent has income. The higher the income of the custodial parent, the lower the support award becomes. Under the Percentage of Obligor Income Model, the custodial parent's income has no bearing on the support award amount.

Named after a Delaware judge, the Melson formula is not a Continuity of Expenditures Model. It first considers the basic needs of the child and each parent. Basic needs amounts relate to the poverty level or a similar subsistence amount. If the obligated parent's income is more than sufficient to cover his or her prorated share of the child's basic needs and the parent's own basic needs, an additional percentage of the obligated parent's remaining income is assigned to child support. This last step allows the child to share in the standard of living afforded by the obligated parent. . . .

Guidelines award amounts among states using the same guidelines model rarely produce identical amounts. As a consequence, one guidelines model does not consistently result in lower or higher support awards than another guidelines model.

It has been nearly twenty-five years since many states first adopted child support guidelines, and most states have conducted several rounds of guidelines reviews since. Some states have made more changes than others. A few states have made no changes to their core formulas/schedules. . . .

Even though most states are based on the same guidelines model, the similarities end there. There are several different studies of child-rearing expenditures underlying guidelines formulas/schedules that vary in age of the expenditure data and economic methodologies, as well as different assumptions about tax rates, what expenses are included or excluded, adjustments for a state's relatively high or low income or housing expenses, and other factors. . . .

States may also benefit from considering whether their current guidelines will serve the future population eligible for child support or required to pay child support. This includes an increasing number of never-married parents and modern family situations, such as three or more legal parents. For example, the shared-parenting adjustment is not often considered in the calculation of support awards for never-married parents, but as demographics and family law change, there may be more pressure to do so.

Pamela Foohey, Child Support and (In)ability to Pay: The Case for the Cost Shares Model
13 U.C. Davis J. Juv. L. & Pol'y 35 (2009)

Since their implementation in the late 1980s, child support guidelines have focused primarily on preserving individual children's economic well-being. With this in mind, current debates about child support guidelines concentrate on how to balance the trade-offs implicit in splitting a single household into two separate households: guidelines balance between not making individual children economically worse-off when their parents divorce, equalizing the economic well-being of the two resulting households, and distributing money to each resulting household based on which household would derive the greatest utility from the money. In so balancing, the debate discounts another consideration that, when taken into greater account, also may advance children's well-being: the ability of parents to pay. . . .

Lowering presumptive child support obligations will make lower-income obligors (payers of child support) better able and thus more likely to pay those obligations, thereby increasing the amount of child support paid to lower-income children, while at most only marginally decreasing the amount of child support paid by middle and upper income obligors, which, when paid at all, usually exceeds the minimum obligations established by current guidelines, and, thus, should remain constant despite lower obligations. Overall, the setting of child support is better approached by incorporating the goal of increasing the total amount of child support paid into the current analysis; this approach has the potential to provide more child support for children on average, thereby advancing the best interests of children, while still preserving the insights into balancing upon which current guidelines are premised. Although new guidelines can be created or current guidelines better tailored to account for the ability of obligors to pay, a guideline already exists for states to implement that incorporates this perspective into the existing analysis: the Cost Shares model, which provides lower child support obligations at almost all levels of obligor income.

The key to maximizing the total amount of child support paid is to explore the payment characteristics of obligors: when they do not pay, when they do pay, and when they pay more than the presumptive obligation yielded by child support guidelines. Research shows that non-paying obligors, generally known as "dead-beat dads" (fathers are the obligors in most cases), do not pay their child support obligations for a number of reasons falling into two broad categories: they do not have the financial resources to pay, or they do not want to and do not intend to pay despite having the financial capacity to do so. Focusing on those who do not have the financial resources to pay, research also shows that these obligors would pay if they had the financial capacity to do so, and that many could afford to pay smaller child support obligations consistently. Accordingly, lowering child support obligations should increase the amount of child support actually paid by lower-income obligors in aggregate, thereby providing more child support for children on average, especially for children from lower-income households.

Moreover, there is evidence that some divorcing and divorced parents mutually agree to deviate upward from the presumptive child support obligation yielded by guidelines in an effort to better reflect the cost of continuing to raise their children at their current standard of living, or otherwise modify their child support arrangement to provide increased monetary support. These deviations are upheld by judges, who also deviate from the presumptive obligations in some situations. In most instances, it is the presence of one or more higher-earning parent that leads parents and judges to deviate from the presumptive obligation — that is, in a percentage of cases (possibly a high percentage of cases) involving middle and high income parents, the guidelines are used merely as guidance. Thus, decreasing child support payment amounts should not cause the actual amount of child support paid by many higher income obligors to decline.

Combining these insights leads to the counterintuitive conclusion that decreasing presumptive child support obligations has the potential to increase the amount of child support paid in aggregate. Indeed, when obligor payment characteristics are explored thoroughly, guidelines that provide lower obligation amounts have the potential to increase the average child support paid per child while only decreasing what some individual children receive in a small percentage of cases. . . .

NOTES AND QUESTIONS

1. *The Formulas Behind the Guidelines.* Which approach is reflected in the Georgia guidelines at issue in *Turner*? How can you tell? Under the flat percentage approach, the court simply calculates a percentage of the noncustodial parent's income to determine the amount owed each month. This approach does not account for the custodial parent's income. Under the income shares approach, the court calculates the parents' combined income, determines the share of the total

contributed by each parent, and then orders the noncustodial parent to pay his or her proportionate share of the child support owed. If the custodial parent, for example, earns $40,000, and the noncustodial parent earns $160,000, the noncustodial parent would be responsible for 80 percent of the child support listed in the guidelines for a family with a combined income of $200,000. The custodial parent, who is responsible for 20 percent of that amount, is presumed to contribute the share directly in goods and services for the child. The income shares approach often allows extraordinary medical expenses and sometimes extraordinary general expenses to be covered by a separate award, again through proportionate shares. The Delaware Melson formula is much more complex and requires many more pieces of information to be considered before an award amount can be determined. Regardless of the approach a state takes, federal law requires that the court specify which parent is responsible for obtaining medical insurance and how that cost is to be paid.[37]

2. *A Rebuttable Presumption.* Under the federal mandates, states must provide that the guideline amount is rebuttably presumed to be correct. In 85 percent of cases, the court orders the guideline amount.[38] The court can deviate upward or downward but only with written findings sufficient to rebut the presumption. Why structure the law this way?

3. *The Mechanics of Child Support.* Child support is typically paid monthly by the noncustodial parent to the custodial parent in a lump sum. What are the advantages of this system rather than, say, having the noncustodial parent pay vendors directly for the child's expenses or reimburse the custodial parent for actual expenditures?

4. *Joint Custody.* The first sets of child support guidelines, from which there has been relatively little change, were developed in the 1980s, before joint physical custody was available in most jurisdictions and certainly before it was popular. Joint custody complicates things in a number of different ways. If each parent is providing in-kind care, should either pay financial support to the other? What if the child will be undergoing a drastic change in the standard of living when going from one residence to the other? Who should pay for the cost of transporting a child? In most states, joint custody is treated as a basis for deviation from the standard guidelines, but little information is given on how to accommodate the residential parenting arrangement.[39] A few states provide special tables for joint custody, which are used if each parent has physical custody for a specific number of days per month, typically

---

37. 42 U.S.C. § 652(f) (2018); 45 C.F.R. § 302.56 (2020). The Affordable Care Act requires that insurance plans with dependent coverage permit dependents to participate until age 26. 42 U.S.C. § 300gg-14 (2018).

38. See Sanford L. Braver et al., Public Intuitions about Fair Child Support Allocations: Converging Evidence for a "Fair Shares" Rule, 20 Psychol. Pub. Pol'y & L. 146 (2014).

39. See Charts, 2018: Family Law in the Fifty States, D.C., and Puerto Rico, 52 Fam. L.Q. 581, 595-98 (2019).

35-40 percent of the total. If joint custody means no child support award (in either direction), should courts be concerned that one parent might insist on joint custody to avoid child support? Or that a parent might insist on joint custody as a legal matter but fail to share it as a practical matter? Custodial "drift" is a well-documented phenomenon in which shared custody arrangements over time begin to resemble more traditional sole custody/visitation arrangements. The drift is usually in the direction of sole custody by the mother.[40] Does that suggest states should be wary of allowing joint physical custody to affect child support guidelines?

2. High-Income Families

CIAMPA V. CIAMPA
415 S.W.3d 97 (Ky. Ct. App. 2013)

CLAYTON, JUDGE: . . .

Peter R. Ciampa and Cynthia L. Ciampa were married in 1988. Three daughters were born of the marriage. In November 2005, they separated and filed for dissolution of the marriage. A decree of dissolution was granted on December 4, 2006. . . .

This issue on appeal is child support. The pertinent history of child support begins with the previously-mentioned property settlement agreement. Therein, Peter agreed to provide Cindy with $6,000 per month in child support for their three daughters. Next, in June 2010, when the parties' oldest daughter turned 18, Cindy made a motion, which among other things, included a request for modification of child support. The family court held a hearing on the various issues including child support. An order was entered on July 6, 2010, wherein the family court made extensive findings regarding reasonable living expenses for the remaining two minor children and ordered that Peter's monthly child support payment remain at $6,000 per month.

Next, in June 2012, Peter moved for a modification of child support because the second daughter would turn eighteen in July 2012, and he would only be responsible for child support for one child. A hearing was held on October 8, 2012. Subsequently, the family court entered findings of fact and an order modifying child support on October 17, 2012. This order reduced the child support monthly payment from $6,000 to $5,800. . . .

Peter now appeals from this order. . . .

The child support guidelines set out in Kentucky Revised Statutes (KRS) 403.212 serve as a rebuttable presumption for the establishment or modification of the

---

40. See, e.g., Eleanor E. Maccoby & Robert H. Mnookin, Dividing the Child: Social and Legal Dilemmas of Custody (1992); Karen Syma Czapanskiy, The Shared Custody Child Support Adjustment: Not Worth the Candle, 49 Fam. L.Q. 409 (2015); Belinda Felhberg & Christine Millwood, Post Separation Parenting and Financial Arrangements over Time: Recent Qualitative Findings, 92 Fam. Matters 29, 32 (2013); Karen Czapanskiy, Child Support and Visitation: Rethinking the Connections, 20 Rutgers L.J. 619 (1989).

amount of child support. Nevertheless, family courts may deviate from the guidelines when they make specific findings that application of the guidelines would not be just or appropriate. KRS 403.211(2). Specifically, the family court may use its judicial discretion to set child support outside the guidelines in circumstances where combined adjusted parental gross income exceeds the uppermost level of the guidelines. KRS 403.212(5).

In the case at hand, Peter is self-employed as an oral surgeon. According to his 2011 tax return, he earned $728,046 in taxable income and $89,627 in tax-exempt income, which combined provided him with a total annual income of $817,673. Cindy does not work outside the home. She provided a 2011 tax return that showed that she had taxable income of $32,681 and tax-exempt income of $19,723, which provides her a total annual income of $52,404.

Consequently, according to the parties' tax returns, their combined income is more than $870,000, which is indisputably outside the income guidelines of the child support charts. The uppermost annual income level listed in the child support guidelines is $180,000. Thus, pursuant to the statutory instructions, the family court "may use its judicial discretion in determining child support in circumstances where combined adjusted parental gross income exceeds the uppermost levels of the guideline table." KRS 403.212(5).

Having determined that the parental income of the parties was outside the child support guidelines, the family court may use its discretion to set the child support amount outside the guidelines as long as it justifies the deviation in writing. Further, if it gives appropriate written reasons, this Court will not disturb the trial court's ruling in this regard.

In the instant case, the family court issued two findings of fact and orders wherein extensive information was provided explaining the family court's rationale for the amount of its child support order. The family court noted the child's reasonable needs were $6,617 per month despite the fact that Cindy submitted proffered expenses totally $9,312.27. . . .

Peter proffers several arguments to undermine the credibility of the family court's decision. We, however, are not persuaded by these arguments. His major concerns are the family court's inclusion of a *future* expense, that is, the purchase of a car when the minor child turns 16; the admissibility of certain evidence provided by Cindy to the family court substantiating the expenses of the child; and, the family court's handling of housing and other expenses as reasonable needs of the child. Further, Peter questions whether the intent of the statute, KRS 403.212(7), is met when the family court ordered only a three per cent reduction in the child support amount and the child support is for one rather than two children.

With reference to the prorated amount for the purchase of a car, we see no reason to second-guess the family court judge. In the interest of fairness, in the December 17, 2012 findings, the family court judge reduced the initial amount requested for the car purchase by prorating the amount of support for the car expenses over 48 months rather than the requested 36 months. Further, nothing prevents Peter from making a motion to be reimbursed for the car expense if Cindy does not purchase the car for the child. . . .

We now address Peter's contention that the family court erred when it included housing and other expenses in its calculus of reasonable needs of the child. Peter's arguments are based primarily on the fact that the amounts were not significantly reduced from 2010 when child support had previously been set. Also, Peter maintains that the family court erred in not imputing income to Cindy.

Again, it is the family court that hears the evidence and knows the situation. Two explanations were provided for the minimal change. First, the expenses for the child have increased over two years. For instance, the tuition to her parochial high school increases each year. Second, Cindy contends that she has researched the actual amount of expenses more extensively than she did for the previous modification hearing.

It is the task of the family court to determine the reasonable portion of housing expenses to allocate for a child when establishing child support. Moreover, reasonable household expenses resulting from a child living in the home are certainly part of the child support equation. Here, Peter has not challenged that the family court has authority to appropriately deviate from the child support guidelines when it provides written findings of fact to support the amount ordered. Having decided that the family court had evidence to support the child support amount that it eventually ordered, we ascertain no abuse of discretion in regard to the amount of household expenses allocated to the child.

With regard to Cindy's employment and income, we observe that the family court included income related to Cindy's tax return. Further, as noted by the family court, imputing income to her based on her job history and qualifications has no impact on the calculations herein. So, regarding imputation of income to Cindy, the family court considered it, made written findings, and did not abuse its discretion in resolving this issue.

In response to Peter's argument that the intent of the statute, KRS 403.212(7), is not met when only a three per cent reduction in the child support amount is ordered and the child support is for one rather than two children, we make several observations. First, KRS 403.212(7) does not express any intentionality but merely lists the amount of child support to be paid when parties' income is not outside the guidelines.

Moreover, parents not only have a universal and moral duty to support and maintain their minor children, but they also have a statutory duty. KRS 405.020. And child support is a statutory duty intended to benefit the children not the parents. The legal obligation to support children remains until the children are emancipated. KRS 403.213(3).

In light of the statutory and moral imperatives for child support, it is the duty of the family court to consider the minutiae and details necessary to fashion a reasonable child support order. It is not the province of an appellate court to delve into these details. Here, the family court made a thorough and conscientious record of the rationale behind the decision, including that the parents' resources were outside the purview of the child support guidelines. For that reason, we hold that the family court's decision regarding the amount of the child support was not unreasonable because it was based on the child's expenses and the parents' resources.

Peter cites often to *Downing v. Downing*, 45 S.W.3d 449 (Ky. App. 2001), as supporting his position that the child support amount was in error. Essentially, *Downing* imposes limitations on the trial court when setting child support in cases where the parties' gross income exceeds the child support guidelines and the parties have not agreed to child support. Peter cites the statement from *Downing* that "[b]eyond a certain point, additional child support serves no purpose but to provide extravagance and unwarranted transfer of wealth," and argues that this is the case here.

But the *Downing* Court explained that "any decision to set child support above the guidelines must be based primarily on the child's needs." It supported the view that children should continue to live at the standard of living to which they had grown accustomed prior to the parents' divorce. And the *Downing* Court further reasoned that the needs of the children should be based on the parents' financial ability to meet those needs.

In essence, our Court in *Downing*, disabused any mathematical calculation extrapolated from the guidelines and provided the following directions:

> [T]he court should take into account any factors which affect the reasonable needs of the child under the circumstances. . . . So long as there is evidence in the record and a reasonable basis for setting child support above the guidelines, this Court will not interfere with the trial court's discretion. But we hold that a trial court abuses its discretion when it relies primarily on a mathematical calculation to set child support without any other supporting findings or evidence.

In its order, the family court found that Cindy submitted expenses in the amount of $9,312.27. The family court, however, determined that the reasonable needs of the child were $6,617 per month and disallowed certain expenses as unreasonable. The disallowed expenses were those related to the child's owning a horse, the purchase of new furniture and redecorating the child's bedroom, employment of a nutritionist and personal trainer for the child, and $100 of the money allotted for the purchase of a car.

Here, the family court considered the reasonable day-to-day needs of the parties' child, the parties' ability to pay, and decided on an appropriate child support amount. Accordingly, we believe that the family court's decision was in keeping with the philosophy found in *Downing* and conclude that its actions comport with the holding in *Downing*. . . .

The family court carefully reviewed the parties' income, lifestyle, and the child's expenses. And it provided written findings to support its order. Legally, the family court has met the statutory and case law requirements for a deviation from the child support guidelines when the parties' income is over the threshold of the child support guidelines. There is no abuse of discretion, and we affirm the decision of the McCracken Family Court.

Maze, Judge, concurring:

I agree with the result reached by the majority, but on slightly different grounds. As the majority correctly notes, Peter agreed to pay $6000 per month for the support of his three daughters. At the time he executed this agreement, he was aware that this amount was in excess of the amount required under Kentucky's Child Support Guidelines. It is well-established that parties may agree to support in excess of the Guidelines. Such agreements are an enforceable contract between the parties, and it is not the place of the courts to disturb it absent some showing of fraud, undue influence, overreaching or manifest unfairness. Peter does not make any such showing.

The difficulty in this case arises because the agreement provides for support in the amount of $6000 for all three children, but does not include provisions for modification of upon emancipation of one or more, but not all of the children. . . . In this case, the trial court properly considered the emancipation of the two older daughters as a basis for modification of the agreement's provisions regarding child support.

Nevertheless, the trial court heard evidence and made extensive findings regarding the reasonable needs of the remaining daughter. . . .

Although the total amount of support for one child seems high to me, I agree with the majority that it was supported by sufficient findings of fact and did not constitute an abuse of discretion.

NOTES AND QUESTIONS

1. *High-Income Families.* Child support tables typically cap out at a certain income level, meaning the mandatory percentage applies only on income up to that level. Courts then have discretion to order additional support from the excess income.[41] Most courts reject the idea that the same percentages should be applied to all available income. What principles should guide the determination?[42] The father in *Ciampa* cited the observation from an earlier case that "[b]eyond a certain point, additional child support serves no purpose but to provide extravagance and

---

41. See, e.g., Tex. Fam. Code Ann. § 154.125 (West 2020) (setting cap); id. § 154.126 (permitting court to award additional support without reference to the guidelines "as appropriate, depending on the income of the parties and the proven needs of the child").

42. See generally Margaret Ryznar, The Obligations of High-Income Parents, 43 Hofstra L. Rev. 481 (2014).

unwarranted transfer of wealth." He was referring to the "three pony rule," which comes from one court's observation that "no child, no matter how wealthy the parents, needs to be provided more than three ponies."[43] Is there an argument that children of divorced or unmarried parents should be the beneficiaries of whatever extravagance would have been bestowed by married parents? How does this view compare with approaches to property division and spousal support in the context of high-income families? Did the *Ciampa* court give good reasons for maintaining the child support amount even after one child left for college?

2. *Low-Income Families.* The questions about whether and how children should share in their parents' excess income occupy a significant place in the child support literature.[44] But what about the problems at the opposite end of the earnings spectrum? Should the guidelines and/or courts take greater care to make sure that the child support obligation can be satisfied without impoverishing the payor parent? Although the original guidelines seemed to increase child support awards on average, the benefits accrued disproportionately to divorced rather than unmarried custodial parents and to non-black mothers rather than black mothers. Children with a noncustodial parent are more likely to live in poverty (24 percent versus 13 percent of all families), and single mothers are more likely than single fathers to live in poverty (27 percent versus 11 percent); the poverty rate also increases with the number of children in the custodial family.[45]

PROBLEM

Former NFL running back Travis Henry has fathered nine children with nine different women (he claims some of the women "trapped" him by lying about birth control). He has a child support order for each child; payments come to some $170,000 per year. He is no longer in the NFL and no longer has a high salary, but he still has significant savings from his NFL earnings. He has fallen behind on many of his obligations, and at least once has had to go to jail for failing to pay.[46] One court issued an order requiring him to put $250,000 in a trust fund to secure future child support payments. Should it be upheld? If so, should the children covered by the other eight orders have any claim to share if he defaults on their support?

---

43. In re Marriage of Patterson, 920 P.2d 450 (Kan. 1996).

44. See Schieffer v. Schieffer, 826 N.W.2d 627, 646 n.15 (S.D. 2013) (Konekamp, J., concurring in part and dissenting in part).

45. See Timothy Grall, Current Population Reports, Custodial Mothers and Fathers and Their Child Support: 2017, at 5 (May 2020).

46. Mike Tierney, With Nine Mouths to Feed, Travis Henry Says He's Broke, N.Y. Times, Mar. 12, 2009, at B14; see also Henry v. Beacham, 686 S.E.2d 892 (Ga. Ct. App. 2009).

3. Post-Majority Support

IN RE MARRIAGE OF CROCKER
971 P.2d 469 (Or. Ct. App. 1998)

ARMSTRONG, J.

Mother and father were divorced in 1987. At that time, the parties' three daughters were ages 11, 8 and 5. The dissolution judgment awarded mother custody of the children and ordered father to pay $200 per month in child support for each child. On mother's motion, the court modified father's support obligation in 1995, ordering father to pay $239 per month in support for each of his minor daughters and $464 per month in support for the parties' oldest daughter, who had turned 18 and was attending school.

In 1997, mother moved to modify father's support obligation to account for the fact that the parties' second daughter had turned 18 and was planning to attend college in California. . . . . [The father challenges the constitutionality of the child support statute.] . . .

ORS 107.108 gives courts authority to order divorced or separated parents to "provide for the support and maintenance" of their children attending school. In doing so, the statute appears to give children attending school whose parents are divorced or separated the privilege of obtaining court-ordered financial support that is not given to children attending school whose parents are or were never married. Conversely, it appears to give an immunity from such a support obligation to married parents and to parents who never married that it does not give to their divorced or separated counterparts. . . .

Considering the statute in context, however, suggests that that may not be the case. ORS 109.155 gives courts authority to order support for children attending school by parents who never married, so that class of parents is in the same position as are the parents in father's class. Moreover, the state suggests that ORS 108.110 could be construed to authorize courts to require married parents of children attending school to support their children. If that were the case, there would be no difference in treatment among the relevant classes of people, because all parents of children attending school would be in the same position as are the parents in father's class.

ORS 108.110 provides in relevant part:

> (1) *Any married person . . . may apply to the circuit court* of the county in which the married person resides or in which the spouse may be found *for an order upon the spouse to provide for support of the married person or for the support of minor children and children attending school, or both* . . . The married person initiating the action for support . . . may apply for the order by filing in such county a petition setting forth the facts and circumstances upon which the married person relies for such order. If satisfied that a just

cause exists, the court shall direct that the married person's spouse appear at a time set by the court to show cause why an order of support should not be entered in the matter. . . .

(2) As used in this section, "child attending school" has the meaning given that term in ORS 107.108.

(Emphasis added.) Although the statute appears to apply to all married people, an examination of its history leads us to conclude that it applies only to married people who are living apart. . . .

[U]nder the statutory scheme, families comprised of married people who live together and who have at least one child attending school are treated differently from those comprised of at least one such child whose parents are married but do not live together, are divorced or separated, or have never married. Relevant to this case, married parents who are living together are given an immunity from an obligation to support their children attending school that is not given to divorced or separated parents. . . .

Because ORS 107.108 can be understood to give an immunity to married, cohabiting parents of children attending school that it does not give to father's "true class," we must determine whether the difference in treatment between the two classes of parents violates Article I, section 20 [of the Oregon Constitution, which provides: "No law shall be passed granting to any citizen or class of citizens privileges, or immunities, which, upon the same terms, shall not equally belong to all citizens"]. Father does not contend, and the trial court did not conclude, that the classifications in this case are based on characteristics that require anything other than an evaluation for whether there is a rational basis for the distinction that the legislature has made among classes of people. Consequently, we consider only whether ORS 107.108 violates Article I, section 20, on the ground that there is no rational basis for the distinction that it draws.

Father does not dispute that the state has an interest in having a well-educated populace. Although children aged 18 to 21 have no general right to have their parents pay for them to attend school, it cannot reasonably be disputed that the state has an interest in having parents support their children in that endeavor. ORS 107.108 advances that interest by providing the means for some children to attend school. The issue, then, is whether the statutory scheme by which the state has chosen to advance that interest—a scheme that distinguishes among true classes—is rational. Father argues that it is not. He notes that many children attending school are in need of financial support and argues that there is no rational reason to target for assistance only those children whose parents are divorced, separated, or unmarried or are married but living apart. The trial court agreed. We do not.

We conclude that the statutory distinction is rational. Even if most divorced or separated parents could cooperate sufficiently to decide whether to support their children attending school, legislators could rationally believe that, because of the nature of divorce and separation, there will be instances in which children will not receive support from their parents to attend school precisely because the parents are divorced or separated, despite the fact that the parents have the resources to provide the support and it is in the children's best interest for them to do so. It might be that, although both parents agree that they should support their child attending school, they disagree on how much each of them should contribute, so that one or both of them contribute nothing. It might be that the nature of the relationship between the parents is so acrimonious that they refuse to agree on anything. It might be that the parent who did not have custody when the child was a minor is unwilling to provide support precisely because he or she did not have custody. It might be that one of the parents who, when married, considered support for his or her child attending school to be a moral obligation, now considers it to be only a legal obligation and, hence, that the parent will provide support only if ordered to do so by a court. In short, legislators could rationally envision situations in which, but for the fact that a child's parents are divorced or separated, the parents would support the child while the child attends school. In that situation, the parents' marital status operates to thwart the state's interest in having parents support their children while the children are attending school. Providing courts with the authority to require those parents to support their children attending school is a rational response to that problem.

Deciding not to give courts authority to require parents from intact families to provide the same support is rational as well. Legislators could rationally assume that, in most instances, parents in intact families will be able to make reasonable decisions about whether to support their children attending school. Moreover, whatever the reasons those parents might decide not to provide that support, legislators could rationally believe that there will seldom be a situation in which, but for the fact that a child's parents are married and living together, the parents would have provided financial support to their child while the child attends school. In other words, the marital status of parents who are living together would not be expected to make them less willing to support their children attending school, but the marital status of divorced or separated parents could have that effect.

In sum, legislators could rationally believe that the most efficient way to advance the state's interest in having parents support their children attending school is to rely on parents to make those decisions in intact families and on courts to make those decision for families that are not intact. That policy decision does not become irrational simply because, on occasion, some married parents who have the resources to support their children attending school will refuse to do so. Nor does it become irrational simply because, under ORS 107.108, on occasion, a court may require separated or divorced parents to support their children attending school even when the parents' refusal to provide that support is for reasons completely unrelated to the separation or divorce. A statute does not have to be perfect in order for it to be rational. In other words, there does not have to be a perfect correlation between the state's interest and the means it uses to advance that interest. . . .

The distinction embodied in the statutes governing support for children attending school is analogous to the distinction that the legislature has made between married and divorced parents with respect to support for their minor children. Every parent has an obligation to care for his or her minor child. The state has a legitimate interest in ensuring that parents fulfill that obligation. Nonetheless, when a child's parents are married, the state generally does not interfere with the parents' decisions on how best to meet their financial obligations to their children. However, when parents divorce or separate, the state assumes that, as a result of the divorce or separation, many of them will no longer be able to work together to make responsible decisions about how to support their children. Accordingly, the state does not wait to see whether, despite the divorce or separation, the parents can decide how to meet their financial obligations to their children. Instead, it steps in to dictate how they will do that by authorizing courts to enter support orders that establish how much money each parent must contribute each month toward the care of the parent's children. Even though some married parents do not make appropriate decisions about how to care for their children and many divorced parents unquestionably do make appropriate decisions, the state has distinguished between parents with respect to their child-support obligations based on their marital status. Although not perfect, the distinction is rationally related to a legitimate state interest. So is the one in this case.

In conclusion, many children pursue some form of education after they reach the age of 18. The state has an interest in having parents support their children in those efforts. In countless situations, children attending school continue to rely on their parents for financial support, whether their parents are married, separated, or divorced or have never married. Unquestionably, there will be occasions when parents from all of those classes will refuse to support their children attending school even though they have the means to do so. Even if ORS 107.108 does not provide a perfect remedy for that problem, it represents a reasonable attempt by the legislature to address the situation in which the refusal by parents to support their children attending school is a direct consequence of the parents' divorce or separation. Therefore, we conclude that the distinction drawn by the legislature among classes of parents has a rational basis and does not violate Article I, section 20, on the ground that it lacks one. . . .

CURTIS V. KLINE
666 A.2d 265 (Pa. 1995)

ZAPPALA, JUSTICE.

In *Blue v. Blue*, 616 A.2d 628 (Pa. 1992), we declined to recognize a duty requiring a parent to provide college educational support because no such legal duty had been imposed by the General Assembly or developed by our case law. As a result of our *Blue* decision, the legislature promulgated Act 62 of 1993. Section 3 of the Act states:

> (a) General rule. —...a court may order either or both parents who are separated, divorced, unmarried or otherwise subject to an existing support obligation to provide equitably for educational costs of their child whether an application for this support is made before or after the child has reached 18 years of age.

The issue now before us is whether the Act violates the equal protection clause of the Fourteenth Amendment of the United States Constitution. The Court of Common Pleas of Chester County held that it did, resulting in this direct appeal....

Appellee is the father of Jason, Amber and Rebecca. On July 12, 1991, an order of court for support was entered on behalf of Appellee's children. On March 2, 1993, Appellee filed a petition to terminate his support obligation as to Amber, a student at Kutztown University, and Jason, a student at West Chester University. After Act 62 was promulgated, Appellee was granted leave to include a constitutional challenge to the Act as a basis for seeking relief from post-secondary educational support....

The essence of the constitutional principle of equal protection under the law is that like persons in like circumstances will be treated similarly. However, it does not require that all persons under all circumstances enjoy identical protection under the law. The right to equal protection under the law does not absolutely prohibit the Commonwealth from classifying individuals for the purpose of receiving different treatment and does not require equal treatment of people having different needs. The prohibition against treating people differently under the law does not preclude the Commonwealth from resorting to legislative classifications, provided that those classifications are reasonable rather than arbitrary and bear a reasonable relationship to the object of the legislation. In other words, a classification must rest upon some ground of difference which justifies the classification and have a fair and substantial relationship to the object of the legislation....

In this instance, we are satisfied that Act 62 neither implicates a suspect class nor infringes upon a fundamental right. Neither the United States Constitution nor the Pennsylvania Constitution provides an individual right to post-secondary education....

Consequently, Act 62 must be upheld if there exists any rational basis for the prescribed classification. It is in this context that we review the Act's creation of a duty, and more significantly a legal mechanism for enforcement of that duty, limited to situations of separated, divorced, or unmarried parents and their children....

The preamble to Act 62 sets forth the legislature's intention "to codify the decision of the Superior Court in the case of Ulmer v. Sommerville, [190 A.2d 182 (Pa.

Super. Ct. 1963] . . . and the subsequent line of cases interpreting *Ulmer* prior to the decision of the Pennsylvania Supreme Court in Blue v. Blue. . . ." It also states:

> Further, the General Assembly finds that it has a rational and legitimate governmental interest in requiring some parental financial assistance for a higher education for children of parents who are separated, divorced, unmarried or otherwise subject to an existing support obligation.

This latter statement begs the question of whether the legislature actually has a legitimate interest in treating children of separated, divorced, or unmarried parents differently than children of married parents with respect to the costs of post-secondary education.

Appellant argues that with the passage of Act 62 the legislature may have chosen to treat the children of married families and divorced/unmarried families differently, not as a preference towards the latter, but out of deference to the Commonwealth's strong interest in protecting the intact marital family unit from governmental interference. Alternatively, Appellant argues that the legislature may have determined that children in non-intact or non-marital families require educational advantages to overcome disadvantages attendant to the lack of an intact marital family. The critical consideration is whether either of these bases or any other conceivable basis for distinction in treatment is reasonable.

Act 62 classifies young adults according to the marital status of their parents, establishing for one group an action to obtain a benefit enforceable by court order that is not available to the other group. The relevant category under consideration is children in need of funds for a post-secondary education. The Act divides these persons, similarly situated with respect to their need for assistance, into groups according to the marital status of their parents, i.e., children of divorced/separated/never-married parents and children of intact families.

It will not do to argue that this classification is rationally related to the legitimate governmental purpose of obviating difficulties encountered by those in non-intact families who want parental financial assistance for post-secondary education, because such a statement of the governmental purpose assumes the validity of the classification. Recognizing that within the category of young adults in need of financial help to attend college there are some having a parent or parents unwilling to provide such help, the question remains whether the authority of the state may be selectively applied to empower only those from non-intact families to compel such help. We hold that it may not. In the absence of an entitlement on the part of any individual to post-secondary education, or a generally applicable requirement that parents assist their adult children in obtaining such an education, we perceive no rational basis for the state government to provide only certain adult citizens with legal means to overcome the difficulties they encounter in pursuing that end.

It is not inconceivable that in today's society a divorced parent, e.g., a father, could have two children, one born of a first marriage and not residing with him and the other born of a second marriage and still residing with him. Under Act 62, such a father could be required to provide post-secondary educational support for the first child but not the second, even to the extent that the second child would be required to forego a college education. Further, a child over the age of 18, of a woman whose husband had died would have no action against the mother to recover costs of a post-secondary education, but a child over the age of 18, of a woman who never married, who married and divorced, or even who was only separated from her husband when he died would be able to maintain such an action. These are but two examples demonstrating the arbitrariness of the classification adopted in Act 62. . . .

Ultimately, we can conceive of no rational reason why those similarly situated with respect to needing funds for college education, should be treated unequally. Accordingly, we agree with the common pleas court and conclude that Act 62 is unconstitutional.

MONTEMURO, JUSTICE, dissenting.

I must dissent. . . .

Act 62 is directed at furthering the education of the citizens of this Commonwealth. It operates on the assumption that divorce necessarily involves a disadvantage to the children of broken families, and is intended to assure that children who are thus disadvantaged by the divorce or separation of their parents are not deprived of the opportunity to acquire post secondary school education. In effect, it attempts to maintain the children of divorce in the same position they would have been in had their parents' marriage remained intact. The Act is not intended to, nor does it, place a premium on the rights of children of divorce while devaluing the same rights for children from intact marriage. It merely recognizes that, in general, divorce has a deleterious effect upon children, which should, insofar as is possible, be redressed. . . .

It would be difficult to argue successfully that the payment of child support is, in general, an obligation freely acknowledged and willingly undertaken by non-custodial parents. The extraordinary amount of time, attention and money devoted by courts, government agencies and legislatures to fashioning and enforcing support orders is testament to the unfortunate fact that the opposite is true. Moreover, the impact of parental non-compliance with support orders on children in need of basic necessities is obvious, hence the stated purpose of the Support Guidelines is to provide for children's reasonable needs which might, and frequently do, absent enforcement of established orders, otherwise go unmet.

It has also been widely acknowledged that among the negative effects of divorce on children are those which concern higher education. Courts faced with cases similar to the one at bar have also noted, over and over again, that in divorce, the normative rules of behavior may no longer apply. Whether because they lose concern for their children's welfare, or out of animosity toward the custodial parent, non-custodial parents frequently become reluctant to provide financial support for any purpose, but are particularly determined to avoid the costs of a college education. Then the custodial parent, who typically has less money than the non-custodial parent, most often becomes the de facto bearer of most, if not all, of the burden of educational expenses, even where the non-custodial parent possesses both resources and background which would inure to the child's benefit were the parents still married. Such parents, are, in addition, even less inclined to assist with the educational expenses of daughters than of sons.

The courts addressing the issue have uniformly decided that equal protection is not offended by an attempt to equalize the disparate situation faced by children of divorce. . . .

What must be remembered, and what the Majority fails to explore, is that Act 62 does not make mandatory the directive to pay child support for college. Section 4327(e) lists standards to assist the court in determining whether or not support is appropriate. Unless these criteria are, in the estimation of the court, met by the parties, no liability exists. . . .

While it does not necessarily follow that in all cases children of divorce are deprived of parental support for college, or that the reverse is true and all children of intact families are provided with the necessary encouragement and finances, children whose parents are still married most often continue to receive support past majority. Equal protection does not demand that every permutation be addressed separately, what is sought is equality not uniformity. . . .

Conventional wisdom once dictated that divorced parents will interact with their children in the same manner as they did during the life of the marriage. Experience has dictated otherwise, viz., the widespread need for enforcement of court ordered support even from parents for whom compliance is not an economic hardship. It is, after all, these parents at whom Act 62 is aimed. Divorce modifies parental behavior in ways which cannot always be anticipated. To ignore the reality of these differences, and the impact necessarily produced upon the children is shortsighted, as the educational achievements of the next generations are critical to the success of this country in an increasingly competitive world.

The law need not, and should not, change direction to comport with every change in the prevailing social winds. Nor is it designed to redress every psychological and emotional ill which trails in the wake of divorce. However, principles of justice require an unwavering commitment to the protection of the weakest members of our society, our children. Refusal to recognize their weakness breaches the social compact, and violates the basic principles of fairness the law is intended to uphold. Given the consequences of divorce, to deprive children of broken marriages of the economic support which they would normally receive from nuclear families is to deny them equal protection. . . . The disadvantage exists; it cannot be ignored or wished away.

If the Majority's view prevails, there is no recourse for these children, who will be victimized twice, first by the disruptions, both financial and psychological, of their parents' divorce, and again by the system which is theoretically designed to protect them. Moreover, such a course will not benefit the children of intact marriages in which, because of a parental disinterest in education or a view that non-support encourages the work ethic, the parents will also refuse to assist their children. The result will be no improvement for anyone.

Once the moral imperative which should motivate parents to fulfill their obligations has dissipated, conscious effort by the state must provide a substitute where it is able to do so. That is what the Legislature wisely has done. By disregarding the rational basis advanced for Act 62, the Majority now transforms this Court into a super-Legislature.

NOTES AND QUESTIONS

1.   *Who Receives Child Support?* The majority of states permit child support to be ordered until a child is eighteen or graduates from high school. In a small number of states, child support extends to age twenty-one.[47] In 1975, the Supreme Court held in Stanton v. Stanton that a law allowing child support to be paid for boys until twenty-one but for girls only until eighteen violated the Equal Protection Clause because it was based on generalizations about boys' need for support during crucial educational and career development years.[48]

The obligation of parents to support children begins from birth. For children of unmarried parents, a court can order child support at any point during the child's minority, and it may be made retroactive to birth depending on the circumstances.[49] Some states, however, expressly prohibit retroactive orders or limit the number of years for a back order.[50] A legally emancipated minor ceases to be eligible for child support, although past-due support can still be collected by the appropriate parent.[51] The law of emancipation is discussed in Chapter 6. A child who deliberately evades parental control may also lose the right of support.[52]

2.   *Measuring Income.* What income and other financial resources count when determining a parent's child support obligation? Most states sweep broadly, counting virtually every source of money as "income" for purposes of determining

---

47. For a recent summary of age cut-offs, see Nat'l Conf. of State Legislatures, Termination of Child Support (Apr. 29, 2019), https://www.ncsl.org/research/human-services/termination-of-child-support-age-of-majority.aspx.

48. 421 U.S. 7 (1975).

49. See, e.g., In re Reitenour, 807 A.2d 1259 (N.H. 2002).

50. See generally Elaine Sorensen et al., Urban Inst., Assessing Child Support Arrears in Nine Large States and the Nation (2017).

51. See, e.g., Ricci v. Ricci, 154 A.3d 215, 230 (N.J. Super. Ct. App. Div. 2017); McKinney v. Hamp, 268 So. 3d 470 (Miss. 2018).

52. See, e.g., Roe v. Doe, 272 N.E.2d 567 (N.Y. 1971).

the payment that should go to the custodial parent. As defined in the Virginia statute, "gross income" includes "all income from all sources, and shall include, but not be limited to, income from salaries, wages, commissions, royalties, bonuses, dividends, severance pay, pensions, interest, trust income, annuities, capital gains, social security benefits, disability insurance benefits, veterans' benefits, spousal support, rental income, gifts, prizes or awards."[53] Income excludes public assistance, federal Social Security disability benefits, and child support received from another parent.[54]

3. *College Tuition.* States vary on whether divorcing or unmarried parents can be ordered to pay for college. In some states, there is no statute addressing the issue. In others, a statute prohibits such orders. In still others, a statute gives courts discretion to order such payments, even if child support otherwise ends at eighteen.[55] The issue of whether and how much parents will contribute to a child's college education is often addressed in separation agreements, rather than as part of a child support order. Is the *Crocker* court right that it makes sense to order payment of college tuition by unmarried or divorced parents even though it wouldn't ask the same of married parents? Or is the majority in *Curtis* right that such a rule gives an unfair advantage to one select group of children, whose needs may not be any different from those not covered by the law? Should states impose obligations on all parents to contribute to post-secondary education to the best of their ability? Would such a statute survive constitutional scrutiny?

4. *The Needs of Adult Children with Disabilities.* Many states give courts discretion to order post-majority support for children with disabilities, with varying definitions and restrictions. Disability in this context is defined by reference to the child's ability to become economically self-sufficient as an adult. Some states permit a court to order post-majority support only where the parents have agreed to be subject to such an order, and others permit an order only if the parents' divorce occurred during the child's minority.[56] Should parents be required to support children into adulthood if they cannot support themselves? On what theory?

---

53. Va. Code Ann. § 20-108.2 (2020).

54. The Supreme Court has held that federal law does not preempt state child support guidelines with respect to disability payments from federal programs. Rose v. Rose, 481 U.S. 619 (1987). States thus have discretion to decide whether to include or exclude payments such as military disability benefits or disability payments under the federal Social Security system.

55. For a current summary of statutes addressing payment of college tuition, see Nat'l Conf. of State Legis., Termination of Child Support, supra note 47.

56. For the laws of each state, see Nat'l Conf. of State Legislatures, Termination of Child Support, supra note 47. See also Karen Syma Czapanskiy, Chalimony: Seeking Equity Between Parents of Children with Disabilities and Chronic Illnesses, 34 N.Y.U. Rev. L. & Soc. Change 253 (2010).

4. New Families and Subsequent Children

As with spousal support and child custody, child support orders are subject to modification. (And unlike spousal support, the parties cannot agree to make child support non-modifiable.) The court retains jurisdiction over a case until the youngest child ceases to be eligible for parental support. What circumstances justify modifying an order? States articulate the standards differently, but, in general, the party seeking a modification must first show changed circumstances to justify reconsidering the child support amount. Per a federal mandate, child support awards cannot be modified retroactively; a new amount can take effect going forward only.[57]

The following case addresses a common modification scenario that courts confront: a parent with a child support obligation having additional children with a different co-parent.

Harte v. Hand
81 A.3d 667 (N.J. App. Div. 2013)

Koblitz, J.A.D.

This appeal raises the issue of how to properly calculate child support for multiple families. Defendant David Richard Hand appeals from two separate child support orders entered on November 7, 2011, and orders denying reconsideration entered on May 25, 2012. . . . The orders regarding support were entered on the same date by the same motion judge and the issues stemming from those orders in the two appeals are identical. We resolve both appeals in this decision, reversing and remanding only for a recalculation of support that takes into account defendant's financial obligations towards all three of his children. . . .

Defendant has three children, each of whom has a different mother. Defendant's oldest son lives with defendant and his current wife. This child's mother lives in Florida and does not contribute to his support. Defendant's younger son lives with his mother, plaintiff T.B. His youngest child, a girl, lives with defendant's former wife, Harte. Defendant was employed as a concrete layer and finisher before he was seriously injured in a 2003 garage collapse at the Tropicana Casino Hotel in Atlantic City. As a result of this injury, he received a settlement of $1.2 million in 2007. He claims to have netted $533,822 after paying several "obligations." At the time of his personal injury settlement, defendant was married to Harte and paying child support to T.B.

After the settlement, defendant agreed to an imputation of $57,200 in annual income when recalculating child support for T.B. Harte and defendant were

---

57. 42 U.S.C. § 666(a)(9) (2018).

divorced in 2008 and defendant again consented to an imputation of $57,200 in annual income as part of their January 2009 final judgment of divorce. In 2011, after a history of enforcement motions by both plaintiffs, defendant unsuccessfully moved to reduce child support for both children, claiming he was unable to obtain through wages and investments the agreed-upon imputed income. The motion judge denied his application, but suggested that if he presented a vocational expert who could demonstrate his lack of ability to earn the imputed income, the judge would consider his application again. . . .

We should not disturb the trial court's findings unless the record does not support the determination with substantial, credible evidence. . . .

The judge calculated child support for the two children not living with defendant based on the individual financial circumstances of the mothers as provided in the Child Support Guidelines. R. 5:6A. In both calculations, the judge entered the undisputed dependent deduction of $177 for the child living with defendant on line 2(d). She determined that it would be unfair to the mothers to designate either order as the initial order, thereby deducting that amount from defendant's available income when calculating the support order for the other child. The judge therefore calculated both support obligations using defendant's imputed annual income of $57,200 as if the only other child defendant supported was the oldest son living with him.

We do not approve the child support calculation method utilized by the motion judge. Equality in treatment for the mothers should not be obtained by requiring the father to pay an inappropriately high level of support for both children. According to Rule 5:6A, the Child Support Guidelines "shall be applied" when a court is calculating or modifying child support. The "guidelines may be modified or disregarded by the court only where good cause is shown. . . ." Although we agree with the judge's concern that the two mothers should not be treated unequally, we do not approve of the method used to achieve equality.

The Guidelines require the court to consider multiple family obligations to obtain an equitable resolution that does not favor any family. The Guidelines also anticipate an adjustment when an obligor must support more than one family. Pursuant to the Guidelines, prior child support orders must be deducted from an obligor's weekly income because such an obligation "represents income that is not available for determining the current child support obligation. . . ." Thus, "the amount of such orders must be deducted from the obligor's total weekly Adjusted Gross Taxable Income." By leaving line 2(b) blank on both the Harte and T.B. worksheets, the judge misapplied the Guidelines.

A later-born child should not be penalized by reducing the obligor's available income by the prior child support obligation. To achieve parity among the children of defendant, we suggest the use of the "prior order" adjustment under the child support guidelines must be modified. For example, here, Guidelines support should be calculated for Harte, first considering her child as having the prior order and listing T.B.'s child as the recipient of the second order; then flipping these positions so the T.B. child is considered the first order and Harte's child considered the recipient of the second order. Similar calculations would be performed in T.B.'s matter, first considering her order as the first entered, then as the second entered. In each calculation, the party receiving the "second" order would have the amount calculated for the "first" order entered on line 2(b) of the worksheet. Then, after the four calculations are prepared, all including defendant's oldest child as another dependent deduction of $177 on line 2(d), the two resulting T.B. worksheet obligations, located at line 27, would be averaged and the two Harte worksheet calculations averaged. Defendant would then be ordered to pay the average of the two support calculations to each plaintiff. This method would ensure that the children were treated fairly regardless of birth order, while not disregarding the father's obligation to pay for all three children. This may well not be the only way to equitably calculate support for multiple families, but we suggest it as one workable method of doing so that is consistent with the Guidelines. We therefore remand for a recalculation of support for the two families.

Importantly, these orders were calculated in the same county at the same time. Even when this does not occur, the Guidelines indicate that an obligor's multiple obligations to different families should be taken into consideration in determining an equitable amount of support for each child. The Guidelines state:

> In some cases, one individual may be obligated to pay child support to multiple families. When the court adjudicates a case involving an obligor with multiple family obligations, it may be necessary to review all past orders for that individual. If the court has jurisdiction over all matters, it may either average the orders or fashion some other equitable resolution to treat all supported children fairly under the guidelines. . . .

Affirmed in part, reversed in part and remanded for a recalculation of child support.

NOTES AND QUESTIONS

1. *New, Blended, and Successive Families.* It is common in the United States for people to remarry after divorce, as well as for people to have children with more than one partner. How should the child support system deal with the competing needs of "first" and "second" families? What policy goals should the system aim to serve?[58] Should the first family have priority? The second or successive ones?

---

58. See generally Adrienne Jennings Lockie, Multiple Families, Multiple Goals, Multiple Failures: The Need for "Limited Equalization" as a Theory of Child Support, 32 Harv. J.L. & Gender 109 (2009); Katherine K. Baker, Homogeneous Rules for Heterogeneous Families: The Standardization of Family Law When There is No Standard Family, 2012 U. Ill. L. Rev. 319.

Should all benefit equally from a parent's income? How can ɛ achieved in practice?

2. *Stepchildren.* Many states have adopted statutes req support stepchildren if the stepparent has received the child any obligation of support terminates with the marriage that ship, and a former stepparent cannot be ordered to pay child s of some basis for assigning legal parentage.[60]

3. *Modifications.* Federal law requires states to build in some mechanism for reviewing and adjusting child support awards over time. The options include: (i) a review of the guidelines themselves every four years, a review of awards in IV-D cases (i.e., cases involving parents receiving government aid) every three years, and individualized review in other cases upon a parent's request; (ii) automatic cost-of-living adjustments in all cases; or (iii) automated adjustments based on information such as tax records.[61]

5. Earning Capacity and Imputed Income

The various child support formulas we discussed entail determining what percentage of a parent's income should be paid to the other parent as child support. But what happens when a parent's income changes? A material increase in the obligor's income can be the basis for a child support modification upward. What about a decrease in income? A court has discretion to impute income to a parent if it determines the parent is unjustifiably unemployed or underemployed. Can courts force a parent to work or to pick a particular job? Under what circumstances should a parent be permitted to forego income in order to stay home to care for the child?

Most states address imputed income expressly in the child support statute. Questions arise as to whether to excuse or modify a parent's obligation to work and, if not, how to calculate the parent's earning capacity. Consider the relevant provisions of Ohio's child support statute:

(9) "Income" means either of the following:
  (a) For a parent who is employed to full capacity, the gross income of the parent;
  (b) For a parent who is unemployed or underemployed, the sum of the gross income of the parent and any potential income of the parent. . . .

---

59. See, e.g., Mo. Rev. Stat. § 453.400 (2020); N.Y. Soc. Serv. Law § 101 (McKinney 2020) (imposing duty of support on stepparents until stepchildren reach age twenty-one). See also Margaret M. Mahoney, Stepfamilies and the Law (1994).

60. See generally Cynthia Grant Bowman, The New Illegitimacy: Children of Cohabiting Couples and Stepchildren, 20 Am. U.J. Gender Soc. Pol'y & L. 437 (2012).

61. 42 U.S.C. § 666(a)(10)(A) (2018).

7) "Potential income" means both of the following for a parent who the court pursuant to a court support order, or a child support enforcement agency pursuant to an administrative child support order, determines is voluntarily unemployed or voluntarily underemployed:

(a) Imputed income that the court or agency determines the parent would have earned if fully employed as determined from the following criteria:

    (i)   The parent's prior employment experience;

    (ii)   The parent's education;

    (iii) The parent's physical and mental disabilities, if any;

    (iv) The availability of employment in the geographic area in which the parent resides;

    (v)   The prevailing wage and salary levels in the geographic area in which the parent resides;

    (vi) The parent's special skills and training;

    (vii) Whether there is evidence that the parent has the ability to earn the imputed income;

    (viii) The age and special needs of the child for whom child support is being calculated under this section;

    (ix) The parent's increased earning capacity because of experience;

    (x)   The parent's decreased earning capacity because of a felony conviction;

    (xi) Any other relevant factor.[62]

Married parents have the autonomy to decide whether and how much to work, how to make tradeoffs between work and other priorities or responsibilities, and how to adjust to a reduction in income. We also presume that parents make decisions that are in the best interests of their children, including those that dictate how much money will be available to the family. An intact family has the luxury of making almost any decision about work, income, and expenditures that it sees fit — so long as these decisions do not constitute "neglect." Bill Gates could have forced his children to assume a middle-class lifestyle, despite having all the money in the world. Why don't divorced or never-married parents have the same autonomy? Are we to assume that they are more likely to behave in ways that are not in their children's best interests?

SHARPE V. SHARPE
366 P.3d 66 (Alaska 2016)

BOLGER, JUSTICE.

A non-custodial parent moved to modify a child support order after she quit her job in Anchorage, moved to a remote village, and adopted a subsistence

---

62. Ohio Rev. Code Ann. § 3119.01 (West 2020).

lifestyle. Although the parent acknowledged that she was voluntarily unemployed, she argued that her decision was reasonable in light of her cultural, spiritual, and religious needs. The superior court disagreed and denied the motion. The parent appeals . . . [W]e affirm the judgment of the superior court.

Jolene Lyon and Jyzyk Sharpe divorced in July 2012. The superior court awarded Jyzyk primary physical custody of the parties' only child and ordered Jolene to pay Jyzyk $1,507.00 per month in child support.

Jolene is a Yup'ik Eskimo who was raised in Nome and has family ties to the native village of Stebbins. When the child support order was issued, Jolene was "living in Anchorage, working at Alyeska Pipeline Service Company, and earning approximately $120,000 a year." In April 2013, she left Anchorage and took up a subsistence lifestyle in Stebbins.

Soon after relocating to Stebbins, Jolene moved to modify the child support order. She alleged that she was "no longer employed," that she was "a full time stay at home mother," and that her only income was her annual Permanent Fund Dividend. These developments, she argued, constituted a material change in circumstances warranting a modification of the child support order. She requested that the court reduce her monthly child support payment to $50 per month, the minimum allowed under Alaska Civil Rule 90.3(c)(3).

Jyzyk opposed the motion, arguing that modification of the child support order was not warranted because Jolene was "voluntarily and unreasonabl[y] unemployed." Although he acknowledged that Jolene was entitled to quit her job and move to a remote community, he argued that the parties' "ten year old daughter . . . should not be required to fund [Jolene's] lifestyle choice."

The superior court held a motion hearing in July 2013. During the hearing, Jolene testified about her life in Stebbins and the benefits she derived from her subsistence lifestyle. She expressed her desire to expose the parties' child to traditional life in Stebbins. And she said that living in Stebbins, a dry community, provided reprieve from an alcohol abuse issue she had experienced during her marriage.

Jyzyk also testified at the hearing. He expressed his belief that the parties' child would benefit from receiving child support from Jolene at its existing amount and noted that these monthly payments "helped with everything [including] rent, groceries, [and] clothes." Jyzyk testified that "[i]n a dream world [he] would bring [the parties' child] to Kotzebue [in the area where he was raised] and raise her on the river," but he recognized that financial constraints prevented him from prudently fulfilling this dream.

After the hearing the superior court denied Jolene's motion. Although the court acknowledged that "[Jolene] is finding sort of a spiritual awakening or reconnecting with Native dance, Native culture, [and] subsistence lifestyle" and that life in Stebbins is "rehabilitative for her," it concluded: "[G]iven [Jolene's] background and her previous earnings I do not agree that . . . she does not have any income capacity simply because she chose to relocate to the village of Stebbins and earn nothing." . . .

When one parent takes primary physical custody of a child after divorce, the non-custodial parent is required to pay child support "equal to the adjusted annual income of the non-custodial parent multiplied by" a specified percentage. Although the "adjusted annual income" is typically calculated using the parent's actual income, under Alaska Civil Rule 90.3(a)(4) "[t]he court may calculate child support based on a determination of the potential income of a parent who voluntarily and unreasonably is unemployed or underemployed." "Potential income will be based upon the parent's work history, qualifications, and job opportunities." As we have noted, the aim of Alaska Civil Rule 90.3(a)(4) "is to give courts *broad discretion* to impute income based on realistic estimates of earning potential in cases of voluntary and *unreasonable* unemployment or underemployment."

Jolene conceded that she was voluntarily unemployed. Therefore, the only issue at the hearing was whether her decision to be unemployed was unreasonable. The superior court concluded that it was. In determining whether a parent is "unreasonably" unemployed, the superior court must look to the totality of the circumstances, including "such factors as whether the obligor's reduced income is temporary, whether the change is the result of economic factors or of purely personal choices, the children's needs, and the parents' needs and financial abilities." But "[b]ecause of the significance of a parent's duty to meet his or her child support obligations, we prioritize fulfillment of that duty over even legitimate decisions to be voluntarily unemployed or underemployed." And we have consistently recognized that, when a child support obligor makes a career change for personal reasons, the superior court should consider the financial impact of this decision on the child.

In *Pattee v. Pattee,* our first case considering imputed income, the noncustodial parent quit his job at a bar in Anchorage and moved to Washington to enroll in Tacoma Community College. 744 P.2d 658, 659 (Alaska 1987). We rejected the notion that a voluntary career change should require an automatic reduction in child support:

> On the one hand, we do not believe that an obligor-parent should be "locked in" to a particular job or field during the minority of his or her children when accepting a lower-paying position may ultimately result in personal or professional advancement. On the other hand, the children of the marriage and the custodial parent should not be forced to finance the noncustodial parent's career change. We believe that the better rule is that stated by the Montana Supreme Court: "[T]he judge [is] to consider the nature of the changes and the reasons for the changes, and then to determine whether, under all the circumstances, a modification is warranted." . . .

The foregoing quote recognizes that a child support obligor should not be "locked in" to a particular career. But this language is in a sentence that implies that a career change must be supported by a "lower-paying position" that will "ultimately result in personal or professional advancement." And this sentiment is immediately followed by the observation that "the children . . . and the custodial parent should not be forced to finance the noncustodial parent's career change." . . .

A few years after the *Pattee* decision, we applied the same rationale to a case where the child support obligor had moved from Alaska to El Paso, Texas to study engineering. *Pugil v. Cogar*, 811 P.2d 1062, 1064 (Alaska 1991). The obligor testified that he decided to change careers because he was "'burned out' on fishing [his prior career] and wanted a safer, less strenuous career." The trial court commended the obligor's pursuit of further education but noted that his plan to enroll as a part-time student and to work as a part-time welder "is not completely realistic" because he could pursue his education while working as part-time fisherman to fulfill his child support obligation. The trial court imputed income to the obligor based on his previous employment in Alaska as a welder and commercial fisherman rather than on his prospective earnings as a welder in El Paso, and we affirmed.

Similarly, in *Olmstead v. Ziegler* we considered the case of a child support obligor who left the practice of law and returned to school to become a teacher. 42 P.3d 1102, 1103-04 (Alaska 2002). The superior court concluded that it was unreasonable for the obligor "to train for a position that is *less* remunerative than that his current education and experience justifies." Though it expressed "[n]o moral criticism of [the obligor's] lifestyle change," the superior court was unwilling to "shift any of the consequent burden [of the career change] to the narrow shoulders of [the] child." We affirmed, noting that the obligor had failed to demonstrate that his career change would benefit his child.

In recent cases, we have repeatedly stated that the "relevant inquiry" when imputing income is "whether a parent's current situation and earnings reflect a voluntary and unreasonable decision to earn less than the parent is capable of earning." And the commentary to Alaska Civil Rule 90.3 specifically requires the superior court to examine the financial impact on the child in deciding whether to impute income: "When a parent makes a career change, [the totality of the circumstances] consideration should include *the extent to which the children will ultimately benefit* from the change." This directive implies that a court may consider the financial impact of a career change on a child, because the amount of child support inevitably affects the child's well-being.

There are certainly cases where we have affirmed child support modifications when a career change was partly motivated by personal factors. But these cases simply illustrate that the superior court has a wide range of discretion when addressing this issue. The fact that some cases have treated relocation decisions as reasonable does not free the superior court from the obligation to consider the financial impact of a career change on the obligor's child. Jolene does not cite any cases where we have held that the consideration of this impact was an abuse of discretion.

In this case, Jolene moved to Stebbins and adopted a subsistence lifestyle without any intention of seeking employment to meet her child support obligation. In support of her request for reduction of her child support obligation, she specifically stated that she had "no intention to return to the work force." The record thus supports the superior court's conclusion that Jolene's decision to leave her employment and move to Stebbins would have an unreasonable financial impact on the resources available to care for her daughter. . . .

In making custody determinations courts must apply the best interests of the child analysis. When a custodial parent seeks to relocate with the child, the court must analyze the reasonableness of the relocation decision to ascertain whether the move has illegitimate motives, such as a desire to prevent contact between the child and the non-custodial parent. If the court finds such illegitimate motives, it must consider them in its best interests of the child analysis. If not, the court cannot hold the parent's decision to relocate against the parent when determining custody.

In contrast, when calculating child support courts do not conduct a best interests of the child analysis. Rather the non-custodial parent's child support obligation is based on a statutorily prescribed percentage of their actual or imputed annual income, as mandated by court rule. . . .

Jolene argues that the superior court . . . gave short shrift to Jolene's religious and cultural needs.

It is true that "the parents' needs" is one of the factors the superior court must consider in evaluating the totality of the circumstances. But the superior court did adequately consider Jolene's needs, and after considering these needs it found that they did not outweigh other concerns, including her daughter's need for financial support:

> [Jolene] finds that [living in Stebbins] is sort of rehabilitative for her from the standpoint of her eliminating . . . some of the poisons of urban life. . . . She is finding sort of a spiritual reawakening or reconnecting with Native dance, Native culture, subsistence lifestyle, all of which is . . . admirable in an abstract sense.
>
> Then again . . . she effectively is . . . taking a vacation from the financial responsibilities that she assumed when she had a child, and the result of her not working and providing financial assistance is that it's going to impose . . . a greater burden on [Jyzyk], but, more importantly, it's going to have an impact over time on the opportunities . . . and resources that are available to take care of [the parties' daughter].
>
> Now, I don't know whether it's realistic to continue child support at [$]120,000 a year, . . . but given her background and her previous earnings I do not agree that it should be that she does not have any income capacity simply because she chose to relocate to the village of Stebbins and earn nothing. . . .
>
> I do find it a difficult choice in this case because [Jolene] does seem to derive some very valid benefits from being in Stebbins, and I'm sure that for the summers [her daughter] derives some benefits there, too, but then there's the other nine months of the year when [the parties' daughter] lives in Anchorage and she'd be getting $50 a month, if that, instead of . . . $1500 a month, which could go a long way toward providing for necessities and also

toward . . . providing for her future needs, educational needs, an
her a good start in life.

The record thus reflects that the superior court adequately
personal needs when it determined that her voluntary
unreasonable.

Despite this consideration, the dissent worries that the superior
ize[s] Alaska Natives' way of life" and "devalues Alaska Natives' cultural, spiritual,
and religious connections to their villages and their subsistence lifestyle." Yet in
reality the dissent's desired outcome would have enormous financial implications
for Alaska Native children. "The primary purpose of Rule 90.3 is to ensure that
child support orders are adequate to meet the needs of children, subject to the ability of parents to pay." Granting either parent absolute freedom to exit the workforce
would undermine this purpose. . . .

CHEN V. WARNER
695 N.W.2d 758 (Wis. 2005)

SHIRLEY S. ABRAHAMSON, CHIEF JUSTICE. . . .
The circuit court granted Jane E. Chen's (the mother's) motion to amend the
child support portion of a divorce judgment to require John J. Warner (the father)
to pay $4,000 per month in child support. The circuit court rejected the father's
argument that the mother's actions constituted "shirking" and declined to use the
mother's earning capacity rather than her actual income in determining whether to
award child support. . . .

The . . . issue is whether the circuit court erred in determining that the mother's
decision to forgo employment outside the home and become an at-home full-time
child care provider was reasonable under the circumstances. . . . [W]e conclude that
the mother's decision was reasonable under the circumstances. . . .

I

The material facts are undisputed. The case at bar arises out of a post-divorce
motion to modify child support. The mother and father, both physicians, were
divorced in 1999 after an 18-year marriage. They have three children, born in 1991,
1993, and 1995.

The judgment of divorce incorporated the parties' agreement. It provided for
joint custody and equal physical placement. The children spent alternating weeks
with each parent. The judgment provided that neither party would pay child support to the other; each would be responsible for the children's daily expenses when
they were in his or her care. Reasonable clothing expenses and other mutually
agreed-upon expenses incurred on behalf of the children were equally divided. The

ather, however, was to pay $400 per child per month into a fund for the children's future education.

At the time of the divorce, both parties were employed full time at the Marshfield Clinic. The mother earned . . . $236,000 per year. The father earned . . . $256,452 per year. Both parents worked outside the home during the marriage.

After the divorce, the mother sought to reduce her employment to be more available for the children, who were of school age or nearing it. Both parents apparently agree that it is in the best interests of their children to have, if feasible, child care provided by a parent. The father testified at the child support modification hearing that, when possible, it was important to have a parent at home full time with the children rather than have someone else care for the children.

The mother voluntarily left her full-time position at the Marshfield Clinic in May 2000 when she was unable to reduce her schedule there to part time.

Leaving her position was not a rash decision. Prior to terminating her employment, the mother had consulted with a financial advisor and was advised that from her $1.1 million savings, she could expect an annual income of about $110,000. This sum was significant, but was less than the income she earned as a physician. The estimate of $110,000 was based on stock market returns over the past 50 years. The mother's estimated budget was $7,000 per month, or $84,000 per year. Because her expected income exceeded her budget, the mother did not seek child support from the father.

The stock market decline in 2001 took a toll on the mother's investment income. That year she earned only $32,000. In response to the income decline, the mother began to look for employment and began invading her assets in order to meet her and the children's expenses. The job search failed to yield any part-time opportunities within commuting distance of her home, although she could have obtained alternating-week work in distant communities. She did not want to live away from home during alternate weeks, so she declined to pursue those opportunities.

In 2002, the mother filed a motion to amend the divorce judgment to require the father to pay child support. She asserted a substantial change in circumstances to justify a child support award. Her income had diminished substantially; the father's income had increased.

Had the mother continued employment at the Marshfield Clinic, she would have been earning $415,000 per year. The father was earning $472,000 per year when the motion was filed in 2002, nearly twice what he earned at the time of the divorce. In addition, his employer contributed $73,000 per year to his retirement plan. The father had assets of $1,218,185, not including securities. He was eligible for nine weeks of paid vacation per year and two weeks of paid meeting time. He maintains three residences.

The father's monthly budget was $8,400, leaving him with discretionary income of $12,000 per month. The mother requested $4,000 per month in child support based on a monthly budget of $7,000.

The circuit court ordered the father to pay child support in the amount of $4,000, but excused him from his obligation to pay $1,200 per month into the children's education fund. Thus, the net effect of the circuit court's order is to require the father to pay an additional $2,800 per month for the children's support.

Not working outside the home full time has enabled the mother to spend significantly more time with the children. This increased time with the children also includes periods during the weeks when the father has placement of the children. She shepherds the children to medical appointments, attends their school activities, does volunteer work at the school, communicates more with their teachers, transports the children to their various extracurricular activities (tae kwon do, ballet, knitting, dancing, piano lessons), and monitors their participation in all their endeavors.

The record is also replete with evidence of the father's involvement in the children's lives.

By all accounts, the children were doing well and their needs were met before the mother left employment at the Marshfield Clinic, and they have continued to do well thereafter.

The father argued in the circuit court and on appeal that the mother's termination of employment in 2000 and her refusal to seek part-time work outside the Marshfield area were unreasonable and amounted to shirking her obligation to support their children.

II . . .

This is a child support modification case. The father asserts that in determining child support the circuit court should have used the mother's earning capacity, not her actual earnings. Obviously, in the present case there is a significant difference between the two numbers. A circuit court would consider a parent's earning capacity rather than the parent's actual earnings only if it has concluded that the parent has been "shirking," to use the awkward terminology of past cases. To conclude that a parent is shirking, a circuit court is not required to find that a former spouse deliberately reduced earnings to avoid support obligations or to gain some advantage over the other party. A circuit court need find only that a party's employment decision to reduce or forgo income is voluntary and unreasonable under the circumstances.

The parties . . . agree that the mother's decision to reduce her income from employment outside the home was voluntary.

The focus of the parties' dispute is whether the mother's decision to forgo employment outside the home to become an at-home full-time child care provider was reasonable under the circumstances. . . .

The test of reasonableness under the circumstances is derived from the case law. . . . [T]he paying spouse should be afforded "a fair choice" of a means of livelihood as well as the ability to pursue what the spouse honestly feels are the best opportunities, even though the present financial return may be reduced from prior employment. The court further said that "[t]his rule is, of course, subject to reasonableness commensurate with [the spouse's] obligations to [the] children and [the former spouse]." The phrase "subject to reasonableness commensurate with a spouse's obligations to the children" has been repeated in numerous shirking cases, including unintentional shirking cases. The phrase "commensurate with a spouse's obligations to the children" does not explicitly refer to obligations of financial support; it includes other obligations, such as child care. . . .

The case law recognizes that the words "subject to reasonableness commensurate with a spouse's obligations to the children" mean that a court balances the needs of the parents and the needs of the child (both financial and otherwise, like child care) and the ability of both parents to pay child support.

Furthermore, Wis. Stat. §767.25(1m)(d) and (e) provide that a court may modify the amount of child support payments under the percentage standard if, after considering the listed economic factors, "[t]he desirability that the custodian remain in the home as a full-time parent," and "the value of custodial services performed by the custodian if the custodian remains at home," the court concludes that the percentage standard is unfair to the child or to any of the parties. Thus the legislature has explicitly recognized that in establishing financial child support obligations a circuit court considers the desirability and value of child care services performed by a custodian. . . .

With appropriate deference to the circuit court's ruling, we now determine the reasonableness of the mother's decision to forgo employment outside the home to become an at-home full-time child care provider.

While a family is intact, the parents' choice of employment, child care, and standard of living are left to the parties, as long as the children's basic needs are met. Upon divorce, however, courts are plunged into the divorced parents' personal lives to ensure that the interests of minor children are protected.

A divorced parent who voluntarily leaves gainful employment outside the home, for however good a reason, may be subject to judicial inquiry into that parent's responsibility to furnish child support. A divorced parent may voluntarily terminate employment but may not do so if the conduct inures to the detriment of child support. There is a limit to the unemployment or underemployment of a parent when the other parent "is presented the bill for the financial consequences."

When a divorced parent decides to forgo employment outside the home to render at-home full-time child care (but not for the purpose of avoiding a support obligation) . . . [a] court must weigh the right of a parent to make such a choice, while keeping in mind the public's interests that children be adequately cared for, that the financial needs of the children be met, and that the financial burdens of child care be apportioned fairly between the parents.

If it determines that a parent's decision to forgo employment outside the home to provide at-home full-time child care is unreasonable, a court can impose an obligation on that parent to support a child by imputing income to the parent based on that parent's earning capacity. . . .

We do not adopt a position favoring or disfavoring a parent's decision to forgo employment outside the home to become an at-home full-time or part-time child care provider. . . .

The factors to be considered in determining the reasonableness of a parent's decision to forgo employment outside the home, become an at-home full-time child care provider, and increase the support obligation of the other parent include, but are not limited to, the following: the number of children at home and their ages, maturity, health, and special needs; the availability of child care providers; the financial needs of the children; any detrimental effect on the child's support level if a parent is a full- or part-time at-home child care provider; the age and mental and physical condition of the parents; the educational background, training, skills, prior employment, and wage earning history of each parent; the earning potential of the parent who forgoes employment outside the home and that parent's efforts to find and retain employment; the status of the job market; the assets and income of each parent and the available resources if a parent is an at-home full- or part-time child care provider; the hardship and burden on the parent employed outside the home caused by the other parent's decision to forgo employment; and any other factors bearing on the needs of the children and each parent's ability to fund child support.

The gender of the parent forgoing employment outside the home to provide at-home full- or part-time child care is not a relevant factor.

The record in the present case supports the circuit court's determination that the mother's initial decision to terminate employment was reasonable. . . .

The question then becomes whether it was reasonable for the mother not to take full- or part-time employment as a physician when the income from her investments fell. It is this decision that precipitated the mother's child support motion and prompted the father's shirking allegation. . . .

The circuit court concluded, and we agree, that a parent's decision to provide at-home full-time child care may but does not, in and of itself, amount to shirking. As the circuit court explained, if the father is right that the mother's forgoing income from employment outside the home to become an at-home full-time child care provider is automatically unreasonable, then every arrangement in which one parent predominantly attends to the children while the other predominantly attends to an income-producing job is shirking. Furthermore, as the circuit court stated, under the father's theory it would no longer be appropriate to impute economic value to child care or homemaking services, as our statutes permit.

The father agreed at trial that if a family unit "can do it," that is, if it is feasible, it is preferable for the children to be with a parent rather than with someone else and that it is preferable to have a parent available as a full-time at-home child care provider rather than have one parent or both parents as part-time at-home child care providers. The father's briefs now seem to assert that the children might have greater opportunities had their mother continued to earn her substantial salary.

The circuit court properly considered the benefits to the children resulting from the mother's decision not to be employed outside the home. The father does not dispute the mother's accounting of her child-related activities, nor does he argue that the children do not benefit from her greater involvement in their lives. Rather, he argues that the benefits are not so great as to render reasonable her decision not to be employed outside the home in the face of her dwindling and inadequate investment returns. The father argues, and the mother does not dispute, that the children were doing well when both parents worked full time outside the home and that the children have no special needs or disabilities. Further, the father points out that the mother worked full time before the children were of school age and now stays home full time while they are in school. The usual practice, he contends, is for a parent to stay home while the children are very young and return to work when they start school.

The father makes good points, but we conclude, as did the circuit court, that the benefits to the children in the present case are a factor to be weighed in favor of the mother's decision not to be employed outside the home. This factor favoring the mother is not, however, determinative of the case.

This case presents the issue of whether it is fair to the father and to the children, in light of the mother's legal obligation to support the children, for a court not to impute to the mother her earning capacity, thereby increasing the father's child support obligations.

The father's key point is that the reasonableness of the mother's decision to be an at-home full-time child care provider should not be based solely on the fact that the father can afford to pay child support. We agree with the father. . . .

Certainly, if a working parent's income were low, that factor would weigh against a finding that the other parent's decision to forgo employment outside the home was reasonable. The converse should also be true.

In the present case the father's ability to make increased expenditures for the children is unusually high. As a result, the effect of increased support of $2,800 on the father's standard of living and financial picture is negligible. The father had monthly discretionary income of $12,000, over and above his monthly expenses and retirement savings. . . .

[T]he father argues that the children will suffer by the mother's decision to forgo paid employment outside the home. He argues that the court has terminated the father's obligation to contribute to the trust accounts for the children's post-high school education, thereby effectively forcing the children to subsidize their mother's early retirement and diminishing the children's funds for post-high school education. We disagree with the father. The mother's decision to forgo employment outside the home to become an at-home full-time child care provider was reasonable considering the present interests of the children and the other factors present in the case at bar. Further, nothing prevents the father from voluntarily continuing to pay $1,200 per month toward the children's education fund. . . .

[W]e conclude that the circuit court correctly concluded that the mother's decision to remain unemployed to be an at-home full-time child care provider was reasonable under the circumstances. . . .

We do not set forth a general rule that it is always reasonable for a parent to terminate employment to become an at-home full-time child care provider when the other parent has the ability to support the children. . . .

We affirm the court of appeals' decision affirming the circuit court's order that the father pay $4,000 per month to the mother as child support.

NOTES AND QUESTIONS

1. *Voluntary Employment Changes.* When an obligor parent loses a job or suffers some other involuntary reduction in income, there is no question that the change can be the basis for a modification of child support. The harder cases are the ones where the parent has voluntarily reduced income because of a career change, pursuit of education or training, or a lifestyle change. What standard should apply to requests for modification in such cases? Should the parent have to show that the reduction in income will ultimately inure to the benefit of the child in some way?

2. *The Case of Incarceration.* Another issue that sometimes arises is whether to impute income to a noncustodial parent who is incarcerated. Prisoners have very limited earning capacity, sometimes earning as little as 25 cents a day.[63] Should courts impute income that could only be earned if the parent were not incarcerated? Some courts have held that the obligor's incarceration is "no justification" for modifying child support on the theory that the parent's criminal conduct was voluntary.[64] Some permit incarceration to serve as the basis for relieving the duty to pay child support, as long as the obligor does not have other available assets.[65] Some treat incarceration as one non-dispositive factor that might support a downward modification.[66] Some defer consideration until the obligor's release to determine what best serves the interests of the child.[67] Which approach is preferable? Professor Ann Cammett argues that the child support enforcement system is detrimental to low-income families in many ways, and that continuing to demand child support from an incarcerated parent who cannot earn the money necessary to pay it "will

---

63. See Esther Griswold & Jessica Pearson, Twelve Reasons for Collaboration Between Departments of Correction and Child Support Enforcement Agencies, 65 Corrections Today 87, 88 (2003).

64. See, e.g., Koch v. Williams, 456 N.W.2d 299, 301 (N.D. 1990).

65. See, e.g., Willis v. Willis, 840 P.2d 697, 699 (Or. 1992).

66. See, e.g., Thomasson v. Johnson, 903 P.2d 254, 256–57 (N.M. 1995).

67. See, e.g., Halliwell v. Halliwell, 741 A.2d 638, 645–46 (N.J. Super. Ct. App. Div. 1999).

not ultimately redound to the benefit of their children."[68] Rather, she argues, harsh and automatic enforcement measures that kick in as arrearages pile up create "perverse incentives that alienate parents from the formal economy and drive them underground — and away from their families."[69]

3. *Gender Roles.* Do you think the court in *Chen* would have ruled the same way if a man had decided to forego a substantial salary in favor of staying home with school-aged children? Was the court influenced by the fact that the husband also made a high salary?

4. *Class Concerns.* The Chen family had the luxury of having ample income available to support the children. What would the case look like if the father was earning $47,200, instead of $472,000? Would it still be deemed reasonable for the mother not to work outside of the home? If not, are families subject to different standards based on class?

PROBLEM

Landon graduated from law school in 2015 and began working as an associate in a large law firm with an annual salary of $140,000. He and his wife, Lucy, got divorced in 2016. Lucy was awarded primary physical custody of their two young children, and Landon was ordered to pay $2300/month in child support. Three years into his legal career, Landon had an epiphany. His work felt meaningless, and he said he was called to a different path. He quit his job and enrolled in seminary school to become a minister. He petitioned for a modification of his child support order on grounds that his desire to shift careers had resulted in a drastic reduction in income (none for the duration of the two-year degree and then an estimated $50,000 per year as a clergy person). Lucy opposed the petition, arguing that their children should not have to suffer because of their father's "mid-life crisis." Who should win and why?

C. Child Support Enforcement

Today, the child support enforcement system is a complicated one due to involvement of federal law, federal and state agencies concerned with the administration of public assistance, state family courts, and criminal law. As you read these materials, consider what the goals of this complex system are. Are they being met?

---

68. Ann Cammett, Deadbeats, Deadbrokes, and Prisoners, 18 Geo. J. Poverty L. & Pol'y 127, 129 (2011).

69. Id. at 130.

1. Criminal Nonsupport

WISCONSIN V. OAKLEY
629 N.W.2d 200 (Wis. 2001)

JON P. WILCOX, J.

We must decide whether as a condition of probation, a father of nine children, who has intentionally refused to pay child support, can be required to avoid having another child, unless he shows that he can support that child and his current children. . . .

I

David Oakley (Oakley), the petitioner, was initially charged with intentionally refusing to pay child support for his nine children he has fathered with four different women. The State subsequently charged Oakley with seven counts of intentionally refusing to provide child support as a repeat offender. His repeat offender status stemmed from intimidating two witnesses in a child abuse case — where one of the victims was his own child. Oakley and the State entered into a plea agreement on the seven counts, but the State, after learning that Oakley's probation in Sheboygan County was in the process of being revoked, moved at sentencing to withdraw the plea agreement. The circuit court for Manitowoc County, Fred H. Hazlewood, Judge, granted the State's motion. . . .

After taking into account Oakley's ability to work and his consistent disregard of the law and his obligations to his children, Judge Hazlewood observed that "if Mr. Oakley had paid something, had made an earnest effort to pay anything within his remote ability to pay, we wouldn't be sitting here," nor would the State argue for six years in prison. But Judge Hazlewood also recognized that "if Mr. Oakley goes to prison, he's not going to be in a position to pay any meaningful support for these children." Therefore, even though Judge Hazlewood acknowledged that Oakley's "defaults, are obvious, consistent, and inexcusable," he decided against sentencing Oakley to six years in prison consecutive to his three-year sentence in Sheboygan County, as the State had advocated. Instead, Judge Hazlewood sentenced Oakley to three years in prison on the first count, imposed and stayed an eight-year term on the two other counts, and imposed a five-year term of probation consecutive to his incarceration. Judge Hazlewood then imposed the condition at issue here: while on probation, Oakley cannot have any more children unless he demonstrates that he had the ability to support them and that he is supporting the children he already had. . . .

II

Oakley challenges the constitutionality of a condition of his probation for refusing to pay child support. The constitutionality of a condition of probation raises a question of law, which this court reviews independently without deference to the decisions of the circuit court or the court of appeals.

Refusal to pay child support by so-called "deadbeat parents" has fostered a crisis with devastating implications for our children. Of those single parent households with established child support awards or orders, approximately one-third did not receive any payment while another one-third received only partial payment. . . . Single mothers disproportionately bear the burden of nonpayment as the custodial parent. On top of the stress of being a single parent, the nonpayment of child support frequently presses single mothers below the poverty line. In fact, 32.1% of custodial mothers were below the poverty line in 1997, in comparison to only 10.7% of custodial fathers. Indeed, the payment of child support is widely regarded as an indispensable step in assisting single mothers to scale out of poverty, especially when their welfare benefits have been terminated due to new time limits.

The effects of the nonpayment of child support on our children are particularly troubling. In addition to engendering long-term consequences such as poor health, behavioral problems, delinquency and low educational attainment, inadequate child support is a direct contributor to childhood poverty. . . . There is little doubt that the payment of child support benefits poverty-stricken children the most. Enforcing child support orders thus has surfaced as a major policy directive in our society.

In view of the suffering children must endure when their noncustodial parent intentionally refuses to pay child support, it is not surprising that the legislature has attached severe sanctions to this crime. This statute makes it a Class E felony for any person "who intentionally fails for 120 or more consecutive days to provide spousal, grandchild or child support which the person knows or reasonably should know the person is legally obligated to provide. . . ." A Class E felony is punishable with "a fine not to exceed $10,000 or imprisonment not to exceed 2 years, or both." The legislature has amended this statute so that intentionally refusing to pay child support is now punishable by up to five years in prison.

But Wisconsin law is not so rigid as to mandate the severe sanction of incarceration as the only means of addressing a violation of § 948.22(2). In sentencing, a Wisconsin judge can take into account a broad array of factors, including the gravity of the offense and need for protection of the public and potential victims. Other factors — concerning the convicted individual — that a judge can consider include:

> the past record of criminal offenses; any history of undesirable behavior patterns; the defendant's personality, character and social traits; the results of a presentence investigation; the vicious or aggravated nature of the crime; the degree of defendant's culpability; the defendant's demeanor at trial; the defendant's age, educational background and employment record; the defendant's remorse, repentance and cooperativeness; the defendant's need for close rehabilitative control; the rights of public; and the length of pretrial detention.

After considering all these factors, a judge may decide to forgo the severe punitive sanction of incarceration and address the violation with the less restrictive alternative of probation coupled with specific conditions. . . .

The statute, then, grants a circuit court judge broad discretion in fashioning a convicted individual's conditions of probation. As we have previously observed, "the theory of the probation statute is to rehabilitate the defendant and protect society without placing the defendant in prison. To accomplish this theory, the circuit court is empowered . . . to fashion the terms of probation to meet the rehabilitative needs of the defendant." *State v. Gray*, 225 Wis. 2d 39 (1999). While rehabilitation is the goal of probation, judges must also concern themselves with the imperative of protecting society and potential victims. On this score, we have explained:

> The theory of probation contemplates that a person convicted of a crime who is responsive to supervision and guidance may be rehabilitated without placing him in prison. This involves a prediction by the sentencing court society will not be endangered by the convicted person not being incarcerated. This is risk that the legislature has empowered the courts to take in the exercise of their discretion. . . .
>
> If the convicted criminal is thus to escape the more severe punishment of imprisonment for his wrongdoing, society and the potential victims of his anti-social tendencies must be protected.

Thus, when a judge allows a convicted individual to escape a prison sentence and enjoy the relative freedom of probation, he or she must take reasonable judicial measures to protect society and potential victims from future wrongdoing. To that end — along with the goal of rehabilitation — the legislature has seen fit to grant circuit court judges broad discretion in setting the terms of probation. . . .

In the present case, the record indicates that Judge Hazlewood was familiar with Oakley's abysmal history prior to sentencing. The record reveals that Judge Hazlewood knew that Oakley had a number of support orders entered for his nine children, but he nevertheless continually refused to support them. He was aware that Oakley's probation for intimidating two witnesses in a child abuse case — where one of the witnesses was his own child and the victim — was in the process of being revoked. Judge Hazlewood was also apprised that Oakley had promised in the past to support his children, but those promises had failed to translate into the needed support. Moreover, he knew that Oakley had been employed and had no impediment preventing him from working. As the court of appeals observed in the witness intimidation case against Oakley, "the refusal to pay the fines and the victim intimidation both show Oakley's cavalier attitude toward the justice system. . . . Oakley needs to be rehabilitated from his perception that one may flout valid court orders and the judicial process with impunity and suffer no real consequence." Given his knowledge of Oakley's past conduct, Judge Hazlewood was prepared to fashion a sentence that would address Oakley's ongoing refusal to face his obligations to his nine children as required by law.

In doing so, Judge Hazlewood asserted that some prison time coupled with conditional probation might convince Oakley to stop victimizing his children. With probation, Judge Hazlewood sought to rehabilitate Oakley while protecting society and potential victims — Oakley's own children — from future wrongdoing. The conditions were designed to assist Oakley in conforming his conduct to the law. In Wisconsin, as expressed in Wis. Stat. § 948.22(2), we have condemned unequivocally intentional refusal to pay child support and allow for the severe sanction of prison to be imposed on offenders. Here, the judge fashioned a condition that was tailored to that particular crime, but avoided the more severe punitive alternative of the full statutory prison term through the rehabilitative tool of probation. At the same time, Judge Hazlewood sought to protect the victims of Oakley's crimes — Oakley's nine children.

But Oakley argues that the condition imposed by Judge Hazlewood violates his constitutional right to procreate. . . . It is well-established that convicted individuals do not enjoy the same degree of liberty as citizens who have not violated the law. We emphatically reject the novel idea that Oakley, who was convicted of intentionally failing to pay child support, has an absolute right to refuse to support his current nine children and any future children that he procreates, thereby adding more child victims to the list. . . .

Oakley fails to note that incarceration, by its very nature, deprives a convicted individual of the fundamental right to be free from physical restraint, which in turn encompasses and restricts other fundamental rights, such as the right to procreate. Therefore, given that a convicted felon does not stand in the same position as someone who has not been convicted of a crime, we have previously stated that "conditions of probation may impinge upon constitutional rights as long as they are not overly broad and are reasonably related to the person's rehabilitation." . . . Applying the relevant standard here, we find that the condition is not overly broad because it does not eliminate Oakley's ability to exercise his constitutional right to procreate. He can satisfy the condition of probation by making efforts to support his children as required by law. Judge Hazlewood placed no limit on the number of children Oakley could have. Instead, the requirement is that Oakley acknowledge the requirements of the law and support his present and any future children. If Oakley decides to continue his present course of conduct — intentionally refusing to pay child support — he will face eight years in prison regardless of how many children he has. Furthermore, this condition will expire at the end of his term of probation. He may then decide to have more children, but of course, if he continues to intentionally refuse to support his children, the State could charge him again under § 948.22(2). Rather, because Oakley can satisfy this condition by not intentionally refusing to support his current nine children and any future children as required by the law, we find that the condition is narrowly tailored to serve the State's compelling interest of having parents support their children. It is also narrowly tailored to serve the State's compelling interest in rehabilitating Oakley through probation rather than prison. The alternative to probation with conditions — incarceration for eight years — would have further victimized his children. And it is undoubtedly much broader than this conditional impingement on his procreative freedom for it would deprive him of his fundamental right to be free from physical restraint. Simply stated, Judge Hazlewood preserved much of Oakley's liberty by imposing probation with conditions rather than the more punitive option of imprisonment.

Moreover, the condition is reasonably related to the goal of rehabilitation. A condition is reasonably related to the goal of rehabilitation if it assists the convicted individual in conforming his or her conduct to the law. Here, Oakley was convicted of intentionally refusing to support his children. The condition at bar will prevent him from adding victims if he continues to intentionally refuse to support his children. As the State argues, the condition essentially bans Oakley from violating the law again. Future violations of the law would be detrimental to Oakley's rehabilitation, which necessitates preventing him from continuing to disregard its dictates. Accordingly, this condition is reasonably related to his rehabilitation because it will assist Oakley in conforming his conduct to the law. . . .

WILLIAM A. BABLITCH, J. (concurring).

This is a very difficult case, one in which courts are understandably reluctant to get involved.

It is important to note at the outset what this case is all about: It is about a father of nine children who intentionally refuses to support them and was convicted of such.

The two dissents frame the issue in such a way that Oakley's intentional refusal to pay support evolves into an inability to pay support. This case is not at all about an inability to pay support; it is about the intentional refusal to pay support. The difference between an intentional refusal to pay support and an inability to pay support is highly significant and, for me, decisive.

If this case was about the right of the state to limit a person's right to procreate based on his ability to pay support, the position articulated by Justice Bradley, I would in all likelihood join her dissent.

If this case was about the right of the state to prohibit a person's right to procreate based on his likely unwillingness or inability to support a child financially in the future, Justice Sykes' position, I would in all likelihood join her dissent.

This case is about a man who intentionally refuses to pay support regardless of his ability to do so. That was the dilemma faced by the sentencing court, and that is what led to the court's order.

I conclude that the harm to others who cannot protect themselves is so overwhelmingly apparent and egregious here that there is no room for question. Here is a man who has shown himself time and again to be totally and completely irresponsible. He lives only for himself and the moment, with no regard to the consequences of his actions and taking no responsibility for them. He intentionally refuses to pay support and has been convicted of that felony. The harm that he has done to his nine living children by failing to support them is patent and egregious. He has abused at least one of them. Under certain conditions, it is overwhelmingly obvious that any child he fathers in the future is doomed to a future of neglect, abuse, or worse. That as yet unborn child is a victim from the day it is born. . . .

ANN WALSH BRADLEY, J. (dissenting).

I begin by emphasizing the right that is at issue: the right to have children.

The circuit court's order forbidding Oakley from having another child until he first establishes his ability to support all his children is unconstitutional. Even the circuit court judge who imposed the condition acknowledged that Oakley will be unable to meet this condition. The probation condition is not narrowly drawn to serve the governmental interest at stake. Additionally, aside from the constitutional infirmities, such a condition of probation entails practical problems and carries unacceptable collateral consequences. . . .

The United States Supreme Court has described the right to have children as a "basic liberty" that is "fundamental to the very existence and survival of the [human] race." *Skinner [v. State of Oklahoma]*, 316 U.S. 535, [541 (1942)]. The right is embodied in the sphere of personal privacy protected from unjustified governmental intrusion by the Due Process Clause of the Fourteenth Amendment. This court, in a case involving involuntary sterilization, has emphasized that the right of a citizen to procreate is central to the zone of privacy protected by the Constitution:

> If the right of privacy means anything, it is the right of the individual, married or single, to be free from unwarranted governmental intrusion into matters so fundamentally affecting a person as the decision whether to bear or beget a child.

Because the right implicated by the condition of probation in this case is one that is central to the concept of fundamental liberty, the state action infringing upon that right is subject to heightened scrutiny.

It is important to bear in mind exactly what the circuit court order proscribed. The circuit court order forbids Oakley from fathering another child until he can first establish the financial ability to support his children. Oakley is not prohibited from having intercourse, either indiscriminately or irresponsibly. Rather, the condition of probation is not triggered until Oakley's next child is born.

Curiously, the condition the majority is upholding is not the condition that the circuit court imposed. Contrary to the majority's characterization of the condition of probation (compare majority op. P6 with P20), the circuit court imposed in its January 13, 1999, Judgment of Conviction and Sentence the following condition:

> Defendant is ordered not to have any further children while on probation unless it can be shown to the Court that he is meeting the needs of his other children and can meet the needs of this one.

The majority and both concurrences frame the condition as if it only forbids an intentional refusal to pay support. This is not the case.

While on its face the order leaves room for the slight possibility that Oakley may establish the financial means to support his children, the order is essentially a prohibition on the right to have children. Oakley readily admits that unless he wins the lottery, he will likely never be able to establish that ability. The circuit court understood the impossibility of Oakley satisfying this financial requirement when it imposed the condition. The court explained that "it would always be a struggle to support these children and in truth [Oakley] could not reasonably be expected to fully support them." Stressing the realities of Oakley's situation, the circuit court explained:

> You know and I know you're probably never going to make 75 or 100 thousand dollar a year. You're going to struggle to make 25 or 30. And by the time you take care of your taxes and your social security, there isn't a whole lot to go around, and then you've got to ship it out to various children.

In light of the circuit court's recognition of Oakley's inability to meet the condition of probation, the prohibition cannot be considered a narrowly drawn means of advancing the state's interest in ensuring support for Oakley's children.

Rather than juxtapose the means chosen in the instant case with the alternatives suggested in *Zablocki v. Redhail*, 434 U.S. 374 (1978), the majority compares the infringement of Oakley's reproductive liberty with the loss of liberty he would suffer had the circuit court chosen to imprison him. It is true that if Oakley were imprisoned he would suffer an incidental inability to exercise his procreative rights. However, the fact of the matter is that Oakley has not been imprisoned. While the State has chosen not to exercise control over Oakley's body by depriving him of the freedom from restraint, it does not necessarily follow that the State may opt to exercise unlimited control over his right to procreate.

The narrowly drawn means described by the Supreme Court in *Zablocki* still exist today and are appropriate means of advancing the state's interest in a manner that does not impair the fundamental right to procreate. These means, as well as other conditions of probation or criminal penalties, are available in the present case. . . .

In light of the constitutional problems and other dilemmas posed by a condition that limits a probationer's right to father a child without first establishing the financial ability to support his children, it is not surprising that the majority is the sole court in this country to conclude that the condition is constitutional. The majority fails to cite any case law in which a court has allowed the right to have children to be conditioned upon financial status. It does not because it cannot. There is no precedent to cite.

Let there be no question that I agree with the majority that David Oakley's conduct cannot be condoned. It is irresponsible and criminal. However, we must keep in mind what is really at stake in this case. The fundamental right to have children, shared by us all, is damaged by today's decision.

DIANE S. SYKES, J. (dissenting).

Can the State criminalize the birth of a child to a convicted felon who is likely to be unwilling or unable to adequately support the child financially? That is essentially the crux of the circuit court order in this case, or at least its apparent practical effect.

Here, as in *Zablocki*, there are less restrictive means available to achieve the State's objectives short of encumbering what everyone agrees is a fundamental human right. As noted by Justice Bradley in her dissent, the circuit court can order Oakley to maintain full-time employment — or even two jobs — as a condition of probation, and to execute a wage assignment to pay off his child support arrearages and satisfy his ongoing support obligations. His tax refunds can be intercepted annually. Liens can be placed on his personal property, and he can be found in civil contempt. He can be criminally prosecuted for any additional intentional failures to support his children, present or future. His probation can be revoked if he fails to maintain employment and make support payments. Granted, Oakley's arrearages are so great, and his history so troublesome, that these means may not ultimately be completely successful in achieving the State's objective of collecting child support. But the same was true in *Zablocki*, and the Supreme Court nevertheless found the statute in that case unconstitutional. I reach the same conclusion here.

This condition of probation subjects Oakley to imprisonment if he fathers another child without advance permission from the State. Illegitimacy and child poverty, abuse, and neglect are among our society's most serious and intractable problems. Conditioning the right to procreate upon proof of financial or other fitness may appear on the surface to be an appropriate solution in extreme cases such as this, but it is unprecedented in this country, and for good reason. The State can order non-custodial parents to financially support their children, and can criminally prosecute those who intentionally do not. The State can remove a child from a parent's custody when the child is in need of protection from parental abuse, neglect, or abandonment, and can criminally prosecute parents who mistreat their children. But I know of no authority for the proposition that the State can order that a child not be conceived or born, even to an abysmally irresponsible parent, unless the State first grants its consent.

Although Oakley is a convicted felon and therefore may constitutionally be subjected to limitations on the fundamental human liberties the rest of us freely enjoy, he cannot constitutionally be banned from having further children without court permission.

NOTES AND QUESTIONS

1. *Constitutionality of Barring Procreation.* In a part of the opinion not excerpted, the majority in *Oakley* sought to distinguish Zablocki v. Redhail, in which the Supreme Court held that a man could not be denied a marriage license due to child support arrearages that resulted in his children's requiring public assistance. Isn't a ban on procreation a more serious intrusion into his protected liberty than the denial of a marriage license? The majority held that the probation condition did not violate Oakley's constitutional rights because it "does not eliminate Oakley's ability to exercise his constitutional right to procreate," as he can "satisfy the condition of probation by making efforts to support his children as required by law." Moreover, the majority characterized the probation term as placing "no limit on the number of children Oakley could have. Instead, the requirement is that Oakley acknowledge the requirements of the law and support his present and any future children." Because, in the court's view, Oakely had the ability to end the condition "by not intentionally refusing to support his current nine children and any future children as required by the law," the procreation term was "narrowly tailored to serve the State's compelling interest of having parents support their children." Are you persuaded by the majority's analysis?

The majority compared probation with conditions to the more physically constraining punishment of prison. Is this comparison apt for determining the constitutionality of the probation condition? In dissent, Justice Bradley asserted that the relevant comparison should be how the encroachment on Oakley's procreative freedom compares to other means short of imprisonment the state might deploy: "It is true that if Oakley were imprisoned he would suffer an incidental inability to exercise his procreative rights. . . . While the State has chosen not to exercise control over Oakley's body by depriving him of the freedom from restraint, it does not necessarily follow that the State may opt to exercise unlimited control over his right to procreate." Elsewhere in her dissent, Justice Bradley pointed to the narrower means described by the Court in *Zablocki* that were available to the state to advance its interest in providing support for children but did not encroach on procreation — measures like garnishment or wage assignment, liens on personal property, and civil contempt.[70]

2. *Federal Criminal Law.* Under the Child Support Recovery Act (CSRA), it is a crime to willfully fail to pay past-due child support for a child who lives in another state.[71] As amended by the Deadbeat Parents Punishment Act of 1998, the failure

---

70. State v. Oakley, 629 N.W.2d 200, 218 (2002) (Bradley, J., dissenting).
71. See 18 U.S.C. § 228 (2018) (support must be unpaid for more than a year and exceed $5000).

to pay for more than two years or a debt greater than $10,000 can be charged as a felony.[72]

3.   *State Criminal Nonsupport.* All states have laws making it a crime for parents to fail to pay child support. Statutes vary in levels of fines and lengths of incarceration, with some, like California, treating nonsupport as a misdemeanor, and others, like Oklahoma, treating it as a felony.[73] Generally, the state must prove that "(1) the defendant acted knowingly or intentionally; and (2) the defendant failed to provide support."[74] Does it matter whether the person alleged not to have paid has the ability to pay? As observed by Professor Courtney Lollar, "[u]nder many state child support laws, judges are not required to determine whether a person alleged to be delinquent on child support payments has the ability to make those payments. Either the fact of a valid child support order or the noncustodial parent's knowledge of such an order is sufficient evidence for a judge to find criminal liability."[75] Do you agree with this approach?

4.   *Civil Contempt.* Contempt proceedings have become a substitute for criminal nonsupport actions. Although contempt is punishable criminally, Professor Elizabeth Patterson notes that "in the child support enforcement system, contempt usually proceeds as a civil rather than a criminal matter."[76] As Professor Elizabeth Katz has shown, in the early twentieth century, family support obligations were routinely enforced under quasi-criminal and criminal laws in courts of domestic relations created primarily for that purpose.[77] Over time, social reformers and legal experts recognized that the costs and stigma of criminal law were counterproductive in securing family support. Consequently, they enacted civil support laws and converted family courts into nominally civil tribunals. The reformed family courts retained the power to incarcerate parents for child support nonpayment, though technically through contempt proceedings that required fewer procedural protections than in criminal prosecutions. Today, both criminal statutes and civil contempt proceedings are available to address child support debt, but criminal law is rarely used. It is estimated that thousands of parents (mostly fathers) are incarcerated for nonpayment of child support through civil contempt hearings each year.[78]

5.   *Punishing Poverty.* To what extent are nonsupport proceedings punishing poor people for having children? Patterson criticizes the use of contempt on these

---

72. See 18 U.S.C. § 228(a)(3) (2018).

73. Cal. Penal Code §270 (2020); Okla. Stat. tit. 21, § 853 (2020).

74. Nat'l Conf. of State Legislatures, Criminal Nonsupport and Child Support (June 8, 2015), https://www.ncsl.org/research/human-services/criminal-nonsupport-and-child-support.aspx.

75. Cortney E. Lollar, Criminalizing (Poor) Fatherhood, 70 Ala. L. Rev. 125, 143–44 (2018).

76. Elizabeth G. Patterson, *Turner* in the Trenches: A Study of How Turner v. Rogers Affected Child Support Contempt Proceedings, 25 Geo. J. on Poverty L. & Pol'y 75, 78 (2017).

77. See Elizabeth D. Katz, Criminal Law in A Civil Guise: The Evolution of Family Courts and Support Laws, 86 U. Chi. L. Rev. 1241 (2019).

78. See id. at 1300.

grounds: "[C]ivil contempt is supposed to be used to coerce a person to do something that he is able, but unwilling, to do. . . . [I]f the contemnor's failure to pay the sums ordered by the court is simply a result of inability to pay, his incarceration can only be characterized as imprisonment for being poor."[79] Does the criminalization of nonsupport further stigmatize poor parents? Consider Lollar's critique:

> [T]he result in Oakley should not be a surprise, as it simply represents the ultimate realization of a criminal-law-based deterrent approach. Criminal convictions are intended to convey moral condemnation and judgment. . . . If a poor father is convicted for engaging in careless sex that resulted in a child he is unable to financially support, he faces not only incarceration but also the fairly unshakeable lifelong stigma of a criminal conviction. We have deemed that to be an appropriate response because of our moral judgments and beliefs about sex and fatherhood.[80]

What social norms are parents, particularly fathers, flouting when they do not pay child support?

6. *Incarceration and Child Support.* While national figures on the prevalence of incarceration from failure to pay child support are not available, a study of county jails in South Carolina found that on a typical day, 14-16 percent of those incarcerated were being held for civil contempt for nonpayment of child support.[81] Nationally, more than half of incarcerated individuals have children under the age of eighteen, with one study showing that a quarter of those incarcerated had a child support obligation.[82] "On average, an incarcerated parent with a child support order has the potential to leave prison with nearly $20,000 in child support debt, having entered the system with around half that amount owed."[83]

2. Civil Enforcement System

When Congress became involved in child support law, it not only aimed to affect the frequency and size of awards, but it also aimed to facilitate enforcement. In 1975, Congress created the Office of Child Support Enforcement as Part D of the Social Security Act ("the IV-D program"). State-based IV-D offices are heavily involved in establishing child support in welfare cases, and they also provide assistance to any payee with a child support order. Since 1975, Congress has amended

---

79. Elizabeth G. Patterson, Civil Contempt and the Indigent Child Support Obligor: The Silent Return of Debtor's Prison, 18 Cornell J.L. & Pub. Pol'y 95, 97–98 (2008).

80. Lollar, supra note 75, at 164–65.

81. Patterson, *Turner* in the Trenches, supra note 76, at 80–81 (discussing surveys from 2005 and 2009 on the number of persons incarcerated on contempt charges based on a failure to pay court-ordered support).

82. Nat'l Conf. of State Legislatures, Child Support and Incarceration (Mar. 4, 2019), https://www.ncsl.org/research/human-services/child-support-and-incarceration.aspx.

83. Id.

the enforcement rules several times to give states added incentives to increase their enforcement efforts and give parents added incentives to cooperate in obtaining orders and enforcing them. Congress has used both carrots and sticks to increase collections. For example, states get performance incentives to improve collection rates. Mothers get incentives if they cooperate in establishing paternity — the first step toward getting a child support award. Responding to those incentives, states have passed tougher laws for parents who do not satisfy their child support obligations. Federal agencies provide technical assistance to states to help locate parents, stay abreast of their employment changes, and coordinate enforcement penalties.

Between federal mandates and state programs, parents who fall into arrears on their child support obligations can face a variety of civil and criminal consequences. A parent who has more than $10,000 in unpaid child support for a child in another state can be charged with a federal felony. Any parent with an existing order can have their wages garnished, so that payments go directly from the employer to the custodial parent. Depending on the state and the circumstances, the obligor may pay the state, who will pass the money along to the custodial parent, which allows the state to track compliance. A parent in arrears can lose a driver's license or other civil privileges, can face civil contempt charges, and can end up jailed for nonsupport. Is jailing a parent for nonpayment of child support a good remedy? Should courts consider the collateral consequences of incarceration, such as the loss of a job, that might impair the parent's future ability to pay support?[84]

In the first decades of Congress's involvement, the push to continually make child support enforcement laws stricter was relatively uncontroversial. Finding and getting money from "AWOL fathers" has been one of the most "successful and bipartisan social policy crusades."[85] The sheriff's office in one New Jersey county conducted a raid after Mother's Day in 1998, arresting 629 "deadbeats" (forty-one were women) and collecting more than $88,000 in back-owed support. Those who couldn't pay up were "sent to jail until they came up with the money or agreed to a payment plan."[86] The Bush Administration heralded a "nationwide sweep" of deadbeat dads conducted by federal agents in 2002, carrying out the President's vow to use federal criminal law aggressively to get men who "repeatedly flouted state court orders."[87] The focus in these raids was on fathers who had the ability to pay, but didn't. But the federal-state child support enforcement system mostly catches poorer parents in its net. A 2007 study by the Urban Institute found that most

---

84. See Frances Robles & Shaila Dewan, Skip Child Support. Go to Jail. Lose Job. Repeat., N.Y. Times, Apr. 19, 2015, at A1.

85. Blaine Harden, Finding Common Ground on Poor Deadbeat Dads, N.Y. Times, Feb. 3, 2002, at D3.

86. Karen Demasters, Deadbeat Dads (and Moms) Are Rounded Up in Raids, N.Y. Times, May 17, 1998, at M6.

87. Robert Pear, U.S. Agents Arrest Dozens of Fathers in Support Cases, N.Y. Times, Aug. 19, 2002, at A1.

arrears were held by parents with no or low income.[88] Congress's original impetus for getting involved in child support was to reduce welfare spending. Under the current system, most of the money collected on behalf of custodial parents who are on public assistance goes to reimburse the government for past assistance.[89] The families get little or no benefit from the enforcement efforts, and sometimes the efforts themselves harm the children by landing their father in legal tangles or even in jail. A commissioner of the federal Office of Child Support Enforcement made the following observation: "While every parent has a responsibility to support their kids to the best of their ability, the tools developed in the 1990s are designed for people who have money. Jail is appropriate for someone who is actively hiding assets, not appropriate for someone who couldn't pay the order in the first place."[90] Do you agree? If so, what tools might be more appropriate?

TURNER V. ROGERS
564 U.S. 431 (2011)

JUSTICE BREYER delivered the opinion of the Court. . .

In June 2003 a South Carolina family court entered an order, which (as amended) required petitioner, Michael Turner, to pay $51.73 per week to respondent, Rebecca Rogers, to help support their child. . . . Over the next three years, Turner repeatedly failed to pay the amount due and was held in contempt on five occasions. The first four times he was sentenced to 90 days' imprisonment, but he ultimately paid the amount due (twice without being jailed, twice after spending two or three days in custody). The fifth time he did not pay but completed a 6–month sentence.

After his release in 2006 Turner remained in arrears. On March 27, 2006, the clerk issued a new "show cause" order. . . . Turner's civil contempt hearing took place on January 3, 2008. Turner and Rogers were present, each without representation by counsel.

The hearing was brief. The court clerk said that Turner was $5,728.76 behind in his payments. The judge asked Turner if there was "anything you want to say." Turner replied:

> "Well, when I first got out, I got back on dope. I done meth, smoked pot and everything else, and I paid a little bit here and there. And, when I finally did

---

88. Elaine Sorensen et al., Urban Inst., Assessing Child Support Arrears in Nine Large States and the Nation 22 (Jan. 14, 2009).

89. Prior to 1996, federal law mandated that states grant a $50/month "disregard," which allowed a parent receiving public assistance to keep the first $50 collected in child support before making any welfare reimbursement. The 1996 welfare reform repealed that mandate; states now have discretion whether to permit any disregard and in what amount. See Personal Responsibility and Work Opportunity Reconciliation Act, Pub. L. No. 104-193, 110 Stat. 2105 (1996).

90. Robles & Dewan, supra note 84 (quoting Vicki Turetsky).

> get to working, I broke my back, back in September. I filed for disability and
> SSI. And, I didn't get straightened out off the dope until I broke my back and
> laid up for two months. And, now I'm off the dope and everything. I just
> hope that you give me a chance. I don't know what else to say. I mean, I know
> I done wrong, and I should have been paying and helping her, and I'm sorry.
> I mean, dope had a hold to me."

The judge then said, "[o]kay," and asked Rogers if she had anything to say. After a
brief discussion of federal benefits, the judge stated:

> "If there's nothing else, this will be the Order of the Court. I find the Defendant
> in willful contempt. I'm [going to] sentence him to twelve months in the
> Oconee County Detention Center. He may purge himself of the contempt
> and avoid the sentence by having a zero balance on or before his release. I've
> also placed a lien on any SSI or other benefits."

The judge added that Turner would not receive good-time or work credits, but "[i]f
you've got a job, I'll make you eligible for work release." When Turner asked why
he could not receive good-time or work credits, the judge said, "[b]ecause that's my
ruling."

The court made no express finding concerning Turner's ability to pay his arrearage (though Turner's wife had voluntarily submitted a copy of Turner's application
for disability benefits). Nor did the judge ask any follow-up questions or otherwise
address the ability-to-pay issue. After the hearing, the judge filled out a prewritten
form titled "Order for Contempt of Court," which included the statement:

> "Defendant (was) (was not) gainfully employed and/or (had) (did not have)
> the ability to make these support payments when due." But the judge left this
> statement as is without indicating whether Turner was able to make support
> payments.

We must decide whether the Due Process Clause grants an indigent defendant,
such as Turner, a right to state-appointed counsel at a civil contempt proceeding,
which may lead to his incarceration. This Court's precedents provide no definitive
answer to that question. This Court has long held that the Sixth Amendment grants
an indigent defendant the right to state-appointed counsel in a *criminal* case. And
we have held that this same rule applies to *criminal contempt* proceedings (other
than summary proceedings).

But the Sixth Amendment does not govern civil cases. Civil contempt differs
from criminal contempt in that it seeks only to "coerc[e] the defendant to do" what
a court had previously ordered him to do. *Gompers v. Bucks Stove & Range Co.*,
221 U.S. 418, 442 (1911). A court may not impose punishment "in a civil contempt
proceeding when it is clearly established that the alleged contemnor is unable to
comply with the terms of the order." *Hicks v. Feiock*, 485 U.S. 624 (1988). And once
a civil contemnor complies with the underlying order, he is purged of the contempt

and is free. *Id.*, at 633, 108 S.Ct. 1423 (he "carr[ies] the keys of [his] prison in [his] own pockets").

Consequently, the Court has made clear (in a case not involving the right to counsel) that, where civil contempt is at issue, the Fourteenth Amendment's Due Process Clause allows a State to provide fewer procedural protections than in a criminal case.

This Court has decided only a handful of cases that more directly concern a right to counsel in civil matters. And the application of those decisions to the present case is not clear. On the one hand, the Court has held that the Fourteenth Amendment requires the State to pay for representation by counsel in a *civil* "juvenile delinquency" proceeding (which could lead to incarceration). Further, in *Lassiter v. Department of Social Servs. of Durham Cty.*, 452 U.S. 18 (1981), a case that focused upon civil proceedings leading to loss of parental rights, the Court wrote that the

> "pre-eminent generalization that emerges from this Court's precedents on an indigent's right to appointed counsel is that such a right has been recognized to exist only where the litigant may lose his physical liberty if he loses the litigation."

And the Court then drew from these precedents "the presumption that an indigent litigant has a right to appointed counsel only when, if he loses, he may be deprived of his physical liberty." . . .

We believe those statements are best read as pointing out that the Court previously had found a right to counsel "*only*" in cases involving incarceration, not that a right to counsel exists in *all* such cases. . . .

Civil contempt proceedings in child support cases constitute one part of a highly complex system designed to assure a noncustodial parent's regular payment of funds typically necessary for the support of his children. Often the family receives welfare support from a state-administered federal program, and the State then seeks reimbursement from the noncustodial parent. Other times the custodial parent (often the mother, but sometimes the father, a grandparent, or another person with custody) does not receive government benefits and is entitled to receive the support payments herself.

The Federal Government has created an elaborate procedural mechanism designed to help both the government and custodial parents to secure the payments to which they are entitled. These systems often rely upon wage withholding, expedited procedures for modifying and enforcing child support orders, and automated data processing. But sometimes States will use contempt orders to ensure that the custodial parent receives support payments or the government receives reimbursement. Although some experts have criticized this last-mentioned procedure, and the Federal Government believes that "the routine use of contempt for nonpayment of child support is likely to be an ineffective strategy," the Government also tells us that "coercive enforcement remedies, such as contempt, have a role to play." South Carolina, which relies heavily on contempt proceedings, agrees that they are an important tool.

We here consider an indigent's right to paid counsel at such a contempt proceeding. It is a civil proceeding. And we consequently determine the "specific dictates of due process" by examining the "distinct factors" that this Court has previously found useful in deciding what specific safeguards the Constitution's Due Process Clause requires in order to make a civil proceeding fundamentally fair. *Mathews v. Eldridge*, 424 U.S. 319, 335 (1976). As relevant here those factors include (1) the nature of "the private interest that will be affected," (2) the comparative "risk" of an "erroneous deprivation" of that interest with and without "additional or substitute procedural safeguards," and (3) the nature and magnitude of any countervailing interest in not providing "additional or substitute procedural requirement[s]."

The "private interest that will be affected" . . . consists of an indigent defendant's loss of personal liberty through imprisonment. . . . Given the importance of the interest at stake, it is obviously important to ensure accurate decisionmaking in respect to the key "ability to pay" question. Moreover, the fact that ability to comply marks a dividing line between civil and criminal contempt, reinforces the need for accuracy. . . . And since 70% of child support arrears nationwide are owed by parents with either no reported income or income of $10,000 per year or less, the issue of ability to pay may arise fairly often.

On the other hand, the Due Process Clause does not always require the provision of counsel in civil proceedings where incarceration is threatened. And in determining whether the Clause requires a right to counsel here, we must take account of opposing interests, as well as consider the probable value of "additional or substitute procedural safeguards."

Doing so, we find three related considerations that, when taken together, argue strongly against the Due Process Clause requiring the State to provide indigents with counsel in every proceeding of the kind before us.

First, the critical question likely at issue in these cases concerns, as we have said, the defendant's ability to pay. That question is often closely related to the question of the defendant's indigence. But when the right procedures are in place, indigence can be a question that in many — but not all — cases is sufficiently straightforward to warrant determination *prior* to providing a defendant with counsel, even in a criminal case. Federal law, for example, requires a criminal defendant to provide information showing that he is indigent, and therefore entitled to state-funded counsel, *before* he can receive that assistance.

Second, sometimes, as here, the person opposing the defendant at the hearing is not the government represented by counsel but the custodial parent *un*represented by counsel. The custodial parent, perhaps a woman with custody of one or more children, may be relatively poor, unemployed, and unable to afford counsel. Yet she may have encouraged the court to enforce its order through contempt. She may be able to provide the court with significant information. And the proceeding is ultimately for her benefit.

A requirement that the State provide counsel to the noncustodial parent in these cases could create an asymmetry of representation that would . . . "alter significantly the nature of the proceeding." Doing so could mean a degree of formality or delay that would unduly slow payment to those immediately in need. And, perhaps more important for present purposes, doing so could make the proceedings *less* fair overall, increasing the risk of a decision that would erroneously deprive a family of the support it is entitled to receive. The needs of such families play an important role in our analysis.

Third, as the Solicitor General points out, there is available a set of "substitute procedural safeguards," which, if employed together, can significantly reduce the risk of an erroneous deprivation of liberty. They can do so, moreover, without incurring some of the drawbacks inherent in recognizing an automatic right to counsel. Those safeguards include (1) notice to the defendant that his "ability to pay" is a critical issue in the contempt proceeding; (2) the use of a form (or the equivalent) to elicit relevant financial information; (3) an opportunity at the hearing for the defendant to respond to statements and questions about his financial status (*e.g.*, those triggered by his responses on the form); and (4) an express finding by the court that the defendant has the ability to pay. . . .

While recognizing the strength of Turner's arguments, we ultimately believe that the three considerations we have just discussed must carry the day. In our view, a categorical right to counsel in proceedings of the kind before us would carry with it disadvantages (in the form of unfairness and delay) that, in terms of ultimate fairness, would deprive it of significant superiority over the alternatives that we have mentioned. We consequently hold that the Due Process Clause does not *automatically* require the provision of counsel at civil contempt proceedings to an indigent individual who is subject to a child support order, even if that individual faces incarceration (for up to a year). In particular, that Clause does not require the provision of counsel where the opposing parent or other custodian (to whom support funds are owed) is not represented by counsel and the State provides alternative procedural safeguards equivalent to those we have mentioned (adequate notice of the importance of ability to pay, fair opportunity to present, and to dispute, relevant information, and court findings).

We do not address civil contempt proceedings where the underlying child support payment is owed to the State, for example, for reimbursement of welfare funds paid to the parent with custody. Those proceedings more closely resemble debt-collection proceedings. The government is likely to have counsel or some other competent representative. And this kind of proceeding is not before us. Neither do we address what due process requires in an unusually complex case where a defendant "can fairly be represented only by a trained advocate."

The record indicates that Turner received neither counsel nor the benefit of alternative procedures like those we have described. He did not receive clear notice that his ability to pay would constitute the critical question in his civil contempt proceeding. No one provided him with a form (or the equivalent) designed to elicit information about his financial circumstances. The court did not find that Turner was able to pay his arrearage, but instead left the relevant "finding" section of the contempt order blank. The court nonetheless found Turner in contempt and ordered him incarcerated. Under these circumstances Turner's incarceration violated the Due Process Clause. . . .

NOTES AND QUESTIONS

1. *Right to Counsel.* Are you convinced that a contempt hearing over unpaid child support is sufficiently simple that a lay person could manage without a lawyer? How might a lawyer's involvement change the nature of the proceeding or the outcome?

2. *Effects of Federal Intervention.* The federal government's involvement in child support enforcement has resulted in an increase in the number of eligible parents with child support awards and in increased collections, but not by leaps and bounds. A 1981 Census report found 8.4 million women raising children with an absent father. Only 59 percent had a child support order in place. Twenty-eight percent of those who were supposed to receive payments that year did not receive a penny.[91] Poor women fared worse; only 39.7 percent of women below the poverty level had an award; and nearly 40 percent of those received nothing at all in 1981.

By 1989, almost 10 million women were raising children as single parents. The child support numbers had improved slightly. Fifty-eight percent of single mothers had a child support award, and of these, only 24 percent were getting nothing. Among poor women, the rate of awards had increased (43.3 percent) and the rate of non-collection had decreased (31.7 percent).[92] The improvement in awards and collections has not been steadily linear. In 2017, the proportion of custodial mothers with a child support award decreased to 51.4 percent, from a high of 64.2 percent in 1994.[93] The proportion of custodial fathers with a support award has held steady around 40 percent, although the number of custodial

---

91. See U.S. Census Bureau, Current Population Reports, Special Studies, Series 9-23, Child Support and Alimony: 1981, at 2 tbl.A (1985).

92. U.S. Census Bureau, Current Population Reports, Series P-60, Child Support and Alimony: 1989, at 4 tbl. B. On general trends, see Ann Nichols-Casebolt & Irwin Garfinkel, Trends in Paternity Adjudications and Child Support Awards, https://www.irp.wisc.edu/publications/dps/pdfs/dp87989.pdf.

93. Grall, supra note 45, at 7. On reasons why so many women do not have child support in place, see Chien-Chung Huang, "Why Doesn't She Have a Support Order?" Personal Choice or Objective Constraint, 54 Fam. Rel. 547 (2005).

fathers has increased.[94] Moreover, custodial parents who had a sup[...]
received no actual support was 30.2 percent in 2017, an increase fr[...]
in 1993.[95] There are significant racial and ethnic variations in thes[...]
non-Hispanic white custodial parents more likely to have an order [...]
to receive support than all other groups.

3. *Visitation and Child Support.* Legally, there is no connection between visitation rights and child support.[96] Among noncustodial parents subject either to an
agreement or order to pay child support, 19.4 percent have neither shared custody
nor noncustodial visitation.[97] Although the causal connection is not well understood, there is a correlation between fathers who have formal custody or visitation
orders and those who fulfill their financial obligations.[98] Some efforts have been
made in recent years to structure the law in such a way as to promote ties between
fathers and their children, and not to focus merely on repaying the government
and punishing wrong-doers. Consider the observations of sociologists Kathryn
Edin and Timothy Nelson, who conducted a field study of fatherhood among the
urban poor:

> Most noncustodial fathers end up contributing very little to the support
> of their children over the eighteen-year span for which society holds them
> responsible. This leads to the question of how these men — who really want
> the kids — view the obligations that the fatherhood role typically carries.
> Almost no one among the fathers we spoke with believe that good fathers
> should "leave everything to the mother." Good fathers, they say, should pro-
> vide. But the definition of good provider is unexpectedly broad. First, in the
> terms used by one father, he must be "all man" and provide for himself, not
> relying too much on his mother or his girlfriend. Though this point may
> seem obvious, it was often made explicit in our men's accounts, presumably
> because for many it is no easy feat. Second, he must mollify those in his cur-
> rent household by paying some of the bills plus a little something for her kids
> now and then. After settling these accounts, he can offer his nonresident
> children some portion of what remains. This sharply abridged sense of finan-
> cial responsibility — "doing the best I can . . . with what is left over" is what
> drives both men's sense of obligation and their financial behavior.

---

94. Grall, supra note 45, at 13.

95. Id. at 7-8.

96. See Ira Mark Ellman, Should Visitation Denial Affect the Obligation to Pay Support?, 36 Ariz. St.
L.J. 661 (2004).

97. Grall, supra note 45, at 7 & tbl. 8.

98. See Chien-Chung Huang, Mothers' Reports of Nonresident Fathers' Involvement with Their
Children: Revisiting the Relationship Between Child Support Payment and Visitation, 58 Fam. Rel. 54
(2009); Lenna Nepomnyaschy, Child Support and Father-Child Contact: Testing Reciprocal Pathways,
44 Demography 93 (2007); Judith A. Seltzer et al., Family Ties After Divorce: The Relationship Between
Visiting and Paying Child Support, 51 J. Marriage & Fam. 1013 (1989); Heather Koball & Desiree Principe,
Urban Inst., Do Nonresident Fathers Who Pay Child Support Visit Their Children More?, Series B., No.
B-44, at 4 (Mar. 2002).

American society tends to assess the unwed father's moral worth with a single question: how much money does he provide? But the men that we interviewed in Philadelphia and Camden vehemently reject the notion that they should be treated as mere paychecks. Instead, they desire, and even demand, at least a slice of the "whole fatherhood experience" in exchange for a portion of their hard-earned cash. When mom acts as gatekeeper or when a child refuses contact, even this relatively weak breadwinner norm can be eroded or nullified.[99]

How might the legal system do better to promote connections between fathers and their children and ensure adequate financial support for the children?

Laurie S. Kohn, Engaging Men as Fathers: The Courts, the Law, and Father-Absence in Low-Income Families
35 Cardozo L. Rev. 511 (2013)

Father-absence is an ever-increasing trend in our country. Exacerbated by poverty, father-absence leaves a disproportionately high percentage of low-income children living with their mothers and enjoying little to no paternal contact. Many sociological, cultural, and economic factors contribute to the likelihood of father-absence and drive fathers away from their children even before they have forged any relationship at all. As such, father-absence is commonly considered to be a non-legal problem. However, the cohort of fathers who become absent only after interactions with the custody and child support systems challenges that characterization and raises questions about the potential relationship between fathers' involvement with the legal system and their subsequent absence.

Engaged fathers can disappear from the lives of their children after custody proceedings or after the imposition or enforcement of child support obligations. Even fathers who litigate aggressively for custody or visitation may retreat from the lives of their children in the aftermath of court proceedings. Mothers who affirmatively support these father-child relationships are left without a meaningful remedy in the face of father-absence. Motions to enforce visitation orders to coerce fathers to spend time with their children rarely prevail in court, nor are they likely to achieve positive father-child engagement. Likewise, though judges are far more likely to entertain contempt actions in the child support system, enforcement seeks child support collection but not healthy father-child involvement. As such, father-absence among this cohort of court-involved families largely evades a litigation remedy to encourage and enhance the paternal relationship. . . .

---

99. Kathryn Edin & Timothy J. Nelson, Doing the Best I Can 206–07 (2013).

The legal system's commitment to enhancing fathers' involvement in their children's lives should derive from a number of sources. First, studies indicate that involved nonresident fathers can be critical to child well-being. Engaged nonresident fathers can play an important role in supporting child development, ensuring academic success, and fostering self-esteem in children. Further, studies illustrate a correlation between negative outcomes for children, such as early sexual activity and delinquency, and father-absence. Second, to the extent that the legal system frustrates a father's pre-existing inclination to positively engage with his children, the system cannot serve the best interests of the child by perpetuating and enhancing barriers to that relationship without further analysis. If fathers enter the legal system with the intention of maintaining relationships with their children, the system is failing children if the fathers' system interaction unintentionally extinguishes that intention. Finally, when custodial mothers seek support from the court to maintain or increase father-presence in the context of a custody or child support action, the court system has an obligation to the well-being of children to minimize its role in impeding that goal. . . .

Although fathers have undertaken increased child-care responsibility over the last four decades, the prevalence of father-absence has been simultaneously increasing. In one large-scale study of the general population of families with nonresident fathers, mothers reported that 34% of the fathers had no contact with the child's household at all. The statistics related to fragile families, in which the parents never marry, paint an even bleaker picture. . . .

Father-absence is less likely in families with mothers who are college graduates. Further, employed fathers are more likely to have regular contact with their children. Other studies have echoed the finding that fathers at higher socioeconomic levels maintain more consistent contact with their children than their counterparts at lower socioeconomic levels. . . .

One study of families with custody orders found that 32% of nonresident fathers had not spent any time with their children in the past year. A study of divorced parents, a group likely to have custody orders in place as part of a divorce action, found that two years after divorce, only one-quarter of noncustodial fathers visited with their children once a week or more. The study reported that between 18% and 25% of those children no longer had any contact with their fathers three years following divorce.

In contrast, studies of fathers' expectations for fatherhood prior to birth foreshadow a different father-child relationship. For example, Kathryn Edin and Timothy Nelson's 2013 publication, Doing the Best I Can: Fatherhood in the Inner City, which draws on seven years of field work delving into the lives of over 100 black and white inner city fathers, reported that, in general, the men in the study were pleased at the news of an impending birth. They noted that "[u]nadulterated happiness — even joy — was by far the most common reaction[.]" . . . Further, multiple studies illustrate that many low-income fathers want to be involved but that economic disadvantages hamper their ability to remain engaged. . . .

The concept of the absent father conjures up images of men who procreate without regard to consequences and disappear without remorse. . . . In fact, however, statistics on father-absence paint a reality in contrast to this picture, suggesting that the causes of father-absence are significantly more complex and varied than assumptions about cultural values, general paternal apathy, and irresponsibility. In fact, by most accounts, African American men are less likely than Caucasian or Hispanic men to be absent fathers. . . . Studies of low-income fathers noted the emotional distress fathers displayed when discussing their absence from the lives of their children.

The quality and nature of a father's relationship with his children's mother as well as his own perception of the relevance of that relationship most significantly affect paternal engagement. Data on absent fathers repeatedly cite the distancing effect men note as a result of a conflictual relationship with their children's mothers. . . .

The relationship between separated parents is self-evidently prone to inherent conflict. First, co-parenting demands parental interaction. Especially when the children are young, interactions between a nonresident parent and his children are often mediated by and intertwined with the custodial parent from a logistical and emotional perspective. Second, after the dissolution of the relationship between the parents, the interaction between parents is often fraught with an emotional complexity and a struggle for control that almost inevitably affects the children. Third, fathers point to conflict produced by new maternal romantic relationships. New romantic partners introduced into a family dynamic that is already fragile can result in increased tension, resentment on the part of the nonresident father, and the deployment of tighter control by mothers. Finally, the court process itself can enhance conflict. . . .

Fathers in low-income families also struggle with multiple structural barriers that impede their relationships with their children. A father with limited resources may not have access to transportation to facilitate frequent visitation, or may be forced to use unreliable transportation that may make him late for visits or that may not be safe or practicable to use to transport children. . . .

Work responsibilities consistently appear on the list of barriers men across the socioeconomic spectrum identify as salient. . . .

Finally, a father who lacks resources may not have an appropriate home to which to bring his children for visitation. . . .

When the court adjudicates custody, court orders seek to render explicit the new structure of parenting relationships. . . . With very few exceptions, court orders refrain from divvying up specific parenting responsibilities, and very few separated parents are able to proactively identify and negotiate such issues on their own. As a result, after the family has dissolved, role ambiguity can predominate.

Low-income fathers report being unsure of what mothers expect of them. . . .

Once the father is no longer part of the original family structure, the time he spends with his children necessarily transforms, whether that time is significant or limited. Engagement with his children is no longer casual, unpremeditated, and spontaneous. Instead, it derives either from a court-ordered schedule or an agreement with the mother, and its time parameters are usually circumscribed. The very nature of this interaction profoundly shifts, and though it may absolve a father of some of the more tedious parenting tasks, it can also transform the relationship into a more superficial one. . . .

Fathers also report that the limited nature of non-primary physical custody or visitation causes them emotional pain that can lead them to reject the visitation altogether. . . .

Finally, a father's discomfort with his new role may stem from feelings of inadequacy in the role of sole care-giving parent. . . .

Social norms can affect behavior within the parent-child structure. The social norms that interfere with the caretaking efforts of fathers who live with their children prior to court action continue to inhibit men from taking advantage of their custody and visitation rights after the dissolution of the family. . . .

[T]he legal system can play a role in reducing barriers to fathers and in facilitating paternal relationships, especially for this group of low-income court-involved fathers. Because the legal system can engage fathers at this critical moment, its role as an inhibitor or facilitator to positive paternal engagement could be influential in arresting the trend of increasing father-absence. . . .

The child support system itself, though largely intended to promote child welfare, can also raise collateral barriers to engagement by low-income fathers that merit consideration in any analysis of the legal system's role in addressing father-absence. In the past fifteen years, government programs to collect child support and to establish parentage, as mandated by both federal legislation and local statutes, have become increasingly aggressive. In addition to establishing criminal penalties for failure to pay child support, some jurisdictions have also conditioned the receipt of public benefits on a mother's cooperation with establishing parentage. While renewed efforts at child support enforcement have been successful on several fronts, current enforcement programs can be more problematic than effective in the population of low-income fathers with little ability to pay in terms of both collection and paternal engagement. Indeed, several years after the implementation of aggressive child support enforcement, a national survey revealed that only 63% of children living below the poverty line in a home with only one parent received child support. Further, data indicate that child support enforcement is negatively correlated with visitation by nonresident fathers. As one father noted, child support enforcement was a continual reminder of state intervention into his private life: "Believe me, I'd pay if they'd leave me alone. It's that I'm 'ordered to pay' that I resent."

Though the child support order for an unemployed father might be as low as fifty dollars per month, such an obligation might still be impossible to meet. Research suggests that the majority of low-income fathers' failure to meet their obligations is not because of their unwillingness to support their children, but because they do not earn enough to satisfy their obligations. When a parent fails to comply with his support obligation, the court can impose job search requirements, require regular enforcement hearings, and ultimately impose sanctions, including criminal contempt. For these fathers, the continual pressure from the government to obtain a job, meet obligations, compensate for arrears, or face sanctions, contempt, or criminal penalties and their collateral consequences can have a significant deterrent effect on paternal engagement. Two specific provisions of child support law, though intended to enhance the support government coffers and to routinize child support payments, also impose particular collateral consequences on paternal engagement that, if addressed, could play a role in reducing the legal system's barriers to paternal engagement.

Under federal and state child support law, current and former recipients of Temporary Assistance to Needy Families (TANF) must assign their rights to child support to the government as reimbursement for benefits. . . .

Welfare cost recovery negatively affects paternal engagement in several ways. First, noncustodial fathers are denied the opportunity to directly benefit their families, often rendering fathers resentful of the government and their families and incentivized to disappear to avoid burdensome and seemingly senseless payments. . . .

Second, family conflict is specifically kindled, rather than tamped, by assignment rules. The mother may not receive any direct support from the father, even if he is meeting his obligations. . . .

Third, assignment deprives parents of the right to negotiate their own child support arrangements, impeding the ability of a family to effectively meet the needs of the children, and eliminating what is often a powerful bargaining tool for mothers. . . .

Assignment renders all of these negotiations and arrangements untenable, since the right to the support belongs to the government. Decisions by the custodial parent to accept informal payments could amount to welfare fraud.

Finally, assignment drives custodial families further into poverty, putting strain on parental relations and negatively affecting paternal engagement. . . .

The legal system is poised to eliminate the negative effects of this program. In order to induce custodial parent cooperation in collecting child support, federal and state law created an exception to the full assignment of child support money. In establishing a pass-through of some portion of child support payments, the government assumed that a custodial parent — who has an interest in the nonresident parent paying child support — would assist the government in locating a nonpaying or unidentified parent and encouraging payment. The government has experimented with several approaches to pass-throughs, and currently guarantees that the federal government will share the cost with the state for the first $100 passed through to custodial parents with one child and $200 to families with multiple children. However, even despite this cost-sharing incentive, fewer than half of the states currently pass-through child support money. . . .

A second aspect of child support law merits consideration from the perspective of both child financial wellbeing and paternal engagement. Child support guidelines currently specify that the payor parent derives no credit for in-kind or informal payments. Informal payments, constituting mere gifts, cannot defray current or past child support obligations. The ban on in-kind payments reflects child support law's unwavering commitment to enforcing monetary obligations against noncustodial parents. While this goal is laudable in seeking to maximize support for children, this inflexible principle can fortify impediments by stoking parental conflict, incentivizing fathers to flee or enter the underground economy, and reinforcing the message that paternal non-monetary contributions are irrelevant. In the end, it likely deprives children of available support. . . .

By taking its role in influencing paternal involvement at the critical moments of child support enforcement, custody, and visitation adjudication more seriously, the legal system can positively affect the social norms that impede paternal engagement. The social norms embedded in our legal system mandate mothers to nurture and fathers to provide support to children, and generally remain silent on paternal caretaking involvement. By adopting some of the mechanisms discussed above to eliminate barriers to paternal involvement, the law and legal system could further support the social norms that value father-involvement.

NOTES AND QUESTIONS

1. *Private Bargaining over Custody and Support.* For unmarried mothers who do not apply for government aid, the state does not unilaterally pursue support enforcement against the father. These parents might not have any interaction with the courts over custody and support. When a married couple wants to dissolve their union, they must obtain permission from a court; the court, in turn, cannot dissolve their relationship without entering custody and support orders if the couple has minor children. But unmarried couples do not need court permission to handle their adult relationship; there is thus no obvious point at which a court would enter custody and support orders. As Professor Clare Huntington asserts, "This means that unmarried partners are left without an effective institution to help them transition from a family based on a romantic relationship to a family based on co-parenting."[100] Should there be a default system of dispute resolution in which

---

100. Clare Huntington, Postmarital Family Law: A Legal Structure for Nonmarital Families, 67 Stan. L. Rev. 167, 171 (2015).

unmarried parents have custody and support determined?[101] Or is there a virtue to the lack of state oversight? Professors June Carbone and Naomi Cahn argue that unmarried mothers and fathers engage in an informal bargain outside the law. They "achieve greater autonomy in structuring relationship terms by evading the law, the courts, and often each other."[102] As they explain, "Many women today create families on their own terms by choosing not to marry, staying away from any form of public welfare, and refusing to seek formal support orders against the fathers of their child."[103] The fathers participate in this bargain by avoiding formal support orders, contributing what they can, and allowing the mothers to control access to the child. Should the law facilitate, or inhibit, maternal gatekeeping in nonmarital families?[104]

2. *Parental Cooperation.* In cases in which the mother and child seek government aid, state child support agencies require mothers to cooperate in identifying and pursuing the child's father. Under Connecticut law, for example, the "mother may be cited to appear before any judge of the Superior Court and compelled to disclose the name of the putative father under oath and to institute an action to establish the paternity of said child."[105] Federal law mandates that states have mechanisms in place to ensure the good-faith cooperation of the custodial parent in establishing paternity, as well as in establishing, modifying, or enforcing a child support order.[106] Why have this type of mandate? What is the punishment for noncompliance? Under the Connecticut statute, the mother who fails to cooperate "may be found to be in contempt of court and may be fined not more than two hundred dollars or imprisoned not more than one year, or both."[107] Do you think state officials are seeking to punish women in this situation? Or might child support enforcement officials simply be using the threat of punishment? Are there some situations in which the mother should be permitted to refuse to cooperate without threat of penalty? Connecticut law, for instance, provides a "good cause" exception, which includes domestic violence or sexual abuse by the father.[108]

NOTE ON CHILD SUPPORT JURISDICTION

The first uniform act designed to deal with interstate child support enforcement issues dates to 1950, but the current one, the Uniform Interstate Family Support Act (UIFSA), was promulgated in 1992 and significantly amended in 1996, 2001,

---

101. See id. at 174 (proposing "the creation of alternative dispute resolution structures" to support co-parenting relationships).

102. June Carbone & Naomi Cahn, Jane the Virgin and Other Stories of Unintentional Parenthood, 7 U.C. Irvine L. Rev. 511, 514 (2015).

103. Id.

104. Compare id., with Huntington, supra note 100, at 173.

105. Conn. Gen. Stat. § 46b-169 (2020).

106. 42 U.S.C. § 654(29) (2018).

107. Conn. Gen. Stat. § 46b-169 (2020).

108. I § 46b-168a (2020).

and 2008.[109] Federal law mandates that all fifty states adopt and follow the 2008 version of UIFSA.[110] Congress also adopted its own law, the Full Faith and Credit for Child Support Orders Act (FFCCSOA), in 1994, which mandates that child support orders be given full faith and credit in the courts of any state if the original court had jurisdiction to issue them.[111] This law works in tandem with UIFSA. "The federal statute lays out jurisdictional requirements for state courts to recognize, enforce, and modify orders of sister states, while the state statute lays out the requirements for the state to make original orders, recognize foreign orders, and modify any outstanding order."[112]

The 2008 revisions to UIFSA are largely devoted to enforcement issues arising from intercountry rather than interstate enforcement. The uniform law is drafted to comply with U.S. obligations under the 2007 Hague Convention on the International Recovery of Child Support and Other Forms of Family Maintenance,[113] which was ratified by the United States in 2016 and entered into force in 2017. Many provisions of this treaty were modeled on the 2001 version of UIFSA, which exerted a "wide influence on the text of the new Convention."[114] UIFSA drafters explained that "[t]he treaty, in essence, establishes the framework for a system of international cooperation by emulating the interstate effect of UIFSA for international cases, especially those affected by the Convention."[115] UIFSA also contains important provisions that control enforcement of child support across state lines.

UIFSA and FFCCSOA give jurisdictional priority to the child's "home state."[116] The home-state court that issues a child support order consistent with the statutory requirements then retains continuing, exclusive jurisdiction to modify the support order as long as the child or any party remains in the state.[117] To receive the benefit of continuing, exclusive jurisdiction, the court issuing the original order must have subject matter jurisdiction over the case and personal jurisdiction over the parties.[118] All told, the statutes together "prohibit a court from entering (and, except under certain limited circumstances, prohibit a court's modification of) a child support order if a sister state's court has already entered a support order involving the same parent and child and the other court's order is, or may be determined to be,

---

109. Unif. Interstate Family Support Act, Prefatory Note (Unif. Law Comm'n 2008) [hereinafter UIFSA].

110. See 42 U.S.C. § 666(f) (2018).

111. 28 U.S.C. § 1739B (2018).

112. Laura W. Morgan, Preemption or Abdication: Courts Rule Federal Law Trumps State Law in Child Support Jurisdiction, 24 J. Am. Acad. Matrim. L. 217, 220 (2011).

113. Hague Conference on Private Int'l Law, Convention on the Int'l Recovery of Child Support and Other Forms of Family Maintenance (concluded Nov. 23, 2007).

114. UIFSA, supra note 109, Prefatory Note.

115. Id. art. 7, intro. cmt.

116. Id. § 207(b)(2)(A); 42 U.S.C. § 1738B(f)(3) (2018).

117. UIFSA, supra note 109, § 205; 42 U.S.C. § 1738B(d) (2018).

118. UIFSA, supra note 109, § 205; 42 U.S.C. § 1738B(c)(1) (2018).

the controlling support order with respect to the parent's duty to support that child or family."[119]

III. Other Questions of Family Support

A. The Obligation of Adult Children to Support Parents

Although we commonly associate the notion of family support with obligations that arise out of marriage (spousal support) or parenting (child support), there are other contexts in which family relationships can be the basis of support obligations. Note our discussion in Chapter 3 of the prevalence of working-age people engaging in care of parents and expected increases in that trend. Under what circumstances should adult children be required to support their parents?

Peyton v. Peyton
8 Va. Cir. 531 (1978)

Charles H. Duff, Judge.

Petitioner [Gordon Peyton] seeks contribution from Respondent [his brother, Randolph Peyton] for one-half of the sum heretofore furnished by the Petitioner for the support and care of their Mother, who he alleges to be in necessitous circumstances. The action was brought pursuant to Section 20–88, Code of Virginia, as amended. . . .

The legal issues are first, whether the admitted receipt by the parties' Mother of Federal Social Security benefits is "public assistance" as that term is employed in Sec. 20–88; and second, whether this action, or any part thereof, is barred by the Statute of Limitations.

The two factual issues for decision are, first, whether the parties' Mother was indeed in necessitous circumstances during the time involved herein; and second, whether the Respondent should be required to contribute support after due consideration is given to the statutory language "after reasonably providing for his or her own immediate family."

With respect to the first legal issue, Section 20–88 specifically provides that it shall not apply to this type of action "if a parent is otherwise eligible and is receiving public assistance or services under a Federal or State program." Respondent

---

119. Morgan, supra note 112, at 222 (quoting John L. Saxon, "Reconciling" Multiple Child Support Orders Under UIFSA and FFCCSOA: The Twaddell, Roberts, and Dunn Cases, 11 Fam. L. Bull. 1, 3 (2000)).

asserts that the only form of public assistance paid from Federal funds direct to an individual is Social Security, and thus the Statute is inapplicable. In my opinion the argument misconstrues the meaning of the words "public assistance."

The Federal Social Security Act, part of the Federal Old Age, Survivors and Disability Insurance legislation . . . establishes a system of social insurance which is financed largely from payroll taxes and which distributes its benefits among numerous classes including the aged, children, disabled, etc. The benefits are not open to all who are needy but are available to those persons eligible for benefits by reason of past employment or relationship to a person who has contributed to the program, etc. In fact, U.S.C.A. Title 42, Sec. 428(d), expressly prohibits the receipt of Social Security payments when the person is receiving assistance under an approved State welfare plan. Virginia has apparently enacted such a plan as Title 63.1, Virginia Code. This plan provides a broad range of welfare assistance for various persons needing public assistance. It is my opinion that this was the intent of the Legislature in referring to public assistance or services in Section 20–88. . . .

Turning now to the factual issues involved, the parties' Mother was adjudged an incompetent by this Court in 1967. Both Petitioner and Respondent are Co-Committees and Co-Guardians of the person and property of their Mother. She has for a number of years been confined to a local nursing home, the expenses thereof being illustrated explicitly by the Accountings filed.

At the hearing there was some testimony with respect to certain jewelry, oriental rugs and other property possibly titled in the Mother's name. Such evidence, however, was not clear and explicit either as to the legal title to the property or the value thereof and I do not find that it is sufficient to outweigh the evidence of necessitous circumstances presented by the Accountings filed and the fact of need of nursing home care.

The final factual issue turns upon the ability of the Respondent to contribute to his Mother's support. A careful evaluation of the needs of the Respondent during the time frame involved, the respective incomes of the parties and the contribution admittedly made by the Petitioner, leads me to the conclusion that the Respondent should be ordered to contribute to the Petitioner the sum of $8,000.00, which sum represents Respondent's proper share of support and maintenance for his Mother from the time covered by the 4th Accounting period through the 10th Annual Accounting period. . . .

AMERICAN HEALTHCARE CENTER V. RANDALL
513 N.W.2d 566 (S.D. 1994)

AMUNDSON, JUSTICE.

Robert Randall appeals the trial court's judgment in favor of Americana Healthcare Center for the costs of care for his elderly mother pursuant to SDCL 25-7-27. We affirm.

Appellant Robert Randall (Robert) is the only child of Harry and Juanita Randall. Although he grew up in Aberdeen, Robert has not resided in South Dakota since in 1954. Robert is now a resident of the District of Columbia.

Robert's father died in 1981. Four years after his death, Robert's mother Juanita hired counsel to draft a trust document entitled "Juanita Randall Maintenance Trust Agreement." This irrevocable trust named Juanita as the income beneficiary and Robert as both trustee and residual beneficiary. The trust principal consisted of Juanita's house which was valued at approximately $30,000 and $100,000 in mutual funds. The trust did not grant the trustee authority to invade the principal for the benefit of Juanita. Juanita was ninety-two years old when she executed the trust document in 1985.

Following an accident which required Juanita's hospitalization, Robert came back to Aberdeen and checked into various nursing homes to place his mother. In the fall of 1990, Juanita was admitted to the Arcadia Unit of Americana Healthcare Center (Americana) in Aberdeen, South Dakota. The Arcadia Unit is specifically designed to deal with individuals who possess mental problems such as Alzheimer's disease. Robert completed and signed all the necessary documents under the power of attorney from his mother and made a two-month advance payment to Americana from his mother's checking account. He also listed himself as the person who should be sent the monthly statements from the nursing home.

At that time, in view of Juanita's limited income, Robert discussed the possibility of financial assistance from Medicaid with various Americana personnel. Later that month, Robert completed an application for long-term care medical assistance for Juanita. In November, the South Dakota Department of Social Services (DSS) denied this application because Juanita had not exhausted all of her assets. At the time, Juanita's only assets were the house and mutual funds which had been conveyed to the trust.

Juanita's bill was two months delinquent at the time Americana learned of the rejected Medicaid application. Americana then contacted Robert about his mother's unpaid bills. Because of Juanita's financial position, Robert, as her legal guardian, filed a . . . Chapter 7 bankruptcy petition which . . . discharged the Americana bill for Juanita individually and Robert, as her guardian, on October 30, 1991. Meanwhile, Americana filed this suit to collect the unpaid bills. . . .

In June of 1991, Robert was requested to remove his mother from Americana because of the unpaid bills. Despite this request, Juanita remained at Americana until her death on December 8, 1991. At the time of Juanita's death, the unpaid balance for her care was $36,772.30. . . .

Prior to trial, the court granted Robert's motion for summary judgment as to Robert Randall as guardian of the person and estate of Juanita because of the discharge in bankruptcy, but denied summary judgment to Robert Randall individually. . . . At the summary judgment hearing, Americana raised its claim under SDCL 25-7-27 for the first time.[20]

On September 3, 1992, Robert renewed his motion for summary judgment on the additional ground that SDCL 25-7-27 was unconstitutional and requested a continuance. . . . The trial court stated that it was premature to rule on the constitutionality of the statute at that time and denied the continuance.

A court trial was held September 22, 1992. At the conclusion of Americana's case, Robert moved for directed verdict on the grounds that Americana had failed to establish either an oral or written contract to act as guarantor for his mother's nursing home bills. . . . The trial court granted Robert's motion for directed verdict on Americana's claims for liability based on an oral or written contract of guarantee. . . . The trial court found in favor of Americana on its SDCL 25-7-27 claim. This appeal followed. . . .

ANALYSIS

Was Robert Randall liable for his mother's nursing home bill under SDCL 25-7-27? . . .

At common law, an adult child was not required to support a parent. Such an obligation could only be created by statute. Such statutes trace their beginnings from the Elizabethan Poor Law of 1601 in England. South Dakota adopted the current version of SDCL 25-7-27 in 1963.

The North Dakota Supreme Court considered a claim premised on a similar statutory provision in *Bismarck Hospital & Deaconesses Home v. Harris*, 280 N.W. 423 (N.D. 1938). That court stated:

> If the person against whom liability is sought to be established refuses to pay for services rendered, an action may be brought against him by such third party. In such action, the plaintiff must establish the kinship of the parties, the financial ability of the person sought to be charged, the indigence of the person to whom relief was furnished, the reasonable value of the services, and that such relief was an immediate necessity.

Id. at 426.

SDCL 25-7-27 requires an adult child to provide support only when they have the financial ability to do so. Robert claims that this is constitutionally defective

---

20. SDCL 25-7-27 states:

> Every adult child, having the financial ability to do so shall provide necessary food, clothing, shelter or medical attendance for a parent who is unable to provide for himself; provided that no claim shall be made against such adult child until notice has been given such adult child that his parent is unable to provide for himself, and such adult child shall have refused to provide for his parent.

because it is unclear when financial ability is to be determined. However, under the facts of this case, a fair reading of the statute shows that the financial ability of the adult child may be determined at any time there is an outstanding debt which has not been barred by the statute of limitations. This certainly seems appropriate where the parent continues to receive care while the child is in control of, and is expending, the parent's assets which are available to pay the debt.

Although Robert could not pay his mother's bills from his own funds, he certainly had the ability to pay after the trust assets had been distributed to him. At trial, it was proven that Robert had received approximately $100,000 in mutual funds from the maintenance trust at his mother's death. Therefore, under the facts of this case, the trial court was correct in holding Robert liable under SDCL 25-7-27.

Does SDCL 25-7-27 deny Robert Randall equal protection of the law?

Robert claims SDCL 25-7-27 violates equal protection because it discriminates against adult children of indigent parents. The trial court held that it did not. Any legislative act is accorded a presumption in favor of constitutionality and that presumption is not overcome until the act is clearly and unmistakably shown beyond a reasonable doubt to violate fundamental constitutional principles. Since Robert challenges the constitutionality of the statute, he bears the burden of proving the act unconstitutional. . . .

No quasi-suspect classification or fundamental right has been implicated in this case, thus, a rational basis analysis will be applied to this support statute. . . .

Under the rational basis test, South Dakota uses a two-pronged analysis when determining whether a statute violates the constitutional right to equal protection under the laws. First, does the statute set up arbitrary classifications among various persons subject to it and, second, whether there is a rational relationship between the classification and some legitimate legislative purpose.

When applying the first prong . . . , it is clear that SDCL 25-7-27 does not make an arbitrary classification. Rather, "it is the moral as well as the legal duty in this state, of every child, whether minor or adult, to assist in the support of their indigent aged parents." *Tobin v. Bruce,* 162 N.W. 933, 934 (S.D. 1917). An adult child is liable under SDCL 25-7-27 upon the same principle that a parent is liable for necessary support furnished to their child. . . .

Robert argues that the only support obligations which are rational are those arising out of a relationship voluntarily entered into. For instance, the obligation to support a child or spouse is at least initially voluntary, therefore, it is rationally based. Robert argues that, since children do not voluntarily enter into the relationship with their parents, it is arbitrary to force this obligation upon them. The fact that a child has no choice in the creation of a relationship with its parents does not per se make this an arbitrary classification. The fact that an indigent parent has supported and cared for a child during that child's minority provides an adequate basis for imposing a duty on the child to support that parent.

Robert also claims that this classification is unconstitutional because it is based on wealth. However, economic-based discrimination has been upheld by this court. . . .

It is certainly reasonable to place a duty to support an indigent parent on that parent's adult child because they are direct lineal descendants who have received the support, care, comfort and guidance of that parent during their minority. If a parent does not qualify for public assistance, who is best suited to meet that parent's needs? It can reasonably be concluded that no other person has received a greater benefit from a parent than that parent's child and it logically follows that the adult child should bear the burden of reciprocating on that benefit in the event a parent needs support in their later years. Consequently, this statute does not establish an arbitrary classification.

The second prong of the test requires a rational relationship between this classification and some legitimate state interest. Clearly, this state has a legitimate interest in providing for the welfare and care of elderly citizens. SDCL 25-7-27 prevents a parent from being thrown out on the street when in need of specialized care. Placing this obligation for support on an adult child is as legitimate as those interests recognized by this court in the past when applying the rational basis test. We have found legitimate state interests to exist under constitutional challenges in the support of children; balancing the treatment of debtors and creditors; education; public safety; preventing the adjudication of stale claims; and protecting the citizens from drunk drivers.

The primary purpose of this statute is to place financial responsibility for indigent parents on their adult children when a parent requires such assistance. Although the legislature repealed similar laws in the past, SDCL 25-7-27 has survived. Therefore, SDCL 25-7-27 serves a legitimate legislative interest, especially under the facts of this case, where indigency was voluntarily created by the trust and there would have been sufficient assets to pay for the parent's care had the trust not been created. Robert has not been denied his right to equal protection under the law. . . .

In conclusion, we affirm the trial court's decision in all respects. . . .

Lee E. Teitelbaum, Intergenerational Responsibility and Family Obligation: On Sharing
1992 Utah L. Rev. 765

The question of what family members owe to each other has become acute for a number of reasons: some demographic; some economic; and some social. The issue, of course, is an old one. During the sixteenth century, support for those who were disabled through youth (typically orphans and abandoned children), age, or infirmity was first a matter for private charity and, when that failed, became a matter of local responsibility. However, the cost of local responsibility was soon recognized, and recognition was swiftly followed by efforts to minimize the public obligation by, for example, punishing those who were "voluntarily" disabled — vagrants and beggars — and shifting to families the primary obligation for support of their disabled relatives.

Although these so-called Poor Laws were adopted in the colonies and have remained on the books in many states, there is little evidence of their widespread use. Public involvement with care of the needy was also scant, particularly during the late eighteenth and nineteenth centuries. Where public assistance was available, it largely took the form of institutional care, particularly for the destitute elderly who were commonly placed in public facilities. Assistance for those who remained in the home was rarely available except from private sources.

With the first third of [the twentieth] century came increased interest in public programs, primarily for children but also for disabled workers. Workers' compensation statutes, although primarily intended to protect employers against large liability awards, provided a limited scheme of protection for employees as well. The effects of the Great Depression substantially accelerated the movement toward public programs while concurrently depleting individual and private resources. Economic collapse limited not only the capacity of citizens to care for themselves, but also the capacities of other private individuals and groups to do so. Private charitable agencies disappeared almost as quickly as private entrepreneurs.

The 1930s, accordingly, saw the creation of the modern social security and welfare system and, with it, the first substantial, direct participation of the federal government in care for the disabled and elderly. Concomitantly, reliance on private and familial responsibility declined. To some considerable extent, these new programs were regarded as a kind of insurance, purchased during employment by workers and their employers and drawn against upon retirement or disability. To the extent that social welfare was need-based, the theory was of societal and intergenerational responsibility rather than familial responsibility. The currently employed would support the elderly or disabled through federal and state taxes, expecting similar assistance from the rising generation when their time of need arrived. And as long as federal support for health and social welfare programs remained substantial, family responsibility laws largely remained dormant.

Conditions, however, have changed. Some of the changes are demographic. The aging of the population is old news. The population in need of support — the very elderly and at least partially disabled — has grown remarkably because advances in health care have extended life spans. Other changes are social in nature. Demographics may describe the larger number of aged citizens, but divorce policy (coupled with differences in remarriage rates for women and men) at least partly explains the larger proportion of single elderly persons (particularly single women) for whom support is especially needed. And some of the changes are economic. On the one hand, social security entitlements have increased since the 1970s, reducing significantly the proportion of elderly persons below the poverty level. At the same time, those who are poor are also highly vulnerable. Federal contributions to federal-state programs such as Medicaid have been restrained, while health care costs have risen enormously. Under these circumstances, and impelled by conservative emphases upon limiting federal (and other governmental) roles in "private" areas of concern, there is once again interest, largely at the state level, in substituting family for local responsibility. . . .

The fact that family members often devote their resources and loyalty to each other rather than to non-family members, and the importance of those special distributions, presents a complex ethical question. On the one hand, discussions of intergenerational responsibility point to these preferences as evidence of a "natural" order of things which can appropriately be employed as a basis for family responsibility laws. On the other hand, commentators from a variety of perspectives regard family loyalty as a serious social and ethical problem.

The desirability of intimate family relations, with the special loyalty and special distributions of resources they may generate, is by no means uncontroversial. Marxists, for example, view the bourgeois family as a vehicle for the accumulation and transmission of capital. In this capacity, it serves not only to reproduce capitalism but to deny authentic liberty to wives and children who are dependent on the income-producing male family head. Habermas, following this view, rejects the conventional portrait of the family as a voluntary, affectionate, inner realm following its own noninstrumental program in favor of an interpretation that emphasizes the conjugal family's function in reproducing capital and its assertion of paternal authority.

For his part, John Rawls, representing ethicists who regard fairness of opportunity as a fundamental aspect of justice, notes that "[t]he consistent application of the principle of fair opportunity requires us to view persons independently from the influences of their social position. . . . It seems that even when fair opportunity . . . is satisfied, the family will lead to unequal chances between individuals. Is the family to be abolished then?" Rawls seems to incline in that direction but ultimately concludes, without much discussion, that the theory of justice as a whole does not make doing so urgent.

Michael Walzer likewise notes that because the family views itself as a special group, radically separated from the general society, it is a perennial source of inequality. Accordingly, he suggests, "the simplest way to simple equality, is the abolition of the family." . . .

Nonetheless, abolition of the family, or even substantial curtailment of its economic significance, has not been widely advocated. The consequence of the special affective relations within the family — a preference for supporting, assisting, and advantaging family members — has sometimes been accepted as a tolerable qualification on the principle of fair opportunity. Preference for family over others has also been treated as an independent principle of justice. . . .

It might further be suggested that the functioning family is, at least within this society, a special relationship. Whereas traditional rights theories emphasize the situation of an individual against the claims of anonymous others, family members do not and cannot suppose any such individualism and anonymity, especially across generations. Indeed, it is not possible to talk about parents without at the same moment having children in mind and vice versa. One term entails the existence of the other, in an ordinary case. Moreover, the identities of parents and children are bound up in such complex ways that it is hard to regard either as an interloper on the other's territory. From this special relationship, perhaps, one might justify a special sense of felt responsibility and obligation within families. . . .

One obvious set of arguments for charging the cost of financial assistance against familial rather than public resources draws on the familiar notion of the family as an economic unit. . . . It may therefore seem appropriate for its members to direct their resources to each other when the need arises.

However, families are least likely to maintain substantial economic relations at just the time support for parents is needed. The parent-child financial relation rarely continues in a substantial way after the children reach majority. As a matter of the production of wealth, family farms and businesses are rare; children who are able to and wish to follow their parents in those enterprises are rarer still. The sources of wealth for family members, therefore, are usually entirely independent of each other.

Nor does the family often continue as a unit of consumption past the adulthood of its younger members. Adult children do not generally continue to live with their parents, even if unmarried. The continuing decrease in family and household size, coupled with the growth of what the Census Bureau unattractively calls "primary individuals" — household heads living alone or with unrelated individuals — reveals the economic and residential separation of family members from each other. Consequently, at the time parents need their children's support, the children will themselves be adults, living in their own households often with their own children, and there will be no substantial economic relationship between them and their parents.

If the enforcement of a family support obligation cannot be justified on the basis of the economic and social relations of families at the time such support is usually needed, it might rest on other traditional grounds. Requiring us to support our parents seems, for example, to express a strong cultural tradition, either in a historical or in some non-historical sense.

The historical tradition would justify such laws as reproductions of a happier world only recently lost — a world where several generations live together, exchanging roles of nurturance and support in a natural way. Family responsibility statutes reflect, accordingly, only a return to previously existing norms that have wrongly been abandoned.

Perhaps unfortunately, however, the historical period to which return is sought is more remote than we imagine. Extended families — three or more generations living in the same household — have been rare in Western Europe for many centuries and never were common in America. Late marriage, late childbearing, early mortality, and geographically diffuse employment patterns after industrialization all conspired to reduce the incidence of three generation families in general and shared residence in particular.

NOTES AND QUESTIONS

1. *Family Support Laws.* A little more than half of states have a statute requiring adult children to provide financial support to their parents in some circumstances.[120] These laws, sometimes called "family support," "parental support," or "filial support" statutes, were more common before the establishment of the social safety net comprised of Medicare (health insurance for the aged), Medicaid (health insurance for the poor and disabled), and Social Security (cash payments for the aged based on contributions during wage earning years). Under a typical statute, the duty to support only arises when the parent is in need (i.e., the parent cannot provide for her own needs and is not eligible for government assistance), and the adult child has the ability to provide after providing for herself and her own dependents. Moreover, some statutes permit an adult child to avoid the duty to support upon proof that the parent wrongfully failed to support the child as a minor. State statutes vary quite a bit on the particulars.[121]

2. *Who Can Sue?* Some of the laws permit a parent to sue an adult child directly for financial support, and some only permit a suit by a third-party creditor who has extended necessary goods or services, such as healthcare, to the parent. Which is the better approach? Where else in family law have we seen a similar doctrine? Some of the filial support laws provide for criminal punishment for nonsupport, in addition to whatever civil liability the statute imposes. What is the theoretical basis for imposing liability on adult children to support their parents, and how does it compare to the basis for imposing an obligation on parents to support their minor children? How does it compare to obligations for support between adults? Does Professor Teitelbaum's account of the cultural traditions surrounding family support resonate with you?

---

120. Katherine C. Pearson, Filial Support Laws in the Modern Era: Domestic and International Comparison of Enforcement Practices for Laws Requiring Adult Children to Support Indigent Parents, 20 Elder L.J. 269 (2013).

121. For a comprehensive overview of current statutes, see id.; see also Jane Gross, Adult Children, Aging Parents and the Law, N.Y. Times (Nov. 20, 2008).

3. *Enforcement.* Filial support laws are rarely enforced, and there are relatively few published cases involving these laws. Why do you think that is? Pennsylvania has been the site of the highest number of cases, in part, because its law is broadly written to impose liability against more people (spouse, adult child, and parent of adult child) in a greater variety of circumstances.[122] Is that a better approach? In the United States, most published cases involve lawsuits filed by nursing homes or medical care providers where large bills were accumulated late in a person's life. As lifespans increase, and people spend more years with large medical expenses, is it fair to distribute to adult children the cost of care their parents could not otherwise afford? Should that responsibility fall to them only if government assistance such as Medicaid is not available? Or is that a burden the state should assume?

B. Incentives for Adult Children to Support Aging Parents

In addition to statutory provisions that might impose a direct obligation on adult children, inheritance and elder abuse laws are a source of more indirect incentives. In all states except Louisiana, parents can freely disinherit their children. Some states provide protection against accidental disinheritance, which may require a parent to expressly disinherit a child in a will, but the substantive power to disinherit is the same. In Louisiana, children who are age twenty-three or younger are entitled to a forced share of a parent's estate, a feature borrowed from inheritance law in civil law countries that give decedents much less discretion over transmission of their property.[123] But even a forced heir can be deprived of his shares (termed "disinherison") if "the decedent has just cause to disinherit him." What constitutes "just cause"? Although this is a statute that applies in only one state, its application sheds light on more general societal expectations for the care and support of aging parents.

AMBROSE SUCCESSION V. AMBROSE
548 So. 2d 37 (La. Ct. App. 1989)

SEXTON, JUDGE.

This is an appeal by two daughters against decedent's spouse seeking to invalidate their disinherison by their father. We affirm.

---

122. Katherine C. Pearson, Filial Support Obligations in Pennsylvania: Adult Children, Parents, and Spouses, in Elder Law in Pennsylvania 957 (Jeffrey A. Marshall ed., 3d ed. 2011); Jared M. DeBona, Mom, Dad, Here's Your Allowance: The Impending Reemergence of Pennsylvania's Filial Support Statute and an Appeal for Its Amendment, 86 Temple L. Rev. 849 (2014).

123. La. Civ. Code Ann. art. 1493 (2020).

Decedent, James Ambrose, who died on February 16, 1987, left a statutory will dated November 15, 1985, in which he sought to disinherit his daughters, Karen Ambrose Hagan Richoux and Loyce Ambrose Forsythe. The disinherison was based on three of the grounds listed in Louisiana Civil Code Article 1621, namely, (1) when a child has been guilty of cruelty to a parent, (2) when a child uses coercion or violence to hinder a parent from making a will, and (3) when a child fails to communicate with a parent for a period of two years after the child reaches majority, without just cause. Mr. Ambrose asserted in the will that his daughter Loyce came by his home and demanded that he make a will authorizing her to manage his separate property. When he refused to do so, she threatened to make his last years miserable. She cursed the decedent and his wife and insulted the decedent, according to his allegations. When asked to apologize, she refused. The parties have not been in contact since 1984.

The testator also asserted that his daughter Karen (also known as Jan) refused to let him see her children and on one occasion became violent and threw her parents out of her home. She has not had contact with the decedent since October 5, 1984. When Mr. Ambrose was hospitalized for lung cancer in 1984, she refused to be present or help her father.

The trial court determined that the facts asserted by the testator were sufficient to raise a rebuttable presumption under LSA-C.C. Art. 1621 that the facts set out in the act of disinherison supported the causes. The court found that the heirs did not carry their burden of rebutting the presumption....

The current total scheme of disinherison is to be accomplished by one of the forms prescribed for testaments. The disinherison is to be by name, expressly done and for a just cause. The current causes for disinherison are only those twelve specifically listed. There is a rebuttable presumption that the facts set out in the act of disinherison are correct. The forced heir has the burden of proving that the cause stipulated for disinherison did not exist or that he was reconciled with the testator after the alleged act at issue.

In the instant case, there is no contest over the form of the disinherison, and it is clear that the causes listed in the instant testament fall within those in LSA-C.C. Art. 1621....

The will sets forth the following facts with regard to Loyce.

> Loyce Ambrose Forsythe, in 1982, came by my home and demanded that I make a will leaving her in charge to manage my separate property. I refused to do so, and she threatened to make my last years on this earth quite miserable. She has cursed me and my wife in person and over the phone, despite our repeated requests that she not do so. The last time being June, 1982, after I returned from the hospital. She called me on the phone and insulted me and cursed me until I began to cry. On September 4, 1984, I was very ill in Lincoln General Hospital, suffering from lung cancer. I called my daughter Loyce and asked her to apologize for things that had taken place in the

past and to come to see me while I was in the hospital. Her response was that she would die and go to hell before she would apologize to me or her mother. I have not seen or heard from her since this incident. Loyce Ambrose Forsythe has been guilty of all of this cruelty on numerous occasions in spite of my efforts to be kind to her. It is my desire that she be disinherited from my estate and deprived of her forced legitime.

The will alleged the following facts with regard to Karen:

On numerous occasions over the previous years, Karen Ambrose Hagan has refused to allow me or her mother to see her children, Darrin and Stephanie. On November 25, 1983, we went to her home in LaPlace, Louisiana, to take the children their Christmas presents. She became violent and we were practically thrown out of her home. She has cursed me a number of times, both in person and over the telephone. She has not called us or had any contact with us since October 5, 1984. During September of 1984 when I was hospitalized for surgery for lung cancer, she refused to be present and offered no help in caring for me after the surgery. Karen Ambrose Hagan has been guilty of all of this cruelty on numerous occasions in spite of my efforts to be kind to her. It is my desire that she be disinherited from my estate and deprived of her forced legitime.

We agree with the trial court that the facts alleged by Mr. Ambrose with regard to Loyce Ambrose Forsythe were sufficient to qualify as an act of coercion which hindered him from making his will. We also agree that the alleged behavior of Karen Ambrose Hagan Richoux rises to the level of cruelty encompassed by LSA-C.C. Art. 1621(2). The statements that on one visit the daughter Karen "became violent" and practically threw her parents out of her home, that she cursed her parent over the telephone, and that she refused to assist her parent either during or after serious surgery are sufficient assertions of cruel treatment under the code article.

As we have determined that the facts alleged by Mr. Ambrose to support disinherison of both of his daughters are sufficient to fall within the pertinent provisions of LSA-C.C. Art. 1621, we now turn to the question of whether or not the daughters rebutted by a preponderance of the evidence the presumption that the causes asserted for their disinherison did not exist. . . .

The evidence as it concerns Loyce reveals that she approached her father in 1982 and demanded that her father alter his will. At that time she threatened to make her father's life miserable if he failed to do so. This statement was overheard by Loyce's mother as well as a relative, Mrs. Barbara Smith, who unknown to Loyce, was in her parents' van. Loyce presented very little evidence to discredit the truth of the testimony of these two witnesses. By her self-serving testimony, she denied making these statements but offered no other evidence sufficient to indicate that the conversation did not in fact take place. The trial court specifically accepted the contrary evidence and we find no error. . . . The trial court finding with regard to Loyce is therefore affirmed.

The alleged facts with regard to Karen present a more difficult issue. The court determined that Karen was guilty of cruelty toward her father based upon the fact that she cursed her father on a number of occasions, she treated her father so badly when he visited her home that he felt unwelcome, she prevented her children from extended visits with her father, she refused to give her father her unlisted phone number, and she failed to visit her father when he was ill.

The allegations set forth by her father were somewhat different. He claimed that on numerous occasions she refused to allow him to see her children. The will stated that he went to her home in LaPlace and she became violent and practically threw him out of her home, that she cursed her parents a number of times, and that she had not called or had contact with her parents since 1984. Also, she refused to be present and offered no help in caring for the father after the surgery.

There was testimony at trial which indicated that Karen (Jan) cursed her father on numerous occasions. . . . There was little evidence presented to indicate that Karen did not use profanity towards her father. Although Karen's son, Darrin, never heard his mother curse his grandfather, his testimony cannot be said to counteract the testimony of other witness[es], some independent, who heard the language when the evidence is viewed as a whole. We cannot find that the trial court erred in finding that Karen failed to rebut the presumption that she in fact regularly cursed her father.

The same is true with regard to the statements alleged by Mr. Ambrose that Karen made him feel unwelcome in her home on Thanksgiving of 1982 and that she failed to give him her phone number. . . .

This evidence as well demonstrates that Karen failed in her burden of showing that she did not make her parents feel unwelcome. . . .

Relevant to the statements that Karen failed to visit her father when she was ill, Karen claims that she visited Mr. Ambrose before he was to have surgery in 1984. The surgery took place a few days later and she was unable to stay. There is evidence in the record that her car was repaired at the end of August and the beginning of September of 1984, the year of her father's surgery. Darrin also indicated that he remembered visiting his grandfather in the hospital once in 1982 or 1983. Ray Hagan, Karen's ex-husband, did remember some time when she did go to Ruston when her father was scheduled to have surgery.

Additional evidence, however, indicated that there were other occasions when Karen refused to visit her father in the hospital. When informed of her father's continuing illness by her ex-husband, she informed Mr. Hagan, "I'm sorry, but that's their problem. I don't have anything to do with them anymore."

Mrs. Barbara Smith witnessed Mr. Ambrose cry after speaking to Karen and asking her to come to the hospital. Tony Holmes, who stayed with Mr. Ambrose in the hospital in 1984, also witnessed Mr. Ambrose crying after speaking with his daughter. Karen presented no evidence in explanation of these events. Therefore, although there are indications that on one occasion Karen may have visited her father, there is independent evidence to indicate that on separate occasions Karen failed to attend her father per his request. The evidence indicates that on at least two other occasions her father requested her presence while he was in the hospital, and all indications support the conclusion that she refused to visit him. Therefore, we cannot find that Karen rebutted the presumption that she failed to visit her father while he was ill in the hospital.

Finally, the trial court found that Karen failed to rebut the presumption that she prevented her father from *extended visits* with her children. However, Mr. Ambrose's allegation in this respect was that his daughter refused to allow him to see her children on *numerous* occasions. The evidence indicates that Karen visited north Louisiana four or five times a year before the problems with her father began. Although the children were allowed to visit the grandparents for extended periods of time before 1985, this ceased to be the case after numerous spats between Karen and her parents.

The evidence, however, indicates that the children were allowed to see their grandparents every time she was in Ruston, although the visits arose from Karen's visits with her sister and not with her parents. Additionally, the evidence shows that her parents were able to see the children on Thanksgiving of 1982. . . . Finally, Mrs. Ambrose admitted that Karen allowed the children to come and spend time with her and her husband but not for more than one-day visits. She admitted that Karen never visited more than twice every year, and that the visits with the children lasted generally no more than 30 minutes.

When all of the evidence is viewed in its entirety, we find that Karen has sufficiently demonstrated that she did allow her children to visit with their grandparents contrary to Mr. Ambrose's assertion. . . .

Although we determine that Karen rebutted the presumption that she failed to allow her children to visit her father, the remaining unrebutted allegations of fact amount to a level of cruelty by Karen towards her father sufficient to trigger the provisions of LSA-C.C. Art. 1621(2). The accumulated acts of constantly cursing her father, making him feel unwelcome in her home, purposefully failing to give him her phone number, and failing to visit him in the hospital after his requests rise to a level of treatment amounting to cruelty. We therefore conclude that the trial court finding is not in error. . . .

NOTES AND QUESTIONS

1. *Neglect of Parents.* What did the court in *Ambrose* label as "cruelty"? Are there certain expectations for how adult children should treat aging parents? Are those expectations universally understood and shared? Louisiana's forced heirship statute specifically permits disinheritance of a child based on the child's failure to

contact the parent for the two years preceding the parent's death.[124] Is mandatory contact a reasonable exchange for entitlement to a portion of the parent's estate?

2. *Unworthy Heirs.* Outside of Louisiana, there is no forced heirship to take away from an unworthy child. But there is another way in which inheritance law might account for the (bad) behavior of an adult child. In most states, a "slayer" is barred from taking the decedent's property through a will or through intestate succession. (The bar may extend to other types of transfers as well, such as an interest in a trust or life insurance.) A slayer is typically someone who has "intentionally and feloniously" killed the decedent, although states vary in the level of culpability necessary to disqualify a person from inheritance as well as in the level of proof required. In some states, the ban on slayer inheritance has been broadened to include a person who did not kill the decedent, but who abused or mistreated the decedent when the decedent was elderly or dependent. For example, Section 259 of the California Probate Code bars inheritance by any person if "[i]t has been proven by clear and convincing evidence that the person is liable for physical abuse, neglect, or financial abuse of the decedent, who was an elder or dependent adult."[125] Do these laws make sense? Are they likely to encourage adult children to care for their aging parents?

3. *Comparative Context.* Many in the United States would be surprised to learn they might have a legal duty to support any relatives other than a spouse or their own children. Inheritance patterns reflect the sense that wealth is to be shared with immediate family, or further down the line of descent, rather than upwards to parents, aunts and uncles, and so on. This is true whether one looks at the rules of intestate succession in every state or at bequests in wills, which predominantly involve gifts to spouses and descendants. Descendants are preferred to ancestors in all situations.

Does the sense of obligation to elder relatives vary by cultural context? Recall our discussion in Chapter 1 of a greater prevalence of multigenerational households among immigrant and some ethnic minority families.[126] In some Asian cultures, for

---

124. On forced heirship in Louisiana generally, see Max Nathan, Jr., Forced Heirship, The Unheralded "New" Disinherison Rules, 74 Tul. L. Rev. 1027 (2000). See also In re Succession of Gray, 736 So. 2d 902 (La. Ct. App. 1999); Succession of Gruce, 683 So. 2d 362 (La. Ct. App. 1996).

125. Cal. Prob. Code § 259 (West 2020). The individual must also have acted in bad faith and been "reckless, oppressive, fraudulent, or malicious" in the commission of the abuse or neglect. Michigan imposes a similar bar to succession, but requires a conviction for the abuse, neglect, or exploitation of the decedent. See Mich. Comp. Laws § 700.2803 (2020); see also Ariz. Rev. Stat. Ann. § 46-456 (2020); 755 Ill. Comp. Stat. 5/2-6.2 (2020); Ky. Rev. Stat. Ann. § 381.280 (West 2020); Md. Code Ann., Real Prop. § 11-111 (West 2020); Or. Rev. Stat. § 112-465 (2020). On these laws generally, see Jennifer Piel, Expanding Slayer Statutes to Elder Abuse, 43 J. Am. Acad. Psychiatry & L. 369 (2015).

126. D'Vera Cohn & Jeffrey S. Passel, Pew Research Ctr., A Record 64 Million Americans Live in Multigenerational Households (Apr. 5, 2018).

instance, a strong tradition of filial piety might shape the behavior of adult children vis-à-vis their aging parents, resulting in greater involvement by adult children in their parents' medical care, particularly at the end of life; a greater likelihood of intergenerational households; and greater sharing of wealth.[127] Should states change laws of inheritance, filial support, or elder abuse to encourage adult children to tend more closely to their aging relatives? Should we think about financial support similarly to other types of care people might also give? Consider this in relation to caregiving for older relatives in general, discussed in Chapter 3.[128]

127. Ju-Ping Lin & Chin-Chun Yi, Filial Norms and Intergenerational Support to Aging Parents in China and Taiwan, 20 Int'l J. Soc. Welfare 109, 110 (2011); Man Guo et al., Filial Expectation Among Chinese Immigrants in the United States of America: A Cohort Comparison, 2019 Ageing and Soc. 1; Sabrina T. Wong et al., The Changing Meaning of Family Support Among Older Chinese and Korean Immigrants, 61 J. Gerontology 4, 5, 8 (2006); Karuna Sharma & Candace L. Kemp, "One Should Follow the Wind": Individualized Filial Piety and Support Exchanges in Indian Immigrant Families in the United States, 26 J. Aging Stud. 129, 129, 130, 137 (2012); Mary B. Ofstedal et al., Intergenerational Support and Gender: A Comparison of Four Asian Countries (1999).

128. Bureau of Labor Stats., U.S. Dep't of Labor, Statistical Am. Time Use Survey, Eldercare in 2011 (2011).

Table of Cases

Index